The Western World

Prehistory to 1715

VOLUME I

Anthony Esler

The College of William and Mary

Prentice Hall, Englewood Cliffs, New Jersey 07632

Library of Congress Cataloging-in-Publication Data

Esler, Anthony.
  The western world : prehistory to the present / Anthony Esler.
    p. cm.
  Includes bibliographical references and index.
  ISBN 0-13-946674-6 (combined); ISBN 0-13-946716-5 (Vol. I);
  ISBN 0-13-946732-7 (Vol. II)
  1. Civilization, Western—History. I. Title.
CB245.E69 1994   93-13253
909'.09821—dc20   CIP

Editorial/production supervisor: *Joan E. Foley*
Acquisitions editor: *Steve Dalphin*
Development editor: *Virginia Otis Locke*
Editorial assistant: *Caffie Risher*
Development assistant: *Asha Rohra*
Cover and interior designer: *Lydia Gershey*
Cover art: *Pieter Bruegel*. Corteo di Nozze. **Maison du Roi, Brussels.**
   Scala/Art Resource
Photo research: *Elsa Peterson/Lorinda Morris-Nantz*
Copy editor: *Anne F. Lesser*
Supplements editor: *Jennie Katsaros*
Production coordinator: *Kelly Behr*

For Steve and Ann, the best Europeans I know.

©1994 by Prentice-Hall, Inc.
A Paramount Communications Company
Englewood Cliffs, New Jersey 07632

Printed in the United States of America
10 9 8 7 6 5 4 3 2 1

ISBN 0-13-946716-5

Prentice-Hall International (UK) Limited, *London*
Prentice-Hall of Australia Pty. Limited, *Sydney*
Prentice-Hall Canada Inc., *Toronto*
Prentice-Hall Hispanoamericana, S.A., *Mexico*
Prentice-Hall of India Private Limited, *New Delhi*
Prentice-Hall of Japan, Inc., *Tokyo*
Simon & Schuster Asia Pte. Ltd., *Singapore*
Editora Prentice-Hall do Brasil, Ltda., *Rio de Janeiro*

Contents

v

Maps

Documents

Preface

Devoting five years of one's life to writing a book like this is not a task to be undertaken lightly. Indeed, not many sane scholars really want to compose a history of the Western world from prehistoric times to the post-modern present. The job absorbs a working teacher's weekends and summers and devours research leaves, year after year. "Still working on The Book?" friends ask, when you come to visit, and shake their heads as you unlimber the ballpoints, writing pads, and packs of four-by-six note cards you are never without, on campus, at home, or abroad. "Why did you ever sign on for such a job?" they ask, and the reader may wonder too.

First, I wrote this book because Prentice Hall asked me to. Second, after teaching the course for thirty years I thought—like most teachers of "Western civ"—that I had something to say about this wide-ranging mural of human history. Third and most important, I thought that, having written a few historical novels, I might be able to produce a textbook that students would find at least occasionally interesting. I have therefore tried to tell the story of Western humankind in a fresh and interesting way that will engage the attention of students without sacrificing necessary depth and detail.

I have tried to tell this history as a story—as a narrative of people and events on the move, of societies evolving through time. At the same time I have allocated a substantial portion of the book to social and cultural analysis, an endeavor on which so much cutting-edge historical research has focused in recent years. I have paid special attention to such sometimes neglected areas as women's history and, in the second volume, to the history of the women's movement for social equality. As the author of an earlier history of the entire world, I have also felt a strong responsibility to deal with the West's repeated encounters with the non-Western world. I have tried to stress not only Western influences on the rest of the world but also a significant Western cultural debt to many non-Western peoples. I have made room here both for a traditional emphasis on conflict between classes, creeds, and nations and for the treatment of that more recently explored sense of community that defines a healthy society. And I have tried to be as up-to-date as the publishing process allows, a feature that seems particularly important in the pivotal 1990s, a watershed decade that could set the historical agenda of the Western world for decades to come.

This book also contains a number of special pedagogical elements that we hope will be helpful to its student readers. Near the beginning of each chapter, a **timeline** gives a sense of sequence in the topics and events to come and of their separate lines of development—broadly, political, economic, and cultural. Scattered through the chapters are no less than six different types of **documents**. Boxes headed *The Rulers and the Ruled* deal with issues of government, politics, and the law; *Mastering Our World* boxes document scientific, technological, and economic evolution; documents headed *The Human Spirit* showcase artistic, literary, religious, and cultural expressions of people throughout history; *War and Peace* documents chronicle military-international interventions and treaties; *Profiles in History* documents offer biographical material; and boxes headed *Probing the Past* examine the study of history. The text contains forty-nine **maps**, and a serious effort has been made to see to it that all places mentioned in the text are shown on these maps.

At the end of each chapter a **topical summary** recaps the major ideas and concepts explored throughout the chapter under such headings as "politics," "economics," "society," "culture," "science," "technology," "war," "art," and "the expanding west." Also at the end of each chapter are an **annotated reading list** and a selection of **key terms** that should help students in their efforts to learn a multitude of new concepts. These terms are repeated, with their definitions, in an alphabetized **glossary** at the back of the book.

A lot of work, in short, has gone into *The Western World*. We hope it helps readers to get a feel for who the members of this world are, where they are in history, and how they got to that point. I would be glad for any feedback teachers or students are willing to provide, and particularly for suggestions of ways to improve the next edition of this book.

Supplements

Accompanying this text is an *Instructor's Manual* that includes chapter objectives, outlines, and summaries, as well as suggested lecture topics, discussion questions, exercises that focus on the relations between the West and the rest of the world, and a guide to video and film resources.

A *Test Item File*, also available to the instructor, contains more than fifty questions (multiple-choice, matching, and essay) per chapter. Questions are based on boxed documents as well as on the text, and special map questions are coordinated with map handouts. The *Test Manager*, a computerized test bank that contains the items from the *File*, allows instructors to edit any items and to add their own questions. *Test Manager* is available for both the IBM and Macintosh computers.

Instructors will also find useful the set of *Map Transparencies* that reproduce every one of the two-color maps featured in the book. For use in exams as well as in student self-tests, a set of blank *Map Handouts* is available.

The two-volume *Study Guide* is designed to make the student's task of mastering the material in this book easier. Chapter objectives, outlines, and summaries provide frameworks for studying each chapter. The *Guide* also includes review questions (multiple-choice, matching) and exercises that require students to think and write about the material covered in the text.

Acknowledgments

In the course of assembling these two bulky volumes, I have accumulated a great many intellectual debts. It is therefore my duty as well as a great pleasure to express my gratitude to at least some of those who have made the book you hold in your hands possible.

First and most of all, I must say thank you again to the scholarly and dedicated Europeanists at William and Mary, with whom I have had the privilege of working over the years—to Professors Maryann Brink, Dale Hoak, Lu Ann Homza, Gil McArthur, Jim McCord, Tom Sheppard, and George Strong, as well as to some who have moved on, especially A. Z. Freeman, Dietrich Orlow, Harold Fowler, and Bruce McCully. Thanks also to the Americanists and the specialists in non-Western history whose knowledge I have drawn upon most frequently—Cam Walker, Ismail Abdalla, Ed Crapol, Craig Canning, and Judy Ewell—and to our classicists, especially Jim Baron and Ward Jones. If I had not known that all these people were willing to let me pick their brains and paw through their books, I would probably never have had the nerve to undertake this project.

Next my gratitude goes to the long-suffering and knowledgeable historians at other universities who accepted Prentice Hall's invitation to read and comment on portions of this book as it has developed. Every page of the book has benefited from their insights, suggestions, and corrections. My thanks then to Achilles Avraamides, Iowa State University; Gayle Brunelle, California State University—Fullerton; John J. Buschen, University of Wisconsin—River Falls; Kevin K. Carroll, Arizona State University; Susan P. Conner, Central Michigan University; Ronald E. Coons, University of Connecticut; Ruth Schwartz Cowan, State University of New York, Stony Brook; Frederic Crawford, Middle Tennessee State University; William M. Delehanty, University of St. Thomas; Marion F. Deshmukh, George Mason University; Barbara M. Fahy, Albright College; Arthur Ferrill, University of Washington; Laura L. Frader, Northeastern University; Henry French, Munroe Community College; Geoffrey Giles, University of Florida; David Gross, University of Colorado-Boulder; Barbara McClung Hallman, California Polytechnic University; Louis Haas, Duquesne University; David A. Hackett, University of Texas—El Paso; Paul Harvey, Pennsylvania State University; Warren L. Hickman, Eisenhower College; Niles R. Holt, Illinois State University; W. Robert Houston, University of South Alabama; David N. Jones, California State University—Fresno; William R. Jones, University of New Hampshire; Konrad H. Jarusch, University of North Carolina; Isabel Knight, Pennsylvania State University; Lloyd Kramer, University of North Carolina; Fred Lauritson, Eastern Washington University; David Lukowitz, Hamline University; John Mears, Southern Methodist University; James Muldoon, Rutgers University; John Kim Munholland, University of Minnesota; Raymond L. Muney, Harding University; Philip C. Naylor, Marquette University; Kenneth Ostrand, Villanova University; James Parry, Seattle University; John F. Robertson, Central Michigan University; Steven Sage, Middle Tennessee State University; Franziska E. Shlosser, Concordia University, Sir George Williams Campus; Peter Stansky, Stanford University; John L. Tevebaugh, Grand Valley State University; Peter Vinton-Johansen, Michigan State University; Allen M. Ward, University of Connecticut; Richard Weisberger, Butler County Community College; Michael Weiss, Linn-Benton Community College; Neil Weissman, Dickinson College; Delno C. West, Northern Arizona University; Merry Wiesner-Hanks, University of Wisconsin. All surviving errors and misinterpretations are of course mine alone.

It is one's students themselves, finally, who deserve any academic writer's gratitude. By bringing their own increasingly international backgrounds to bear on classroom discussions or simply by asking the hard questions that send the teacher back to the sources, they contribute immeasurably to the education of their instructors. I thank all my own students, past and present.

At Prentice Hall, the most professional and hard-working selection of editors I have ever known labored over this book. It would never have been written at all if Executive Editor Steve Dalphin, who recruited me for the last one, hadn't pried me away from another project to try my hand at this one. Two enormously skilled and understanding development editors, Cecil Yarbrough and Virginia Otis Locke, gave the project the benefit of their knowledge of books, book-making, and much else. Cecil guided me through the first draft of the book. Ginny worked with me on the final revision of the entire manuscript, seeing it through to production. Despite my sometimes negative reactions to all the rethinking and rewriting both of these editors suggested, the book is deeply in their debt. Joan Foley handled production deftly and bore with my seemingly congenital inability to respond to deadlines on time with remarkable calm. For excellent copyediting I am grateful to Anne Lesser and especially to Ann Hofstra Grogg, who proved amazingly able to pluck out inconsistencies a hundred pages apart.

Finally, I would like to acknowledge a few personal debts that can never be adequately repaid. I would like to thank my parents, Jamie Arthur and Helen Kreamer Esler for raising me with an awareness that thinking is part of life and that there is a larger world out there waiting. Thanks to my first wife Carol Clemeau Esler and to my sons Kenneth Campbell Esler and David Douglas Esler for being wonderful travelers and for finding plenty to like in European cities and villages. And thanks again to my wife Cam—Professor Helen Campbell Walker—for many years of insights and for everyplace from Skara Brae to wherever next year.

Anthony Esler
Jamestown Road
Williamsburg, Virginia

 *The New York Times* **Program**

Introduction
What Is the Western World?

You may think that a strange question to ask, for most of us think we know the answer. If, just to be sure, we look into a dictionary or two we are not surprised to note that as far back as Shakespeare's day, *Western* referred to "Western or European countries" and that more recent usage defines *the West* as "Europe and the Americas." There is much more, however, to any attempt to understand the Western world today and as it has evolved throughout the past. *The West, Western civilization,* and *the Western world* are in fact among the slipperiest historical, geographical, and cultural concepts in common use today.

The West, for instance, is not simply a piece of geography whose history can readily be traced back down the centuries. It is true that this term has been used for hundreds of years as a synonym for Europe, geographically the western portion of the enormous continent of Eurasia. But in the twentieth century, the most powerful of Western nations has certainly been the United States, located on an entirely separate continent and on the other side of the Atlantic from Europe. Moreover, some nations found on still other continents, such as Argentina and Australia, are usually also considered part of the modern West.

The Western world is also not a unique form of society, readily distinguishable from all others. Through most of its history, in fact, Western society has been structured much like other societies around the world. Like other great cultures, the civilization that emerged in Europe and spread across the world developed complex economies and social systems and built cities, states, and empires. Historically speaking, westerners are more like other peoples than they sometimes seem to think.

Nor is the Western world easily defined in terms of a body of characteristic ideas and ideals, that is, a common culture to which all Western peoples have historically adhered. Admittedly, Westernness is frequently seen as a matter of allegiance to a common heritage often defined as Judeo-Christian and Greco-Roman and as including belief in democratic government, individual rights, and free enterprise. As this book will reveal, however, many of these concepts and cultural commitments hardly existed through significant portions of Western history.

Nevertheless, the elusive conception of Westernness has both historical meaning and value for us as we try to understand the Western world, past and present. To disentangle that meaning we must reject all efforts to establish a final, fixed definition of Western civilization or to separate the West from the rest of the world. It is by defining the West in terms of *growth* rather than fixed boundaries, of *dynamic change* rather than stasis, and of *interaction* with others rather than isolation that we may make some sense out of Western history and achieve a better understanding of the place of the West in today's multicultural world.

In the simplest territorial sense, the Western world is seen in this book as a *growing* thing. It has expanded and spread throughout its history, swelling from the little Greek world of 2500 years ago to the mighty array of modern nations scattered around the globe today.

In social and cultural terms, the Western world is also a *dynamically changing* thing. If the ancient Greeks had never heard of the Judeo-Christian tradition, the ancient Romans had, for it was in Roman times that the West began to absorb the stream of religious belief that acquired a central place in Western life. If the society of the Middle Ages, in turn, had little knowledge of such scarcely developed modern concepts as political liberty and social equality, it was the eighteenth-century movement known as the Enlightenment that fostered the key role of these values in subsequent Western civilization. Over thousands of years the West has continued to evolve, each phase of its history building on the one that preceded it.

Finally, this process of territorial growth and cultural evolution has been accompanied by a third important characteristic: fertile *interaction* with many non-Western cultures. For the West has not evolved in splendid isolation, preserving its principles and customs free of external influence. On the contrary, from the very beginning Westerners have interacted with other peoples with often extremely valuable results.

Beginning in the first few chapters of this book we will see how ancient Egypt and the Near East helped to shape Greece during the earliest stages of Western history. We will visit a Roman Empire that included sizable portions of North Africa and Western Asia. In the Middle Ages, we will find Byzantines, Muslims, and Mongols both threatening and influencing European society. And in modern times, we will see an imperial West coming into what was often oppressive but also mutually influential contact with other peoples all around the world. Peoples from all parts of the globe have helped to build the West as we know it today, both by providing ideas, labor, and goods and by contributing energetic new citizens to many Western nations.

As the Western world has grown, changed, and interacted with other peoples it has also contributed many creative achievements to the history of humankind. For example although derived in part from the thought of other peoples, the physical sciences as we know them emerged in their modern form in the sixteenth-century West. Most of the political, economic, and social ideas that underlie the structures of modern states around the world are also Western in origin. The ongoing industrialization of the globe began in eighteenth-century Europe. And it was the West that forged the world market, thus bringing all the world's peoples into closer contact than any of our ancestors had ever experienced. These are not, it must be admitted, insignificant contributions to the world's store of achievements.

In the chapters that follow we begin with a few small communities in a fertile river valley and continue to expand our subject until half the globe seems to be in some sense "Western." We envision the Western world as a dynamically developing civilization that has always been part of a larger society. And we follow throughout the line of historical evolution and achievement that provides the flexible yet solid core of Western identity today.

Part I

The Ancient West

During the long millennium that stretched from approximately 800 B.C. to A.D. 500, Western civilization began to take shape in southern Europe, around the Mediterranean Sea. Borrowing from the earlier and more developed civilizations of the Near East and Egypt, Greece and Rome between them laid the foundations of the Western world.

The Greeks developed the first Western city-states, and the Romans built the largest of ancient Western empires, encompassing the shores of the Mediterranean and including much of western Europe. Both the participatory democracy developed by Athens and other Greek city-states and the order, prosperity, and sheer scale of imperial Rome greatly impressed and influenced later Western peoples.

Economically, the Greeks and Romans moved from peasant farming to large-scale commercial agriculture. They also developed handicraft industries and building skills of great sophistication. Both were trading peoples: Greek commerce spread around the Mediterranean and Black seas, and the Roman Empire became part of an intercontinental network of trade that reached as far as China.

In terms of social structure, the ancient West developed a complex range of castes and classes. Most people were probably peasant farmers, slaves or, especially in Roman times, urban poor. There were important merchant and artisan classes in the cities, and the hereditary aristocracy of large landowners and political officeholders played the leading role in the histories of both Greece and Rome.

Culturally, the Greeks are usually seen as more innovative, more intellectually adventurous, and more artistically creative than the Romans. In philosophy, science, art, and literature Greek civilization influenced all later Western cultures. The Romans, on the other hand, were masters of such practical arts as engineering, law, and government. And it was during the period of Roman rule that Christianity was born and spread from the Near East into the Western world.

A look at a map (Map 6.1, p. 162) indicates how this first formulation of Western society and civilization had spread by the time Rome fell in the fifth century A.D. Greek trade and colonies were scattered from the western end of the Mediterranean to the eastern end of the Black Sea. The mighty Roman Empire had conquered almost all the peoples around the Mediterranean Sea, extending its rule well into the Near East and across North Africa. Rome had then extended its sway northward across Europe, absorbing Celtic and Germanic peoples and spreading through France, Spain, and the Balkans all the way to northern England.

The West of ancient times must have been a very different place from the Western world we know. Its centers were its cities, with their temples, law courts, market places, amphitheaters, aqueducts, and large tenement neighborhoods. But most early Western people, like most people everywhere in the world, lived in the country, farming or herding, following the round of the seasons to produce the food, clothing, and other things that all societies need. The Greek philosopher Socrates debating basic human values in the Athenian marketplace, Augustus Caesar ruling the Western world from the seven hills of Rome, and the unknown millions whose labor built both Athens and the Roman Empire were all part of the founding generations, the first builders of the Western world.

The history of Western civilization began before the invention of civilization and outside the confines of the Western world altogether. Like other developed societies, the West built on foundations laid down by prehistoric peoples. And like most other civilizations, Western society also drew significantly on the civilizations of other peoples, in early times the ancient Near East and North Africa. These prehistoric and non-Western roots of Western history are the focus of this first chapter.

The first ancestors of all human beings apparently appeared several million years ago in southeastern Africa. Over many thousands of generations, these early prehumans evolved and spread until modern human beings were found around the world. While our ancestors were developing biologically they were also evolving culturally. The earliest peoples were food gatherers and hunters who made tools out of stone and lived in small roving bands. Later generations discovered how to produce their own food and settled in small agricultural villages. From these beginnings the ancient cities and larger states in which civilization was born developed not much more than five thousand years ago.

These first civilizations emerged in the fertile river valleys of Mesopotamia—now Iraq—and Egypt. Around these first cities, kingdoms, and empires, many Near Eastern peoples developed their own societies: among these were the Hittites, the Phoenicians, the Persians, and the Hebrews. From the pattern of culture that took shape among these peoples around the eastern end of the Mediterranean Sea, the Greeks and the Romans, the first peoples to be considered "Western," drew freely in building their own civilization.

Queen Nefertiti. c. 1360 B.C. Painted limestone. Ägyptisches Museum, Staatliche Museen, Berlin

Our Prehistoric Ancestry

In the raw, stony gash of Olduvai Gorge in Tanzania, East Africa, a visitor can easily pick up—but will not be allowed to keep—fossil-bearing rock from the slopes and trails. Fossilized bone and chipped flint tools make up the majority of the evidence we have about prehistory, and Olduvai Gorge is one of the most famous of all quarries of such remains. It was the renowned archaeologist team of Mary and Louis Leakey who in 1959 uncovered in this maze of sun-bleached, broken stone the fossil evidence that established what is believed to be the African genesis of the human race.

	3500 B.C.		3000		2500	
POLITICAL, MILITARY, AND DIPLOMATIC EVENTS	**c. 3500**	Sumerian city-states	**c. 3000**	Upper, Lower Egypt	**2700–2300**	Old Kingdom Egypt
			c. 2850	Menes unifies Egypt	**c. 2300**	Sargon of Akkad
SOCIAL AND ECONOMIC DEVELOPMENTS	**c. 3500**	First cities	**by 3000**	Mesopotamian irrigation	**by 2500**	Egyptian irrigation
	c. 3500	Mesopotamians develop bronze working				
ART AND LITERATURE, SCIENCE, PHILOSOPHY, AND RELIGION	**c. 3500**	Mesopotamian cuneiform writing			**c. 2700**	Pyramids at Giza

A brief introduction to our prehistoric ancestors follows. It is a story that will take us from the first chippers of flint to the people who reared the walls and towers of the earliest human civilizations.

The Birth of the Human Race

Scientists and scholars in many fields have contributed to modern knowledge of the prehistoric past. The first fossil remains of prehistoric human beings to be recognized as such were found not in Africa but in a cave in Germany's Neander Valley in 1856. There workers discovered the rude remains that gave the name Neanderthal to one of the most celebrated of prehistoric peoples. In later decades came the important finds of the Cro-Magnon people of France, Java Man of Southeast Asia, Peking Man of China, and the Taung Baby of South Africa. Since World War II, a rash of discoveries in East Africa have included the Leakeys' finds in Tanzania, some of which go back almost two million years, and Donald Johanson's "Lucy," a skeleton that is well over three million years old, found on a rocky slope in Ethiopia (see box, "Finding Lucy").

Experts in other fields have helped to frame our current understanding of our human and prehuman origins. Geologists and physicists, for instance, have been able to date bones and stone tools by analyzing the rock layers in which these bits of evidence are found or by measuring the dwindling radiation of carbon (*carbon dating*) in the relics themselves. Anatomists and biochemists have established the close kinship between human beings and their near relatives in the nonhuman animal world by analyzing anatomical structures, blood groups, and chromosome patterns. Ethologists, who study the behavior

4

2000	1500	1000	500 B.C.

2050–1800 Middle Kingdom Egypt
c. 1900 Hebrews leave Mesopotamia
1792–1750 Hammurabi
1750–1530 Old Babylonian Empire
1700–1200 Hittite Empire

1570–1100 Egyptian New Kingdom and Empire
1503–1482 Hatshepsut
1469–1436 Thutmose III
1379–1362 Aknaton
c. 1300 Moses
1100–604 Assyrian Empire
1000–960 David
1000–750 Phoenicians
960–933 Solomon

612–539 New Babylonian Empire
539 Cyrus founds Persian Empire

---

c. 2000 Middle Kingdom trade

c. 1500 New Kingdom trade

c. 1200 Hittites introduce ironworking
1000–750 Phoenician commercial predominance

c. 750 Coinage in Lydia

c. 500 Jewish diaspora begins

---

c. 1750 Hammurabi's Code

c. 1300 Ten Commandments
c. 1000 Phoenician Alphabet
c. 950 Solomon's Temple

c. 600 Hanging Gardens of Babylon
8th–4th centuries Hebrew prophets

---

of animals, have drawn illuminating parallels between human behavior and that of other creatures. And despite controversy over the validity of their method, cultural anthropologists have studied food-gathering peoples that have survived into the twentieth century, such as the Australian Aborigines, in order to expand our understanding of prehistoric society and culture.

Our prehistoric ancestry apparently goes back tens of millions of years to small lemurlike creatures who lived by picking fruit and catching insects among the branches of primeval forests. The descendents of these furry tree dwellers include many now extinct genera and species of the broad family of *hominids*, or humanlike creatures. One of the oldest of our clear precursors, an ungainly creature who flourished in Asia perhaps twelve million years ago, was christened *Ramapithecus* after a mythic Hindu hero. Much later, about four million years ago, a number of prehuman types emerged in Africa, including the australopithecines, or "southern apemen," and the beginnings of the genus *Homo*—our own direct ancestors. Along this latter line of development came *Homo habilis* ("the toolmaker"), dating from approximately two million B.C.; *Homo erectus* ("one who walks erect"), emerging more than 1.5 million years ago; and finally *Homo sapiens* ("wise or thinking human being"), perhaps two hundred thousand years ago. The two types of *Homo sapiens* known to us are the *Neanderthals* (c. 125,000–35,000 B.C.) and the *Cro-Magnons*, found at least as far back as 40,000 B.C. The Cro-Magnons are usually seen as our own direct ancestors: biologically, we differ scarcely at all from these people of forty millennia ago.[1]

Specific connections between these groups and subgroups—and others that fell by the wayside down the long evolutionary road—are much debated by the experts. The overall pattern of develop-

PROBING THE PAST Finding Lucy

Donald C. Johanson (1949–   ), a leading student of the prehistoric past at the University of California at Berkeley, was only thirty-one when he discovered the oldest extant skeleton of an erect-walking hominid, the celebrated "Lucy" (named for the Beatles song played during the all-night celebration at Johanson's camp that followed the discovery). Standing no more than 3 feet high and weighing perhaps 60 pounds, Lucy lived and died at what is today the Hadar site in Ethiopia some 3.4 million years ago. The moment of discovery, after many long days under the broiling African sun, comes vividly to life in Johanson's account:

> The gully in question was just over the crest of the rise where we had been working all morning. . . . As we turned to leave, I noticed something lying on the ground part way up the slope.
> "That's a bit of a hominid arm," I said. . . .

"What makes you so sure?" he said.

"Jesus Christ," said Gray. He picked it up. It was the back of a small skull. A few feet away was part of a femur: a thighbone. . . .

An unbelievable, impermissible thought flickered through my mind. Suppose all these fitted together? Could they be parts of a single, extremely primitive skeleton? No such skeleton had ever been found—anywhere.

"Look at that," said Gray. "Ribs."

A single individual?

"I can't believe it," I said. "I just can't believe it."

"By God, you'd better believe it!" shouted Gray. "Here it is. Right here!" His voice went up into a howl. I joined him. In that 110-degree heat we began jumping up and down. With nobody to share our feelings, we hugged each other, sweaty and smelly, howling and hugging in the heat-shimmering gravel, the small brown remains of what now seemed almost certain to be parts of a single hominid skeleton lying all around us.

Source: Donald Johanson and Maitland Edey, *Lucy: The Beginnings of Humankind* (New York: Warner Books, 1981), 16–17.

---

ment, however, seems fairly clear. It is a pattern of slow biological evolution in response to major environmental changes.

Over several millions of years the earth has experienced a series of long periods of low temperatures alternating with much shorter spans of warmer climate. Periods of global cooling led to the buildup of glaciers in the north. These periods also saw a drying out of much of the rest of the world, as water was absorbed into the glaciers, and the resulting extinction of many species of animals and plants. It may have been in response to such a drastic shrinking of forest areas in Africa that the ancestors of the first australopithecines abandoned their life in the trees and adapted to a new life on the sunny African savannah. Here they began the gradual evolution that produced the human race as we know it today.

Feet evolved from the gripping paws still found on arboreal monkeys to the heel, arch, and balancing toes that made it easier to walk on the earth. By rising upright and balancing on their two hind feet—perhaps originally to peer over the waving grasses—prehumans freed their forepaws for carrying food and for manipulation. It was from these first fumbling be-

ginnings that our unique human combination of fingers and opposing thumb gradually took shape. Most important, the brain of these prehumans began to grow in size and subtlety. This growth in the brain's capacity introduced an unprecedented feature into the evolution of humanity: the potential for significant *cultural* rather than purely *biological* development.

During the later phases of this evolutionary process, furthermore, our ancestors began to move from one place to another. Then as now, we were a migrating species, and the long trek from our prehistoric roots to the beginnings of recorded history was a journey across the globe as well as down the centuries.

Half a million years ago, the glaciers that had built up in the arctic began to expand once more, inching slowly southward across Eurasia and North America. Glacial meltwater during the summer months and soil ground up by the advancing glacier itself turned relatively barren terrain into lush grasslands on which grazing animals flourished. Huge herds of woolly mammoths, shaggy bison, horses, and deer browsed the well-watered prairies in the glacial zone. These great herds in turn attracted predators, among them the saber-toothed tiger, the cave bear, and our own hominid forebears.

The journey out of Africa that thus began a few hundred thousand years ago took our ancestors northward through the Near East, west into Europe, and then east across the vastness of Asia. More recently, only a few tens of thousands of years ago, wandering bands of hominids migrated across the seas to the Americas and to Australia, completing their colonization of the globe.

Two fundamentally different ways of life evolved among these prehistoric hominids. The earliest was the food-gathering mode, which prevailed during the *Paleolithic,* or Old Stone Age (*paleo* derives from the Greek for "ancient"; *lithos* is the Greek word for "stone") that lasted from several million years ago until perhaps 10,000 B.C. The later and much shorter phase of our prehistoric social evolution was the food-producing stage called the *Neolithic,* or New Stone Age, between perhaps 10,000 and roughly 3500 B.C.

Food-Gathering Peoples

Our earliest, tree-dwelling forebears were probably primarily vegetarians, eating mainly nuts and berries and other fruit among the branches. When they descended from the trees, they began to eat more meat, though they continued to collect and consume vegetable food.

To operate this simple subsistence economy, these prehistoric populations made a major breakthrough early in their cultural evolution: they invented tools. At least two million years ago, Paleolithic prehumans were fashioning primitive implements out of chipped stone, later of bone and wood as well. Our Stone Age ancestors actually made a fine art out of the flaking of flint into sharp-edged instruments, from hand axes and scrapers to spearpoints. Especially in the later Paleolithic period, "tool kits," as archaeologists call them, included sharp awls for piercing animal hides, bone sickles for cutting wild grains, stone chisels for working with wood, and spearpoints and arrowheads made of flint.

Paleolithic people responded to the periodic descent of the glaciers with another whole range of ingenious and practical inventions. Having first simply wrapped themselves in animal skins, they learned to construct Eskimo-style parkas, with clearly shaped arms and legs and in some cases hoods. They learned to preserve and then to kindle fire, both for cooking and for warmth. They not only turned caves and other rock shelters into homes, but built stone huts and rude tents out of hides draped over poles, stones, or the bones of large animals they had killed.

The evolution of prehistoric hunting technology clearly illustrates this pattern of increasing ingenuity. In the later Paleolithic period, the range of the simple spear was extended first by the *atlatl,* or throwing stick, then by the bow and arrow. Fishhooks and even harpoons were used by shore-dwelling peoples. Pit traps were employed to catch some game, and other animals were driven over cliffs or into swamps to provide Stone Age hunters with a feast.

Modern views of the social organization of Paleolithic peoples, based often on analogies with surviving food gatherers, are more debatable. It seems likely, however, that the basic food-gathering band probably comprised two or three dozen people for most of prehistory, perhaps increasing to seventy-five or a hundred in some communities in the later Paleolithic period. These small groups probably lived in relatively egalitarian societies. Where there was so little material wealth or political power to contend for, there was probably also comparatively little exploitation or oppression of one person by another. Human beings, some anthropologists have urged, did not develop strong hierarchical distinctions based on class or gender until they had developed more complex societies.

Such hunter-gatherer bands, however, probably inaugurated the basic division of labor, primarily by gender, that is still found among foraging peoples today. Women, girls, and the younger boys may have been responsible for the daily gathering of vegetable foods such as fruit, nuts, and edible roots. And it seems likely that it was the men and older boys who would rise in the predawn hours to hunker down around a distant water hole, waiting for deer or smaller game to come within reach of their spears. Thus women may have dominated the base camp and men the hunting grounds.

At the same time, men and women both contributed to the social cohesion of the group as a whole. Thus Paleolithic men, operating as hunters, may have learned very early the value of teamwork. Like a wolf pack or a pride of lions today, hominid hunters probably worked together to corner and destroy their larger or faster prey. Probably, too, they divided up the meat thus secured as hunting peoples in Africa and elsewhere do today, awarding different portions of the kill to each member of the band according to a code based on kinship or other traditional rules. Such sharing, like teamwork in the hunt, helped to strengthen the group's social bonds.

Operating out of the base camp, meanwhile, women as gatherers probably provided the more dependable source of food for the entire band. The berry bushes, after all, were there every morning: whether the deer came by the water hole or not was more problematical. In addition, women, who bore children and had the major burden of raising them, were probably the primary educators in many basic matters. Presiding over the family and providing the largest part of the food supply, women made a further contribution to the sense of community that could mean survival itself to the isolated groups in which prehistoric peoples lived.

Beyond these important economic, technological, and social developments, the Neanderthal and Cro-Magnon peoples in particular produced some surprisingly impressive artwork and the beginnings at least of religious beliefs. An early expression of an aesthetic sense, for example, was the development of personal adornment. It is believed that Old Stone Age people may have painted or tattooed their bodies, as many peoples have since. In addition, large numbers of prehistoric beads and other articles intended to adorn the person have been found. And if what sculpture we have from the period is to be trusted, some Paleolithic women bound their hair up in buns behind their heads, whereas others wore it in a frizzy style that resembled some modern-day hairdos.

More striking artistic achievements include the famous cave art of our Cro-Magnon forebears. The walls of caves like those at Lascaux in the Dordogne region of southwestern France and Altamira in northern Spain, for instance, glow with paintings dating to 30,000 B.C. and earlier. Simple relief carvings, clay sculpture, and carved stone, bone, and ivory also reveal the artistic impulses and talents of our ancestors. Depictions of animals predominate, including such large game as horses, deer, bison, and mammoths. People are also represented, though less naturalistically, often as stick figures. Not infrequently, however, the contour of a reindeer horn or the bulge of a painted bison's shoulder reveal both the painter's familiarity with the prehistoric world and genuine artistry.

Early religious beliefs may have included the worship of some of these animals. Among the Neanderthals, for example, the careful placement of cave-bear skulls in niches or other prominent places may indicate a "bear cult" as far back as 100,000 B.C. The fact that some of the animals painted on Cro-Magnon cave walls thirty thousand years ago are pierced by spears or arrows may reveal belief in "sympathetic magic" of the sort often practiced by hunting peoples in later times. According to this ancient faith, if the shaman or priest draws an arrow piercing a pictured animal, a real arrow will strike home in the field the next day. Small stone "Venus figurines" of women, who were often depicted as big breasted and pregnant, may be symbols of fertility designed to bring about human and animal births as well as the growth of food plants. Such fertility cults were also found among many later peoples.

As early as Neanderthal times, finally, the dead of both sexes were sometimes buried in clothing decorated with beads, surrounded by especially fine tools and weapons, and painted with red ocher or even sprinkled with flowers. Such practices seem to suggest reverence and affection, perhaps even an intuition of personal immortality, an afterlife in which beaded finery and the best tools might be of use to the departed. Beliefs that would become widespread throughout human history may thus predate the birth of civilization by many thousands of years.

The Neolithic Revolution

Cro-Magnon people carried the culture of food-gathering humanity about as far as it could go. A great change was coming as the prehistoric period drew to a close—a change so startling that it is sometimes described as the first genuine revolution in the history of the human race.

V. Gordon Childe, one of the twentieth century's most influential authorities on prehistory, coined the term *Neolithic Revolution* for this vast social change that put our species on the last lap to civilization. It was not, of course, a political upheaval—there were no political institutions to revolutionize in those simpler societies. It was, however, a drastic transformation in the economy, technology, and social and cultural life of humankind. Its primary achievement, in Childe's view, was the invention of agriculture.

Recent archaeological finds suggest that the hunter-gatherer peoples of later Paleolithic times had actually begun to develop more complex societies before the birth of agriculture. The ivory beads and other decorative objects possessed by some western European food gatherers more than thirty thousand years ago are cited as evidence of the existence of a primitive social hierarchy. More than twenty thousand years ago, some Paleolithic peoples in central

The story of the Western world, like that of people everywhere, began with the prehistoric family. In this model of a Neolithic household, what evidence do you see of the early, hunting way of life?

the cooler climate. Another view emphasizes the human contribution to the exhaustion of the game: the killing off, first of larger animals, then of the smaller prey by increasingly skilled and deadly prehistoric hunters. Whatever its cause, the declining supply of meat would have put heavier pressure on the collectors of vegetable food to make up the difference—a powerful incentive for the invention of agriculture.

Some authorities also see the more settled food-gathering societies just described as contributing to the development of full-scale agriculture. The greater efficiency of settled food-gathering may have produced at least a modest increase in population, thus further increasing pressure on the existing food supply. This pressure, in turn, may have impelled Neolithic people to experiment with techniques of cultivation and domestication that evolved into agriculture.

The resulting agricultural revolution probably began hind end foremost—that is, with harvesting rather than with planting. "Food gathering," after all, is simply the harvesting of food plants found growing wild in nature. Food gatherers, who had learned when each fruit or root or wild grain would ripen, could easily have noticed that a little care—such as watering and weeding—produced a more bountiful harvest. They might also have noticed the sprouting of kernels of wild wheat or barley where grain had been stored or cast aside unconsumed. With the herds they preyed on dwindling, perhaps with the population growing, some groups of prehistoric people decided to settle down and tend the richest crops right through the growing season, from sowing time to harvest.

The most likely architects of this crucial transformation of human life were women, who as food gatherers were most likely to understand the life cycles of vegetable foods. We may imagine these prehistoric gatherers, then, watering wild barley when the band arrived at the end of a scorching summer, pulling weeds or plucking insects from the leaves, and scattering a portion of the harvest on the ground—perhaps as a form of sacrifice—to be rewarded by a new crop in the next growing season.

Although the cultivation of the soil was central to the agricultural revolution, the domestication of animals was almost equally important. Animals, like plants, could be tended and kept under human control, rather than sought out in the wild. The people of the New Stone Age thus came to herd and pen up animals and to slaughter them as needed rather than when they could be found. Sheep, goats, and pigs were among the first beasts to be domesticated in this way.

Russia seem to have forsaken caves for semipermanent shelters built of mammoth bone and to have engaged in forms of trade or gift exchange with neighboring peoples that brought them raw materials from several hundred miles away. Some thirteen thousand years back, the Natufian food-gathering people of what is today Israel lived in rude stone huts, carefully stored the wild grain they gathered, and made tools like mortars and pestles to process the food they foraged. The full-fledged agricultural villages that were the core of the Neolithic revolution probably evolved out of such relatively advanced late Paleolithic settlements.

The great change itself, however, was the major shift from food *gathering* to food *producing,* a process involving both the cultivation of the soil and the domestication of animals. This shift apparently occurred first in the Near East as early as 10,000 B.C.

Some attempts to explain the agricultural revolution have stressed the end of the last ice age, that is, the shrinking of the glaciers northward that began about this time. This in turn, it is postulated, led to another major ecological change: big game were drawn further north, following the grasslands and

Over the brief five or six thousand years of the Neolithic period in the Near East, our ancestors acquired an amazing amount of information about what could be done with both plants and animals. Stone Age farmers, for instance, understood the value of manuring the soil to increase fertility. They learned to breed animals and plants selectively for larger yields or more meat on the bone. And they began to make systematic use of animal byproducts, such as milk and eggs.

The invention of crop cultivation and animal husbandry were major achievements for the human race. By freeing people from the Paleolithic routine of hunting and gathering, Neolithic technologies liberated people to develop a variety of new skills and crafts. And because cultivation of the soil and the domestication of animals yielded much more food per acre than food gathering, the human population grew, slowly peopling villages, cities, and then great empires. The sense of land ownership and the willingness to fight to defend one's land or to conquer new territory may also be traced to Neolithic recognition of the value of fertile land and lush pastures. More complex societies, larger political units, private property, and warfare may thus all be traced back to this crucial breakthrough twelve thousand years ago.

Laboring in the fields with crude hoes or digging sticks and grinding grain with stone tools was no easier than hunting and gathering. But the discovery of food production did open up new styles of life to our Neolithic ancestors. And the first form of that new life was the society of the agricultural village.

Food-Producing Peoples

The buried ruins of Neolithic farming communities have been uncovered in many parts of the Near East. On the West Bank of the Jordan River in modern Israel you can look down on the walls of Jericho, now some 45 feet below the level of the sunbaked land around it. In the lowest of Jericho's eight excavated levels of habitation, carbon dated to 7800 B.C., as many as two thousand farmers lived in round clay houses topped with conical roofs. Prehistoric Jericho was surrounded by a town wall, and in its center was a pillared temple garnished with sculptures of animals and of gods who were half human and half animal.

At Çatal Hüyük on the Anatolian plateau of southern Turkey, archaeologists have uncovered the ruins of a town of farmers and shepherds some 32 acres in size and dating back to 6500 B.C. A village discovered at Jarmo, in modern Iraq, had a population of no more than 150. Both of these towns were considerably smaller than ancient Jericho, but size was not the key achievement of these Neolithic communities. A flint-edged sickle made around 4500 B.C. at Tepe Yahya in Iran, a plow used in 3500 B.C. in Iraq provide proof of much more crucial accomplishments in the life of the agricultural village.

Stone was still the primary hard material used for tools by Neolithic peoples, and textiles and ceramics also came into use during this period. The knives they carved with, the sickles they used to cut their grain were still bladed or edged with stone. But it was stone worked to a new standard of excellence, no longer chipped and rough edged, but carefully smoothed and polished. The people of the New Stone Age, furthermore, learned to make pots out of clay—at first coiled by hand, then shaped on the potter's wheel—to produce ceramic jars for both cooking and storing food. The craftspeople of Neolithic times also discovered the art of weaving animal hair or vegetable fibers into cloth, and the resulting wool and linen textiles slowly replaced animal hides as human clothing.

It is likely that society remained very close knit in Neolithic agricultural villages, despite their larger populations and greater social complexity. Family and clan ties were as important as they had been in the Paleolithic period. Labor was probably still divided between the sexes, as it had been in food-gathering bands. Men now probably did much of the agricultural labor, though women joined them in the fields, and children could herd sheep or goats on the surrounding hillsides.

Distinctions of wealth and power perhaps began to emerge this early. Impressive collections of ornaments and other objects buried with some of the dead suggest that at least a few people had greater wealth than others. Private ownership of property, however, may not always have been recognized. Among Neolithic remains in Egypt, for instance, archaeologists have found what appear to have been communal granaries. Power also was probably much less clearly defined or widely exercised than it was in later centuries. To judge from the situation at the beginning of recorded history, prehistoric village elders probably did make some decisions for the village as a whole, but these decisions were likely to be based on tribal traditions understood by all. And such crucial matters as when to sow and when to reap may well have been decided by consensus rather than by leaders.

By this time, finally, there were substantially increased contacts between villages and even between one region and another. The discovery of cowrie shells in villages far from the water, for example, probably indicates some form of commercial exchange or at least ritualized gift giving between peoples. And the fact that the earliest settlement at Jericho was walled and moated makes it likely that warfare of some sort had also come into the Neolithic world.

To the modern eye the painting and sculpture of the early agricultural villages constitute no great artistic advance from that of the caves. A human skull from Jericho with a face plastered onto the front of it and cowrie shells for eyes may strike us as rather more bizarre than artistic. The still rough statuettes and wall paintings of female figures from Neolithic times are generally recognized as fertility symbols, for the fertility of crops and herds remained as important to food producers as to food gatherers.

We also know that personal adornment, music, and dancing flourished among these last generations of prehistoric people in the Near East. Although their tools were still of stone, they were already decorating themselves with beads made out of copper. We have pictures on roughly plastered walls of men dancing, beating what appear to be tambourines and waving what are clearly bows. It is apparently a hunting dance among a people who had not yet entirely abandoned the ways of their ancestors.

We may, finally, carry our educated guesses about Neolithic religion beyond what the artifacts reveal. Though the approach is somewhat controversial, we may draw once more upon parallels with later peoples at a similar stage of social evolution. Religion among preurban Native Americans or African agricultural villagers, for instance, tends to be animistic. Animists see all nature—plants, animals, streams, mountains, stars—as living beings, and as in some sense divine. Some of the earliest rituals and hymns of ancient civilizations also invoked, not anthropomorphic gods and goddesses, but spiritual presences within the forces of nature. The sun's warmth, the fertilizing power of rain, the beneficence of the harvested grain itself were worshiped by the people of the first Near Eastern city-states. Thus it

seems quite likely that Neolithic farmers also prayed to the forces of nature, much as their Paleolithic ancestors had sought through the shaman's magic to bring the deer to the hunter's spear.

Women may have played an important part in this religious and ritual activity. Images at Çatal Hüyük show women disguised as vultures engaged in formal rites and rituals. There is some evidence of archaic religions in the Mediterranean region centered on a mother goddess, later shouldered aside when predominantly male-run city-states absorbed the surrounding villages. The priestesses who served this primordial goddess may have presided over annual sacrifices to ensure good harvests and abundant flocks. They may also have been charged with last rites for the dead—the Çatal Hüyük vulture-figures were performing funeral rites—or have been shamans, serving as spirit mediums through whom the dead communicated with the living.

If "Lucy" is the most impressive Paleolithic find thus far, perhaps the most astonishing Neolithic discovery is the "Iceman." Found frozen in an Alpine glacier by German hikers in 1991, this wizened, battered Stone Age man probably died of exposure some 5,300 years ago. The body, "freeze-dried" and covered with snow, was found largely intact, his clothing, tools, and other gear scattered around him. Clad in leather and woven grass, he had flint tools, a copper ax, a bow and arrows, a backpack, and leather boots. He may also have been carrying hot coals for a fire and bits of tree fungus containing "natural antibiotics" as medicine. "The Iceman" apparently fell asleep at his campsite in the Alps a thousand years before the pyramids were built. He is today "the nearest we may ever come to meeting a real person from the Stone Age."[2]

It is a long way from the earliest hominids to the last prehistoric people—the distance from Olduvai Gorge to the Dordogne. A replica of the skull of *Homo habilis* grins at you in the tiny museum on the cliff overlooking Olduvai. Across the rocky ravine outside, shining under the African sun, you can just see the bungalow from which Mary Leakey sets out daily in a Land Rover for her work. Far to the north, in the Dordogne region of southwestern France, a statue of a Cro-Magnon man on a hotel terrace welcomes visitors to the few prehistoric caves still open. From Olduvai to Lascaux is a two-day journey now, a jouncing ride over African roads, a day's flight north, and then the train from Paris in the morning. It took prehistoric humankind five hundred thousand years—a hundred times the length of human history—to make that journey the first time from Africa to western Europe, from *Australopithecus* to us.

The Emergence of Civilization

Who has not felt the fascination of buried cities and lost civilizations? Mounds of earth, swarms of workers, and a handful of people in Bermuda shorts and pith helmets—this is archaeology, as we have come to know it from countless films, television programs, and the *National Geographic Magazine*. And in fact much of what we know about the first civilizations comes from the work of archaeologists like Sir W.T. Flinders Petrie and J.H. Breasted. Men and women of many nations have been excavating ancient Near Eastern sites like Ur and Babylon or Egypt's Karnak and the Valley of the Kings for the past century and a half.

From Mesopotamian times on, furthermore, we begin to have written records of past events: prehistory gives way to recorded history. The invention of

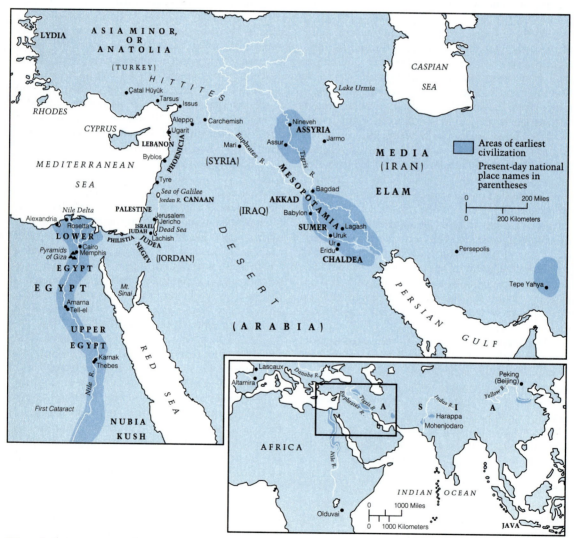

Map 1.1 Early Centers of Civilization

writing was a major achievement of the first civilized peoples, and the written material that survives provides the documentation on which historians have traditionally depended. From the clay tablets of Mesopotamia to Egyptian papyri, ancient tax rolls, religious texts, and the annals of royal conquests tell us much of what the builders of the first cities and empires did, thought, and believed.

From these two types of sources, archaeological and documentary, we may thus conjure up at least a hazy vision of the first civilizations. To make sense out of this evidence, however, more theoretical analysis is also necessary. A key question, for instance, is why did it happen? Why did human beings move out from Neolithic villages and form cities and civilizations in the first place?

Among likely causes of the emergence of the civilized state, theorists stress such factors as population growth, war and conquest, social stratification and exploitation, and charismatic leadership. Population growth was certainly part of the expansion from villages to cities, in the Near East as elsewhere. Denser concentrations of people probably occurred in river valleys as swamps along the rivers dried out, producing rich farmland that could be watered from the rivers themselves. Expanding populations may also have led to feuds between cities over arable land, to wars of conquest, and hence to still larger political units, the first empires. These larger polities also typically came to be dominated by upper classes, an elite who sought to strengthen the state and to control and exploit their neighbors to advance their own interests.

As important as any of these causal factors, finally, were the state-building efforts of such charismatic leaders as Hammurabi of Babylon and Cyrus, the founder of the Persian Empire. As we will see, kings were frequently war leaders, and their victories and conquests not only expanded their realms but strengthened royal government. A militarized aristocracy and a large royal army also undoubtedly added to the power of the central state. But governments also undertook the large-scale flood control and irrigation works that made the ancient river valleys so abundantly productive. The benefits conferred on all by the control of the river further encouraged people to accept the authority of the state. Both the defense and expansion of the realm and the irrigation of the valley by autocratic rulers could make any return to village autonomy very unlikely indeed.

The result of the coming together of all these elements, however, was more than a larger, stronger state: it was the birth of civilization itself. *Civilization* is a word of many meanings. It is sometimes used to describe virtually any culture, from surviving food gatherers to the modern urban-industrial state. Here, however, the term is used in a strictly technical sense. Civilization, in a single somewhat unwieldy sentence, was a new stage of human social and cultural evolution that produced larger and more complex political, economic, and social structures, more elaborate systems of thought and belief, and a broader range of artistic expression than was possible in earlier, simpler societies.

From the beginning, civilization thus defined added many things to human experience. With civilization was born the city and such larger political units as the city-state and the empire. Autocratic rulers usually presided over these states, generally working closely with priests and claiming divine sanction for their rule. Bureaucracy developed with the officials and scribes who administered the state. Social classes emerged, based on the development of private ownership of land and on the diversity of social functions required by a more complex economy.

Another prime characteristic of civilization was a much greater diversity of crafts and skills: the early civilizations introduced metalwork, large-scale building, long-distance trade, and writing. Metals—bronze beginning around 4000 B.C., iron after 1200 B.C.—replaced stone in the manufacture of tools and weapons, and metalworkers were among the first artisans to develop specializations, trade secrets, and handicraft guilds. Local exchange of goods expanded among civilized peoples into long distance trade in such essentials as oil and metals and in such manufactured goods as fabrics and ceramics. Monumental edifices such as city walls, temples, palaces, and tombs provide impressive evidence of the technical virtuosity of early civilizations. And writing—on clay, stone, parchment, and other materials—comes as close as any single skill can to drawing a line between civilized and precivilized peoples.

All these features—the city and the state, autocracy and bureaucracy, social classes and complex crafts and skills—were found in the Eastern civilizations that first appeared in the fourth millennium B.C. They were also characteristics of the Western societies that evolved substantially later, in the first millennium before Christ.

Mesopotamia and the First Cities

Civilization as we know it was born in the curving swath of fertile land that ran from the Persian Gulf around through Syria and Palestine and down the length of Egypt. The new society first arose in Mesopotamia, the wide valley running northwest from the head of the gulf in what is today Iraq. The fact that the valley was watered by two rivers, the Tigris and the Euphrates, led the ancient Greeks to give this civilization the descriptive name, *Mesopotamia,* "the land between the rivers." This ancient river valley provided fertile soil for agriculture and the basis for a city-based society far more complex than the agricultural villages that had preceded it.

The City-States of Sumer

The Tigris and Euphrates rivers rise in the mountains of Turkey and flow southeast, through Iraq, to the head of the Persian Gulf. Before human beings attempted to control them, the two rivers produced erratic and destructive flooding, ending in a plain of reedy swamps and pools at their juncture near the gulf. Once tamed by human works, however, the waters of the two rivers began to turn the wide flat valley between them into enormously productive agricultural land.

The great rivers had other values for those who mastered them. As rafts and then oar-driven boats and sailboats were invented, the rivers became arteries of trade and communication, linking the cities of Mesopotamia together. The rivers thus shaped the lives of all who lived along their banks, creating over centuries a unified culture, from the shores of the Persian Gulf to the Anatolian uplands more than 500 miles to the northwest.

Stone Age agricultural villages had developed as early as 8000 B.C. in the grassy uplands of northern Mesopotamia, in an area known as the Syrian steppe. Here were rain enough for farming, wild plant and animal food to fall back on as needed, and rivers that allowed for some tentative experimentation in irrigation when the rains failed. Between 5000 and 4000 B.C., some of these Neolithic farmers moved on down the rivers into the region of Sumeria, or Sumer, the southern portion of the land of the two rivers, taking with them grains and flocks of sheep and goats. Here they could harvest dates from the palm trees and spear fish in the marshes. Here too a little diking and draining produced rich soil, bountiful crops of wheat and barley, and a swelling population. And here in ancient Sumer the first cities in the world—Ur and Uruk, Eridu and Lagash and Akkad—gradually took shape.

Specialization of labor developed as the villagers built temples to offer thanks to the gods for their prosperity. That portion of the villagers' produce intended for the gods was channeled by priests to people who, freed of agricultural labor, began to specialize in craftwork. One of the first technological breakthroughs that resulted from this specialization of labor was the production of bronze. This alloy of copper and tin proved hard enough to replace stone in tools, weapons, and other useful objects. Thus, about 4000 B.C., the Stone Age gave way to the Bronze Age, during which craftworkers began to produce beautiful jewelry, fabrics, and other luxury goods. Some of these products, furthermore, went to traders, often agents of the temples. This new class of merchants exchanged these goods with other peoples for such basic raw materials as wood and building stone, for Sumer's only natural resources were rich soil and plenty of water.

As opportunities for trade grew, people developed new and better methods of transportation. At first, merchants used mules and other beasts of burden to carry their goods. The invention of the wheel, either in Sumeria or earlier, in Neolithic times, enabled people to construct carts that could carry much greater loads. Traders also probably constructed crude rafts or early boats of reeds or inflated bladders, though the Nile would be the first real home of larger vessels propelled by sails.

It was around the temples of Mesopotamia that the first cities emerged about 3500 B.C. These growing communities of priests, artisans, and traders, including both their homes and places of work and worship, were protected by high walls. Some cities had popular assemblies dominated by groups of elders, a legacy from the agricultural village. City assemblies, however, served in a primarily judicial function; they had little real political power. For centuries, it was the priests, as servants of the gods, who were the most powerful element in the typical city.

Gradually, however, city governors, usually successful war leaders, overshadowed their rivals and assumed the leadership of the cities. Attacks by nomads from the Arabian desert or the Syrian steppe to the west, or from the mountains of Iran to the east, strengthened the authority of these military leaders.

Gods of ancient Sumer, the oldest of all human civilizations. When Sumerian armies captured a neighboring city-state, they triumphantly carried off such clay representations of their enemies' gods into "captivity."

In time, the city governors made their power hereditary and announced that they were the chief stewards of the gods on earth. These new rulers took the title of *lugal* (literally "big man") and became the first kings in history.

The cities lugals governed dominated the surrounding villages both politically and economically. The result was a combination of metropolitan center and agrarian hinterland called the city-state. By 3000 B.C., small states of this type were established across both Sumer and Akkad, in the central region of the Mesopotamian valley. There were perhaps fifteen or twenty such city-states, each with its urban core and agricultural hinterland. Most had populations of between twenty and thirty thousand people, and few were more than a hundred square miles in extent, the size of a modern county.

A developed Mesopotamian city was laid out on a rectangular plan, with high walls, watchtowers, and tall gates. Its distinctive stepped pyramids called *ziggurats,* each crowned with a shrine to a god or goddess, dominated temple complexes and threw long shadows over the city walls and the land beyond. The sprawling royal palaces, built around a series of courtyards, included impressive throne rooms and many private chambers, thick walled, dim, and cool. Wealthy nobles and merchants lived in similarly elaborate homes. Broad avenues intended for ceremonial processions bisected the metropolis. Most streets, however, were narrow winding lanes, and most houses were little more than cubicles, crammed as close together as the citizens of medieval Baghdad or modern Cairo.

Beyond the city walls, the tiny farming villages along the rivers were now enmeshed in a network of dikes, canals, and irrigation ditches. Wheat and barley, date palms and fruit trees stood tall against the rainless blue sky. On the road, a creaking two-wheeled cart or a caravan of donkeys laden with goods might pass. On the river, one might see a raft with a flapping sail. More rarely, there might be soldiers with long spears, or a nobleman borne in a sedan chair on the shoulders of his servants. This was the physical reality of early civilization as archaeologists have been able to reconstruct it. Unraveling the political realities of the fourth and third millennia before Christ, however, is another and more difficult problem.

The Empires of Ur and Babylon

The names of city-states and kings filter down to us across the centuries, inscribed on stone or incised in clay. Although it is difficult to place people and events with precision in so distant a past, we do know that cities like Uruk and Lagash and Ur rose in the early Sumerian centuries, around 3000 B.C.

We even have the likenesses of some of the long forgotten kings of these cities, and records of the deeds of which they were proudest. There is, for instance, a broken bronze head that may represent the hawklike face of Sargon of Akkad, history's first great conqueror. Sargon, around 2300 B.C., led his Semitic peoples down from the central reaches of the Tigris and Euphrates rivers into the Sumerian cities, where they established a short-lived Akkadian rule over the southern plain. There are stubby, round-faced statues of Gudea of Lagash, who imposed his authority on many of his Sumerian neighbors sometime around 2100 B.C. And we have fragments of a law code promulgated by Shulgi of ancient Ur about the year 2000 B.C.

The much excavated city of Ur seems to have been a splendid example of the developed Mesopotamian city-state. The largest of the early Sumerian cities, Ur had an elaborate system of dikes and canals that irrigated the surrounding fields. The merchants of Ur traded northward up the rivers and eastward, across the Arabian Sea, with other city-states that had sprung up along the Indus River in what is today Pakistan. The kings of Ur enforced laws, collected taxes, and around 2000 B.C. exercised a brief hegemony over the surrounding Sumerian cities.

Hammurabi of Babylon (r. 1792–1750 B.C.), however, has over the centuries become the most famous of all Mesopotamian kings. He was the ruler of the Amorites—like the Akkadians, a Semitic people—who had established themselves at Babylon, in central Mesopotamia, where they were in a position to dominate the entire valley between the two rivers. The records we have of Hammurabi's reign illustrate the functioning of the developed Mesopotamian monarchy at its best.

We have royal correspondence on clay tablets that shows Hammurabi supervising his scribes, a small but recognizable government bureaucracy. His public inscriptions declare that in addition to meting out royal justice and defending the state he built roads and kept up the all-important system of irrigation canals. But the great Babylonian ruler is best known for his code of almost three hundred laws—the Code of Hammurabi.

Hammurabi's Code has survived in the form in which he presented it to his people, inscribed on a stele (a stone slab or pillar) crowned with carvings of the king himself and of the god in whose name he claimed to speak. The legal principles thus set out included some very brutal punishments clearly aimed at retribution rather than reform. The code also emphasized class differences, prescribing one punishment for a noble, another for a commoner, and a third for slaves. Women and men of the same class, on the other hand, tended to get the same legal treatment.

But Hammurabi's Code meant more than institutionalized vengeance and rigid social hierarchy. It incorporated a sense of justice and tried to make the punishment fit the crime. Women had independent legal standing, and the laws even gave them rights against their husbands (see box, "Women and the Law of Hammurabi"). There were economic regulations too, dealing with business contracts, debt, minimum wages, and irrigation practices. Many of these regulations were clearly built on centuries-old Mesopotamian traditions. For some historians, however, the very fact that this ancient law code was displayed in a public place, rather than remaining the special concern of magistrates or priests, is evidence that Hammurabi was a genuine reformer. There may be at least a modicum of truth in the Babylonian king's summation of his own achievements: "I promoted the welfare of the land . . . I made the peoples to rest in friendly habitations. . . . I have governed them in peace; I have sheltered them in my strength."[3]

The Assyrian Empire

An Assyrian wall panel excavated from the palace of the legendary conqueror Sennacherib at Nineveh in northern Mesopotamia might appear uninteresting at first, even boring—a jumble of flat stylized figures carved in stone. Look more closely at this depiction of the Assyrian assault on the walled city of Lachish in 701 B.C., however, and you may pick out some vivid details: protruding cheekbones, heavy brows, jutting curly beards, and long arrows slanting up toward the walls of the city. Below are the results of the battle: hapless prisoners streaming in a long line toward exile—parents and children, camels and oxen and two-wheeled carts. Sennacherib (r. 705–682 B.C.), himself

THE RULERS AND THE RULED
Women and the Law of Hammurabi

The Babylonian Code of Hammurabi sheds some light on the status of women in one of the earliest civilizations. In this set of laws, which dates from about 2000 B.C., a number of regulations specifically relate the behaviors of men and women to each other. Note that although punishment for infractions of the moral code by women could be very harsh, a woman's oath had weight at law, and divorce seems to have been almost as easy for women as for men. What do you deduce from the radically different punishments decreed for the two types of incest described in rules 154 and 157?

129. If the wife of a seignior [a noble, or lord] has been caught while lying with another man, they shall bind them and throw them into the water. If the husband of the woman wishes to spare his wife, then the king in turn may spare his subject.

131. If a seignior's wife was accused by her husband, but she was not caught while lying with another man, she shall make affirmation by god and return to her house.

138. If a seignior wishes to divorce his wife who did not bear him children, he shall give her money to the full amount of her marriage-price and he shall also make good to her the dowry which she brought from her father's house and then he may divorce her.

142. If a woman so hated her husband that she has declared, "You may not have me," her record shall be investigated at her city council; and if she was careful and was not at fault, even though her husband has been going out and disparaging her greatly, that woman, without incurring any blame at all, may take her dowry and go off to her father's house.

154. If a seignior has had intercourse with his daughter, they shall make that seignior leave the city.

157. If a seignior has lain in the bosom of his mother after the death of his father, they shall burn both of them.

Source: *The Code of Hammurabi*, trans. J. Mook, in *The Ancient Near East: An Anthology of Texts and Pictures*, ed. J. B. Pritchard, (Princeton, N.J.: Princeton University Press, 1958), 139.

watches the fall of the city from a three-step throne, surrounded by his bodyguards, his war chariot ready at hand.

The center of Mesopotamian power moved slowly up the two rivers, from Sumer in the southeast to Babylon in central Mesopotamia and finally to Assyria, in the hilly northwestern reaches of the valley of the two rivers. From their capital at Nineveh, within marching distance of the eastern Mediterranean, the Assyrians were well situated to strike at the other city-states and kingdoms that had emerged in the Near East and North Africa by this time. The Assyrian rulers thus built an empire that reached well beyond the confines of Mesopotamia early in the first millennium B.C.

During the period of greatest Assyrian power, from 900 to 600 B.C., war leaders like Sargon II (r. 722–706 B.C.) and Ashurbanipal (r. 668–627 B.C.) were the terror of their Near Eastern neighbors. These aggressive rulers made annual military campaigns a primary activity of the state. To acquire the rich booty depicted by their wall sculptures, to glorify their chief god Ashur, and perhaps to erect a wall of fear that would keep their enemies at bay, the Assyrian kings marched out each year to fight.

From Babylon around to Egypt, Assyrian power grew. The Assyrian campaigns of the ninth century B.C. were apparently little more than raiding expeditions. In the eighth and seventh centuries B.C., however, incessant fighting imposed a semipermanent Assyrian suzerainty over a curving band of cities, farms, and grazing land around the southeastern corner of the Mediterranean. Governors and garrisons imposed a loose but centralized administrative system supervised by the "King of the World" in Nineveh. The most famous Assyrian monarchs were also great builders: Sennacherib built a famous aqueduct, and Ashurbanipal constructed a library containing more than twenty thousand clay tablets dealing with learned subjects from history to astronomy. It is generally agreed that these rulers brought city-state civilization to northern Mesopotamia. They also probably contributed to the painful process of accustoming the Near East as a whole to a larger imperial authority—a valuable lesson, in view of the empires to come.

Among contemporaries, however, it was the pain that was remembered. The militaristic Assyrians littered their path through history with flaming cities, deported populations, and the spectacle of leading citizens impaled, flayed, or burned alive in front of their own shattered city gates. There was no

the celebrated "hanging gardens," a terraced ziggurat-style royal park considered one of the wonders of the ancient world.

High Culture Between the Rivers

We know more about the ancient Mesopotamians, however, than the physical appearance of their cities and the names and deeds of a scattering of kings. From the ruins of this oldest of civilizations, archaeologists and historians have sifted the evidence of religious beliefs, scientific discoveries, architecture, art, and literature—the cultural achievements, in short, of this vanished civilization.

Mesopotamian religion, like that of most early civilizations, was polytheistic. The people of the Mesopotamian city-states worshiped such divinities as Enlil, "lord wind," the chief divinity of ancient Sumer; Anu, the god of the sky; Ninhursag, "lady of the mountain"; Enki, lord of the waters; and Ishtar, the "queen of heaven" and goddess of war, identified with the planet Venus. Over centuries, individual divinities acquired broader religious meanings. Thus Ishtar, originally a goddess of Semitic invaders, blended with the Sumerian goddess of love, Inanna, and came to preside over love, fertility, and creative power. Each city-state had its own patron divinity, and when one city triumphed over the others, its principal god was soon recognized as chief among the heavenly host. Thus the Assyrian sun god, Assur, enjoyed preeminence during the Assyrian ascendency, as did Marduk, the patron god of Babylon, during the New Babylonian Empire.

Besides the great gods and goddesses, there were large numbers of spirits, demons, and other supernatural entities to be placated, consulted, and feared. Particularly in hard times, when floods or wars devastated the land, people flocked to their temples, consulted astrologers and diviners, and went in terror of demonic forces. Even in the best of times, Mesopotamians would not embark on a commercial venture or a military campaign, shape a brick, or bring forth a child without consultation with stargazers or prayers to the gods.

Yet Mesopotamians were also scientific observers of the heavens, creative mathematicians, and the inventors of the first developed system of writing. The ancient Sumerians were the first people we know to map the night sky, and the Babylonians were as celebrated for their astronomical knowledge as for their alleged astrological insights. They charted

It is traditional to call this bronze head Sargon of Akkad, history's first empire-builder, although we do not know that this casting of an Akkadian ruler is actually Sargon. The hawk-like visage and intricately dressed beard do give this face an aura of power, perhaps even menace.

weeping when, in 612 B.C., an alliance of rival powers finally overwhelmed Assyria, and Nineveh itself was sacked and burned.

Chief among those who brought Assyria down was the last Mesopotamian power to rule the Tigris-Euphrates valley: the New Babylonian, or Chaldean, Empire. Flourishing briefly during the late seventh and the first half of the sixth century B.C., this second Babylonian hegemony extended almost as far as the Assyrian Empire had, around the Fertile Crescent through Syria and Palestine to the frontiers of Egypt. The greatest ruler of the New Babylonian Empire, Nebuchadnezzar II (r. 604–562 B.C.), defeated the Egyptians at Carchemish, captured Jerusalem, and carried the Jews into their Babylonian captivity. He built and refurbished many temples, raised the famous walls of Babylon, and constructed

the constellations of the zodiac, noted the movement of the planets, and developed a calendar and a water clock to measure time. The Mesopotamian peoples invented a number system based on multiples of six and twelve and were the first to divide the circle into 360 degrees and the hour into sixty minutes, mathematical conventions now accepted around the world. Most important, about 4000 B.C. the Sumerians developed the first true system of writing, the cuneiform ("wedge-shaped") script with which they wrote on clay.

Writing was not invented for literary purposes. Oral literature, sung by bards, told by storytellers, or recited as part of temple liturgy, long predated the invention of writing. In fact, the scribes who developed the first form of writing had nothing more artistic in mind than counting sheep. Sheep, cattle, measures of grain, and jars of oil changed hands repeatedly through sale, taxation, the collection of "temple fifths," and in other ways. Writing was originally a simple tally system for recording these transactions. It began with a quick picture of a sheep, followed by a mark for each animal that passed through the gate. As civilization grew more complex and the necessary records more complicated, the number of symbols grew. The little pictures became a few conventional strokes that caught the essence of the idea: each symbol represented a thing. To these symbols were soon added characters that stood for the sounds of syllables in spoken Sumerian. Both symbols of things and symbols of sounds could then be combined to represent longer words. It is easy to see why such a system required study at a special school.

Although it was the temple, the palace, and the bazaar that utilized writing first, in time cuneiform script did begin to be used to record early types of literature. Some of these ancient Mesopotamian literary forms were also found later in the Bible. For example, Mesopotamian proverbs foreshadow those attributed to King Solomon, Mesopotamian songs find an echo in Hebrew psalms, and there are hero tales in the writings of both peoples. Not surprisingly, the Mesopotamians, who lived in fear of river flooding, produced a flood story comparable to that of the Bible's Noah. And among the earliest pieces of literature in the world that can be attributed to a known author is a hymn to the goddess Inanna, ascribed to the poet Enheduana, the daughter of Sargon of Akkad.

The most famous Mesopotamian hero tale, however, is more often compared to the myths of the Greeks and Romans than to biblical accounts. In the *Epic of Gilgamesh* a "Mesopotamian Hercules" kills monsters, defies the powerful goddess Ishtar, and finally sets out for the end of the world in search of the secret of eternal life. Gilgamesh fails in his quest, for he is mortal and must die; but his heroic failure remains a powerful example of human courage in the face of an inexorable fate.

Egypt and the Growth of Centralized Monarchy

West of Mesopotamia, at the northeastern corner of Africa, lay the second great center of ancient Near Eastern civilization: Egypt. In Egypt, however, social evolution beyond the village level produced not a culture of separate city-states but a strongly centralized monarchy. Under the autocratic rule of the kings who would come to be called *pharaohs,* the land of the Nile thus became the home of a relatively united people shortly after 3000 B.C.

A Kingdom Emerges Along the Nile

Like Mesopotamia, Egypt grew and flourished in a fertile river valley. The Nile valley, however, provided an even more ideal environment for the rise of a great civilization. Even without much human improvement, the Nile flooded evenly, coating the land with a rich silt accumulated over its long journey north from the lakes of central Africa. Further improved by the irrigation works of the pharaohs, the great river produced two crops a year and made Egypt the breadbasket of the Mediterranean world down to Roman times. (For an idea of the great importance of the Nile to the people of its valley, see the box titled "A Hymn to the Nile, from Whom All Blessings Flow.")

The Nile valley also differed from the valley created by the Tigris and Euphrates in its configuration: it was not wide and flat but long and narrow. For most of the 750 miles of its course from the waterfalls of the first cataract to the Mediterranean, the habitable valley was seldom more than 10 miles wide. The Nile Delta, where the river broke into many mouths as it reaches the sea, did broaden out into a fan-shaped marshy area like that of Sumer. The rest of ancient Egypt, however, wound like a serpent between the Libyan desert to the west and the Arabian desert to the east. The crushing heat, the almost total lack of water or vegetation in these neighboring "red lands" made the fertile "black lands" along the river all the more precious to the Egyptians.

The narrowness of the valley and its total dependence on the Nile discouraged the development of separate centers of political power like the Mesopotamian cities. Villages lay close together all along the river, all within easy reach of the power of the ruler. There was little need for cities to develop as independent commercial centers because, at least in early times, this most fortunate of lands needed little from abroad. Thus because there were neither political nor economic reasons for the emergence of urban centers, Egypt was able to move beyond the city-state and develop a centralized monarchy larger and more long lasting than anything in the Near East.

In Egypt as in Mesopotamia, archaeology has taught us most of what we know about early development. Shortly after Neolithic farmers settled in Mesopotamia, others drifted into the Nile valley. Agricultural villagers from the Sudan and inner Africa settled the upper reaches of the river, while Mediterranean peoples established themselves in the delta. Small territorial units comprising several villages developed along the river, each probably dominated by its priests and united by allegiance to a totemic animal with which the people felt a special kinship. There was also some loyalty to the "two lands," the two main geographical regions of the country as a whole: Lower Egypt, meaning the broad delta area, and Upper Egypt, the long narrow valley to the south. Cultural and social evolution along the Nile proceeded as it had along the Tigris and Euphrates. And by approximately 3150 B.C., after a long interregional struggle, Menes, a prince of Upper Egypt, had conquered Lower Egypt, established his capital at Memphis in the delta, and become the first king of a united country.

Egypt remained a unified nation for most of the next three thousand years. The ancient territorial units became administrative districts, and the kings of Upper and Lower Egypt came in later centuries to be called by the more familiar title of *pharaoh*. Thirty-one dynasties of pharaohs—three successive historical *Kingdoms* called Old, Middle, and New—ruled the valley of the Nile. Traditionally, the Old Kingdom is said to have lasted from approximately 2700 to 2200 B.C., the Middle Kingdom from 2050 to 1800, and the height of the New Kingdom and the Egyptian Empire from 1570 to about 1100 B.C.

A long decline characterized most of the next one thousand years. There were breakdowns in order, notably during the intermediate periods between the Kingdoms. There were foreign invaders, especially after 1000 B.C., who conquered and ruled the land. But until Egypt became a province of the Roman Empire in 30 B.C. the kingdom of the Nile remained the most favored of nations and Egyptians,

THE HUMAN SPIRIT

A Hymn to the Nile, from Whom All Blessings Flow

The hymn reproduced here was probably sung at ancient Thebes as part of the religious ceremonies held to greet the annual flooding of the Nile. This expression of veneration for the great river illustrates several aspects of the religious sensibility of the ancient Near East. Can you see evidence of worship of the forces of nature here? Do you detect a tendency to bargain with anthropomorphically conceived divinities, offering sacrifices for services rendered, and an awareness of the crucial role the river played in the lives of all the people?

Praise to thee, O Nile, that issueth from the earth, and cometh to nourish Egypt.... That watereth the meadows, he that Re hath created to nourish all cattle. That giveth drink to the desert places.... If he be niggardly the whole land is in terror and great and small lament.... When he riseth, the land is in exultation and every body is in joy. All jaws begin to laugh and every tooth is revealed.

He that bringeth victuals and is rich in food, that createth all that is good. The revered, sweet-smelling.... That createth herbage for the cattle, and giveth sacrifice to every god, be he in the underworld, in heaven, or upon earth. ... That filleth the storehouses, and maketh wide the granaries, that giveth things to the poor.

When the Nile floodeth, offering is made to thee, cattle are slaughtered for thee, a great oblation is made for thee. Birds are fattened for thee, antelopes are hunted for thee in the desert. Good is recompensed unto thee.

Source: Adolph Erman, *The Literature of the Ancient Egyptians*, trans. A. M. Blackman (London: Methuen, 1927), 146.

in the eyes of their neighbors, the most fortunate of peoples.

Old Kingdom Egypt: The Pyramid Builders

The basic pattern of Egyptian civilization was established during the Old Kingdom dynasties that followed Menes. The Old Kingdom pharaohs were the pyramid builders, and their age was a kind of golden age of peace, plenty, and social justice, at least according to Egyptians of later centuries.

The Egyptians went the Mesopotamians one better in the crucial matter of divinely sanctioned rule. Mesopotamian rulers claimed to be stewards or bailiffs of the gods, but pharaohs were themselves gods. Each pharaoh was in fact identified with more than one Egyptian divinity. Born the son of Re, the all-powerful sun, the pharaoh was also an incarnation of the sky-god Horus and in death would be united with Osiris, the divine king of the underworld.

With such divine connections, pharaohs could claim truly awesome powers. The pharaohs' word was law to all their people, and their will was carried out by a large bureaucracy of trained scribes who collected taxes, supervised the irrigation system, exercised the royal monopoly of foreign trade, organized and equipped the royal armies, and built enormous public works, including royal palaces, temples, and tombs. The pharaohs themselves performed religious ceremonies that were believed to cause the Nile to flood on time and to ensure peace and order. Like Mesopotamian rulers, the pharaohs redistributed much of the wealth of the land through gifts to nobles and officials and through payments to artisans, builders, and others.

The power of Egypt's god-kings was so great that, at least in Old Kingdom times, the development of other potentially important segments of society was significantly stunted. In these early centuries, the organized priesthoods of Re and other gods were properly subservient to the god who walked among them. The small merchant class had little prominence or social prestige, since the lucrative long-distance trade was run by scribal bureaucrats. The largest structures in Egypt were the royal

The pyramids of Giza loom massively above the desert outside of Cairo. The largest of these gigantic tombs was built more than four thousand years ago for the pharaoh Khufu, a great ruler of the Old Kingdom.

pyramid tombs built by pharaohs Khufu, Khafre, and Menkaure at Giza between 2600 and 2500 B.C. And the highest ambition of the greatest officials and most noble princes in the land was to merit a tomb in the shadow of the pharaoh's.

It was as autocratic a society, in short, as any in ancient history. But like Hammurabi's Babylon, it was not a society without a sense of justice and human decency. Since the pharaoh's word itself was law, there was no need for codes like Hammurabi's. But the pharaoh was expected to rule according to the principles of *ma'at*, a combination of social justice, order, and truth that added up to what the Egyptians saw as righteousness. If individual kings fell short of this social ideal, so have rulers in many times and lands. And there was always another pharaoh coming, a new son of Re to bring health and vigor once more to the land and its people.

Between the pharaohs and their hierarchy of power on the one hand and the masses they ruled on the other, there were intermediate social ranks. Skilled artisans worked in bronze, copper, and the precious metals, as well as some of the hardest stones, to produce tools, weapons, and elegant luxury goods. There were workers in cloth, ceramics, wood, and other basic materials. But no one in these middle ranks would dream of aspiring to even a modest tomb in the shadow of the god-king's.

Egyptian peasants, like their distant descendants the *fellaheen* who till the soil today, lived a life of productive toil. Some authorities see them as little better than serfs on the lands of nobles or temples, or forced laborers under the eyes of royal overseers. They did owe large chunks of their produce to the state, and, even more than Mesopotamian peasants, gave much labor to irrigation works or to building temples and future tombs for reigning pharaohs. On the other hand, labor on public works seems to have been paid, and hours were sensibly limited, given the blistering heat of the Egyptian sun.

Women also enjoyed more independent status than they did in some later societies. Female members of the royal family had important administrative duties; other women had leading positions in temple cults. Further down the social scale, some women practiced such skilled trades as textile manufacturing or served as priestesses in the temples, while others worked beside men in the fields. From the Old Kingdom to the end of Egyptian history, women had legal and property rights equal to men's. Daughters could inherit just as sons could, and women were paid equally for equal work. They were

even called up for compulsory labor on government works just as male peasants were, evidence that women were considered as autonomous persons, not as dependents of men.

Middle Kingdom Egypt: The Transition

Toward the end of the third millennium B.C.— around 2200—this ordered system began to crumble. The so-called First Intermediate Period was perhaps triggered by an unprecedented stretch of low Niles that left the black lands unwatered and the granaries empty. Feuds within the ruling dynasty weakened the central government, and provincial governors grew rebellious. Foreign tribes drifted in from Palestine and from Syria further to the north, sometimes challenging local authorities. Law and order broke down, and the people complained of violence, poverty, and official oppression.

After two troubled centuries, however, the First Intermediate Period ended with the reestablishment of the pharaohs' authority. As in the days of Menes, it was a dynasty from Upper Egypt that swept down the length of the river to power. Amenemhet I (1991–1962 B.C.) and his successors of the twelfth dynasty moved the capital upriver from Memphis to Thebes, where the priests of the new sun god, Amen, supported their bid for power. The result was what later scholars have called the Middle Kingdom, which lasted from around 2050 to shortly after 1800 B.C.

The pharaohs of the Middle Kingdom do not seem to have enjoyed the unquestioning reverence that the people had apparently felt for the rulers of the Old Kingdom. Nobles now exercised a good deal of independent regional power. Scribes in the bureaucracy could also become powerful, rising to eminence on the basis of the mastery of the sacred art of writing, administrative efficiency, or political skill. To compensate for the decline in reverence for the monarchy, however, there seems to have been an enhanced sense of justice and public welfare. Officials were exhorted to govern fairly, to reject bribes, and to care for the people according to the ancient principle of *ma'at*. The pharaohs themselves were often depicted in sculpture with brows furrowed with care for their subjects.

The Egyptians were an intensely conservative people, far more given to looking backward to past glories than forward to the future. The Middle Kingdom, however, revealed new tendencies that, in retrospect, clearly pointed to a greatness to come. In both military and commercial affairs, the pharaohs of the period around 2000 B.C. presaged the vaster achievements of the New Kingdom of the next millennium.

One hears more of the pharaoh's armies in the Middle Kingdom period, and foreign trade expanded. The Egyptians fought both their African neighbors to the south and the Semitic peoples of Palestine. As early as the Old Kingdom, furthermore, Egyptians had carried the art of shipbuilding beyond the rafts and reed boats of the earliest centuries of civilization to plank-built wooden sailing ships. During the Middle Kingdom, they sailed these vessels out of the Nile and around the eastern Mediterranean. Egyptians not only developed the copper mines of the neighboring Sinai area but traded with the emerging culture of the island of Crete, where— as we will see in the next chapter—the seeds of Western civilization were being planted by the seagoing Minoans. What gave the Middle Kingdom its distinctive character was this foreshadowing of a more expansive era—of empire building, far-reaching trade, and foreign conquest.

New Kingdom Egypt and the Egyptian Empire

Shortly after 1800 B.C., the Middle Kingdom collapsed as the Old Kingdom had, in a welter of weak government and rebellious nobles and governors. The domestic problems of the Second Intermediate Period that followed were compounded by a wave of intrusions by a nomadic Near Eastern people called the Hyksos. Equipped with fast war chariots and bronze weapons, the Hyksos seized power in the delta and ruled much of the country for a century. They were expelled around 1600 B.C., once again by an aggressive princely house from Upper Egypt led by the brothers Kamose and Ahmose, the younger of whom pursued the Hyksos all the way back to their base of support in Palestine.

The Egyptian victory gave the people of the Nile a new taste for foreign wars and conquests. A succession of militaristic pharaohs, including Thutmose III (r. 1469–1436 B.C.) and Ramses II (r. 1290–1224 B.C.), assembled a formidable empire for the New Kingdom. In so doing, they also created a new public image for the pharaohs of Egypt: the god-king as warrior, crushing his foes under the churning wheels of his chariot.

A militarized nobility eager for glory, powerful priesthoods pleased at the prestige accumulating to their victorious gods, and a nation dazzled by success and greedy for booty all supported the ambitions of the pharaohs. Equipped with light war chariots, bows, and bronze swords modeled on those of the Hyksos, the armies of Thutmose III repeatedly defeated other peoples northward through Palestine and on into northern Mesopotamia. Thutmose also pushed south of the Nile's first cataract into the land of the Nubians, Egypt's nearest African neighbors, and conquered the Kingdom of Kush, today's Sudan. In the north, Ramses II fought the iron-armed Hittites to a standstill at Kadesh and later divided Syria with them. At its height, the Egyptian Empire encompassed Nubia and Kush, Palestine, Syria, and the northern reaches of the Euphrates. "I made the boundaries of Egypt as far as . . . the sun encircles," boasted one royal conqueror. "I made Egypt the superior of every land."[4]

Foreign trade also expanded as the Egyptian Empire grew. The pharaohs dispatched caravans and fleets of ships to bring back copper from Sinai, gold from Nubia, and exotic animals from the land of Punt far down the Red Sea. Slaves and tribute poured in from the empire, and the divine rulers and their nobles lived luxurious lives in brightly decorated palaces and country estates.

One of the most aggressive traders among the pharaohs was Hatshepsut (r. 1503–1482 B.C.), the only woman ever to govern the New Kingdom Empire in her own right. Thrusting her way to power as daughter of one pharaoh and widow of another, Hatshepsut appointed talented, ambitious newcomers to high office, encouraged foreign commerce, and was a great builder of public monuments. The trading expedition she dispatched to Punt was described admiringly by the chroniclers. There were more victories and more conquests to come, but Egypt was never wealthier and more splendid than under its great queen Hatshepsut.

Another colorful ruler of the New Kingdom was Akhenaton (r. 1379–1362 B.C.), the strange "heretic pharaoh." In an almost universally polytheistic world, Akhenaton became a monotheist, a believer in an obscure sun god called Aton. Gripped by the zeal of a convert, he denied the existence of all the other gods and sought to replace their temples, cults, and priesthoods with the worship of Aton. He prayed in open-roofed temples to the one god, visualized not in human or animal form, but as the sun disk itself as it soared over Egypt each day.

To escape the influence of the powerful priests of Amen-Re, Akhenaton abandoned Thebes for a new city, built in the desert near what is today Amarna, which he intended as the center of his new cult. Here there flourished for a brief time a new, more human and realistic style of art, the Amarna school. Among the monuments of this style are convincing sculptures of Akhenaton's own ungainly, large-featured face and lovely likenesses of his swan-necked queen, Nefertiti, who played an important part in the new religion.

Even a pharaoh, however, could not crush so powerful an establishment as the ancient priesthoods of Egypt. After the heretic pharaoh's death, it was Aton's temples that were destroyed and Akhenaton's name that was struck from the monuments and the lists of kings. Perhaps the strangest fate, however, was reserved for Akhenaton's hapless young heir, Tutankhamen (r. c. 1361–1351 B.C.). Abandoning Amarna and returning to Thebes, Tutankhamen died there while still in his teens, a thoroughly insignificant pharaoh. More than three thousand years later, the 1922 discovery of King Tut's tomb, crammed with exquisitely crafted artifacts, gave the world its most dazzling glimpse of the vanished splendor of the pharaohs.

Egypt's imperial greatness was gone by 1000 B.C. During the centuries that followed, Egypt, weakened by feuds between pharaohs and priests, became itself the victim of a series of foreign conquerors. The African kings of Kush, upriver in the Sudan, had ancient cultural ties with Egypt and strove to preserve its traditions. Most of these invaders, however, were foreign foes, including the Assyrians, already discussed, the Persians, to be surveyed shortly, and such later Western invaders as the Macedonians of Alexander the Great and the Romans of Julius Caesar.

Egyptian political greatness thus waned after 1000 B.C. Egyptian civilization, however, remained a beacon to later peoples, including the founders of Western civilization, the ancient Greeks.

The Culture of the Nile

The Egyptians shared the common polytheism of most early peoples. Some of their divinities were animals—cats, cows, crocodiles, hippopotamuses, hawks—creatures familiar in their land, perhaps originally the totemic animals of the villagers along the river. The chief Egyptian gods, however, were often

anthropomorphic, human in shape, though they frequently retained animal heads.

The Egyptian pantheon served the human and political needs of ancient Egypt. A sun god—first Re, then Amen, and more briefly Aton—occupied the chief place. Osiris, ruler of the spirits of the dead who dwelt in the underworld, was the object of special devotion among Egyptians, who believed profoundly in life after death. Osiris's divine queen, Isis, who was believed to have brought her husband back from the dead after his murder by the evil god Set, gave hope of eternal life to growing numbers of Egyptians. Horus, the hawk-shaped sky god, was the incarnation of the living pharaoh, who was identified after death with the divine Osiris as king of the underworld. Anubis, the jackal-headed god of the graveyard, weighed the souls of the dead before Osiris and cast them into the waiting jaws of the crocodile-headed Heart Eater if they were found wanting.

Awareness of death occupied a central place in the worldview of the Egyptians. They developed the craft of mummification in order to preserve the body for the use of the soul, or *ka*, after death. The famous Egyptian *Book of the Dead* detailed the progress of the spirit through the underworld and described the responses that the soul should properly make to all the deities encountered along the way. Wealthy or powerful Egyptians filled their tombs with sometimes exquisite objects, from statuettes of servants to life-size chariots, for their use after they had departed. The walls of tomb passages and grave chambers were brightly painted with pictures of earthly pleasures, from banqueting to hunting, that the dead might hope to enjoy again in the other world. Even the drinking songs of the Egyptians often expressed a related theme:

> Put song and music before thee
> Behind thee all evil things
> And remember thou only joy
> Till comes that day of mooring
> At the land that loveth silence.[5]

Another central quality of Egyptian art is a profound conservatism. Egypt's formal writing system of hieroglyphics, inspired in part by Mesopotamian cuneiform, differed in preserving many of its pictorial elements unchanged for thousands of years. Egyptian "wisdom literature" ran heavily to proverbs on the virtues of tradition and obedience and encouraged the ambitious to emulate the wise men and famous scribes who had gone before. Egyptian

With this pose, Pharaoh Menkaure and his queen, Khameremebty, set a tradition that other rulers followed for centuries. What evidence do you see that this royal pair of the Old Kingdom may have been quite fond of one another? [Mycerinus (Greek version of pharoah's name) and Wife (Queen), 4th Dynasty, Old Kingdom, Slate. Courtesy Museum of Fine Arts, Boston]

painting followed the same formal rules century after century, depicting the human figure in profile with the eyes and shoulders shown frontally. Perhaps most strikingly, statues of pharaohs sitting with feet planted on the ground, hands resting on their knees, and wearing the traditional false beard and ancient crown of Upper and Lower Egypt look pretty much alike down the dynasties. Only during the radical

Amarna period of the New Kingdom, mentioned earlier, was some effort made to capture the individuality of a ruler.

A third quality was monumentality, a combination of grand scale and simplicity that has made Egyptian architecture as awesome to modern as to ancient visitors. The 80-foot columns of the great hall of the temple at Karnak in Upper Egypt made this the largest temple ever built in the ancient world. Towering Egyptian obelisks have been carried off as trophies to cities as far away as Paris, London, and New York. And the three looming pyramids at Giza, on the outskirts of modern Cairo, still dwarf the antlike streams of tourists, the hawkers of souvenirs and camel rides who throng around them today. Napoleon, who fought his Battle of the Pyramids within sight of these monumental tombs, estimated the stone that made up the Great Pyramid of Khufu alone would suffice to build a 3-foot wall entirely around France.

Egyptian civilization was highly developed technologically. Egyptians constructed sundials, water clocks, and a calendar of 365 days. They seem to have understood the basic principles of the right-angle triangle, later formulated by the Greek Pythagorus, and were famous for their medical skill, up to and including brain surgery. The engineering genius demonstrated by this ancient people was quite remarkable. For Khufu's pyramid alone, 6 million tons of stone were carved from the living rock, moved hundreds of miles downriver and overland by barge and sledge, roller and lever, and then raised on ramps to a height of almost 500 feet above the desert. And there they sit today, incredible monuments to the engineering skills, the social cohesion, and the focused will of the ancient Egyptians.

Persia Unites the Near East

If the ziggurat and the pyramid epitomize the achievements of the fourth and third millennia B.C., perhaps the bronze-tipped spear or iron arrowhead most vividly symbolizes the tumultuous changes of the second and first millennia. The age of the founders of civilization in Mesopotamia and Egypt was succeeded by an epoch of sweeping military conquests and of ever vaster empires built by force of arms.

The apotheosis of force embodied in a Hittite iron dagger or a Persian bow was only one element in the turbulent history of these centuries, but it was an element of central importance. The peaceful uses

Columns at Karnak, in Upper Egypt, tower over a modern visitor and his guide. Can you see why structures like this, built many centuries before the first Greek cities, impressed the ancient Greeks? [Courtesy of TWA]

of bronze and iron and the remarkable expansion of Phoenician trade in fact represented more long-lasting contributions to human civilization. To contemporaries, however, the rise of unprecedented empires built and maintained by military force was the most astonishing phenomenon of the age. In this section we look at both the peaceful evolution of society and the warfare and struggle that led to empire building.

The Near East in Tumult

In 3000 B.C., Mesopotamia and Egypt were the only centers of civilized living in the world. After 2000 B.C., however, two things happened: A number of other peoples began to build cities and to develop new skills, from writing and metalwork to larger social organization. And still other peoples took a more direct route to the luxuries of civilized living: they seized them by force.

Some of these invaders were heirs of the two original civilizations, for example, the Assyrians of northern Mesopotamia and the pharaohs of New Kingdom Egypt. Other ambitious peoples, however,

were also pouring into the Near East: the nomads of the desert and the steppe. Of these, the Hittites were the first to forge and wield iron weapons, while the Persian troops of Cyrus and Darius the Great built the largest empire in history up to that time. In addition, the period from approximately 2000 to 500 B.C. saw the rise of such dynamic new peoples as the far-trading Phoenicians and the Hebrews, whom we discuss in the last major section of this chapter.

One thing that many of the peoples who so vigorously shook up the Near Eastern world after 2000 B.C. had in common was nomadic roots and a willingness to venture into new lands, as the originally nomadic Hittites and Persians did. The Phoenicians, though not nomads, pioneered long-distance trade from the Mediterranean out into the Atlantic. This urge to pack up and move on merits a brief discussion before we turn to a more detailed look at each of these vigorous new peoples.

Pastoral nomadism represented a late-developing style of life for humankind. Some groups of human beings had been unable—or unwilling—to make the full transition from the food–gathering mode to farming. Pressed by stronger neighbors into

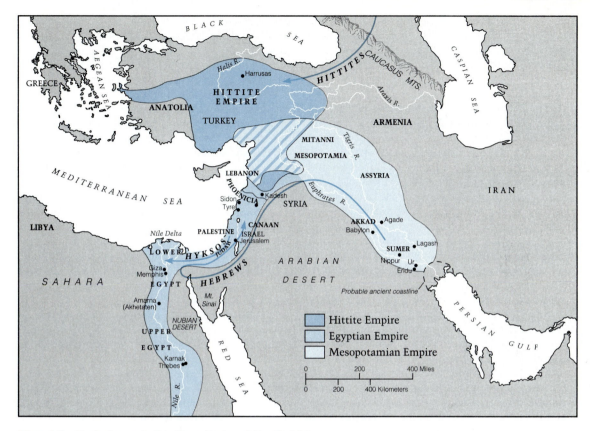

Map 1.2 Turbulence in the Near East and North Africa

land too poor for cultivation or simply rejecting the hard labor of farming, pastoral nomads derived their livelihood from the tending of sheep, goats, cattle, horses, and other animals. Because their herds or flocks had to be moved incessantly over their marginal land in search of pasture and water, the herders moved too. Organized in clans, highly mobile, toughened by their hard life, and led by resourceful men used to making rapid decisions in unfamiliar territory, they were dangerous enemies. Not infrequently, they cast covetous eyes on the well-watered farmland and the material plenty of the city-based civilizations.

Two groups of nomads threatened the ancient Near East: those who spoke Semitic tongues and those whose languages were Indo-European. Semitic groups included the Akkadians, the Amorites of the Old Babylonian Empire, and the empire-building Assyrians of northern Mesopotamia, all originally invaders from the dry Syrian steppe. Indo-European intruders included the Hittites and the Persians, both of whose ancestors were probably originally nomads of the vast Eurasian grasslands. Both Semitic and Indo-European groups continued to spread

across the Old World, so that today both Arabs and Jews speak Semitic languages, whereas most European tongues, Persian, and Indian Sanskrit are Indo-European languages.

These restless, aggressive, often remarkably creative peoples of the steppes were at the heart of the turbulence that characterized the second and much of the first millennium before Christ. We conclude this overview of these earlier civilizations from whom the West learned so much with some account of the Hittites, the Phoenicians, the Persians, and the Hebrews.

The Hittites and the Phoenicians

Difficult as it is to choose among the teeming peoples of the ancient Near East, the Hittites and the Phoenicians, for very different reasons, must clearly be mentioned. The Indo-European Hittites had migrated down from the Eurasian steppes into the area of modern Turkey during the earlier part of the second millennium B.C. In their new home, the Hittites had established a powerful empire, fighting the New Kingdom pharaohs to a draw and oppressing the early Assyrians. The great Hittite contribution to the history of civilization, however, was the introduction of a new technology into the Fertile Crescent: the working of iron.

The Iron Age, inaugurated by the Hittites around 1200 B.C., depended on a process of pounding and then quick quenching heated ore that produced a "semi-steel" hard enough for a strong tool or a sharp-edged weapon. Before the introduction of Hittite iron technology, most weapons had been made of bronze, an alloy made chiefly of copper and tin. Since iron was much more plentiful than copper, ironworking made it possible to outfit much larger armies. Thus the bronze-armed aristocratic chariot fighters who dominated battlefields down through New Kingdom Egyptian times were replaced, in the days of Persian power, by much larger armies of iron-armed infantrymen.

The Phoenicians, a Semitic people who lived in cities along the coast of modern Lebanon, developed a brilliantly successful commercial culture in the early part of the first millennium B.C. Phoenician merchant seamen from Tyre and Sidon traded the length of the Mediterranean and even beyond the Straits of Gibraltar into the Atlantic, voyaging as far as Stone Age Britain for tin. Paper from the Phoenician city of Byblos was so famous that the very name became synonymous with *book*—and the source of our word *Bible*. Overall, the Phoenicians were the greatest traders on the Mediterranean before the Greeks.

A major Phoenician contribution to Western history was the simplest system of writing yet devised. The short easy-to-use Phoenician alphabet of twenty-two letters did not, like the Mesopotamian and Egyptian scripts, require advanced training to master. Borrowed by the early Greeks, this simple Phoenician alphabet became the basis for all Western forms of writing down to the present day.

The Persian Empire

Around the middle of the first millennium before Christ, another new people came to dominate the Near Eastern world: the Persians. The Persians and their close allies, the Medes, were a semicivilized Indo-European people from the mountains of Iran whose forebears had been nomads on the Eurasian steppes. Originally the Medes were the dominant group. In the middle 500s, however, a leader emerged among the Persians who made them the builders of the largest empire in history up to that time.

Cyrus the Great (r. 559–530 B.C.)—Cyrus the Shepherd to his own people—was one of the most successful conquerors in history. He led his tough cavalry, equipped with short powerful bows, to an astonishing series of victories. In 550 B.C. Cyrus overthrew his overlord, Astyages, the king of the Medes. Another early victim was Croesus of Lydia, the first ruler to produce gold coins as a medium of exchange, reputed to be the richest ruler in the world. After the conquest of Lydia in 546 B.C., the Persian warrior-king fought his way from the Anatolian plateau of what is today Turkey to the far cold mountains of Afghanistan. Returning to the civilized lands of the Near East, Cyrus led his battle-hardened host south to Babylon. That richest of cities, languishing under the unworthy regent Belshazzar, shrewdly opened its gates to the Persians in 539 B.C.

When Cyrus died, fighting once more on his eastern frontiers, his son Cambyses (r. 530–521 B.C.) led the Persian host still further southward to victory on the Nile. After a brief struggle for power, a third emperor, Darius the Great (r. 521–486 B.C.), carried Persian rule further yet, west along the North African coast and north across the Hellespont into the Balkans, the southeastern corner of Europe.

By approximately 500 B.C., then, the Persians governed an empire that dwarfed anything seen in the world before. It included the whole sweep of the Middle East, from the shores of the Mediterranean to the banks of the Indus in what is today Pakistan. All this, plus northeastern Africa and a bit of southeastern Europe, acknowledged the authority of the "king of the four quarters of the world" in the splendid new Persian capital of Persepolis, in what is now Iran.

Persian power was probably not much better organized than that of the Assyrians had been, but it was generally less violently enforced. The wide empire was ruled by a score of local governors called *satraps,* or "petty kings," who enjoyed a large degree of autonomy under the crown. The power of the Persian army, built increasingly now on its heavy infantry and the noble bodyguard called the Immortals, continued to be respected. There was a centralized administration, including a body of inspectors—or spies—to keep tabs on the satraps. A royal system of roads, some common laws, and a common coinage were also unifying factors. In general, however, the diverse subject peoples, including

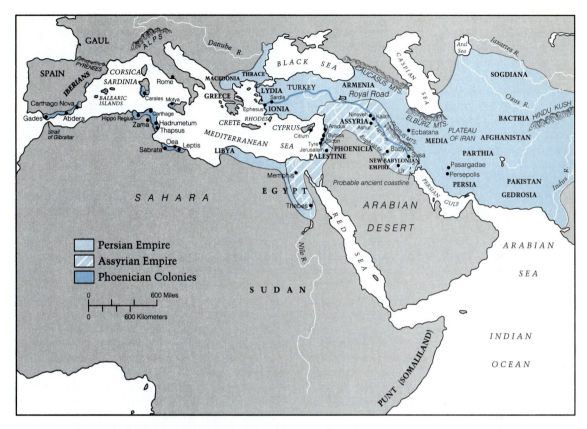

Map 1.3 Spread of Near Eastern and North African Civilizations

Egyptians and Babylonians, Greek settlements in western Turkey, and nomads in central Asia were allowed to keep their old ways and to a large extent run their own affairs.

Like the Assyrians and the New Kingdom pharaohs, the Persian emperors faced not only foreign foes but repeated rebellions and secessions. Like other early empire builders, the Persians demanded mostly taxes and tribute, and the royal writ ran no further than fear of the Persian army. Still, for more than two hundred years after the conquests of Cyrus in the sixth century B.C., the power of the Persians was awesome to behold.

They also became one of the most civilized of ancient peoples. Persian rulers built impressively, as the ruined pillars of the great palace at Persepolis remind us even today. A remarkable religious movement also took root among the hard-fighting Persian nobility, the monotheistic faith of the sixth-century B.C. religious leader Zoroaster. Zoroaster preached a militant religion that pitted the god of light Ahura Mazda and his divine champion Mithras against the prince of darkness, Ahriman. Roman legionaries later learned to worship Mithras, and Ahriman served as a model for the Christian Satan.

Persian arms remained potent long after Cyrus's day. A painted relief of one of the royal guards called the Immortals shows a short trimmed beard and an elaborately decorated ankle-length robe, a wide-bladed spear, and a capacious quiver of arrows. These crack troops would soon confront the brash challenge of the Greek city-states in one of the epic confrontations of Western history. And nobody would have bet on the Greeks.

The Hebrews and Ethical Monotheism

Of all the early Near Eastern civilizations, finally, that of the ancient Hebrews was the most influential on the future history of the Western world. The Hebrews were the founders of one of the world's oldest cultures and the ancestors of the modern Jewish community. Most important, they were the shapers of Judaism, a religion ancestral to both Christianity and Islam. In the Judaic tradition, the Hebrews gave the world the earliest form of *ethical monotheism*, a faith that emphasized morality and justice rather than sacrifice and ritual, and a religion that worshiped one God rather than a pantheon of divinities. In all these ways, the ancient Hebrews made major contributions to the historical evolution of Western life and culture.

The Rise of the Hebrews

As the Bible makes clear, the Hebrews were nomadic herders on the desert fringe of the civilized Near East during the second millennium before Christ. They came out of Mesopotamia in the days of the patriarch Abraham, perhaps about 1900 B.C., and their wanderings down the centuries took them as far as New Kingdom Egypt. There they apparently became exploited laborers, a state of oppression out of which the great leader Moses led them (in "the Exodus") probably sometime around 1270 B.C. Thereafter, most of their history was lived in Palestine, the land they believed their god Yahweh had promised them.

Here they established themselves after 1200, first fighting and then settling down beside other peoples, including the Canaanites and the Philistines. Here the Hebrews' traditional leadership of priests and judges—the latter also serving as war leaders—gave way to a typical Near Eastern monarchy around 1000 B.C. The initiator of this Israeli drive for power was King Saul (r. c. 1020–1000 B.C.), whose aggressive policies laid the foundations for the achievements of his successors. Under David (r. c. 1000–960 B.C.) and his son Solomon (r. c. 960–933 B.C.), the new nation of Israel flourished for most of the tenth century B.C. David built a capital at Jerusalem, and Solomon constructed an impressive temple there for the worship of Yahweh.

King Solomon was the most brilliant of these rulers. Revered for his wisdom in later centuries, he was in his own time a shrewd and successful Near Eastern monarch. Besides his vast temple in Jerusalem, Solomon constructed fortifications and even whole cities elsewhere in Israel. He strengthened the royal administration, fostered the use of iron for both agricultural tools and weapons, and expanded foreign trade. In the international arena,

All that remains today of Solomon's Temple, seen here in a reconstruction, is the so-called "Wailing Wall" in old Jerusalem, where devout Jews still pray daily. In its original glory, the Temple must have been one of the most magnificent sights in the ancient Near East.

Solomon forged a marriage alliance with Egypt and took advantage of the weakness of both the Hittites and the Assyrians in his time to project Israel into the forefront of Near Eastern affairs.

Internal discord strained the new institutions, however, and before 900 B.C., the kingdom had split into two parts, Israel in the north and the smaller state of Judah around Jerusalem in the south. Both states were subsequently swallowed up by more powerful neighbors, Israel falling to the Assyrians in the eighth century B.C., Judah to the New Babylonian Empire in the sixth century. When Cyrus the Persian conquered Babylon in 539 B.C., he allowed Hebrews who so desired to return to Palestine and establish a small client state of the Persian Empire there. Thereafter, however, Israel would enjoy only brief periods of independence from the days of David and Solomon until the twentieth century A.D.

Hebrew Society

Thanks particularly to the unique collection of evidence provided by the Bible, scholars have assembled a convincing picture of the social evolution of this Near Eastern people. Herders and wanderers throughout much of the first thousand years of their history, the Hebrews found a primary sense of identity in the so-called twelve tribes of Israel, which traced back to the twelve great-grandsons of Abraham. Once the Hebrews had settled in Palestine, however, paramount authority became localized in the male heads of individual households. These heads of families controlled their wives' property and had absolute power over their children. Men and women had their assigned tasks in the fields; boys and girls watched the flocks that still remained important in the economy.

After 1000 B.C., as the Hebrew monarchy took shape and Jerusalem and other towns flourished, the life of the people became still more complex. Village headmen and royal officials began to usurp much of the authority formerly exercised by the heads of tribes or families. Among the Hebrews as among other ancient peoples, small family farms began to give way to large estates owned by nobles and worked by laborers and slaves, while in the towns, artisans practiced many crafts. After their return from Babylon about 500 B.C., some Jews became widely traveled merchants in the first of the many *diasporas* (dispersal or exile) that would take them to all the lands of the Western world in centuries to come.

Within this society, women were encouraged to fill two traditional roles—those of wife and mother. The chronicles of the Hebrews in the Old Testament do, however, reveal an awareness that women possessed skills beyond the family circle. Women of the lower classes might function as cooks or bakers, midwives, nurses, professional mourners, and in other capacities. Hebrew women generally enjoyed property rights and increased protection within marriage. From the sixth century B.C., at any rate, Hebrew women owned property, engaged in business dealings, and took cases to court in their own names. And the Book of Proverbs hails above all the more practical skills of the "good wife":

> She considers a field and buys it; with the fruit of her hands she plants a vineyard.
> She girds her loins with strength and makes her arms strong.
> She perceives that her merchandise is profitable.[6]

It was a life, in short, rooted in the family and the household, but sometimes extending well beyond it.

The Prophetic Age

Through all their trials and tribulations, the Jews continued to elaborate a monotheistic, increasingly moral religion. In its own right and as a source for both Christianity and Islam, Judaism would prove to be one of the most powerful of all religious visions.

Yahweh, as the Hebrews first understood him, was not unlike the gods of other ancient peoples. The divine patron of the Hebrew people was a god of storm and war. The Hebrews carried his sacred relics about with them in a chest called the Ark of the Covenant, symbolizing his agreement to guide and protect them. They worshiped him with ceremonies and sacrifices, as gods were worshiped everywhere.

A particularly powerful element in this early Hebrew religion was Jewish law. Central to the traditional Hebrew code were the thirteenth-century B.C. Ten Commandments that Yahweh was believed to have given to Moses on Mount Sinai after the Jews' Exodus from Egypt. These basic commandments glorified God, requiring his people to worship no other gods before him and forbidding them to represent him in statues or other images. The Ten Commandments also forbade a number of crimes, including murder, theft, lying, and even desiring the lands or wife of another. Over the centuries, furthermore, the Hebrews developed an intricate array of other laws, covering not only criminal offenses and civil disputes but religious duties, dietary regulations, relations with foreigners, and much else. This ancient Hebrew law had much of the rigor of Hammurabi's Code, demanding an eye for an eye and providing such harsh penalties as death by stoning for adultery.

Important advances in this religious view were initiated by spiritual teachers called *prophets* between the eighth and the fifth centuries B.C. The Hebrew prophets were not members of the priesthood but laymen inspired by the will of Yahweh. They went among the people preaching, castigating them for

iniquity, warning them of impending peril, or proph-
esying renewal and inspiring hope.

Yahweh as the prophets saw him was clearly
more than one divine patron among many. He was
the only real God: all the gods of the Egyptians, the
Mesopotamians, and the rest were mere images of
wood and stone. This one true God was also the creator of the universe and the divine will that determined the course of history (see box, "Judah, Behold Your God!").

The God of the Hebrews demanded a good
deal more of his followers than sacrifices, ritual worship, and observance of the letter of the law. The
God of the Hebrews required both personal morality
and social justice, and he punished those who committed crimes or oppressed their neighbors. The

prophet Elijah, a powerful preacher in the 800s B.C.,
thundered against the priests of Baal, a god many Is-
raelites had come to worship, and denounced an oppressive Hebrew king for stealing another man's
land. In the 700s B.C. Isaiah warned that God would
send the Assyrians against the chosen people if they
did not turn from their wicked ways. Jeremiah
(about 626–586 B.C.) urged social and political as
well as religious reform, exhorting the people to love
God in their hearts, and warning of the Babylonian
danger even as it swept over Israel.

The Yahweh of Abraham and Moses was an
awe-inspiring lord, condemning the worship of all
other gods, concerned above all with his chosen people. The God of the prophets was clearly the only
god and was more dedicated to fairness, compassion,

THE HUMAN SPIRIT   Judah, Behold Your God!

This portion of the biblical book of Isaiah was
probably composed by a Hebrew prophet living at
the time of the captivity in Babylon (550–538
B.C.). During this period, when the Hebrew states
of Judah and Israel had been absorbed by Assyrian
and Babylonian conquerors and many Hebrews
were living in exile in the New Babylonian Empire,
the future of the Hebrews must have seemed very
dim indeed. At such a time, the powerful preaching of Isaiah revived their confidence that their
God would save them in the end.

To what does Isaiah compare the God of the
Hebrews when he wants to emphasize his *care* for
his chosen people? What in the Hebrews' past way
of life made this an effective comparison? How
is the *greatness* of the Lord expressed by the
prophet Isaiah? Why would the ringing assertion
that worldly power is vain and that divine power
will strengthen true believers appeal to the Hebrews in Babylon? To Christians in Rome centuries
later?

> O Zion, that bringest good tidings, get thee
> up into the high mountain; O Jerusalem, that
> bringest good tidings, lift up thy voice with
> strength; lift it up, be not afraid; say unto the
> cities of Judah, Behold your God!

Behold, the Lord God will come with strong
hand, and his arm shall rule for him, and his work
before him.

He shall feed his flock like a shepherd; he shall
gather the lambs with his arm, and carry them in
his bosom, and shall gently lead those that are
young.

Who hath measured the waters in the hollow
of his hand, and meted out heaven with the span,
and comprehended the dust of the earth in a
measure, and weighed the mountains in scales,
and the hills in a balance? . . .

Behold, the nations are as a drop of a
bucket. . . . All nations before him are as nothing; and they are counted to him less than nothing, vanity. . . .

It is he that sitteth upon the circle of the earth
. . . that bringeth the princes to nothing; he
maketh the judges of the earth as vanity. . . .

But they that wait upon the Lord shall renew
their strength; they shall mount up with wings as
eagles; they shall run, and not weary; and they
shall walk and not faint.

Source: *Isaiah* 40, 9–15, 17, 22–23, 31. *The Holy Bible* (Cambridge, England: Cambridge University Press)

morality, and justice. Throughout their history, the Jews practiced a monotheistic, morally sensitive religion, first in the time of Moses and then in prophetic times. On these Judaic foundations Christianity rose in its turn to become the religion of most Western people in later ages.

By 500 B.C., when our survey of the Eastern origins of Western civilization draws to a close, there were city-states, nations, and empires in many parts of the world. Rajahs ruled a number of states along the Ganges in northern India. The kingdoms of northeastern China were locked in a long period of wars from which the Chinese Empire would emerge. African kingdoms flourished up the Nile and along the Mediterranean coast, and Native Americans were raising huge temples in Mexico and Peru. In Europe, meanwhile, the Greeks had become the first of Western peoples to build cities and to learn to write, work metals, and meditate on the largest questions, human and divine. We will turn in Chapter 2 to these first builders of the Western world.

A Topical Summary

Politics: The scale on which prehistoric humanity lived in Paleolithic bands or Neolithic villages was too small to generate political activity. The earliest civilizations, however, produced several forms of political organization. The first city-states arose in Mesopotamia, the first larger state formed in Egypt, and both these river valley civilizations produced early empires. Government by divine sanction was common throughout the ancient Near East and northeastern Africa, and the first bureaucracies were organized to carry out royal commands.

Economics: The peoples of the Old Stone Age were food gatherers and hunters, whereas New Stone Age people settled down to cultivate the land and used domesticated animals. Along the Tigris and Euphrates rivers in Mesopotamia and in the valley of the Nile River in Egypt, large-scale irrigation projects made it possible to expand grain production, develop handicraft industries, and engage in long-distance trade. With these developments, populations grew.

Society: Prehistoric society may have been relatively egalitarian, but with the earliest civilizations came a full array of social classes, from slaves and peasants through artisans and merchants to an aristocratic elite. Gender-based social roles in prehistoric times evolved into patriarchal societies in the early civilizations, though women still performed many tasks and retained some rights.

Technology: In both the Old and New Stone ages, people depended on stone tools, but they developed ceramics and weaving in the Neolithic period. Civilization brought a much wider array of skills and tools, including the working of bronze and iron, boats and carts, large-scale building, and control of the great rivers around which the early civilizations emerged.

Culture: Such basic aspects of high culture as art and religion may be traced back to prehistoric times. The earliest civilizations took a giant leap forward with such achievements as the hanging gardens of Babylon, the Egyptian pyramids, and early developments in astronomy, mathematics, and medicine. Most important in terms of long-range impact on Western civilization, however, was the birth of ethical monotheism among the ancient Hebrews.

Some Key Terms

atlatl 7	*hominid* 5	Paleolithic 7
civilization 13	*lugal* 15	prophets 31
diaspora 31	*ma'at* 22	*satraps* 28
Cro-Magnon 5	Neanderthal 5	*ziggurat* 15
ethical monotheism 30	Neolithic 7	

Notes

1. Recent research suggests that because our ancestors shared the world with the Neanderthalers for thousands of years and because the two species differed little from each other biologically, we may be carrying some Neanderthal genes along with our primary Cro-Magnon heritage.
2. Boyce Rensberger, "'Iceman' Offers Look at Stone Age Moment," *Washington Post*, October 15, 1992, pp. 1, 22–23.
3. James B. Pritchard, ed., *Ancient Near Eastern Texts Relating to the Old Testament* (Princeton: Princeton University Press, 1950), 178.
4. J. H. Breasted, *Ancient Records of Egypt*, vol. 2 (Chicago: University of Chicago Press, 1906), 40.
5. W. M. Flinders Petrie, *Social Life in Ancient Egypt* (New York: Cooper Square, 1970), 106.
6. *Proverbs*, 31, 10, 16–18.

Reading List

ALDRED, C. *Akhenaton, Pharaoh of Egypt: A New Study.* London: Thames and Hudson, 1968. Expert evaluation of the monotheist pharaoh.

———. *The Egyptians.* New York: Praeger, 1973. Highly recommended overview. See also T. G. H. James, *Pharaoh's People: Scenes from Life in Imperial Egypt* (Chicago: University of Chicago Press, 1984). Vignettes with translations from surviving papyri.

COHEN, M. N. *The Food Crisis in Prehistory: Overpopulation and the Origins of Agriculture.* New Haven: Yale University Press, 1977. Important contribution to our understanding of a crucial topic.

COOK, J. M. *The Persian Empire.* London: Dent, 1983. Narrative and analytical history of Persia, based on Greek historians, inscriptions, and recent archaeology. See also M. A. Dandamaev and V. G. Lukonin, *The Cultural and Social Institutions of Ancient Iran,* translated by P. L. Kohl (New York: Cambridge University Press, 1989).

DAHLBERG, F., ed. *Woman, the Gatherer.* New Haven: Yale University Press, 1983. Valuable collection of essays reassessing the role of women in prehistory.

EDWARDS, I. E. S. *The Pyramids of Egypt.* Harmondsworth, England: Penguin, 1961. Standard work on the best known ancient Egyptian monuments.

HODDER, I. *The Domestication of Europe: Structure and Contingency in Neolithic Societies.* Cambridge, Mass.: Blackwell, 1990. Sophisticated analysis of prehistoric society and culture. See also B. Campbell, *Mankind Emerging* (Boston: Little, Brown, 1979). A clear account of human evolutionary development.

JACOBSEN, T. *The Treasures of Darkness: A History of Mesopotamian Religion.* New Haven: Yale University Press, 1976. Learned and thoughtful analysis of the development of early religious thought. See also the older classic, H. Frankfurt et al., *Before Philosophy* (Harmondsworth, England: Penguin, 1949). A classic study of the myth-making mind of the ancient Near East.

JOHANSON, D., and M. ELDER. *Lucy: The Beginnings of Humankind.* New York: Warner, 1981. Discovery, dating, and analysis of one of our oldest ancestors.

KRAMER, S. *History Begins at Sumer.* 2d rev. ed. Philadelphia: University of Pennsylvania Press, 1981. Authoritative and well-written overview, emphasizing Sumerian firsts in history.

LAESSOE, J. *The People of Ancient Assyria.* Translated by F. S. Leigh-Browne. New York: Barnes and Noble, 1963. What we can learn from surviving letters and inscriptions.

LERNER, G. *The Creation of Patriarchy.* New York: Oxford University Press, 1986. Exploration of the emergence of male dominance in ancient society. See also B. Lesko, *The Remarkable Women of Ancient Egypt* (Berkeley: Scribe, 1978). Pioneering study of celebrated Egyptian women.

LICHTHEIM, M., ed. *Ancient Egyptian Literature: A Book of Readings.* 3 vols. Berkeley: University of California Press, 1973–1980. Translations of hieroglyphic texts, representative and readable.

MOSCATI, S. *The Phoenicians.* New York: Praeger, 1968. The first great seafarers and their colonies.

OATES, J. *Babylon.* London: Thames and Hudson, 1986. Excellent survey of Babylonian history and society.

OPPENHEIM, A. L. *Ancient Mesopotamia.* Chicago: University of Chicago Press, 1964. Good survey of history and culture.

PETTINATO, G. *The Archives of Ebla: An Empire Inscribed in Clay.* Garden City, N.Y.: Doubleday, 1981. The recently discovered Syrian center of early Near Eastern civilization.

PRITCHARD, J. B., ed. *Ancient Near Eastern Texts Relating to the Old Testament.* Princeton: Princeton University Press, 1969. Standard collection of readings from both Mesopotamia and Egypt. See also H. W. F. SAGGS, *The Encounter with the Divine in Mesopotamia and Israel* (London: Athlone, 1978). Stimulating cross-cultural comparisons of religious experiences.

SAGGS, H. W. F. *Civilization Before Greece and Rome.* New

Haven: Yale University Press, 1989. The ancient Near East, surveyed by a mature scholar writing for the non-specialist. See also R. DE VAUX, *The Early History of Israel* (Philadelphia: Westminster Press, 1978). A solid history of the ancient Hebrews.

WALKER, C. B. F. *Reading the Past: Ancient Writing from Cuneiform to the Alphabet.* London: British Museum, 1990. Stimulating introduction to the earliest forms of writing in western Eurasia.

The admiration of later Western peoples for "the glory that was Greece"[1] generally relates to the shining achievements of the fifth century B.C. in Athens and, to a lesser degree, to the Hellenistic period that followed. These were the centuries, after all, that produced the Greek democracy, philosophy, art, literature, and science that form such an important part of Western culture. Recently, however, historians have become increasingly enthusiastic about exploring the accomplishments of the Greek peoples *before* 500 — the subject of the present chapter.

Thanks to new archaeological evidence and new methods of analyzing old evidence, not one but several earlier periods of impressive Greek achievement have been revealed. The first to be uncovered were the Minoan and Mycenaean civilizations, dating from the third and second millennia B.C., whose ruins have been excavated over the past hundred years. The Minoan paintings of the "bull leapers" at Knossos and the golden face of a Mycenaean chieftain called "the Mask of Agamemnon" have come to stand for exotic pre-Greek cultures very different from the columned temples of the Classical Age. Most recently, we have found unexpected qualities in the period of Greek revival and expansion that directly preceded the fifth century B.C. The development of the unique Greek form of the city-state, the spread of Greek colonies and trade all around the Mediterranean, and some real cultural breakthroughs make the eighth, seventh, and sixth centuries B.C. look in some ways more revolutionary than the fifth.

It is this exciting Greek Awakening — the Greek world from perhaps 750 to 500 B.C. — that concerns us throughout most of this chapter. We begin, however, by examining the earlier world of the Minoans and Mycenaeans, which lasted from about 2600 to about 1100 B.C.

The Rampin Head. c. 560 B.C. Musée du Louvre, Paris

Minoans and Mycenaeans

It is a real question whether the world of the Minoans and the Mycenaeans belongs to the history of Greece or to that of the ancient Near East. The geographical center of the Minoan-Mycenaean world was not the Greek peninsula, after all, but the Aegean Sea, which lies between Greece and Asia Minor (today's Turkey). The Minoan heartland in particular was the large island of Crete on the south-

Like "Sargon," in Chapter 1, this famous "Mask of Agamemnon" is a traditional attribution. Even if it does not represent the Mycenaean king who led the Greeks against Troy, it evokes an image of the ancient warlords as they raced their chariots across Greece and ran their long ships up on the Agean shore before Troy.

The Greek World—Mountains and Sea

From a rooftop terrace in a hill village on the Greek island of Evvia—ancient Euboea—you can look out today across a microcosm of the Greek world of ancient times. Before you, the hills slope rapidly down through cypresses and eucalyptus trees to a curving bay and the Aegean beyond, the "wine-dark sea" of which Homer sang. Out on the water, smaller islands fade to the horizon. Behind you, the hillside scales up to mountains sown with olive trees, shepherds, and sheep. Just over a rocky shoulder, there is an ancient quarry with a half-finished column, cut from the surrounding stone two thousand years ago, lying in the gorse. It is all there: the world the Greeks inhabited and a hint of what they made of it.

It was a poor land of thin soil over rock, indifferently watered—quite unlike the rich river plains of Mesopotamia and Egypt. Most people of ancient Greece were farmers, like people everywhere, but few were rich by Near Eastern standards. And most of the time there was not enough surplus product to support so large an elite as the aristocracies, priesthoods, and monarchies of the Near East. Many Greeks had to find some other means of livelihood than the land, like handicrafts or commerce on the sea. Others were eventually driven to leave Greece entirely, establishing colonies across the Aegean or still farther away, across the Mediterranean or the Black Sea.

The sea played a crucial role in the history of the Greeks. In their divided homeland of peninsulas and islands, water was never far away. The relatively calm Mediterranean linked the early Greeks as much as it divided them, for they became seafarers early, as they are to this day. The ancient Minoans were sailors and traders, and the Mycenaeans were traders and pirates. The economic heart of the Greek revival that began about 750 B.C. was trade and overseas colonization. The Greeks overcame the huge Persian Empire at sea, and the Athenian Empire of the fifth century flourished all around the Aegean Sea. The greatest Greek epic poems, Homer's *Iliad* and *Odyssey,* focused on the Trojan War, in which a Greek armada crossed the Aegean to destroy the city of Troy (whose prince had stolen away a Greek queen, known thereafter as "Helen of Troy"), and on the adventures of the Greek hero Odysseus on his long voyage home.

The world of the Greeks was thus both united and divided. Unlike the unified river valleys in the ancient Near East, the land of the Greeks was broken up by mountains and small valleys, peninsulas, and

ern perimeter of the Aegean, between Europe and Africa. Culturally, furthermore, these Bronze Age peoples of the Aegean clearly owe more to the developed Near Eastern civilizations that we looked at in Chapter 1 than to the village societies of contemporary southern Europe.

What has strengthened the connection between the Minoan and Mycenaean cultures and the later Greek civilizations is the accumulating archeological evidence unearthed by scholars since the latter part of the nineteenth century. Among these revelations were Heinrich Schliemann's discovery of the ruins of ancient Troy, and of Mycenae itself, in the 1870s and Sir Arthur Evans's excavation of the palace of Knossos, the Minoan capital on Crete, in the early 1900s. No less intriguing was the 1952 decoding, by the young British architect Michael Ventris, of the Mycenaean script known as *Linear B,* which revealed that the Mycenaeans spoke an early form of Greek.

From this very limited documentary evidence, from continuing archeological endeavors, and from the distorted reflection preserved in myth and literature, it is thus possible to conjure up at least something of the first civilizations in Western history.

islands. It was easy and natural for Greek city-states to maintain their independence, to produce no all-powerful pharaohs or kings of kings, and to feud with each other throughout their history. These divisions also bred deep loyalty to one's own city, one's own small country of a few thousands or tens of thousands of people. At the same time, the very geographical separateness and isolation of the Greeks may have made them cling to the common Greek culture that united them.

Hellenism, the culture of the Hellenes, as the Greeks called themselves, was thus not loyalty to a political state, but a shared set of attitudes and values. Certain distinctive qualities—independence of mind, rationality, aesthetic sensitivity, and more dubious traits like sharp trading and contentiousness—linked all Greeks, however far they were scattered across the earth.

This world of mountains, valleys, islands, seacoasts, and the sea later on produced the pillared temples of the Athenian Acropolis and the marketplace below, where the philosopher Socrates argued basic values with all comers. But the story of Greece takes us back to a very different world from the Athens of Socrates. It takes us back to Minoan Crete, to the warlike Mycenaeans, and to the cultural context within which both of these earlier peoples lived.

The Cultural Context

Although the geographical framework of early Greek history is important, the cultural context in which Western civilization got its start is even more crucial. To understand this context, we must return to the pre-Greek world of the ancient Near East and North Africa outlined in Chapter 1. We must also begin the examination of relations between the Western world—at this point consisting of a handful of Greek city-states—and the non-Western world at large, to which we will return throughout this book.

Greeks of the Classical Age—discussed in Chapter 3—were well aware of their debt to older civilizations. Philosophers like Plato and historians like Herodotus honored the Egyptian and Near Eastern forerunners of their own culture. And modern archaeologists have found ample evidence of contacts between the early Greeks and their neighbors to the south and east. Some modern scholars, emphasizing the "Afro-Asian roots" of classical civilization, have suggested that the emerging West borrowed much more extensively from neighboring cultures than had been believed. We need not abandon the Western claim to fundamental originality to recognize that, from the very beginning, Western civilization grew in a profitable symbiotic relationship with other cultures.

Examples of the exchange of art and handicrafts between early Greeks and their neighbors abound. For example, a collection of silver vessels decorated in styles indigenous to the Aegean area and dating back to 2000 B.C. was found in the ruins of an Egyptian temple. Thus it seems very likely that there were commercial relations between the Minoan trading empire and Middle Kingdom Egypt. Egyptian artifacts found in both Crete and mainland Greece and Egyptian tomb paintings representing both Minoans and Mycenaeans, all dating from around 1500 B.C., give evidence of further trade and perhaps diplomatic contact between these peoples. After 1000 B.C., as we will see, Greek traders and soldiers penetrated both Egypt and the Near East, settling along the coast of Asia Minor and in the Nile Delta, trading, fighting, and learning from these other cultures.

From all these contacts, the Greeks who laid the foundations for Western civilization derived many benefits. From the Near East, as we will see, they took the Phoenician alphabet and Lydian coinage. From Egypt they learned artistic styles and techniques, such as the creation of large imposing statues. Some scholars have further suggested that the Greeks may have derived important legal, scientific, and philosophical ideas from Egyptian sources, though the evidence for this is less clear.

Above all, perhaps, as we trace the emergence of a distinctively Greek culture, we should be aware of the larger cultural context in which this process takes place. European civilization did not spring full blown out of barbarism or prehistory. When the first Indo-European ancestors of the Greeks and the Romans moved down into the Mediterranean basin, civilization around the eastern end of the Mediterranean was already many centuries old. The Minoans, the Mycenaeans, and the early Greeks were all beneficiaries of these older venturers into civilization.

The Minoan Sea Kings

Before the Minoans and the Mycenaeans there were much older settlers on both the Aegean islands and the Greek mainland, Paleolithic and Neolithic peo-

2500 B.C.   2000

**POLITICAL,
MILITARY,
AND
DIPLOMATIC
EVENTS**

c. 2500–1500   Minoans in Crete

**SOCIAL
AND
ECONOMIC
DEVELOPMENT**

2500–1500   Minoan commercial
empire in Aegean

**ART AND
LITERATURE,
SCIENCE,
PHILOSOPHY,
AND RELIGION**

---

ples who occupied the region as early as the third millennium B.C. These prehistoric dwellers built agricultural villages, learned to work metals, and exchanged raw materials and finished goods. Some chieftains among them lived in clay-brick houses and accumulated stores of gold and silver jewelry. Around 2000 B.C. the region was invaded from the north by the first of several waves of Indo-Europeans whose original home had been the Eurasian steppes. These intruders destroyed much of the simple society they found and then settled down to live with the survivors. These Indo-European invaders were probably the earliest ancestors of the original Greeks but they remained a relatively underdeveloped culture until the coming of the Minoans and Myceneaens in the second millenium B.C.

This early invasion did not cross the Aegean to Crete, however. There, a more developed commercial society was already taking shape. The people of Minoan Crete may themselves have been immigrants from the Near East, coming from either Egypt or Asia Minor (modern Turkey). Whatever their ethnic derivation, they certainly acquired crafts and ideas from Asia Minor, Syria, Egypt, and North Africa. Throughout some half-dozen centuries after 2000

B.C., however, the Minoans developed a unique civilization of their own.

The Minoan hegemony of the Aegean (c. 2000–1500 B.C.) was labeled "Minoan" by archaeologist Arthur Evans after the mythical King Minos of Crete, whose wife was said to have given birth to the monstrous Minotaur. Like the empire of the Hittites, Minoan civilization was unknown before twentieth-century archaeologists recovered it from the earth. Almost all we know about it rests on archaeological evidence, for the few inscribed tablets that have been found are written in a script called *Linear A*, which no one has as yet succeeded in deciphering. What the archaeologist's spade has turned up, however, is astonishing enough.

Evans divided Minoan history into three major periods: Early Minoan (c. 2600–2200 B.C.), Middle Minoan (c. 2200–1500), and Late Minoan (c. 1500–1200). These divisions, however, are of value primarily as a scale for dating the artifacts uncovered by archaeologists. The political history of the island empire must remain unknown until someone as skilled at cryptography as Michael Ventris deciphers the Linear A clay tablets. For the moment, we can only say that the seaborne Minoan culture rose late in

c. 1500 Destruction of Knossos	**c. 1198** Fall of Troy	**750–500** Greek city-states emerge
1500–1100 Mycenaeans in Greece	**1100–750** Greek Dark Age	**600–500** Tyrannies
	c. 1000 Dorian conquest	**c. 594** Solon's reforms in Athens
		546–527 Pisistratus

1500–1100 Mycenaeans as pirates and traders		**750–500** Greek commercial expansion
		750–500 Greek colonies

	c. 800 Homer	**c. 600** Sappho
	c. 700 Hesiod	
		c. 600–500 Archaic art
		550–500 Milesian philosophers

the third millennium B.C., flourished through the early second millennium, and suffered some mysterious catastrophe about the beginning of the first millennium before Christ.

The Minoan Empire was primarily a commercial predominance, with a center at the city of Knossos on Crete. It had trading posts and commercial contacts around the Aegean, including some on the Greek mainland, as well as in Egypt, Syria, and elsewhere in the Near East. Minoan cities seem to have done without walls and moats, indicating either that their hegemony was a peaceful one or that they depended on their fleets for defense. Recent discoveries of fortifications and evidence of early destruction on the island indicate that the Minoans may have experienced more violence than was once thought. Still, there are no artistic representations of King Minos charging into battle and no evidence of a militarized aristocracy. The overwhelming impression is of a trading people like their contemporaries the Phoenicians, or like the later Greeks.

Minoan culture resembles that of the Near East in only the most general ways. First, the Minoans lived in cities—the first cities in Europe, not to be matched elsewhere in the West for a thousand years.

Leading citizens dwelt in multistoried houses built around courtyards, and royal palaces like that at Knossos were labyrinths of rooms with courtyards at their centers. Minoan writing appears to have developed much as Near Eastern scripts did, from pictures to a kind of writing based on syllables, and it was inscribed on clay tablets in the Mesopotamian fashion. The rulers of Minoan Crete may also have been indebted to the Near East for models of the centralized bureaucratic government that some archaeologists believe they imposed on the island.

In a larger sense, however, Minoan culture seems quite unique. The sprawling, many-chambered royal palace at Knossos boasts a stately staircase and a red-columned throne room. There are charming wall frescoes of landscapes, the sea, and the lives of the ruling caste. There seem to have been few large temples in Crete, though sections of the palace were clearly intended for religious purposes, and other sacred ceremonies apparently took place on mountaintops and in caves. The Cretan aristocracy, if we are to believe the frescoes, lived an idyllic life, strolling in flower gardens, sipping wine, or practicing the startling sport of bull leaping, in which young men and women vaulted

41

over the horns of bulls and danced on their backs, perhaps, again, as part of a religious ceremony. Even the recently disclosed evidence of occasional human sacrifice has done little to undermine the general impression of a normally peaceful and pleasant society.

It is above all through its art that Minoan civilization projects such an exotic and appealing image. Minoan artists, men and women, produced eggshell-thin pottery decorated with flowing pictures of sea creatures and other animals and plants. Small figurines of ivory depict athletes or goddesses, sacred snakes, and the double-ax motif found everywhere in the island. The pastel wall paintings seem especially bright windows into the vanished Minoan past.

That the Minoan civilization did vanish, perhaps as early as 1450 B.C., perhaps as late as 1100, is clear. It also seems certain that it perished in violence. The source and nature of the cataclysm that swept the Minoan world away, however, remains in dispute. Some historians attribute the sudden end to this world to some natural catastrophe, such as an earthquake or a volcanic eruption. Others interpret the visible evidence of burning and widespread destruction as proof that the state fell to foreign invaders, probably the Mycenaeans from the mainland.

Whatever happened, life did not end in Crete. Villages survived, and some of them grew prosperous enough to trade beyond the islands again. But the wealthy commercial cities and cool palaces of the Minoan traders who once dominated the Aegean were gone forever.

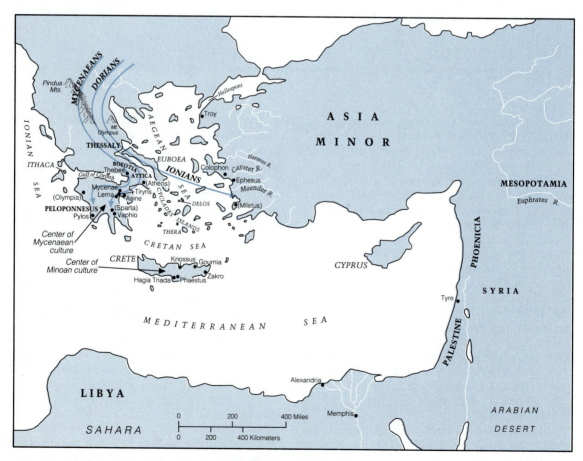

Map 2.1 Minoans, Mycenaeans, and Neighboring Peoples

The Mycenaean Warriors

A rival power had been growing on the mainland for several centuries before the fall of Knossos. The Mycenaean hegemony (c. 1500–1100 B.C.), based on the Peloponnesian peninsula of southern Greece, was cruder and more violent than the Minoan empire. The famous Lion Gate at Mycenae, crowned with rough-hewn relief sculptures of rearing lions, does have a raw strength about it. But there is none of the smooth sophistication of the frescoes of Knossos. In general, it is strength rather than beauty that characterizes the civilization of the Mycenaeans.

The Mycenaean people may have come down into Greece as another wave of invaders from the north. As we have already noted, they spoke an early version of Greek. Warriors and traders, they established a power structure in southern Greece that has been called the *palace system*. In this system, scattered fortresses at Peloponnesian sites like Mycenae, Pylos, and Tiryns and at Athens and Thebes in central Greece dominated the countryside. These roughly built stone "palaces" were linked by roads over which the heavy chariots of Mycenaean merchants and warlords rattled with a flash of bronze armor and a glitter of weapons. The bulk of the mainland population, however, still lived in small agricultural settlements where they labored, with the help of slaves taken in raids across the sea, to support themselves and their overlords.

The Mycenaeans, like the Minoans, were at home on the sea. Their trading ships plied the waters of the Aegean and the Mediterranean beyond, but they were at least as likely to come ashore with weapons as with merchandise. Knossos may have fallen victim to one such massive Mycenaean raid. So, as we have noted, did the Near Eastern city of Troy.

On one level, Mycenaean civilization, with its palace system and endless wars, was a coarse-grained military oppression. Yet when archaeologists have probed the graves of the Mycenaean warlords they have found startling treasures. There were game boards made of ivory, birds of crystal, gold jewelry, and golden face masks, including the flat grim countenance of what Heinrich Schliemann named the Mask of Agamemnon after a Greek leader in the Trojan War. The immense beehive-shaped *tholos* or tombs of Mycenae were the largest structures to be found in Europe in that early age, and the colonnaded palaces themselves were the largest such structures that were ever built in ancient Greece.

The Mycenaean kings had royal administrators who kept records in Linear B, in which the Mycenaean version of Greek was written. Mycenaean pottery actually circulated farther around the eastern end of the Mediterranean than Minoan ware, but it was not as delicate, and its decorative patterns were copied with increasing crudity from earlier work. If Minoan culture was a golden age, the Mycenaean epoch was an age of bronze.

Sometime between 1200 and 1100 B.C., still more waves of intruders came down from the north. Some of these invaders infiltrated into the existing society gradually, but others raided and destroyed Mycenaean settlements. Mycenae, Pylos, and other fortresses of the lords of the Lion Gate were put to the torch. The last group of intruders—known to tradition as Dorians—were once again Greek-speak-

The Lion Gate at Mycenae, which originally fronted a massive palace, is set in a doorway topped by a *lintel* or cross-beam, a basic architectural form the Greeks used throughout their history. What do you think the two lions carved in the triangular stone slab above the lintel stood for?

ing Indo-Europeans, probably pastoralists who soon occupied the southern part of the Greek mainland. Their coming brought a new era to Greece and another ratchet downward for Greek culture. The Greek Dark Age had begun.

The Greek Dark Age

The next few centuries are known as the Greek Dark Age (1100–750 B.C.). Under the impact of the Dorian onslaught, the Mycenaean kings and their palaces vanished, and with them the arts they had sponsored. The craft of writing, probably known only to royal scribes, passed away with them. Even the practice of agriculture seems to have vanished in some places, giving way to the livestock raising of the nomadic invaders.

Fleeing Greeks were scattered to the islands and to the coasts of Asia Minor, giving the whole area a homogeneity it had probably lacked before. But for the time being, it was a homogeneous culture at a low ebb indeed. Stimulating contact with the world beyond the Aegean was largely lost. In the vivid Greek imagination, the outside world was soon populated with monsters, and the past became a time when gods and heroes walked the earth.

Politically, economically, and socially, there was almost nothing left of the commercial hegemony of the Minoans or the military rule of the Mycenaeans. What little did remain was so reduced that it lost all significance in the diminished Dark Age world.

The mainland, the islands, and the farther coasts were divided politically into tiny territories, clusters of villages dominated by local strongmen. These local war leaders often still called themselves kings, but they had neither the power nor the trappings of their Mycenaean predecessors, let alone the greatness of contemporary monarchs in the Near East. Like the rulers of a more famous Dark Age—Europe's early Middle Ages—these petty kings fought and feasted and listened enraptured to the bards who chanted the glorious deeds of their ancestors. And although they liked to claim descent from the great sky-god Zeus, they often labored in the fields with the common folk at harvesttime.

The economy of Greece seldom produced lavishly, even at the best of times, but it must have been difficult simply to survive in the Dark Age economy.

Knowledge of agriculture did survive (or revive) in most places, and it was during this period that iron tools and weapons replaced bronze. But there were no cities, no commercial sector to speak of, and little production of handicrafts beyond objects for local use. It was life at subsistence level: days bending in the fields or climbing the rocky slopes with flocks of sheep and goats. Olive trees and grapevines grew in the light, dry soil, varieties of wheat in the small fields. It was the world of the poet Hesiod's (fl. c. 700 B.C.) *Works and Days,* when the height of human wisdom was knowledge of soil and seasons, flocks and vines (see box, "Pray to the Gods and Follow the Plow").

The social structure of this rude society was based on clan affiliation, age group, and family; it was a structure whose roots stretched back into prehistory. An area no larger than a county today might be divided among several clans, each clan consisting of a number of powerful families who claimed descent from a common ancestor. The fighting-age youth of such a group were often organized into *phratries,* or "brotherhoods." These groups of young men of the same age dined and trained together and fought side by side. The family, however, remained the fundamental building block of society. The father ruled the family unit, serving as its spokesman and defender in society at large and as its intermediary with the gods.

As in many preurban societies, the individual existed only as part of a defining group—phratry, family, clan. Most members had little say in their own lives. Fathers of families, leading families within a clan, and local petty kings held sway. But even they were rigorously guided by tradition and taboo.

Much had obviously been lost since Minoan aristocrats strolled in their gardens or Mycenaean kings made the earth shake under their chariot wheels. On the other hand, some of these apparent losses turned out to be significant advantages for the future growth of Greek institutions and ideas. Almost certainly, for instance, the reduction of monarchy to a shadow of its former greatness made it relatively easy for the Greek city-states to do without kings in later centuries. Moreover, the assignment of most religious functions to petty kings and heads of families reduced the importance of priests, so that organized priesthoods never had the power or prestige in Greece that they enjoyed in the Near East. Even the lack of material wealth during the Dark Age may have helped nurture a basic leveling

The Greek Awakening

The Greek Dark Age was followed by a dynamic revival that was clearly the work of the historic Greeks. This Greek Awakening encompassed about two and a half centuries, from 750 to 500 B.C. During this period the Greeks recovered the arts of civilization, spread well beyond their Aegean homeland, and laid the foundations for the classic Greek civilization to come. Thus the Classic Age that followed, in the fifth century B.C., was the mature expression of a culture whose revolutionary breakthroughs came two centuries earlier.

Sources of Revival

In seeking the sources of the Greek Awakening, it is important to note that the Dark Age itself was not without its productive consequences. The links between the agricultural village of the Dark Age and the city-state, or *polis,* of the ages that followed are not easily traced, but some parts of the causal chain between them are becoming clear. A probing of Greek graveyards, for instance, finds them substantially fuller in the eighth century, concrete evidence of rapid population growth. The building of temples and indeed of cities themselves reveals increasing productivity, the achievement of a surplus beyond the daily needs of the population. And the discovery of Greek pottery and other products at sites in many parts of the Mediterranean world gives us evidence of the rapid growth of long-range trade once more.

Even the evolution of military technology and organization helps to illuminate the origins of the new social order. For it is during this time that the infantry phalanx replaced the war chariot as the Greeks' most effective fighting unit. The *phalanx* was a heavily armored infantry formation that fought in close battle order, each infantryman protecting the man beside him, all pushing together for a breakthrough. The armor of this heavy infantryman, or *hoplite,* including breastplate, helmet, shield, and greaves to protect the legs below the knee, could only be afforded by middle-rank or wealthy men— merchants, skilled artisans, well-off farmers. Not surprisingly, these well-to-do defenders of the polis came to dominate the emerging city-states in political and other ways. The close-order combat and the drill necessary to make the phalanx work, some have sug-

---

MASTERING OUR WORLD
Pray to the Gods and Follow the Plow

The eighth-century B.C. poet Hesiod may have started out life as a farmer in Boeotia, north of Athens. In his *Works and Days* he recounted many now well-known myths—such as the story of Pandora's box, the opening of which released all troubles into the world—and he advanced a theory that the world had passed through five ages, from the golden age to his own, a grim age of iron. The poet also offered more practical advice. What evidence do you see that Hesiod believed in an industrious, frugal, and devout life? What prudent advice on how to survive on a hardscrabble farm in Dark Age Greece do you see here?

Mark when you hear the voice of the crane who cries year by year from the clouds above, for she gives the signal for ploughing and shows the season of rainy winter:

Pray to Zeus of the Earth and to pure Demeter to make Demeter's holy grain sound and heavy, when first you begin ploughing, when you hold in your hand the end of the plough-tail and bring down your stick on the backs of the oxen as they draw on the pole-bar by the yoke-straps. Let a slave follow a little behind with mattock and make trouble for the birds by hiding the seed; for good management is the best for mortal men as bad management is the worst. In this way your corn-ears will bow to the ground with fullness if the Olympian himself gives a good result at the last, and you will sweep the cobwebs from your bins and you will be glad, I ween, as you take of your garnered substance. And so you will have plenty till you come to grey springtime.

Source: Hesiod, *Works and Days,* in *The Homeric Hymns and Homerica,* trans. Hugh G. Evelyn-White (Cambridge, Mass.: Harvard University Press, 1922), 37–39.

---

tendency in Greek society, a sense that no person is or should be vastly greater than his or her neighbor. This impulse toward equality played an important role in the emergence of a new social order in later Greek centuries.

gested, both reflected and generated a strong sense of community responsibility and loyalty, attitudes that could have had much to do with the success of the Greek city-state.

By 750 B.C., furthermore, this more numerous, better off, and considerably more sophisticated people were also developing a new set of political institutions. At first this was not a revolutionary process. Traditional institutions like the clan and the phratry, for example, were not abolished but were absorbed into the new system, where they had new functions but kept much of their old prestige. The leaders of the old clans, many of whom had become wealthy landowners, had leading roles in the new order too. Respect for this old aristocracy was a continuing force in politics even in more democratic later times. In some places, even the title of king remained, frequently as the designation for an official charged with officiating at religious ceremonies. In general, however, kings no longer had any real authority in the Greek world.

Origins of the Greek City-State

The Greek city-state that began to evolve toward the end of the Dark Age had some things in common with the city-states of the Near East. Like them, the Greek *polis* was small in size and population. An average Greek city and its hinterland approximated the territorial extent of the Dark Age district that had preceded it. Natural frontiers, however, were perhaps more common than in the East: the boundaries of a city-state were often defined by valley walls, the angle of a coastline, or the extent of a small island. The population could run to tens, even hundreds of thousands for a city and its surrounding villages: Athens, at its height during the Classical Age, may have had three hundred thousand residents.

The Greek city-states were, however, more numerous than their Mesopotamian or Phoenician precursors. Hundreds of them were distributed over the mainland, the islands, and the neighboring coasts of the Aegean. Each city presided over a number of villages in the surrounding countryside. Most Greeks, in fact, still lived in villages that were surrounded by pasture or farmland and came into the city only to trade, to participate in traditional religious ceremonies, or to take part in the new political functions of the citizenry.

The physical structure of the Greek city had its special features, just as the ancient Mesopotamian city did. Although organized priesthoods were not as powerful among them as among the Mesopotamians, Greeks traditionally centered their urban growth around a hill dedicated to the gods, particularly to the patron god or goddess of the state. This *acropolis,* or "high city," could also serve as a refuge in case of foreign attack. Below it was the equally essential *agora,* or marketplace. The agora too had other functions: it was a place for lounging and gossip, for political and later philosophical discussion.

What was strikingly original about the early Greek city-state, however, was not its physical plan, but its political institutions. Most city-states had an assembly, a council, and a number of elected officials. Assemblies of warriors or heads of family and councils of elders had been common in preurban village communities in many parts of the world. In Greek cities, the assembly was composed of citizens with political rights, which meant free adult males, often members of the phalanx, and property owners. Excluded from political rights were women, resident foreigners, slaves, and the poor. Limited as it was, however, this politically active Greek citizen body encompassed a larger portion of the population than enjoyed political power anywhere else in the Mediterranean.

Political power in Greek city-states included the right to vote on major matters of public policy, to elect officials to carry out those policies, and to serve as an official if chosen. As issues grew more complicated, a council evolved to guide the deliberations of the full assembly. The council might be chosen from the assembly itself and do little more than set the agenda. Or it might be composed of members of the old aristocratic families and end by dominating the political life of the state.

Elected officials of the city-state, finally, could include war leaders or generals, officials entrusted with religious observances, judges, and civil authorities like the Athenian *archons,* whose political clout could be substantial. These officials tended to be chosen for short periods, often only a year. In the confident early centuries of the Greek Awakening, political problems did not seem too large for a few untrained officials to handle or too complicated for an assembly of ordinary citizens to understand.

Not all Greek states developed the structured government by assembly, council, and elected officials we have just outlined. In Sparta, for instance,

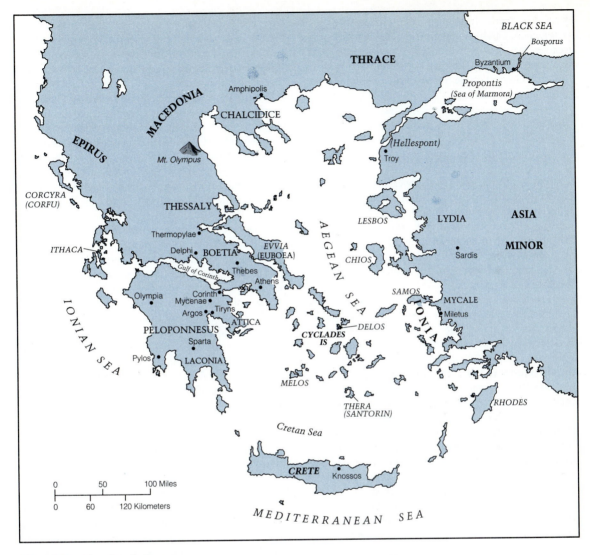

Map 2.2   The Greek Aegean

authority was much more centralized. A conservative and militaristic state, Sparta even retained the monarchy, having not one but two kings, who served as generals and performed religious functions. Five officials called *ephors,* however, wielded much of the power. The *gerousia,* a council composed of twenty-eight elder statesmen plus the two kings, also had much influence. The assembly was summoned only to elect officials or to vote yes or no on proposals offered by the rulers. This system, which the Spartans attributed to a semimythical lawgiver named Lycurgus, was actually developed as a means of controlling masses of forced laborers called *helots*

who did most of the work in Sparta. No other city-state retained so much of the political authoritarianism of earlier times.

The principles on which the Greek political system was normally based seem to have included an impulse toward equality and a sense of civic responsibility. There was also an emphasis on the importance of justice, meaning the even-handed application of the traditional laws and customs, lists of which began to be inscribed on stone in public places. These principles were, of course, often breached in practice. But they led to further development of both Greek political institutions and the political ideas that undergirded them. Influential later Greek studies of government, such as Plato's *Republic* and Aristotle's treatise on *Politics* with which political scientists wrestle to this day, had their roots in several centuries of Greek experience with this uncommon system of governance.

The Greek Colonies

To understand the rise of self-governing city-states in Greece, we need to look beyond the history of the polis itself to the economic growth and colonial expansion that accompanied and supported the political innovations of these centuries. Intertwined with all three of these forces we find the continuing fact of population growth—further evidence, perhaps, of the vitality of the Greeks.

From 750 B.C. on, the population increase that crowded the small cities of Greece and the Aegean drove many Greeks out of that world altogether. People who simply could not support themselves at home set out to trade and settle on the far coasts of the Mediterranean and beyond. This wave of colonization lasted through the seventh and sixth centuries B.C. and even on into the Classical Age that began around 500. It was a great diaspora, and it established Greek cities as far afield as Spain and the Black Sea. We will survey the major areas of colonization here, emphasizing the scope of Greek colonial expansion, and then attempt some analysis of this Greek version of colonialism.

Not long after 800 B.C., Greek traders had begun to follow the path earlier taken by Minoans and Mycenaeans to the sources of civilization in the Near East. Settlers in what is sometimes called East Greece established themselves on the southern shores of Asia Minor and on the large island of Cyprus. Over the next two centuries they moved on to Syria, where they accepted the overlordship of the Assyrian kings, and to Egypt, where the pharaohs sternly limited them to a single port. In this ancient part of the world, even the brash Greeks were impressed by the polished craftware of Syria and the monumental architecture of Egypt.

In the eighth century B.C., the Hellenes also turned their eyes west and began the great wave of colonization in earnest. They settled most thickly in southern Italy and Sicily, a region that became known as *Magna Graecia*, Great Greece, so many

were the Greek cities flourishing there. In Sicily, the Greeks began a long feud with the Phoenicians, who had already settled on the island. In southern Italy, Greek settlers helped to instruct the early Romans in the arts of civilization.

Further west, Greek colonies were established in southern France, notably at Massilia (Marseilles today) and more sparsely in southern Spain, including a settlement at Gades (Cadiz). Greek settlements appeared in Libya, in North Africa, and on the straits leading into the Black Sea. Greeks also established settlements around the Black Sea itself in what are today northern Turkey and southern Russia. The Greek way of life, however, does not seem to have fared as well in these northern climes as it did around the warmer southern seas.

Not all Greek city-states dispatched bands of colonists to far places: Athens, the greatest Greek city-state, sent out none during this period, and Sparta only one. But some highly developed states that had less territory at home to feed their growing numbers did seize on this expedient. Corinth, then more prosperous than Athens or Sparta, founded many colonies. So did cosmopolitan Miletus, on the Asia Minor side of the Aegean. Some of the colonial offshoots themselves also became famous cities, like wealthy Syracuse in Sicily, or Byzantium on the Bosporus, the city that later became Constantinople.

These Greek settlements were similar in some ways to the overseas colonies founded by European empire builders in modern times but differed from them in at least one important way. The process was certainly as deliberate among the Greeks. Once a city-state had decided to establish a colony, the city gathered colonists—every family might be required to supply one—appointed a distinguished leader, collected ships and supplies, and consulted merchants or others with overseas experience on a likely site. The city might offer support while the colonists raised the walls of their new settlement, apportioned fields, awed the indigenous people with the strength of the phalanx, and began the building of houses and temples. Thereafter, however, the mother city most commonly made no effort to retain control of the colony but allowed it to become an independent state. Ties of sentiment and commerce might bind the two, but in most cases no more than that. It was not Greek power that spread around the Mediterranean, but Greek civilization.

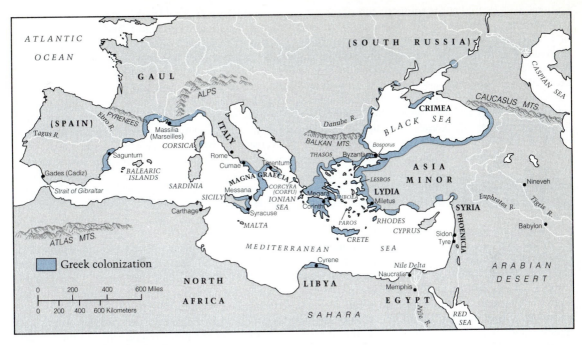

Map 2.3   Greek Colonization

Greek Commercial Expansion

Beneath the excitement of political change and colonial expansion lay the booming Greek economy. These three forces were interrelated, and all three were related to population growth. To feed the swelling numbers that did not seek new homes overseas, the Greek city-states imported wheat from as far away as southern Russia, and they pulled fish from the seas in increasing quantities. Most important, Greek farming at home expanded into every bit of usable land. Beyond the town and its surrounding fields of grain, grapevines and olive trees spread up the dry, rocky slopes, providing Greek cities with wine and oil, essentials of their own diet and major export items as well. Shepherds still watched their flocks on the higher slopes in the time-honored way, but large-scale commercial agriculture was transforming the village hinterlands below.

In the cities, the manufacture of pottery, textiles, and metalware also expanded rapidly. Many of the skills of Greek metalworkers, potters, weavers, and other artisans had originally been borrowed from the Near East. But the aesthetically and commercially precocious Greeks were soon producing and selling more than their mentors. Greek vases, for example, have been found among non-Greek peoples all around the Mediterranean. So great was the demand that Greek workshops developed a rudimentary division of labor, one artisan shaping the pot on the wheel, another painting its decorative design, and a third firing it in the kiln. When even this effort to speed up productivity could not keep up with demand, slaves were purchased and settled in many Greek cities to provide an additional work force.

Commerce evidently expanded as industrial and agricultural production did. New and larger ships were built, propelled by sails and by fifty or more oarsmen. Again, technical borrowings from the Near East helped. The art of writing, lost through the Dark Age, was once more imported into the Greek world, this time from their commercial rivals, the Phoenicians. After 800 B.C., a modified Phoenician alphabet of twenty-four letters spread among the Greeks. Coinage was invented around 650 B.C. in Lydia, a wealthy monarchy in Asia Minor, and the Greeks were stamping rude coins of their own by 600.

A leading example of this vigorous economic growth, as well as of the related wave of colonial expansion, was the booming cosmopolitan city of

Corinth. Well located at the southern end of the narrow isthmus that linked the Peloponnesus to the rest of Greece, this city had commercial outlets on both the Gulf of Corinth to the west and the Aegean Sea to the east. Corinthian artisans were celebrated bronzeworkers, and they also produced a much admired style of pottery. Corinthian shipbuilders were unexcelled. As we have seen, the Corinthians founded a number of colonies, including the Ionian island of Corcyra (Corfu today) and the great city of Syracuse on the island of Sicily, off the toe of the Italian boot. As we will see, Corinthian wealth and prestige gave that city a prominent part in the struggles and achievements of the next two hundred years.

Economic expansion was the key, however. Relatively free enterprise developed among the Greeks as it seldom had in the Near East, where royal or priestly overseers, royal monopolies and commercial expeditions, and other forms of government involvement in the economy were ancient traditions. Other peoples found the Greeks sharp traders, and their own poets noted the glitter of greed in the eye of the new entrepreneur, whether he was an aggressive merchant or an aristocratic landowner who financed overseas commercial ventures. But he was also very frequently successful.

Tensions and Reforms

There were a number of social and political consequences of the new wealth, and not all of them were positive. Elements of the growth and change that we have discussed had their darker side. By the sixth century B.C., the strains of rapid social transformation had begun to show. To cope with these inevitable social dislocations, two new types of Greek leader emerged: reformers and tyrants. Let us begin, however, with a look at the problems Greek society faced at the end of two centuries of drastic change.

The rough egalitarianism we associate with Greece had never been absolute, even in the depths of the Dark Age. Among the migrating tribes who repeatedly invaded the area, some groups had always had more land than others. Furthermore, the new affluence of the eighth, seventh, and sixth centuries B.C. stimulated an intensified acquisitiveness among the Greeks. The competitive spirit sometimes led to ruthless greed. As a result, brutal social exploitation often accompanied dynamic growth.

Exploitation could take many forms. Landowners who had more arable land to begin with or who were more alert to the export market got richer and expanded their holdings. Less successful farmers went into debt to their neighbors, paid huge interest, and sometimes even had to sell themselves and their families into slavery to pay their debts. In cities, manufacturers of pottery, metalware, and other goods and commercial entrepreneurs competed feverishly to please the growing market with more novel and beautiful designs. But these same aggressive spirits exploited their laborers and imported increasing numbers of foreign slaves to keep up with the demand.

Even among the better off, competition led to social resentments. The old landed aristocracy, particularly those who had seized the opportunities of the new era and had grown with the times, maintained and even enhanced their traditional preeminence in the new city-state. Their arrogance in society and their political domination of the council, the assembly, and the traditional judicial institutions sometimes stirred bitter resentment in other classes.

Resentment was often especially widespread among the middling, or hoplite class. As we have noted, the middle ranks of farmers had now been joined by representatives of the new industrial and commercial wealth to form an increasingly important bloc in society. These people, the backbone of the economy and the defenders of the state, sometimes challenged the older wealth and power of the aristocracy. And the increasing desperation of the lowest classes, from landless farmers to rowers in the ships of the merchants, added to the growing tension.

Thus economic exploitation, class conflict, and political factionalism grew along with the new wealth. One response was to attempt to reform the laws of the city-state to remedy social evils. Shortly before 600 B.C., for instance, the city of Athens commissioned a nobleman named Draco to codify its laws. Draco's efforts, although they were so rigorous that harsh regulations are still often described as "draconian" measures, did result in the publication of fixed laws under the jurisdiction of the government. This was at least an advance over clan retribution or ad hoc rulings by aristocratic elders serving as judges.

A generation later (the traditional date is 594 B.C.), the Athenians chose a widely respected aristocrat named Solon (c. 638–c. 558) as sole archon, or chief civil authority, to reform the laws once more.

Solon's reforms, which were economic as well as political, prohibited debt slavery and stimulated economic growth by encouraging production of olive oil and pottery for export and by standardizing the Athenian systems of weights and measures to conform to those of Corinth and the Near East. On the political side, Solon divided the population into four classes based on landholding, assigning each grade a place in the political structure. The upper two classes could hold the chief offices, both as archons and as members of the *Areopagus,* the traditional noble council, which also functioned as the highest court of law. Even the lowest rank of landholder could vote in the citizens' assembly and sit on the new *heliaea courts* of law, which in the next century challenged the aristocratic Areopagus for legal jurisdiction in Athens.

Solon's reforms were moderate, involving no such fundamental changes as land redistribution or genuine democracy. He did, however, begin to replace family connections with civic responsibility and aristocratic predominance with rule by public officials and popular participation in political affairs. "My strong shield guarded both sides equally," wrote Solon, "and gave to neither unjust victory."[2]

The Greek Tyrants

A more widespread response to social strain, however, was the seizure of power by tyrants. To the Greeks, *tyranny* meant not so much brutal oppression as illegitimate rule by individuals who held power through demagogic appeal, political intrigue, force, or a combination of all these. The tyrants of the sixth century B.C., however, had a larger part to play in Greek history than the furtherance of their own political ambitions. Though normally of aristocratic birth, they commonly presented themselves as champions of the middle orders of society and protectors of the poor. To win the support of these groups, tyrants enacted reforms. They thus frequently undermined the power of the ruling class from which they sprang, advanced the interests of the hoplite classes, and even eased the burdens of the lowest ranks of society. When tyrants were overthrown after a generation or two, as typically they were, they often left the state further along toward a fairer society.

The tyrants who arose in Corinth, Athens, and other city-states imposed such social changes as the division of large estates among poor peasants, the encouragement of handicraft manufacturing, and the development of overseas markets. They also earned support by waging successful wars against neighboring city-states, building magnificent temples, and patronizing poets and artists who celebrated their greatness as benefactors of the state.

Peisistratus and his son Hippias, who dominated Athens in the second half of the sixth century B.C., were celebrated examples of the Greek tyrant of this period. A nobleman and a war hero who made his fortune in foreign mining, Peisistratus (r. 546–527 B.C.) seized power three times in Athens, in 560, 556, and finally, with the help of an army of mercenaries, in 546 B.C. He drove rivals such as the Alcmaeonid family into exile, and by strengthening Athenian government, weakened the traditional influence of the aristocracy.

Peisistratus rebuilt the agora and expanded the wine and oil trade. It was about his time that Athenian "owls," coins stamped with the image of the bird sacred to Athena, the patron goddess of

This Athenian "owl" was the most respected currency of its time. The West has had a number of internationally accepted monetary units down the centuries, including the Byzantine bezant, the Florentine florin, the British pound and, most recently, the American dollar. [Kunsthistorisches Museum Vienna, Austria. Erich Lessing/Art Resource, New York]

Athens, were first minted. These coins came to be widely accepted throughout the Greek world. This Athenian tyrant earned the support of the masses by redistributing land confiscated from noble rivals to the small farmers, and by providing work for the poor on large building projects. By erecting new temples and sponsoring such civic and religious celebrations as the festival of Dionysus, he also gained a reputation for piety.

Peisistratus's beautification of Athens and his support for dramatists, poets, and artists earned the city much of the prestige it enjoyed in the next century. His support for the lower echelons of society against his fellow aristocrats and his preservation of at least the forms of citizen participation in government laid the foundations for the democracy that was to be Athens's glory.

Peisistratus was succeeded by his sons Hippias (r. 527–510 B.C.) and Hipparchus (r. 527–514). The brothers, who ruled jointly, followed their father's benevolent policies for over a decade but after Hipparchus's murder in a private quarrel, Hippias grew increasingly suspicious and cruel. In 510 B.C. the Alcmaeonid family returned with a powerful Spartan army and overthrew Hippias, ending the tyranny in Athens. It is worth noting, however, that Cleisthenes, a member of the Alcmaeonid family who became a primary architect of Athenian democracy, built on some of the foundations laid by the tyrant Peisistratus.

Early Greek Society and Culture

A bustling, aggressive, self-confident new society had thus taken shape over much of the Greek world by 500 B.C. Greeks everywhere shared many of the same values and believed in the same gods. Yet Greeks fought Greeks in petty wars and competed fiercely with their fellow townspeople in the marketplace and the assembly. It was a dynamic balance of forces, a society of contrasts.

It was also a society in the grip of rapid cultural transformation. Recent research and revaluation of the cultural remains of the period called here the Greek Awakening have led students of the era to see it in a new light. Such terms as *renaissance* and even *revolution* have been used to describe the rapid development of a distinctively Greek culture during these centuries before 500 B.C. Much of the evidence remains skimpy—fragments of poetry, thoughts of the first philosophers preserved in the books of later

writers, rare and too often broken statues. The foreign influence already noted also evidently played an important role as inspiration and as a culturally liberating force, loosening up more rigid and formal early Greek styles. But most scholars also see in the art and thought of this period both the rational structure and the irrepressible vitality of the Classic Greek civilization that was about to emerge.

Unity and Diversity

The Greek world, as we are reminded at every turn, was a divided one. But there was a unity in this world as well, a common culture that transcended yet was enriched by the variety it encompassed. The diversity of Greek society, which was both geographical and political, was perhaps more evident to contemporary Greeks than it can ever be to us. How many differences, after all, will a future historian see among the English-speaking capitalist democracies of the twentieth century—the United States, the United Kingdom, Canada, and Australia? Yet the differences are real and clear enough to us. And so it was with the Greek city-states in their smaller world.

That world, as we have seen, was geographically widely dispersed by the end of the sixth century B.C. There was mainland Greece itself, divided into a number of regions and states, as well as the islands of the Aegean, the Ionian coast of Asia Minor, and Greek colonies in other parts of the Mediterranean and around the Black Sea. On this foundation of geographic dispersion grew the political divisions of the Greeks. Athens emerged as the metropolis of Attica, which lay north of the Gulf of Corinth in central Greece. Sparta became the great power in the Peloponnesus, south of the gulf. Corinth was commercially the most successful state, and Miletus was the greatest city in Ionia. In the Dark Age, wars between petty kings might have been no more than raids for slaves or cattle. In the Greek Awakening that followed 750 B.C., city-states fought more seriously for every stretch of mutually claimed arable land. Civic loyalty to a particular city-state became a passionately lauded virtue.

Yet there was an underlying cultural unity as well. They were all *Hellenes*, descended from a common mythic ancestor, and in their own eyes thoroughly superior to the "barbarians" around them. These neighbors might be highly civilized, like the Egyptians or the Persians—*barbarian* did not mean crude or uncivilized but rather non-Greek. A number of factors encouraged these feelings of common Greekness.

All the Greeks, to begin with, spoke the same language, though there were many Greek dialects. The Doric accent of the Peloponnesus was associated with the terse speech of the Spartans, the dialect of sophisticated Ionia with the first Greek philosophers, and the Attic speech of Athens became the literary language. But the basic common tongue gave all Greeks a sense of being one people, no matter how far they wandered or how bitterly they quarreled with each other.

Religion was another force for unity. Each polis had its own patron divinity, but all Greeks believed in the same pantheon, the great gods traditionally believed to dwell on Mount Olympus in northern Greece. Headed by Zeus, this celestial company included gods and goddesses of love and war, grain and wine, the sea and the hearth of home—things that mattered intensely to all Greeks. If the Hellenes were not as single-mindedly religious as some Near Eastern peoples, familiarity with the same ancestral gods served to bind the peoples of the many Greek city-states together.

Other cultural elements, some of them related to religion, also drew the Greeks together. There were Panhellenic athletic contests, of which the Olympic Games, believed to have been founded in 776 B.C., were the most famous. At Olympia in the Peloponnesus, Greeks from many cities gathered every four years to race on foot and in chariots, hurl the discus and the javelin, wrestle, and box in fierce but peaceful competition. Other all-Greek sports meets included Corinth's Isthmian Games and the Pythian Games held at Delphi, site of Greece's famous oracle.

The shrine at Delphi, high in the mountains north of the Gulf of Corinth, also helped to remind Greeks of their common heritage. Here priestesses of Apollo responded to the questions of individuals or delegations from city-states with what were believed to be divinely inspired prophecies. All Greeks, finally, also shared a repertoire of artistic styles and common tastes. As we will see, Greek temples have a family likeness, and all Greeks revered Homer as the most inspired of poets.

Social Classes and Gender Roles

The evolution of the social structure of the Greeks, from Dark Age poverty and village culture to the competitive and exploitative class system of the age of the Greek Awakening, has been briefly traced. It will be useful now, however, to outline the basic structure of fully developed Greek society, for the interplay of social groups had much to do with the subsequent unfolding of Greek history.

With the passing of the Dark Age kings, the landed aristocracy claimed the highest prestige in society. Most Greeks probably accepted these claims to social preeminence based on respectable agricultural wealth, family names long eminent in the state, and descent from semidivine heroes. As Greece grew wealthier, some aristocrats developed a taste for luxury—for racehorses and Corinthian vases, elegantly dressed hair and oriental oils and perfumes. These hereditary nobles did not, however, lose touch with the older virtues of their ancestors. These included courage, honor, justice as they understood it, rivalry within their own ranks for leadership, and loyalty to their class against all others.

Next down the social scale were the middle levels of society, the hoplite class, including well-off farmers and newly wealthy men of business. This diverse group probably did not feel much unity, for although farming was a traditionally respectable occupation, trade was not. Nor were the middle classes normally eager to shoulder the old aristocrats aside and rule in their place; they were much more likely to imitate the tastes and manners of their social superiors. Still, there were resentments when aristocratic cabals prevented the "new people" from having their say in the assembly or twisted the laws in their own interests.

We know much less about the poorest classes and their views. In this period, poor farmers and laborers in the workshops, rowers on Greek ships, helots in Spartan fields, and slaves engaged in other labor had no part in the political life of the state. Furthermore, it is not likely that they aspired to a share of political power or to economic or social equality in any modern sense. Fairness, evenhanded enforcement of the laws, and changes in the laws when abuses were too gross were probably the extent of their social philosophy.

Another aspect of early Greek social history about which we know less than we would like is gender roles—the differing parts played by men and women in this first of Western societies. It seems likely that the status of women was relatively high among the first people in this corner of the world, the ancient Minoans. Their chief divinity was probably female, a Great Goddess or Great Mother whose worship has

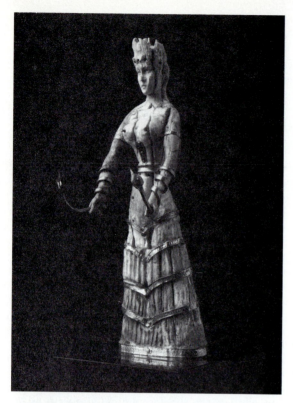

The flounced skirt of this ivory-and-gold Snake Goddess from Minoan Crete (c. 1500 B.C.) is ringed with gold, and the snakes that encircle her arms and rear their heads toward her are also gold. The figure's timeless beauty and strength presages the glory of Athens and ancient Greece that was to come. [Snake Goddess, Minoan, from Crete. About 1600–1500 B.C. Gold and ivory. H: 6½ in. Gift of Mrs. W. Scott Fitz. Courtesy Museum of Fine Arts, Boston]

been detected all over the Mediterranean in early times.

Women were also prominent among the elite pictured on Minoan walls, and young women were apparently as free as young men to take part in the sport of bull leaping. The Minoan society was matrilineal, so that inheritance was through the female rather than the male line. Minoan women could own property in their own names, and some women may have worked at crafts like pottery.

Of women in Mycenaean times and in the Greek Dark Age that followed we know as little as we do of most things from those periods. It seems likely that the northern invaders who populated the Greek lands, from the Mycenaeans on, were a patriarchal people who relegated women to lower status. Though half the original twelve Olympians were fe-

male, Zeus was their imperious king. Homer's epic poetry of the late Dark Age included such prominent women as the beautiful Helen of Troy, but the poems were primarily stories of male adventure.

There is at least some evidence of the status of women in society as the Greek Awakening reached its climax in the sixth century B.C. The rights and activities of upper-class women in particular were clearly limited. Greek men believed that their honor required them to protect—or control—all the women in their households. For this reason, wives, daughters, and other female relatives were cloistered in a special section of the house. They did their share of the work—spinning and weaving were main occupations for women—but always in this protected enclave. Only a poor man would send his wife out to work in a market stall.

Greek women in the sixth century B.C. were probably freer to own property, had more rights in marriage, and may have been more prominent in society and in some religious cults than they had been in the Dark Age. Nevertheless, the wives of Athenian citizens probably enjoyed fewer of these and other signs of social status than Minoan court ladies had a thousand years before in ancient Crete.

Religion and Philosophy

Closely interwoven with the Greek society we have sketched was a polytheistic religion similar to those that flourished among Near Eastern peoples. In the Greek world, however, alternative explanations for the nature of things began to crop up in the sixth century B.C. The first Greek philosophers began to speculate about the accuracy of traditional wisdom.

Greek religion, like that of many peoples, came in layers. At the top were the cults of the Olympians, the great gods whose genealogies had been chronicled in Hesiod's *Theogony*, whose temples still draw tourists and whose statues grace our museums today. Much less public were the folk beliefs and mystery religions that probably tell us more about the depths of Greek religious feeling.

Zeus was universally recognized as the king of the gods and the final arbiter of human destinies. But his queen, his brothers, and his children, the other Olympians, had crucial functions too. Zeus's brother Poseidon was god of the sea, and his daughter Athena was the goddess of wisdom, the crafts, and sometimes military strategy. Apollo reigned as lord of poetry, music, law, and prophecy. Aphrodite was the goddess of beauty and love, Ares lord of the battlefield, and Artemis goddess of the hunt.

The Olympians were very human gods and goddesses. They were more powerful than mortals and gifted with eternal life, but otherwise they ate and drank, loved, hated, and intrigued much as humans do. They often came down to earth to interfere in human lives. Indeed, Zeus had a number of sons with earthly women. These semidivine offspring were the heroes of Greek myth—Herakles (Hercules) who slaughtered more monsters than Gilgamesh did, Theseus who killed the Minotaur of Crete, Achilles, perhaps the greatest of all the heroes of the Trojan War, and others.

These gods and heroes were honored with beautiful temples and celebrated in annual festivals by the newly wealthy city-states. Choral odes were chanted to them, parades held in their honor, unblemished cattle sacrificed to win their favor. Priests, however, did not gain powerful positions in Greek society because kings, officials, and heads of families presided at these ceremonies. Indeed, the cults of the Olympian gods sometimes seem rather like civic celebrations, the temples and statues evidence of the wealth of the city as much as of its piety.

Yet there was a deeper layer of religious life among the Greeks. Particularly in the countryside, ancient fertility cults still existed, and the forces of nature were embodied in local spirits of the place. Female spirits called naiads inhabited brooks and streams, and dryads, or wood nymphs, roamed the forests. Centaurs and satyrs (half man-half horse and half man-half goat, respectively) capered and pranced on the hills or at least through the dreams of farming folk and shepherds.

Sometimes newer cults captured the imagination of even the most sophisticated. Among these were the cults of Dionysus and Demeter, the divinities who were responsible for the harvest of grapes and grain. The belief in the goddess Demeter was a fertility cult celebrating the growing of the grain. Demeter also promised eternal life to initiates who attended the Eleusinian mysteries, religious ceremonies centering on rituals and dramatic spectacles so secret that they remain unknown to this day. The followers of Dionysus worshiped a god of grapes and wine whose death and rebirth also symbolized the annual rebirth of the crops apparently with ecstatic rites including midnight revelry and feasting on the raw flesh of a sacrificial animal. Yet Dionysus was also honored more publicly and sedately at a great annual festival at Athens, where the Greek theater was born.

These emotional, ecstatic discharges of energy in the name of religion reveal a startlingly irrational side to the Greek character. The early Greeks, however, are still seen as a significantly rational people, apostles of logic and common sense. Both early Greek science and the thought of the first philosophers support this more traditional view.

Greek science flourished more vigorously in later centuries, but its beginnings are worthy of note, particularly in light of the special concern of contemporary philosophers with the natural world. There is evidence, for instance, that the Minoans understood the decimal system, and Homer, writing in the Greek Dark Age, alluded to some fairly sophisticated surgical treatment of war wounds. In the sixth century B.C. Greeks built sundials, observed the properties of magnets, understood how veins and arteries worked, and hypothesized that life on earth had evolved from amphibians some twenty-five centuries before Charles Darwin proposed his theory of evolution. Although they were wrong about some things—they saw the earth as a disk rather than a globe, for example—their interest in science bore rich fruit in later Greek centuries.

Philosophia, literally "love of wisdom," referred in ancient Greece to freewheeling speculation on the nature of things and on the proper conduct for human beings. The first such independent thinkers were Ionians, citizens of the rich and sophisticated city of Miletus. The Milesians and their immediate successors seem to have devoted their energies to trying to understand the ultimate nature of the world around them. They expressed their views in sometimes poetic works that survive only in fragments; yet even a superficial glance at the range of their thinking reveals the speculative reach of the Greek intellect.

Thales of Miletus (c. 625–547 B.C.), the first Greek philosopher, believed that all things ultimately reduce to water, an idea perhaps derived from Egyptian or Mesopotamian thought. Others suggested that either air or fire was the ultimate substance, and Thales's pupil Anaximander (c. 610–c. 547) urged that the world is best defined in terms of the four basic qualities of hot and cold, moist and dry.

Some of the followers of these thinkers in the early fifth century B.C. went considerably beyond these early efforts. Pythagoras (c. 580–500), best known for his contributions to geometry, asserted that the essence of the universe lay in numerical relationships. He formulated the famous Pythagorean theorem concerning the hypotenuse of the right triangle (another concept known earlier to the Egyptians), and recognized that the pitch of a vibrating string on a musical instrument is directly related to its length. As a philosopher, however, he went much further, declaring that all of nature is permeated by such numerically based cosmic harmonies.

Heraclitus (c. 540–450 B.C.), recognized in his own time as the most difficult of the Ionian thinkers, seems to have believed that the essence of reality is change. The world, he said, is like a leaping flame or a flowing river in which nothing is ever the same. Parmenides (born c. 515 B.C.), by contrast, became the true founder of philosophical metaphysics by demonstrating that beneath all appearances of difference and change lies pure being, eternal and immutable. Parmenides saw understanding of this ultimate ground of reality, comprehensible only through human reason, as the true goal of philosophical inquiry.

The Greeks thus moved in a few generations from folk wisdom to full-fledged philosophy. Many of the answers they produced were far from simple, and some were contradictory: Heraclitus and Parmenides could scarcely both be right. But then, metaphysical questions like these still await definitive answers some twenty-five centuries later.

Art of the Archaic Age

Over the centuries of the Greek Awakening the arts of painting, sculpture, and architecture all evolved. Moving from generally primitive beginnings in the Dark Age, the plastic arts went through a phase of what is called "orientalizing" in the eighth and seventh centuries B.C. to a thoroughly Greek sixth-century climax in what is traditionally known as the Archaic style.

Nearly all the early Greek painting that survives is found on a wide range of pottery—from huge funerary urns and storage vessels to large jars for mixing wine and water and wide elegant cups for drinking the result. At first, during the Dark Age, these vessels were decorated in a geometric style, covered with lines, zigzags, triangles, and other patterns. Simple line drawings of animals repeated in a frieze were gradually admitted to the geometric decoration. But then from East Greece came a startling new style, full of flowers and animals, of rosettes, lions, griffins, sphinxes, and other motifs picked up in the Near East.

Liberated by this immersion in oriental themes, potters at Corinth, Athens, and elsewhere turned to

the subject that would always fascinate Greek artists more than any other: the human figure. Pictures of gods and goddesses, scenes from famous myths or from the battles of the Trojan War soon became common on Greek vases. So did scenes from every-

Compare this Archaic Greek statue of a young woman with that of Queen Khamerernebty standing with her husband in Chapter 1. Can you see similarities in the pose and details (fingers, feet) of the two statues that suggest that this early Greek sculpture had an Egyptian model?

day life, of women talking at the well or men at drinking parties. Two basic techniques evolved: *black figure,* in which the figures were painted in black on the reddish background of the clay, and *red figure,* in which the entire vase was painted black, leaving the figures in the reddish color of the original clay. The figures evolved slowly toward naturalism, though they retained simple line drawing and exaggerated poses in profile. By 500 B.C., Greek painters had developed a masterly control of flowing line, ingenuity of composition, and a vigor of presentation that would seldom be excelled.

Greek sculpture also made a major leap ahead under the influence of the ancient East. Thus the crude stick figures cast in bronze during the Dark Age were replaced during the Greek Awakening by Eastern griffins and lions, much more fully rounded and convincing, in both bronze and stone. And again Greeks turned their attention to the human figure. Carved in the white marble so common in the rocky islands and hills of Greece, these life-size brightly painted figures were clearly influenced by ancient Egyptian models. The typical young man, or *kouros,* stands naked, facing you rigidly, hands at his sides, one foot advanced. The young woman, or *kore,* is fully clothed, her figure concealed in the stiffly formal folds of her gown. Both wear the strange "Archaic smile," created by the way the curve of the cheek meets the angle of the lips. We have seen those fixed poses before, in the more smoothly carved stone of Egyptian statues many centuries older. Greek sculpture, as it developed, took that art along roads never before trodden.

Greek architecture also emerged under Egyptian influence in the seventh century B.C. Accustomed to simple structures of stone and mud brick, with porches or roofs sometimes supported by wooden pillars, the Greeks were awed by Egypt's huge columned stone temples. By the mid-sixth century B.C., newly wealthy Greek city-states were building temples in stone too. These structures were simple in design, house-shaped structures with pillared colonnades and relief sculpture under the eaves and along the sides above the fluted pillars. The capitals of the columns were of two sorts, the simpler Doric and the more elaborate Ionic, inspired by Ionian contacts with Near Eastern architecture. The basic structure remained simple post and lintel, a matter of pillars and crossbeams, like that of earlier Greek buildings. But the Greek genius explored the subtle possibilities of this architectural form all the way to the Parthenon.

Poetry in the Age of Homer

Poetry is actually older than prose as a literary form. Greek poetry was invented before Greeks learned to read and write. It evolved as an oral tradition roughly comparable to the folk songs and balladry of many peoples. In the Dark Age, bards chanted epic war poems; in the seventh and sixth centuries B.C., lyric poems were sung by soloists or choruses to the sound of a lyre. Both epic and lyric were composed and recited in a rhythm based on the length of the vowel sounds rather than on accentuation of syllables, as in later Western tradition. The Greeks thus learned to construct a gripping narrative, compress a powerful emotion into a turn of phrase, and put into

Here the bard Homer seems to be seeking another audience for the works he recited in village squares or palaces. Carved centuries after the blind poet wrote the *Iliad* and the *Odyssey,* the statue reflects the Greeks' continuing veneration of Homer. What helps us feel the poet's blindness?

words "the way life is" when literature was still a performing art, and everyone read aloud even when alone. From the earlier, epic tradition, we have one giant: Homer. Of the later, lyric poetry, many fragments survive, but again one poet stands out: Sappho.

Homer was hailed by the ancient Greeks as their greatest poet, his *Iliad* and the *Odyssey* as sacred books. Homer was traditionally described as blind and as having lived in Ionia, probably around 800 B.C. Classicists dispute Homer's dates, and some have questioned whether Homer ever lived at all, suggesting that the poems were really a compilation of the work of several people. Most authorities feel, however, that the order and development imposed on these two novel-length poems must be the work of a single mind, although the author was almost certainly working with traditional tales of that most popular of Greek myth cycles, the story of the Trojan War.

This legendary conflict pits a Greek army against the Near Eastern city of Troy in a ten-year struggle, a conflict ignited by the seduction of the Greek princess Helen by the Trojan prince Paris and ending with the destruction of his city. Homer's *Iliad*—the *Poem of Ilios,* or Troy—deals with a single series of events in the tenth year of the war. It is the story of "the wrath of Achilles," who was the greatest of the Greek heroes. Because of a falling out with the Greek king, Agamemnon, Achilles turns his back on the war,

WAR AND PEACE   The Black Earth Ran Blood: Achilles on the Battlefield

Homer's *Iliad,* the epic of the siege of Troy, climaxes with Achilles's return to the battlefield to avenge the death of his friend Patroclus. The bard's audience around 800 B.C. probably knew battle wounds, and they got them here in profusion and with anatomical precision. The first great Western poet also used what became known as *Homeric simile,* an example of which can be seen in the excerpt quoted here. Homer makes an extended comparison between the enraged hero, Achilles, and an uncontrollable and destructive force of nature, a forest fire, as he describes Achilles's rampages across the battlefield.

> Then Achilleus swooping on Dardanos and Laogonos, sons both
> of Bias, dashed them to the ground from behind their horses,
> one with a spearcast, one with a stroke of the sword from close up.
> Now Iros, Alastor's son . . .
> he stabbed with his sword at the liver
> so that the liver was torn from its place, and from it the black blood
> drenched the fold of his tunic and his eyes were shrouded in darkness
> as the life went. Next from close in he thrust at Moulios
> with the pike at the ear, so the bronze spearhead pushed through and came out
> at the other ear. Now he hit Echeklos the son of Agenor
> with the hilted sword, hewing against his head in the middle
> so all the sword was smoking with blood, and over both eyes
> closed the red death and the strong destiny. Now Deukalion
> was struck in the arm, at a place in the elbow where the tendons
> come together. There through the arm Achilleus transfixed him
> with the bronze spearhead, and he, arm hanging heavy, waited
> and looked his death in the face.
>
> As inhuman fire sweeps on in fury through the deep angles
> of a drywood mountain and sets ablaze the depth of the timber
> and the blustering wind lashes the flame along, so Achilleus
> swept everywhere with his spear like something more than a mortal
> harrying them as they died, and the black earth ran blood.

Source: Homer, *The Iliad,* translated by Richmond Lattimore (Chicago: University of Chicago Press, 1951), 416–417.

and it is not until his best friend Patroclus has been killed trying to take his place that Achilles returns to the battlefield. There he takes a bloody revenge in a rampage that climaxes with his killing of the greatest Trojan hero, Hector. (For a vivid scene from this rampage, see the box titled "The Black Earth Ran Blood: Achilles on the Battlefield.")

In Homer's *Odyssey,* we follow the Greek hero Odysseus (Ulysses) home from Troy. Odysseus's ten-year wandering around the Mediterranean brings him encounters with monsters and magic, seductive sirens, and bloody violence enough to satisfy any modern audience's hunger for excitement. All these adventures are presided over by the very human gods and goddesses who decide in the end who is to live and who is to die. Most strikingly, even amid the carnage and the marvels, there are moments of tenderness and truth that have spoken down the centuries to later generations. Hector saying goodbye to his wife and child before going out to the battle from which he will not return, Odysseus's faithful wife Penelope staving off a horde of ambitious rivals by an ingenious ruse, even the aged dog that recognizes the returning hero are touches of human warmth in a world of violence and death.

Sappho stood firmly and passionately for life. "Some say a cavalry corps, some infantry . . . are the finest sight on the dark earth," she says in a famous fragment, "but I say that whatever one loves is."[3] We know more about Sappho than we do about Homer, but she, too, has been a controversial figure. We know she was an aristocratic woman who lived on the island of Lesbos off the Ionian coast around 600 B.C. She was one of the lyric poets of the seventh and sixth centuries B.C. whose verse dealt often with religious and patriotic themes but who also wrote love poems, drinking songs, satires, and other brief expressions of strong feelings.

Sappho surrounded herself on Lesbos with admiring young women, and some of her love poems may have been directed to them. The term *lesbian* used today to refer to women whose sexual preference is for other women derives from her Greek island. What Sappho's own sexual preferences may have been we cannot know. She had a daughter, and thus may have had a husband, and some of her poems sing the praises of handsome men rather than the beauty of girls. But for readers of poetry, the poet's own feelings are less important than the words she left us.

Sappho wrote of a light step, a look, a laugh

Sappho, the Greek poet, is shown here with Alcaeus, another celebrated Greek bard of the island of Lesbos. The Greeks honored their poets as much as they did their philosophers, political leaders, and war heroes. Can you think of any poet of the modern West who receives this sort of adulation?

that stops the heart. She wrote of her love for her child, a "golden flower" for whom she would not take a kingdom. She hymned the beauty of the Greek islands, turning moonrise over the sea into words that defy the translator yet. All we have of her verse is fragmentary, sometimes no more than a single vivid image. Yet such is the power of these shards of poems—they are so compact, direct, and delicate—that no one questions Sappho's right to stand with the greatest. She certainly spoke for herself when she wrote "They will remember us."

A Topical Summary

Politics: First the Minoans and then the Mycenaeans dominated the Aegean Sea, the Minoans largely through commercial expansion, the Mycenaeans primarily by force. After the Greek Dark Age, a period of regression to village life, major city-states emerged on the Greek mainland as well as on the islands of the Aegean and the surrounding coasts. Through the efforts of political reformers and ambitious tyrants, the city-state evolved into a relatively self-governing community in a world made up largely of autocratic monarchies.

Economics: Commerce was an important part of both the Minoan and Mycenaean cultures, but during the Greek Dark Age people returned essentially to subsistence agriculture. With the Greek Awakening came industrial and commercial expansion, and by 500 B.C. Greek prosperity could be seen in the presence of Greek ships, colonies, and products—wine, oil, jars and other, handcrafted articles—all over the Mediterranean world.

Society: Although they were divided politically, Greeks were united by a common language, religion, and other shared beliefs and customs. Greek society revealed a full range of class differences, despite its relatively democratic political system, and imposed distinct limits on the roles of women and the lower classes.

Technology: Bronze Age skills were part of the Minoan and Mycenaean cultures, but it was not until the Greek Dark Age that Greek peoples began to use iron as well as bronze and not until the Greek Awakening that they began to make large ceramic storage vessels, to build ships that were propelled by sails and oars, and to construct the first of the temples for which Greece is famous.

Culture: A new vitality combined with shrewd borrowings from Near Eastern and Egyptian models to produce the culture of the Greek Awakening. Ceramics and architecture in particular owed a considerable debt to these neighboring civilizations. Greek philosophy, however, moved in original directions, and the poetry of Sappho and Homer celebrated such eternal human experiences as love and war.

The Expanding West: The Greeks who descended from the northern grasslands into the Greek peninsula soon spread to the islands of the Aegean. From the eighth century on Greek traders and colonists expanded the Greek world still further around both the Mediterranean and the Black Seas. A pattern of expansion thus emerged as an integral part of Western history from its very beginnings.

Some Key Terms

agora 46	Hellenes 52	palace system 43
archon 46	*helot* 47	*phalanx* 45
Areopagus 51	*hoplite* 45	*phratry* 44
black figure ware 57	*kore* 57	*polis* 45
ephor 47	*kouros* 57	red figure
gerousia 47	Linear A, 40	ware 57
heliaea court 51	Linear B 38	

Notes

1. Edgar Allen Poe, "To Helen."
2. "The Lawgiver's Boast," trans. Gilbert Highet, in *The Oxford Book of Greek Verse in Translation*, ed. T. F. Higham and C. M. Bowra (Oxford: Clarendon Press, 1938), no. 159.
3. Mary Barnard, *Sappho* (Berkeley: University of California Press, 1966), no. 30.

Reading List

BERNAL, M. *Black Athena: The Afroasiatic Roots of Classical Civilization.* 2 vols. New Brunswick, N.J.: Rutgers University Press, 1987–1991. Controversial study of Egyptian and Near Eastern influences on early Greek culture.

BOARDMAN, J. *The Greeks Overseas: Their Early Colonies and Trade.* Rev. ed. London: Thames and Hudson, 1982. Thorough study of early Greek expansion.

CHADWICK, J. *The Mycenaean World.* New York: Cambridge University Press, 1976. Perhaps the best socioeconomic survey of the Mycenaean period.

CRAIK, E. M. *The Dorian Aegean.* London: Routledge and Kegan Paul, 1980. Scholarly guide to the society and culture of the Dorian peoples.

EMLYN-JONES, C. J. *The Ionians and Hellenism: A Study of the Cultural Achievement of the Early Greek Inhabitants of Asia Minor.* London: Chapman and Hall, 1980. Focuses on the artistic and philosophic contributions of Ionia to early Greek culture.

FINLEY, M. I. *The World of Odysseus.* Rev. ed. Harmondsworth, England: Penguin, 1979. The Homeric world and its worldview, by a leading authority.

FORREST, W. G. *A History of Sparta, 950–192 B.C.* New York: Norton, 1969. Excellent general history.

GUTHRIE, W. K. C. *The Greeks and Their Gods.* Boston: Beacon, 1955. Religion and its many roots in a society often thought of as notably secular.

HAMPE, R., and E. SIMON. *The Birth of Greek Art from the Mycenaean to the Archaic Period.* London: Thames and Hudson, 1981. Urges continuity between the Mycenaeans and the Greeks who succeeded them as masters of the Aegean world.

HOMER. *The Iliad.* Translated by R. Lattimore. Chicago: University of Chicago Press, 1951. Powerful poetic rendering by a noted Greek scholar who is also a modern poet.

JEFFREY, L. H. *Archaic Greece: City-States ca. 700–500 B.C.* New York: St. Martin's Press, 1978. Political history of the period.

MURRAY, O. *Early Greece.* Atlantic Heights, N.J.: Humanities Press, 1980. Archaic Greece in the eastern Mediterranean context.

PALMER, L. R. *Mycenaeans and Minoans.* 2d ed. Westport, Conn.: Greenwood Press, 1980. Revisionist approach to the two most ancient cultures of the Greek world.

POMEROY, S. B. *Goddesses, Whores, Wives, and Slaves: Women in Classical Antiquity.* New York: Schocken, 1975. A celebrated feminist survey of women's place in Greece and Rome.

RICHTER, G. M. A. *Archaic Greek Art Against Its Historical Background.* New York: Oxford University Press, 1949. Still a good survey.

SAPPHO. *The Songs of Sappho in English Translation by Many Poets.* Mount Vernon, N.Y.: Peter Pauper Press, 1946. Literary versions that capture the spirit of the poet better than more literal translations of the often fragmentary surviving poems.

SNODGRASS, A. *Archaic Greece: The Age of Experiment.* London: J.M. Dent, 1980. Essays on various aspects of the period of the Greek Awakening.

STARR, C. G. *The Economic and Social Growth of Early Greece, 800–500 B.C.* New York: Oxford University Press, 1977. Good summary, with some emphasis on Near Eastern influences.

VERMEULE, E. *Greece in the Bronze Age.* Chicago: University of Chicago Press, 1972. Scholarly treatment of Mycenaean Greece.

WILLETTS, R. F. *The Civilization of Ancient Crete.* Berkeley: University of California Press, 1977. The story of the island culture from Minoan to Roman times.

WOODHOUSE, W. J. *Solon the Liberator.* London: Oxford University Press, 1938. Goals and achievements of the Athenian reformer.

The fifth century B.C. has a symmetry and a tragic climax that give it a powerful dramatic appeal. It is the story of a genuine golden age bracketed by two terrible wars. It was once customary for historians to present this drama as a clear-cut struggle between good and evil. Its heroes were the freedom-loving Athenians, depicted as winning a great war against the barbarous East, bringing freedom, truth, and beauty to the West, and then going down to tragic defeat at the hands of their fellow Greeks, the militaristic Spartans. The story thus had a clear beginning, middle, and end: the Persian War of the early fifth century, the Periclean Age of the middle decades, and the wars between the Greek city-states that brought the century to its tragic close.

It still makes sense to divide the century into these three parts, though none of the parties involved look as simply good or bad as they once did. The Persians may not have been the barbarians, the Spartans the single-minded militarists, or the Athenians the pure champions of freedom we once imagined. But however we reinterpret the political history of the century, the cultural accomplishments of the age still stand out. There is little doubt that without the civilization of fifth-century B.C. Greece, Western thought and art could scarcely have evolved as they have for the past 2,500 years.

Athena Lemnia. Roman marble copy after an original of c. 450 B.C. by Phidias. Museo Civico, Bologna, Italy

The Persian Wars

A classic definition of tragedy explains it as a story that begins gaily and ends gravely; a comedy goes just the other way. If we imagine the history of the Greek fifth century B.C. as a tragedy in three acts, the first act clearly fits this pattern. It is the story of the greatest victory in Greek history: the triumph of the small Greek city-states over the Persian colossus, at that time the world's largest empire.

The Persian Threat

When Apollo's sun chariot rose each morning, it traveled first across the vast lands of the Persians, a people who had never yet lost a war. *Yet,* of course, was not very long: the Persian Empire had been founded only a couple of generations earlier. Cyrus the Great seized power among the Medes and the Persians in 500 B.C. and marched into Babylon in

539. His son Cambyses conquered the other primary center of ancient civilization by overrunning Egypt in 525 B.C., and Cambyses's son Darius, the third of the Achaemenid line, took over the leadership of the empire after a brief civil war in 521. Persia was, in short, a young and still dynamic state in 500 B.C. and one whose power had been built on the battlefield.

Darius (r. 521–486 B.C.), who like his grandfather Cyrus was known as "the Great," organized the conquests of his predecessors and, in attempting to preserve them, brought the empire into conflict with the Greeks. Darius's subjects included Mesopotamians, Egyptians, Syrians, Hebrews—historically known as Jews from about this time—the Greeks of East Greece, and all the other civilized peoples of the Near East. They also included the agricultural villagers and pastoral nomads of the less developed northern tier of the Middle East, today's Turkey, Iran, Afghanistan, and Pakistan. Darius himself pushed the frontiers of his empire into the Balkan corner of Europe and beyond Egypt into Libya.

To impose the authority of a limited number of Persians on so vast and disparate an array of peoples, Darius granted considerable autonomy to his provincial satraps, or governors, and to many of the conquered peoples themselves. Subject peoples often retained their traditional institutions while recognizing the emperor's overlordship. In Egypt, for example, the Persian king of kings was pharaoh. He was the favored choice of Marduk, the patron god of Babylon, and among the Persians, he was divinely chosen by Ahura Mazda, the god of the Zoroastrian religion. All subjects of the empire, however, were required to pay tribute, contribute troops to the army, and acknowledge the absolute sovereignty of Darius the Great.

The Greek city-states of Ionia, scattered down the Aegean coast of Asia Minor, were only a small part of this huge agglomeration of peoples. Suiting his rule to their traditions, Darius appointed tyrants (in the Greek sense of the term) to govern the Ionian states, choosing men who would be properly subservient to local satraps. He also imposed his authority on the Greeks of Cyprus, the Egyptian delta, and the other Greek colonies. In the north, he crossed the Hellespont—the narrowest part of the straits linking the Aegean and Black seas—to conquer the seminomadic Scythians and the region of Thrace on the northern coast of the Aegean. There he collected tribute from the partially hellenized Kingdom of Macedonia, just north of the mainland Greek city-states. Even before the great struggle began, then, the Greeks of the mainland and the Aegean islands could feel the hot breath of Persian expansion on their necks.

When, in 499 B.C., the Greek cities of the Ionian coast rebelled against the Persian king, they began a struggle that lasted twenty years and engulfed the entire Greek world. Indeed, the Persian wars in the eastern Mediterranean dragged on for half a century. Confronting the Persian foe across their narrow island-strewn sea, the Greeks might well be apprehensive. When at one point the worried Athenians sent an embassy to ask the oracle at Delphi what to expect, the priestess's response was terrifying. "Why sit you, doomed ones?" she demanded of the delegation:

> Fly to the world's end, leaving
> Home and your city. . . .
> All is ruined, for fire and the headlong
>   God of War
> Speeding in a Syrian chariot shall bring
>   you low.[1]

The First Persian Invasion

As early as 510 b.c., smoldering resentment among the Ionian Greeks had inspired an abortive revolt based on an inaccurate report of Persian defeats elsewhere. Then in 499 b.c., a much larger and more consequential rebellion broke out, led by Miletus, the wealthiest, most sophisticated of all the Ionian cities. The insurrection was sparked by the Milesian tyrant, Aristagoras, who had not advanced as he hoped in the service of Darius. But it also reflected real dissatisfaction among the restlessly independent Greeks. And it looked for a time as though the revolt might have a future.

Inspired by the defiant example of Miletus, Greek cities up and down the eastern Aegean coast, from the Hellespont in the north to the island of Cyprus in the south, overthrew their Persian-backed tyrants and prepared to fight. Envoys were dispatched to mainland Greece requesting the assistance of their brothers across the sea. Of the Greek city-states, only Athens and its neighbor, Eretria, responded with a few ships and men. Nevertheless, in 498 B.C., the Athenians, the Milesians, and their allies marched inland, pushing the local Persian troops aside, and capturing and burning the provincial capital of Sardis.

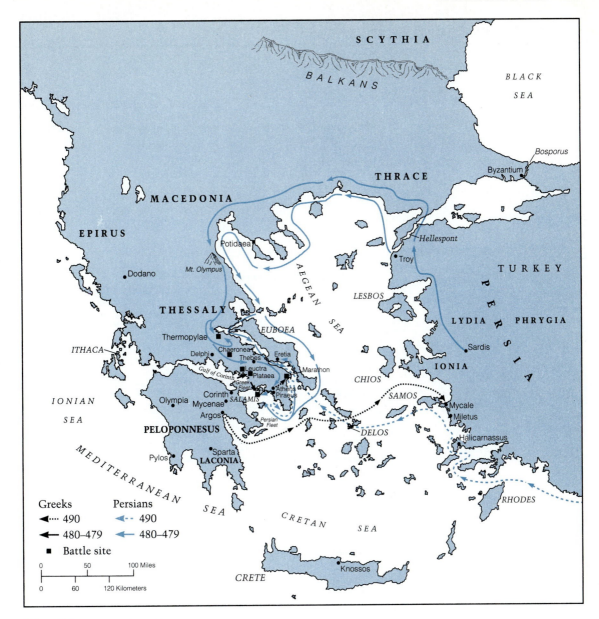

Map 3.1 The Persian Wars

Then things began rapidly to go wrong for the rebels. More substantial Persian forces defeated them on land and sea. Their Greek allies departed for home. And in 494 B.C. the Persians besieged Miletus itself. They captured and destroyed the city, enslaved some of its surviving population, and sent the rest off into exile in southern Mesopotamia.

In Athens, there was mourning for fellow Hel-lenes. In his many-columned throne room at Perse-polis, Darius determined to discourage a recurrence by making an example of the two Greek states that had dared to aid his rebellious Ionian subjects.

In 490 B.C. a Persian expedition involving hun-dreds of ships and perhaps fifty thousand men threaded its way through the islands of the Aegean to its targets in central Greece. Eretria, on the long

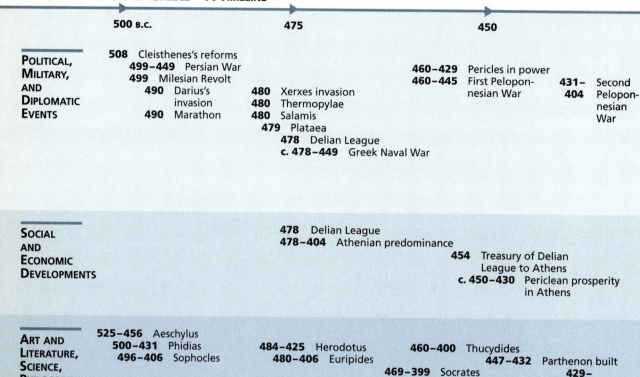

500 B.C.   **475**   **450**

POLITICAL, MILITARY, AND DIPLOMATIC EVENTS

- 508 Cleisthenes's reforms
- 499–449 Persian War
- 499 Milesian Revolt
- 490 Darius's invasion
- 490 Marathon
- 480 Xerxes invasion
- 480 Thermopylae
- 480 Salamis
- 479 Plataea
- 478 Delian League
- c. 478–449 Greek Naval War
- 460–429 Pericles in power
- 460–445 First Peloponnesian War
- 431–404 Second Peloponnesian War

SOCIAL AND ECONOMIC DEVELOPMENTS

- 478 Delian League
- 478–404 Athenian predominance
- 454 Treasury of Delian League to Athens
- c. 450–430 Periclean prosperity in Athens

ART AND LITERATURE, SCIENCE, PHILOSOPHY, AND RELIGION

- 525–456 Aeschylus
- 500–431 Phidias
- 496–406 Sophocles
- 484–425 Herodotus
- 480–406 Euripides
- 460–400 Thucydides
- 469–399 Socrates
- 447–432 Parthenon built
- 429–347 Plato

offshore island of Euboea, was taken and burned. Then the Persians crossed the narrow strait to the mainland and drew their ships up on the shore of the mountain-fringed coastal plain of Marathon, 26 miles northeast of Athens.

The Athenians had found few Greeks willing to stand with them against the great power of the East. Sparta, which had the most powerful army of any Greek state, had agreed to send support but not until after an important religious festival. Even some Athenians counseled submission, or at least fighting only within sight of their own city walls. In the end, however, perhaps nine thousand Athenian troops marched up the coast to Marathon to face the fury of the Persians.

Reconstructing ancient battles is not easy. All versions of this one, however, stress the contribution made by the Athenian general Miltiades (c. 554–489 B.C.), who combine a shrewd tactical sense with firsthand knowledge of the Persians, whom

he had served in earlier years in Asia Minor. All authorities agree that the Greeks were outnumbered, that they attacked the Persian camp in a line of battle that was weak in the center but strong in the wings, and that it was these latter troops who drove back the Persian flanks and then closed on the Persian center, which broke and fled. When the day's fighting was over, the Greek historian Herodotus assures us, six thousand of the invaders had fallen, but fewer than two hundred Greeks.

The Second Persian Invasion

Ten years later, in 480 B.C., the Persians came again, but this time they mounted a full-scale invasion by land and sea. Darius began preparing for this invasion shortly after the defeat at Marathon, but the

415 Syracuse expedition

404 Defeat of Athens by Sparta

384–322 Aristotle

new offensive was delayed first by Darius's need to put down a rebellion in Egypt and then by his death. Xerxes (r. 486–465 B.C.), Darius's young son, then took up the plans for the Persian conquest of the West. By the autumn of 481 B.C., Xerxes had assembled an enormous army that may have included as many as 150,000 men and a fleet of more than six hundred ships. It was certainly the largest military force the Western world had ever seen. From Sardis and the Ionian coast, Xerxes began to move north and west toward the Straits and the lands of the Hellenes beyond.

The Greeks, in the meantime, had made plans of their own, determining this time to hang together rather than separately. The Athenians had turned against Militiades after a military failure that followed Marathon, and he had died rejected by his own people. But Athens had produced another leader of genius: Themistocles (c. 527–460 B.C.), the city's most ardent advocate of sea power. Themis-

tocles was logical, persuasive, and obsessed with the crucial role he believed Athens's "wooden walls," the stout sides of its long oar-driven warships, would play in its future defense. He argued his fellow citizens into fortifying Piraeus, the harbor of Athens, and into using the windfall discovery of a rich silver lode in the mines at Laurium to build a fleet of two hundred fighting ships. These ships—called *triremes* for their three rows of oars, one above the other—ultimately provided the backbone of the Greek navy that faced the Persians in the coming war.

With the armed might of the East streaming across a double bridge of boats at the Hellespont into the land that later became Europe, however, the Greek states that wanted to fight turned first to the famous Spartan army. In a meeting at Sparta, some thirty city-states formed a defensive league and chose the Spartans as their leaders, although the Athenian fleet gave Athens a voice almost equal to Sparta's in some key decisions. Many Greeks favored abandon-

In this bas relief from Persepolis, the Persian emperor Darius the Great receives his son and heir Xerxes, who stands behind his father. Notice that both are larger, more fully bearded, and slightly elevated above the other figures. Compare the dressing of their beards with that of Sargon of Akkad (Chapter 1).

ing the north and making a stand on the narrow neck of land that joined the wide Peloponnesian peninsula to the rest of Greece. The Athenians, however, did not want to abandon their home in central Greece without a fight, and argued successfully for an attempt to hold farther north. The Spartan king Leonidas (r. 490–480 B.C.) thus set out with three hundred Spartans and a force of several thousand other Greeks to face an army of perhaps 150,000 at the narrow northern pass of Thermopylae. Today a statue there shows the Spartan leader, long-faced and hugely helmeted, stone lips curving upward in an Archaic smile.

The pass at Thermopylae (literally, "the hot gates") is in some places less than 50 feet wide. The Greeks held the Persians there for two scorching days in August of 480 B.C. Then a traitor showed the invaders a mountain path that enabled them to outflank the defenders. Leonidas, seeing the impending disaster, ordered most of the other Greeks to withdraw while he, his Spartans, and a handful of others stayed, fought, and died. "Go tell them at Sparta, passerby," runs the famous epitaph for the three hundred at Thermopylae, "that here, obedient to their will, we lie."

Offshore, meanwhile, the Greek fleet held the much larger Persian force at bay while late summer storms destroyed several hundred of the Persian armada. There was now no hope of successful resis-

tance north of the Gulf of Corinth, however, and most of the Greeks retreated to the isthmus at the eastern end of the gulf to defend the Peloponnesus. The Greek fleet, however, anchored in the strait between the offshore island of Salamis and the mainland, only a few miles west of Athens. They were close enough to see smoke rising from the temples on the Acropolis as the Persians swarmed through the abandoned city.

It was Salamis that became the key to victory. Themistocles succeeded in tricking the Persian fleet into attacking in the narrow straits between the island and the mainland, and there, in a long and bloody day's fighting, the Greeks destroyed perhaps two-thirds of the Persian ships. Emperor Xerxes, who had set up his throne on a seaside hill to observe his victory, watched the sun set on the remnants of his fleet as it fled eastward. He knew that without his navy, which was essential to protect his supply lines, his huge army could scarcely survive in an enemy land.

The Persian emperor therefore took much of his army home with him that fall. And when hostilities began again in the spring of 479 B.C., things went decisively against him. The sizable contingent he had left in central Greece was crushed by an army under the Spartan general Pausanias at Plataea. The Athenian-dominated Greek fleet, meanwhile, crossed the Aegean, attacked the great Persian naval base at My-

Athena, patron goddess of Athens, leans on her spear in this relief sculpture from the Acropolis. This traditional "Mourning Athena" pose probably indicates that inscribed on the stele in front of her is the annual list of Athenians who died for their country in war in the year just ended.

cale, and literally wiped out the Persian navy. It was a disastrous end to the second major effort of the heirs of Cyrus to overrun the West.

Today, you can picnic among the olive trees at Thermopylae or stand on the memorial to the Greek dead at Marathon and see where the Persian ships lay drawn up on the shore and where the Greeks advanced. More important, from our vantage point in time, we can see even more clearly than they could the magnitude of their achievement. For the Persians came no more to Greece. The eastern frontiers of the Western world had been established by those twenty years of struggle with the most powerful empire of the age.

The Greek Naval War

The war still had thirty years to run, but it now became a very different kind of struggle. The Greeks were on the offensive, their victorious fleets the essential instrument of their continuing success.

Despite their defeats in 490 and 480–479 B.C., the Persians still occupied the northern shores of the Aegean and ruled the Ionian states. In 478 B.C., therefore, Athens and a number of other seacoast and island states organized a military alliance to carry on the war. Meeting on the sacred island of Delos, the founders of the *Delian League* swore to fight shoulder to shoulder to defend the independence of the Greek cities from the Persians. Other goals included the liberation of the Ionian Greeks and the expulsion of Persian power from the entire Aegean Sea area. In fact, the League did achieve the latter two goals. It proved more difficult, however, to maintain the independence of individual city-states within a league overwhelmingly dominated by Athens, now the greatest sea power in the Greek world.

From the beginning, the Athenian fleets provided the core of the Delian League's military forces, though the other allies made contributions in ships, goods, or—most often—in cash. For much of the period, furthermore, operations were directed by the Athenian admiral Cimon (c. 512–450 B.C.), a skilled diplomat as well as a generally effective military leader. Under his guidance, the Greek peoples of the northern and eastern shores of the Aegean were freed from Persian domination. There were some substantial setbacks, including the loss of more than two hundred Greek vessels sent to support an Egyptian rebellion against Persia. There were also great victories, like the destruction of the rebuilt Persian fleet in 469 B.C. The long wars finally ended in 449 B.C. with a Persian agreement to keep their navy out of Greek seas and to refrain from oppressing the Ionian city-states. In the eyes of the Greeks, at least, the peace was a victorious one, for they had accomplished their war aims.

Explanations for the triumph of the smaller and disunited Greeks over the sprawling might of the Persian Empire vary. Herodotus, like many Western historians since, saw it as a victory of free men over the slaves of an Eastern despot. He also depicted it as divine punishment for the hubris, or overweening arrogance, of the Persian emperor. More practical explanations point to Greek military superiority in some key areas. For example, the Greek soldier, who wore a heavy metal breastplate, helmet, and shield, had obvious advantages over the Persian infantryman

This reconstruction of a Greek trireme shows the oars that provided the ship's primary motive force in battle as well as its deadly beak, used for ramming. When triremes pulled parallel in combat, oarsmen were often hacked to death by the swords of battling soldiers or crushed by the butts of splintering oars.

protected only by leather and fabric. The well-drilled Greek phalanx often stood firm against Persian charges.

Greek *triremes,* with their 150 oarsmen and metal beaks in the prow for ramming other ships, were extremely maneuverable. A devastating tactic was to swing alongside an enemy vessel, ship oars at the last moment, and sheer off those of their foes, leaving them helpless in the water and vulnerable to ramming. When, as at Salamis, large numbers of troops were carried on each Greek warship, they could swarm aboard an enemy vessel and slaughter the rowers.

Whatever the causes of the Greek victory, it did more for Greece than free it from the Persian threat. Victory gave Greeks in general, and Athenians in particular, the self-confidence, power, and wealth that carried them to the splendid accomplishments that began in the middle decades of the century. At the same time, that confidence could turn to over-confidence, to hubris among the Greeks in their turn, and bring them to as great a fall as their Eastern foes before them.

The Age of Pericles

Athens had been a relatively slow starter among the Greek city-states. At the start of the fifth century B.C., Sparta, despite its old-fashioned monarchical form of government, was probably the most admired of the Greek states. Athens, however, moved quite quickly to the forefront in many areas. Pericles's reference to his city as "the school of Greece" (see box, "Athens Is the School of Greece") was not merely rhetoric, nor did it refer only to cultural achievements. Both Athens's international position and its political constitution deserved the attention they got from contemporaries and from historians and political theorists in later times.

The second act of the drama, then, concerns itself with Athens's predominance among the Greek city-states, its role among nations, and the evolution of its relatively democratic government. This section also centers on the man who contributed more than any other to establishing Athenian preeminence—Pericles, who gave his name to the pivotal middle third of the fifth century B.C.

The Evolution of Athenian Democracy

Since the time of Solon who, about a hundred years before the Persian War, instituted major reforms in the laws of Athens (Chapter 2), the Athenian political system had been evolving in a more or less liberal direction. Although the Athenian democratic ideal was less inclusive than that of more modern democracies, political power did spread among a larger and larger percentage of the people. The chief builders of this Athenian democracy were the reformer Cleisthenes, whose constitutional innovations were instituted in 508 B.C., and Pericles, who made democracy work in the thirty years during which he dominated the political life of the city, from 461 to 429.

During the sixth century, Solon had tried to be fair to all classes of society, whereas the tyrant Peisistratus had set himself up as a champion of the middle and lower ranks. The city-state had an assembly, or *ecclesia,* of all male citizens over eighteen, for which something between thirty and fifty thousand people qualified; a council of four hundred inherited from Solon's reforms; a board of nine archons, or executive officials; and the traditional court, or Areopagus, which was composed of former archons and dominated policy-making. Nevertheless, tribal and other traditional factions, the strong influence of the old landowning clans, and high income qualifications for officeholding all limited political power to a small minority of the citizen body. Thus the Athens of the late sixth century B.C. remained a society dominated by ancient territorial, social, and economic distinctions and allegiances.

Cleisthenes thrust his way to the front rank of Athenian politics soon after the fall of Peisistratus's son Hippias in 510 B.C. Born of an aristocratic clan himself, Cleisthenes sought power through popular dissatisfaction with the policies of his aristocratic rivals. In return, he offered a genuine break with the past and a real division of political power among the people.

Cleisthenes's approach was to break up the old centers of political power and replace them with new political units. A key change was the creation of the *deme,* a new political subdivision about the size of a country village or a ward within the city itself. The 175 demes that eventually evolved in Athens became the basic units of Athenian political life, replacing the aristocratic phratry. Unlike the phratries, the demes involved artisans and other ordinary citizens in local affairs, for all citizens—free adult males—were inscribed on the deme rolls. Another major change was to replace the ancient ethnic tribes with ten political "tribes." The members of the new tribes were drawn not only from Athens's demes but from all the main regions of Attica; they came from the poorest hill villages, well-to-do farms on the plains, and the most prosperous city wards. The new political tribes were thus balanced socially, economically, and regionally.

On this basis, a new council of five hundred, the *boule,* was formed. This council was composed of fifty representatives from each of the ten new tribes, all chosen by lot by the demes. Each tribe's delegation to the council of five hundred was given a turn at guiding the council's deliberations and the general operations of the government for one-tenth of the year. A major step was thus taken toward replacing traditional factions and the power of local magnates with a broader loyalty to the city-state as a whole and a wider distribution of power in the state. Another step in this direction was the decision in 501 B.C. to reorganize the army into ten regiments, one from each of the new tribes, each electing its own general. These ten elected generals became increasingly important as the fifth century advanced.

Two more general developments did much to advance the principles and practices of democracy. One was the increasing importance of the navy, in which even the poorest Athenian citizens could participate as rowers. As defenders of the state, the lower classes could now justify claims to a share in its political life, as aristocrats and the middle classes had done before them. Another important factor was the change in the means of choosing many officials, including even the prestigious archons, from election to selection by lot. This reform opened these positions up to any enfranchised citizen. This change also decreased the power and prestige of the Areopagus, which was composed of former archons. With the lower classes participating in policy-making and the bastions of aristocratic authority weakened, democratic reforms could not long be resisted.

By about the middle of the fifth century B.C., the Areopagus had become a law court with limited jurisdiction, and the property qualifications for magistrates had been lowered. In addition, financial allowances were provided for members of the council, and citizens who served in the large popular courts were paid, as were those who served in the army or navy. Because most offices were now filled by lot, and because terms of office were short—usually a year or less—almost everyone had some government service. Voting continued for the board of ten generals, which increasingly replaced the archons as the executive heads of the government. And the device of ostracism, introduced during the Persian Wars, allowed the assembly to send anyone perceived as a threat to the welfare of the state into honorable exile for ten years by simple majority vote.

The result was a rough-and-ready system of direct rather than representative democracy. The assembly of all citizens, which served as both the legislature and the chief court, met every ten days or so,

while one-tenth of the council of five hundred were always on duty, as were archons, generals, and lesser officials. In practice, an assembly of thousands of farmers, traders, perfumed aristocrats, and sweaty laboring men must have been a bit unwieldy: a quorum, after all, was six thousand people. Despite the agenda prepared by the council, the assembled citizens tended to listen to whoever could hold their attention. Established leaders could get a hearing more easily than others, old aristocratic names still often commanded respect, and demagogic appeals swayed audiences all too frequently. Still, if we set a vision of this milling, raucous crowd alongside the bas-reliefs of Persepolis that show Darius in his embroidered robe sitting stiffly on his throne while satraps bow and marching lines of tribute-bearing subjects parade into the royal audience hall, it seems clear that Athens came a good deal closer than Persia to the modern notion of democratic government.

Pericles

The structure of Athenian democracy was thus essentially complete. The most effective leader of the period was Pericles (c. 490–429 B.C.), who dominated Athens during the middle decades of the fifth century B.C.. An aristocrat and friend of such leading cultural figures as Sophocles the playwright and Phidias the sculptor, Pericles also had a reputation for honesty in financial matters and a gift for oratory. From the 460s to the 430s B.C., these qualities won him repeated election to the board of generals and swayed the assembly to accept his proposals and follow his policies. Pericles is thus generally credited with transforming midcentury Athens into the most honored and powerful of Greek states, both in his own time and in the collective memory of the West.

As a democrat and a patriot, Pericles combined a lifelong commitment to a broader sharing of political power in Athens with an aggressive dedication to the greatness of his city in the Greek world. His institutional contributions were modest, though they included the introduction of payment for public service so that the poor could take part as mentioned earlier. This commitment to democracy was reflected in a famous speech in praise of Athens given toward the end of his life: "Our constitution," he told his fellow citizens, "favors the many instead of the few." The laws of Athens, he said, "afford equal justice to all," while "advancement in public life falls to reputation for capacity, class considerations not being al-

Pericles of Athens, the most celebrated statesman of ancient Greece, broods on the fate of nations in this idealized funerary sculpture. Is this a realistic representation? Look particularly at the hair, beard, and eyes.

philosophy during the fifth century B.C.. Indeed, the Athens he described in the speech just cited as "the school of Hellas" was in large part a city of his own building, the achievement which has led historians to affix his name to the age in which he lived.

The Athenian Empire

There was, however, another side to Pericles's patriotic dedication to Athenian supremacy. He more than any other turned the Delian League against Persia into an Athenian Empire. This surge of Athenian imperialism overseas both put the capstone on Athenian preeminence and sowed the seeds of its undoing.

Though organized as a voluntary alliance, the Delian League was dominated by Athens from the beginning. A council of representatives of the allied states was supposed to set general policy, and the treasury of the league was established at the shrine of Apollo on the sacred island of Delos. In practice, however, the treasurers were appointed from Athens, and the allied navy was commanded by an Athenian admiral. No doubt the Athenians saw this as only fair, inasmuch as they provided the bulk of the league's navy and bore the brunt of the battle.

Over the quarter century that followed the founding of the league in 478 B.C., however, Athenian "leadership" became something more than that. After 470, no member was allowed to withdraw from the alliance, and some that tried were militarily punished and required to pay heavy indemnities. Greek cities liberated from the Persian yoke were encouraged to join the Delian League, and some other areas, including cities on the large offshore island of Euboea, were forcibly enrolled in the grand alliance. Athens even converted some lesser states into tribute-paying colonies of its own. Some of these territorial acquisitions, furthermore, were on the Greek mainland and seemed to have little to do with the struggles of Delian League on the Aegean. Still, the Athenians may have justified their actions as necessary in the broadest sense, since a strong Athens was clearly essential to the victory of the common cause.

From the 460s B.C. on, Athens was more often dictating to its allies than consulting them. In 454 B.C. the treasury of the league was moved from Delos to Athens; the reason given was greater security. The annual contributions of the members, however, were soon being used to pay the salaries of oarsmen

lowed to interfere with merit; nor again does poverty bar the way."[2] It was an idealized portrait of Athenian society, but a clear statement of Pericles's ambition for his people.

Pericles presided also over the rebuilding of Athens, physically shattered by Persian attacks in 480 and 479 B.C.. His inspiration is often seen behind the construction of the gleaming marble temples on the Acropolis, the elaboration of public festivals, even the flowering of Athenian drama and

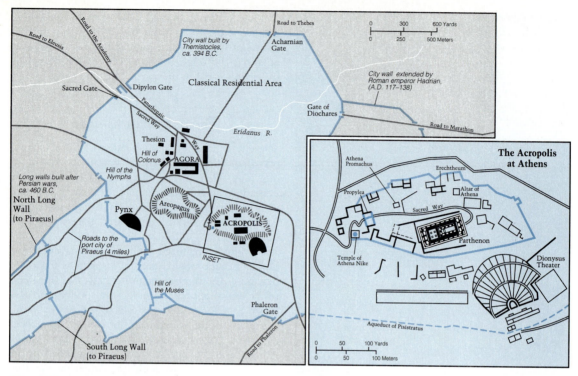

Map 3.2   Athens in the Fifth Century B.C.

in Athenian triremes, and even to build Pericles's new temples on the Athenian Acropolis. As the century advanced, the assembly at Athens passed laws that became binding on all members of the league. For example, Athens legislated a common set of weights and measures as well as the use of Athenian coinage—the Athenian owl that we already mentioned—all over the Aegean. Again, such measures could be justified by their improving the region's economy as a whole, thus further strengthening the league for the great struggle.

When the wars with Persia ended in 449 B.C., however, the Greeks were confronted with the undeniable reality of the Athenian Empire. It included most of the Aegean coastal states, from Attica and Thessaly on mainland Greece to Thrace in the north and on around to the shores of the Hellespont and the Ionian city-states of Asia Minor. Almost all the islands were members, from huge Euboea and tiny Delos in the west to such celebrated homes of Greek civilization as Lesbos and Rhodes in the east. All told, some 170 separate city-states with a combined population of perhaps two million were ruled by a

few tens of thousands of Athenian citizens who were guided in their turn by the powerful voice of Pericles.

Imperialism had its critics. In Attica itself, conservative landed elements in the countryside, less directly involved in the new commercial wealth and imperial grandeur of Athens, attacked the oppression of fellow Greeks as a matter of principle. Many of Athens's "allies" were bitter over the loss of their much prized Greek independence. This resentment frequently obscured both the fact that Athens encouraged democracy among its subject peoples and the evidence of increased prosperity among merchants and artisans from other cities, especially those who moved to Athens to ply their trades.

Perhaps the most striking thing about the Athenians' experience with democracy and imperialism, however, is that they did in fact thrash out in public these fundamental questions concerning the morality of their policies. The Greeks had plenty of vices, including those we have highlighted, but one of their virtues was a passionate commitment to freedom of thought.

The Peloponnesian Wars

The third act of the Greek tragedy that played itself out throughout the fifth century B.C. was yet more war. The Peloponnesian Wars, whose main phase lasted from 431 to 404 B.C., were not great patriotic struggles of Greeks against a foreign foe, nor were they studded with glorious victories. These wars were fratricidal conflicts that pitted the Hellenes against each other. Greece could only emerge the loser.

We have noted the contentiousness of the Greeks before. This combativeness may have been rooted in their geographically divided land of valleys, islands, and peninsulas and in the intense loyalty Greeks felt for their separate city-states. The economic and political competitiveness of their commercial, relatively democratic society may also have bred rivalrousness among them. In fact, Greeks competed everywhere, from the law courts to the Olympic Games. As long as they faced a powerful common foe like Persia, these internal rivalries could be suppressed. Once Persia was effectively repulsed, however, the leading city-states turned once more to the inter-Greek quarrels that finally climaxed in the terrible Peloponnesian Wars.

The chief antagonists in this unhappy struggle were Athens, the great naval power of central Greece, and Sparta, the greatest of Greek land powers, which ruled the Peloponnesus in the south. We have already traced Athenian political evolution and the growth of the Athenian empire. Let us now examine the unique Spartan state and its rise to power.

The Rise of Sparta

The image conjured up by the term *Spartan* has, since ancient times, been that of a man in arms. The Spartan peers out at us through the bronze of an ancient statue, a warrior swathed in a dark cloak, his face almost entirely concealed by a masklike helmet topped with a spreading crest. The seventh-century Spartan poet Tyrtaeus (fl. c. 650 B.C.), who lived and wrote about the same time as Sappho, expressed the idea with force:

> For no man ever proves himself a good
> man in war
> unless he can endure to face the blood
> and the slaughter
> go close against the enemy and fight with
> his hands.[3]

A Spartan soldier, helmeted and wrapped in his cloak. Something of the fearsome reputation of Greece's most implacable fighters comes through in this miniature bronze figure. [Draped Warrior, 510–500 B.C.. Greek, Bronze, 5¹⁵⁄₁₆ in. high. © Wadsworth Athenum, J. Pierpont Morgan Collection]

In large part, that was what Spartan life, Spartan society, and Spartan history were all about: producing the finest fighting machine that Greece had ever known. But this approach to life cost Spartans something.

The Spartans were apparently among the last of the Dorian invaders to drift down into Mycenaean Greece, in the southern Peloponnesus, during the Greek Dark Age. Lovely ivory carvings and the stirring poetry of Tyrtaeus indicate that Sparta's history continued to resemble that of other city-states into the Greek Awakening. Two crucial wars, however, sent the course of Spartan development in unique directions.

In the later seventh century B.C., driven by overpopulation and hunger for land, the Spartans attacked and conquered their neighbors, the Messenians. In the sixth century, these same people rebelled and had to be suppressed. Both of these wars lasted for decades and strained the Spartans to the breaking point. After the first Messenian war, the Spartans converted the entire Messenian population into serfs called helots. After the second, they restructured their own society to ensure that the helots would never revolt again.

In the sixth century B.C., then, Sparta established a government that, although it superficially resembled those of other city-states, was actually a rigid oligarchy bolstered by vestiges of the old-fashioned monarchy that had perished elsewhere during the Greek Dark Age. As we noted in Chapter 2, there were not one but two kings in Sparta, both of whom were primarily war leaders who also had important religious duties.[4] A council, or *gerousia*, composed of the two kings plus twenty-eight men over age sixty, prepared proposals that were submitted to an assembly of all male citizens over thirty, who could vote on the proposals but not discuss them. Five elected administrators, called *ephors*, maintained social traditions and oversaw the conduct even of the kings.

What made Sparta unique, however, was not its government but its social structure. Perhaps 90 percent of the population were serflike helots, assigned to work the fields of the citizens. To keep this large oppressed majority in line, Sparta built a garrison state. At the age of seven, a Spartan male child left his parents for a state school, where he was taught basic reading and writing, turned into a perfect physical specimen, and drilled in military skills. At twenty, he joined the army, where he served for the next forty years. He could marry at eighteen but had to live in the barracks until he was thirty, slipping home in secret to visit his wife. He continued to eat with his messmates until he was sixty when, at last—if he lived that long—he was excused from further military service and allowed to return permanently to his family.

Spartan men were thus denied any real family life. They were not allowed to farm (helots did that), to engage in trade (Spartan money consisted of unwieldy iron bars), or to practice any craft other than fighting. The arts rapidly withered in Spartan society, and Sparta played little part in the cultural explosion that we discuss later in this chapter. It should be noted, however, that Spartan women seem to have enjoyed some advantages unique to the Greek world. Perhaps because men were so preoccupied with military matters, the women of Sparta owned and managed two-fifths of the property. They were also encouraged to participate in sports and to grow strong—in order to bear healthy sons for the state.

Sparta thus succeeded in molding its citizens into a unique society. Conservative in their social beliefs, devoted to old-fashioned virtues like respect for age, religion, and tradition, inured to hardship, and committed above all to courage, duty, self-denial, and love of country, the Spartans were much admired by many Greeks. They were also widely feared, both at home and abroad, as the most effective fighting force in the Greek world.

Toward the end of the sixth century B.C., the Spartan fighting machine began to impose its power on new neighbors. These peoples, called *perioici* ("dwellers around"), were not enslaved but were required to aid the Spartans in war. This century also saw the organization of an even larger Spartan-dominated alliance of Dorian city-states known as the *Peloponnesian League.* Members accepted Spartan leadership in foreign affairs and sent contingents to support the Spartan army in war but were otherwise self-governing. Until the Delian League was formed in the next century, the military force that Sparta assembled by drawing on the *perioici* and the Peloponnesian League was the largest such force ever gathered in Greece.

According to one of many anecdotes illustrating Spartan hardihood, courage, and dedication to the service of the state, a good Spartan mother handed her son his shield with the admonition to come back "with your shield—or on it." Because a Greek shield was heavy, it was the first thing a fleeing warrior threw away. The shield was also large: a dead soldier could be carried home on it. There was no question which course Sparta expected of its citizens: recall the example of Leonidas and the three hundred at Thermopylae.

Greeks Against Themselves

The common danger of Persian conquest had brought Athens and Sparta together in the opening decades of the fifth century B.C. But during the middle years of the century, while Pericles guided Athens to imperial supremacy over the Aegean, the Spartans looked on with increasing alarm. Shortly before mid-century, as the Persian Wars wound down, the First

Peloponnesian War broke out. This conflict was triggered by the defection of the state of Megara from the Peloponnesian League and its alliance with Athens, threatening to tip the power balance in Athens's favor. Sparta declared war in 460 B.C., and the war ended in 445, with a peace and an agreement to negotiate future disputes. Athenian expansionism, however, continued to bring Periclean Athens into conflict with other mainland Greek peoples, including Sparta and its allies.

In the 430s B.C., then, new crises arose. In 433, Athens supported Corcyra in a naval struggle with Corinth, a prominent member of the Peloponnesian League. The following year, the Athenians supported the revolt of Potidaea, a Megarian colony, by closing all the ports of the Delian League to Megara. Pressured by Corinth, Megara, and others, the Spartans were persuaded in 431 B.C. to again declare war on the Athenians. Announcing that they fought, as before, for Greek freedom, the Spartans marched north.

The Second Peloponnesian War lasted for a quarter of a century, from 431 to 404 B.C., although a truce was declared between 421 and 416. During the first phase, an indecisive struggle between a sea power and a land power, neither side was able to get close enough to the heart of enemy strength for a fatal blow. The Athenians struck by sea, raiding the coasts of the Peloponnesus and even establishing bases around its shores. They could not get at Sparta itself, however, which was located well inland. Raiding deep into Attica, the Spartans besieged Athens but, finding the city connected by long walls to its port at Piraeus, were unable to cut Athens off from the grain supplies and imperial revenue that continued to arrive by sea.

When the entire population of Attica crammed into the besieged city, however, a plague swept through Athens, killing tens of thousands, including Pericles himself. After the great leader's death, there was a split in Athenian leadership between a war faction led by the successful general Cleon (d. 422 B.C.) and a peace party under the more cautious Nicias (d. 413 B.C.). The Spartans, meanwhile, could not make good on their promises to break up the Athenian Empire because they had no fleet to reach Athens's overseas possessions.

In 421 B.C. Nicias, who emerged as Pericles's temporary successor, negotiated the Peace of Nicias, but it was a peace born of frustration rather than one that reflected a settlement of issues. Sparta had accomplished too little, and Athens had lost too little. Moreover, there were those in both camps who urged that with one more push wonders might be achieved. This time it was the Athenians, their imaginations fired with enthusiasm for new conquests, who plunged the Greek world into fratricidal conflict once more.

The evil genius of Athens during this second phase of the war was a brilliant but self-indulgent and unstable young aristocrat named Alcibiades (c. 450–404 B.C.). This ultimately unscrupulous young man became the main spokesman for a new grand scheme: the conquest of Syracuse, the powerful Greek city in Sicily. Indeed, all Sicily might be theirs, Alcibiades told the Athenian assembly, as well as the cities of southern Italy—in short, Great Greece itself might be brought under Athenian rule. His dazzled fellow citizens voted huge resources for the venture and in 415 B.C. dispatched two hundred ships and tens of thousands of Athenians and others westward. But the expedition was poorly led and executed. Syracuse proved too powerful, and the result was the worst disaster of the war—the loss the following year of the entire Athenian fleet and army. Alcibiades, after being summoned home, defected to Sparta.

Things went from bad to worse for the Athenians. From 412 B.C. on, another major player reentered the game, tilting the odds still more heavily against Athens. Persia offered to subsidize a fleet for Sparta in exchange for a free hand in reconquering the Greek cities in Ionia, on the eastern edge of the Aegean. To the dismay of Athenians and other Hellenes, the Spartans accepted the offer. The self-proclaimed defenders of Greek liberties were thus revealed as willing to sell Greek cities for Persian aid against a fellow Greek power. Athens's moral position, however, was somewhat weakened by the fact that it had also sought Persian help in this terrible and corrupting struggle.

For some time the Athenians, crippled as they were after the Sicilian fiasco, were still able to beat the inexperienced Spartans on the sea. Then in 405 B.C., another large Athenian fleet fell to the enemy, this one seized by the Spartans on the shores of the Hellespont while its ill-disciplined crews were inland on a foraging expedition. This humiliating defeat left Athens helpless, and the Spartan commander, the great general Lysander (d. 395), followed up on his advantage at once. Quickly recrossing the northern Aegean, he laid siege to Athens once more—this time by sea as well as by land. The Athenians starved through a brutal winter rather than surrender, but in the spring of 404 B.C. they laid down their arms at last.

There were many among the embittered Spartan allies who wanted to see Athens destroyed utterly after the long and desperate struggle. This, to their credit, the Spartans refused to do. But they did require the Athenians to destroy the long walls that linked Athens to its vital port and that had made it impossible to break the city by siege for so long. The Athenians were also compelled to give up their empire and what remained of their navy. And the Spartans imposed a government of Athenian puppet rulers known as the *Thirty Tyrants* on what had been the most democratic people in the Greek world.

The Effects of Civil War

At the level of grand strategy, the Peloponnesian Wars pitted the two Greek leagues headed by Athens and Sparta against each other. At a deeper, more disastrous level, the wars turned allies against allies, social classes and fellow citizens against one another, and Greeks against their own traditions.

Both leagues were shaken by the struggle, and at the end of it the Delian League was disbanded. The gropings toward a larger Hellenic unity that might have prevented so much future bloodshed

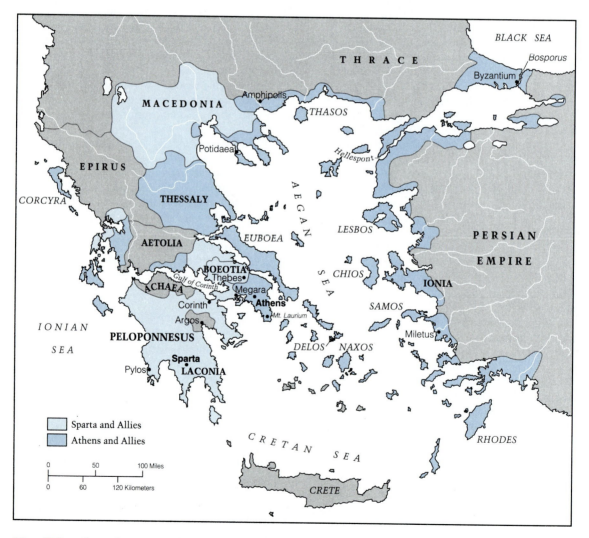

Map 3.3   The Peloponnesian Wars

were throttled. Thereafter, as we shall see, first Sparta and then other powers as well repeatedly tried—and failed—to impose an outright hegemony on all the Greeks, rather than promote an alliance of supposed equals.

Many Greek cities were also divided internally in the course of the conflict. Thucydides, the great historian of the Peloponnesian Wars, pointed out that in many city-states, leaders of local democratic and oligarchic factions turned on each other. Oligarchs, who favored Sparta, worked for the domination of society by its older families and more well-to-do citizens; democrats, supporters of Athens, demanded more power for the masses of the people. The two factions often carried the feuds of the assembly into the streets. The Athenians even encouraged a revolt of the Spartan helots against their masters, and the Spartans did the same with the Athenian slaves. Mob violence and murder created mutual hatreds that would last for generations.

Both sides, finally, betrayed their own oldest and highest ideals of civilized behavior in the maelstrom of bloodshed that the wars became. It was bad enough that Greeks fought Greeks on so huge a scale. Even worse were the violations of truces, the execution of hostages, and even in some notorious cases the massacre of all male citizens and the enslaving of the women and children of a defeated city-state. Sparta did this first at Plataea in 427 B.C., and the Athenians followed the same savage policy at Melos in 415.

All these internal divisions manifested themselves in Athens, where the death of Pericles opened the way for a succession of lesser leaders. These demagogues turned the poor against the rich and generated a struggle between oligarchs and democrats that actually led to a short-lived oligarchy around the year 410 B.C. Worse still, the Thirty Tyrants that the Spartans forced on Athens in 404 B.C. instituted a reign of terror, executing hundreds of leading democrats. When democracy was finally restored, the democrats in their turn carried out reprisals against people suspected of undemocratic views. The most notorious of these reprisals was the trial and execution in 399 B.C. of Socrates, the greatest philosopher of the Periclean age.

Like all great tragedies, the Greek drama of the fifth century B.C. was thus in the final analysis an internal one. The heroic allies of the Persian War turned savagely against each other in the Peloponnesian conflict, betraying in the process the ideals they had once shared.

Society and Economics

The broken temples of the Acropolis rising above the haze of modern Athens can give us only the most fragmentary sense of the ancient city. Today, on an average summer afternoon, the hilltop is wiltingly hot, a dazzle of sun on white stone, a surge of fellow tourists, and a babble of languages never heard in ancient Greece. Beyond the white-pillared buildings and fallen columns, the colorful shirts and designer sunglasses, you look down through the trees to streets full of automobiles. Yet the strident noise and bustle of modern Athens is not so alien to the city's ancient realities as we might think. The Greeks of Pericles's century were no less busy and active than their modern descendants. Theirs too was a hustling society, alert to the main chance, and as full of incongruities as any in our age.

In many ways, Greek society of the Classical Age embodied the social and economic trends of the period of the Greek Awakening that preceded it. In this section we discuss some changes, such as shifts in trade patterns and expansion of the public sector of the economy. But we also investigate continuing social realities, including class structure, gender roles, and the place of slavery in the Greek world.

Private and Public Economy

The economic prosperity of the Greek Awakening certainly roared on through much of the fifth century B.C. Especially after the victory over Persia and during the period of Athenian preeminence, the overall economic picture remained extremely favorable. Some aspects of the economy did change, however, and we will take a look at these.

Throughout much of Greece, agriculture continued to be primarily small-scale subsistence farming, although there were some substantial landowners. Some of the latter produced crops for the city market and for export. Wheat and barley, onions, garlic, and other vegetables tended to be sold locally, while grapevines and olive trees still provided wine and oil, much of it for overseas export.

Business and industry also continued with little change. Most handcrafted products were produced in home workshops and sold in a street of similar shops; this pattern, common in the bazaars of the ancient Middle East, recurred later in the guilds of medieval Europe. Workers in bronze and marble, potters, carpenters, sculptors, and shoemakers filled the narrow streets with the sounds and smells of industry. In such shops, the artisan proprietor usually worked beside his laborers, though there were some larger "factories" that employed large numbers of handworkers.

Long-distance commerce was still expanding, though major routes and distribution centers did change. Timber, grain, and other staples were imported, particularly into Athens, which could not supply its swollen population from the agricultural produce of even so substantial a hinterland as Attica. Oil and wine, exquisite red-figure jars and vases, and luxury goods of various sorts were common exports. Of the major trading cities, Corinth and the Ionian city-states suffered a decline. In the west, Syracuse waxed exceedingly rich, though wars were endemic in Sicily, and the whole of Great Greece — Sicily and southern Italy — felt the growing competition of the North African metropolis of Carthage, of which we will hear much more in chapters to come. The clear center of the continuing commercial boom, however, was now Piraeus, the port of Athens. Its wharves and warehouses were the most jammed and bustling, its harbor the most crowded with shipping of any in the Greek world.

An aspect of the economy that loomed increasingly important in the fifth century B.C., especially in Athens, was the public sector. Most Greek city-states had minimal government revenues — minor fines, tolls, and fees. They depended instead on the *liturgy*, the "public service to the gods" expected of the rich, who were expected to make large voluntary contributions to pay for an annual festival or a warship intended for the city's defense.

Periclean Athens, however, had at its disposal the huge contributions paid in annually by the members of the Delian League. A large portion of these revenues went for an enormous public works program. The league's money put many thousands of craftsmen and laborers to work on the long walls, the agora, the theater, the temples on the Acropolis, and other large-scale Athenian structures. Pericles himself showed a clear awareness of the economic importance of his lavish plans to beautify the city, pointing out to the assembly the jobs that would result, not only for workers directly involved, but for shippers, for what we might call subcontractors, and for other artisans. As his Roman biographer Plutarch clearly saw, "these public works distributed plenty through every age and condition" for many prosperous years.[5]

Citizens, Aliens, Slaves

Trade and war not only brought Greek citizens into direct contact with foreigners but brought many foreigners to Greek cities. As a result, Greek society in the fifth century B.C. was composed of three major groups: citizens with or without political rights, *metics*, or resident aliens, and slaves.

Politically enfranchised citizens were normally native born and always male and free.[6] Such a citizen might be wealthy, but he might also be a man of middling means or relatively poor. Such citizens had legal and political rights and a military obligation. Frequently they were farmers, the oldest and most respectable occupation. The better off city-dwelling citizens gave much of their time to government service, athletics, and such other activities as drinking parties or philosophical discourse.

Most Greek wives and daughters of the citizen class led house-bound, legally limited lives. They could not own or manage property, participate in politics, or be seen in public except at funerals and a few religious ceremonies. Their very exclusion from public life may have reinforced the tendency of Greek men to consider women of lower status, in view of the average male citizen's concern with public affairs. In addition, the extreme difference in age between the typical husband and wife (a groom was likely to be thirty, a bride around fifteen) may have encouraged a belief that women were less knowledgeable than men, and thus limited their lives to child rearing and household management.

Aliens were more commonly either artisans or merchants. They were required to register with the city, pay a modest tax, and sometimes serve in the military. They were not allowed to own property, participate in the deliberations of the assembly, or hold public office. Some resident aliens practiced exotic crafts indigenous to their homelands but rare and in demand in their new homes. Others were shrewd merchants, sometimes with foreign business contacts — hustling immigrants who invigorated the market economy of the city-state. What they were denied in political rights they compensated for by making a lot of money.

Although the topic of slavery in ancient Greece has been discussed repeatedly, there is very little we can say about it with certainty. We do know that slaves were frequently foreigners, men and women imported to the Greek city-states as prisoners of war.

If they were freed by their masters, all slaves, native or foreign born, were automatically classified as aliens. A slave's legal status was comparable to that of a citizen's tangible property or his domestic animals. The average Greek thought of slaves as "naturally" subservient and accepted slavery as a normal social institution.

Slaves do not, however, seem to have played as important a part in Greek society as they did elsewhere in the ancient world. They were not employed in large numbers as agricultural field hands, for instance, as they were later in Rome. They were not as numerous in Greece as they were elsewhere: by one estimate, they constituted no more than a third of the population of Athens, less in most other Greek states. Slaves usually competed with free labor for work and labored, as free workers did, beside their masters. However, the conditions of their lives varied according to the type of work they performed. Slaves who worked in the state silver mines at Laurium lived a wretched life, whereas those who worked as house servants in Athens or Corinth were often part of a family. Nevertheless, slave labor undoubtedly helped citizens find the time to participate in the civic institutions of which they were so proud.

Art and Thought in Classical Greece

The Greek cultural achievement comprises one of the most astonishing bodies of seminal art, literature, and thought in Western history. Greece, which had already produced some of the most admired of all Western poetry, gave birth in the fifth century B.C. to some of the most powerful dramas ever produced anywhere. The first historians in the world were fifth-century Greeks, and the Greek fifth and fourth centuries nurtured three philosophers—Socrates, Plato, and Aristotle—whose ideas are still debated today. In the arts, the realistic yet idealistic style of sculpture invented by the Greeks of the Classical Age also became the core of a central Western tradition. Even the ruins of the buildings Pericles raised on the Acropolis are crowded with visitors today.

The Athenian Acropolis. Few monuments of any age so clearly symbolize Western civilization as the white marble columns of the Parthenon, shown at the right center. What qualities of Greek culture, what aspects of Greek history are illustrated in this picture?

Greek Values

Ancient Greeks, like all peoples, shared certain common values, general attitudes toward the world and beliefs about how one ought to behave in it. Some of these basic Greek values—for example, loyalty to the state—became part of an ongoing, evolving set of Western values that have survived to this day. Others, such as acceptance of homosexuality, have fared less well in later periods.

Two widely admired qualities of character among the classical Greeks were the use of reason and loyalty to the city-state. To the average Greek, reason might mean no more than common sense, a kind of overarching rationality that made a person stop and think, or talk things over with his fellow citizens, before plunging into some impulsive action. The Greeks were not in fact always as rational as they liked to think they were. But Greek belief in the importance of reason, particularly as elaborated by Greek philosophers like Plato, became a fundamental characteristic of Western culture.

Loyalty to the city-state resembled modern patriotism in some ways, but differed crucially in others. First of all, it was focused on a much smaller community and based on face-to-face relationships and strongly felt ties to familiar land, streets, and places. It was also a kind of civic piety, rooted in popular devotion to patron gods and goddesses and memories of heroic ancestors. Such loyalty exerted a powerful force on Greeks, compelling citizens to put their lives on the line for the city and moving the rich to make large voluntary material contributions, the liturgies, to the welfare of the community.

Some of the most admired moral qualities among the Greeks were what came to be called the four "cardinal virtues": wisdom, justice, courage, and temperance or moderation. Again, not all Greeks lived up to these lofty ethical imperatives. It is hard, for instance, to think of the aggressive, hard-driving Hellenes as devoted to moderation and a sense of limits. Still, these virtues become part of the Western ideal code of values in later centuries.

The Greeks also entertained distinctive attitudes toward love and sex. Sexual relations generally were discussed at least as openly among the ancient Greeks as they are in the twentieth century. They were the subjects of jokes, bawdy humor being a staple of the Greek comic theater. The passion we call "romantic love" between men and women seems sometimes to have been considered a form of madness. In Euripides's play *Medea*, for instance, love drives Medea, the foreign wife of the Greek hero Jason, to murder her own children as an act of vengeance for her husband's infidelity. On the other hand, tomb inscriptions hint at real affection between many husbands and wives.

We also should note here that Greek intellectuals seem often to have taken a much different view of women in general than most of their countrymen did. Socrates, for instance—or Plato speaking through him—thought that women were the intellectual equals of men and should be as well educated. The playwright Sophocles created powerful female characters like Antigone, who defends principle against the state with incomparable vigor (see the section "The Greek Theater"). Euripides's *Medea* and his *Trojan Women* passionately denounce the wrongs done to women.

Greek literature also includes many references to homosexual love. From Sappho's lyrics to Plato's *Symposium,* passionate and overtly sexual feelings between people of the same sex were enthusiastically expressed and praised. Some saw such ties as a good basis for a teaching relationship between a young person and an older one. In practice, homosexuality was probably much more common among aristocrats, who were so rigidly separated from the opposite sex in home and society. It was also widespread in the segregated society of Sparta. Most of the time, however, homosexual relationships seem to have been limited to adolescence and youth, giving way in later life to the heterosexual relations seen as necessary for a stable family and for the production of heirs to the family name and fortune.

The Greek Historians

A sense of the past, like a sense of values, has developed among most peoples. The Greeks, like their Near Eastern predecessors, fitted their own human story and the heroic deeds of their ancestors into a larger framework of myths and legends, gods and goddesses. In the fifth century B.C., however, this first of Western peoples broke with supernatural accounts of human affairs to produce the systematic, critical investigations of the human past we call history. The pioneers of this breakthrough in human self-understanding were Herodotus, the "father of history," and Thucydides, often hailed as the greatest of all ancient historians.

Herodotus of Halicarnassus (c. 484–c. 425 B.C.) and Thucydides the Athenian (c. 460–c. 400) had a good deal in common. Both were historians of great wars—Herodotus of the Greek struggle with Persia, Thucydides of the Peloponnesian Wars. Both therefore concentrated heavily on political and military events and on the doings of kings, statesmen, and generals. Both also wrote about contemporary or recent events, carrying out most of their research by talking to participants or to people possessing knowledge of the recent past. Because both were sophisticated, widely traveled men, they were critical of their sources and suspicious of bias and error, as a good historian should be. Both were also men of letters, however, skilled writers who gave dramatic accounts of such dramatic events as the victory at Marathon or the Sicilian disaster. Like other historians of ancient times, they also salted their narratives of true events with orations and debates which, while not verbatim transcriptions, did offer vigorous literary presentations of the views of leading actors or of the issues at stake.

Herodotus's *Persian War* stands out as the work of a gifted storyteller, a genial Ionian who had traveled everywhere and was as fascinated by the exotic customs of Eastern peoples as by the motives of Xerxes in attacking the Greeks. In its vast canvas and vivid vignettes of kings and battles, the book is often compared to a Homeric epic. Herodotus was also still religious enough to see divine punishment in the defeat of Persian hubris, and patriotic enough to see the war as a triumph of Greek freedom over Eastern despotism. His *Persian War* was an "investigation," the original meaning of *historia*, but it was a moral tale too, with a fine upbeat theme.

Thucydides's *Peloponnesian War* was the product of very different times and a very different man. Thucydides was an Athenian aristocrat and general who, exiled during the first phase of the war in punishment for a military failure, turned his attention to chronicling the struggle, a task for which his military experience and many contacts among Greek leaders qualified him eminently. His *Peloponnesian War* sees the defeat of his native Athens rooted in the failure of its democracy as the feckless multitude proved unable to carry on without the guiding genius of Pericles. As a skeptical Athenian of the later fifth century B.C., furthermore, Thucydides saw no supernatural forces at work, only fortune and human folly. With scientific objectivity, he detailed the horrors of the plague at Athens and the brutalization of the Athenians, offering no moral to his story save the grim awareness that, in real history, men are often wolves to one another.

Philosophy: The Sophists and Socrates

The first Greek philosophers aimed at a deeper understanding than that. Sixth- and early fifth-century B.C. Ionian thinkers like Heracleitus (c. 540–c. 470 B.C.) and Parmenides (b.c. 515 B.C.) had founded the subtle branch of philosophy known as metaphysics, which tries to understand the ultimate nature of the world. During the later fifth and the fourth centuries B.C., Greek philosophers not only speculated more deeply about metaphysical matters but turned their attention to ethics and politics as well, formulating immensely influential theories about human moral and social conduct. Three men contributed more than any others to these developments: Socrates, Plato, and Aristotle.

The way for these major thinkers, however, was paved by a controversial breakthrough movement in fifth-century Greek thought, the rise of the *Sophists*. The Sophists were popular teachers, men who—for a fee—undertook to instruct the young sons of well-off Greeks in the sort of worldly wisdom that would guarantee them success in later life. The heart of the Sophists' formal teaching was rhetoric, or the art of winning oratory. A master of the rhetorical arts, they assured their pupils, could always win his case before the courts, carry his motion before the assembly, and win the sort of prominence in the state that every well-born youth coveted. Less exclusively success-oriented minds growled that they were teaching the young to use tricky argument to make the worse cause seem the better one.

Some Sophists were openly skeptical of the beliefs of their forefathers. They doubted the existence of the gods and questioned the laws of the city-state. Greeks are no better than Persians, they said, and all things are relative. In such a world, where moral imperatives are matters of opinion, success is what counts. Conservatives expressed their displeasure, declaring that the youth were being corrupted. Opposition to the subversive teachings of the Sophists spread even to the views of such a thoroughly principled a philosopher as Socrates.

A stonemason by trade, Socrates (469–399

Socrates the philosopher is depicted here as ancient tradition describes him, as a physically unprepossessing person. Does anything of the passion for truth that animated the man himself come through in this bust from a Roman museum?

B.C.) spent little time carving stone. He was an overweight, unprepossessing cracker-barrel philosopher, normally to be found lounging in the shady colonnades around the agora arguing with judges, poets, the young, the old—anyone, in fact, who wanted to talk about the largest questions in life. Judge, what is justice? Poet, what is beauty? Council member, how *should* the ideal state be run? When in the nightmarish aftermath of the Peloponnesian Wars Athens could no longer stand a questioning voice, Socrates was condemned to death for corrupting the youth. On the day of his execution, he convened his friends to discuss what seemed to him an appropriate question: *Is there life after death?*

Socrates saw his role in society as that of an intellectual gadfly, stinging his fellow citizens into serious thought about serious matters. The *Socratic method*, often imitated by talented teachers since, consists in rational disputation, with the object not of defeating the opposition but of searching for mutual enlightenment. If we argue it out, the Athenian philosopher suggested, maybe we will both learn something new. "The unexamined life," said Socrates, "is not worth living." His lifelong commitment to free discussion of the central values and institutions of his time provided an admired model for future generations of Western people.

Philosophy: Plato and Aristotle

One of Socrates's most admiring students was a young man of noble lineage and poetic inclinations named Plato. Plato (429–347 B.C.) became the most influential philosopher in Western history. After Socrates's execution in 399 B.C., Plato wrote the *Dialogues*, which tell us most of what we know about his master's ideas. But Plato also used the *Dialogues* to express his own original concepts, putting them into the mouth of Socrates. Among Plato's original concepts, the *Theory of Ideas* (or the theory of forms or absolutes) has been of central importance to Western thought.

Beyond the flux and flicker and rumble of things, Plato agreed with Parmenides, there lies permanence—an unchanging, higher reality. That world of eternal truths Plato called the realm of Ideas—not Ideas in your head, but Ideas with an independent existence of their own, in their own separate world of being. It is, he said, a transcendent realm, not made of matter or accessible to the senses. The eternal Ideas that lie behind this illusory world of change can only be apprehended by human reason and thus only by a true lover of wisdom—a philosopher.

These Ideas, however, give form and meaning to all the particular things in this material world of change and diversity. Things in the everyday world around us—or "particulars," as Plato called them—reflect, embody, or "participate in" the platonic Ideas. Individual human beings, for example, are human because they participate in the *Idea* of humanity. A triangle on a blackboard reflects the ideal *form* of the triangle. A poem or a statue is beautiful to the extent that it embodies the *absolute* beauty to be found only in the transcendent realm of Ideas.

On this foundation of what is sometimes called the "two-story universe"—Ideas above, particulars below—Plato based his social and ethical views. All ethical values, he declared, are absolute—*not* relative—because they reflect forms or Ideas in that transcendent world. Human justice is an approximation of absolute justice, your courage or mine a pale imitation of ideal courage. Again, only the philosopher is capable of directly apprehending values in themselves; only the philosopher can achieve an almost mystical vision of the form of pure goodness.

In his most famous work, *The Republic,* Plato urged that because of their superior understanding, philosophers should be the rulers of the ideal state. Under their wise rule, the other members of society would perform the lesser tasks they were best fitted for. Peasants would farm, and soldiers would defend the state. The result would be the best of all communities, the perfect republic guided by "philosopher kings" with a unique insight into the realm of eternal truths.

A critic of the theory of Ideas might suggest that Plato's absolutes are really only definitions based on the observation of a lot of particulars and have no independent existence at all—that there is, in short, no upper story on the universe. In defense of the independent existence of Ideas, a Platonist might invoke the modern example of the suspension bridge: What holds the San Francisco Bay Bridge up? Steel cables, or the mathematical formulas of weight and strain, tension and tensile strength embodied in this monument of modern engineering? And which is closer to eternal—the steel cables or the mathematical Ideas?

Historically speaking, it is the influence of Plato's Ideas that matters. In chapters to come, we will see Plato's notions shaping the thoughts of the fathers of the Christian church. We will see Michelangelo chiseling away Renaissance marble to release the absolute beauty Plato said lay therein. And, as we will see, philosophers from the fourth century B.C. to the nineteenth century A.D. would continue to find converts to the Platonic notion that Ideas are more real than things, that reason lies at the heart of the universe.

Plato's most famous pupil and greatest rival down the centuries was Aristotle (384–322 B.C.). Son of a physician, Aristotle became tutor to Alexander the Great and founder of his own school of philosophy in fourth-century Athens. Aristotle, whose knowledge was encyclopedic, left us his ideas in the form of lecture notes on logic, rhetoric, metaphysics, physics, biology, ethics, politics, and art, to name just a few of the subjects he mastered. In the Middle Ages, when Aristotle's works made up a large part of the university curriculum, he was described as "the master of those who know."

A practical man with an empirical bent and a lifelong interest in biology, Aristotle developed his own theory of Ideas. For him, Ideas are real enough, but they exist *within* the particulars, not in some transcendent, nonmaterial realm of being. His forms, furthermore, are active forces, purposive drives in nature. These *entelechies,* as they are sometimes called, impel all things to develop to predestined ends. The best example of an Aristotelian entelechy is thus not a triangle or a suspension bridge but an acorn, within which the form of the oak tree is laboring to achieve its indwelling purpose.

Even a brief catalog of Aristotelian insights gives some sense of the range and variety of his many-sided intelligence. Aristotle's ideal state, for instance, would not be ideal but practical. He favored a balanced mix of democracy and oligarchy, dominated by a stable middle class. His ethical theory urged the *golden mean,* "moderation in all things." Virtue, he said, is not the opposite of vice, but a mean *between* vices: courage is a virtue, but both cowardice and foolhardy recklessness are vices—all extremes are wrong. Aristotle's definition of artistic beauty as "the imitation of nature," his claim that great literature produces a *catharsis,* or purging of emotional tensions, his definition of a tragic character as a noble nature doomed by a single flaw—all are familiar theories today. Aristotle's metaphysics and logic did for medieval Scholastic theology what Plato's did for the fathers of the Christian church. His scientific views prevailed until the scientific revolution of modern times.

The Greek Theater

Philosophy was for the favored few, but Greek theater was for the multitudes. People poured into the open-air theater carved out of the south side of the Acropolis hill, as many as thirty thousand strong, at the annual spring festival in honor of Dionysus. The amphitheater had a round stage with a central altar to Dionysus set in front of a series of columns and a background painting of a temple or a palace. The actors wore carved masks equipped with speaking tubes so they could be heard across the huge audience and stood on high clogs so they could be seen. They shared the stage with a chorus, who spoke for the author or reacted for the audience, commenting on the unfolding story. The chorus danced and sang or chanted, the actors sometimes sang, sometimes spoke, a vigorous thrust and counterthrust of formal argument. We really have no modern equivalent of

Greek theater, but the opera probably comes closer than any other present-day theatrical form.

Greek plays were presented in groups of three tragedies, sometimes a trilogy on a single subject, all by the same author. Prizes were awarded for those judged best, not by theater critics, but by a representative sample of the audience. The stories of the plays usually came from Greek mythology, so that everyone knew how they came out. This familiar material, however, was used to illustrate such themes of eternal human concern as the family and society, morality, religion, or human destiny. Frequently, too, these dramatic treatments reflected the concerns, attitudes, and moods of the period in which they were presented. Thus Aeschylus's *Persians* hails the Greek

triumph over their foes, whereas Euripides's *Trojan Women*—discussed below—challenges the myth of Greek heroism in the middle of the brutal Peloponnesian Wars.

The three most honored tragedians of the fifth century—and the only ones whose plays have survived—were Aeschylus, Sophocles, and Euripides. Aeschylus (525–456 B.C.) pioneered in developing the Greek theater. For example, he added to the number of actors permitted on stage so as to heighten conflict. And conflict there was, not simply between good and evil but often between two choices so terrible that there is no "lesser of the two evils." In the *Oresteia,* the only complete trilogy we possess, the hero Orestes can avenge the murder of his father, who

---

THE HUMAN SPIRIT The Clash of Principle

Sophocles's *Antigone,* first performed about 440 B.C. at the height of the golden age of Pericles, centers around the powerful confrontation of King Creon and Antigone, a strong-willed woman who will not compromise her principles. Antigone's two brothers have been killed in an attack on their city, one defending it, the other fighting on the side of the attackers. King Creon orders that the traitor be left unburied, his soul thus denied rest in the underworld. Antigone, who loves both her brothers, defies king and country to perform the pious act of interment. Sentenced to death for her act of defiance, she defends her decision:

> ANTIGONE: Now you have caught, will you do more than kill me?
> CREON: No, nothing more; that is all I could wish.
> ANTIGONE:
> Why then delay? There is nothing that you can say
> That I should wish to hear, as nothing I say
> Can weigh with you. I have given my brother burial.
> What greater honour could I wish? All these
> Would say that what I did was honourable.
> But fear locks up their lips. To speak and act
> Just as he likes is a king's prerogative.
> CREON: You are wrong. None of my subjects thinks as you do.

> ANTIGONE: Yes, sir, they do; but dare not tell you so.
> CREON: And you are not only alone, but unashamed.
> ANTIGONE: There is no shame in honouring my brother.
> CREON: Was not his enemy, who died with him, your brother? You honour one, and so insult the other.
> ANTIGONE: He that is dead will not accuse me of that.
> CREON: He will, if you honour him no more than the traitor.
> ANTIGONE: It was not a slave, but his brother, that died with him.
> CREON: Attacking his country, while the other defended it.
> ANTIGONE: Even so, we have a duty to the dead.
> CREON: Not to give equal honour to good and bad.
> ANTIGONE: Who knows? In the country of the dead that may be the law.
> CREON: An enemy can't be a friend, even when dead.
> ANTIGONE: My way is to share my love, not share my hate.
> CREON: Go then, and share your love among the dead. We'll have no woman's law here, while I live.

Source: Sophocles, *Antigone,* in *The Theban Plays,* trans. E. F. Watling (Baltimore: Penguin, 1961), 139–140.

THE HUMAN SPIRIT
The Good Things of Life

This expression of Aristophanes's comic view of the typical Athenian comes from a play called *The Peace,* which was produced in the middle of the Peloponnesian Wars. Here Athens's leading comic dramatist represents the average citizen as less concerned with democracy and patriotism than with enjoying the good things of life and the creature comforts that poured into the wealthiest of the Greek city-states. Compare this frank materialism with Pericles's view of Athenian character and values.

> Moreover we pray that our marked-place may
> Be furnished each day with a goodly display,
> And for garlic, and cucumbers early and rare,
> Pomegranates, and apples in heaps to be there,
> And wee little coats for our servants to wear.
> And Boeotia to send us her pigeons and widgeons,
> And her geese and her plovers: and plentiful creels
> Once more from Copais to journey with eels
> And for us to be hustling, and tussling, and bustling,
> With Morychus, Teleas, Glaucetes, all
> The gluttons together besieging the staff,
> To purchase the fish . . . .
>
> What a pleasure, what a treasure,
> What a great delight to me,
> From the cheese and from the onions
> And the helmet to be free.
> For I can't enjoy a battle,
> But I love to pass my days
> With my wine and boon companions
> Round the merry, merry blaze. . . .

Source: Aristophanes, *The Peace,* trans. Benjamin Bickley Rogers, in *Aristophanes,* ed. E. Capps, T. E. Page, and W. H. D. Rouse (Cambridge, MA: Harvard University Press, 1927), lines 999–1009, 1127–1135.

Sophocles (497–406 B.C.), a contemporary and friend of Pericles, is often seen as representing the mature genius of the Greek theater. In his plays, gods are less likely to appear on stage, and fate works itself out through human character. Aristotelian tragic flaws in otherwise noble characters doom such powerful protagonists as Oedipus and Antigone.

Sophocles's treatment of the story of Oedipus, in *Oedipus the King,* revolves around the moral blindness of a noble ruler. Oedipus simply cannot bring himself to believe that he has unknowingly committed the two terrible sins of murdering his father and marrying his mother—even though, as a foundling, he could not have been expected to recognize his true parents. In *Antigone,* the heroine's crime is her stubborn defiance of her ruler in order to bury both of her brothers—a sacred obligation—even though one was killed while defending their city and the other, a traitor, while attacking it. Tradition would grant one brother an honored funeral, the other the terrible punishment of lying unburied, food for dogs, his soul to wander forever without finding rest in the underworld. But Antigone loves and honors both her brothers and will die rather than neglect her duty to them as she sees it. The great king Oedipus and the noble heroine Antigone thus face moral dilemmas that have no easy solutions, yet their nobility stays with us after the final choral ode (see box, "The Clash of Principle").

The plays of Euripides (485–407 B.C.) were very different. Imbued with the skepticism of the Sophists and the bitterness engendered by the Peloponnesian Wars, Euripides was an angry man, looking reality in the face and seeing no gods to come to the rescue, no noble human characters shining through. One of his plays that is still frequently performed illustrates the dark temper of his times. In *The Trojan Women,* based once more on the Greek national epic of the conquest of Troy, Euripides chose to explore not the deeds of Homer's heroes but the fate of the women of Troy, who, after seeing their husbands and sons struck down, are themselves dragged off into slavery in a strange land. The play, with its empathy for women, foreigners, and the defeated and its angry contempt for the brutality of the Greek "heroes," demonstrates both sensibility and honesty.

To get away from such murderous contemplation of the unthinkable you might try a comedy—but if it was by Aristophanes (450–385 B.C.) you would not get away from larger concerns and public issues. The most famous writer of the Old Comedy of fifth-century Greece, Aristophanes wrote a great deal

was killed by Orestes's mother, only by committing the equally terrible crime of matricide. Aeschylus, however, was as convinced of the underlying justice of the divine order and of Greek society as Herodotus was. He introduces the goddess Athena and even a trial before the ancient Areopagus court, resolving the tension with the forgiveness of Orestes and the taming of the spirit of traditional revenge.

of social satire (see box, "The Good Things of Life"). He lampoons some of the greatest public figures, such as Pericles, as well as colorful characters like Socrates, whom he depicts, in *The Clouds,* hanging from the ceiling in a basket, floating in clouds of muddled philosophical speculation and teaching young people ridiculous arguments that would turn them against their parents. In *Lysistrata,* written 2,400 years ago, Aristophanes solved the problem of war by having the women of Greece rebel, seize the Acropolis, and refuse to have sex with their husbands until the bloody-minded male half of the population yields to an even deeper biological need than bloodlust and makes peace.

The Living Art of the Acropolis

The Greek theater was for rare occasions. The city itself, with its temples, monuments, and statues, was there all the year round to give pleasure to its citizens. It is easy to become accustomed to art that is always before our eyes, so familiar that we scarcely see it at all. Pericles, however, did not think this would happen to Athenians, confronted with "beauty in our public buildings to delight the eye" and "falling in love" with the city as they saw it day by day.

Architecture, sculpture, and painting evolved throughout the fifth and earlier fourth centuries B.C. and reached their pinnacle in this Classical Age. Many Greek artistic achievements, such as the Parthenon sculpture Lord Elgin brought back to the British Museum, grace the museums of the Western world today. But the Greeks were a gregarious, public people, living much out-of-doors in the Mediterranean style, and a better way to see their art would have been as they did: surging through the streets and up the winding way to the temple-crowned Acropolis in the great parade of the Panathenic festival, the annual celebration in honor of the city's patron goddess Athena.

The private houses the Athenians would pass were plain mud-brick structures built around a central court, set close together along the winding dusty lanes. But the public buildings, Pericles's glory, crowding the crest of the Acropolis or clustered around the agora at its base, would gleam ahead against the blue Mediterranean sky.

The clamorous agora, with market stalls, tombs of heroes, and halls of the council and the magistrates would be left behind on a feast day. Up the winding path through pines and cypresses, the singing throng would emerge into the city of the gods, bringing Athena her new robe for the coming year. Through the pillared Propylaea Gate, past the towering bronze statue of Athena, the people would move. They would pass the elegant little temple of Athena Nike (Athena Victorious) and the Erechtheum with its portico of caryatids—supporting columns in the shape of maidens—guarding the goddess's sacred olive tree. At last they would arrive at the Parthenon itself, the temple of Athena Parthenos (Athena the Virgin) to deliver the sacred garment. Through the columns, they would see Phidias's 40-foot gold and ivory statue of the goddess of the city, gazing nobly out at the assembled worshipers.

The Parthenon was a simple rectangular building framed with columns, with painted relief sculpture beneath the gently sloping roof. On such an occasion, Athenians might not notice the subtle variations from straight lines and equal distances that make the Parthenon one of the most brilliantly designed pieces of architecture in the Western world. But their eyes would react with pleasure to the subtle curves and slanting lines just the same, as Pericles's builders had intended.

Greek sculpture of the Classical Age had also reached a level of balanced excellence—a combination of realistic representation with the idealization proper to gods and heroes—that would never be excelled. Earlier fifth-century B.C. examples survive from the temple of Zeus at Olympia in the western Peloponnesus, including the often reproduced statue of Apollo, perfectly proportioned, his handsome young face radiating the grave, emotionless certainty appropriate to the god of light and truth. The most admired sculptural find of our times is the larger-than-life bronze Zeus recovered from an ancient shipwreck off the coast of Euboea. Arms extended, bearded face, and empty eye sockets once set with precious metal or special stones to imitate living eyes, it is an impressive representation of divine power.

The goal of the classical style was to represent in bronze or marble the inner spiritual realities that Plato called Ideas, forms, absolutes. Hence the classical style eased the rigid poses of earlier figures, perfected the idealized proportions. In Myron's *Discus Thrower,* this style gave us the perfect athlete poised for action, while Polyclitus's naked youths and gods radiate a spirit of strength and the potentiality of youth.

Greek painters, Aristotle tells us, mastered such techniques as shading, foreshortening, and other modern devices common in Western painting since the Renaissance, but no examples have survived. Greek vases of the classic period do remain to us, however. These impressive examples of red-figure ware were decorated with graceful figures depicting a heroic Achilles or Sappho at her lyre. Private homes were also enlivened by gorgeous textiles, a lost art that once glowed on curtains, cushions, and clothing and is now only hinted at in representations on Grecian urns. Again we have hints and fragments of an amazing cultural achievement—our gift from the very beginnings of Western civilization.

A Topical Summary

Politics: Greek political history of the fifth century B.C. falls into three distinct periods. During the first decades of the century, all Greece rallied to repel the Persian invasion. Throughout the midcentury Age of Pericles, Athens towered over the other city-states. In the last period, the fratricidal Peloponnesian Wars turned Greek against Greek: in the end, Athens and the cities allied with it went down to defeat at the hands of Sparta and its allies. Despite these events, government did become more democratic in many city-states, at least for the minority of inhabitants who were citizens.

Economics: The economic boom of the Greek Awakening continued during the Classical Age, fueled by expanding trade by Greeks around the Mediterranean. A good deal of wealth that accrued to individual city-states went into the coffers of the Delian League and was then channeled by Periclean Athens into impressive public works.

Society: Male citizens enjoyed relative equality in many city-states, but women were limited to the private sphere of the family. Foreigners did well economically but had no political rights, and slaves or helots did much of the work of the society.

Technology: There was little significant technological change during the golden age of Greece. An abundance of labor, perhaps, made technological innovation unnecessary. The warships called triremes, however, provided a strong foundation for Athenian sea power, and large workshops employing many artisans enhanced the productivity of the city-state.

Culture: Classical Greece generated an unexcelled outpouring of original art and ideas. Greek tragedy, sculpture, and architecture inspired centuries of imitation. Greek historians, the first in the Western world, chronicled the stirring events of the century. And the Greek philosophers of the fifth and fourth centuries B.C., especially Socrates, Plato, and Aristotle, influenced all later periods of Western thought.

Some Key Terms

boule 71
Delian League 69
deme 71
ecclesia 71
entelechy 85

golden mean 85
liturgy 80
metic 80
Peloponnesian League 76
Socratic method 84

Sophists 83
Theory of Ideas 84
Thirty Tyrants 78
trireme 70

Notes

1. Herodotus, *The History of the Persian War*, trans. Aubrey de Selincourt, rev. A. E. Burn (Harmondsworth, England: Penguin, 1972), 488.

2. Thucydides, *The Peloponnesian War*, trans. Richard Crawley (New York: Random House, 1951), 104.

3. *Greek Lyrics,* trans. Richmond Lattimore (Chicago: University of Chicago Press, 1955), 14.

4. We do not know the reason for Sparta's dual monarchy. Among the possibilities that have been suggested are an attempt to blend a native monarchy with an invading Dorian one, a solution to the rivalry of two aristocratic families, or a way to prevent the tyranny of a single ruler.

5. Plutarch, "Pericles," *The Lives of the Noble Grecians and Romans,* trans. John Dryden, rev. Arthur Hugh Clough (New York: Modern Library, 1932), 162.

6. For some legal purposes, Athenian law declared that *both* a citizen's parents must have been citizens, by this prescription including the politically disenfranchised mother.

Reading List

DE SAINTE CROIX, G. E. M. *The Class Struggle in the Ancient Greek World.* Ithaca: Cornell University Press, 1981. Strains in a slave society seen as class conflict.

DODDS, E. R. *The Greeks and the Irrational.* Berkeley: University of California Press, 1951. Classic investigation of supernatural beliefs among a people renowned for their rationality.

FINLEY, M. I., ed. *The Legacy of Greece: A New Appraisal.* Oxford: Clarendon Press, 1981. Historic contributions—and limitations—of the founders of Western civilization.

FROST, F. *Greek Society.* Lexington, Mass.: D. C. Heath, 1980. Brief introduction.

GARNSEY, P., ed. *Trade in the Ancient Economy.* London: Chatto and Windus, 1983. Articles on many facets of Greek commerce, drawing on both archaeological and documentary evidence.

GRENE, D., and R. LATTIMORE, eds. *The Complete Greek Tragedies.* 3 vols. Chicago: University of Chicago Press, 1960. Vigorous translations of Aeschylus, Sophocles, and Euripides.

GUTHRIE, W. C. K. *The Greek Philosophers: From Thales to Aristotle.* New York: Harper, 1960. Survey by a leading authority, with emphasis on Plato and Aristotle.

HEALY, J. F. *Mining and Metallurgy in the Greek and Roman World.* London: Thames and Hudson, 1978. Profits, administration, and working conditions.

HERODOTUS. *The Histories.* Translated by A. de Selincourt. Rev. ed. Baltimore: Penguin, 1972. Clear modern translation of the history of the Persian Wars.

HOOKER, J. T. *The Ancient Spartans.* London: J. M. Dent, 1980. Spartan political history in its geographical and cultural framework, stressing foreign relations.

KAGAN, D. *Pericles of Athens and the Birth of Athenian Democracy.* New York: Free Press, 1991. Enthusiastic account by a distinguished historian of ancient Greece.

KITTO, H. D. F. *The Greeks.* Chicago: Aldine, 1964. Personal view of the Greek cultural achievement by an eminent scholar.

LACEY, W. K. *The Family in Classical Greece.* Ithaca, N.Y.: Cornell University Press, 1968. Older but valuable contribution to the study of family history.

PERADOTTO, J., and J. P. SULLIVAN, eds. *Women in the Ancient World: The Arethusa Papers.* New York: SUNY Press, 1984. Pioneering articles from the classical journal *Arethusa.* See also M. R. Lefkowitz, *Women in Greece and Rome: A Source Book in Translation* (Baltimore: Johns Hopkins University Press, 1982). Vignettes from literature and life across the class spectrum.

ROBERTSON, C. M. *A Shorter History of Greek Art.* Cambridge: Cambridge University Press, 1981. Shorter version of Robertson's *History of Greek Art* (1975), with splendid illustrations. See also J. Boardman, *Greek Art* (New York: Praeger, 1973).

SEALEY, R. *A History of the Greek City-States ca. 700–338 B.C.* Berkeley: University of California Press, 1977. The roots of political life in the city-state, stressing regional and personal rivalries rather than class conflicts.

STOCKTON, D. *The Classical Athenian Democracy.* New York: Oxford University Press, 1990. Readable and valuable analysis of Athenian democracy in action, stressing participation and sense of community. See also J. K. Davies, *Democracy in Classical Greece* (London: Fontana, 1978). Fifth-and fourth-century democracy in its economic, social, and cultural frame. J. Ober, *Mass and Elite in Democratic Athens: Rhetoric, Ideology, and the Power of the People* (Princeton: Princeton University Press, 1989). Uses the rhetoric employed by the elite to communicate with the citizen body to illuminate the practice of democracy.

THUCYDIDES. *History of the Peloponnesian War.* Translated by R. Warner. Rev. ed. Baltimore: Penguin, 1972. Literate translation of the best of ancient histories. See also D. Kagan's four-volume history of the war, from *The Outbreak of the Peloponnesian War* (Ithaca, N.Y.: Cornell University Press, 1969) to *The Fall of the Athenian Empire* (Ithaca, N.Y.: Cornell University Press, 1987).

VLASTOS, G. *Socrates: Ironist and Moral Philosopher.* Ithaca, N.Y.: Cornell University Press, 1991. Highly praised study by a leading authority. See also I. F. Stone's readable—if debatable—*The Trial of Socrates* (Boston: Little, Brown, 1988).

WILCOXON, G. D. *Athens Ascendant.* Ames: Iowa State University Press, 1979. Athenian history from Solon to Pericles.

WYCHERLY, R. E. *The Stones of Athens.* Princeton: Princeton University Press, 1978. Sprightly guide to ancient Athens, with discussion of housing, streets, and temples.

The Greek world that emerged from the brutal experience of the Peloponnesian Wars was a different place politically, militarily, economically, socially, and culturally. Throughout the fourth century B.C., Greeks struggled to come to terms with new, often disturbing realities. Among these was the rising power of the Macedonian dynasty of Philip and Alexander the Great, which we will explore at some length. Thanks in large part to Alexander's far-reaching conquests, Greece entered a new phase of its history—the *Hellenistic Age. Hellenistic,* which means "Greek-like," describes the wider world of the Mediterranean, North Africa, and the Near East that came under powerful Greek influences in the wake of Alexander's conquests. The Hellenistic era lasted from Alexander's death in 323 to the death of the famous Egyptian queen Cleopatra in 30 B.C.

Perhaps the most obvious difference between this complex period and those that preceded it lay in the political dimension. The fourth century B.C. and the Hellenistic Age saw the Greek city-states lose their primary place in Western society to larger powers. First, Philip and Alexander of Macedon (Macedonia) became masters of Greece in the later fourth century. Thereafter, the Hellenistic monarchies that succeeded Alexander dominated the Mediterranean world—and much of the ancient Middle East as well—until the Roman Empire absorbed both monarchies and city-states in the second and first centuries B.C.

In economic, social, and cultural terms, this was an expansive and challenging time. Under the aegis of the new monarchies, Hellenistic Greeks embarked on an even greater territorial expansion than that of the Greek Awakening. Greek communities were soon scattered far across western Asia and northeastern Africa, from Persia down into Mesopotamia and Egypt. For much of the period, the wealth of this expanding Greek zone, evidenced by booming trade and lavish building, was greater than it had ever been before. Stimulated by this cosmopolitan new environment, Greek art and intellectual inquiry also took startling new directions in the Hellenistic Age.

The Macedonian Hegemony

The political history of Greece in the fourth century B.C. centers on the coming of the Macedonians. Through the first two-thirds of the century, the city-

Head of a Poetess. Nineteenth century copy of a Greek original. The St. Louis Art Museum

400 B.C.   300

POLITICAL, MILITARY, AND DIPLOMATIC EVENTS

404–338	Sparta, Thebes, Athens struggle for hegemony
359–336	Philip of Macedon
338	Chaeronea
336–323	Alexander the Great
336–325	Conquest of Persia
307–301	Antigonus I
305–280	Seleucus I
305–283	Ptolemy I
c. 300–270	Arsinoë II

SOCIAL AND ECONOMIC DEVELOPMENTS

320–220	Economic growth in Hellenistic monarchies
320	Rise of Alexandria begins

ART AND LITERATURE, SCIENCE, PHILOSOPHY, AND RELIGION

460–377	Hippocrates
400–325	Diogenes
342–292	Menander
341–270	Epicurus
335–263	Zeno
323–50	Hellenization of Near East and Egypt
310–250	Theocritus
295–214	Apollonius of Rhodes
287–212	Archimedes
275–194	Eratosthenes
c. 270	Aristarchus

states continued to fight among themselves for a position of prominence. In 338 B.C. Philip of Macedon imposed Macedonian predominance on all of them. Four years later, his son Alexander led a Macedonian and Greek army into Persia, beginning a campaign that established Greco-Macedonian rule all across the ancient Near East. It was thus above all the impact of Alexander of Macedon that turned Greek life in new directions and moved Greece into the last period of its ancient history.

Greece Divided

"The powerful exact what they can, and the weak grant what they must."[1] These words of a grim Greek general, recorded by the historian Thucydides, sum up the harsh lesson of the Peloponnesian Wars. All Greece learned these rules of the power game during the long duel for supremacy between Athens and Sparta. And unhappily for Greeks, that conflict was not ended by the Spartan victory. Leading city-states continued to struggle for power in the Greek world: Sparta, Thebes, Athens, and even Syracuse, in Sicily, fought for *hegemony,* the predominant position in Greek affairs. Persia also continued to intervene in Greek politics with bribes, alliances, and edicts. There was, finally, a continuing struggle for power within many individual city-states, divided more than ever before by embittered factions.

Continued military conflict was not surprising. Decades of struggle in Greece had largely replaced the citizen armies of earlier centuries with professional soldiers who fought for pay. These hired troops were led by experienced military commanders to whom war was a way of life. The first loyalty of such commanders was often to their little armies rather than to the city-states they were hired to defend. And fighting was their business.

In addition, many of the city-states' political leaders saw power as essential to their own or their constituents' interests. At the beginning of the

47–30   Cleopatra VII
30   Rome takes Egypt

220–50   Economic decline in Hellenistic monarchies
200–50   Social tensions increase

c. 200   *Winged Victory*

fourth century B.C., after the long struggle with Athens, Spartan leaders like Lysander (d. 395 B.C.) were convinced that only a Spartan hegemony could guarantee Sparta's security. By midcentury, defenders of Athenian democracy like Demosthenes (384–322 B.C.) were urging war to save Greece from the Macedonians. In Syracuse, the long-ruling tyrant Dionysius the Elder (r. 405–367 B.C.) seems to have been most concerned with establishing his own power and that of his city in Great Greece, to the west. All these leaders thus saw plenty of good reasons for the wars to continue.

The seemingly endless struggle for power within the city-states also had its roots in profoundly held beliefs and essential group interests. Most of the larger states were torn by feuding factions. One continuing division was that between oligarchs and democrats, who typically represented the interests of more and less prosperous citizens, respectively. Some of these factions also believed that Greece would be better off if one or another of the major contending city-states was dominant. Aegean and Ionian merchants were thus willing to accept Athenian protection once more, but others of a more conservative bent saw in Sparta the defender of sterner old Greek virtues. There were thus as many reasons for coups and revolutions within the city-states as there were for wars between them.

Beneath this tangle of ideals and ambitions, loyalties and interests, however, two other options for the organization of power in Greece intruded slowly upon Greek consciousness during the course of the fourth century B.C. Both options were based on a notion virtually unthinkable in 404 B.C.: the recognition of a higher political authority than that of the individual city-state. One possibility was either federation of the city-states into leagues, like those headed by Athens and Sparta in the preceding century, or some degree of unity among all the Greek states. A leading Athenian orator, Isocrates (436–338), for example, proposed a pan-Hellenic alliance dedicated to a war against Persia. The other option, anathema to the independent-minded Greeks, was what seemed increasingly likely — a Greece dominated by hereditary monarchy, either Persian or Macedonian. In the end, the Macedonian royal house did impose its hegemony on all the Greeks — and mobilized them for the assault on Persia that Isocrates had urged.

The Struggle for Power

The struggles of the chief city-states for the leadership of Greece filled the first half of the fourth century B.C. with intrigues, alliances, and wars. After its victory in the Peloponnesian Wars, Sparta remained the dominant power for more than thirty years, from 404 to 371 B.C. Thebes succeeded Sparta for a decade, from 371 to 362, but Athens organized a new alliance based on sea power and fought to reassert its predominance over the Aegean. To the west, Syracuse laid waste its neighbors in Sicily and southern Italy. But the center of Greek history remained on the mainland of Greece and in the Aegean, with the rivalry of Sparta, Thebes, and Athens at its heart.

Spartan hegemony was expressed in such unpopular institutions as compulsory tribute from its allies, the installation of Spartan governors and military garrisons in some cities, and the encouragement of oligarchic pro-Spartan factions in others. Sparta also became increasingly involved in military interventions in other Greek states. Sparta even sought alliance with Persia, returning Ionian cities to Persian control and serving as the enforcer of a temporary peace settlement imposed on Greece by the Persian emperor. Spartans thus alienated even those Greeks who had originally rallied to them in reaction to the Athenian imperialism of the preceding century.

A leader of the anti-Spartan reaction was the city-state of Thebes in the region of Boeotia, just west of Athens. A Spartan military seizure of the city's citadel outraged Thebans and fired a liberation movement that freed the city in 379 B.C. Theban armies then broke Sparta's rule over Boeotia and, in 371, they crushed the Spartans at Leuctra in a defeat so decisive that the Spartan predominance in all of Greece was effectively ended.

Theban hegemony, however, proved to be even more short lived than the Spartan predominance it replaced. Thebes organized a Boeotian League to serve as an expanded power base and in its turn solicited and won the support of Persia. Theban power was based in part on military reforms and tactical innovations, but it was also the work of talented leaders like the widely admired general Epaminondas. In 362 B.C., however, Epaminondas was killed at the battle of Mantinea, fighting an unlikely alliance of convenience between the old rivals Athens and Sparta. The Thebans won the battle, but their claims to supremacy dissolved thereafter.

Athens, meanwhile, had long since reestablished itself as one of the most powerful of the city-states. Defeat in the Peloponnesian Wars, followed by a Spartan garrison at Athens, the Spartan-supported Thirty Tyrants, hundreds of executions, and thousands of exiles had ignited a powerful Athenian freedom movement. Within three years after their defeat in 404 B.C., the Athenians had overthrown the Thirty, and in the next decade they rebuilt their walls and their fleet and began to reconstruct their Aegean empire. Thereafter, Athens capitalized on the growing antipathy to Sparta by organizing a new naval confederacy and taking a leading part in the last rounds of struggle for hegemony. By the 350s, after the Spartan and Theban bids for power had collapsed, Athens was ready to spearhead a very different struggle. The greatest of Athenian orators, Demosthenes, became the leading spokesman for the effort of the city-states to maintain their independence against the colossus of the north, the looming power of Macedonia.

Philip of Macedon

Macedonia, in northern Greece, has some breathtaking mountain vistas, but to civilized Greeks Macedonia in the fourth century B.C. was the backwoods, a rugged half-developed land stretching across the northern frontiers of the Greek world. A hereditary monarchy ruled by the descendants of tribal chiefs, it was much larger than any city-state and was generally considered only about half Greek and one-quarter civilized.

Macedonian rulers in the fifth and fourth centuries B.C. tried to hellenize their court with imported talent and built a few new cities that somewhat resembled those of their southern neighbors. Philip, King of Macedonia in the 350s, had lived for several years in Thebes and professed a great admiration for Greek culture. His son Alexander, who succeeded him in 336 B.C., had no less a tutor than the philosopher Aristotle and was an ardent reader of Homer. Still, Macedonians were scarcely considered Hellenes even if they did speak the Greek language, and their admission to the Olympic Games was a bit of a concession.

Ambitious, ruthless, shrewd, and violent, Philip of Macedon (r. 359–336 B.C.) has traditionally been seen by historians as the quintessential man of power. By an efficient combination of political reorganization, shrewd and unscrupulous diplomacy, and brilliantly applied military force, Philip succeeded in imposing his authority, and a new political order, on Greece. More recent opinion, however, suggests that Philip was less a man of iron will than a man under immense pressures, from both within his own country and abroad. In this view, Philip fought his way to success in response to problems that could be solved in no other way. Whichever formula best explains what happened, the view of Philip's contemporaries is clear: Greece, as one commentator declared, had never produced a man like him before.

Philip came to power in his large loosely organized country in his early twenties when the reigning king, his brother, died in battle, leaving Philip as regent for his nephew. Philip soon thrust the young heir aside, outmaneuvered and outmuscled several rivals for the throne, and made himself king. He then set to work to reorganize both his army and his nation, always with one eye on the world of the city-states to the south.

Both the country and its military machine were substantially transformed during Philip's twenty-two-year reign. The new king reasserted Macedonian control over the seacoast of the northern Aegean, expanded trade, developed gold mines, built new cities, modernized his capital city, Pella, and got a famous Greek philosopher to educate his son. More important for his international ambitions, Philip constructed a new, genuinely national army. His rambunctious nobles still formed an elite cavalry corps called the royal Companions. A large infantry of tough Macedonian peasants was also organized, however, drilled in a more open formation than the Greek phalanx and armed with a 13-foot spear that far outreached anything in use in Greece. Strengthened by experienced mercenary adjuncts and the latest siege machinery, the Macedonian army was a formidable fighting force.

Greeks looking north grew more and more nervous as Philip expanded and modernized his country, frightening all his neighbors. The voice raised most insistently and eloquently against him was that of the Athenian orator Demosthenes (384–322 B.C.). In a series of public denunciations of the northern threat, scathing speeches that came to be known

Demosthenes, the orator who warned Athens of the danger of Philip of Macedon, does not really look the heroic statesman in this Hellenistic statue. Do you think a picture or statue should resemble the person depicted, or is it better to represent people who accomplish great things as physically impressive also?

as *Philippics*, this last defender of the independent city-states tried to rally both his own countrymen and the other states to take a stand against Philip. In the end, his passionate if perhaps self-interested urgings outweighed the voices of other leaders, like Isocrates,

Map 4.1   The Struggle for Greek Hegemony and the Rise of Macedonia

who felt that only decisive leadership like that of the Macedonian king could put an end to the fratricidal strife of the Greeks. Whether we see Demosthenes as a demagogic defender of the self-destructive city-state system or a last voice of freedom crying in the wilderness, however, the end result was the same.

After years of maneuvers and countermaneuvers, the Macedonian host finally moved south in force to confront the best alliance Demosthenes had been able to put together, composed primarily of Athenians and Thebans. At Chaeronea in 338 B.C., the Macedonians smashed the Greek armies and opened the way for Macedonian domination of all Greece. A key figure in the victory, commanding on the left flank, was Philip's teenage son Alexander, whose troops shattered the Thebans and annihilated their crack "Sacred Band."

A barbaric stone lion still broods today over a field of flowers where the Sacred Band were buried at Chaeronea. The rest of Greece accepted the inevitable: Macedonian hegemony. Thebes was occupied by Macedonians and, after a subsequent revolt, leveled. Athens made terms with the victor. Most of the city-states were organized at last into a single alliance, the *League of Corinth,* sponsored and led by Macedonia. Philip, eager for still larger conquests, graciously accepted the league's request that he lead a combined Macedonian-Greek army in an invasion of the ancient common enemy, the Persian Empire.

In 336 B.C., however, the Macedonian monarch was stabbed to death by a vengeful nobleman, whether in a personal vendetta or on behalf of political rivals we do not know. Luckily for history, if not for Persia, Philip left an heir behind who was more than capable of taking over from his father.

Alexander the Great

Alexander's mother Olympias was estranged from her husband and devoted to her son and his future. When Philip took another wife, raising the possibility of a rival heir, Olympias, apparently a strong-willed, ambitious woman herself, angrily withdrew from the royal court, taking the young Alexander with her. Philip, however, had already given his son at least two things of value: the tutorship with Aristotle, which engendered a love of all things Greek, and essential on-the-job training in the fundamentals of military command. The noble Companions who surrounded Alexander when he led Philip's left wing at Chaeronea became the commanders of Alexander's own troops. Only twenty when his father was assassinated in 336 B.C., Alexander was ready to assume Philip's mantle.

The thirteen-year reign of Alexander the Great (r. 336–323 B.C.) was one long military campaign. After burying his father, Alexander dealt firmly with rumblings of rebellion in Greece and with an untimely barbarian incursion from the north. He then set off for the East to launch the invasion of Persia that Philip had planned to lead.

It was an excellent time to strike at this traditional enemy of the Greeks. The world's largest empire was clearly in decline. The royal court of Darius III (r. 336–330 B.C.) was riddled with factions, and the satraps in the provinces were rebellious. Nevertheless, the empire still stretched for 2,500 miles, across western Asia from the Mediterranean to the Indus. Alexander spent the next dozen years fighting his way across it.

The young king's first victory, in 334 B.C. on the Granicus River just across the Hellespont, was typically headlong and impetuous, Alexander leading the charge in person. Thereafter, the Macedonians marched down through the ancient Near East, defeating Darius at Issus in 333, capturing Tyre after a costly siege in 332, and continuing south through Palestine to Egypt. Returning northward, Alexander crushed Darius's army a second time at Gaugamela in 331 and took Babylon and the Persian capitals of

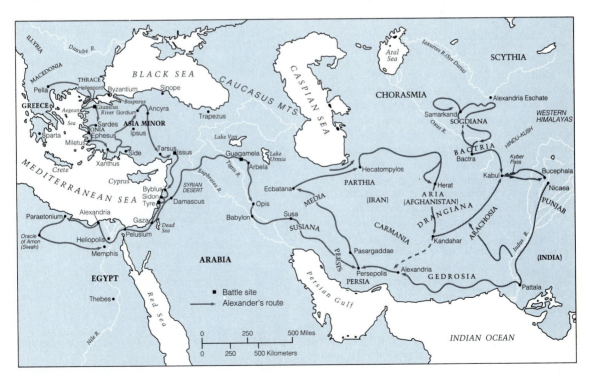

Map 4.2 Alexander's Campaigns

Susa and Persepolis, looting and burning the latter. He then pursued the king of kings so relentlessly that one of the Persian's own satraps, ambitious to replace the defeated ruler, left Darius's corpse on a road in Media for the advancing Macedonians to find.

But the wars of Alexander were not over. In 330 B.C. he led his troops on to the east, up into the barbaric lands of central Asia, and then down through the Khyber Pass into India. In 326, now beyond the Indus in the Punjab, the Macedonians fought the powerful Indian army of King Porus (d. 321 or 315 B.C.), whose cavalry rode on elephants. Then at last Alexander's army had enough. Worn out, ragged, thinned in numbers, they insisted on turning back across the scorching wasteland north of the Arabian Sea and traveling up the Persian Gulf toward Babylon.

There, within a year of his return, Alexander the Great died in 323 B.C. of a sudden fever. At thirty-two, he was master of all the civilized world he knew. Asked by hovering lieutenants to whom he wished to leave his immense empire, the dying Alexander is supposed to have replied, "To the strongest."[2]

A Megalomaniac or a Man with a Dream?

Alexander was short, strong, and probably not as good-looking as the handsome beardless portrait heads that are to be found all over the ancient world. What else do we know about him? He could be chivalrous, as when he spared the royal family of Darius. He could be brutal, as when he murdered a close friend in a drunken rage. He was famous for sharing the rigors of campaigning with his soldiers. He worshipped the legendary Achilles and often charged into battle at the head of his troops.

He was also apparently a shrewd military commander. He laid out a grand strategy to close all the ports of the Near East to Persia and succeeded in doing so, though it took him three years and a brutal siege of Tyre to accomplish it. Recent research shows how carefully he also planned his long marches. His troopers slogged a total of more than 20,000 miles back and forth across the Middle East, yet he planned wells, forage, and food so meticulously that an army of as many as thirty thousand men seldom went hungry on the endless campaign. His tactics for each of his major battles have been traced admiringly in military history books ever since. And he never lost a battle.

Alexander's larger political goals remain much more controversial. Some historians have seen him as a man with a dream, a vision of an empire in which Greeks and Persians—Europeans and Asians— shared power, intermarried, and fused their cultures. Others have seen Alexander's intention as a precursor of that more recent dream, the federation of the world (see box, "Alexander's Vision of One World United"). A new generation of historians, however, has read the skimpy record differently. Recent biographies have suggested, for example, that Alexander may have had a hand in his father's murder and agree with ancient critics that he was an alcoholic and a megalomaniac. These authorities see him as a man

---

WAR AND PEACE
Alexander's Vision of One World United

In the following passage, Plutarch (c. A.D. 46–c. 120) implies that Alexander's vision was of a united world—"the whole inhabited earth" should be fatherland to all. But according to Plutarch, although Alexander treated all people equally, he also believed he ruled by divine right and that his rule was supreme. So *was* Alexander a man with a global vision? Or was he merely hungry for power over all peoples?

> Alexander did not follow Aristotle's advice to treat the Greeks as if he were their leader, and other peoples as if he were their master . . . But, as he believed that he came as a heaven-sent governor to all, and as a mediator for the whole world, those whom he could not persuade to unite with him, he conquered by force of arms, and he brought together into one body all men everywhere, uniting and mixing in one great loving-cup, as it were, men's lives, their characters, their marriages, their very habits of life. He bade them all consider as their fatherland the whole inhabited earth, as their stronghold and protection his camp, as akin to them all good men, and as foreigners only the wicked.

Source: Plutarch, *Moralia*, in W. W. Tarn, *Alexander the Great*, vol. 2 (Cambridge: Cambridge University Press, 1948), Appendix 25, vi.

Alexander the Great, hectic and passionate, charges into battle against the Persian emperor in this Roman wall painting. Although created hundreds of years after Alexander's death, the picture captures something of the headlong rush into history that characterized the young Macedonian's meteoric career.

of blood and conquest, very unlikely to have entertained any dreams of power sharing and global federations.

Yet Alexander did do more than defeat his enemies wherever he found them. As his father had founded new towns in Macedonia, Alexander also sowed the route of his long march with settlements patterned on Greek cities, naming many of them after himself. The most important of these Alexandrias was in Egypt; within a century it became the greatest city in the Western world. As the years passed, furthermore, the Macedonian king adopted some Near Eastern ways. He wore Persian costume and allowed his subjects to prostrate themselves before him in the Persian style. He married a Middle Eastern princess named Roxane and encouraged his officers to marry Persian aristocrats. And he recruited large numbers of Persian and other Asian troops. All these policies have led some very realistic historians to see his ultimate goal as a fusion of peoples and cultures.

Alexander had divine honors voted him by Greek cities, and he may have believed the assertions of Egyptian priests that he was the son of Amen, an-

cient Egypt's sun god, whom the Greeks were beginning to equate with Zeus. To some historians this is evidence that Alexander verged on megalomania. Certainly he expected obedience from East and West alike: according to Arrian, our best ancient authority, he prayed for "harmony and fellowship in the empire between Macedonians and Persians."[3] Perhaps there is a clue for us in the phrase "in the empire," which Alexander himself expected to rule for many years more.

The consequences of Alexander the Great's policies, as we shall see, differed from anything he could have imagined. As for his intentions, since no new evidence is likely to become available and the authorities are so drastically divided, it may be best simply to admit that we will probably never know.

The Hellenistic Monarchies

"The name of Alexander," wrote the distinguished German historian Johann Gustav Droysen, "signifies

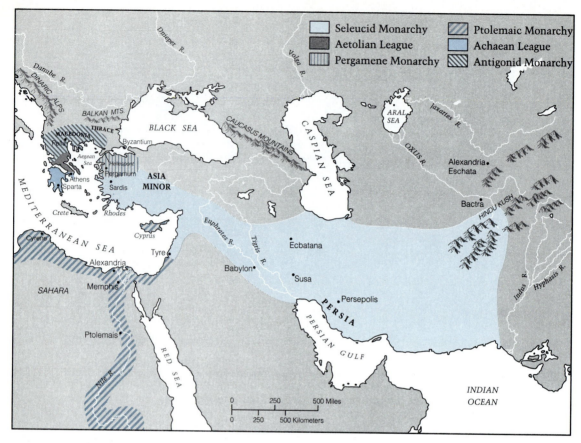

Map 4.3   The Hellenistic Monarchies

the end of one epoch of world history and the beginning of a new one."[4] Alexander's conquest of the East marked the beginning of the Hellenistic Age, and the history of this period was clearly that of Alexander's heirs and of his legacy. This section looks first at the successor states to Alexander's empire, the realms of the Hellenistic kings. It then surveys the expansion and contraction of Hellenistic trade and the resulting social tensions that beset Hellenistic society. Finally, we will examine what has often been considered the greatest legacy of the Macedonian conquest—the spread of Greek culture through nearby regions of western Asia and northern Africa.

The Successor States

Whatever Alexander intended to do, he left behind a new state system stretching from Greece and Egypt across much of the Middle East. These new nations were hereditary monarchies and much larger than the Greek city-states, but they were every bit as rivalrous. The political history of the Hellenistic world was therefore in very large part the history of conflicts between the Hellenistic kings and queens for a larger share of the world they had inherited from Alexander.

In the beginning, there was apparently some effort on the part of Alexander's Macedonian commanders to hold what they had conquered for the Macedonian royal house. But the palace intrigues of the Macedonian monarchy had often been bloody, and Alexander's direct heirs—an incompetent half brother and an unborn child in the womb of Queen Roxane—were in no shape to assert their claims forcefully. The generals' plan for holding things together, finally, boiled down to appointing themselves governors of various portions of the wide empire.

Within less than two decades, all of Alexander's family, including his mother and his sisters, died by violence, as did several of his generals and many of the soldiers who had marched with him. By 300 B.C., three of the chief Macedonian commanders had divided the lion's share of the empire up among themselves and were squabbling over the spoils.

Antigonus I, the One-Eyed (382–301 B.C.), the grizzled veteran among the generals, came closest to taking it all. In the end, however, the *Antigonid dynasty* he founded had to be satisfied with Macedonia itself, Asia Minor (Turkey), and intermittent hegemony over mainland Greece. Seleucus I (c. 358–280), the youngest of Alexander's marshals, claimed most of the enormous expanse of the old Persian Empire. Yet in the next century, eastern Persia and even the central provinces cast off the Macedonian yoke, leaving the *Seleucid monarchs* mostly ancient Mesopotamia. Ptolemy I (c. 367–283), finally, whose memoirs, as drawn upon by Arrian, tell us most about Alexander, successfully established himself and his descendants as the thirty-first, *Ptolemaic dynasty* of Egyptian pharaohs. Cleopatra, who ruled some three hundred years later, was the last of the Ptolemies and the last independent ruler of ancient Egypt as well.

Most of the old city-states of mainland Greece reorganized themselves one last time into two large confederacies. The *Aetolian League* north of the Gulf of Corinth and the *Achaean League* south of it were both normally under the overlordship of the Macedonian Antigonids. Only a few city-states, including the wealthy island of Rhodes and the city of Byzantium on the Bosporus, managed to remain independent.

Among the most famous later rulers of Hellenistic dynasties were the queens of Ptolemaic Egypt. It became the custom there for the Ptolemies, like some of the earlier pharaohs, to marry their sisters, some of whom turned out to be the stronger rulers. Daughters and widows of male rulers also could and did exercise an important share of power in Egypt.

Among the most successful of these Hellenistic queens was Arsinoë II (r. c. 299–c. 279 B.C.). A powerful personality, she dominated the nation for three decades in the third century and, in a victorious war with Seleucid Persia, expanded Ptolemaic Egypt to its greatest size. Commonly seen as the ruler who inaugurated the golden age of the Ptolemies, Arsinoë II had an Egyptian province and Greek cities named after her and was worshiped after her death.

Less successful but better known was Cleopatra VII (r. 50–30 B.C.), Egypt's last hope for freedom from the expanding Roman Empire. Inspired by the historic accomplishments of earlier Egyptian queens, Cleopatra committed her energies and talents to a last-ditch effort to resist Roman domination. This she sought to accomplish through successive alliances with two of the most powerful Roman leaders of the time, Julius Caesar and Mark Antony. Only the death of one of her Roman allies and the defeat of the other frustrated Cleopatra's efforts. She died by her own hand—to become a legendary name in history.

Wars loomed very large in the history of the successor states. Of all the conflicts among the Hellenistic rulers, however, the only ones that have real historical significance for us are the final confrontations in which each ruler, in turn, succumbed to the expanding might of Rome—to be dealt with in the next chapter. We turn now, therefore, from the endless struggles of Alexander's heirs to the broader aspects of his legacy—the nature of the Hellenistic monarchy itself and the adoption of Greek culture by the former Persian Empire.

The Image of the New Rulers

The successors of Alexander in Persia, Egypt, Macedonia, and elsewhere ruled in a style and on a scale that had no precedent in the Greek past. They assumed grand titles like Savior, Benefactor, and The Great. They built themselves huge palaces, contributed lavishly to the beautification of Greek cities and famous shrines, and staged spectacular public festivals. In the old Near Eastern style, they made law by decree and assembled hordes of officials and armies of unprecedented size to carry out their will. Frequently, like Alexander himself, they followed the ancient Eastern practice of calling themselves gods and establishing cults in their own honor. It was enough to make the democratic Greeks of an earlier age turn over in their graves.

Practices differed from one kingdom to another, and evidence is more voluminous for some states than for others. Industrious scribes and the dry air of Ptolemaic Egypt have combined to preserve written records that give us a detailed picture of Egyptian government, and archaeological excavations in Asia Minor reveal something of the splendor that surrounded the monarchs there. From a variety of sources, historians have thus assembled a picture of the prototypical *Hellenistic monarchy,* a new and startling phenomenon in the Western world.

The typical Hellenistic monarch surrounded himself or herself with royal "Friends," what later ages would call courtiers. The monarch's Friends were both social companions and willing instruments in all matters of government. Below these fortunate few who basked in the sunshine of royal favor, there were the professional bureaucrats. These scribes may have been inherited from the old Egyptian or Persian regimes, but they soon had Greek replacements or supervisors. In the service of the new, richer monarchies of the Hellenistic Age, the size of the Hellenistic administrative system in fact grew beyond anything seen before.

Hellenistic monarchs were apparently also chief judges, at least in Egypt, where we have the best evidence. They collected taxes and coined money in much larger quantities than governments had before in western Eurasia. They were commanders in chief of the armies, leading the troops in person and advertising their victories in the high style that went back to ancient Egypt, Assyria, and beyond. And indeed style was a central feature of the Hellenistic monarchy. The Hellenistic kings projected a powerful public image of being both ever victorious and the restorers of peace, of possessing immense wealth and of spending it lavishly on a mix of courtly splendor, public festivals, and gifts of theaters or temples to favored cities. They spent freely as patrons of the arts also, and consulted judiciously with celebrated philosophers.

Of central importance in establishing an image of charismatic leadership were the royal cults. The Greeks had long recognized the divine descent of mythic heroes like Achilles, of Dark Age petty kings, and of aristocratic families, but not, until Alexander's day, of living individuals. The line between "public honors" and real worship may have remained fuzzy even in Hellenistic times, but the new royal cults did boast statues and altars, priests, sacrifices, feasts, hymns, and invocations of the divine ruler. It was at this time, then, that the idea of the divinely sanctioned monarch, which had been developed by Near Eastern people, became a part of Western political thinking.

Altogether, the splendor of the new state was unprecedented. The Ptolemies of Alexandria dwelt in palaces that impressed even the Egyptians, who had three thousand years of pharaohs for comparison. The famous Mausoleum, the tomb of King Mausolus (d. 353 B.C.) of Caria, in Asia Minor, was hailed as one of the wonders of the world in its time and has given us the word *mausoleum,* still used for an impressive tomb today.

The grandeur of the new monarchies has overshadowed in history another important political fact of the age: the survival and in some ways the flourishing condition of the city-states. There were still many of them, from the ancient states of Greece and the Mediterranean to cities founded by Alexander across the Middle East. A few, as we have seen, were still entirely independent. Many more accepted the protection of the Hellenistic monarchies, receiving their "freedoms" back at royal hands. Rhodes, the island that served as the financial center of the Hellenistic world and raised the huge bronze statue called the *Colossus of Rhodes* in its harbor, was only a city-state. Athens retained its assembly and its orators and was still the "school" of Greece, famed for its philosophers as far away as Rome. Nevertheless, the city-state was no longer the norm for political organization in the Greek world. That honor now belonged to the semidivine monarchies that were the political legacy of Alexander's great adventure.

Wealth and Poverty

Greek society as it evolved in the Hellenistic period boasted not only strikingly autocratic government but distinctive economic and social features. From an economic point of view, the Hellenistic world appears to have been more prosperous than any Greek age before it. And the condition of women was probably better than at any earlier time. However, the gulf between the richest and the poorest yawned wider than it ever had, and tensions between the classes increased.

The economic history of these centuries is not all of a piece. The hundred years or so after Alexander's death in 323 B.C. seem to have comprised a period of impressive economic expansion. The period following this prosperous third century, however, appears to have been a time of economic decline.

As early as the fourth century B.C., Greek merchants became even more skilled and businesslike. Trade revenues were apparently higher, and into the third century the upper classes of the cities were increasingly well off in spite of the incessant wars. The

Macedonian conquest had opened the well-filled Persian treasuries, and the new Hellenistic monarchs stamped large quantities of new coins with their own features. As a result, cash replaced barter almost everywhere and prices rose rapidly, both boons for business. In addition, the Greek-Macedonian predominance created new demands for Greek goods in the East, further expanding the volume of trade. This commercial expansion was also encouraged by the building of larger merchant ships and better harbors equipped with stone quays and lighthouses like the famous Pharos of Alexandria. Banking also became more professional, though interest rates were extravagant, often running above 25 percent a year.

The Mediterranean market thus grew busier than ever before. Such established Greek exports as wine, olive oil, and pottery were still in great demand. Luxury goods like glass, jewels, perfumes, incense, and papyrus came from the Near East. Commodities such as timber, metals, and wheat were also widely exchanged. By this time wheat was drawn from Sicily as well as from Egypt and the Black Sea. Slave labor continued to be imported from the less developed fringes of the Greek world. Meanwhile, Mediterranean merchant adventurers reached still further out during the expansive Hellenistic Age. Mariners explored the coasts of the Caspian Sea, circumnavigated Britain, and pushed down the African coast as far as the Cape Verde Islands. Though Seleucus I feuded with the Indian empire builder Chandragupta (r. c. 321–c. 297 B.C.) over territory in what is today Pakistan, trade with India brought jewelry and spices along the Persian caravan routes and by sea up the Persian Gulf and the Red Sea.

After the third century, however, the economy began to shrink again, and social discord intensified once more. Inflation and the endless wars drained the wealth of the Hellenistic monarchies. Cities still glittered as relative beacons of prosperity, but the countryside sank deeper into poverty. And in the cities too the gap between rich and poor continued to widen.

Government, especially in the Near East, still played a large part in the economic life of the period. In Ptolemaic Egypt especially, government officials continued to extract rent, taxes, and compulsory labor from the peasantry, and Greek innovations increased their burdens. The Greeks built better roads and introduced iron tools and new crops to the Egyptian community. They ran the agricultural economy even more tightly, telling the peasants exactly what to plant, providing seed in proper quantities, and collecting the grain for overseas export to enrich the treasuries of the Ptolemies. Basic industries like the production and distribution of wine, beer, and salt also remained highly profitable government monopolies.

Individual entrepreneurs—middle-class traders and artisans as well as aristocratic investors—continued to be common in the older Greek world around the Aegean. There were entrepreneurs also in the newer Greek cities of Seleucid Persia and its neighboring states. But the Hellenistic monarchies generally regulated and profited from the economic productivity of their countries as their predecessors in the Near East had done.

This conjectural rendering of Alexandria's great lighthouse, the Pharos, gives at least some sense of the scale and grandeur of Hellenistic building. Of course, Egypt's own tradition of building on the grand scale predated the Macedonian conquest by many centuries.

Social Tensions

In this enlarged Greek-dominated world of new
monarchies and surviving city-states, of boom times
and bad times, social discontent flared once more. If
anything, the bitterness between the classes was
worse throughout most of the Hellenistic period
than it was in the Classical Age. The old loyalty to
the city-state that had somewhat mitigated class conflict had been badly undermined by the Peloponnesian Wars and the fourth-century B.C. struggle for
hegemony in which rich and poor so often found
themselves on opposite sides. The individualism of
some of the philosophical schools also undercut the
growth of a community spirit that might have
bridged class differences and conflicting economic
interests. During most of the fourth century, furthermore, the great colonization movement of earlier periods seemed ended, so that there was little in
the way of a safety valve for excess and discontented
populations.

As pressures mounted in the fourth century
B.C., conflicts between the wealthy few and the poor
majority grew more virulent. The common people
demanded such drastic reforms as the cancellation
of debts and the redistribution of the estates of large
landowners among poor peasants. The more privileged classes set up associations and clubs dedicated
to the maintenance of oligarchic power in their own
hands.

There was some improvement in the later
fourth century. Alexander's conquests of the 330s
and the 320s B.C. opened up vast new lands for
Greek emigration and exploitation. The economic
boom of the third century further eased the pressure. The rich stayed rich, but the poor were fewer
and not so badly off. Judicious distribution of festivals and other favors added to the less rebellious
mood of the masses.

Then in the second and first centuries B.C., the
end of Hellenistic prosperity rekindled social tensions. The wealthy, not willing to give up their privileged position, tended to make up for worsening
economic conditions by expanding their landholdings at the expense of hard-hit peasants. The peasants and the urban poor responded by slacking off
in their work and even by refusing to work at all—
an early form of industrial strike. In Greece particularly, the cities echoed once again to the shouts of the
factions whose political slogans often reflected the bitter antagonisms of the social classes. If we add to this

picture the tensions between Greek rulers and the
non-Greeks they ruled in the East, we can see clearly
the sources of weakness in Hellenistic society.

Only one bright spot remained in this picture of
increasing social conflict and exploitation: the legal,
educational, and economic conditions under which
women lived improved dramatically in Hellenistic
times. Hellenistic women had more rights in marriage than they had in earlier periods, and in some
parts of the Greek world, women had as much right
to own property as men did. Greek women of good
family were also no longer uniformly confined to the
"private sphere" of the home but moved into the
larger world once reserved for men. Hellenistic
women thus held public magistracies and other official positions in some city-states. There were women
doctors, musicians, and painters and at least one
woman architect. Women raced on foot and in chariots at the Olympic Games, and statues of victorious
women began to appear at the great shrine of Apollo
at Delphi.

The Hellenization of the East

The Near East in our time is a welter of cultural
overlays. Arab, Turkish, Roman, Persian, and Egyptian ruins lie scattered in waste places or loom above
the noise and color of the modern bazaar. In such a
tangle of past cultures, the Greek element is not the
first to leap to the traveler's eye. Yet the impact of
Hellenistic Greece continues to be a significant topic
of scholarly discussion, and the *Hellenization* of the
East is considered by many to be the most important
consequence of the Macedonian conquest.

The opening of western Asia and northeastern
Africa to Europeans did bring Greeks in unprecedented numbers into the ancient East. They came to
serve in the armies and the governmental administrations of the new Macedonian rulers, as well as to
trade and to settle. And to some degree, at least,
they brought Greek ways with them.

The Greek city was one center of the Greek
presence in the East. Alexandria, the Ptolemaic capital situated in the Nile Delta, was both the cultural
capital of the Hellenistic world and the largest city in
the West before the rise of Rome. Scores of other
Greek cities were established as military colonies all
across the former Persian domains, where the Seleucids provided land, housing, and money in return for
military service from the Greek colonists. There may
have been as many as seventy or eighty of these new

towns, some built in conjunction with existing native settlements but all dominated by a Greek ruling class.

Greek bureaucrats, soldiers, and traders further increased the Greek presence in the conquered lands. In Egypt, the ancient scribal bureaucracy of the pharaohs was now run by Greek-speaking people from the West, while for generations only Macedonians and Greeks served in Ptolemaic armies. When we add to these the great increase in the numbers of Greek merchants and artisans in Near Eastern cities, there is no doubt that the Greco-Macedonian element in these Asian areas was significantly strengthened. And Greeks in the East could of course depend on the support of the Hellenistic monarchs.

The newcomers brought to the East as much as they could of the life they had lived around the Aegean—their language, their religion, their culture. These Greek settlers had their own political organization and their own courts of law. They continued to read Homer and to attend performances of the revived plays of fifth-century B.C. Athenian dramatists in the hot valley of the Nile or on the barren uplands of Iran.

This Greek style of life undoubtedly had some impact on the older world around these Western enclaves. Hercules carved in stone turns up along the Persian Gulf, and statues of Buddha in far-off India reflect the influence of Greek techniques. In Egypt, the separation between Greeks and Egyptians eventually broke down sufficiently to allow Egyptians to serve in the army and even to permit some intermarriage between Greeks and Egyptians. Hellenized Egyptians, Syrians, or Mesopotamians probably became more acceptable in Greek society as the generations passed. There was even some cultural influence in the other direction. Such Eastern religious faiths as Persian Zoroastrianism and the cult of the Egyptian goddess Isis, as we will see, found followers first among the Greeks and later among the Romans.

An important example of the disturbing and disorienting impact of Hellenistic Greek influences is to be found in Palestine, now part of the Seleucid empire. Many upper-class Jews of this period seem to have taken eagerly to everything Greek, from language and literature to art and athletics. Others, however, bitterly resisted Hellenization, some demanding political independence, others simply asserting their right to practice their ancient faith. A Seleucid attempt to suppress Judaism altogether in the second century B.C. triggered a determined Jewish revolt led by Judas Maccabeus (d. 160 B.C.). The resulting restoration of Judaism in Jerusalem is still celebrated in the Jewish feast of Hanukkah.

Though Jewish resistance to Hellenization was exceptionally strong, Western influence on the ancient East was perhaps nowhere quite as deep or as long lasting as some historians have suggested. Even at its height, Hellenization tended to be limited to urban areas or coasts. The Seleucids surrendered most of Persia to Asian rulers in less than a century, and the Ptolemies lost Egypt to the Romans in three centuries, though the Romans provided support for a continuing Greek presence along the Nile. Within a few more centuries, non-Western regimes and Asian faiths completely reclaimed North Africa and the Near East.

Yet though the Greek predominance ended and Greek cities built of brick crumbled to dust, archaeologists still find in a broken column or a scattering of Greek coins evidence of the ancient impact of the West on the East. And Western scholars in modern times found that stories about the great conqueror "Iskander" were still being told in Asian marketplaces more than twenty centuries after Alexander rode that way.

Hellenistic Culture

In the arts, literature, science, religion, and philosophy, the fourth century B.C. and the Hellenistic Age that followed constituted an immensely impressive, sometimes quite startling period. Hellenistic high culture can be seen as largely a response to this exotic new world of autocratic monarchies, enormous wealth, sharpened class differences, and disorienting contrasts between Greek ideas and Asian or North African cultures. Artists and writers contributed to this complex reaction by representing their world in both realistic and romantically escapist ways. Greek scientists tried to explain the world in realistic terms. By contrast, philosophers and religious thinkers sought escape from troubled and confusing times in the philosophic quest for peace of mind or in the ecstatic release of cult worship.

The Arts: Realism and Sentimentalism

Greek artists plunged eagerly into the celebration of the new era. The splendor of the Hellenistic monar-

The soft flesh of Aphrodite, the Greek goddess of love (known later to the Romans as Venus) pulses with warmth and life in this Hellenistic rendering. The heads and arms of statues, often carved from separate pieces of stone, were easily broken off by vandals.

great leader. In Hellenistic sculpture, however, the idealized proportions and Olympian calm of fifth-century statues were replaced by precise anatomical accuracy and careful delineation of individual character. Realism became an end in itself, not a means of communicating a larger truth.

Aphrodite, the goddess of love, was sculpted naked now, with a body so smooth and subtly modeled that it would be quite easy today to confuse a photographic close-up of a tautly sculptured calf or a fold of flesh with a photo of the real thing. Sculptors also showed what they could do by flinging these accurately rendered bodies into violent, twisting motion, as in the famous group of Laocoön and his sons crushed in the serpent's coils. Or they used swirling, clinging draperies to define the moving bone and muscle beneath, as in the great *Nike of Samothrace*, known as the *Winged Victory*, glowing today in a pool of light at the end of a long gallery in the Louvre in Paris.

Realistic portraiture in stone flourished as never before. Hellenistic sculptors bring the living faces of contemporaries before us, from the sensitive Antiochus I the Great to a thuglike king of Bactria, from a thin and somber Demosthenes to an anonymous drunken old lady, every wrinkle and swollen vein in evidence. Even Socrates was sculptured as overweight and unprepossessing, as he apparently was in life, rather than as a great philosopher ought to have looked.

Another oddly contrasting element in Hellenistic style was a longing for *escape* from the very realities that this style was so good at depicting in painful detail. Sentimental subjects were as popular as realistic portraits. The public loved tragic depictions of the Dying Gaul, but also appealing statues of children in various poses, including the cliché carving of a small boy plucking a thorn from his bare foot. Equally trivial and equally charming were genre figures made of clay, like the Tanagra figurines. These miniatures of ordinary ancient Greek people go about their everyday business still: a slender young woman wears a mantle and a fashionable hat; an old lady walks a baby that will not fall asleep. Later ages would also sentimentalize such things, but few young women in any age can have been quite so softly feminine, few grandmothers or babies so sweet.

It was in building, however, that Greek artistry rose most magnificently to the challenge of the new age of the Alexandrian successor states and their deified kings. Whether their clients were city-states

chies, subsidized by Persian gold and the endless bounty of the Nile, produced an unprecedented flow of commissions for statues, temples, palaces, and even new cities. Classical traditions combined with a new sense of grandiloquent scale and an enthusiasm for novelty to generate a distinctive Hellenistic style in the arts.

One element in that style was a new zeal for realism. Although the sculpture of the Classical Age was the most realistic to date in Western culture, fifth-century B.C. sculptors went only so far with naturalistic representation as they needed to make their symbolic points—for example, to show Zeus as the incarnation of power or Pericles as the image of the

Why might the unknown Hellenistic artist have created this simple statue of a boy pulling a thorn out of his foot? The fact that the talent that was once reserved for important figures was in this period lavished on everyday subjects tells us something about the artistic taste of this less heroic age.

seeking to preserve their heritage or monarchs aiming to awe the masses, Greek builders were equal to the task.

The Greek cities distributed across the Middle East had to have their temples and their agoras like those at home, their theaters and gymnasiums dedicated to sound minds in sound bodies. Greek elites everywhere prided themselves on decorating their cities, and Hellenistic kings demonstrated their beneficence by giving a new theater or a new stoa, or pillared portico, to a favored city.

Some Hellenistic cities were dazzling sights, with their walls and terraces and two-storied stoa, their hilltop temples and palaces. Pergamum in Asia Minor set the standard for splendor, with its colonnaded agora, its great altar of Zeus and its temple of Athena, its royal palace crowning the hill, and an open-air Greek theater that held ten thousand spectators.

Most splendid of all was Alexandria. The main harbor, with the Pharos, its 400-foot lighthouse, symbolized the commercial wealth of the city, its palaces and temples the presence of the divine Ptolemies. Perhaps most famous, however, were Alexandria's cultural institutions, the zoological and botanical gardens and, especially, the museum and libraries—the latter containing perhaps 400,000 books. Public buildings like these stood several stories high and were elaborately decorated with painted sculptures.

Reality and sentimental dreams met and mingled in these metropolitan complexes. The reality of Hellenistic power merged with the romantic dream that Classical Greek culture could be preserved forever in these exotic new homes in Asia and Africa.

Literature: From Comical to Pastoral

In Hellenistic literature, the tension between a hankering for realism and romantic escapism showed as clearly as it did in sculpture. Drama, poetry, and prose all reflected these divergent tugs on the Hellenistic psyche.

Realism was evident in such new forms as the *Characters* of Theophrastus (c. 372–287 B.C.), pithy thumbnail sketches of all-too-human types with their foibles on display. And racily realistic dialogue began to appear in some popular theatrical entertainment. Even scholars followed the trend. Polybius (c. 200–c. 118 B.C.), the most famous historian of the second century B.C., made absolute objectivity his goal. His *Histories* recounting the rise of Roman dominance in realistic terms declared that it was not so much the favor of the gods as armed might that was making Rome master of the Western world.

Perhaps most vividly, however, the comic plays of Menander (342–292 B.C.), written around 300 B.C., put ordinary people of the Hellenistic world on the stage. The New Comedy, of which Menander was the foremost practitioner, differed from the Old Comedy of Aristophanes in that it deliberately eschewed large issues and political positions. Menander's characters—slaves, prostitutes, and pastry cooks, ordinary Greeks who would not know Homer from Hercules—face problems having more to do with sex, love, and money than with the great issues of the day. The actors in these plays still wore masks, though they also wore ordinary street clothes. They still spoke in verse but in a rhythm that approximated everyday speech. Menander's characters were comic stereotypes, and his endings were invariably happy, but his people were closer to real Greeks and real problems

Scholars of many persuasions gathered at the great library of Alexandria in Hellenistic times. Notice the form the "books" these people read took and the way the manuscripts were stored. Why did historians in later centuries mourn the loss of this library and its contents to fire in ancient times?

than Aristophanes's Socrates with his head in the clouds or *Lysistrata*'s women taking over the Acropolis to put an end to war.

Yet the urge to escape from reality was there too, in scholarship and literature. The museum and libraries of Alexandria were frequented by the leading scholars of the day, many of them subsidized by the Ptolemaic government. A major focus of Alexandrian scholarship was the thought and literature of the Greek past. Homeric studies flourished, producing learned and abstruse commentaries on the greatest Greek poet. These scholarly treatises, though detailed and ingenious, lacked a realistic sense of Homer's Dark Age world. Such scholarship is also often seen as escapist because these Hellenistic scholars buried themselves in the literature of the

past instead of facing the disturbing realities of their own times and producing a living literature of their own.

It was, however, the formalism of the Alexandrian poets and the idyllic pastoral poetry of Theocritus in particular that best illustrated this longing to slip away from the way life was into a variety of never-never lands. *Formalism*, or art for its own sake, became a literary cult among the poets of sophisticated Alexandria. Their goal was not to offer inspired truths or insights into the human condition but to produce perfect poems. Technical perfection meant mastery of metrical forms, rhetorical devices, and all the classical models back to Homer. From this distillation of the poetic discoveries of past centuries, the Alexandrian formalists generated verse of a polished simplicity and an allusive wit that was quite beyond any ordinary Greek—beyond anyone, in fact, except their fellow poets.

This dream of escape to unlikely, idealized realms of poesy also affected the subject matter of Hellenistic verse. Apollonius of Rhodes (295–214 B.C.) revived the epic form of Homer in his *Argonautica* to tell, not a war story, but a love story. The story of the Greek hero Jason's many adventures in his quest for the Golden Fleece in his ship, the *Argo,* and of his love for the Asian sorceress Medea might sound a bit like Odysseus's long voyage home. But Jason is no rough-hewn Homeric hero, and his voyage is so heavy with learned commentary on the local antiquities that it sometimes sounds more like a journey through a museum than a cruise to the mythical kingdom of Colchis.

The Alexandrian poet Theocritus (c. 310–250 B.C.) gave expression to a more obvious escapism in his thirty *Idylls,* short poems evoking an "idyllic" pastoral world of shepherds and shepherdesses. The meticulously crafted songs of these simple folk on such subjects as love, death, and the beauties of nature could take the cosmopolitan reader far from the thronged streets of Alexandria to the half-imaginary groves of Theocritus's youth in his native Sicily. The rustic accents of the shepherds and the Sicilian settings based on his own early years were realistic elements in Theocritus's poetry. But the longing of the city dweller to get back to nature and the belief that peasants, or farmers, are morally superior and lead happier, more aesthetically pleasing lives was to become a staple of literary escapism in Western culture.

The Hellenistic period also saw a significant increase in the availability of education for women. Some schools seem to have been coeducational, and a highly literate female aristocracy developed. This in turn led to the appearance of a number of women writers and to the presence of women in the philosophical schools.

On the literary side, the poetic legacy of Sappho was taken up several centuries later in the larger Hellenistic world. A number of Hellenistic women were honored by their cities for their poetry. Erinna of Telos, perhaps the most revered woman poet of the period, was compared to Sappho by her contemporaries. Erinna mastered the complexities of Greek verse forms at a remarkably early age and wrote the much admired *Distaff,* in which she lamented the death of a friend. Dead herself by the age of twenty, Erinna was mourned in turn by her peers.

Science: The Hellenistic Flowering

During the Hellenistic period, Greek scientists achieved enormous advances in human understanding of the material world. There had been some investigation of the nature of the physical world in earlier Greek centuries. The Milesian philosophers of Ionia, the Pythagoreans, Plato, and Aristotle all speculated on the ultimate nature of the world around us. In the sixth century B.C., Pythagoras (c. 580–500 B.C.) offered mathematical insights, including the famous "Pythagorean theorem," or the formula for determining the hypotenuse of the right triangle. In the fifth century, Hippocrates (460–377 B.C.), the most famous of Greek doctors, inspired new directions in medicine and proposed the Hippocratic oath, which is still taken by doctors today.

The greatest Greek breakthroughs in mathematics, astronomy, physics, and biology, however, came in the fourth and third centuries B.C. Fusing Greek and Near Eastern scientific insights and exchanging ideas in the stimulating atmosphere of Alexandria, Hellenistic scientists learned more about the universe than the West learned for the next two thousand years. It took the modern scientific revolution to match—and exceed—the Hellenistic achievement.

It was during the Hellenistic period that Euclid (fl. c. 300 B.C.) summed up Greek geometrical knowledge in his *Elements of Geometry.* Euclid's elegantly logical mathematical demonstrations communicated the Greek rational spirit as effectively as Aristotle's logic did to later generations of Western people, and his book was used in schools even into the present century. Other Hellenistic Greeks studied the mathematical characteristics of circles, spirals, and conic sections.

Archimedes of Syracuse (287–212 B.C.) and other Hellenistic scientists made basic discoveries in several areas of physics, including optics, acoustics, hydrostatics, and mechanics. Archimedes calculated the value of *pi*—the ratio between a circle's circumference and its diameter—and formulated the basic principle of the lever, asserting with typical Greek panache that if he were given a long enough lever and a place to stand, he would literally move the world. Proudest of his discoveries in abstract mathematics, Archimedes was also traditionally credited with designing ingenious war machines for the defense of his city. In the end, however, he is perhaps most famous for a single word, shouted as he raced home dripping from the public baths with a new insight into the displacement of water by his own body. His cry of *"Eureka!"* ("I have found it!") is often taken as the quintessential expression of the Greek passion for truth.

In biology, the wide-ranging philosopher Aristotle recognized the relationship between groups and families of living things. His empirical observations were sharp and generally so accurate that later scientists hesitated to challenge him even when he was in error. His pupil Theophrastus, author of the satirical *Characters* that we have already mentioned, also developed a method of categorizing plants that remained standard well into modern times. With the medical insights achieved by Hippocrates and by Galen (129–c. 199 A.D.) later on, this biological research reflected an empirical spirit that would scarcely be seen again until the birth of modern science.

Greek scientists made their most impressive discoveries in the study of the earth and the heavens—in geography and astronomy. With their new access to Babylonian astronomical data and with the great Alexandrian libraries to draw on, the Hellenistic Greeks had a sounder empirical basis for speculation in this field also.

Greek scholars came to realize that the earth is a sphere and divided its surface into degrees of longitude and latitude. Eratosthenes (275–194 B.C.) calculated the size of the earth and Hipparchus (c. 190–126 B.C.) the length of the year with remarkable accuracy. The astronomer Aristarchus (c. 310–230 B.C.) deduced that, though the heavenly bodies all seem to revolve around the earth, the sun is actually the center of the planetary system and the earth merely one of the planets (see box, "A Greek Precursor of Copernicus"). It was Hipparchus's earth-centered explanation of the structure of the universe, however, that won general acceptance. And this erroneous view—in the learned, mathematically sophisticated form proposed by the astronomer Ptolemy in the second century A.D.—was reverently accepted until Copernicus's day.

Religion and Philosophy: Mystery Cults, Stoics, Epicureans, and Cynics

Accompanying the rise of Greek science were serious doubts about the traditional gods, already questioned by the Sophists of the fifth century B.C. Sophisticated people were amused by the mythical amours of Zeus, and some suggested that all the gods and goddesses might be legends based on half-

forgotten kings and heroes. Confronted with the possibility that the gods of their fathers might never have existed at all, many people prayed instead to Fate or Fortune, to whom statues and temples were solemnly raised. Hope for good fortune was embodied in the particularly popular cult of Tyche, or Luck, conceived of as a goddess like Athena or Aphrodite.

Other Hellenistic Greeks, unable to confront the grim possibility that life really might be a matter of blind chance, turned to astrology, magic, and a growing number of oriental religions. Astrology built on the scientific recognition that the sun does affect the moon, the tides, and growing things, insisting that stars and planets could affect the course

---

MASTERING OUR WORLD
A Greek Precursor of Copernicus

So many ancient books have been lost that much of what we know about Greek ideas comes from references or quotations in other books that *have* survived. So it is with Aristarchus's heliocentric view of the structure of the universe, first proposed in the third century B.C. His theory is recounted here in the writings of his better known contemporary, Archimedes. What shape do you think "most astronomers" believed the earth itself to be?

Now you are aware that "universe" is the name given by most astronomers to the sphere whose center is the center of the earth and whose radius is equal to the straight line between the center of the sun and the center of the earth. This is the common account, as you have heard from astronomers. But Aristarchus of Samos brought out a book consisting of some hypotheses, in which the premises lead to the result that the universe is many times greater than that now so called. His hypotheses are that the fixed stars and the sun remain unmoved, that the earth revolves about the sun in the circumference of a circle, the sun lying in the middle of the orbit, and that the sphere of the fixed stars [is] situated about the same center as the sun.

Source: Archimedes, "The Sand Reckoner," in Dagobert D. Runes, *A Treasury of World Science* (Paterson, N.J.: Littlefield, Adams, 1952), 38–39.

of human life as well. Many, including highly educated people, consulted astrologers for guidance before undertaking any serious project, just as their ancestors would have consulted oracles.

The Eastern *mystery cults,* meanwhile, came closer to replacing the Olympians than they had ever done (see also Chapter 2). The faiths of Dionysus and Demeter, going back to the Greek Awakening, had never had so many initiates. Of the newer religions, the cults of the Egyptian goddess Isis and of Cybele, the Earth Mother from Asia Minor, were the most successful.

The worship of Cybele and her consort Attis revived once more the ancient spirit of the fertility cult. Cybele's rituals involved ecstatic violence, climaxing on the annual "Day of Blood," when priests slashed themselves with knives and those of the higher ranks castrated themselves before screaming crowds. The religion of Isis, bringer of eternal life, and Osiris, lord of the underworld, which went far back in Egyptian history, was encouraged by the Ptolemies as a national religion. For many, Isis became the incarnation of all the gods, the "Goddess of Ten Thousand Names," the repository of all wisdom. Above all, she was the merciful divinity who brought salvation and eternal life to those who believed in her.

These oriental cults of the Hellenistic epoch thus offered the greatest escape of all from the harsh realities of life: communion with a deity who promised another, better life to true believers. Elaborate processions through the streets, ritual dramas enacting the rebirth of the god, secret initiations, hymns, and ecstasies all revealed the profound emotional hungers that "realism" could not satisfy.

For the more intellectually inclined, however, escape from a world of meaningless splendor might be found in the new philosophies. Of these, Epicureanism and Stoicism had the greatest influence, though Cynicism produced perhaps the most colorful gurus. The goal of all the new schools may be summed up, however, in a single phrase: "withdrawal from reality to find peace of mind."[5]

Zeno (335–263 B.C.), the founder of *Stoicism,* taught in the columned stoa around the marketplace at Athens. Urging that a rational principle orders all things in nature, Zeno concluded that all people, sharing in this basic rationality, were fundamentally equal. Slaves, women, and even foreigners were thus brothers and sisters under the skin. This was a valuable insight for Hellenistic Greeks who, unlike their ancestors, often lived in North Africa or the Near

Isis, the Egyptian goddess of ten thousand names, absorbed the qualities of many other divinities and came to be worshiped all around the Hellenistic Mediterranean. She is shown here with a cow's horns—her sacred animal and a symbol of beauty—framing the solar disk.

East, surrounded by people very different from themselves.

The fundamental Stoic concern, however, was to find a way of life that would help people escape the misfortunes that beset all human lives. Admitting that human affairs were often beyond human control, Zeno preached duty and emotional disengagement from the world around us. By overcoming fear, desire, and other human feelings, his followers sought what they called *apathy,* an "emotionless-ness" that would free them from the worst the world could do. Thus purged of their emotions, they could do their duty and confront whatever came quite calmly—as we still say, stoically.

Epicurus (341–270 B.C.), the founder of *Epicureanism,* agreed with his contemporary Zeno on the harsh nature of life in this world, but he disagreed about the formula for escape from it. Epicurus adopted the *atomism* of the philosopher Democritus (c. 460–370 B.C.) as his metaphysical foundation. Everything, he said, even a god, is made of tiny identical particles of matter called atoms, drifting through space, encountering and linking up by pure chance to form the material world we know. By the philosophically dubious introduction of a willed "swerve" in the drift of atoms, however, Epicurus gave us some control over our own lives. And he told his followers how to exercise that control: through the pursuit of pleasure.

But the pleasure Epicurus preached was no eat-drink-and-be-merry sensual hedonism; it was simply the absence of pain. "The end of all our action," he declared, "is to be free from pain and fear, and once we have attained all this, the tempest of the soul is laid."[6] Death itself need hold no terrors, for it involved no afterlife but simply the dispersal of the atoms of our bodies into the universe. For this life, Epicurus and his disciples retreated to a walled garden on the edge of Athens, where they found approved pleasures in friendship, music, poetry, and the fragrance and colors of the flowers.

The ultimate philosophical withdrawal, however, was that of the Cynics, who sneered at society, rejected material comforts, and sought salvation in forms of "natural living" so crude that they outraged their contemporaries. The most notorious of the *Cynics,* Diogenes (c. 400–c. 325 B.C.) jeered at money, marriage, education, and "social conventions" like the taboos on incest and cannibalism. Diogenes lived in a large jar instead of a house and, rejecting all political allegiance, declared himself a "citizen of the world." His total lack of inhibition and his refusal to be enslaved by Hellenistic social conventions earned him the contempt of many but an admiring epitaph: "Your fame will live forever, Diogenes, because you taught humankind the lesson of self-sufficiency."[7]

Among the philosophers, a number of women were disciples of Pythagoreans and some were followers of Plato, but the Stoics and the Epicureans, distinctively Hellenistic schools, offered them the warmest welcome. Epicurus saw women as fellow seekers, while Stoics recognized the divine spark of rationality in people of both sexes. There were even women in the ranks of the Cynics, perhaps the most radical of the new schools. They were apparently not always accepted easily among the disputants at the feet of the various masters. But Hipparchia the Cynic responded with proper philosophical serenity when challenged as to why she had abandoned her weaving to join the search for truth: "Do I seem to you to have come to a wrong decision, if I devote that time to philosophy which otherwise I should have spent at the loom?"[8] She might have been speaking for philosophers of both sexes who sought escape from the workaday world in the search for a higher reality.

A Topical Summary

Politics: The continuing struggle for hegemony among Greek city-states ended when Philip of Macedon and his son Alexander the Great subdued all the feuding Greek states and then went on to conquer the Greeks' ancient enemy, Persia. But Alexander's immense empire quickly fragmented into feuding Hellenistic monarchies in which the once independent Greeks became subjects rather than self-governing citizens.

Economics: For a century after Alexander's conquests the economy of the Mediterranean and the Near East was extremely prosperous. Then a sharp decline set in, and the gulf between rich and poor expanded dramatically.

Society: Social tensions built steadily during the Hellenistic Age. Cultural differences between Greeks and non-Greeks and class conflicts between rich and poor challenged the cosmopolitan order. Women's role in society expanded somewhat in the later Greek centuries.

Technology: The scale of Hellenistic building dwarfed all earlier Western efforts. Monarchs expanded their palaces and cities, and the increased trade during the early part of the period led to the building of larger harbors, with solid stone docks and towering lighthouses like the Pharos at Alexandria.

Culture: Hellenistic rulers built splendidly to project an image of their own greatness. Hellenistic science expanded Western knowledge in the fields of astronomy, physics, biology, and medicine. Much of the period's literature, sculpture, philosophy, and religion, however, often reflected a need to escape from the tensions of Hellenistic society into sentimental art, ecstatic cults, or inward-turning systems of thought.

The Expanding West: A striking feature of the Hellenistic Age was the spread of both Greek power and Greek culture across much of the Near East and parts of North Africa. Following Alexander the Great's epic march to India, Macedonian sovereigns ruled Persia for a century and Egypt for three. These and other Hellenistic monarchies encouraged the cultural Hellenization of the eastern end of the Mediterranean from the fourth century on.

Some Key Terms

Achaean League 103
Aetolian League 103
Antigonid dynasty 103
atomism 114
Cynics 114
Epicureanism 114

formalism 110
hegemony 94
Hellenistic Age 93
Hellenistic monarchy 103
Hellenization 106
League of Corinth 98

mystery cults 113
Philippic 97
Ptolemaic dynasty 102
Seleucid monarchs 102
Stoicism 113

Notes

1. Thucydides, *Peloponnesian War,* vol. 5, trans. Benjamin Jowett (Oxford: Clarendon Press, 1900), 89.
2. Diodorus Siculus in Claire Preaux, *Le Monde Hellénistique: La Grèce et l'Orient, 323–146 av. J.-C.,* vol. 1 (Paris: Presses Universitaires de France, 1978), 127.
3. Arrian, *Anabasis Alexandri,* trans. E. I. Robson (New York: Putnam's, Loeb Classical Library, 1929–1933), 7.11.1.
4. Johann Gustav Droysen, *Geschichte des Hellenismus* (Tubingen: Wissenschaftliche Buchgemeinschaft, 1952), 1.
5. Michael Grant, *From Alexander to Cleopatra: The Hellenistic World* (London: Weidenfeld and Nicolson, 1982), 234.
6. Epicurus, *Letters,* in Grant, *Alexander to Cleopatra,* 240.
7. Grant, *Alexander to Cleopatra,* 245.
8. Diogenes Laertius, *Lives and Opinions of Eminent Philosophers,* vol. 6, 96–98, quoted in G. W. Botsford, *Hellenic Civilization* (New York: Columbia University Press, 1920), 665.

Reading List

Bosworth, A. B. *Conquest and Empire: The Reign of Alexander the Great.* Cambridge: Cambridge University Press, 1988. Clear, detailed account by a leading authority.

ELLIS, J. R. *Philip II and Macedonian Imperialism.* London: Thames and Hudson, 1976. The achievements of the first great Macedonian.

GRANT, M. *From Alexander to Cleopatra: The Hellenistic World.* New York: Scribner's, 1982. Colorful evocation of the age by a prolific classicist.

GREEN, P. *Alexander of Macedon, 356–323 B.C.* Berkeley: University of California Press, 1991. Sharply critical of the Macedonian conqueror. For an older, more laudatory view, see W. W. Tarn, *Alexander the Great* (Boston: Beacon Press, 1956).

GRUEN, E. S. *The Hellenistic World and the Coming of Rome.* Berkeley: University of California Press, 1984. Hellenistic Greek intrigues and entanglements pave the way for Roman domination of the Mediterranean.

HADAS, M. *Hellenistic Culture.* New York: Norton, 1972. Interpretive study by a leading modern scholar.

HAMILTON, C. D. *Sparta's Bitter Victories: Politics and Diplomacy in the Corinthian War.* Ithaca, N.Y.: Cornell University Press, 1979. Political rivalries and military clashes between the city-states in the decades after the Peloponnesian Wars.

HAMMOND, N. G. L. *Alexander the Great: King, Commander, and Statesman.* London: Chatto and Windus, 1980. Balanced evaluation of the famous commander, seen here as a statesman as well.

——. *A History of Macedonia.* 3 vols. Oxford: Clarendon

Press, 1979. Basic book on Macedonia, before and after Alexander.

HANSEN, M. H. *The Athenian Democracy in the Age of Demosthenes: Structure, Principles, and Ideology.* Translated by J. A. Crook. Oxford: Blackwell, 1991. Describes participatory democracy operating more effectively than most would have expected.

HAVELOCK, C. M. *Hellenistic Art.* Greenwich, Conn.: New York Graphic Society, 1970. The art of the Hellenistic Greek world and of early Rome, from Alexander to Augustus. See also T. B. L. Webster, *Hellenistic Poetry and Art* (New York: Barnes and Noble, 1964).

HORNBLOWER, S. *The Greek World 479–323.* New York: Methuen, 1983. Survey of Greek history in the fifth and fourth centuries, with many interpretive insights.

KLEIJWEGT, M. *Ancient Youth: The Ambiguity of Youth and the Absence of Adolescence in Greco-Roman Society.* Amsterdam: J. C. Gieben, 1991. Upper-class families and career-oriented youth.

LLOYD, G. E. R. *Greek Science After Aristotle.* New York: Norton, 1973. Clear presentation of scientific theories for the nonscientist. See also his *Early Greek Science: Thales to Aristotle* (London: Chatto and Windus, 1970).

LONG, A. A. *Hellenistic Philosophy: Stoics, Epicureans, Sceptics.* London: Duckworth, 1986. Covers the major Hellenistic schools.

ONIANS, J. *Art and Thought in the Hellenistic Age: The Greek World View 350–50 B.C.* London: Thames and Hudson, 1979. Hellenistic art and thought as related by contemporary artists and critics.

OWENS, E. J. *The City in the Greek and Roman World.* London: Routledge, 1991. Ancient cities as public places, sacred shrines, seats of royal power, and as sites of other human activities.

POMEROY, S. B. *Women in Hellenistic Egypt.* New York: Schocken, 1985. Study of women's roles by an authority on women in antiquity.

ROSTOVTZEFF, M. I. *The Social and Economic History of the Hellenistic World.* Oxford: Clarendon Press, 1941. Old but thorough study by a celebrated classical historian.

SAMUEL, A. E. *From Athens to Alexandria: Hellenism and Social Goals in Ptolemaic Egypt.* Challenges traditional view of cultural cross-fertilization between Greeks and Egyptians, asserting persistent separation of the two peoples and cultures.

WALBANK, F. W. *The Hellenistic World.* Cambridge, Mass.: Harvard University Press, 1982. Excellent survey of the period.

Rome: The Republic

Bust of a Roman. First century B.C. Marble, 14⅜". The Metropolitan Museum of Art. Rogers Fund, 1912

The great achievement of the Romans was building and ruling a vast empire. They were never quite the artists or the original thinkers that the Greeks were. But they did manage to bring not only most of western Europe but the Near East and North Africa as well under a single government. It is the only time in history this has happened.

The long-range consequences of this achievement were equally remarkable. The Romans left to later Western centuries a legacy that included not only Roman culture but much Greek and some Near Eastern civilization as well. Roman law, Greek philosophy, and the Judeo-Christian religious traditions all reached the medieval and modern West in large part through Rome. If Greece was the originator, Rome was the consolidator of what is properly called the Greco-Roman heritage, a major component of Western civilization.

The thousand-year span of Roman history, roughly 500 B.C.–A.D. 500, divides in the middle at about the time of Christ. During most of the first five centuries of this history, the period of the *Roman Republic,* Rome was governed primarily by its aristocracy, the patrician ruling class that sat in the Senate and held most of the executive offices. During the second half of Roman history, the period of the *Empire,* hereditary emperors ruled the state, and the Senate became little more than a rubber stamp for imperial decrees. Both these periods, however, shared in Rome's epochal achievement, the building of a *territorial empire* encompassing western Europe and the Mediterranean basin. The present chapter surveys the history of the Republic and the emergence of the Roman territorial empire. Chapter 6 traces the development of the Empire as a form of government and the climax, decline, and fall of Rome's territorial empire in the West.

Other common achievements besides the building of an immense territorial state link the two periods. Travelers in later times sense these long-range accomplishments as they walk beneath triumphal arches that once celebrated Roman victories, stroll the forum where Roman orators once thundered, gaze up at aqueducts that still stand as symbols of Roman engineering genius. The Romans may not have matched the mind of Plato or the hands that carved the *Winged Victory,* but they were great conquerors, rulers, and builders, and as such they have left their mark on history.

The Roman forum as it looks today. Here powerful orators thundered denunciations of national enemies or demanded political reforms, and huge crowds cheered. Now of this center of Roman public life only scattered columns, the shells of public buildings, and a single triumphal arch (left) remain.

Roman Beginnings

Not all the remains of the ancient West lie open to the Mediterranean sun. You can also find ancient history under the Church of San Clemente in Rome. While Catholic services are chanted in the nave above, you pass down through level after level of history. There is an ancient Roman church beneath the floor of the modern one. Still further down, there lies a temple of Mithras, the Persian god adopted by the Roman legions. At the deepest level, finally, dark waters swirl through a second-century alleyway far below the traffic of modern Rome. Such a descent into the past may also point you still further back— back to a time before the city of Rome existed at all— back to a handful of villages scattered over green hills under a blue Italian sky.

Rome and the Mediterranean

Geography played as important a part in Roman history as it did in the history of the Greeks. The city of Rome, to begin with, evolved from a group of villages on the river Tiber in central Italy, and Italy is the central landmass in the Mediterranean Sea, two geographical facts that help explain Rome's rise to mastery of the Mediterranean. Another aspect of Italian geography that helped determine the course of Roman history was the fact that the Italian land is not chopped up into tiny mountain valleys or narrow promontories as Greece is. Because their land was not divided, it was much easier for Romans to move beyond the city-state than it was for the Greeks to do so. The Apennines mountain range does run the

| | 500 B.C. | | 400 | 300 |

POLITICAL, MILITARY, AND DIPLOMATIC EVENTS

509 Roman Republic founded

494 Lex Hortensia

490s Alliances with Italian peoples

484–287 Struggle of the Orders

450 Twelve Tables

445 Lex Cornuleia

396 Capture of Veii

336 First plebeian consul

SOCIAL AND ECONOMIC DEVELOPMENTS

484–287 Plebeians demand rights

CULTURE: THE ARTS, PHILOSOPHY, SCIENCE AND RELIGION

length of Italy, but it leaves large arable plains, especially in the Po River valley in the north and down the western side of the peninsula. This fertile soil, combined with much more abundant rain than Greece enjoys, could support a larger population than the Greek mainland.

At the same time, a lack of good harbors—except in the south, where Greek colonies were already established—limited Rome's interest in the sea and the world of commerce, where Greeks excelled. Though Rome's empire ringed the Mediterranean, and Rome later built fleets and imported heavily from overseas, it was always essentially a land power. Romans became famous as builders of roads, not ships.

The Mediterranean—*mare nostrum*, "our sea,"

as the Romans later came to call it—did offer Rome some rich targets for conquest. The Mediterranean is the core of a water system some 2,500 miles long and includes such tributary bodies of water as the Adriatic, Aegean, and Black seas. Its coasts are eminently livable, with a subtropical climate, sufficient pasture to support cattle, horses, mules, sheep, and goats, and fertile land enough to cultivate a variety of grains and fruits. And the sea itself had for centuries served as an avenue of trade for Phoenicians, Greeks, and others, and as a stimulus for cultural development through easy intercourse between peoples.

By 500 B.C., then, the eastern half of the Mediterranean Sea was already bordered by flourishing civilizations. From the Nile valley in North Africa around to the Turkish Straits, which separate Asia

Timeline

200	100	1 A.D.

157–86 Marius
137–78 Sulla
106–48 Pompey
106–43 Cicero
100–44 Julius Caesar

287 Measure passed by Assembly of Tribes becomes law
279 "Pyrrhic victory"
265 Rome rules all Italy
264–241 First Punic War
245–183 Hannibal
218–201 Second Punic War
216 Cannae
202 Zama

149–146 Third Punic War
133–31 Civil War
133, 123 Tiberius and Gaius Gracchus consuls

60 First Triumvirate
43 Second Triumvirate
31 Actium
31–41 Rule of Augustus Caesar

from 150 Rise of equestrians
from 150 Slave population grows
from 150 Eastern wealth floods Rome
from 133 Class conflict in Rome

70 Spartacus slave revolt

254–184 Plautus
190–159 Terence
from 150 Hellenization of Rome
106–43 Cicero
96–55 Lucretius
84–54 Catullus

---

from Europe, lay the high cultures of the Near East. The cities of the Greek world stretched from the Ionian coast of Asia Minor westward across the Aegean and Adriatic seas all the way to the colonies of Sicily and southern Italy. The western half of the Mediterranean was more sparsely civilized, but it too was dotted with cities, many of them Phoenician and Greek colonies along the coasts of modern France, Spain, Morocco, Tunisia, and Algeria. As Rome grew stronger, furthermore, the Mediterranean as a whole was growing richer. Wealth piled up in the Hellenistic monarchies to the east; prosperous cities like Syracuse in Sicily or Carthage in North Africa glittered within easy reach of Roman power.

The Mediterranean basin, as we have seen, had become over three thousand years one of the great-est centers of civilization in the world, as highly developed as the Hindu-Buddhist culture of India and the Confucian civilization of China. To impose political unity on one of the most affluent and brilliant centers of world civilization was Rome's first historic accomplishment.

The First Romans

The Romans certainly did not look like a people of destiny in 509 B.C., the traditional date of the founding of the Republic. They were only one of a number of peoples living on the Italian peninsula, most of them culturally unimpressive by Greek standards.

And as far as we can tell, they were until that year firmly under the thumb of a more civilized people to the north, the mysterious Etruscans.

According to one Roman legend, the first founder of Rome was a Trojan prince named Aeneas who escaped from burning Troy and crossed the Mediterranean to settle in Italy. Another story tells how Aeneas's descendant Romulus laid out the original walls of the city of Rome itself and then struck his own brother Remus dead for jumping over the line, thus giving fair warning of the fate that awaited anyone so foolish as to cross a Roman wall again. Still another story has the city that Romulus built ruled by the Tarquins, kings of the neighboring Etruscan people, until the Etruscan ruler raped Lucretia, a Roman woman of high degree. The resulting revolt expelled the last king and created the Roman Republic in 509 B.C. The reality was apparently less dramatic, but the historic forefathers of the Romans, like Aeneas, Romulus, and the Tarquins, did step upon the stage of history with weapons in their hands.

The pre-Roman inhabitants of Italy seem to have been rather slow to move out of prehistory. The Neolithic agricultural revolution, which began around 10,000 B.C. in the Near East, did not reach Italy until 2500. The age of copper and bronze, which began in the Near East before 3000 B.C., did not get started in Italy until 1500. And it was not until approximately 1000 B.C. that the ancestors of the Romans migrated down from the north.

These invaders were Indo-European peoples, whose dialects eventually evolved into Latin and the related languages of neighboring Italic tribes. As a whole they were a tough, warlike people who moved rapidly from using excellent bronze weapons to wielding even more successful iron ones. At first pasturing flocks on the high slopes of the Apennines, they only gradually descended to seize the farmlands of the native Bronze Age peoples of the Italian plains.

Thus by about 750 B.C. the peoples who were to become Romans were living in thatch-roofed villages among the seven hills beside the Tiber where the great city later stood. They had selected a good location for their settlements, with defensible hills and a river ford, 15 miles in from the sea, that marked a key juncture on the main north-south road. The fields around their hills were fertile, and the early Romans exerted a growing influence on most of the less strategically located Latin-speaking peoples around them.

Etruscan Predominance

A more developed people, however, soon imposed their authority on many of the Latin peoples, including the early Romans. Evidence of the Etruscan culture begins to appear in the archaeological record around 800 B.C., and from all we can tell the Etruscans developed a sophisticated urban civilization, centered just north of Rome in what was called Etruria, now Tuscany. We do not know where they came from, but their language was not an Indo-European one, and their burial and sacrificial practices point to the Near East. From the ruins of their cities and the strikingly beautiful artifacts in their tombs, however, archaeologists have deduced a good deal about the economic, social, and cultural nature of Etruscan civilization.

The Etruscan cities were apparently ruled by kings, at least in the early centuries. They established a loosely linked league of cities between the Arno and the Tiber, the rivers on which Florence and Rome stand today. Etruscan power, however, sometimes reached as far north as the Po valley and as far south as the Bay of Naples. Skilled metalworkers and merchants, the Etruscans traded with the Greek colonies still further south. And as soldiers and pirates, they formed a military ruling class, forcing other Italian peoples to work their fields, mine their metals, and serve in their armies.

The Etruscans borrowed a good deal from the Greeks to the south, from building methods and weaponry to anthropomorphic gods and a version of the Greek alphabet. But they had their own unique cultural characteristics as well. An intriguing feature of Etruscan society, for instance, seems to have been relative equality between the sexes. Their own religion apparently revered the Great Mother whose worship was found in other parts of the Mediterranean, and their society may have been to some degree matrilineal. To judge from their tomb paintings and bas-reliefs, women shared meals and in other ways stood on a basis of parity with men.

The early Romans learned a great deal from their Etruscan neighbors and overlords. During the sixth century B.C., when Etruscan kings called the Tarquins did apparently rule them for a time, the villages that lay scattered among the seven hills were fused into a small city. The Romans built temples, public buildings, and walls, all centered on the Capitoline Hill where the Temple of Jupiter was

An Etruscan couple recline on their sarcophagus, together in death as they were in life. Compare this Etruscan pair with the statues of Pharaoh Menkaure and Queen Khamerernebty in Chapter 1: here again, what makes us feel there was genuine affection between the husband and wife portrayed?

built. They drained a swampy bit of low ground that had been used as a cemetery and turned it into the forum, a market and public meeting place like the Athenian agora. Like the Etruscans, furthermore, the early Romans began to exchange goods with the colonies of what they called Great Greece, or *Magna Graecia*, further south. In fact, it was the Latin term *Graeci* that gave us the name "Greek" for the people who called themselves the Hellenes.

But it was the Etruscan influence that was paramount among the earliest Romans. Jupiter and Juno, the king and queen of the Roman pantheon, were originally Etruscan gods, though they later acquired Greek characteristics. Some Roman styles in building, including the arch and the vault, were modeled on those of Etruria. The Romans adopted the alphabet that the Etruscans had borrowed from the Greeks, and it was this Roman version that became the basis for the alphabet used later by western European languages, including English.

Even the oppressive Etruscan monarchy left its mark on the political organization of the Roman Republic that resulted from the rebellion against the Etruscans in 509 B.C. The Roman Senate, for example, was originally an advisory body to the Etruscan

king of Rome. The consuls, Rome's chief magistrates, took over the Etruscan symbol of ultimate authority, the bundle of rods and the ax, together called the *fasces*, representing the king's power to order corporal punishment and execution. Even the white gown called a toga, the badge of citizenship in the Roman Republic, was borrowed from the Etruscans.

When the Romans overthrew their last Etruscan ruler—called Tarquin the Proud by Roman historians—they were thus a very different people from the agricultural villagers the Etruscans had found in the seven hills near the Tiber. The Romans who began their independent history shortly before 500 B.C. were still a relatively simple folk. But they were now rulers of a city-state, able to read and write, trading for pottery with Great Greece, and possessed of a clear national character of their own.

A Tough-Minded Conservative Society

Even after they had developed an urban center among the seven hills, the Romans continued to cultivate the qualities of their warlike peasant forebears.

Most Romans remained farmers and soldiers for centuries after 500 B.C. They continued to be a tough-minded lot, more concerned with justice than with mercy, with discipline than with independence of mind. A realistic and practical people, they reformed their constitution when the necessity for change became overwhelming, but because of their instinctive conservatism they made such changes sparingly. In undertaking such reforms, they tended to balance advantages granted one segment of society with limiting powers in the hands of others.

The social structure of the earliest Romans, like that of most preurban peoples, was based on a family unit over which the father had absolute authority. Broader units of social organization included the *gens* or clan, composed of a number of families claiming common—sometimes divine—ancestors. Larger still was the tribe, based on birth or place of residence; evidence from the third century B.C. indicates that there were at least thirty-five tribes in early Rome.

Relations between the sexes were strongly patriarchal. Roman women of the Republic were usually subject to male guardianship. Patriarchy was enshrined in the ancient *patria potestas,* the father's life-and-death power over the rest of the family. The father's legal authority included the right to arrange a daughter's marriage, to sell any member of the family into slavery, or to sentence a wife, child, or slave to death.

On the other hand, a Roman woman did acquire considerable status when she married, and the "Roman matron" could be as much admired a figure as the father of the family. Female virtues were defined in the context of family life, as in an admiring tomb inscription: "She loved her husband with her whole heart . . . cheerful in conversation, dignified in appearance, she made wool."[1] Yet women could inherit property in their own names, had the legal right to refuse a marriage arranged for them by their parents, and could even obtain a divorce relatively easily, especially in the looser atmosphere of the later Republic.

On top of older divisions based on family relations, newer social classifications founded primarily on landed property had emerged by 509 B.C. There were two such social classes in the early Republic: patricians and plebeians. The *patrician* minority boasted the most distinguished ancestors, owned the largest farms, and were the recognized leading citizens of the state. The rest of the people were *plebeians,* most of whom were poor farmers. Some plebeians, however, became men of wealth and ambition themselves in later years. The development of the early Roman constitution resulted primarily from conflict between these two classes, or "orders," of Roman society.

Rich and poor apparently shared a common loyalty to Rome. Like the Greeks in the heyday of the Greek city-state, Romans felt strong ties to the community that bred them. This rough equivalent of modern patriotism was encouraged by the beliefs and folkways of the Romans, by veneration of ancestors and ancestral gods, and by respect for law, tradition, and custom. Both the success of Roman arms and the relatively restrained nature of the "struggle of the orders" between Rome's social classes owed something to this widely shared allegiance to the Republic.

Early Political Institutions

The government of the early Roman Republic resembled that of the Greek city-state. There were executive magistrates, a Senate corresponding to a Greek council, and not one but several popular assemblies. Perhaps the best place to begin a look at government is with what was originally the most powerful of these assemblies, the *comitia centuriata.* Typically drawn up at a trumpet blast on the Field of Mars in a bend of the river northwest of the Capitoline Hill, the comitia centuriata, or "assembly of the centuries," was composed of hundred-man units in the Roman army. Like the early Greek assemblies, this gathering of Roman males under arms met periodically on their drill field to elect magistrates, pass laws, and decide basic questions of policy, including war and peace. The assembly of the centuries, however, was organized ultimately on the basis of wealth, with the most affluent units—the cavalry—voting first and frequently influencing the votes of the rest.

There were other assemblies, of which the most important was the *comitia tributa* (assembly of the tribes). The assembly of the tribes, in which the citizens were organized simply by birth or residence, played an important part in the constitutional struggle that arose in the later years of the Republic, replacing the assembly of the centuries as the most important of Roman popular assemblies.

The council called the *Senate* was officially only an advisory body, a council of elders that offered advice on government affairs to both the assemblies and the magistrates. In fact, however, these three hundred men were the real rulers of the state. Originally heads of the wealthiest clans and members of ancient patrician families, senators were also often former magistrates and senior statesmen. As aristocrats and former holders of high office, they wielded great influence in the assemblies. Because they spoke for the patrician ruling classes, senators tended to be conservative; because they held their Senate seats for life, they could afford to take the long view. The power of the Senate thus militated against both innovation and impulsive policy decisions. In times of peril, senators could provide strong and steady leadership; confronted with a need for change, however, they often resisted reform.

Of the Roman magistrates, the most powerful were the *consuls,* a pair of elected officials who enjoyed the *imperium,* the absolute power, that had been wielded by the banished kings. Imperium, symbolized by purple robes and the rods and the ax, conferred the crucial authority to command armies in the field as well as the power to punish any citizen. The consuls were elected by the assembly for only a single year. In the early days, however, they were always patricians who could look forward to advancing to the Senate immediately upon completing their year's consulship.

Other magistracies also developed in Rome. Praetors served as judges, military commanders, and provincial governors. Censors conducted military censuses and evaluated individuals' fitness for political office on moral as well as other grounds. And elected officials called dictators might replace consuls in command of troops in the field for limited periods.

The system was not what we would call a democratic one. Throughout the history of the Roman Republic, noble or wealthy families exercised a disproportionate influence. The Roman system of clientage, which we will discuss later as a key feature of the social system, helped extend the political influence of the great families. Under this system, Romans of lower degree frequently became clients of the great houses, offering their support and service in return for protection and economic help from their noble patrons. And one situation in which an ambitious patron was likely to call on his clients for support was in voting on measures in which the patron had a particular interest or in supporting the patron's candidacy for office.

Voting in the assemblies, furthermore, was by group rather than by head, another factor significantly affecting the distribution of political power. A voting majority was the majority of centuries or tribes voting a particular way, not the majority of individual votes cast. This practice probably went back to such primitive practices as having troops express their support for a commander by responding one unit at a time with shouts of approbation.

In later Roman times the tribe became the unit for voting in all Roman assemblies, and this group vote meant that two tribes with only a small number of voters present could outvote one much larger tribe. As Rome acquired new territories far from the city and, gradually, extended the vote to its new peoples, dozens of new rural tribes easily outvoted the four urban tribes of the city of Rome. Conservative and agrarian elements controlled the countryside, where the system of clientage was strong, and as a result these elements exercised a powerful force in politics. Although as we will see, the Roman system permitted a significant degree of popular participation in political decision making, the preponderance of power remained in the hands of the senators, the leading citizens of the Roman Republic.

The Struggle of the Orders

The first couple of hundred years following the overthrow of the kings saw a long intermittent struggle by the Roman plebeians to claim a larger share of political power. This conflict, called the *struggle of the orders,* lasted through the fifth and fourth centuries B.C. and into the third. It brought significant change to Roman political life.

In asserting and expanding their rights, the plebeians were strengthened by the fact that their service and loyalty were needed as Rome attempted to gain control of the Italian peninsula. During this period, the state was frequently at war and always dependent on the army to hold what had been gained. Disaffection among the troops and the threat of mass mutiny therefore became powerful weapons in the political conflict between the orders. More than once, apparently, the plebeians staged a secession or general strike to get their way. But because their goal was neither to seize power from the traditional leadership nor to destroy the state, practical compromise solutions were ultimately worked out.

The first clash between the orders came in 494 B.C., when the plebeians threatened a secession and won the right to elect two magistrates of their own, called *tribunes*. Over generations, these tribunes, whose number increased to ten, acquired extraordinary powers. They could countermand the decisions of consuls, veto legislation, and appeal any case directly to the Senate. Most important, the person of a tribune was deemed sacred, and he was thus safe from bodily harm throughout his tribuneship. As we will see, later reformers claimed this same immunity, though not always successfully.

Another advance for the plebeian majority came in 450 B.C., when political pressure forced the publication of the laws for the first time. Inscribed on twelve wooden tablets, these *Twelve Tables* made public the traditional laws, customs, and legal procedures that only patrician magistrates and senators had mastered before. There was a good deal of common sense in these laws, along with some harsh punishments and sometimes invidious distinctions between classes and sexes. But their public display at least told ordinary Romans what their rights were.

Other reforms followed, some of them clearly directed at raising the status of the wealthier plebeians to parity with that of the established patrician families. In 445 B.C., for example, the *Lex Canuleia* (named for its sponsor), by legalizing intermarriage between the two orders, made it possible for wealthy plebeians to marry into the prestigious patrician clans. In 367 the Licinio-Sextian laws opened the consulship to plebeians. And in 287, after another defiant challenge by the lower social orders, the *Lex Hortensia* decreed that laws passed by the assembly of the tribes were legally binding on the whole Roman people. Not only were the highest offices and the upper classes now open to ambitious and successful plebeians, but the plebeian assembly could contribute directly to shaping the law of the land.

The final outcome, however, was not democracy in the modern sense. The Senate continued to make major decisions involving war, peace, and financial matters and to guide the decisions of the assembly through personal influence, money, and even threats. The assemblies met rarely, so the Senate and the magistrates largely ran the country. But the advance of the well-to-do plebeians, who could now infiltrate the senatorial classes through marriage or the consulship, was a substantial change. As a result, a new, broader but still conservative, senatorial elite of old patrician and newer plebeian families came to dominate political life.

The Expansion of Rome

While the Romans were shaping a government that suited their conservative, pragmatic character, they were also embarking on a larger historical enterprise: the building of an empire. During the five centuries of the Roman Republic, the area under Roman control came to girdle the Mediterranean. What began as petty strife on the hills and plains of central Italy ultimately made Romans masters of their world.

Causes of Roman Expansion

Why did Romans apparently seek to conquer the world they knew? One of the more paradoxical modern explanations for Roman empire building has been the suggestion that the Romans conquered their neighbors essentially in self-defense. This view asserts that the Romans most commonly began their wars, not out of lust for conquest, but in defense of their own interests or those of their allies. Each Roman victory, this interpretation suggests, led to further expansion of Roman frontiers or to more Roman client states and thus to more international interests and responsibilities. These in turn led to more wars and more conquests.

There are simpler explanations, however. There was booty to be had, from the flocks of nearby villages to the plunder of an Etruscan city or, in later centuries, the amazing wealth of the Hellenistic East. There was glory too, for Roman aristocrats eager to add to the family laurels and lead a triumphal procession through the cheering streets of Rome. Political ambition was also increasingly a motive, especially during the later Republic, when political careers could be decisively advanced by foreign conquests. At the bottom of it all, finally, were some basic Roman assumptions which fewer modern people seem to share: that war is a natural and honorable human activity, for instance, and that foreign conquests make a nation stronger.

The instrument that built the empire was the famed Roman army, one of the most admired military forces in history. Like the armies of the Greek city-states, the army of the early Republic was a citizen force, composed of farmers who owned at least enough property to afford their own weapons. Organized in the style of the Greek phalanx that the Etruscans had borrowed from the city-states of southern Italy, Roman infantrymen were armored with helmets and breastplates and armed with shields

This Roman legionary from the last days of the Republic is fully armed for battle with spear and shield, light armor, helmet, and the famous Roman short sword. The large shield and spear, strengthened by Roman discipline, made the Roman phalanx a nearly impenetrable wall, while the short sword was deadly for close-in fighting.

Other factors contributed to the high proportion of Roman victories. The methodical care they took to build a fortified camp every night on the march made it hard to catch them unprepared. The military colonies they established in conquered lands and the all-weather military roads that could bring rapid aid to a besieged garrison meant that a Roman conquest was likely to be for keeps. Underlying all these elements was Roman discipline, tenacity, and a chauvinistic sense of Roman superiority that made Roman armies frequently victorious and almost sure to come back again when they were not.

In the following pages, the campaigns and conquests of the Republic are grouped under three headings. We will look first at the wars of the unification of Italy, next at the crucial conflict with Carthage, and then at Rome's final advance to mastery of the Mediterranean.

The Conquest of Italy

Roman accounts of their own early history are legendary and were recognized as such by Roman historians like Livy, who composed his epic *History of Rome from Its Foundations* in the days of Augustus, five centuries after the founding of the Republic. These stories were clearly intended to be inspirational. There was brave Horatius defending a bridge across the Tiber, holding a whole army at bay (see box, "Horatius at the Bridge"). There was noble Cincinnatus, the hero who abandoned the plow for the battlefield but, unlike later leaders who used their military triumphs as springboards to political power, returned to his simple farm as soon as victory was won. Such legends do, however, provide a broad outline of the expansion of Roman power up and down the peninsula.

Rome's first foes included many peoples who shared the peninsula of Italy with this growing city-state, as well as people who had settled on the large island of Sicily to the south. Around fifth-century B.C. Rome on the hills and plains of Latium in central Italy were Latin tribes and other speakers of Italic languages (the languages of ancient Italy) whose ancestors had moved into the peninsula at about the same time as the Romans' forebears. To the north and south were the most advanced urban peoples of Italy: the Etruscans north of the Tiber and the Greeks around the heel and toe of the Italian boot and on Sicily. Farther north, in the fer-

and spears in the hoplite style. Divided into the hundred-man units called *centuries,* the early army also included some cavalry and some lighter infantry. In the hill wars of the early Republic, however, Roman commanders learned to break up the phalanx into small independent blocks of troops called maniples, armed with javelins rather than spears.

THE RULERS AND THE RULED   Horatius at the Bridge

The patriotic Roman historian Livy (59 B.C.–A.D. 17) consciously set out to highlight the heroism and integrity of the Romans of the early Republic, hoping thus to provide models for his Augustan contemporaries. This account of the courageous stand of Horatius Cocles against an Etruscan army—an incident known to later generations as "Horatius at the Bridge"—admirably illustrates this vision of Rome's noble past. Notice not only Horatius's patriotism and bravery but also the very modest reward he accepted from his fellow citizens: eternal honor but only as much land as he could plow himself.

> When the enemy appeared, the Romans all, with one accord, withdrew from their fields into the City, which they surrounded with guards. Some parts appeared to be rendered safe by their walls, others by the barrier formed by the river Tiber. The bridge of piles almost afforded an entrance to the enemy, had it not been for one man, Horatius Cocles; he was the bulwark of defence on which that day depended the fortune of the City of Rome. . . . He . . . warned and commanded them to break down the bridge with

steel, with fire, with any instrument at their disposal; and promised that he would himself receive the onset of the enemy, so far as it could be withstood by a single body. Then, striding to the head of the bridge. . . he covered himself with his sword and buckler and made ready to do battle at close quarters, confounding the Etruscans with amazement at his audacity. . . . With a shout they cast their javelins from every side against their solitary foe. But he caught them all upon his shield, and, resolute as ever, bestrode the bridge and held his ground; and now they were trying to dislodge him by a charge, when the crash of the falling bridge and the cheer which burst from the throats of the Romans, exalting in the completion of their task, checked them in mid-career with a sudden dismay. Then Cocles cried, "O Father Tiberinus, I solemnly invoke thee; receive these arms and this soldier with propitious stream!" So praying, all armed as he was, he leaped down into the river, and under a shower of missiles swam across unhurt to his fellows, having given a proof of valor which was destined to obtain more fame than credence with posterity. The state was grateful for so brave a deed: a statue of Cocles was set up in the comitium, and he was given as much land as he could plough around in one day.

Source: Livy, *History of Rome*, vol. 1, trans. B. O. Foster (Cambridge, Mass.: Harvard University Press, 1961), 249–253.

tile Po valley, were the ruder settlements of the warlike Gauls, a Celtic people some of whom had settled in what was called Cisalpine Gaul, on the Roman side of the Alps. Farther south, sharing Sicily with the Greeks, were enclaves of settlers from the old Phoenician colony of Carthage, in North Africa.

The Romans began to fight almost as soon as they were free. Under Etruscan tutelage, they had attained a predominant position among their Latin neighbors, and they wanted to retain that position. Moreover, there was also a very real possibility of reconquest by the Etruscans. For both these reasons, in the first few years of the fifth century B.C. the Romans imposed alliances on the other peoples of Latium in central Italy. They also began to chop away at Etruria to the north, and in 396 B.C., after a long siege, they destroyed a major stronghold of Etruscan power, the great city of Veii.

Half a dozen years after this victory, however, the Romans suffered the greatest defeat in the history of the early Republic. Around 390 B.C., a marauding army of wild Gauls from the north overwhelmed a Roman army and sacked, looted, and held the city for ransom. The Romans picked themselves up, rebuilt their city and their alliances, and reconquered lost ground. When the Gaulish raiders next came south, they were repulsed. Rome's ultimate revenge was even sweeter, for in later centuries Roman legions marched north to conquer not only Cisalpine Gaul but the Gauls' homeland beyond the Alps in what is now France.

Meanwhile, Rome continued to absorb neighboring Italian peoples and soon found itself intervening in the affairs of the Greek city-states to the south. One of these, the city of Tarentum, summoned a Greek king from across the Adriatic, Pyrrhus (319–272 B.C.) of Epirus, to its aid. Pyrrhus had a famous mercenary army, and he beat the Romans twice at great cost to himself. In 279 B.C., surveying a battlefield littered with casualties, Pyrrhus is supposed to have groaned, "One more victory like this over the Romans, and there'll be nothing left of us." By 275 he had departed, leaving the Greeks of southern Italy to Rome and the grim phrase "a Pyrrhic victory" (a victory that is too costly) to history.

Roman Rule in Italy

By 265 B.C. Rome was the master of Italy from just south of the Po valley to the toe of the Italian boot. But territorial expansion meant more than winning wars. It was also a matter of organizing both their newly conquered lands and their new client states into a durable structure of power. Roman tenacity in war was matched by a pragmatic trial-and-error approach to imperial organization. What worked, they tried again; what did not, they abandoned. The result was an assemblage of colonies and alliances that proved remarkably resilient and long lasting.

Some lands won in war—for example, the city of Veii, whose territories doubled the size of Rome—were promptly parceled out among Rome's own rapidly growing population. Any people who lost to the Romans could expect to lose about a third of their land to Roman military colonists, who paid for their farms by providing military garrisons for the conquered territory.

Such losses were undoubtedly resented. But there was much to be gained by becoming, willingly or not, part of the growing Roman confederation of Italian peoples and cities. Those who accepted the status of Roman ally got Rome's protection from foreign aggression in return for providing troops for the Roman army. More fortunate peoples were made partial citizens of Rome, that is, citizens who could trade and marry in Rome but could not vote or otherwise take part in political life. As partial citizens, these people both paid taxes and provided troops to Rome. The most trustworthy of the Italian peoples absorbed by Rome were made full citizens, living henceforth under Roman law, voting, and holding office like native-born Romans, in addition to accepting the citizen's obligation to pay taxes and serve in the army.

An important feature of this system was that communities and peoples brought under Roman sway could advance up the scale of membership, to achieve in time full citizenship in the empire. Given the growing wealth and power of Rome, this was a prize worth having and one that subject peoples came to clamor for, sometimes in the teeth of opposition from the Romans themselves. Down the centuries, defections from this structure of imperial power were remarkably few, even in Rome's hours of greatest trial—one of which was about to burst upon Italy even as the confederation was completed in the middle of the third century B.C.

The Wars with Carthage

The dramatic image of Hannibal crossing the Alps with his African army, complete with elephants, was a nightmare that haunted Romans for generations. And the three *Punic Wars* (from *Poeni* or *Puni*, the Roman word for the Phoenician ancestors of the Carthaginians) in fact constituted the most dreadful military ordeal in the history of the Republic.

Carthage lay in what is today Tunisia, in North Africa, less than 100 miles across the narrow waist of the Mediterranean from Sicily. It was thus only 400 miles from Rome. Since the fall of the Phoenician city-states in the sixth century B.C., Carthage had established an extensive commercial empire of its own. By the third century, this seaborne Carthaginian Empire encompassed most of the coasts and islands of the western Mediterranean, including the North African Maghreb (stretching from Tunisia to Morocco), southern Spain, the large islands of Corsica and Sardinia, and the western part of Sicily. Besides its powerful navy, Carthage had a strong mercenary army, a great harbor, famous walls, and a government run by old commercial families through the familiar system of assembly, council, and magistrates.

Dominating trade at the western end of the Mediterranean as the Greeks led commerce in the east, the Carthaginians had fought more than one war with their Greek commercial rivals. But they had never yet come to blows with the Romans, who waged their battles on land and were not heavily involved in maritime trade. Conflict between an expansionist Rome and the empire that dominated the western Mediterranean was as likely, however, as big-power contests have been in many periods of history.

The First Punic War (264–241 B.C.) erupted over Sicily, the Greek buffer zone between Roman Italy and Carthaginian North Africa. The conflict began when Carthage and Rome intervened in the is-

Map 5.1 Roman Expansion in Italy Under the Republic

land to support different factions of a gang of Italian mercenary soldiers who had seized the city of Messina in northern Sicily. The Roman Senate hesitated to get involved, for Rome lacked a fleet and had, moreover, no quarrel with the Carthaginians. In the end, however, the Romans voted to build a fleet and plunged into a war that lasted twenty-three years and was the start of Rome's territorial expansion beyond the Italian peninsula.

It was a long brutal struggle. There were pitched battles at sea, in Sicily, and in North Africa, as well as Carthaginian raids on the coast of Italy. In 241 B.C., Carthage, perhaps only slightly more exhausted than Rome, made peace and surrendered Sicily. Three years later, Rome intervened in revolts by Carthaginian mercenaries in Sardinia and Corsica and acquired these two large offshore islands as well. But the rivalry between Carthage and Rome had only begun.

In the decades that followed, Rome added to its power, notably by overrunning the Po valley and imposing Roman rule at last on the Cisalpine Gauls. The Romans also learned to govern their most recent acquisitions in a new way, as provinces with appointed Roman governors; this was the beginning of Roman imperial organization.

The Carthaginian Empire, meanwhile, sought to compensate for its losses by expanding and strengthening its hold on southern Spain, and it was here that the Second Punic War (218–201 B.C.) broke out, two decades after the first. Again, intervention in the affairs of other states led to a conflict between the great powers. It began with clashes in Spain between the Roman client state of Saguntum and some tribal allies of Carthage. Carthage seized Saguntum, and the Romans mobilized against the North Africans. According to a traditional Roman account, Hannibal, the Carthaginian commander in Spain, had planned a campaign of revenge against Rome for some time. Whether or not this was true, Rome declared war in March of 218 B.C., and as soon as the snows began to melt in the mountain passes of the Pyrenees, Hannibal began his overland march toward Italy with a large army, including war elephants brought around the Mediterranean from Africa.

Hannibal (245–183 B.C.) is commonly ranked with Alexander the Great as one of the most successful military commanders in history. His father Hamilcar (c. 270–229 B.C.) had led the Carthaginian forces in the First Punic War and, according to tradition, had made the boy swear an oath on the altars of the gods of Carthage "to prove himself . . . an enemy

of the Roman people." For the Romans, the war Hannibal brought them was "the most memorable of all wars that were ever waged."[2]

It was because the Roman fleet, built during the first war with Carthage, still controlled the seas that Hannibal had to reach Italy by land from Spain. He accomplished this rather astounding feat, which involved a march of 1,000 miles across the Pyrenees, the Rhone River, and finally the mighty mountain barrier of the Alps, by the fall of 218 B.C. Arriving in the Po valley with an army of more than twenty-five thousand men, he easily rallied Rome's newest subjects, the Gauls, to his cause and devised a simple but devastating plan. His aim would be to meet and defeat Roman armies as often as possible, until the Roman confederation rose in revolt against its weakened overlords, destroying Roman power forever. Over the next fifteen years of fighting up and down the Italian peninsula, the African commander very nearly accomplished his goal.

In every encounter, Hannibal was the better general, commanding an experienced army supported by large numbers of Gaulish auxiliaries. With brutal regularity, he defeated every Roman army sent against him. At Cannae in 216 B.C., he inflicted the worst defeat Rome had ever suffered. Allowing the Romans to advance against his center, the African general sent his cavalry galloping around the Roman rear, then crushed the Roman flanks and closed in on the Roman center with the wings of his own infantry force, where he had deliberately concentrated his strength. He thus annihilated the legions in a "double envelopment"—first cavalry, then infantry—a maneuver often described as one of the most brilliant in the annals of warfare. As the defeats piled up, the Romans were reduced to arming slaves to defend the city and even resorted to human sacrifice to win back the favor of their relentless gods.

The one thing they did not do was surrender. For years they simply avoided meeting Hannibal in the field, devoting their energies instead to whipping their allies back into line whenever they wavered. In fact, the central Italian core of the confederation remained loyal throughout the ordeal. And Hannibal, the lord of the battlefield, did not have the manpower or the siege engines to capture a major walled city like Rome. As long as Rome's allies remained loyal, final victory in Italy thus remained beyond the Carthaginian's reach.

In 209 B.C. a young Roman general named Scipio (236–184 B.C.) seized the main Carthaginian base in Spain. And when Hannibal's brother

Hasdrubal led a relief force into Italy in 207, the Romans intercepted and destroyed it. This victory they announced to Hannibal by hurling his brother's head into the Carthaginian camp.

The long debilitating struggle came to an end soon thereafter. In 204 B.C. Scipio landed with a Roman army in North Africa. Hannibal returned to defend his homeland the following year. And there, at Zama in 202, Scipio earned the additional name of "Africanus" by defeating the greatest general of his age in a victory at least partially due to the defection of some of Hannibal's mercenary troops.

Rome emerged from the Second Punic War with the rest of Carthage's island holdings and southern Spain, although the Roman legions had to fight another long and savage guerrilla war to impose Roman rule finally on the fierce Spaniards. In the course of the war with Hannibal, Rome had also seized the Dalmatian coast of the Balkans, directly across the Adriatic to the east. After 202 B.C. the Carthaginian Empire was no more, and Carthage was reduced to little more than a second-class power.

One more bloody war remained to be fought, however, before the vendetta between the two peoples ended at last. The Third Punic War (149–146 B.C.) was one-sided and merciless. It was motivated by Roman nervousness over a Carthaginian economic revival and by the vindictiveness of Roman politicians like Cato the Elder (234–149 B.C.), who made the slogan "Carthage must be destroyed" his bitter watchword in the Senate. This third war consisted essentially of a Roman siege of the great city of Carthage itself. Led by Scipio Aemilianus (185–129 B.C.), an adopted grandson of Scipio Africanus, the Romans captured the city, destroyed parts of it, and sowed salt in the plowed-up ruins, a symbolic assertion that Carthage would never rise again. After 146 B.C., the Romans had a new province to add to their list, this one beyond the Mediterranean Sea in Africa.

The Conquest of the East

Meanwhile, with startling rapidity, Rome had been advancing eastward around the Mediterranean, imposing its will on the world of the Hellenistic Greeks. The Roman intrusion began in 200 B.C., just two years after the defeat of Hannibal at Zama. Within a dozen years, the fact of Roman military

supremacy in the East had been established. By 133, the lands of the eastern Mediterranean had been largely converted into Roman colonies or protectorates.

The Roman hero Quinctius Flamininus (c. 227–174 B.C.), proconsul in Greece, explained Rome's invasion of the Hellenistic East in highly idealistic terms. Rome, he told the Greeks assembled for the Isthmian Games, was the "one people in the world which would fight for others' liberties at its own cost, to its own peril . . . ready to cross the sea that there might be no unjust empire anywhere and that everywhere justice, right, and law might prevail."[3] The reality was a bit more complicated than that. Idealism may have played some role in Roman expansion into Greece itself, for many Roman aristocrats were admirers of Greek culture. Rome's early interventions in the East as a whole, however, were motivated primarily by a determination to defend Roman interests. Subsequently, the Romans were drawn in deeper by their own earlier commitments, and by frustration with halfway solutions to the problems those involvements created. An increasingly powerful motive, finally, was greed as the Romans glimpsed the dazzling wealth of the East that was clearly theirs for the taking.

Rome established its paramount military position in the eastern Mediterranean by defeating the ambitious and long-reigning rulers of the two most powerful of the Hellenistic monarchies, Philip V (r. 221–179 B.C.) of Macedonia and the Seleucid king Antiochus III (r. 223–187 B.C.). The Romans fought no less than four "Macedonian" wars with Philip V and his successors between 215 and 146 and one decisive "Syrian" war (192–189 B.C.) with Antiochus. It was a complicated and protracted struggle, and a good illustration of the complexity of diplomatic and military relations in the ancient world.

Rome's first clash with Macedonia came during the Second Punic War, when Philip V opportunistically allied himself with Hannibal after the Carthaginian's great victory at Cannae. The resulting First Macedonian War (215–205 B.C.) was a Roman holding action in which Rome organized an alliance of Greek states to restrain Philip while Rome itself struggled for survival against Hannibal. The Romans were drawn into the Second Macedonian War (200–197 B.C.) by the pleas of Athens, Pergamum in Asia Minor, and the island city-state of Rhodes, the financial center of the Hellenistic world. These wealthy little states sought to redress the balance of power

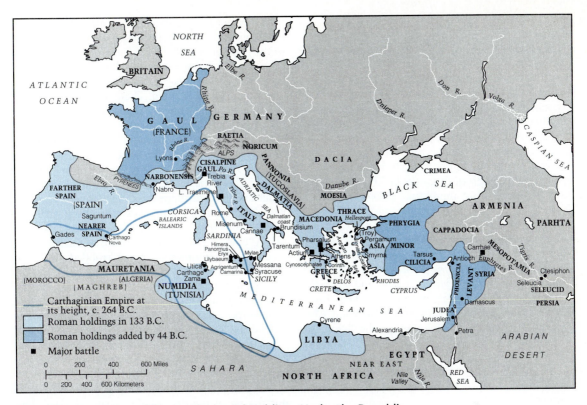

Map 5.2   Expansion of Roman Territorial Holdings Under the Republic

against the aggressive Macedonian ruler, a goal that was also in Rome's interests. In the brief ensuing struggle, Quinctius Flamininus led a Roman army toughened by the long conflict with Carthage to victory over Philip V at Cynoscephalae (196 B.C.).

From Syria, meanwhile, came a new threat in the person of the ambitious young Seleucid prince Antiochus III, who sought to revive the greatness of the Alexandrian successor state of Seleucid Persia. When Antiochus invaded Greece from the east, Rome was once again summoned to redress the power balance. While Roman and Rhodian fleets controlled the seas, a Roman army under Cornelius Scipio and his brother Scipio Africanus, conqueror of Carthage, crushed Antiochus at the Battle of Magnesia in 190 B.C.

Later victorious struggles with real and false heirs of Philip led first to the breakup of the Macedonian monarchy into parts and finally to the absorption of Macedonia as a Roman province in 148 B.C., just two years before the destruction of Carthage. In 133 King Attalus of Perga-

mum submissively left Rome his entire country in his will. Four years later, Pergamum became the core of a Roman province encompassing all the western part of Asia Minor. From the Greek city-states around to Egypt, the rest of the area was converted into a string of client states of the great city on the Tiber.

The Romans did not want the cost and responsibility of governing the East. But they did require respect for their interests and, when it came down to it, obedience from smaller allies. Too often, however, Roman interests were flouted and Roman requests were ignored. The Greeks frequently saw the Romans as they had the Macedonians of Alexander the Great's time: less as liberators from menacing Eastern monarchs than as semicivilized invaders themselves. Thus confronted by resistance and repeated upheavals, the Romans fought war after war in the eastern Mediterranean, gradually transforming their role from that of ally and defender of the international order to that of imperial master.

A Century of Civil Strife

The last century of the Republic was the century of the *Roman Civil War.* It was an epoch dominated by larger-than-life characters: the reforming brothers Tiberius and Gaius Gracchus, the feuding warlords Marius and Sulla, Cicero the orator, Julius Caesar, dashing Mark Antony, and wily little Octavian, who became Augustus Caesar, the second founder of Rome. From the challenge to the traditional power structure triggered by the Gracchi brothers in 133 B.C. to the triumph of Augustus in 31 B.C., this was also one of the most tumultuous periods of ancient history.

As it happens, this is also a period for which evidence is particularly abundant. We have Roman histories and biographies, among them Plutarch's *Parallel Lives of Greeks and Romans* and Suetonius's colorful *Lives of the Twelve Caesars,* and even the writings of leading participants, including Julius Caesar's own accounts of the *Gallic Wars* and *Civil War* and the voluminous writings of the Republic's most eloquent champion, the orator Cicero, whose collected letters are an invaluable source. When we add the insights of modern historians into the many-layered social turmoil of the time, we have a feast of history.

Not, of course, that it seemed that way to the Romans as they saw all their achievements threatened by riot, conspiracy, and civil war. Old Rome, the Rome of the Republic, was dying around them. They could not know that a new and in many ways greater Rome, the Empire of Augustus and his successors, was also being born.

Social Strains

The defeat of Carthage and the rapid imposition of Roman hegemony on the Hellenistic East transformed Roman society. This lunge into overseas imperial expansion gave Romans more power and wealth than any Western people had ever had. These events, however, also created problems beyond the capacity of the Republic to manage. The foreign victories of the third and second centuries thus paved the way for the domestic catastrophes of the first century B.C.

The changes in Roman society were interlocking and complex. Most simply phrased, the rich grew vastly richer while many of the poor became desti-tute. The senatorial elite gained profitable access to the grain fields of North Africa, Sicily, and Spain and to the movable wealth of the Hellenistic monarchies. They used their increased capital to expand their estates in Italy, buying up the farms of the hapless smallholders around them. These small farmers, once the backbone of Rome's agrarian economy and of the Roman army, had spent so much time campaigning in foreign lands that they could not maintain their farms. As a result they were particularly vulnerable to takeovers by the aristocracy. Thus dispossessed, these peasants, many of them veterans, sought new opportunities in the cities, particularly in Rome itself. Finding little work there, they settled at last into the crowded multistory tenements called *insulae* ("islands") in the poor sections of the city, lived on a government grain dole, and brooded over their wrongs.

While the aristocracy built new mansions on the Palatine Hill and a growing class of urban poor inhabited the slums of the Aventine or the lower areas around the forum, two new groups arose to complicate the struggle between the Roman social classes. These were the equestrian order and an expanding population of slaves.

The equestrian order challenged the wealth, if not the social prestige, of the senatorial class. The *equestrians,* meaning "horsemen" or "knights," actually made their money from manufacturing, trade, and moneylending at home and from tax gathering, grain growing, and other forms of exploitation in the provinces. To their enemies, they seemed more concerned with moneymaking than with the traditional aristocratic career in politics and public service. The equestrians, for their part, resented senatorial political predominance and neglect of equestrian interests. The mutual dislike of the two groups became a fertile source of discord.

At the bottom of society, meanwhile, immense numbers of slaves, many of them prisoners taken in the wars, were brought back to Rome. Slaves soon replaced free labor on noble estates. In the cities, they were employed in the workshops and did manual labor, thus closing off these options for landless peasants. And though some slaves, notably house servants, had quite acceptable accommodations and sometimes warm relationships with their owners, others quite literally groaned under the lash. The contemporary Roman historian Diodorus Siculus thus described the lot of the most brutalized of slaves, those who worked in the mines:

As a result of their underground excavations day and night they become physical wrecks, and because of their extremely bad conditions, the mortality rate is high; they are not allowed to give up working or to have a rest, but are forced by the beatings of their supervisors to stay at their places and throw away their wretched lives.[4]

Slaves were also trained in gladiatorial schools to fight each other at the public games that grew increasingly common. Slave rebellions thus became an even more feared form of social violence than the riots of the urban poor that erupted with increasing frequency in the last century of the Republic.

At the heart of the Roman state, senatorial families feuded for political power with a new bitterness. As the population grew and as Roman citizenship was extended to other Italian peoples, there were more people to compete, not only for the honor and authority of magistracies and military commands, but for the riches of the newly conquered provinces. Increasingly, then, the upper classes resorted to violence themselves. Senators organized mob violence against political enemies; generals dared to bring their armies back from foreign conquests to crush political foes in Rome itself. Their troops, dreaming of booty, served as pawns in the ambitious gambits of their commanders.

Add to this explosive mix the unhappy fact that the Romans, so successful in organizing Italy, had not yet learned how to rule the larger Mediterranean world they now dominated. Administrators of far provinces, who typically stayed only a year, took as much as they could get in bribes, gifts, and other profitable rewards before hurrying home to get on with their political careers. Equestrian exploiters squeezed taxes, lucrative contracts, and other revenues out of the conquered. At the same time, the client states were alienated by ill-conceived policies aimed at keeping them powerless while minimizing Roman responsibility for their fate. Even Rome's oldest allies, the Italian peoples of the confederation, felt cheated of their fair share of land and loot and looked down upon by the arrogant new conquerors in Rome. They too simmered toward revolt.

The result was a violent century of civil strife (see box, "Horrors of Civil War"). Between 133 and 31 B.C. the Republic was torn by foreign wars, imperial revolts, slave rebellions, and riotous mobs. Armies were constantly on the march, demagogues shouted in the forum, and intrigue abounded in the Senate house. Attempting to guide the whirlwind were the power brokers of this age of civil war whose plots and acts of violence we will chronicle shortly. Between them, they shattered the Roman Republic and brought the Roman Empire—Rome of the emperors—to birth.

The Gracchi

Grandsons of the great Scipio Africanus, Tiberius (163–133 B.C.) and Gaius (154–121 B.C.) Gracchus were heirs of one of the noblest houses in Rome, yet they took up the cause of the most distressed. The tradition of aristocratic leadership for popular causes reaches back to Periclean Athens and up to the America of the Roosevelts. Charges of demagoguery have generally accompanied popular political movements, and there have indeed often been political motives mixed with nobler impulses. There are no better exemplars of this mix of popular reform with personal political ambition than the Gracchi.

"Tiberius," wrote Plutarch in his biography of the brothers, "was gentle and composed, alike in cast of features, expression, and demeanor, whereas Gaius was highly strung and impassioned." Addressing the people, Tiberius stood quietly and spoke calmly, moving his hearers to pity for the misery he sought to alleviate. Gaius, younger by nine years, "was the first Roman to stride up and down the rostra [the speaker's platform in the forum] and wrench his toga off his shoulder" in his zeal to stir his audiences to action.[5] Tiberius challenged the system first, in 133 B.C.; Gaius ten years later, in 123.

Tiberius Gracchus had seen and claimed to have been moved by the condition of peasants who had lost their lands and particularly by the plight of dispossessed veterans who, he reminded the people, though "they are called the masters of the world do not possess a single clod of earth which is truly their own."[6] Elected tribune in 133 B.C., he proposed a radical land redistribution bill that would reclaim public lands currently held by large landowners and parcel them out among the poor.

Tiberius's allies in the Senate included his own powerful kinsmen, the Claudian clan, who supported his land bill in hopes of gaining support for their faction rather than out of concern for landless veterans. But the bill would hurt so many wealthy senatorial families that Tiberius had far more enemies than friends in the Senate. Many senators were also disturbed at Tiberius's defiance of traditional constitutional practice, as when he led the assembly to vote a hostile tribune out of office and then ran for tribune a second time himself. Above all, the senatorial elite feared Tiberius Gracchus's popularity with the plebeian masses, seeing in him a revolutionary demagogue moving to subvert the Roman constitution.

Tiberius got his bill passed and some land redistributed. But as he tried to speak to an election crowd in his second campaign for the tribuneship, a mob of senators and their supporters burst into the meeting. In the melee that followed, the reformer's enemies beat him to death with clubs and pieces of broken furniture. In other parts of the city, several hundred of his followers also perished in an outbreak of political violence that itself shockingly subverted the constitution.

The stunned younger brother, Gaius Gracchus, who had helped with the land distribution, withdrew from politics for a decade. Then, his plans carefully laid, he took up his slain brother's populist cause and perhaps his political ambitions once more.

Gaius moved from the family home on the aristocratic Palatine Hill down into the poor quarter around the forum. Elected tribune in 123 B.C. and again in 122, he had a party of supporters that included all the other tribunes elected his first year in office. To maximize popular support, he proceeded to reactivate the land distribution commission and to pass a law to regulate the price of grain sold to the urban masses. To win the backing of the equestrians, he sponsored legislation opening the new provinces in Asia Minor to their ministrations as private tax collectors. He also introduced a bill creating equestrian courts to try aristocratic governors accused of malfeasance, thus pitting the two highest orders of society against each other.

Building on these achievements, Gaius Gracchus launched a much broader reform campaign than that of his late brother. He sponsored bills to build new roads to bring farm produce to larger markets. He urged the establishment of urban colonies for those of the poor who did not want to return to farming. And he campaigned for citizenship for the Italian allies, a move that turned out not to be popular among Romans of any class.

Gaius's enemies in the Senate at first responded rather more subtly than they had to Tiberius's challenge. They outbid the younger Gracchus for votes

PROBING THE PAST
The Horrors of Civil War

The savagery of Rome's century of civil strife is disturbingly evoked in the following extract from Appian's *History of Rome.* Although he condemns the spreading violence in strong terms, the second-century A.D. historian also expresses particular outrage at the breakdown of civil order and the unseemliness of factional conflict in such formerly sacrosanct places as temples or assemblies. Worst of all, he suggested, was revolt against Rome itself by those who should have been its defenders. Does Appian, like Livy, see earlier times as better times?

There were chiefs of factions in different places aspiring to supreme power, some of them refusing to disband the troops intrusted to them by the people, others levying forces against each other on their own account, without public authority. . . . The sword was never carried into the assembly, and there was no civil butchery until Tiberius Gracchus, while serving as tribune and bringing forward new laws, was the first to fall a victim to internal commotion; and many others besides, who were assembled with him at the Capitol, were slain around the temple. Sedition did not end with this abominable deed. Repeatedly the parties came into open conflict, often carrying daggers; and occasionally in the temples, or the assemblies, or the forum, someone serving as tribune or praetor or consul, or a candidate for those offices, or some person otherwise distinguished, would be slain. Unseemly violence prevailed almost constantly, together with shameful contempt for law and justice. As the evil gained in magnitude, open insurrections against the government and large warlike expeditions against the country were undertaken by exiles . . . or persons contending against each other for some office or military command. . . . Whichever of them first got possession of the city, the others made war nominally against their adversaries, but actually against their country. . . . Ruthless and indiscriminate massacres of citizens were perpetrated. Men were proscribed, others banished, property was confiscated, and some were even subjected to excruciating tortures.

Source: Appian, *The Roman History,* vol. 2, trans. H. White (London: Macmillan, 1899), 1–2.

by offering a larger number of urban settlements than he had proposed. They exploited the unpopularity of the offer of citizenship to other Italians in order to undermine Gaius's standing among the Roman poor. Then, responding to an outbreak of violence in the popular assembly, the Senate declared martial law in the city and ordered the consuls to use all necessary force to restore order.

Where a few hundreds had perished with Tiberius, several thousand people were now slaughtered, many in the tenement streets of the Aventine. Gaius Gracchus asked one of his own followers to strike him down lest he die at the hands of his enemies. "He lost his life," wrote a second-century A.D. Greek historian, "in consequence of a most excellent design, which, however, he pursued in too violent a manner."[7]

Whatever their true motivation and however excellent or unconstitutional their designs, the Gracchi had failed, and their effort left a violent legacy. Roman blood had been shed in political quarrels for the first time, it was said, since the fall of the Etruscan kings. The equestrians and the senatorial elite were thereafter at each others' throats. The masses brooded over the economic relief they had almost had, and looked for new opportunities to express their discontent. Senate conservatives had successfully defended the constitution—and their own property and powers. But they had done so at great cost.

Marius and Sulla

Marius and Sulla seized center stage from a very different direction than that attempted by the Gracchi. Famous generals, ambitious politicians, both were willing to use their troops to settle their political feuds in the streets of Rome.

Gaius Marius (157–86 B.C.), a "new man" of equestrian stock, was a political outsider whom the old senatorial ruling-class elite never trusted. A brave soldier and the rebuilder of the Roman army, Marius was also an opportunistic careerist who ended his days conducting summary executions in the streets of the capital. Lucius Cornelius Sulla (137–78 B.C.), descended from an ancient but no longer wealthy patrician family, remained a staunch supporter of the Senate. Twenty years Marius's junior, Sulla had an ironic wit, preferred the company of actors to that of

respectable citizens, and climaxed his career by plunging all Italy into civil war.

The two men served together in the war with Jugurtha (r. 118–105 B.C.), the North African king of Numidia (part of Libya today), a tedious guerrilla contest that lasted from 111 to 106 B.C. Marius, who was in command, shattered the enemy forces; but it was young Sulla, his lieutenant, who engineered the betrayal of Jugurtha himself into Roman hands. Marius was welcomed home in triumph by the people, but Senate insiders said Sulla had been cheated of his due credit. From this, Roman historians suggested, grew their twenty-year rivalry.

Both men went on to more commands and more celebrated victories. Marius rescued Rome from foreign foes by repulsing an invasion of Germanic peoples from the north, the Cimbri and Teutones, in 101 B.C. Sulla helped save the state as one of the commanders who won the Social War (91–88 B.C.), a rebellion by Rome's oldest Italian allies, bitter at being denied citizenship and otherwise discriminated against. In politics, Marius appealed to the popular assembly and dabbled in the politics of reform, while Sulla stood firmly with the conservative majority in the Senate.

Both men made long-term if not always intentional contributions to Rome's future. While Sulla hunted the last rebels in the Social War among the crags of the Apennines, the government, shaken by the revolt, pragmatically granted their allies the citizenship they asked for. Within a couple of generations, Rome and its former allies were thus welded into one nation, and Italy as a whole became the political base for Roman domination of the Empire for the next five centuries.

Marius contributed more directly to Rome's imperial future by guiding the reorganization of the Roman army into the classic *Roman legion*. From the year 100 B.C. on, each legion came to number five thousand men organized in ten cohorts, uniformly armed with javelin and shortsword. The army borrowed the famous shortsword used for close-in work from its Spanish foes. The legion was normally supported by archers, slingers, and mounted cavalry, the latter often recruited from the more flamboyant, less disciplined barbarian lands on the edge of the empire.

Even more important, soldiers no longer had to be even small landholders. They were henceforth paid regular salaries, a lure that drew many poor men into the service. But the new legions also became increasingly dependent on their commanders to lead them to rich pickings and to coerce the government into voting them land allotments on their return from the wars. The result was a more professional, full-time army, but one whose primary loyalties were more likely to be to the legions themselves or to successful generals than to the Roman state.

What this could mean became apparent when the competition between Marius and Sulla burst into the open at the end of their lives, during the violent decade between 88 and 79 B.C. The trouble began when a Near Eastern monarch named Mithridates (r. 120–63 B.C.) rose to challenge Rome's dominance of its client states and provinces in the East. Sulla, a consul for the year 88 B.C., was set at the head of the army dispatched to handle the matter. Then Marius emerged from retirement, rallied equestrian support, and got the assembly to vote him the command instead. Sulla's response was to bring his army to Rome, drive Marius and his allies from the city, and then turn east once more. Soon thereafter, however, Marius and his faction returned, reestablished their power in Rome, and executed a number of their political enemies after thoroughly illegal trials. Marius, then in his seventieth year and seventh consulship, and perhaps no longer quite sane, died before he could perpetrate further outrages.

In Asia Minor, Sulla slowly beat back Mithridates and suppressed a series of insurrections the Near Eastern ruler had set off among the Greeks. Five years after Marius's death, Sulla returned to Italy, fought a gory civil war with the popular leaders who had succeeded Marius, and finally established himself as dictator in Rome itself. Soon tablets with lists of "proscribed" popular leaders went up in the forum, invitations to any citizen to bring in the outlawed politicians for a price. Again, thousands of equestrians and even some scores of senators died.

Taking a constitutional reform as his mandate as dictator, Sulla proceeded to strengthen the Senate while opening it to equestrian membership, and to weaken the power of the tribunes and the assembly. His main concern, however, was to see to it that the lands confiscated from the proscribed were divided among his soldiers, more than one hundred thousand in number. Once he had accomplished this, he turned the government back over to the Senate, settled into a luxurious retirement, and died within a year. Like Marius, he did not long outlive his brutal triumph. Nor did his governmental changes survive him by a dozen years. But the example he had set of

building political power on military victories and deploying troops to impose his will on Rome itself was duly noted by more than one ambitious younger man.

The Rise and Fall of Julius Caesar

The Republic was now within two generations of its end. The giants of the penultimate round of clashing ambitions and crumbling ideals were Pompey, Cicero, and Julius Caesar. The lesser figures that swirled around them were many, their maneuvers intricate and unending. What follows can only be a summary account of a dying age and the men who tried to save it or to bring it down.

Gnaeus Pompeius (106–48 B.C.)—Pompey the Great, as he came to be called—was a protégé of Sulla's and followed the latter's road to fame and fortune until he reached the sticking point. In the two decades following Sulla's death—the 70s and 60s—Pompey earned a reputation as Rome's most successful military commander. He crushed an attempted uprising near Rome and suppressed a revolt in Spain. He helped to smash the great slave rebellion of 73 B.C. led by Spartacus, the gladiator who raised tens of thousands of slaves and terrified all Italy before the legions broke him. Pompey also swept the pirates off the sea, finished off King Mithridates in the Near East, expanded and reorganized Rome's empire at that end of the Mediterranean, and returned home triumphant in 62 B.C. There, however, he fell afoul of politics, and discovered that he didn't have Sulla's stomach for shredding the constitution with Roman shortswords.

Pompey wanted a land distribution for his men and a formal ratification of his new order in the Near East. The Senate, fearful of his popularity and his army, hesitated to make him greater still by granting all his demands. Pompey waffled, backed away from deploying brute force, and looked around for political allies instead. He wanted to be hailed in triumph by the Republic, not to destroy it.

Marcus Tullius Cicero (106–43 B.C.) wanted very much to save the battered Republic and, again, to rise as high among its elite as he could. Trained in law, oratory, and philosophy in both Rome and Greece, Cicero was a man of immense talent. But because he was descended from equestrian stock, he was doomed to be all his life a "new man," the first in his family to rise to offices and honors. Nevertheless, his skill at public pleading made him an extremely well-off lawyer with a mansion on the Palatine. His energy, administrative ability, and sheer oratorical brilliance carried him from one magistracy to another, until, in 63 B.C., he was elected to the consulship.

By the late 60s, then, Cicero had reached the highest offices in the Republic. He had also worked out an idealistic formula for the salvation of the state. The key, he felt, was "the harmony of the orders," by which he meant collaboration rather than conflict between the equestrian and senatorial classes to rule in the best interests of all Romans. For the next twenty years, as senator, writer, and even in his private correspondence, Cicero preached his belief in Roman law and Roman freedoms, in responsible ruling classes and the best traditions of the Republic.

The enigmatic face of Julius Caesar—soldier, statesman, and the man many thought would be king in Rome—gazes out at us from this bust. Murdered in the Senate house, Caesar left his name and legend to a line of emperors.

Gaius Julius Caesar (100–44 B.C.), probably the most famous Roman of them all, was certainly one of the hardest to figure out. He had brains, courage, ambition, and perhaps most important, imagination. Descended from the ancient patrician Julian clan—they traced their ancestry back to Venus by way of Aeneas—and a relative by marriage of Marius, Caesar plunged into the political maelstrom in the 60s, just as Pompey and Cicero were reaching the height of their careers.

Julius Caesar was probably the second most eloquent man in Rome after Cicero, and he proved a greater general than Pompey. Of the three, he was the only one with the imagination to see that the Republic had become a hollow sham, a cloak for the ambitions of its rulers, and the only one who was willing to take a sledgehammer to the foundations of the state.

Caesar rose slowly. In the 60s, he made an informal political alliance with Pompey and a third, very wealthy politician named Crassus (c. 115–53 B.C.) to advance their mutual interests. Cicero, who might have made a fourth partner, refused to join the cabal. Thanks to this so-called *First Triumvirate*, however, Pompey got the land for his troops and his Asian settlement ratified, and the other two got the military commands they wanted, for Caesar had seen that Pompey's was a surer road to success than Cicero's. Pompey then rested on his laurels, and Crassus died fighting the Parthians in the East. Caesar spent most of the 50s conquering Transalpine Gaul (roughly coterminous with modern France) for Rome.

Caesar returned to Italy in 49 B.C., facing the same fear and hostility from the Senate that Pompey and Sulla had confronted before him. The Senate demanded that he lay down his command before he returned. Caesar's response was to cross the Rubicon, the river in northern Italy marking the legal limits of his authority in Gaul, at the head of his legions. Announcing "the die is cast," he marched against his political foes.

The Senate ordered Pompey himself to defend Rome against Caesar. Caesar routed his old ally, pursued him to Greece, and crushed his army there in 48 B.C. Pompey fled further still, to Egypt, where agents of the next-to-last Ptolemaic pharaoh cut him down, a sacrifice to Caesar's rising star. When Caesar arrived, he installed the last of the Ptolemaic line, the intriguing Cleopatra, as ruler of Egypt. He then swept victoriously across North Africa, from the Near East to Spain, and returned to Rome to decide the fate of the Republic itself.

Caesar had a sense of theater. When he reached the capital in 46 B.C., he mounted parades to celebrate not one but four consecutive triumphs for his conquests in Gaul, Egypt, Asia, and Africa. One parade included a decorated wagon with the famous battle report: *Veni, Vidi, Vici!*—"I came, I saw, I conquered!" Celebrating his victories in Asia, Caesar climbed the steps of the capital between two rows of forty elephants holding aloft torches to light his ascent. At the same time, he pardoned all his enemies and laid on public festivals and grain distributions of unprecedented lavishness. Then he set to work to see what he could do with the shambles of the Republic.

Caesar began by assuring his own grip on power. He accumulated a number of important offices himself, including dictatorship for life in 45 B.C. He expanded the number of magistracies and the size of the Senate and packed both with his old officers. And he provided military colonies for his troops in many parts of the empire.

A stable structure of authority thus established, he turned to more substantive changes. He divided Italy into municipal districts for more efficient administration. He extended Roman citizenship to a number of deserving regions. He announced a program of public works to repair the ravages of civil war and put the poor to work. He even found time to reform the calendar, replacing the hopelessly inaccurate lunar year with the solar calendar which, with but a single correction fifteen centuries later, we still use today.

Time, however, was the one thing Caesar did not have. Rumors that he planned to have himself crowned king were all over Rome. The autocracy he had already put in place had destroyed the traditional power of the Senate. Some, like Cicero, opposed him as a matter of principle, others because he had shattered the political futures they had planned for themselves. And Caesar, whether from undue self-confidence or indifference bred of illness and weariness after the long struggle, had dismissed his bodyguard.

"The Ides of March have come," he called to an augur who had warned him of danger on that day as he entered the Senate on March 15, 44 B.C. "Ay, they have come," the soothsayer replied, "but they have not gone."[8] The conservative conspirators, led by two of Caesar's trusted aides, clustered around as if to greet him. And then the dagger blows rained down. He fell, the Roman historians tell us, at the

very foot of a statue of Pompey the Great. (For more grim details of this famous assassination, see the box, "The Ides of March Are Come.")

PROFILES IN HISTORY
The Ides of March Are Come

Few political assassinations have caught the imaginations of later generations like that of Julius Caesar. The following convincingly circumstantial account comes from the Roman historian Suetonius's (A.D. 75–140) *Lives of the Caesars.* Most English-speaking people get their impression of Caesar's murder from William Shakespeare's *Julius Caesar.* How do the dying man's last words in Shakespeare's play—"Et tu, Brute?"—"And you too, Brutus?" spoken in Latin—contrast with the closest approximation recorded by Suetonius?

> As soon as Caesar took his seat, the conspirators crowded around him as if to pay their respects. Tullius Cimber, who had taken the lead, came up close, pretending to ask a question. Caesar made a gesture of postponement, but Cimber caught hold of his shoulders. "This is violence!" Caesar cried, and at that moment one of the Casca brothers slipped behind and with a sweep of his dagger stabbed him just below the throat. Caesar grasped Casca's arm and ran it through with his stylus; he was leaping away when another dagger caught him in the breast. Confronted by a ring of drawn daggers, he drew the top of his gown over his face, and at the same time ungirded the lower part, letting it fall to his feet so that he would die with both legs decently covered. Twenty-three dagger thrusts went home as he stood there. Caesar did not utter a sound after Casca's blow had drawn a groan from him; though some say that when he saw Marcus Brutus about to deliver the second blow, he reproached him in Greek with, "You too, my son?"
>
> The entire Senate then dispersed in confusion, and Caesar was left lying dead for some time until three of his household slaves carried him home in a litter, with one arm hanging over the side.

Source: Suetonius, *The Twelve Caesars,* trans. Robert Graves (Harmondsworth, England: Penguin, 1957), 43–44.

The Triumph of Augustus

So Rome's civil wars were not over after all. The ultimate round of intrigues and battles dragged on for thirteen years more. In the end, only two contenders for the leadership of the Roman world remained. But to get to that point, many had to fall.

In the first dizzying moment after Caesar's death, Senate conservatives like Cicero may actually have thought it possible to restore the Republic as it had been. The assassins, led by Caesar's lieutenants, Marcus Brutus (85–42 B.C.) and Cassius Longinus (d. 42 B.C.), saw themselves as liberators and expected to be applauded by the people. The most vigorous voice in the days after the assassination, however, was that of another of Caesar's followers, Mark Antony, who knew the people better than the conspirators did. All but ignored on the fringe of things was eighteen-year-old Octavian, Caesar's grandnephew, adopted son, and heir. Of all the contenders, only the last two had a chance.

Mark Antony (82–30 B.C.), Plutarch reports, was "a brilliant soldier," immensely popular with the troops, among whom he ate, drank, and joked about their love affairs. He had a thick beard, an aquiline nose, and "a certain bold and masculine look, which is found in the statues and portraits of Hercules." It was an image Antony assiduously cultivated, wearing "his tunic belted low over the hips, a large sword at his side, and a heavy cloak."[9] His swaggering self-confidence, his gift for bringing the Roman populace around to his point of view, and his quick action in getting hold of Caesar's papers all made him seem a likely candidate for the next dictator of Rome.

Octavian (63 B.C.–A.D. 14), as Suetonius describes him in later life, was considerably less prepossessing. Augustus's eyes were "clear and bright," the author of *The Twelve Caesars* hastens to assure us, "and he liked to believe that they shone with a sort of divine radiance." But "his teeth were small, few, and decayed; his hair yellowish and rather curly; his eyebrows met above [his] Roman nose."[10] He was short, he sometimes walked with a limp, he could not stand heat or cold, he had nasty coughs and frequent stomachaches. In 44 B.C. he was a sickly teenager with no military experience, and the knives were already out. When he set out for Rome to claim his inheritance, even his mother begged him not to do it.

The last act of the savage ballet began with Mark Antony dominating center stage, repelling all invaders. By manipulating Caesar's last will and testament and stirring up the passions of the populace, he quickly extinguished the assassins' dreams of glory and sent them scuttling off to governorships in the East. For a time, he dallied with the senatorial conservatives; but Cicero could see that Antony was no man of principle, and the Senate backed away. Antony rejected Octavian's claims almost contemptuously, refusing him his inheritance and even hinting darkly that the boy might have had something to do with his granduncle's assassination. For a hushed moment, Antony stood alone, and it looked as though Caesar had found his real inheritor in the new Hercules.

But Octavian's ambition was made of sterner stuff, however feeble his physical equipment. Retreating to a military colony south of Rome, he told Caesar's veteran troops that his name too was Caesar. With troops and the magic name, he was soon back to demand a place at the bargaining table. The upshot was the *Second Triumvirate,* a formal public alliance this time, between Octavian, Antony, and Lepidus (d. 18 B.C.), the late Caesar's Master of the Horse.

The three proceeded to purge even more of their enemies than Sulla had done, including thousands of equestrians, hundreds of senators, and Cicero himself, who was murdered by Antony's minions as he sought to leave for Greece. The Triumvirate, officially charged to "put the Republic in order," formally deified the murdered Caesar in the Hellenistic manner, outlawed his assassins, and headed east to get them.

The army of the triumvirs met the forces led by Caesar's assassins at Philippi in Macedonia in 42 B.C. Octavian, now twenty-one but no more martially inclined than he had been, remained in his tent while Antony led the troops to victory. Brutus and Cassius took their own lives. "Very few indeed of the assassins," according to Suetonius, "outlived Caesar for more than three years, or died naturally."[11]

As was common with alliances of political convenience in those last days of the Republic, the Triumvirate proved not much more durable than the lives of the conspirators. Lepidus was shunted off to Africa. Antony took a command in the rich eastern provinces for his share of the spoils, fought new wars with the Parthians, and fell in love with Queen Cleopatra of Egypt. Cleopatra, determined to save Egypt for the Ptolemies, pinned her final hopes on the swaggering soldier who still looked most likely to emerge with Julius Caesar's bloodstained mantle around his husky shoulders.

Octavian, meanwhile, returned to Rome and plunged into politics. Although he never became a great military leader, he at least organized and dispatched the forces that defeated one rival after another. He thus put down a revolt led by Antony's brother and his ex-wife Fulvia in Italy as well as a naval assault commanded by Pompey's son Sextus. Octavian also faced the hatred of the people whose land he had to confiscate to reward his troops and the despair of starving Romans when Sextus Pompey cut off the city's food supply. Older and wiser, he began to see the value of stability, traditional values, and old Roman ways. By the mid-30s B.C., he was halfway from anemic, ambitious youth to the Augustus Caesar of history.

Augustus Caesar in a typically imperial pose. The armor, the staff of office, the commandingly upraised arm all embody the force of character and confident authority that made Augustus not merely another clever politician but the first emperor of Rome's golden age.

But the great problem still remained: the ever-popular Antony, now ruling all the East conjointly with the scheming and clever Cleopatra. Octavian began cautiously and shrewdly with a propaganda campaign claiming that Mark Antony, drunk with love, had surrendered Rome's eastern empire to the Serpent of the Nile. He then raised a huge military force and turned one more weary time to march around the eastern Mediterranean.

He did not have so far to go. The last battle was fought by sea off Actium in western Greece in 31 B.C. Antony's fleet, weakened by a plague and outmaneuvered by Octavian's forces, was bottled up and beaten. Cleopatra, who had come west with her husband, hurried back to Egypt, and Antony, for once in his life, fled the battlefield and followed her.

Octavian continued his eastward progress unopposed. Mark Antony committed suicide at Alexandria and Cleopatra, learning that Octavian wanted her alive to grace his triumphal procession through Rome, took her own life too. The last Hellenistic monarchy died with her. The Roman Republic, undermined by generations of corruption, class conflict, political feuds, and civil wars, was already dead.

Society and Culture Under the Republic

As Rome grew from a cluster of hill villages to a huge city and the hub of an empire, the society and culture of the Romans changed too. An increasingly elaborate class system and a powerful Greek influence on Roman culture are only the most obvious examples of these changes. Still, the conservative Romans did cling to some social patterns and cultural traits. In many ways, in fact, the conflict between old ways and newfangled innovations defined the sociocultural scene in the Roman Republic.

The Impact of Wealth and Power

The Roman social ideal under the Republic was practically Jeffersonian in its simplicity: every man a farmer, every woman a spinner of wool. Even a large landowner was supposed to toil beside his tenants and slaves under the Italian sun: the conservative statesman Cato did so as late as the second century B.C. Even a wealthy woman was theoretically expected to produce homespun clothing for her family: Augustus Caesar required the women of his household to do so even as the Republic passed away.

Neither aspect of this social ideal in fact matched the realities of life in the Rome of Cato's or Augustus's day. Sprawling in its teeming hundreds of thousands, its temples and tenement blocks, across the seven hills, Rome at the end of the Republic was a very different place from what it had been like in the beginning. Both class relations and gender roles had evolved far beyond the nostalgic thatched-roof ideal.

As we have seen, early class divisions between patrician and plebeian, or large and small farmer, had developed into a much more complicated structure. In early republican times, the struggle of the orders had opened the senatorial class to penetration by the wealthier plebeians. Thereafter, the growth of the Roman Empire had increased the wealth of the senatorial class, spawned an upwardly mobile new equestrian order, turned small farmers into an urban proletariat, and flooded farms and workshops with slaves. The result was not so much class conflict with battle lines clearly drawn as a network of traditional social relationships under strain. For there were also forces that worked to hold the Republic together for the better part of the republican period.

Among the traditional relationships that bound the orders of society together, the highly developed system of *clientage* was central. In the earliest days and at the lowest level, this meant the almost feudal obligation of plebeians to work the estates of a patrician landowner, who in turn was obliged to protect and support his plebeian clients. In the more complex society of later republican times, clientage bound less affluent and prestigious Romans to support the political ambitions of the great, while the latter advanced the more modest political aspirations and economic interests of their clients.

Similar ties across class lines often bound masters and slaves, the power of the owner being balanced to some degree by responsibility to support the unfree worker. Frequently, furthermore, slaveowners freed their slaves in later life; and such a manumission, rather than ending a relationship, created a new one, between master and freedman. A freedman's contract, in fact, often required continuing payments or other services to the former master. Nevertheless, many gravemarkers erected by grateful freedmen to former masters seem to reflect genuine feelings of affection and respect.

Relations between the sexes also evolved under the pressures of the later Republic. Aristocratic women often exercised considerable political influence over their male compatriots, especially during the disturbed later years of the Republic. Patrician women could draw on Roman traditions of female heroism that went back to Rhea Sylvia, the mother of the city's legendary founders, Romulus and Remus, as well as on the prestige and family power that accompanied the status of the Roman matron. A woman of the upper classes could also become extremely wealthy by inheritance, especially during the long and bloody civil wars, when so many of the senatorial elite perished. Bringing family influence, wealth, and political savvy to bear on the political and military infighting of the first century B.C., such women were often in the thick of the struggle to preserve or advance the interests of husbands or families. As we shall see, they gained even greater power during the period of the Roman Empire.

At bottom, finally, the Republic held together as long as it did because for several centuries basic loyalty to the state was strong enough to resist the economic and political forces that threatened to pull society apart. Even a late republican figure like Livy, born just ten years before Caesar crossed the Rubicon, began his history of Rome by announcing that his goal was to record "the story of the greatest nation of the world." Although he admitted that "of late years, wealth has made us greedy and self-indulgence has brought us [to] every form of sensual excess," he nevertheless firmly believed that over the centuries "no nation has ever been greater or purer than ours, or richer in good citizens or noble deeds."[12] This sort of allegiance, cultivated by patriotic legends, public ceremonies, and histories like Livy's, was another force binding the destinies of Romans of all classes. During the successful centuries that began with Augustus, that loyalty was rekindled and helped hold the Roman world together despite continuing differences between the orders of society.

The Hellenization of Rome

Roman culture, like Roman society, also felt great pressures for change over the history of the Republic. In this instance, however, a good case can be made that the forces of innovation swept all before them.

The great force for cultural change in the Roman Republic was the highly developed civilization of its Greek neighbors. It has been said that the

Romans conquered the Greeks and then fell captive to their new subjects—captivated by the entrancing art and startling ideas of the Hellenistic Greek world.

The Romans had begun to learn from the Greeks—either through Etruscan intermediaries or directly from the Greek city-states of southern Italy—as early as the sixth century B.C., when Greece was in its great Awakening. The Roman alphabet and the hoplite-style phalanx are important examples of this early influence. Even the chief gods of the Roman state, Jupiter and Juno, Mars and Venus and the rest, soon came to resemble the Greek Olympians, Zeus and Hera, Ares and Aphrodite. Following this productive stimulus in Etruscan times, however, the Romans seem to have been isolated from Greek influences during the early centuries of the Republic. Too busy building their own power base in Italy, too culturally unsophisticated to be fascinated by the artistry of Sophocles or the philosophical problems that absorbed Plato, Romans were not ready to learn more from the Hellenes.

It was in the third and second centuries B.C., as

their imperial horizons widened to include overseas territories, that the Romans really discovered Greek culture. It was Hellenistic Greek art and thought by this time, and Roman aristocrats seized on it with avidity. Shiploads of Greek statues were brought back for display in Roman public squares and buildings. Whole libraries of Greek books flooded into Rome, and a more cosmopolitan Roman elite learned Greek the way later Europeans learned French, as the necessary "second language" for the cultured. Greek philosophers came to lecture in Rome, and Greek rhetoricians were hired to sharpen the oratory of the sons of the senatorial class.

The result, at one level at least, was a massive transplant of Greek culture westward to Rome. The ideas of the Greek philosophical schools, especially the Hellenistic schools of Stoicism and Epicureanism, found new homes in Roman minds. Roman poets wrote verses in Greek meters and in the pithy, witty style of the Alexandrians. The oratory of Cicero echoed the rhetorical patterns of Demosthenes and the lessons of Greek writers on

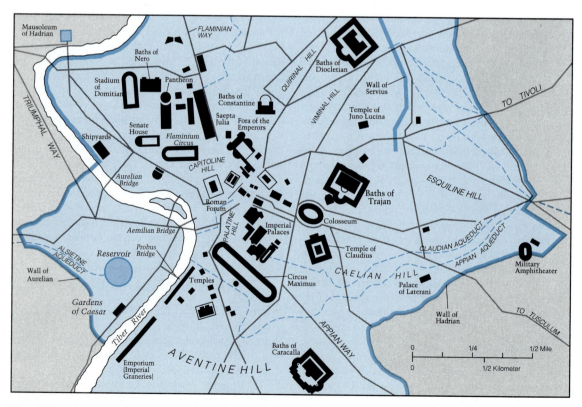

Map 5.3   The City of Rome in Ancient Times

the art of rhetoric. The Hellenistic Greeks had never had a realistic chance against the Roman legions, but they won the hearts and minds of the Roman elite with ease.

There was some resistance, of course. Cato, the orator who insisted that Carthage must be destroyed, also fulminated against the Hellenization of Roman culture. His school of conservatism, however, did not achieve much long-term success. Other Roman aristocrats took eagerly to the new ideas. Cornelia, daughter of Scipio Africanus and mother of the Gracchi, was a much admired matron of the old school. But she read and wrote Greek as well as Latin, shared her father's enthusiasm for Greek culture, and remained a widely respected figure in the most cultivated Roman and international society. The charm of novelty and the eagerness to be "up with the latest" thus combined with genuine appreciation for the Greek cultural achievement to transform Roman culture.

What resulted, however, was not mindless imitation, but a synthesis of Greek ideas and techniques with the Roman spirit. As American culture in later centuries differed in tone and spirit from the European culture from which it grew, so Romans subtly but significantly transformed their Greek heritage. In some cases, Roman versions were to be more influential later on than the Greek originals were. The most famous Epicurean, for instance, was the Roman Lucretius, the most celebrated Stoic the later Roman emperor Marcus Aurelius. It was the Roman Vergil, deeply inspired by Homer, who taught later centuries how to write epic poetry, not Homer himself.

Most important of all, however, the Romans made Greek culture their own, writing in Greek meters or meditating on Platonic Ideas as naturally as the Greeks themselves did. The result was a merged Greco-Roman culture that had already taken shape by the end of the Republic and advanced to even more spectacular achievements in the Augustan Age that followed.

Roman Literature in the Age of Cicero

In the later centuries of the Republic, Romans, stimulated by their brilliant neighbors, began to show what they themselves could do in art and thought. From poetry to oratory, from impressive building to highly individualized portraits in stone, they did very well indeed.

As befit an imperial people, the Romans built on a grand scale. By the end of the Republic, their columned temples were already as impressive as those of the Greeks, their open-air theaters on the Greek model already held thousands of spectators, and their aqueducts marched proudly across the countryside, bringing water to Roman cities. Greek sculpture had excited Roman emulation, but the Romans were producing portrait sculpture that had its own qualities. They learned naturalism, a passion for lifelike detail, from Hellenistic carving, but they infused a sense of character and individual humanity into the faces of men and women that was their own. Some of the most striking examples are not the statues of the great names, but the tombstone busts of citizens of the middle rank, perhaps based on death masks but filled with the life that once was there. The stern face of the head of a great patrician family, or the affection of an elderly couple holding hands in Roman marble, vividly embody the personalities and the personal relations of these citizens of a long-vanished empire.

Among the Roman literary voices who drew on Hellenistic models yet produced something distinctly Roman were the comic dramatists Plautus (254–184 B.C.) and Terence (190–159 B.C.). They modeled their plays, not on the social satire of Aristophanes, but on the New Comedy of Menander, full of Hellenistic stage conventions and sentimental situations. Yet they managed to impose a full-bodied Roman flavor on the usual star-crossed lovers, cases of mistaken identity, and slaves who were inevitably cleverer than their masters.

The most admired literary lights of the Republic, however, clustered in the first century B.C., flourishing even as the Caesars and their rivals connived and fought for power. It was a striking illustration of the thesis that it is frequently not peaceful times, but times of turmoil and conflict that produce great art.

One of the greatest poets of the period was Lucretius (96–55 B.C.), whose book-length epic *On the Nature of Things* summarized the Epicurean atomist view of the nature of the universe. Profoundly aware of the violent tenor of the times, Lucretius sought to free his fellow Romans from their fear of death and supernatural forces by revealing an antiseptic universe of drifting atoms and empty space. In the end, however, his work was less philosophy or science than a great poem, replete with vigorous flashes of imagery that can still raise a living picture in the mind twenty centuries later.

The greatest lyric poet of the age was Catullus (c. 84–c. 54 B.C.). Drawing his predilection for short poems and verbal wit from the Alexandrians and his subjects and themes from the corrupt high society of the last years of the Republic, Catullus transcended both his models and his subjects. His verses ranged from ribald insults directed at fellow men-about-town to passionate expressions of love for a very sophisticated woman who already had more lovers than she knew what to do with. The fashionable cynicism of the age is clearly reflected in his recognition of what his beloved's protestations of love are worth:

> My woman says she'd prefer to marry no one
> but me, even if Jupiter asked for her love.
> Ah yes: but what a woman says to an eager lover,
> write it on running water, write it on air.[13]

Yet Catullus was also capable of writing the moving elegy composed over his brother's tomb in Asia Minor, at the far edge of the Empire, that begins:

> Through many nations, over many seas, I traveled
> to pay this service, brother, with my tears. . . .[14]

The most admired literary voice of those last tense decades, however, was of a very different sort: the sonorous voice of Cicero, conservative statesman, eclectic philosopher, and the greatest orator of his time. The dozens of his speeches that survive from the law court and the Senate house, as well as his treatises on such weighty topics as duty and friendship, religion and government, show the influence of Greek rhetoric and philosophy. But the rolling cadences that made him the most revered and imitated of all Western orators boomed with the rhythms of the Roman tongue. And the subjects he returned to again and again—freedom under law, the "harmony of the orders," and the essential soundness of the Republic—reflected a distinctly Roman dream.

Risking his life to attack the ambitions of Mark Antony, Cicero prayed "that in dying I may leave the Roman people free—the immortal gods could grant me no greater gift."[15] A year later he was dead at the hands of Antony's officers, his severed head nailed to the rostra in the forum where he had so often spoken. If the Republic for which he died seems unworthy of his sacrifice, yet the dreamer was not diminished thereby.

The Rise of Christianity

The best-known ancient name of all today, however, lived far from the capital of the Western world. Jesus of Nazareth, born under Augustus, executed under his successor Tiberius, lived and died unknown except to the Jewish population of Palestine and the Roman governor and garrison who ruled there. Even Pontius Pilate does not seem to have heard of Jesus before he was brought up for trial. Yet the religion founded by Jesus Christ outlasted the fall of both the Roman Republic and the Roman Empire to provide the spiritual core of the next age of Western history.

In this section we will examine the life of Christ and the sources of Christian ideas; in the final section of Chapter 6 we will look at the rise of the Christian church in the days of the Caesars. In this survey of the origins of Christianity, however, we will be laying the foundations for much more than the history of Roman Christianity. Jesus never saw a medieval cathedral spire or heard a modern Christian hymn, but without him neither the spires nor the hymns of many later centuries would have risen against Western skies.

Religion, Philosophy, and Cults

The Roman world into which Christ was born was not in a literal sense a religiously impoverished society. Traditional polytheistic religions, Greek philosophical schools, and the Hellenistic mystery cults were all flourishing. All of these, particularly in their weaknesses, in fact prepared the way for the spread of the Christian religion in the Roman Empire.

During the last centuries before Christ and the opening centuries of what was to become the Christian era, Romans continued to honor and sacrifice to Jupiter, Mars, Venus, and the other gods and goddesses of their ancestors. But the worship of these divinities was "essentially a public religion," not concerned with "private . . . religious commitment."[16] The gods were conceived of as primarily concerned with the success and prosperity of the Roman state, and important religious functions were assigned to magistrates and to the Roman Senate. In the late Republic, furthermore, rival political factions were not above manipulating religion in order to present themselves as the chosen instruments of the gods. The worship of the official pantheon thus lacked the spiritual warmth and power that many Romans needed in those tumultuous times.

For the cultured few, as we have seen, the Greek philosophical schools still offered thoughtful answers to the large questions of life. Stoicism became particularly popular among the Romans, with two special emphases. Roman Stoics like Cicero replaced the passive tone of Stoic "apathy" with a stress on doing your duty, come what might, clearly a valuable virtue for the rulers and soldiers responsible for holding the empire together. Roman Stoicism also emphasized the universalist side of this teaching, the belief that there is an indwelling rational spirit at the heart of the universe that dwells also in each of us. All human beings, of whatever race, class, or gender, are brothers and sisters under the skin because of this spark of rationality in us all. For the masters of so many peoples, this belief in universal brotherhood was very useful too.

Platonism underwent even more remarkable changes, particularly in the *Neoplatonism* ("New Platonism") taught by the influential philosopher Plotinus at Alexandria in the third century A.D.

Plotinus (c. 205–c. 270) asserted that the greatest of all the transcendent Platonic forms (or Ideas or absolutes) was what he described as the One, the central source of all being and all values, from which these qualities radiated like light from its source. The more distant one was from the spiritual source, the less reality and the less value anything had. The material world, Plato's old world of particulars, was the furthest removed from the One, hence the least good and the least real of all. But the human soul was spiritual too, despite its confinement in the prison of the body, and might reach the spiritual center of all things through philosophical study, meditation, and mystic vision.

Many people, however, found the philosophers too intellectual, too coldly logical, to satisfy their religious needs. Such people frequently went back to the Greek mystery religions, to the fertility cults of the ancient Near East and North Africa. Among the *mystery cults* that drew large numbers in Roman times were the religions of the Greek Dionysus (Bacchus to the Romans), the militant Persian Mithras (a favorite of Roman legionaries), the

Roman women celebrate secret rites of the cult of Dionysus in this wall painting from Pompeii. A young matron clings to an older woman for moral support, while a celebrant clashes cymbals to the rhythm of the orgiastic dance. What elements give the painting a feeling of graceful movement?

Egyptian Isis, and Cybele, the "Great Mother," from Asia Minor.

A number of the mystery religions focused on a dying divinity who was resurrected, like Dionysus or Osiris, the latter brought back to life by Isis. A major appeal of these cults, as noted earlier, was their offer of eternal life to their initiates. Among the rituals of these foreign faiths, baptism and communion were common. Initiates into the cult of Mithras, for example, were baptized by being washed in the blood of a sacrificed bull, a ceremony that was believed to open the road to salvation. Isis offered a symbolic communion feast for believers, in which they believed they became one with the Goddess of Ten Thousand Names.

Christianity too would preach a risen God who guaranteed eternal life, would baptize believers (though only rhetorically "in the blood of the lamb"), and would offer communion with God through a sacred meal. Christianity would thus meet many of the spiritual needs that the popularity of the mystery cults had revealed in the Roman world.

Judaism and Jesus

One important key to understanding the life and message of Jesus Christ is to remember that he was born and raised a Jew. The Hebrews, whose dedicated monotheism had made them stand out among the polytheistic Near Eastern societies of ancient times, seemed just as exotic in the Greco-Roman world. The Jews, as the Hebrews had come to be called around 500 B.C., were a thorn in the side of the Romans. Insular, rebellious, swept by fevers of what must have seemed like religious fanaticism to their rulers, most Jews refused to be assimilated into the world empire. To many Romans, the Christian sect looked like more of the same, only worse.

Since their captivity in Babylon during the sixth century B.C., the Jews had been a subject people most of the time, governed by Babylonians, Persians, Ptolemaic and Seleucid Greeks, and, since the 60s B.C., by the Romans. Under the Greeks and Romans, some Jews did become increasingly hellenized and romanized, accepting the language and customs of their rulers, reading Greek philosophy or Latin literature. Under King Herod I the Great (r. 37–4 B.C.), the ruler in whose reign Jesus was born, Roman influence was particularly strong. There were also communities of westernized Jews living in cities

across the Near East and around the Mediterranean, the Jews of the *diaspora*, or "dispersion," who, while they continued to practice their religion, were open to the culture of their neighbors.

Beneath this veneer, however, the old faith still burned fiercely—and with it, the spirit of rebellion. The Jews rebelled against the Seleucids, who had tried to install Zeus in the temple at Jerusalem. They revolted again on the death of King Herod, the cruel ruler who was Rome's puppet in the region. They asked for direct Roman rule then, rather than another domestic tyrant, got troops and a Roman governor, and soon began to protest against his rule. They rose in revolt against Nero in the 60s A.D. and against other emperors in later centuries.

The Jews of Jesus's time still believed in one God, Yahweh, invisible and all-powerful, creator of the world, whose chosen people they believed themselves to be. They still affirmed that God required not only ritual practices, but also rigorously ethical conduct. The personal morality prescribed by the Ten Commandments and the sense of social justice urged by the prophets were central to the Judaic faith. Much of what Jesus later preached was part of his Judaic heritage, studied in the temple of his childhood, breathed in with the religiously charged air of this corner of western Asia. "Do not think that I have come to destroy the law or the prophets," Jesus declared. "I have not come to destroy, but to fulfill."[17]

Judaism in Jesus' time, however, included a number of other, more controversial doctrines that also became part of Christian belief. Many Jews, perhaps influenced by the Zoroastrianism of their former Persian rulers, had come to believe in the resurrection of the dead and in everlasting life for the righteous, damnation for the sinner. There was also a widely held belief in a coming savior or *Messiah*. Most Jews saw the Messiah as a political liberator from foreign oppression. Some, however, expected a spiritual savior, a divine Chosen One who would inaugurate a kingdom of righteousness on earth. Again, Jesus must have absorbed all these beliefs as he studied the scrolls and talked with the priests of Galilee.

There were also a number of sects and a continuing tradition of prophetic inspiration in the land of Jesus' birth. The most important sectarian groups were the Sadducees, the Pharisees, and the Essenes. The aristocratic Sadducees, leading citizens and priests of the temple, were supporters of the status quo, even if it meant coming to terms with their

Roman rulers. The more popular Pharisees were vigorous defenders of ritual perfection and the Law of Moses, which governed every aspect of their lives. Condemned as hypocrites in the New Testament for their "holier than thou" attitude, the Pharisees were popular preachers in the synagogues of Jesus' day. The Essenes, finally, were monkish communities, dwellers in the desert whose beliefs were revealed in detail for the first time by the discovery of the Dead Sea scrolls at Qumran in Jordan in the 1940s. These Essenes had withdrawn entirely from society to await the coming Messiah and the triumph of righteousness over wickedness, when humble and ascetic spirits like themselves should inherit the earth.

This was the Palestine into which Jesus was born, somewhere between 8 and 4 B.C., while Augustus Caesar ruled at Rome and the Roman golden age was just beginning.

The Message of Christ

Standing on the Arbel cliffs in northern Israel, with the flat blue Sea of Galilee spread out below you and the twin-peaked mountain called the Horns of Hattin behind, you are looking out over the green land where Christ lived and preached. Beyond the hills to the west lies Nazareth. Below, on the western shore of the Sea of Galilee, the village of Capernaum, where Jesus recruited Peter, the fisher of men, nestles among cedars and orchards on the lake shore. Among these hills and along these roads, Jesus preached for most of his three years' ministry, before taking the long hot road south to Jerusalem.

Looking down at this first countryside to hear his words, you are struck with a sudden sense of the intimacy, the humanity of this level of communication. Word spreading from that village over there to that one just down the road. Words spoken eye to eye in the grateful shade of a palm tree tossing in the breeze from the Mediterranean. A real man walking real roads, speaking to small groups among low stone houses roofed with thatch, with the lake shore just beyond. A real man, touching the sick among the cook fires, or fixing with a gaze full of sudden force those few who would rise from their labors and follow him.

We have no contemporary accounts of Jesus' life or character. Paul's epistles are the earliest Christian writings, and Paul did not come on the scene until Jesus had passed from it. The four Gospels probably date to the latter part of the first century or the early decades of the second, perhaps between A.D. 70 and 120. Since Jesus was crucified in A.D. 29 or 30, the Gospels probably reflect living traditions about the founder current among Christians at that time, rather than eyewitness testimony. It is important to note also that all these early documents are the work of believers, and thus testaments of religious faith as much as historical documents. Nevertheless, they tell us all we are ever likely to know about the founder of one of the world's great religions.

Jesus was born at the end of the reign of Herod the Great in Judea, but grew up in Galilee, in the northern part of Palestine. Jesus' family were apparently people of the artisan class, Joseph being a carpenter. His mother's name was Miriam, Mary in English. The first thirty years of his life are largely a blank in the record. What is recorded, including his studies in the temple as a boy and his confounding the priests with his knowledge of the faith, indicates that he was an extremely religious youth. When he was about thirty, not young in those days, he was baptized in the Jordan River by John the Baptist, a popular lay preacher in the ancient prophetic tradition. Thereafter, Jesus took up his own religious calling and began to preach to the people in his turn.

Jesus' mission probably lasted about three years, though even that is not certain. He spoke in the synagogues and disputed points of doctrine with priests and Pharisees and gained a larger following by his open-air sermons in the fields and streets of Galilee. He spoke to ordinary men and women, even to children, and offered consolation to sinners, tax collectors, non-Jews, and others whom the rigidly righteous shunned as impure. Stories of miracles followed in his footsteps: he turned water into wine, fed multitudes on a few fish and loaves of bread, cured the sick, restored sight to the blind, raised the dead. Disciples gathered around him. Many who heard him speak thought the Messiah had come at last.

Jesus' words moved people of all kinds, including, the Gospels assure us, an occasional Roman. His message, as Christians would later come to understand it, included the two "great commandments": Love God, and love thy neighbor as thyself. He declared that the will was as important as the deed, that a sin committed in the heart was no less sinful than the act of adultery, robbery, or murder. Perhaps most exciting to those who saw and heard him speak, he announced that the moment foretold had

In this early Christian picture, Christ displays the words, "I am the Way to Truth and Life." The words, the halo, and the cross continued to be part of the image of Christ over time. What differences do you see between this figure and both medieval and modern images of the founder of Christianity?

indeed come, that "the time is fulfilled, and the kingdom of God is at hand. Repent and believe."[18]

Most importantly, Jesus presented himself, not as another prophet, but as a divine being, the Son of God. And he declared that to believe in him was the only road to salvation: "I am the Way." *Christ*, the Anointed One, the Messiah so long prophesied, had come to earth. He offered to those who accepted his teaching the supreme gift of eternal life.

The last days of Jesus' own life are reported in more detail than any other part of it in the Gospels. The story, familiar everywhere in the Western world, tells how he went south from Galilee down into Judea, entered Jerusalem to the cheers of thousands, defied the priestly hierarchy in the temple, ate a last supper with his dozen chosen disciples, was betrayed by one of them, convicted by the priests for blasphemy, and executed by the Romans for treason. Pontius Pilate, the Roman governor of Judea, had a crude sign nailed up on the cross on which Jesus was crucified, derisively labeling him "the king of the Jews." The Romans, outsiders in Palestine, probably could not distinguish between the various meanings of the term *Messiah* among the Hebrews.

And that should, by all practical Roman common sense, have been that. But history sometimes transcends common sense, and it is in fact from the crucifixion of Jesus that we date the most far-reaching spiritual transformation in the history of the Western world. We take up the spread of Christianity in the next chapter, on the Roman Empire in its prime and in its decline.

A Topical Summary

Politics: The political history of the Roman Republic began with the emergence of the self-governing city-state of Rome in central Italy around 500 B.C. Centuries of war and territorial expansion carried Roman rule around the Mediterranean and into parts of western Europe. Political and social conflict, however, plunged Rome into a long Civil War that transformed the Roman Republic, dominated by its upper classes, into the Roman Empire. The Empire was founded by its first emperor, Augustus Caesar, shortly before the birth of Christ.

Economics: The expanding Rome of the Republic grew rich from the conquest of the Carthaginian commercial empire and the wealthy Hellenistic monarchies of the eastern Mediterranean. Loot,

taxes, and slaves from the provinces made the city of Rome splendid but undermined the social cohesion of the state.

Society: Originally a conservative social order composed of sturdy peasants and a stern patrician ruling class, Roman society deteriorated under the impact of the new wealth and foreign influences. The rich got much richer while many of the poor, driven from their farms by slave-run latifundia, swarmed into the slums of Rome. The resulting social tensions, heightened by the reforming efforts of popular tribunes like the brothers Tiberius and Gaius Gracchus, made their contribution to a century of civil strife.

Technology: The Romans learned many practical skills from their neighbors and one-time rulers the Etruscans, as well as from the more developed peoples they conquered. By Augustus's time, they had built the huge city of Rome, and their military technology was extensive, including weapons design, naval construction, and the military roads that linked the Empire.

Culture: Roman culture was enriched during the period of the Republic by the influence of the Hellenistic civilization of the conquered Greeks. Greek statues, books, and ideas flooded the Republic, but the Roman spirit suffused much of the work of comic dramatists like Plautus and Terence and the stirring oratory of Cicero. Roman religion and philosophy did not, however, provide spiritual satisfaction for many Romans, and in the last years of the Republic a new faith destined to spread across the Western world emerged—the religion first preached by Jesus Christ among the Jews of Palestine.

The Expanding West: Roman conquests reached much further and went much deeper than Greek expansion had. As the history of the Roman Republic drew to a close, Rome's imperial provinces ringed the Mediterranean and included parts of Spain, France, and other European lands. Although the Roman Empire was established by conquest and early Roman governors exploited the new provinces without mercy, the Republic laid strong foundations for the Empire that was to come.

Some Key Terms

century 127
clientage 143
comitia centuriata 124
comitia tributa 124
consul 125
Empire 118
equestrians 134
fasces 123
First Triumvirate 139

imperium 125
insulae 134
Messiah 148
mystery cults 147
Neoplatonism 147
patria potestas 124
patrician 124
plebian 124
Punic Wars 129

Republic 118
Roman Civil War 134
Roman legion 137
Second Triumvirate 141
Senate 124
struggle of the orders 125
tribune 126
Twelve Tables 126

Notes

1. John Edwin Sandys, ed., *A Companion to Latin Studies* (Cambridge: Cambridge University Press, 1935), 185.
2. Livy, *History of Rome,* vol. 2, trans. D. Spillan et al. (New York: American Book, n.d.), 14.
3. *Livy,* trans. E. T. Sage (Cambridge, Mass.: Loeb Classical Library, 1935), 33.33.5–7.
4. Diodorus Siculus, *Bibliotheca Historica,* in Ian Jenkins, *Greek and Roman Life* (London: British Museum Publications, 1986), 66.
5. Plutarch, *Makers of Rome: Nine Lives by Plutarch,* trans. Ian Scott-Kilvert (Harmondsworth, England: Penguin, 1965), 154–155.
6. Ibid., 162.
7. Appian, *Roman History,* trans. Horace White (New York: Macmillan, 1913), 35.
8. Gaius Suetonius Tranquillus, *The Twelve Caesars,* trans. Robert Graves (Harmondsworth, England: Penguin, 1957), 45.
9. Plutarch, *Makers of Rome: Nine Lives by Plutarch,* trans. Ian Scott-Kilvert (Harmondsworth, England: Penguin, 1965), 274.
10. Suetonius, 94–95.
11. Ibid., 49.
12. Titus Livius, *The Early History of Rome: Books I–V of the History of Rome from Its Foundation,* trans. Aubrey de Selincourt (Harmondsworth, England: Penguin, 1960), 18–19.
13. Catullus, No. 70, in Gilbert Highet, *Poets in a Landscape* (Harmondsworth, England: Penguin, 1959), 32.
14. No. 101, ibid., 21.
15. M. Tullius Cicero, "Second Philippic Against Antony," in *Selected Works,* trans. Michael Grant (Harmondsworth, England: Penguin, 1960), 153.
16. Mary Beard and Michael Crawford, *Rome in the Late Republic* (Ithaca, N.Y.: Cornell University Press, 1985), 30.
17. Matthew 5:17.
18. Mark 1:15.

Reading List

BRADLEY, K. R. *Discovering the Roman Family: Studies in Roman Social History.* New York: Oxford University Press, 1991. Sees Roman family feeling undermined by death, divorce, variety of care providers. See also B. Rawson, ed., *The Family in Ancient Rome: New Perspectives* (Ithaca, N.Y.: Cornell University Press, 1986).

BURKERT, W. *Ancient Mystery Cults.* Cambridge, Mass.: Harvard University Press, 1987. Brief but readable and expert account, with some attempt to explain the appeal of the cults.

CRAWFORD, M. H. *The Roman Republic.* London: Fontana, 1978. Succinct and lively survey, laced with quotes and interpretations of debated points.

FREDRIKSEN, P. *From Jesus to Christ: The Origins of the New Testament Image of Jesus.* New Haven: Yale University Press, 1988. Scholarly and readable work, part of a recent upsurge in books about the historical Jesus.

GELTZER, M. *Caesar: Politician and Statesman.* Translated by P. Needham. Oxford: Blackwell, 1968. Authoritative political biography.

GRANT, M. *The Etruscans.* New York: Scribner's, 1980. Archaeological investigation of this mysterious people, for the general reader. See also P. M. OGILVIE, *Early Rome and the Etruscans* (Atlantic Highlands, N.J.: Humanities Press, 1976).

HARRIS, W. V. *War and Imperialism in Republican Rome, 327–70 B.C.* Oxford: Clarendon Press, 1979. Argues that Roman expansion was a deliberate policy rooted in the political ambitions of the Roman aristocracy.

HOPKINS, K. *Conquerors and Slaves.* New York: Cambridge University Press, 1978. Relations between owners of large estates and their work force.

KEPPIE, L. *The Making of the Roman Army: From Republic to Empire.* London: Botsford, 1984. The evolution of the Roman military machine.

LAZENBY, J. F. *Hannibal's War.* Warminster, England: Aris and Phillips, 1978. Geography, logistics, strategy and tactics. See also N. Bagnall, *The Punic Wars* (London: Hutchinson, 1991) for a military history of all three wars.

LEFKOWITZ, M. R., AND M. B. FANT. *Women in Greece and Rome.* Toronto: Samuel Stevens, 1977. Valuable overview of the lives of women in both societies. See also S. B. Pomeroy, *Goddesses, Whores, Wives, and Slaves: Women in Classical Antiquity* (New York: Schocken, 1975).

LIVY. *The Early History of Rome.* Translated by A. de Selincourt. Baltimore: Penguin, 1960. Readable modern translation of the patriotic early books of Livy's History.

MITCHELL, T. N. *Cicero, the Senior Statesman.* New Haven: Yale University Press, 1991. The defender of the Republic in his most influential years. See also his *Selected Political Speeches,* translated by M. Grant (Baltimore: Penguin, 1977).

NICOLET, C. *The World of the Citizen in Republican Rome.* Translated by P. S. Falla. Berkeley: University of California Press, 1980. Sees the citizen as an active participant in the life of the state.

SCULLARD, H. H. *A History of the Roman World, 753–146 B.C.* 4th ed. London and New York: Methuen, 1980. Old-fashioned narrative history at its best.

SEAGER, R. *Pompey: A Political Biography.* Berkeley: University of California Press, 1979. The struggle with Caesar from Pompey's point of view. See also A. KEAVENEY, *Sulla, the Last Republican* (London: Croom and Helm, 1982).

STAMBAUGH, J. E. *The Ancient Roman City.* Baltimore: Johns Hopkins University Press, 1988. Useful if sometimes idealized introduction.

STOCKTON, D. *The Gracchi.* New York: Oxford University Press, 1979. The reforming brothers seen against the social crisis of their times.

SYME, R. *The Roman Revolution.* London: Oxford University Press, 1967. Brilliant if still controversial interpretation of the Roman Civil War. For a more recent analysis, see M. BEARD and M. H. CRAWFORD, *Rome in the Late Republic* (Ithaca, N.Y.: Cornell University Press, 1985).

TAYLOR, L. R. *Party Politics in the Age of Caesar.* Berkeley: University of California Press, 1966. Classic study of political factions and tactics at the end of the Republic.

VANDERBROECK, P. J. J. *Popular Leadership and Collective Behavior in the Late Roman Republic (ca. 80–50 B.C.).* Amsterdam: J.C. Gieben, 1987. Sometimes debatable analysis of plebeian political activism.

WARDMAN, A. *Rome's Debt to Greece.* New York: St. Martin's Press, 1976. The impact of Greek culture, with attention to the ambivalence of Roman attitudes.

We move now from the period of the Roman Republic, dominated by the ruling classes and the Senate, into the period of the Empire, in which Rome was ruled by hereditary emperors. Romans always said they detested kings, and Augustus and his immediate successors were satisfied to be called *princeps*—"first citizen." The first two centuries of the Empire are technically called the *principate*, the period in which republican forms were preserved while in fact emperors ruled. The third century saw an anarchic period of warring generals and short-lived military emperors, rather like the Roman Civil War of the first century B.C. Following this near breakdown of central authority, Diocletian and Constantine reorganized the Empire in the fourth century, adopting more of the trappings of imperial state as a means of welding the Empire together.

The story of the revival of Rome under Augustus, the two centuries of peace that followed, the violent third-century breakdown, the fourth-century reconstruction, and the fifth-century A.D. decline and fall has an epic feel. It is an account of the triumph and decay of the only empire ever to rule the West. Our narrative also recounts the expansion of Western civilization northward into Europe beyond the Alps. During Roman times, this outreach remained rather tentative, with the Mediterranean continuing to be the center of the Western world. Following the fall of Rome, however, the center of historical gravity shifted definitively to the north in medieval times. Altogether, the history of Rome under the emperors spanned a half millennium of triumph and tragedy, in which the Romans completed the process of laying the ancient foundations for later Western history.

Young Girl with Stylus. First century A.D. Museo Nazionale, Naples, Italy

The Roman Peace

A visit to Pompeii is the best way to get a sense of life as it was lived in imperial Rome. This Roman provincial city of twenty thousand, located in southern Italy near Naples, was buried in an eruption of Mount Vesuvius in A.D. 79. Excavated in the nineteenth century, Pompeii's grid of streets, walls, and buildings lies in ruins, overgrown with weeds, yet it communicates the feel of life in Rome's golden age as no book can. An old market town in a prosperous agricultural area that exported wool, olive oil, and wine, the city was besieged by Sulla, flourished under Augustus, and disappeared under a rain of lava and ash at the height of the era known as the *Pax Romana,* the Roman Peace. You can walk today among its public squares and temples, its amphitheater, public baths, brothels, and taverns. Murals in the villas of the wealthy and election posters on public walls project a vivid impression of urban life in ancient Rome.

The two centuries that followed the triumph of Augustus, from 31 B.C. to A.D. 180, were in fact Rome's true golden age. During the first emperor's own reign, now known as the *Augustan Age*, the framework of the peace, prosperity, and civilization that followed was constructed. As we will see, some of the early emperors were tyrants or worse, but the Empire itself was well enough hammered together to survive even a Nero. By and large, it seems safe to say that the two hundred years from Augustus's triumph over his rivals in 31 B.C. through the reign of the philosopher-emperor Marcus Aurelius in the second century A.D. were not only the best of Roman times, but some of the best years the Western world has ever known.

Augustus and the Golden Age

The Roman world at the end of the Civil War, however, was a shambles; and it was as the rebuilder of Rome that Augustus Caesar would earn his distinguished place in history. He wasn't Augustus yet: a compliant Senate would vote him that title four years later. In 31 B.C. he was Octavian still, the thirty-two-year-old politician who had parlayed the Caesarian legacy and his own shrewdness and determination into total victory. An unpromising teenager when Julius Caesar died in his own blood on the floor of the Senate house, Octavian returned to Rome thirteen years later with an army of grim-faced veterans and the glint of a winner in his eye. He had never been any sort of general: his skilled commander Agrippa had done his fighting for him. But the challenges that Octavian faced now were political, constitutional, economic, and social, the kind of problems that he could handle very well.

To deal with the accumulated miseries of several generations of social dislocation and civil strife, Octavian had Julius Caesar's willingness to undertake sweeping reforms, modified by his own dozen years of experience and strong awareness of the need to preserve traditional forms. More practically, he

commanded an immense army and was extremely rich. And he had the war weariness of all Romans working for him. People longed for peace and order once more, even if it meant sacrificing something in the way of Roman liberties.

Octavian's first priority was to establish his own power on unshakable foundations. Over the next few years, he succeeded in maintaining his position as the only warlord left in the field after the Civil War by retaining command of the army and direct rule over Syria, Egypt, Gaul, and Spain. By pyramiding his civil offices, he also acquired enormous political power, including the imperium of the consul, the immunities and popular image of the tribune, and even the religious authority of the *pontifex maximus,* chief priest. By acquiring such honorific titles as *Augustus*—meaning "revered, blessed, and inspired ruler"—he added to his air of *auctoritas*, the prestige and confidence of the maximum leader.

Even as he built his own real power, however, Augustus piously preserved the forms of republican government so dear to the conservative Roman heart. Consuls, tribunes, and other magistrates continued to be elected, though not until the "first citizen" had endorsed their candidacies. The Senate and the assemblies continued to meet, but under the guidance of special steering committees chaired by Augustus and his followers. Decisions were issued as they always had been—By Order of the Senate and the Roman People—but they were decisions formulated in Augustus's home on the Palatine Hill.

Broader political reorganization was also necessary, however, to establish real order in the territorial empire the Romans had thrown together over the preceding two centuries. Augustus reshaped the Senate by replacing unindustrious patricians with vigorous "new men" from the equestrian order. To administer the state, he also appointed energetic equestrians to important posts and made much use of talented freedmen and slaves, the core of Rome's future professional bureaucracy. In the capital, he took steps to make the streets and tenements of the city safe by providing police and fire protection for the first time. In the provinces, he firmly asserted the right of Roman governors to enforce the laws, collect taxes, and defend the borders, but he supervised them much more closely to prevent extortion of the sort that had flourished under the Republic. A good deal of power, in fact, was left to traditional provincial authorities and ruling classes.

Augustus's economic reforms included new but fair taxes on land and other property based for the

	1 A.D.	100	200

POLITICAL, MILITARY, AND DIPLOMATIC EVENTS

31 B.C.–A.D. 180 Roman Peace	
r. 31 B.C.–A.D. 14 Augustus	
r. 14–37 Tiberius	
r. 41–54 Claudius	
r. 54–88 Nero	
97–180 "Five Good Emperors"	
r. 98–117 Trajan	
r. 117–138 Hadrian	
r. 161–180 Marcus Aurelius	
180–284 Third-Century Breakdown	
r. 193–211 Septimius Severus	

SOCIAL AND ECONOMIC DEVELOPMENTS

31 B.C.–A.D. 180 Economic Revival	
4 B.C.–A.D. 29/30 Jesus	
64 Nero's persecution	
d. about 67 Paul of Tarsus	
180–284 Economic Breakdown	

CULTURE: THE ARTS, PHILOSOPHY, SCIENCE AND RELIGION

70 B.C.–A.D. 19 Vergil	
65 B.C.–A.D. 19 Horace	
57 B.C.–A.D. 17 Livy	
43 B.C.–A.D. 18 Ovid	
31 B.C.–A.D. 14 Augustan Age	
5 B.C.–A.D. 65 Seneca	
55–115 Tacitus	
165–255 Origen	

first time on regular censuses of population and wealth. His great programs of public works and rebuilding after the long wars put large numbers of jobless plebeians to work, and he provided land allotments for one hundred thousand military veterans out of his own pocket. He improved the road system and established a sound imperial coinage to encourage trade. Beyond such basic measures, however, he kept economic regulation to a minimum. With order and confidence restored, the economic life of the Empire was soon booming again.

To protect the state he was reviving, the first Roman emperor deployed an enormous army of more than a quarter of a million men along 4,000 miles of frontier. He organized a volunteer army with a twenty-year term of enlistment, better pay, and a retirement bonus equal to more than half a soldier's earnings for his quarter century of service. Stationed in frontier fortresses, Roman soldiers also built roads, aqueducts, and other public works. In addition, Augustus founded the Praetorian Guard, nine thousand highly paid elite troops, one-third of whom served as an imperial bodyguard, a source of trouble for later rulers but a guarantee of order in Augustus's day.

Roman arms were not always victorious. The romanized German leader Arminius, for instance, shattered three legions in the Teutoburg forest during Augustus's last years. But for two centuries at least, Rome's legionaries generally defended the frontiers successfully.

Augustus also encouraged social and cultural reform and revitalization. He sponsored legislation against unduly luxurious living and in favor of decent treatment for slaves. He promoted laws that punished marital infidelity and supported marriage and the family. As high priest, he built scores of temples and encouraged the restoration of traditional religious practices. He allowed himself to be formally deified in the eastern provinces, which we have seen .

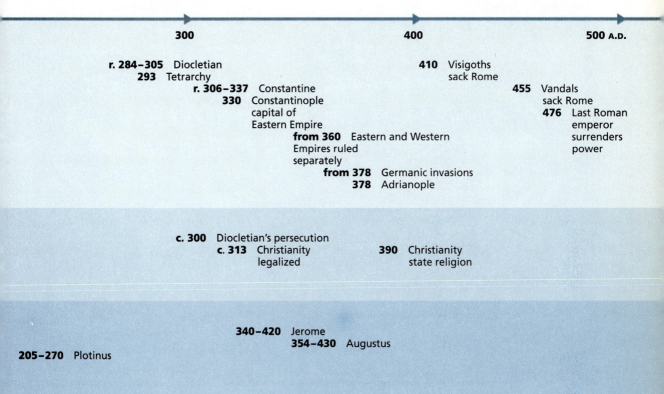

300		400		500 A.D.

r. 284–305 Diocletian
293 Tetrarchy
r. 306–337 Constantine
330 Constantinople
capital of
Eastern Empire
from 360 Eastern and Western
Empires ruled
separately
from 378 Germanic invasions
378 Adrianople

410 Visigoths
sack Rome
455 Vandals
sack Rome
476 Last Roman
emperor
surrenders
power

c. 300 Diocletian's persecution
c. 313 Christianity
legalized

390 Christianity
state religion

340–420 Jerome
354–430 Augustus
205–270 Plotinus

was customary with Hellenistic rulers. To show his enthusiasm for Greek culture, he had himself inducted into the Eleusinian mysteries and built a temple to Apollo outside his own home on the Palatine. In Rome, he set a high moral tone by his exemplary married life with his wife Livia. He patronized writers and artists and encouraged the poet Vergil to work on the *Aeneid*, his patriotic epic on the founding of Rome by the Trojan hero Prince Aeneas.

No wonder they voted him *pater patriae,* "father of his country," and praised him as "the savior of all mankind":

> For both land and sea are at peace, the cities are teeming with the blessings of concord, plenty, and respect for law, and the culmination and harvest of all good things brings fair hopes for the future and contentment with the present.[1]

Augustus has been seen as ruthlessly ambitious, which he surely was, and coldly hypocritical, which he probably was not. Physically unprepossessing, he yet developed the air of authority that impressed Romans. On his deathbed, after forty-five years in power, he is supposed to have asked those clustered round if he had acted his part well. The answer can only be yes. His legacy was the Pax Romana, the Roman Peace that would last for two hundred years.

The Dynasts of the First Century

The history of the first and second centuries A.D. may look a little seamy close up. Roman historians enjoyed collecting shocking stories about the scandalous lives of their rulers, and there were plenty of scandals to record. We will take a look at these rulers and the colorful lives they led at the top of the Roman Empire before turning to the more substan-

An altar dedicated to the "Roman Peace." The central figure is probably Ceres, goddess of grain and agricultural fertility. The two other large figures seem to represent the land and water over which Rome presides. Can you think of any familiar statue that represents "American Freedom" in the same symbolic way?

tial achievements of the Roman government as a whole during Rome's greatest age.

Two dynasties ruled the Empire for most of the century after Augustus's death in A.D. 14: the Julio-Claudians and the Flavians. Both ruling houses included more than their share of incompetent and even vicious leaders. The second century after Augustus, the period from 96 through the death of Marcus Aurelius in 180, was by contrast hailed as the era of the "five good emperors."

The dynasts of the first century A.D. established hereditary monarchy in all but name, passing on the power of imperium and the title of *imperator* (the source of our word "emperor") from one generation to the next within the ruling family. The half century after Augustus saw the reigns of four Julio-Claudian rulers of varying quality and character—Tiberius, Caligula, Claudius, and Nero—before the dynasty collapsed in the bloody rivalry of the "year of the four

emperors" in A.D. 69. Of the four Julio-Claudians who followed Augustus, only Claudius showed any of the qualities of Julius and Augustus Caesar. The next three decades were dominated by the even briefer Flavian dynasty, composed of the tough military commander Vespasian and his two sons Titus and Domitian. Though they usually still went through the motions of consulting the Senate and the traditional magistrates, all these men were autocrats, some of them as oppressive as any Eastern potentate.

Augustus's stepson Tiberius (r. A.D. 14–37) tried for a decade to imitate the *pater patriae* but thereafter fell victim to paranoia and debauchery at his notorious retreat on the isle of Capri in the Bay of Naples. Caligula (r. 37–41), quite possibly insane and undoubtedly tyrannical and incompetent, was assassinated after less than four unsettled years in power. Claudius (r. 41–54), though lame, afflicted with a speech impediment, and happiest when studying ancient history, proved a much more conscientious ruler. During his dozen years in power, he drained swamps, raised aqueducts, and built a seaport for the capital at Ostia. He followed Augustus in staffing an increasingly professional civil service with his own Greek freedmen and organized them into functional bureaus. He made a mistake, however, in marrying his niece Agrippina and adopting her son Nero as his heir. Claudius's subsequent death was probably engineered by his unscrupulous wife in order to raise her son to the throne.

The emperor Nero (r. A.D. 54–68) proved a feckless and dissolute young man whose only goals in life were to win public approbation as an athlete and a singer. For these purposes he opened a private chariot track and a private theater where he could practice his crafts before select audiences of servile flatterers. He also gave himself up to debauchery colorful enough to rival that of Tiberius or Caligula. One typically flamboyant "entertainment" was held on a fellow reveler's private lake, where the boats were fitted with gold and ivory, "their rowers were degenerates assorted according to age and vice," and the quays were lined with "brothels stocked with high-ranking ladies" and "naked prostitutes, indecently posturing and gesturing."[2]

Of the crimes most often charged against him, Nero probably was responsible for the murder of his mother five years after he came to the throne she had won for him. He did not set fire to the city and "fiddle while Rome burned," despite the rumors that he retired to his private stage to strum his lyre and sing of the destruction of Troy while his own capital burned around him. But he did try to pin the blame for the great fire of A.D. 64 on the secretive and unpopular Christian sect, executing large numbers of them to appease the people's need for scapegoats for this destructive conflagration.

The reign of Nero, however, was beset by still greater disasters. There were major rebellions in provinces as far apart as Britain and Palestine. In England, Queen Boudicca (d. A.D. 60), a towering red-haired woman furious at Roman treatment of her daughters and her country, led the Celtic tribes in a desperate, if ultimately unsuccessful effort to hurl the legions into the sea (see box, "Boudicca Fights for Freedom"). In Palestine, the Jews revolted against the Empire because of perceived challenges to their religious beliefs and wiped out a Roman garrison. When Spain and Gaul also proved unstable and Nero's own troops turned against him, he was deposed by the Senate and finally took his own life.

In the ensuing confusion, the "year of the four emperors" saw the commanders of four provincial armies compete to seize the throne by force. The survivor was Vespasian (r. A.D. 69–79), an efficient military man whose sons Titus (r. 79–81) and Domitian (r. 81–96) succeeded him. Vespasian was a no-nonsense autocrat who suppressed rebellions, further reduced the power of the Senate, and strengthened the authority of the *imperator*. Titus's short reign saw two disasters: the destruction of the temple

WAR AND PEACE
Boudicca Fights for Freedom

The Roman order did not always look so ideal from the conquered provinces as it did from Rome. In the following passage from Tacitus's (5 B.C.–A.D. 65) *Annals of Imperial Rome*, written half a century after the events, the British rebel leader Boudicca rallies her people to expel the Roman army of occupation. Her people pillaged, her daughters raped by Roman soldiers, Boudicca fought a bloody war of retribution, burning and looting Roman garrisons and cities. What effect does the fact that the Roman historian allows her to speak for herself and her cause in an oration to her troops have on you as a reader? Why do you think Tacitus quotes her?

"We British are used to woman commanders in war," she cried. "I am descended from mighty men! But now I am not fighting for my kingdom and wealth. I am fighting as an ordinary person for my lost freedom, my bruised body, my outraged daughters. Nowadays Roman rapacity does not even spare our bodies. Old people are killed, virgins raped. But the gods will grant us the vengeance we deserve! The Roman division which dared to fight is annihilated. The others cower in their camps, or watch for a chance to escape. They will never face even the din and roar of all our thousands, much less the shock of our onslaught. Consider how many of you are fighting—and why! Then you will win this battle, or perish. That is what I, a woman, plan to do!—let the men live in slavery if they will."

Source: Tacitus, *Annals of Imperial Rome*, trans. Michael Grant, in A. F. Scott, *The Roman Age: Every One a Witness* (London: Scott and Finlay, 1977), 43–44.

at Jerusalem during the suppression of a Jewish revolt and the disappearance of Pompeii in the eruption of Vesuvius. Domitian, finally, was another dictatorial paranoid, whose real enemies in the end struck him down in a palace coup.

The Five Good Emperors

By good fortune, a new pattern emerged in imperial politics during the second century A.D., the century of what are traditionally called the "five good emperors." As it happened most of the "good emperors" did not prove adept at producing biological heirs; they therefore adopted adult heirs to succeed them. The practice of imperial succession by adoption rather than by blood ties made it possible for reigning emperors to select and groom suitable successors to carry on their work. This procedure began following Domitian's assassination, when the Senate itself selected the first of these rulers, Nerva (r. A.D. 96–98). An elderly upright man without direct heirs, Nerva selected a famous general to succeed him. The four rulers who followed Nerva—Trajan, Hadrian, Antoninus Pius, and Marcus Aurelius—all proved extremely able and successful.

Trajan (r. A.D. 98–117), raised in Rome's Spanish provinces, won victories as far away as Dacia (Romania today), Mesopotamia, and Persia. A great builder, Trajan left monuments to his reign in a bridge across the Danube, a new city in Algeria, and a 100-foot column sculptured with his victories that can still be seen in Trajan's Forum in Rome today. Trajan also prepared his successor Hadrian for the awesome job he was to inherit by providing him with broad administrative experience.

Born in Spain like his mentor, educated at Rome, in love with Greek culture, and experienced in fighting the German barbarians, Hadrian (r. A.D. 117–138) was a man for all seasons. Over his twenty years as emperor, he undertook a number of reforms. He definitively reshaped the Augustan administrative system into a thoroughly professional civil service, including many career-minded equestrians. He encouraged the codification of the Roman laws, granted women equal legal status with men, and improved the legal condition of slaves. He also traveled the Empire, spending almost half his reign outside Italy in Britain, France, Spain, North Africa, and the Near East. He

Hadrian's Wall still winds across the countryside in the border country between England and Scotland, where it was originally designed to keep pre-urban tribes from overrunning the lands of the Roman Empire. Do you know of a great wall built in Asia for a similar purpose?

built such fortifications as "Hadrian's Wall," intended to keep the Scottish Celts out of northern England, and another line of defenses linking the fortified Rhine and Danube rivers to hold back the Germans. He also reorganized the border garrisons, requiring that most garrison troops be recruited in the provinces they were to defend.

Hadrian had his limitations as a ruler. He governed by decree, without even pro forma consultation with the Senate. His insensitive policies in Palestine triggered two Jewish revolts. Like his predecessors, he sponsored bloody gladiatorial shows to win popularity with the masses. Yet he was a man of wide culture, a serious administrator, and another great builder—the Roman Pantheon, the round temple to "All the Gods" that remains so remarkably preserved today, is mostly his work.

The reigns of the last two "good emperors," Antoninus Pius (r. A.D. 138–161) and the Stoic Marcus Aurelius (r. 161–180), are often considered together as four decades of exemplary rule. Antoninus Pius presided over one of the most peaceful periods in Roman history, Marcus Aurelius over one of the most prosperous. But pressures mounted in the latter's reign, so that the Stoic emperor spent years fighting on Rome's frontiers. His armies defeated the Parthian cavalry in Persia, but they also brought back a mysterious plague that caused many deaths in Europe. Toward the end of his reign, he had to face a potentially more dangerous threat on the Rhine-Danube frontier where he himself campaigned frequently against the Germans. Beset by many problems, Marcus Aurelius found in Stoicism both the strength to persevere while there was hope of success and the courage to accept inevitable setbacks when they came. His volume of *Meditations* has always been one of the most widely read of Stoic tracts.

Imperial Government: The Hub

Strong leaders, however, come only sometimes into any nation's history. What the Romans had in these first two centuries of the Empire was a system, an evolving political structure that could carry them through the profligates and tyrants, providing at least some degree of justice and prosperity no matter what scandalous behavior went on in the palaces on the Palatine or the imperial retreat on Capri.

To understand the new system of governance introduced by Augustus and developed by his successors, we have to look at two things: relations between the new emperors and the old ruling class, and the continuing development of the Roman governmental administration.

Much of the trouble at the center during the first century of the Roman Peace came from the mutual hostility of the emperors and the old senatorial ruling class. The senatorial elite continued for generations to dream and scheme for a restoration of what they thought of as "Roman liberties," meaning mostly their own right to run the Empire as the senatorial aristocracy of the Republic had done. The autocratic new order, however, which had been brought to power specifically by the failure of the old system, could not permit this. A destructive interaction thus emerged. The old elite whispered behind their hands and plotted in secret; the new rulers deployed their spies and ordered executions. Luxurious living and flagrant immorality, meanwhile, continued to infect both the imperial and senatorial elites.

By the second century A.D., however, this cycle had been largely broken. Most of the five good emperors not only chose their successors wisely but won their acceptance by the senatorial class, the army, and other segments of society. Succession was thus free of uncertainty and violence, and relations between the emperors and the ruling class became much easier. Meanwhile, the emperors had been building an imperial bureaucracy that took over much of the business of ruling and did it much more efficiently than it had been done under the Republic. The Augustan civil service had replaced many of the rapacious senatorial exploiters of the provinces with Octavian's slaves and freedmen or with ambitious equestrians who could be much more rigorously controlled. Under Claudius in the middle of the first century, another step was taken with the introduction of specialized bureaus charged with such functions as the administration of justice, finances, records, and correspondence. Under Hadrian, in the first half of the second century, hardworking equestrians became even more important in the civil service, and carefully graded career ladders in civil and military administration were opened up.

The result was an increasingly efficient system of government. The imperial bureaucracy maintained armies on the far frontiers and kept the huge capital city supplied with food from as far away as Egypt. It was the hub of a structure of increasingly uniform administration not to be matched in the West for many centuries.

Imperial Government: The Wheel

As important as the strength of the Roman central government was the length of its reach across the Roman world. The Roman Empire was the largest state the West had seen or would see again until the emergence of modern continental powers like the United States. This was also one of the few times in Western history that such a variety of peoples were brought together under a single Western government. When we add to the equation the advantages the Romans did *not* have, above all the technology that enables a modern state to function, their achievement becomes all the more astonishing.

If Rome was the hub, the Empire was the wheel. And the spokes that connected them included defense, politics, and social integration. The Roman

Empire continued to expand during the first two centuries of the imperial period. In Europe, it came to include not only England, France, Spain, and the Low Countries, but Austria and Switzerland and the central European and Balkan territories of modern Hungary, Yugoslavia, Romania, Bulgaria, Albania, and Greece. In the East, Rome ruled most of what is today Turkey, Syria, Israel, and Jordan, as well as parts of northern Mesopotamia. In Africa, Roman authority stretched from Egypt to Morocco, from the Nile to Gibraltar. The result was an empire of unprecedented size, still roughly centered on the Mediterranean but stretching from the North Sea to the Black Sea, from the Rhine-Danube line to the Sahara. The Roman Empire at its height was over 3 million square miles in area, approximately the size of the continental United States today, and had a population variously estimated at between 60 and 100 million people.

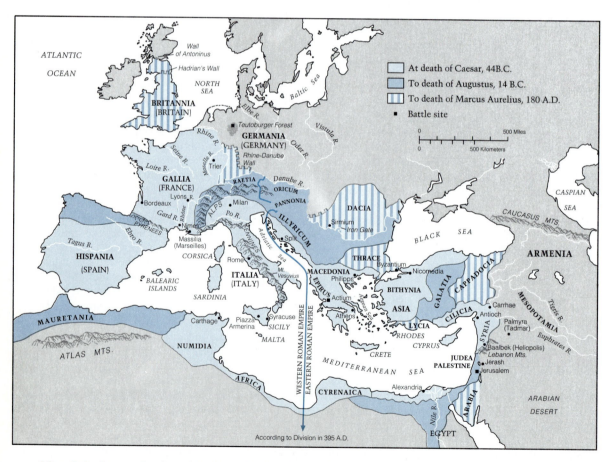

Map 6.1   Roman Territorial Holdings Under the Empire

The legions had conquered all this territory, and they defended it. The process of conquest was a brutal one, involving both bloody imperial wars and subsequent suppressions of rebellions. Massacres were perpetrated on both sides, and "barbarians" were sold as slaves in Rome in large numbers. In crushing Boudicca's revolt in Britain, the Romans—as a Roman commentator disgustedly put it—"made a desert and called it peace." The Jews on Mount Masada, during a bitter revolts preferred mass suicide to surrender to the Romans.

With the passing of the generations, however, areas firmly absorbed into the Empire became the beneficiaries of Roman military power. By the second century A.D., conquered peoples were beginning to staff the legions themselves, and all Roman subjects enjoyed security, relative prosperity, and generally less oppressive government than they had experienced before the Romans came.

The conquered lands were absorbed into the Roman political system as well. At first, traditional rulers were left largely in control of local affairs. As the Roman administration developed more real power, however, the old local elites were increasingly absorbed into the central imperial structure. The Roman Senate itself was slowly expanded to include senators from Gaul and Spain, from the Near East, and from North Africa, until by the second century A.D. half the Senate was provincial. Roman citizenship too was extended, slowly and grudgingly at first, but then more broadly. By 212, all freeborn subjects had both the rights and the obligations—such as paying taxes—of citizenship in the Empire.

Like other empire builders before them, the Romans tolerated a large degree of cultural diversity among their various subject peoples. Most Roman subjects worshiped their own gods, had their own social systems, and spoke their own languages. Among the wealthier and more educated elements of the provincial populations, however, a romanized stratum did evolve. The ruling classes of many lands came to dress like Romans, speak Latin, read Roman literature, and sponsor Roman-style chariot races and gladiatorial shows for the masses. The Roman Peace of the first two centuries A.D. thus became more than a matter of military protection and political administration: it generated the beginning of a common society as well.

The Pax Romana was the longest period of relative peace the Western world had yet known or would know again. The history of Europe, North Africa, and the Near East in modern times has been scarred by many terrible wars, climaxing in the world wars of the present century. When Roman legions guarded frontiers that reached from London to Constantinople, life was much more peaceful for a lot of people in between.

Decline and Fall

In the third century A.D., it all began to come apart. In the fourth, they shored it up again. But in the fifth century, the whole elaborate structure collapsed, and with it the ancient Western world. That, in three sentences, is the story to be told in the following pages. Explaining the disaster will require a more analytical approach—and more pages. Let us begin, however, with a brief survey of the events themselves.

The Third-Century Breakdown

During the third century A.D., an interwoven series of misfortunes battered the Roman Empire. Some of these, like the political collapse at the center and the first waves of foreign incursions, are clear enough on the record. Others, such as economic decline and social demoralization, have been largely brought to light by the researches of modern historians. Together, they add up to a near collapse of the Empire two centuries before that event actually took place.

The trouble began under the last of the five good emperors, Marcus Aurelius (A.D. 161–180). The Stoic emperor had to face barbarian assaults from the West and plague spreading from the Near East. His greatest misfortune, however, was to father a son. Since he had a natural heir, he broke with the second-century practice of nominating successors of proven ability, selecting instead his own son Commodus (180–192), the first of a disastrous line to follow. For neither Commodus nor most of his third-century successors proved worthy of their heritage.

One obvious symptom of this is the sudden multiplication in the numbers of emperors, from five in the second century to dozens in the third. Most of these very short-term rulers were generals who, in the old pattern of the Roman Civil War, bribed their troops to support them in a bid for power only to be toppled in a few years (or months) by new contenders. The Praetorian Guard, stationed in Rome itself, played a particularly active role in the making and unmaking of emperors.

Equally disturbing was the increase in the num-

This statue of the emperor Marcus Aurelius, one of the few equestrian statues to survive from ancient times, challenged Renaissance artists to do as well. Notice also that the entire mass is really balanced on only two of the horse's hooves.

plex of factors that we will explore shortly. And with all these disasters came the sort of social dislocation and psychological malaise that, though hard to footnote, can insidiously undermine an already weakened society.

Over the century between Marcus Aurelius's death in A.D. 180 and the accession of Diocletian, who would finally halt these debilitating trends, in 284, some competent rulers at least struggled to reestablish control. Septimius Severus (r. 193–211), a successful general from North Africa, strengthened both defense and administration, advancing equestrian administrators still further at the expense of the old senatorial elite. During and after his reign, Septimius Severus's wife and widow, Julia Domna, her sister Julia Maesa, and the latter's daughter Julia Mamaea had considerable power, sometimes exercised through unworthy male relatives, sometimes directly. They took charge of official correspondence, signed official decrees, and destroyed political opponents as ruthlessly as other third-century politicians.

Septimius Severus's successor Caracalla (r. A.D. 211–217) extended citizenship to almost all free inhabitants of the Empire and built the huge Baths of Caracalla in the capital. Aurelian (r. 270–275), hailed as "restorer of the world" during his brief reign, built new walls around the city of Rome, turned back Germanic invasions into Italy itself, and defeated the formidable Queen Zenobia (r. 267–272) of Palmyra, a Near Eastern metropolis of great wealth.

The best efforts of the Severans and of rulers like Aurelian, however, proved unable to stem the tide. Under pressure from within and without, the Roman Empire looked to be on the edge of final collapse as the third century stumbled toward its close.

ber of successful incursions by "barbarians." These invaders ranged from the thoroughly civilized people of the Sassanian Persian Empire in the East to Germanic tribes who had not yet learned to build cities or empires in the West. The Sassanians, able to face the Romans on a much more equal footing than the Parthians had, recaptured eastern Roman provinces taken from their predecessors. In A.D. 260 they even defeated and captured a Roman emperor. In central and western Europe, meanwhile, the hard-fighting if undisciplined Germanic tribes broke through the Roman defense lines to occupy the Balkan provinces and raid across the Rhine into Gaul.

Demographic and economic blows also rained down on the Empire. Though reliable statistics are few, there seems to have been a sharp population decline in the third century A.D. This was apparently due as much to foreign and civil wars as to recurring bouts of what may have been bubonic plague, an Asian killer that would return even more devastatingly at the end of the Middle Ages. Economic production also went down at this time, due to a com-

Fourth-Century Restructuring

Two remarkable emperors finally brought recovery in the decades around A.D. 300. Diocletian (r. 284–305) and Constantine (r. 312–337) reassembled at least a facsimile of the old system that held for another century. Both share responsibility for the establishment of this later Roman Empire; indeed, it is often not certain which of them instigated which reform during the half century bracketing the year 300. Both were dedicated to rigorously authoritarian rule and rigid social conservatism. Diocletian, who usually gets the lion's share of the credit, was a Balkan provincial who had risen through the army. He imprinted his personality on the time by building huge imperial palaces and by transforming the imperial government at last into a full-fledged Eastern monarchy. Diocletian received prostrate petitioners in elaborate silken robes heavy with gold and jewels, gold dust gleaming in his hair, wearing the purple boots that would thereafter be the symbols of imperial authority. Constantine, who fought his way to power, was considerably more of a military man than his predecessor. He is best remembered for two historic acts: legalizing the Christian church after three centuries of intermittent persecution, and founding the city of Constantinople on the Straits connecting the Mediterranean with the Black Sea. Both events had immense consequences for the history of the Middle Age, the next stage of Western history.

These two men faced successively the host of problems produced by the third-century breakdown. They tackled them in the tried and tested imperial manner, beginning at the center. But they carried the imperial solution—more power to the center—further than any of their predecessors had dreamed of doing.

Diocletian's original solution, usually called the *Tetrarchy* ("Rule of Four") seemed at first to involve a division of power rather than further centralization. To protect the buckling frontiers, four imperial rulers divided primary responsibility among them: two senior rulers called Augusti and two Caesars, co-rulers and heirs apparent to the older men. This system, however, collapsed in Constantine's day into a four-way struggle, from which he emerged as sole ruler in A.D. 324.

More important was the great expansion and elaboration of the imperial administration. Under Diocletian and Constantine, the historic provinces were replaced by a system of four large prefectures, twelve dioceses, and ninety-six much smaller provinces. A hierarchic administration beginning with a group of imperial advisers comparable to a modern cabinet spread down through a bewildering array of grades and specializations to the local level. Among the new civil servants were numbers of spies and government agents who would be called secret policemen in a later century.

An important feature of the system was the division of civil from military authority, intended, like the subdivision of the old provinces, to prevent provincial military commanders from acquiring political power. The army itself was also reformed once more. Now staffed almost entirely with provincials, it was subdivided between fixed garrisons and mobile

This monumental head of the Emperor Constantine once topped a colossal thirty-foot statue long since broken in pieces. The broad face represents a later Roman symbolic style of sculpture. The simplified planes perhaps also reflect the fact that, when the head was in place on the huge body, the face would have been seen from far below.

units poised to reinforce them. Heavily armored cavalry began to usurp the central place once granted to the infantry phalanx. In numbers, the army of the later Empire approached and may have exceeded the half-million mark.

To support the top-heavy new bureaucracy and army with which they proposed to restore order and security, Diocletian and Constantine attempted social and economic regulation so rigid that it has been called totalitarian. Some of it, including a misguided attempt at price regulation that sparked riots in the cities, had to be abandoned. But serious and sometimes painfully successful efforts were made to fix everyone in a hereditary economic slot—peasants to stay on the large estates, carpenters to ply their fathers' trade. Equally unpopular were regulations that forced people of substance to accept local government appointments their ancestors would have been honored to receive. In both cases, the primary goal was to establish a firm tax base for the expanded administration and defense establishment, as well as for the dazzling new round of imperial building that announced the new Rome to the world.

Fifth-Century Collapse

It was a good try, and for the bulk of the fourth century A.D. the new authoritarianism seemed to be holding the Empire more or less together and keeping potential invaders out. But there was plenty of instability in the later 300s, and in the next century the Empire crumbled.

Despite Constantine's reestablishment of rule by a single emperor, the east-west division of authority and responsibility reasserted itself soon after his death. The job was simply too big for one man, and there was no lack of candidates for the imperial purple. From the 360s on, therefore, there were frequently separate emperors for the western and eastern halves of the Empire, one centered at Rome, the other at Constantinople. Imperial authoritarianism continued to be capricious and cruel and exactions of imperial officials oppressive, undermining the people's political faith and draining their economic wealth. As a result, the political decline of the Roman Empire was far advanced before the climactic round of barbarian invasions got under way.

That round began, not on the European frontiers of the Empire, but far away on the steppes of Asia, where restless nomads were on the move once more. The triggering event was the westward thrust of a Mongol people called the Huns, who had reached the region north of the Black Sea in the fourth century A.D. and pushed on into Europe in the fifth. This mounting pressure from the East, furthermore, set the Germans on the Roman borders into motion in their turn. In the fifth century, both the Huns and the much more numerous Germans breasted and broke through the frontiers of the Western world.

They were two very different peoples. The Huns were pastoral nomads from the Asian grasslands who lived on their horses and were furious cavalry fighters. The Germanic peoples—Goths, Franks, Vandals, Saxons, and others—were village-dwelling forest tribes who inhabited much of Europe east of the Rhine and north of the Danube. More will be said of the Germanic peoples in the early Middle Ages and of the Mongols when they returned toward the end of the medieval period. For now, we need only consider the invasion of the Roman Empire, which brought the ancient history of the Western world to an end.

The term *invasion,* however, which raises an image of marching armies bristling with spears, seriously misrepresents what actually happened. These intruders came not as conquering armies, but as migrating peoples—women and children, wagons and flocks, as well as men with weapons. Some of these intruders had been infiltrating the Empire for centuries, coming to live and work in the civilized zone. What took place in the latter part of the fourth century, the fifth century, and the earlier sixth century A.D. was rather the cresting of a wave of migration than a sudden assault. Nevertheless, these massive incursions were accompanied by battles and plundering. And they did undermine Roman institutions and ways of life the Romans had introduced into Europe over the preceding four hundred years.

In this chapter, we simply outline the collapse of the political structure of the Roman West under the weight of the Germanic invasions. The long-term impact of these barbarian intrusions into western Europe must wait until the next chapter, when we look at the new order that slowly emerged.

The first major breakthrough came in the Eastern Empire in the 370s, when a Germanic people called the Visigoths, driven from their own lands west of the Black Sea by the invading Huns, sought sanctuary inside the Roman defense lines. Admitted to the Empire and then unmercifully exploited by Roman soldiers and officials, the Visigoths revolted. In 378 they defeated a Roman army and killed the Eastern Roman emperor in the Battle of Adrianople, only 100 miles or so from Constantinople itself. It was the beginning of a century of barbarian triumphs.

Arrows on a map show the confusion of the folk wanderings that followed. The Visigoths themselves pillaged their way across the Balkans and down into Italy, where in A.D. 410 their leader Alaric shocked the Roman world by plundering Rome itself. From Italy, the Visigoths turned back north and west once more, crossing Gaul to found a Visigothic kingdom in what had been Roman Spain. Further to the north, the Vandals, also jarred loose from their ancestral lands in eastern Europe by the Huns, crossed Germany, burst through the Roman frontiers, and moved on through Gaul, Spain, and the Straits of

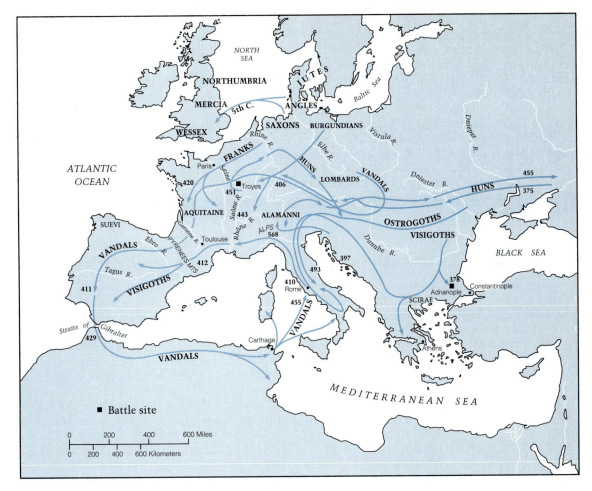

Map 6.2   Germanic Invasions of the Roman Empire

Gibraltar to establish a Vandal kingdom in North Africa, around Roman Carthage. From this base, they crossed the narrow waist of the Mediterranean to sack Rome yet again in 455. When the Romans withdrew their legions from Britain to deal with these disasters, Saxons from north Germany and Angles and Jutes from Denmark crossed the Channel in increasing numbers to invade southeastern England, where a new scattering of Germanic kingdoms soon appeared.

The Huns themselves, meanwhile, after pausing on the Danube plain, moved on into Roman Europe under the leadership of Attila (r. 434–453), who soon became known to the partially Christianized West as "the Scourge of God." Turned back by Roman troops in Gaul, the Huns headed south into Italy to pillage the rich heartland of the Empire and to camp threateningly within sight of the walls of Rome. A plague that decimated their numbers as well as Attila's own death finally turned them back into Asia. Within decades, however, they were succeeded in Italy by more Germanic peoples. And in A.D. 476 the last Western Roman emperor, a youth named Romulus Augustulus, surrendered power to the German mercenary Odoacer (c. 433–c. 493), who became the first Germanic king of Italy.

There were others still to come. The hosts of Theodoric the Ostrogoth (c. 454–526) soon entered from the east and became masters of Italy in the 490s. The Lombards followed in the next century, and the region of Lombardy in northern Italy is called after them still. In the north, two powerful tribes of

Franks pushed into northern Gaul and defeated the last Roman governor in the 480s. The Franks established the most powerful of the Germanic kingdoms in Gaul, which came to be called France after these conquerors.

The Eastern Roman Empire, with its capital at Constantinople, survived the fall of the Western Empire. Traditionally, however, the passing of the last Roman emperor of the West in 476 has been considered to mark the end of the Roman imperium that had begun to take shape almost a thousand years before, and with it the end of the domination of the evolving West by the ancient civilizations of Greece and Rome.

Why Did Rome Fall?

Historians are concerned not just to find out what happened in the past, but to figure out why. They have learned, furthermore, that to understand a major historical event such as a great war or a revolution one must look, not for one cause, but for a complex of interrelated historical events and conditions that together brought about the event under consideration. An event as awesome as the collapse of Rome and the end of the ancient world has given historians plenty of food for debate. These scholarly disputes have produced a long list of likely causes — as well as some cogent objections to many of them.

Clearly, for instance, there were military causes for the fall of Rome. The Germanic invasions, sparked by the Hunnish intrusion from the East, broke through the frontiers and fragmented the Western Empire politically. But there had been pressure on the frontiers before: why did the Roman army fail this time? There are technical explanations, including settling the troops too comfortably into the local population and assigning them too many nonmilitary functions, from contract work for the army to subsistence farming and herding for themselves. There also seems to have been more activity among the nomadic peoples of inner Eurasia than there had been for some centuries, a new testing of Roman defenses that a weaker Empire failed. An older, less convincing contention is that non-Italian legions lacked Roman skills or commitment to Rome. But there were many successful German, Balkan, and other provincial commanders, and Roman blood did not confer a monopoly on courage or military skill.

Political causes are also easy to point to, though some of these too are doubtful. During the last century of their history, as we have seen, Roman emperors became noticeably more authoritarian and withdrawn as a matter of policy. Officials also grew increasingly oppressive, rapacious, and numerous, and there was an almost totalitarian effort to fix society in rigid social patterns. These policies may have undermined popular dedication to the defense of a realm that must have looked as tyrannical to many as the barbarian alternatives. Yet the staffing of the bureaucracy with efficient if sometimes officious Greeks and Near Easterners seems unconvincing as a cause of political decline. It was, as we shall see, precisely the Near Eastern Greek-speaking half of the Empire that survived.

Many twentieth-century historians have been particularly interested in the part played in human affairs throughout history by economic forces. Certainly economic and social factors contributed significantly to the disastrous decline of the Roman Empire. Increased taxation to support a top-heavy bureaucracy and an enormous military establishment undoubtedly drained the Empire economically. Government exactions that drove peasants to flee left land unworked, while tax penalties for success may have discouraged the growth of a productive middle class. The tendency of poor farmers to seek the protection of a powerful landowner, on whose lands they accepted the serflike status of *coloni,* tended to break the Empire up into local economic units at the expense of the larger imperial economy and the state it supported.

More fundamental economic difficulties may have been rooted in Rome's heavy dependence on slave labor, which discouraged technological development. An abundance of manpower made labor-saving devices a low priority in the ancient West. The fact that slaves did much of the handicraft manufacturing and other work in the cities may also have inhibited the growth of a business middle class. A system based heavily on slavery, furthermore, would have faced a dangerous labor shortage when wars of conquest, which brought in plenty of slaves, were replaced by less profitable defensive struggles on the frontiers. Although there were many free farmers and a middle class that included many freedmen, this economic deterioration surely helps to explain the overall decline of the Empire.

What we may term ecological causes, often closely related to the state of the economy, have also been adduced. Thus droughts, climatic variations, and overworked land may have contributed significantly to shrinking agricultural productivity. The plague and other epidemic diseases may help to explain the decline in the Roman population that apparently took place, though the Germanic invaders, dependent on primitive small-scale agriculture and pastoralism, undoubtedly remained much less numerous than the Romans. The claim that use of lead-lined vessels for food and water by the aristocracy led to slow sterilization and decline in the size of the ruling classes has not found widespread acceptance, since such vessels were also used in the Eastern Roman Empire, which survived handily.

Some writers have suggested that moral or ethical decline contributed heavily to the failure of the Roman Empire. For example, many have asserted that the Roman aristocracy was fatally undermined by luxurious living and debauchery. As we have seen, however, such practices were common among some elements of the Roman elite even during Rome's golden age, making it unlikely that they were a determining factor in the Empire's collapse. Another frequently cited source of moral decline, in this case among the lower classes, is "bread and circuses," the provision of free food and entertainment for tens of thousands of Rome's jobless tenement dwellers. Though this policy may have undermined a sense of public responsibility and stifled initiative, even the most enfeebled ward of the government might have felt some impulse to defend the state that provided the bread and circuses.

Still another much-debated source of diminishing concern for the survival of the Empire is the rise of Christianity. Edward Gibbon, in his classic eighteenth-century account of *The Decline and Fall of the Roman Empire,* was one of the first to allege that the new religion drew intelligent energetic leaders away from the declining state to the rising church. The Christian faith may also have turned some people's minds from this world to the next, leaving them unconcerned for the salvation of the earthly kingdom, since eternal salvation in the heavenly kingdom lay ahead. Some early Christians and Jews did refuse both military service and the requirement that citizens express allegiance to the ruler by throwing incense on the altar of the emperor's "genius." Again, however, the Eastern Roman Empire, which became as strongly Christian as the Western Empire, found leaders and soldiers enough to preserve it for ten more centuries. Nor, as we will see in later chapters, did Christian belief inhibit the development of an aggressively military ruling class in medieval Europe.

One of Gibbon's broadest assertions about the decline and fall, finally, has considerable appeal, though it would certainly be hard to document. This is the suggestion that the Empire as a whole was simply too large to survive. It had too much land, too many people to rule and defend. It devoured its resources on an unprecedented scale and had not the technical means to replenish them. A dinosaur among the nations, the Roman Empire simply fell of its own weight. The problem, as Gibbon pointed out, was not to explain the decline and fall of the Empire, but to understand how it lasted as long as it did.

Roman Achievements

The social and cultural achievements of imperial Rome were in many ways more impressive than those of the Republic. Through the first two centuries, especially, the Roman Empire achieved a remarkable level of economic productivity, social stability, and intellectual and artistic accomplishment. There was a scale, a sense of grandeur to Roman literature, sculpture, architecture, and engineering that is every bit as impressive as the cultural scintillation of the Greeks before them. And the international economy fostered by Roman rule, the majestic edifice of the Roman law had few parallels in Western history.

Economic Expansion

The economic life of the Empire followed the pattern of its political evolution, booming under Augustus and the "good emperors," declining as the Empire did thereafter. It was the framework of Roman rule, after all, that made prosperity possible. Thanks to Roman legions on the frontiers, the network of Roman roads across Europe, and the protected sea lanes crisscrossing the Mediterranean, farmers, artisans, and merchants could carry on their business in safety and confidence. The whole of western Europe and the Mediterranean basin became a vast integrated economy.

The energies of all the Roman peoples were thus unleashed in a surge of productivity and ex-

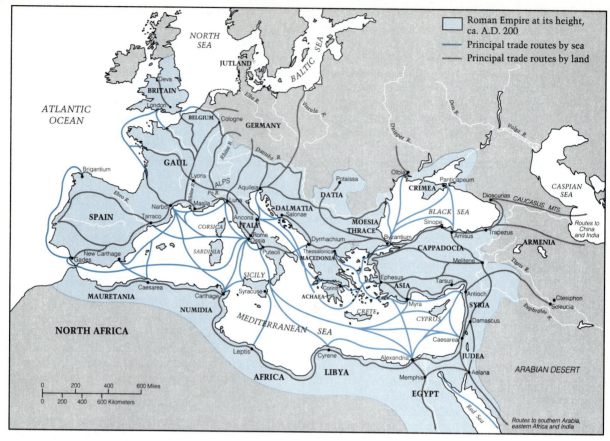

Map 6.3 Roman Economic Development

change. Across seas scoured of pirates, over stone roads maintained by legionaries flowed the wealth of the Empire. Grain, fruit, oil, and wine; marble, metals, timber, wool, and other raw materials; pottery, glassware, textiles of all sorts, tools, weapons, utensils, sculpture, jewelry now circulated freely around the Roman world.

This integrated Western economy also reached out beyond the Western world to import goods from farther south and east. Trade goods came up the Nile from inner Africa, or across the Sahara on Bedouin camels. As many as 120 ships a year left Egypt for India by way of the Red Sea and the Indian Ocean; Near Eastern merchants brought goods from China along the Asian caravan trail called the Great Silk Road. From Africa came wild beasts for the arenas, ivory, gold, papyrus, purple dye, and the crystalline stone called porphyry. From Asia came spices, cottons, and precious stone from India, silks and porcelain from Han China, metals

and textiles from the Near East. The Asian imports in particular represented a substantial drain on Rome's supply of gold and silver, an unfavorable balance of payments with the East that worried some Roman commentators.

Most Romans lived on farms, but cities were more numerous than ever before. On the agricultural side, the huge estates called *latifundia*, established during the Republic, continued under the Empire. Aristocratic landowners stressed diversified agriculture on these plantations, combining olive trees and fruit orchards, grape vines and pasture for cattle and sheep. They largely abandoned commercial grain production to Sicily and Egypt.

The competition of the huge latifundia tended to drive small farmers out of business and into the cities. The Roman Peace, however, had meant fewer wars, hence fewer captives to provide slave labor. As a result, many estates shifted to tenant farming. In the later Empire, tenant farmers on self-sufficient estates called *villas* accepted the serflike status of *coloni*. Bound to the land if not to the landowner, *coloni* received the protection of the landlord in a time when the government no longer seemed able to guarantee security. It seems likely that the isolated self-sustaining manor of medieval times evolved from the villa, which made little effort to produce for the larger market.

Urban living, however, remained the ancient ideal, and cities spread far across western Europe under the protection of Rome. The towns of the western parts of the Empire were small but numerous. Army garrisons, market towns, administrative and later ecclesiastical centers, they rose across Spain, France, England, and elsewhere north of the Alps, at the same time continuing to develop around the Mediterranean. It was possible in Hadrian's day to find a Roman magistrate or a regulated marketplace, to see a play or a gladiatorial contest anywhere from North Africa to northern England.

In the older parts of the civilized Mediterranean zone, cities were much larger, wealthier, and more cultured. Metropolises like Alexandria and Carthage in North Africa and Antioch, Ephesus, and later Constantinople in the Near East held populations of hundreds of thousands of people. Rome itself may

---

THE HUMAN SPIRIT   The Perils of the Roman Streets

The second-century A.D. satiric poet Juvenal was less concerned with Roman ideals than with Roman realities. His *Third Satire: Against the City of Rome,* quoted here, describes the bustling sprawling city on the Tiber, not as it looked from an elegant house on the Palatine Hill but as experienced by an ordinary citizen who had to fight his way through the streets. Do you think Roman streets were more or less crowded than our own? More or less dangerous?

Here in town the sick die from insomnia mostly.
Undigested food, on a stomach burning with ulcers,
Brings on listlessness, but who can sleep in a flophouse?
Who but the rich can afford sleep and a garden apartment?
That's the source of infection. The wheels creak by on the narrow
Streets of the wards, the drivers squabble and brawl when they're stopped . . .

When his business calls, the crowd makes way as the rich man,
Carried high in his car, rides over them, reading or writing,
Even taking a snooze, perhaps, for the motion's composing.
Still, he gets where he wants before we do; for all of our hurry
Traffic gets in our way, in front, around, and behind us.

Somebody gives me a shove with an elbow, or two-by-four scantling.
One clunks my head with a beam, another cracks down with a beer keg.
Mud is thick on my shins, I am trampled by somebody's big feet.
Now what?—a soldier grinds his hobnails into my toes . . .

Look at other things, the various dangers of nighttime.
How high it is to the cornice that breaks, and a chunk beats my brains out,
Or some slob heaves a jar, broken or cracked, from a window . . .
There your hell-raising drunk, who has had the bad luck to kill no one,
Tosses in restless rage, like Achilles mourning Patroclus,
Turns from his face to his back, can't sleep, for only a fracas
Gives him the proper sedation. But any of these young hoodlums,
All steamed up on wine, watches his step when the crimson
Cloak goes by, a lord, with a long, long line of attendants,
Torches and brazen lamps, warning him, *Keep your distance!*
Me, however, whose torch is the moon, or the feeblest candle
Fed by a sputtering wick, he absolutely despises . . .

Source: Juvenal, *Third Satire: Against the City of Rome,* in *The Satires of Juvenal,* trans. Rolfe Humphries (Bloomington: Indiana University Press, 1958), 42–44.

have harbored a cosmopolitan population of one million. It was in these older cities, and particularly in the city of Rome itself, that imperial splendors were most profusely and massively on display.

Social Life Under the Empire

Social life in Rome, the capital of the Western world, was as varied and colorful, corrupt and fascinating as that of any metropolis of later times. Upper and lower classes, men and women, for all their differences, shared many of the pleasures and problems of urban living. (On some problems, see box, "Perils of the Roman Streets.")

For the lower orders, problems included such basics as housing, food, and employment. Compelled by poverty to live in overcrowded tenement buildings, the Roman masses took advantage of the warm Mediterranean climate to spend much of their time in the city's bustling streets. We have pictures of them drinking and gambling with dice, and in the ruins of Pompeii and Herculaneum, we can see the roofless remains of food stalls and cafes where ordinary citizens found refreshment. For main meals, food staples were provided at government expense in a grain dole that expanded to include free cooking oil and wine. Employment, however, the Romans never managed to generate for much of the idle urban populace. These dangerous classes were therefore kept fed and entertained, the "bread and circuses" many governments have found it expedient to offer people not absorbed by the economy.

By way of entertainment, emperors and other wealthy citizens sponsored costly public spectacles. Instead of the intellectually demanding plays put on in ancient Athens, Roman entertainments favored bloody gladiatorial conflicts and spectacular chariot races. Tens of thousands swarmed into the Colosseum, the model for all such sports stadiums since, to watch professional gladiators, prisoners of war, slaves, and condemned criminals fight each other to the death. Even larger numbers flooded the Circus Maximus to watch two- and four-horse chariots race around a 5-mile track and honored winning drivers as the Greeks had Olympic athletes, with cheers, gifts, and public monuments.

The Roman upper classes, the patricians and equestrians, enjoyed an even more exciting social life than had their precursors of the late Republic. There were still theaters in which those with a more sophisticated taste might see tragedies and comedies of the sort described in the previous chapter. A major import from Greece were public baths, huge buildings including hot and cold pools, steam rooms, gymnasiums, and refreshment booths, with separate areas for men and women. Banquets and dinner parties also grew in popularity among the upper classes. In these gatherings, men and women shared soft couches, gourmet meals prepared by foreign chefs, musical and other entertainment, wine, and conversation.

Wealthy women seem to have lived more pleasant, luxurious lives than they had even in the late Republic. They could own large amounts of property in their own right, and their husbands were often pleased to have them show off their wealth. Divorce, more difficult under Augustus, became easier later. From statues, histories, and the writings of Roman satirists, we have a vivid picture of conspicuous consumption under the Empire. Wives and daughters of great houses dressed in imported silks and expensive jewelry, carefully made up with cosmetics, unguents, and perfumes, spending hours having their hair dressed in the latest fashion in order to be properly dazzling at the banquet, the theater, or the reserved seat in the amphitheater.

Roles for upper-class women in the more serious world included social and cultural patronage and important functions in a number of the religious cults. Wealthy women, like wealthy men, earned popular acclaim and social prestige by subsidizing public entertainments or feasts, or by erecting monuments and even temples. Many daughters of good families seem to have been educated, either with their brothers or separately, and some of these women became patrons of literature and the arts. Julia Domna (c. 167–217), daughter of a Syrian high priest and wife of the emperor Septimius Severus, surrounded herself with artists and intellectuals and was herself called "Julia the Philosopher." In the religious sphere, the worship of the many female divinities was in women's hands. Particularly important was the worship of Vesta, goddess of the hearth, whose imperial shrine was tended by the Vestal Virgins, women of unrivaled prestige in Rome. A number of the foreign goddesses worshiped in the Empire, including Isis and Cybele, had female priests, as did Fortuna, the all-important incarnation of good luck.

Roman Law

A major achievement of Roman society was the impressive edifice of the Roman law. Shaped slowly

On this elegant Roman tomb, a mother and child await food brought to them by a servant. Note the details of furniture and clothing, the woman's elaborately dressed hair, and the pet animals, all indications of wealth and a comfortable family life.

over centuries in typically conservative Roman fashion, it constitutes an important part of the Roman legacy.

The oldest Roman laws, the famous Twelve Tables, had been officially published in the fifth century B.C., at the beginning of the recorded history of the Republic. As the Roman Empire grew, however, interacting with other nations and acquiring subject peoples of many nationalities, these original laws proved increasingly inadequate. Changes were therefore gradually introduced. This process took place particularly during the period between the second century B.C., the time of the Gracchan reforms, and the second century A.D., when Hadrian's codification of the laws slowed the process of change appreciably.

New laws and legal principles were added through three procedures. Especially under the Republic, legislation passed by the Roman assemblies provided new laws. During the imperial period, the decrees of successive emperors acquired the force of law. And throughout Roman history, the pronouncements of magistrates and legal experts reshaped the law generation by generation. Thus the edict issued by the praetor, the government's chief legal officer, summed up the legal principles he would follow during his term of office. Even more

influential were the opinions of jurisconsults, legal advisers to magistrates, whose informed judgments carried great weight in Rome.

Through legislative action, imperial decree, and the pronouncements of legal authorities, then, Roman law changed to meet its growing and increasingly complex obligations. These changes were influenced by both the specific legal traditions of subject peoples and the thinking of Greek philosophers on law in general. Roman magistrates often had to deal with legal disputes between subject peoples of widely differing Asian, African, and European customs and traditions. To adjudicate in such instances, the Romans developed some general principles called *ius gentium,* "law of the peoples," many of which eventually came to be applied to Roman citizens as well. These general principles, originally compromise attempts at fairness, were in time philosophically undergirded by the view of Greek Stoics that there exists an *ius naturale,* "natural law," transcending mere human legislation. This was conceived of as a higher law, derived from the indwelling rational principle that Stoics believed gave order to the cosmos. This natural law, no less a Roman lawyer than Cicero believed, should be basic to any human legal system.

To these foreign challenges and inspirations, finally, should be added the powerful Roman sense of equity. Justice—not mercy, but basic fairness—was a fundamental Roman value: "Let justice be done," the Roman legal maxim ran, "though the heavens fall." The resulting system, as we shall see, became a cornerstone of Western legal codes and thought in both medieval and modern times.

Literature and History

The two greatest ages of Roman culture stand back to back in the late Republic and the early Empire. The Augustan Age that followed Octavian's victories was marked by a surge of patriotic enthusiasm for Augustus's effort to rebuild the shattered Empire. Thereafter, however, as the later emperors and the Roman people themselves failed to live up to the Augustan promise, a somber and even cynical note became increasingly evident in Roman thought and art. Vergil, the greatest of Roman poets, and Livy, Rome's most inspiring historian, illustrate the enthusiasm of the earliest Empire; other poets, historians, and philosophers express the later mood.

Vergil—Publius Vergilius Maro (70–19 B.C.)—earned his place in cultural history with one great poem, his epic of Rome's mythic beginnings, the *Aeneid*. A sensitive, immensely gifted country squire, Vergil wrote other poems, including his *Georgics*, a celebration of the simple country life that sophisticated urban Romans loved to read about. But he spent the latter part of his life writing the story of the hero Aeneas in majestic hexameter verse. The *Aeneid* was clearly inspired by Homer's epics, but it is in many ways a much more polished literary production than the vigorous early Greek original. The poem of Rome's founding was also encouraged by Augustus himself, who could see the value of a good patriotic epic at this stage.

The *Aeneid*, read in Latin classes to this day, narrates the adventures of the Trojan prince Aeneas, whom most Romans believed to have been their earliest ancestor. Vergil follows his hero's wanderings over the Mediterranean in search of a new home after the fall of Troy and his struggle for a place in Italy for himself and his descendants. In one famous episode, the future founder of Rome has a tragic love affair with Dido, queen and founder of Carthage—which in later centuries became Rome's greatest foe. In another, Aeneas journeys through the underworld of the dead, where his father's spirit pre-

dicts Rome's future greatness as ruler of the Western world. Throughout the *Aeneid*, Roman readers felt the powerful presence of a hero with a Roman sense of mission. Augustus hoped they would be moved to develop a similar sense of dedication in their own times.

Vergil's contemporary Horace (65–19 B.C.) was actually a late convert to the Augustan Empire, having fought for years on the side of the Republic. His poems praised Augustus and Roman virtues like courage and friendship, while satirizing the lives of less noble Romans. They also demonstrated a rare mastery of poetic form that has stirred the admiration of Latin scholars and later poets ever since.

Livy's *History of Rome*, also inspired by Augustus's triumph, is quite a different production from the Greek histories of Herodotus and Thucydides. Like Herodotus, Livy (57 B.C.–A.D. 17) was celebrating a great national achievement; but unlike his Greek predecessors, he attempted to cover, not a single recent event, but the whole history of his country. Drawing on existing historical accounts as well as on myths and legends, he set out to narrate in many volumes the whole story of Rome's rise to mastery of the Mediterranean world. Like Vergil, however, Livy focused on earlier times—in Livy's case on the early days of the Republic, when, he believed, civic pride and patriotism had flourished. His hope was that remembering the achievements of the founding fathers might rekindle virtue and love of country in Romans of his own age.

There were too many rulers like Nero among the next few emperors, however, and the luxury and corruption of the Roman elite seemed as flagrant as ever. Among the writers who responded to this side of the history of the first and second centuries A.D. were the poet Ovid, the historian and moralist Tacitus, and the playwright and philosopher Seneca.

Ovid (43 B.C.–A.D. 18), only a generation younger than Vergil, was born too late to take the aging Augustus seriously. Ovid's *Metamorphoses*, retelling in urbane verse many of the ancient myths (especially those involving supernatural transformations), has been a mine of Roman mythology ever since. His poetry often had a flippant, cynical ring, particularly his most widely read work, *The Art of Love*. This guide to the fine art of seduction in imperial Rome got him peremptorily exiled for the rest of his life to the remotest Black Sea outpost Augustus could come up with.

Seneca (5 B.C.–A.D. 65), a leading philosophical, literary, and political figure of the middle of the first century, had the frustrating experience of trying to tutor the future tyrant Nero in the path of Stoic virtue. An eclectic Stoic philosopher, a believer in humane treatment even for slaves and gladiators, Seneca wrote essays on ethics, scientific treatises, satires, and tragedies. Seneca's tragic dramas influenced the revival of theater in the days of Shakespeare and Racine. Underlying his satire and his moral essays, however, ran the Stoic philosopher's somber conviction that his was the worst of times.

The historian Tacitus (A.D. 55–c. 115) was even more firmly of this opinion. His *Annals* of the Empire is often contrasted with Livy's *History* of the Republic. Tacitus's pithy prose contrasts sharply with his predecessor's rolling cadences, as his dark view of first-century Rome does with Livy's noble vision of Rome's past. In a famous essay, *Germania,* Tacitus characterized the lives of the "barbaric" Germans as superior to those of supposedly civilized Romans. Convinced that absolute rule corrupts absolutely, he salted his *Annals* with the crimes and scandals of the emperors.

Sculpture, Architecture, and Engineering

A sometimes harshly honest people, the Romans had their portraits done realistically in stone in the Empire as they had in the Republic. There were exceptions: the physically unimpressive Augustus had himself depicted as a much more handsome man than he was, some of his statues modeled perhaps on idealized images of Alexander the Great. In the later Empire, a monumental stylization crept in, illustrated by the huge oddly blank face of Emperor Constantine, looking more like a symbol of imperial power than a specific human being. But most of the uncountable Roman portrait heads in museums large and small across Europe are clearly likenesses of real people: this is how Gaius really looked, wrinkled in old age, veins a bit swollen in his neck, and his wife, Portia, who was younger than he when she died.

Roman building provided a framework for the lives of such people. As architects, the Romans went beyond the Greeks in developing the arch, the vaulted hall, and the dome in order to roof the vast spaces of imperial bathhouses, basilicas, or temples. The splendor of Roman cities lay in these public structures: public baths, law courts, temples, palaces, circuses, theaters, triumphal arches, monuments. The city of Rome itself in the days of the Empire was

a world's wonder. Augustus boasted that he found Rome brick and left it marble—and he was only the first emperor.

The same array of solid practical construction can be found across the Empire. You can walk across the valley of the river Gard in southern France on top of a towering Roman aqueduct—or drink water still brought into the city of Segovia through one in Spain. You can stroll on the rough remains of the Appian Way in Rome, or look down at a similar bit of pavement behind the German cathedral of Cologne. You can turn off a highway in North Africa and be confronted by Roman walls and columns, or find yourself staring down at a Roman manhole cover in a ruined city in western Asia.

For all this building, Romans developed engineering techniques of immense ingenuity and practicality. Roman construction typically combined stone facings with concrete, thus lightening the weight of the walls. Roman engineers developed basic pulleys and cranes of sorts in use as recently as the nineteenth century. They deployed temporary wooden scaffolding to facilitate construction, as modern builders do. They learned to drain water from portions of rivers and bays in order to lay the foundations of bridges, aqueducts, and harbor works. The best Roman roads were built on a yard-deep substructure of gravel and concrete and topped with foot-and-a-half thick paving stones. They were far superior to any roads built in Europe until modern times.

The range of Roman public structures clearly emphasizes the practical concerns of this most hardheaded of ancient peoples. Besides such infrastructure as harbors and roads, Romans built many bridges, granaries, reservoirs, and sewers. Fourteen huge aqueducts brought enough water into the city of Rome itself to slake the thirst and wash the bodies of a million people every day. Even the *Cloaca Maxima,* the main sewer under the streets of the capital, was not matched in the Western world until the nineteenth century.

Old Rome has largely vanished under the jammed thoroughfares of the modern city, but we can still visit that ancient world in the excavated ruins of Pompeii. Sitting on a bench in the Street of Tombs outside the city gate, beside the road that once led to Herculaneum and the sea, you think of how ancient these vine-grown sepulchers were even in A.D. 79. How permanent too the city itself must have seemed. What could happen, after all, to such a solidly built, crowded, living reality as Pompeii and the Roman world of which it was a part?

The arches of this Roman aqueduct still tower over the city of Segovia in Spain, once a province of the Roman Empire. Like Roman roads and Roman law, Roman cities, with their many amenities, were major benefits of the only period in which the Western world has enjoyed political unity.

The Christian Church Takes Shape

Among the things that the Pompeiians could never have known was the date of the disaster that destroyed them. For A.D. 79—*Anno Domini,* the year of the Lord—is, of course, a date in a calendar not yet invented when Mount Vesuvius erupted and destroyed Pompeii. Fifty years after the crucifixion of Jesus in A.D. 29 or 30, his teachings were just beginning to spread around the Mediterranean. In the following pages, we trace the rise of the Christian church through the first five centuries A.D.—a crucial part of the legacy of the Roman period to future ages.

Mission to the Gentiles

In the wake of the crucifixion, a shock wave spread through the ranks of what is sometimes called the "Jesus Movement" to distinguish it from the full-fledged Christian church that followed. The faithful scattered, and many of the disciples fled. To most, it must have seemed that the dream of the Messiah had died upon the cross. Pontius Pilate went back to the problems of trying to govern a people who were likely to riot if Roman legionaries marched through Jerusalem with their metal standards—"graven images" of eagles—uncovered.

Then the rumors began again. We cannot hear them whispered up the narrow whitewashed streets, discussed behind closed shutters, spoken at last in public places. But the Gospels tell the story those voices told.

He had risen from the tomb. He had shown himself to his disciples, had eaten with them and opened his wounds to doubting fingers. He had ascended into heaven to be with his Father. And he would come again. The faith was alive once more: alive and spreading.

Jesus had told his disciples to spread the Gospel, the "Good News" of his coming. Their faith restored by what they profoundly believed they had experienced, they proceeded to do just that. The Acts of the Apostles, as recorded in the New Testament, include the martyrdoms of many, and the birth of a network of what the later world would call churches. The greatest of Christian missionaries, however, was a man who had never seen the living Jesus: Paul of Tarsus.

Paul (c. A.D. 36–c. 67), a Hellenized Jew of the diaspora, had his own spiritual experience of the Anointed One, a vision on the road to Damascus that changed his life. Formerly a persecutor of the new sect, he became a dedicated proselytizer for Christianity. And because of his immersion in Greco-Roman culture, he was able to reach the non-Jewish population of the Mediterranean world more effectively than the more provincial Jews who had known Jesus personally could have done.

A tireless traveler, preacher, organizer, Paul carried his message through Syria, Asia Minor, Macedonia, and Greece to Rome itself, establishing churches as he went and maintaining correspondence with all of them. Inevitably, Paul's own understanding of Christian doctrine became part of the faith as he spread it. From him came a heavy empha-

sis on sin as the natural human condition, a wickedness inherited from the original sin of Adam. Paul stressed three particular virtues: *faith* in the truth of Christianity, *hope* of salvation through Christ, and, above all, *love* of God. In the end, however, he saw salvation not as something to be "earned" by Christian living, but as a gift of God, conferred only by divine grace.

Above all, the mission of Paul to the Gentiles—the vast non-Jewish majority of the Empire—represented a fundamental step in the spread of Christianity: the decision to reach out beyond the Mediterranean Jewish community to all humankind. This, Paul profoundly believed, had been the intention of Christ, the divine son of the creator of the world, the God of all peoples. Nevertheless, for a faith nurtured in the intensely inward-looking world of Palestine, this was an unprecedented step. It changed the history of the Western world.

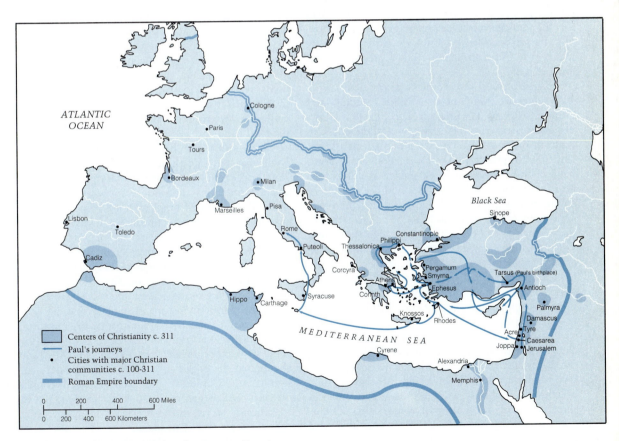

Map 6.4 Christianity Under the Roman Empire

Christianity Under the Sign of the Fish

Most of the earliest converts were urban dwellers, frequently the poor and humble, though some wealthier people accepted the new religion as well. The most wretched of Rome's subjects found consolation in a religion that promised a better life to come. The more cultured could listen with interest to the arguments of a Hellenized, educated Christian like Paul. First in the Near East, from Palestine through Asia Minor, then through Greece to Italy and, more slowly, to the western parts of the Empire, the new sect spread.

For Christians in early centuries, the essence of Christ's message was summed up in the Sign of the Fish. The fish was an ancient religious symbol often associated with commemoration of the dead. Christians adopted it because the letters that composed the word *ICHTHYS*, "fish" in the Greek lingua franca of the Hellenistic East, were the initials of the key phrase: *Jesus Christ, Son of God, Savior.* This was the message of the enigmatic sign, a rude drawing of a fish scrawled on a wall or above a door, by which early Christians indicated their presence to fellow believers.

Christian rites were simpler and perhaps warmer with fellowship than those of other contemporary Western religions. Christians were baptized as Christ had been, symbolically washing away their sins with water in order to begin a new life in Christ's spirit. They met in private homes for religious feasts commemorating Christ's own last supper of unleavened bread and wine, feeling as they did so a sense of communion with Jesus, who had said that the bread and wine were his flesh, his blood. The sacrament of the Eucharist, or holy communion, was thus born. Celebrants also prayed, sang hymns, perhaps read early versions of the Gospel story, or a letter from the indefatigable Paul. Early Christians shared their personal property in some places, and the wealthier members sometimes paid for the communion feast they all consumed.

It sounds a harmless regimen; yet trouble came almost at once to the new religion. Like the Jews, the Christians rejected all other gods except their own, and thus looked almost like atheists to their polytheistic neighbors. They refused to perform even the formal religious gesture of allegiance to the emperor by casting incense on the imperial altar, and thus came to be suspected of disloyalty and sedition.

They met in private, a privacy that turned into secrecy as their neighbors' suspicions exploded into persecution. And secrecy, in turn, encouraged rumors that they practiced shocking rites, including incest and ritual murder. As political and social troubles developed in the later Empire, followers of the new faith were often made scapegoats for any great misfortune, human or natural. Because of their "monotheistic exclusiveness" Christians were believed to endanger "what the Romans called the *pax deorum* (the right harmonious relationship between gods and men)" and thus "to be responsible for disasters which overtook the community."[3]

For three centuries, then, Christians were an often despised minority, attacked by mobs in the cities, expropriated and executed by the Roman government. Responsible Roman officials like Pliny the Younger (A.D. 62–c. 113) asked only that suspects deny the charge they were Christians in order to be set free. Nero, by contrast, sent them into the arena with wild beasts, or, in the aftermath of the great fire, turned them into human torches to light his gardens. In the disastrous third century particularly, efforts were made to destroy the now widespread sect. Officials confiscated church property, deprived upper-class Christians of government positions, enslaved lower-class ones, and sometimes condemned hundreds to death. Many Christians welcomed and even sought such martyrdom as a way of testifying to their faith, sure they would awaken from their suffering on the right hand of the Lord.

The worst of the persecutions came under Diocletian, the late third-century emperor who restored order to Rome at the cost of rigid authoritarianism. Under his successor Constantine, however, the suffering of the Christians at last come to an end. According to Christian chroniclers, Constantine, on the eve of a crucial battle in his long struggle for power, saw in the sky a great cross and heard the words "In This Sign Conquer." He thereupon ordered his soldiers to inscribe the cross on their shields, marched on to victory, and was converted to the faith. Modern historians suggest that he may have hoped to use the commitment, organization, and growing wealth of the church to help hold the Empire together. While he does not seem to have abandoned the pagan cults, he did end the persecution of the Christians and even returned church property and began to build churches himself. In 313, finally, he issued the Edict of Milan, decreeing official toleration of Christianity.

Most of the succeeding emperors were themselves Christians, and the church grew rapidly in size, wealth, and prestige. In the 390s, finally, Emperor Theodosius I (r. 379–395) declared Christianity the state religion of the Roman Empire. In 394 he began the official persecution of the pagans.

The Emergence of the Church

One reason for the survival of the new religion was that Christian communities had from early times developed rudimentary organization, and this in turn evolved into a structured Christian church. This ecclesiastical organization, paralleling the secular government of the Empire, existed when Constantine legalized the church in A.D. 313. It had only to come into the open to become a powerful force in the Western world.

Even a spontaneous gathering of Christians was likely to produce leaders. Jesus' brother James (d. c. 62) led the faithful in Jerusalem. Peter (d. c. 64) is traditionally believed to have headed the church of Rome itself. Smaller communities also had their spiritual guides and chief members. As early as the second century, furthermore, a larger hierarchy of leadership was emerging. Each local congregation had its priest. The priest derived his authority from a higher official called a bishop, the recognized head of all the Christians in a diocese, a particular city or region. Bishops in turn traced their spiritual authority back to the apostles who had founded their churches, and thus to Christ himself. By the third century, the Christians of the Empire owned sacred texts, ritual objects, churches, and other property. They had also established ecclesiastical courts to enforce the doctrinal and moral principles of Christianity.

Women played an important part in the early life of the Christian church. Some were widely admired leaders, prophetesses who claimed divine inspiration. Some Christians thought that these vessels of the Holy Spirit, rather than the emerging structure of bishops, should be the chief guides of the church. In many local churches, women's organizations had important functions. Groups of celibate women, virgins or widows, handled much of the material side of the church's activities, from charity to property. Their "house churches" served as central places for religious feasts and refuges for wandering preachers. Women church leaders also took charge of the conversion, indoctrination, and baptism of women converts. In later centuries, women encouraged pilgrimages and the veneration of saints. Constantine's

This wall painting, which may be an early Christian representation of the Virgin Mary and the child Jesus, dates from the late third century A.D., only a few decades before Diocletian's last terrible persecution of the Christians and Constantine's legalization of the church in the early fourth century.

mother Helena was believed to have played a leading part in encouraging the veneration of Mary, which played such an important role in medieval and later Christian worship. The Christian assertion that in Christ "there is neither Jew nor Greek . . . neither bond nor free . . . neither male nor female"[4] continued to win the devotion of many women to the church.

As Christianity emerged from the shadow of persecution shortly after A.D. 300, its organizational structure developed still further. Among the many independent bishops, a few who presided over the largest cities in the Mediterranean world acquired a higher authority than others. Known as archbishops, they became the ecclesiastical heads of regions containing the churches of a number of bishops. Some few archbishops, finally, claimed even larger authority. These included the heads of the churches of Alexandria, Antioch, Constantinople after it became an imperial capital, and, most important, Rome. The bishop of Rome based his claim to primacy on the fact that Peter, the disciple on whom Jesus had said he depended to build his church, had been the founder and first bishop of Rome. In addition, both Peter and Paul were believed to have been martyred there by Nero. And the city itself still enjoyed immense prestige as the ancient imperial capital and the largest city in the West. By the fifth century, the bishop of Rome was increasingly granted priority among the others, and the foundation of the Roman Catholic papacy had been laid.

Heresy and Schism

A central and continuing problem that beset the new church perhaps even more after it was legalized was the problem of heresy. Any system built on ideas, from ancient philosophies to modern ideologies, tends to generate a variety of interpretations of its basic principles. This in turn often leads to feuds between proponents of various views and even to splits, or schisms, in the organization itself. In a religious organization like the Christian church, which offered eternal life to those who followed the true teachings of Christ and warned that eternal punishment awaited those who were seduced by false doctrines, distinguishing orthodoxy from heresy became a matter of paramount importance.

By the time the church was legalized in A.D. 313, the life of the historical Jesus was three centuries in the past. Councils of church leaders and scholars had already decided which accounts of his life and teachings were "canonical"—orthodox and true—and thus established the official text of the Bible. As a *historical* event, the words and deeds of the founder of the faith were thus firmly established. As a *spiritual* event, however, the life and character of Christ remained a very controversial issue. Church thinkers, often drawing on Greek philosophical concepts and other sources of ancient wisdom, attempted to explain "the nature of the Incarnation"—that is, what it *meant* to say that Christ was the Son of God. Some of the resulting theories were accepted and be-

came basic Christian doctrine; others were rejected as inaccurate and heretical. In these disputations among church thinkers was born Christian theology, the effort to understand long-past historical events in profounder philosophical terms than the traditional accounts contained in the Bible.

A familiar, thoroughly orthodox example may be found in the Gospels themselves, in the enigmatic opening words of the Gospel of John (1:1), probably written about A.D. 100: "In the beginning was the Word, and the Word was with God, and the Word was God." In Greek, the language of the New Testament, the word here translated as "Word" was *Logos,* and *Logos* was a philosophical term long used by Stoics to denote the active spiritual force emanating from the rational principle of the universe. Referring to the historical Jesus of Nazareth in such terms helped to explain what had happened in Palestine by identifying the divine nature of Jesus with a familiar philosophical concept.

Not all such attempts, however, found favor with the leaders of the church. An early heresy was the view of the Near Eastern Gnostics, Christians who believed they possessed a "secret wisdom" (*gnosis* in Greek) concealed from others. According to the *Gnostics,* Christ, since he was divine, must have been a purely spiritual being, in no sense material. A purely spiritual being, however, could not have been crucified upon a material cross, could not have suffered or died as Jesus was reported to have done. Gnostics also believed that the human soul is consubstantial with, or of the same spiritual substance as God, and that salvation comes not through reading or hearing the Word preached, but only through mystic revelation of the gnosis.

A different but equally heretical view was that of the *Arians,* followers of the Alexandrian priest Arius (c. A.D. 280–336). Arius insisted that if Christ was God's "begotten Son," then he could not be identical with God, as monotheistic orthodoxy asserted. Christ should be seen, then, as a creation of God's, as not eternal (since he was begotten in time), and as in some sense dependent on the Father. If the Gnostics emphasized the gulf between Christ and humanity, the Arians sought to broaden the gap between Christ and God.

To both, the church replied that Jesus Christ had been both God and man, divine and human. And if this was a mystery beyond our human comprehension, it was also a mystery that Christians were not at liberty to doubt.

A heresy with even broader application, with

roots outside Christianity itself, was Manichaean dualism. This widely influential doctrine, which drew on the teachings of the Persian Zoroaster, was preached by a third-century Near Eastern prophet named Mani (A.D. 216–276). Attempting to deal with the age-old problem of evil—how a good and powerful God could be responsible for a universe filled with suffering and sin—the *Manichaeans* absolved God of responsibility by declaring that *another* power produced the evil in the universe. This approach, depicting good and evil as independent forces in the cosmos, saw the universe as a combat zone between the two. It also, however, tended to give Satan (the Zoroastrian Ahriman) something like parity with God. This view too was rejected as heretical by the church, which characterized Satan as merely one of God's fallen angels, in no sense an equal-but-opposite power.

There were a number of other such attempts at reinterpretation, and the Christian church was soon as full of sectarian divisions as Judaism had been in the time of Christ. It was a serious problem, and one that would recur throughout the history of Christianity.

To deal with such disputes on an authoritative level, bishops would often meet in councils, thrash out differences of opinion, and issue joint statements on policy or theology. At the first ecumenical council called by Emperor Constantine at Nicaea near Constantinople in A.D. 325, the Arian theory was declared heretical. Even more important, however, the council issued the Nicene Creed, a brief statement of orthodox Christian belief that was used as a standard for many centuries. Church councils became an essential instrument for settling disputes and solving problems within the church from 325 to the most recent such meeting, the reforming Vatican Council of the 1960s.

The Fathers of the Church

The very vigor of these disputes over doctrine in the early church honed some exceptional minds. The most influential of these early scholars and preachers, who included both Greek and Latin writers, became known as the fathers of the church.

The Greek fathers had the advantage of being able to read both the New Testament and the ancient philosophers in their original Greek. Such scholars as Clement of Alexandria (c. A.D.

150–211), Origen (c. A.D. 185–254), and Basil of Cappadoccia (c. A.D. 329–379) could both expose the errors of Greek mythology and philosophy and use the techniques of Greek thinkers to explore Christian theological problems in more depth. They were thorough biblical scholars, and Origen, perhaps the most admired of the Greek fathers, was especially celebrated for his textual study of the Hebrew Old Testament.

The Latin fathers included Jerome, Ambrose, and above all Augustine. Jerome (c. A.D. 340–420), an immensely learned man, was most famous for his translation of the entire Bible from Hebrew and Greek into Latin. This *Vulgate* version (so called because it was in the "vulgar," or popular Latin of his day) was the text used by scholars in the West throughout the Middle Ages.

Ambrose of Milan (c. A.D. 340–397) was a much-admired preacher and, as bishop of that north Italian city, a powerful church administrator. Among his theological contributions, two stand out. He took from Cicero a Stoic emphasis on doing one's duty, but elevated it by emphasizing duty to God rather than the civic duty stressed by the Stoics. More important, Ambrose became a vigorous advocate of the power of the church over that of the secular authorities. In one celebrated instance, Ambrose excommunicated Emperor Theodosius himself for having massacred the population of a rebellious Greek city, refusing to readmit the emperor into the good graces of the church until he had repented and done penance for his sin. This demonstration of the superiority of priestly over royal power was cited in later centuries by powerful medieval popes and by reformers like John Calvin in support of their assertions of the supremacy of religious over secular authority.

The most influential of all the *church fathers,* however, was Augustine (354–430), bishop of Hippo in North Africa. Augustine's life is almost a model of the discovery of Christianity by the Roman world.

Raised by a Christian mother and a pagan father in Roman North Africa, Augustine was an eager student of pagan learning throughout his youth and young adulthood. A particular admirer of Plotinus and the Platonists, he believed even in his later life that their teachings had opened the way to Christian understanding for him: "Having then read those books of the Platonists," he wrote in his *Confessions,* "and thence been taught to search for incorporeal [nonmaterial] truth, I saw Thy invisible things."[5] In his youth, he was also much impressed by the teachings of the then fashionable Manichaeans, whose hard line between spirit and flesh and condemnation of sex in particular remained with him all his life.

A successful student and then teacher of rhetoric, Augustine moved from his home near Carthage to Rome and then to Milan, where, inspired by the eloquences of Ambrose and by the Scriptures themselves, he was converted to Christianity. (For his own memories of this turning point in his life, see the box, "The Conversion of St. Augustine.") Thereafter, he became a prolific Christian writer himself, crusaded vigorously against various heresies, was appointed bishop of Hippo in his native North Africa, and died there even as the barbarian Vandals closed around his city.

Augustine's books on many aspects of Christian life and belief provided guidance for priests and inspiration for laypeople throughout the Middle Ages. His uniquely personal *Confessions*, virtually the only such autobiography we have from ancient times, traced his spiritual pilgrimage from paganism and heresy to the true faith. His *City of God* sought to explain all history in Christian terms, and particularly to answer the pagan charge that it was the conversion of the Empire to Christianity that had brought Rome defeat at the hands of the barbarians. Influential theological positions taken by Augustine included his conviction that salvation comes only through divine grace, not through human virtue, and his opposition to sexual pleasure as a sin of the flesh—two points of view that Paul had also preached. Believing that God's grace was the sole source of salvation, Augustine also came to believe in predestination—that an all-powerful God has destined every human soul for salvation or damnation, and that "good works" cannot affect the outcome. The Roman Catholic church rejected this view, insisting on the equal importance of faith and works on the road to life eternal. In the early modern period, however, Protestant reformers like Luther and Calvin found warrant for their own predestinarian views in the writings of Augustine.

The history of Rome thus ended with the Christian church institutionally developed and intellectually vigorous. The Roman state withered and collapsed under the assault of less developed peoples from the north and east. The Christian faith survived, expanded still further by converting its barbarian conquerors, and emerged as the dominant force in the next stage of Western history, the age of medieval Christendom.

PROFILES IN HISTORY
The Conversion of Saint Augustine

The *Confessions of Saint Augustine,* written around A.D. 400, is one of the earliest and most admired autobiographies in Western history. In this book, the future saint offers an account of his sinful early life, his search for a truth to live by among the pagan intellectual currents of a dying empire, and his final coming to Christ in his thirty-second year. The *Confessions* thus gives us a glimpse of the sort of personal experience that many ordinary Christians must have shared during the early centuries of the spread of Christianity across the Western world. Does the author's preliminary lament increase the impact of his subsequent revelation?

O Lord, how long? how long, Lord, wilt thou be angry forever? Remember not our former iniquities, for I felt that I was held by them. I sent up these sorrowful words: How long, how long, "tomorrow and tomorrow"? Why not now? why not is there this hour an end to my uncleanness?

So was I speaking and weeping in the most bitter contrition of my heart, when lo! I heard from a neighboring house a voice, as of boy or girl, I know not, chanting, and oft repeating, "Take up and read; Take up and read." Instantly, my countenance altered, I began to think most intently whether children were wont in any kind of play to sing such words: nor could I remember ever to have heard the like. So checking the torrent of my tears, I rose; interpreting it to be no other than a command from God to open the book and read the first chapter I could find. . . . Eagerly then I returned to the place where Alypius was sitting; for there I had laid the volume of the Apostle when I arose thence. I seized, opened, and in silence read that section on which my eyes first fell: Not in rioting and drunkenness, not in chambering and wantonness, not in strife and envying; but put ye on the Lord Jesus Christ. . . . No further could I read, nor needed I, for instantly at the end of this sentence, by a light as it were of serenity infused into my heart, all the darkness of doubt vanished away.

Source: Augustine, *The Confessions,* trans. E. P. Pusey (New York: Pocket Books, 1952), 147–148.

A Topical Summary

Politics: Augustus Caesar and the emperors who succeeded him presided over the two most successful centuries in Roman history. The third century A.D., however, saw a partial breakdown of the Empire, followed in the next century by a more rigorous imperial administration under Diocletian and Constantine. Finally, in the fifth century, the Empire crumbled under a combination of internal strains and Germanic invasions from without.

Economics: The Roman Empire, linking the economies of western Europe with those of North Africa and the Near East, brought two centuries of prosperity to the region. The breakdowns of the third and fifth centuries A.D., however, were as much economic as political in nature, and with the fall of Rome, Europe lost its profitable contact with neighboring continents for centuries to come.

Society: Like Rome of the Republic, the Roman Empire saw its upper classes flourish while large numbers lived on the dole in cities or labored, often as tenant farmers, in the fields. Women at the top of society, at least, had more legal rights and broader access to social life. Roman law, which evolved slowly over the centuries, became one of the world's great legal codes and has continued to influence the law of the Western world down to the present.

Technology: Romans were great builders, dotting western Europe with cities and harbors, crisscrossing the land with roads and aqueducts. Roman technology ranged from architecture based on the arch and dome to impressive systems of water supply and sewage disposal.

Culture: Among the cultural achievements of Rome in the period of the Empire were the poetry of Vergil, the histories written by Livy and Tacitus, and some of the most accomplished sculpture in Western history. The spread of Christianity, however, had more far-reaching consequences. The ideas of Paul and the church fathers expanded the range and influence of Jesus' teachings until Christianity became the central religion of the Western world.

The Expanding West: The golden age of the Roman Peace encompassed not only the Greco-Roman Mediterranean, North Africa, and varying portions of the Near East, but much of Britain, France, Spain, Switzerland, the Balkans, and the rest of western Europe. For two hundred years, the Western world thus included a temporarily unified zone still centering around the Mediterranean Sea but including much of Europe's future heartland as well.

Some Key Terms

Arians 180	*imperator* 158	*pax deorum* 178
Augustan Age 155	*ius gentium* 173	*Pax Romana* 155
church fathers 181	*ius naturale* 173	*pontifex maximus* 155
coloni 171	latifundia 170	*principate* 154
Gnostics 180	Manichaeans 181	Tetrarchy 165
ICHTHYS 178	*pater patriae* 157	villas 171

Notes

1. *Ancient Greek Inscriptions in the British Museum* (Oxford: Oxford University Press, 1893), No. 894, trans. by David Magie, *The Roman Role in Asia Minor,* vol. 1 (Princeton: Princeton University Press, 1950), 490.
2. Tacitus, *The Annals of Imperial Rome,* trans. Michael Grant (Harmondsworth, England: Penguin, 1956), 321.
3. G.E.M. de Ste. Croix, "Why Were the Early Christians Persecuted?" *Past and Present,* 26 (1963), 24.
4. Galatians 3:28.
5. *The Confessions of Saint Augustine,* trans. Edward B. Pusey (New York: Pocket Books, 1952), 124.

Reading List

BRADLEY, K. R. *Slaves and Masters in the Roman Empire: A Study in Social Control.* Brussels: Latomus, 1984. Relations between owners and slaves, with an interesting attempt to penetrate the minds of the latter.

BROWN, P. *Augustine of Hippo.* Berkeley: University of California Press, 1967. Imaginative life and times of the most influential of the fathers of the church.

———. *The World of Late Antiquity: From Marcus Aurelius to Muhammad.* London: Thames and Hudson, 1971. Popular presentation by a gifted scholar.

CHAMBERS, M., ed. *The Fall of Rome—Can It Be Explained?* New York: Holt, Rinehart and Winston, 1970. Many theories, few certainties on this much debated historiographical question. See also A. TERRILL, *The Fall of the Roman Empire: The Military Explanation* (London: Thames and Hudson, 1986), and R. MACMULLAN, *Corruption and the Decline of Rome* (New Haven: Yale University Press, 1988).

COPLEY, F. O. *Latin Literature: From the Beginnings to the Close of the Second Century A.D.* Ann Arbor: University of Michigan Press, 1969. Survey of Roman literature by a leading translator.

DRINKWATER, J. F. *Roman Gaul: The Three Provinces, 58 B.C.–A.D. 260.* Ithaca, N.Y.: Cornell University Press, 1983. Ancient France under the Romans.

DUNCAN-JONES, R. *The Economy of the Roman Empire: Quantitative Studies.* London: Cambridge University Press, 1974. Essays on agriculture, cities, prices, and other aspects of the economy, heavily supported by statistics.

GARZETTI, A. *From Tiberius to Antoninus: A History of the Roman Empire A.D. 14–192.* Translated by J. R. Foster. London: Methuen, 1974. Massive history of the centuries of the Roman Peace after Augustus. See also the more recent study by C. B. WELLS, *The Roman Empire* (London: Fontana, 1984), stressing economic and social affairs.

GRANT, M. *Saint Paul.* New York: Scribner's, 1976. Highly readable life of the "second founder" of the Christian church.

HALLETT, J. P. *Fathers and Daughters in Roman Society: Women and the Elite Family.* Princeton: Princeton University Press, 1984. Suggests that aristocratic women exerted significant influence on affairs. See also J. P. V. D. BALSDON's pioneering *Roman Women* (New York: John Day, 1963).

JONES, A. H. M. *Augustus.* New York: Norton, 1971. Excellent overview of the rise, rule, and reforms of the first emperor, by an authority.

LEVICK, B. *Claudius.* New Haven: Yale University Press, 1990. Impressive life of the misfit who became one of Rome's greatest rulers.

LEWIS, N. *Life in Egypt Under Roman Rule.* New York: Oxford University Press, 1983. Stylish and scholarly picture of life in this African province of the empire.

MARKUS, R. A. *Christianity in the Roman World.* New York: Scribner's, 1974. Christian values shape a self-confident sense of Christian identity as the Empire crumbles. See also W. H. FREND, *Martyrdom and Persecution in the Early Church* (Grand Rapids, Mich.: Baker, 1981).

SPEIDEL, M. *Roman Army Studies.* Amsterdam: Grieben, 1984. Short papers on many aspects of the Roman military system.

SUETONIUS. *Lives of the Caesars.* Translated by R. Graves. Baltimore: Penguin, 1957. Colorful, critical Roman biographies, translated by a celebrated modern writer. For a more recent study of one of the more notorious emperors chronicled here, see M. T. GRIFFIN, *Nero: The End of a Dynasty* (New Haven: Yale University Press, 1984).

THOMPSON, E. A. *Romans and Barbarians: The Decline of the Western Empire.* Madison: University of Wisconsin Press, 1982. Essays on the decay of the Roman imperium in the provinces; witty and learned. See also B. CUNLIFFE, *Greeks, Romans, and Barbarians: Spheres of Interaction* (New York: Methuen, 1988). An analysis of relations between the Mediterranean world and the rest of Europe in terms of a southern economic "core" and a northern "periphery."

———. *Romans and Blacks.* Norman: University of Oklahoma Press, 1989. Exemplary study of the evidence and the scholarly literature on race relations, which seem not to have been a problem in Rome. See also F. SNOWDEN's seminal work, *Before Color Prejudice: The Ancient View of Blacks* (Cambridge, Mass.: Harvard University Press, 1983).

WEBSTER, G. *Boudicca: The British Revolt Against Rome, A.D. 60.* Totowa, N.J.: Rowan and Littlefield, 1978. Brief, archaeologically informed study of the English queen and her challenge to Rome.

WILLIAMS, S. *Diocletian and the Roman Recovery.* New York: Methuen, 1985. Well-written life of the emperor who shared with Constantine the task of pulling Rome together after its third-century decline. See also, for administrative and historiographical analysis, T. D. BARNES, *The New Empire of Diocletian and Constantine* (Cambridge, Mass.: Harvard University Press, 1983), and T. D. BARNES, *Constantine and Eusebius* (Cambridge, Mass.: Harvard University Press, 1981), an authoritative narrative of the emperor's life and reign.

Part II

The Centuries of Christendom

The Middle Ages, roughly from A.D. 500 to 1500, marked a new beginning for Western history. As we have seen, the Roman Empire and civilization collapsed in the fifth century under both internal and external pressures. Over the next thousand years, Western peoples began again with simple agricultural villages and slowly learned to rebuild cities and larger political units. During this second cycle of Western history, which we explore in the next five chapters, Western society expanded economically and technologically once more, and constructed a sophisticated culture in which the Christian religion played a central role.

After the disintegration of the Roman Empire, medieval people had to start from scratch to build political institutions. With the disappearance over much of the former Roman world of cities and central government, political power fell into the hands of feudal barons, who had only a limited personal allegiance to more powerful nobles. Yet after several hundred years, more sophisticated and larger territorial units did emerge. New forms of the city-state, often dominated by merchants and artisans, took shape, and in time monarchies developed, loosely governed countries that provided the basis for the nation-states of the future.

The economy of the medieval European state evolved gradually from subsistence agriculture on simple manor farms to an integrated regional or even international economy. Merchant companies and craft guilds rebuilt the cities as centers of production and commerce. And trade expanded well beyond the West, reaching to North Africa, the Near East, and ultimately as far as China.

Socially and culturally, there were significant differences between the ancient and medieval West, but there were important similarities as well. Most peasants were still bound to the land they tilled, not outright slaves but serfs owing the lord of the manor both unpaid labor and payments in kind. However, there were now several elite classes—the older landed aristocracy, the emergent urban middle classes, and the upper ranks of the church hierarchy—and they often feuded. Still, this period is usually seen as Europe's great Age of Faith, when Christian beliefs infused Western thought and art. The most learned people in the Western world were religious thinkers, and the tallest building in any city was the cathedral.

Traditionally, the medieval period—once referred to as the Dark Ages—was seen as a time of slow growth, when the West was a relatively underdeveloped part of the globe. But the seeds of later territorial expansion were there. Although North Africa and the Near East, once part of the Roman Empire, were now absorbed into the rival Muslim family of nations that stretched from Africa to India, the West's ambitious kings, merchants, crusaders, and missionaries expanded its boundaries to include more of central and eastern Europe.

Throughout the medieval period the West was influenced by many non-Western peoples: pagan Vikings from the north, Arabs from the south, and nomadic peoples from the steppes of Eurasia. The Byzantine Empire, survivor of the eastern half of the Roman Empire and centered at Constantinople, was medieval Europe's earliest important trading partner, and the West soon learned to trade profitably with the Muslim world as well. From many of these peoples came valuable cultural borrowings, including the Arabic numerals we use today.

Traditionally, the Middle Ages has meant castles and cathedrals, warrior kings like Charlemagne and Richard the Lion-Hearted, and saints like Francis of Assisi or Joan of Arc. It also meant city streets full of busy artisans, clusters of peasant huts surrounded by fields and pastures, and isolated monasteries and convents where monks and nuns worked and studied, preserving the cultural life of the West. All contributed to the ongoing life of the Western world, and all made their contributions to our evolving Western heritage.

Head of Sigtuna. Antikvarisk Topografiska Arkivet, State Historical Museum, Stockholm

Western civilization experienced the worst setback in its history during the five centuries between A.D. 500 and 1000. This European "Dark Age" comprises the first half of the larger cycle of Western history called the Middle Ages. Such periods, when things fall apart, are not, unhappily, unusual in the histories of civilizations. The West had already had its share, in the Greek Dark Age and Rome's chaotic third century A.D. But the Western world had never seen a setback to prosperity, stability, and high culture like the early Middle Ages, the centuries of political disorder and social and economic decline that followed the crumbling of the Western Roman Empire.

Civilizations, however, have a sometimes astonishing capacity to bounce back. As we will see in later chapters, medieval Christian civilization demonstrated such resilience in the High Middle Ages, the new cultural flowering of the eleventh, twelfth, and thirteenth centuries. In this chapter, however, we are concerned primarily with the medieval West's early efforts to survive and regroup after its collapse.

During these early medieval centuries, the elements of a new, more broadly European culture than that of the Mediterranean basin were slowly assembled: wider lands, new peoples, and the evolving Christian church. But waves of new migrants overwhelmed the efforts of the Germanic monarchies, first to preserve what remained of Roman civilization and then to build anew. Even the period's greatest effort to restore order, the Carolingian Empire of Charlemagne, faded away in a few generations.

What *was* accomplished during the early medieval period was the stabilizing of a much looser order of society than that of ancient Rome. The feudal political structure was a ramshackle affair, but it did either stem or absorb wave after wave of barbarian invaders. The manor system was essentially a subsistence economy, but it fed at least some of the people much of the time. And throughout these centuries, the church and its influence grew and spread. The papacy, the monastic system, and the cultural life of Christendom were beacons that flared against the darkness of the early Middle Ages.

Europe Before the Romans

In this second major phase of Western history, the stage and most of the actors are relatively new to us. It is therefore useful to survey the territory that lay

	400	500	600

POLITICAL, MILITARY, AND DIPLOMATIC EVENTS

378–532 Germanic Invasions	**476** Fall of Rome		
r. 440–462 Leo the Great	**r. 481–511** Clovis		
	r. 489–526 Theodoric		
	500–751 Merovingians	**r. 590–604** Gregory the Great	

SOCIAL AND ECONOMIC DEVELOPMENTS

from 400 Fusion of Roman and Germanic Elements	**from 500** Decline of Cities	
	from 500 Emergence of Manorialism	
	529 Emergence of Monasticism	

CULTURE: THE ARTS, PHILOSOPHY, SCIENCE AND RELIGION

c. 480–c. 524 Boethius	**597** Augustine to England
c. 480–c. 580 Benedict	**664** Synod of Whitby
c. 490–543 Cassiodorus	
c. 500 Brigid in Ireland	
538–594 Gregory of Tours	

north of the Mediterranean basin, and to understand the peoples who lived in what is Europe today as the old order crumbled. The center of the Western world was moving northward, and we must move with it. We begin with a look at the territorial and human foundations of the lands north of the Alps that were about to become the new center of Western civilization.

A Divided Continent

Perhaps the best way to get a sense of the European land today is to get off the airplanes and even the trains and hike, bike, or drive it. Go the youth–hostel route, have wine, bread, and cheese in a field for lunch, and find the cheapest menus outside the brasseries and trattorias for supper on the village square. All of a sudden Europe isn't just the Tower of London, the Louvre, and the Trevi Fountain. It's dusty roads and olive trees, a curve of the Rhine and a castle on a crag, or snowballs in the Alps. It's wine country and grain country, lakes and fjords and

forests. From Ireland to the Urals, from the Mediterranean to the Arctic Circle, there's a lot of country there.

The very variety of the continent makes describing its basic geography in words no easy task. Still, we should make some effort to develop a sense of the geographical outline of this new and larger stage of Western history before we focus on what was happening there fifteen hundred years ago.

There are a few basic facts, easily enough assimilated. Europe consists of the western fifth of the double continent of Eurasia. It is generally defined as the territory running from the Atlantic Ocean east to the Ural Mountains and the Turkish Straits. The Black Sea and the Mediterranean mark its southern frontier, the arctic reaches of Scandinavia and Russia its northern one. In area, it is somewhat larger than the United States.

If you were to cut out a map of Europe, it would take you quite a long time, because of the many ins and outs of its coastline. Scandinavia, the Iberian countries, Italy, and Greece are all huge peninsulas, and there are many large islands in both the Mediterranean and the Atlantic, including coun-

700   **800**   **900**   **1000**

711–925 Arab, Magyar, Viking Invasions

732 Battle of Tours

r. 747–768 Pippin the Short

751–987 Carolingians

r. 771–814 Charlemagne

843 Treaty of Verdun

r. 871–899 Alfred the Great

r. 1014–1035 Canute

by 850 Emergence of Feudalism

c. 680 *Beowulf* composed

c. 673–735 Venerable Bede

735–804 Alcuin of York

c. 750 Lioba in Saxony

c. 780–c. 840 Carolingian Renaissance

try-sized ones like Great Britain and Ireland. Inland too, Europe is broken up by massive mountain chains—the Pyrenees, the Alps, and the ranges of the Balkans and the Caucasus. The continent is marked also by long river valleys, like the Seine in France, the Po in Italy, the Rhine-Danube line that formed the Roman frontier, or the Elbe, Dnieper, Volga, and other rivers of eastern Europe.

Western Europe in particular is a tumbled land, folded and wrinkled, with only a few plains and plateaus like those in Spain and France. The real "great plains" of Europe lie in the central and eastern parts of the continent: a drive from Berlin to Moscow can remind you of nothing so much as a trip from Chicago to Kansas, leaving out most of the towns. But much of the rest of Europe has mountains on the horizon, gleaming rivers winding down a glen, or church spires showing over rolling hills.

In ancient and medieval times, this European land was a good deal less tidy than it looks now. Forests were heavy over much of the continent, and there was much more undeveloped wasteland—undrained marshes, rocky hills, or open grasslands untenanted save by nomadic herdsmen. The great

mountain ranges, not yet sown with picture-postcard ski resorts, loomed as cold and forbidding barriers to trade and travel.

There was immense potential in that black European earth, heavier than that of the Mediterranean but capable of producing bumper crops once the forests were pushed back, the swamplands drained. Properly exploited, those endless coasts and rivers were made for trade, the streams that fed them for turning water wheels. There was as much building stone north of the Alps as south of them, and minerals sleeping under the earth, waiting for a later age to turn them into buildings and bridges, machinery and structural steel. And the climate—albeit colder and wetter the farther north you went—might serve to brace people to their duties rather than to slow their efforts.

The familiar political divisions of today were not yet there, of course. Such twentieth-century powers as Germany, France, Britain, and Russia did not exist. There were no tidy groupings of other nations, from the Scandinavian countries to the Balkans. Still, the mountain ranges, river valleys, and winding coastlines that defined later political frontiers were there. Geography was as important to Europe's future politics as to its economic future.

To turn Europe into one of the most successful areas of human habitation on the globe was the labor of many centuries. Much of the rest of this book is in fact devoted to exploring the achievements of these European generations. We begin here with a closer look at the people who initiated that long labor.

Early Europeans

Around 30,000 B.C., western Europe was one of the bright spots on the prehistoric cultural map of *Homo sapiens*. It was in Europe that Cro-Magnon humanity brought the Old Stone Age to a brilliant climax in the caves of Lascaux and Altamira. Thereafter, however, the cutting edge of human cultural evolution shifted to the east. Agriculture, cities, and civilization were all invented in the Near East and North Africa and flourished in India, China, and the Mediterranean basin before they found their way to Europe north of the Alps.

The European land was inhabited from Paleolithic times onward, though the hunters and food gatherers who lived there were scattered rather thinly between the Atlantic coast and the plains of European Russia. It was a long time after the Paleolithic climax at Lascaux before the Neolithic agricultural revolution reached Europe beyond the Mediterranean basin. For one thing, the arts of cultivating the soil, domesticating animals, building villages, and working metals could not simply be taken over wholesale from the Near East. Soil, animals, and building materials were different in the forests of central Europe or the fens of Britain. Contacts were also minimal between the Near Eastern civilized zones and the vast preurban world of food-gathering humanity north of these islands of urban living. Still, basic techniques did trickle west and north, along the Danube and the Rhine into Europe.

At first it was a slash-and-burn agricultural world. Prehistoric Europeans used ax and fire to make a clearing in the woods and enrich the soil with the ashes, exhausted the land in a few seasons, then moved on to slash and burn again. It was a very different style of food producing from the armies of organized peasants who labored in the irrigated river valleys of Mesopotamia or Egypt. And there were other differences as well. Most European houses were built of rough stones or logs and thatch rather

than baked brick or stone blocks. Cities, literacy, and other civilized complexities did not come north until Roman armies did. And many Europeans continued to live as their ancestors had, by hunting, fishing, and gathering fruit, nuts, tubers and natural grains in season.

Still, Europe to the north was not standing entirely still while the pyramids, the Parthenon, and the Colosseum rose around the Mediterranean. As early as the sixth millennium B.C., Neolithic people were beginning to grow crops in central Europe; by the middle of the fourth millennium, there were farm hamlets as far north as Britain. And there were monuments in northern lands as well: the megalithic tombs and the circles and lines of huge stones raised for religious purposes all across Eurasia, from Ireland to Korea. Circular arrangements like Stonehenge in England featured huge vertical slabs of rock called *megaliths,* some with horizontal capstones linking pairs; and there were long avenues of standing stones like those of Brittany in western France. These open-air cathedrals were no mean achievements for small populations of illiterate agriculturalists.

Meanwhile, however, Europe was sharing at least one experience with the more developed societies to the south: invasions from the Eurasian steppes. Waves of migrating peoples have flowed slowly from east to west across Eurasia through much of recorded history. Pastoral herders rather than settled farmers, these nomadic peoples were set in motion sometimes by overpopulation, sometimes by the drying out of the marginal grasslands where they lived, sometimes by the pressure of other moving tribes. They drifted west because the western steppes were greener and better watered. In the end, many of them found their way to Europe.

The great Eurasian migrations of historic times may be divided into two groups: those of the Indo-Europeans and those of the Turko-Mongol peoples. The *Indo-European peoples* probably originated around the Caspian Sea in southern Russia and spread south and west to India, Persia, and Europe. Waves of Indo-European invaders migrated into Europe from the second millennium B.C. until the time of the fall of the Roman Empire. The *Turko-Mongol* peoples came from further east, from Mongolia and the barren lands north of the Great Wall of China. They repeatedly invaded Europe and the Middle East, beginning with the Huns in the last days of the Roman Empire and ending with the Mongol followers of Genghis Khan in the later Middle Ages.

Indo-European immigrants had probably re-

Amid stone circles and other monolithic groupings like these at Stonehenge, in England, prehistoric people held religious ceremonies long before Roman cults or Christianity. The stones were often aligned with the position of the sun at the summer solstice or with other astronomical configurations detectable by early observers of the night skies.

placed most of the prehistoric inhabitants by A.D. 500. The Greeks and Romans of the Mediterranean, the Celts, Slavs, and Germans to the north all spoke Indo-European languages. These peoples, who built Western civilization in its varying forms, grew in numbers and sank deep cultural roots into the land. As a result, the Turko-Mongol nomads who followed them were seldom more than raiders into most of Europe. Their settlement areas were limited to the continent's eastern fringes, including Hungary, Russia, and Ukraine. Even the vast Mongol Empire of Genghis Khan, which in the thirteenth century included China and much of the Middle East, penetrated the West no further than European Russia.

Of the major groups of Indo-Europeans, the Celtic peoples who once populated France, Germany, and even northern Italy were by early medieval times being pushed back toward the western edges of Europe by advancing Germanic tribes. The Celts raised their megaliths and left some striking jewelry and lovely legends, but in medieval times they were largely limited to Brittany on the French coast, western Britain, and Ireland. The Slavs, meanwhile, dominated the eastern half of Europe, from the Baltic Sea and the Balkans to the Ural Mountains. These Slavic tribes were the forebears of the Russians, Ukrainians, Poles, Czechs, and most of the other peoples of eastern Europe. Western and central Europe, finally, were dominated by the Germanic peoples who had swamped the Roman Empire. These Germanic tribes—the ancestors not only of today's Germans but of French, English, and other peoples of medieval and modern Europe as well—will be our focus in this chapter.

Germanic Society

Historians once drew a hard line between the civilized Romans and the German barbarians who shattered the Roman order. Further research has rendered the line between the two cultures much less clear. The very word "barbarian," with its pejorative connotations and its stress on sharp cultural differences between the Roman and Germanic worlds, must now go in quotation marks, along with such old-fashioned terms as "Dark Ages." What we have, in fact, is a slow transition rather than a total destruction, a melding of cultures rather than the simple replacement of one by the other. Still, we should look at the distinctive society the Germans brought to the mix before analyzing the fusion.

In late antiquity and early medieval times, as noted above, perhaps three-quarters of western Europe was covered with trees. In clearings scattered through the forests, the *Germanic peoples* lived in tiny villages of one-room log huts or shanties of wattle and daub, mud over interwoven poles. They grew barley and oats, grazed a few cattle, worked metals, and fought among themselves with heavy swords and spears.

Among the Germans, as among preurban peoples in other parts of the world, women sometimes did more physical labor than men did, particularly managing the fields and tending the herds while the men were away at war. The Germanic peoples were also polygamous, a feature of their culture that much disturbed medieval Christian missionaries. Yet Romans thought they detected among the Germans a sense of equality between men and women and, as we will see, something like this may well have influenced the relatively positive attitudes of early medieval people toward women in leadership roles.

The Germans had no political structure beyond assemblies of warriors, councils of elders, and elected war leaders, though the latter did sometimes emerge as kings in the simplest sense—that is, as fighting leaders and chief priests. As everywhere in the preurban world, clan and family inspired the strongest feelings of loyalty, and immemorial custom served in lieu of law. The German tribes believed in great gods to whom chiefs sacrificed, but also in a multitude of nature spirits. Trees were sacred, pools and streams were inhabited by spirits, and all nature was alive, as it had once been to all peoples. Until they encountered Christianity, in short, the Germans entertained a thoroughly animistic worldview that filled rustling leaves and moving waters and empty sky with spiritual presences.

The Germans tended to be taller than Italians or Greeks and were believed to look very picturesque in furs and barbaric gold jewelry. As the box "Ancient Germans as Noble Savages" suggests, Tacitus saw them as a moral cut above the "decadent" Romans

PROBING THE PAST
Ancient Germans as Noble Savages

The Roman historian Tacitus had never seen the empire's Rhine frontier when he composed his work *On Germany* shortly before A.D. 100. One of his primary objectives seems to have been moral rather than historical: he sought to condemn what he saw as the decadent society of contemporary Rome by contrasting it with the simple free lives of the "noble savages" of the German forests. Yet Tacitus had talked with Roman military commanders and provincial administrators who had visited the Germanic tribes beyond the Rhine, and his essay gives us a striking picture of life among the ancestors of the builders of medieval Europe. What Roman vices are suggested by the virtues commended here? What Germanic values are apparent in this account?

In every house the children grow up, thinly and meanly clad, to that bulk of body and limb which we behold with wonder. Every mother suckles her own children, and does not deliver them into the hands of servants and nurses. No indulgence distinguishes the young master from the slave. They lie together amidst the same cattle, upon the same ground, till age separates, and valour marks out, the freeborn. The youths partake late of the pleasures of love, and hence pass the age of puberty unexhausted: nor are the virgins hurried into marriage; the same maturity, the same full growth, is required: the sexes unite equally matched, and robust; and the children inherit the vigour of their parents.

Source: John Louis Beatty and Oliver A. Johnson, eds., *Heritage of Western Civilization* (Englewood Cliffs, N.J.: Prentice-Hall, 1982), 255–256.

despite their barbarism. Yet there were elements in the culture of these people of the whispering trees that blended well with a Roman legacy to shape some of the basic institutions of medieval Europe. And the cross-fertilization began long before Rome fell.

The Rhine-Danube line had protected the Roman Empire from invasion, but it had not kept Germans out. They entered the Empire as slaves, as settlers pleading for protection from other tribes, as

Ancient & Medieval Art

Western civilization, like the other great civilizations of the world, has left a record of its views and values, its dreams and deepest beliefs, in the enduring works of art that survive to us from each stage of Western history. These color pages and those in other parts of the book will offer a selection of the more typical, more revealing, or simply most admired art of the Western world.

This first portfolio includes both ancient and medieval Western art. Samples of the art of the Greeks and Romans and their Near Eastern and African predecessors reveal something of the majesty and beauty these cultures commanded. The art of the early, high, and later Middle Ages shows Mediterranean and northern European cultures merging, the impact of Islam and Byzantium, and above all the shaping influence of the Christian religion on Western culture during this period.

Hatshepsut Enthroned. From Thebes, Deir el Bahri, Temple of Hatshepsut. Indurated limestone, painted; height about 77" (195 cm). The Metropolitan Museum of Art, Rogers Fund and Contribution from Edward S. Harkness, 1929

Hatshepsut, queen and pharaoh, declared herself the daughter of the sun god Re and assumed the double crown of upper and lower Egypt. Despite her traditional costume and pose, her individuality comes through in this formal portrait sculpture.

Spring. Detail of fresco from Thera, Greece. Athens Museum

The lifestyles of the ancient Minoans, the earliest forerunners of the Greeks, seem reflected in lovely wall paintings like this. Like other Mediterranean peoples, the Minoans apparently lived out of doors much of the time and particularly enjoyed their gardens.

Warrior Figure. Riace Bronze. Archaeological Museum, Reggio Calabria, Italy

This majestic fifth-century Greek warrior, who may have held a shield in his left hand, appears powerful and alert today despite twenty-five centuries under the sea. The figure is one of two bronze statues found buried in the sand of the ocean floor off the coast of southern Italy and near the site of an ancient Greek colony. These statues are thought to represent art of the time just preceding the Classical period.

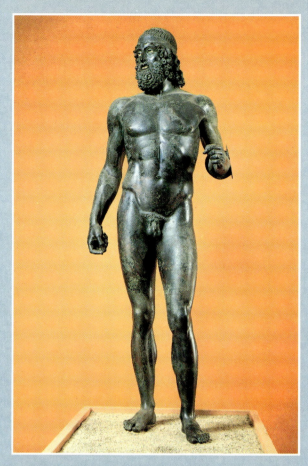

below: Instruction in Music and Grammar. Red figure. Greek kylix. c. 480 B.C. Bildarchiv Preussischer Kulturbesitz, Berlin

This red-figure picture is part of the design of a Greek cup that depicts the arts and sciences—such as poetry, dance, and history—presided over by the nine Muses.

Bust of Julia Domna. Capitoline Museum, Rome

Julia Domna (d. 217), of Syrian birth and the wife of the Roman emperor Septimus Severus (r. 193–211), was a powerful figure in the regime of her son, the emperor Caracalla (r. 211–217). According to some authorities, Caracalla left her in charge of much of the civil administration of the empire when he went on campaign. Apparently Julia learned of her son's murder during such an absence and chose then to take her own life.

below: Wall painting from the villa of Livia at Primaporta. Museo delle Terme, Rome

Most ancient painting has disappeared with the walls on which it was done, but excavations at Pompeii in southern Italy have revealed how sophisticated the Romans had become in this art. Murals like this one show an understanding of landscape and perspective.

GIOVANNI PAOLO PANNINI. C. 1740. *The Interior of the Pantheon.* Oil on canvas. Samuel H. Kress Collection. © 1993, National Gallery of Art, Washington, D.C.

The Roman Pantheon drew many admiring tourists as far back as the eighteenth century, when the Italian artist Giovanni Paolo Pannini created this painting. With its multi-colored marbles and lofty dome rising almost 150 feet above the floor this is the best preserved of all ancient buildings.

Procession of the Virgins. Sant' Apollinare Nuovo, Ravenna. Italy

This procession of Virgin Martyrs from Sant' Apollinare in Ravenna, dating from the sixth century, shows the saints holding their crowns of martyrdom as they advance. Light reflecting off the *tesserae* gives the mosaic a shimmering, appropriately unearthly look.

Front cover of the *Lindau Gospels*.
© The Pierpont Morgan Library 1993.
New York

Elaborate covers were made even in early medieval times for hand-written copies of the Gospels. Precious metals and costly jewels were used lavishly to glorify these accounts of the life of Jesus Christ.

Rose window, Sainte Chapelle. Paris

The intricate tracery of stone and glass that gives Gothic architecture such a light, upward-reaching feel is beautifully illustrated in the royal Sainte Chapelle in Paris. This twelfth-century chapel reflects both the piety and the wealth of medieval France.

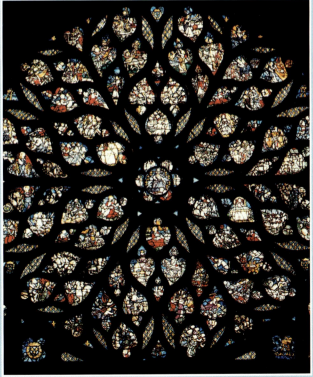

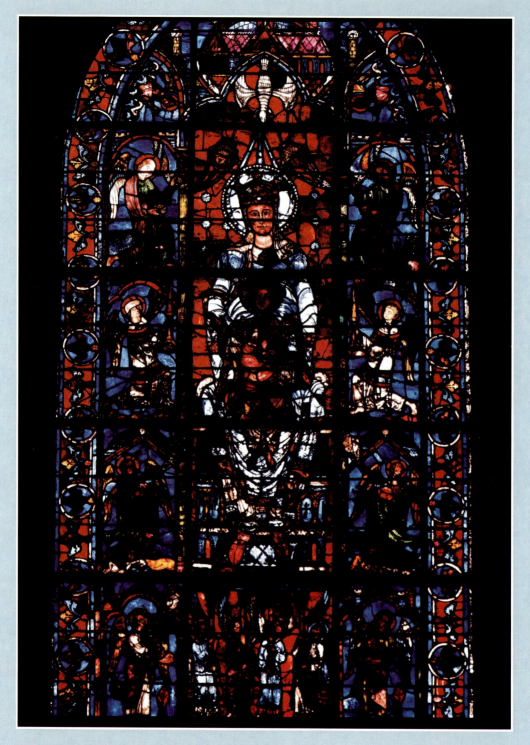

Notre Dame de Belle Verrière, Chartres Cathedral, France

The timeless beauty of this twelfth-century stained glass window from the cathedral of Chartres is hard to reproduce on paper. Only with sunlight glowing through the figures of Mary, Jesus, the Holy Spirit, and the surrounding angels do the images come to life as the artists intended.

Title page of the Gospel of St. John (with depiction of St. John the Evangelist), *Lindisfarne Gospels.* British Library, London

The medieval art of book illumination, like much other medieval art, was highly decorative. Emphasizing line and color, the monks who crafted copies of sacred texts made the few hand-copied books that were available into works of art.

below: Mosque of Suleiman. Istanbul

Muslim mosques were as majestic and beautiful as medieval Christian churches, though built in a very different style. Like Christian emperors and kings, Muslim caliphs and sultans advertised their piety and glorified their reigns by raising such immense houses of worship as this Mosque of Sultan Suleiman in the former Constantinople.

Our Lady of Tenderness, XVC. Pscor School of Icon-Painting. Tretyakov Gallery, Moscow

The Orthodox Church of eastern Europe produced many *icons* like this one, representations of sacred figures intended to serve as foci for religious worship. Both the chapels of princes and the huts of peasants reserved places of honor for these religious artifacts.

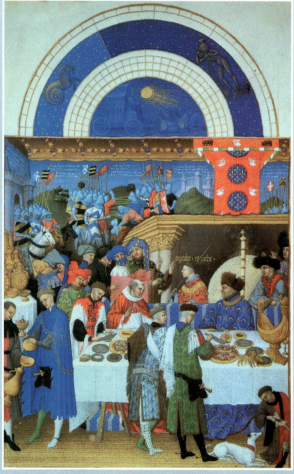

Très Riches Heures du Duc de Berry. January. The Duke at the Table. Musée Condé, Chantilly

The skill of late medieval illustrators is well represented in this picture by Pol de Limbourg from the Duke de Berry's fifteenth-century *Book of Hours.* The duke (in fur hat) dines in his castle hall as courtiers test his food and play with his dogs. The tapestry on the rear wall depicts a battle.

mercenary soldiers ready to fight in Roman armies. Even those who stayed in the woods beyond the line watched and learned from the world across the river. In later Roman times, many abandoned their animist creeds for Christianity, though often in the Arian form, which was heresy in Rome from the early fourth century on.

So romanized were Germanic peoples like the Goths, who had lived on the Roman frontiers for centuries, that historians now suggest they probably shared a basic popular culture with the illiterate masses within the Empire. And as we will see, some of the Germanic kings tried to preserve as much as they could of the Roman way of life even after the Roman Empire had fallen.

Elements of the Germanic culture, however, exercised a crucial influence on the new world that slowly took form after 500. There were, for example, aspects of the social and political organization of the Germans that found an echo in coming centuries. The divine ancestry claimed by German war leaders and their role as chief priests, for instance, contributed to the claims of medieval kings to rule by divine right. The oath of the German chief's *comitatus,* his war band of chosen companions, sworn to fight and die with their leader, looked ahead to the

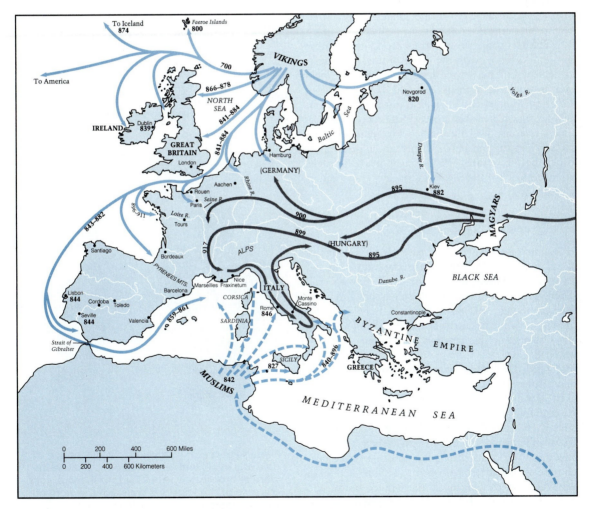

Map 7.1   Invasions of Europe, Seventh Through Eleventh Centuries

feudal allegiance sworn by vassal nobles to their medieval superiors. The fact that Germanic chiefs had no power to make laws and had to make important decisions in consultation with councils of elders helps to explain the limited authority of medieval rulers and the emergence of royal councils and parliaments.

Such Germanic legal institutions as the groups of twelve sworn men who decided the guilt or innocence of a person accused of an offense inspired the later Western system of trial by jury. It is possible to trace such a fundamental medieval economic institution as the craft guild back to social organizations among the Germans. Even the medieval practice of dividing farmland up into long narrow strips rather than rectangular fields may go back to the difficulty of turning the heavy Germanic plow at the end of a furrow, which made fewer and longer furrows a labor-saving device.

The Germanic peoples thus brought a number of useful practices with them out of the dark forests of ancient Europe. In the long run, Christian ideas and institutions, Roman law and language, even Greek philosophy and art had as much to say about the directions later Western civilization took as Germanic customs did. But in the early centuries especially, when survival rather than high culture was at issue, the life ways of the Germans made a crucial contribution to the evolving society of Western Christendom.

Centuries of Struggle

It was not for want of leadership that the kings of the early Middle Ages failed to reestablish strong and lasting government in Europe after Rome's fall. There were men of energy, determination, and intelligence, though seldom with much book learning, among early medieval rulers. People like Theodoric the Ostrogoth, Charlemagne, and Alfred the Great also had a genuine desire to recapture what had been lost when the Roman order passed, or to establish a viable substitute. But neither attempts to maintain a tribal monarchy in the old Germanic style nor efforts to establish a new royal authority by force proved strong enough to overcome the early medieval drift toward fragmentation and anarchy. When we add to this the waves of barbarian invasion that broke over Europe with shattering force in the fifth and sixth centuries and then again in the eighth, ninth, and later centuries, the failure of central government is scarcely surprising.

Germanic Kingdoms: From England to Africa

The fourth-century incursion of the Asiatic Huns, as we saw in the last chapter, had set the Germanic peoples also in motion westward into Roman lands. The Huns, though they established themselves for decades on the Danube plains and drove deep into Roman Gaul and Italy, never set up a permanent state. Even under their great fifth-century leader Attila (r. 434–453), they remained true to the nomadic traditions of many generations, raiders rather than conquerors. It was the Germans they had dislodged who conquered and ruled in Europe and beyond.

The first of these were the Visigoths. After defeating the Eastern Roman emperor at Adrianople in 378 and sacking Rome itself in 410, the Visigoths pushed still farther west to establish a kingdom in Spain and southern France by 418. As Arian Christians, they had some difficulty with their Catholic Christian subjects until a sixth-century Visigothic king accepted conversion to Catholicism. Though its rulers faced many rebellions, the Visigothic Kingdom of Spain survived for three hundred years, until

These sixth-century Ostrogothic eagles, made of gold and inlaid with semi-precious stones, were worn as brooches. The bold patterning and vigorous style of this jewelry is typical of the work of the Germanic nomads who descended upon Europe from the Eurasian steppes.

it was swept away by the Arab invasion of the eighth century.

Other Germanic peoples or federations of Germanic tribes forged less long-lived kingdoms in the part of Roman Gaul that later became France. The Alamanni ruled on the upper Rhine by 420, the Burgundians dominated southeastern France from 443, and the Franks settled in the northern part of the country during the fifth century. Of these peoples, Burgundy enjoyed varying degrees of independence through most of the Middle Ages, though it ultimately became a province of France. Of them all, however, the Franks, who crushed the Alamanni, expelled the Visigoths, produced the famous Charlemagne and gave their name to modern France, had by far the longest future.

To the south, the Vandals passed across Spain and the Straits of Gibraltar to found a short-lived kingdom in North Africa. They settled in modern Tunisia, around ancient Carthage, by 429. The Vandals made their name a synonym for random destruction by recrossing the Mediterranean to ravage Rome itself in 455. Within a few generations, however, they were overwhelmed in their turn by the armies of the Byzantine (Eastern Roman) emperor Justinian (r. 527–565).

In the north, the Angles, Saxons, Jutes, and Frisians invaded what had been Roman Britain. Though they came first as raiders and pillagers, after 550 they founded a number of small kingdoms in England, referred to as the *Heptarchy,* or "Seven States." These "Anglo-Saxon" conquerors pushed the older Celtic inhabitants to the western margins of the islands, back into Scotland, Ireland, Wales, and other regions of the so-called *Celtic fringe.* Even within the Heptarchy, division prevailed for the next three centuries, until one state among them, Alfred the Great's Wessex, provided the power base for a serious attempt to unify England.

Germanic Kingdoms: Ostrogoths and Franks

There was still much fighting ahead—there would be no end of it, really, over the next five centuries—but some of the new rulers were trying to act more like kings than warlords. In this effort, they often invoked the only model of more sophisticated government they knew, that of the Roman Empire which had just fallen to pieces under their hands. Most of the early German kings at least formally acknowl-

edged the superiority of the surviving Eastern Roman, or Byzantine, Empire and its emperor in Constantinople.[1] In the mid-sixth century, furthermore, the most famous of these emperors, Justinian, temporarily succeeded in reconquering much of the Mediterranean rim, including Ostrogothic Italy, Vandal North Africa, and the southern part of Visigothic Spain. Nor were these the last efforts to imitate or to reassemble the once mighty empire of the Romans. Yet none succeeded. Two major examples from these earliest medieval years illustrate the reasons why.

Theodoric (r. 493–526), often called the Great, established the first Germanic kingdom in Italy in the late fifth century and ruled it for thirty years, almost half its history. Theodoric had already led his Ostrogoths—"Eastern" or "Shining" Goths—from their home in the Balkans to attack Constantinople. There, however, a shrewd Byzantine emperor had turned him westward against Rome. When he arrived in Italy in 488, complete with horses, wagons, herds, and two hundred thousand Ostrogoths—his entire nation— he found Italy in the hands of a fellow German, Odoacer, who had replaced the last Roman emperor only a dozen years before. After a bloody and devious struggle, Theodoric captured and killed his rival. He then set to work to rule the heartland of old Rome in peace and in a thoroughly Roman style. "An able Goth," after all, he declared, "wants to be like a Roman; only a poor Roman would want to be like a Goth."[2]

Theodoric acknowledged the overlordship of the Byzantine emperor at Constantinople and left the Roman administration in control of Italy itself. He even abandoned the law of the Ostrogoths and imposed Roman law on his own people—the only Germanic king to do so. He extended preferment and royal favor to Roman scholars and civil servants like Boethius, whose labors, as we will see in a later section, preserved considerable portions of the classical heritage for later centuries. Seeking to reestablish a Roman peace over as much of the rest of Europe as he could, Theodoric dictated terms to some of his fellow Germanic rulers and arranged marriage alliances with others.

In the end, however, his best efforts proved vain. He had two strikes against him from the beginning. He was a Goth, and thus never really acceptable to the Roman aristocracy he sought to win over. And he was an Arian Christian, a believer that Christ was not of one substance with God, but subordinate to him. This view made Theodoric and his Ostrogoths heretics in the eyes of the Roman pope, the patriarch at Constantinople, and the Christian Italians he ruled. Theodoric's tentative efforts to impose some peace and order on Europe also failed as his and his successors' power to enforce their will declined. The Franks to the north were soon defying him openly, and not long after his death the armies of Justinian invaded Italy from the east, followed soon thereafter by the last of the Germanic invaders, the Lombards.

The Lombards, in fact, overran most of the Italian peninsula after 568, establishing a kingdom in the fertile northern region along the Po River—Lombardy today—and scattering disunited lesser states down the peninsula. With the Eastern Roman (Byzantine) Empire still controlling coastal enclaves and the popes occupying a special position in Rome, Italy a century after Theodoric was once more a divided land.

A similar fate awaited the Frankish king Clovis (r. 482–511), who also failed to impose a fundamentally new order, either in the Kingdom of the Franks (the core of modern France) or in a larger sphere. Clovis was the founder of what is usually considered France's first royal dynasty, the Merovingians. He began his career as a Germanic war chief, leading his long-haired Salian ("Salty," or Seacoast) Franks into battle and scheming shrewdly against rival German princes. From their homeland in the lower Rhine valley, two confederations of Frankish tribes had pushed into Roman Gaul in the fifth century. By intrigue, murder, and election, Clovis made himself king of all the Franks. By victories in war, he imposed his rule on the old Gallo-Roman population, on other Germanic tribes in Gaul—Alamanni, Burgundians, Visigoths—and on parts of western Germany as well. His Frankish kingdom became the most powerful of the German successor states to the Western Roman Empire.

In some ways, Clovis showed himself more realistic than Theodoric. Recognizing that the Roman order was dead and could not be revived, Clovis attempted to build a new one. Instead of depending heavily on the old Roman aristocracy in Gaul, he sought to form a new Frankish landholding elite loyal to the crown. To this end, he appointed many of his own royal companions as "counts" to rule large tracts of land in the king's name. Rather than feud with the Roman Catholic religious establishment, as Theodoric had, Clovis converted from paganism to Catholic Christianity. By doing so, he not only conformed to the religion of the people he ruled but forged a firm alliance with the church. He and his successors were thus able to draw on the church's educated and wealthy bishops and its growing numbers of monasteries, which were also centers of agricultural skill, wealth, and learning.

The Merovingian dynasty that Clovis founded flourished for several generations. Within a hundred years, however, it had become a byword for feebleness, his successors "do-nothing" kings of a hopelessly divided realm. Neither Clovis's Germanic tribal vision of what he was doing nor his innovations proved adequate to the task of state building.

In the first place, Clovis and those who followed him had no clear idea of the state at all. They were kings of the restless Franks, without a fixed capital city, clear frontiers, or any sense of the territorial nation. The Merovingian Frankish kings treated the lands they had conquered as a personal estate, dividing the country up among their heirs. Even the counts they appointed to rule the provinces soon became established local rulers, the ancestors of feudal nobles, with little feeling of allegiance to the crown. Because the Merovingians did not forge a civil service of their own and the Roman provincial administration soon ceased to function, little governing was actually done.

It was two and a half centuries before a Frankish king who had Clovis's energy but more vision made a serious effort to rule, not only France, but much of Europe. This was Charlemagne.

Charlemagne's Empire

Charles the Great—Carolus Magnus in Latin, Charlemagne to French- and English-speaking people—is probably the most famous of all medieval kings. His contemporary biographer, his godson Einhard, has left us a clear picture: "Charles was strong, and of lofty stature [six feet three, as was discovered when his tomb was opened in the nineteenth century] . . . his eyes very large and animated, nose a little long, fair hair, and face laughing and merry." He had a "belly rather prominent" and wore the traditional Frankish clothing: a fringed tunic and hose, a coat of otter and marten fur, a blue cloak; "and he always had a sword about him, usually one with a gold or silver hilt."[3]

The king, Einhard further reports, loved to have family, friends, and dependents around him and made decisions surrounded by a motley collection of advisers in the old Germanic way. He was intelligent, spoke Latin and some Greek, was fascinated by astrology, and worked very hard at learning to write, though he made little progress because, his biographer says, he took it up too late in life. The monasteries he encouraged and the scholars who frequented his court—which he moved about but eventually centered at Aachen in the Rhineland—became the center of a revival of Western culture and scholarship known as the Carolingian Renaissance.

The Kingdom of the Franks that Charlemagne ruled was the largest and most powerful state in Europe in 800. He made it considerably larger and more powerful. If anyone could give direction to the chaotic drift of the times, Charles the Great was surely the one.

Charlemagne's ancestors had been "mayors of the palace," chief court and administrative officials to Clovis's descendants, the later Merovingian rulers of the Frankish state. Some of these officials had enhanced their own power by regulating the distribution of royal lands to other Franks or by making war on other Germanic peoples and forcing them to acknowledge Frankish authority. Charlemagne's forebears had also strengthened their ties with the Roman Catholic church by supporting missionary efforts and by serving as the pope's special protectors against the Kingdom of the Lombards in northern Italy. Charlemagne's grandfather, Charles Martel ("Charles the Hammer," r. 714–741), had performed a notable service by turning back the Muslim Arabs in the Battle of Tours in 732. Charlemagne's father, Pippin III the Short (r. 741–768), had won papal sanction for the transfer of the Frankish crown itself from the feeble Merovingian line to the virile new Carolingian dynasty, as the family came to be called after Charlemagne.

Charlemagne (r. 768–814) not only dressed like a Frank, but was a war leader in the old Frankish tradition. He reigned for forty-six years and fought in more than fifty military campaigns. Another contemporary account offers a picture of Charlemagne as he looked to his enemies, in this case the Lombards of doomed Pavia in northern Italy, that differs strikingly from Einhard's jolly, convivial ruler:

Then they beheld Charlemagne, the man of iron, in his iron helmet, his arms covered with iron casing, his iron breast and his broad shoulders protected by an iron armor; his left hand raised up the iron lance, while the right was ever ready to grip the victorious steel. . . . His horse as well was iron in color, iron in its courage. . . . Oh, the iron. Alas for the iron! This was the

desperate cry of the inhabitants [as the] iron shook the firmness of their walls and the courage of [their] youth.[4]

"Oh the iron—alas for the iron" indeed! In his endless wars, the emperor of the Franks crushed the Lombards, the Saxons, and the Bavarians. He conquered Brittany and Aquitaine. He drove the Arabs back beyond the Pyrenees and decimated the Avars—Turko-Mongol heirs of the Huns—on the Danube plain. He was capable of hanging four thousand Saxons in a single day. His grandson remembered him as a man whose "tempered severity" made "the hearts of both Franks and barbarians" tremble.[5] But by the

Charlemagne, looking almost larger than his horse in this bronze sculpture of the period, wears the crown and holds the orb of imperial authority. Note the heavy sword under the monarch's cloak, a symbol of his many victories and conquests. Notice also the monumental feel of this representation, which is in fact only a small figurine.

early ninth century, Charlemagne's empire included most of western Europe: modern France, Belgium, the Netherlands, and Switzerland, as well as major portions of Germany, Italy, and Spain.

It was an empire scarcely to be matched in Europe until Napoleon's day. And the Frankish king made a serious attempt to rule what he had conquered. He did this by pragmatic responses to problems as they came up and by tinkering with existing institutions, rather than through detailed planning or broad reorganization. The dukes and counts he appointed served as jacks-of-all-trades; they were mili-

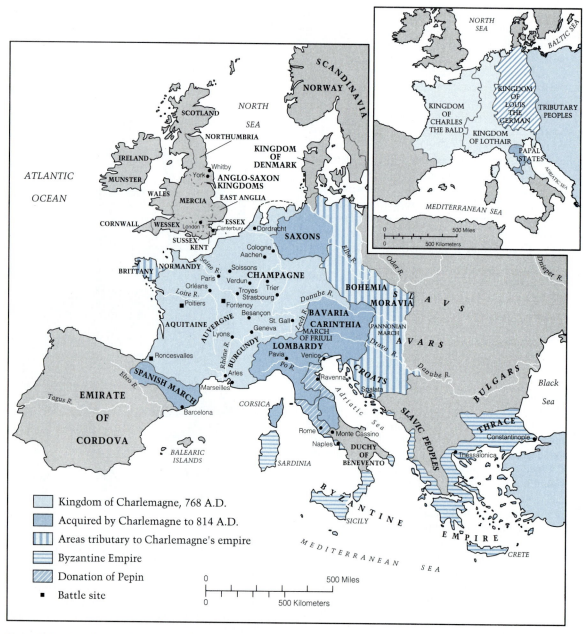

Map 7.2 Carolingian Empire and Anglo-Saxon England

tary, judicial, and administrative officials of the crown in the countryside. The roving representatives, called *missi dominici,* whom he dispatched to inspect the counties, kept a check on both civil and ecclesiastical authorities and promulgated royal directives of all sorts. He also gathered the chief men of the realm, churchmen as well as nobles and royal appointees, to report to him and to hear royal decrees, called *capitularies* (see box, "Charlemagne on Good Government").

On Christmas Day in the year 800, the capstone was placed on this structure of power when Pope Leo III, grateful for Charlemagne's help against his enemies, crowned him emperor and Augustus, Christian heir of all the Caesars. The imperial title made Charlemagne equal to the Byzantine emperors in Constantinople and superior to all European rulers. It further cemented the vital alliance between the French crown and the church, linking the destiny of the still undeveloped medieval monarchy with the much more sophisticated structure of the Christian church.

But this impressive achievement, like the other Germanic kingdoms, did not last. Charlemagne died in 814, leaving his empire to his son Louis the Pious (r. 814–840), who proved more interested in cultivating his own soul than in carrying on his father's imperial tradition. In 843 Charlemagne's three grandsons divided the empire among them in the old Germanic way (see map 7.2 inset), and it was soon subdivided still further. The counts and dukes ceased to be royal appointees and became hereditary local magnates instead. Charlemagne's empire had, in fact, depended as much on his endless military campaigns and on his distribution of conquered lands among his nobles as on structured administration. As a result, the Carolingian Empire scarcely survived his death.

Charlemagne's legacy was nonetheless substantial. He had successfully reasserted the importance of strong central government. Much of later medieval government drew on this Carolingian model. And even the division of Charlemagne's lands by his grandsons revealed trends of great future significance. At Strasbourg in 843, two of the grandsons, Charles the Bald (823–877) and Louis the German (c. 804–876), joined forces against the third, Lothair (795–855), and took a solemn oath of mutual support. Each swore in the language understood by the other's soldiers, and the languages the two allies used were clearly the ancestors of modern French and German. The political emergence of these two nations lay far in the future, but the cultural foundations were already being laid in the ninth century.

THE RULERS AND THE RULED
Charlemagne on Good Government

The following extract from Charlemagne's *capitularies,* or royal decrees, for the year 802 gives some indication of how seriously the Carolingian emperor took the governance of the realm. These paragraphs are taken from the official instructions to Charlemagne's *missi dominici,* the powerful royal agents dispatched to check on the nobles who ruled the provinces of the empire. These injunctions are thus less likely to be pious homilies or public relations ploys than to reflect serious government policy.

The most serene and most Christian lord emperor Charles ... would have all the various classes of persons mentioned in the following sections live strictly in accordance with the law. Moreover, where anything which is not right and just has been enacted in the law, he has ordered them to inquire into this most diligently and to inform him of it; he desires, God granting, to reform it. . . .

And let the *missi* themselves make a diligent investigation whenever any man claims that an injustice has been done to him by any one, just as they desire to deserve the grace of omnipotent God and to keep their fidelity pledged to him, so that in all cases, everywhere, they shall, in accordance with the will and fear of God, administer the law fully and justly in the case of the holy churches of God and of the poor, of wards and widows, and of the whole people.

Source: Norton Downs, ed., *Medieval Pageant: Readings in Medieval History* (Princeton: D. van Nostrand, 1964), 68–70.

Raiders and Settlers: Vikings, Arabs, Magyars

Meanwhile, new threats to western Europe had been gathering around the unsteady states that succeeded the Roman imperium. From north, south, and east, new and even more savage invasions knifed into Christendom in the eighth and ninth centuries. The most important of these were the Magyars, who came galloping out of the Asian grasslands, the Arabs from the southern deserts, and the Vikings, the sea kings who sailed down from the north in their long black dragon ships.

The Magyars, like the Huns before them and the Mongols still to come, were steppe nomads. Breeders of beautiful horses, taking no prisoners in combat, they were powerful cavalry soldiers. Advancing westward from the Black Sea, they established themselves in the wide valley of the Danube, modern Hungary. From this base in eastern Europe, they raided central and western Europe. In the later eighth and earlier ninth centuries, Germany, France, and Italy all suffered from Magyar depredations. Their goal was plunder, and by slaughtering whole villages they put such fear into the hearts of Europeans that other settlements bought them off with tribute without a fight. For those who resisted, there was the edge of the sword, or perhaps an Eastern slave market waiting.

From the desert lands of Arabia and North Africa to the south came Arab warriors. These invaders, however, were impelled by religious motives as well as by hope of pillage. And in some places, they came not merely to raid, but to stay.

In the early seventh century, a great religious leader named Muhammad (570–632), called the Prophet by his followers, arose in Arabia. Welding educated oasis Arabs and fierce desert Bedouins into one people with the new faith of Islam—discussed in the next chapter—Muhammad unleashed a powerful new force across western Asia and northern Africa. And less than a century after his death in 632, Muslim armies were moving against Europe as well.

Arab-led Berber forces from North Africa crossed the Strait of Gibraltar in 711, overwhelmed the Kingdom of the Visigoths in Spain, and pushed on over the Pyrenees into the Kingdom of the Franks. In 732 they were finally stopped at Tours in western France by Charles Martel, Charlemagne's grandfather; but not even Charlemagne was able to drive these invaders out of Spain. In the ninth century, meanwhile, Muslim forces from Tunisia invaded Sicily, attacked southern Italy, raided and established bases in southern France, and sacked Rome in 846. Becoming good sailors, these former desert dwellers also plundered merchant shipping up and down the Mediterranean.

Many of the Muslim invaders, however, were not merely looters, but conquerors and builders. We will look later at the civilization they constructed across Asia, Africa, and parts of Europe. As we will see, one of its centers was in Spain, where Muslims ruled throughout the Middle Ages, contributing a great deal to European culture. But in the eighth and ninth centuries, Europeans saw nothing but flashing scimitars and knew nothing of Islam but the onrush of its armies. "Fight those who do not believe in Allah," the Prophet had declared, "until they pay tribute out of hand."[6] His followers were doing just that.

The most feared of all these intruders, however, were neither Magyars nor Arabs but European enemies, the Vikings or Northmen who came pouring out of Scandinavia. "Good Lord, deliver us," Christians devoutly prayed in the depths of that violent age, "from the fury of the Northmen." We see them still in a rude Anglo-Saxon carving at Lindisfarne Abbey in Britain—appropriately enough on a tombstone—swinging swords and battle-axes as they advance.

Scholars dispute the causes for the Viking explosion out of Norway, Sweden, and Denmark in the eighth and ninth centuries. Suggested motives include overpopulation due to the widespread practice of polygamy; the inability of their cold northern lands, almost as unproductive as the steppes or the deserts, to feed the population; the tendency of an overthrown Viking leader to prefer emigration and foreign conquests to a subordinate position at home; and, of course, the ancient lure of plunder there for the taking.

The means they used are better understood. The Vikings were Europe's greatest seafarers and shipbuilders. They built fleets of 50-foot "dragon ships," lined with shields, propelled by long oars and a single square sail. These they manned with two- or three-score seaborne warriors to whom rivers and bays, seas and even the Atlantic Ocean were a second home. Like their warrior gods roistering in Valhalla overhead, they were joyful, savage fighting men. The toast *"Skol!"* really does mean "skull"; according to legend, it was a toast drunk from the metal-lined skull of a Viking's slain foe.

The image of the Viking wading ashore with horned helmet and unkempt beard blowing in the wind, whirling a long-handled battle-ax does, however, require considerable qualifying. The Northmen were far-ranging traders before they were pirates, and they became settlers afterward. They bartered fur, slaves, and their own ironwork as far as Baghdad and northern India. Their vessels had crossed the Atlantic by 1000, establishing settlements in Iceland, Greenland, and North America. Like the Arabs, however, they made their most vivid early impact on medieval Europe as raiders and pillagers.

In the ninth century particularly, Northmen raided the coasts of England, Ireland, France, and

Spain and probed major rivers like the Rhine and the Seine. They also traveled from Scandinavia down the Dnieper and Volga rivers across Russia to the Black Sea and on from there to strike Constantinople. Like the Magyars, they slaughtered, looted, and wrung tribute from their victims. Like the Arabs, however, they also sometimes settled down to stay. In 866 they established a kingdom in eastern England. In 911 a Frankish king bought off the Norse leader Rollo (c. 860–c. 932) with a wide swath of northwestern France that came to be known as Normandy. In the southern part of what became Russia, the Northmen imposed their rule on the indigenous Slavs and organized the first Russian state, a loose confederation of princes centered at Kiev in today's Ukraine.

As the dust of this last and most violent of the great invasions began to settle in the later ninth and early tenth centuries, the Magyars were emerging as the aristocratic rulers of what became Hungary; the Arabs governed Spain and dominated Sicily; and the Northmen controlled southern Russia and substantial parts of England and France in addition to their native Scandinavia. As the violence ebbed for the second time, there was a chance again to restore order to the battered Western world.

Efforts at State Building: Alfred and Canute

Two men who tried to reestablish a structure of authority in their overlapping areas of western Europe were the English ruler Alfred the Great and the Danish king Canute. Alfred and Canute lived a century and a half apart and were on opposite sides in the wars of their age. Yet both tried hard to build states that could survive the tumult of the times.

As we have seen, the Romans had abandoned England early in the fifth century, leaving the land open to Germanic raids from the mainland that slowly turned into permanent settlements. Roman civilization vanished as Angles, Saxons, Jutes, and other tribes established their rule on the island. Missionaries, however, brought Christianity back to England as early as the sixth century. And by the eighth century, the dozens of divisions into which the land had at first fissured had coalesced into seven tribal kingdoms, the Heptarchy. In the ninth century, then, even as Viking attacks gathered force, the ruler of one of these seven little kingdoms took upon himself the double task of unifying Anglo-Saxon England and turning back the Danish invaders. This

was Alfred, king of the West Saxon region of Wessex, in southeastern England.

Alfred the Great (r. 871–899) probably did more to establish a stable state in the teeth of internal disunion and foreign assault than any ruler since Charlemagne. He imposed the authority of the house of Wessex on most of England outside a Danish enclave in the northeast. He organized a more efficient and mobile army and built ships and fortifications to protect his embryonic country. His struggle with the Danes ended less decisively, though they agreed to limit themselves to the region they had already settled, known as the Danelaw, and came to accept Christianity. Like Charlemagne and Theodoric, Alfred also encouraged scholarship and sponsored a cultural revival in southern England.

Much of what Alfred had accomplished survived for the better part of a century; he may even be said to have laid the foundations for an English nation. But the times were not propitious for nation building. Disorder and violence were still too rampant for a central government to succeed.

In 991 a successor of King Alfred's had to agree to pay tribute to the increasingly aggressive Danes, for which purpose a tax was levied on England, the much resented Danegeld. Then in 1013 King Sven of Denmark invaded and overran the kingdom. Four years later, the Anglo-Saxon royal council, or *witenagemot,* itself elected Sven's son, King Canute of Denmark, king of England also. The emergent nation of Alfred's day had become once more a province of another's empire.

Canute (r. 1017–1035), however, was another ruler dedicated to imposing central authority on a divided and unstable realm. He governed a far-flung and geographically divided empire, including Denmark, Norway, and Iceland as well as England. And he proved as able a ruler as Alfred had been, confronting forces of disunion that were perhaps even greater.

Canute had the vision to see England, rather than Denmark, as the center of his scattered realm and worked hard at building unity there. He gathered a mixed council of Danes and Englishmen to advise him and sought to encourage peace and even a merging of the Danish and Anglo-Saxon populations. He also worked closely with the Roman church, became a Christian himself, and promoted that religion among the Northmen. As Theodoric had accepted Roman law, so Canute sponsored and encouraged a revival of Anglo-Saxon law and presented himself as ruler in that tradition.

Yet when Canute died in 1035, he left no viable heir to his fledgling empire, and it collapsed like a house of cards. Denmark and Norway went their separate ways, and the house of Wessex reclaimed the English throne. Within a generation, however, that house was also extinguished as a new foreign dynasty swept to power. The new invaders were led by William the Conqueror, who, as we will see in a later chapter, finally began the building of a unified England in an era of strong kings and resurgent central government.

Early Medieval Society

In the broadest sense, European society in the early Middle Ages experienced political changes that were quite different from those that occurred in ancient Greece and Rome. Medieval people did not see one form of government give way to another, as when Greek city-states lost power to Hellenistic monarchies or the Roman Republic gave way to the Roman Empire. The early medieval period experienced a general decay of all government. These northern European peoples were for several centuries simply unable to generate centralized political institutions strong enough and long lasting enough to provide a stable framework for living in the teeth of internal disintegration and external assault. Functions that had once been performed or fostered by governments thus fell into other hands.

The feudal system, which we will examine shortly, offered at least a modicum of military protection. The medieval manor farm produced a subsistence-level food supply. The church became the most impressive of all medieval institutions, contributing not only a desperately needed faith but, as we will see, some practical supports for society as well. Between them, feudalism, the manor system, and the church held the early medieval world together through these dangerous centuries.

The Successor States

As we have already noticed in particular cases, the Germanic successor states that replaced the Roman Empire brought their own ideas of government to the region. At the same time, however, German kings came to terms with and even borrowed from the Roman legal and political structure they found in their newly conquered lands.

The Germanic peoples were normally governed by codes of customary behavior binding on all descendants of a common divine or semidivine tribal ancestor. For their new subjects, however, and for disputes involving both Germans and Romans, the Germanic kings issued a number of legal codes based on residency rather than descent and combining Germanic, Roman, and Christian concepts. The earliest of these, the *Lex Visigothorum,* was promulgated in 483, and others were issued by the Burgundian, Anglo-Saxon, and Merovingian Frankish rulers.

The larger structure of government in the Germanic successor states is best illustrated by the empire of Charlemagne around 800. The Frankish emperor claimed for himself supreme secular and religious power, portraying himself as the heir of both the Roman Caesars and the biblical kings David and Solomon. Crowned the successor to Augustus by the pope, he saw himself as the "anointed of God," much as his Germanic ancestors had seen themselves as descendants of their own gods. The Christian doctrine of the divine right of kings to rule had first crystallized in the West in Visigothic Spain, where kings were crowned by priests. After Charlemagne's coronation by the pope in 800, divine sanction became the central justification for royal power in the Middle Ages.

For policy-making, Charlemagne summoned an annual assembly of nobles and high-ranking churchmen. This assembly was not a lawmaking body like later parliaments or other legislative assemblies, but it served nevertheless as a model for these later institutions. Like later medieval monarchs, furthermore, the Carolingian emperor usually decided what he wanted to do before he convened his advisers. He then summoned these leading dignitaries of church and state primarily to get their formal commitment to royal policies.

Below the divine-right ruler and his chief advisers, Charlemagne's administrative structure, like that of his Merovingian predecessors, was headed by members of his own household. Personal servants with governmental functions included the seneschal who managed the royal estates, the chamberlain in charge of the royal treasury, the marshal of the royal armed forces, and a chaplain who was both spiritual guide and chief secretary to his majesty. Far from the court, finally, the counts and dukes who exercised primary power in distant provinces and the *missi dominici* who carried royal authority to these outlying areas were also the monarch's personal appointees. Unlike the specialized bureaucratic jobs of later centuries, most of these functions were easily interchangeable in the early Middle Ages.

The duties of the early medieval officials, at least by the standards of modern governments, were minimal. They had to organize military campaigns, maintain a few royal law courts, collect royal tolls, build and repair the few forts, roads, and bridges for which the monarchy was responsible. Kings claimed authority in executive, legislative, and judicial affairs, with no division of powers. Strong government—where it did emerge—was essentially the execution of a monarch's decisions by his personal servants and by nobles bound to him by oaths of personal allegiance.

Women may have been accepted more easily in leadership positions in early medieval times than later on. The relative equality of husband and wife among the Germanic tribes had generated important roles for the wives of Germanic chiefs and led to the emergence of some women rulers. Among the early Angles and Saxons, for instance, women of rank were sometimes employed to negotiate peace between hostile peoples. The readier acceptance of women in positions of political authority in the Germanic kingdoms is best evidenced by the tone in which early chroniclers recount their accomplishments. Merovingian queens like Fredegund (d. 597), who began life as a servant, intrigued and fought their way to power like third-century Roman empresses. Alfred the Great's daughter Aethelflaeda (d. 918) ruled northern England very successfully, fought the Danes, and recovered and fortified as much territory as her famous father had. And all this political activity was recorded by the chroniclers as evenhandedly as they recounted the deeds of male rulers. It was only in later medieval centuries that such exploits by a woman began to be seen as unnatural, as "manlike" or "above the nature of her sex."[7]

Feudal Politics

Despite law codes, civil servants, assemblies of notables, and monarchs making claims to great personal authority, however, strong government was not common in early medieval times. In its place a far less centralized political structure known as feudalism gradually evolved in many parts of early medieval Europe.

The concept of feudalism is much debated among modern historians, and the discussion that follows must be understood as a set of very sweeping generalizations, not as a description of any uniform or universal medieval system of feudal relations. At least in its earlier forms, feudalism may be best understood as an effort to provide minimal governmental functions—mostly military defense and police protection—over local areas when central government could no longer guarantee even these essentials. With the passing of Roman government and the failure of the Germanic successor states to provide an adequate substitute, local magnates with military experience often recruited a few lesser landowners, also trained to the sword, to defend their holdings and to restore some semblance of order. Thus elite cadres of men devoted to arms and to the land and power they could accumulate with their weapons came to dominate Europe. They were the West's early medieval substitute for government and, as such, essential to the survival of the Western world.

Within this military caste evolved a loose hierarchy of authority called *feudalism.* Less powerful knights and nobles offered their services to more powerful ones in return for protection and land. In a formal ceremony of *homage and investiture,* the less powerful fighting man took an oath of personal allegiance to the more powerful leader and was invested with a *fief*—an estate that included both an expanse of land and the villages full of laborers who worked it. The dependent was henceforth known as the *vassal* of the man to whom he had pledged his service and whom he then recognized as his *feudal lord.* The roots of this system of personal allegiance went back to the old Germanic *comitatus* or war band and even to the Roman system of patron and client. Feudalism thus defined became common first in France and the Low Countries, later over much of medieval Europe.

The participants in the ceremony of homage and investiture probably saw it in different ways. For the lord, it was the homage that counted: the lord's military clout was increased by the addition of the new vassal with his handful of trained soldiers. For the vassal, the investiture was the heart of the matter, conferring upon him a valuable fief that would support him, his family, and his armed retainers. Feudalism was, in short, a system of land tenure based on military service. But it also meant protection for all concerned. The lord's private feudal army of vassals and their men-at-arms was so much the larger. The individual vassal could depend on his lord for help, and the peasant labor force had at least a small resident garrison of experienced fighters to guard it.

Early in the evolution of the feudal system, the lord might simply take his new man into his own household and provide him "food and clothing" directly; or there might have been a simple money payment. The basic feudal relationship thus came into existence before the key later feudal institution of the fief. In time, however, the feudal contract became more complex and specific, involving a variety of obligations on both sides.

In developed feudalism, the vassal was required to provide his lord with military service, including a specified number of armed retainers, for a particular number of days, often forty, of fighting per year. The vassal also came to owe "aids," or money payments, on the occasion of his lord's oldest son's knighthood, his oldest daughter's marriage, his own departure for a foreign war, or his ransom if the fortunes of war went against him. Loyal vassals were expected to attend the lord's court, to provide wise advice, and to help try vassals who had failed in their trust. For feudal loyalty remained the essential cement that held the entire rickety system together, and breaches of fealty had to be punished.

But there was opportunity in this system for vassals to do well too. With a fief, they acquired not only labor and land but the right to establish a local law court and collect fees and fines, the right to charge tolls, and in later times, to coin their own money. Some vassals, furthermore, collected a number of such fiefs and parceled some of them out to vassals of their own, thus becoming great men in their turn. Some took fiefs from several lords, creating awkward conflicts of interest if any two of their lords should fall out between themselves. To deal with this contingency, vassals had to recognize one overlord as their *liege* lord, meaning that they would rally to his cause even against another lord to whom they had sworn loyalty (see box, "An Oath of Homage"). At the top of this rickety pyramid of power, meanwhile, the feudal allegiance of the greatest lords to their royal sovereigns was often more a formality than a political fact, a fiction cloaking a rough parity of power, negotiated alliances, or open enmity. The system became, in short, tangled and unstable. In the early Middle Ages, however, it did give Europe a loose yet flexible substitute for government, with military protection, local authority, and sometimes local baronial courts and currency as well.

The lady of the manor—the lord's wife—also played an important part in the functioning of the feudal system. Her marriage was arranged for her and had more to do with family alliances or transfers of property than with love. The crude castle she lived in was dominated by males whose main concerns were weapons and horses, hunting and fighting. And her husband, at least in the early Middle Ages, seems to have been able to treat her pretty much as he pleased, which sometimes meant brutally. A nobleman could

PROFILES IN HISTORY
An Oath of Homage

This example of a feudal oath, which dates from the thirteenth century, illustrates the complexities of developed feudalism. Here a French nobleman, John of Toul, pledges his primary allegiance and military service to Beatrice, countess of Troyes. Because John has sworn homage to several other magnates as well, however, he must also specify the tortuous procedures by which he will attempt to honor his various oaths of allegiance if any of his overlords should find themselves in conflict with each other. Do his plans for balancing his feudal commitments sound practical to you? Does this suggest any weaknesses in the feudal system?

I, John of Toul, make it known that I am the liege man of the lady Beatrice, Countess of Troyes, and of my most dear lord, Theobald, count of Champagne, her son, against all persons living or dead, except for my allegiance to lord Enjorand of Coucy, lord John of Arcis and the count of Grandpré. If it should happen that the count of Grandpré should be at war with the countess and count of Champagne on his own quarrel, I will aid the count of Grandpré in my own person and will send to the count and the countess of Champagne the knights whose service I owe them for the fief which I hold of them. But if the count of Grandpré shall make war on the countess and the count of Champagne on behalf of his friends and not in his own quarrel, I will aid in my own person the countess and count of Champagne and will send one knight to the count of Grandpré for the service which I owe him for the fief which I hold of him, but I will not go myself into the territory of the count of Grandpré to make war on him.

Source: Thomas C. Mendenhall, Basil D. Henning, and A. S. Foord, eds., *Ideas and Institutions in European History 800–1715* (New York: Holt, Rinehart, and Winston, 1948), 11.

cast off his wife for adultery or failure to produce an heir, while he himself often kept concubines.

Yet the lady of the manor had important responsibilities. Most of our evidence comes from the later Middle Ages but probably applies as well to the earlier centuries. A lord's wife had first of all to provide a male heir for her husband's lands: female heirs were less acceptable because they could not perform the military service on which most land tenure depended. The lady of the manor also had a house to run—a large one, though she had servants to help. More importantly, however, like her Germanic forebears she had the responsibility of defending the estate when her husband was off at the wars. Since wars were common and vassals were often called on to fulfill their military service obligations, women not infrequently had to direct the defense of feudal castles and lands.

The idea and the very term *feudal system* were invented long after the Middle Ages by seventeenth- and eighteenth-century scholars who were trying to explain the remnants of feudal relations that survived in their time. So confused is the chronology, so diverse the phenomenon of historical feudalism that some recent historians have suggested simply abandoning the notion of a feudal "system" altogether. These revisionists would replace sweeping generalizations on the subject with a rich variety of "detailed descriptions of areas characterized by different forms of government and social structure."[8] In the broadest textbook perspective, however, the concept of feudalism still seems to have much to recommend it as an introductory approach to early medieval government.

Manorial Agriculture

From the top of early medieval society, we turn now to the bottom. From lords and their vassals, we shift our focus to the relationship between these members of the upper class and the serfs who labored for them.

Vassals and serfs were both committed to the service of others, but there the similarity ended. The vassal was a soldier and a landholder, committed by his own free oath to his overlord, and part of the medieval political elite. The serf was a peasant farmer, bound by tradition and law to the land he worked, and the hard-working basis of the medieval economy. Serfs provided the labor on which everything else rested. They also constituted the large majority of medieval people, 90 percent of whom lived and worked all their lives on manorial estates.

The *medieval manor,* like the feudal system, had its origins in both Roman and Germanic practices. Medieval serfs were the descendants of Roman *coloni* who had surrendered independent peasant status to a Roman landed magnate in return for land and protection. Though they were not slaves, *coloni* were bound to cultivate the land they worked as tenants or sharecroppers. From the fourth century on, they were forbidden to leave that land, as medieval serfs were later on. The early medieval manor village was thus patterned to some degree on the Roman villa or estate. But the lord of the manor also derived much of his traditional authority over his serfs from the powers enjoyed by the chief of a Germanic village. From the mixture emerged a set of agrarian institutions that were unique to medieval Europe.

This manorial pattern of agriculture took shape first in parts of France, Germany, and Italy and spread to many other parts of the continent. Peasant life on the Celtic western fringe or in Slavic eastern Europe, in sheep-herding or wine-growing areas, developed very different forms of organization. Yet the

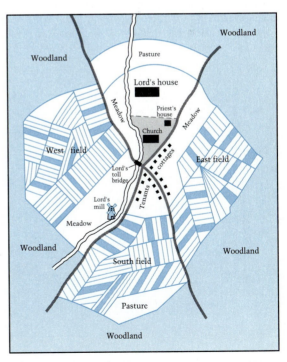

Map 7.3   Plan of a Manor

manor was prevalent enough in much of Europe to warrant our focusing on it here.

A look at a manor village from the top of a neighboring hill would not show anything like an American farming county, each substantial farmhouse and barn isolated among wide, rectangular, fenced-in fields. All the peasants on a medieval manor commonly lived together in a village. All their fields, laid out in unfenced strips, were spread out around the tiny hamlet. In northern Europe, such strips were frequently about 220 yards long (a furrow's length, or furlong) by 16 feet wide. The length, as we noted, was determined by the distance a draft animal could pull without tiring and the width by the space needed to turn the animal and plow around. Four such furlong strips added up to an acre, the modern unit used to measure land.

The typical village consisted of some dozen one-room thatched-roof huts, a small church, perhaps a mill by the stream, a bakehouse, and a brewhouse in northern Europe, a winepress in the south. On the hill, the lord of the manor's stronghold in the early Middle Ages looked more like a log fort in Daniel Boone's America than the elaborate Norman castle of later medieval centuries. Inside the manor house, the lord had two rooms instead of the peasant's one. There was an all-purpose "great hall," where the men-at-arms would eat and sleep, play with the dogs, perhaps clang through a practice bout, and

wait for a war. And there was a "chamber," where the lord's wife, family, and serving women could get some peace and quiet. The manor house was probably as damp and drafty as the serf's hut. For lord and serf alike, there were a minimum of material things: benches, stools, trestle tables, mugs, spoons, knives, homespun clothing, leather harness, weapons, and tools.

Serfs belonged to the manor itself: to its land, its fields, its community, its customs. Though they could not be bought and sold like chattel slaves, serfs could not leave the estate without the lord's consent. They were subject to the lord of the manor's will in many other ways too, for he had the right to impose the discipline necessary to ensure they performed their many labor obligations. Normally serfs worked perhaps three days a week on the lord's land but did extra work at harvest time. They also kept roads and bridges in repair and did other work around the manor, an obligation known as *corvée* labor that long outlasted serfdom itself. With what time was left them, they tilled their own strips of land. There were still some free peasants among them, and a few outright slaves. But serf labor was the backbone of the system, the bone and muscle of the manorial economy.

Serfs had other obligations too. They paid the lord a percentage of their harvest and perhaps a small head tax, or *taille*, as well. They paid a tithe—proba-

Medieval European peasants, most of them serfs bound to the land, instituted a number of valuable advances in agricultural technology, including the heavy plow shown here. In this English manuscript illustration from the later Middle Ages, the woman goads the oxen as the man guides the plow.

bly not literally a tenth even then—to support the church and the local priest, who probably also worked his own strips of land. They paid for the services of the mill, the bakehouse, the winepress—all of which were owned by the lord. They paid him to marry outside their tiny community or to inherit the hut and the family strips, and they paid fines to his bailiff when they were caught poaching and hauled up before the lord's court. All payments were in kind, of course: chickens, fruit, honey, a measure of grain for the lord, a loaf of bread left to pay the baker. Peasants at the Abbey of St. Germain des Prés outside Paris, for instance, owed their landlords "three chickens and fifteen eggs, and a large number of planks to repair . . . buildings" as well as "a couple of pigs . . . wine, honey, wax, soap, or oil"; "women were obliged to spin cloth or to make a garment for the big house every year."[9]

Life on the Manor

Life on the medieval manor was life lived close to the heavy earth, the meadows, the woods to which the peasant family tramped every day. The children could gather cow dung in the meadow and spread it on the fields, collect firewood (only fallen limbs—no cutting the lord's trees), or watch the pigs grub for roots and acorns in the woods. The husband leaned on the wooden plow, which was further weighted by a heavy stone, while his wife wielded a goad to keep the oxen pulling.

To preserve fairness, the land was either parceled out into strips as the arable land was, or used communally, as was normally the case with pasture and forest. Everybody's animals grazed and rooted on the commons, each family had some strips of the best land down by the stream, the rocky land up the hillside, and the marshy bit at the edge of the fens. The lord's strips too were typically scattered among those of his serfs.

The peasants decided together when to plow, sow, and harvest each field. They knew, as tillers apparently had since Neolithic times, that crops need to be rotated, land left fallow to recover its fertility. As the Middle Ages advanced, a three-field system became more common. Instead of half the land lying unused each year, a third was left fallow, a third planted in winter wheat, and another third in soil-replenishing beans, peas, or barley.

Peasant women shared the labor that was the common lot. Wives frequently worked beside their husbands in the fields. They always ran the basic social unit—the family—which of course meant more

work. Women prepared food, bore children and cared for them, made clothing, fed chickens, milked the cow, and did a great deal more besides. A medieval writer described some of a housewife's problems in the Middle Ages:

> And how, I ask, though it may seem odious, how does the wife stand who when she comes in, hears her child scream, sees the cat stealing food, and the hound at the hide? Her cake is burning on the stone hearth, her calf is sucking the milk, the earthen pot is overflowing into the fire.[10]

There seem to have been fewer women serfs than men. This disturbing statistic may reflect female infanticide or perhaps the debilitating effect of childbearing coupled with hard labor. Yet even in reduced numbers, women fed their families, made the clothes on their backs, and still found energy to work in the fields. Neither they nor their husbands had any choice about the work that was the common lot.

Medieval men drank huge quantities of beer and wine and apparently were often drunk. Women were frequently accused of being scolds and shrews. Life was so difficult on the medieval manor that it is hard to blame either of them.

Expanding Christendom

Out of the tumultuous times between the fifth and the tenth centuries, only one institution in western Europe emerged clearly stronger, larger, and with a more powerful grip on the minds and lives of Western peoples. This was the Roman Catholic church. Building on intellectual and institutional foundations laid down in Roman times, the church survived the passing of the Western Roman Empire, responded vigorously to new circumstances, and carved out a unique position at the center of Western life in the Middle Ages.

Early Medieval Popes— Gregory the Great

The primacy of the popes, or the bishops of Rome, in Western Christendom took centuries to establish. As we have seen, Rome had some advantages from the beginning: it was the imperial see, the largest and richest diocese of the church, and the city where Peter was martyred and both Peter and Paul were buried. As early as the fourth century, the popes had begun to cite Matthew 16:18—"Thou art Peter and upon this rock I will build my church"—as evidence of Christ's intention to make the diocese of which Peter had been the first bishop the center of the entire church.[11]

During the fifth century, several aggressive and powerful popes advanced claims to papal supremacy within the church. Pope Leo I the Great (r. 440–461) urged the spiritual identity of the popes with Peter when speaking on religious matters. He also obtained an imperial edict from one of the last Western Roman emperors establishing papal jurisdiction over all Western bishops. He rejected claims of superiority advanced on behalf of the patriarch of Constantinople and dictated imperiously to church councils. Leo's alleged role in persuading Attila the Hun to spare the city of Rome also added to papal prestige. A generation later, Pope Gelasius I (r. 492–496) declared papal superiority to both the Eastern Roman emperors and church councils where matters of faith and morals were concerned. The "Gelasian doctrine" of the supremacy of priestly power over secular authority gave later medieval popes a claim to higher power than that of kings and was a crucial contribution to medieval political theory.

Perhaps the largest early medieval contribution to the rise of papal power, however, was that of Pope Gregory I the Great (r. 590–604). An ivory carving dating from the ninth or tenth century shows Pope Gregory as a saintly looking tonsured monk, writing with a quill pen in a book while a dove whispers divine inspiration into his ear. The most influential pope of these five centuries was in fact bald, dark, and hook-nosed, and at least as likely to be organizing disaster relief or negotiating with barbarians as writing his famous books. But he had been a monk, and his book *Pastoral Care* certainly seemed inspired to many later leaders of the church.

Once the prefect, or chief administrative official, of Rome, Gregory later served as the Roman church's envoy to Constantinople. By all accounts, he was a hard-driving, highly organized, and exceedingly capable man. He elevated the secular position of the papacy by feeding the populace in time of siege, caring for the sick in plague time, organizing the defense of the city, and then negotiating peace with the advancing Lombards. A prolific writer, he produced a commentary on the Bible and lives of the early saints in addition to his *Pastoral Care,* which offered guidance to bishops in the nurturing of their flocks.

As a former monk, Gregory encouraged the spread of monasticism—see below—which was

Pope Gregory I—St. Gregory the Great—was an influential Christian thinker and a gifted writer, using the spoken Latin of his day as the model for his widely admired prose style. As the fourth Father of the Roman Church, he was represented many times in medieval western European art.

coming to be seen as the most perfect form of Christian life. He also vigorously fostered missionary activity, also surveyed below, which by the year 1000 had brought most of the population of Europe at least nominally within the Christian fold. So impressive was Gregory's contribution that he came to be considered one of the fathers of the church, though he lived two centuries after the other Latin fathers, Augustine, Jerome, and Ambrose.

The rise of papal supremacy in the Western church was subsequently strengthened by the alliance between the papacy and the powerful Frankish Empire, especially under the Carolingians. Pippin the Short's donation of a large portion of central Italy to the see of St. Peter in 756 gave the popes a valuable territorial base. Charlemagne's acceptance of an imperial crown at the pope's hands in 800 seemed to indicate that the papacy had the power to confer imperial sovereignty over the Western world on a favored ruler.

The spread of the institutional power of the popes over the Christian churches of western Europe thus took several hundred years to develop. Meanwhile, the early Middle Ages saw two other major trends in the history of the church, both encouraged by Gregory and his successors. These were the missionary conversion of Europe and the rapid growth of the monastic movement.

Missionaries

Christianity, which had girdled the Mediterranean in Roman times, had spread much more thinly into Europe north of the Alps. The coming of the Germanic invaders, who were pagans or, almost worse, Arian heretics, had smothered most of what Christian communities there were in Roman provincial cities. And in A.D. 500 there were still large numbers of Germanic, Celtic, and other Europeans beyond the Rhine-Danube line who had never yet been touched by the Gospel.

A major achievement of this first half of the Middle Ages was the conversion of many of these inhabitants of western Europe to the unifying Roman faith. A great step toward this goal came in 597, when Pope Gregory the Great dispatched an embassy headed by Augustine (d. 604), the first archbishop of Canterbury, to convert the pagan Anglo-Saxons of England. Augustine succeeded in bringing about the conversion of King Ethelbert of Kent (r. 560–616), who was followed to the baptismal font by his chief men and ultimately by all his people. Roman missionaries faced vigorous competition for British converts from the Irish church, which had survived the Germanic invasions but differed from Rome on key points of ritual. At the Synod of Whitby in 664, however, the Roman rite triumphed, assuring its eventual victory over the British Isles as a whole.

Thereafter, Britain became a key base for missionary expeditions back to the continent, particularly to the Germanic tribes. But whether they came from Italy or Britain, early medieval missionaries tended to follow the procedure laid down by Augustine, converting kings first and then their peoples. Only after winning this profession of adherence to the new faith did the church proceed to the much longer, slower business of turning pagans into real Christian believers.

Women played an important part in this missionary effort. Among the unsung martyrs of the early spread of the faith were Christian women who married pagan kings in hopes of converting their husbands. Other women conducted more orthodox missionary activity, running monastic establishments in pagan areas and making many converts. Some of these, like St. Brigid in Ireland around 500 or St. Lioba, the eighth-century missionary to Saxony, were among those who attained the church's highest honor—canonization as saints.

The actual conversion of pagan populations took centuries and may never have been as total as the church desired. But through sermons and catechisms, through the legends of the saints and sharp examination of the moral and spiritual condition of Christians, priests all across Europe labored at the task. And if peasants would persist in murmuring a pagan invocation as they passed an oak tree that had once been sacred, or in leaving a bite out for the little people, lest the horses' manes be tangled in elflocks or the milk sour in the morning—well, there were more serious problems in the world of the early Middle Ages.

Monks and Nuns

The monastic life was much admired by medieval Christians, even if they could not all achieve it themselves. For monks and nuns were people who had committed their whole lives to Christ.

The ascetic tradition—withdrawing from the world into seclusion and denying the pleasures of the flesh in order to focus entirely on the spiritual life—was not unique to Christianity. There were Buddhist monks and nuns already, and there would be Muslim ascetics too. In the Christian church, the movement began in late Roman times. In Egypt, Palestine, and Syria, pious souls as early as the third century turned their backs on a society in decline and retreated to the desert to live as solitary hermits. In time, however, ascetics began to band together into communities rather than live in isolation, and the practice spread from the Near East to Europe.

The father of Western monasticism was St. Benedict of Nursia (c. 480–c. 543), the leader of a community of monks at Monte Cassino in south central Italy. Benedict compiled a set of rules for his community that, because of its logic and practicality, came to be used by monasteries all over Europe.

The *Benedictine Rule* required monks and nuns to give up the ordinary life of getting and spending and commit themselves to a lifetime of piety and labor. A day in a monastery or convent was divided into periods for worship, work, and study. There were half a dozen religious services over the twenty-four-hour day. Daily manual labor in the fields, gardens, or monastery buildings was required of everyone. And time was set aside for reading, copying, and meditating on the Scriptures and other sacred writings.

Three great vows were also required of the holy brothers and sisters: obedience, poverty, and chastity. The first meant absolute obedience to the abbot or abbess who headed the monastery or convent, although these authorities were expected to consult with their communities on important decisions. The vow of poverty required complete abandonment of worldly possessions: even the robes and sandals that monks and nuns wore were issued by the institution. Perhaps most admired by medieval people was the vow of chastity, which in time came to be taken by all priests in the Roman Catholic church.

It was a hard and demanding life. Benedict's *Rule* avoided the extreme practices that some ascetics had adopted to tame fleshly desires, such as fasting, all-night vigils, hair shirts, and even self-flagellation, lashing themselves with whips. Though some still adopted these extreme measures, the system as a whole made no such demands, channeling religious energies into the labor, study, and prayer that St. Benedict had prescribed.

Thousands of monasteries and convents, some large, some small, grew up across Europe. Monastic establishments performed many pious, charitable, and socially useful functions, from providing hospitality for travelers to caring for the poor and sick and converting the heathen. Because their people worked so hard, monasteries also made major contributions to the clearing and draining of land and to valuable experimentation with crops and breeding. Because monks had to study edifying literature, monasteries became centers of literacy and refuges for bits and pieces of classical literature as well. And because they were so much admired, monasteries and convents received many gifts and bequests, often in land, from pious Christians. As a result, orders of monks and nuns sworn to poverty came into possession of some of the largest landholdings in medieval Europe.

It was also behind convent walls that women found their most common escape from patriarchal medieval society. Women could not serve as priests in the Christian church, as they often had in pagan cults, but the monastic system was open to them. Convents theoretically accepted women of all social

Benedictine nuns listen intently to their abbot in this English medieval manuscript. Among the monks and nuns who spent much of their lives copying and illuminating manuscripts were some great artists. Can you tell what this anonymous artist has done to make this picture lively and exciting? [Courtesy of his Grace the Archbishop of Canterbury and the Trustees of Lambeth Palace Library.]

classes, but in fact they were often largely populated by the daughters of the well-to-do, who could contribute land or other gifts to the institution. In some of these establishments, capable and ambitious women presided as abbesses over hundreds or even thousands of people and vast acreages of convent lands.

The monastic establishment, like the manor, was a self-sufficient agricultural community, and as such it fitted the needs of the times perfectly. Islands of peace in a violent age, monasteries and convents also gave a refuge to human beings who were not suited to life leaning on a plow, coping with a household, or swinging a sword. Most important to contemporaries, monastic houses were seen as vessels of the Holy Spirit, ideal communities where men and women could lift their eyes and hearts to a higher and better world than that in which they lived.

Early Medieval Culture

Like the culture of the Greek Awakening, the art and thought of the early Middle Ages was perhaps most important as the foundation for a later cultural flowering. The high medieval glories of the Gothic cathedral, Scholastic thought, and the Renaissance of the twelfth century had their roots in the early Middle Ages. Yet there was a vitality, a stirring of the spirit among these early artists and thinkers that belongs to this age alone.

Germanic Decorative Arts

When the Germanic tribesmen who overran the Roman Empire attempted to imitate Greco-Roman naturalistic art, the results were typically crude. A gingerbread man in low relief with a large sword, button eyes, and one hand raised to comb his hair, a symbol of manly vigor, looks more like an Easter Island primitive than a piece of Western art. But when they practiced the traditional arts of their own people, the decorative skills their Indo-European ancestors had brought down from the steppes, it was another story.

Medieval jewelry, regalia, and decorated useful objects all vibrate today with the vitality of the earlier peoples of the forest and the steppe. Metalwork, especially gold, and large brightly colored precious stones were favorite media. Among natural objects, animals were most widely and successfully represented, from horses to eagles and wolves. No attempt was made at realistic representation of even these admired creatures. Instead, as in the animal art of earlier steppe peoples, the bodies and limbs were stylized and reshaped into sweeping curves and abstract patterns of striking beauty.

Early medieval kings, like their nobles, reveled in heavy gold jewelry garnished with rough colored stones. The Iron Crown of Lombardy carried off by Charlemagne is actually only lined with iron: the outside is gold and set with huge jewels. The crown of the Visigothic kings of Spain, unearthed from a treasure trove near Toledo, gleams today with intricately worked gold and agates, sapphires and pearls. Charlemagne's own cross and orb is a symbolic globe surmounted by a cross, again gleaming with precious metal and encrusted with jewels.

Looking at brooches or belt buckles today, we find the metal restlessly alive with interlacing lines, symmetrically curving linear patterns that in later centuries became a defining feature of Gothic art. Crude and bold, intricate and intertwined, Germanic art influenced future styles, but no future age could match its barbaric strength.

Early Medieval Literature and Scholarship

Literature and thought also altered drastically in character in the early Middle Ages. The replacement of an educated Roman aristocracy by a largely illiterate warrior nobility and of Greek philosophy by Christian theology was bound to transform the intellectual life of the new Europe.

A vigorous oral literature, now largely lost, was sung or chanted in the halls of Europe's new rulers. Little of this was written down in continental Europe, where the few literate people were perhaps too awed by their Latin literary predecessors to set down their own efforts. From the British Isles, however, comes one Anglo-Saxon epic at least, the hero tale of *Beowulf,* dating from the seventh or eighth century. Everything about the poem is debated by scholars, but the story itself, of the hero Beowulf's killing of the monster Grendel and then of Grendel's even more ferocious mother, at least suggests something of the taste in tales of the Anglo-Saxon warrior elite.

Most of those who could read and write were now in the church, many of them monks, and they tended to produce books of religious edification more than anything else. St. Augustine's *City of God* remained immensely popular, as did Gregory the Great's study of the Book of Job and his collection of saints' lives.

Even books on subjects that would once have been thoroughly secular, like history, showed strong religious influences in medieval times. Thus the *History of the Franks* by Gregory of Tours (538–594) and the *Ecclesiastical History of the English Nation* composed by the Venerable Bede (c. 673–735) both reveal a historian's concern for evidence and accuracy and are essential sources for the history of the period. Yet both accept miracles in large numbers as a matter of course, and Bede became the first scholar to utilize a chronology beginning with the birth of Christ and to use the A.D. (*Anno Domini*—"Year of the Lord") dating system in a major work. History, in short, was no longer a secular subject, but part of the great intellectual crusade to glorify God in the age of faith.

Fortunately for future scholarship, there were also efforts to preserve enough classical writing to instruct churchmen in basic Latin, the language of the church. A major contributor to this preservation of at least some of the classical heritage for religious purposes was the scholar-administrator Boethius (c. 480–c. 524) who lived in the Rome of Theodoric the Ostrogoth. Boethius compiled large collections of classical learning, ranging from the sciences to Aristotelian logic. His most famous work, *The Consolation of Philosophy,* shows how much he was a man of an earlier, pre-Christian age. Writing the book in Theodoric's prison, under sentence of death, Boethius sought consolation in the ideas of ancient philosophers rather than in the Scripture that was then sweeping all other ideas aside.

Cassiodorus (c. 490–580), another of Theodoric's ministers of state, was more directly concerned with educational reform and dreamed of establishing an academy of classical studies in Ostrogothic Rome. When this proved impossible after the Byzantine invasion that toppled the Ostrogothic kings, Cassiodorus retreated to his own estate in southern Italy and founded a monastery. Here he taught his monks Greek and the Greek and Latin classics and produced an *Introduction to Divine and Human Studies,* describing the major works of classical antiquity and explaining how the methods of classical scholarship could be used to explain sacred texts. Cassiodorus's work was used as a textbook throughout the Middle Ages.

The Celtic Flowering

Not all the art, literature, and scholarship of early medieval times was Germanic in origin. Indeed, the most brilliant early flowering of medieval culture came on the far western edge of Europe's Celtic fringe, in Ireland.

The Irish Celts remained relatively untouched by invading peoples through much of the early Middle Ages. Neither the Romans nor the Anglo-Saxons pushed beyond the Irish Sea, and the Vikings did not establish even a temporary settlement in Ireland until the end of the eighth century. Ireland in earliest medieval times, then, developed its own society and culture. Irish social and political institutions were as simple as those of other preurban peoples, a loose structure of clans and petty kings who often feuded with each other. Culturally, however, this politically undeveloped land became a radiant center of early medieval art, literature, and learning.

One element of the larger European culture that did reach Ireland was Christianity, which followed its own line of development after its arrival in the island in the fifth century. Irish monasteries became paramount centers of learning in early medieval Europe. Irish missionaries carried their version of the faith to Scotland in the sixth century and on into the Germanic forests of continental Europe. Though Roman Catholic Christianity eventually displaced Celtic forms of worship, Irish missionaries had made an important contribution to the Christianization of Europe.

During this period, Irish decorative arts reached their peak and a unique literary tradition developed. Celtic decorative artists specialized in illuminated manuscripts like the gorgeous eighth-century *Book of Kells,* a version of the Latin Gospels with elaborately decorated capitals and illustrations for each chapter. Drawing upon Germanic styles encountered in Anglo-Saxon Britain, Irish craftworkers produced beautiful metalwork like the Ardagh chalice, an early eighth-century masterpiece of exquisitely worked silver and glass. Old Irish literature also flowered in these early centuries. Irish kings kept bards at their courts to sing the legends of their heroic ancestors. These and later sagas and hero tales, legends of early saints, lyric poems, and poetic evocations of the Irish countryside were written down in the High Middle Ages to become part of an enduring legacy of Irish history and culture.

The Carolingian Renaissance

The best examples of the sort of learning and art admired by early medieval rulers come from the Kingdom of the Franks, particularly during the Carolingian Renaissance sponsored by Charlemagne. Seeing himself as a sort of a Christian Augustus Caesar, Charlemagne seems to have taken the patronage of culture seriously. He also apparently saw the practical value of education for officials of both the state and the church. He therefore imported scholars from various parts of Europe and urged the production of holy books, the establishing of schools, and other cultural activities.

The emperor's chief cultural mentor was an English churchman, Alcuin of York (735–804). Alcuin headed the Palace School at Aachen and guided the preparation of new editions of St. Jerome's Latin Bible and of St. Benedict's *Rule,* which became the standard versions of these two key medieval texts. Charlemagne's interest in schooling also led to the establishment of some monastery schools and to efforts to provide book learning for the children of the Frankish nobility in the Palace School. According to his biographer Einhard, the towering emperor of the Franks did not hesitate to administer physical punishment personally to children of his greatest nobles who got their grammar wrong.

Two apparently modest scholarly achievements of the Carolingian Renaissance, however, actually had more far-reaching consequences. One of these was a determined effort to standardize church Latin. This reform gave the Roman church an international language at a time when Europe was becoming increasingly divided linguistically as separate national languages emerged. The other surprisingly valuable accomplishment of this scholarly revival was the development of a new standard script for books that added lower-case letters to the Roman capitals used up to that time. These *Carolingian minuscules* became the model for the lower-case alphabet still in use today.

This fragment of a manuscript includes examples of two important medieval innovations—Carolingian minuscule, or lower-case, lettering and the form of illustration called *illumination.* Illuminated capitals like this one, mingling pictures with the letters themselves, are among the glories of medieval art.

A Topical Summary

Politics: During the first half of the Middle Ages (roughly A.D. 500–1000), invasions by Goths, Franks, Arabs, Vikings, and others combined with the weakness of the Germanic monarchies that replaced the Roman Empire to shatter political order in Europe. Despite the best efforts of such state builders as Clovis, Charlemagne, and Alfred the Great, Europe sank into disarray, a society dominated by feudal lords loosely linked by oaths of personal allegiance to warlords stronger than they.

Economics: The collapse of the Roman Empire with its integrated economy and access to the larger world reduced most of western Europe to subsistence agriculture. Like feudalism, the manor system made life at the minimal level possible. On the economic side this meant a return to the agricultural village.

Society: Early medieval society was much simpler than that of ancient Rome. Most people were serfs, peasant laborers ruled by the feudal aristocracy and spiritually dominated by an expanding Christian church. Women may have enjoyed more authority in this loosely structured society than they did in later medieval times.

Technology: The material framework of society declined drastically in the early Middle Ages as roads decayed, cities crumbled, and technical skills that had been developed in Greco-Roman times were lost. Only basic agricultural techniques and such related skills as those of the blacksmith and the miller survived.

Culture: Early medieval art and thought were shaped by Germanic styles, Christian ideas, and what remained of classical learning. Under the patronage of the church and of such would-be revivers of Roman traditions as Charlemagne, vigorously decorative art pointed toward Gothic styles to come. The writings of Christian thinkers, from Gregory the Great to Alcuin of York, became medieval classics.

Some Key Terms

Benedictine Rule 209
capitulary 199
Carolingian minuscule 213
Celtic fringe 195
comitatus 193
feudalism 203
feudal lord 203

fief 203
Germanic peoples 192
Heptarchy 195
homage and investiture 203
Indo-European peoples 190
Lex Visigothorum 202
medieval manor 205

megalith 190
missi dominici 199
taille 206
Turko-Mongol peoples 190
vassal 203
witenagemot 201

Notes

1. The city of Constantinople had originally been the Greek city of Byzantium, from which the medieval Byzantine Empire, originally the eastern half of the Roman Empire, derived its name.
2. Quoted in Michael Grant, *Dawn of the Middle Ages* (London: McGraw-Hill, 1981), 6.
3. Einhard, *The Life of Charlemagne,* trans. Samuel Epes Turner (Ann Arbor, Mich.: Ann Arbor Paperbacks, 1960), 50–51.
4. Einhard and Notker the Stammerer, *Two Lives of Charlemagne,* trans. L. Thorpe (Harmondsworth, England: Penguin, 1969), 163–164.
5. Quoted in J. Kelley Sowards, ed., *Makers of the Western Tradition: Portraits from History,* 4th ed. (New York: St. Martin's Press, 1987), 145.
6. Sura 2, verses 29 ff., quoted in Grant, *Dawn of the Middle Ages,* 63.

7. Betty Bandel, "English Chroniclers' Attitude Toward Women," *Journal of the History of Ideas,* XVI (1955), 114–115.
8. Elizabeth A.R. Brown, "The Tyranny of a Construct: Feudalism and Historians of Medieval Europe," *American Historical Review,* 79 (1974), 1987.
9. Eileen Power, *Medieval People* (Garden City, N.Y.: Doubleday, 1955), 19.
10. Lina Eckenstein, *Woman Under Monasticism* (Cambridge: Cambridge University Press, 1896), 327.
11. The name translated into English as "Peter" was the Aramaic word *kepa,* which meant "rock." What Jesus was apparently saying was that Peter's name symbolized his character and that therefore Jesus would lay the responsibility for the building of his church on this person of rocklike strength. *New Catholic Encyclopedia,* vol. 11 (New York: McGraw-Hill, 1967), 244.

Reading List

BEOWULF. Translated by E.T. Donaldson. New York: Norton, 1975. The Anglo-Saxon epic, with useful background material and critical analysis.

BLOCH, H. *Feudal Society.* Translated by L. A. Manyon. Chicago: University of Chicago Press, 1961. Major

work by a great historian seeking to recapture the "total social environment" of the age.

BULLOUGH, D. A. *The Age of Charlemagne.* London: Elek, 1965. Illustrated account for the nonspecialist that puts Charlemagne in the context of his times.

DOEHAERD, R. *The Early Middle Ages in the West: Economy and Society.* Translated by W. G. Deakin. New York: North-Holland, 1978. Agriculture, trade, population, and scarcity in the early medieval economy.

DUBY, G. *Rural Economy and Country Life in the Medieval West.* Columbia: University of South Carolina Press, 1968. Classic account by a pioneer of the sophisticated new social history, drawing on quantification and social science to create a living picture.

DUCKETT, E. T. *Alfred the Great.* Chicago: University of Chicago Press, 1958. Scholarly, highly readable study.

HOYT, R. S. *Feudal Institutions: Cause or Consequence of Decentralization?* New York: Holt, Rinehart and Winston, 1963. Focuses on feudalism as a rival to the slowly emerging centralized monarchy.

JONES, G. *A History of the Vikings.* 2d ed. New York: Oxford University Press, 1984. Exploits archaeology, art history, and other disciplines to construct a vivid narrative account.

LEYSER, K. G. *Rule and Conflict in Early Medieval Society: Ottonian Saxony.* London: Edward Arnold, 1979. Essays on divine sanction of these German rulers, on women's wealth, and on other subjects.

LOURDAUX, W., AND D. VERHELST, eds. *Benedictine Culture, 750–1050.* Louvain: Leuven University Press, 1983. Essays that explore the culture and intellectual contributions of the monastic life in its broader historical and social contexts.

MARENBON, J. *Early Medieval Philosophy (480–1150): An Introduction.* London: Routledge and Kegan Paul, 1983. Christian thought under the influence of Boethius and St. Augustine.

MCKITTERICK, R. *The Frankish Kingdoms Under the Carolingians, 751–987.* New York: Longman, 1983. Stronger on cultural matters than on political history, with revisionist emphasis on lesser Carolingians.

RANDERS-PEHRSON, J. D. *Barbarians and Romans: The Birth Struggle of Europe, A.D. 400–700.* Norman: University of Oklahoma Press, 1983. Very well-written survey, including encounters with leading personalities of this pivotal period.

RANDSBORG, K. *The Viking Age in Denmark: The Formation of a New State.* New York: St. Martin's Press, 1980. The rise of the Danish empire, based as much on archaeology as on historical documents.

RICHARDS, J. *The Pope and the Papacy in the Early Middle Ages, 476–752.* Boston: Routledge and Kegan Paul, 1979. Sees early medieval popes as more important than traditional concentration on the developed papacy of the High Middle Ages would allow.

RICHE, P. *Daily Life in the World of Charlemagne.* Translated by J. A. McNamara. Philadelphia: University of Pennsylvania Press, 1978. Class, gender, and other social relationships.

THOMPSON, E. A. *The Early Germans.* New York: Oxford University Press, 1965. Summarizes what can be deduced about this preliterate people from the writings of the Romans.

WEMPLE, S. F. *Women in Frankish Society: Marriage and the Cloister, 500–900.* Philadelphia: University of Pennsylvania Press, 1981. Engagingly written study of women's lives from the Germanic invasions to the Carolingians.

WILSON, D. M. *Anglo-Saxon Art from the Seventh Century to the Conquest.* London: Thames and Hudson, 1984. Well-illustrated survey of an impressive sample of early medieval art.

WOLFRAM, H. *History of the Goths.* Berkeley: University of California Press, 1988. Thoroughly researched study of Gothic tribes in Roman and early medieval times. See also T. S. Burns, *The Ostrogoths: Kinship and Society* (Wiesbaden: Franz Steiner Verlag, 1980). A brief account of the Germanic conquerors of Italy, drawing on anthropology, archaeology, and geographical studies.

From a world of castles and manor villages, we move now to very different realms. This chapter focuses on the eastern edge of the Western world: on the glittering metropolis of Constantinople, the steppes and forests of Russia, and the desert lands of the medieval Arabs. In political terms, this means a survey of the Byzantine Empire, Slavic Europe, and the expanding Islamic zone.

It is unfamiliar territory for most Americans, so we will refer from time to time to the chapter maps at the beginning of each major section. As for the time frame, we find ourselves once more moving across the early medieval centuries; but we start a bit later and carry our coverage a century or so further along. Byzantine history can be most usefully begun with Justinian and Theodora in the sixth century and Islamic history with Muhammad in the seventh, while the Russian past has few historic names before the coming of the Vikings in the ninth century. And we follow all three of these stories up to 1100 or later.

In each of these cases, we are dealing with neighboring or related cultures whose destinies were intricately intertwined with that of western Europe. The Byzantine, or Eastern Roman Empire was the great protector, stimulus, yet sometimes rival of the West. Arab Islam, though a powerful influence on Europe's later medieval revival, was the great adversary of medieval Christendom. And Slavic eastern Europe was the other half of the medieval Western world itself.

The Virgin of Vladimir. Early twelfth century. Dormition Cathedral, Moscow

The Byzantine Empire

Long vanished from the modern map, the *Byzantine Empire* was at its height in the sixth century under Justinian, when its territories reached around the Mediterranean. The historic core of the Byzantine Empire, however, was the region that survived by approximately the year 1000: the area that includes modern Turkey, Greece, and the eastern Balkans. Its center was one of the Western world's most valuable waterways, the Straits between the Mediterranean and Black seas, comprising the Dardanelles, the Sea of Marmora, and the Bosporus. The Byzantine capital, located on the Bosporus near the Black Sea, was the great and ancient city of Constantinople.

No serious effort can be made in these few pages to outline the thousand-year history of the

	500	**600**	**700**
POLITICAL, MILITARY, AND DIPLOMATIC EVENTS	**r. 527–565** Justinian **by 565** Reconquest of Roman Empire **5th and 6th centuries** Slavic migrations	**r. 610–641** Heraclius **632–661** Rightly Guided Caliphs **661–750** Umayyad Caliphate **570–632** Muhammad	**r. 714–741** Leo the Isaurian **732** Battle of Tours
SOCIAL AND ECONOMIC DEVELOPMENTS		**6th century** Silk culture brought to Byzantium	
CULTURE: THE ARTS, PHILOSOPHY, SCIENCE AND RELIGION	**533** Justinian's Code **535** Hagia Sophia	**By 632** Muhammad's Koran	

Byzantine Empire. After a glance at the general contour of that history and a glimpse of a powerful Byzantine personality or two, the bulk of our time must go to anatomizing this exotic world of clamoring bazaars and golden churches on the near edge of Asia. We will try, however, to communicate a hint of the glamour of that city of gold at the end of the world as it must have looked to medieval Europeans ten centuries ago.

A City, an Empire, a Civilization

This Christian empire of the East had at least two names, and its fabulous capital city had three. The city on the Straits between the Mediterranean and Black seas was founded in the seventh century B.C. as a Greek colony called Byzantium. It came to be called Constantinople after the Roman emperor Constantine refounded it in the fourth century A.D., and it has been known by its modern Turkish name of Istanbul for the last fifty years or so. The empire itself was still commonly called the Eastern Roman Empire in ancient times and the Byzantine Empire in the Middle Ages.

This tangle of names reflects the complex culture of the Empire itself, in whose history Greek, Roman, and Near Eastern elements are intertwined. Some attention must therefore be given to the basic shape of Byzantium—the city, the empire, and the civilization (see map 8.1).

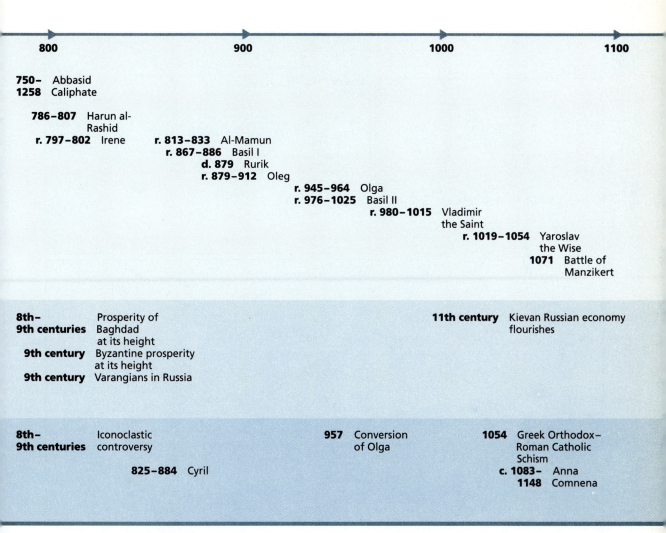

| 800 | 900 | 1000 | 1100 |

750– 1258 Abbasid Caliphate

786–807 Harun al-Rashid
r. 797–802 Irene
r. 813–833 Al-Mamun
r. 867–886 Basil I
d. 879 Rurik
r. 879–912 Oleg
r. 945–964 Olga
r. 976–1025 Basil II
r. 980–1015 Vladimir the Saint
r. 1019–1054 Yaroslav the Wise
1071 Battle of Manzikert

8th– 9th centuries Prosperity of Baghdad at its height
9th century Byzantine prosperity at its height
9th century Varangians in Russia
11th century Kievan Russian economy flourishes

8th– 9th centuries Iconoclastic controversy
825–884 Cyril
957 Conversion of Olga
1054 Greek Orthodox– Roman Catholic Schism
c. 1083– 1148 Anna Comnena

Constantinople was one of the great cities of the world in the Middle Ages. The original Greek settlers, with a shrewd eye to the commercial possibilities, had sited the city perfectly on the Straits that separate Europe from Asia. Emperor Constantine saw the military advantages of this location as a center of defense for the richest and most populous part of the Roman Empire against Germans from the north and Persians from the east. He and his successors had therefore built huge walls to supplement the water that protected the city on three sides. After the fall of the western half of the Roman Empire, Constantinople's commercial wealth, military strength, and political stature as capital of the surviving half of the Empire stood it in good stead. A metropolis of perhaps three hundred thousand peo-

ple, it easily dwarfed any other city in the Christian world.

Constantinople remained a beacon of civilization and wealth through most of the Middle Ages. The Empire it ruled was much less stable and subject to distinct ups and downs over the centuries. Over the millennium of Byzantine history, from the fall of Rome in the fifth century to that of Constantinople in the fifteenth, the Empire fluctuated strikingly in size. At the time of the fall of the West, the Eastern Empire encompassed only the crescent of land from Greece through Asia Minor (modern Turkey) around to Egypt. Under Emperor Justinian in the sixth century, this area was vastly expanded by the reconquest of Italy, southern Spain, and much of North Africa. By the year 1000, however, all these

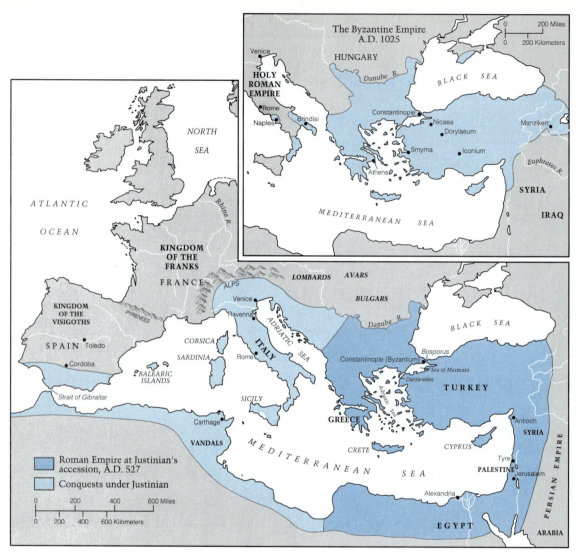

Map 8.1   The Byzantine Empire

lands had been lost, along with much of the original Eastern Empire. Perhaps the best way to define the Byzantine Empire, then, is simply as the area ruled by Constantinople (Byzantium), waxing and waning with the centuries and the fortunes of many wars.

The multilayered complexity of Byzantine civilization was also rooted in the accumulating contributions of the peoples who lived in the Empire and ruled it. From the Greeks came the original business savvy and some of the subtlety of Greek Orthodox theology. From the Romans derived the autocratic central government and perhaps a gift for bureaucratic organization. In the Hellenistic Near East, we may find the origins of divinely sanctioned monarchy and of the oriental splendor of Byzantine palaces and churches. But the whole is clearly greater than the sum of its parts. The golden halo crowning a Byzantine saint, the roar of a race track crowd as the chariots thundered past, a line of emperors who professed to speak with God's own voice—these are unique to this, the most autocratic, affluent, and ascetic city in Christendom.

Byzantine Origins

Despite their exotic Eastern aura, both the Byzantine state and the *Greek (Eastern) Orthodox Church* evolved gradually from Western beginnings. Beyond the broadest contributions of ancient Greece and Rome just mentioned, the early history of Byzantium shows clearly its development out of the world of Western antiquity.

The beginning of the Byzantine state may be traced back to the administrative division of the Roman Empire by Diocletian (r. 284–305) in the late third century or to the construction of much of Constantinople by Constantine (r. 312–337) in the early fourth. The latter's official transfer of the imperial capital to his new city in 324 is often considered to mark the beginning of Byzantine history. But Constantine and other early Eastern Roman emperors saw themselves as rulers of the whole Empire, not merely its eastern provinces. Not even the Germanic occupation of the Western Roman Empire in the fifth century could shake this conviction. Justinian, the great Byzantine emperor of the sixth century, continued to speak Latin and labored mightily to liberate the Western provinces from their conquerors. By the reign of Heraclius I in the seventh century, however, all the elements of medieval Byzantium were clearly in place, from oriental ceremony and autocracy to the predominance of the Greek language and the Greek Orthodox church.

The Orthodox church also took shape gradually out of origins shared with the Roman Catholic church of western Europe. From the time of Constantine's legalization of the Christian religion in 313, the bishops of Constantinople refused to recognize the growing authority of the bishops of Rome. Partly because of the growing wealth and political importance of Constantinople, its bishops, called *patriarchs,* acquired an ascendancy over the bishops of the other Eastern cities roughly comparable to the authority of the Roman popes over Western bishops. The split between the Eastern and Western churches did not become official until the eleventh century, but in fact the two main divisions of Christianity had drifted apart long before.

During the late Roman and early medieval centuries, this Eastern Empire, like western Europe, underwent significant changes. Eastern Roman emperors from Constantine in the fourth century to Heraclius in the seventh managed to turn back or divert the Germanic and Turko-Mongol invaders who so drastically transformed the West. But the Byzantine Empire of the Middle Ages was, as we shall see, a very different entity from the Roman Empire of the Caesars.

Justinian and Theodora

In the sixth century, Byzantium produced its greatest rulers. In Emperor Justinian (r. 527–565) and his empress, Theodora, Byzantium in fact gave the world one of the most impressive and controversial royal couples in history.

The contemporary Byzantine historian of the reign, Procopius, has left us not only valuable accounts of the emperor's wars and of his great building program, but also a scurrilous *Secret History* full of court scandals and scathing attacks on the characters of the emperor and his consort. The details of this *History* may be no more reliable than the average tabloid gossip column today. But the book does give us a privileged look at the human beings behind the monumental stiffly posed mosaics of Justinian and Theodora.

Justinian inherited the throne from his uncle, Justinus I (r. 518–527), after serving as his junior colleague for some years. Procopius tells us that Justinian was "neither tall nor short, but of normal height . . . rather plump, with a round face." He was extremely accessible—the palace was always swarming with people—"easily led astray" and "easy meat" for deceivers, above all for his controversial wife Theodora.[1] Daughter of a circus animal trainer, Theodora was a famous dancer and a celebrated courtesan when Justinian met her and fell hopelessly in love with her. She had, the historian admits, "an attractive face and a good figure," but "not a particle of modesty."[2] She scandalized high society by her shocking stage performances before Justinian married her and elevated her with him to the imperial throne.

Justinian seems to have had a compulsive dedication to restoring the vanished grandeur of Rome. For thirty years, he labored to rebuild a united Empire, to codify its vast body of laws, and to turn Constantinople into a "New Rome" worthy of the Empire's ancient traditions. Sometimes faulted for exhausting the resources of the Eastern Empire in a hopeless effort to recover the West, Justinian nevertheless left behind him one of the most beautiful cities in the world and one of the most influential codes of laws in history.

Yet he might never have had the chance to do any of these things if it had not been for Theodora.

The great sixth-century Byzantine emperor Justinian stands at the center of this mosaic in the church of San Vitale in Ravenna, the northern Italian city that was the western capital of Justinian's expanded Eastern Roman Empire. Can you see both secular and church figures in the imperial retinue?

"She was extremely clever," even Procopius admitted.[3] And it was she who, when a wave of political rioting threatened to drive the young Justinian from his throne, stiffened his backbone and kept him there. A tough outsider who had made it to the top and did not propose to let go, she declared: "If flight were the only means of safety, yet I should disdain to fly. Death is the condition of our birth, but they who have reigned should never survive the loss of dignity and dominion. . . . For my own part, I adhere to the maxim of antiquity, that the throne is a glorious sepulchre."[4]

Justinian's efforts to reunite the Roman Empire required many years of massive military campaigns by land and sea. His most successful generals, Belisarius (c. 505–565) and the eunuch Narses (c. 480–574), did in fact accomplish more than anyone could have dreamed possible. The Vandal regime was shattered in North Africa and almost all the southern coast of the Mediterranean reclaimed. A large slice of Spain was recaptured from the Visigoths. Most important, a pincer movement by fleets and armies liberated the old Roman heartland of Italy from the Os-

trogoths and established a Byzantine viceroy at Ravenna. These wars, accompanied by long campaigns against Persia in the East, dragged on for most of Justinian's reign, exhausted even the Byzantine treasury, and left Italy in particular devastated by decades of war. At his death, a Roman Empire once more ringed the Mediterranean; but both the New Rome and the old had paid in terrible effusions of blood and treasure.

Justinian's codification of Roman law proved a far more lasting achievement. Roman law had been accumulating for almost ten centuries since the Twelve Tables of the early Republic. It included legislation, imperial edicts, and the legal opinions of centuries of Roman jurists. Justinian appointed a series of commissions to tackle the huge job of bringing order into this rich jumble of legal materials. The result was the *Corpus Iuris Civilis,* literally the "Body of the Civil Law," sometimes called simply Justinian's Code. The three most important elements of Justinian's Code were the *Codex* of carefully organized edicts of the emperors, the *Digest* of the legal opinions of Rome's greatest legal minds, and the *In-*

stitutes, a basic guide to the law for students. The *Corpus Iuris Civilis,* compiled in the sixth century, reached the medieval West in the eleventh century and became the basis for the laws of a number of the new nation-states emerging in the High Middle Ages. Roman legal principles also influenced both the ecclesiastical law of the Roman Catholic church, as it began to take definitive shape in the twelfth century, and modern international law, when it began to emerge at the end of the sixteenth.

Justinian was also, finally, the greatest builder of all the Byzantine emperors. Much of this construction was composed of necessary public works across the expanding Empire: law courts, public baths, aqueducts, roads, and fortifications. He also built schools, orphanages, hospices for the sick, public recreation areas, and extensions on his own royal palaces. Above all, however, Justinian built churches. His church-building program extended from Egypt and Palestine to Greece and Italy, where such gems of Byzantine architecture as San Vitale in Ravenna and, later, St. Mark's in Venice, were constructed in the Byzantine style. Constantinople itself, however, was Justinian's special concern: his architects raised or refurbished three dozen churches in the city, including by far the largest church in the medieval world: Hagia Sophia, the Church of the Holy Wisdom.

The Eastern Emperors

Of the many emperors who succeeded Justinian on the throne of the Byzantine Empire, only a few can be touched on here. Their reigns highlight a brief survey of the five centuries between Justinian's reconquest of much of the West in the sixth century and increasing Western encroachment on Byzantium in the eleventh.

Heraclius I (r. 610–641) both reorganized the Empire administratively and fought valiantly to stem a tide of Asian assaults on it, including one that proved a major threat to Christendom as a whole. The core of Heraclius's administrative restructuring was the *theme system,* perhaps borrowed from his Persian opponents, combining provincial political reorganization with a more effective military defense. Under Heraclius, soldiers were granted land in various provinces of the Empire in return for accepting a hereditary military obligation. The commanders of these farmer-soldiers soon became the chief administrative authorities

in the provinces where they settled, and the term *theme,* originally denoting a military unit, came to be applied to the provincial divisions of the Byzantine Empire. The Roman imperial administration established by Diocletian and Constantine thus gave way to a military-based structure of provincial government more suited to a time of mounting military pressure.

Among the invaders Heraclius had to face were the nomadic Avars who had entered eastern Europe from the Eurasian steppes; Persians under the powerful Sassanid dynasty dedicated to reviving ancient Persian greatness; and the first wave of Muslim Arab expansion. He successfully weathered the Avar onslaught from the Balkans to the north and decisively rolled back a Persian advance out of Iran to the east. In the last years of his reign, however, he lost much of his Near Eastern territory to Arab hosts fired by the new faith of the Prophet Muhammad—a harbinger of troubled times to come.

Over the following century, the Arabs pressed the Empire hard, while a new threat from the steppes emerged in the Bulgars, founders of an aggressive Bulgarian Empire in the Balkans. The Arabs besieged Constantinople itself for five years in the 670s, and Byzantine rulers were forced to deal with both of these menaces for centuries.

One who dealt firmly with the Arabs was the celebrated military emperor Leo III the Isaurian (r. 717–741). Leo broke a second major Arab siege of Constantinople in 718. More disruptive in the long run, however, was the beginning of a violent religious dispute within the Empire, the *iconoclastic controversy.* The pious Leo issued decrees forbidding icons—images of God, the Virgin Mary, or the saints used to stimulate devotion—on grounds that they encouraged idol worship. Byzantine monks and many Orthodox Christians bitterly opposed this view and resisted its implementation for the next hundred years.

Religious issues and relations with eastern and western Europe played a large part in Byzantine history over the following century. The iconoclastic controversy ended in 843 with the restoration of the veneration of images, though the emperor's power over the church continued. During the 860s, Byzantine missionaries carried the Orthodox faith to Moravia (later, Czechoslovakia), while the emperor himself presided over the conversion of the Bulgarian ruler. Disputes between Eastern Orthodox and Western Catholic Christianity, however, grew steadily worse, and in 867 the patriarch of Constantinople angrily rejected papal claims of supremacy over all Christian churches.

The reign of Basil I (r. 867–886) saw the Byzantine Empire at its height—wealthy, freed of internal religious friction, and victorious over foreign foes. Basil proved a good administrator and a successful general. He reformed the army, the navy, and the legal system, and defeated the Arabs on land and sea. The Byzantine Empire continued its feud with the Catholic West, however, occupying territory in southern Italy and continuing to reject the religious supremacy of Rome.

During the hundred years after Basil I, challenges once more multiplied from within and without. Internal resistance to imperial authority now came, not from the monks, but from rapacious noble landholders. These magnates grew wealthy by exploiting the peasantry and became powerful enough to put armies in the field against the emperor. From outside the empire, the threat of Arab power declined, but the Bulgars grew more aggressive. At the same time, Turkish raiders from the East and Norman knights from western Europe put pressure on Byzantine lands in Turkey and southern Italy.

Basil II (r. 976–1025), called "the Bulgar Slayer," made a determined effort to deal with both foreign and domestic enemies. Basil launched a broad-gauge counterattack against the landed aristocracy, defeating them in battle and confiscating many of their estates, some for redistribution to the peasants. He also pushed the frontiers of the Empire eastward once more and resisted European encroachments, defeating a joint force of Normans and Lombards in Italy and decimating a Bulgar army. It was this latter victory, from which he sent back thousands of captured Bulgar warriors with their eyes put out, that earned Basil II his grisly nickname. In this sea of violence, the achievement that had the greatest long-range significance, as we will see, was the conversion of Kievan Russia to Orthodox Christianity in the later 980s.

If the reign of Basil I in the ninth century marked a high point in Byzantine history, that of Basil II in the eleventh was followed by a decline in the fortunes of the Eastern emperors. In 1054 the schism between Eastern and Western Christendom reached its climax as pope and patriarch severed relations and excommunicated each other. In 1071 the Seljuk Turks, who had replaced the Arabs as the most militant of Muslim peoples, administered a catastrophic defeat to the Byzantine army at Manzikert. And in 1081 Byzantium's landed magnates rallied sufficient strength to put one of their own, Alexius I Comnenus (r. 1081–1118), on the imperial throne. Alexius faced a hostile world, with Turkish power growing to the east, Norman knights more aggressive to the west, and increasing numbers of Italian merchants, drawn by the wealth of Byzantium, threatening his control at home. The Byzantine Empire still had more than four hundred years of history ahead of it—but they were hard centuries.

Autocracy and the Army

Despite these high and low points, the Byzantine Empire generally exhibited enviable political stability and military strength under pressure. Individual emperors came and went, sometimes toppled by palace coups, not infrequently facing popular, aristocratic, or even ecclesiastical opposition, but generally more stable than Western rulers. Byzantine armies lost battles, but they performed their primary function of preserving the state. Institutionally, certainly, the Byzantine government and military were stronger than anything western Europe saw for centuries.

There was no question that the Byzantine government governed. The West would not see so successful an autocracy until the reign of Louis XIV in the seventeenth century. *Autocrat* was in fact one of the official titles of the Byzantine emperor, and the source of the word as we use it. The emperor also inherited the Roman power of imperium, granted to him on his accession by the army, which elevated him on a shield to indicate its acceptance of him as commander in chief. Perhaps even more important, the Byzantine autocrat enjoyed the Hellenistic monarch's aura of divinity conferred on him by the Greek Orthodox church, which anointed him with holy oil in recognition that he ruled by divine right, as God's viceroy on earth.

The exalted position of the Byzantine emperor was embodied in the high-flown titles and elaborate court ceremonials that surrounded his person. Anyone who entered the imperial presence had to prostrate himself full length before the emperor. Hymns and trumpet flourishes heralded the emperor's approach when he went forth among his people. The emperor of Byzantium's day was one long ceremony in his own imperial honor.

Byzantine emperors asserted a far-reaching authority over many aspects of the lives of their people. They regulated the economy and took a liberal share of the gross national product through taxes, customs duties, and government monopolies like the prof-

Empress Theodora is shown here surrounded by her entourage. Although the mosaic form, in which small pieces of colored stone or glass are arranged to make pictures, does not lend itself to fine detail or excessive realism it can produce a jewel-like splendor comparable to stained glass.

itable silk industry, a technology that imperial agents had smuggled out of China. The emperors also claimed to be heads of the Orthodox church, appointing bishops, calling ecclesiastical councils, and passing on the resulting decisions. The autocratic claims of the emperors extended to empresses like Irene (r. 797–802), a contemporary of Charlemagne's, and the sisters Zoe (r. 1028–1055) and Theodora (r. 1055–1056), who guided the affairs of state as autocratically as male rulers.

To turn their authoritarian claims into realities, the Byzantine rulers had a professional civil service with a tradition that went back to the days of the Roman Caesars. The treasury, staffed with shrewd products of the Greek business community, was particularly efficient at extracting taxes from the wealthy cities of the Empire. The diplomatic and intelligence services of the Byzantines were also justly famous, creating puppet rulers and supporting pro-Byzantine factions among the peoples on their frontiers.

When such intrigues failed, finally, the armed forces could generally handle the situation. Building on a Roman tradition of military excellence, Byzan-

tine troops were normally well trained and organized, in possession of the latest intelligence on the enemy, and equipped with such up-to-date devices as signal mirrors and "Greek fire," a flammable chemical mixture sprayed on enemy vessels to set them ablaze. Undergirding these tactical advantages was the theme system of regional military organization we already mentioned. Troops and fleets defending their own farms and ports proved more effective in the field than the mercenary or even slave soldiers who preceded them.

The political and military strength of the Byzantine Empire preserved it for many centuries in the face of increasingly long odds against its survival. The power of the Empire had an additional effect, however: it protected the weakened West by stopping invaders from the East before they could reach western Europe. During the centuries between 500 and 1000, when the West was most fragmented and disorganized, this defensive function was particularly valuable. By the time the Byzantine Empire finally fell to foreign conquerors at the end of the Middle Ages, Europe was strong enough to stand alone.

The Wealth of Constantinople

Economically and socially, the Byzantine Empire was as successful as it was in the political arena. And this success also benefited the economically underdeveloped nations of the West.

The distinctive feature of Byzantine society was its urban development. And the twin keys to the prosperity of its cities were foreign trade and handicraft manufacture, which flourished there as nowhere else in Christendom.

The Byzantine Empire, unlike western Europe, inherited an urban society from Greco-Roman antiquity and preserved this legacy throughout the medieval period. Besides the capital Constantinople, Byzantine cities in the earlier period included Egyptian Alexandria, Beirut, Tyre, and Antioch on the eastern Mediterranean, and Trebizond on the Black Sea. They were crowded tangles of palaces and slums, churches and bazaars, with high walls, teeming ports, and caravansaries where caravans unloaded. They had all the problems of metropolitan areas before and since, from plague and fire to violent street crime. But they also had the capacity to generate wealth, the intellectual sophistication, and the sheer vitality of cities throughout history.

The Byzantine capital was built on one of the world's greatest natural harbors, the Golden Horn. Even more important, Constantinople was located on the narrow bottleneck of East-West trade, the most important commercial connection in the world. Goods came by caravan along the Great Silk Road from China, by sea across the Indian Ocean, down the rivers of Russia, or across the eastern Mediterranean from Europe to pour in a golden flood into the bazaars of Byzantium.

Into the markets of Alexandria and Antioch, Trebizond and Constantinople flowed the wealth of the world. From western Europe came textiles and weapons, iron and wood. From eastern Europe came furs and amber, wheat, honey, and slaves. Enamels, glassware, and brilliantly dyed and decorated fabrics from the Near East splashed color across the bazaars. All the way from India and Southeast Asia came precious stones, pearls, carved ivory, and the spices that scented and flavored the lives of the wealthy—nutmeg, cloves, cinnamon and ginger, pepper and sugar, aloes and musk. And from China and the Far East the most valuable of all trade items took the better part of a year to reach Byzantium: silk to clothe the bodies of the richest of the rich.

In Constantinople and other Byzantine cities, furthermore, street after street of skilled guild crafts-people labored to produce some of the finest craftware in the world. Goldsmith work, carved ivories, jewelry, and their own gorgeous purple silks were shaped by sensitive hands in Byzantine workshops. Illuminated manuscripts for scholars, incense and beautiful vestments for churches were handcrafted for local and foreign markets. Golden cups and tableware for the wealthy, icons and relic boxes for the pious, gold and silver rings, necklaces and pendants—the dazzling list had no end.

Constantinople's slums were the densest, its palaces and churches the most gorgeous. The crowds that filled the sixty thousand seats of the Hippodrome, the race track and sports stadium behind the imperial palace, could terrorize the streets if their favorite chariot drivers lost. Merchants from all parts of Eurasia had their own national enclaves in Constantinople, with their own warehouses, stables, hostelries, churches, mosques, or temples, all tolerated—if carefully policed—by the Byzantine authorities. And visiting envoys from kingdoms of Franks and Goths and Slavs prostrated themselves in awe before an emperor whose throne was flanked by handcrafted clockwork lions and shaded by a gilded tree in which sang artificial birds of bronze and gold.

"There is no estimating," said the Western chronicler Geoffroi de Villehardouin (c. 1150–c. 1213), "the quantity of gold, silver, rich stuffs [fabrics] and other valuables" in Byzantium.[5] That wealth played its part in Western history too. In the High Middle Ages, as we see in a later chapter, trade with the Near East did much to revive Western commerce and to stimulate the revival of cities across Europe. And the source of much of that stimulus was the handicraft industry and the international trade connections of the workshops and bazaars of Constantinople.

From a rooftop in today's Istanbul, the view across the busy stretch of water called the Golden Horn is one of Muslim domes and spires rising among modern European buildings. The skyline of medieval times was quite different, of course, but one thing was as true of the medieval as of the modern city. The harbor was thick with the spars and masts of ships, the Grand Bazaar and the mercantile houses crowded with people haggling over the price of goods—just as they do today.

Byzantine Art and Thought

Byzantine palaces and craftwork were splendid, but, as in medieval Western Christendom, it was the church that dominated the intellectual and creative life of this society. The spirit of the Greek Orthodox church infused Byzantine culture from basic political concepts and scholarship to graphic arts and architecture.

A distinctive feature of the Orthodox church was the power of the Byzantine emperors to regulate its affairs. Since Constantine had sat in council with Christian bishops to rule on theological disputes in the fourth century, the rulers of the Eastern Empire had claimed supreme power over the church. Eastern emperors, while they were not priests, directed and deposed patriarchs, summoned and supervised church councils, and played a leading part in bringing about change in church practice and even in theological interpretation. The Roman popes, after the fall of the Western emperors, were free to construct a "papal monarchy" in the West; but in the East the emperors still ruled, dominated the patriarchs, and treated the church as if it were a branch of the state.

Interestingly, this policy of imperial control of the religious establishment, called *caesaropapism,* did not lead to the secularization of religion. Emperors were often thoroughly informed on theological matters and took very seriously the religious obligations suggested by another of their imperial titles—"Equal to the Apostles." *Caesaropapism* actually reflected the intense religiosity of the Byzantines, the conviction that the Orthodox faith was the only true one, the Byzantine emperor God's chosen representative on earth, every war a Crusade, and Constantinople itself "the city protected by God."

In a realm so glutted with wealth, it is perhaps not surprising that people were particularly impressed by individuals who could resist material temptations. Monks, whose monasteries were often in the heart of the cities, were thus both leading figures in the church hierarchy and popular heroes as well. In later Byzantine times, when the Empire's worldly fortunes declined, monks and other pious individuals turned increasingly to mysticism, abandoning the material world altogether in order to find in meditation a means of direct spiritual contact with God. For the majority, however, beautiful churches, impressive services, and moving hymns provided means of mass communion with the deity.

In an atmosphere so charged with religious feeling, theological disputes were also particularly passionate. One of the few occasions on which the Orthodox church resisted the emperors was, as we have seen, the iconoclastic debate, which also helped bring about the schism between the Greek Orthodox and Roman Catholic churches. Other theological disputes between the Eastern and Western churches had to do with differences in the liturgical ceremonies of the two churches, and/or with such practical matters as the marriage of priests, sanctioned in the East but, by the High Middle Ages, forbidden in the West. Another much-argued point was the Catholic inclusion of the word *filioque* in the Creed, indicating that the Holy Spirit proceeds from both God the Father "and the Son"—heresy in Constantinople. It was over the *filioque* issue that the final split between the Eastern and the Western churches took place in 1054.

In a society where monks were popular leaders and theological disputes the "great debates" of the time, it is not surprising that religious literature dominated the field. Saints' lives were as popular in the East as in the West, the most celebrated poets wrote hymns, and immense quantities of biblical commentaries, theological tracts, and other devotional works were produced. Paradoxically, however, Byzantine scholarship also treasured its heritage from ancient—and thoroughly pagan—Greece. Practically all the earliest manuscripts we have of the Greek philosophers, dramatists, and poets are Byzantine copies of long-vanished originals. The Byzantine intelligentsia seem to have been enthusiastic readers of Homer and Plato. And they certainly did the West an incalculable service by preserving this common Western heritage of Greek art and thought through centuries when even kings in western Europe were often illiterate.

Education was widespread in Byzantium. There were universities in a number of cities, special schools for officials, church schools to train priests, and monastic schools. Some basic education was also available to the lower orders, especially through the craft guilds. Girls as well as boys attended some of these educational institutions. Most schools stressed secular learning: Roman law and Greek philosophy, rhetoric, medicine, and the sciences.

Original scholarship and art also flourished in the Byzantine Empire. An outstanding example is Anna Comnena's *Alexiad,* the epic history of the reign of her father, Emperor Alexius I (r. 1081–1118). Composed in verse, Comnena's work combines thoughtful analysis with vivid description. She offers, for instance, a candid characterization of the flower of Western chivalry marching through Byzantium on their way to fight the Turks. The "Franks," as Near Easterners called Europeans, were described as famed for "their irresistible manner of attack" but also for "their unstable and mobile character" and for being "always agape for money."

All the spirituality and all the artistry of the Byzantines combined to produce the unique beauty of the Byzantine church. Gorgeous silk wall hangings, sculptured ivory, wall paintings, and mosaics all glorified the house of God. Byzantine mosaics often used small blocks of colored glass, sometimes dusted with silver or gold, instead of bits of colored stone to form their pictures. The same formal composition was used in these mosaics whether the figures looking out from the wall were divine or human, God or the emperor. Such images drew a powerful parallel between God enthroned upon the world and surrounded by the heavenly hosts and the emperor of Byzantium flanked by his imperial court. The parallel between divine and earthly power was not lost on the multitudes who flocked to the many churches of the Empire.

When Justinian opened Hagia Sophia, his great Church of the Holy Wisdom, in 535, it was recognized at once as a masterpiece. Combining the oblong nave of a basilica church with the cross-shaped domed plan, it miraculously suspended a dome more than 100 feet across over the central altar. The vast open space within, framed by gigantic piers and pillars, glowed with colored marble, gleaming mosaics, and silken hangings, purple and green, silver and gold. "But who could fittingly describe the galleries?" wondered Procopius, "the beauty of the columns and the stones with which the church is adorned [like] a meadow with its flowers in full bloom?"[6] The dome of Hagia Sophia was imitated a hundred times in Christian churches and Muslim mosques in later centuries. But only the original is regularly compared with the Parthenon, St. Peter's in Rome, and Chartres Cathedral as among the indisputably great buildings of the Western world.

Kievan Russia

The neighbors who most resembled the western Europeans during the Middle Ages were the Slavs and other peoples of eastern Europe (see map 8.2). Sprawling over most of the continent east of the Elbe and the Danube, the Slavic peoples in particular were the largest of all the Indo-European groups who had populated the continent. They were also, however, culturally cut off from Europeans who spoke Germanic or Romance languages instead of Slavic ones, and who were Roman Catholic rather than Greek Orthodox. Until quite recently, these differences led to a tendency on the part of Western

historians to neglect the Slavic and other eastern European contributions to European history. To do so was to leave out a significant part of the story, for eastern Europe is as much a part of the historic West as the central and western portions of the European continent are.

Eastern Europe and Its Peoples

It is easy to see the eastern half of Europe as "Slavic Europe": most of the modern countries of this region, after all, do have substantial Slavic populations. The majority of the citizens of the former Soviet Union, for instance, are Great Russians, Ukrainians, or White Russians—all Slavic peoples. So are most of the inhabitants of Poland, Bulgaria, and the recently dissolved states of Czechoslovakia and Yugoslavia, along with substantial minorities elsewhere in the region. On the other hand, most Hungarians, Romanians, and Albanians do *not* speak Slavic languages or consider themselves Slavs, and there are non-Slavic minorities in many other eastern European lands. Despite a substantial Slav majority, in short, this half of Europe, like the western portion, is more accurately envisioned as a mosaic of peoples. In the Middle Ages, this collection of east European peoples stretched from the Baltic to the Balkans, bordered on the west by the German-speaking countries, on the north by Scandinavia, and on the south by Greece and Turkey.

You can get a bus in Brussels or a train in Paris that will take you all the way to Moscow via Berlin and Warsaw. You will ride for whole days through grassy plains and mosquito-ridden pine forests between such cities as Warsaw, Minsk, and Smolensk, all substantially rebuilt after their destruction in World War II. And there is no better way to get a feel for the big skies and Kansas-like landscape of much of eastern Europe.

Geographically, most of this half of Europe is the east European plain. This immense geological formation, which can actually be traced as far west as France or even southeast England, flows almost uninterrupted across German-speaking central Europe and east Europe all the way to the Ural Mountains. It is an enormous area. From Warsaw to the Urals is about as far as from Chicago to the Pacific, and there are no great natural barriers, like the Alps or the Pyrenees, to divide it. As a result, in early times Slavic peoples were able to migrate easily from one part of eastern Europe to another. By the same token, there was little to keep other peoples out of the

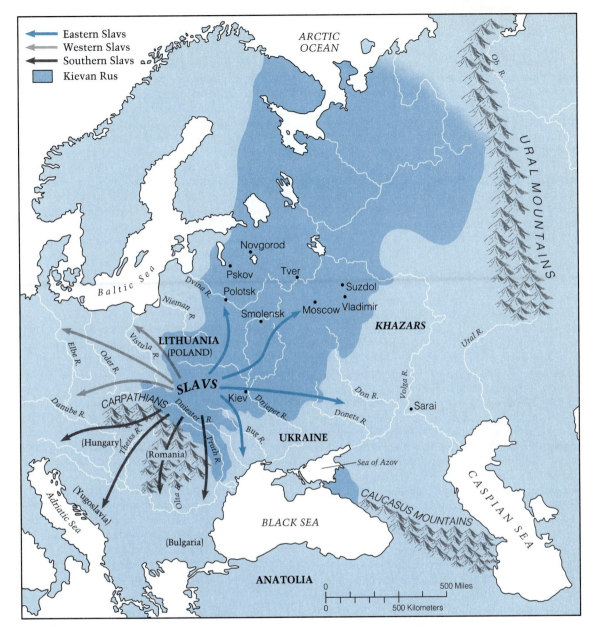

Eastern Slavs
Western Slavs
Southern Slavs
Kievan Rus

Map 8.2 Spread of the Slavs and the Kievan Rus

area. In this chapter, we see Viking intrusion from the north and Byzantine cultural penetration from the south, both of which made important contributions to the development of Slavic society and culture. We also note the appearance of Magyars in Hungary, Vlachs in Romania, and other peoples from further east who played a major part in the history of the region. In subsequent chapters, we deal with later medieval invasions by the Germans from the west and the Mongols from the east, both crucial formative experiences for the future nation of Russia.

A dozen centuries ago, much of this east European plain was rolling grasslands, the lush western steppes that haunted the dreams of Eurasian nomads farther east. The northern portion, however, was colder and thickly forested, a less hospitable climatic zone as far north as Canada's Hudson Bay. Linking these two zones of forest and steppe were a number of great rivers running north and south, particularly the Dnieper flowing into the Black Sea and the Volga into the Caspian.

The major exception to this pattern is the mountainous corner of southeastern Europe known as the Balkans. A drive south from central Europe to Greece through the Carpathians is more likely to remind you of Colorado than of Kansas. Here in particular you encounter non-Slavic languages and the descendants of Avars and Magyars and Vlachs. We focus on the Slavs in the present section, which is concerned primarily with the early history of Russia. But the descendants of Asian nomads, as well as Germans, Scandinavians, and Greek-speaking peoples, also play their part in these and later pages.

The Spread of the Slavs

The earliest speakers of Slavic languages seem to have lived in the area that is today eastern Poland and western Ukraine. From this center, three great branches of the original Slavic people moved east, west, and south in the fifth and sixth centuries of the Christian era. The *West Slavs* populated twentieth-century Poland and Czechoslovakia, perhaps the most westernized of eastern European countries. The *South Slavs* filtered down into the Balkan peninsula to become the basic populations of twentieth-century Yugoslavia (which means "South Slav"), Romania, Bulgaria, and other Balkan nations. The *East Slavs*, finally, occupied European Russia and became the ancestors of the Russians, Ukrainians, and Bela-, or White, Russians of today. It was a folk wandering as great as that of the early Germans, and as fraught with significance for later history.

We have no Tacitus to give us tantalizing glimpses of life among the preurban Slavs, and so we must make do with scattered foreign testimony and with what the archaeologists can tell us. From these sources we learn that the West Slavs were traders and fighters, quite as willing to do battle with each other as with the Germanic peoples they encountered. The Polish plains became known as the "land of forts." South and west of this Polish region, in what became Czechoslovakia centuries later, a ninth-century empire of Great Moravia flourished briefly. Perhaps most important for the future of the Slavic people as a whole, this Moravian Empire became the first Slavic nation to receive Greek Orthodox missionaries from Byzantium.

The South Slavs inexorably filled the mountain valleys and eastern plains of the Balkans, but tended to be ruled by other peoples. They were absorbed by the Greeks, conquered by the Bulgars, and enslaved by both Byzantines and western Europeans; the very word *slave*, meaning an unfree laborer, derives from "Slav." In Yugoslavia on the Adriatic, however, the South Slavs remained independent, though divided among themselves.

The largest branch of the parent stem, the East Slavs, occupied much of the huge area between the eastern Baltic and the Black seas. They were for the most part agricultural villagers, living in huts that were often built half-underground for warmth during the long Russian winters. Their family structure was patriarchal; the families of several brothers often shared the same dwelling area. Leadership for the village as a whole—which tended to be considerably larger than the typical western European village—was provided by a chief and a council of elders.

The East Slavs practiced slash-and-burn agriculture in the northern forests, where the population was thickest. North and south, they tilled the land with heavy horse-drawn plows and traded, among other things, in slaves. Like most preurban peoples, they worshiped the spirits of the natural world around them—of the woods and the flowing rivers—and a great god of thunder over the Russian plains. At some village sites, we can trace the post holes of large circular temples built of wood. Byzantines who visited the living villages described the Slavs as a friendly, clean, hospitable people who loved music but could be fierce fighters.

In modern terms, they were a preurban, preliterate culture, a people vast in numbers and occupying more territory than any other Indo-European people, yet unorganized beyond the level of the chiefdom. They were a people, in short, who were potentially far more than they had yet become. Newcomers from the north and south helped to set them on their road.

The Varangian Princes

From the north came the Varangians, Vikings following the rivers down from Scandinavia. From the south, the culture of the Byzantine Empire and its metropolis of Constantinople spread up into the lands of the Eastern Slavs. During the ninth and tenth centuries, these two forces stimulated the emergence of a new culture and even of a loose political unity among the Slavs.

Wherever there was water, the Vikings were at home. Down the Dnieper and the Volga and their tributaries, through the dark pine forests of the north and across the golden plains of Ukraine drifted the dragon ships. Here and there they went ashore and built forts. A reconstructed tapestry from the ninth century shows baggy pants, elaborately carved horse-drawn wagons for overland transport, and heavy swords and spears. An Arab trader who met some Varangians at the mouth of the Volga on the Caspian Sea in the tenth century "admired their fine physique, though deploring their highly defective personal hygiene"—a striking contrast to the Slavs, who loved nothing better than a good hot bath.[7]

The Varangians used their forts as bases for trade and tribute-gathering among the Slavic villages. They took home furs, honey, and slaves. But many of them stayed, married Slavic women, lost their Scandinavian identity, and became the progenitors of Russia's emerging nobility, the *boyars*. They played an important part in the building of the first sizable trading towns in Russia, including Novgorod in the northern forests and Kiev on the southern steppes, both founded in the ninth century.

The Varangians also brought more extensive political organization to the East Slavs, though again the details are obscure. According to the *Primary Chronicle*, the greatest example of early medieval Russian historical writing, around 860 the feuding citizens of Novgorod petitioned the Vikings to restore order and become their rulers, and a Varangian named Rurik (d. c. 879) answered the call. This *calling of the princes* paved the way for Varangian political suzerainty. Rurik's successor Oleg (r. c. 879–912) united the northern and southern trading centers of Novgorod and Kiev in a loose alliance of Varangian princes that ruled all the land between. Oleg made his residence at Kiev, so that the political center of this first Russian state shifted south to Ukraine, and the Varangian-dominated Slavic principality became known as the *Kievan Rus*. The term *Rus*, apparently originally applied to the Varangians as a people, became in later centuries the root of the name of the Russian nation itself.

The Impact of Byzantium

The establishment of the Varangian capital at Kiev had significant and unforeseen consequences. The original intention was probably to bring the Varangians within trading and raiding range of the

Black Sea and especially of Constantinople. Viking fleets did in fact strike the Byzantine metropolis several times. But the move also brought the center of the Kievan Rus within easier reach of Byzantine influences. These influences from the civilized south proved to be perhaps even more important than the impact of the Vikings in shaping emerging Slav society. The Vikings had come with their swords and brought political unity; the Byzantines came with a missionary faith and brought a whole culture.

Greek Orthodox Constantinople became the missionary center for Slavic eastern Europe, as Rome had been for Germanic western Europe. Byzantium's first missionary efforts, however, were directed toward the West and South Slavs rather than to the East Slavs in the Rus. In 862 the ruler of the West Slav state of Moravia, in today's Czech Republic, fearful of the subversive influence of the Roman Catholic Christianity of his German neighbors, asked the Byzantine emperor to send some holy men to teach them the Greek Orthodox version of Christianity. The mission sent out to them was headed by two brothers, Cyril (c. 827–869) and Methodius (c. 825–884), later known as the "Apostles to the Slavs." The two men spoke Slavic and devised an alphabet for their converts; a somewhat later version, based on Greek and known as Cyrillic, became the Russian script of today. In the later ninth century, Bulgaria, with some reluctance, accepted Greek Orthodoxy, as in time did most of the Slavic peoples. Ironically, the Czechs, like their Polish neighbors, were eventually converted to Roman Catholicism. These peoples thus became the core of an enclave of Roman Christianity in predominantly Greek Orthodox eastern Europe.

The conversion of the East Slavs of Kievan Russia did not come until the end of the tenth century. In 957 the reigning princess of Kiev, Olga (r. 945–964), who "always sought wisdom in this world," was baptized a Christian in Constantinople.[8] (See box, "The Conversion of Olga.") When Olga's grandson Prince Vladimir the Saint (r. 980–1015) also accepted the Orthodox faith in 988, the elite of the Rus and most of the populations of the trading towns followed him into the church. The bulk of the Slavic peasantry probably remained pagan long after these royal conversions, as peasants did in western Europe. Nevertheless, the influence of the new religion, and of the intensified contact with Byzantium that accompanied conversion, was far-reaching.

The religion itself, of course, was central. Greek Orthodox priests and services were exported to Russia. Orthodox monasteries, which played an impor-

PROFILES IN HISTORY
The Conversion of Olga

The conversion of Olga, grand duchess of Kiev, to Orthodox Christianity in 957 was as important as that of western European kings to Roman Catholicism in earlier centuries. Beginning in the reign of Olga's grandson Vladimir the Saint (r. 980–1015), much of Russia's medieval culture followed the new faith from Byzantium to the Russian steppes. This version of the duchess's conversion, which comes from the *Primary Chronicle* (c. 1100), depicts this early Russian heroine as both admired by and getting the better of the Byzantine emperor.

The reigning Emperor was named Constantine, son of Leo. Olga came before him, and when he saw that she was very fair of countenance and wise as well, the Emperor wondered at her intellect. He conversed with her and remarked that she was worthy to reign with him in his city. When Olga heard his words, she replied that if he desired to baptize her, he should perform this function himself; otherwise, she was unwilling to accept baptism. The Emperor, with the assistance of the Patriarch, accordingly baptized her.

When Olga was enlightened, she rejoiced in soul and body. The Patriarch, who instructed her in the faith, said to her, "Blessed art thou among the women of Rus, for thou has loved the light and quit the darkness. The sons of Rus shall bless thee to the last generation of thy descendants." He taught her the doctrine of the Church, and instructed her in prayer and fasting, in almsgiving and in the maintenance of chastity. She bowed her head, and like a sponge absorbing water, she eagerly drank in his teachings. . . .

After her baptism, the Emperor summoned Olga and made known to her that he wished her to become his wife. "How can you marry me, after yourself baptizing me and calling me your daughter? For among Christians that is unlawful, as you yourself must know." Then the Emperor said, "Olga, you have outwitted me." He gave her many gifts of gold, silver, silks, and various vases, and dismissed her, still calling her his daughter.

Source: Samuel Hazzard Cross and O. P. Sherbowitz-Wetzor, trans. and eds., *The Russian Primary Chronicle* (Cambridge, Mass.: Medieval Academy of America), 82.

tant part in the religious life of Byzantium, were founded in growing numbers among the East Slavs, and monks became the most revered holy men in Russia as they were among the Byzantines. Reverence for the religious images called icons also passed from Byzantium to the Russian Orthodox faithful.

Larger cultural influences accompanied the new faith. Literacy and the use of the Cyrillic alphabet spread not only among churchmen but among Russia's rulers and business community as well. The arts also benefited: churches were built inspired by those at Constantinople, and the making of icons became a fine art in Russia as it was in Byzantium. In centuries to come, this long-lasting Byzantine connection brought the Russians some influential Byzantine political ideas, notably the belief in political autocracy. In the tenth century, however, the confederation of princes centered at Kiev was not strong enough to attempt to model itself on the autocratic emperors at Constantinople.

The Age of Yaroslav the Wise

The Kievan Rus reached its height in the early eleventh century. The presiding spirit of this Kievan golden age was Yaroslav the Wise (r. 1019–1054), perhaps the greatest prince to rule the first Russia, revered today especially in the new independent state of Ukraine.

Yaroslav, son of the convert Vladimir, was a hero of the *Primary Chronicle*. He turned back a wave of invaders from the eastern steppes and expanded his own frontiers northward into territories formerly held by the Finns. He had the traditional laws of the East Slavs assembled and codified for the first time. He achieved the formal separation of the Russian Orthodox church from the Greek Orthodox parent body in Constantinople. He made the principality of Kiev known in western Europe and negotiated alliances with some of Europe's ruling houses. Under Yaroslav, Russia was in closer contact with the western half of the continent than it was again until modern times, when Russian czars reached out once more for contact with the West.

The success of the Kievan Rus, however, was more than the achievement of one ruler, or even a succession of them. Built on solid economic foundations, this society generated some surprisingly liberal political institutions, and may have been freer than the western Europe of its day.

The economy of the East Slavs was based on agriculture but featured a bustling commercial sector as well. Russian peasants grew enough wheat to export it in significant quantities. The trading towns on the Russian rivers shipped other things too, including honey, amber, and furs. The Byzantine Empire remained the Rus's main trading partner, but Russians also exchanged goods with western Europe through Scandinavia, with Asia through the steppe nomads, and even with the Arabs, who had by that time conquered most of the Middle East in the name of Islam.

The structure of Kievan society was less rigid in

It is hard to say whether Yaroslav the Wise, portrayed here in one of a series of seventeenth-century paintings of early Russian, Muscovite, and Kievan rulers, was a Russian or a Ukrainian hero. Ukraine is now of course an independent state. In any case, he played an important part in the early history of both Russia and Ukraine.

some ways than that of contemporary Western Christendom. Most Russian peasants were free, though there were slaves and some serfs among them. The boyar nobility was normally attached to the retinue of a regional prince, but there was no established feudal system, and boyars could take their services wherever they pleased. Most promising, perhaps, the trading towns had free institutions, notably a municipal council, or *veche,* which governed the city with little princely or boyar intervention.

Like Charlemagne and Alfred the Great in western Europe, Yaroslav and his heirs sponsored a cultural flowering during the brief period of Kievan hegemony. Greek artisans were imported to decorate the scores of churches that sprang up in Kiev, including the Church of the Holy Wisdom, which is still to be seen there. Like their English or French contemporaries, scholarly Russian monks like Hilarion— metropolitan (bishop) of Kiev from 1051 to 1054— wrote religious tracts, including many lives of the saints. Historical writing included the *Primary Chronicle,* which, like contemporary western European histories, had a religious core, emphasizing the conversion of Russian princes and their subsequent victories over their pagan foes.

Yaroslav himself had the reputation of being a great reader, writer, and translator of works of religious edification from Byzantine Greek into the Church Slavonic used in Russia. Monastery schools apparently taught the Cyrillic alphabet to some of the children of princes and nobles. Indeed, the aristocracy of Kiev may have been more literate than the contemporary western European nobility: "For great is the profit of book-learning," as the *Primary Chronicle* says.[9]

Like the kingdoms of early medieval peoples in western Europe, however, these first state-building efforts of the East Slavs did not last. The Rus remained a loose confederation of princes in spite of the recognized headship of the prince of Kiev. A particularly unfortunate feature was the lack of a clear line of succession. In the generations after Yaroslav, an elaborate system of allotting domains to various princes on the basis of their seniority and the relative wealth of their regions led to disputes and even to wars between rulers. This system had the same effect as the division of France among Frankish princes, fragmenting the state into smaller pieces. When a powerful new nomadic people appeared out of the East in the thirteenth century, the Mongols of Genghis Khan, the divided and rivalrous princes of Kiev stood little chance against them.

The Empire of the Arabs

South of the Byzantine Empire lived another people who, like the Slavs, were largely undeveloped at the beginning of the Middle Ages. These were the Arabs, and the force that was to give them direction was one of the world's great religions—Islam.

Islam, still a living force in the world today, ought to be more familiar to us than the vanished civilization of Byzantium or the ill-documented early history of the Slavs. Late twentieth-century impressions of Arabs and Islamic movements, however, may actually hamper our understanding of the golden age of Arab Islam. Headlines about oil sheiks and terrorist groups scarcely prepare us for the civilizing vision of Muhammad, the Arabian Nights

Hagia Sophia, the sixth-century Church of the Holy Wisdom at Constantinople, was grander than any other cathedral in Christendom when it was built by Emperor Justinian. Converted into a mosque and then a museum, the church is still one of the most marvelous sights of modern Istanbul.

splendor of old Baghdad, or the spiritual peace still to be found in the courtyard of an ancient mosque.

Though there are similarities between the militance of those days and ours, a more useful comparison might be drawn between the zeal of medieval Christian Crusaders and that of the Muslim conquerors of that same period. As we see in a later chapter, both Christians and Muslims in those days saw paradise opening to the holy warrior, and neither was averse to wading through blood to reach the golden gates. At the same time, both were capable of profound spirituality and a deep appreciation of beauty. It is perhaps worth noting that when the Muslims finally captured Constantinople, they did not destroy Hagia Sophia, the greatest church in Christendom, but instead converted it into a mosque.

The Desert Peoples

The world in which the religion of the Prophet Muhammad was born was very different from the sophisticated cities of the Byzantine Empire or the steppes and forests of Russia. Islam grew up among the sun-dazzled sands and palm-fringed oases, the dry wadis and jutting crags of Arabia. This region, which lay south of the Byzantine Empire, had by the seventh century A.D.—the first century of the Muslim calendar—produced a society as distinctive as either of the other two surveyed.

On today's map, Arab countries stretch from the Near East all across North Africa—through Egypt, Libya, Tunisia, Algeria, Morocco—to the Strait of Gibraltar and beyond. Arabia itself, the Arab homeland, spreads southward from the ancient Fertile Crescent between the Red Sea and the Persian Gulf into the Indian Ocean. Here around A.D. 600 the last of the great world religions emerged among a people who had thus far, like the Slavs and Germans, lived on the fringes of history. For them, like their northern neighbors, all that was about to change.

The twin settings of pre-Islamic Arab society were the oasis and the desert. At oases, some of which were large enough to accommodate several villages, the water table lay close enough to the surface to permit the digging of wells and the cultivation of crops, especially dates and wheat. The much larger desert areas of Arabia, by contrast, depended largely on the skimpy spring rains to produce enough grass to feed the sheep, asses, camels, and other animals herded by nomads. At the oases, farms, towns, and settled society developed; on the desert, nomadic Bedouins evolved a society always on the move to keep up with the sparse water and pasturage on which their flocks depended.

Linking the two cultures was a remarkable animal: the camel. Capable of carrying heavier loads than any beast of burden except the elephant, able to survive for long periods without water, and surprisingly fast-moving when goaded to a gallop by its Bedouin master, the camel was ideally suited to this desiccated land. Bedouin Arabs rode and herded camels, lived off their milk and meat, and used them for the rapid cavalry raids that were central to their style of fighting. Oasis Arabs used camels to import what they could not make for their own use, and for the long-distance trade in which the oases served as way stations and markets. The camel was also central to the symbiotic relationship that developed between oasis and desert: oasis Arabs bought their camels from Bedouins, and Bedouins used the camel to conduct profitable raids on the caravans of oasis-bound merchants.

Transcending these differences, however, were the cultural features shared by all Arabs. Like many peoples early in their histories, the Arabs of the seventh century were a tribal or clan-based society with an animistic religion and a vigorous oral literature. The family was the building block of Arab society, with large clans and larger tribes claiming common, often divine ancestors. The religious life of the Arabs before Muhammad centered on spirits and demons called *djinn* and on more important gods, often the patron divinities of particular clans. All these supernatural presences were associated with such natural objects as palm groves, oddly shaped rock formations, or bright stars. An immensely popular art form, finally, was Arabic oral poetry. Chanted by professional bards in fixed poetic meters, these popular ballads dealt with the blood feuds of the clans and the deeds of heroic Bedouins.

The southern sands, like the northern steppes, were a unique world and had produced a culture well adapted to this environment, if distinctly limited by it. Despite its uniqueness, however, Arabia was not cut off from the rest of the Middle East. Arabs traded and raided in the Byzantine and Persian empires and had regular contact with Palestine and Syria. They were well aware of the monotheistic religions of Judaism and Christianity that flourished in these regions. There were, in fact, scattered communities of Jews and Christians living in Arabia itself. Contact with these monotheistic peoples had already begun to make some Arabs ponder even before Muhammad came on the scene, bringing with him the third great faith to be born in this narrow corner of the Near East.

The Vision of Muhammad

In the Name of God, the Merciful, the
  Compassionate
Praise belongs to God, the Lord of All
  Being,
The All-merciful, the All-compassionate,
The Master of the Day of Doom.

Thee only we serve, to Thee only we pray
  for succor.
Guide us in the straight path,
The path of those whom Thou hast
  blessed,
Not of those against whom Thou art
  wrathful,
Nor of those who are astray.[10]

The man who heard these words echoing through his head and later spoke them in the market town of Mecca was in his forties, black-bearded, with intense dark eyes. Sitting alone on a mountain outside the town, he sometimes saw "a waking vision of a gigantic being on the horizon—on every horizon—on every horizon to which [he] turned his eyes—who spoke to him the words he must say."[11] His enemies among the Arabs accused him of being possessed by a djinn; more worldly Byzantines claimed he was an epileptic. The consensus of modern scholarship is that he was in any event profoundly sincere.

The Prophet Muhammad (570–632), of the Hashim clan of the Quraysh tribe, grew up as a marketplace orphan in the caravan oasis town of Mecca in west-central Arabia, not far from the Red Sea. Mecca, on the main north-south caravan route, was also a pilgrimage center, famous for its pagan religious shrine, the Kaaba, where idols and other sacred objects were gathered for veneration by many clans. In this atmosphere of caravans and pilgrims Muhammad grew up and became a respected businessman. He married a wealthy businesswoman named Khadijah (d. 619),

The angel Gabriel inspires the prophet Muhammad to write the Koran, the holy book of Islam. Muhammad, who clearly had some familiarity with both Judaism and Christianity, saw himself as God's last messenger to the human race.

who considerably enhanced his position in the trading community, and with her he had a half-dozen children. Then, in his fortieth year, he began to have visions.

Muhammad had probably encountered both Christianity and Judaism in his travels with the caravans. In middle age, he began to withdraw to a mountain overlooking the city to meditate. It was here, around 610, that he heard the great voice he identified as the angel Gabriel telling him to recite to others the religious revelations that would be vouchsafed to him. Over the next twenty-two years, Muhammad did so, reciting to growing numbers the rhythmic, vivid Arabic verses of the *Koran*, the Muslim holy book. (For an extract, see the box, "The Holy Koran Promises Salvation.")

He spoke first to his own family, and his wife Khadijah became the first convert to the new religion. A few others, many of them young and not of the wealthiest classes, began to listen to him too, and

then one or two of the most powerful. Most of the leading citizens of Mecca, however, were unreceptive to Muhammad's new faith, a militant monotheism that seemed to challenge all the pagan cults which drew the lucrative pilgrim trade. After a dozen years of preaching, therefore, the Prophet and his embattled followers left Mecca and moved 250 miles north to another city, subsequently renamed el-Medina, "The City," the first community to accept the Prophet's message. This "flight to Medina" became known as the *Hegira,* and the year of the Hegira, 622 by the Christian calendar, is the year 1 for Muslims everywhere.

For the last ten years of his life, Muhammad developed his ideas in the more practical atmosphere of guiding the affairs of the city that had accepted his leadership. Reaching out to the desert Bedouins, he also became more aggressive, urging believers to fight for their faith against unbelievers, something the feuding, raiding desert nomads were quite will-

THE HUMAN SPIRIT
The Holy Koran Promises Salvation

The Islamic faith shared some basic attitudes with its medieval rival, the Christian religion. In the following passages, the Koran praises one God, creator of heaven and earth, and describes how God sent his emissary to preach salvation for those who worship their maker and care for the neediest of his children. Note also the expectation that unbelievers would in time be converted to the true faith, a missionary impulse that medieval Islam also shared with Christianity.

IN THE NAME OF THE MOST MERCIFUL GOD

Whatever is in heaven and earth praises God; the King, the Holy, the Mighty, the Wise. It is he who hath raised up amidst the illiterate Arabians an apostle from among themselves, to rehearse his signs unto them, and to purify them, and to teach them the scriptures and wisdom, whereas before they were certainly in a manifest error and others of them have not yet attained unto them, by embracing the faith, though they also shall be converted in God's good time; for he is mighty and wise. This is the free grace of God: he bestoweth the same on whom he pleaseth: and God is endued with great beneficence. . . .

Whatever is in heaven and earth celebrateth the praises of God; his is the kingdom, and unto him is the praise due for he is almighty. It is he who hath created you. . . . He hath created the heavens and the earth with truth; and he hath fashioned you, and given you beautiful forms; and unto him must ye all go. . . .

By the brightness of the morning; and by the night, when it groweth dark; thy Lord hath not forsaken thee, neither doth he hate thee. Verily the life to come shall be better for thee than this present life: and thy Lord shall give thee a reward wherewith thou shalt be well pleased. . . . Wherefore oppress not the orphan; neither repulse the beggar; but declare the goodness of thy Lord.

Source: *The Koran,* trans. George Sale (New York: American Book Exchange, 1881), Chapters 62, 64, 93.

the shrine of the Kaaba of its idols, retaining only the holiest of its relics, a black stone of meteoric origin, which he said was sacred to the one God, Allah. By the time of the Prophet's death in 632, two years after his triumph in his own city, virtually the entire population of Arabia had accepted his message.

The message of the Koran is summarized most simply by the two linked propositions: "There is no God but Allah, and Muhammad is his Prophet." *Islam* means "submission" to the will of God, and Muhammad's Koran explained Allah's basic requirements of the faithful. These included belief in the one God and his Prophet, in personal immortality, heaven and hell, and a Day of Judgment. Good Muslims were required to pray five times daily, to fast during the daylight hours of the month of Ramadan, to try to make a pilgrimage to Mecca, and to give alms to the poor. There were also some dietary regulations, including the prohibition of alcoholic beverages. Some of these ideas may have their roots in Judaic or Christian teachings, and Muhammad actually saw himself as a prophet in the line of Moses and Jesus, whose inspiration he did not deny.

On the broad social level, Muhammad, like the Hebrew prophets and Jesus of Nazareth, condemned some of the common practices of his day as immoral and unjust. Female infanticide and charging usurious rates of interest, for example, were declared to be sins in the eyes of Allah. Polygamy was permitted up to four wives, though few men could afford more than one; and women, though they lived secluded lives in the women's quarters, often found it easier to inherit and retain control of property in the Islamic world than they did in medieval Europe. The Koran and the large body of Muslim law that grew up in later centuries also offered rules for family life, for business relations, and a criminal code—a blueprint for Muslim society as a whole. From the visions that came to Muhammad on his mountain flowered a vigorous prescription for life on earth as well as a glimpse of paradise.

The Arab Conquests

It would not have looked like a flowering if you had been a Persian, a Byzantine, a North African, or a southern European over the next hundred years. For from the Prophet's death in 632 dates the first terrifying explosion of *jihad,* the Muslim holy war.

ing to do. In a long series of skirmishes and battles, the Muslims brought one Arabian tribe after another over to their side. Eight years after the Hegira, then, Muhammad had developed sufficient strength to return and set his own terms with Mecca. He cleansed

The motive force behind the jihad, like that of the Christian Crusades to come, was certainly in part religious. Death while fighting for Allah, Muslims believed, would be rewarded by an eternity in the gardens of paradise. But, like the later European Crusaders, the jihad also had more material motives, including the traditional Bedouin raider's enthusiasm for booty. It also seems likely that overpopulation of their unproductive desert homeland encouraged Arab armies to set out, sword in hand, in search of new living space.

They found it, with a vengeance. Unified for the first time by their common faith, oasis Arabs and Bedouins of many tribes made a powerful new force in the world. Sticking largely to the hit-and-run tactics of their raiding days, they repeatedly caught their enemies off balance, wore them down, and destroyed them. Another factor in their long string of victories was the weakness of their most formidable foes, the Byzantines and the Persians, exhausted by their own long wars. The result was a wave of conquest of almost unparalleled speed and success. (See map 8.3.)

Within a dozen years, Arab armies had surged out of their sunbaked peninsula to seize the coastal provinces of Syria and Palestine and to capture Egypt—all three parts of the Byzantine Empire—and had overrun all of Sassanid Persia. As the seventh century wore on, the Arabs pushed westward across Byzantine North Africa to the Atlantic and east as far as the frontiers of India. Early in the following century, they drove on into central Asia and swung around through Asia Minor, the Byzantine heartland, to besiege Constantinople itself in 717. In the West, a force of Arabs and North African Berbers crossed the Strait of Gibraltar in 711, smashed the Visigothic Kingdom in Spain, and moved across the Pyrenees into France in 725.

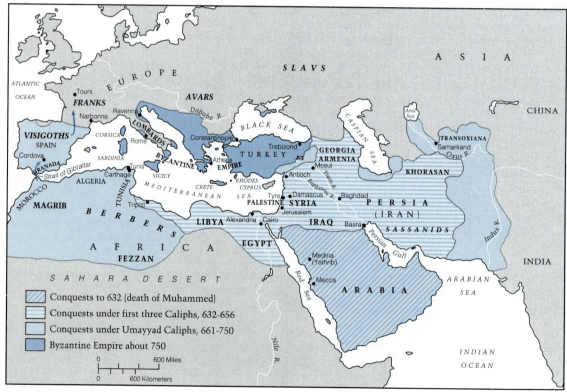

Map 8.3 The Expanding Muslim Zone

Thus in the early eighth century, less than a hundred years after the death of Muhammad, Christendom found itself caught in a gigantic vice as Muslim forces pressed in on the Christian zone from both ends of the Mediterranean. With Arab armies roving through western France and camped outside the walls of Constantinople, the very survival of the West seemed questionable.

At this juncture, however, both the Byzantine Empire and the emergent Carolingian dynasty in France rose up and turned back the Arab advance. The Byzantines broke the siege of Constantinople in 718 and pushed the Muslims back to a slowly stabilizing frontier in the middle of Asia Minor. And in 732, Charles Martel defeated the Arabs at Tours. He then began the process, which his grandson Charlemagne completed, of harrying them back to a fixed frontier along the Pyrenees.

By this time, however, the Arabs had built fleets and had begun to raid Europe's southern coasts, establishing bases in Sicily and southern France, looting Rome and even raiding across northern Italy to catch Alpine merchant caravans unaware. The pagan Vikings and the Magyars, who also looted Christian lands in the eighth and ninth centuries, converted to Christianity, settled down, and became part of European society. But the Muslim world, rallying around its own potent monotheistic faith, was intact and threatening still when the medieval period ended and the modern age began.

The Arab Caliphs

The political history of this powerful rival of medieval Christendom was as violent as that of the West itself in the early Middle Ages. Like the Byzantine Empire, however, the world of Islam achieved economic and cultural heights that were the envy of their Western rivals.

The centuries of Arab domination of the Islamic zone date roughly from 600 to 1050, though nominal Arab rule lasted until 1250. During this age of Arab supremacy, the chief Muslim political and religious leaders were the *caliphs,* the "successors to the Prophet." The most important of these were the "rightly guided" caliphs (632–661), who directly succeeded the Prophet, and two longer ruling dynasties, the Umayyads (661–750) and the Abbasids (750–1258). Outside the realms of this central line of caliphs, a number of Muslim secession states also emerged during these early centuries.

The four rightly guided caliphs presided over an unstable alliance of Bedouins and oasis Arabs and a growing variety of conquered peoples. As spiritual heirs of Muhammad, they also had to help shape a still unsettled religious tradition. It is perhaps not surprising that violent disputes arose and three of the Prophet's first four successors died by violence. Yet most made their own contributions too. Thus Abu Bakr (r. 632–634), Muhammad's oldest disciple, stood for the principle of a single successor and for the rejection of "false prophets" speaking in the founder's name. Omar (r. 634–644) launched the first wave of Muslim expansion. Othman (644–656) sponsored the official version of the Koran and pointed toward the triumph of the dynastic principle by notoriously favoring his own family during his tenure of power. Ali (r. 656–661), finally, was the unwitting source of Islam's longest and deepest schism. A cousin of the Prophet, he won the support of the *Shiite* faction, who insisted that the leadership of the faithful should be vested only in members of Muhammad's own family. Ali, however, was assassinated in a struggle that saw the powerful Umayyad clan seize the caliphate, which they held for the next hundred years. The conflict between the Shiites and the orthodox *Sunni,* or traditional majority, which we discuss in the next section, has continued down to the present day.

The Umayyads, as we have seen, carried the first great wave of Arab conquest to its climax in the early eighth century, overrunning Spain and besieging Constantinople. They also moved the capital of the caliphate from Mecca to Damascus (today the capital of Syria) and significantly transformed the caliph's effective role in Islam. Without abandoning their religious titles, the Umayyad caliphs increasingly left religious matters in the hands of Islamic judges and theologians. Their own court at Damascus became both more secular and more sophisticated, tendencies that accelerated under their successors.

The Abbasid dynasty came to power on a tidal wave of religious and political resentment of Sunnite theology and Arab oppression. Supported by Shiites and outsiders among the conquered, Abu l'Abbas (r. 750–754) seized control of the caliphate in a bloody coup that left almost all the Umayyad princes dead. The new dynasty, however, did little to change the direction of development laid down by its predecessors. Moving the capital once more, this time to the new city of Baghdad (the capital of modern Iraq), the Abbasids built over the next three centuries a metropolis to rival Constantinople in size, opulence, and culture.

The most renowned of the Abbasid caliphs were celebrated for their wealth and sophistication. Harun al-Rashid (r. 786–809), known to the West as the caliph of the *Arabian Nights* tales, fought the Byzantines but also imported Greek manuscripts from them and commissioned scholars to translate the wisdom of these ancient pagans for his cosmopolitan elite. The reign of Al-Mamun (r. 813–833), Mamun the Great, was even more splendid. Mamun built libraries, a center for theological study, and an astronomical observatory, and encouraged all the sciences and many arts.

Throughout the centuries of Arab rule in Islam, the real political power of the caliphs over the far-flung community of Muslim believers was quite limited. As we see in the next section, separate caliphates flourished in Spain, Egypt, and elsewhere during this period. The hegemony of the Arabs even in the Middle Eastern heart of the Muslim zone was challenged in the eleventh century when the Seljuk Turks seized Baghdad. The later Abbasids thus became essentially figureheads in their own capital. The power of Islam, however, continued to grow under first the Seljuk and then the Ottoman Turks, who continued to threaten—and to influence—the West well into the early modern period.

Divisions in the Muslim World

Rather than trace the rise and fall of the caliphates in more detail, we first analyze the sources of the divisiveness that rent the fabric of the Arab Empire, then the deeper roots of Islamic unity. Several forces, to begin with, contributed to the pattern of divisive violence within the Empire. One was the ancient Arab tradition of vendetta and blood feud between tribes and clans. Another was the inevitable tension between Arab conquerors and the peoples they conquered. Some heirs of proud civilizations were made to feel like second-class citizens even when they converted to the Muslim faith. Another, more diffuse source of discord was the growing gap between haves and have-nots as Muslim society grew richer and more urbanized. Most important, however, were the sectarian differences and religious schisms that arose in medieval Islam.

It took the most determined efforts of the early caliphs—and the lure of endless victories and booty—to hold the feuding Arabs together even in the early days of the movement. Family feuds were crucial to the rise of both the Umayyads and the Abbasids. When the founder of the latter dynasty seized power in 750, he made a determined effort to exterminate the entire Umayyad clan—and the one who got away fled to Spain and founded what became a rival caliphate at the other end of the Mediterranean.

Political secession became endemic under the Abbasids as regional culture and local interests came to outweigh the power of the distant Abbasid ruler. Much of North Africa followed the Spanish example before the eighth century was over: Spain revolted against the Abbasid dynasty in 755; Morocco, just across the Strait of Gibraltar, rebelled in 788; and Tunisia followed in 800. In the ninth century, Middle Eastern centers of ancient civilizations also asserted their political independence—Persia in 820 and in 868 Egypt, which also established an independent caliphate.

In the long run, however, the most potent force for civil disorder proved to be religious disagreements. Medieval Islam, like medieval Christendom, was divided by disputes over the meanings of the faith. One strong challenge to the established order came from the Sufi movement. The Sufis, like monks in contemporary Christendom, were devout ascetics committed to meditation and mysticism. In particular, they cultivated an emotional form of Islam that appealed to the feelings through music, movement, chants, and ecstatic trances. Condemning the worldliness and wealth of Muslim princes and caliphs, the Sufis found many followers among the have-nots, the masses of the Muslim faithful.

The greatest force for schism in Islam, however, was the Shiite movement, which began in the days of the rightly guided caliphs. Shiite Muslims shared many basic beliefs with mainstream Sunni Muslims, just as Roman Catholic and Greek Orthodox Christians shared a common core of doctrine. But the differences between Shiite and Sunni Islam also ran at least as deep as those between Catholic and Orthodox Christians.

Sunni Muslims, of course, recognized the Koran as the central source of religious truth. But they also venerated the Sunna, the body of traditions concerning the deeds and sayings of the Prophet and his companions that Islamic scholars had accepted as authentic. And Sunni Muslims normally accepted the legitimacy of rule by caliphs, successors to the Prophet with at least an aura of religious sanction.

Shiites, by contrast, rejected the Sunna as a source of spiritual guidance. Even more important, they believed the leadership of the Islamic world had been usurped by worldly caliphs from the beginning. They insisted that only truly holy men directly descended from the blood of the Prophet should rule the Muslim world. Their heroes were the martyred leaders of the early Shiite movement, like the murdered fourth caliph Ali, and martyrdom became an immensely honored destiny among them. Many believed that Allah had designated a succession of inspired leaders called *imams,* all descended from Ali. These men, not the caliphs, were the true heads of the community of the faithful. The twelfth, or "hidden," imam, who disappeared in the 870s, would one day return to bring justice and righteousness to the world at last.

The Shiite movement focused the resentments of non-Arabs and of the poor and oppressed in many parts of the Muslim world. The movement itself split over centuries into a number of conflicting tendencies. By the end of the Middle Ages, however, the Shiite phenomenon was centered in what is now Iran—then Persia—where it is still dominant and a source of militance and discord within the Muslim world.

The Unity of Islam

The forces that made for a larger unity in the Muslim world, however, outweighed all these sources of discord. And though, as we have seen, religious differences were important sources of conflict, the primary unifying forces in the Muslim zone were also rooted in the Muslim faith. In the end, religion itself was the great bond that held Spaniards and Egyptians, Persians and Turks together culturally if not politically.

Arabic, for instance, the common language of the Muslim world, was introduced initially for religious reasons. During the early centuries, Arabic, of course, was the language of the conquerors and rulers of the Empire. More important, however, was the Islamic requirement that the Koran be read in Arabic, as the Prophet had written it, and all services in mosques be conducted in that language. From this beginning, Arabic became the language of business, literature, and government in many countries, and therefore a language many non-Arabs hastened to acquire.

Another unifying element was a common law—again, rooted in the Islamic religion. Though the

Arab Empire in the literal sense of a unified caliphate crumbled rapidly under the Abbasids, the basic Muslim law, the *sharia,* continued to be applied in all Muslim lands. This elaborate structure of legal principle and rules for living was based primarily on the Koran; but partly also on the Sunna, the traditions about the Prophet's views and actions; partly on analogies that could be drawn with his recorded views; and partly on the consensus of leading Islamic theologians and jurists. The sharia was administered, not by a formal system of courts, but by Muslim judges called *kadis.* The criminal code of the sharia could be harsh, the business law acute—Muhammad himself, after all, had been a merchant. Muslim law and tradition also governed family relations. Though polygamy was countenanced and women confined to the private sphere of the harem, women were also allowed con-

The splendor of the far-reaching Muslim zone was seldom more dazzlingly displayed than here, in the Alhambra, palace of the Moorish rulers of Granada in fourteenth-century Spain. The Lion Court lies straight ahead, through the elegant arches. The palace is cool in the noon-day heat, bright with flowers, garnished with reflecting pools.

trol of their own property and had the right to divorce their husbands. The sharia was recognized and enforced all across the Muslim world. Wherever you went, you knew the rules and the penalties—again, a feature that helped bind all these peoples.

Travel and trade also acted as connecting links, giving Muslims a sense of belonging to a single international community. Many Muslims traveled to fulfill their religious obligation to make the once-in-a-lifetime pilgrimage to Mecca. Many more traveled for commercial reasons. With their conquests across the center of the Old World, Muslims became masters of the Eurasian trade routes. West of China, the Great Silk Road and other caravan roads were now operated largely by Muslims. Lateen-rigged Arab dhows plied the sea routes across the Indian Ocean, from India and Ceylon to the Persian Gulf or the Red Sea, whence it was only a short haul overland to the Mediterranean. With a common language and law in force, with habits of hospitality and the customs of the caravansaries and bazaars much the same whether one was in Alexandria or Damascus, Basra or Samarkand, it is not surprising that trade flourished.

This surge of trade and the continuing richness of Near Eastern craftwork under Muslim auspices also had the unintended effect of helping stimulate the commercial revival of Christendom in the High Middle Ages. For the Crusades brought large numbers of Europeans into contact with oriental luxuries and created a demand for them in quantities that even the Byzantine Empire could not supply. And neither Muslim nor Christian merchants hesitated to trade with the enemy between holy wars.

Linked by bonds of language and law, travel and trade, many Muslims seem to have had a strong sense of the unity of the Islamic world that transcended its political divisions. This feeling of pride in and allegiance to a larger, transnational unity was further strengthened by the brilliance of Islamic culture in the golden age of Arabic Islam.

The Arab Golden Age

The cultural evolution of the Arabs was as rapid as their conquests had been. The illiterate Bedouin of Muhammad's day, about 600, would have been totally out of place in the Umayyad capital of Damascus around 700. And he would have been as hopelessly lost in the vast Baghdad of Harun al-Rashid in 800 as he would have been in Byzantium.

What the Arabs had done was conquer the an-

cient centers of Near Eastern and North African civilization, areas that had also absorbed a Greek cultural legacy in Hellenistic times. And the Arabs learned very rapidly. In some areas of art and thought, their religion limited what they could absorb. More often than not, however, toleration left the way open for profitable contact with Persian art or Greek philosophy. And in the end, it was precisely the Arabic and Islamic traditions of the conquerors that inspired their most remarkable cultural achievements.

As with Byzantium, we must look first at the cities, the treasure troves of Islamic culture. The

PROBING THE PAST
Ibn Khaldun's View of History

The degree of civilization reached by medieval Islam may be gauged by the level of historical understanding of which the Muslim golden age was capable. The highly sophisticated view of history expressed here was formulated by Ibn Khaldun (1332–1406), a North African scholar and statesman whose seven-volume *Universal History* was immensely admired by the twentieth-century British global historian Arnold Toynbee (1889–1975). While most medieval chroniclers stuck to relatively simple narratives, Ibn Khaldun here proposes a much broader and more analytical approach to the human past.

It should be known that history, in matter of fact, is information about human social organization, which itself is identical with world civilization. It deals with such conditions affecting the nature of civilization as, for instance, savagery and sociability, group feelings, and the different ways by which one group of human beings achieves superiority over another. It deals with royal authority and the dynasties that result (in this manner) and with the various ranks that exist within them. (It further deals) with the different kinds of gainful occupations and ways of making a living, with the sciences and crafts that human beings pursue as part of their activities and efforts, and with all the other institutions that originate in civilization through its very nature.

Source: Ibn Khaldun, *The Muqaddimah*, trans. Franz Rosenthal, ed. N. J. Dawood (Princeton: Princeton University Press, 1967), 371.

desert Bedouin who captured cities like Alexandria and Antioch had a distrust of such places and lived instead in camps outside the ancient metropolises. But the caliphs soon not only moved into cities, but began to build their own. Mecca remained the sacred pilgrimage center, but the Umayyad caliphs moved to Damascus, and the Abbasids turned Baghdad into a city as glorious in wealth and color and sheer sprawling immensity as Constantinople itself.

The Baghdad of Harun al-Rashid was a metropolis of palaces and mosques, libraries, scholars, and poets as well as of teeming bazaars, craftshops, and caravansaries. It was said that you could buy anything in the world in the bazaars of Baghdad, and the streets described in Scheherazade's tales do echo with the polyglot life and excitement of the cities of the early caliphates.

There is little left of the monuments of old Baghdad today, and even the exquisite craftwork of Persian, Byzantine, or Syrian artisans that was once on sale there is in shorter supply now than we would like. But the elegant pillars and courtyards, the fountains and flowering gardens of the Alhambra in Spanish Granada at the other end of the Mediterranean give a sense of what a medieval Muslim palace could be like. And the surviving ivory and metalwork, brilliantly illuminated Arabic manuscripts, and exquisite textiles indicate something of the luxury of the life of the Arab princes.

Caliphs also became eager patrons of scholarship and literature, and Arab scholars and poets took almost too enthusiastically to these pursuits. Thus histories of Muslim cities, books of travel through the Muslim world, and lives of Arab heroes and Muslim saints appeared along with the theoretical tracts of theologians and students of the sharia. (See box, "Ibn Khaldun's View of History.") But the newly civilized Arabs also became intrigued by Greek and even Indian philosophy and science. Greek ideas on medicine set the Muslims thinking, and they soon became the best doctors in western Eurasia. The study of Hellenistic science and mathematics and the far more efficient Indian system of numbers—including that marvelous aid to calculation, the zero—was permitted. And so Arabs became famous astronomers, mathematicians, astrologers, and alchemists—all valued scholarly specialties in the Middle Ages. But pagan philosophers like Plato and Aristotle raised serious problems for Muslim thinkers. The study of Greek philosophy led some Arab commentators to wonder if human reason might not be as good a tool for uncovering truth as divine revelation. It was

a point of view as controversial in Islam as it was in the Christian West.

In literature, the newly sophisticated Arabs were soon moving in directions that ranged from frivolity to downright immorality. Stories like those of the *Arabian Nights,* culled from Greek, Asian, and other exotic sources and recounted by professional storytellers, were sometimes risqué and seldom spiritually elevating. Arab poetry moved from the old hero tales of blood feuds to court poetry in praise of good wine and the banquet table, or to thoroughly erotic love poetry.

Once more, the Arabs were going to pass on much of this body of achievement to their Christian rivals. Christian scholars, as hungry for new truth as Western merchants were for trade, crossed the Pyrenees to study Greek philosophy and science and learn the mysteries of "Arabic" numbers at the feet

The golden-roofed shrine of the Dome of the Rock in Jerusalem marks the spot from which Muhammad is believed to have ascended into heaven. Located in modern Israel, this seventh-century building is still a sacred place to the world's Muslims. Note the elaborate decoration and the absence of statues or pictorial representations of sacred figures.

of Muslim scholars in Spain. And Arabic love poetry, serenades, and even the lute filtered insidiously across the mountains to inspire the troubadour love poetry of southern France that we look at in a later chapter.

The Muslim world, however, did not abandon its religious faith in the bright new world of urban sophistication and secular culture. Some of the most distinctive and beautiful Muslim art was actually shaped by Islamic religious requirements. Islam, for instance, prohibited images of divine personages or human beings on religious or other public buildings. While Muslims enjoyed wall paintings or illustrated books in private, mosques and palaces were therefore decorated with beautiful nonrepresentational patterns of arabesque and filigree. Designers often used Arabic script itself as a decorative motif, thus communicating a message from the Koran while patterning a wall, a textile, or a silver plate.

Most important, however, the requirements of Muslim worship created the *mosque.* There were other religious structures, including schools for religious study, tombs of saints, and shrines like the Dome of the Rock in Jerusalem, whose golden dome sheltered the spot from which Muhammad was believed to have ascended into heaven. But mosques were everywhere, with their tall minarets from which the faithful were summoned to prayer, their fountains for ceremonial ablutions, the large courtyard or hall where the believers gathered, and the glowingly decorated *mihrab,* the niche indicating the direction of Mecca, toward which Muslims faced when they knelt to pray. All these were lovingly crafted to create an atmosphere of cool peace out of the blazing sun, a twilight world conducive to religious devotion.

Even a non-Muslim can sense that peace today sitting on a worn carpet in the ninth-century mosque of Ibn Tulun in the medieval section of Cairo. Birds dart among the columns through which one can look across the courtyard at the rare stepped minaret rising against the blue. In such a place, with the sounds of Egyptian traffic muted by the heavy walls, it is easy to feel the presence of the generations of believers who for eleven hundred years have found comfort and peace among these columns.

A Topical Summary

Politics: The three eastern civilizations that bordered western Europe in the earlier Middle Ages—the Byzantine Empire, Kievan Russia, and the Muslim zone of Eurasia and North Africa—exhibited very different political structures. The Byzantine emperors were rigid autocrats ruling a strongly centralized state. Kievan Russia was ruled by a loose alliance of Varangian, or Viking, princes. The Arab caliphs who succeeded the Prophet Muhammad presided over a politically divided, although spiritually unified, realm.

Economics: The Byzantine Empire, with its great port at Constantinople at the narrow juncture of trade between East and West, was one of the most industrially and commercially developed states in the world in this period. The Slavic peoples of eastern Europe, peasant agriculturalists through most of the early Middle Ages, generated a flourishing urban commercial sector around 1000. The Arabs, caravan traders and pastoral Bedouins in the Prophet's day, emerged as masters of great cities and far-reaching trade routes linking northern Africa, western Asia, and parts of southern Europe.

Society: Socially, the Byzantine Empire was dominated by its sophisticated urban population, in which merchants, artisans, and, paradoxically, monks played leading parts. In eastern Europe, foreign elites often dominated—Magyar or Bulgar invaders from the steppes or, in Russia, a boyar aristocracy of Viking descent. In the Muslim zone, a conquering Arab alliance of oasis dwellers and Bedouins ruled a variety of peoples from Persia to Spain, gradually merging with local elites to form a cultured upper stratum of society.

Technology: The Byzantines inherited the crafts, building skills, and other technological capacities of the ancient world and developed a range of intricate technical devices of their own, from "Greek fire" to mechanical birds. In eastern Europe and the Islamic zone, Slavs and Arabs acquired technological skills from Byzantines, Persians, and other older peoples. They created, particularly in Constantinople, Damascus, and the Baghdad of Harun al-Rashid, urban environments as advanced as any in the world.

Culture: Scholarship, literature, and art were much

influenced by religion in all three of these ancient societies. Historical writers like Anna Comnena and Ibn Khaldun were much more sophisticated than the authors of Russia's *Primary Chronicle,* but Kiev's Church of the Holy Wisdom is as beautiful if not as large as Constantinople's Hagia Sophia or the Muslim Dome of the Rock in Jerusalem. Most widely influential of all were Muhammad's Koran and the body of law and tradition, popular Sufi religion and beautiful mosques produced by the Arab golden age.

Some Key Terms

autocrat 224
boyar 231
Byzantine Empire 217
caesaropapism 227
caliph 239
calling of the princes 231
Corpus Iuris Civilis (Justinian's Code) 222
djinn 235

Greek (Eastern) Orthodox Church 221
Hegira 236
iconoclastic controversy 223
imam 241
Islam 237
jihad 237
kadi 241

Kievan Rus 231
Koran 236
mihrab 244
mosque 244
patriarchs 221
sharia 241
theme system 223
veche 234

Notes

1. Procopius, *The Secret History,* trans. G.A. Williamson (Harmondsworth, England: Penguin, 1966), 78–79.
2. Ibid, 83, 84, 91.
3. Ibid., 83, 127.
4. Edward Gibbon, *The Decline and Fall of the Roman Empire* Vol. 2 (New York: Modern Library, 1932), 491.
5. Ibn Fadlan, in Michael Grant, *Dawn of the Middle Ages* (London: McGraw-Hill, 1981).
6. *Buildings,* vol. 1, trans. H.B. Dewing (Loeb Classical Library) (Cambridge, Mass.: Harvard University Press, 1940), i, 58–59.
7. In Grant, *Dawn,* 187.
8. Samuel Hazzard Cross and Olgerd P. Sherbowitz-Wetzor, trans. and eds., *The Russian Primary Chronicle* (Cambridge, Mass.: Medieval Academy of America, 1953), 83.
9. Ibid., 137.
10. *The Koran Interpreted,* trans. Arthur J. Arberry (London: Oxford University Press, 1972), 1 (sura 1, verses 1–9).
11. Marshall G.S. Hodgson, *The Venture of Islam: Conscience and History in a World Civilization,* vol. 1 (Chicago: University of Chicago Press, 1974), 161.

Reading List

BECKWITH, J. *The Art of Constantinople.* New York: Phaidon, 1968. Beautifully illustrated survey of Byzantine art.

BROWNING, R. *Justinian and Theodora.* London: Weidenfeld and Nicolson, 1971. Well-written account for the nonspecialist.

COLLINS, R. *The Arab Conquest of Spain, 710–797.* Cambridge, Mass.: Blackwell, 1989. Integrates narrative history with a critique of source materials. See also A. D. Taha, *The Muslim Conquest and Settlement of North Africa and Spain* (New York: Routledge, 1989) and A. G. Cheyne, *Muslim Spain, Its History and Culture* (Minneapolis: University of Minnesota Press, 1974).

CORMACK, R. *Writing in Gold: Byzantine Society and Its Icons.* London: George Philip, 1985. Byzantine religious art as a product of Byzantine society.

DONNER, F. M. *The Early Islamic Conquests.* Princeton: Princeton University Press, 1981. Valuable analysis of the Arab conquests, including discussion of weapons, tactics, and motivation.

FEDOTOV, G. P. *The Russian Religious Mind.* Woodside, N.Y.: Northland, 1976. Focuses on the mind of the Kievan Rus.

FINE, J. V. A. *The Early Medieval Balkans: A Critical Survey from the Sixth to the Late Twelfth Century.* Ann Arbor: University of Michigan, 1983. Overview of five centuries, from the Byzantine supremacy to the rise of independent Balkan states.

GEANAKOPLOS, D. J. *Interaction of the 'Sibling' Byzantine and Western Cultures in the Middle Ages and Italian Renaissance (330–1600)*. New Haven: Yale University Press, 1976. The first part of the book traces cultural relations between Roman Catholic and Greek Orthodox zones during medieval times.

HODGSON, M. G. S. *The Venture of Islam: Conscience and History in a World Civilization*. Chicago: University of Chicago Press, 1974. Impressive three-volume exploration of Muslim history, the first volume focusing on the medieval Arab Empire.

HUSSEY, J. M. *The Orthodox Church in the Byzantine Empire*. Oxford: Clarendon Press, 1986. Summarizes beliefs and controversies in the framework of Byzantine history.

LEWIS, B. *The Arabs in History*. Rev. ed. New York: Harper & Row, 1960. A brief introduction.

NICKEL, H. L. *Medieval Architecture in Eastern Europe*. Translated by A. Jaffa. New York: Holmes and Meier, 1983. Stresses interweaving of Byzantine styles with regional Slavic traditions.

NORMAN, D. *The Arabs and Medieval Europe*. 2d ed. New York: Longman, 1979. Emphasizes conflict over cultural interaction.

OBOLENSKY, D. *The Byzantine Inheritance of Eastern Europe*. London: Variorum, 1982. The long-term consequences of the vanished Byzantine supremacy on the eastern edge of the Western world.

OSTROGORSKY, G. *History of the Byzantine State*. Translated by J. Hussey. Oxford: Blackwell, 1968. Impressive summary of a thousand years of complicated history in a single volume.

PASKIEWICZ, H. *The Rise of Moscow's Power*. Translated by P. S. Falla. Boulder, Colo.: East European Monographs, 1983. The core of modern Russia takes shape.

RUNCIMAN, S. *The Byzantine Theocracy*. New York: Cambridge University Press, 1977. Stresses religious foundations of Byzantine imperial power.

VERNADSKY, G. *Origins of Russia*. Oxford: Clarendon Press, 1959. Older but still stimulating analysis of political, cultural, and other factors that shaped medieval Russia.

YOUNG, M. J. L., J. D. LATHAM, AND R. B. SERJEANT, eds. *Religion, Learning, and Science in the Abbasid Period*. London: Cambridge University Press, 1990. Authoritative essays on the civilization of Europe's highly developed neighbor.

CHAPTER 9

The High Middle Ages: Cities and Kings

Head of St. Joseph. Reims Cathederal, Reims, France

The slice of time between 1000 and 1300 marked the climax of medieval history. During this period, called the High Middle Ages, Western civilization not only recovered lost ground but expanded and explored new terrain. The era saw economic recovery, the reestablishment of strong government, and the zenith of medieval Christendom's central institution, the Christian church.

In this chapter we deal with the reestablishment of the basic political and economic parameters of a successful civilization as coins clinked from hand to hand once more and kings brought barons to heel. In the chapter that follows we look at religion, society, culture, and European expansion during the High Middle Ages, the age of cathedrals and Crusades.

The Revival of Europe

It is easier to recognize recovery than it is to explain it. The combination of circumstances that finally brought medieval people out of the long doldrums of the early Middle Ages is still subject to much speculation and dispute. We therefore work as much with hypotheses as with generally accepted views, examining some of the *possible* factors in the transition from a world bounded by the woods and wasteland around a tiny manor village to one in which proud cities and prouder kings emerged once more.

Sources of Change

Modern people like to see themselves "in control" of what happens to them, directing their own fates. Frequently, however, circumstances entirely beyond our control contribute significantly to what happens to us. This was certainly the case with medieval civilization.

A modest improvement in the climate from Britain to German-speaking central Europe, for instance, played a significant part in the economic and social achievements of the era. A grinding retreat of the polar ice seems to have begun as early as the ninth century. The concomitant warming trend in the European climate lasted through the twelfth century at least. As a result, Western people enjoyed more bountiful harvests, ate better, and lived longer during the High Middle Ages. Population growth led to increased economic demand. Increased demand, in turn, played a vital role in the economic recovery of this period, stimulating both agricultural expansion and the revival of commerce and handicraft industry.

Another long-term change beyond the control of feudal Europe was the end of the second wave of raids and invasions that had ravaged the West during the eighth and ninth centuries. Vikings, for example, increasingly came to settle and rule rather than to plunder and destroy. Thus, as we have seen in earlier chapters, the Northmen were fitted into the feudal system of France as Normans, became the Varangian rulers and later the boyar nobility of Russia, and temporarily incorporated England into Canute's Danish Empire. To the east, invaders from the Eurasian steppes were absorbed into the Slavic population, as the Bulgars were, or became a ruling elite, like the Magyars in Hungary. Along Europe's southern fringes, the Saracens, as Europeans called the soldiers of the Arab-dominated Muslim world, ruled much of Spain and still raided Western shipping on the Mediterranean. But the great Arab invasions of the seventh and eighth centuries were in the past.

The easing of this burden of endless war saved many regions from periodic devastation. Peace also allowed European politics to evolve beyond a purely feudal structure based on the necessity for local defense. The growth of both the European economy and royal governments thus benefited from the settling down of the restless raiders of earlier centuries.

Other factors also contributed to an improvement in the quality of life. Feudal barons and manor serfs who cleared new land to grow more crops made their contribution. So did the merchants and artisans who organized guilds and raised the walls of medieval towns. Kings who strove to control the feuds of their vassals, royal administrators who labored to bring centralized government and stability to their people—all played a part in the shaping of the High Middle Ages. A change in the weather and a transformation of the lifestyles of aggressive neighboring peoples thus combined with perhaps even more important changes in the political and economic climate to transform the lives of Europeans in the three centuries immediately following 1000.

Revival in the Tenth Century

The urge to rehabilitate ages formerly dismissed as "dark" seems to be a recurring theme among historians. We have seen, for instance, how the Greek Awakening has been pushed back three centuries before Pericles. The historiography of the Middle Ages shows a similar trend. Once shrugged off as a thousand-year "Dark Age" between the glittering civilization of Rome and that of the Renaissance, the medieval period has been definitively lightened by what is called the twelfth-century Renaissance of the High Middle Ages and, to a somewhat lesser extent, by the Carolingian Renaissance that centered around 800. Most recently, some medieval historians have also offered evidence that the period between the Carolingians and the twelfth century was not as unrelievedly dark as had been assumed. The tenth century in particular seems to have produced some impressive achievements that continued to bear fruit in the climax of medieval culture that followed.

Even proponents of this view admit that the period of the greatest victories of the Vikings and the final collapse of the Carolingians was in many ways a "dim, grim, and dark" age.[1] But the tenth century did also see the beginning of some of the most important trends of the next three hundred years, including religious reform, commercial revival, the founding of governments that would last, and some remarkable cultural accomplishments. A survey of some of these fleshes out this contention that the tenth century was not the darkest of centuries, but a harbinger of things to come.

Political and constitutional developments during this period appear to have been largely, though not entirely, on the local level. In France, for example, the decline of Carolingian power allowed the emergence of fully developed feudalism dominated by powerful dukes and counts. In Germany, ancient tribal loyalties and surviving Carolingian military leadership combined to produce such states as the duchies of Saxony and Bavaria. In Italy, independent cities flourished under the aegis of powerful bishops. In England, traditional Anglo-Saxon administrative subdivisions called shires (counties) and officials called *shire-reeves*, or *sheriffs*, survived intact through the period of Danish rule.

Some local or regional power centers, like the German duchies, resisted the impending rise of royal power. Others, like the Anglo-Saxon shires, actually proved useful to royal rulers seeking to expand their

	900	1000
POLITICAL, MILITARY, AND DIPLOMATIC EVENTS	**r. 936–973** Otto the Great **962** Holy Roman Empire founded **r. 987–996** Hugh Capet	**r. 1056–1106** Henry IV **r. 1066– 1087** William I the Conqueror **1066** Hastings
SOCIAL AND ECONOMIC DEVELOPMENTS		**11th century** Revival of trade **11th century** Many towns founded in Italy and Low Countries

authority in later centuries. The feudal system itself could be manipulated by shrewd monarchs to provide a foundation for centralized government. And as early as the tenth century a start was made at restoring kingly rule, with the founding of the German Holy Roman Empire in 962 and the accession of the Capetian dynasty to the French throne in 987.

European commerce also began to revive in the tenth century. The leading spirits in this first resurgence of trade were peoples with ties outside Europe in the relatively prosperous East or people whose seafaring style of life was conducive to trade.

Commercial exchange had declined precipitously with the fall of the Roman Empire in the fifth century, the disintegration of its city-based civilization, and the temporary severing of major Mediterranean trade routes by the Muslims in the seventh century. Most of Europe, as we have seen, reverted to a subsistence agricultural economy. The early Middle Ages did see continuing commercial exchange of some items, however. These included salt, the only known preservative for meat, and such luxury goods as silks, spices, gold plate, wine, and swords, all prized by the early medieval Germanic elite.

The source of supply of most luxury products lay outside Europe entirely, in the Middle East and beyond. Most early medieval traders in these goods therefore were people with Middle Eastern connections, including Jews, Syrians, and Greeks. Jews, being neither Christian nor Muslim, proved ideal intermediaries. "These merchants," a Muslim commentator noted, "speak Arabic, Persian . . . the Frank, Spanish, and Slav languages. They journey from West to East, from East to West, partly on land, partly by sea. . . . Some make sail for Constantinople . . . others to the palace of the king of the Franks to place their goods."[2]

Another source of Eastern imports was found in northern Italy. Cities like Venice remained part of the Eastern Roman, or Byzantine, Empire and maintained at least limited commercial ties with Constantinople. In the High Middle Ages, this avenue of trade became an important stimulus to Europe's real commercial revival.

Other leading early medieval traders were North Sea fisherfolk, who served as part-time merchants, and the Vikings, who combined trading with raiding as they ranged around the Western world. Viking voyagers took furs from northern Europe and slaves captured in their piratical raids down the rivers of Russia or through the Mediterranean to exchange for Near Eastern luxury products. These products in

r. 1073–1085 Gregory VII
1077 Canossa

r. 1152–1190 Frederick I, Barbarossa
r. 1154–1189 Henry II
r. 1180–1223 Philip II Augustus
r. 1199–1216 John
r. 1212–1250 Frederick II
Stupor Mundi
1214 Bouvines
1215 Magna Carta
r. 1226–1270 Louis IX

12th–13th centuries Agricultural improvements
and expansion
Commercial Revolution
at height
New towns built across Europe
Population expands

turn found their way back into Europe at the hands of the Northmen.

Over most of Europe, however, trade remained very limited in the tenth century. Much of what commercial exchange there was took place at regional fairs. Here traveling merchants joined the motley throngs of local lords, artisans, peasants, entertainers, and horse traders, offering exotic products from far away to princes, nobles, bishops, or other notables. Peddlers might also show up in isolated villages with a modest pack and news picked up on their travels. It was from such simple beginnings, from goods transported by Jews, Italians, Vikings, and peddlers of all nations, that a roaring commercial revival evolved during the next three centuries.

Religious and Cultural Renewal

The major religious change of the tenth century was the reform of the monastic system pioneered by the Abbey of Cluny in southern France. The original Benedictine monasteries, islands of culture and agricultural growth in earlier medieval times, had declined as Carolingian power faded and new pagan invaders swept over the land. Many monastic estab-

lishments were looted and destroyed. Others were taken over by local barons who appointed their own kin as abbots in order to milk the wealth of the monasteries. As a counter to this corruption of some monastic communities, Duke William the Pious of Aquitaine (d. 918) in 910 established what became a model monastery at Cluny.

The key to Cluny's success and enormous influence was its independence from local lay control, a unique feature of the duke's foundation. Liberated from worldly entanglements and obligations, Cluniac monks followed a revised form of the Benedictine Rule (see Chapter 7) that stressed personal piety and a daily routine dominated by liturgical services. The first three abbots of Cluny, furthermore, were able administrators and men of deep religious commitment, exemplars of the Cluniac ideal. As the reputation of this citadel of revived Christian piety spread, monasteries all over Europe sought to follow the example of Cluny. Many accepted the direction of its abbots, creating a Europewide network of Cluniac houses. By the end of the tenth century, the Cluniac reform had spread to more than a thousand monastic establishments, where holy offices were chanted and prayers raised to heaven on a scale that deeply impressed the medieval world.

Even high culture found a place in that century as civilization fumbled toward new beginnings. A scattered handful of religious thinkers, for instance, continued to explore philosophical questions as they understood them from the works of Boethius and St. Augustine. The science of musical notation spread widely in the ninth and tenth centuries, preserving medieval music for us a thousand years later. And mathematics began to be taught at a higher level of sophistication than it had been at the height of the Carolingian Renaissance.

Another feature of tenth-century culture was the reappearance of lay patronage of the arts after centuries of primarily ecclesiastical support. The church continued to be the most important patron of the culture of Christendom throughout the High Middle Ages. But the tradition of aristocratic and princely patronage, reestablished in the tenth century, resumed its central place in early modern times.

The tenth was a threshold century. It was, as a leading medieval historian puts it, "a vital period of transition; many of its achievements had their roots in the earlier Carolingian period and bore fruit in the eleventh and twelfth centuries."[3] It was as yet a trickle of change only, but the full flood followed soon thereafter.

The Revival of Trade and Towns

The heart of the economic recovery that fueled the High Middle Ages was the revival of long-distance trade. Commercial exchange, in turn, stimulated the development of handicraft industry, the rebirth of cities, and a commercial revolution of immense long-range importance for the future economic history of the West. Underlying all these remarkable achievements, however, were important changes in medieval agriculture, to which we turn first.

Agricultural Changes

When we last looked in on a medieval manor, sometime before 1000, the serfs were working their narrow strips of land with a simple heavy plow made of wood and pulled by slow-moving oxen. A few centuries later, however, there were significant changes in European agrarian life, and in its consequences.

The plow used in the later Middle Ages typically had an iron blade to open the clay soil more efficiently, a moldboard to turn it over, and wheels to make the whole process easier. Horses often replaced oxen, for they plowed faster and pulled harder. When they were shod with iron horseshoes made in a village smithy, horses could get better traction and were less likely to injure their hooves. When the medieval horse collar over the shoulders with a strap across the chest was introduced in later medieval times, horses could put their full weight into the operation. Other improvements included the invention of the windmill where no stream flowed fast enough to turn a water mill effectively.

The manor fields in which ninth-century serfs worked, furthermore, were frequently more extensive than they had been. Peasants in the years after 1000 cleared wooded land, drained swamps, and brought pasture under the plow. The acreage of arable land in use and the resulting production thus grew rapidly in the eleventh, twelfth, and thirteenth centuries. The peasants were opening up north temperate Europe to agricultural development at an unprecedented rate. As a result, there might be a score of huts in the village now instead of a dozen, and more children wrestling and tumbling in the street, for later medieval agriculture supported a growing population. There might also be a few coins in the peasant's hut and a market day in a nearby town—a town that hadn't even been there in earlier centuries.

A number of other changes besides technical improvements helped account for this boom in agriculture. The cessation of Viking, Muslim, and Magyar incursions, for one thing, simply made life safer than it had been, and the harvest surer, encouraging people to plan and work for a more expansive future. There were other incentives too, rooted in social changes. By clearing new land, for instance, a hard-working peasant might produce a large enough surplus to purchase his freedom from serfdom, even to make him a man of means in his little village.

The status of the peasantry as a whole began to change too. In western Europe, at least, serfdom itself was largely phased out by the end of the High Middle Ages. Lords commuted the traditional labor obligations of their peasants to rent payments instead, using the rent to pay for the luxuries they were beginning to covet. In so doing, they converted serfs bound to the land into tenants and hired laborers on a large scale.

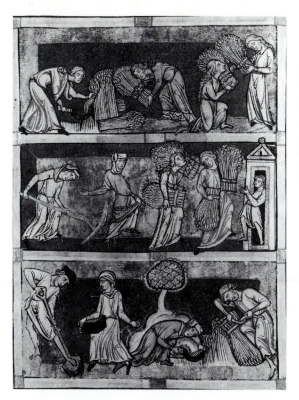

German peasant women sow seed, harvest grain, and take the grain to the mill in these pictures from the Rhineland. What familiar tools are being used in this medieval agricultural community?

Some of the old labor requirements and seigneurial rights survived, such as the peasant's obligation to do corvée work, repairing roads and bridges on the estate, or the lord's exclusive right to hunt. More important, the fundamental place of the peasantry, subservient to the landed aristocracy and providing the agricultural labor on which the rest of society depended, remained unchanged, as it did through most of modern history. Nevertheless, free peasants did often become more vigorous and more productive. And some of them left the land entirely to follow other lines of work, from commerce and handicraft industry to soldiering, which the new agricultural surpluses made possible.

The peasant was still there, and his work still fed his world. But it was a more varied, more challenging, and more rapidly changing world than that of his ancestors in earlier medieval times.

The Resurgence of Trade

The evolution of medieval commerce from the isolated peddler with his pack to commercial caravans, crowded fairs, and merchant vessels under sail is well illustrated in the life of a medieval saint whose early years were devoted to worldly pursuits. According to the *Life of St. Godric,* this humble peasant lad "chose not to follow the life of a husbandman [farmer]" but turned instead to "the merchant's trade." He therefore

> began to follow the chapman's [peddler's] way of life, first learning to gain in small bargains and things of insignificant price; and thence, while yet a youth . . . to buy and sell and gain from things of greater expense. For, in his beginnings, he was wont to wander with small wares around the villages and farmsteads of his own neighborhood; but, in process of time, he gradually associated himself by compact with city merchants.[4]

With his new associates, organized for mutual protection into a company of merchants, Godric traveled "through towns and boroughs, fortresses and cities, to fairs and to all the various booths of the marketplace, in pursuit of his public chaffer [trade]." He even bought a ship and embarked upon still wider commerce, as so many merchants did in later medieval and modern times.

The world of Godric, with its merchant guilds and shipping, its fairs and cities, was evidently very different from the early medieval world of isolated manor villages and untraveled wilderness. Yet the whole elaborate structure of commercial and urban civilization must have been largely the work of clever, energetic, and profit-conscious spirits like Godric, building from "small bargains" to the bustling fairs and market towns of the High Middle Ages.

A major stimulus to this process was the trade by sea with the Byzantine Empire mentioned earlier. The sea lanes of the Mediterranean had been the center of Roman commerce, and some of this maritime trade had survived the fall of the Roman Empire in the West. Most important, the Italian port of Venice at the head of the Adriatic Sea had maintained a "special relationship" with Constantinople throughout the early Middle Ages, importing at least

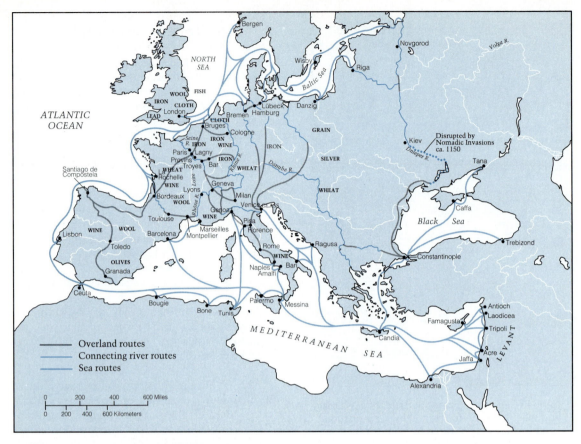

Map 9.1 Medieval Cities and Trade Routes

a thin stream of luxury goods for churchmen and aristocrats in the days of Ostrogothic, Lombard, and Frankish control of northern Italy. As Viking and Arab depredations decreased and population and production grew once more, this thin stream swelled into a broad current of commercial exchange, reaching into northern Europe and encouraging further trade all along the line.

The chief artery of European commerce in the High Middle Ages flowed north and south, from Italian ports like Venice, Naples, and Genoa up the Rhone River into France or across the Alps and down the flourishing Rhine valley to the Low Countries (the Netherlands and Belgium today). From the Low Countries, goods passed by sea to Britain, Scandinavia, and the north German towns on the Baltic. At the southern end of this commercial axis, trade also expanded, from the original Venetian connection to other ports around the Italian peninsula and beyond to southern France and Spain. Subsidiary routes developed by sea around the west coast of Europe and by land or river transport across France, German-speaking central Europe, and Slavic eastern Europe. Additional distribution centers emerged in what became the nations of Czechoslovakia and Poland, and goods were also dispersed down the river routes of European Russia.

The goods that passed over these increasingly well-traveled routes included a great deal of local agricultural produce exchanged for basic necessities like clothes and tools or for the wool and iron from which these were made. Long-distance trade also included commodities, such as grain, timber, and furs from the Baltic, raw wool from England, and grain and wine from southern Europe. Among the most popular European manufactured goods to flow through this commercial network were woolen textiles, often woven in the Netherlands and then finished by skilled workers in the Italian cities. From Asia, finally, came the luxury items so much prized by the emerging affluent classes of Europe: spices and precious stones; illuminated manuscripts, carved ivories, and goldsmith work; and silks, linens, and cotton cloth, often exquisitely brocaded or embroidered.

Along the high roads, over the Alpine passes and down the Rhine, caravans of well-dressed merchants and laden pack mules thus traveled from fair to fair, spreading out a dazzling array of goods for peasants and nobler customers who had gathered to celebrate some local saint's day. For safety's sake, and to collect as wide a variety of goods as possible, traders organized themselves into merchant companies called *guilds* and journeyed together, making an annual circuit of major fairs from spring to fall. On

the Mediterranean or the Baltic, trading vessels also coasted the ragged shores of Europe. High, round, single-masted vessels with large square sails in the north, three-masted ships with lateen (triangular) sails in the southern sea, these medieval cargo carriers fed the burgeoning commercial activity on land.

Godric and his kind risked exorbitant local tariffs and tolls, as well as bandit attacks, when they traveled by land, storms and pirates by sea. The roads were dusty or muddy tracks, the seas still unfamiliar and dangerous to Europeans. But if they succeeded, they could become wealthy men. They could build a world for themselves separate from the manor village or the feudal castle. The world they built was the relatively free, immensely dynamic, solidly bourgeois world of the medieval city.

Medieval commerce centered in the cities and was frequently conducted by water, the cheapest mode of transport. This Flemish picture shows some chests of goods and a number of bales of cloth being loaded for shipment abroad.

The Growth of Cities

It was once believed that virtually no towns remained after the barbarian invasions of the fifth century, and that only the twelfth-century commercial revolution restored both cities and long-distance trade to the West. We now believe, however, that a number of Roman cities remained standing in long urbanized southern Europe, notably in Italy, Spain, and southern France. In northern France, England, the Low Countries, and southern Germany, the skeletal remains of scattered towns survived, at least as fortified areas or ecclesiastical administrative centers. Only in northern Germany, Scandinavia, and eastern Europe, where the Romans had not penetrated, did the agricultural village remain the largest concentration of population at the beginning of the Middle Ages.

Still, for reasons that remain subject to debate, major urban growth did not come until the eleventh, twelfth, and thirteenth centuries. The twentieth-century Belgian historian Henri Pirenne proposed an elaborate thesis linking the rebirth of city life directly to the revival of trade. As Pirenne saw it, the original merchant companies typically moved from place to place all summer, selling their goods at local fairs and markets. In the winter, however, they settled under the walls of a fortified castle or a bishop's palace to wait until the roads became passable again in the spring. These merchant settlements grew, attracted more free population, built permanent shops and defensive walls, and became the towns and cities of the High Middle Ages.

The Pirenne thesis thus saw towns growing up largely as the result of long-distance trade. Italian seaport cities—Venice first of all, then Naples, Pisa, and Genoa flourished as entry points for Eastern goods. Marseilles in southern France, Barcelona in Spain, Bruges in the Low Countries, and Lübeck and Danzig on the Baltic also grew with the golden touch of trade. River ports too swelled with the coming of commerce, including Cologne, Frankfurt, and other Rhineland cities, and Novgorod and Kiev on the Dnieper route in Russia. Wherever main highways met, where rivers could be bridged or forded, and on bays and sheltered inlets—wherever resurgent trade flowed naturally—cities took root and grew.

Carcassonne in southern France is an excellent example of the medieval walled city. Originally built in the thirteenth century, these double walls were restored to their medieval splendor in the nineteenth century.

More recent scholarship, however, has both challenged Pirenne and gone considerably beyond him. Some medieval historians, for example, point out that Pirenne drew conclusions for Europe as a whole from studies really limited to the Low Countries and northern France. Others note that the collapse of trade during the early Middle Ages was not so complete as was once thought, indicating that other new forces besides a commercial revival may be needed to explain the urban resurgence. It has also been suggested that the local market may often have played a larger part than long-range trade in the growth of towns, many of which were dominated by local traders.

More centrally, Pirenne tended to see medieval cities as growing up essentially in opposition to their rural surroundings, having nothing in common with the older medieval world of lords and peasant villages. We now have evidence, however, that both shrewd local barons and feudal monarchs fostered trade and founded protected markets around which towns might grow. Many historians, furthermore, now dispute the notion of a separation between urban and rural society as a whole, urging that it took a prosperous hinterland to provide food, customers, and excess population for a growing city. Recent urban studies, furthermore, stress a continuing connection between the countryside from which immigrants typically come and the cities where they settle. Such newcomers to the city often retain close ties with the villages of their birth and draw further immigrants from the same area in later generations.

The motives of those who make this rural-to-urban migration usually include both a "push" and a "pull." A number of forces do in fact seem to have pushed some medieval people out of the countryside. One obvious source of discontent was the relative poverty of village life, even during a time of agricultural expansion. Another was the desire of some peasants to escape the life of servitude that bound them to the manor. And even among the aristocracy, it often happened that the law of inheritance called *primogeniture* assigned an entire estate to the oldest son of a family; the younger sons then had to make their way elsewhere, sometimes in the commercial world of the city.

On the "pull" side, these discontented elements could often find comparative freedom and opportunity in the new towns. The medieval German saying "city air makes free" referred specifically to freedom from serfdom, traditionally conferred if a peasant lived openly and unchallenged in a city for a year and

a day. But the freedom of city life included much more for its merchant elite and for immigrants of all social classes. Urban freedom included the opportunity to rise by one's own efforts unfettered by a previous condition of servitude. And though medieval values were not the same as modern ones, personal freedom and the profit motive probably had some appeal even this far back in Western history.

Guilds and City Government

The dominant organizations in most medieval cities were the *merchant guilds* whose members had founded the city in the first place. As the wealthiest men in town and the ones who dominated the marketplace, these merchant guildsmen were the recognized urban power elite. In Florence, the members of the seven merchant guilds were called the "fat people," the plutocracy who ran the city. In Venice, the great commercial families had their names inscribed in a "golden book" that entitled them to elect the city's *doge,* or duke, and to have a voice in government.

In time, however, medieval artisans also organized guilds to manage their affairs. These *craft guilds* were traditionally run by the guild masters, skilled artisans who owned their own workshops. The masters employed workers called journeymen to help them and took on apprentices as trainees, and these people were also members of the guild. Journeymen could aspire to become guild masters themselves if they could produce a piece of work that would satisfy the guild as to their skill and could accumulate sufficient capital to open their own shops. Apprentices signed on for a term of years—typically seven—during which time they were given bed, board, and training in return for their labor.

Guilds performed a number of important functions in medieval cities besides producing needed goods. They kept up the quality of manufactures by certifying only artisans who had proved their skill to practice in the city. They controlled competition by allowing no one who was not a certified member of the guilds to open a shop. They often set wages and prices and regulated their own marketplaces. Guilds also provided a number of social services for members and their families, including basic education for children, funeral expenses for members, and support for widows and orphans. And they played an important part in the religious and community life of the

A French artisan family at work. The man is plan-
ing a piece of wood, the woman drawing out
thread from her distaff preparatory to spinning
it. Even the child seems to be clearing up below.
Throughout most of history, the family itself was
the primary economic unit.

town, participating in church festivals and giving
banquets for their own members. Guilds were thus
in many ways central to the economic and social life
of the medieval city.

But the evolving towns quickly came to need
more than these fundamentally economic organizations; they needed political institutions as well. This
was particularly so because the mushrooming cities
of the High Middle Ages were a departure from the
norm in that still feudal world. City dwellers were
neither feudal lords nor feudal vassals, neither lords
of the manor nor peasant laborers. They needed a
kind of law that was different from feudal law or the
baron's manorial justice, and different courts to enforce it. They needed commercial law to regulate a
world defined by business contracts, and a stiff criminal code to protect property that consisted of movable goods rather than land. And they required their

own local knowledgeable administrators to govern
their city.

Townspeople secured the right to shape their
own law and government independent of the feudal
system only after sometimes bitter struggles with the
traditional local authorities. If the town had grown
up around a bishop's palace, citizens might rally to
the cause of a religious reformer to shake the
bishop's power. If a feudal baron was the local magnate, townsmen might make common cause with a
distant monarch who was trying to impose his authority on the nobles from above. The towns provided financial revenues and experienced administrators—often lawyers skilled in manipulating the new
laws—for the royal government. In return, monarchs
conferred royal charters guaranteeing the independence of medieval cities.

On the basis of such constitutional guarantees,
medieval cities organized governments typically
composed of city councils or boards of aldermen and
of magistrates, who served as both judges and administrators. They passed their own laws, including
stern criminal codes and detailed codes of business
law. They taxed themselves to keep the city walls in
repair and to build almshouses for the poor, hospitals
for the sick, and a guildhall for the town's leading
citizens.

These urban centers of handicraft production
and commercial exchange, however, nurtured two
very different attitudes toward society, each with important long-range consequences. The social ethic of
the craft guild reflected the general medieval emphasis on sociability, group responsibility, and corporate
identity, the tendency of medieval people to see the
individual as primarily a member of a larger group or
collective whole. The town government and many of
its laws, however, dominated by an *urban patriciate*,
or elite, of leading merchants, tended to emphasize
individual rights and liberties, the foundations of a
more competitive, individualistic society to come.

The ideals of the craft guilds included "social
solidarity, . . . brotherhood, friendship, and mutual
aid."[5] From this sense of group solidarity sprang the
guilds' protectionist opposition to outside competition, and indeed to anyone among themselves getting more than his "just share" of the town's business. From the general communitarian orientation of
the guilds came, not only their own social services
for members, but also the urban measures just mentioned, a "volume of social legislation" that one historian sees as "inviting comparison with modern
welfare socialism."[6]

The foundations of a more competitive modern social order, by contrast, were laid by the emergence of personal freedom and private property as the modern West came to know them. Feudal vassals and manor serfs normally held their fiefs or strips of farmland only on condition that they performed the military or agricultural service required of them. The vast lands of the church were owned, not by an individual, but by the institution as a whole. In cities, however, freehold property did emerge. It was subject to the state's right of "eminent domain" to limit or control its use, as private property still is. But it was land that could be bought and sold, inherited, or otherwise disposed of freely by the owner and embodied the concept of private property as we know it.

Personal freedom was also greater in towns than in other medieval institutions. Obedience to a superior was a matter of honor to a knight, of piety to a monk, and was rigorously imposed on the peasant majority. But the medieval maxim "city air makes free," as we have seen, summed up the greater degree of independence from both social superiors and the customs of one's own group.

Medieval cities were by no means democratic societies. They often called themselves "republics," but the term did not connote popular sovereignty. Since only property owners, guild masters, or members of the town corporation could vote or hold office in a medieval town, cities were actually oligarchies run by the established business and professional elites. Still, cities were less rigidly authoritarian than most medieval institutions. And in centuries to come, commercially developed countries like England and the Netherlands were among the first to develop more liberal institutions at the national level.

As we shall see, craft workers and town governments, the work force and the merchant patriciate, were vigorously at odds even in the later Middle Ages. In modern times, the two social ideals of "working-class" community and "bourgeois" individualism evolved along very different paths. In the towns of the High Middle Ages, however, the ideals of freedom and group solidarity coexisted in some degree of harmony.

The Commercial Revolution

Of more immediate importance, medieval cities produced the *commercial revolution,* a collection of business practices and policies that became the foundation of modern capitalism in the West. A fundamental step toward a modern capitalist economy was the increasingly widespread use of money once more. Merovingians, Carolingians, and other early medieval rulers had minted coins, but the barter system, the exchange of gifts, and the direct provision of food and clothing to feudal subordinates were much more common than commercial exchange in early medieval times. From the High Middle Ages on, however, coins were in common use again in the West. Kings, nobles, and others had the right to mint their own coins, which found their way into the humblest manor villages. The Florentine gold *florin,* accepted everywhere for several centuries, was a sort of international standard currency in the later Middle Ages, like the British pound sterling in the nineteenth century or the American dollar in the twentieth. This return to a money economy added immensely to the flexibility and sophistication of business life.

A related development was the gradual acceptance of the ancient practice of lending money at interest. In the Middle Ages, the Christian church officially condemned most moneylending for a profit as immoral "usury." To many medieval people, interest for loans seemed rather like getting something for nothing. Christian merchants, however, found ways of getting around this prohibition. One method was to claim that substantial risk was involved, as it frequently was if the money was invested in trade over bandit-infested roads or stormy seas, and then to charge extra as a compensation for the risk factor. Another common expedient was to arrange repayment in another country and another currency, profiting both from the fee for money-changing and from the differences in rates of currency exchange. As the church grudgingly came to accept interest as a legitimate source of income, some merchants became essentially bankers, earning the bulk of their incomes from moneylending and other financial operations.

Other technical advances that made business more efficient included letters of credit, bills of exchange, and double-entry bookkeeping. When a business involved a number of stages, as was the case with the manufacture of woolen cloth, a merchant might hesitate to carry bags of coins about with him, preferring to establish a credit relationship with the shearers, spinners, weavers, dyers, and many others through whose hands the wool passed. Similarly, a merchant trading in a distant country might take a bill of exchange from his own banker to a bank in the city to which he was traveling, rather than risk carrying coins on the dangerous roads. And such bookkeeping improvements as the use of Arabic numbers instead of Roman numerals and the balancing of credits and debits on a regular basis made any business more efficient.

A major step forward, finally, was the appearance of various forms of what was later called the *joint-stock company.* Such a company pooled the cap-

ital of a number of merchants for great commercial ventures that no one of them could finance alone (see box, "Medieval Investment Advice"). This practice also reduced business risks because each investor committed only a portion of his total wealth. Originally, such companies were established only by members of a single family or for a single enterprise. Medieval joint-stock companies, however, were the precursors of early modern trading combines, like the European East India Companies, and of the huge corporations of our own day.

A word or two should also be said about the vigorously competitive spirit of some medieval businessmen. The craft guilds in particular do not look very competitive; as we have seen, a basic purpose of the guild system was to regulate business and limit competition. Competition between leading family firms or individual merchant princes, however, could be as cutthroat as that of any nineteenth-century "robber baron." In this way also, the commercial revolution of the High Middle Ages pointed toward future trends.

MASTERING OUR WORLD
Medieval Investment Advice

This Norwegian trader's advice to his son seems to suggest a balanced portfolio, including local and long-distance trade in different markets and even investment in land, a flexible response to changing economic conditions. Elsewhere this medieval capitalist urges a careful selection of business partners, adding that the successful trader should "always let almighty God, the holy Virgin Mary, and the saint whom you have most frequently called upon to intercede for you to be counted among your partners."

If you have much capital invested in trade, divide it into three parts: put one-third into partnerships with men who are permanently located in market boroughs, are trustworthy, and are experienced in business. Place the other two parts in various business ventures; for if your capital is invested in different places, it is not likely that you will suffer losses in all your wealth at one time; more likely it will be secure in some localities though frequent losses be suffered. But if you find that the profits of trade bring a decided increase to your funds, draw out the two-thirds and invest them in good farm land, for such property is generally thought the most secure, whether the enjoyment of it falls to oneself or to one's kinsmen. With the remaining third, you may do as seems best—continue to keep it in business or place it all in land. However, though you decide to keep your funds invested in trade, discontinue your own journeys at sea or as a trader in foreign fields, as soon as your means have attained sufficient growth.

Source: L. W. Larson, trans., *The King's Mirror* (New York: American Scandinavian Foundation, 1917).

The Emergence of Feudal Monarchy

The story of the political revival of the High Middle Ages is the history of how princes—emperors, kings, dukes, or other independent rulers—gradually imposed political order on substantial portions of Europe after the year 1000. There were false starts, wrong turns, and failures on that road to political recovery, but to the degree that these rulers succeeded their story has a larger historic significance. They could not know it, but these medieval monarchs were building the European nation-states of modern times.

We recount, in this section and the three that follow it, some of the failures of will and fruitless conflicts that marked the path to nationhood. Our emphasis, however, falls where it should: on the emergence of strong royal governments in at least some parts of Europe during this period.

The Rise of Royal Power

Before we look at the political histories of France, England, and Germany between 1000 and 1300, however, let us attempt a social science model of what was going on *in general* here. Like all ideal models, this one fits no specific case exactly. But it may provide a map of sorts through the tangle of events that follows.

In the first place, remember that rulers with nicknames and titles like William the Bastard, St. Louis, Frederick Redbeard, and Richard the Lion-Hearted were not modern politicians. Medieval kings expanded their domains with no notion of such modern concepts as "balance of power" and "natural frontiers" and built their embryonic bureaucracies without ever having seen an organization chart. They fought their wars for thoroughly medieval reasons—to gain knightly honor and renown, to assert feudal rights over territory, to settle a long-standing vendetta with a dynastic rival. They tried to govern with whatever instruments came to hand: personal servants and private secretaries, shrewd churchmen, powerful nobles, and lawyers from the newly emergent cities.

The Europe out of which the more successful of these medieval princes carved their kingdoms was in theory a united Christendom. In fact, it was a feudal patchwork of small political units, overlapping loyalties, and conflicting ambitions. Early medieval kings were typically feeble do-nothing monarchs without the means to govern effectively. Real power was held at the local level, by counts and dukes, bishops and abbots, and by the wealthy cities just emerging along the trade routes. Everywhere, too, power relations were complicated by an international church whose authority reached across all frontiers and a feudal system that could make even a king the vassal of another ruler for at least some of his territories.

In this jungle of claims and counterclaims, powerful magnates and porous frontiers, ambitious monarchs had to make their way. Typically, they tried to milk the wealth of the towns, exploit the church, and force their noble vassals to acknowledge the authority of the crown. Commonly also, they sought to expand their realms, augmenting their own greatness at the expense of their neighbors.

Sources of Royal Power

Ramshackle as the feudal order was, it tenaciously resisted efforts to expand monarchical power. Barons bitterly fought attempts by kings to be more than "first among equals." The church, under a series of strong-willed popes, asserted papal primacy over kings and emperors. Even the towns sometimes resisted royal ambitions, taxation, and territorial claims.

In the long run, successful princes achieved their ends both by manipulating the feudal system and by reaching outside it. They insisted on their own place at the top of the feudal hierarchy, and they called arrogant barons to account for violations of feudal principle. At the same time, they sought help outside the old political-military structure of power. Tapping the riches and administrative know-how of the church and the emerging cities, they depended increasingly on salaried bureaucrats and hired mercenary soldiers.

Most of these royal manipulators were men. We will be looking at the aggressive careers of many of them, from William the Bastard, better known as William the Conqueror of England, to Frederick Barbarossa ("Redbeard"). But there were also a number of successful women rulers during the Middle Ages. In the eleventh century, William the Conqueror's wife Matilda governed Normandy most efficiently while he was bringing England to order. In the twelfth century, women like Eleanor of Aquitaine, her daughter Marie of Champagne, and Alix de Vergy of Burgundy governed a large part of France. And the renowned Hermengarde, countess of Narbonne, ruled her territories for half a century alone, fighting wars, succoring the poor, protecting the church, and earning a reputation as a shrewd judge in tricky problems of feudal law.

Male or female, these architects of a new power structure depended on more than shrewdness, manipulation, and force. They built their power on a rationale as well. Medieval monarchs justified their claims to power by appeal to two principles: hereditary succession and divine sanction.

The new monarchies established the principle of hereditary succession, not from older to younger brother or by division of the realm between brothers as in earlier times, but by primogeniture. This approach, which as we have seen was also followed by the barons on their own estates, sometimes caused resentment and rebellion by younger sons. But it offered a better prospect of orderly succession to power and of keeping large political units intact from generation to generation than any other expedient available to them.

Even more important, kings justified their expanding lands and powers by insisting on *divine sanction* for their authority. Basing political power on divine authority was a practice as old as ancient Babylon, but it took a uniquely Christian form in the medieval West. Medieval kings found support for the practice in the Old Testament assertion that God had sanctioned the rule of judges and kings over his people in biblical times. Crowned by archbishops or even popes, anointed with holy oil in cathedrals while hymns rose to the vaulting overhead, medieval monarchs saw themselves as God's viceroys in this world.

Feudal Monarchy in France

The Capetian dynasty of France, which ruled for well over three centuries, from 987 to 1328, provides one of the best illustrations of nation building and the aggrandizement of royal power by a feudal monarchy. The Capetians succeeded the heirs of Charlemagne when his Empire fell apart under the later Carolingians. Divided among three of Charlemagne's grandsons in 843, pummeled by Viking, Muslim, and other invaders, the Empire disintegrated into several states, including the precursors of modern France and Germany. In the area that later became France, Hugh Capet was chosen king by the powerful feudal nobility following the death of the last Carolingian in 987. The Capetians reigned for the next three and a half centuries, throughout the High Middle Ages. Under such talented rulers as Louis VI in the twelfth century, Philip II Augustus in the twelfth and thirteenth, and Louis IX in the thirteenth century, the Capetian kings built the French feudal monarchy into one of the most powerful in Europe.

The Rise of the Capetians

When Hugh Capet (r. 987–996) was chosen king by the French nobility, he had very little power; indeed, this was one reason why he was chosen. The real authority of the early Capetian kings extended only to a small royal domain called the Ile de France, the region around the city of Paris on the Seine River in the north central part of the modern nation. This domain was surrounded by the much larger territories of powerful dukes and counts, nominally the king's vassals but in fact quite willing to defy and even make war on him. During their 340 years in power, however, the Capetians expanded their territories west to the English Channel and south to touch the Pyrenees and the Mediterranean. Perhaps even more important, thanks to an improved if still simple administrative system, they actually ruled the lands they claimed.

It was not an easy job. The assembling of a nation-state out of the scattered fiefs of many vassals may be compared to putting a jigsaw puzzle together—always remembering, of course, that medieval monarchs had no clear idea of what the picture would look like when they were done. And indeed, for two centuries the Capetians added very little to the royal domain—the territory they governed directly through salaried employees. Most of their land was parceled out to noble vassals, who offered oaths of feudal allegiance to their sovereigns in return. These vassals actually governed most of the land the French king claimed. To the north, Flanders (Belgium today) became one of the most prosperous commercial and urban areas in Europe. Elsewhere, Burgundian dukes went forth to rule Portugal, Normans to conquer Sicily. Most disturbing, as we see in the next major section, the French king's most powerful vassal, Duke William of Normandy, seized the throne of England, and through marriage and inheritance his heirs acquired a good deal of France as well.

The checkered career of Eleanor of Aquitaine (1122–1204) provides a good illustration of the complexities of medieval politics. At age fifteen, Eleanor inherited the titles of Duchess of Aquitaine and Countess of Poitou, and with them more land than the Capetian King Louis VI had. When Louis, her guardian under feudal law, arranged her marriage to his son and heir, Louis VII (r. 1137–1180) and then died, Eleanor became queen of France itself. When she failed to provide her husband with an heir, however, Louis VII had the marriage annulled. This proved to be a mistake, for Eleanor promptly married Henry II of England, adding her lands to his. In later years, she both ruled her own vast domains and served as regent for her famous son Richard the Lion-Hearted of England, proving a continuing thorn in the sides of both the French and English monarchies. The Capetian kings in particular still had a long way to go in building a viable government for France.

The Growth of Royal Government Under the Capetians

Beneath this feudal tangle, however, the Capetian rulers had been laying at least the foundations for

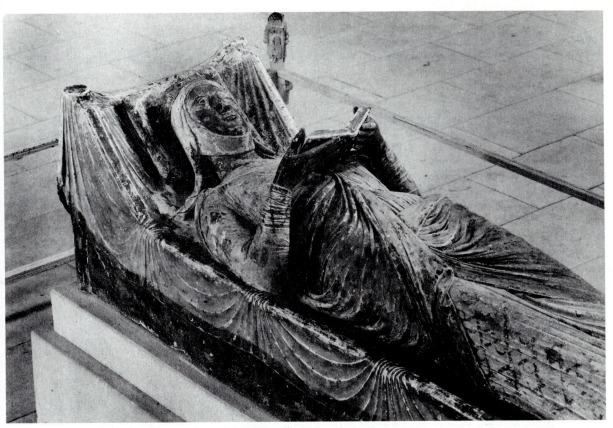

The tomb of Eleanor of Aquitaine at the abbey of Fontevrault in France depicts the former queen of both France and England reading a sacred text. Later medieval tomb effigies offered much more realistic images of the dead than this idealized likeness.

royal power in France. Reign after reign, they built popular acceptance of the dynasty, earned the support of the church, and even manipulated the feudal system itself to their own advantage. In these often undramatic but extremely important endeavors, a number of Capetian kings played a part.

An early step toward obtaining recognition of royal power was the establishment of the house of Capet's hereditary right to the throne. Hugh Capet had been elected king by the nobles. For the next two centuries, however, the Capetians saw to it that their eldest sons were elected and duly crowned while their fathers still lived and reigned. By so doing, they established in the Capetian line the traditional right of succession by primogeniture from father to oldest son.

Another important step in the expansion of royal power was the generally close working relation-

ship that the French kings maintained with the church. Close ties between the French crown and the Roman church went back to the conversion of Clovis and the coronation of Charlemagne. In the eleventh, twelfth, and thirteenth centuries, the Capetians accepted some of the most vigorous papal claims without sacrificing their own interests. Popes, for example, invested French bishops with their offices and powers—but French kings invested them with their lands and got an oath of loyalty from them in return. As a result of such compromises, the strength of the monarchy was augmented by the support of the church and by the services of such able churchmen as the twelfth-century Abbot Suger of St. Denis as royal ministers of state.

Another approach to the problem of increasing royal power in the teeth of feudal opposition was to manipulate the feudal system itself in royal interests.

The Capetians, like other medieval monarchs, nominally occupied the apex of a feudal pyramid of power. The greatest lords in the land held their vast lands as vassals of the crown. The king's royal council, the *curia regis,* summoned several times a year to advise their sovereign, was composed of both the chief barons and the leading churchmen in France. The greatest nobles, however, were so powerful, so rich in lands and vassal knights, that the kings had to play the game of feudal politics very skillfully if they were to turn their claims of royal power into realities.

Capetian kings were alert to every opportunity to exploit the vagaries of the system. They were quick to reclaim fiefs when a noble family that held its lands directly from the crown died out. They organized the marriages of heiresses of great estates to their own trusted adherents, and they stepped in at once to seize the lands of "contumacious" vassals who defied their authority. A powerful king like Philip Augustus even attempted to compel the vassals of the great magnates to take an oath of direct allegiance to the crown in order to undermine the authority of their more immediate overlords.

Most important, however, the Capetian kings over several hundred years pieced together the beginnings of a real royal bureaucracy. Frequently drawn from the towns and including increasing numbers of lawyers, this early civil service collected royal revenues, administered the king's justice, and kept him informed on what was happening in the provinces far from the royal court. Though churchmen and members of the lower aristocracy continued to play their part in government, it was less common for great nobles to function as the king's most important advisers.

By the beginning of the twelfth century, Louis VI (r. 1108–1137), called "the Fat," was garnering the sort of support among the governed that the dynasty would need if it was to exercise genuine dominion. Louis sought and won the cooperation of the church, the merchants, even the peasantry. He employed both ecclesiastics and townsmen as royal officials while his noble vassals faced increasing pressure to bow to the royal will. Louis realized that good relations with most of these groups were vital to the continuing growth of monarchical authority.

As the twelfth century drew toward a close, then, the Capetians had laid the groundwork for the achievements of two of France's greatest kings: Philip II and Louis IX. The former greatly increased the size of the royal domain; the latter elevated the prestige and authority of the French throne beyond anything it had known before.

Philip Augustus and the Expansion of the Royal Domain

Philip II (r. 1180–1223), a contemporary recorded, had "a bald pate, ruddy complexion," and was "given to drink and food" and "prone to sexual desire."[7] More important for history, he was "skilled in stratagems," a shrewd political intriguer, a skillful diplomat, and a good organizer of armies, though he was more interested in military engineering than in chivalric escapades. He was, in sum, just the man to begin the long process of building the French nation.

Philip continued the strengthening of the royal bureaucracy begun by his predecessors. Many of the traditional Capetian local magistrates and tax gatherers, called *prévôts,* had turned their offices and the lands granted for their support into inherited rights and became local magnates themselves rather than dependable royal servants. Philip Augustus remedied this with his usual vigor, dispatching a new breed of enforcer of the royal will to the provinces, officials called *baillis* in northern France, *sénéchals* in the south, who supervised the work of the *prévôts.* Because *baillis* and *sénéchals* were paid salaries and were not then granted lands, and because they were moved around frequently enough to prevent their developing local ties, they tended to remain firmly attached to the interests of their royal master.

Philip's greatest territorial concern was with the English domination of the western half of France. He therefore proceeded to weaken the English, first by supporting Henry II's rebellious sons, Richard the Lion-Hearted and John, against their father, and then by intriguing with John against his older brother when the latter became king. When John in his turn finally inherited the English throne in 1199, Philip Augustus caught him in a high crime under feudal law—marrying a woman already pledged to another of Philip's vassals. Philip used this offense as an excuse to confiscate many of John's French possessions—Normandy, Anjou, Brittany, and other English holdings north of the Loire. John responded by allying himself with other princes opposed to the French king's expanding power, including the German emperor and the count of Flanders, and launched an attack. At the Battle of Bouvines in 1214, however, Philip Augustus defeated his foes and made

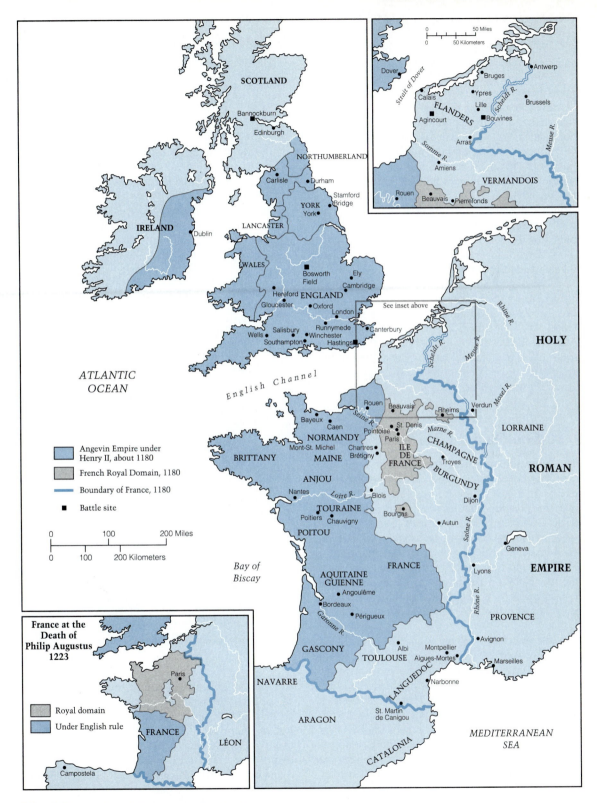

---

good his claim to the northern half of England's possessions in France.

Philip also began the process of imposing the authority of the house of Capet on southern France. The southern regions had become infested with religious heretics of the Cathar or Albigensian sect — discussed in the next chapter — and the nobles had tolerated and even supported the movement. When the militant Pope Innocent III urged the eradication of this heresy, Philip's northern barons swarmed into the south, as much to plunder the wealth of the southern nobles as to fight heretics. In the last year of his life, Philip himself sponsored a royal expedition against the Albigensians aiming at the imposition of royal authority on the south. This intervention, continued by the next two French kings, did in fact bring most of southern France under the French crown by the middle of the thirteenth century.

The English still controlled much of southwestern France, and there were other powerful vassals, like the dukes of Burgundy, who defied the French kings in later medieval centuries. But Philip Augustus had acquired much land to the west and south of his hereditary domain around Paris and had established a precedent of royal expansion that later French kings followed.

St. Louis and the Throne of France

The most admired of all the Capetian kings, however, was Louis IX (r. 1226–1270), who was canonized as St. Louis by the Roman Catholic church less than three decades after his death. A rare combination of personal piety, a strong sense of justice, and political acumen made Louis IX perhaps the most revered of all France's medieval monarchs. The prestige of the royal saint, in turn, greatly strengthened the hold of the monarchy on the loyalty of the French people. For an example of Louis's relationship with his subjects, see the box, "A Medieval King Administers Justice."

The grandson of Philip Augustus, Louis IX projected a very different image from that of his worldly and not overly scrupulous grandfather. Raised by a strong-willed, intensely devout mother, Blanche of Castile (1188–1252), Louis became famous for keeping the peace and meting out equal justice to rich and poor. As France's ruler, he surrounded himself with holy friars and completed the suppression of the Albigensian heretics. In foreign affairs, he personally led two Crusades to North Africa, part of medieval

PROFILES IN HISTORY
A Medieval King Administers Justice

Jean de Joinville's (1224–1317) *Life of St. Louis* (1309), commonly regarded as the first great biography in a modern European language, depicts the French king Louis IX as a model medieval monarch. Joinville, who fought beside King Louis in the Sixth Crusade (see Chapter 10), characterizes his sovereign as a valorous knight, a pious Christian, and, in the following paragraphs, as ruler concerned for the welfare of his subjects. Like the chieftains and kings of earlier, simpler ages, Louis IX here presides over an open-air court where any good subject might come to have a case judged or a dispute decided.

Ofttimes it happened that he would go, after his Mass, and seat himself in the wood of Vincennes, and lean against an oak, and make us sit round him. And all those who had any cause in hand came and spoke to him, without hindrance of usher, or of any other person. Then would he ask, out of his own mouth, "Is there any one who has a cause in hand?" And those who had a cause in hand stood up. Then would he say, "Keep silence all, and you shall be heard in turn, one after the other." . . . Sometimes I have seen him in summer go to do justice among his people in the garden of Paris, clothed in a tunic of camlet, a surcoat of tartan without sleeves, and a mantle of black taffeta about his neck, his hair well combed, no cap, and a hat of white peacock's feathers upon his head. And he would cause a carpet to be laid down, so that we might sit round him, and all the people who had any cause to bring before him stood around. And then would he have their causes settled, as I have told you before he was wont to do in the wood of Vincennes.

Source: Jean de Joinville, *Chronicle of the Crusade of Louis IX,* trans. Frank Marzials, in *Memoirs of the Crusades* (New York: E. P. Dutton, 1908), 149–150.

Europe's long campaign against the Muslim peoples of northern Africa and western Asia (see Chapter 10).

For all his Christian piety, Louis IX was also, and just as importantly, a strong defender of royal authority. He maintained the traditional alliance between church and state while firmly asserting royal rights over French bishops and archbishops. He did not seek confrontation with his great vassals, but he did outflank them by forbidding private warfare between them and by hearing legal appeals from their local baronial courts. He also began the useful practice of issuing royal decrees that were binding on all his vassals after consulting with only a select few of them.

To the bureaucracy he inherited from Philip Augustus, Louis IX added a new layer by appointing roving officials called *enquêteurs* to travel the land checking up on the work of the *baillis*, *sénéchals*, and *prévôts*. He also minted a royal coinage good

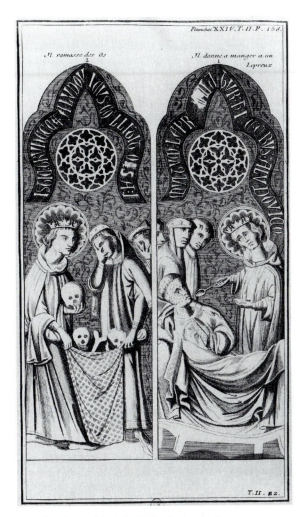

King Louis IX's saintliness is shown here on a page of manuscript that describes his departure for the Seventh Crusade. On the left, he is gathering up sacred relics; on the right, he feeds a leper.

throughout the realm and issued royal ordinances that were valid throughout the country. Humble as he was before the Lord, he was firm on his own rights here on earth. He did not accept the traditional view that kings were only "first among equals" when surrounded by their feudal vassals. "There is," he said, "only one king in France."[8]

During the thirteenth century also, specialized groups of officials emerged to supervise such crucial governmental functions as revenue gathering and the administration of justice. On the revenue side, the origins of the royal treasury or Chamber of Accounts are usually traced back to specialists in government finances in the reign of Philip Augustus. Royal justice was strengthened by special meetings of the *curia regis*, or royal council, devoted to judicial proceedings, sessions that led some royal advisers to become legal specialists. Neither the Chamber of Accounts nor the *Parlement de Paris*, the central French law court, was officially chartered until the next century. But the French monarchy had at least begun to build centralized legal and financial institutions before 1300, in the reigns of Philip Augustus and Louis IX.

Feudal Monarchy in England

Another of the major feudal monarchies evolved in England. In this relatively small and self-contained area, the Normans who conquered the country in the eleventh century were able to construct almost a model feudal monarchy over the next three hundred years. At the same time, other political changes in feudal England laid the foundations for the British constitutional monarchy of much later centuries.

William the Conqueror and the Norman Conquest

The Norman and the related Angevin dynasties ruled England from the late eleventh century through the fourteenth (1066–1377). Like the Capetians in France, these English kings forged a feudal monarchy that had considerable real power over the realm. William I the Conqueror crossed the Channel from Normandy to impose his rule on

England by force in 1066. A century later, in 1154, Henry II, son of William's granddaughter Matilda and Geoffrey of Anjou, came to the throne as the first ruler of the Angevin (from Anjou) line. Among England's leading rulers of the twelfth and thirteenth centuries were Richard I the Lion-Hearted, John of Magna Carta fame, and Edward I, in whose reign the English Parliament began to take its modern shape. These Norman and Angevin kings between them laid the foundation of the modern English nation.

It was once commonly asserted that the Normans simply imported developed feudal monarchy from France to England. Now, however, historians see the process as a more incremental one, in which the Norman and Angevin kings built on the administrative foundations and governmental traditions already established in Anglo-Saxon times. There was thus as much historical evolution as there was traumatic change in the origins of English government.

Still, the figure of William the Conqueror (r. 1066–1087), sometimes called William the Bastard in his own day, does loom large in any history of England. Of illegitimate birth—a serious problem in that age of hereditary power—William was hardened by the rough-and-tumble of Norman politics in his long struggle to establish his title to the dukedom. He was a great fighter, shrewd and tenacious; he was also greedy and brutal. The sort of person who gets described in the shorthand of the history textbook as a "strong king," William of Normandy both conquered England and imposed order upon it. "No one however powerful dared do anything against his will," reports the *Anglo-Saxon Chronicle* for 1087, and as a result "any honest man could travel over his kingdom without injury with his bosom full of gold, and no man dared strike another."[9]

The Norman conquest clearly illustrates the most obvious method of medieval nation building— by the edge of the sword. But there were political and social complexities behind even this relatively simple medieval decision by force of arms. The duchy of Normandy that Duke William ruled in the middle of the eleventh century was itself an extremely successful exercise in state building. Founded by Viking settlers, nominally a vassal state of the French monarchy, the duchy included much more of northwestern France than the Normandy peninsula that juts north into the English Channel today. The Norman dukes had built a strong feudal state, developed their own domestic economy, and fostered trade with England and Scandinavia. Ties between Normandy and England

were close. Norman nobles often traveled across the Channel; and Harold the Saxon, whom William faced at Hastings in 1066, had probably visited him in Normandy only two years before.

England itself under the last descendants of Alfred the Great was a land torn by faction feuds and violence, haplessly presided over by King Edward the Confessor (r. 1042–1066), England's own royal saint. When Edward died in the fatal year 1066, there were three claimants, all armed and ready to fight for his throne: the Saxon Harold (c. 1022–1066), who was the late king's brother-in-law; Duke William of Normandy, who claimed Edward had named him as his successor; and King Harold Hardraada of Norway. All three were ambitious men, and all had wrongs to avenge, scores to settle, or feudal rights to assert.

The Norwegian king struck first, landing in northern England in September, and was resoundingly defeated by Harold the Saxon. Immediately afterward, in October, William of Normandy landed on the south coast with an army of vassals and soldiers of fortune to assert the right to the crown of England that he believed had been conferred on him.

Harold the Saxon, wearied by his victory in the north, where he had left many of his troops, and from his rapid journey south, was surprised by the Norman host a few miles from Hastings on the morning of October 14. Harold planted the Dragon Banner of Wessex and his personal standard of the Fighting Man on the crown of a hill and prepared to receive the Norman onslaught, deploying his local recruits and his faithful household troops, armed with their traditional battle-axes, in close formation.

The duke of Normandy depended on his armored cavalry of Norman barons, armed with long lances and experienced in massed cavalry charges, supported by archers and infantrymen. According to a famous story that may even be true, the French minstrel Taillefer led the first Norman charge, singing war songs and tossing his sword into the air and catching it again as he rode. William himself galloped into battle with a string of holy relics around his neck and, despite setbacks, directed the struggle very efficiently throughout the day.

Harold the Saxon died fighting late in the afternoon, felled by an arrow through the head. The Normans hunted and slaughtered his scattered troops until nightfall, when William called them off. But that day's fight, and that fatal arrow, had redirected the course of English history.

English Efforts at Expansion

Crowned King William I on Christmas Day of 1066, the Norman conqueror still had hard fighting ahead of him. He passed out land and loot to his followers and set out to pacify the country by force. It took him five years of cruel campaigns to extinguish the last sparks of organized resistance. When the north of England erupted in rebellion, for instance, he simply destroyed their crops and left them to starve. But by 1071, he had accomplished the remarkable feat of conquering a kingdom of more than a million English people with only a few thousand Norman knights.

Such a triumph was awesome, and there were other conquests to come. Later additions to the territories of the English monarchy came with Henry II in the twelfth century and with Edward I in the thirteenth. But of course there were losses too.

Henry II (r. 1154–1189), William the Conqueror's great-grandson, was, as we have seen, the prime architect of England's enormous but short-lived Angevin Empire. Most of Henry's vast territorial acquisitions came through two determined women: Matilda of Anjou (1102–1167) and Eleanor of Aquitaine. Matilda, Henry's mother and a granddaughter of William the Conqueror, promoted her son's right to the English throne through an anarchic decade and a half. Young Henry himself married the tempestuous Eleanor of Aquitaine, recently divorced from the French king Louis VII, who brought her own extensive lands in the south of France to her English marriage. When Henry finally inherited the English throne two years after his marriage, he thus ruled not only England but the entire western half of France, from Normandy in the north through Anjou to Aquitaine in the south. To this he added by force of arms a substantial slice of eastern Ireland. The Angevin dynasty Henry established in England in the twelfth century thus for a time controlled more of western Europe, from Ireland to central France, than Britain would ever rule again.

Within half a century, however, this immense heritage had begun to crumble. This reversal of fortune was due in significant part to Henry II's family problems, a reminder of how personal a form of government feudal monarchy really was. Henry's repeated infidelities caused Eleanor to return to southern France, where she governed Aquitaine and made it a haven of medieval courtly culture. Henry's sons Richard the Lion-Hearted and John rebelled against him and fell in with the intrigues of the great enemy

of his later years, Philip Augustus of France. After Henry's death, Philip bested King Richard and King John one after the other and ended by recapturing Normandy, Anjou, and the rest of the northern half of England's French empire at Bouvines in 1214.

At the end of the thirteenth century, however, King Edward I (r. 1272–1307) made further additions to the English realm, some of which remained within it. A major acquisition was the conquest of the ancient Celtic enclave of Wales, in western England. By naming his eldest son prince of Wales and by garrisoning the green hills with castles he bound the Welsh lands to Britain for the next seven centuries. Edward also campaigned against the Celtic Scots in the rugged north, and for a time he succeeded in imposing his will on Scotland, though English rule there did not long outlive King Edward himself. Complete control of Ireland and union with Scotland came only in modern times.

The Organization of Royal Administration

The Norman and Angevin monarchs constructed a system of centralized government in England that was in many ways even more effective than that of the Capetians in France. But England in the twelfth and thirteenth centuries also saw constitutional developments that pointed toward a very different future for the English political system.

As in France, the growth of English royal power involved conflicts with other powerful elements in medieval society, such as the feudal nobility and the church. In the island kingdom also, a relatively efficient bureaucracy took shape to advance royal interests. Two factors made these steps easier in England, however: the beginnings of national organization inherited from Anglo-Saxon times and the application of principles of centralized feudalism already developed in Normandy.

William the Conqueror left the Anglo-Saxon system of shires intact and continued to utilize the traditional sheriffs as local administrators and law enforcers. The *witenagemot,* the chief Anglo-Saxon council, was replaced by its continental equivalent, a *curia regis.* From the continent also came the feudal structure of vassals and subvassals in its Norman form, with the monarch himself firmly established at the apex of the feudal pyramid. William required both his own chief barons and all their vassals to swear direct allegiance to him in a mass oathtaking

Harlech castle in Wales, built by King Edward I, illustrates the fully developed fortress of the High Middle Ages. Intended to guard frontiers or garrison conquered territories, castles like this could withstand long sieges.

on Salisbury Plain, thus weakening the power of the great lords, whose feudal supporters now owed a higher loyalty to their king. To strengthen his hand still further, the new king prohibited private wars between the barons and required open access to every fortified castle in England.

In his dealings with the church, William returned the ecclesiastical lands he had conquered and appointed an able Italian, Lanfranc (c. 1005–1089) to be archbishop of Canterbury, the highest church post in England. Lanfranc effectively reorganized the dioceses and introduced continental church practices into the country. On the other hand, the king would not do homage to the pope for his new kingdom, and he insisted on a royal say as to whether the English church should accept papal decrees.

As a step toward increasing royal revenues, in 1086 William ordered a national census of population and property, the first such national survey in any European country. This much-resented compilation, known as the *Domesday Book*, attempted to list every feudal lord and field hand, every acre of arable

land, plow, and pigsty the compilers could find. The *Domesday Book* has been a gold mine of information for historians in later centuries.

William I's successors carried these policies further. The royal council evolved toward greater specialization. Thus a secretariat charged with foreign correspondence emerged and a treasury department called the Exchequer grew up. A tax called *scutage* ("shield money") was levied on vassals who preferred money payments to military service. In order to avoid conflicts of loyalty between church and state, Norman kings shied away from using churchmen in administrative positions, employing laymen instead. They also began to reward their full-time officials with salaries instead of grants of land, thus encouraging them to remain royal servants rather than adopt the viewpoint of local landowners.

The greatest English legal and administrative reformer of the High Middle Ages was Henry II, who added so much to England's territorial holdings. In the late twelfth century, Henry built on traditional institutions and the work of his Norman predecessors a framework of law and law enforcement that had far-reaching consequences.

To make royal justice available to his people—and to bring legal fees into the government—Henry II dispatched itinerant judges, called *justices of eyre* (*eyre* meant "to travel"), to circulate through the shires trying cases. These circuit judges followed a traditional procedure of calling up groups of informed local people to give information about cases brought before them and to indicate who they thought was responsible, the origin of the modern jury trial. The royal justices also sometimes summoned groups of citizens to report all crimes in a district since the judge's last visit, the forerunner of the grand jury system of today. The judgments offered by these royal judges, furthermore, grew into a body of legal precedent and principle rooted in local practices, yet applicable all over England—the beginnings of the English *Common Law.*

This systematic extension of royal justice brought the king into competition with existing baronial and ecclesiastical legal systems. Henry made no effort to close down the local courts of the barons, but he did try to offer an alternative that would draw as much legal business as possible into the royal courts. Henry proved unable to escape confrontation with the rival system of church law, however, and the result was one of the most famous church-state conflicts of the Middle Ages, the bitter struggle between King Henry II and Archbishop Thomas Becket (c. 1117–1170).

King Henry appointed Becket, his boon companion and former royal chancellor, archbishop of Canterbury. Becket's primary loyalties, however, turned out to be to his church rather than to his king. The two fell out particularly over *benefit of clergy,* the principle of the church's canon law that all clergymen be tried in church courts. Henry, declaring that the punishments prescribed by ecclesiastical courts were too mild, decreed that in the future churchmen might be retried in royal courts. Becket insisted on the church's right to try its own. The dispute led to the archbishop's excommunication of those who supported the king and to bitter threats from the impatient Henry. Just before Christmas in the year 1170, four of Henry's knights took his angry wish to be rid of this defiant priest as their command. They stabbed Thomas Becket to death one night after vespers in his own cathedral at Canterbury.

The martyred Becket, however, won the last round. Public outrage and papal pressure forced the king to abandon his efforts to bring the clergy under English law, and to do humiliating penance for the crime. Becket himself was canonized two years after his murder, and Canterbury almost at once became a major center of miracles and pilgrimage.

Magna Carta and the Model Parliament

Despite such setbacks, by 1200 England's kings had built one of the strongest royal governments in Europe. During the next century, however, another trend emerged in English constitutional history: the imposition of legal limits on royal power, and the suggestion that others might have a say in the increasingly centralized government of England.

The two most important early steps toward a broadening of English government were the Great Charter—*Magna Carta* in Latin—extracted from King John by his barons in 1215, and the beginnings of the English Parliament in the later 1200s. Both grew from problems and practices common to other medieval monarchs. Neither transformed government in medieval England. But these two thirteenth-century innovations emerged over time as cornerstones of English liberties and representative government.

The troubles between King John (r. 1199–1216) and his barons grew partly from the fact that he was arrogant, oppressive, and much less heroic than his knightly brother Richard the Lion-Hearted (r. 1189–1199). When he inherited the throne, John also found that Richard's chivalric adventures in foreign wars had left the royal treasury empty. Once in power, John was forced to back down in a struggle over an appointment to the archbishopric of Canterbury by one of the most powerful of medieval popes, Innocent III (r. 1198–1216). And as we have seen, King John was outplotted and outfought by Philip Augustus in a feud that cost England half its French empire. It was in the wake of this last debacle that King John's own nobles called him to account at Runnymede.

The parchment they set before him in that famous meeting in a field beside the Thames in June of 1215 was a purely feudal document. The Great Charter, to which he was to affix the royal seal and which he was then to circulate to every shire in England, was a royal agreement to refrain from exploiting the traditional feudal payments of scutage and feudal aids and from conducting illegal trials of his noble vassals. The charter also required him to recognize the liberties of the towns and the right of the church to choose its own bishops (see box, "Royal Power Is Limited"). By and large, however, the confrontation at Runnymede was a demand by the king's vassals for redress of feudal grievances. If anything, given the trend toward greater royal power, it was a backward-looking document, strengthening the hand of the old nobility.

The meanings of historic events, however, often change with the passage of time. Revised more than once after 1215 and seen increasingly as a basic constitutional document, Magna Carta really began to have a larger significance during the great seventeenth-century struggle between king and Parliament in England. It was then that constitutional lawyers and political reformers began to expand the meanings of the Great Charter. If feudal aids might not be levied "except by the common consent of the realm," this later age insisted, then *all* forms of taxation required consent, not just of the barons, but of the seventeenth-century Parliament. Further, if the charter protected the liberties of barons and boroughs, it protected *everyone's* freedom. In this way, by broad construction and argument from analogy, Magna Carta came to be accepted as a fundamental guarantor of the rights of freeborn Britishers and of their constitutional descendants in other lands.

A similar future significance lay ahead for the English version of the common medieval practice of summoning leaders of the main "estates"—churchmen, nobles, and the wealthier commoners—to consult with the monarch, especially when royal revenues were involved. In thirteenth-century England, such meetings were often called parliaments, meaning "discussions." Besides bishops and titled nobility, lesser landed aristocrats and leading citizens of the increasingly prosperous English towns might also be asked to attend such gatherings, to discuss policies and agree to finance them.

The thirteenth century actually saw increasing royal demands for financial aid from royal vassals and from the wealthy towns. The king's expenses, particularly during wars, simply outran the income that could be derived from the royal estates. The regular revenues that a feudal monarch could collect from his subjects were few and specifically defined: there was no generally recognized governmental right to tax the nation in order to carry on the business of government. Hence English kings had frequent occasion to summon the leading citizens to explain the necessity for yet another royal exaction.

THE RULERS AND THE RULED
Royal Power Is Limited

These excerpts from the English Magna Carta indicate some of the major groups and institutions whose "rights and liberties" the English barons compelled King John to recognize at Runnymede in 1215. These selected clauses remind us that in the Middle Ages even royal power was limited by the traditional powers and prerogatives of other elements in medieval society. The Magna Carta also points ahead to the broader structure of rights and freedoms for all citizens that reformers in later centuries erected on the foundation of this "Great Charter."

John, by the grace of God king of England, lord of Ireland, duke of Normandy and Aquitaine, count of Anjou: to the archbishops, bishops, abbots, earls, barons, justices, foresters, prevosts . . . and all . . . faithful subjects, greeting. Know that . . .

1. First of all [we] have granted to God, and for us and for our heirs forever, have confirmed, by this our present charter, that the English church shall be free and shall have its rights intact and its liberties uninfringed upon. . . .

13. And the city of London shall have all its old liberties and free customs as well by land as by water. Moreover we will and grant that all other cities and burroughs and towns and ports, shall have all their liberties and free customs. . . .

28. No constable or bailiff of ours shall take the corn or other chattels of anyone except he straightway give money for them, or can be allowed a respite in that regard by the will of the seller. . . .

39. No freeman shall be taken, or imprisoned, or seized, or outlawed, or exiled, or in anyway harmed—nor will we go upon or send upon him—save by the lawful judgment of his peers or by the law of the land. . . .

63. Wherefore we will firmly decree that . . . the subjects of our realm shall have and hold all the aforesaid liberties, rights and concessions, duly and in peace, freely and quietly, fully and entirely, for themselves and their heirs, forever, as has been said. . . . Given through our hand, in the plain called Runnimede between Windsor and Stanes, on the fifteenth day of June, in the seventeenth year of our reign.

Source: Ernest F. Henderson, ed. and trans., *Select Historical Documents of the Middle Ages* (London: George Bell and Sons, 1910), 135–148.

Constitutional historians have generally felt that it is the summoning of townsmen and "knights of the shire," or country gentry, as well as the nobles and bishops, that turned a feudal court into a parliament. This happened in England in the thirteenth century, most notably at the so-called *Model Parliament* called by Edward I in 1295. Edward, whose conquest of Wales and wars in Scotland and France were costly, often had need at least to give the impression of consulting before announcing that further funds would be necessary. He therefore summoned representatives of church, aristocracy, and the upper ranks of the commoners. On occasion, he even made concessions to landholders or rich merchants to encourage their agreement to his demands.

Again, it was the trends of later centuries that made these occasional gatherings and the precedent they set significant. In later medieval and early modern centuries, parliaments became increasingly common, and their membership became fixed. Titled aristocrats and high churchmen met together as the House of Lords; two knights from each shire and leading citizens from selected cities sat in the House of Commons. For a long time, however, Parliament remained what it had been in its beginnings: a conclave of England's ruling classes, of nobles and bishops, country squires and leading townsmen. It was not until the nineteenth century that membership in the House of Commons expanded to include representatives of most of the general population, not until the twentieth that women were allowed to serve as members of Parliament. Only then, when Parliament had come to stand as a symbol of democracy, did the full significance of England's expanded feudal courts of eight centuries earlier become apparent.

Germany Under the Holy Roman Empire

The *Holy Roman Empire* that sprawled across German-speaking central Europe was potentially the greatest, but ultimately one of the least successful feudal monarchies. The emperors became the titular rulers of the German states and expanded into Italian and Slavic areas as well. During the High Middle Ages, they made Germany one of the great centers of medieval Western civilization. Yet in the end, they failed to impose centralized imperial authority of the sort that other feudal monarchs established in their domains.

The Birth of the Holy Roman Empire

The German medieval empire was a strange beast. It was not even officially referred to by its full title of Holy Roman Empire for centuries after it began to develop in central Europe. An eighteenth-century wit said that it was in fact neither Holy nor Roman nor an Empire, and he was essentially correct. Though they were traditionally crowned by popes or papal representatives, the Holy Roman emperors were no more *holy* than English or French monarchs who were crowned by archbishops. The claim of these German rulers to be *Roman* emperors was equally spurious, though they did seek to expand their power down into Italy, the center of ancient Roman power. And despite their best efforts at state building, the German rulers never built an *empire* comparable to strong centralized imperial structures in other times and places.

Nevertheless, three successive dynasties contributed to the effort of the German emperors to expand their territorial holdings and strengthen their authority by establishing a new empire in Europe. These were the tenth-century Saxons (919–1024), the eleventh-century Salian house of Franconia (1024–1137), and in the twelfth and thirteenth centuries the great house of Hohenstaufen (1152–1254). And in the early days, while the French and English monarchies were still in the early stages of their development, these German rulers had considerable success.

Leading monarchs of these three dynasties included the Saxon Otto I the Great, who founded what would later be called the Holy Roman Empire in 962; the Salian Henry IV, who fought the great Pope Gregory VII to a standstill in the eleventh century; and the powerful and colorful Hohenstaufen emperors Frederick I Barbarossa in the twelfth century and Frederick II, called the Wonder of the World, in the thirteenth. Each of these three ruling houses, as we shall see, had its roots in a different part of German-speaking central Europe. But like their contemporaries in France and England, these German rulers all labored to impose centralized authority on a substantial portion of Europe.

The Holy Roman emperors, however, faced powerful opposition from the rulers of the great duchies that had survived the collapse of Carolingian power east of the Rhine. These duchies—Saxony, Bavaria, Franconia, Swabia, and Thuringia—were subsequently joined by large numbers of smaller feudal fiefdoms, both baronial and ecclesiastical; by free knights on their individual estates; and by the new commercial cities. All these political units defended their autonomy with vigor. The result was that, although officially they presided over most of central Europe, the Holy Roman emperors failed to erect a structure of royal power comparable to that achieved by French and English monarchs.

Other factors also inhibited the power drive of the emperors. For one thing, the predominantly German-speaking region of medieval Europe they sought to rule was a good deal larger than the Germany of later centuries and commensurately harder to control. In the High Middle Ages, the German emperors claimed an area that stretched from the Baltic Sea down to the Adriatic and included, besides today's Germany, large parts of what are today eastern France and northern Italy. Their aspirations were thus not limited by such "natural" frontiers as the Rhine and the Alps: the Rhone, not the Rhine, was their French frontier, and they intervened vigorously in the affairs of Lombardy and Rome, well south of the Italian Alps.

Not only geography, but great differences of economic and social development divided these far-flung lands. The duchies of the eastern Carolingian Empire had been much less developed than those of the west. There were fewer towns in the German territories than on the French side, less cultivated land, more forest and marsh. These old lands of the Germans had also missed five centuries of Roman civilization, which constituted at least a recoverable heritage in France. Nor did the half-developed duchies north of the Alps have much in common with the bustling urban areas of Lombardy, which the emperors also claimed, or with medieval Rome, now the city of the popes.

Unifying such a diversity of peoples, spread over an area larger than France and England combined, was not going to be an easy job. And the course of early German history did not make it any easier.

When the last Carolingian to rule in the eastern part of Charlemagne's empire died in 911, the great duchies just mentioned emerged as the real powers in Germany. These duchies were once seen as expressions of resurgent German tribal identity after centuries of Carolingian imperial domination. In fact, the dukes were originally Carolingian military commanders, charged with defending the eastern frontiers of the Empire. They were willing to accept the weak Carolingian kings who succeeded Charlemagne in the east as long as there were any, and they elected one of their own as king when Charlemagne's blood line failed. They objected, however, when their new kings, chosen mainly to lead them in their long wars with the Magyars, tried to impose real royal power on them.

In the tenth century, therefore, the duchies asserted their autonomy from the crown. The dukes identified their regimes increasingly with the peoples they ruled, consulting with local assemblies and rapidly emerging as Saxon or Bavarian rulers rather than Carolingian military leaders. Like nobles and kings elsewhere, they took over the local church, nominating bishops in their duchies and taking a share of ecclesiastical revenues. The great German magnates thus acquired a sense of independence that proved very difficult for German emperors to overcome.

The tenth-century Saxon dynasty, however, took a serious stab at it, particularly during the reign of Otto I the Great (936–973). The house of Saxony in general and Otto I in particular labored to establish the supremacy of the elective royal crown over German principalities. They won acceptance of the hereditary principle as the Capetians did, by seeing to it that the heir to the throne was duly elected by the nobles and even publicly acclaimed while his father still ruled. In fact, however, both these German kings and the Holy Roman emperors who succeeded them were formally chosen by seven princely "electors" right up to the Empire's dissolution in 1806.

Otto the Great, like so many of the founders of feudal monarchies, was also a famous fighter. He crushed the Magyars after a long struggle and garrisoned the frontiers against future intrusions. In the 950s, he led his armies over the Alps, beginning three centuries of German imperial intervention in the affairs of Italy. At home, Otto also strove to rule with a strong hand. He established his own relatives as rulers of the other German duchies. He brought the German church under imperial patronage and control, using bishops as imperial administrators, drawing freely on church revenues, and in return supporting the bishops' independence from noble control. He also encouraged the spread of Christianity among the Slavs on the eastern frontiers—the beginning of Germany's traditional *Drang nach Osten,* the "drive toward the East" into Slavic lands.

The founding of the Holy Roman Empire itself

by Otto the Great in 962, finally, seemed to put the capstone on the edifice of royal power in the German states. Otto, like Charlemagne a century and a half before, went to Rome a king and returned an emperor crowned by the pope in return for Otto's support in a local struggle with the Italian nobility. The new emperor may have seen himself as having a special mission to protect the Christian church, as Charlemagne apparently did. But the primary result of his coronation as emperor was to exalt him above all other European monarchs. The imperial title brought no new powers, but it gave Otto the Great and his successors unrivaled prestige in tenth-century Europe.

The Salian emperors of the eleventh century developed this position of leadership still further. During that century, regional differences in Germany declined somewhat under the impact of travel, trade, and cultural interchange between the great duchies. The emperors continued to draw on the wealth and administrative talents of the church. Some of the Salian rulers, however, began to make use of lowborn laymen as royal bureaucrats. These *ministeriales,* whose dependence on the crown was absolute, were much resented by the German magnates whose traditional power they usurped.

Tensions between the emperors and the German nobility, in fact, intensified during the eleventh century. The internal conflict burst into the open in 1075 when imperial ambitions in Italy ran afoul of a new breed of pope in Rome.

The Struggle Between Emperors and Popes

A topic like the *investiture controversy* has a hopelessly medieval sound to it. Ostensibly, the controversy dealt with the question of who had the right to invest a new bishop with the ring and staff that were the symbols of his office—the pope or the emperor. But much more was at issue during the struggle over lay investiture that raged for half a century around 1100. This conflict brought to a head the long effort of the German emperors to master northern Italy. And it very nearly dumped them into the trashbin of history.

The investiture issue is often included in an account of the long-running struggle between popes and emperors in the High Middle Ages. There were, however, four parties to this intense power struggle: the German emperors and the autonomous German magnates, the Roman popes and the northern Italian cities.

The Empire's Italian policy, which went back to Otto the Great, is often seen by historians as a disastrous obsession, draining German resources to no purpose. At the time, however, it probably looked sensible enough. On a highly principled level, the Holy Roman emperors saw themselves as the Holy Father's natural protectors. They therefore expected the same sort of subservience from the pope that monarchs and nobles expected from "their" bishops or village priests. On the level of power politics, the emperors believed that if they did not step into the power vacuum in northern Italy, others would. There were even economic reasons, for the northern Italian cities were among the richest in Europe. In this context, the repeated Italian interventions of Otto I, Henry IV, Frederick I, and Frederick II, which we look at shortly, are quite understandable.

In the eleventh, twelfth, and thirteenth centuries, however, this policy brought the German emperors into head-on conflict with a militant revival of papal power. Church reform and the rise of the "papal monarchy" are dealt with in the next chapter. For now, let us briefly preview these issues: from Gregory VII in the eleventh century to Innocent III in the thirteenth, the popes felt they had every right to defend the church from worldly corruption and exploitation by secular powers. What this meant to the revived Empire was a stiffening of will in Rome, a papal refusal to accept imperial "patronage." It also meant a series of *papal* interventions in *German* affairs that, responding to imperial intrusions into northern Italy, came near to shattering the Empire.

The confrontation between Emperor Henry IV (r. 1056–1106) and Pope Gregory VII (r. 1073–1085) stands with that between Henry II of England and Thomas Becket as a vivid symbol of church-state conflict in the heart of the age of faith. Gregory was a longtime crusader for both church reform and papal power. Henry favored the first but angrily rejected the second as a challenge to his control of the German church and to his claims to superiority over the Roman popes. The issue came explosively into the open in 1075, when Gregory VII officially condemned the widespread practice of lay investiture, by which secular princes invested bishops with their ring and staff of office. Gregory was determined that laymen should no longer control the appointment of churchmen, that henceforth only the pope should invest bishops with the symbols of their spiritual authority. Henry IV responded by convening his German

Map 9.3 Medieval Germany and Italy

bishops to reject the papal decree, and by contemptuously dismissing Gregory—a former Cluniac—as "no longer pope, but false monk." Gregory reacted even more violently, announcing that the German emperor was excommunicated from the church and deposed as emperor, and that his subjects were absolved from any obligation to obey him.

The German princes and barons listened to this furious war of words with growing enthusiasm. They favored virtually anything that weakened imperial power. They saw a possibility of reestablishing their own control over local bishops once imperial control over them was ended. And the papal absolution of any German subject who refused to obey the emperor was a virtual invitation to rebellion. Within months, much of the nobility of Germany, led by the duke of Saxony, was up in arms.

The barons announced that they fully supported the pope's decree and demanded the emperor submit to His Holiness and get the ban of excommunication lifted. They called an assembly of the German nobility to pass final judgment on their imperial overlord—and asked the pope himself to take the chair. Gregory, a hot-eyed crusader for his cause, accepted with alacrity and set out for Germany.

Henry's response to this unheard-of challenge was either brilliant or humiliating, depending on your interpretation of the event. What he did was intercept the pope at Canossa in northern Italy, plead for absolution, and wait for three days in the snow, clad in sackcloth and humility, until Gregory perforce relented and lifted the ban of the church. The vivid image of an emperor submitting to a pope for many centuries embodied the power of the medieval papacy, the triumph of religion over the secular state. From the point of view of the immediate political situation, however, Henry had effectively deprived the pope of his most powerful weapon by getting the excommunication lifted. And he had kicked the ideological props out from under the rebellious German magnates.

After the high drama at Canossa, the struggle blazed briefly into violence and then dwindled away to end in a compromise solution decades later. The insurrectionary German barons rebelled and were suppressed. Henry resumed his defiance of Pope Gregory and ended by driving him into exile, where one of the most famous of all popes died an embittered man. Early in the following century, Pope Calixtus III (r. 1119–1124) worked out a compromise solution whereby the church invested bishops with the symbols of their spiritual office, while the secular authority conferred the territorial fiefs that supported them.

The German nobility, meanwhile, remained discontented, and the power of the emperors declined once more. By the middle of the twelfth century, the bishops had ceased to serve as instruments of imperial policy. Enfeebled emperors had lost control even of the *ministeriales,* the bureaucrats their predecessors had depended on when ecclesiastical administrators failed them. The Hohenstaufen dynasty that came to power in the mid-1100s was thus deprived of both ecclesiastical and lay support as it faced renewed rebelliousness among the princes and revived conflict in Italy. As it happened, however, that dynasty produced two of the greatest of all Holy Roman emperors during the hundred years between 1150 and 1250: Barbarossa and Frederick II.

Barbarossa, Frederick II, and the Dream of Imperial Order

The great twelfth-century German emperor Frederick I, popularly known as Barbarossa ("Redbeard"), and his grandson Frederick II, labeled *Stupor Mundi,* "Wonder of the World," by a thirteenth-century chronicler, were as different as two powerful men can be. Both struggled for stronger central government against mounting tides of resistance. Both became fatally entangled in the affairs of Italy. In the end, neither was able to forge a united German empire.

Frederick Barbarossa (r. 1152–1190) was a powerful, full-bearded man. Genial and enthusiastic, he seems to have combined some shrewd geopolitical instincts with medieval confidence in the Crusades and his own divine right to rule. On the practical side, he worked steadily and effectively to rebuild imperial power in Germany. Less realistically, he also ordered the Saracens to surrender the Near East to him as the legitimate heir of the Caesars and set off for the Holy Land in the conviction that if the Holy Roman emperor could ride through the streets of Jerusalem, the Second Coming could not be far behind.

The disintegration of the German empire was well advanced when Barbarossa came to the throne in 1152. In addition to a crumbling bureaucracy, nobles who resisted his authority, and popes who challenged it, he had to face growing resistance from the north Italian cities and a renewed tendency toward *particularism,* or strongly felt regional loyalties, in Germany. The emperor met these challenges over his forty-year reign by laboring to restore the imperial image, to reorganize Germany along the lines of a classic twelfth-century feudal monarchy, and to establish imperial dominion over northern Italy once and for all. His overall vision seems to have been of a vast empire, centered in Switzerland and extending from the Danish frontier in the north to the Papal States in central Italy.

A variety of measures contributed to the restoration of imperial prestige. These included Frederick I's proper coronation in Rome, an official canonization for his imperial predecessor Charlemagne, vigorous support for the revival of Roman law now being taught again in Western law schools, and the first actual use of the name *Holy Roman Empire* for the empire of the Germans. Frederick's reorganization of his German possessions included both reconstruction of the imperial administration and the establishment of a feudal hierarchy, exalting the great dukes and other higher ranking German magnates well above the rest of the nobility as his own chief vassals and giving them responsibility for controlling their own lands. In this attempt to reestablish his power in Germany, Frederick's main opponent was Henry the Lion (c. 1129–1180), the duke of Saxony and a longtime foe of the house of Hohenstaufen. When Henry hesitated to join the emperor in his Italian campaigns, however, he was declared an unfaithful vassal and driven into exile, his immense lands confiscated by the triumphant emperor.

But once again Italy proved the great stumbling block to imperial success. Barbarossa's dream of imperial order required a strong royal domain, including his hereditary duchy of Swabia north of the Alps, Burgundy to the west, and the rich towns and croplands of Lombardy south of the mountains. With this core secure, he hoped to be able to extend his real authority out to the north German and central Italian fringes of his empire. Swabia was a family possession; the emperor acquired Burgundy by marriage; and he set out to win control of northern Italy by force. He was opposed by popes in the tradition of Gregory VII and by the proud merchant aristocracy of the north Italian cities, led by Milan. It was an alliance of these towns, the *Lombard League,* that finally checked the imperial effort at hegemony south of the Alps by administering a crushing defeat to Barbarossa's army at Legnano in 1176.

In his last years, however, the irrepressible emperor found new worlds to conquer. In 1190 he enthusiastically joined the Third Crusade to free the Holy Land from the Seljuk Turks. A profound believer in the Crusade, he knew also that it would enhance imperial prestige if the Holy Roman emperor led the Christian host. He was, however, a very old man, and he never reached Palestine. Confident to the last, Frederick Barbarossa drowned fording a river in Asia Minor.

A few years before his death, however, Frederick I had arranged a shrewd dynastic marriage for his son Henry (1165–1197) to Constance (1154–1198), heiress of the Kingdom of Sicily, a feudal monarchy centered in Sicily but including the southern half of Italy also. Barbarossa's canny eye saw the papacy caught in a vice between a Hohenstaufen empire in the north and a Hohenstaufen kingdom in the south. It is unlikely, however, that he could have envisioned the product of this marriage of diplomatic convenience—Frederick II (r. 1212–1250), the wonder of his world.

More than one historian has suggested that Frederick II would have been more at home in the Renaissance than in the High Middle Ages. Raised in Sicily, he was a man of wide culture and curiosity, literate in six languages, a patron of poets and scholars, a reader of Aristotle, tolerant of Muslims (of whom there were many, descendants of Arab invaders, in Sicily). Where his famous grandfather had been a bluff, hearty warrior, the second Frederick was a shrewd, subtle diplomat. At least one pope suspected him of being the Antichrist, and he had the distinction of being excommunicated no less than four times.

A fascinating individual and an excellent ruler of Sicily, Frederick II proved a disaster for the Holy Roman Empire. Sicilian born and bred, he constructed a tightly organized nation-state in his southern Italian realm, tried hard to win control of the rich northern Italian cities, and came into repeated conflict with the Roman popes between. He spent as little time in his enormous German possessions as he could, however, and took little interest in German affairs.

Compelled to agree to a Crusade as the price of his coronation by Pope Innocent III, Frederick postponed the holy war as long as he could and then ended it by negotiating a treaty with the Turks allowing Christian pilgrims access to the shrines in Palestine. To buy peace in the Empire so he could get on with his elaborate Italian policies, Frederick literally gave away most of the powers his imperial predecessors had fought so hard for. He granted charters of liberties to German cities from Switzerland to the Baltic and recognized Bohemia as an independent kingdom. Most disastrous for prospects of German unity, he granted first the

German bishops and abbots, then the princes and nobles, almost total freedom from imperial control. They were allowed to mint their own coins, operate their own courts, collect customs duties at their frontiers, and run their own states without imperial interference. For himself, he claimed only the imperial title and the right to control foreign policy—mostly in the interest of his grand scheme for Italy. And even in the south, his Italian-centered vision of

royal power failed: Frederick died in 1250 still struggling to force the Lombard cities to accept his rule.

From the mid-thirteenth century onward, therefore, the Holy Roman Empire was really little more than a loose confederation of great duchies, baronial holdings, ecclesiastical states, free cities, and even individual knightly estates under the emperors. There was to be no truly unified German nation until the latter part of the nineteenth century.

A Topical Summary

Politics: During the High Middle Ages—the eleventh, twelfth, and thirteenth centuries—Europe rediscovered strong central government in the form of feudal monarchies. Royal governments based on hereditary succession and divine sanction began to assemble administrative systems capable of reining in the power of the feudal nobility. Monarchs as different as Philip Augustus and St. Louis in France and as aggressive as William the Conqueror and Henry II in England fought and feuded, laying the foundations of modern nation-states to come. Equally talented and hard-driving rulers like the Holy Roman emperors Frederick Barbarossa and Frederick II *Stupor Mundi,* however, proved unable to create more than a shadow empire in the German states.

Economics: On the reborn long-distance trade routes of Europe, cities reappeared in the High Middle Ages. Merchant companies settled around

existing religious or military centers, evolved into merchant guilds, spawned craft guilds, built city walls, and developed city government. And in these bustling new urban centers, a "commercial revolution" forged many of the techniques and tools of modern capitalism.

Technology: Technological improvements over the simple skills of the manor village emerged in both the countryside and the new cities of the High Middle Ages. Peasant villagers developed the heavy iron plow, the horse collar, the horseshoe, and the windmill. Medieval guild masters specialized in a growing variety of handicraft techniques for making everything from cloth and candles to wagon wheels, swords, and jewelry. And medieval masons began to build again, raising city walls and towering churches on a scale scarcely seen in the West since Roman times.

Some Key Terms

bailli 264
benefit of clergy 271
commercial revolution 259
Common Law 271
craft guild 257
curia regis 264
divine sanction 261
Drang nach Osten 274

enquêteur 267
florin 259
Holy Roman Empire 273
investiture controversy 275
joint-stock company 260
justice of eyre 271
Lombard League 278
Magna Carta 271
merchant guild 257

ministeriale 275
Model Parliament 273
particularism 277
prévôt 264
primogeniture 257
sénéchal 264
urban patriciate 258

Notes

1. Geoffrey Barraclough, *The Crucible of Europe: The Ninth and Tenth Centuries in European History* (London: Thames and Hudson, 1976), 7.
2. Ibn Khurdhadbah, *Book of Routes* (846), in Salo

Wittmayer Baron, *A Social and Religious History of the Jews,* vol. 4, 2d ed. (New York: Columbia University Press, 1957), 181.
3. Rosamond McKitterick, *The Frankish Kingdoms*

Under the Carolingians (London and New York: Longman, 1983), 228.

4. *Life of St. Godric,* trans. G.G. Coulton, in *Medieval Europe,* eds. William H. McNeill and Schuyler O. Houser (New York: Oxford University Press, 1971), 91–92.

5. Antony Black, *Guilds and Civil Society in European Political Thought from the Twelfth Century to the Present* (Ithaca, N.Y.: Cornell University Press, 1984), 13–14.

6. Ibid., 46.

7. *Chronicon Sancti Martini Turonensis,* in John W. Baldwin, *The Government of Philip Augustus* (Berkeley: University of California Press, 1986), 356.

8. Quoted in Robert Fawtier, *The Capetian Kings of France: Monarchy and Nation, 987–1328* (London: Macmillan, 1962), 26.

9. Quoted in D.C. Douglas, *William the Conqueror: The Norman Impact upon England* (Berkeley: University of California Press, 1964), 373.

Reading List

BALDWIN, J. W. *The Government of Philip Augustus: Foundations of French Royal Power in the Middle Ages.* Berkeley: University of California Press, 1986. Imaginative interweaving of narrative and institutional analysis.

BARON, S. W. *A Social and Religious History of the Jews.* 18 vols. 2d ed. New York: Columbia University Press, 1952–1983. Standard work on the subject, with detailed coverage of the Jews in medieval Europe.

BARRACLOUGH, G. *The Origins of Modern Germany.* Oxford: Blackwell, 1949. Older and controversial, but still perhaps the best place to begin on medieval Germany.

BLACK, A. *Guilds and Civil Society in European Political Thought from the Twelfth Century to the Present.* Ithaca, N.Y.: Cornell University Press, 1984. Provocative study of competition between corporate, fraternal ethos and individualistic, competitive ethic of modern capitalism—both with origins in the medieval towns.

BOLTON, J. C. *The Medieval English Economy, 1150–1500.* London: J.M. Dent, 1980. Best survey of English economic development. See also H. E. HALLAM, *Rural England, 1066–1348* (Atlantic Highlands, N.J.: Humanities Press, 1981), summarizing the literature on manor farming, with attention to ecology and technology.

CHIBNALL, M. *Anglo-Norman England, 1066–1166.* New York: Blackwell, 1986. Up-to-date overview of England after the Conquest, by a leading authority.

CONTAMINE, P. *War in the Middle Ages.* London: Blackwell, 1984. Highly recommended general study of medieval warfare.

DOUGLAS, D. C. *William the Conqueror: The Norman Impact upon England.* Berkeley: University of California Press, 1964. Excellent study of William I and his achievement.

DUBY, G. *The Three Orders: Feudal Society Imagined.* Translated by A. Goldhammer. Chicago: University of Chicago Press, 1980. Stimulating analysis of medieval social theory as it developed in France.

ENNEN, E. *The Medieval Town.* Translated by N. Fryde.

New York: North-Holland, 1979. Excellent overview, with attention to regional differences.

FAWTIER, R. *The Capetian Kings of France: Monarchy and Nation, 987–1328.* Translated by L. Butler and R. J. Adam. New York: St. Martin's Press, 1966. Older but scholarly survey of the rise of the French monarchy.

GILLINGHAM, J. *The Angevin Empire.* London: Arnold, 1984. Clear and challenging introduction to the history of England's medieval empire. On the Angevin civil service, see R. V. TURNER, *Men Raised from the Dust: Administrative Service and Upward Mobility in Angevin England* (Philadelphia: University of Pennsylvania Press, 1988).

HERLIHY, D. *Opera Muliera: Women and Work in Medieval Europe.* Philadelphia: Temple University Press, 1990. Concentrates on work that was performed outside the home.

HILLGARTH, J. N. *The Spanish Kingdoms, 1150–1516.* 2 vols. Oxford: Clarendon Press, 1978. Most thorough account of political, economic, and cultural changes.

JORDAN, W. C. *Louis IX and the Challenge of the Crusade.* Princeton: Princeton University Press, 1979. The saintly king and French social ideals.

KELLY, A. *Eleanor of Aquitaine and the Four Kings.* Cambridge, Mass.: Harvard University Press, 1957. Combines scholarship with readability.

PACAUT, M. *Frederick Barbarossa.* Translated by A. J. Pomerans. London: Collins, 1970. A clear exposition of the long conflict between popes and emperors.

SPUFFORD, P. *Money and Its Use in Medieval Europe.* New York: Cambridge University Press, 1988. Thoroughly researched study of the medieval money economy.

STRAYER, J. *The Medieval Origins of the Modern Nation State.* Princeton: Princeton University Press, 1970. The rise of the medieval kingdoms from which the nation-states evolved, by a noted medievalist. See also H. A. MYERS, *Medieval Kingship* (Chicago: Nelson-Hall, 1982).

UNGER, R. *The Ship in the Medieval Economy, 600–1600.* London: Croom Helm, 1980. Useful overview, based on underwater archaeology as well as written sources; notes both Byzantine and Muslim influences.

Queen of Sheba. Twelfth century. Musée du Louvre, Paris

The interior of a Gothic cathedral is like a high-vaulted cave. Clustered piers rise into the dimness, shadowy figures move in the aisles, feet scrape on stone. There are tombs, massive sarcophagi on which knights and ladies repose, hands folded, stone eyelids closed seven centuries ago. Hushed voices, flickering candles, altars and crucifixes emerge from the shadows. Above the portals and the pillared aisles glows the jewel-like radiance of stained glass.

But look more closely at the sculptured stone scenes from Scripture and saints' lives, turn up the carved wooden seats in the choir, and you may see a very different world. Here is a simple peasant plowing, or an impudent Eve; there a crouching ape, or a devil with his tongue sticking out. Above you, leaves, flowers, and other realistically rendered vegetation cluster around the capitals of columns. But if you climb the endless narrow stone stairs to the roof, you can share the view of modern Paris with the gargoyles, fantastic stone monsters that look like nothing ever seen on land or sea.

If you feel a bit confused as you emerge into the twentieth-century sunlight, the milling crowds and honking cars and postcard stands, it is understandable. You have just had a tour of the distinctly unmodern mind of the Middle Ages.

Probably more than most moderns, medieval people felt a religious dimension to their society—and a social function for religion. We return to this interpenetration of the spiritual and the material shortly, when we analyze the medieval worldview in properly theoretical terms. But in a sense this entire chapter must be an excursion through that medieval twilight zone where the material world of every day and the radiance of a more spiritual realm met and mingled. It was a world where God was in his heaven, angels and demons were real, and the Blessed Virgin could always be counted on for comfort and help. In this chapter about society and religion in the High Middle Ages, the first thing to remember about them both is that they fitted together more perfectly than at any other time in Western history.

The Church Triumphant

The world the kings and tradesmen made in the eleventh, twelfth, and thirteenth centuries was one in which religious organizations and church leaders played a central role. These high medieval church leaders did not believe in separation of church and state, in religious toleration, in religion without dogma or heaven without hell. They were human beings doing a job, one they believed was more important than any other task could possibly be. Believing, they thrust their way into every sphere of life, challenging kings and tending lepers, reforming religion and inventing the Inquisition.

Corruption in the Church

The medieval church was not always a triumphant institution of powerful popes and towering cathedrals. At the beginning of the High Middle Ages, in fact, it was as deeply sunk in weakness and worldly corruption as it would ever be.

The root of the trouble was a rather too close relationship between church and society. Corruption, worldliness, and secular control seemed to be all bound up together. *Simony,* the buying and selling of church offices and priestly services, and *nepotism,* the appointment of relatives to clerical positions, put the church at the beck and call of the wealthy. Clerical marriage, or concubinage, through which priests indulged their sexual natures, was a surrender to the needs of the flesh. Lay investiture, by which secular rulers invested bishops with their spiritual authority, elevated the powers of this world over that of the church, as Roman popes recognized in the investiture controversy dealt with in the last chapter. It was in a fierce determination to redress this balance in favor of the spiritual realm, to exalt God and his church over wealth and power and fleshly weakness, that the great reform movement of the eleventh and twelfth centuries was born.

The problem went back to the beginnings of the Middle Ages, but it had become particularly acute since the decline of the Carolingian Empire— the church's great protector—and the ravages of Vikings, Magyars, and Arabs in the ninth and tenth centuries. The raiders had looted churches and leveled monasteries. Feudal barons and monarchs had offered protection, but at a price: if the secular powers were to respond to the church's need, the church must serve the needs of its lay patrons in return. Thus, in the eyes of the reformers, the seeds of worldly corruption entered into the soul of the Christian church.

The need for reform was apparent at every level of society. At the village level, the knight who built a small church for his peasants expected to name the parish priest who would officiate there. The person he chose might be a relative of his—but then, why shouldn't a man take care of his family? If the priest was illiterate—even if he lived with a woman—he was no different from all the other peasants in the village. As long as the bishop had properly consecrated him, such a priest had all the spiritual power the church could confer.

The great nobles, the French counts and dukes and the lords of the great German duchies, took much the same attitude at a higher level. They appointed their kin as bishops and abbots, and in so doing tapped the wealth of the episcopal sees and the great monasteries. Again, they saw this as a perquisite that went with their titles, like the loyalty of their knights or the labor of their peasants.

As we have seen, Christian monarchs assumed the right to control the churches within their own realms. Like lesser magnates, they too appointed their followers to high church offices and took a share of ecclesiastical revenues. But their needs were more complex. Monarchs often made use of educated and able clerics as administrators in the royal governments; to be sure of the loyalty of these ecclesiastics, princes coveted the power to appoint them in the first place. As royal government grew, increasing conflicts of interest, for example, between royal and ecclesiastical courts, brought monarchs into head-on confrontation with the papacy itself.

By 1000, worldliness and corruption had reached as high as the see of St. Peter itself. The Donation of Pippin in 756 had conferred a substantial slice of central Italy upon the popes. Some pontiffs became more deeply involved in the secular affairs of these lands, known as the Papal States, than in the spiritual affairs of Christendom. Worse yet, with the passing of the Carolingian Empire, the popes lost the imperial power that had protected them from their political enemies in Italy. The papacy became a prize to be competed for by powerful Italian noble families, or even a hostage to urban rebellion within the city of Rome itself. Some popes behaved more like local politicians than like the spiritual heirs of St. Peter.

Even the monastic establishments in which particularly devout Christians had sought to escape from this world all too often became sunk in worldliness. Many monks and nuns were actually the children of aristocratic families who sought an honorable place for a second son who would not inherit land or for a daughter they could not provide with an adequate dowry. Such people brought their aristocratic and thoroughly worldly lifestyles with them into the

	900		1000	
POLITICAL, MILITARY, AND DIPLOMATIC EVENTS	**10th century**	Spanish Reconquista begins German *Drang nach Osten* begins		
SOCIAL AND ECONOMIC DEVELOPMENTS			**r. 1049–1054** Leo IX **r. 1073–1085** Gregory VII	
CULTURE: THE ARTS, PHILOSOPHY, SCIENCE AND RELIGION			**1073–1109** St. Anselm **c. 1079–1144** Abelard	

cloisters. Even the most dedicated religious came in temptation's way. Benedictines worked hard on monastery lands, as the Rule prescribed, brought in bumper crops—and made money. Cluniac houses renowned for their piety attracted huge gifts from Christians who admired them or who hoped to ease their own way into heaven by a pious donation. The church already owned a large portion of Europe's agricultural land. As European trade revived in the High Middle Ages, ecclesiastical institutions grew even wealthier and sometimes more worldly.

In the twelfth and thirteenth centuries, some Christians began to do something about it. Some of those who demanded change were later canonized as

saints. For others, a grimmer fate was in store: condemnation and punishment as heretics.

The Challenge of Heresy: The Albigensians

The religious revolutionaries came first, in the twelfth century. The church reformers who were hailed as saints came later, in the thirteenth. The two groups differed in doctrine, but they shared a visceral revulsion at the degradation into which the church had sunk and an emotional commitment to their faith. Both groups evolved out of the same surge of

1095–1099 First Crusade
1099 Crusaders capture Jerusalem

1138–1193 Saladin
1147–1149 Second Crusade
1187 Turks recapture Jerusalem
1189–1192 Third Crusade
1202–1204 Fourth Crusade
1204 Crusaders seize Constantinople
1208 Albigensian Crusade
1212 Children's Crusade
1220–1263 Alexander Nevsky
1248–1254 and 1270 Louis IX's crusades

1098 Cistercians founded
1098–1179 Hildegard of Bingen

1171–1221 St. Dominic
1181–1226 St. Francis
r. 1198–1216 Innocent III
1210 Franciscan order founded

12th century Song of Roland
1090–1153 St. Bernard
1119 University of Bologna founded
late twelfth century Marie de France flourished
1163–1235 Notre Dame Cathedral built
1167 Oxford University founded
1126–1198 Averroes
1130–1204 Maimonides
1150 University of Paris founded
fl. 1170 Chrétien de Troyes
1200–1280 Albertus Magnus
1225–1274 Thomas Aquinas

religious feeling that later transformed the papacy, built the cathedrals, and set the Crusaders on the road to the Holy Land.

The religious revolutionaries, condemned by the church as heretics, were people of all classes of society—men and women, nobles and knights, rich merchants and the urban poor. Many of them were city people, and this first great wave of medieval heresy centered in southern Europe, in the south of France and in Italy. An early heretic to achieve widespread notoriety, for instance, was a wealthy merchant named Peter Waldo (c. 1140–c. 1218) from the city of Lyons in southern France. Waldo got religion, gave away all his worldly goods, and took to the roads to preach. The *Waldensians,* as his followers were called, circulated portions of the Bible in a translation the people could read, rather than in St. Jerome's Latin version, the *Vulgate,* available only to clerics. They urged the clergy to set aside worldly possessions and return to the simple life of the Gospel age.

A more elaborate and more challenging heresy was that of the Cathars ("purified ones" in Greek). Better known as *Albigensians* from the city of Albi, a major center of Albigensian activities in southern France, these dissenters flourished in the twelfth and early thirteenth centuries. Their faith may have had non-Christian Near Eastern origins, their lives were extravagantly ascetic, and their opposition to the organized church was absolute.

The Albigensians were dualists, seeing not one great, good power, God, ruling the universe, but two titanic forces in conflict, God and Satan. God was the spirit of goodness, light, and spirit; the Devil was lord of evil, darkness, and this world. This doctrine went back to Persian Zoroastrianism, with its struggle between light and darkness, and to the early heresy of the Manichaeans, condemned in Roman times. In the minds of medieval Christians, this dualism produced some clearly unorthodox beliefs. Satan, Albigensians believed, had created and ruled the material world. Christ was pure spirit, and so had never been "made flesh" at all, nor really crucified. The goal of the religious life was the freeing of the pure spirit from the prison house of the body.

The purified Cathar elite, called *perfecti*, rejected the world, the flesh, and the Devil with a vengeance. They did not eat meat, marry, or produce children. They could often outargue priests, and they had a wide reputation for leading pious and highly moral lives. They found many followers in the easygoing, sensual cities of southern France and the commercial centers of northern Italy, and knights and nobles often supported them as an excuse to appropriate church property. But the root of their appeal lay in the spiritual hunger of the times, and in the anticlericalism that resulted from the failure of the church to meet that need.

Wandering Friars: Franciscans and Dominicans

Revulsion against worldly corruption inspired more orthodox Christians to action too. The first fruit of this reaction was a great revival of the monastic impulse. Now, however, the sort of pious Christian who had accepted the Rule of St. Benedict or the model of Cluny in earlier centuries supported new monastic orders and an entirely new approach to the religious life—the wandering life of the friars.

By the eleventh century, Cluniac monks were hiring servants to do their required labor for them, and the mother house at Cluny had the largest church in Christendom, and one of the most gorgeous. When the fervent Cluniacs had become more famous for wealth than for piety, it seemed like time for a new start.

One new beginning came at Cîteaux in Burgundy, where the *Cistercian* order was founded in 1098. The Cistercian goal was to escape from worldly temptations by rejecting the opulent style of life of other orders. There were few statues and pictures in Cistercian churches, no beautiful vestments used in their services. From Spain and Portugal to northern England, they applied the Benedictine labor requirement with a vengeance, recruiting many lay brothers to help with the work. A thoroughly disciplined labor force, the Cistercians soon made large tracts of land bloom—and brought themselves once more within reach of temptation.

More than a hundred years later, at the beginning of the thirteenth century, a daring new approach to the challenge of living an ascetic, spiritual life emerged. Franciscan and Dominican friars did not flee to isolated monasteries, but lived and worked among the suffering, sinning masses of humanity, protected from contamination only by the armor of their faith. They lived like monks, but in the world, not out of it. And they brought to the

These nuns are Poor Clares, members of the second order of St. Francis. This religious order for women was founded by the noblewoman Chiara (or Clare) di Favarone with Francis's encouragement three years after Francis's own order had been accepted by the pope.

new commercial cities of the West a powerful revivalist spirit that stirred the hearts of many.

St. Francis of Assisi (c. 1181–1226) challenged the worldliness of the increasingly prosperous West head on, with a reassertion of the Gospel spirit and the monastic ideal. Son of a well-to-do cloth merchant in the northern Italian town of Assisi, Francis aspired first to chivalric fame in a local war, and only then to the poverty and spiritual perfection of the religious ascetic. Obeying a visionary call to "repair God's church," Francis developed a unique style of life based on absolute poverty, service to one's fellow beings, and joyous love of God. He also expressed a childlike love of the natural world, manifested in a sermon to the birds or in a hymn to the sun (see box, "St. Francis's 'Canticle to the Sun'").

Begging and preaching his way through Italy, Francis won thousands of converts to his way of life, and in 1209 or 1210 *the Franciscan order* was officially recognized by Innocent III. This was the first order of friars, and soon Francis's followers were carrying his message of humility and love across Europe. Later, Francis himself tried to reach Jerusalem and to convert the Muslims to Christianity, but he failed in these efforts. During his last years, according to those who knew him, he received the *stigmata*, the wounds of Christ, in his hands, feet, and side. Though many in the hierarchy feared that Franciscan poverty and humility might be seen as a rebuke to the triumphant material splendor and power of the high medieval church, the order survived, and Francis of Assisi himself has always been among the most loved of Catholic saints.

St. Dominic (1171–1221) faced another difficult problem—the spread of heresy, which itself was in considerable part kindled by revulsion against wealthy prelates and a worldly church. Like Francis—whom he much admired—Dominic founded a men-

THE HUMAN SPIRIT   St. Francis's "Canticle to the Sun"

It may seem surprising that a Christian saint should compose a hymn to the beauty of this world in the heart of a medieval age dedicated to otherworldly faith. St. Francis, however, saw in all God's creations a mirror of the Creator and admired "Brother Sun" and "Sister Moon" as naturally and joyfully as he fed the birds who flocked around him. But this "Canticle to the Sun" is not the simple-minded effusion of a simple soul. Notice the structured way in which the author praises first God, then the heavenly bodies, the four elements, the tribulations of human life, death itself, and finally God once more.

Most High, Omnipotent, Good Lord.
Thine be the praise, the glory, the honour, and
  all benediction.
To Thee alone, Most high, they are due, and no
  man is worthy to mention Thee.

Be Thou praised, my Lord, with all Thy creatures, above all Brother Sun, who gives the day
  and lightens us therewith.
And he is beautiful and radiant with great splendour, of Thee, Most High, he bears similitude.

Be Thou praised, my Lord, of Sister Moon and
  the stars, in the heaven hast Thou formed them,
  clear and precious and comely.

Be Thou praised, my Lord, of Brother Wind, and
  of the air and the cloud, and of fair and of all
  weather, by the which Thou givest to Thy creatures sustenance.

Be Thou praised, my Lord, of Sister Water, which
  is much useful and humble and precious and
  pure.

Be Thou praised, my Lord, of Brother Fire, by
  which Thou hast lightened the night, and he is
  beautiful and joyful and robust and strong.

Be Thou praised, my Lord, of our Sister Mother
  Earth, which sustains and hath us in rule, and
  produces divers fruits with coloured flowers and
  herbs. . . .

Be Thou praised, my Lord, of our Sister Bodily
  Death, from whom no man living may escape,
  woe to those who die in mortal sin. . . .

Praise ye and bless my Lord, and give Him
  thanks, and serve him with great humility.

Source: *The Mirror of Perfection*, trans. Robert Steele, in *The Little Flowers of Saint Francis* (New York: E. P. Dutton, 1910), 387–389.

dicant, or begging, order. *Dominicans,* however, took as their particular mission the preaching of true doctrine to combat heresy and save souls from hell. This goal in turn required Dominic's followers to study theology; and in the next century it produced such brilliant theologians as Thomas Aquinas. Dominicans, renowned for their struggle against heresy, also became leading figures in the Inquisition, the church's agency for the suppression of unorthodox religious beliefs.

For despite their common origins in the new burst of religious feeling, orthodox and dissenting religious movements inevitably came into conflict. Faced with an upsurge of heresy, the church developed a powerful new instrument of interrogation, persuasion, and punishment—the Inquisition. Heresy, the refusal to accept orthodox Christian views, was seen as threatening both the soul of the heretic and the salvation of all who might be corrupted by exposure to heretical doctrine. In 1233 Pope Gregory IX therefore founded the Holy Office of the Inquisition, delegating ecclesiastical judges to work with local bishops to ferret out spiritual contagion. And these judges were usually Dominican or Franciscan friars.

The Inquisition became notorious in later centuries for its persecution, not only of medieval heretical sects, but also of Jews, witches, and others whose real or alleged views differed from those of the church. The inquisitors' methods of procedure, including unspecified accusations, secret testimony from unidentified witnesses, and torture to secure confessions, became unacceptable to modern courts. The punishments inflicted, which included fines, imprisonment, and, for lapsed heretics (those who repented but later returned to their heretical views), public execution by burning at the stake, have also shocked people of later centuries. Such methods and punishments, however, were not unknown to secular courts in that age. And the goal of enforcing orthodox doctrine on which salvation itself depended probably seemed quite legitimate to the crowds of true believers who gathered to watch such executions in that religiously exalted age.

Reforming Popes: Leo IX and Gregory VII

The swelling demand for religious renewal, reflected at the grass roots by Albigensians and Waldensians,

monks and friars, also found ardent champions at the center of Latin Christendom in Rome. The transformation of the papacy, sometimes called the *Gregorian Reform* because of the central role played by Pope Gregory VII, actually stretched over more than two hundred years. It climaxed in an unprecedented assertion of papal preeminence in the pontificate of the most powerful of medieval popes, Innocent III.

The beginnings of the revival of the papacy came in the middle of the eleventh century, under Pope Leo IX (r. 1049–1054). The papacy in 1050 was in desperate need of regeneration. Noble Roman clans fought for the papal office. Holy Roman emperors intervened to depose popes and to impose pontiffs of their own choosing. Popes lived luxurious lives, ignoring the religious mission that their predecessors had asserted for the see of the St. Peter. Pope Leo, in the brief five years of his pontificate, made an impressive beginning at setting things right.

Leo, a German, was appointed by the Holy Roman emperor Henry III (r. 1039–1056). Although the great reform eventually took a distinctly anti-imperialist direction, Leo's very foreignness enabled him to cut through the tangle of Roman corruption without compunction. And he came from a German Empire in which the new religious fervor was spreading. A deeply religious man himself, he plunged into a whirlwind effort to spread that fervor, not only to Rome, but throughout Western Christendom.

Leo IX's particular targets were those ancient vices, simony and clerical marriage. Both the buying and selling of church offices and the sexual indulgence of priests seemed to him to reveal the corruption of the spirit by the flesh. To mobilize the forces of godliness against these vices, Leo gathered like-minded spirits, including Cluniac monks, at Rome and gave them important positions in the church. To spread his gospel of reform, he traveled across Europe, holding church councils to condemn simony and punish laxity among the bishops themselves. Where he could not go to correct abuses, he sent legates, papal emissaries with full powers to act in the pope's name. Europe was thus made aware of the new spirit in Rome, of the new determination of the popes.

That spirit and determination survived Leo's time in the band of dedicated reformers he gathered around him. This group, sometimes called the Hildebrandine party (after Hildebrand, a leader in the movement), turned its attention particularly to strengthening the power of the papacy. A major breakthrough was the establishment in 1059 of the right of the College of Cardinals, a body of leading Roman churchmen, to elect future popes. The goal of an independent papacy, free of noble or imperial control, was thus materially advanced. A second manifestation of this preoccupation with papal power was less happy: the formal break with the Eastern Orthodox church in 1054. Due at least in part to the new zeal in the West, the long simmering *filioque* controversy (Chapter 8) and the differing attitudes of the two churches toward married priests flared up. And it was one of Leo IX's own reforming zealots, Cardinal Humbert (c. 1000–1061), who delivered a bull of excommunication, as if expelling a sinner from the church, to the Greek patriarch Michael Cerularius

(c. 1000–1059) in Constantinople. The head of Greek Orthodox Christianity responded by excommunicating the Roman pope in his turn, completing the great divide in medieval Christendom.

In the last quarter of the eleventh century, that crusading zeal brought the reformer Hildebrand himself to the papal throne as Gregory VII (r. 1073–1085). A volatile, driven man who had been associated with Cluny and had served as one of Leo IX's secretaries, Gregory had been the heart and soul of the reform effort for twenty years before his election as pope. Hot tempered, unbending, and absolutely convinced of the righteousness of his own cause, Gregory was "eaten up with . . . one burning passion: to restore the glory of the Apostles" Peter

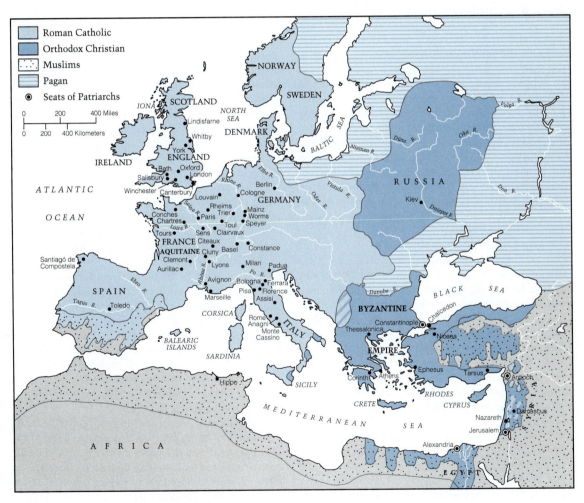

Map 10.1 Medieval Christianity

and Paul, both buried at Rome—to establish, in short, the power of the popes.[1]

Absolutely committed to the moral regeneration of the church under papal leadership, Gregory also clearly believed that the papacy should play a leading role in the life of Christendom at large, in secular as well as in religious affairs. Exactly how he envisioned the relationship between the popes and the increasingly powerful feudal monarchs is not certain. Some historians believe Gregory sought only to assert that there were two different sorts of authority in the world and that priestly power in general was superior to secular power. Others believe he meant to claim that the pope was the source of *all* authority on earth, including that of kings. Whatever his precise view, he challenged the greatest of earthly powers, the Holy Roman emperor, in what proved to be the crucial conflict of his pontificate.

As we saw in the last chapter, Gregory's demand for an end to lay investiture seemed a direct challenge to the secular monarchs' sovereign power to run their own states. To the pope, it was a matter of establishing papal sovereignty over the international church. To get his way, Gregory made use of powerful but purely spiritual weapons: *excommunication,* expelling the emperor from the church, and *interdict,* forbidding the performance of any church services anywhere in Henry's realms. Both were powerful because medieval Christians believed that the popes, as vicars of St. Peter, held the keys to salvation—and because the German princes could use this condemnation of the emperor as a pious excuse to rebel against him.

When in 1077 Emperor Henry IV "went to Canossa" to beg, in sackcloth and ashes, for papal absolution, he may in fact have outfoxed Gregory by getting him to lift the excommunication that provided Henry's barons with their excuse for rebellion. In the end, Henry IV had the troops, and he used them to drive Pope Gregory into exile in southern Italy where he died, lamenting the earthly fate of those who fight for righteousness. Still, the spiritual weapons of papal power had brought an emperor to his knees, however temporarily. And the power of the papacy had not yet reached its height.

The Power of the Papacy

The exile and death of Gregory VII represented a setback for the resurgent power of papal Rome.

Within ten years, however, a new pope had caught the imagination and seized the leadership of Christendom. In 1095 when Pope Urban II (r. 1088–1099) preached the First Crusade, he provided a release for still-building religious passions and rekindled popular support for the reformed papacy. The popes, who a century before had been pawns in the political games of German emperors or Roman noble clans, were now capable of mobilizing the chivalry of Christendom for a holy war, the first of the great Crusades (discussed in the last section of this chapter).

A more practical twelfth-century development that greatly strengthened the papacy was the codification and widespread application of the church's *canon law.* It was at this period that Christian scholars set out to establish an organized body of legal principles based on authoritative Christian sources. Inspired by the recent establishment of law schools like that at Bologna which taught Justinian's code of Roman law, the architects of church law set out to codify Christian doctrines that had accumulated over centuries. This meant collecting, comparing, and validating scriptural injunctions, decisions of church councils, papal decrees, and statements of the fathers of the church and other respected Christian thinkers. Where there were apparent differences of opinion, canonists fixed on the principle that whatever view had earned papal approbation was probably the correct one.

The process was a long one, though the cornerstone of medieval canon law, Gratian's *Concordance of Discordant Canons,* was published at Bologna shortly before 1150. From this growing edifice of ecclesiastical law, the papacy gained both a valuable instrument of control and the prestige of having been recognized as the ultimate authority on church law. Papal power also grew in other ways. The compromise solution to the dispute over lay investiture, effected by Pope Calixtus II in 1122, gave the papacy much more control over the appointment of bishops than it had before. Rome also established firm control over the canonization of saints at this time, replacing a rather casual earlier process by which a local reputation for sanctity might be enough to earn one sainthood.

Marshaling Christian armies and codifying Christian law, the papacy built its power. Then at the very end of the twelfth century came a pontiff who both articulated and wielded that authority as the arbiter of Christendom: the most powerful of all medieval popes, Innocent III.

The Most Powerful Pope: Innocent III

A thirty-seven-year-old canon lawyer, unanimously elected by the cardinals of the church, Innocent III (r. 1198–1216) had an exalted sense of the papacy's place in Christendom. He described his position as that of "the vicar of Jesus Christ, successor of Peter . . . set between God and man, lower than God, but higher than man, who judges all and is judged by no one."[2] Kings, he said, shone with reflected light, like the moon; the papacy was the sun. So extravagant was his language at times that some historians have suggested he was actually proposing that secular authority should be replaced by that of the church. It is certainly safe to say that he was an aggressively activist pope who saw the papacy as the final arbiter in secular as well as in spiritual matters. During his eighteen years on the throne of St. Peter, he enacted further church reforms, fought heresy, and interfered in the affairs of the greatest princes in Europe.

Innocent's major contribution to church reform came at the end of his pontificate, when he summoned the Fourth Lateran Council (1215), a gathering of leading churchmen as important in the history of the church as the fourth-century Council of Nicaea. The *Fourth Lateran Council* produced the definitive list of seven sacraments, the sacred rites of the church, in which a Catholic must participate to be saved. The council also offered an official explanation of the most important of the sacraments: the Mass, or communion service, was defined as a mystical transformation of the communion wafer and wine into the spiritual body and blood of Christ. The thrust of all the council's decisions was to further elevate the position of the clergy, for only priests could perform these sacred and essential rites.

Innocent also took strong steps to curb the heresies that had spread rapidly in recent decades, particularly the Albigensian movement already discussed. He favored preaching and example as means of bringing heretics back into the fold, and to this end he officially recognized the Franciscan and Dominican orders of friars. The "purified ones," however, proved difficult to win over, and they were too popular and too often protected by nobles to be easily weeded out. In 1208, following the murder of a papal legate, Innocent therefore proclaimed a holy war against both the Albigensians and the Waldensians that effectively—and bloodily—suppressed the heretics. Innocent also authorized the Fourth Crusade

This painting by the early Renaissance artist Giotto shows Pope Innocent III granting St. Francis official permission to found the Franciscan order in 1209. Francis's faithful followers kneel behind him.

in 1204, and when the crusaders seized and plundered Greek Orthodox Constantinople instead of attacking the Muslim Turks, he saw in the incident God's hand smiting the Orthodox heretics.

Several of Innocent III's clashes with the kings of this time have already been touched on. He intrigued vigorously to manipulate the Holy Roman emperors, including the most brilliant of them, Frederick II. In England, Innocent compelled the hapless King John to accept a papal nominee as archbishop of Canterbury by a combination of spiritual and diplomatic ploys, laying England under interdict and then offering to support an invasion by Philip Augustus of France. In spite of these bouts of power politics, however, Innocent also dreamed of putting an end to war between Christian sovereigns—a project in which he failed.

Endlessly active, the vicar of Christ came down heavily on monarchs for moral infractions, excommunicating even the great Philip Augustus to compel him to take back the Danish wife he had set aside. Innocent imposed his advice on princes from

Spain to Scandinavia. And within the church, he continued the vigorous moral crusades begun in the days of the Gregorian Reform against simony, clerical marriage, and other forms of conduct unbefitting the church as he envisioned it.

High Medieval Society

The narrator in William Langland's late medieval poem *Piers the Plowman* had a dream. In it, he saw "a fair field full of folk" stretching from the Tower of Truth to the Vale of Death.[3] The dream was allegorical, but the medieval folk who swarmed in Piers's bright vision were real enough: plowmen and pilgrims, kings and knights, beggars, jesters, and fools. Let us look next at these medieval people, at the way they lived and the ways they related to each other at the high noon of medieval history.

Principles of Social Organization

Three important principles governed the social organization of the Middle Ages: a strong sense of community, a clear recognition of social hierarchy, and, during the later medieval period at least, a surge of social mobility and change.

The medieval sense of identification with the community and of the importance of the group over the individual has often been contrasted with the more individualistic outlook of modern times. Modern Western peoples have come to believe that society exists to provide a good life for its individual members. Medieval people, by contrast, seemed scarcely able to conceive of the individual except *as* a member of a church, class, or local organization. Excommunication or outlawry, which expelled the individual from the church or from the protection of secular society, were thus terrible punishments indeed.

The small size of the village, where a few dozen families had known each other for generations, helps explain this sense of society as a close-knit web of relationships. By the High Middle Ages, however, the sense of community had expanded beyond the village. Society was bound by a spectrum of face-to-face groups, which included the family and the manor community, but also the organized craft guild, and even the medieval city, which typically had only a few thousand inhabitants. Then there were the three "estates," or broad social classes: church

people, aristocrats, and commoners. And there was the Christian church as a whole, into which every individual was baptized at birth.

The power of these communities over the individual could be tyrannical, regulating behavior by rigid taboos, suppressing free thought, and ignoring individual talents. Most people lived as their parents had, accepted the conventions of their community, and would never have dreamed of aspiring to anything different. On the other hand, medieval people also had the social and emotional support that comes with being part of a stable community. They could depend on the family, the village, or the guild to take care of their needs. They knew their place in God's world and their immortal destiny. Few medieval men or women had to ask themselves the questions often heard in modern atomized societies: Who am I? Where am I going? What shall I do with my life? They knew.

The sense of hierarchy, and the belief that hierarchy was natural and normal, was also highly developed among medieval people. Society itself was conceived of hierarchically, in terms of the three broad estates: the church was the highest estate; the feudal aristocracy came second; and the rest, from the richest merchant to the poorest serf, came last. Within each community, too, there were clearly established hierarchies. The relations of bishop to priest, of lord to vassal, of lord of the manor to peasant laborer, or of guild master to journeyman were all relationships of superior to inferior, of domination and subordination. If there was any equality, it was only in the afterlife—and even there angels and demons were conceived of as grouped in nine orders hierarchically arranged. Although today we may find this rejection of human equality objectionable, to medieval people it seemed quite natural, part of the immutable structure of God's world. Ambition to get ahead was a sin: the good Christian accepted his or her divinely allotted place in society humbly and obediently.

And yet social mobility was an increasingly visible reality in the High Middle Ages. Agricultural growth and the decline of serfdom allowed some peasants to become relatively well-to-do and others to leave the land and make other careers for themselves. The revival of trade and towns produced not only the conservative guilds but also merchant princes driven by a vigorous capitalist spirit. Yet medieval people tended still to condemn such unnatural behavior. They passed laws prohibiting wealthy merchants from dressing more expensively than knights, their traditional social superiors. They also preached sermons on the sin of greed and the virtues of monkish humility.

We will look at the lives of medieval people in proper medieval order, dealing first with churchmen, then with knights, and finally with the common folk of village and town. All three of the tendencies just mentioned, however—community and change as well as hierarchy—are visible shaping the basic patterns of medieval life. All are seen in the complicated interactions of Langland's field of folk, "all manner of men, the mean and the rich, working and wandering as the world asketh."[4]

A More Sophisticated Clergy

The lives of the clergy became much more sophisticated in the High Middle Ages. From the simple culture of Benedictine monks and illiterate priests emerged the reformed and cultured church of Gregory VII and Innocent III.

The life of the church was transformed from top to bottom by the Gregorian reform and the elaborate bureaucratic machinery of what is sometimes called the "papal monarchy" of Innocent. Great abbey churches like Cluny, the cathedrals and palaces of bishops, and the growing splendor of the papacy in Rome were visible symbols of the new ascendancy of the church. Its wealth grew with the revenues of its enormous landholdings, with the tithes and other payments forwarded to Rome by bishops, with fees and fines from ecclesiastical courts. Bishops and archbishops, no longer beholden to secular lords, became powerful men themselves. And even if a pope did not really rule the world, emperors did hold the pope's stirrup and bend to kiss his slipper.

To staff the growing ecclesiastical administrative machinery—which quickly outgrew that of any secular monarch—canon lawyers and accountants proliferated in the church, men more at home with numbers and complicated points of law than with theology or liturgical observances. It was at this time too that the first universities emerged, under church sponsorship, staffed by philosophers and logicians exploring religious truth with the help of abstruse Aristotelian logic. And with the new sophistication came some of the new morality that Leo IX had worked for in the eleventh century. The great prelates of the thirteenth-century church might be proud men, but they were not so likely to succumb to the fleshly sins, and the buying and selling of offices was the exception rather than the rule.

Comparable changes were felt among the lower ranks of the church hierarchy. The nuns and prioresses, priests and pardoners and other clerics of Chaucer's *Canterbury Tales* only a century later are a bewildering reminder of the complexity of the new church. The lives of parish priests themselves were changing. Not only cathedrals, but countless village churches were built at this time. The priests who officiated there were also increasingly likely to be literate, products of the new cathedral schools. And they were much less likely to be living with women as clerical celibacy became not only the ideal but the rule in the Roman church in the High Middle Ages.

Even the life of the monastic houses was affected by the new wealth and sophistication. Monks still chanted the prayers and psalms prescribed by the Benedictine Rule, raising their voices to God seven times every day. But monasteries encompassing hundreds of monks and dozens of manor farms also demanded managerial skills. In addition, some monks specialized in hand printing and illustrating holy books or in the study of canon law. As for the physical labor originally required of the religious, much of that was now performed by illiterate lay brothers recruited from the peasant classes.

Women also played a variety of roles in the renovated church. This came about in spite of the fact that the ecclesiastical developments of the High Middle Ages sometimes seemed to undermine women's place in the church. The rejuvenated papacy of Gregory VII and Innocent III, for example, took control of local church affairs out of the hands of landed magnates—some of whom were women—and emphasized the role of the ordained priest, a role closed entirely to women. The Gregorian reforms closed down double monasteries, which included women as well as men, and put convents under the supervision of male church officials. The rise of cathedral schools and universities, by shifting the center of medieval learning from monasteries and convents to all-male episcopal establishments, closed the doors of scholarship to many women. Even the new orders of wandering friars discouraged female involvement, frequently asserting that a life of begging and service was too hard for women.

But there were orders of nuns still, and women heretics too. In the mid-thirteenth century, there were five hundred convents in Germany alone. Many of these nunneries followed the rigid rule originally devised by Hildegard of Bingen (1098–1179), a widely admired writer, mystic, and adviser to popes. Though the mendicant life was closed to women,

This picture of Trotula, renowned teacher of medieval medicine, shows that in the Middle Ages a few talented women found places in the intellectual firmament. [Courtesy the Trustees of the Wellcome Trust, London]

Franciscan and Dominican religious houses for nuns did in time emerge. There were also independent groups of dedicated laywomen called Beguines who labored to help the poor in Rhineland cities.

Other women, denied scope for their talents in the Catholic church, were swept up in heretical movements. The Waldensians encouraged women to preach publicly. Among the Albigensians of southern France, there were female as well as male perfecti, and some women were leaders of the movement. In the desperate defense of Toulouse against the anti-Albigensian forces, women and young girls fought with the men, and the leader of the attackers,

Simon de Montfort (c. 1165–1218), was killed by women.

Both women and men, in short, played a part in this colorful and exciting time. In these centuries, the medieval church both came to terms with and played a leading role in an increasingly complex society. For people who thought the church was becoming too concerned with its new secular responsibilities, the Franciscan friars embodied the best tradition of simple piety which, in a simpler age, had been all that was required of a servant of the Lord. The flexibility and rich variety of the thirteenth-century church is well illustrated by the fact that Innocent III—canon lawyer, diplomat, and power broker—could see the value to the church of the simple friar from Assisi.

The Chivalric Code and Courtly Love

The second estate in medieval society was its hereditary landed aristocracy, the military elite of knights and titled nobles. These feudal descendants of the Germanic warriors of Roman times had provided most of what real power there was in the earlier Middle Ages. In the eleventh, twelfth, and thirteenth centuries, wealthy towns and ambitious monarchs challenged this noble preeminence. Yet the feudal aristocracy was still both powerful and respected. Building on a basic style of life that went back for centuries, this militarized ruling class developed during the High Middle Ages a unique code of conduct known as *chivalry*. The ladies of this class, meanwhile, formulated a doctrine of *courtly love* intended to improve relations between the sexes.

A twelfth-century knight had an increasingly heavy investment in his military tools. He had to own a heavy two-handed sword, long lances, perhaps a battle-ax, mace, or other hand weapons, shield and helmet, chain mail and later heavy plate armor, and a strong war horse to carry the load. If he was powerful enough, he might have a huge stone castle built on the Norman model, with battlemented walls, towers, and a defensive moat. He might still be illiterate, but he trained with his weapons throughout his youth, kept in trim by hunting on horseback, and participated in mock combats called tournaments and jousts to keep his military skills honed. And while knocking another man off a horse with a stick may look silly in a modern cartoon, in fact it took skill as well as strength to direct the point of a long lance to the essential point of impact when riding at full gallop and peering through a narrow slit in a heavy iron helmet.

There was plenty of fighting to do also. A young knight sometimes went looking for combat, wandering around Europe joining local wars and having the sorts of adventures that youth often covets. In later years, established as the lord of a manor, a knight might have to settle a feud with a neighbor by force of arms. His feudal overlord could also call on him at any time to serve his forty days a year. No self-respecting knight or noble refrained from joining battle if his king became involved in war, and Crusades, as we will see, could take him off to fight exotic foes beyond the seas.

A feudal baron had other responsibilities too, of course. Besides providing protection for all his dependents, he had economic, legal, and political tasks to perform. Even if he assigned the day-to-day operation of his estates to managers called bailiffs, he himself was ultimately responsible for the cultivation of his fields. Despite the spread of royal and ecclesiastical courts, the local baron's court still handled many offenses. And a true vassal was expected to provide his overlord with good political advice, while the most powerful feudal lords took major parts in the political intrigues and conflicts of the day.

These were the real military and political responsibilities of Europe's medieval ruling class. Over the medieval centuries, meanwhile, an idealized code of aristocratic conduct had been evolving: the *code of chivalry*. In its first form, chivalry was a largely military and feudal ethic, prescribing proper conduct for a good knight and vassal. Feudal chivalry, which had developed by the eleventh century, required a number of military qualities—courage, strength, and skill with weapons—usually summed up as chivalric prowess. In addition, a true knight was expected to follow certain "rules of the game" on the battlefield. Thus it was considered wrong to attack an unarmed or injured opponent, to gang up on a single foe, or otherwise to take unfair advantage. Other elements of feudal chivalry focused on the knight's feudal and manorial responsibilities. Feudal loyalty was a crucial virtue, since only the network of feudal allegiances held the whole system together. Lavish hospitality, sometimes called *largesse*, was also much praised, even though the expense of entertaining in baronial style could be ruinous.

On this foundation of feudal and military virtues a broader set of chivalric obligations was imposed by the church of the High Middle Ages. The gentle perfect knight, churchmen urged, had obligations that extended beyond his relations with his fellow feudal aristocrats. According to this view, the first duty of the military aristocracy was to serve and defend the Christian church. A second social duty was to serve his prince and defend the state. A third duty of a knight was to take women, churchmen, and civilians generally under his protection, rather than rape or loot as many did on military expeditions. Equipped with these broader commitments, going well beyond purely military skills, the barons of the twelfth century were as useful to the new age of towns, emerging monarchical states, and the resurgent church as they had been to a less complex society in earlier centuries.

Most striking, finally, was the medieval cult of *courtly love* that was grafted onto the chivalric ethic in the twelfth century, originally by the aristocratic women of southern France. Affectionate and sexual relationships between women and men in medieval times, particularly between husbands and wives, seem to have been frequently unsatisfying to women. Knights apparently did not hesitate to beat their wives, or to cast them off entirely because they failed to produce an heir or because a more profitable match turned up. Knights and nobles often seem to have saved their passion for mistresses, concubines, and prostitutes, all common around feudal courts. This situation led some noblewomen in the twelfth and thirteenth centuries to attempt to broaden the concept of chivalry to incorporate the notions of courtesy, tenderness, and romantic love that the often itinerant ballad-singers called troubadours were making a significant part of medieval culture (see pages 306–307).

The perfect knight, the doctrine of courtly love urged, was first of all a faithful lover. He adored a high-born lady, not some lower-class light-of-love, and his passion was the most powerful emotion in his life. His love enhanced his other chivalric qualities, doubling his prowess (especially in a tournament that his lady watched) and strengthening his loyalty (at least to his lady). Of more immediate interest to most noblewomen, however, he developed courtesy and sophistication. He washed more often, dressed elegantly, and learned to be polite and to talk wittily and entertainingly. He learned to dance. He even learned to write love poems, or at least to sing them, accompanying himself on a lute.

The courtly love ethic was propagated at the courts of women like Marie of Champagne

meulp adiufee et fi remerchies
de voftre deliurance monfeigneur?
de bourboy et monfeigneur de
coucy car ils ont moult fort en
tendu pour vous. Et auffi la
conteffe de fainct pol car la bon

ne dame fen eft moult grande
ment acquittee de vous aydier.
¶ Le feigneur de clary ref
pondy en telle maniere et dift
grans mercis a meffeigneurs
mais ie audoie auoir bien fait.

The martial splendor of a medieval tournament is colorfully depicted in this book illustration. Note the gaudy pavilions and the expensively decked out war horses astride which the pride of medieval chivalry demonstrated their skills.

(1145–1198), who in the twelfth century gathered young knights, ladies, and noble youths in so-called courts of love to listen to troubadour songs and to debate intricate questions of courtly love and knightly honor. And although these efforts probably did not transform male conduct, the tradition of courtly behavior did survive and flourish during the Renaissance and in later centuries as well.

It is unlikely that even Chaucer's "perfect knight" approximated all the ideals of chivalry. But there were brave and skillful knights, there were knights who went off to the Crusades primarily for religious reasons, and there were probably knights who loved truly and faithfully. And if we today feel revolted at the slaughter of noncombatants, or think it is right to serve one's country, or admire a debonair lover, our feelings have their roots in these medieval cults of chivalry and courtly love.

Peasant Life and City Life

The third estate in medieval society included the vast peasant majority, which ranged from 75 percent of the population even in heavily urbanized parts of Italy to more than 90 percent in many parts of Europe. It also included the widely varied populations of the towns, from rich merchants to apprentices and beggars. The makeup of the third estate was so broad, in fact, that it is very difficult to generalize about it.

In recent decades, however, social historians have learned much more than was once thought possible about the masses of medieval humankind. From wills and court records, from sermons and tracts on household management, from parish registers and business records, from archaeological and anthropological analysis, social historians have assembled a vast array of new data. From these sources we can get some sense of what life was like for those millions who were never candidates for canonization and made no claims to chivalric perfection.

From birth to death, the course of a peasant's life reveals some features that must seem quaint to us and some that look grotesque. Yet the basic elements of our common humanity stand out too. For example, infanticide, which was probably practiced in earlier medieval times, may have declined in the High Middle Ages, yet infant mortality was probably still quite high, given medieval techniques of midwifery, which included vigorously shaking the woman in labor to hasten delivery. If the child made it into this world, it faced other traumas. Infants were often very casually attended to by their hard-working parents, and many accidental deaths are reported. To keep them out of trouble, babies were frequently swaddled—wrapped like little mummies in yards of cloth, an approach to child care which, psychologists tell us, may have produced some very submissive or some very troubled children.

A child's working life began as soon as it could walk and handle things without dropping them. (For a description of some peasant working skills, see box, "Country People: The Ploughman and the Dairy Maid"). First around the hut and then in the fields, boys and girls learned from their father and mother. When they didn't learn quickly or well, they were hit or beaten. On the happier side, there were church festivals in the village for each season of the year and sometimes a fair celebrating the birthday of a local saint. Such occasions featured booths and jugglers and dancing, eating and drinking too much, and, for youths and maids, discovering the joys of sex.

Church records of marriages and first births seem to indicate that, in some parts of Europe at least, it was customary not to get married until a young woman was pregnant. Once married, a peasant woman was likely to be pregnant often, a fact that, coupled with the hard work she shared with her husband, probably shortened her life. In these expansive times, peasant women also often took over the working of the family's traditional strips of land around the village while their husbands cleared or

MASTERING OUR WORLD   Country People: The Ploughman and the Dairy Maid

Originally intended as a list of the "offices" or duties and ideal qualities of the functionaries who ran a medieval manor, these profiles offer more than that to twentieth-century readers. In these paragraphs we have concrete descriptions of the ways in which medieval people spent their days. In addition, we get a glimpse of the skills and responsibilities of these agricultural workers, too often dismissed as "ignorant peasants," who lived and worked half a dozen centuries ago.

THE OFFICE OF THE PLOUGHMAN

The ploughmen ought to be men of intelligence, and ought to know how to sow, and how to repair and mend broken ploughs and harrows, and to till the land well, and crop it rightly; and they ought to know also how to yoke and drive the oxen, without beating or hurting them, and they ought to forage them well, and look well after the forage that it be not stolen nor carried off; and

they ought to keep them safely in meadows and several pastures, and other beasts which are found therein, they ought to impound.

THE OFFICE OF DAIRYMAID

The dairymaid ought to be faithful and of good repute, and keep herself clean, and ought to know her business and all that belongs to it. She ought not to allow any under-dairymaid or another to take or carry away milk, or butter, or cream, by which the cheese shall be less and the dairy impoverished. And she ought to know well how to make cheese, and she ought to save and keep the vessels of the dairy, that it need not be necessary to buy new ones every year.

The dairymaid ought to help to winnow the corn when she can be present, and she ought to take care of the geese and hens and answer for the returns and keep and cover the fire, that no harm arise from lack and guard.

Source: James Bruce Ross and Mary Martin McLaughlin, eds., *The Portable Medieval Reader* (New York: Viking Press, 1949), 133–136.

drained new acreage. The work of both partners might now include some handicraft industry carried on in the cottage for sale in a larger town nearby— perhaps carving wood or spinning thread and weaving cloth on contract for a city merchant. By the twelfth century, there were many local market towns where peasants took produce to sell and bought tools or a rare treat.

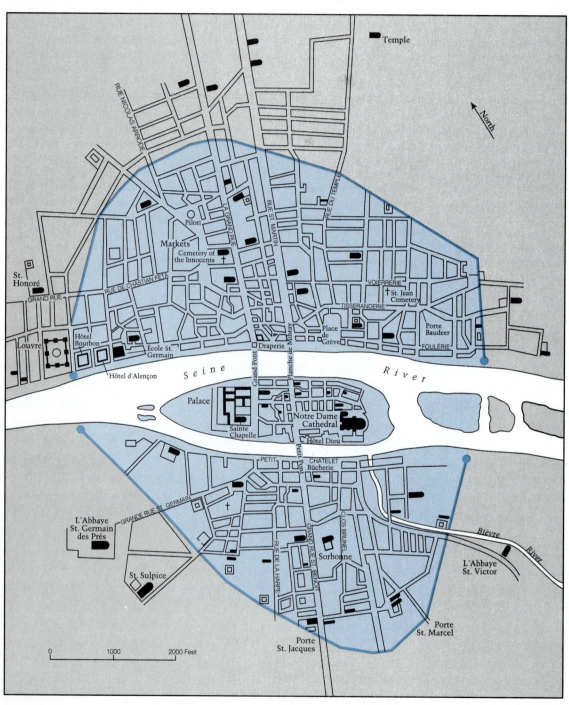

Map 10.2 Thirteenth-Century Paris

Violence was less universal than it had been in the early Middle Ages, and people tended to live a bit longer, though peasants were still not likely to survive much past forty. They were buried in the yard around the church, close to that symbol of their hope for a better life to come. And despite all the priest could do, new generations of youths and maids danced and sang among the graves on feast days.

A day in the city was an exciting event for village peasants, but the townspeople themselves were probably blasé about their urban style of life. Despite its walls, the city was not cut off from the countryside. There was no smog, you could see the environing hills clearly between the rooftops, and it was only a short walk to green fields. A fine town had perhaps ten thousand inhabitants; the largest cities in Europe did not run much over a hundred thousand.

It is common to analyze social groups in terms of power relations of oppressors and oppressed, noting who gives orders and who takes them. A day in a guild workshop, however, would probably reveal as much cooperation and sharing as domination and subordination. The master craftsman, his family, and his unmarried journeymen and apprentices probably all lived together in a tall house jammed against the house next door in a very narrow street. The upper stories tended to project out over the street, making it quite dim even at midday. If it was a particularly successful town, the narrow lane might be paved with cobblestones and have an open sewer running down the middle of it. The ground floors of most of the houses in an artisans' quarter were given over to shops and workrooms, all handcrafting the same product, one shoemaker next to another. Thus whole streets were filled with goldsmiths or swordsmiths, barrel makers or candle dippers. There might be a citadel at the end of the high street, or a new cathedral church. But the business of the city was business, and shops, with living quarters on the premises, predominated within the walls.

People rose early, washed from a basin, cleaned their teeth with a twig, and dressed for the day. Downstairs, servants who worked for little more than bed, board, and clothing started the fire and swept the floor. The wife of a well-to-do merchant might go to Mass at the church, but many wives had no time. With a servant, they would set off early to shop, going from one marketplace to another and dealing with fishmongers, butchers, bakers, and vegetable sellers for each item of the daily diet.

Some wives and daughters, however, worked in the shop with the master and his assistants. Some

guilds were in fact entirely composed of women, while in others a widow could inherit not only her husband's shop but his place in the guild as well. In hard times, however, women might be prohibited from doing guild work, which journeymen in particular saw as depriving them of jobs that should be theirs.

Thus through the average day, journeymen, apprentices, and perhaps some members of the family labored in the shop. The master worked with them or sat in the open-fronted stall facing the street, dealing with customers. The main meal of the day came at midday or even earlier, and was often substantial. Thick soup and crusty bread, fish, meat, spicy sausage, and wine or beer were consumed in hefty quantities. The master presided while the mistress directed the servants. And the family, journeymen, and apprentices ate just as they worked, together.

When it got dark, everyone went to bed, apprentices and journeymen sharing one room, the family another. The unlit city was soon asleep.

The Jews in Medieval Society

Outside these homogeneous neighborhoods and manor villages, one group constituted a genuine social and cultural minority: the Jews of the diaspora. During the High Middle Ages, Europe's Jewish communities faced a time of crisis and transition. Small in numbers but well established in many parts of western Europe, they now encountered mounting religious persecution, and many migrated into eastern Europe or even beyond.

The Jewish diaspora, or "dispersal," of Roman times had taken many Jews far from their Palestinian homeland. Jews settled across the Near East and North Africa and moved into Roman Europe. Most, however, remained south and east of the Mediterranean, in areas that were overrun by the Muslim followers of the Prophet Muhammad in the seventh century. In the earlier Middle Ages, perhaps 90 percent of the Jewish people lived in the Muslim zone rather than in Christendom. Settled in self-governing communities under the overall authority of their Muslim rulers, they did well in commerce and various crafts.

The Jewish communities of Europe, however, also enjoyed a considerable degree of liberty and relative prosperity in the early medieval period. As mentioned in Chapter 9, they sometimes functioned as traders between Europe, the Near East, and Africa. Jews in some parts of Europe enjoyed the special protection of rulers who valued the skills of a disciplined, literate people and the wealth some of them accumulated. Under the Carolingians, for instance, Jews often held high government posts and were protected in their rights to own land and other wealth.

Excluded from the feudal hierarchy and from Christian manorial villages in many places, however, Jews moved into a variety of commercial and handicraft industrial trades in Europe as they did in the Muslim zone. They also practiced medicine, served as bankers, and often engaged in small-scale moneylending. Living in close-knit communities, separate from Christian neighborhoods even in cities, they formed an anomalous group in medieval Christendom.

From the tenth century on, however, popular antipathy to Jews in the Western world became more apparent. The religious resurgence of the High Middle Ages fostered feelings of Jewish inferiority to Christians and bred dark suspicions that Jews were agents of Antichrist. The identification of Jews with moneylending added to their unpopularity, and they often became scapegoats for natural disasters like famine or epidemic disease.

The High and late Middle Ages brought traumatic times to the Jewish people. During this period, Jews in both Muslim and Christian lands encountered increasing hostility and even violent persecution. In the Christian West, major persecutions coincided with the Crusades that began shortly before 1100, holy wars against Islam that often began with massacres of Jews in Europe itself. Another dark period of persecution was triggered by the Black Death, the terrible plague that reached Europe just before 1350, for which the Jews were often quite irrationally blamed.

One consequence of these medieval persecutions was the further spread of Jewish communities across the Western world and beyond. Expelled by royal decrees from England in the thirteenth century, from France in the fourteenth, and most disastrously from Spain in the later fifteenth century, Jews moved steadily eastward. Some found new homes in the emerging civilization of Poland and other Slavic lands. Others drifted as far as Constantinople, the polyglot Byzantine metropolis, where Jewish literacy, discipline, and efficiency enabled them to flourish once more. Jews did not return to western Europe in large numbers until modern times.

The Gothic Age

The large majority of medieval people, however, were Christians, and this became one of the great ages of Western Christian culture. The age of the Twelfth-Century Renaissance, Scholastic thought, the chivalric epic, and the cult of courtly love, the culture of the High Middle Ages is perhaps best characterized by a single adjective: *Gothic*.

The term was originally coined by Renaissance intellectuals who despised the art of the medieval cathedral as crude and inharmonious, the work, they said, of "Gothic" barbarians. As used today, however, *Gothic* has broader and more positive meanings. The dynamic restlessness of the Gothic style does go back to the art of the steppe-dwelling Germanic barbarians who flooded across Europe at the beginning of the Middle Ages. But the underlying logical structure of Gothic art may be traced through Scholastic philosophy to Aristotle. And the upward thrust of the Gothic cathedral reflects the heavenly aspirations of a profoundly Christian age. The label *Gothic* thus encompasses the uniquely medieval fusion of Germanic, Greek, and Christian elements that reached its climax in Europe in the twelfth and thirteenth centuries.

Medieval Religious Culture

The precise nature of the Christian religious culture of the medieval majority deserves at least a cursory survey before we go on to some of its more impressive intellectual and artistic manifestations. This section looks at religious culture in the anthropological sense of the term, as a mix of beliefs, attitudes, and practices. For it was this living faith, interwoven with the lives of medieval people, that gave the age its unique tone and character.

Over the millennium between Jesus' time and the High Middle Ages, the Christian story had acquired a rich incrustation of new meanings. The core of this traditional Christianity had been developed by Christian thinkers over the centuries. The popular faith of the medieval masses, however, was also shaped by prevailing social attitudes and integrated into the social life of the villages and towns of medieval Europe.

The center of the Christian religion remained salvation through Christ. Adam and Eve had sinned by defying God's commandment in the Garden of Eden, and all their descendants had inherited this primal sinfulness and its awful punishment—liability to eternal damnation. But Christ, by taking the sins of the human race upon his shoulders and suffering for all humanity on the cross, had made salvation possible for those who would follow him. Sinners still went to hell, but those who lived Christian lives and died in a state of grace, at peace with God, would find bliss in paradise. At the end of the world, often imagined as near at hand, Christ would descend to earth a second time and pass a final judgment on all the living and the dead.

Christ's mother, Mary, and a multitude of saints also loomed large in the medieval mind. The saints were the great martyrs, preachers, and spiritual leaders of the past, from Peter and Paul in Gospel times to Francis of Assisi in their own days. Patrons of every Christian people, every region, craft, and condition of men, the saints were omnipresent. Their relics, from the crown of thorns and the holy lance that had pierced Christ's side to the heads, hands, or bones of apostles and martyrs, were preserved in jeweled reliquaries and housed in churches. These saintly remnants had power to cure the sick and work miracles, and the roads of Christendom filled with pilgrims every spring, traveling to their shrines.

In the High Middle Ages, however, none could match the glory and power of the Virgin Mary. The Mother of Christ, the Queen of Heaven, Mary was the great intercessor, pleading at the throne of God for suffering sinners here below. Most of the great cathedrals were dedicated to her, and were therefore called *Notre Dame*, churches of Our Lady. Mary was more often represented in stone and paint and stained glass than Christ himself, and stories of her infinite mercy, her miracles, and her comforting of mortals were the most popular of all the miraculous tales in the age of faith.

The religious life for most Christians was centered around a series of moments of contact between the material and spiritual worlds in the rites of passage called the seven *sacraments*. The seven, formalized by Innocent III's Fourth Lateran Council in 1215, were baptism soon after birth, confirmation as a member of the church in adolescence, marriage for most young adults, ordination for priests, the Mass or communion service, confessions of sins and penance, and the last rites for the dying. At each of these important moments in a human life, hymns and priestly words and gestures, holy water, holy oil, or the consecrated wine and wafer inspired a sense of contact with the realm of the spirit.

The sacrament of baptism washed the soul of the child clean of the sin of Adam and Eve. Marriage forged an alliance between the families of bride and groom and was in fact "the preeminent method of bringing peace and reconciliation to the feuds of families and parties, the wars of princes, and the lawsuits of peasants."[5] Death brought whole villages together in an elaborate social ritual including the laying out of the body, public mourning, the funeral procession, burial in the churchyard, and a wake or funeral feast. Even sin and its forgiveness was not a personal matter only, but a social problem, threatening the whole community with God's anger and purged by public absolution of the sinner.

A reconstruction of the supreme sacrament of the Mass or communion service, as celebrated in a medieval church, gives a sense of this social dimension of medieval religion. "One should imagine a good deal of noise," one authority suggests, "people coming late, walking or shuffling about, some talking, the occasional argument." Only the "unusually devout" would be "praying in corners" while the priest chanted in Latin and consecrated the communion wafer and wine. "For the devout as for the average soul," however, "the elevation of the Host was a moment of transcendental experience" as the bell rang, all knelt, and the officiating priest raised the wafer "round and white in the priest's fingers"— God himself summoned down into the sacred bread.[6]

It is a vivid image of the West in the grip of a great world religion. In recent years, however, a serious scholarly challenge to this traditional view of the Middle Ages as an age of Christian faith has emerged. Study of Inquisition records and medieval sermons has unearthed a surprising amount of pre-Christian folklore and magical practice among medieval Europeans. These discoveries have led some scholars to postulate the existence of not one but two religious communities in the Middle Ages.

At the top, the historical revisionists suggest, there was a small Christian elite, literate, city-based, and clerical. Among the unlettered peasant masses, however, there flourished a "'folklore' culture best likened to that observed by anthropologists in Third World countries" today. This non-Christian majority faith, some feel, was based on "forms of primitive magic" that can be traced back to Indo-European folk beliefs older than Western civilization itself.[7] Seen in this perspective, what has been regarded as a period of near-universal Christian faith looks more like an age of priestly oppression of a popular culture based on pre-Christian spells and charms.

That pre-Christian folk beliefs survived in larger

numbers than was once suspected now seems indisputable. To suggest, however, that Christianity scarcely reached beyond a priestly elite seems to most medieval historians to be going too far in the other direction. It suggests replacing a questionable vision of a body of undiluted Christian faith with an equally unconvincing model of two religious communities in conflict over a thousand years of Western history. Empirically speaking, furthermore, evidence for the existence of popular Christian belief, particularly after 1000, seems too massive to be ignored.

For medieval people life was a hard physical struggle, each individual soul a battleground between angelic and demonic forces. To face the myriad material and spiritual problems of life, Christian faith seemed as essential to most medieval men and women as any physical tool or social structure of the age.

Gothic Architecture and Art

The most impressive expressions of this faith of medieval Christendom were the great *cathedral* churches of the High Middle Ages. The art of the Gothic Age found varied expression in its *cathedrals*, which incorporated not only brilliant architectural design but sculpture, stained glass, and other arts. Sometimes called "Bibles in stone," these churches used the arts to tell Bible stories and saints' lives and to communicate basic doctrines such as the sovereignty of God and the coming Last Judgment. They provided spiritually uplifting places for worship and impressive settings for colorful religious services.

The basic ground plan of the cathedral, a long nave crossed by a transept, represented the cross of the crucifixion; the soaring Gothic arches, like praying hands, pointed the way to heaven. "We understand a piece of wood or stone," declared a ninth-century Christian thinker, "only when we see God in it."[8] It seems very likely that many medieval people did in fact think they saw God in the stone, carved wood, and glowing glass of the great cathedrals.

Churches were built in astonishing numbers during the High Middle Ages. In France alone, eighty cathedrals and five hundred other large churches were constructed, along with many thousands of parish churches. The city of York in northern England had more than forty churches to serve a population of no more than ten thousand—one for every 250 people. Cathedrals were the largest buildings in the West since Roman times: the cathedral at

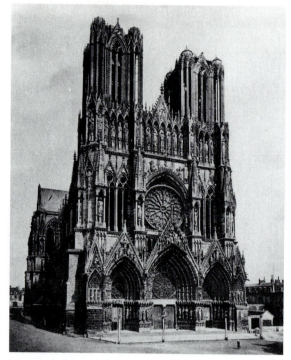

Reims cathedral, where France's medieval kings were crowned, towered above the city. Notice the twin towers, the three portals, and the round rose window over the central portal.

Amiens, with 200,000 feet of floor space, could hold the city's entire population. Built by master masons using the best artisans and skilled labor, these religious structures did not come cheap. They represented massive commitments of money, labor, and skill.

Such costly efforts could only be undertaken where money was available. Hence most cathedrals were raised along a north-south axis that ran from Bologna through Paris to London, with a parallel swath up the Rhine valley—the wealthiest and most commercially developed parts of medieval Europe. The money for a new church came from the prosperous diocese where it was to be erected, from gifts made in return for perpetual prayers for the soul of the giver, from offerings at shrines, and from the sale of *indulgences* of sins to pious Christians.[9] The motives of those who paid were diluted by other impulses too: the ambition of a bishop to outdo his neighbor, or the civic pride of a wealthy city. Nevertheless, it should be pointed out that the results were still churches, not imperial palaces or skyscrapers full of business offices. The sensibility of the Middle

Ages was a religious one, and its arts reflected this fact.

The style of building changed significantly during this period, from Romanesque during the tenth and eleventh centuries to Gothic in the twelfth and thirteenth. The Romanesque style, in which such monastic churches as that at Cluny were built, was characterized by massive walls and round arches. The weight of the roof, however, imposed strict limits on the size of such churches, and they tended to be lower and dimmer, with fewer windows (which would weaken the walls) than those that followed.

Gothic churches, by contrast, combined three features—the pointed arch, ribbed vaulting, and the flying buttress—to create larger and much loftier buildings. Ribbed vaulting, running up clustered piers and crisscrossing the ceiling, carried much of the weight of the roof, and graceful flying buttresses provided further bracing from the outside. The pointed arch lifted the roof still higher and gave the cathedral its sense of upward reaching. Since the ribs and buttressing supported so much of the weight, the walls could be pierced for large areas of stained glass. The typical Gothic church, finally, had three arched portals or doorways in the west front, flanked by two huge towers, a long high-arched hall or nave with arched aisles on either side, a spire over the altar where the nave intersected with the transept, and a choir at the east end.

Elaborate carved stone decoration covered all exterior surfaces, including prominent sculptural groups around the portals. These representations of Christ, Mary, and other biblical personages, of saints and kings, featured relatively realistic proportions and graceful draperies, but displayed more concern with idealized beauty than with individualized faces or figures. This is true even of tomb sculpture and statues of identifiable kings and queens. It was what these people stood for, or how the figure strengthened the verticality of a column or the curve of an arch, that mattered, not precisely what they looked like.

The most beautiful stained glass windows were assembled like mosaics of separate pieces of colored glass fitted between leadings to form a picture, which was then set in an iron frame to fit the window space. The stained glass itself was mixed with oxides to create brilliant ruby reds, emerald greens, or blues unreproducible today. The huge arched windows glowed with a radiance like precious stones when the sun shone through them, as they still do.

Any tour of Gothic cathedrals should include the first, Abbot Suger's abbey church of St. Denis located in what is now a grimy Paris suburb; Notre Dame de Paris on its island in the Seine; and perhaps Westminster Abbey in London. Connoisseurs will also urge you to visit Reims, where the kings of France were crowned; St. Louis's *Sainte Chapelle* in Paris, where the walls of colored glass shine like a giant jewel box; and the immense cathedral of Cologne. But all pilgrim roads lead at last to Chartres, where classic sculpture frames the portals and Our Lady of the Beautiful Glass looks down from the most gorgeous window in the world.

Some spiritually minded Christians, like St.

The interior of Reims cathedral reveals the powerful vertical thrust of the Gothic style. The rose window shows here too over the portal at the far end.

Bernard of Clairvaux (1090–1153), opposed spending so much on churches while there were still beggars in the streets. "The church is resplendent in her walls," Bernard said, "beggarly in her poor; she clothes her stones in gold, and leaves her sons naked."[10] It is an eternal argument, and it applies as much to the Acropolis and the exploration of space as to the cathedrals. It seems, however, that human beings experience more than one kind of hunger; in some sense, at least, Our Lady of the Beautiful Glass has fed many people.

The Twelfth-Century Renaissance

The lust for new lands and new products, the hunger for faith and beauty of the High Middle Ages was accompanied by a growing desire for knowledge. In part, this quest had a practical basis. The expanding bureaucracies of the revived church and the feudal monarchies required educated administrators. To meet this demand, new educational institutions evolved in Europe: the first universities.

In the early Middle Ages, most education was offered by monastery and cathedral schools. These schools taught Latin and a smattering of what were called "the seven liberal arts"—the *trivium* of grammar, rhetoric, and logic; and the *quadrivium,* arithmetic, geometry, astronomy, and music. Guilds provided practical training, and in Italy city schools founded by wealthy philanthropists emerged. It was these twelfth-century cathedral and municipal schools that evolved into the ancestors of modern universities.

The word *universitas* was first used for educational institutions around 1200, to describe organizations established by students in southern Europe, by teachers in the north. Students, gathering in growing numbers to hear famous lecturers, banded together to force the professors to cover the material and to treat them fairly on examinations, as well as to fight high room rents and food prices in university towns. Professors organized into four faculties based on their specialties—law, medicine, philosophy, and theology—in order to maintain control over curriculum and teaching degrees. Teaching was normally done in a hired hall, and students paid their teachers directly.

University teaching meant primarily lecturing on a set text. The professor both read the text aloud and commented on it while the students dutifully copied everything down. This made sense, for it was the only way poor students were ever going to get copies of expensive handwritten books. After several years

of study, students presented themselves to boards of professors who examined them orally for the bachelor's, master's, or doctor's degree in a given subject, much as guild masters tested the skill of journeymen who sought the status of master.

In this way, then, a flood of new knowledge began to pour into Europe in the twelfth and thirteenth centuries. During this *Twelfth-Century Renaissance,* as the movement is sometimes called, Europe began to recover a substantial portion of the wisdom of the ancient Greeks and Romans that had been preserved among Europe's more civilized neighbors for centuries. From Byzantium came Roman law, in the form of Justinian's Code, first taught at the University of Bologna, which went on to become the greatest law school in Europe. As we have already noted, church scholars were soon at work constructing canon law on the Roman model. From Muslim Spain came much of the philosophy and science of ancient Greece, including the voluminous works of Aristotle, for medieval students "the master of those who know." Aristotle quickly became the backbone of the philosophy course and profoundly influenced theology as well. Thus the University of Paris, Europe's most celebrated theology school, also specialized in Aristotelian philosophy.

Dozens of universities were founded in Europe in the High and later Middle Ages, including Paris, Montpelier, and Bordeaux in France; Oxford and Cambridge in England; Heidelberg, Cologne, and Prague in the Holy Roman Empire; Bologna, Padua, and Naples in Italy; and Seville and Coimbra (founded at Lisbon) in Spain and Portugal. Western scholars took advantage of the toleration of the Muslim regime in Spain to travel to Toledo to study Aristotle's philosophy, Ptolemy's astronomy, and Greek mathematics or medicine at the feet of Muslim professors. Students, usually young men in their twenties or thirties, also often traveled, going from one European university to another to hear celebrated lecturers in the fields in which they were interested.

University students, though they typically came from families of merchants or modestly endowed knights, were usually poor. They were often accused of intoxication and riotousness, charges supported to some degree by legal and university records and by surviving collections of student songs. Many were serious students, however, working for a bachelor's degree in order to find a position as a canon lawyer under Innocent III or as an administrator for Philip Augustus or Frederick II. Others, probing deeper into philosophy and theology, became the intellectual leaders of their age.

In this medieval university classroom, as in its many descendants of our own time, the teacher lectures and the students take notes. Unlike today's typical college student, however, the students here are all men and mostly mature individuals with careers already begun in the church.

Scholastic Thought

The most important of the *Scholastic* philosophers—men like Albertus Magnus ("Albert the Great") and Thomas Aquinas—are known as the "doctors" of the church. They were the most influential Christian thinkers between the fathers of the church in late Roman times and the Reformation preachers of the early modern period. Their intellectual milieu was the University of Paris, the Athens of the High Middle Ages. The air of the rude lecture halls in the "Latin Quarter" on the left bank of the Seine, where students sat in the straw to take notes and professors began to lecture at five in the morning, was electric with intellectual excitement. The source of this explosion of philosophical and theological enthusiasm was the coming together of two great streams of Western thought: the Judeo-Christian tradition and Greek philosophy, particularly the works of Aristotle. The pagan reasoning of the Greeks sometimes seemed to challenge Christian faith, but the Scholastics insisted that philosophy

could in fact illuminate faith, bringing new depth to Christian understanding. What Plato had done for the fathers of the church, Aristotle thus did for the doctors. He offered stimulating new ideas and methods of analysis that led to a new synthesis of Christian thought.

Valuable as these ancient ideas were, the tension between pagan and Christian was still there. By studying pagan thinkers, the Scholastics were working on the razor's edge of heresy, as conservatives like St. Bernard loudly reminded them. The danger was doubly great because Aristotle's works came from Spain with the commentaries of Muslim scholars like Averroës (1126–1198). The Averroist thesis that a proposition might be true in philosophy even if it was *not* true in revealed religion was as heretical in Islam as it proved to be in Christian thought. Nevertheless, the pioneer Aristotelian Albertus Magnus (c. 1200–1280) dared to assert that, while "in matters of faith and morals Augustine is to be believed rather than the philosophers," nevertheless, "if one speaks of medicine, I should rather believe [the Greeks] Galen or Hippocrates, or if of the nature of things, I believe

Aristotle . . . who is expert in the nature of things."[11] The brilliant French iconoclast Peter Abelard (c. 1079–1144) noticed that there were conflicts even between Christian authorities, such as that between the Scripture and the church fathers. In *Sic et Non,* he listed arguments pro and con for more than 150 important points of doctrine.

A new synthesis of Augustine and Aristotle, of faith and reason, emerged in the works of Thomas Aquinas (c. 1225–1274), later canonized for his religious insights. In his *Summa Theologica* and many other works, Aquinas sought to provide a summation, in Christian terms, not only of Christian thought but of all knowledge. To accomplish this feat, he and others made use of what became known as the Scholastic method of analysis. Based on Aristotelian logic, this approach proceeded through precise definition of terms, clear distinction between parts of a problem, consideration of authoritative views on each side of the issue, and the use of rigorous formal logic to reach what seemed to the *Scholastics* to be irrefutable conclusions. In constructing his magisterial *summa,* Aquinas admitted there were some truths that were accessible only to faith. Thus the nature of the Trinity, the Three—Father, Son, and Holy Ghost—who are yet One God, must remain forever a mystery. But there were other areas of understanding, including the powers of God and the natural world, that could and should be understood by reason. The resulting attempt to summarize all knowledge has earned Aquinas the title of "the Angelic Doctor" in the calendar of saints.

Scholastic philosophy acquired in later centuries an undeserved reputation for nit-picking and logic-chopping, for pursuing such pedantic and pointless inquiries as "how many angels could dance on the head of a pin." Some of the problems these medieval thinkers probed, however, were so profound that they remain unresolved to this day. The *problem of universals,* for instance, raised the issue of whether broad abstract categories possess independent reality, or whether only individual things exist. Is there such a thing as "humanity," or are there really only millions of individual human beings? Is "courage" a reality, or is it just an abstraction based on observation of a large number of individual courageous acts? One school, the *realists,* said that so-called abstractions are spiritual realities, like Plato's eternal Ideas. Others, the *nominalists,* declared that such general concepts are only names, words, a breath of air. The nominalist view, however, came too close to questioning the reality of the spiritual world to be a com-

fortable one for many thinkers in the High Middle Ages.

And such disputes could matter. Aristotle, for example, helped Christian thinkers explain the most important of all the sacraments, the communion service. The wafer and the wine look and taste no different after the priest consecrates them than before: in what sense, then, have they been transformed into the body and blood of Christ? The answer, in Aristotelian terms, was that the *essential* qualities, or spiritual substance, of these things have been replaced by the spiritual substance of Christ; but their *accidental* material qualities remain unchanged. Leading Christian thinkers continued to debate this issue at least through the Reformation, but Aristotle seemed to some of the best medieval minds to have pointed the way to a solution.

There were those who said with Anselm (c. 1033–1109), archbishop of Canterbury, "I believe in order that I may understand." And there were others, like Abelard, drunk on Aristotle's logic, who passionately declared, "I understand in order that I may believe." But whether they put faith or reason first, the Scholastics produced an intellectual synthesis of the two that satisfied the finest minds of the age.

Chivalric Epics and Troubadour Poetry

Most serious writing in the High Middle Ages was in Latin, the international language of the church and of culture generally. The language of Augustine and Aquinas was, however, incomprehensible to most Europeans, who spoke the "vernacular" languages, early versions of English, French, German, Italian, Spanish, and the other tongues of modern Europe. For these people, ranging in social class from nobles to peasants, an impressive literary tradition after 1300 produced such masters as Chaucer and Dante. Even during the High Middle Ages, however, early vernacular writers developed literary genres with a wide popular appeal—and produced an occasional masterwork.

As popular literature, these genres spoke to the interests of a variety of medieval audiences. The tales and fables called *fabliaux* poked often bawdy fun at such leaders of society as rich merchants and fat monks. Miracle and morality plays, put on in the church, communicated simple Bible stories or the lives of saints to mass audiences. A ballad tradition celebrated such folk heroes as Robin Hood. The most highly developed literary forms, however, were the feudal epics called *chansons de geste* ("songs of deeds"), the courtly love lyrics originally composed by troubadours, minstrels, and *minnesingers,* and the more elaborate romances that followed.

The songs of knightly deeds were intended for audiences of old-fashioned fighting barons, whose literary interests did not go much beyond heroic bloodshed. Epic cycles evolved around famous knights like Charlemagne's *paladins,* the French equivalents of King Arthur's knights of the round table, with unscrupulous Saracens (Muslims) playing the villains. The virtues celebrated were those of feudal chivalry—courage and skill, honor and loyalty. Thus the most famous of the chivalric epics, the *Song of Roland,* narrates the heroic death of the French paladin Roland, who is ambushed while leading the rear guard of Charlemagne's army returning through the Pyrenees after a campaign against the Muslims in Spain. In high chivalric style, Roland refuses to use his great horn to call for help until his troops have been wiped out and he himself is mortally wounded. But the twelfth-century soldier's view of combat as a matter of personal honor is vividly expressed by the hero's words, addressed to his sword as he raises it for the last time:

> Ah! Durendel, how beautiful you are, how clear,
>   how white! How you flame against the
>   sun! . . .
> Ah, Durendel, how beautiful and holy you are!
>   Your golden hilt is full of relics. . . .
> May you never fall into the hands of a coward![12]

The love poetry of the troubadours, composed originally in the Provençal language of southern France, was further developed by northern writers in French. Both the forms and sentiments of these lyrics may derive from the Arab love songs of Moorish (Muslim) Spain. In the medieval context, however, they became associated with the cult of courtly love and with the whole idea of romantic love as it evolved in Western culture.

To the ancients, sexual love tended to mean bawdy jokes or erotic madness, like the passion that drove Dido to commit suicide for love of Aeneas. To most medieval Christians, sexual passion was a sin: the only proper reason for intercourse was procreation. The passionate love the troubadours sang about was therefore illicit and frequently unhappy, for the woman was usually married and in any case rejected the lover's suit pitilessly. But it was a love, heavy with sensuality and sadness, that particularly moved the hearts of the gay, warmly human society of France's sunny south.

In the hands of a skilled poet like Chrétien de Troyes (fl. 1170), the troubadour spirit could transform the old fighting epic. Chrétien's poetic narratives based on the Celtic legends of King Arthur and his round table of knightly heroes are romantic tales of chivalry in which love may play as important a part as combat. Such central Arthurian themes as the great Sir Lancelot's tragic passion for Arthur's queen, Guinivere, and the mystic quest for the Holy Grail—Christ's cup at the Last Supper—go back to this medieval French poet. And the lays of the twelfth-century poet Marie de France mingled the realities of court life with chivalric legend in a way that a romantic age found particularly intriguing. In poetic tales like *The Two Lovers,* Marie depicted love as a powerful psychological force driving men and women to joy, despair, and even crime.

Medieval Jewish Culture

Outside the Christian community entirely, finally, Europe's most important minority produced its own vibrant intellectual life during this period. Despite increasing persecution, Jewish medieval culture bloomed in the Christian West. Learned rabbis studied the *Torah,* a body of holy wisdom centered on the first five books of the Hebrew Bible (the Christian Old Testament), which they saw as the foundation of all Judaic thought. Jewish thinkers also immersed themselves in the *Talmud,* a massive body of rabbinical writings based on close reading of the Torah. And like both Muslim and Christian scholars, some Jewish students mined the thought of Plato and Aristotle for philosophical insights that might illuminate their own faith. Academies for Judaic studies were established in Italy, Germany, and Spain. Other Jewish intellectuals and artists produced history, philosophy, poetry, and some baffling mystical insights.

Medieval Jewish culture north of the Mediterranean flourished most brilliantly outside Christendom, in Muslim Spain. The *Sephardic Jews* of Spanish Andalucia, led by a "courtier class" of Jewish administrators in the service of the Muslim rulers, generated a remarkable outpouring of scholarship and literature. The freewheeling intellectual life engendered by this cross-fertilization of cultures produced a range of outlooks among sophisticated Jews, from secular rationalism to profound religious devotion. In the twelfth century, however, waves of Muslim fanaticism destroyed this island of civilized living, converting Jews by force or driving them into exile, as a similar surge of religious hysteria was doing in Christian Europe at the same time.

One who fled from Spain in the later twelfth century was the most honored of all medieval Jewish thinkers, Moses Maimonides (1130–1204). A brilliant scholar and religious philosopher, Maimonides wandered across North Africa and the Near East before settling in Cairo. There he wrote a series of books that spread among Jews all around the Mediterranean and earned him a reputation as a controversial sage. After making contributions to the study of logic, astronomy, ethics, the Talmud, and the Torah and composing an unrivaled multivolume commentary on Jewish Law, Maimonides wrote his most controversial work, the *Guide of the Perplexed*. Drawing on biblical and rabbinical ideas, the *Guide* explored a wide range of intellectual concerns, from the relative value of faith and reason to prophecy, divine providence, and the existence of God. Maimonides's daring ideas outraged some rabbis in his own time but have earned him an unrivaled place among Jewish thinkers ever since.

An Expanding Society

Human energy, once unleashed, is not easily focused or kept within bounds. It is not surprising, then, that the economically booming, culturally dynamic society of twelfth-century Europe, gripped by a great religious resurgence, should turn aggressive eyes toward the rest of the world. The result was a burst of territorial expansion that climaxed in the famous Christian holy wars called the Crusades. The High Middle Ages thus saw Europe's most vigorous wave of foreign conquests between the Roman Empire in ancient times and the beginnings of modern Western imperial expansion in 1492.

The Medieval Expansion of Europe

A sense of movement, hustle, and drive pulses through the history of the eleventh, twelfth, and thirteenth centuries. We have seen it in the building of cities and the emergence of the feudal monarchies. It is evident in the revival of the medieval church and in the immense enlargement of the reach and power of the papacy.

Other forms of expansive energy have also been noted along the way in these last two chapters. Population, for example, almost certainly expanded substantially. Statistics are extremely spotty, but wherever available, they show patterns of growth. People were living a bit longer; total populations, rural and urban, were increasing. Overall production figures also expanded. The reclamation of land and the birth of urban craft guilds produced more crops and more things to serve the needs of more people.

But Europe was part of a larger world. To the north was only ice, to the west the Atlantic, one of the stormiest oceans in the world, great gray billows that only a mad Viking would challenge. But east and south, in Asia and Africa, there lay new worlds to conquer.

In the early Middle Ages, Europe had been feeble and backward by comparison with its glittering neighbors, the Byzantine Empire and the far-spreading world of Islam. Through the first half of the medieval period, the Byzantines had provided a protective bulwark for Western Christendom and a stimulus for the gradual revival of trade. The Muslims of Asia and North Africa had been a looming threat, battering at the gates of Constantinople, hovering behind the Pyrenees—yet at the same time stimulating the revival of twelfth-century culture in the West.

Europe, in short, had been in somewhat the position of an underdeveloped nation today, fearing its more powerful neighbors yet drawing on the economic and cultural achievements of more technically advanced peoples. In the twelfth century, however, this relationship between the West and the near ends of Asia and Africa began to change.

In the later Middle Ages, western Europeans pushed south, reconquering Sicily and most of Spain from the Muslims. European soldiers and settlers moved east to colonize the edges of the east European plain with German knights and peasants. Above all, they launched the great Crusades into the Near East and North Africa, temporarily conquering Constantinople, occupying Palestine, and repeatedly invading other Muslim kingdoms. For the first time since Roman days, the larger world had reason to fear the peoples of the West.

The *Reconquista* and the *Drang nach Osten*

We are not dealing here merely with the ambitions of individual monarchs or even of dynasties, but with movements that took centuries and involved whole societies. Thus the Spanish reconquest of the Iberian peninsula, known as the *Reconquista,* began as early as the tenth century and did not end until the fifteenth. The German penetration of Slavic eastern Europe, called the *Drang nach Osten,* or "drive toward the East," also began in the tenth century and is sometimes seen as continuing even into Hitler's invasion of Russia in the Second World War. Each of these movements, however, involved a major surge during the High Middle Ages.

Germany's *Drang nach Osten* began in the reign of Otto the Great, the founder of the Holy Roman Empire. In 955 Otto had definitively defeated the marauding Magyars of Hungary at the Battle of Lechfeld. To strengthen the frontier against renewed incursions, he established fortified colonies and marches, or military border lands, running from the western Baltic in the north down to the head of the Adriatic. He then supported church efforts to move into the area to convert the pagan Slavic population to Christianity. A degree of economic integration also resulted, since both the German military and the monastic establishments made use of Slavic labor, while German cities grew up near the Baltic, serving as bases for further German expansion.

For the next three centuries, this broad eastward push continued. As was true in Otto's time, a variety of forces contributed. As the agricultural expansion of the High Middle Ages got under way, some German lords and peasants, seeking new lands to develop, moved into the territories beyond the Elbe. In the twelfth century, Frederick Barbarossa's great rival, Henry the Lion, duke of Saxony, moved with many of his followers into the eastern frontier area and continued the process of Germanization. In the thirteenth century, Frederick II helped establish the Teutonic Knights, a chivalric order based in the region known in modern times as Prussia, that very soon became more interested in conquering land than in spreading the faith. Generation after generation, the Germans thus pushed east along the shore of the Baltic and down the Danube, until by the end of the thirteenth century the border wound from the mouth of the Vistula in the north down to the neighborhood of modern Trieste on the Adriatic.

Whether the invaders were knights or monks, farmers or traders, this slow expansion had a cruel effect on those whose lands were colonized. The Slavs resisted the intruders and rebelled against the occupiers. A first hint that the Westerners might meet their equal in these eastern lands came when a Russian prince, Alexander Nevsky (c. 1220–1263), grand duke of Novgorod, defeated the German knights on the ice of Lake Peipus in 1242, temporarily stalling the German drive. In the next century, however, the Hanseatic League of German trading cities formed on the Baltic, and Prussia, the core of modern Germany, emerged there in early modern times.

The Western drive into the south took the form of military invasion of the peninsulas and islands of the western half of the Mediterranean, a region occupied in earlier centuries by Arab and Berber conquerors. Again, a variety of elements of European society participated in the southern push and exploited the conquered lands in different ways.

Restless land-hungry Norman knights first invaded Sicily in the later eleventh century, five years before the Norman conquest of England, thirty-five years before the First Crusade. It took the Normans decades to conquer the large triangular island off the toe of the Italian boot, then dominated by Muslims and Byzantines. In the early twelfth century, however, the Normans added the southern half of Italy itself to their new domain. As they did in England, the Norman conquerors combined imported feudalism with existing governmental institutions. In this case, they used the Muslim system of acquiring government revenues to create a most efficient feudal monarchy, the Kingdom of Sicily.

Further to the west, meanwhile, naval assaults launched from the Italian trading cities of Genoa and Pisa had seized other Mediterranean islands from the Arabs, including the large island of Sardinia between Italy and Spain. It was in Spain itself, however, that the European southern push centered.

In a sense the Reconquista *was* the history of medieval Spain. Muslim invaders from North Africa drove into Visigothic Spain in 711, and the last of them were not expelled from Spanish soil until 1492, the year Columbus sailed. Most of the area of modern Spain and Portugal, however, was reconquered during the thirteenth century.

The liberators were primarily the hard-bitten Spanish kings who had been hurled back into the Pyrenees but never entirely overcome by the Muslim invaders. These "warrior lords" formed a strong alliance with the church, fighting their war of reconquest as a holy war against the Moors. In the course of this centuries-long struggle, furthermore, powerful and independent groups of Spanish knights grew up, fierce fighters dedicated to "honor and faith," to fighting the enemies of Christ and liberating Spanish land. In addition, the petty Spanish kings offered land to other Europeans who came to join the struggle south of the Pyrenees.

By 1250, when Cadiz was conquered, the Moors were penned into a southern strip of land running from the mountains around Granada down to Gibraltar, an area they occupied for the next three centuries. On the liberated land, three major Christian kingdoms emerged: Castile, Aragon, and Portugal. The victors, however, were unable to impose the sort of unity the Normans had developed in southern Italy. They faced powerful impediments to centralized government in the independence of the Spanish knights and the Spanish church. The allies who had come for land free of feudal obligations also resisted royal power. And the Spanish kings' own policy of offering self-government to Jews and Muslims in return for their surrender undercut monarchical authority. As a result, the rulers of the Iberian kingdoms, like the kings of England, began to consult with representatives of their subjects. Thus the regional *cortes*, the rough equivalent of an early English parliament, became a feature of government in this zone of European expansion.

The Crusades

The most important manifestation of the medieval expansion of Christendom, however, was the crusading movement that began at the end of the eleventh century and lasted through the thirteenth. Indeed the Christian world had never seen a movement quite like it.

"A grave report has come from the lands around Jerusalem and from the city of Constantinople," Pope Urban told the huge crowd, "that a foreign race, a race absolutely alien to God . . . has invaded the land of those Christians, has reduced the people with sword, rapine, and flame . . . and has . . . razed the churches to the ground. . . . On whom, therefore, does the task of avenging this fall . . . if not on you, upon whom . . . God has bestowed outstanding glory in arms?"[13] So Robert of Reims recorded the Pope's words 900 years ago.

The pope had announced a public session for the last day of the Council of Clermont in 1095, and French clergy and laymen alike had gathered in such numbers that the cathedral could not hold them. The papal throne had therefore been set up on a

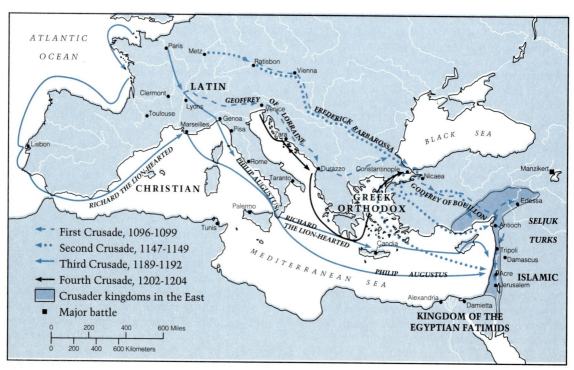

Map 10.3   The Crusades

platform in the fields outside the east gate of the city. The crowd was huge and pressing close.

"This land you inhabit," the pope went on, "is . . . overcrowded by your numbers; it . . . scarcely furnishes food for its farmers alone. This is why you . . . fight one another, make war and even kill one another. . . . Stop these hatreds among yourselves. . . . Take the road to the Holy Sepulcher, rescue that land from a dreadful race and rule over it yourselves." This, he explained, was quite legitimate, "for that land *that,* as Scripture says, *floweth with milk and honey* was given by God as a possession to the children of Israel."[14] And were not Christians the new children of Israel, God's chosen people?

"When Pope Urban had with urbane delivery said these things," the chronicler reports, "everyone, moved by the same feelings, shouted in unison, 'God wills it! God wills it!'"[15] A venerable French bishop knelt before the pontiff to beg permission to go, and hundreds more surged forward. These details may not be strictly accurate, even though the author was there, but this account does capture the spirit of the First Crusade.

Like many other momentous events in history, the crusading movement had many causes, and they were probably more complicated than Pope Urban said or understood. Going back centuries into the past, these causal factors were deeply rooted in the societies of the two contending peoples.

The *Crusades* are sometimes described as "armed pilgrimages." The tradition of Christian pilgrimage to Palestine went back at least to the fourth century, when a Frenchwoman named Egeria had made the journey to pray at Jerusalem and Bethlehem. The Muslim Arabs had conquered the area in the seventh century but had generally tolerated Christian visitors. Christians, after all, were "people of the Book" too, and Muhammad had recognized Jesus as a fellow prophet. In the eleventh century, however, more militant tendencies emerged in both the Christian and Islamic worlds.

We have seen the upsurge of religious feeling in the West and noted the role of religion in the campaigns against the pagan Slavs and the Muslims in Spain. In the Islamic world, the Seljuk Turks, steppe nomads and new converts, had just established their suzerainty over the Near East. In 1071 they had crushed the Byzantine army at Manzikert, and in 1095 the Byzantine emperor, Alexius I Comnenus (r. 1081–1118), had pleaded with Pope Urban to send help before Constantinople, the bastion of Christendom, should fall.

The idea of a holy war in the East also looked like a solution to a number of social problems that plagued Europe in the eleventh century. Overpopulation and resulting pressure on the food supply, as the pope indicated, militated in favor of seizing a land flowing with milk and honey. The endemic violence of the military aristocracy, particularly of younger sons who could not inherit estates, also needed an outlet—and what better one than fighting the Muslims instead of each other? As the Crusades continued, furthermore, clearly mercenary motives became increasingly evident. Italian trading cities provided transport, supplies, and naval support in exchange for commercial concessions in Muslim lands. Even crusading knights like the Templars, so called because their headquarters was set up next to the Temple of Solomon in Jerusalem, became very wealthy by exploiting their position as the protectors of the Holy Land.

Yet the *First Crusade* seems to have been driven to a great extent by the religious motives unleashed by Urban at Clermont and by more popular preachers elsewhere in Christendom. The pope offered full absolution of sins to any Crusader who gave his life for the cause: they would be holy martyrs ascending to the right hand of the Lord. The religious feeling that was raising the popes to unprecedented heights and covering the land with churches stirred many simple Christians to "take the Cross" (*Crux* in Latin) and become *Crus*aders. Donning shirts marked with the cross of Christ, they set out for the Holy Land. One modern authority suggests that some may have confused the Jerusalem in the Near East with the heavenly Jerusalem described in the Bible's Book of Revelation: "They believed that they were marching directly to the city of eternal bliss."[16]

In fact, two crusading hosts set out in 1095: the so-called People's Crusade, an ill-organized horde led by charismatic orators like Peter the Hermit (c. 1050–1115), and four contingents of heavily armed knights from Normandy, Flanders, southern France, and Sicily. The People's Crusade, composed of peasants and the very poor, some on the edge of starvation, turned into a riotous, thieving mob as it crossed the Balkans and the Byzantine Empire. The Byzantines, horrified at this invasion by what must have looked like the dregs of Western Christendom, expedited their passage across the Bosporus into Asia, where the Turks slaughtered them.

The real army, which came soon after, also had its problems with its Byzantine allies. "The Franks," as Near Easterners called them, expected transport and supplies from the Empire they had come to save;

they also hoped to carve out kingdoms for themselves in Muslim lands. The Byzantine emperor took advantage of this situation. In return for his cooperation, Emperor Alexius I required the Western knights to swear vassal homage to him for any lands they conquered. The Crusaders agreed, but grudgingly.

This Western army was not led by half-mad hermits, but by soldiers like Godfrey of Bouillon (c. 1060–1100) and his brother Baldwin (c. 1058–1118), Raymond of Toulouse (1042–1105) from the south of France, and Bohemond (c. 1050–1111) from Taranto in Italy. These were experienced fighting men, hungry for loot. They also caught the Muslims at a moment of division and relative weakness. The new Turkish hegemony was still disputed by the older Arab regime, and conflict between the rival Sunnite and Shiite sects flared. Despite hardships and some resistance, then, the Crusaders won victory after victory.

They defeated a Turkish army in Asia Minor and seized enough treasure to encourage them to proceed. The ancient city of Edessa in Syria surrendered without a fight, and the great port of Antioch was taken after a half-year siege. Finally, in the summer of 1099, the Crusaders captured Jerusalem. What happened thereafter is often cited as a vivid illustration of the savagery of holy wars. As the author of the standard three-volume history of the Crusades describes it, "The Crusaders, maddened by so great a victory after such suffering, rushed through the streets and into the houses and mosques killing all they met, men, women, and children alike. All that afternoon and all through the night the massacre continued."[17] One knight, going the following morning to visit the temple where Christ had walked, "had to pick his way through corpses and blood that reached up to his knees."[18] (For an eyewitness account of one such massacre, see box, "Crusaders Wade in the Blood of the Unbelievers"). Later Frankish rulers tried to work out ways of living with the Muslims and Jews—many of the latter had also been killed—in Jerusalem; but, as in the Byzantine Empire, the First Crusade had sown the seeds of future discord in the Holy Land.

The Crusader States

Nevertheless, the First Crusade had achieved its primary objective. The victorious Crusaders established a string of small feudal kingdoms along the eastern end of the Mediterranean. Over the next two centuries, there were more campaigns, including attacks on Egypt and the Maghreb as well as in the Near East. But there were never victories like those of the First Crusade, and by the thirteenth century the crusading ideal itself was seriously corrupted by an admixture of more worldly motives.

The *Crusader States* ruled by their Christian conquerors stretched from Syria in the north to the Sinai in the south. The Kingdom of Jerusalem, ruled by Baldwin and his heirs, was the largest, the others fiefs of the king of Jerusalem. The frequently hostile Byzantine emperor, however, still claimed suzerainty over them all. And all around them, from Gibraltar to the Ganges, stretched the enormous lands of the Muslims.

The Crusader States were thus essentially outposts of Christendom in the Near East and as such required constant garrisoning. To defend a 500-mile-long strip of land, much of it desert, the conquerors built isolated castles like the famous *Krak des Chevaliers* in Syria. But these fortifications were too widely scattered to be an effective line of defense. The most powerful fighting forces in the Christian enclave were the knightly crusading orders including the Templars and the Teutonic Knights. The Templars, the best known, were an order of soldiers sworn to monkish vows and dedicated to defense of the routes into Jerusalem and of the pilgrims. Within a few generations, however, the Templars became better known as financial agents in the Near East and landholders in Europe.

The knights and the states also tended to squabble among themselves in the time-honored way of feudal barons, sometimes even forming alliances with neighboring Muslim rulers to support their claims against each other. Most important, perhaps, the Franks always remained a small military elite ruling a conquered people. For unlike eastern Europe and Spain, the Near East never drew significant numbers of western European settlers.

It is not surprising, then, that once the Muslims achieved some degree of unity and developed strong leadership, the position of the Crusader States deteriorated rapidly. And later Western Crusades proved unable to shore up this crumbling position.

When in the 1140s the County of Edessa in Syria fell to the Muslims, St. Bernard of Clairvaux preached the Second Crusade, and the king of France and the Holy Roman emperor responded. Superior force on the Muslim side and division among the Christians, however, led to an ignominious failure.

In the 1180s, the great Muslim leader Salah ad-Din (1138–1193), known to the West as Saladin, decisively turned the tide. Uniting Egypt, Mesopotamia, and Syria, he closed in on the Crusader States and overran the Kingdom of Jerusalem itself in 1187. This time the three most powerful rulers in the West responded: the German emperor Frederick Barbarossa and the French and English kings Philip Augustus and Richard the Lion-Hearted all joined the *Third Crusade*. But Barbarossa drowned in Asia Minor; and Philip and Richard, archfoes at home, could not work together against the common enemy in the Near East. In the end they took the port of Acre but could not retake Jerusalem. Nevertheless, the chivalrous Saladin agreed to allow pilgrims access to their holy places once more.

The worst debacle of all occurred in 1204, when the *Fourth Crusade,* preached by Pope Innocent III, turned to attacking Christians instead of Muslims. The knights who set out for the Holy Land this time were first diverted by the Venetians, who offered to cancel the bill for transporting the Crusaders east if the new army would capture a rival trading city called Zara across the Adriatic. Having accomplished this, the Crusaders next agreed to help a pretender to the Byzantine throne, Alexius IV Angelus, to win his empire—a project the Venetians, alert to the possibility of a trade monopoly in Constantinople, eagerly supported. Alexius offered supplies and support for the Crusade, and the Western knights succeeded in occupying his capital for him. Alexius, however, proved unable to provide the promised aid, and was subsequently overthrown and killed by a rival (1204). The Crusaders thereupon sacked Constantinople and took over the Byzantine Empire themselves. The results of the Fourth Crusade thus included a sixty-year Latin Empire in Byzantium—the Byzantine emperors recaptured their capital in 1261—and an expanded Venetian commercial empire stretching from the Dalmatian coast to Crete and including a number of islands in the Adriatric and the Aegean seas. Innocent III excommunicated the Crusaders, who never did make contact with their Muslim foes.

The thirteenth century, finally, saw the crusading ideal lose all credibility in a series of "internal" Crusades, fought by Europeans against each other. A number of popes thus promised remission of sins for the Albigensian Crusade against the heretics in southern France in 1208, and then for wars against their political enemy, Frederick II, after 1220. Yet the faith of France's King Louis IX—St. Louis—was still strong: he led a Crusade to Egypt in the 1250s and one to Tunis in 1270, where he died. In Palestine, meanwhile, the Muslims were mopping up most of the remnants of the Crusader States. They recaptured Antioch in the 1260s, Tripoli in the 1280s, and

Acre in 1291, massacring tens of thousands of Christians in the process.

Balance Sheet

In the early years at least, the Crusades were a genuinely popular movement. Besides ambitious kings and land-hungry knights, many other Europeans "took the cross" as well. Peter the Hermit's ragtag horde came to a tragic end, but others followed. In 1212 the so-called Children's Crusade mobilized the poor and the young in a spontaneous campaign that got no further than the shores of the Mediterranean. There, when the waters failed to part allowing them to walk across to Palestine as promised by one of their boy prophets, the band broke up. There is evidence also that women Crusaders marched on the Holy Land. Thus the Arab chronicler Imad ad-Din testified (disapprovingly) that "among the Franks there were indeed women who rode into battle with cuirasses and helmets . . . and acted like brave men although they were but tender women, maintaining that all this was an act of piety."[19]

By the end of the thirteenth century, however, the crusading impulse was waning, and the dynamic expansionism of the High Middle Ages had largely run its course. What had come of it?

Some historians feel that the costs, particularly in the case of the Crusades, outweighed any gains. The Crusades were immensely expensive in lives and money, and they led to no lasting territorial gain. The religious element in all these expansionist wars turned the pious enthusiasm of the twelfth and thirteenth centuries into bigotry and savage persecution. German conquerors treated the Slavs as brutally as Spanish and Norman knights treated Muslims. The Spanish Inquisition, forged in the effort to pacify conquered Muslims and Jews, was the most feared persecutorial body in Europe in later centuries. Even in the Middle Ages, Crusaders sometimes began their holy wars with pogroms against Jewish communities in Europe, while the Albigensian Crusade bathed the soil of southern France in blood.

Nevertheless, there were some gains for the West from this high medieval burst of expansion. In eastern Europe, the size of the Holy Roman Empire doubled between the tenth and thirteenth centuries. Land brought under cultivation by more efficient western European agricultural methods produced crops more abundantly. By 1300, the prosperous towns of the Hanseatic League were emerging on the Baltic, and the Teutonic Knights, returned from the Holy Land, were laying the foundations for what became modern Prussia.

Most of the Iberian peninsula had been reoccupied by Christian Europeans by the end of the thirteenth century. Centralized monarchies were beginning to take shape there, though the two modern states of Spain and Portugal did not emerge as strong nations until the fifteenth century. Like Prussia, both Spain and Portugal played important parts in modern Western history—particularly in the new burst of expansionism that began in 1492.

In the Near East, as we have seen, the Crusades had failed to establish a lasting Western presence. Yet some material benefits did accrue to Europe. Trade, already revived by the Byzantine connection, was further stimulated by the establishment of Christian distribution centers in the Crusader States. Italian cities such as Venice and Genoa particularly profited, as did Marseilles, from which a heavy pilgrim traffic sailed annually for the Holy Land. In their efforts to finance Crusades and commerce with Palestine, furthermore, Western merchants developed their skills in handling large amounts of money over long distances through such devices as bills of exchange and letters of credit. To pay for royal Crusades, Western governments also ventured into the complicated business of levying direct taxes—and their peoples began the painful process of learning to accept the occasional necessity for such taxes. In general, Westerners gained some experience with organizing large-scale overseas ventures—experience that became useful three centuries later when the West began to expand once more, this time on a global scale.

A Topical Summary

Society: The High Middle Ages saw increased sophistication in all three "estates" of medieval society. In the church, papal power reached its zenith under Gregory VII and Innocent III. Both new mendicant orders, like the Franciscans and the Dominicans, and new heretical movements, such as the Albigensians, revealed the depth of religious renewal. The feudal ruling class developed the chivalric code and the cult of courtly love. The pace of both peasant and city life picked up appreciably under the stimulus of economic growth.

Culture: The eleventh, twelfth, and thirteenth centuries also produced a cultural flowering that was deeply imbued with the religious culture of the age but reflected other social and intellectual influences as well. Gothic art and architecture dominated the huge cathedrals that rose across western Europe during this period. Scholastic thought evolved a new synthesis of faith and reason. And popular literature

created bawdy tales, heroic songs of knightly deeds, and tender love poetry.

The Expanding West: For the first time since the days of the Roman Empire, Western civilization began to expand again in the High Middle Ages. The Spanish *reconquista* and the German drive eastward into Slavic lands reinforced the major European outreach of the period—the Crusades. And though the Crusader States in Palestine survived less than a century, they prepared the way for the great imperial expansion of the West in modern times.

Some Key Terms

Albigensian 285
canon law 290
cathedral 302
chanson de geste 307
Cistercians 286
code of chivalry 295
courtly love 295
Crusader state 313
Crusades 311
Dominicans 288
Drang nach Osten 309

excommunication 290
First Crusade 311
Fourth Crusade 313
Fourth Lateran Council
  291
Franciscans 287
Gothic style 300
Gregorian reform 288
nepotism 283
problem of universals 306
quadrivium 304

Reconquista 309
sacraments 301
Scholastics 306
Sephardic Jews 307
simony 283
stigmata 287
Third Crusade 313
trivium 304
Twelth Century Renaissance 304
Waldensians 285

Notes

1. Richard Southern, *The Making of the Middle Ages* (London: Hutchinson, 1967), 139.
2. "Sermon on Consecration of a Pope," in *The Crisis of Church and State, 1050–1300,* trans. Brian Tierney (Englewood Cliffs, N.J.: Prentice Hall, 1964), 132.
3. William Langland, *The Vision of William Concerning Piers the Plowman,* ed. Walter W. Skeat (London: Oxford University Press, 1924), line 17.
4. Langland, lines 20–21.
5. John Bossy, *Christianity in the West, 1400–1700* (New York: Oxford University Press, 1985), 20.
6. Ibid., 67–68.
7. John van Engen, "The Christian Middle Ages as a Historiographical Problem," *American Historical Review,* 91 (1986), 519.
8. John Scotus Erigena, in Andrew Martindale, *Gothic Art* (London: Thames and Hudson, 1986), 9.
9. The sale of indulgences, offering the remission of punishment for sins in return for money contributions, was developed to help finance the Crusades. It was strongly protested at the time of the Reformation.
10. In G. G. Coulton, *The Fate of Medieval Art in the Renaissance and Reformation* (New York: Harper and Brothers, 1958), Appendix 26, vi.
11. In *New Catholic Encyclopedia,* vol. 12 (New York: McGraw-Hill, 1967), 1156.
12. *Chanson de Roland,* vol. 1, ed. Joseph Bédier (Paris: Édition d'Art, n.d.), 175–179.
13. Robert de Reims, *Historia Iherosolimitana,* in Louise and Jonathan Riley-Smith, *The Crusades: Idea and Reality, 1095–1274* (London: Edward Arnold, 1981), 44.
14. Ibid.
15. Ibid.
16. Hans Mayer, *The Crusades,* trans. John Gillingham (London: Oxford University Press, 1972), 12.
17. Steven Runciman, *History of the Crusades,* vol. 1 (Cambridge: Cambridge University Press, 1951), 286–287.
18. Ibid.
19. *History of the Conquest of Jerusalem,* in Francesco Gabrielli, *Arab Historians of the Crusades* (London: Routledge and Kegan Paul, 1984), 207.

Reading List

BENSON, R., et al., eds. *Renaissance and Renewal in the Twelfth Century.* Cambridge, Mass.: Harvard University Press, 1977. Authoritative essays on many aspects of the Twelfth Century Renaissance. See also the pioneering work of C. H. HASKINS, *The Renaissance of the Twelfth Century* (Cambridge, Mass.: Harvard University Press, 1977).

BROOKE, R. C. *Popular Religion in the Middle Ages: Western Europe 1000–1300.* London: Thames and Hudson, 1984. Introduction to a burgeoning field of research.

DUBY, G. *The Age of the Cathedrals: Art and Society, 980–1420.* Translated by E. Levieux and B. Thompson. Chicago: University of Chicago Press, 1981. Stimulating impressionistic study of the cathedrals as products of a shift in medieval mentality.

ERLER, M., AND M. KOWALESKI, eds. *Women and Power in the Middle Ages.* Athens: University of Georgia Press, 1988. Essays on the exercise of power by medieval women of different social classes. See also S. M. STUARD, ed., *Women in Medieval Society* (Philadelphia: University of Pennsylvania Press, 1976), on the many roles women played in medieval society.

HANAWALT, B. *The Ties that Bound Peasant Families in Medieval England.* New York: Oxford University Press, 1986. Uses official records and literary sources to recreate daily lives in convincing detail. See also C. N. L. BROOKE, *The Medieval Idea of Marriage* (Oxford: Oxford University Press, 1989), a synthesis of legal, social, and religious ideas.

HASKINS, C. H. *The Rise of the Universities.* Ithaca, N.Y.: Cornell University Press, 1957. Classic account of the emergence of the first universities in the Western world.

HERLIHY, D. *Medieval Households.* Cambridge, Mass.: Harvard University Press, 1985. Family structure and social class in a world of growing populations and a limited food supply.

KEAN, M. *Chivalry.* New Haven: Yale University Press, 1984. Positive evaluation of the cult of chivalry. See also C. S. JAEGER, *The Origins of Courtliness: Civilizing Trends and the Formation of Courtly Ideals, 939–1210* (Philadelphia: University of Pennsylvania Press, 1983), which sees chivalry as restraining knightly proclivities toward violence.

KEDAR, B. Z. *Crusade and Mission: European Approaches Toward the Muslims.* Princeton: Princeton University Press, 1984. Valuable synthesis of views on relations between the Western and Muslim worlds in the Middle Ages.

LE GOFF, J., ed. *The Medieval World.* Translated by L. G. Cochrane. London: Collins and Brown, 1990. Scholarly essays on medieval social ideas.

MATHEW, D. *The Medieval European Community.* New York: St. Martin's Press, 1977. Sees an emerging community conducive to productivity and progress, led by religious reformers, artisans, entrepreneurs, and other self-confident, creative people.

PELIKAN, J. *The Christian Tradition: A History of the Development of Doctrine.* 5 vols. Chicago: University of Chicago Press, 1971–1983. Volume 3 of this standard survey deals with medieval religious thought from 300 to 1300.

PHILLIPS, J. R. S. *The Medieval Expansion of Europe.* Oxford: Oxford University Press, 1988. Useful survey of the activities of crusaders, merchants, missionaries, and other forerunners of later Western imperial expansion.

PRAWER, J. *The Latin Kingdom of Jerusalem: European Colonialism in the Middle Ages.* London: Weidenfeld and Nicolson, 1972. Sees the most developed crusader state as the model for later Western colonies overseas.

REYNOLDS, S. *Kingdoms and Communities in Western Europe, 900–1300* (New York: Oxford University Press, 1984). Focuses on the traditional sense of community in village, guild, and parish and the medieval consensus on good government and royal power.

RUNCIMAN, S. *A History of the Crusades.* 3 vols. New York: Harper & Row, 1967. Old standard, lengthy but extremely readable narrative history. See also D. E. QUELLER's scholarly account of *The Fourth Crusade: The Conquest of Constantinople, 1201–1204* (Philadelphia: University of Pennsylvania Press, 1977).

STRAW, C. *Gregory the Great: Perfection in Imperfection.* Berkeley: University of California Press, 1988. Sophisticated exploration of Gregory's contributions to Christian thought and sensibility.

ULLMANN, W. *The Growth of Papal Government in the Middle Ages.* London: Methuen, 1955. Institutional development and growing power of the papacy. On the complicated struggle between Rome and secular rulers, see U.-R. BLUMENTHAL, *The Investiture Controversy: Church and Monarchy from the Ninth to the Twelfth Century* (Philadelphia: University of Pennsylvania Press, 1988).

WARNER, M. *Alone of All Her Sex: The Myth and Cult of the Virgin Mary.* New York: Knopf, 1976. Well-written and provocative interpretation of the medieval cult of the Virgin.

WEINSTEIN, D., AND R. M. BELL. *Saints and Society: The Two Worlds of Western Christendom, 100–1700.* Chicago: University of Chicago Press, 1982. Computer-based study of the saintly qualities admired by medieval Europeans.

Nicholas Gerhaert. *Self Portrait*. Notre Dame, Strasbourg, France

Day of wrath and doom impending
Heaven and earth in ashes ending . . .

Dies Irae ("Day of Wrath"), a thirteenth-century hymn commonly sung in services for the dead, powerfully expressed the sense of overwhelming disaster in which the Middle Ages ended. For in the fourteenth and the earlier fifteenth centuries, it seemed very much as if God's wrath was indeed pouring down upon Christendom, as if the Day of Judgment was at hand, the Four Horsemen of the Apocalypse thundering across the sky.

Even a brief catalog of the major disasters to be confronted in this chapter should give some sense of the precipitous decline that ended the second great cycle of civilization in Western history. Perhaps the best known catastrophes of the period between 1300 and 1453 were the plague called the Black Death, the Hundred Years' War between England and France, and the capture of Constantinople by the Turks. When we add tumult and schism in the Catholic church, a late-medieval economic decline, civil strife in the new cities and nations of the West, and a steep decline in European population, the Western preoccupation with death and judgment during these centuries is clearly understandable. If there was ever an age that looked like the end of the world, surely this was it.

And yet, as we see in Chapter 12, a new stage in the history of the Western world was coming into existence even as the Middle Ages sank into chaos. The great social and cultural revival known as the Renaissance was in fact beginning in Italy in the fourteenth and fifteenth centuries even while medieval institutions and cultural forms fell into disarray in the countries north of the Alps. There were even some signs of renewal in northern Europe during this period of collapse and decay. The south had the beginnings of Renaissance painting and poetry in Giotto and Petrarch; the north had Flemish painting and Geoffrey Chaucer to its credit. Nevertheless, it is the terror of God's wrath, the sense of doom impending that must concern us most as we see this second great phase of Western history coming to its end.

Famine, Pestilence, and Strife

In this first section, we explore some of the economic, social, and ecological elements in this complex of catastrophes. It is a complicated network of factors, including poverty and civil strife as well as climatic changes, epidemic disease, and population decline. When things started to come apart in the late Middle Ages, they came apart everywhere at once.

Famines and Plagues

In recent years historians have devoted a good deal of study to what we may call the ecological dimension of history. The relations of human beings to their natural environment and to other living things, from crops to disease germs, help to explain much of the human story. Certainly they help us to understand what went wrong in fourteenth-century Europe.

During the first half of this century, repeated waves of local famine and epidemic disease swept over various parts of Europe. We know something of the likely causes of each, of the relations between them, and of their impact on the even more terrible years to come.

Famine erupted at different times in different places, most devastatingly in northern Europe between 1315 and 1317 and further south around 1340. Hunger, of course, was not rare in medieval Europe, even during the High Middle Ages. In the spring, when the preceding year's crops were running out and winter wheat was not in yet, human beings and animals began to lose their natural reserves of fat. But these early fourteenth-century peri-

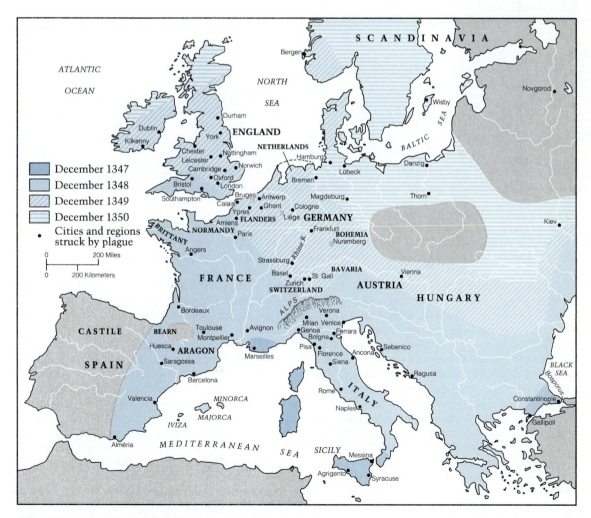

Map 11.1 Spread of the Black Death

	1200		1300	

POLITICAL, MILITARY, AND DIPLOMATIC EVENTS

r. 1206–1227 Genghis Khan
1220s–1240s Golden Horde invades Russia

r. 1300–1326 Othman
1302 *Unam Sanctam*

SOCIAL AND ECONOMIC DEVELOPMENTS

1305–1378 Avignon papacy
1315–1340 Famines

CULTURE: THE ARTS, PHILOSOPHY, SCIENCE AND RELIGION

c. 1260–1328 Meister Eckhart
1265–1321 Dante
1320–1384 Wycliffe

ods of starvation were much worse than normal. What statistical evidence there is suggests that some areas experienced population declines as high as 10 percent.

The immediate causes were local periods of bad weather, particularly storms that destroyed grain crops. The famines also seem to have coincided with the end of the high medieval expansion in the amount of land under cultivation and the cessation of land reclamation through clearing forest and scrub and draining swamps. In a sense, medieval people may have been the victims of their own success. The demographic growth of the High Middle Ages may simply have resulted in overpopulation relative to the land and agricultural methods available to feed the people. A few bad harvests could wreak much greater havoc in a swollen population than they might have in a smaller, more thinly spread one.

Closely related to the spread of local and regional starvation was the surge of epidemic disease. These epidemics included animal infections of various sorts, which seriously depleted the livestock in some places. This probably led to even more human suffering and death, not because it deprived humans of food—most medieval people ate very little meat—but because oxen and horses were needed for labor, sheep for the wool they produced. Without these animals, farmers and shepherds could not earn a livelihood.

For the human beings, typhoid fever was apparently epidemic in the early fourteenth century. Disease commonly follows famine, for undernourished populations are more vulnerable to infection. But the Middle Ages may again have been paying for its own earlier achievements. Epidemic diseases are much more common in large populations, especially in cities where people are packed close together and contagion can spread rapidly. The population growth and the growth of cities in the high medieval centuries may thus have prepared the way for increasing populations of germs and viruses. But a new killer was coming that would dwarf these disasters.

r. 1327–1377 Edward III
1337–1453 Hundred Years' War
1346 Crécy
1356 Poitiers

r. 1413–1422 Henry V
1413–1431 Joan of Arc
1415 Agincourt
1451–1481 Muhammad II
1453 Constantinople falls
1455–1485 Wars of the Roses

1348–1350 Black Death
1350–1400 Economic decline
1358 Jacquerie
1378 Ciompi Revolt
1378–1417 Great Schism
1381 Wat Tyler's revolt
1395–1456 Jacques Coeur
1400–1450 Economic stagnation

1340–1400 Chaucer
1364–c. 1431 Christine de Pisan
1369–1415 Hus
c. 1373–c. 1440 Kempe
1380–1471 Thomas à Kempis
1395–1441 Jan van Eyck
c. 1400–1464 Rogier van der Weyden
1413–1463 Villon

The Black Death

In the fourteenth century, a microscopic creature now called *Yersinia pestis* inhabited the digestive tract of the flea that lived in the fur of small rodents like the Asian black rat, native to the eastern end of Eurasia. One might think that medieval Europeans half a world away would have been safe from micro-infected rats native to the crowded cities of China. This bacillus, however, was about to undergo one of the great ecological odysseys of human history and to devastate medieval Europe. The Chinese were already dying in large numbers when the whole ecological complex began to move west.

Some of the fleas changed hosts, transferring to the clothes, packs, and persons of busy East Asian merchants who traveled the Silk Road from China to central Asia and the Middle East. Other fleas continued to inhabit the fur of rats who found new homes in the small wooden cargo vessels of those times, especially those carrying shipments of grain. In 1347 a grain ship from the Crimea in southern Russia carried rats, fleas, and bacilli over the last leg of their journey, across the Black Sea and the eastern Mediterranean to the port of Messina in Sicily. From there, thanks to the busy roads and sea lanes of Europe's commercial revolution, rats, fleas, and their microbial parasites spread to a whole new world of human habitations as densely populated as the cities of East Asia.

Everywhere the fleas once again shifted to human hosts, and when their insect jaws punctured human skin, the bacilli passed into the bodies of medieval people. The infection spread through the lymphatic system. Painful swellings, the *buboes* for which the *bubonic plague* was named, appeared at the throat, under the arms, in the groin. Soon, black patches or spots of blood appeared under the skin. In the variant known as *pneumonic plague*, the bacilli spread through the bloodstream to the lungs, causing pneumonia. The infected person was racked by terrible coughing and spat blood; sputum, sweat, and feces emitted a strong smell. Medieval people called it *atra mors*—"the dreadful death"—a phrase later mistranslated as "Black Death," the name it has been known by ever since (see box, "The Black Death").

In the Western world, pain, terror, pandemonium reigned. Where the plague escalated to the pneumonic strain, coughing spread the bacilli directly through the air. One flea bite thus rapidly infected a whole household, and the household in turn infected the narrow street outside. Friends who came to help, priests who administered the last rites, all carried the fleas or the bacilli away with them to their own households and to the next home they visited. Recognizing the pattern, people shunned the homes of the sick, leaving family after family, street after street to care for its own—and die. Cities were filled with fear and funeral corteges; mass graves were opened up for the dead.

Those who died in largest numbers were city dwellers and the poor, who lived most closely packed together, and the caring citizens who continued to bring them comfort. The wealthy and others who could afford to leave abandoned the cities and waited for the infection to pass. No one knew the cause of the plague, which was blamed on a variety of factors from "bad air" to the wrath of God punishing humankind for its sins. Equipped with very limited medical knowledge, city and royal governments were helpless. And the plague advanced inexorably northward across Europe. After decimating a few Italian coastal cities in 1347, it moved on to Italy, France, and Spain in 1348, to England and western Germany in 1349, and to Scandinavia and the Baltic in 1350. Naples, Rome, Florence, Marseilles, Paris, Barcelona, London, Vienna, Hamburg—the cities that had been reborn in the preceding three centuries were stricken one by one. Medieval statistics remain patchy and unreliable, but the most common estimate is that a third of the population of Europe died of the Black Death.

The epidemic waned after 1350, but it was not gone. The plague returned in the 1360s and the 1370s, and again around 1390. This was in fact the beginning of a pandemic of bubonic plague, which would recur again and again over the next three centuries. One of the most vivid documentary-fictional accounts of a city gripped by the contagion is Daniel Defoe's *Journal of the Plague Year*, written in the seventeenth century, more than three hundred years after the arrival of the pestilence. The impact was greatest during the late medieval period, however, when everything from economic life and social relations to culture and religion was affected by one of

MASTERING OUR WORLD
The Black Death

Giovanni Boccaccio (c. 1313–1375) set his famous collection of tales, *The Decameron* (c. 1350), in the time of the Black Death. His graphic description of the plague gives some sense of the horror it inspired in its victims. Note also what attempts medieval people—doctors, priests, civic authorities, and others—made to deal with the pestilence. Given their lack of understanding of the role of microorganisms in the spread of disease, do their efforts to defeat or escape from the plague sound sensible to you?

In Florence, despite all that human wisdom and forethought could devise to avert it, as the cleansing of the city from many impurities by officials appointed for the purpose, the refusal of entrance to all sick folk, and the adoption of many precautions for the preservation of health; despite also humble supplications addressed to God, and often repeated both in public procession and otherwise, by the devout; towards the beginning of the spring of the said year the doleful effects of the pestilence began to be horribly apparent by symptoms that showed as if miraculous.

. . . in men and women alike it first betrayed itself by the emergence of certain tumors in the groin or the armpits, some of which grew as large as a common apple, others as an egg, some more, some less, which the common folk called gavoccioli. From the two said parts of the body this deadly gavocciolo soon began to propagate and spread itself in all directions indifferently; after which the form of the malady began to change, black spots or livid making their appearance in many cases on the arm or the thigh or elsewhere, now few and large, now minute and numerous. And as the gavocciolo had been and still was an infallible token of approaching death, such also were these spots on whomsoever they showed themselves. Which maladies seemed to set entirely at naught both the art of the physician and the virtues of physic; indeed, whether it was that the disorder was of such a nature to defy such treatment, or that the physicians were at fault . . . and, being in ignorance of its source, failed to apply the proper remedies; in either case . . . almost all within three days from the appearance of the said symptoms, sooner or later, died. . . .

Source: Giovanni Boccaccio, *The Decameron*, vol. 1 (New York: Dutton, 1930), 5.

"The Triumph of Death," as this painting is called, was a common theme in the later Middle Ages. Here corpses laid out for burial force these aristocratic passers-by to confront the fact that the same fate awaits even the most fortunate.

the most terrible calamities ever to afflict the Western world.

The most obvious consequences of the loss of a third of the labor force were economic. Production declined drastically in many places. Laborers profited from the situation by demanding and often getting much better terms from employers and landlords, but the latter suffered commensurately. And with the cost of labor going up, prices went up too. The Black Death thus played a large part in the economic dislocations discussed in the next section.

Religion and the church, so central to medieval life, were also profoundly affected. A large proportion of the most devoted priests and nuns died caring for the sick in Italy, Germany, and elsewhere. Church affairs, it has been suggested, were thus too often left in the hands of survivors, more self-concerned and less dedicated to their religious callings. This in turn may well have contributed to the decline of the church in the late Middle Ages that is explored later in this chapter.

The whole tone of society was colored by the omnipresence of death. In a stricken city, many abandoned their shops, their homes, and their responsibilities and gave themselves over to alcohol and debauchery. Others, seeing the plague as a divine punishment, turned to extreme mortification of the flesh. Wandering through the land in long lines of flagellants, they lashed themselves with whips as penance for the sins of the world. A powerful new theme emerged in the art of the age: the *Dance of Death*, depicting dancing skeletons leading aristocrats and merchants, peasants and paupers alike to their graves—a grim reminder that death spares neither high nor low. Tomb sculpture often reflected a bizarre fascination with death and decomposition. In place of the dignified representations of the dead on earlier tombs, realistically carved corpses now began to appear on the lids of sarcophagi.

Economic Decline and Stagnation

In this time of famine and plague, the medieval economy also reeled toward collapse, declining drastically during the later fourteenth century and stagnating through the first half of the fifteenth. It seems likely that the economic expansion of the High Middle Ages had in fact reached its natural limits by 1300, before the disasters of the fourteenth century

These German flagellants wandered the roads bearing the cross and lashing themselves with whips in order to share the suffering of Christ, atone for the sins of the age, and win remission of the miseries that afflicted their land.

struck. A population decline of more than 30 percent left many fields unworked, goods unsold in every shop. Agricultural and handicraft-industrial production, as well as volume of trade, declined precipitously, international commerce perhaps by as much as 60 percent. But this decline in production and commerce was only the most evident of the economic problems of the age.

Although more people in the lower classes died from famine and disease, those who survived found themselves in a fortunate economic situation. The drastic shortage of labor meant that farm workers could demand excellent terms from their landlords to keep them on the land. It meant that urban workers could get much higher wages—sometimes three or four times what they had been paid before. The labor shortage also led to a greater mobility of labor, as workers moved in search of the most favorable terms. It even gave some of the surviving laborers access for the first time to such luxuries as meat, fruit, and good wine and beer.

On the other hand, the economic crisis hurt landlords and merchants, for both of whom labor costs were rising rapidly at a time of sharply declining demand. Knights and noblemen were caught in a vise between the chivalric virtue of largesse and the baronial lifestyle on the one hand, and dwindling returns from their land on the other. Businesses that had prospered in the twelfth and thirteenth centuries collapsed during the fourteenth as labor costs rose, the number of customers diminished, and profit margins shrank.

Under these circumstances, landholders and merchants fought back in a variety of ways. Landed aristocrats discovered that by converting labor-intensive arable land into sheep pastures, they could cut their need for expensive labor to a few shepherds. This of course meant depriving many peasants of their homes and livelihoods. In the towns, guilds began to limit membership—often to the relatives of existing masters—in order to restrict destructive competition. Again, this hurt journeymen who had hoped to rise in the business and outsiders who could not even be admitted to apprenticeship.

European political leaders did try to deal with the economic chaos, usually by attempting to defend the old system. The governments of England and France and of the kingdoms of Castile and Aragon in Spain passed laws regulating wages and limiting worker mobility. Italian towns and some other cities outlawed journeymen's associations, workers' organizations intended to fight guild control. The Hanseatic League of Baltic German towns, like other associations of commercial cities, tried to establish a trade monopoly of its region and to bargain as a group with trading partners elsewhere. Typically, the league's functions were defensive: to protect the interests of Lübeck, Bremen, Cologne, Hamburg, and other members in troubled economic times.

Between the landed aristocracy and the peasantry, between the merchant oligarchies of the towns and their work force, bitter social tensions thus emerged in the fourteenth century. In this way, class conflict was added to the list of woes besetting the people of the later Middle Ages.

Social Disarray

Medieval people had little understanding of economic issues. If one had asked a fourteenth-century merchant or landlord about the economic trends of the times, he would very likely have complained that everything favored the greedy lower orders these days. In fact, however, merchants and landholders remained substantially better off than the lower orders. If, on the other hand, one had asked a peasant or a journeyman laborer about the economic situation, he or she would probably have explained that the masters were doing everything possible to deprive the workers of the "just wage" laborers had come to expect. Actually, thanks to the labor shortage, artisans of this time were probably better off economically than any of their ancestors.

It was, in short, a conflict between a status quo under attack and a revolution of rising expectations. The result was a series of peasant revolts and urban rebellions in some of the most economically developed parts of Europe in the course of the fourteenth and early fifteenth centuries. Specific issues differed from one time and place to another, but the underlying circumstances and the resulting social conflicts were much the same.

Peasant revolts had occurred even in the High Middle Ages, but they became more common and more violent in the later medieval centuries. Two of the most terrible were the French *Jacquerie* of 1358 and the Peasants' Revolt in England in 1381.

"Jacques Bonhomme" ("Jack Goodfellow") was a nickname coined by the French upper classes for their stereotype of the good-hearted average peasant—a decent fellow, basically satisfied with his lot. Great was the horror, then, when thousands of Jacques Bonhommes revolted in 1358, attacking and burning chateaus, killing landlords, raping their wives, and leaving a trail of death and destruction across northern France. As the box on the "Peasants' Revolt" suggests, the peasantry, already ravaged by the Black Death and frustrated in their demands for improved labor conditions, were pushed beyond the limits by the Hundred Years' War (see next section), which brought high taxation, the ravages of mercenary armies, and unsuppressed banditry.

Unfortunately, the French peasants had little effective leadership and no clear program for social change. Although the aristocracy were caught off balance by the suddenness and savagery of the outburst, they soon rallied and crushed the rebellion, massacring perhaps as many as twenty thousand peasants in the process.

The even larger Peasants' Revolt in England more than two decades later grew from some of the same economic discontents, although the English

WAR AND PEACE
The Peasants' Revolt

The pressures of the Hundred Years' War, added to the normal problems and privations of peasant life, triggered revolts by the laboring poor of the countryside on both sides of the English Channel. In the excerpt here, Jean Froissart (1337–1410), a well-known chronicler of knightly deeds, is clear on the violence of the French Jacquirie. Why do you suppose he shows so little understanding of the grievances of the peasants?

Some of the inhabitants of the country towns assembled together in Beauvoisis, without any leader: they were not at first more than one hundred men. They said, that the nobles of the kingdom of France, knights, and squires, were a disgrace to it, and that it would be a very meritorious act to destroy them all. . . .

They then, without further council, collected themselves in a body, and with no other arms than the staves shod with iron, which some had, and others with knives, marched to the house of a knight who lived near, and breaking it open, murdered the knight, his lady, and all the children, both great and small; they then burnt the house. . . .

They did the like to many castles and handsome houses; and their numbers increased so much, that they were in a short time upwards of six thousand: wherever they went, they received additions, for all of their rank in life followed them, whilst every one else fled. . . .

These wicked people, without leader and without arms, plundered and burnt all the houses they came to, murdered every gentleman, and violated every lady and damsel they could find. He who committed the most atrocious actions, and such as no human creature would have imagined, was the most applauded, and considered as the greatest man among them.
. . .

When they were asked for what reason they acted so wickedly; they replied, they knew not, but they did so because they saw others do it; and they thought that by this means they should destroy all the nobles and gentlemen in the world. . . .

Source: Jean Froissart, *Chronicles of England, France, Spain, and the Adjoining Courtries from . . . Edward II to . . . Henry IV*, tr. Thomas Johnes (London; William Smith, 1844), pp. 240–41.

The savage reaction triggered by the Jacquerie was in many places more violent than the original revolt. Why would the knights tend to have the better of it when the lower classes revolted?

peasants framed their issues more clearly and demanded specific social changes. The immediate causes of this revolt included new taxes, the ravages of the war and other rural violence, and the reluctance of landlords to modify manorial labor obligations. These deeper grievances were further expressed in peasants' demands for a final end to serfdom and for the confiscation of the wealth of the church. Their leaders, about whom not much is known, included a laborer named Wat Tyler and a popular priest called John Ball whose social radicalism was expressed in the jingle:

> When Adam delved and Eve span [spun wool],
> Who was then the gentleman?

In 1381, then, peasant rebellion exploded across southeastern England, the normally prosperous area around London. A peasant army burned manor houses, killed a number of leading citizens, including the archbishop of Canterbury, and attacked royal of-

ficials. In this desperate situation, King Richard II (r. 1377–1399), still a youth of fifteen, risked his life by going to the peasants with an appeal to disperse and a personal assurance that their demands would be met. When they did disperse, however, England's landholding elite counterattacked and slaughtered many of the rebels. Both Tyler and Ball were executed. And King Richard, feeling that commitments made to a rabble under duress need not be binding, quickly forgot his promises of social change.

In both the Jacquerie and the Peasants' Revolt, elements of the urban population supported the rural rebellions. In Paris, a merchant named Etienne Marcel (c. 1316–1358) engineered a widespread strike and called for the removal of unpopular royal advisers. In London and other English cities, journeymen and apprentices rebelled, demanding that their opportunities to advance through the guilds be unblocked once more. But urban discontent did not need the excuse of rural violence. Violent social conflict also broke out in the handicraft-industrial cities of Flanders (modern Belgium) and in Florence in the 1300s, climaxing in the Florentine Ciompi Revolt of 1378.

Conflict between artisans and merchant elites exploded at the very beginning of the fourteenth century in Flanders. Artisans of the three great wool-producing cities of Bruges, Ypres, and Ghent bitterly resented the defensive policies of merchant oligarchs, who kept wages low, outlawed journeymen's associations, and blocked efforts on the part of the poorer industries to organize guilds of their own. Two outside feudal powers also played a part in the struggle: the counts of Flanders, who used the artisans' cause as an excuse to try to impose their authority on the merchant oligarchy, and the king of France, whose help the merchants sought.

In 1302 the artisans of Bruges murdered their royal governor and a number of the town's leading merchants, and even defeated a French army in the field. A quarter century of class conflict followed, before an alliance of the merchant elite, the French king, and the count of Flanders—who had changed sides—defeated an artisan army and massacred many workers. Despite this setback for the rebels, the bloody struggle dragged on through most of the rest of the century, until a paternalistic duke of Burgundy intervened to foster the development of the lucrative wool-producing cities as a whole in the 1380s.

Florence, the wealthiest of Italian cities at the beginning of the fourteenth century, was also torn by simmering social conflict that lasted for decades.

Florence was dominated by an oligarchy of woolen cloth manufacturers, bankers, and export merchants, who operated through the city's wealthiest merchant guilds and controlled city government. The poorer and less prestigious guilds and the poorest day laborers, the *ciompi,* or wool carders, struggled for the political power necessary to improve their economic standing. Feeling the economic pinch of the century, the Florentine business elite laid off workers, clamped a ceiling on wages, and, like the merchants of Flanders, prohibited laborers' associations. An initial revolt as early as the 1340s was firmly suppressed, but the coming of the Black Death later in that decade contributed to the growing tensions.

The climax came with the Ciompi Revolt of 1378, when the poorest workers seized the city hall and forced the oligarchy to accept their terms. These included increased production (which increased the number of jobs available), the legalization of new guilds among the *ciompi* and their allies, and the appointment of some of the poorest guild workers to government offices. Again, however, the workers' gains did not prove lasting. Within four years, the city's patrician overlords had outmaneuvered the inexperienced rebel leaders, regained control of the government, and begun to renege on earlier concessions. The bitterness continued into the following century, until the Medici family, Renaissance Florence's most famous bankers and political bosses, saw the need to take the interests of the lower orders into consideration as well.

Demographic disaster and economic decline thus combined with the policies of landlords and merchant oligarchs to touch off both peasant and urban rebellion. But there was violence on a larger scale too, for this period also witnessed a sudden international upsurge in warfare and political disorder.

The Hundred Years' War

The widespread wars and political dislocations of the fourteenth and fifteenth centuries, like the demographic, economic, and social disasters, centered on one or two major events. What the Black Death and the contraction of the late medieval economy were to the social and economic history of the period, the Hundred Years' War was to the military and political trends of the times. For that prolonged struggle helped to weaken governments, generate what has been called bastard feudalism, and kindle civil wars in the most unified and powerful of medieval nations.

The direct impact of the war itself was traumatic enough. King Philip VI of France (r. 1328–1350), famous for organizing jousts and tournaments for his nobles, was a true representative of the age of chivalry; Edward III of England (r. 1327–1377) was equally dedicated to the chivalric ideal. These men and their successors into the next century, including England's youthful warrior-king Henry V and France's saint in armor, Joan of Arc, fought the longest and bloodiest of medieval conflicts, the Hundred Years' War (1337–1453). It was a struggle that came close to extinguishing the French monarchy, in the end did destroy the English empire in France, and effectively ended the long-standing domination of European battlefields by armored knights on horseback. The result of this thoroughly chivalric struggle was thus as great a disaster as plague, famine, or economic decline for late medieval people.

Causes of Conflict

A search for the deeper causes of the catastrophe has uncovered a variety of causal factors. Medieval people saw the issues as dynastic, a feud between two royal houses. Modern historians have emphasized economic causes. And a new and imponderable causal element was the first glimmering of national feeling in both England and France.

Proponents of the old dynastic interpretation point out that in the early fourteenth century, the king of England still controlled Gascony and other territories in southwestern France. He was, however, the French king's vassal for these lands, and frictions inevitably developed between a French ruler trying to assert his authority over his vassals and an English ruler demanding his feudal right to govern his French fiefs as he saw fit. The tension increased when the ancient French royal house of Capet failed to provide an heir, and the crown was therefore assigned to a first cousin of the last of the Capetians, Philip VI (r. 1328–1350) of the house of Valois. Among the disappointed claimants to the throne, however, was Edward III of England (r. 1327–1377), a nephew of the last Capetian king. Edward's claim was tainted in feudal eyes by the fact that it came through a woman, his French mother, but the English king continued to assert his rights with vigor. This agitation, combined with conflict over administration of England's French territories, escalated into a struggle for the French crown itself— and moved from the law courts to the field of battle.

Recent historians, however, have noted some important economic motives, including Anglo-French rivalry over the wealthy cities of Flanders. The French kings, as overlords of the county of Flanders, demanded their rightful dues from the region. The Flemish nobility resisted these demands and turned for help to England, which depended on the area as a market for English wool and a source of finished woolen cloth. This lucrative economic connection repeatedly involved English kings in the political struggles of the Flemish cities and in the feuds between Flanders and the French monarchy.

A third important motive, particularly for the continuation of the war once it was begun, was the development of something resembling modern nationalism in both England and France. Each royal contender quickly attributed the war to the perfidy, greed, and cruelty of the other side and spread this version through official pronouncements, church sermons, and by other means. The people of both countries rallied to popular war heroes like Edward III, Henry V, or Joan of Arc, whom they increasingly saw as symbols of the nation as a whole. The two peoples also groaned under the heavy burdens imposed by the war, from loss of property and human life to the immense financial costs—all of which they tended to blame on the national enemy rather than their own rulers. This traumatic national experience thus produced the rudiments of national feeling which, combined with a passion for chivalric glory and a lust for loot, helped to perpetuate the war for half a dozen generations.

Edward III and English Victories

With beating drums and blaring trumpets, fluttering pennants and flapping banners, the kings of England and France thus went forth to war. France, three times as populous and much richer than the island nation of England, looked far the stronger. But the English benefited from a series of alliances with rebellious French subjects—in this first phase, with the wool towns of Flanders. Their chances were also improved by better leadership and discipline, and by the deployment of an unexpectedly potent weapon: the English longbow. Six feet long, requiring a strong arm to draw and years of practice to master, this traditional English peasant weapon could be fired three times as fast as the crossbows used by the French infantry and had the power to penetrate all but the heaviest plate armor. It was not superior English chivalry that won

the day in battle after battle in France, but sturdy English peasants wielding this fearsome medieval missile weapon.

Over the first twenty years of the war, then, the armies of Edward III won one encounter after another. In 1340 the English triumphed in the naval battle of Sluys, winning the control of the channel Edward needed to operate across the water in France. In 1346 the English met the French knights at Crécy in northern France in what became the paradigm battle of the war. The French were worn out from their hot pursuit of the invaders, yet hurled themselves upon the foe with the sort of impetuosity that minstrels and troubadours admired. The English simply held firm while a blizzard of arrows littered the field with screaming horses and helpless or dying French knights. The following year, the key port of Calais fell to the English, giving them ready access to northern France for future campaigns.

The coming of the Black Death caused a temporary halt in the human carnage, but ten years later, in 1356, the English won an even more stunning victory at Poitiers in central France. The rain of English

This picture of the great battle of Crécy, taken from a medieval chronicle, clearly distinguishes between the French standard on the left and the English one on the right, between French crossbows and English long bows, and between the heavily armored, mounted knights and the more lightly armed archers on both sides.

arrows took an even greater toll than at Crécy. Knights, nobles, and even allied sovereigns perished, and the French king himself—Philip's successor John (r. 1350–1364)—was taken prisoner and held for an enormous ransom.

Edward III died in 1377 after a fifty-year reign, leaving England exhausted by decades of war. France, meanwhile, though even more battered by the long conflict, had acquired one of the more competent French rulers of the war, Charles V the Wise (r. 1364–1380). Thanks also to a series of financial and governmental reforms and to the skill of one of France's greatest commanders, Bertrand du Guesclin (c. 1320–1380), the French pushed the English back. By 1380, England held only a string of French port cities along the Channel, from Calais down to Bordeaux. Both sides, however, were nearing collapse from the terrible strain of the contest. As a result, both avoided major campaigns for the next thirty-five years, though an endless series of raids, sieges, and skirmishes continued.

Henry V, Joan of Arc, and the Turn of the Tide

It would have been an excellent time to bring the struggle to an end, with honor satisfied on both sides. Efforts, indeed, were made in that direction, including the marriage of an English prince to a French princess in 1396. Early in the next century, however, a fiery new English king, seeing France convulsed by what amounted to a civil war, was tempted across the Channel once more.

Charles the Wise had been succeeded by the intermittently insane Charles VI (r. 1380–1422). With a mental incompetent on the throne, ambitious French princes of royal blood were soon feuding for power. One of these, Louis, duke of Orléans (1372–1407), gained effective control over the king himself; the other, John the Fearless, duke of Burgundy (1371–1419), promptly allied himself with the English. Against this background, England's young King Henry V (r. 1413–1422) resolved to reassert his rights in France.

In 1415 Henry invaded Normandy and met the French army in the celebrated battle of Agincourt. Even without the support of the Burgundians, the French substantially outnumbered the English. But the field was thick with mud, slowing the French cavalry charges, and the deadly hail of English arrows rained down once more. The French were routed again, the victorious invaders proceeded to overrun the rest of Normandy, and the Burgundians occupied Paris.

Henry V then showed himself as shrewd a diplomat as he was a successful military commander. By the Treaty of Troyes (1420), Charles VI agreed to legitimize all Henry's conquests in northern France, disinherited his own son, and named the young English king heir to the throne of France. For a dazzling moment, it looked as if the most extravagant dreams of Edward III were to be realized at last, as if a single monarch might come to rule both of the most powerful nations in medieval Europe.

Two years later, however, both the feeble-minded French sovereign and the virile young English monarch died within a few months of each other. The new English king, Henry VI (r. 1422–1471), was an infant, unable to assert his rights under the Treaty of Troyes. Charles VI's disinherited son declared himself King Charles VII (r. 1422–1461) but seemed militarily incapable of making good his claim in the face of the powerful English-Burgundian alliance. The stage was set for more decades of grinding war.

Into this hopeless situation came what seemed to the French like a miracle from heaven—the young girl known to history as Joan of Arc (c. 1412–1431). Daughter of a devout and prosperous farming family from the village of Domrémy in Lorraine, Joan began in her teens to hear the voices of saints and angels summoning her to save France from the unending wars. With the English and their Burgundian supporters occupying northern France—including Paris—and much of the southwest as well, Joan's mission could only be accomplished by force. And the only source of an army was the apparently feckless Charles VII, still uncrowned seven years after his father's death, his troops dispirited, his cause seemingly hopeless. Nevertheless, it was to Charles that the seventeen-year-old peasant girl turned in the spring of 1429.

What Joan accomplished in less than a year was, in its way, as miraculous as her later reputation. It is doubtful that she really convinced Charles and the worldly men around him that she was, as she said, "the Maid sent from God."[1] Still, Charles allowed her to ride out with the soldiers that he sent to relieve the besieged city of Orléans, as she had asked. She certainly had a galvanizing effect on the troops, who broke the English siege. And when Joan returned victorious, she moved Charles himself to risk everything by marching off—under her escort—to

This is Joan of Arc as she appears in a contemporary sketch in the corner of a court record. Does this figure, complete with sword and banner but otherwise very young and unwarlike, look like your impression of the warrior maid?

forces had driven the English out of both Normandy in the north and Gascony in the south, leaving the invaders only the isolated port of Calais to show for 116 years of intermittent warfare.

Joan had not lived to see the glorious French victories. In 1430, the year after her triumphs at Orléans and Reims, she had been captured by the Burgundians. Turned over to the English, she was tried for witchcraft and heresy by the French ecclesiastical courts in the occupied zone. She was convicted and burned alive in 1431, still insisting her inspiration was divine, not diabolical.

An illiterate peasant demanding the right to command armies, a girl who cut her hair and wore men's clothing, a teenager who led her elders by the nose, Joan remains in some ways one of the most astonishing of medieval people. In one great respect, however, she was not atypical at all: true believers in divine inspiration never seemed to be in short supply in the age of faith.

Marauding Mercenaries and Bastard Feudalism

Violence, too, was never lacking in the Middle Ages; yet there seems to have been even more of it than usual during the fourteenth and fifteenth centuries. Besides the major campaigns of the Hundred Years' War, later medieval times were afflicted by baronial factionalism, bastard feudalism, and marauding mercenaries. Once the dogs of war were unleashed, they could not easily be brought to heel, as even the most powerful monarchs soon learned.

Mercenary soldiers—called *free companies* because they had no fixed feudal ties but sold their services to the highest bidder—multiplied during the Hundred Years' War. Both sides found these professional troops, efficiently commanded by captains with an eye out for profit, to be more effective fighting forces than the traditional feudal levies. The free companies, however, tended to live off the land, showing no more respect for the people they were defending than for their enemies. During the long periods between campaigns, furthermore, mercenaries often turned into bandits, establishing themselves in fortified castles, imposing tribute on the surrounding countryside, and frequently robbing travelers and looting villages and even cities. It was a throwback to the anarchistic days of the early Middle Ages, and it devastated parts of France for generations.

The feudal system itself was corrupted during

be crowned king at last in the traditional ceremony in the cathedral at Reims, in the heart of the English-occupied zone.

Anointed and crowned, with the miraculous maid by his side, Charles VII suddenly began to look like a king to the French people. From that point on, things moved slowly but inexorably in his favor. In the 1430s, he made at least a temporary peace with the duke of Burgundy and began the reorganization of the French army. Garrisoning his cities with regularly paid soldiers, he also provided them with a new weapon more devastating than the English longbow: artillery. Gunpowder, known in China centuries before, found military application in Europe in the early fourteenth century, although cannons did not become effective weapons of war until the fifteenth. Charles VII's new army included professional artillerymen and trains of siege guns. By 1453, his

the fourteenth and fifteenth centuries into what is sometimes called *bastard feudalism*. The feudal bond, once based on a personal oath that often reflected genuine respect and loyalty to one's overlord, became in later medieval times increasingly a matter of cash payments. Nobles, like kings, simply hired fighting men, clothing them in their own colors and maintaining them at their own expense. They used these private armies both to meet their feudal military obligations to their overlords and to settle disputes in their own provinces by force of arms. Feudal display had never been more grand, outdoing even that of the High Middle Ages with lavish feasts, elaborate tournaments, new knightly orders, and other manifestations of enthusiasm for the chivalric ideal. Too often, however, a veneer of chivalry concealed crass mercenary greed or unseemly aristocratic ambition.

Not surprisingly, baronial factionalism also experienced a powerful resurgence in the later Middle Ages. The most successful high medieval monarchs had worked hard to bring their vassals to heel, suppressing private feuds and fortified castles. But a century of intensified warfare, inevitably accompanied by defeats for one king or the other, brought feudal rebelliousness and factional conflict back with a vengeance, as we will see in the next section.

The Monarchies Challenged

In these strained and war-torn times, finally, the feudal monarchy itself seemed to be under fire. The Hundred Years' War and the ensuing climate of social disarray, mercenary violence, and bastard feudalism all contributed to this challenge to royal power. Even more important was the rebelliousness of ambitious nobles, whose intrigues and private wars divided not only royal courts but whole countries. Beyond this, it has been suggested, lay structural problems of the medieval monarchy as an institution. Among these were the loose feudal organization of much political power, the limited authority of monarchs to tax wealthy landholders, and the decline of landed wealth itself under the impact of war, plague, and general economic decline.

These historic disasters and institutional weaknesses interacted with the personal failings of individual rulers to bring the powerful monarchies of earlier centuries to a low ebb in the 1400s. This happened not only in war-ravaged France and England, but also in Spain, the Holy Roman Empire, and parts of

eastern Europe. Let us glance briefly at three of these areas.

In France, the English more than once encouraged the great royal vassals to defect from the French king, promoting secession by wealthy Flanders, by the peninsular duchies of Normandy and Brittany, and most importantly by the ambitious dukes of Burgundy. The French royal court became a hotbed of intrigue, and powerful nobles and royal favorites plundered the country remorselessly. The policies of the French rulers themselves also contributed to the crumbling of royal power over the great fiefholders. Attempting to keep their vassals in line, French monarchs gave large areas of land to princes of royal blood. These became the most aggressive and ambitious of all the "overmighty subjects" who challenged the authority of their sovereigns.

In the early fifteenth century, then, with the mentally incompetent Charles VI as France's nominal ruler, the dukes of Burgundy and Orléans were able to divide much of the French ruling class into two bitterly opposed factions. Louis, duke of Orléans, was assassinated in 1407; John the Fearless, duke of Burgundy, in 1419; and all France was plunged into civil war even as the country reeled under the renewed English invasion led by Henry V. Under Joan of Arc's protégé Charles VII, the French monarchy began to recover and then to extend the centralizing power it had enjoyed in the twelfth and thirteenth centuries. But the challenge of the fifteenth century brought France's kings very low indeed before recovery began.

England also suffered from feudal factionalism and royal weakness during the 1400s. Military setbacks and the immense cost of the war enabled the ambitious English noble house of Lancaster to overthrow Edward III's incompetent successor Richard II in 1399. Half a century later, in the wake of its final expulsion from France, England also slid into a prolonged bout of civil strife known as the *Wars of the Roses* (1455–1485). For three decades, the powerful baronial houses of Lancaster and York, symbolized by red and white roses respectively, fought each other up and down the land.

The strongest champion of the house of Lancaster was Queen Margaret (1430–1482) wife of the Lancastrian king Henry VI (r. 1422–1461), the heroic Henry V's mentally incompetent son. A strong-willed dynast, Margaret fought doggedly for many years to hold the throne for her family. The Yorkist claimant Edward IV (r. 1461–1483) seized

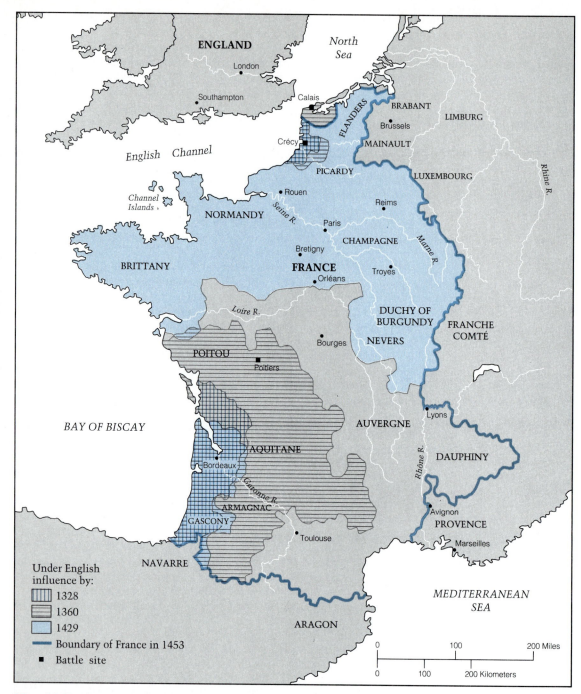

Map 11.2 The Hundred Years' War and English Rule in France

power after a series of bloody battles, but was himself for some years seen as a virtual puppet of the ambitious "kingmaker" Richard Neville, earl of Warwick (1428–1471), who had helped the young king to his crown. Warwick subsequently fell out with Edward, shifted to the Lancastrian camp, and briefly restored Henry VI to the throne in 1470. But Edward and the Yorkists recovered and counterattacked; Warwick died in battle, and hapless Henry VI in the Tower of London.

The climax of this carnival of civil strife came in the brief, bloody reign of Richard III (r. 1483–1485), Edward IV's brother and the last Yorkist king. Richard, the witty hero-villain of one of Shakespeare's most popular plays, imprisoned and probably murdered Edward's young son and heir Edward V (1483), along with a number of other Yorkist rivals. It was only when Richard himself fell on the battlefield at Bosworth (1485) to another Lancastrian claimant, Henry Tudor, that a dynasty capable of reasserting royal authority emerged once more in England.

In the German states of the Holy Roman Empire, meanwhile, central power also continued to deteriorate rapidly in the later Middle Ages. In this vast, predominantly German-speaking area of central Europe, as we have seen, the emperors had failed to establish strong royal government in the fourteenth century. The fifteenth saw the decline of political power at the next level down, among the great princely families who had defeated the centralizing efforts of the emperors. Ruling families like the Habsburgs of Austria and the Wittelsbachs of Bavaria still suffered from the old German custom of dividing the realm among the various members of a princely clan. In addition, all the German princes faced aggressive challenges from below as insurrectionary nobles and knights, independent towns, and rebellious peasants repeatedly rose against them.

The election of Frederick III (r. 1440–1493) of the house of Habsburg as Holy Roman emperor in 1452 brought to the German imperial throne a family that continued to hold that title until the Empire itself was abolished in the nineteenth century. Earlier Habsburgs had ruled Austria and other German states, as well as Hungary and Bohemia, but had been handicapped by feuds within the family and by the opposition of other German rulers. Only with the reunion of the Habsburg territories and the ascendancy of Emperor Maximilian I (r. 1493–1519) did the power and prestige of the German emperors begin to grow once again.

The Church Divided

Even in the worst of times, afflicted by wars, rebellions, and the decline of royal power, medieval people had their religion to console them. At the end of the Middle Ages, however, even that consolation seemed to be denied them as the papacy sank into division and disrepute and heresy stalked the land once more.

The Avignon Papacy

By the beginning of the fourteenth century, the Roman church was once again in need of rehabilitation. The great days of the Gregorian reform were more than two centuries in the past. High offices were once again bought and sold, and worldly friars were as common as worldly monks. It was at this juncture that the most outspoken of all champions of papal supremacy challenged one of the most determined builders of royal power—and lost.

Boniface VIII (r. 1294–1303) was not a pope of the stature of Gregory VII or Innocent III. Deeply involved in Roman aristocratic politics and the butt of scandalous rumors, he nevertheless responded vigorously when King Philip IV the Fair (meaning "Handsome") of France (r. 1285–1314) challenged papal control over the Catholic church in his country. Without prior consent of the pope, Philip attempted to tax the French church to pay for royal wars. When Boniface forbade the tax, Philip responded by prohibiting the export of gold and silver from France, effectively cutting off all papal revenues from Europe's richest country. Boniface gave way, allowing the king to levy a tax on church property, at least in a legitimate emergency such as a just war.

But Philip the Fair went further: he brought a French prelate to trial for treason in a French court. Philip thus raised again the vexing question of clerical immunity from trial in secular courts. And this time Pope Boniface did not back away. He issued instead the most sweeping of all assertions of papal supremacy over secular rulers, the bull *Unam Sanctam* in 1302. (A bull is an official document or decree, often one issued by the Church; the term is derived from the word *bulla* for the imperial seal affixed to such a document.) The sword of secular authority wielded by earthly monarchs, the pope decreed, was subordinate to the sword of spiritual power held by the heirs of St. Peter. "Therefore we declare, state, define, and pronounce that it is altogether necessary to salvation for every human creature to be subject to the Roman Pontiff."[2]

King Philip, a notable aggrandizer of royal power in France, did not hesitate to strike back at the great monopolist of international power. Conspiring with the pope's enemies in Rome, he dispatched a band of royal agents led by Guillaume de

Nogaret (c. 1260–1313) to seize Boniface at Anagni in 1303 and bring him to trial as a false pope. The scheme misfired as ordinary Italian townsmen rallied to the pope and expelled the foreigners. But Boniface, a man in his sixties, psychologically and perhaps physically battered by Philip's henchmen, died within a month of their visit.

But the relentless French king was not through. To prevent further papal interference, he engineered the election of a Frenchmen, Clement V, to the papacy in 1305 (r. 1305–1313). Clement, furthermore, did not go to Rome, but settled at Avignon, on what was then the southeastern border of France. Thus began a seventy-year period of papal exile from Rome (1305–1378) known as the *Avignon papacy*.

Seven French popes ruled the church from the sunny southern city of Avignon, on the Rhone. Seen by many Christians as a "second Babylon" of worldliness and corruption, Avignon did become the site of a splendid new papal palace and a brilliant court. Through the first half of the Hundred Years' War, the English and others declared that the Avignon popes were captives of the French king. But Avignon was not part of France; it was a papal enclave. And the popes of this exile, though they appointed many French cardinals, seem to have worked for the interests of the church as a whole. Nevertheless, the reputation of Avignon damaged papal prestige.

Another charge leveled against the Avignon papacy had more substance. The Avignon popes were widely seen as worldly, even venal men, more concerned with squeezing the Christian faithful for church revenues than with providing spiritual leadership. And in fact the Avignon papacy did help to develop the well-oiled machinery of church administration, a primary purpose of which was the collection of revenues from the international church and its holdings. These revenues, furthermore, were often used for such unspiritual ends as maintaining cardinals in splendor at Avignon or armies to defend the Papal States in Italy. Altogether, even if Avignon was not as sunk in corruption as its enemies averred, it was not the fount of spiritual guidance and consolation many Christians needed in those tortured times either.

Strolling the streets and squares of Avignon today, you will find one of the most pleasant of the cities of Provence, France's sunny south. The palace of the popes, with its crenellated towers and its peaceful view across the river Rhone, looks thoroughly medieval. Little remains of the sinful city condemned by the fourteenth-century poet Petrarch or of the throbbing center of papal administrative organization extolled by modern historians. But Avignon was both, and the Avignon papacy opened the way to an even more disturbing chapter in the history of western Christendom.

The Great Schism

When the papal sojourn in Avignon ended in the later 1370s, it was replaced by something even worse: the *Great Schism* (1378–1417). Pope Gregory XI returned to Rome, where he died in 1378. Under pressure from a Roman mob determined that the papacy should not again repair to Avignon, the predominantly French College of Cardinals elected an Italian pope, Urban VI (r. 1378–1389). Urban, however, immediately launched a hot-tempered assault on the luxurious living, financial abuses, and other sins of the ecclesiastical hierarchy. The French cardinals thereupon withdrew from Rome, elected a new, French pope, Clement VII (r. 1378–1394), and returned to Avignon. Urban, meanwhile, appointed an Italian College of Cardinals and remained in Rome.

Western Christendom was thus confronted by the disturbing spectacle of two popes, each claiming to be the legitimate heir to St. Peter, the bearer of the keys to heaven. Both demanded revenues from the churches of the West. Each excommunicated the other, putting the soul of any Christian who supported the wrong claimant in mortal danger. It was precisely what a Europe reeling under the hammer blows of famine, plague, and war did not need.

Rulers and their nations had to choose a pope to support: the French defended the Avignon line; the English accepted Rome; the Holy Roman Empire favored first one and then the other. Many Christians, already dismayed at the worldliness into which the church was sinking once more, turned away from the official church to private devotions or even to new heresies. Many others must have lapsed into deep cynicism at the spectacle.

Yet most Christians, including their rulers, remained profoundly troubled. The only practical solution religious thinkers and leaders could come up with was the *conciliar movement* of the first half of the fifteenth century. The conciliar movement was based on the conviction that a church council could both end the Schism and reform the church, and that conciliar government might even replace papal rule in the Western church. Such gatherings as the

Council of Nicaea of 325 and Innocent III's Fourth Lateran Council of 1215 had successfully resolved great problems before. Surely God would inspire such a conclave in this dark hour of Christendom.

In the first half of the fifteenth century, a series of councils was held. The first, the Council of Pisa in 1409, did not augur well for the conciliar approach. After firmly announcing that both the Roman and Avignon popes had been deposed, the assembled dignitaries chose a new one. Unfortunately, neither the Roman nor the Avignon pontiff accepted his dismissal, and western Europe had three popes instead of two.

The Council of Constance (1414–1418) was somewhat more productive. Called at the insistence of the Holy Roman emperor and supported by such powers as the kings of France and England, this gathering of theologians and princes of the church did succeed in at least some of its objectives. The council managed to depose both the Roman and Pisan popes, and by depriving the Avignon papacy of all support, forced its collapse within a dozen years. These actions paved the way for a conclave that elected a new pope, Martin V (r. 1417–1431), who settled a single papacy once more in Rome. On the other hand, the Council of Constance did not effect any reforms, since the new pope promptly dissolved it. Nor did conciliar authority ever replace papal power in the church.

Mysticism, Lay Piety, and Resurgent Heresy

Even in this dark, bewildering time, however, religion did not perish. In many parts of Europe, Christians found their way to a sense of God's presence in their lives through mysticism, private devotions, or the new heresies of Wycliffe and Hus (explored later). Religious belief survived, but the isolated mystic, the small groups of devout laypeople, and the peasants who responded to the anticlerical preaching of the new heretics all in their various ways challenged the unity of medieval Christianity, for they sought God outside the traditional framework of the Roman church.

Individual people who were towers of religious strength and often had a highly developed mystical gift were found in many lands. In the fourteenth century, the Italian St. Catherine of Siena (1347–1380) and St. Bridget of Sweden (c. 1303–1373) took leading roles in bringing the papacy from Avignon back to Rome. In the fifteenth

century, the earthy English mystic Margery Kempe (c. 1373–c. 1440) chronicled her visions and pilgrimages—which took her as far as Rome and Jerusalem—in a popular autobiography that became one of the first classics of the genre in English. But it was in the Low Countries and in Germany that the revival of religious devotion found its most intense and influential expression.

In the shadows of the great cathedrals that followed the winding course of the Rhine from the Netherlands down through western Germany, individuals and small groups of Christians now lived an intense religious life, but in private homes. Mystical spirits like Master Eckhart (c. 1260–c. 1328) urged the faithful to find God within themselves through meditation or, in the words of an immensely popular tract attributed to Thomas à Kempis (c. 1380–1471), through a personal *Imitation of Christ* (1425). Theologically orthodox, these spiritual leaders pointed out an emotional path to the religious life that transcended dogma and had no need of relics or pilgrimages, priests or prelates.

Emotional religiosity and private devotions also characterized the movements toward lay piety called the *devotio moderna*, the "modern devotion" that flourished in the Low Countries and the German states. The most famous of these movements, the Brethren of the Common Life, was patterned on the teaching of the Flemish mystic Gerard Groote (1340–1384), "the apostle of his country," as a follower described him, "who kindled the fires of religion in the cold hearts of men."[3] The Brethren, living communally, breaking bread and working together, encouraged each other in prayer and fasting, study and worship. The Sisters of the Common Life were also disciples of Groote and of his successor as leader of the movement, Florence Radewijns (1350–1400), who restructured and expanded the array of brother and sister houses. Although these groups functioned outside all the official monastic orders, they lived much like monks and nuns, and because their views were orthodox, the church could not move against them. Yet the humble piety of these laymen did contrast disturbingly with the worldly lives and theological quibbles of the feuding followers of the rival popes.

Other individuals and groups who carried their search for God over the line into heresy did incur the wrath of the authorities. (For a medieval justification of this practice, see the box titled "Thomas Aquinas Defends the Persecution of Heretics.") Wycliffe in England and Hus in Bohemia (the Czech Republic today) followed this dangerous road. Both men were university professors who stirred less educated Christians to religious dissent.

John Wycliffe (c. 1320–1384) of Oxford University declared that faith bloomed in the hearts of those who were divinely predestined to salvation. He believed that all religious truth was to be found in Scripture rather than church dogma, and that priests had no special spiritual powers that were not available to any Christian. Writing in the middle of the Hundred Years' War, Wycliffe particularly denounced the Avignon papacy, urging that Englishmen refuse to contribute revenues to a sinful papal court that danced to the tune of the French king. Wycliffe's message, however, went far beyond war-kindled patriotism, moving men and women of the lower orders of society to read translations of Scripture and to probe their own souls for signs of predestined salvation without the help of the official church. This underground movement, called *Lollardy*, survived to provide support for the Reformation two centuries later.

Jan Hus (1369–1415) of the University of Prague was a student of Wycliffe's views but developed his own passionate style, denouncing the wealth and corruption of the church to *Hussite* crowds of Bohemian townsmen and peasants. Like Wycliffe, Hus insisted that priests were not a separate caste with special prerogatives and powers. His demands for

PROFILES IN HISTORY
Thomas Aquinas Defends the Persecution of Heretics

The Inquisition, whose aggressive prosecution of the war against heresy darkened the last centuries of the Middle Ages, would find few defenders today. In medieval times, however, the practice of punishing religious dissenters made eminently good sense even to the best minds. Here Thomas Aquinas, the most admired of medieval religious thinkers, argues for the suppression of heresy. Given medieval assumptions, do you see merit in the view expressed here?

ARTICLE III. *Whether heretics should be tolerated. I reply that,* with regard to heretics, two considerations are to be kept in mind: (1) on their side, (2) on the side of the Church.

(1) There is the sin, whereby they deserve not only to be separated from the Church by excommunication, but also to be shut off from the world by death. For it is a much more serious matter to corrupt faith, through which comes the soul's life, than to forge money, through which temporal life is supported. Hence if forgers of money or other malefactors are straightway justly put to death by secular princes, with much more justice can heretics, immediately upon conviction, be not only excommunicated but also put to death.

(2) But on the side of the Church there is mercy, with a view to conversion of them that are in error; and therefore the church does not straightway condemn, but *after a first and a second admonition,* as the Apostle teaches (*Tit.* iii. 10). After that, if he be found still stubborn, the Church gives up hope of his conversion and takes thought for the safety of others, by separating him from the Church by sentence of excommunication; and, further, leaves him to the secular court, to be exterminated from the world by death.

Source: Thomas Aquinas, *Summa Theologica*, ii, Q. xi, Art. 111, in Henry Bettenson, *Documents of the Christian Church* (London: Oxford University Press, 1961), 186–187.

Heresy often came to a swift and painful end in the Middle Ages. Here Jan Hus the Bohemian heretic is burned at the stake in Switzerland in 1415 while secular and religious authorities look on.

church reform and his doctrinal heresies brought him into conflict first with his archbishop and then with the Council of Constance. Although the council's members shared Hus's dedication to reform, they rejected his theology, and in the age of faith, this rejection was paramount. Hus was condemned and burned for heresy in 1415.

Wycliffe and Hus both encouraged the use of the living vernacular languages in religion, rather than church Latin, and followers of Wycliffe translated the Bible into English. The new heretics, like the mystics and the Brethren of the Common Life, were strongly anticlerical, rejecting priestly mediation between God and the individual worshiper and condemning the wealth and worldly concerns of the church. Despite their deeply religious nature, then, both the heresies and the lay piety of the later Middle Ages reflected the crumbling of the religious unity of the Roman church—another symptom of the decline of medieval Christendom.

Mongol and Muslim Attacks

Against a Europe thus weakened and divided in so many ways came perhaps the greatest threat of all in the later Middle Ages: invaders from Asia. From the four-fifths of the Eurasian continent that lay east of the Urals came waves of Mongol horsemen and the powerful armies of the Ottoman Turks. Between them they shattered both of the medieval "shields of the West"—Kievan Russia and the Byzantine Empire. As the medieval cycle of Western history drew to a close, it did not seem at all unlikely that the story of Western civilization might be ending too.

The Decline of Kievan Russia and the Byzantine Empire

We have encountered these peoples of the Eurasian steppes before. The Indo-Europeans who populated most of Europe were originally steppe nomads who penetrated Europe and the Near East in the second millennium before Christ. Turko-Mongol invaders from the steppes had included the Huns who reached the walls of Rome in the last days of the Empire. In the thirteenth, fourteenth, and fifteenth centuries, however, the most formidable of all these Asian intruders broke into eastern Europe: the Ottoman Turks, marching under the banner of Islam, and the *Mongols* of Genghis Khan.

The realms of Eastern Christendom against which they marched no longer constituted the substantial bastions they had once been. The Kievan Rus, never strongly unified, was even more divided and weakened by outside pressures when the Mongols appeared out of the Eastern grasslands in the thirteenth century. The Byzantine Empire, powerful enough in Justinian's day to undertake the reconquest of the Mediterranean, was only a narrow strip of land on each side of the Bosporus when the Ottomans moved against it in the fourteenth and fifteenth centuries. A brief look at the decline of Eastern Christendom on the eve of invasion helps to explain the terrifying breakthroughs of Turks and Mongols at the end of the Middle Ages.

Even in the great days of Yaroslav the Wise in the eleventh century, the Kievan Rus had been more an alliance of princes than a centralized monarchy. The practice of parceling out royal lands to princely heirs had proved as fatal to national unity in Russia as in western European nations. As early as the eleventh century also, Turkish nomads called the Cumans had begun to raid the southern steppes, the heartland of Kievan Russia. Instead of uniting to resist these incursions, however, feuding Russian princes had often taken them on as mercenaries in their endless petty wars with their neighbors.

By the twelfth and thirteenth centuries, many East Slavs were withdrawing to the west and north to escape the Cumans and the endemic warfare of the steppes. Those who moved westward became the ancestors of the White Russians (or Belarussians) and the Ukrainians of modern times. In the late Middle Ages, however, they fell temporarily under the rule of the Catholic Kingdom of Poland or the still pagan Grand Duchy of Lithuania and were thus lost to Russia for hundreds of years. East Slavs who moved northward to settle in the scantily populated forests contributed to the development of the great Russian trading city of Novgorod and founded other cities, including Moscow. In this forest zone of European Russia, Muscovy soon emerged, the core of modern Russia. But first there was the Mongol conquest to face and endure.

The Byzantine Empire far to the south had, as we have seen, already lost large portions of its territory. The Arabs in the seventh century and the Seljuk Turks in the eleventh had conquered most of the Near East. In 1204 the Fourth Crusade had turned against its Byzantine allies and occupied the truncated Empire itself through the first half of the thirteenth century. Even after the restoration of the

Greek emperors by Michael VIII Paleologus (r. 1259–1282) in 1261, bitter struggles between rival claimants to the throne undermined the political strength of the Empire. Economically, meanwhile, Venetian and other Italian merchants had come to dominate the commerce of Constantinople, while oppressive imperial tax collectors and the reduction of the peasantry to serf status by rapacious landlords had further weakened the state.

Religious disputes completed the disarray of the Empire that claimed the leadership of the Greek Orthodox world. The split between the Greek Orthodox and Roman Catholic churches had been made official by mutual excommunications in 1054. Byzantium's need for Western aid in the face of military threats from the East, however, kept alive the issue of reunification with the Roman half of Christendom, a dispute that caused bitter divisions in Constantinople. Even more disturbing, the Orthodox church was riven by a resurgence of mysticism and the rise of new monastic movements in the fourteenth century. The most important of these, called *Hesychasm,* the search for inner peace, centered around the ancient tenth-century monasteries on Mount Athos in Greece. The monks of Mount Athos—who are still there—cut themselves entirely off from the surrounding countryside, excluded women and even female animals from their mountaintop cloisters, and gave themselves up wholly to meditation and scholarship. New monastic foundations in Constantinople itself divided between those devoted to the preservation of their cultural heritage, including ancient Greek philosophy and literature, and those committed to a mystical search for a spiritual "inner light" of salvation. Still other Byzantine religious thinkers, meanwhile, saw signs of the impending end of the world—a presentiment that, as far as the Byzantine Empire was concerned, was not far from right.

The Yoke of the Golden Horde

Mongolia today is a barren land between Russia and China. Modern cities and collective farms have largely squeezed out the herding, tent-dwelling life led by Mongols well into the present century. Looking at a forlornly flapping felt tent on that cold northern plain today, it is hard to remember that seven centuries ago the ancestors of these people built the largest empire the world had ever seen.

Turko-Mongol peoples had for hundreds of years harassed the ancient civilizations of Asia just as the Germanic peoples had harassed the Roman Empire. Pastoral nomads, expert archers, and totally at home on their shaggy Mongolian ponies, these tribes and clans of the northern steppes had repeatedly broken through the Great Wall of China or pushed through the passes of the Northwest Frontier into India. Then, shortly after 1200, a remarkable leader arose among them: Temujin, hailed by his followers as Genghis Khan, Lord of All Men. Genghis Khan (r. 1206–1227) imposed unity and organization on the Mongol peoples for the first time and led them in a series of sweeping conquests where they had only conducted sporadic raids before. Within a couple of generations, he and his successors had overrun the Chinese Empire, central Asia, the Muslim Middle East, and a substantial chunk of eastern Europe.

A probing expedition penetrated into Kievan Russia in 1223, defeating the Russian princes in a battle on the Kalka River near the Sea of Azov. In the 1230s, after Genghis Khan's death, his grandson Batu Khan (r. 1235–1255) led a major invasion of the lands of the East Slavs, devastating Kiev and many other Russian cities in 1240 and galloping on to burn and pillage in Poland, Hungary, and Bohemia. Thereafter, the Mongols established a capital at Sarai on the Volga and settled down to exploit a conquered Russia.

The Mongols were skillful and ruthless fighters, plundering and putting captured cities to the torch, slaughtering whole populations in order to fill their enemies with fear. Europeans, like the Chinese and Muslim peoples who faced them, recounted stories of half-human savages destroying all in their path. Ruling an empire that stretched from China to the frontiers of the Holy Roman Empire, from Moscow to Baghdad, they certainly looked unstoppable.

Once victorious, the Mongols proved less oppressive than might have been expected. The *Golden Horde,* as the Mongol khanate that governed Russia was called, actually required little of their Slavic subjects beyond regular tribute, occasional drafts of Russian recruits for their armies, and the humble submission of each Russian princeling before he could exercise authority over his city or principality. Still, the two centuries of the Mongol yoke did cut most of Russia's budding commercial ties with the West. Mongol rule also habituated the Russians to a more rigorously authoritarian rule than most European peoples experienced. For the Golden Horde—so called from the color of their tents—

Map 11.3 Mongol and Ottoman Turkish Invasions of Eastern Europe

were always ready to ride when any Russian principality was dilatory with its tribute or slow to make submission. And raids into other eastern European lands continued, putting the fear of the Mongols into European hearts well beyond the khanate of the Golden Horde.

Over Eurasia as a whole, however, the most important consequence of the Mongol predominance was the reopening of the trade links between East and West that had flourished in ancient Roman times. Protected by Mongol rulers whose linked realms stretched from China to Russia, merchants once again traveled the Silk Road from China through central Asia and down through the Middle East to the Mediterranean and the Muslim and Christian worlds of western Eurasia and North Africa. It was, as we see, a harbinger of better times for Europeans as well as for Asians.

The Fall of Constantinople

Another and even more terrible threat, however, seemed to loom over Christendom as the Middle Ages drew to a close. This was the menace of the Ottoman Turks, the third great wave of followers of the Prophet Muhammad, after the Arabs and the Seljuk Turks, to march against the West.

The collection of Turkish clans that would come to be known as the *Ottoman Turks* descended from the steppes of central Asia into the Muslim Middle East in the thirteenth century. Refugees like many others from the irresistible advance of the Mughals of Genghis Khan, they were nomads and spoke a Turko-Mongol language. Eastern Islam remained in the hands of the Seljuk Turks against whom the Crusades had been launched a century earlier, though an Arab caliph still presided as a figurehead in Baghdad. Converting to the Muslim faith, the Ottoman Turks followed the pattern of their predecessors, serving in the wars against Byzantium, carving out a place for themselves in the violent world of the *ghazis,* the Muslim frontier fighters who pushed insistently against the eastern wall of Christendom.

In 1300 their great leader Othman (r. 1300–1326) became an independent sultan and founded the Ottoman dynasty. His son Orkhan (r. 1326–1360) conquered much of Anatolia, the plateau of inland Turkey today, and then went on to take most of what remained of the Byzantine Empire in Asia. The Anatolian peasantry, who had been oppressed by Byzantine officialdom, found life easier under the Ottomans. Some accepted conversion to Islam; many learned the Turkish tongue. In return, they taught the Turks the arts of agriculture and settled living. From the Byzantines too, the Ottomans learned the subtleties of governmental administration—a skill for which they showed a notable knack. It was, for instance, Othman's son Orkhan who first organized the *janissary corps.* These Christian slaves, converted to Islam and trained from childhood as an elite corps of soldiers and administrators, played a key role in the great Ottoman Empire to come.

In the middle of the fourteenth century, the Ottomans reached the Straits west of Constantinople, and in 1354 they captured Gallipoli on the European shore. Having outflanked the Byzantine capital, they began to push northward, up through the Balkans toward central Europe. The great Battle of Kossovo in 1389, in which they defeated an alliance of Bulgarians, Romanians, and Serbs (founders of twentieth-century Yugoslavia), gave them most of the Balkans. As they paused on the borders of Hungary, a crusading army from France and the German states rushed to the aid of the Hungarians. The Ottomans wiped them out.

At the beginning of the fifteenth century, there seemed little to stop the advance of Turkish Islam into the heart of Christendom. An unexpected reprieve, however, came in the person of yet another legendary Asian warrior: Timur the Lame, better known as Tamerlane (1336–1405). Descending out of central Asia with his own powerful Mongol army, he conquered northern India and then swung westward into the Near East. In 1402 he met and crushed an Ottoman army at Ankara in central Turkey. But Tamerlane was soon on his way back to his home in Samarkand, leaving little but corpses and looted cities in his wake. And the Ottomans, who had grander ambitions, were on the move once more by the 1430s.

This time they turned their attention to the areas they had bypassed earlier. In the 1440s they completed the conquest of Greece. In the 1450s they marched against the fragment of the Byzantine Empire that remained—the legendary city of Constantinople.

In Europe, desperate efforts were made to bolster the ancient outpost of Christendom. Once more there were attempts to reunify the Catholic and Orthodox branches of Christendom, stirring up renewed sectarian bitterness in Constantinople. Military expeditions were dispatched, but too little and too late. Under a twenty-three-year-old sultan, Muhammad II (r. 1451–1481), known thereafter as the Conqueror, the Ottomans closed in on their prize.

It was no nomadic horde that moved against Constantinople in the spring of 1453. The Ottoman Turkish force was by this time a well-organized army, equipped with the largest siege guns in the world. It advanced with skill and prudence, fortifying the Straits to prevent resupply by water and ringing the walls of the city with seventy thousand veteran soldiers. The Turks even transported a fleet overland into the Golden Horn, Constantinople's famous harbor, a remarkable feat for the military engineering of the time.

At the end of May, the huge Turkish artillery breached the walls, and the Turks poured in. The last Byzantine emperor, Constantine XI (r. 1449–1453), died fighting. Muhammad the Conqueror rode through the carnage to Justinian's great Church of the Holy Wisdom, where he heard an Islamic sermon even before the building was reconsecrated as a mosque.

The year 1453 is often used to mark the end of the Middle Ages. To thunderstruck Christians in the West, the fall of Constantinople seemed to threaten more than the end of an age. It seemed to presage a renewed Muslim assault that could sweep all Christendom into the trash bin of history.

The Survival of the West

Plague, Famine, War, and Death were the Four Horsemen of the Apocalypse. Rising from the pages of the New Testament's Book of Revelation, they thundered across the skies of the late medieval imagination, terrifying images of a world declining toward its end.

Confronted not for the first time with impending doom, however, Western humanity once again demonstrated a remarkable range of survival skills. In one area of human endeavor after another, later medieval people adapted, coped, and even developed in response to the shocks of the fourteenth and fifteenth centuries. In the last section of this chapter, we will outline some of the positive achievements of the time in the fields of government, society, and the arts.

The Growth of Government

The kings who fought so many wars also had countries to run, and some did so with growing efficiency

under the pressure of war and their own ambitions. At the same time, however, governmental institutions increasingly reflected the interests of such other powers in medieval society as the aristocracy, the towns, and the church. It was in fact the very extravagance of royal ambitions that gave these other powers the leverage they needed to establish a place for themselves in the evolving structure of royal government.

Later medieval rulers continued the efforts of their predecessors to strengthen royal bureaucracy, particularly in the fields of law and finance. In France around 1300, Philip the Fair employed growing numbers of *gens du roi*—king's men—to impose his will. In particular, he sent his own judges and lawyers from the Parlement of Paris fanning out over the country to establish the preeminence of the king's justice and to undermine the surviving baronial courts. In England in the mid-1300s, Edward III used different means to achieve the same end, appointing local landowners to serve as his *Justices of the Peace* with a combination of judicial and administrative duties. These "JPs" were to serve for centuries as royal agents in the shires. On the financial side, both English and French monarchs were compelled by their long wars to increase their revenues drastically. Despite the resistance of traditionalists who thought that kings should live on the profits of their own estates, Charles VII secured the right to levy a regular tax, or *taille,* on the whole French nation. By Henry V's time, the English royal budget was six times what it had been before the Hundred Years' War began. As far away as eastern Poland and Hungary, as far south as the Kingdom of Naples, monarchs worked to expand their administrative power and their financial resources.

The increasing need for money, however, also led the kings of the late Middle Ages to make concessions to the wealthiest and most powerful of their subjects. These concessions frequently took the form of granting a voice in the royal government itself to these traditional enemies of centralization. In France, the power-hungry Philip the Fair convened the first French *Estates General* in 1302 in order to get these great men of the realm to vote him taxes for a war. This assembly, purporting to represent all three estates of medieval society—clergy, knights, and commoners—in fact resembled the original English Parliament, which had also consisted of three groups: the leaders of the church, bishops, and abbots; dukes, counts, and other landed magnates; and merchants and lawyers from wealthy towns.

The Parliament in England, established in the

preceding century, grew stronger, particularly during Edward III's long war-torn reign. During this period, Parliament divided into upper and lower chambers—the House of Lords, consisting of the church hierarchy and the nobility just mentioned, and the House of Commons, where townsmen and untitled country gentry met together, beginning a partnership of historic significance. During this period also, the parliamentary practice of petitioning the king evolved into genuine legislation as those petitions the king granted were duly registered as laws. Perhaps most important, the House of Commons acquired the exclusive right to initiate revenue bills. This *power of the purse* gave Commons a great deal of political clout in centuries to come.

In later medieval and earlier modern times, monarchs normally manipulated these occasional conventions of their ruling classes in their own interests. The powerful prelates, landed aristocrats, and wealthy merchants assembled in the Parliament, the Estates General, the Spanish *Cortes,* and similar bodies seldom seriously challenged the authority of the crown. In one case, however, the great magnates were able to extract major concessions from a monarch as early as the fourteenth century. This occurred in the Holy Roman Empire, where the emperor surrendered most of the real power to the individual German states by the *Golden Bull* of 1356.

The basic pattern for the delegation of imperial power had been established in the thirteenth century by the formidable emperor Frederick II, whose main interests lay in Italy and who willingly sacrificed power in Germany to free himself for an active policy in the south. In the mid-fourteenth century, Emperor Charles IV (r. 1355–1378), whose primary concern was to strengthen his hereditary kingdom of Bohemia, won the consent of the German princes to his efforts by issuing the Golden Bull. This fundamental document formally granted the right to choose each successive emperor to seven princely electors—the duke of Saxony, the count palatine of the Rhine, the margrave of Brandenburg, the king of Bohemia, and the archbishops of Cologne, Mainz, and Trier. It also vested broad independent powers in all the German princes and lesser magnates, including rights to coin money, run their own courts, control mineral rights, and otherwise operate free of imperial intervention.

In the fifteenth century, finally, the Habsburg dynasty of Austria—whose members were elected Holy Roman emperors from 1452 until the abolition of the Empire in 1806—followed the policies estab-lished by Frederick II and Charles IV. The Habsburgs thus concentrated on building the power of the dynasty in its hereditary domains, centered this time in Austria, and allowed the princes, nobles, churchmen, knights, and towns of the Holy Roman Empire almost complete autonomy to run their own domestic affairs.

Business Recovery

The fourteenth-century depression and the stagnation of the economy through the first half of the fifteenth century was an economic and social calamity for most Europeans. Yet there were some business-people who managed to prosper even in hard times. In so doing, furthermore, they added significantly to the West's economic base and to its armory of business skills and techniques.

Despite the passing of the expansive economy of the High Middle Ages, it was still possible for an aggressive entrepreneurial spirit like the French merchant, manufacturer, and financier Jacques Coeur (1395–1456) to grow very rich indeed. Born poor, this late medieval merchant prince rose through the mining industry, textile manufacturing, and Mediterranean trade to become one of the richest men of his time. He built an immense mansion, dressed in velvets and multicolored robes like a nobleman, and became a financier to kings. His financial empire was finally destroyed by political enemies, who charged him with extortion, poisoning, and other offenses. Jacques Coeur may have lacked political savvy, but no one questioned his ability to make money, even in depressed times.

Other businessmen also built themselves private palaces, erected impressive Gothic guildhalls, and continued to contribute lavishly to civic charities and church building. They stayed afloat and even prospered by fine-tuning business techniques developed earlier, by moving into new lines of profitable endeavor, and by building new and more dynamic centers of business activity in hitherto less economically developed parts of Europe.

Thus partnerships and larger companies began to be established on a more permanent basis and to employ professional agents in distant cities to further their interests. Improved bookkeeping methods, letters of credit, and bills of exchange became more common, the use of Arabic numerals even more widespread. Some merchant families began to circulate Europewide newssheets, precursors of today's business press, to help them keep abreast of changing conditions in those politically and economically troubled times.

New businesses also emerged in the late Middle Ages. These included the development of luxurious new fabrics in the wool-manufacturing towns of the Low Countries, an immense armaments industry in Milan, and mining and metallurgy in Austria and Hungary. Most important was the expansion of banking and other financial operations. These included collecting taxes for kings and princes, serving as financial agents for the church, currency dealing, and of course moneylending at a healthy rate of interest. Such loans could go spectacularly bad, especially when bankers financed the sometimes extravagant ambitions of kings. But they could also make a financier like Jacques Coeur extremely rich.

Even in times of economic decline or stagnation, some parts of Europe exhibited real economic growth. Southern Germany and Switzerland, for example, developed extensive commercial and financial sectors in this period. Flanders gradually gave way to the Netherlands as a center of industry and commerce, and Bruges took second place to the bustling Dutch city of Antwerp. On the Baltic, as noted, the Hanseatic League made the fortunes of Lübeck, Hamburg, and dozens of other cities.

Some European merchants, finally, found ways to take advantage even of some of the more disturbing trends of their times. A few European traders explored the Eurasian caravan routes reopened by the Mongols. The Venetian Marco Polo (c. 1254–c. 1324) was the most famous merchant traveler to take that long road east and back again. With his father and his uncle, Marco Polo journeyed across the Middle East and central Asia to China, where for some years he served the most famous Mongol ruler of China, Kublai Khan. Polo's account of the wonders of the Asian civilizations he had seen during his seventeen years at the other end of Eurasia influenced Christopher Columbus, Vasco da Gama, and other European explorers who set out to reach East Asia by sea at the end of the fifteenth century.

Most Europeans remained inward looking and parochial, battered by the late medieval economic decline, as the Middle Ages drew to a close. The conservative guilds of earlier centuries survived to protect the interests of most urban craft workers, and the vast majority of peasants never looked beyond the village and the economic niche in which they were born. But the future belonged to those who were willing to take a chance on something new.

Late Medieval Art

Even in a Europe under siege from so many directions, finally, art and literature did not vanish. As long as there were wealthy merchants, self-glorifying kings, and popes in Rome or Avignon, artists found work.

Gothic cathedrals continued to be built, some of them exploding into the elaborate *flamboyant* ("flaming") style, a profusion of stone traceries, fan vaulting, buttressing, turrets, and finials. The Gothic style also spread to secular structures, including guildhalls, urban mansions, and the castles of great magnates. We have only an exquisite miniature painting of the long-vanished palace of the fourteenth-century French duke of Berry, for example, but it shows the fairy-tale elaboration of towers and turrets that gave their special charm to the chateaus of the fifteenth and later centuries.

Architecture, the dominant art in the days of the high medieval cathedral builders, lost its central place in the fourteenth and fifteenth centuries. Among arts now developing rapidly was painting, the fine art that would play a central role in the Renaissance. A major technical breakthrough was the fifteenth-century invention of oil painting, a medium that was thick, slow drying, and exceptionally rich in color, giving the artist greater control and an expanded chromatic range. Another change was the final abandonment of the flatness and linear quality of Byzantine mosaics, stained glass, and earlier medieval miniature painting, which now gave way to fully rounded, carefully modeled faces and figures. Details of clothing, furniture, and other accessories of daily living were also rendered with meticulous realism. Still rare, however, was the concern with underlying anatomy and convincing perspective that came to distinguish the painting of the Renaissance.

Late medieval painting north of the Alps reached its highest development in Flanders, especially in the work of such masters as Jan van Eyck (c. 1395–c. 1441) and Rogier van der Weyden (c. 1400–1464). The fidelity of Flemish artists to realistic detail made them the most admired painters of portraits, a new and burgeoning field. They also did altarpieces and other religious paintings, however, which shine with the spirit of the lay piety that also flourished in the Low Countries. Van der Weyden's *Descent from the Cross,* for instance, centers on Christ's gaunt body being lowered from the cross. Yet it is the bowed heads and lowered eyes, the sense of deep sorrow and devotion imbuing the figures who surround him that give the picture its somber power—and that express most movingly the spirit of the *devotio moderna.*

The Climax of Medieval Literature: Dante and Chaucer

A later medieval development that had a profound impact on Western literature was the emergence of the vernacular, or modern languages, as literary vehicles. This change made possible the rise of national literatures in the West, including the work of such brilliant later medieval writers as Dante and Chaucer, François Villon and Christine de Pisan.

Latin remained the language of serious thought in the church, the universities, and the scholarship of

This portrait of Dante, the work of one of Giotto's students or imitators, has some of the somber, even dark qualities we may imagine in the creator of the Divine Comedy.

the emerging Renaissance. From the thirteenth century on, however, some versions of the spoken tongues of the European peoples began to be recognized as legitimate "literary languages" also. Literary traditions thus grew up in the dialect of the Paris area of northern France, in the Tuscan Italian spoken in Florence, in the southeastern English of London, in the Castilian Spanish of Spain's leading kingdom, and so on. Literature in these languages had the advantage of being available to a much broader cross section of the national population than the handful of churchmen and scholars who were literate in Latin. The new vernacular literatures thus played an important role in the slow development of national cultures and national consciousness in Europe.

Dante Alighieri (1265–1321), universally hailed as Italy's greatest poet, was the son of a bourgeois family in the wealthy commercial city of Florence. Drawn into the feuds of the papal and imperial political factions that divided northern Italy, Dante was driven into exile for the rest of his life in 1302. His works included a eulogy of the Italian language and a thoughtful tract *On Monarchy* discussing the relative claims of pope and emperor to the allegiance of contemporary Europeans. One of his most popular works was his *Vita Nuova* ("New Life"), a poetic evocation of the beauty and virtue of Beatrice Portinare (1266–1290), whom he loved all his life and converted into a symbol of idealized perfection.

It was his epic poem, *The Divine Comedy* (1312–1321), however, that earned Dante his place among the three or four greatest of Western poets. This vision of a journey through Hell, Purgatory, and Heaven offers a panoply of medieval people, real and fictional, facing the consequences of their earthly lives in the other world. Sinners, saints, and many in between, they are assigned their punishments and rewards with Scholastic logic and depicted with vivid imagery, some condemned to the subterranean circles of the inferno, others exalted to the heavenly spheres beyond the stars. Introduced to the other world by the Roman poet Vergil and guided by his beloved Beatrice to his final discovery of celestial bliss, Dante offers an unparalleled journey through the spiritual "other world" of the age of faith.

Geoffrey Chaucer (1340–1400), England's most admired poet before Shakespeare, was, like Dante, of middle-class origins. Descended from a family of London leatherworkers and winemakers, Chaucer himself became a royal civil servant under Edward III and his successors. Around a successful career as a diplomat and comptroller of customs, he produced poems that combined earthy humor with love and high idealism. Drawn like Dante to the great literature of ancient times, the English poet produced a translation of Boethius's *Consolations of Philosophy* and a tragic love story in verse, *Troilus and Criseyde*, set against the background of the Trojan War. Far and away his most popular work, however, is his *Canterbury Tales*, dating from the 1390s. Here again, a motley array of medieval people of all sorts and conditions pass before our eyes, this time not in the other world but threading a very real pilgrim road from a London suburb to Canterbury Cathedral. The tales the Canterbury pilgrims tell to pass the time range from sermons to animal fables, from chivalric romances to bawdy stories. Each is suited to its teller, each a further revelation of the range and humanity of Western people as a second great cycle of Western history wound toward its end.

In the French poets Christine de Pisan (1364–c. 1431) and François Villon (1413–1463), we have two strikingly original spirits whose writing expressed awareness of deep currents of distress in the fifteenth century. Christine de Pisan was a woman intellectual whose verse and prose commanded respect. Her allegorical *Book of the City of Ladies* (1405) raises such startlingly modern issues as education for women and the sexual double standard, which condemns women for sexual behavior that is acceptable for men. Villon was even further out of the mainstream of courtly verse and chivalric romances. Born in poverty, he discovered his intellectual gifts as a roistering university student, became a bandit, and was nearly executed for murder. His poems, written in the slangy French of the late medieval Parisian underworld, give us a glimpse of that community of the damned—criminals, prostitutes, beggars, and others who lived their lives at the bottom of society. A modern note—the celebration of society's victims—is clearly struck once more. Yet there is a sense of loss here also, of a medie-

---

THE HUMAN SPIRIT
The Last Days

The darkening mood of the end of the Middle Ages was reflected in the widespread belief that the end of the world itself was near. The events of the biblical Apocalypse were frequently pictured on church walls, and poems like this ballade "Against the Present Time" by the French writer Eustache Deschamps (1346–1407) expressed the prevailing sense of social decay and doom impending:

> Time of mourning and of temptation,
> Age of tears, of envy and of torments,
> Time of languor and of damnation,
> Age of declining nigh to the end,
> Time full of horror which does all things falsely,
> Lying age, full of pride and of envy,
> Time without honor and without true judgment,
> [Ours is an] age of sadness which shortens life.

Source: Eustache Deschamps, in Johan Huizinga, *The Waning of the Middle Ages* (Garden City, N.Y.: Doubleday, 1956), 33.

---

val world as much myth as reality, indubitably vanishing as the fifteenth century wore on, in Villon's most haunting refrain: "But where are the snows of yesteryear?"[4] (For another poetic reflection of this mood, see the box titled "The Last Days.")

An age was dying. Despite the sulfurous imagery of Dante and the flame-lit Last Judgments on the walls of late medieval churches, however, the end of the world was not yet. The Four Horsemen took their toll, yet in the end they passed by.

A Topical Summary

Politics: Wars ravaged Europe during the fourteenth and fifteenth centuries, the period that included the Hundred Years' War between England and France, the Mongol domination of Russia, and the Ottoman Turkish capture of Constantinople. Some late medieval rulers strengthened their governmental machinery. Institutions speaking for the wealthiest and most powerful of their subjects, however, including the English Parliament and the Estates General in France

and elsewhere, exploited the royal need for funds in order to increase their own rights and powers too.

Economics: Famine and plague, particularly the Black Death, reversed the demographic growth of the High Middle Ages, destroying perhaps a third of the population and triggering a deep economic downturn. The depression of the later fourteenth century turned into economic stagnation in the earlier fifteenth century. Individual merchants like Jacques Coeur, however, continued to flourish, and new industries and more effective business organization did strengthen the economy in the fifteenth century.

Society: The ravages of war and the shrinking late medieval economy also led to violent conflicts between social classes in many parts of Europe. Peasant revolts and urban rebellions thus added to the disarray of the late medieval centuries. The Great Schism in the Roman Catholic church, when two or even three rival popes claimed to be St. Peter's heirs, also contributed to the social confusion of a dying age.

Technology: Military technology made especially significant advances in this war-torn age. Particularly important was the development of artillery, which was effectively deployed in both the Hundred Years' War and the Turkish conquest of Constantinople.

Culture: The waning of the Middle Ages produced some elaborate late Gothic churches and guildhalls, and some new art and literature pointed toward the work of early modern times. The latter included the realistic art of the Low Countries and the poetry of Dante, Chaucer, and other writers in the vernacular, or modern languages.

Some Key Terms

Avignon papacy 334	free company 330	Justices of the Peace 341
bastard feudalism 331	*gens du roi* 341	Lollardy 336
bubonic plague 321	Golden Bull 342	Mongols 337
ciompi 327	Golden Horde 338	Ottoman Turks 340
conciliar movement 334	Great Schism 334	power of the purse 342
Dance of Death 323	Hussites 336	*taille* 341
devotio moderna 335	*Jacquerie* 325	*Unam Sanctum* 333
Estates General 341	*janissary corps* 340	Wars of the Roses 331

Notes

1. *The Trial of Jeanne d'Arc,* trans. W.P. Barrett (London: Routledge, 1931), 165.
2. *Unam Sanctam,* in *The Crisis of Church and State,* trans. Brian Tierney (Englewood Cliffs, N.J.: Prentice Hall, 1964), 189.
3. Maurice Keen, *The Pelican History of Medieval Europe* (Harmondsworth, England: Penguin, 1968), 283.
4. "Ballade des Dames du Temps Jadis," in *Oeuvres,* ed. André Mary (Paris: Editions Garnier Frères, 1951), 31.

Reading List

ABU-LUGHOD, J. *Before European Hegemony: The World System A.D. 1250–1350.* New York: Oxford University Press, 1989. Emphasizes the role of the Mongol Empire in establishing an economic world system in late medieval times.

ATKINSON, C. W. *Mystic and Pilgrim: The Book and the World of Marjorie Kempe.* Ithaca, N.Y.: Cornell University Press, 1983. The work and milieu of the remarkably worldly late medieval mystic.

CHAUCER, G. *The Canterbury Tales.* Boston: Houghton Mifflin, 1974. Medieval people brought vigorously to life by a master of characterization as well as of Middle English verse.

DANTE ALIGHIERI. *The Divine Comedy.* Translated by J. Ciardi. New York: Norton, 1970. Poetic modern rendering of the great Italian poet's imagined journey through the other world.

FOURQUIN, G. *The Anatomy of Popular Rebellion in the Middle Ages.* New York: North-Holland, 1978. Survey of mass uprisings—religious, social, and political—during the fourteenth and fifteenth centuries.

GIES, F. *Joan of Arc: The Legend and the Reality.* New York: Harper & Row, 1981. Many views of the most famous of French saints.

GOTTFRIED, R. S. *The Black Death: Natural and Human Disaster in Medieval Europe.* New York: Macmillan, 1983. Relates the bubonic plague to human ecology and outlines the broad economic and psychological circumstances in which it occurred.

GUENEE, B. *States and Rulers in Later Medieval Europe.*

Translated by J. Vale. New York: Blackwood, 1985. Comparative study of royal governments in western Europe.

HOLMES, G. *Europe: Hierarchy and Revolt, 1320–1450.* London: Harvester Press, 1975. Brief yet comprehensive overview of the end of the Middle Ages, with glances ahead at the early modern period.

HOWELL, M. C. *Women, Production, and Patriarchy in Late Medieval Cities.* Chicago: University of Chicago Press, 1986. Productive women in male-dominated institutions.

HUIZINGA, J. *The Waning of the Middle Ages.* Garden City, N.Y.: Doubleday, 1956. Famous portrait of a dying age, focusing on France and the Low Countries.

LAMBERT, M. *Medieval Heresy: Popular Movements from Bogomil to Hus.* New York: Holmes and Meier, 1976. Broad historical summary of the major medieval heresies.

LEFF, G. *The Dissolution of the Medieval Outlook: An Essay on Intellectual and Spiritual Change in the Fourteenth Century.* New York: New York University Press, 1976. Brief but illuminating interpretation of late medieval thought.

LE ROY LADURIE, E. *Montaillou: The Promised Land of Error.* Translated by B. Bray. New York: Braziller, 1978. Startling account of life in a late medieval village, including candid confessions of heretical beliefs and sexual peccadillos, based on Inquisition records.

NICOL, D. M. *The Last Centuries of Byzantium, 1261–1453.* London: Hart-Davis, 1972. The decline of the Byzantine Empire to its final fall to the Ottoman Turks.

PERROY, E. *The Hundred Years War.* Translated by W. B. Wells. London: Eyre and Spottiswoode, 1951. Best short account, putting military events in their political and social context.

ROSS, C. *Richard III.* Berkeley: University of California, 1961. Good introduction to a controversial ruler of England.

SEWARD, D. *The Hundred Years War: The English in France, 1337–1543.* New York: Atheneum, 1982. Clear and informed narrative account of the war, stronger on events than analysis.

TURBERVILLE, A. S. *Medieval Heresy and the Inquisition.* Hamden, Conn.: Archon, 1964. Balanced account. R. I. MOORE, *The Formation of a Persecuting Society: Power and Deviance in Western Europe, 950–1250.* (New York: Blackwell, 1987) sees religious persecution as intrinsic to medieval society.

VALE, M. *War and Chivalry: Warfare and Aristocratic Culture in England, France, and Burgundy at the End of the Middle Ages.* London: Duckworth, 1981. Sees more vitality in fifteenth-century chivalry than is commonly believed.

Part III

The West Reborn

The modern age, as the majority of historians conceptualize it, began earlier than most people think. Admittedly the boundary between medieval and modern times is hazy, more a matter of gradual change than of ends and beginnings, but today it is typically set at the time of the European Renaissance, rather than in the eighteenth century when modern industry and many modern ideas first took shape.

The early modern period, with which this part of the book is concerned, is commonly dated from the fifteenth century for Europe and from a slightly earlier time for Italy, where the rebirth of arts and letters called the Renaissance began. Just as the fall of Rome in the fifth century has traditionally been seen as marking the divide between the ancient and medieval periods, so the fall of Constantinople in 1453 has often been taken as a convenient point at which to end the Middle Ages and begin the modern age. As we will see, the early modern period gives way somewhere in the eighteenth century to a more recognizably modern age. We follow the common practice of marking the end of early modern history with the reign of the great French king Louis XIV, who died in 1715. Thus we deal with the 1400s, 1500s, and 1600s in this part of the book.

For the now rapidly expanding Western world, these were the turbulent centuries of such innovative spirits as Columbus, Martin Luther, Copernicus, Isaac Newton, Leonardo da Vinci, and William Shakespeare. They were times of change and challenge not only for the West but for humankind itself.

In the political arena, the early modern period saw the development of the strongest central governments since ancient Rome in the "new monarchies" of the fifteenth and sixteenth centuries and the "absolute monarchies" of the seventeenth. But the seventeenth century also witnessed the emergence in England of the constitutional monarchy, the forerunner of more democratic forms of government. And these were the centuries of the birth of Europe's vast overseas empires, which brought much of North, South, and Middle America under western European rule. With these and other intercontinental empires came a global exchange of goods that became known as the world market. Imperial Europe was the center of a flow of silk, spices, and slaves from Asia and Africa and of gold, silver, sugar, and tobacco from the Americas.

Looked at through the prism of social history, the European core of the Western world exhibited a new fluidity after 1500. Few European peasants were serfs any longer, and the commercial middle class gained a new importance. A few brilliant individuals mastered so many arts and skills that we still reserve the label "Renaissance person" for an individual with a multiplicity of interests and talents.

It is the intellectual and artistic life of this period that has most dazzled later observers. The Renaissance revitalized Western culture, partly by a major recovery of ancient arts and ideas, partly by inventing new art forms of its own. The Reformation divided western Europe spiritually but ended by fostering a spirit of toleration not seen in the West since ancient Rome.

In terms of territorial expansion and of contacts with non-Western peoples, the early modern period marked a great leap forward. In the sixteenth century, as we have noted, Spain and Portugal conquered large tracts of the New World; Portugal in particular established colonies and trading posts in many parts of Africa and Asia. In the seventeenth century, the English, French, and Dutch carved out smaller settlements and commercial empires in North America, the Caribbean basin, India, and Southeast Asia, with outposts as far east as China and Japan. Although even in the Americas much of this expansion was limited to coastal areas and islands, and by 1715 Africa remained largely unpenetrated and Asia unconquered, the mere presence of Western soldiers, traders, settlers, and missionaries in so many parts of the world was unprecedented. The global rise of the West had begun.

The Western world got a new start in the centuries around 1500, and the core of that new beginning was a remarkable social and cultural revival we call the *Renaissance*. The word *renaissance* means "rebirth," and the period carrying that name, which began in Italy in the 1300s and climaxed across much of western Europe in the 1500s, has often been seen as the springtime of the modern world. Although this view has been challenged and reinterpreted by a number of historians over the past century and a half—and we will explore some of these objections—the fundamental strength of this conception justifies structuring this and the next chapter around the notion of a Western rebirth.

In the present chapter we deal with the aggressive "new monarchs" of the Renaissance who restored political power to the center of European states and with the economic expansion and social dynamism of the age as a whole. Then we turn to the great cultural achievements in thought and scholarship, literature and the arts for which the Renaissance is renowned. Later chapters in this part focus on other innovative, even revolutionary events that owe at least part of their impetus to this period of reawakening and rebirth.

Andrea del Verocchio. *Lorenzo de' Medici*. National Gallery of Art, Washington, D.C. Samuel H. Kress Collection

The Renaissance in History and Historiography

Let us begin with some historiographic considerations. The Renaissance is, after all, an interpretive concept, not a "fact" like a battle or an election or a day in your life. Much of our understanding of the past, as we have seen, hinges on such historiographic or interpretive theories, and the closer we get to the present day, the thornier the problems of interpretation seem to get. The many questions surrounding the idea of the Renaissance comprise one of the most challenging of these problems of historical interpretation.

The Idea of the Renaissance

Probing the past for historical understanding is a little like detective work, sifting detailed bits and pieces of evidence in search of larger truths. In this case, the evidence ranges from yellowing manuscripts and old account books to antique weapons, early printed

	1300	1350	1400

POLITICAL, MILITARY, AND DIPLOMATIC EVENTS

1389–1464   Cosimo de' Medici

SOCIAL AND ECONOMIC DEVELOPMENTS

1348   Black Death

1400–1450   Rise of Medici business empire

volumes, and whole palaces full of art. And the goal is not to understand a single historical figure like Alexander the Great or to trace the emergence of a single nation-state, such as England or France, but to establish the existence and define the nature of an entire epoch of Western history.

Western historical awareness of the *Renaissance* evolved slowly, from the first intuitions of contemporaries through the sweeping interpretations of the nineteenth century to the more critical analyses of our own times. Here we first trace the development of the theory that a new age began around 1500 and then, after looking at some challenges to this view, outline the historiographic assumptions this book makes in the chapters that follow.

Five hundred years ago, some European artists and intellectuals began to feel that theirs was a special time. "This century, like a golden age," wrote the Florentine philosopher Marsilio Ficino in the late 1400s, "has restored to light the liberal arts, which were almost extinct: grammar, poetry, rhetoric, painting, sculpture, architecture, music. . . . Achieving what had been honored among the ancients, but almost forgotten since, the age has joined

wisdom with eloquence . . . recalled the platonic teaching from darkness into light. . . ."[1] Intellectuals then and in the following centuries compared the Renaissance to such cultural high points in Western history as the Augustan Age in ancient Rome and the Age of Pericles in ancient Athens. They also tended to contrast their own enlightened times with what they saw as the "dark ages," the thousand years between the fall of Rome and the modern period.

The notion of a Renaissance, or "rebirth," of European civilization in the fifteenth century was given its most influential form by the nineteenth-century Swiss historian Jacob Burckhardt in his book *The Civilization of the Renaissance in Italy* (1860). Burckhardt defined the Renaissance as the period in cultural history that began with the poet Petrarch in Italy in the fourteenth century and climaxed in the early sixteenth, the age of such artistic giants as Leonardo da Vinci and Michelangelo. Burckhardt stressed the influence of classical culture in the Renaissance revival but also detected such uniquely modern attitudes as belief in human individualism and love of the natural world.

Later historians added other dimensions to this

r. 1461–1483 Louis XI
r. 1462–1505 Ivan III
r. 1469–1492 Lorenzo dé Medici
r. 1474–1504 Isabella
r. 1479–1516 Ferdinand
r. 1485–1509 Henry VII
1492 Charles XII invades Italy
r. 1492–1503 Alexander VI
r. 1493–1519 Maximilian I
r. 1503–1513 Julius II
r. 1509–1547 Henry VIII
r. 1515–1547 Francis I
r. 1519–1555 Charles V

1450–1500 Economic recovery
1460s–1520 Rise of Fugger businesses
1492 Moors, Jews expelled from Spain
Columbus reaches America
1498 Vasco da Gama reaches India
c. 1500 Population returns to 1348 level

theory of a cultural rebirth five centuries ago. Politically and economically too, some thought, the Western world underwent significant change in the fourteenth, fifteenth, and sixteenth centuries. A leading twentieth-century student of the Renaissance as a concept thus summed up "the distinguishing characteristic of the Renaissance" as "the change from a natural economy to one based on money, from a rural society to one in which the influential classes dwelt in cities and drew their wealth directly or indirectly from trade."[2]

A Historiographic Construct?

A number of historians have challenged this image of a golden springtime for the modern world. Some criticisms focus on specific points, denying the central role of classical culture or the essential role of Italians as the first modern people. Experts on the Middle Ages have understandably objected to having their period characterized as "dark" by contrast to the Renaissance. But there have been even more probing questions concerning the chronology, basic

characteristics, and very existence of what is, after all, a historiographic construct, a historical theory about the past.

Simply dating this age of rebirth proved awkward. If we describe the revival as beginning in Italy in the fourteenth century, we must note that it takes place at exactly the time when the rest of Europe was going the other way, sinking into the wave of late medieval disasters described in the last chapter. The end of the Renaissance also overlaps the Reformation in the sixteenth century: Michelangelo shared the earlier 1500s with Martin Luther, and England's Renaissance—the Elizabethan Age of Shakespeare—came in the late 1500s. Some of these chronological difficulties can be overcome by seeing the Renaissance as a trend that *spread* from fourteenth-century Italy to Europe north of the Alps in the fifteenth and sixteenth centuries. And the Renaissance overlap with the Reformation at the other end has led many historians to think of the first stage of modern history as the age of both the Renaissance *and* the Reformation, an approach that is also reflected in this book.

The specific definition of the Renaissance also posed problems. Was it really a rebirth of ancient

Map 12.1 Italy in the Fifteenth Century

culture—or the *birth* of new and unprecedented modern directions of development? The best answer may be that the Renaissance was both. Much Renaissance art and literature was clearly based on ancient models, but Renaissance artists like Leonardo and writers like Shakespeare were original talents, redefining painting and the drama for the modern age.

Most difficult of all, perhaps, is defending the whole notion of beginnings and endings in history. As we noticed in connection with the decline and fall of the Roman Empire, the tendency today is to stress continuities and transitions, rather than to draw hard lines between historical eras. In the case of the Renaissance and Reformation, there are certainly clear continuities with the Middle Ages. The feudal monarchies and commercial towns of the medieval period, for example, were the direct ancestors of the strong Renaissance monarchies and prosperous cities

we discuss in this chapter. There were strong individualists in the Middle Ages, yet people continued to see themselves as parts of communities, classes, and other collectivities through the Renaissance and beyond.

The fourteenth, fifteenth, and sixteenth centuries were undoubtedly a period of transition, but so are all historical periods. In the case of this passage from medieval to modern, the contrasts seem stark enough to justify looking at the Renaissance as a new beginning. The catastrophes of the later Middle Ages really were devastating, and there were many startling differences between the twelfth and the sixteenth centuries, the High Middle Ages and the High Renaissance. The new arts of Leonardo and Shakespeare, the Reformation split in Western Christendom, and such contemporary events as the discoveries of Columbus and Copernicus and the growth of Western overseas empires and of a Western-dominated world market all make the medieval Europe of 1200 look quaint, provincial, and far away. Thus, all things considered, *Renaissance,* implying both recovery and new beginnings, is not too strong a term for what happened in western Europe in the centuries around 1500.

Economics, Politics, and Culture

The idea of the Renaissance was originally a cultural one, defining early modern developments in the history of ideas, literature, and the arts. Yet the present chapter is concerned almost exclusively with economic and political trends during these centuries. What is the relevance of economics and politics to the study of a cultural golden age?

Culture, like most other things, costs money. Pictures and statues must be paid for, poetic and architectural masterpieces commissioned by a patron or a public wealthy enough to afford these luxuries. One might assume that cultural golden ages would also turn out to be ages of affluence, when there is plenty of extra money around to pay for art. At first glance, the Renaissance—or at least its seminal early stages—does not seem to meet these conditions.

It is true that an economic revival began in the later fifteenth century and crescendoed in the sixteenth. We discuss this economic upturn in the sections that follow. But the fourteenth and fifteenth centuries, the first half of the Renaissance as it is traditionally defined, saw Europe sink into a deep depression followed by a long period of economic stagnation. How, then, do we account for the cultural flowering that began in Italy as early as the 1300s?

A number of explanations have been suggested. For one thing, the European depression was not uniform. Some regions and some sectors of the economy were spared, and some—for example, insurance—even boomed. What money there was, furthermore, could be monopolized by successful individuals, giving a few merchant princes plenty of money to spend on artistic wall paintings or collections of elegantly hand-copied books. Even a trend toward smaller families could contribute to this concentration of wealth in a few hands, as we will see.

The tendency to spend money on culture also seems to have been growing, and here the political framework becomes important to our understanding of Renaissance culture. The rulers of Renaissance cities and states, it has been suggested, may have

been willing to invest lavishly on guildhalls, town halls, and other civic structures as an expression of their confidence in the state and its future during hard times. Renaissance political leaders, furthermore, may have patronized culture as a way of winning public approbation and acceptance into the cultured elite. Many Renaissance princes, as we will see, were self-made rulers who could not claim an ancient noble name or a hereditary throne. By subsidizing famous writers or great artists, they gained reputations as people of cultured taste and as patrons of "higher things."

The emergence of this educated elite, ending a thousand years of church domination of culture, meant that what money did reach a Renaissance

Jan van Eyck's *Marriage of Giovanni Arnolfini and Giovanna Cenami* depicts the fashionable wedding of a prominent Italian businessman who lived and worked in the Netherlands to a woman from his home town of Lucca. Van Eyck's picture reminds us of the close ties between the Netherlands and Italy, the two wealthiest parts of Europe in the fifteenth century.

prince or merchant prince was increasingly likely to be spent on classical relics or contemporary art. "Culture," as one authority puts it, "tended to become the highest symbol of nobility, the magic password which admitted a man . . . to the elite ground. Its value rose at the very moment that the value of land fell."[3] The old political ruling class, basing its claim to political power on feudal landholding, thus made room for a new aristocracy claiming to be people of culture and capacity and justifying that claim by supporting the cultural rebirth of western Europe.

We concentrate in this chapter on economics and politics, in the next one on art and literature. But the connections between the material and cultural spheres of human life were as intricate and important at the beginning of the modern era as they are today.

Economic Revival

The economic history of the Renaissance period is one of dynamic change after the decline and stagnation of the later Middle Ages. Demographically, commercially, financially, and in terms of overall production, the West was expanding once more in the later fifteenth and sixteenth centuries, as it had been in the twelfth and thirteenth. A good deal of this renewed growth was rooted in the new and unprecedented overseas expansion of the Western peoples that began with the voyages of Christopher Columbus and Vasco da Gama in the 1490s. But the renewed material and economic growth of the West began before the overseas empires took shape, and it is these earlier Renaissance developments that concern us here.

"Put money in thy purse," says one of Shakespeare's shrewder if less savory characters, and all things will be possible.[4] Certainly the turbulent history of the Renaissance was to a significant degree built on this great early modern expansion in the material wealth of the West.

Renewed Population Growth

A primary source of this first modern surge of productivity and power may be found in the demographic statistics of the age. The population of the West, which had grown rapidly in the centuries between 1100 and 1350, had been flung into a precipitous decline by the plagues, famines, and wars of the later Middle Ages. Around 1450, however, a demographic recovery began that was to last some two hundred years. By 1500, Europe's population was probably approaching that of 1350 once more. By 1600, population gains of perhaps 50 percent had been registered across much of the Western world.

Cities grew particularly rapidly. Only four European cities had populations of over 100,000 in 1500, three of them—Venice, Milan, and Naples—in Renaissance Italy. By 1600, five cities—those just listed plus London and Paris—had more than 150,000 people. Several others, including Rome and Palermo in Italy, Antwerp and Amsterdam in the Low Countries, and the Spanish and Portuguese imperial ports of Seville and Lisbon, now had populations over 100,000. The population of London alone may have multiplied as much as four times—from 50,000 to 200,000—in the course of the sixteenth century.

Although these numbers sound convincing, it should be emphasized that all such figures for this early period are estimates at best. The study of demography, which has undergone something of a methodological revolution in recent decades, has developed some ingenious techniques for reckoning populations and determining population trends before the nineteenth century, when comprehensive census taking began. Tax records, for instance, provide valuable guides, though these are often based on households rather than individuals. More detailed statistical studies of sample communities may be derived from the registers of births, marriages, and deaths kept in parish churches. Yet the evidence remains scattered and fragmentary. And when one factors in the wide local and regional variations, all statements about population trends in the early modern centuries must remain tentative.

Nevertheless, if the demographic recovery and advance just outlined is even broadly accurate, its impact on the Western economy must have been considerable. More mouths to feed necessitated expanded agricultural production. Handicraft manufacturing and larger industrial ventures were also stimulated by increased demand. And commercial exchange inevitably expanded to effect the necessary distribution of this increased production to the growing numbers of customers. The rapid economic expansion of the Renaissance was thus in large part caused by the increased demand created by population growth.

Agriculture, Trade, and Technology

Other factors besides growing demand contributed to the widespread revival of Europe's economic life in the fifteenth and sixteenth centuries. In both agriculture and industry, continuations of progressive medieval trends combined with innovative methods to trigger a new surge of productivity and exchange.

European agriculture grew in part because of demographic recovery. With more people to feed, woodlands, swamps, and rocky hillsides abandoned by farmers when the Black Death swept through were once again brought under the plow. Especially notable was land reclamation from the sea. Centering in the Low Countries—the Netherlands and Belgium today—this campaign by lowland dwellers to push back the sea produced large amounts of new arable land in northwestern Europe. Methodical and determined, the Dutch in particular had been raising dikes and draining land since the High Middle Ages. By the sixteenth century, these massive engineering projects had reclaimed thousands of acres of *polders,* table-flat land scored by irrigation canals, guarded by immense dikes, and drained by slowly turning windmills.

Dutch engineers were soon being hired to help the English and other coastal peoples expand the areas they too had recovered from the sea. The Dutch have continued this work over the centuries, turning marshy river deltas and intrusive arms of the North Sea into fertile farm and pastureland, much of it below sea level.

Another factor in the agricultural growth of this period was the controversial type of land organization often called *enclosure.* Under this system, lands formerly plowed in uneconomical strips by medieval villagers were enclosed in large blocks by landowners for more efficient utilization. Enclosure usually involved a shift from cropping the land to pasturing sheep for wool production. The enclosure system required less labor—only a few shepherds rather than villages full of peasants. This feature proved a great advantage after the Black Death had drastically reduced the size of the peasant work force available in the mid-fourteenth century. The lower labor bill also made enclosures more profitable for landowners in later periods. Enclosures, which spread in the sixteenth century and continued to become more common, especially in England, made land more economically productive than it had been.

There were important drawbacks. The Spanish

Pol de Limbourg's illustration of harvest and sheep-shearing time at the Duke de Berry's chateau near Poitiers shows men cutting grain and women clipping wool off the backs of sheep in the fifteenth century.

Mesta, or sheep raisers' association, made stock breeding so profitable that other productive sectors were drastically neglected. Even more disturbing, in a Europe whose population was growing once again, enclosures had the unfortunate effect of driving large numbers of peasants off the land where their labor was no longer required. These "sturdy beggars" (so called to distinguish them from cripples who begged because they were not physically able to work) thronged the roads and swelled the populations of the cities, creating new social tensions there.

A more positive consequence of enclosure was a renewed expansion of cloth manufacturing, the oldest and largest of Western industries. Production not only of woolens but of linens, silks, and other fabrics grew. An increasing variety of qualities and types of cloth emerged, including worsteds (tightly woven wool), fustians (mixing linen and cotton imported from the Near East), and luxurious velvets, brocades, and cloth-of-gold. Some of this hand manufacturing was cottage industry, done on cottage looms and spinning wheels by peasants. Their labors were coordinated by traveling merchants who provided the raw materials and picked up the roughly woven cloth in what became known as the *putting-out system*. This form of domestic production presided over by a merchant capitalist is, as we will see in a later chapter, often described as *proto-industrialism,* the precursor of the Industrial Revolution. In the Low Countries and in the southern German states, this boom in the clothmaking trades also stimulated the renewed growth of handicraft industry in the towns. In northern Italy, crafts connected with the finishing of rough cloth continued to prosper in the cities, along with wool and silk manufacturing.

Metallurgy was another industry that made great strides in the later fifteenth and sixteenth centuries. Technical innovations contributed largely to these advances. New techniques for driving mine shafts deep into the earth, for shoring them up against cave-ins and pumping out water seepage made possible the exploitation of iron, copper, silver, and other metals from strata that were unreachable before. Advanced smelting technology used large bellows to increase the heat of furnaces that separated ore from slag or silver from lesser metals. Heavy mechanical hammers were developed to pound metal into required shapes. Water wheels, long used for grinding grain, were brought into play here to provide power for draining mines and operating bellows and triphammers in foundries. (For other uses of the water wheel, see box, "Renaissance Water Wheels.") Mining and metalworking thus reached new levels of productivity, especially in Germany, Hungary, Bohemia (the Czech Republic of today), and other parts of central Europe.

The life of the miner or the metalworker was a hard one, but the economy of Europe as a whole benefited significantly from technological breakthroughs in these fields. Among the consequences were higher grade iron, larger quantities of bronze, and silver production that may have multiplied five times even before the beginning of large silver imports from the Americas in the early 1500s. Bronze for cannons—and Renaissance statues—silver for coinage, which itself stimulated the economic recov-

MASTERING OUR WORLD
Renaissance Water Wheels

The eminent French historian Fernand Braudel here describes the level of technological development achieved in the West by the beginning of modern times. All the devices listed could be powered by one of the oldest power sources, the water wheel. How rare such technology was, however, is made clear by the wondering description of an early power saw included in this account.

> The uses of the waterwheel had become manifold; it worked pounding devices for crushing minerals, heavy tilt-hammers used in iron forging, enormous beaters used by cloth fullers, bellows at iron-works; also pumps, millstones to grind knives, tanning mills and paper mills, which were the last to appear. We should also mention the mechanical saws that appeared in the thirteenth century. . . .
>
> But mechanical saws were still no everyday sight. When Barthélemy Joly crossed the Jura and arrived at Geneva in 1603, he noticed mills in the Neyrolles valley at the outlet of the lake of Silan handling "pine and fir wood which is thrown from the top of the precipitous mountains to the bottom, with a pleasing device by which several movements [of the saw] from bottom to top and in the opposite direction proceed from a single wheel turned by water, the wood moving forward of its own accord . . . and another tree following in its place with as much method as if it were done by men's hands." It is obvious that this was indeed an unusual sight, worthy of inclusion in a travelogue.

Source: Fernand Braudel, *Capitalism and the Material Life 1400–1800,* trans. Miriam Kochan (New York: Harper & Row, 1967), 261.

ery, and other essential products poured forth in unprecedented quantities.

Renaissance Cities

With both population and productivity growing rapidly once more, commerce also flourished in the Renaissance. Merchants were the middlemen who got goods from producers to consumers, stimulating both production and consumption, and growing exceedingly rich in the process. Italy was the center of this resurgent capitalism, but cities flourished in the north as well.

Commercial methods originally pioneered in the Middle Ages were further developed. Coinage itself, reestablished in Europe during the twelfth-century commercial revolution, expanded further in the fifteenth century, thanks to the increased amount of silver available. With this monetary expansion came a gradual inflation in prices and a commensurate increase in the profits of merchants. Such business practices as the letter of credit—safer than carrying coins—and double-entry bookkeeping were also more widely used, and commercial insurance for long and dangerous trading voyages became common. The family firms and joint-stock companies of the fifteenth century, sometimes smaller than their medieval predecessors, were better organized to respond flexibly to changing times. And as we will see, some Renaissance entrepreneurs established commercial networks that reached across much of Europe.

Cities remained the centers of Renaissance trade, and their growth reflected the commercial expansion of the era. Though the medieval urban centers of the Low Countries, the Rhineland, and elsewhere flourished, Italian commercial preeminence continued throughout the fourteenth and fifteenth centuries. Among the large and prosperous Italian cities of the Renaissance were Milan, Genoa, Naples, Rome, and most admired of all, the venerable commercial metropolis of Venice and the newer center of wealth and culture, Florence.

The Venetian Republic, a key connection between Europe and the Near East since the Middle Ages, now commanded a coastal and island empire that stretched from northern Italy down the Adriatic and across the eastern Mediterranean as far as Cyprus. It still imported luxury goods from the Near East and beyond. Its industries included the famous Venetian arsenal, dedicated to shipbuilding and weapons manufacture for defense, which employed some ten thousand men and women by 1500, making it the largest single employer in Europe.

The city of canals that the tourist sees today, with its splendid townhouse facades and tangled commercial streets, dates largely from this period. Venice's Palace of the Doges, at the entrance to the Grand Canal, is thick with statues, paintings, and gilded decoration, a weight of opulence that reaches its climax in the hall where the General Council of more than a thousand merchants once met. It is an immense chamber, floored with multicolored marble, lined with carved oak seats, its walls and vast ceiling covered with glowing Renaissance paintings framed in carved and gilded rectangles, half circles, and ovals. Even the most blasé American visitor may pause before going out for a fantastically expensive drink in the piazza San Marco to reflect on the splendor in which the Venetian Republic conducted its affairs in its golden age.

Most dazzling of all, however, was Florence, the economic as well as the cultural capital of Renaissance Italy. Still a major trade emporium and a center of woolen manufacture and other handicraft industries, Florence in the fifteenth century was also perhaps Europe's leading banking and financial center.

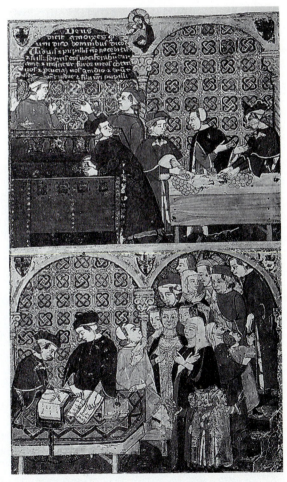

This Italian bank of the late fourteenth century is crowded with customers. Business leaders found financial dealings more profitable than either manufacturing or commerce. What do you miss in this bank that you would expect to see in modern ones?

The Florentine florin was an international currency, the dollar of its day, and branches of Florentine banks were found in all the great cities of Europe.

Ringed in by hills on the Arno River in northern Italy, about halfway between Rome and Venice, the city of Florence was famed for its beautiful churches, palaces, public buildings, and squares. Its patrician business community included some of the leading patrons of Renaissance art and learning, wealthy people who surrounded themselves with mural paintings and statuary of bronze and marble and who subsidized poets and philosophers. A Florentine urban *palazzo*, or mansion, might be rough stone on the outside, facing the turbulent streets of the city; but its inner courtyards, halls, and chambers were magnificent reflections of the taste of the city's mercantile elite.

In northern Europe, the revival of commerce was perhaps most vividly embodied in the rise of Antwerp, which emerged as the trading center of the Netherlands in the later fifteenth century. Like Venice, Antwerp benefited commercially from its location at the meeting of major trade routes. The city stood at the northern end of the Rhine-Alpine axis,

with easy access to the North Sea and the merchant roads of Germany and northern France. Again, however, a farsighted business community made a central contribution. In particular, Antwerp's merchant patriciate opened what became Europe's most famous *Bourse,* or stock exchange and money market, in the early sixteenth century. Inscribed with the welcoming slogan "For the use of merchants of all nations and tongues," the Antwerp exchange swarmed with merchants and bankers from Britain, France, the cities of the Hanseatic League and of south Germany, the Italian city-states, Spain, and Portugal. Antwerp thus became the leading commercial and financial center of northern Europe in the 1500s, and the Gothic townhouses of its merchant rulers were as impressive in their very different style as the marble halls of Florentine palazzi.

The Medici and the Fuggers

Two of the greatest names among Renaissance merchant bankers were the Italian Medici family of Florence and the German house of Fugger, headquar-

Florence in 1490—the Florence of Lorenzo de' Medici—stretched along the Arno river in north central Italy. The cathedral of Florence, with the first dome raised in the Western World since ancient Rome, stands in the center of the picture. The cloth manufacturing district is on the other side of the river, in the industrial suburbs.

tered in Augsburg. The former were among the most successful businessmen in fifteenth-century Italy; the latter were the wealthiest financiers in all Europe in the sixteenth century. These dynasties of merchants and bankers illustrate this stage of mer-

cantile capitalism, which was laying the foundation for the industrial capitalism of a later century while bringing unexampled wealth to Renaissance Europe.

The Medici, the best known of Renaissance business clans, rose to prominence in the early 1400s

Jacob Fugger with his chief accountant. The labels in the background are the names of major European cities, beginning with Rome and Venice, where the great international house of Fugger had commercial and financial dealings.

when they began to give more of their attention to banking than to their established trading activities. In the middle of the century, the most successful of them, Cosimo de' Medici (1389–1464), made the Medici bank one of the biggest in Renaissance Italy and the centerpiece of an international business empire. Enjoying membership in three of the Big Seven merchant guilds of Florence, the Medici family was involved in such key industries as wool processing and silk manufacture and in foreign trade, from the importation of Near Eastern spices to the large-scale export of cloth to France. Above all, however, their wealth was built on the far-flung branches of the family bank, which were to be found not only in the Italian metropolises of Venice, Milan, and Rome, but north of the Alps in the southern French cities of Lyons and Avignon, in Bruges in the Low Countries, in the Hanseatic city of Lübeck, in London and Barcelona and elsewhere. These extensive commercial and financial enterprises were bound together by family ties and interlocking partnerships. Branch managers were often both relatives, by blood or by marriage, and partners in the Medici bank in Florence. Profiting from loans to businessmen, noblemen, princes, and popes, the fifteenth-century Medici earned their reputation as the greatest financial dynasty in Renaissance Italy. And in the strong, deeply wrinkled face of Cosimo, hailed by his fellow citizens as *pater patriae,* "the father of his country," we see reflected the strength of will and care for detail that made these merchants and bankers a driving force in early modern history.

The Fugger family of Augsburg, in southern Germany, became Europe's most successful financiers in the 1500s. Jakob Fugger (1459–1526), called "Jakob the Rich," who had learned his trade in Venice, built the fortunes of the family. Their enterprises eventually stretched from Naples to Flanders and from Spain to Poland and deployed ten times the capital of the Medici bank in its heyday. Leading manufacturers of linen and fustians, masters of the iron, copper, and silver mines of central Europe, and traders in spices, jewels, and other luxury products, the Fuggers, like the Medici, still made most of their money from the trade in money itself. As international bankers, they lent money to businessmen, notably to German miners. They were most famous, however, for their loans to the ruling houses of Europe, particularly to members of the Habsburg family, who by the sixteenth century included both Holy Roman emperors and kings of Spain. Fugger money paid for military campaigns and for the elaborate ceremonial occasions beloved of Renaissance sovereigns, bribed the electors who chose Habsburg emperors, and influenced the election of popes.

By going into politics, the Medici clan continued to play an important part in European history for more than a century after their relative financial decline. The Fuggers remained singlemindedly committed to business; and a series of bad loans, particularly to royal governments, brought the house to ruin early in the seventeenth century. The city of Augsburg had to construct an expanded debtors' prison to hold the numbers of business associates and bank depositors who followed the house of Fugger into bankruptcy. Nevertheless, by capitalizing many industrial and commercial ventures and by financing the wars and political ambitions of princes, the Fuggers, like the Medici, had helped shape the history of Renaissance Europe.

Renaissance Princes

The most famous of Renaissance political thinkers, Niccolò Machiavelli (1469–1527), whose views are discussed in the next chapter, is best known for a brief manual of statecraft called *The Prince.* By "prince," Machiavelli did not mean the son of a king and queen, but simply an independent ruler, of either sex and any title. The duke of Milan, the Holy Roman emperor, Queen Elizabeth, and the pope were all "princes" in this sense. Because Renaissance politics revolved around such leaders, we pay considerable attention here to princes in all their decadence and grandeur.

Let us look first at the emergence of the princes often called "Renaissance despots" in the city-states of Italy and then at the "new monarchs" of the nation-states north of the Alps. The achievements of these first modern rulers provide a useful framework for the economic, social, and cultural explorations that follow.

The Revival of Political Power

The power of the new rulers of the Renaissance was built on medieval foundations. As in the Middle Ages, a good deal of independent authority remained in the hands of the great nobles and the church, of distant provinces with traditional laws, of self-governing towns, guilds, and other constituent parts of the realm. In theory, a healthy commonwealth was run by a variety of hierarchies, each with its own sphere of operations—the aristocracy, the church, the law, the town corporations, and so on—establishing between them a balance of rights and obligations. The Renaissance despots of the south and the new monarchs of the north, however, possessed a larger share of power than their predecessors had. And both types of Renaissance ruler continued to expand the authority of the central government at the expense of other political subdivisions throughout the early modern period.

The strength of Renaissance rulers of the fifteenth and earlier sixteenth century lay partly in personal traits. Princes like Cosimo and Lorenzo de' Medici in Florence, Louis XI of France, Ferdinand and Isabella in Spain, and Henry VII in England tended to be shrewd political manipulators and hard-working heads of state. They often took a pragmatic view of power and of the means necessary to achieve it. They paid somewhat less attention to such medieval concerns as royal piety or chivalric show. Getting the job done was what mattered to these tough-minded rulers.

Renaissance princes governed through both formal and informal institutions. Among the central institutions of early modern government was the informal gathering of power brokers and cronies called the *princely court*. More formal and more lasting were the growing centralized administrations and the beginnings of modern diplomatic corps, armies, and navies.

The courts of princes were social institutions that gathered the chief people in the realm about the ruler. Ministers of state, great noblemen, ambitious soldiers of fortune, charming hangers-on, the prince's friends and lovers, artists, entertainers, and servants in large numbers clustered around a powerful ruler. They came to make their fortunes—to become princely favorites (or favorites of favorites), to acquire lucrative posts or lands, to win knighthoods or noble titles. In return, they were willing to serve the prince by doing the work of government—some as judges or treasury officials or royal secretaries, others by carrying out diplomatic missions or commanding armies in the field.

Competition for royal favor and rewards was rife at court, and competing factions could paralyze a government or divide a nation. A shrewd ruler, on the other hand, could play chief favorites off against one another and get the most work out of all of them. Women found more power at court than elsewhere, either as sovereigns themselves or as wives or mistresses of princes. Satirists like the Italian wit

Aretino (1492–1556)—a onetime courtier himself—sneered at princely hangers-on as sycophants condemned to "wait at table, stand about at their master's pleasure in a state of exhaustion, clean out privies [or] pimp for a happy young lord."[5] Moralists denounced the Renaissance court as a cesspool of worldliness and vice. Nevertheless, the courts got much of the governing done in early modern times.

Among the more formal institutions, courts of law and departments concerned with princely revenues continued to develop as they had in the medieval period. The handling of government business was increasingly routinized, a commonly cited sign of professionalization. The sheer number of officials grew, and their work was more and more specialized. It was increasingly common to make a lifetime career as a public official, as it had been in ancient Rome. Both at the center of power at the court or capital and in far-off provinces, professional administrators began to make the will of the prince a reality once more.

Foreign Relations

Foreign relations were the heart of statecraft as Renaissance rulers understood it. Thus it is not surprising that both the modern diplomatic corps and the military services began to take shape in these centuries.

In medieval as in ancient times, an ambassador had been an envoy dispatched on a particular mission: to seek help, demand submission, declare war, or negotiate an alliance. Only in the early modern period did major powers begin to post resident ambassadors in the capitals of other states. Combining intelligence gathering with diplomatic efforts to advance the interests of their sovereigns, these permanent representatives abroad created something that had never existed before in the West—a web of continuous interstate relations.

It was during the Renaissance, furthermore, that foreign secretaries at home and ambassadors in other lands first began to conceive of foreign relations not only as an instrument to advance their own national interests but as a means of preventing aggression by others through the maintenance of a rudimentary *balance of power* (see box, "The Balance of Power in Italy"). One celebrated early example of embryonic balance-of-power thinking was the effort of the Medici in Florence in the 1400s to organize a power balance among the Italian states. Another was the

PROBING THE PAST The Balance of Power in Italy

Francesco Guicciardini (1483–1540), politician and diplomat, was perhaps the best historian produced by the Italian Renaissance. His work is distinguished by its critical assessment of sources and by its broad awareness of the international context of events. In this passage from his *History of Italy,* Guicciardini outlines the "balance of power" among fifteenth-century Italian city-states and other principalities. "Lorenzo" is Lorenzo de' Medici, the Florentine banker and political leader. How did the "jealousy and rivalry" of the powers contribute to the peace of Italy?

> Since there was the same will for peace in Ferdinand, Lodovico, and Lorenzo—partly for the same and partly for different reasons—it was easy to maintain an alliance in the name of Ferdinand, King of Naples, Giovan Galeazzo, Duke of Milan, and the Florentine Republic for the mutual defense of their states. This treaty, which was entered into many years before and subsequently interrupted for various reasons, had been renewed in 1480 for twenty-five years with the adherence of nearly all the small states of Italy. Its principal

object was to prevent the Venetians from increasing their power, for they were undoubtedly greater than any one of the confederates, but much less so than all of them put together. They kept their own counsel, hoping to increase their power through friction and disunity among others, and stood ready to profit by any event which might open the way for them to the domination of the whole of Italy. It had been clear on more than one occasion that this was what they sought, especially when, on the death of Filippo Maria Visconti, Duke of Milan, they attempted to seize that state under color of defending the freedom of the Milanese: and more recently when in open war they tried to occupy the Duchy of Ferrara. It was easy for the confederation to curb the greed of the Venetian senate, but it did not unite the allies in sincere and faithful friendship because—full of jealousy and rivalry—they constantly watched one another's movements, mutually thwarting every design whereby any one of them might increase its power or reputation. This did not make the peace any less stable, but rather inspired each with a greater promptness to put out any sparks which might be the origin of a new outbreak.

Source: Francesco Guicciardini, *History of Italy and History of Florence,* trans. Cecil Grayson (New York: New English Library, 1966), 88.

"common cause" of Protestant states headed by Queen Elizabeth against Catholic Spain in the later sixteenth century. We will look at both of these efforts in a little more detail shortly. This use of the Western state system itself as a device for restraining aggression led in later centuries to powerful alliances against the France of Louis XIV and Napoleon, against both imperial and Nazi Germany, and most recently against the Soviet Union.

The alternative to peace, of course, was war; and like their medieval forebears, many Renaissance rulers thought of warfare as a particularly princely business. In early modern times, however, the medieval feudal levies of armed vassals and their henchmen were largely replaced by increasingly professional and well-equipped fighting forces.

These were not yet standing armies or full-fledged navies. Few early modern nations could afford the luxury of keeping any substantial number of men sitting idly under arms, waiting for a war. Mer-

cenary troops, often German or Swiss, were as readily available as they had been in later medieval times. The landed aristocracy still saw warfare as a gentleman's occupation, but they now raised a regiment, not by calling on the feudal allegiance of vassals, but by paying soldiers, often out of their own resources. They continued, however, to command their troops in the field in order to win honor as their ancestors had. The regiment of several thousand men in fact became the basic military unit: the Spanish regiments, the *tercios,* comprised the most experienced, effective, and feared national army in sixteenth-century Europe.

The "art of war," as it was increasingly called, saw a number of significant changes. The battlefield was no longer dominated by cavalry as in the Middle Ages, but instead by infantrymen armed with long spears called pikes. Supporting troops deployed new and still comparatively ineffective gunpowder weapons. Thus companies of musketeers increasingly replaced bowmen, though their many varieties of long gun—musket, arquebus, matchlock—were unrifled, lacking the spiral grooves inside the barrel that impart a spin to the bullet fired from a modern firearm, and hence uniformly inaccurate. The cannon of the age still fired solid balls of metal rather than explosive shells, but like the musket was a harbinger of things to come. The Renaissance also gave much more attention to defensive fortifications and to logistics and supply, although in practice the outcome of a siege tended to depend on hunger within the town and disease on both sides. And despite plans and allocations for supplies, most armies on the move ended up living off the countryside.

Navies evolved even more slowly than armies, perhaps because of the cost of ships. Venice and other Italian coastal city-states had oared galleys that practiced naval maneuvers together. Northern powers had powerful new *galleons*, primarily sail-driven warships capable of operating on the stormy Atlantic, but few monarchs could afford more than a handful of them. Equipped with several masts and sails, these vessels were much more maneuverable than earlier European ships. With cannons mounted on their fore- and aftercastles as well as on "gun decks" below, they became floating gun platforms, capable of crippling or even sinking other ships while still hundreds of yards away. The Dutch and British were the most successful naval powers, though most of their ships were privately owned, sailing under *letters of marque* by which their sovereigns empowered them to seize enemy shipping and to keep most of what they found on board for themselves.

Italian Renaissance Princes

Italy, in Roman times creator of the greatest political unity Europe had ever known, was one of the continent's most divided zones at the beginning of modern history. Like the autonomous German states of the Holy Roman Empire, the loosely linked Swiss cantons, and the provinces of the Low Countries, most of Italy was a patchwork of small states in the Renaissance. Yet in the fourteenth and fifteenth centuries particularly, the Italian city-states produced a new type of ruler who became a model for the new monarchs of the nation-states to the north: the Italian Renaissance despot.

Like tyrants in ancient Greece, the *Renaissance despots* of early modern Italy were not necessarily cruel or oppressive rulers. *Despot*, like *tyrant* in ear-

lier centuries, meant simply an illegitimate ruler, one who governed without a traditional or constitutional basis for power like that enjoyed by the hereditary, divinely sanctioned monarchs of the north. Of the five most powerful Italian states in the later fifteenth century, the Duchy of Milan was ruled by the Sforza family, founded by a mercenary captain who had seized power; the Republic of Florence was dominated by the Medici bankers; the Republic of Venice was governed by the old established merchant families; the Papal States in central Italy comprised the worldly domain of the heads of the Roman Catholic church; and the Kingdom of Naples was ruled by foreigners related to the Aragonese dynasty of Spain.

The Italian political scene was changing over the fourteenth and fifteenth centuries, and many despots were the products—or the perpetrators—of those changes. In the High Middle Ages, the long struggle for control of Italy between the Holy Roman emperors and the Roman popes had the effect of preventing

Andrea del Verrocchio's statue of the military captain *Colleoni* was one of the first large equestrian statues made since Roman times. What do you think gives the statue the feeling of aggressive power it seems to radiate?

either from establishing an undisputed hegemony. The resulting power vacuum had fostered the growth of a large number of small but prosperous commercial and handicraft-industrial city-states. At the same time, however, these urban republics, or *communes*, were often torn by internal feuds between upper and lower classes and between partisans of either the pope or the emperor. In addition, they tended to be violently competitive and were frequently at war with each other, hiring mercenary companies to do most of the fighting but suffering themselves from sieges, unsafe roads, and ravaged countryside.

To restore order, the city-states sometimes turned to powerful autocratic rulers. In other cases, the head of one faction or a hired mercenary commander, a *condottiere*, might seize power. One way or another, during the Renaissance, despotism increasingly replaced the oligarchic merchant republic of the High Middle Ages. In the fourteenth and fifteenth centuries, furthermore, these local despots often moved to expand their control over neighboring cities. The results included a decrease in the number of independent city-states, the emergence of relatively stable dynasties, and the predominance of the five large regional powers mentioned earlier, the "great powers" of Renaissance Italy.

In order to rule without clear constitutional sanction, the Italian despots became skilled practitioners of the art of politics. They imposed their will through military or monetary power, through political intrigue and manipulation. Some dominated politics by their personal popularity or by engaging in lavish programs of public building. Some used art patronage for political purposes, lavishing largesse on poets and artists who glorified them in verse and prose, paintings and statues. This was the political scene that Machiavelli observed around 1500, the world whose fundamentally amoral tone he communicated with such startling honesty in *The Prince*. It was a political world with no chivalric illusions, no lingering sense of the unity of Christendom, dedicated to the single-minded pursuit of power through war and politics (see box, "Machiavelli's *Prince*").

THE RULERS AND THE RULED Machiavelli's *Prince*

Niccolò Machiavelli's shrewd analysis of Renaissance government, *The Prince*, has been seen by some as a recipe for political chicanery and tyranny, by others as a realistic description of power politics in any age. Using political success as his standard, Machiavelli here suggests that, human nature being what it is, the beloved prince who never lies to his people may not prove as effective a ruler as one who bases his power on fear and deception. Such "Machiavellian" policies have been attributed to many powerful rulers in later centuries.

This leads to a debate: Is it better [for a ruler] to be loved than feared, or the reverse? The answer is that it is desirable to be both, but because it is difficult to join them together, it is much safer for a prince to be feared than loved. . . . Because we can say this about men in general: they are ungrateful, changeable simulators, runaways in danger, eager for gain; while you do well by them,

they are all yours; they offer you their blood, their property, their lives . . . when need is far off; but when it comes near you, they turn about. A prince who bases himself entirely on their words, if he is lacking in other preparations, falls. . . . Men have less hesitation in injuring one who makes himself loved, for love is held by a chain of duty which, since men are bad, they break at every chance for their own profit; but fear is held by a dread of punishment that never fails you. . . .

I conclude then . . . that, since men love at their own choice and fear at the prince's choice, a wise prince takes care to base himself on what is his own, not on what is another's. . . .

How praiseworthy a prince is who keeps his promises and lives with sincerity and not with trickery, everybody realizes. Nevertheless, experience in one time shows that those princes have done great things who have valued their promises little, and who have understood how to addle the brains of men with trickery; and in the end they have vanquished those who have stood upon their honesty.

Source: Niccolò Machiavelli, *The Prince*, in *The Chief Works and Others*, trans. Allan Gilbert, vol. 1 (Durham, N.C.: Duke University Press, 1965), 62, 64.

The Medici and the Borgias

The "new politics" of the Italian Renaissance became in a sense the school for Europe in matters of state. A look at two or three Renaissance Italian despots will illustrate the sort of lessons the West learned from the Italian political scene.

The great city of Milan in the fertile Po valley of northern Italy was internationally known for the manufacture of cloth, arms, and armor. A leader in the struggle of the north Italian cities against imperial control from beyond the Alps, Milan came under the domination of two successive military clans, the Visconti in the 1300s and the Sforza after 1450.

Gian-Galeazzo Visconti (r. 1378–1402) converted the city-state from a merchant republic to a dukedom, thus legitimizing one-man rule, and expanded Milanese power over most of Lombardy. Francesco Sforza (r. 1450–1466), the most famous condottiere of his time, allied Milan with Florence in a political coalition that, with the help of Naples in the south, maintained a balance of power in Italy for decades. Francesco's son, Lodovico "the Moor" Sforza (r. 1481–1499), engaged Leonardo da Vinci to cast his father's statue in bronze and was an international intriguer shrewd enough to earn the admiration of Machiavelli. In the end, however, Lodovico's intrigues failed to save him from the bigger battalions of the French. The latter came pouring down through the Alps at the end of the century to inaugurate a violent period of European big-power warfare over Renaissance Italy.

The Papal States, stretching across central Italy from Rome to the Adriatic, had largely slipped out of papal control during the Avignon papacy and the Great Schism. In the later 1400s and the early 1500s, however, a series of thoroughly worldly and politically ambitious popes turned their attention to recovering control of the Papal States, adding the neighboring lands of the Romagna, and feuding with other Italian rulers. Popes like Sixtus IV (r. 1471–1484) and Innocent VIII (r. 1484–1492) taxed harshly and sold church offices in order to send armies against Naples, Venice, Florence, and other rival principalities.

One of the most aggressive of these political popes was the notorious Borgia pontiff, Alexander VI (r. 1492–1503). Scion of a Spanish family and father of the much romanticized Cesare and Lucrezia Borgia, Pope Alexander founded a family that became notorious for plots, poisons, and alleged sexual irregularities. He spent lavishly and intrigued ruthlessly to reassert papal power in central Italy and to impose papal authority on the lands and mountain strongholds of the neighboring Italian nobility.

Cesare Borgia (c. 1475–1507), an unprincipled politician and celebrated soldier, became duke of Romagna and looked to Machiavelli like a man who might have it in him to unite all Italy, as in the days of the Roman Caesars. Lucrezia (1480–1519), lovely in her youth and devoutly religious in her later years, married three times in order to advance the family's dynastic ambitions, and was more likely a pawn than a participant in her relatives' nefarious schemes. Only the sudden death of Pope Alexander—attributed by many to poison—and Cesare Borgia's subsequent imprisonment and later death in battle put an end to the ambitious machinations of the Borgias. Mean-

Giorgione's portrait of Cesare Borgia captures some of the energy and shrewdness of this ambitious Renaissance intriguer. How do the angle of the head, the background, and the clenched fist in the foreground contribute to our impression of Borgia's character?

while, Julius II (r. 1503–1513), the "warrior pope," completed the reconquest of the Papal States. The volcanic Julius has become famous also for his disputes with the equally strong-willed Michelangelo over the painting of the Sistine ceiling. In his own day, Julius was accused by his enemies of taking unfair advantage in the Italian wars by blessing the cannon he turned against his foes.

The most famous of Italy's Renaissance rulers, however, were the heads of the Medici family of Florence, among them Cosimo de' Medici (1389–1464). Cosimo built his political power on the family's wealth. Following his father's advice (see box, "Death of a Medici"), he dominated political life by appealing to the less prestigious craft guilds while playing leading businessmen off against each other in the ruling councils of the Florentine Republic. In foreign affairs, it was Cosimo who organized the triple alliance of Florence, Milan, and Naples that restrained the more aggressive, expansionist power of Venice and the Papal States for more than forty years, from 1450 to 1492.

Cosimo's grandson Lorenzo (r. 1469–1492), called "the Magnificent" for his style of life and lavish art patronage, found both political power at home and the international balance of power harder to maintain. A rebellion in Florence led by a rival banking family and a war with both the Papal States and Naples, Florence's erstwhile ally, scarred the middle years of Lorenzo's tenure of power. Like his grandfather, however, he continued to rule, without doing drastic violence to the republican constitution of Florence, through influence, intrigue, and manipulation. Subsequent Medici formalized their power by turning Florence into a dukedom and going on to provide both queens and popes for sixteenth-century Europe.

The New Monarchies

The kings of the north also prospered during the Renaissance period. Reestablishing the royal power that had been shaken by the troubles of the later Middle Ages, they laid solid foundations on which later monarchs might build. It is with the first of these, the so-called *new monarchs* of the late fifteenth century, that the present section is concerned.

These royal rulers had taken up the drive of high medieval kings to establish their own real authority in the lands they ruled. Their newness lay in their sometimes ruthlessly pragmatic policies, their growing tendency to claim absolute power over their subjects, and their sheer success as builders of cen-

---

THE RULERS AND THE RULED
Death of a Medici

Giovanni di Bicci de' Medici, head of the rich and powerful Medici family of Florence at the beginning of the fifteenth century, here offers some deathbed advice to his two sons. He begins with the economic preeminence of the Medici clan in Renaissance Florence and Tuscany but emphasizes the political tactics that made the family powerful, including the cultivation of popularity with the masses, a modest demeanor with other Florentine leaders, and such fundamental political goals as peace and prosperity. The older of Giovanni's two sons, Cosimo de' Medici, followed this advice with consummate skill, laying the foundations for two centuries of Medici power.

"Beloved sons, neither I nor any man born into this world should feel grief at exchanging worldly cares for perpetual repose. I know that the last days of my life are nigh . . . . I leave you in possession of the great wealth which my good fortune has bestowed upon me, and which your good mother and my own hard work has enabled me to preserve. I leave you with a larger business than any other merchant in the Tuscan land, and in the enjoyment of the esteem of every good citizen, and of the great mass of the populace, who have ever turned to our family as their guiding star. If you are faithful to the traditions of your ancestors, the people will be generous in giving you honors. To acheive this, be charitable to the poor, kindly and gracious to the miserable, lending yourselves with all your might to assist them in their adversity. Never strive against the will of the people, unless they advocate a baneful project. Speak not as though giving advice, but rather discuss matters with gentle and kindly reasoning. Be chary of frequenting the Palace [the center of government in the Florentine Republic]; rather, wait to be summoned, and then be obedient, and not puffed up with pride at receiving many votes. Have a care to keep the people at peace, and to increase the commerce of the city. Avoid litigation or any attempt to influence justice . . . . I depart joyfully and with more happiness if you do not enter into party strife . . . . I commend to you Nannina my wife and your mother . . . . Pray to God for me, my sons, that my passage may be crowned by the salvation of my immortal soul. Now take my blessing. . . ." Saying this, he passed from this life.

Source: Giovanni Cavalcanti, *Istorie Fiorentine* (1838). In *The Lives of the Early Medici as Told in Their Correspondence*, Janet Ross, ed. and trans. London: Chatto and Windus, 1910. P 6.

tralized government. Some gave at least lip service to the chivalric and crusading ideals of their medieval predecessors, but almost all were primarily dedicated to expanding the power of the monarchy in the Renaissance world.

The tendency toward a revival of royal authority in the later 1400s was evident in some of the oldest of European nation-states, including France and England, and in some of the newer nations that would play key roles in modern history—most notably Spain and Russia. There was also an abortive drive toward centralization of power in the Holy Roman Empire, the politically divided German-speaking area in central Europe that would not in fact be united until the later nineteenth century.

France Under Louis the Spider

Of all the celebrated sovereigns whose names and fame come crowding at us out of this segment of the past, Louis XI of France (r. 1461–1483)—the Spider King—was one of the least glamorous. Where other princes gloried in feats of arms and royal pageantry, King Louis preferred manipulation and intrigue, bribing allies and waiting out his foes. Modest in manner, assiduously cultivating the great of his own and other nations, collecting information, organizing and conspiring, he wove intricate webs that were sometimes too clever to succeed. But his approach was far more suited to the times than was the much admired chivalry of his great rival, Charles the Bold (r. 1467–1477) of Burgundy, and Louis's other independent-minded vassals. In the end, the unimpressive French king bested them all.

With the English invaders of the Hundred Years' War expelled from France by Louis's predecessor, Louis XI's most dangerous antagonist was his powerful vassal Charles, duke of Burgundy. The ambitious duke had a grand scheme: to construct a new state stretching north and south along the Rhine between France and the Holy Roman Empire. Supported by the fighting prowess of the Burgundian knights and the wealth of the Netherlands, also ruled by the house of Burgundy, it was not an impossible dream. Had Charles succeeded, he could have stripped the French monarchy of half its lands and created a powerful new state in the heart of Europe.

Louis the Spider, however, responded to Charles's martial challenge by subsidizing the redoubtable Swiss, then the most effective mercenaries in Europe, who were also threatened by Burgundian expansionism. The Swiss, then, did the French king's

fighting for him, defeating Charles the Bold three times. They finally killed him at the Battle of Nancy in 1477, while Louis sat smiling in the center of his web, reaching out to absorb most of Burgundy once the duke was dead.

Additional territorial acquisitions under Louis XI included the large Angevin lands in the west and south, which he inherited, and two provinces pried away from Spain. He thus left the French monarchy twice the size of the kingdom he had inherited.

Louis also left it stronger and more centralized. He reasserted his authority over the remaining lands held by independent princes of the blood, promoted and supported middle-class officials, and expanded the royal army (though he tended to keep it in reserve rather than committing it to battle). He increased taxation and encouraged the development of handicraft industry in France. He left the country prosperous and powerful, fully recovered from the disasters of the Hundred Years' War.

England Under the First Tudor

England also recovered from its late medieval trauma of foreign and civil strife. The Wars of the Roses, which had seen the land torn by factions of feuding nobles led by the houses of Lancaster and York, ended dramatically with the Battle of Bosworth Field in 1485. The victor was the Lancastrian Henry Tudor, a shrewd, industrious Welshman much closer in spirit to Louis the Spider than to the chivalrous warriors of the Middle Ages.

Henry VII (r. 1485–1509) had an unimpressive hereditary claim to the throne of England. Nevertheless, with his Yorkist rival Richard III dead on the field at Bosworth, the crown Henry Tudor allegedly plucked from a bush on the battlefield was clearly his by right of conquest. The royal house of Tudor that he founded became England's most admired—and romanticized—dynasty: Henry VII was the father of Henry VIII and grandfather of Queen Elizabeth I. The first Tudor spent his quarter of a century on the throne strengthening and enriching the kingdom they would inherit.

Henry suppressed the rivals who sought to reopen the Wars of the Roses with firmness and a certain imaginative flair, setting one pitiful Yorkist claimant to working in the royal kitchens. Like Louis XI, Henry VII generally preferred diplomacy to warfare. He strengthened England's international position by marrying his daughter Margaret (1489–1541) to James IV, king of Scotland (r. 1488–1513), and his son Arthur to Catherine of Aragon (1485–1536), daughter of the powerful King Ferdinand and Queen Isabella of Spain.

To promote domestic tranquillity, Henry VII himself had married Elizabeth (1465–1503), the heiress of the house of York. He also suppressed the private armies that the barons of both factions had been accumulating since the Hundred Years' War. To strengthen his own hand, he increased the powers of the justices of the peace in the shires and promoted burghers and churchmen to high official posts in the central government.

Coming from the unprosperous land of Wales, Henry Tudor was particularly conscious of the importance of money. He worked diligently with his councilors to expand the wealth of both the kingdom and the monarchy. Through the confiscation of the lands of rebels against the crown and through the heavy exactions imposed by his notorious Court of the Star Chamber, he accumulated an unprecedented treasury surplus of more than a million pounds. He also provided official support for the cloth trade, England's biggest export, and signed commercial treaties with states as far away as Florence. Like Louis XI, Henry VII thus left his country unified and prosperous.

Spain Under Ferdinand and Isabella

As medieval monarchies that had been evolving for hundreds of years, France and England were old players of the power game. Two newer powers emerged in the fifteenth and sixteenth centuries, however, that came to rival the older monarchies. These two new nations, taking shape at the southwestern and northeastern ends of Europe, were Spain and Russia. Spain emerged as a great power as it achieved nationhood through the union of the Iberian principalities of Castile and Aragon in the 1470s. Modern Russia, by contrast, was only beginning to take shape with the triumph of the medieval duchy of Muscovy over all rivals in the late 1400s. In both cases, however, the rise of strong centralizing rulers was facilitated by the final defeat of non-European peoples who had invaded these areas during the Middle Ages—the Moors in Spain and the Mongols in Russia. Each of the new powers, finally, reached out across continents and seas—Spain almost at once, Russia more slowly—assembling empires of unparalleled size.

The first Iberian kingdom to attain unified statehood, however, was not Spain but its small neighbor Portugal. The kings and fighting nobility of Portugal had expelled the Moors—Muslim Arabs and Berbers—from their territory as early as the High Middle Ages. In 1385 the Portuguese successfully resisted the growing power of Spanish Castile. King John I the Great (r. 1385–1433) then established a strong monarchy in Portugal more than half a century before the process was begun in Spain. By winning the support of the church, establishing a small royal army and navy, organizing royal courts and promulgating a national law code, John's Aviz dynasty took firm control of the country. By encouraging both trade and the formation of a strong middle class, the Portuguese rulers had forged a prosperous state by the end of the fifteenth century. And in 1415 under Prince Henry the Navigator, this small country became, as we will see, the first Western nation to launch a calculated campaign of expansion overseas.

The unification of the rest of the Iberian peninsula into the much larger Kingdom of Spain took longer. Surrounded on three sides by water (the Atlantic, the Strait of Gibraltar, and the Mediterranean), the territory that became Spain was isolated from the rest of Europe by the Pyrenees mountain range. Overrun by the Moors in the eighth century, divided geographically, linguistically, and politically, and home to Christians, Muslims, and Jews alike, this corner of Europe had experienced none of the unifying trends of medieval France and England. Isabella of Castile (r. 1474–1504) and Ferdinand of Aragon (r. 1479–1516), whose marriage began the process of Spanish unification, had their work cut out for them.

Married as teenagers in 1469 in what may have been that rarity among royal marriages, a love match, the two inherited the thrones of their respective kingdoms in the 1470s. The result was a personal, but not an institutional, union of the two largest Iberian monarchies. Castile, by far the larger, and Aragon remained separate entities, each with its own internal administration, regional characteristics, and independent feudal nobility. Two unifying factors, however, did bind Castilians, Aragonese, and most other Spaniards: a common enemy in the Moors, who still ruled the Kingdom of Granada in the south, and the loyalty of a crusading people to the militant Catholic church. Isabella's intelligence and religious piety and Ferdinand's crafty aggressiveness helped them to parlay these factors into strong royal government and international power.

To bring their feudal aristocracy under royal control, the new rulers minimized noble participation in the *cortes* (assemblies) of Castile and Aragon,

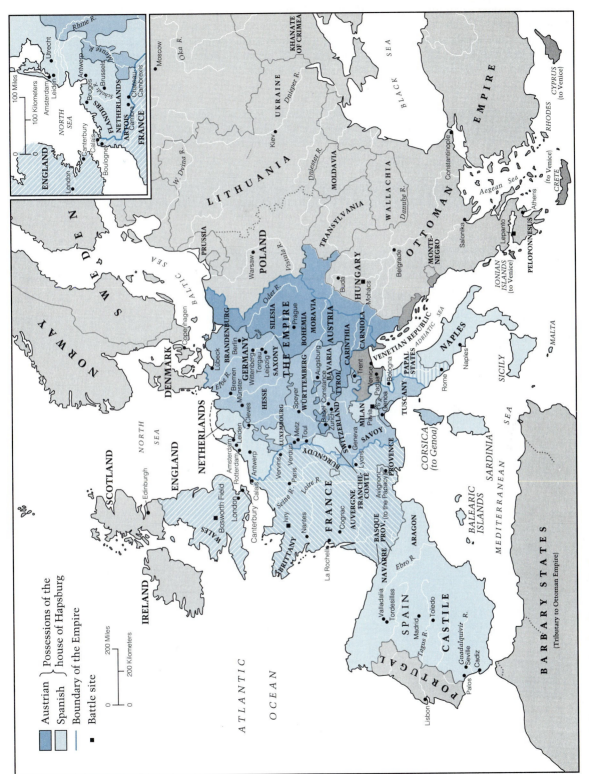

Map 12.2 Europe in the Sixteenth Century

Legend:
- Austrian — Possessions of the house of Hapsburg
- Spanish — Possessions of the house of Hapsburg
- Boundary of the Empire
- ■ Battle site

and Isabella appointed her husband grand master of the Castilian orders of chivalry. To control the towns, the determined pair appointed royal officials to replace elected magistrates and councils in Spanish cities. Ferdinand and Isabella also created a group of powerful councils on the national level to deal with finances, justice, and international and religious affairs. Staffing the new councils mostly with lawyers, they ruled in large part through these central institutions. Even as they developed relatively modern governmental structures, however, *los reyes católicos*—"the Catholic kings," as they came to be called—used medieval religion and the church to strengthen the state. They made good use of Isabella's astute chief adviser Cardinal Ximenes, transforming the Spanish

Inquisition into a virtual branch of the government. And by equating Christianity with patriotism, the Catholic kings used the strong religious feelings of the people as an ideological cement to hold the new nation together.

In the 1480s, the new rulers gained a special grip on the loyalty of most Spaniards by launching a crusade to expel the last Muslims from western Europe. They achieved this goal with the conquest of Granada in 1492, the same year in which Isabella received the aspiring navigator Christopher Columbus for the first time—in her camp outside the walls of the last Moorish stronghold—and provided the support that led to the founding of the huge Spanish Empire in the New World. Ferdinand, meanwhile, ex-

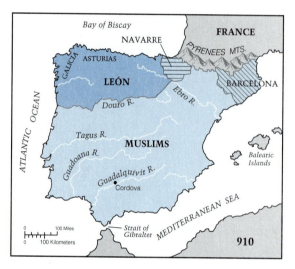

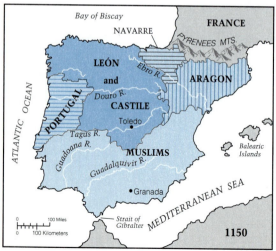

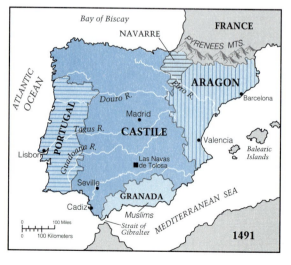

Map 12.3   Unification of Spain

panded the Aragonese power base already established in Naples and Sicily into a greater Spanish presence in Renaissance Italy. The Spanish sovereigns also arranged a series of carefully calculated diplomatic marriages into the ruling houses of France, England, and the Holy Roman Empire. Through war, diplomacy, and gambling on Columbus, they thus elevated their still only half-unified nation to the rank of one of Europe's greatest powers. In the sixteenth century, under their Habsburg grandson and great-grandson, Emperor Charles V and King Philip II, Spain emerged as the greatest of Western powers, and one of the greatest nations on the globe.

Ferdinand and Isabella implemented a fiercely orthodox religious policy, and one that is difficult for us to understand today. They required the large Muslim and Jewish populations to convert to Christianity, persecuted them through the Inquisition, and finally expelled both groups. The expulsion of the Jews in particular cost Spain many of its wealthiest merchants, most skilled artisans, and most brilliant intellectuals. But the rigorously Catholic nation that remained, though economically weaker, may have been politically stronger, solidified and strengthened internally. It was certainly prepared to lead the forces of Western Catholicism in the impending struggle with the Protestant Reformation and to launch the conquest of the pagan New World with special zeal.

The First Czar of Russia

On the other side of Europe, across the wide east European plain and down into the mountain ranges of the Balkans, the Slavs and other peoples of Eastern Christendom had evolved their own monarchies by the end of the Middle Ages. By far the most important of these in the long run was the new state of Muscovy just taking shape in northern Russia. At the time, however, a number of their neighbors looked at least as important as emerging Russia.

Among the most prominent eastern European nations, Poland, Lithuania, Hungary, and Bohemia shared some common problems and patterns of development. Most of these states faced foreign pressure, either from the Germans of central Europe or from the Ottoman Turks advancing up the Balkan peninsula after their conquest of Constantinople. Thus the Teutonic Knights—a crusading order of chivalry that had turned to fighting pagans along the Baltic Sea—harassed both the Poles and the Lithuanians. Bohemia was part of the German-ruled Holy Roman Empire—a rebellious part after the Hussite religious revolt (discussed in the last chapter) exploded in 1415. The Turks, meanwhile, invaded and raided Hungary, Poland, and much of the rest of eastern Europe in the earlier 1500s.

Most of these states also felt the familiar strains of conflict between ambitious monarchs and the traditional noble ruling class. In Poland, the nobles succeeded in largely emancipating themselves from their kings, gaining tax exemptions, absolute authority over their peasants, and legislative supremacy through the *diet*, or assembly, which they controlled. In Hungary, the gains of the Magyar nobles were only temporarily reversed by King Matthias Corvinus (r. 1458–1490). This strong-willed, shrewd Renaissance prince built up his army and his financial strength, imported Italian artists and scholars to glorify his capital at Buda, and for a time made Hungary the most powerful nation in eastern Europe. In spite of powerful rulers like Matthias Corvinus, however, the determination and power of the Magyars made the Hungarian nobility a potent factor throughout their country's modern history.

But the future lay with the slowly stirring might of Muscovy. The new nation just unfolding around Moscow in the forests of northern Russia grew over centuries to become the largest country in the world. The slow crumbling of the hegemony of the Mongol Golden Horde left two north Russian states as the most likely candidates for supremacy: Novgorod and Moscow. Novgorod in the northwest, with access to the Baltic Sea, developed as a typical medieval commercial city, with a patrician merchant class running the expanding principality through its assembly, the *veche*. Moscow, more centrally located in European Russia, evolved in closer contact with the Mongols and under the influence of Byzantium.

A fourteenth-century prince of Moscow, Ivan I (r. 1328–1341), known as "Moneybags," became chief collector of revenues for the Golden Horde and made Moscow the wealthiest of all the Russian states. Another Muscovite prince, Dmitri of the Don (r. 1359–1389), earned an immense reputation by defeating the Mongols at the Battle of Kulikovo in 1380. It was a century later, however, before Ivan III the Great (r. 1462–1505) turned back the last Mongol advance on Moscow in 1480, emerging as the first real ruler of the state that became the core of modern Russia. Ivan the Great also established Russia's claim to be the true heir of the Byzantine tradition. He married a niece of the last emperor of Constantinople, took the imperial titles of autocrat and caesar, or *czar*, and established the Byzantine policy of caesaropapism,

Isabella of Castille and Ferdinand of Aragon, whose marriage had unified most of Spain, here accept the surrender of Granada, the last Muslim enclave in the land, in 1492. From a contemporary viewpoint, this was a much more important achievement than their financing of Columbus's expedition the same year.

or subordination of the Russian Orthodox church to the czarist state. It was Ivan, finally, who first declared that Muscovite Russia was the "Third Rome," the modern heir to ancient Rome and medieval Byzantium, with a comparable right to universal and absolute authority.

Under Ivan III, the ambitious Muscovite state overwhelmed and absorbed the rival principality of Novgorod in the 1470s. In so doing, Moscow added substantially to its territory, which Ivan expanded still further by seizing parts of eastern Lithuania and Poland. The result was a Muscovy extending as far north as the Arctic and as far east as the Ural Mountains. Perhaps more important, however, the victory of Moscow over Novgorod meant the virtual severing of Russian contact with western Europe. Novgorod's Western-style commercial middle classes, with their local assembly and trade with the West,

gave way to a more autocratic regime with traditions rooted in Russia's unique connections with the Mongols and Byzantium.

Russian autocracy in 1500, however, was in some ways more claim than reality. Although Byzantine court ceremonies, hierarchy, the theories of autocracy and caesaropapism emerged early, the actual power of the Moscow czars grew more slowly. Ivan the Great attempted to undercut the self-destructive old princely tradition of dividing the state among male heirs, but a clear line of undivided succession was not established until the reign of Ivan the Terrible in the later 1500s. Russia's boyar nobility also clung to its traditional right to hold land free of military service or to change princely overlords at will, prerogatives that also erode slowly over the sixteenth century. Even the caesaropapist Russian Orthodox church defended its lands against czarist encroachment. And the first of the major government administrative departments, which subsequently grew into the huge czarist bureaucracy, did not even come into existence until the early 1500s. A direction had been laid down by the Muscovite czars; but it took centuries to build the czarist state that had the reputation of being the most autocratic in the Western world.

The Holy Roman Empire

"The Holy Roman Empire of the German Nation," as it was first officially called in the fifteenth century, had never attained a centralized organization comparable to that of England or France. Germany did produce a strong—if in the end less successful—ruler in this period. The Austrian Habsburg emperor Maximilian I (r. 1493–1519) was a new monarch of the old school. By temperament a medieval king, a chivalric ruler who loved the knightly virtues, Maximilian displayed an old-fashioned idealism that made him much more popular than either Louis XI in France or Henry VII in England. But the Austrian emperor also saw the need for more centralized authority over his ramshackle confederation of principalities, free cities, and independent knights and bishops, and he labored toward that end. His greatest successes, paradoxically, were achieved not by the military ventures he embarked on with such enthusiasm, but by a series of diplomatic marriages.

Maximilian's centralizing efforts were aimed at imposing imperial authority on the *Reichstag*. This assembly, inherited from the earlier fifteenth century, brought together the seven imperial electors, the chief German princes, and the leaders of the free cities of Germany. The emperor's new schemes for governmental reform included an imperial council with real executive powers over the separate German states, imperial law courts and coinage, an end to private wars, and even a system of imperial taxation. The courts and the imperial council were in fact cre-

ated, but because these institutions were largely controlled by the electors and the princes, they did not increase the power of the Holy Roman emperor after all.

In the tradition of his medieval predecessors, Maximilian led a series of imperial armies over the Alps into Italy. These indecisive campaigns added little to his international position, at least in material terms of territory or wealth. Through a series of fortunate diplomatic marriages, however, he did lay the groundwork for the Habsburg international supremacy of the sixteenth century. His own marriage to Mary of Burgundy (1457–1482), daughter of Charles the Bold, brought him the wealthy commercial and industrial centers of the Netherlands. The marriage of his son Philip (1478–1506) to Juana the Mad (1479–1555), daughter of Ferdinand and Isabella, brought the vast Spanish possessions in Europe and the New World into the hands of the Habsburgs in the next generation. Through such politically astute marriage alliances, the Habsburgs, who could not impose centralized authority on the German states, nevertheless emerged as the most powerful dynasty in Europe as the sixteenth century began.

There was a bustle and a stirring among the political rulers of the West in 1500. Despots in Italy and the new monarchs in Europe north of the Alps were laboring mightily to establish more powerful governments than the most successful of medieval sovereigns. Yet there was a sweaty intensity, a driven quality about this commitment to power that disturbed at least one shrewd contemporary commentator. They were, admitted the Spider King's biographer Philippe de Commines (c. 1447–1511), "great men [who] labored so much to aggrandize themselves and to acquire glory." And yet, he wondered, "would it not have been better, both for them and all other princes, and for men of middling rank who have lived under these great men . . . if they had . . . striven less hard, . . . undertaken fewer enterprises and . . . been more afraid of offending God and of persecuting their subjects and neighbors?"[6]

A Topical Summary

Politics: Renaissance rulers restored centralized political power to the growing nation-states and smaller principalities of Europe in the fourteenth, fifteenth, and sixteenth centuries. Italian Renaissance despots like the Medici in Florence often shunted aside

the business oligarchies that had dominated medieval city-states. Aggressive "new monarchs" like the Valois in France, the Tudors in England, and Isabella and Ferdinand in Spain acted similarly toward independent-minded nobles and began to build stronger administrative institutions to rule their countries.

Economics: Later fifteenth- and sixteenth-century Europe experienced a vigorous economic revival after the late medieval depression triggered by the Black Death. Populations began to grow again, creating both demand for products and a labor force to supply them. Enclosure made land use more efficient, though it undermined the traditional agricultural village. The volume of trade expanded, cities

began to grow once more, and merchant bankers like the Medici and the Fuggers led the West into an era of expanding mercantile capitalism.

Technology: Technological developments made an important contribution to the Renaissance economic revival. The putting-out system increased the productivity of cottage industry, especially in textile manufacturing; new machinery helped to expand mining and metallurgy.

Some Key Terms

balance of power 363
Bourse 360
commune 366
condottiere 366
czar 373
enclosure 357
galleons 365

letter of marque 365
los reyes católicos 372
Mesta 357
new monarchs 368
palazzo 360
polder 357
proto-industrialism 358

putting-out system 358
Reichstag 375
Renaissance 351
Renaissance despots 365
tercio 364
veche 373

Notes

1. Marsilio Ficino, *Opera Omnia,* trans. Mary Martin McLaughlin, in James Bruce Ross and Mary Martin McLaughlin, *The Portable Renaissance Reader* (New York: Viking Press, 1953), 79.
2. Wallace K. Ferguson, *The Renaissance* (New York: Holt, 1940), 8.
3. Robert S. Lopez, "Hard Times and Investment in Culture," in Anthony Molho, *Social and Economic*

Foundations of the Italian Renaissance (New York: Wiley, 1969), 112–113.
4. Iago in *Othello,* I, iii, 344 ff.
5. John Larner, "Europe of the Courts," *Journal of Modern History,* 55 (1984), 676–677.
6. *Memoirs: The Reign of Louis XI,* trans. Michael Jones (Harmondsworth, England: Penguin, 1972), 417–418.

Reading List

BELL, J. N. *Markets and Merchants: The Expansion of Trade in Europe, 1500–1630.* New York: St. Martin's Press, 1977. Sixteenth-century commercial expansion, with due reference to European political conflicts, Italian business methods, and the influence of precious metals from the New World.

BONNER, R. *The European Dynastic States 1494–1660.* Oxford: Clarendon Press, 1990. A valuable volume in the *Oxford History of the Modern World* series.

BRAUDEL, F. *Afterthoughts on Civilization and Capitalism.* Translated by P. M. Ranum. Baltimore: Johns Hopkins University Press, 1977. Briefly summarizes the main themes of Braudel's multivolume study of *Materialism and Capitalism* between 1400 and 1800.

BREISACH, E. *Caterina Sforza: A Renaissance Virago.*

Chicago: University of Chicago Press, 1967. Life of an exceptional Renaissance woman with a surprisingly modern view of "woman's place."

BRUCKER, G. *The Civic World in Early Renaissance Florence.* Princeton, N.J.: Princeton University Press, 1977. Public life in the most renowned of Renaissance city republics. On class conflict between the urban patriciate and working-class neighborhoods, see S. K. COHN, *The Laboring Classes in Renaissance Florence* (New York: Academic Press, 1980).

BURCKHARDT, J. *The Civilization of the Renaissance in Italy.* Oxford: Phaidon, 1951. Illustrated edition of Burckhardt's classic, which shaped our image of the Renaissance for more than a century.

CHRIMES, S. B. *Henry VII.* London: Eyre Methuen, 1977.

History of Henry VII's reign by a constitutional historian.

FARR, J. R. *Hands of Honor: Artisans and Their World in Dijon, 1550–1650.* Ithaca, N.Y.: Cornell University Press, 1988. Working men and women, with emphasis on sense of community, the "cohesive culture" of sixteenth- and seventeenth-century artisans.

FERGUSON, W. K. *The Renaissance in Historical Thought: Five Centuries of Interpretation.* Boston: Houghton Mifflin, 1948. The evolution of historical understanding of the Renaissance period as a reflection of the shifting perspectives of later centuries.

FLINN, M. W. *The European Demographic System, 1500–1820.* Baltimore: Johns Hopkins University Press, 1981. A summary of research on population trends and their causes.

GUTMAN, M. P. *Toward the Modern Economy: Early Industry in Europe, 1500–1800.* Philadelphia: Temple University Press, 1988. Interaction of popular attitudes and social structures with economic and demographic factors contributing to the rise of proto-industrialism. See also F. F. MENDELS's seminal "Proto-industrialization: The First Phase of the Industrialization Process" (*Journal of Economic History,* vol. 1 [1972], 241–261).

HILLGARTH, J. N. *The Spanish Kingdoms, 1250–1516.* 2 vols. Oxford: Clarendon Press, 1988. A comprehensive survey: see Volume 2 for the fifteenth century and the "Catholic monarchs."

HOLBORN, H. *A History of Modern Germany.* 3 vols. New York: Knopf, 1959–1970. Volume 1 of this excellent general history deals with early modern Germany.

HOOK, J. *Lorenzo de' Medici.* London: Hamilton, 1984. Recent and readable brief life.

KENDALL, P. M. *Louis XI: 'The Universal Spider.'* London: Allen and Unwin, 1971. Skillfully written life by the biographer of a number of fifteenth-century rulers.

KLARWILL, V. von. *The Fugger News-Letters.* Translated by P. de Chary. London: John Lane, 1928. An ancestor of the modern newspaper, the Fugger in-house commercial publication mixed hard news with rumors, comets, and two-headed calves.

MATTINGLY, G. *Renaissance Diplomacy.* Harmondsworth, England: Penguin, 1973. Basic study of the subject by a historian who can make institutional history intriguing reading.

MISKIMIN, H. A. *The Economy of Later Renaissance Europe, 1460–1600.* New York: Cambridge University Press, 1977. Recovery and new growth in the economic life of the Renaissance, with reference to the impact of plague, population growth, and overseas expansion. For authoritative essays on many aspects of the subject, see E. E. RICH and C. H. WILSON, eds., *The Cambridge Economic History of Europe,* vol. 5, *The Economic Organization of Early Modern Europe* (New York: Cambridge University Press, 1977).

THOMPSON, J. A. F. *Popes and Princes, 1415–1517: Politics and Polity in the Late Medieval Church.* London: Allen and Unwin, 1980. The Renaissance papacy between the Schism and the Reformation, emphasizing the growth of royal power in church affairs.

VERNADSKY, G. *Russia at the Dawn of the Modern Age.* New Haven, Conn.: Yale University Press, 1968. Standard account by a leading historian specializing in earlier Russian history.

WARNICKE, R. M. *Women of the English Renaissance and Reformation.* Westport, Conn.: Greenwood, 1983. A scholarly survey of famous women in Tudor times, stressing the emancipating impact of humanist education and the Reformation.

The *Renaissance* has as romantic and colorful a reputation as any age of Western history. It conjures up images not only of ambitious despots and aggressive merchant princes but of brilliant painters, impassioned poets, and daring thinkers. It was, we are told, a time of exaltation and excess when artists and writers dared to dream of rivaling the ancients—and in fact produced a new beginning in Western culture. It was an age that said yes to life with a throbbing conviction that less self-confident later centuries might envy.

This stirring vision of Renaissance society does fit such choice spirits of the age as the feverishly ambitious Cesare Borgia, the passionate and brilliant sculptor Benvenuto Cellini, and even some of Shakespeare's more colorful contemporaries in Elizabethan England. The majority of Renaissance people, of course, like the majority of people today, led considerably less exciting and creative lives. Yet on the pedestrian labors of this majority were built the wealth and power, the brilliant lives and splendid cultural achievements of the age. A look at Renaissance society combined with a survey of Renaissance high culture will thus illuminate both the social foundations and the cultural peaks of Western civilization in this age of transition from medieval to modern.

An Evolving Society

In recent decades, historical analysis of past societies has improved considerably in depth and subtlety. By borrowing techniques from other social sciences, including economics, sociology, and anthropology, historians have learned to see society as more than a collection of individuals, or even a simple hierarchy of social classes. Women and men, people of different ethnic backgrounds, urban and rural people now find important places in our anatomies of the cultures of yesterday just as they do in our efforts to understand our own time. The use of the computer has also made a major contribution, bringing unaccustomed precision to the colorful but impressionistic visions of traditional social history. Historians themselves, finally, have developed such analytical concepts as the structures and mentalities of society, illuminating the social organization and thought processes of peasants or townspeople in other centuries. In the overview of Renaissance society that follows, we draw on all these techniques in attempting to understand the lives and minds of at least some Renaissance people.

Leonardo da Vinci. *Mona Lisa*. c. 1503–05. Musée du Louvre, Paris

	1300	1350	1400	1450
POLITICAL, MILITARY, AND DIPLOMATIC EVENTS				
SOCIAL AND ECONOMIC DEVELOPMENTS		**1320–1340s** Jews persecuted in France and German states		**1430s– 1440s** Vittorino da Feltre's school
CULTURE THE ARTS, PHILOSOPHY, SCIENCE AND RELIGION	**1267–1327** Giotto **1304–1374** Petrarch **1313–1375** Boccaccio	**1341** Petrarch crowned poet laureate	**c. 1386–1466** Donatello **1407–1457** Valla **1433–1499** Ficino **1444– 1510** Botticelli	

The New Aristocracy

A distinguishing characteristic of the ruling class of Renaissance society was a renewed emphasis on secular learning. For the first time in a thousand years, the Western world had an educated upper class. In this way, the Renaissance elite—including patrician townspeople as well as landed aristocrats—resembled the rulers of the Greco-Roman world more than it did the feudal rulers of the Middle Ages. Medieval elements, however, remained strong in the training and lifestyles of this early modern elite. And some traits of character that were particularly admired in the Renaissance set the ruling class of this era off from both these earlier ages. For example, the admiring phrase "Renaissance man" described someone who was skilled and well versed in many if not all of the arts

and sciences. There were Renaissance women too, as we see in the next section, though their roles were more restricted by the temper of the times.

The age's social ideal was outlined in so-called *conduct books.* Most of these were Italian, and the most famous of all was Baldassare Castiglione's (1478–1529) *Book of the Courtier* (c. 1516). According to Castiglione, such medieval physical skills as mastery of sword and spear, stylish horseback riding, hunting, and other sports like wrestling and tennis (played with smaller rackets and on an indoor court) were essential parts of the genteel life. The perfect Renaissance gentleman was also expected to have the social graces first cultivated in the high medieval courts of love: the ability to sing, play the lute or some other musical instrument, dance such athletic Renaissance dances as the galliard, and perhaps most of all, carry on the sort of elegant, witty

r. 1469–1492 Lorenzo
de' Medici

r. 1558–1603 Elizabeth I

1455 Gutenberg
Bible printed
  1492 Jews expelled
from Spain

1527 Castiglione's
Book of the Courtier

1452–1519 Leonardo da Vinci
  1463–1494 Pico
  1466–1536 Erasmus
  1469–1536 Machiavelli
  1471–1528 Dürer
  1475–1564 Michelangelo
  1478–1535 More
    1483–1553 Rabelais
    1483–1520 Raphael
    1487–1576 Titian
      1500–1571 Cellini

1525–1594 Palestrina
  1533–1592 Montaigne
  1541–1614 El Greco
  1547–1616 Cervantes
    1564–1593 Marlowe
    1564–1616 Shakespeare

conversation fashionable in Renaissance princely courts.

The major new emphasis, however, was the requirement that a Renaissance gentleman possess a civilized knowledge of the "humane letters," meaning the ancient classics. The Renaissance aristocrat was also expected to understand and participate in the literary and artistic explosion of his own time. He should thus be both familiar with the revival of classical studies called *humanism* and sensitive to the art and literature of the Renaissance itself, subjects that are explored in later sections of this chapter.

It was a tall order, more often praised than achieved. But there was more, a list of broader virtues and personal qualities, some of which we still admire. Most widely hailed at the time was honor, meaning a well-deserved reputation for courage, integrity, and the classical virtues generally, plus a will-

ingness to defend this reputation with sword and dagger in a duel. Less openly discussed but also much admired was success itself—high position in one's city or princely court, victory in war, even vast wealth conspicuously displayed in lofty mansions and retinues of liveried servants. All these virtues, furthermore, were to be worn with a certain ease of manner called *sprezzatura* in Italian, the nonchalance of the casually superior person who is master of every situation.

Two qualities of Renaissance character, finally, have been perhaps clearer to modern historians than they were to Renaissance people themselves. The first of these was a widely admired blend of individualism and what Machiavelli called *virtù*—a combination of the ability to stand on one's own feet and the will and capacity to fight one's way to the top. Though the Renaissance condemned social climbing in theory, successful climbers were often admired, and suitably aristocratic ancestors could usually be found for the individual who did win high place and reputation without the advantage of gentle birth. Most striking, though, is the many-sidedness of such rare Renaissance individuals as Leonardo da Vinci, versatile geniuses whose many talents have earned them the label of "universal." Leon Battista Alberti (1404–1472), for instance, was a multifaceted Florentine, perhaps best known as an architect and the author of books on the subject, but also celebrated for his writings on painting, moral philosophy, geography, language, and secret codes! When we call a contemporary a *Renaissance person* today, it is this quality that is usually meant: a dazzling mastery of many fields which expands our sense of human capabilities.

Did Women Have a Renaissance?

The position of women in the Renaissance has become a subject of debate in recent years. An older view stressed the intellectual and cultural achievements of individual Renaissance women and at least implied an improvement in the personal status of women in general. More recently, however, it has been suggested that women were actually less free and respected in the Renaissance than they had been in the Middle Ages. In fact, the picture may be more complicated than either of these conflicting interpretations would suggest.

The ideal education of a Renaissance lady in many ways resembled that of a Renaissance gentleman. She too could study the ancient poets and philosophers, learn to play, sing, dance, and draw and to excel in the elegant, urbane conversation of the court. Many upper-class women also acquired skill in riding, in hunting with hawks, and in other vigorous activities.

There, however, the resemblance ended. Women did not engage in the more violent sports or learn to use weapons. Instead, the Renaissance lady, like her medieval forebear, was encouraged to practice such "feminine accomplishments" as skilled needlework and embroidery. A number of traditional personal qualities were also part of the image of the ideal woman around 1500. Religious piety, moral virtues, and social submissiveness to parents and husbands were still commonly praised traits. Even the learning and social skills the Renaissance lady acquired, it has been suggested, were essentially decorative, fitting her to preside with proper grace and elegance over her husband's home or court. Some preachers and public moralists even urged that women were not really capable of serious learning. Others thought the main purpose of education for women was to make them better mothers for their sons. Even where they enjoyed an education comparable to that of Renaissance gentlemen, the training that enabled men to rule an increasingly complex world was designed to prepare their ladies for traditional roles as hostesses, wives, and mothers.

Joan Kelly-Gadol, in her classic essay "Did Women have a Renaissance?" drew on a close reading of literary evidence to suggest that the Renaissance actually represented a net loss in power and prestige for women.[1] The ladies of medieval romances, Kelly-Gadol urged, at least commanded the devoted service of enamored knights. The more decorative, less active ladies in Renaissance courtly literature did not. The Renaissance also saw an upsurge in moralistic bourgeois tracts praising female obedience, chastity, and piety, all virtues suitable to a burgher's submissive wife or daughter.

Underlying these differences in the literary image of women, Kelly-Gadol detected a decline in real power for both noble women and the women of the urban patriciate in the Renaissance. There was a decline in the weight of hereditary claims, which had been a chief source of female authority in the Middle Ages. At the same time the rise of despotic princely power seized by force or guile and most often exercised by men led to an increasingly passive and subservient role for women in Renaissance society. There was a revival of the ancient Athenian distinction between "an inferior domestic realm of women" and a "superior public realm of men," a "division between personal and public life" that became the basis for "the modern relation of the sexes" for the next five centuries.[2]

As in many other areas of the relatively new field of women's history, the evidence on the status of women in the Renaissance is not all in yet. The list of Renaissance thinkers who admired the intellectual capacities of women includes such luminaries as Erasmus and Thomas More; yet even such an intellectual rebel as Martin Luther insisted that women's education was primarily to strengthen the hand that rocked the cradle. On the eve of the reign of Queen Elizabeth, the woman who was to guide England to peace, prosperity, and immense cultural productivity, the powerful Calvinist preacher John Knox thundered in *The Monstrous Regiment [Rule] of Women* that "it is . . . a monster in nature that a woman should reign and bear empire above man."[3]

And yet, despite the commonplace that woman's role was subordinate, aristocratic gentlemen and ladies are depicted as exchanging wit and repartee on a basis of evident equality in such popular Renaissance works as Shakespeare's plays and the bawdy tales of the Italian writer Boccaccio. The celebrity of these famous Renaissance authors surely indicates that the situations they described had at least some basis in both social reality and popular attitudes toward women.

Certainly more respect and admiration seem to have gone to gifted women in the Renaissance than in the Middle Ages, and there were probably more powerful women in the later period too. Queen Elizabeth herself was fluent in a half-dozen languages, including Latin and Greek, and Thomas More's

daughter Margaret Roper attained an international reputation for her learning. Italian Renaissance ladies like Isabella d'Este (1474–1539), hailed by poets as "first lady of the world" for her exquisite taste, were among the most discriminating collectors of antiquities and patrons of Renaissance art. Caterina Sforza (1463–1509), countess of Forlì, is cited in Kelly-Gadol's essay as a female Renaissance prince who rose through "skill, forcefulness, and ruthless ambition" like her great adversary Cesare Borgia.[4] The women of Venice's urban patriciate, their large dowries and other property protected by law, had "a substantial economic impact" through loans and investments and an even more important political one, "strengthening and stabilizing ties . . . among patrician lineages and within the patriciate generally."[5] And however much their enemies might rail against "the monstrous regiment of women," Renaissance sovereigns like Queen Elizabeth I of England and others, dealt with in the next chapter, probably changed the history of their times more than any medieval queen did.

The Family

We have thus far been concerned in considerable part with social ideals and stereotypes. Our attitudes toward ourselves and others do of course help to guide our social behavior. Much else besides, however, goes into shaping the complexities of a living society. Several of the following sections draw on some of the newer social history to illuminate the life of the family, the community, and the psychological underpinnings of Renaissance culture.

It is perhaps too easy in a time when the family plays a less central role in society than it once did to underestimate its significance in the Renaissance. During this period the family firm and the family farm were still commonplace, people inherited property and status through families, and hereditary monarchies and diplomatic marriages governed and linked the nations. Even an ordinary family raised its own children, arranged apprenticeships or marriages for them, and cared for the elderly at home. The family was the basic block of society, responsible for its individual members in law, taxed as a unit, often involved in traditional alliances or feuds with other families that lasted for generations. It was, in short, a key early modern institution, well worth the investigation it has begun to get in recent years.

The average Renaissance family was apparently

Leonardo da Vinci's drawing of the celebrated Renaissance patron of the arts, Isabella d'Este, seems to combine a thoughtful, contemplative air with vigorous awareness. How do Leonardo's "smoky" shading and the pose of the hand help us to read her character in this way?

much closer in size to the twentieth-century nuclear family than was once thought. Although the families of the well-to-do were considerably larger than our familiar small unit of parents and children, the families of urban poor and rural people were typically small.

Among the urban patriciate, the landed gentry, or the nobility, the family unit often included uncles and aunts, grandparents, cousins and other kin, not to mention several categories of servants. Such a large Renaissance household resembled the extended family still found in some preindustrial societies today. Among the peasantry and the city poor, however, infant mortality, late marriage, and the difficulty of supporting large numbers of children kept family size down. Peasant farmers might have four children but lose two before they were grown up; a family of four was in fact about all the average peasant plot of land could support. City populations also sometimes reveal average family sizes of no more than three or four people. In fifteenth-century Florence, for example, men were often not financially able to marry until they were in their thirties. They married girls in their middle teens, and not infrequently died as early as forty. Such couples produced few children during their relatively brief married lives.

The physical structures in which Renaissance families lived displayed at least some improvement over medieval housing. Window glass began to appear in the north of Europe, for instance, and the stove, more efficient than the fireplace, was invented in Germany. Both aristocratic and patrician middle-class homes began to display paintings, vases and other art objects, solid but elaborately carved chests, wardrobes, and other furniture, porcelain, and glassware. And the Italians, who preferred not to get their fingers greasy during the meat course, invented the fork.

Legally and traditionally, the husband and father was the head of the family, the master of the house. (For a rather different view, as expressed by one writer, see the box titled "Husbands and Wives in the Sixteenth Century.") As in earlier times, however, his orientation was normally outward: he went daily to the fields, to the shop out front or downstairs, or sometimes to a place of work still farther away. Peasant women, urban housewives, and ladies of the manor still ran the basic building block of society, whether it meant cuffing children and shooing chickens or directing the activities of dozens of servants. All this, of course, was still combined with the

THE HUMAN SPIRIT
Husbands and Wives in the Sixteenth Century

Steven Ozment, professor of history at Harvard and a leading authority on this period, argues that patriarchy was neither universal nor necessarily tyrannical. The popular broadside poem he quotes here suggests that husbands were urged to respect and work with their wives in a genuinely companionate marriage during the early modern period. "Why should we quarrel and bare our teeth," the poem urges further on, when "this brings us only disrespect" in the community. Does the recipe for living together offered here sound patronizing to you? Does it sound as though it might have worked in the sixteenth century?

> My good fellow, mark well what I say.
> You young husbands are too ill-tempered,
> Petulant, mad, stupid, and shameless.
> When your wife displeases you,
> Or fails to agree with your point of view,
> Or overrides your wishes on a matter,
> Or has not yet learned to make a proper home,
> You want to correct everything with blows.
> No honorable man would ever behave this
>   way. . . .
>
> Therefore, punish your wife
> Only with kind and understanding words,
> Spoken together in private.
> [Say to her]: "My dear wife, this you should not
>   do,
> It is not fitting for you,
> And it is shameful and harmful.
> If you want my favor and good will
> You must learn to obey me.
> In return I will obey you
> By not doing those things that ill befit me
> And conduct myself as an honest man.
> I will speak no more unkind words to you.
> We shall live together as friends. . . .
>
> When something disturbs you, bring your complaint directly to me,
> And when something bothers me, I shall speak
>   directly to you.
> I forbid you to stand before me in fear.
> There is no one else we can trust completely.

Source: Steven Ozment, *When Fathers Ruled: Family Life in Reformation Europe* (Cambridge, Mass.: Harvard University Press, 1983), 53.

time-honored commitment of women to their half of the world's labor.

Attitudes toward children differed, but some Renaissance people at least seem to have had a sense of the child as something special, as something to cherish. It is often pointed out, for instance, that in works of art of this period the Christ Child begins to be represented as a recognizable infant, rather than as a small adult figure, and that the plump baby angels and cupids still popular on greeting cards today made their first appearance in Renaissance painting and sculpture. Teachers and child-rearing manuals urged rigor, insisting that sparing the rod inevitably spoiled the child; but some parents were apparently inclined to coddle their offspring, making these endless injunctions on the virtues of discipline necessary. Only the well-to-do had the wherewithal to pamper their children, of course, and the modern celebration of childhood and the joys of family life did not come until the late eighteenth century. But in the early modern family there does seem to have been more expression of affection toward children than was once thought.

Cities and Villages

The larger community, whether it was an agricultural village or a bustling city, was also of great importance to Renaissance people. Indeed, our awareness of Renaissance individualism and the glittering achievements of individual Renaissance rulers and artists has perhaps blinded us to the strongly felt

This detail from Leonardo's *Virgin and Child with St. Anne and John the Baptist* shows the faces of Mary and Anne by graceful shading and mastery of the underlying bone structure. [Leonardo da Vinci. Detail of *The Virgin and Child with St. Anne and John the Baptist*. c. 1499. Charcoal and Chalk. Reproduced by courtesy of the Trustees, The National Gallery, London]

need for involvement in the community that was as characteristic of Renaissance as of medieval times.

The homes of early modern villagers showed few advances beyond those of their medieval forebears, though chimneys and snug rainproof thatching were more common in the north. The watermill or windmill, the smithy, and the parish church still stood out among the clustered huts, and there was often a manor house or castle on a neighboring hill. But there were also more deserted villages, thanks to enclosure. "Sheep are devouring people," they grumbled in England as villages emptied of people and sheep proliferated in the fields the villagers had once tilled. Beggars and bandits who had once been hard-working peasants thus joined the mendicant friars, wandering students, military companies, and merchant caravans on the crowded roads.

The rediscovery of the ancient Roman writer Vitruvius's *On Architecture,* with its emphasis on the functional layout of streets, squares, walls, and sewage disposal, led to a rash of city planning. The main squares of such cities as Florence were rendered much more splendid, but few new towns were actually built. Most Renaissance cities rose on medieval or even ancient foundations. Clustered thickly around crossroads, riverbanks, or hilltops, their streets, houses, churches, and public buildings were crammed within a second, third, or fourth concentric ring of expanding city walls. Cobblestoned streets and multistoried buildings were common by now. Italian cities were often lower and more open, with airy squares and two-story buildings predominating; French or German cities had taller overhanging houses shading their narrow medieval lanes.

Neighborhoods were still often defined by the guilds that practiced there, and towering churches were still the main landmarks, proudly added to by guilds and merchant princes. City halls, guildhalls, hospitals, almshouses, schools, and buildings used by the community at large also reflected the intensity of civic pride. North and south, however, cities still had close contact with the surrounding countryside. Such swollen metropolises as London and Paris were accused of draining the country for many miles around. Everywhere, fruit, vegetables, and grain were brought in daily from the farms and hills clearly visible beyond the walls. Vegetable gardens were sandwiched in between the houses, and chickens, goats, and milk cows were raised in crowded city streets. The result was a colorful if not always healthful scene as garbage and sewage still lay heaped in city streets or trickled along open sewers.

Power relations in both villages and cities also resembled their medieval precursors. Though serfdom had largely vanished from western Europe in the Renaissance, peasant villages were still often dominated by local landowners. In many places, the lord's bailiff still administered local justice, and compulsory corvée labor and other holdovers from the medieval manor were still common. The relative political independence characteristic of medieval cities persisted, and the superior quality of urban life continued to draw immigrants from the countryside. For the urban patriciate, political participation through elected councils and magistracies was further encouraged in some places by the new familiarity with the ancient city-states and the Roman Republic gained through education.

The sense of community was widely expressed in the public celebrations, civic functions, church festivals, and popular entertainments of all sorts that frequently filled the streets of Renaissance towns. Crowds gathered for weddings and funerals, for the installation of officials and the arrival of visiting dignitaries, and for the whipping, mutilation, or execution of criminals. Processions, feasts, and festivals highlighted the church calendar also, celebrating saints' days of local significance, Christmas and Easter, the New Year, Epiphany, and especially the gaudy carnival time that preceded Lent. Such occasions were celebrated with elaborate processions and feasts, with entertainment in the form of plays, puppet shows, jugglers, and acrobats. There was also plenty of dancing and singing, drunkenness, casual sexual encounters, and sometimes wanton violence. These public celebrations served as occasions for the release of sexual or aggressive impulses that were normally repressed within the framework of the social system.

Renaissance Mentalities

Beneath idealized models of the Renaissance lady and gentleman, beneath the social realities of the family and community, lie the most elusive layers of the life of the Renaissance: the mental, emotional, and psychological substratum on which all else was built. This is the level of conventional beliefs, popular attitudes, and ways of thinking and feeling often referred to collectively as the *mentalité* ("mentality") of a people. Mentalities encompass the traditional values, the worldview, the cast of mind and patterns

Map 13.1 Culture of Renaissance Italy

of thought of a people, class, or other subgroup in society. Far more than the high culture of Renaissance thought and art surveyed later, the regional and class mentalities of Renaissance people sometimes had deep roots in cultures older than Western civilization itself. Through the study of popular culture, the analysis of festivals like those described in the preceding section, and the perusal of legal or ecclesiastical records containing testimony from ordinary citizens of the Renaissance world, it is possible to reconstruct something of even this deepest level of Renaissance consciousness.

What is revealed is sometimes startlingly at variance with the orthodox and formal beliefs of the age. In the sixteenth century, for instance, when religious issues were widely discussed because of the Reforma-

tion conflict, a belligerent Italian miller called Menocchio testified before the Inquisition to religious beliefs that fitted neither Catholic nor Protestant orthodoxy. Rejecting Scripture as lies and priests as corrupt and irrelevant, the miller asserted that God was made of the four elements—earth, air, fire, and water—that heaven is "like being at a feast" and hell "a priestly invention," and that the world had come into existence out of primal chaos by spontaneous generation, like cheese riddled with worms—the angels in Menocchio's muddled metaphysics![6]

When manifestations of popular feeling like the great annual festivals are analyzed anthropologically, as ritualized expressions of a mentality, they may reveal many levels of meaning below the generalized sense of community mentioned earlier. During the Mardi Gras festival preceding Lent, for example, when gluttony, drunkenness, and sexual license held sway, the normal ordering of society was magically suspended. Lords of Misrule reigned over the carnival; satirical songs and skits attacked the church, the civil authorities, and the wealthy; men dressed as women and women as men; cocks and bulls were sacrificed to the public pleasure; and masks and costumes protected the perpetrators of every enormity from the consequences of such behavior. Analysis of such festivals suggests pagan as well as Christian roots, seasonal and agricultural significance, half-concealed venting of social antagonisms, and other levels of meaning. Some historians have seen in these annual suspensions of social order such varied elements as the inversion of gender roles, the upsetting of the cosmic order of the universe, and the reversal of time itself.[7]

Such analysis makes it clear that the "Renaissance mind," like the mind of most people in most times, is a far richer stew than we had imagined, and that the Renaissance challenge to orthodoxy was not limited to artists and thinkers. But there were some Renaissance Europeans who were not part of the orthodox majority at all.

The Jews in the Renaissance

The most important minority in the Western world in early modern times was the widely scattered Jewish community. European Jews suffered repeatedly from violent persecution during the late medieval and early modern centuries. Paradoxically it was also during this period that some more learned members of the Christian majority developed a new interest in what to them were the mysteries of the Hebrew holy books.

As noted in earlier chapters, the hysteria accompanying religious crusades and the disasters that threatened medieval Christendom in its last centuries often led to violent attacks on the Jews of Europe. Long blamed for the death of Christ, suspected of bloody secret rites, and resented as moneylenders, Jews were particularly made to serve as scapegoats to satisfy the desperate need for someone to blame when the world goes wrong.

As early as the thirteenth century, Louis IX of France—St. Louis—had rigorously enforced anti-

Jewish regulations, and in 1290 the Jews were expelled entirely from England. In the fourteenth century, Jewish minorities were blamed by terrified Christians for the horrors of the Black Death. Waves of persecution included exile from France, first in 1306 and again in 1394, massacres of Jews in France in 1320, killings by gangs of German *Judenschläger* ("Jew beaters") in the 1330s and 1340s, and even in once tolerant Spain, which saw the murder of many Jews in a wave of forced conversions in the 1390s. These compulsory converts *(Marranos)* were, however, widely suspected of practicing their old faith in secret, and in 1492 Ferdinand and Isabella ordered both them and the remaining Jews expelled from the kingdom.

Even through these violent centuries, however, successful Jews played important roles in the business, professional, and political life of the West. France repeatedly had to allow the return of exiled Jews because of the skills and wealth they brought with them. Highly placed "court Jews" helped finance the Holy Roman Empire, and Jews like Don Isaac Abranavel (1437–1508) were among the most trusted advisers of Ferdinand and Isabella of Spain. In Spain and particularly in Italy, highly educated Jews pursued successful careers in government service, law, the universities, and in other professions and crafts. Rome under the Renaissance popes around 1500 became a haven for Jewish scholars of serious learning.

Learned Renaissance Christians, furthermore, added to their passion for the pagan Greco-Roman classics a new interest in the Hebrew language and the Hebrew Old Testament. Renaissance scholars like Pico della Mirandola became fascinated by the Jewish mystical tradition of the *Cabala*, which sought occult meanings in the sacred writings of ancient and medieval Judaism. Lorenzo de' Medici supported Jewish scholarship as well as Greek studies. Some Jews accommodated their own faith to the worldly Renaissance values of the sixteenth century and mixed easily with the Christian elites of commercial cities like Venice.

In the later sixteenth century, however, the intensified religious feeling kindled by the Protestant and Catholic Reformations led to renewed persecution of Jews, even in Italy. Harried from country to country and always under threat of confiscation of property or personal attack, the oldest Western minority managed only by a remarkable tenacity of purpose both to survive and to preserve its faith intact.

The New Humanism

"The rebirth of literature and art" is a highly mis-leading definition of the Renaissance, for both had flourished, though in different modes and styles, in the Middle Ages too. Still, there is no denying that in both realms of creativity, Western culture looked very different after the Renaissance than before. The next three sections survey the writing and art of the three centuries that began with the poetry of Petrarch and the painting of Giotto in fourteenth-century Italy and climaxed in the work of Michelangelo and Shakespeare in the sixteenth.

It is in the manipulation of the written word, from poetry to political thought, that the Renaissance was most clearly a revival of ancient culture. We look first at humanism, the conscious effort to recapture the vanished literary glories of the "wise ancients." But Renaissance writers were creative people too, and soon new literary forms took shape in the vernacular languages, and great names emerged who, like Shakespeare, had "little Latin and less Greek."

Rediscovering the Classics

The *humanist movement* was not a school of literature in the normal sense. It was a shared passion for the ancient classics and a determined effort to recover—and to imitate—lost masterpieces. Humanist writers spent little time on metaphysics, logic, and theology, which were the central concerns of the medieval university. Instead, they concentrated on what seemed to Renaissance scholars to be more "human" literary subjects: poetry and rhetoric, ethics, history, and government. The new movement thus became known as *studia humanitatis*—"human studies" or as we say today, "the humanities"—and those who pursued these studies were called humanists.

The original goal of humanism was to imitate rather than create from scratch. The typical humanist was an ink-stained scholar, learned in Latin, Greek, and sometimes Hebrew. He was often a teacher or tutor of aristocratic children, a secretary to Renaissance princes or ruling councils, or perhaps a glorified toastmaster providing orations and poems on public occasions in exchange for princely patronage. Yet the humanist enthusiasm for the 5-foot shelf of Greco-Roman masterworks had a profound effect not only on Renaissance literature but on Reforma-

tion religion and on education, society, and social thought in early modern times.

What the humanists set out to do, and largely achieved, was to recover most of the classical literary heritage from the neglect into which it had fallen over the preceding thousand years. Some Latin writers, like Vergil, had been known in some form all through the Middle Ages. Greek science and Aristotelian philosophy had been reimported into high medieval Europe through Venetian contact with Byzantium and through Muslim Spain. But it was the humanists who restored the larger part of Latin and much Greek literature to the mainstream of Western culture.

Humanist scholars began as early as the fourteenth century to dredge up forgotten manuscripts of Latin classics from dusty monastery shelves. These rare finds—a hitherto unknown oration of Cicero, a lost book of Livy's history of Rome—were edited and annotated by their triumphant discoverers. Thereafter, copies were carefully deposited in the libraries of famous patrons of scholarship and art like the Medici, or in the Vatican Library, founded by Pope Nicholas V (r. 1447–1455). As printing presses—discussed later—sprang up in many European cities, publishers like the Aldine Press of Venice made printed copies of these works available to students, teachers, and an increasingly literate aristocracy. For those whose Latin was not up to the originals, translations into the major languages were made, and collections of selected literary gems and wise sayings were widely published.

The Greek classics reached Europe via a different route in the fifteenth century. During those unhappy last decades of the Byzantine Empire, Greek scholars from Constantinople migrated westward to Renaissance Italy, bringing copies of Greek tragedies and Platonic dialogues with them. The learned Byzantine Manuel Chrysolorus (c. 1353–1415), who taught ancient languages in Italy, urged the preparation of translations that would communicate the spirit rather than merely the literal meaning of the classics. Since even educated Renaissance people seldom went beyond Latin to study a second ancient language, such translations of Greek works into Latin and then into modern languages were a major means of expanding European awareness of the Greek contribution to our Greco-Roman heritage.

Humanists carefully polished their own Latin to resemble that of the classic authors, reviving the literary Latin of ancient writers instead of the simpler Latin of the medieval church. More important in the long run, they were transforming the educational institutions and expectations of western Europe. As private tutors or heads of elite schools, humanists taught the ancient classics to Europe's aristocracy. Renaissance despots and the new monarchs alike, meanwhile, demanded higher education in their officials and ministers of state, who had to cope with the increasingly complex business of governing a modern state.

Thus for the first time since antiquity, Europe acquired an educated ruling class. The aristocracies of all nations, moreover, shared the same store of historical knowledge, literary taste, and philosophical insights. A core of classical culture thus became one of the distinctive unifying features of the modern West, thanks to the humanists of the Renaissance.

Humanists from Petrarch to Erasmus

The first humanist was Francesco Petrarca (1304–1374), known as Petrarch in English, a dedicated poet and scholar often described as the first "Renaissance man." Trained in the law at Bologna, Petrarch was much more interested in poetry. A great admirer of Vergil's heroic epic, the *Aeneid*, and of Cicero's moral writings, Petrarch wrote orations, treatises, and epistles after the style of Cicero and attempted a Vergilian epic called *Africa*, the story of Scipio Africanus's victory over Hannibal. Petrarch pioneered in two basic humanist directions: ferreting out manuscripts of ancient Roman writers, and writing original works in classical literary Latin rather than in the church Latin of the Middle Ages. Yet he had a strong medieval otherworldly streak himself and was as great an admirer of St. Augustine as of Cicero and Vergil. His fame as scholar, moralist, and poet was so great that King Robert of Naples (r. 1309–1343) revived the ancient custom of rewarding excellence with a laurel crown to make Petrarch the first modern poet laureate in 1341.

It was Petrarch's influence more than any other single factor that turned other scholars to the study of the classics. The collective weight of the new movement stimulated the Italian aristocracy to begin collecting manuscripts, coins, statuary, and other survivals of Roman greatness. A vast work of recovery and revival thus got under way. Among the leading humanists who carried on the effort in the fifteenth century were Valla, Ficino, and Pico della Mirandola.

Lorenzo Valla (1407–1457) epitomized the new movement at its most daring. He feuded with ri-

THE HUMAN SPIRIT
Pico on the Dignity of Man

The humanist enthusiasm for the human potential found no more eloquent spokesperson than the brilliant fifteenth-century Italian scholar Pico della Mirandola. Here Pico builds on the view urged by the Platonic philosopher Marsilio Ficino that human nature falls in the middle of the created world, halfway between angels (purely spiritual beings) and animals (purely material creatures). But Pico goes one step further, celebrating God's gift to humankind of free will, the capacity that only human beings possess to choose their own destinies. Do you think we are as free to become whatever we want to be as Pico believed?

Now the highest father, God the master-builder, had, by the laws of his secret wisdom, fabricated this house, this world which we see . . . [Thereafter] He took up man, a work of indeterminate form; and, placing him at the midpoint of the world, He spoke to him as follows:

"We have given thee, Adam, no fixed seat, no form of thy very own, no gift peculiarly thine, that thou mayest . . . possess as thine own the seat, the form, the gifts which thou thyself shalt desire. A limited nature in other creatures is confined within the laws written down by Us. In conformity with thy free judgment, in whose hands I have placed thee, thou art confined by no bounds, and thou wilt fix limits of nature for thyself. I have placed thee at the center of the world, that from there thou mayest more conveniently look around thee and see whatever is in the world. Neither heavenly nor earthly, neither mortal nor immortal have we made thee. Thou . . . art the molder and maker of thyself; thou mayest sculpt thyself into whatever shape thou dost prefer. Thou canst grow downward into the lower natures which are brutes. Thou canst again grow upward from thy soul's reason into higher natures which are divine."

O great liberality of God the Father! O great and wonderful happiness of man! It is given to him to have that which he chooses and to be that which he wills. . . . If he cultivates sensation . . . he will become a brute. . . . If intellectual, he will be an angel and the son of God. . . . Who does not wonder at this chameleon . . . ?

Source: Giovanni Pico della Mirandola, On the Dignity of Man, trans. Charles Glenn Wallis (Indianapolis: Bobbs Merrill, 1940), 4–5.

val humanists, criticized medieval Scholastic philosophers like Thomas Aquinas for poor style, and offered corrections of St. Jerome's Latin translation of the Bible, standard throughout the Middle Ages. He produced a philosophical dialogue in which one of the speakers urged the totally unchristian theory of the ancient Epicureans that pleasure is the true goal of life. And in a notorious challenge to papal authority, Valla demonstrated through stylistic analysis of the text that the Donation of Constantine, which had provided a basis for the pope's claims to rule the Papal States and to possess a larger temporal sovereignty over Christendom as a whole, was a forgery. Marsilio Ficino (1433–1499) studied Greek as well as Latin, translated Plato's works, and founded the Platonic Academy in the Florence of the Medici. Ficino believed that Platonic philosophy provided powerful intellectual support for revealed religion. He also explored the ideas of the third-century Neoplatonic philosopher Plotinus and fathered the influential notion of "platonic"—really Neoplatonic—love, a spiritual passion of one person for another, which at its highest level is transmuted into the soul's love for God.

Giovanni Pico della Mirandola (1463–1494) was an intellectual prodigy who died at thirty-one yet found a unique immortality: "Pico" is today the name of the largest crater on the moon. The son of a noble family, Pico della Mirandola studied law at Bologna, philosophy with Ficino, and theology in Paris. He also immersed himself in Hebrew and Arabic as well as Latin and Greek. His most famous work was the *Oration on the Dignity of Man* (1486), in which he praised humankind's divinely granted freedom, the unique capacity of human beings to make of themselves whatever they wished, from animals to angels (see box, "Pico on the Dignity of Man"). This was the humanist message at its most exalted: a confident assertion of pride in human achievement and of conviction that human beings are masters of their fates.

By Pico's time, humanist writing and scholarship had also spread to the northern countries. *Northern humanism,* however, had a different tone and focus. It is often described as less pagan and worldly, more moralistic and overtly Christian than the humanism of the sunny south. In fact, Italian humanists were much less pagan than their more daring tracts sometimes sounded. Still, there was a larger concern for the Christian classics—the Scriptures and the writings of the church fathers, for instance—among the northern humanists. Their work

was actually laying the scholarly foundation for the Reformation.

The most famous of these northern scholars was Desiderius Erasmus (1466–1536) of Rotterdam, sometimes called the prince of humanists. Born in modest circumstances, educated by the Brethren of the Common Life, the Dutch Erasmus spent some time in a monastery and studied theology in Paris. He led a wandering life, traveling over much of Europe, enjoying the patronage of the great, and earning the reputation of being the most distinguished intellect in the Western world.

Erasmus's *Adages* (1508) made the wisdom of the ancients available in pithy sayings for less scholarly Renaissance people. In the *Complaint of Peace* (1515), he made the pacifist case against war long before there was an antiwar movement. His most famous work was the satirical oration called the *Praise of Folly* (1509), which exposed the follies of sixteenth-century people of every class and condition. Erasmus's major concern, however, was to apply humanist scholarship to the great books of the Christian tradition. He published what were for his time

This picture is one of many portraits of Erasmus of Rotterdam, the most admired intellectual of his day. Which portrait do you think is more successful at capturing the intelligence of the subject—this one, or that of Isabella d'Este?

definitive editions of Augustine, Jerome, and others of the church fathers. His edition of the Greek New Testament was used by leaders of the Reformation to bolster their arguments from Scripture and as the basis for their vernacular translations of the Bible.

Erasmus himself propounded what he called "the philosophy of Christ," based on faith, Christian love, and ethical behavior rather than on dogma and ritual, and applied this humanistic creed to the education of European aristocrats and rulers in such books as *The Handbook of the Christian Knight* (1503) and *The Education of a Christian Prince* (1516). A correspondent of the founder of Protestantism, Martin Luther, and a friend of the Catholic martyr Thomas More, Erasmus refused to take sides in the struggle over the Reformation that, as we will see, bitterly divided sixteenth-century society. Though he had satirized the vices of churchmen and debated Luther on the freedom of the human will, in the end the prince of humanists stood alone, defending his own intellectual independence above all else.

Humanist Social Thought

Modern social thought can be traced to humanist origins in the fifteenth and sixteenth centuries. In Italian civic humanism and in two unique works by humanists, Machiavelli's *Prince* and More's *Utopia,* lie the origins of some basic modern ideas of how human society is or should be run.

A clearer idea of how society really works is evidenced in the revival of history writing as a serious intellectual discipline. Developed first by the Greeks and Romans but like most other disciplines reduced to the role of adjunct to theology during the Middle Ages, history once more achieved autonomy and developed critical insight at the beginning of the modern era. Perhaps the best known Renaissance practitioner of the craft was Francesco Guicciardini (1483–1540). A Florentine diplomat and papal administrator, Guicciardini produced two histories of Florence and a *History of Italy* in his own time that made discriminating use of documentary evidence in a thoroughly modern critical spirit.

Civic humanism is a term for the ideas of political participation put forward in fifteenth-century Florence. In this city republic, which traced its roots back to Roman times, the humanist Leonardo Bruni (c. 1370–1444) and others urged that it was the duty

of educated people to put their knowledge at the service of the commonwealth by participating in government. Bruni claimed that this was the oldest Roman tradition, the tradition of the self-governing Rome of the Republic. Government, he asserted, should welcome such citizen participation. The educated, furthermore, had an obligation to turn from the selfish joys of scholarship to the nobler duty of government service.

Niccolò Machiavelli (1469–1527), an admirer of the ancients and author of the famous *Discourses on Livy,* the Roman historian, developed a rather different impression from Leonardo Bruni's. After fifteen years as secretary to the ruling council of Florence and a good deal of diplomatic work, Machiavelli, as noted in the previous chapter, knew the leading statesmen of the Age of the Renaissance despots and new monarchs. Losing his post when the Medici clan, temporarily expelled from Florence in the 1490s, returned to power in 1512, Machiavelli retired to the country. During this enforced retirement, he proceeded to tell all: the truth about government, not as it ideally ought to be, but as it really was in practice.

The Prince (1513) was conceived as a manual of statecraft, part of a late medieval tradition of "mirror of princes" books listing the skills and virtues a perfect ruler should have. Erasmus's *Education of a Christian Prince* updated the genre by urging Greco-Roman classics as well as Christian works as guides to governance. Machiavelli's list of princely qualities, however, owed less to classical or Christian models and more to close and honest observation of politics as it was practiced in his day. Niccolò Machiavelli's *Prince* immediately earned a reputation for cynicism and wickedness that made "Machiavellian" shorthand for devious treachery and "Old Nick" a nickname for the devil himself.

The best place to begin to understand this little book is not with the prince but with his people. Machiavelli's view of humankind was actually orthodox enough: as Adam's seed, we are all sinners, feckless and faithless, responsive only to bribery or force, each class and faction determined to advance its own interests at all costs. In such a world, Machiavelli felt that only a shrewd and ruthless prince could govern successfully. He therefore advised such unchristian, unplatonic policies as brutal repression (fear is more dependable than popularity); governmental deception (lying may be necessary to gain the prince's ends); lavish rewards to the ruler's supporters (what Jacksonian democrats would later call the spoils system); manipulation of religion and law to keep the people in order and to improve the prince's image; and so on down a chillingly realistic catalog of maxims that never found their way into a civics textbook.

Machiavelli did in fact have his political ideals. He admired the love of country shown by Livy's idealized Romans. He had served the Florentine Republic and remained a strong believer in republican institutions and civic loyalty all his life. Yet he voiced a passionate hope that Italy might find some prince—perhaps the likes of Cesare Borgia—strong enough to resist the foreign invaders who were devastating the land. Such a prince would have to play the fox and the lion, sly and strong enough to survive in the jungle of politics and international relations. For if half our human destiny is determined by *fortuna* or luck, the other half is determined by *virtù*, a much-

admired quality of character including willpower, courage, intelligence, and ability but lacking many distinctly Christian virtues. Cesare Borgia was his idea of the man of virtù. *The Prince* is a book about this sort of political power, a manual of statecraft without a moral, and the rumored bedside book of every modern autocrat and dictator from Frederick the Great to Stalin.

The *Utopia* of Thomas More (1478–1535) was all moral—an account not of the way things are, but of how an ideal state *ought* to be run. It established a genre of modern fiction that traces its roots to Plato's *Republic* and has continued into our own century. Yet like Machiavelli's *Prince*, More's *Utopia* (1516) was unique.

A lawyer and an admired humanist, a family man who educated his daughters in classics as if they were sons, a high public official who sometimes

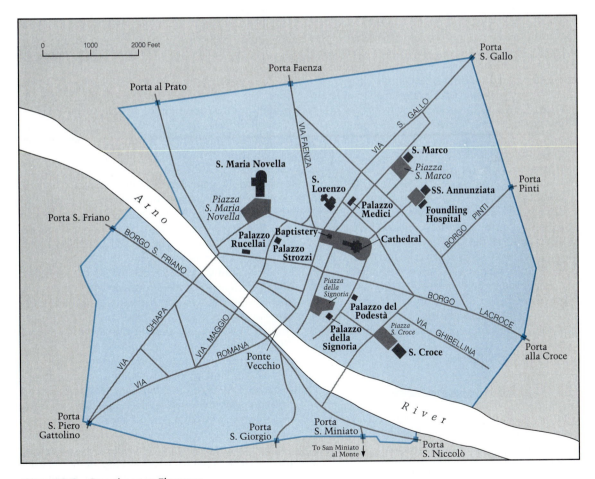

Map 13.2   Renaissance Florence

wore a monkish hairshirt under his robes of state, More himself was a true original. Erasmus's friend and Henry VIII's chancellor, he tried to put his ideals into practice. Like Thomas Becket dealing with Henry II in an earlier century, however, Thomas More discovered there was a point at which his religious commitments outweighed loyalty to his king. For refusing to renounce the pope and accept King Henry's headship of the English church during the Reformation, More was beheaded in 1535.

More's *Utopia* is divided into two parts. The first is a discussion of the scholar's duty to serve the state, even though princes will probably ignore his good advice, preferring war to peace and a lavish princely lifestyle to the popular welfare. The second part describes the ideal state, imagined as an island in the Ocean Sea, where so many new discoveries had been made in recent decades. More's Utopians demonstrated an almost monastic willingness to share and contempt for worldly wealth: material possessions were owned in common, and gold was used for such ignoble purposes as making chamber pots. Reason, education, and social discipline had turned Machiavelli's feckless mob into a happy, hard-working, well-ordered community in More's Utopia.

The weakness of More's glowing vision, however, was revealed in the title itself. *Utopia* means "Nowhere." As critics have repeatedly pointed out, there was no such community. To label a social ideal as "utopian" has thus been to dismiss it as unrealistic—as a social vision too perfect for this world— ever since.

All three of these Renaissance views of society had great influence on Western social thought. Civic humanism reintroduced the Greek and Republican Roman ideal of the good citizen to the modern West. Machiavelli initiated a very different tradition, one of hard-boiled analysis of political relations with an emphasis on power, conflict, and expediency. More created yet a third tradition, the utopian view of society that challenged the inevitability of "the way things are" by exploring the possibilities of a better world.

Schools and Books

This new wave of interest in the life of the mind, finally, was advanced by two related developments. These were the creation of new schools and theories of education by the humanists themselves and the development by German artisans of the first of the modern media of communication, the printed book.

Humanists, as mentioned, often served as tutors to the children of the ruling classes. As teachers and scholars, they soon evolved theories of education markedly at variance with the practice in the church-related educational institutions inherited from the Middle Ages. In the early fifteenth century, Pietro Paolo Vergerio (1370–1440), a professor at the University of Padua, wrote perhaps the first influential tract on teaching, *On Gentlemanly Manners and Liberal Studies.* Vergerio urged training of body, mind, and spirit, stressing a broad introduction to liberal arts rather than professional training. Vittorino da Feltre (1378–1446) put some of these pedagogical ideals into practice in a school he opened outside Mantua. Intended originally for the children of the ruling Gonzaga family and of the nobility of Mantua, the school also took in poor but capable students. A dedicated humanist and a legendary teacher, Vittorino emphasized Greek and Latin but also included plenty of physical exercise and a heavy admixture of moral and spiritual instruction.

The new approach to education spread to northern Europe also. Humanists taught the classics to the offspring of princes and ambitious nobles there too, and some humbler institutions were infected with their ideals. Future sovereigns like Henry VIII and Queen Elizabeth were taught ancient languages and literatures. Among the best known schools to appear beyond the Alps were those run by the Brethren of the Common Life in the Netherlands, whose graduates included Erasmus himself. Among northern educational theorists, finally, the Spaniard Juan Luis Vives (1492–1540) urged such radical changes as the use of the modern languages (rather than Latin) in schools, and education on an equal basis for women and men.

Humanist education remained for the most part elitist, teaching great ideas to the children of princes, the nobility, or the urban patriciate. A second development with a much wider reach and an even larger impact, however, also came in the fifteenth century. This was the invention of movable metal type and the advent of the printed book in Western history.

The technology of papermaking and woodblock printing originated in China and reached Europe through Muslim Spain in the High Middle Ages. The next step was the use of movable type—tiny metal letters that were arranged to form sentences and pages of text, locked in a frame, inked, pressed against paper to make a printed page, and then removed from the frame to be rearranged in new sentences and used to print another page. This process was developed in the German city of Mainz in the 1440s, probably not by Johannes Gutenberg (c. 1390–1468), traditionally considered the inventor of printing, but by a group of ingenious Rhineland printers including Gutenberg. The result, in any case, was revolutionary. Movable type made it possible to reproduce books much more cheaply and in much greater numbers than ever before. Gutenberg's first Bible came out around 1455, and by 1500 there were millions of books in the hands of Europeans.

The development of the art of printing was the second great breakthrough in the history of human communications. The first was the invention of writing itself in ancient times; the third is taking place today as film and the electronic media evolve into the twenty-first century.

Renaissance Literature

The writers of the Renaissance include some of the great names of English, French, Spanish, and Italian literature. We begin by looking at some of the general characteristics of Renaissance writing. In the sections that follow, we will explore the contributions of some of the most celebrated writers of this earliest modern literature.

Traditional Forms

Both in form and content, Western literature at the beginning of the modern period aimed at truth and beauty rather than at originality. The grip of conventional wisdom and inherited genres was strong. Drawing on the ideas of the early Christian fathers and the Greco-Roman classics, with a chivalric inspiration or two, Renaissance writers tended toward tried-and-true themes and subjects: great kings and heroic captains (with an occasional Falstaff-like buffoon thrown in), courtly love and bawdy jokes, noble Romans and wise Greeks, human wickedness and divine retribution filled the pages of their books. They wrote epic and lyric poetry, tragic and comic drama, orations and epistles, and pastorals, social satire, and moral philosophy because the Greeks and Romans had. Literature was in some ways a performing art, the goal being to express the eternal verities in appropriate style, to move readers to feel their truth once more.

Reading Renaissance literature, then, requires some of the background knowledge and literary taste of Renaissance readers. Familiarity with the Bible and with ancient history and mythology is a great help. Renaissance writers used references to Venus and Mars, crossing the Rubicon, and cutting the Gordian knot as shorthand for abstractions like love and war, a political gamble, or the bold decisiveness that wins. A taste for metaphor, allegory, and symbol is also useful. Renaissance readers could get as bored as modern ones with *golden* hair, teeth like *pearls*, or a *storm* of sighs. But they appreciated a well-worked-out metaphor, and they liked to see vices and virtues personified and acting out their qualities in allegorical fashion.

An ear for rhyme and the rhythm of language also helped them enjoy periodic prose and the intricate rhyme schemes and meters of traditional poetry. For poet and reader alike, the fourteen lines of the sonnet form, the fixed number of beats per line, and the required pattern of rhyming words were simply the rules of the game. And the skillful manipulation of a five-beat line of iambic pentameter moved them as the beat in music might. The meter certainly plays a large part in the effectiveness of lines like

> Was *this* the *face* that *launch'd* a thousand ships
> And *burnt* the *top*less *towers* of *Ilium?*[8]

Rephrase this passage as

> Did this face cause a thousand ships to be
> launched
> And the towers of Ilium to be burned?

and you may not have changed the meaning, but the power of Helen's beauty, the images of the huge Greek fleet putting to sea and of Troy in flames somehow lose a lot of their impact.

Innovative Spirits: Petrarch to Cervantes

Even in an era that strove so hard to imitate its predecessors, there were innovators and original spirits. A brief look at some of the great names of Renaissance literature illustrates the variety and uniqueness as much as the conventions of this age of effervescent Western creativity. And Petrarch and Boccaccio in Italy, Rabelais and Montaigne in France, and Cervantes in Spain are all among the greatest names in continental European literature of any age.

The two most critically acclaimed and influential of Italian Renaissance writers both wrote in the fourteenth century, at the beginning of the new era. Petrarch, already discussed, was not only the founding father of Latin humanism but an enormously influential poet in Italian. His fame in Italian literature was based on his *Sonnets to Laura* (1360), a collection of lyrical love poems addressed to the great love of his life, who had died in the plague. This most admired of all collections of Renaissance sonnets reflected the divide in Petrarch's psyche between his sensitivity to physical beauty and his belief in the superiority of spiritual things. The Laura of these poems is both physically beautiful and the symbol of a higher perfection. This intriguing duality, and the beauty of Petrarch's verse, won him hordes of imitators all over Europe. By the end of the Renaissance, the Petrarchan conventions of golden hair and hopeless love began to seem a little silly even to Renaissance readers, and poets like Shakespeare satirized them. But for a number of generations, Petrarchism in poetry was as satisfactory to that age as the romantic conventions of our time are to us.

A very different attitude toward love and sexual passion was taken by Petrarch's contemporary and friend Giovanni Boccaccio (1313–1375). Son of a Florentine merchant, bored with business and law, Boccaccio gave himself over to a life of pleasure and poetry in Renaissance Naples. Returning to Florence in time to witness the ravages of the Black Death in 1348, Boccaccio soon thereafter wrote the *Decameron,* the collection of one hundred witty, often bawdy tales on which his reputation largely rests. Presented as stories told by ten spritely young ladies and gentlemen who have fled the ravages of the plague to a country retreat, the book has a vitality that earned it immense popularity both during and long after the Renaissance. Boccaccio also wrote a great deal of poetry and, under the influence of Petrarch, became a respected humanist in his later years. But it is the bawdy tales from the *Decameron* that are still reprinted commercially today.

The most famous French writer of the first half of the sixteenth century, François Rabelais (c. 1483–1553), also earned a reputation for earthy humor. But there is much more to Rabelais's multivolume *Gargantua and Pantagruel* (1532–1552) than the gross passages that used to be replaced by asterisks in Victorian editions. An unenthusiastic monk, a successful physician, a learned humanist, and a robust

wit, Rabelais brought out the successive volumes of his comic masterpiece in spite of the opposition of the church. There is much of the tall tale in Rabelais's stories: Gargantua and his son Pantagruel are fairy-tale giants, and Paul Bunyan style exaggeration is one of the author's favorite devices. But there is a joy in the play of language for its own sake and an endless inventiveness that, along with the scatological humor, made these books bestsellers. For the more sophisticated reader, there were stinging satires on the pretensions of just about every distinguished profession, including law, medicine, theology, scholarship, war, and the monastic vocation. The famous Rabelaisian "Abbey of Thélème" was described as a very worldly miniutopia, a secular retreat for the "well born, well educated, and well endowed" of both sexes where the Benedictine rule has been replaced by a Renaissance maxim: "Do As You Wish!"

Michel de Montaigne (1533–1592), as great a name in the French literature of the second half of the century as Rabelais was in the first half, was a very different sort of person, yet every bit as original a mind. A gentleman, a judge, and mayor of Bordeaux, Montaigne showed few signs of literary aspirations until he retired to his country chateau to jot down his thoughts on life—the three volumes of *Essays* (1572–1580) that became French classics and established the essay as a literary genre. Montaigne's *Essays* offer, first, a living self-portrait of a late Renaissance man, more skeptical and less self-confident than Petrarch or Pico and thoroughly Erasmian in his refusal to take sides in the Reformation struggles currently tearing his country apart. In addition, however, Montaigne brought his substantial classical learning to bear on the world around him, providing thoughtful comment on everything from friendship and skepticism to the new fashion of horse-drawn coaches and the nature of the New World's "noble savages." Montaigne's motto, "What Do I Know?" reflected the maturity of an age whose early aspirations had been called into question by competing fanaticisms but whose choicer spirits were coming to terms with human fallibility.

Miguel de Cervantes (1547–1616), the greatest Spanish writer of this "golden century" in the history of Spain, said goodbye to his age with a laugh. Cervantes himself had aspired to military glory, fighting the Turks in the great naval battle of Lepanto, but he ended his military career as a prisoner of war. He dreamed of literary fame and fortune but he scraped along most of his life as an underpaid civil servant and author of brief tales and short plays. In the two vol umes of *Don Quixote* (1605), however, Cervantes created one of the great books and two of the archetypal characters of modern fiction. The insanely idealistic knight Don Quixote and his peasant squire Sancho Panza who set off in search of chivalric adventures in a thoroughly postchivalric century are the stuff of great comedy, from slapstick to social satire. That may in fact have been all that Cervantes consciously intended. But the dreaming knight and his hapless squire have ever since been unforgettable symbols of the fate of high ideals in a real world where there are no more magic dragons to slay. Don Quixote has for four hundred years embodied the nobility of dreams and "quixotic" quests in a world of tawdry realities.

Shakespeare and the English Renaissance

The Renaissance came late to Britain, Europe's offshore islands to the west. But the literary flowering of the Elizabethan Age (1558–1603) was worth waiting for. Swashbuckling gentry like Sir Philip Sidney and Sir Walter Raleigh were themselves writers of distinction. Edmund Spenser, sometimes called the "poets' poet," Francis Bacon, who magnificently declared that he "took all knowledge to be [his] province," and Christopher Marlowe, the playwright of the "high aspiring mind," all reflect the scope and energy of the time. And in the plays and poems of William Shakespeare of Stratford-upon-Avon, the age of Elizabeth produced the best writing the English language has yet seen.

Edmund Spenser (1552–1599), a poet first, last, and always, is almost never read today outside English classes. To Elizabethans, he was a glittering manipulator of intricate patterns of verse, a clever constructor of intriguing allegories, and—surprising though it may seem to more recent readers—a master storyteller. The popularity of his epic *The Fairie Queene* (1590–1596) owed much to that aristocratic enthusiasm for chivalry that Cervantes laughed to scorn a few years later. The interwoven adventures of the Red Cross Knight, Prince Arthur, Britomart the Maiden Knight, and many others questing through a dreamlike land of wonder and romance held readers enthralled quite as much as the underlying allegories teased the Elizabethan mind.

Christopher Marlowe (1564–1593), Kit to his drinking and writing friends, was one of the first literary bohemians. Defying the orthodox and the rigidly righteous, he was reputed to be an atheist, may have

been an agent for Queen Elizabeth's secret service, and was certainly the finest English dramatist before Shakespeare. Dying young in a tavern brawl, he left half a dozen plays that incarnated the overweening self-confidence and exalted aspiration of the Renaissance. Marlowe's *Tamburlaine the Great* (1587)—the Tamerlane of history—wants to conquer the world. His millionaire Barabas in *The Jew of Malta* is the merchant prince reveling in his millions. And *Dr. Faustus,* Marlowe's version of the medieval legend of the man who sold his soul to the Devil, exults in the supernatural power to master time and space, tweak the pope's nose, and summon up Helen of Troy from the distant past to grace his bed. Yet Faustus's career, like young Kit Marlowe's, has its terrible end when Faustus faces death and eternal hellfire in an anguished final hour on earth that finds powerful expression in Marlowe's mighty lines.

William Shakespeare (1564–1616), his fellow playwright Ben Jonson said with much truth, was "not for an age, but for all time." Still, Shakespeare does reflect some aspects of his age. His plays included historical epics, rollicking comedies, and brooding tragedies that eminently suited the taste of his contemporaries. His plot lines were very often borrowed from history books or the works of earlier writers. His characters—in *Romeo and Juliet, Macbeth, Henry V, Richard III, Hamlet, Julius Caesar, Othello, King Lear, The Tempest,* and so many others—while larger than life, were also embodiments of passions that were not new to the Elizabethan stage: love, ambition, heroism, jealousy, revenge.

What makes Shakespeare's plays special is that dramatically they *work*, and poetically they say things as well as they have ever been said. When modern directors regularly adapt Shakespeare for the present-day stage, turning his plays into operas, musical comedies, or movies, they find again and again that, from the broad structure of each play to the construction of each taut scene, the Elizabethan dramatist knew precisely what he was doing. He knew how to build the tragic tension, how to relieve it with a comic interlude, how to plunge his characters into the ordeal that will test them to the utmost, and how the story must end. Imagine the masterful tyrant Richard III dying with a plea for mercy, or the star-crossed lovers Romeo and Juliet happily married at the final curtain!

The poetry remains to be read, or heard, on the lips of the most celebrated actors of each age in turn. Even the twentieth-century ear, too often tone deaf to poetry, takes Shakespeare in and cannot get him out. To be or not to be, that *is* the question—how many have asked it since Hamlet? It is the east, the passionate lover cries, and Juliet is the sun. Caesar—and how many great men since?—doth bestride the narrow world like a colossus. Henry V's stirring exhortation at Agincourt, Once more into the breach, dear friends! was read aloud to British troops storming ashore in Normandy on D-Day in World War II. Out, out, damned spot! (Who would have thought the old man to have so much blood in him?)—Lady Macbeth's tormented dreams have ever since been the most terrible expression of guilt, of the blood that will not wash away. And in the end, how many have found that Life *is* but a walking shadow, a poor player that struts and frets his hour upon the stage, and then is heard no more . . . a tale told by an idiot, full of sound and fury, signifying . . . nothing. There is something in Shakespeare for all times, even our own.

Renaissance Art

We may have to hone some skills we do not often use to read Renaissance literature, but there are no such barriers between us and the art that made the Renaissance famous. When we think of the Renaissance, most of us probably think first of the *Mona Lisa* or the *Last Supper*, or of God giving life to Adam on Michelangelo's Sistine ceiling. The appeal of these works is perhaps more immediate than anything we have seen since ancient Greece and Rome, and we do not really need a book to tell us we like them. Still, a little historical explanation does not hurt, and it may help to illuminate the period as much as the art itself.

Renaissance artists, like Renaissance writers, tried to learn from ancient models. In architecture particularly, they borrowed heavily and praised what they learned. Ancient sculpture was also an inspiration, and Michelangelo did statues of fauns and Bacchus before he turned to *Moses* or the Medici. In painting, which played as central a role in the arts of the Renaissance as architecture did in the Middle Ages, Renaissance artists were innovators of the first order. Beginning in Italy once more, let us look at the most familiar achievement of the age: the art that produced the Mona Lisa smile, the dome of St. Peter's, and a dazzling array of other masterpieces.

Renaissance Painting

In painting and other graphic arts, Renaissance artists had little choice but to be original. No ancient paintings had survived to be imitated—or none that the Renaissance knew about, since the buried city of Pompeii still slumbered unknown under many feet of volcanic ash. The fundamental goal that Renaissance painters set for themselves was that urged by Aristotle and illustrated by ancient sculpture: art as the imitation of nature. Individual artists would go far beyond mere representation, seeing beauty where the ordinary eye saw none and imposing their own individual styles on the world they painted. But the contemporary art historian Giorgio Vasari (1511–1574) offered as his highest critical commendation the accolade of "lifelikeness," and much of the innovative energy and originality of the age went into perfecting new techniques to achieve this end.

A basic method pioneered in the Renaissance was drawing and sketching from life. It was said of Leonardo da Vinci that "whenever he saw a strange head or beard or hair of unusual appearance . . . he would follow such a person a whole day, and so learn him by heart, that when he reached home he could draw him as if he were present"[9] and you can still learn to draw horses from his close-up sketches of their heads, legs, hooves, and rumps. Among the artists of the northern Renaissance, Albrecht Dürer's often-reproduced praying hands are as utterly convincing in their gnarled piety as they were when he drew them four and a half centuries ago. Another technical innovation was the careful exploitation of highlights and shadows—*chiaroscuro*—as form-revealing elements. Shadows defining the folds of clothing or the curve of a painted cheek make Renaissance faces and figures stand out in naturalistic relief from the surface of canvas or wall.

Two basic devices above all, however, made Renaissance painters the masters of graphic realism. These were anatomically accurate figure drawing and a firm command of perspective.

Really convincing *figure drawing* became a prerequisite for success in painting for the first time in the early modern centuries. Renaissance artists sketched from the living model, learning through many painstaking hours of practice to render human bodies convincingly. Leonardo initiated the practice of studying the mechanics of human anatomy by sketching dissected corpses, and living models posed routinely in Renaissance studios. The result was an unprecedented skill at painting human faces and

Raphael's *School of Athens* shows the great philosophers of ancient Greece grandly if inaccurately framed by huge Roman arches. Notice how the receding lines of perspective focus the viewer's eye on the greatest of the Greek thinkers, Plato and Aristotle, in the center of the picture.

bodies as they really were. Figures depicted nude or partially clothed thus looked far more lifelike; but so did figures swathed in heavy robes, since clothing hanging from realistically conceived bones, muscles, and flesh was inevitably more convincing.

Behind this emphasis on the human figure lay the Neoplatonic belief that the body is the vessel of the soul, the most perfect of created things. But artists did not need Greek philosophical theories to move them to explore the new methods eagerly. They gloried in their newfound mastery for its own sake, and practiced it as no painters had before.

The art of *perspective* drawing was another part of the course of study at the new art academies that sprang up for the first time in the sixteenth century. Artistic perspective may be defined as the technique of creating the impression of a three-dimensional world on a flat surface. There are many ways of doing this, most of them discovered during the Renaissance.

Atmospheric perspective, for instance, enables the artist to give a picture depth by depicting distant objects as dimmer, grayer, and bluer than people and things in the foreground. The dust and moisture in the air have these effects on what the eye sees in real life, after all: all mountains are blue in the distance. The basic techniques of perspective drawing, however, involve various forms of linear or mathematical perspective. This approach is based on the easily observable fact that, as the eye perceives them, parallel lines do in fact meet this side of infinity—at the horizon. This phenomenon can most easily be observed in nature by looking along a straight stretch of road or a railroad track running to a flat horizon. Then imagine the whole of the level land before you as a vast checkerboard on which you stand, watching the squares diminish as they recede from you toward the edge of the earth, and you are in the wonderful artistic world of horizon lines and vanishing points called mathematical perspective. By imposing this sort of grid on the world as they sketched and painted it, Renaissance artists learned to represent figures, buildings, and cities with proper placement and foreshort-

Zephyrs waft the newborn Venus, goddess of love, across the Mediterranean to shore in Botticelli's *Birth of Venus.* Contrast the linear quality of this picture with the paintings by Leonardo Da Vinci shown earlier in this chapter.

ening and in the correct relative size depending on their distance from the observer.

The result of combining this array of skills was art with a new degree of lifelikeness. With the exception of the great modernist rebellion of our own century, Western artists have been using these Renaissance techniques ever since.

Italian Painters: Giotto to Titian

Leonardo da Vinci and Michelangelo, Raphael and Titian were unquestionably the giants among the painters of the High Renaissance. Their predecessors of the fourteenth and fifteenth centuries, however, also deserve a place in any overview of this crucial period in the history of Western art.

Giotto di Bondone (c. 1267–1337), whose life overlapped that of Petrarch, is sometimes heralded as the first Renaissance painter. His series of frescoes depicting the life of St. Francis, on the walls of the Arena Chapel in Padua, broke with the flat style of medieval painting. Neither perspective nor anatomical detail are strongly evident in Giotto's pictures, yet their solidity and the use of chiaroscuro cause his people to stand out from the surface of the wall. In the next century, Masaccio—whose real name was Tommaso Guidi (1401–1428)—made major contributions to the

new style during his short life. His *Adam and Eve Expelled from Paradise* shows a remarkable skill in anatomy and foreshortening as well as a sense of the terrible drama of the moment. His *Holy Trinity with the Virgin and St. John* adds a sense of perspective, achieved through a vaulted hall in the background and the figures of the couple who commissioned the picture kneeling outside the frame in the foreground.

One of the most controversial painters of the end of the fifteenth century was Sandro Botticelli (c. 1444–1510). Profoundly affected by the humanistic, philosophical, and religious currents of his time, Botticelli is now best known for his *Birth of Venus* from the sea and his *Primavera (Springtime)*. Both were symbolic, almost allegorical paintings, done with a nearly calligraphic line. The elegant goddesses have a freshness that often seems to radiate the enthusiasm of the Renaissance Florence of Botticelli's patron, Lorenzo de' Medici.

The most famous of all Renaissance painters was Leonardo da Vinci (1452–1519). A many-sided genius, Leonardo combined scientific speculation with artistic brilliance, a light hand on a lute with the strength to bend an iron bar. If his white-bearded head in a famous sketched self-portrait looks bitter, it is perhaps because so few of his many projects came to fruition. His speculative designs for such technological breakthroughs as flying machines and submarine

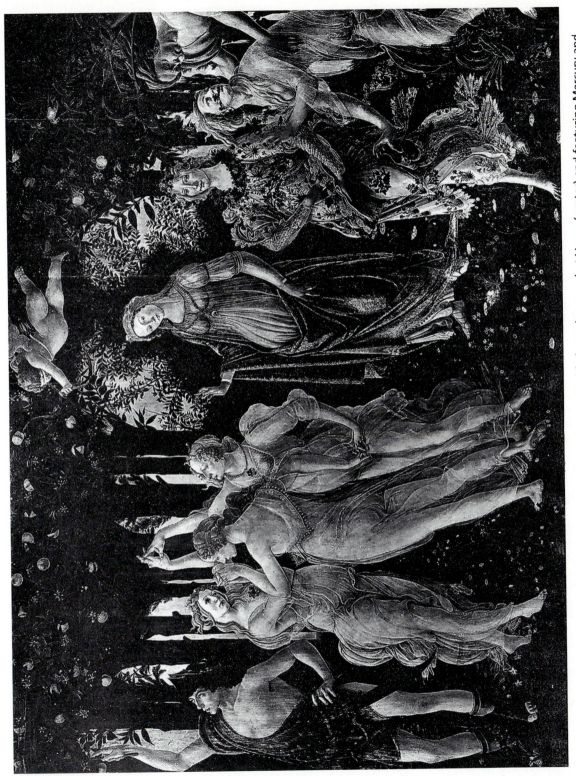

Botticelli's *Primavera* (Springtime) is a typical Renaissance allegory presided over by a modest Venus (center) and featuring Mercury and three dancing Graces (left), the passing Hours (flowered dress), and Flora, goddess of spring (right). This happy Renaissance recovery of a classical heritage soon collided head on with the Reformation suspicion of such pagan subjects. [Sandro Botticelli. *Allegory of Spring* (also called *Primavera*). Uffizi Gallery, Florence, Italy]

Michelangelo's *Creation of Adam* from the ceiling of the Sistine Chapel in Rome is one of the best-known of all Western paintings. The throbbing vitality of God's extended forefinger contrasts strikingly with the languid finger of Adam waiting for the ultimate gift of life.

boats remained unknown until others had developed more practical designs. The full-sized model of his proposed equestrian statue of the duke of Milan was used for target practice by invading French soldiers.

But Leonardo's surviving work both illustrates and transcends the artistic trends of his age. His sketchbooks include many anatomical drawings and some rough perspective studies for paintings, in which the checkerboard grid is clearly visible. His smoky chiaroscuro shows in the enigmatic *Mona Lisa,* the portrait of a lady whose smile has become the best known in Western art. And though his *Last Supper,* done with experimental pigments that failed, began to flake off the wall even during his own lifetime, the composition of this great picture remains intact. Christ looks straight out at you from the center while the twelve apostles, in groups of three, turn to each other in stunned disbelief at the master's announcement that one of them will betray him to his enemies. The picture embodies Leonardo's conviction that everything—expression, gesture, even the model chosen, costume, and accessories—should help to convey the artist's message.

Michelangelo Buonarotti, despite his lifelong concentration on sculpture, also painted some of the most magnificent of Renaissance frescoes in the Sistine Chapel of the Vatican in Rome. His immense panorama of the biblical book of Genesis, from the

creation through the flood, on the ceiling of the Sistine took four years of excruciating labor to create. But when the irascible Pope Julius demanded to know when the great work would be finished, Michelangelo answered in words that many a more modern artist might have used: "It will be finished when I have satisfied myself!"[10]

The 350 biblical and classical figures were deliberately executed with bodies hugely out of proportion, in order to radiate superhuman spiritual power. A recent restoration, intended to reveal the bright original coloring, has seemed a brilliant restoration to some, a desecration to others. But the immense shapes remain. And the most famous composition, God infusing life into Adam with the touch of a finger, is still perhaps the most widely reproduced detail in Renaissance art. (For an appreciation of another famous painting from the Sistine Chapel, see the box titled "Michelangelo's *Last Judgment.*")

The sixteenth century flung up so many famous names in Italian painting alone that it is hard to keep the list of greats from growing into a catalog. Raphael Sanzio (1483–1520), best loved for his charming Madonnas, is admired by critics for his large compositions. *The School of Athens* gathers all the great philosophers and scientists of ancient Greece, with Plato and Aristotle in the center, majestically framed by a series of monumental Roman arches receding in

PROFILES IN HISTORY Michelangelo's *Last Judgment*

Giorgio Vasari, whose collection of the lives of Renaissance Italian artists has been a gold mine for art historians, was himself an artist and the founder of an early academy for the training of artists. Here Vasari offers an informed contemporary appreciation of Michelangelo's *Last Judgment* on the end wall of the Sistine Chapel in the Vatican—a hall already glorified by the artist's earlier ceiling paintings of scenes from *Genesis*. Notice the qualities Vasari admired in the art of his own time: general lifelikeness, anatomical accuracy, perspective ("foreshortening" of figures), and the convincing depiction of emotions, virtues, and vices in human figures. What would a modern abstract painter say about these standards? Are Vasari's the criteria you would use to judge a picture, or would other qualities be more important to you if you were choosing a picture to hang on your wall?

It is impossible to describe the variety in the heads of [Michelangelo's] devils, veritable monsters of hell. The sinners display their sin and fear

of damnation. The whole work is finely and harmoniously executed, so that it looks as if it had been done in one day, and no illuminator could have equalled its execution. Indeed, the number of figures and the force and grandeur of the painting are such that it is impossible to describe it. Every human emotion is represented and marvelously expressed. The proud, envious, avaricious, luxurious, and others may be recognized . . . from their attitudes and treatment. It is marvelous that this great man who was always wise and prudent and had met many people, could have acquired a practical knowledge of the world such as is gained by philosophers by means of speculations and books. A man . . . who understands painting will see the tremendous power of art in the thoughts and emotions of the figures. . . . Here are foreshortenings which seem in relief, done with softness and harmony, while his treatment of the parts shows what paintings may be when executed by good and true masters. . . . [Michelangelo] labored upon this work for eight years and uncovered it in 1541, I think on Christmas Day, to the marvel of all Rome and the whole world. I was at Venice, and when I went to Rome to see it, I was thunderstruck.

Source: Giorgio Vasari, *The Lives of the Painters, Sculptors, and Architects*, vol. 4 (New York: J. M. Dent, 1927), 143–144.

Renaissance perspective into the background. Titian, or Tiziano Vecellio (c. 1487–1576), was one of the most long lived and successful of all artists. A leader of the Venetian school of "colorist" painters, he was as interested in rich hues as in perfect forms. In his many brilliant portraits, living faces look out at us with a realism that goes beyond the physical to give us a sense of the personality of the individual before us.

Northern Painters: Dürer to El Greco

In the sixteenth century especially, Renaissance Italian styles in painting and the other arts spread out across Europe, as classical humanism and Italian literature had before them. As they spread, Renaissance artistic styles both evolved and interacted with such powerful currents as the Protestant and Catholic Reformations in the lands beyond the Alps. The result was an enriched and distinctive art of the Northern Renaissance.

The greatest German artist of the age was Albrecht Dürer (1471–1528), sometimes called "the German Leonardo." Son of a Nuremberg goldsmith, an eager learner during visits to Italy in the 1490s and again soon after the turn of the century, Dürer combined German, Italian Renaissance, and Reformation influences in his work. As a goldsmith, book illustrator, painter, and man of intense curiosity about the natural world, the German shared some of the universality of Leonardo. Master above all of a restless Gothic line, Dürer produced hundreds of woodcuts and copper engravings that were widely published across Europe. His passion for Renaissance naturalism shows in his famous small paintings of some of nature's more modest creations—a large brown hare, a tuft of grass—infused with trembling life by Dürer's sensitive brush.

Deeply disturbed by human weakness and fallibility in a world largely beyond human control, Dürer was an admirer of Martin Luther and became a Lutheran during his later years. In enigmatic allegorical works like *The Knight, Death, and the Devil* and powerful evocations of such religious themes as *The Four Horsemen of the Apocalypse*, he combined a Renaissance eye for accurate detail with a Reformation awareness of the supernatural forces, divine and diabolical, that the people of his century imagined all about them.

In his clear and brilliant portraits, Hans Holbein the Younger (c. 1497–1543) contemplated his age, producing vivid likenesses of leading humanists, leaders of the Reformation, and others who surrounded the rising new monarchs of the Renaissance. Born in Augsburg and a student of both Flemish and Italian naturalism, Holbein painted such luminaries as Erasmus and, during his long sojourn as court painter to England's Henry VIII, Thomas More and King Henry himself.

The greatest Spanish painter of the sixteenth century was born Doménikos Theotokópoulos in Crete, studied in Renaissance Venice, and lived and worked for forty years in Spain, where he was known as El Greco—"The Greek" (1541–1614). El Greco's paintings illustrate the late Renaissance style called *mannerism*—an abandonment of the classic harmonies of High Renaissance art for strikingly personal styles, aiming at singularity and strangeness. El Greco's mannerist style achieved disturbingly abnormal effects with devices such as unnaturally elongated forms, sour colors, and dramatic contrasts of light and shadow. The narrow hands, flamelike figures, and cold greenish skin tones for which he is famous also served as compelling expressions of the spiritual exultations of the Catholic Reformation. His *Burial of Count Orgaz* contrasts the earth where the funeral takes place with heaven above—opening in triumph to receive the soul of the pious count—in a work of medieval force and mannerist expressiveness. More eye-catching today is his phantasmagoric *View of Toledo;* seen under swirling black clouds and the glare of lightning, it is the first great landscape in modern Western art.

Architecture and Sculpture

The Renaissance Italian ruling classes began the practice of collecting not only the manuscripts of ancient books but statuary and other artifacts dating back to classical times. In the palaces and villas of Italy, princes, prelates, and cultivated urban businessmen built collections that were of great value to Renaissance artists as models of ancient styles. Interest also grew in Roman ruins, especially in the city of Rome itself, where whole buildings like the Pantheon had survived virtually intact. The writings of the Roman architect Vitruvius were taken up and studied by Renaissance builders. The result was a wave of emulation of Roman architecture and Greco-Roman sculpture that transformed the art of early modern times.

The humanist Leon Battista Alberti was also an architect and the author of books on Roman architecture. Other Renaissance architects also rediscovered the beauty of the classical orders of columns and colonnades and the Roman art of roofing vast spaces with huge domes. With the Pantheon as a living model, Filippo Brunelleschi (1379–1446) raised a dome over the cathedral of Florence that proved the possibility of building such structures once more and inspired many imitators. The Gothic church silhouette, with its emphasis on towers and spires, was replaced by a Renaissance and later baroque profile dominated by the dome. In time, the basilica ground plan, with its long nave and crossing transept symbolic of the cross of Christ, was also significantly modified. More and more churches were designed on an equal-armed Greek cross plan roofed by a dome. With the spaces between the short arms filled in by separate chapels, a floor plan emerged that, based on the circle, the "perfect figure," could be seen as symbolizing God himself.

The most influential Renaissance architect was Andrea Palladio (1508–1580), whose palaces and country villas, churches and government buildings rose in a number of north Italian cities. In Palladio's work, stately colonnades and elegant Ionic and Corinthian capitals once more featured prominently. In later centuries, his widely read *Four Books on Architecture* (1570) spread such influential devices as the Palladian portico—a porch graced by two-story columns—as far north as the stately homes of Britain and as far west as the white-pillared mansions of the American south.

The most admired single architectural achievement of the Renaissance, however, was Michelangelo's dome on St. Peter's Church in Rome. Designed in the master's later years and erected after his death, the dome towers 435 feet above the floor, setting the scale of a church designed for giants. The majesty of the great dome is a fitting legacy from the Renaissance to the age of the baroque that followed, combining Roman majesty with the power of the Catholic Reformation in which baroque art was born.

Map 13.3 Culture of Renaissance Europe

Once inside St. Peter's cathedral, furthermore, new splendors loom overhead. If visitors do not have an aching neck from staring up at the Sistine ceiling, they will get one quickly enough in St. Peter's, gazing upward at the race of larger-than-life statues that inhabit the great church. And in sculpture as in architecture, a modern tradition grew from the Renaissance fascination with the Greco-Roman legacy.

In the fifteenth century, Donatello (c. 1386–

Michelangelo's dome crowns St. Peter's church in Rome. Some art critics feel that later additions, including the facade and the curving colonnade in front, undermine the effect Michelangelo intended. Try covering the lower part of the picture to see the building as it looked in the sixteenth century.

1466), the first great Renaissance sculptor, produced statues very different in spirit and technique from their medieval predecessors. In his *Gattamelata,* a bronze glorification of a celebrated condottiere, Donatello cast the first large equestrian statue made since ancient times. His series of statues of *David* offered the first great free-standing male nudes since antiquity. Andrea del Verrocchio (1435–1488), Leonardo's early master, rivaled Donatello, particularly in his powerful equestrian statue of the condottiere *Colleone,* who, glaring down at you over a heavily armored shoulder, looks as though he would as soon ride you down as look at you. At least as impressive, however, was the sculptural range of Benvenuto Cellini (1500–1571). In his colorful *Autobiography* (1558), Cellini reveals a vivid Renaissance personality combining vanity, sensitivity, and even mysticism. He also gives us some idea of the labor and difficulty of casting a huge bronze statue in the sixteenth century. His famous representation of *Perseus,* showing the mythical hero with sword in hand, raising the severed head of the monster-woman Medusa, offers a mix of Greek anatomical realism with the distinctive grace of the later Renaissance. Cellini also worked in

gold, fashioning for King Francis I of France the world's most celebrated saltcellar. In this foot-wide masterpiece, a reclining Neptune and a sea goddess confront each other across a miniature world of curling waves, seahorses and mermaids, a tiny temple, and a minute boat (for the salt) wrought of gold, jewels, and shell.

But the greatest of Renaissance sculptors, perhaps the greatest of all carvers of stone, was Michelangelo Buonarotti (1475–1564). The young Michelangelo studied ancient statuary in the gardens of Lorenzo the Magnificent in Florence and did early statues of classical subjects. His view of art was shaped by Platonic and Neoplatonic doctrines, which led him to declare that the "form" of the statue was already present in a block of marble before he laid a chisel to it. Inspired by a Platonic vision of the beauty within, he saw the artist's job as simply to chip away the excess stone to lay bare that perfect indwelling form.

Michelangelo was, however, a devout Christian, and his most famous work is on Christian themes. His remarkable early *Pietà*—Mary mourning over the body of the crucified Christ—shows a youthful

One of the undisputed masterpieces of the Renaissance is Michelangelo's *David*. How do the hands and head contribute to our sense of the young man's strength? If the figure were not identified as a biblical character, could you see it as a Greek or Roman god?

and lovely Virgin with the Savior stretched across her lap, a totally unlikely pose, yet compositionally perfect and deeply moving. His taut *Moses* incarnates the fierce power of the Old Testament patriarch, from the turn of the bearded head to the great hands clutching the Tablets of the Law. And Michelangelo's giant *David,* three times the size of a normal man, combines youth and strength, the face of a classic Apollo with the hard-fingered hands of the shepherd boy who struck down Goliath. If any single work of art may be said to embody the proud confidence of the High Renaissance, it is the *David* of Michelangelo.

The Birth of Modern Music

Modern music was also born during the Renaissance, building on late medieval polyphonic church music and evolving to the eve of the modern opera by 1600. The unfolding of this whole new world of sound was one of the most irresistibly appealing artistic accomplishments of the age.

In contrast to the pattern in other Renaissance arts, the new music began in the north and spread south of the Alps. Renaissance music evolved in the Low Countries, where medieval music had achieved its climax, and reached Italy in force only in the sixteenth century. Late medieval polyphonic music was, however, enriched in the Renaissance by elaborate harmonies and the development of counterpoint, seeking to give maximum scope to each component voice without losing the impact of the whole. Religious and secular music influenced each other, producing magnificent masses and other church choral music as well as tuneful songs and madrigals for an evening's entertainment.

A wealth of new and modified instruments was also introduced in this inventive age. These included such keyboard instruments as the virginal and clavichord; wind instruments from the recorder to the sackbut (an early trombone); strings like the lute and harp; and the booming king of percussion, the kettledrum. Composers favored the keyboard instruments because of their range, but the favorite instrument of accompanists and many amateurs was the universally popular lute, the guitar of its day.

During the earlier Renaissance, wealthy Flemish and Dutch cities like Antwerp trained professional singers and musicians in their cathedral schools. In the sixteenth century, the princely courts of Italy made concerts by singers accompanied by lutenists part of the aristocratic lifestyle. Music also played an important part in dramatic productions, both between the acts and as part of the play itself. The first modern operas evolved out of such drama-with-music in the 1590s, and Claudio Monteverdi's *Orfeo,* which can still be seen today, was first performed in 1607.

The coming of the two Reformations, Protestant and Catholic, in the sixteenth century further encouraged the development of music. Luther composed moving hymns, and Calvinists who sniffed idolatry in the other arts made room for music in their services. The hymn sung by the Protestant congregation as a whole, rather than by the priest and the choir, as in the medieval church, thus became an important expression of the shared faith of many Protestant communities. The Catholic Reformation also mobilized music to move the hearts of the faithful. In Giovanni da Palestrina (c. 1525–1594), the

Catholic Reformation produced the most admired composer of the century. Working in Roman churches and building on Flemish counterpoint, Palestrina produced pieces so stirring that the church officially endorsed his work as the model for sacred music. Before the century was over, Catholic south Germany—Austria and Bavaria—had also begun their long love affair with the sound of music, producing songs, masses, and many other forms in profusion for increasingly cultivated ears.

The centuries of the Renaissance and Reformation thus took Western music to the brink of the greatest musical flowering in Western history—the modern musical world of opera, ballet, symphony, and much more.

The Artist and Society

During the Renaissance the artist's place in society was only beginning to approximate the place that such gifted men and women enjoyed in later centuries. Although poets and thinkers had been honored in the West since ancient times, artists, particularly during the medieval period, had occupied a much lower place in public esteem. Because they worked with their hands, whereas theologians, philosophers, and poets worked with their minds, people who carved stone, painted pictures, and practiced other arts were considered an inferior breed, "mere" manual workers. Artists were thus generally seen as little more than artisans. They were in fact members of craft guilds, apprenticed and trained like other craftspeople, paid by the hour, and treated like servants even in the fourteenth and fifteenth centuries.

It was the immense personal prestige of sixteenth-century artists like Leonardo, Michelangelo, and Titian that elevated the status of painters, sculptors, and other practitioners of the "fine arts," as they came to be called. Highly paid and widely ad-

mired, honored by emperors, kings, and popes, such men successfully laid claim to parity with writers and thinkers. Trained in new art academies featuring theoretical subjects like perspective, proportion, and the complexities of bronze casting, artists insisted that they too were "brain workers," to whom the brush or the chisel was no more important than the pen in the hand of the poet. In idolized giants like Michelangelo, finally, the fine arts produced their first modern "geniuses." Such men, whose talents seemed to transcend the natural order, earned reputations for integrity, dedication, and spiritual superiority once reserved for saints and prophets.

The position of women in Renaissance art deserves special note. Although women have excelled in all the arts in later modern times, there are few female names in the lists of Renaissance painters and other artists. This fact has provided further evidence for those who question whether the Renaissance was a period of rebirth for women at all. There is, in any case, an obvious social explanation. Women were not apprenticed to the goldsmiths' and other guilds that traditionally trained artists during the Renaissance period, nor were they admitted to the later Renaissance art academies. They were not allowed to learn figure drawing by sketching male nudes as men did. Since the ordinary avenues of artistic training were closed to them, only a few exceptional women managed through special circumstances to learn these professions.

One of these was Sofonisba Anguissola (c. 1532–1625). The talented daughter of a northern Italian nobleman, she moved beyond the sort of amateur skill at art Castiglione recommended for young ladies and gentlemen to become a successful professional painter. Her work, mostly portraiture like *The Artist's Sisters Playing Chess,* was characterized by vivid personal expression. Michelangelo offered critiques of her work, and she was finally summoned to Madrid to become a court painter to Philip II.

A Topical Summary

Society: A literate new elite emerged in Renaissance Europe, people—from both the aristocracy and the urban patriciate—who were broadly educated and skilled in many areas. Although some educated Renaissance ladies were honored by society, in general the role of women was severely restricted. The Jews suffered intermittent persecution, but some Renaissance intellectuals were intrigued by ancient Judaic ideas. Most Renaissance people were still the products of the family and the village or neighborhood community in which they lived. Yet underlying Renaissance mentalities reveal half-conscious ambivalence about the norms of class and gender, about religion and the morality of everyday life.

Culture: The Renaissance humanist movement exercised a central influence on the cultural flowering of the fourteenth, fifteenth, and sixteenth centuries. Humanists like Petrarch and Erasmus turned to ancient Latin and Greek classics to provide guidance for the new society and the new culture of early modern times. The ideas of intellectual leaders like Erasmus and of such challenging social thinkers as Machiavelli and the civic humanists were also spread through humanistic education and by the newly developed printing press.

Literature: Renaissance writers in the modern languages often employed Greco-Roman literary forms. Innovative spirits like Montaigne and Shakespeare, however, developed such new literary forms as the essay and the Elizabethan stage play; the unique talents of Rabelais and Cervantes produced such inimitable classics as *Gargantua* and *Don Quixote*.

Art: Renaissance artists both drew on ancient models in architecture and sculpture and invented their own forms, as in painting and music. As with so much else in the period, the naturalistic and classically oriented styles of Renaissance art took shape first in Italy and then spread north of the Alps. The masterpieces of Leonardo, Michelangelo, Dürer, El Greco, and their contemporaries transformed the art of the West and set stylistic standards that predominated for four centuries after 1500.

Some Key Terms

chiaroscuro 398	*mentalité* 386	Renaissance person 382
civic humanism 392	northern humanism 391	*sprezzatura* 381
conduct book 380	perspective 399	utopia 394
mannerism 404	Renaissance 379	*virtù* 381

Notes

1. Joan Kelly-Gadol, "Did Women Have a Renaissance?" in *Becoming Visible: Women in European History,* 2d ed., eds. Renata Bridenthal, Claudia Koonz, and Susan Stuard (Boston: Houghton Mifflin, 1987).
2. Ibid., 177, 197.
3. Quoted in J.E. Neale, *Queen Elizabeth I: A Biography* (Garden City, N.Y.: Doubleday, 1957), 63.
4. Kelly-Gadol, 186.
5. Stanley Chojnacki, "Patrician Women in Early Renaissance Venice," *Studies in the Renaissance,* 21 (1974), 198–200.
6. See Carlo Ginzburg, *The Cheese and the Worms: The Cosmos of a Sixteenth-Century Miller,* trans. John and Anne Tedeschi (New York: Penguin, 1982), 65, 76–77, 55 ff.
7. See, for instance, Emmanuel Le Roy Ladurie, *Carnival in Romans,* trans. Mary Feeney (New York: Braziller, 1979), 305–324.
8. Christopher Marlowe, *Dr. Faustus,* V, i, 97–98. By eliding the second syllables in *towers* and *Ilium,* you get twice the stress where you need it. For best effect, read it aloud, with feeling.
9. Giorgio Vasari, *Lives of the Artists,* trans. E.L. Seeley (New York: Noonday Press, 1957), 148.
10. Vasari, 301.

Reading List

BARKER, P. *Popular Culture in Early Modern Europe.* New York: New York University Press, 1978. Sees the period 1500 to 1800 as the golden age of local popular culture, from folk songs and dances to carnival entertainment, before modern homogeneous mass culture overwhelmed this authentic popular expression.

BENEVOLO, L. *The Architecture of the Renaissance.* Translated by J. Landry. London: Routledge and Kegan Paul, 1978. Comprehensive coverage, with many illustrations, plans, and maps.

CERVANTES SAAVEDRA, M. DE. *The Portable Cervantes.* Harmondsworth, England: Penguin, 1976. Includes *Don Quixote* and other vigorous Renaissance writing by Cervantes.

CRAVEN, W. G. *Giovanni Pico della Mirandola: Symbol of His Age.* Geneva: Droz, 1981. Revisionist view of the famous humanist, whose celebration of the dignity of man is here deemphasized.

EISENSTEIN, E. L. *The Printing Press as an Agent of Change: Communications and Cultural Transformations in Early Modern Europe.* 2 vols. New York: Cambridge University Press, 1979. Assigns a crucial role in both the Renaissance and the Reformation to the new communications technology produced by the invention of movable type.

FEBVRE, L. *The Problem of Unbelief in the Sixteenth Century.* Cambridge, Mass.: Harvard University Press, 1982. Trailblazing study that analyzes a Renaissance attitude through the writings of Rabelais.

GINZBURG, C. *The Cheese and the Worms: The Cosmos of a Sixteenth-Century Miller.* Translated by J. and A. Tedeschi. Baltimore: Johns Hopkins University Press, 1980. Cosmology from the bottom up, probing deeper meanings of a plain-man view of the world.

HUIZINGA, J. *Erasmus of Rotterdam . . . With Selections from the Letters.* Translated by F. Hopman and B. Flower. London: Phaidon, 1952. A classic life of the Dutch humanist by a great Dutch historian.

JORDAN, C. *Renaissance Feminism: Literary Tastes and Political Models.* Ithaca, N.Y.: Cornell University Press, 1990. Renaissance discussions of the position of women as precursors of modern feminist ideas.

KELSO, R. *Doctrine for the Lady of the Renaissance.* Urbana: University of Illinois Press, 1956. Discussion of male-female equality among the Renaissance elite.

KEMP, M. *Leonardo da Vinci.* London: Dent, 1981. Illustrated life of the famous artist.

KLAPISCH-ZUBER, C. *Women, Family, and Ritual in Renaissance Italy.* Translated by L. Cochrane. Chicago: University of Chicago Press, 1985. Quantitative, ethnographic, and other studies by an expert in the new social history.

KRISTELLER, P. O. *Renaissance Thought.* 2 vols. New York: Harper, 1961–1965. Lucid essays on humanism and related major trends in Renaissance philosophy.

LIEBERT, R. S. *Michelangelo.* New Haven: Yale University Press, 1983. A scholarly account. See also U. BALDINI, *The Complete Sculpture of Michelangelo* (London: Thames and Hudson, 1982).

MACHIAVELLI, N. *The Prince, Selections from 'The Discourses,' and Other Writings.* Translated by A. Gilbert. London: Fontana, 1972. Good selection of representative works.

MORE, T. *Utopia.* Edited by E. Surtz and J. H. Hexter. New Haven: Yale University Press, 1965. Impressive scholarly edition, Volume 4 of *Complete Works.*

RABELAIS, F. *Gargantua and Pantagruel.* Translated by T. Urquhart and P. Motteux. Chicago: Encyclopedia Britannica, 1952. Old but vigorous translation.

SHAKESPEARE, W. *The Complete Works.* Edited by C. J. Sisson. London: Oldhams Press, 1953. Includes authoritative introductory essays. Any paperback edition of individual plays, however, will serve the purpose, especially if read aloud.

TILLYARD, E. M. W. *The Elizabethan World Picture.* Harmondsworth, England: Penguin, 1963. Brief but valuable presentation of the traditional hierarchical view of the universe and society.

VALENCY, M. *In Praise of Love: An Introduction to the Love Poetry of the Renaissance.* New York: Macmillan, 1961. Useful approach to an immensely popular Renaissance theme.

WHITE, C. *Dürer.* Oxford: Phaidon, 1971. Many drawings by the German master of expressive line.

Martin Luther. National Museum, Stockholm

The Age of the Reformation resembled the Renaissance it overlapped chronologically in one more substantive way: the Reformation also constituted a rebellion against the orthodoxy of the Middle Ages—in this case, in religion. As a result of the Protestant Reformation, much of the northern half of western Europe seceded from Roman Catholic Christendom. The Catholic church, partially in reaction against the Protestant revolt, proceeded to transform itself in the Catholic Reformation. The reigns of most of the later new monarchs of the sixteenth century were shaped by the strains and conflicts generated by the conflicting Reformations, and in the end much of western Europe was swept by terrible wars of religion.

From another perspective, however, the Reformation represents less an extension of Renaissance rebelliousness into religion than a resurgence of medieval religious fervor and a reaction against the worldliness of the Renaissance itself. Preachers like Martin Luther and John Calvin, despite their disputes with the popes, were reasserting the medieval priority of spiritual over secular concerns, of the next world over this one.

In the broadest of modern perspectives, finally, it is possible to see the Reformation as the first of a series of great revolutionary movements rooted in ideas that surged across the modern Western world. In the case of the Reformation of the sixteenth century, the informing ideas were of course religious in nature. In the Enlightenment and the Age of Democratic Revolutions of the later eighteenth and earlier nineteenth centuries (see particularly Chapters 20–22), the guiding ideas were primarily political and constitutional. And in the upheavals of the twentieth century (see Chapters 29, 30, and 32), social and economic ideas played a central role. From this point of view, the Reformation in religion may be defined as a prototype and paradigm of the ideological revolutions to come.

The present chapter focuses on the Protestant and Catholic Reformations and on their impact on the nations and the international relations of the period. The larger significance of the Reformation as a paradigm of modern ideological conflict should be kept in mind, however. Paradoxical as it may seem, such later true believers as Robespierre in the French Revolution of 1789 and Lenin in the Russian Revolution of 1917 may make more sense seen as the intellectual—and psychological—heirs of Martin Luther and John Calvin, the religious radicals of the 1500s.

The Lutheran Revolution

The Lutheran revolt that set off the Protestant Reformation is one of the most dramatic of historical confrontations between rebellious ideas and established institutions. Both sides based their stands on Christian beliefs. In both cases, however, other elements also entered into the struggle. Martin Luther's ringing defiance of Emperor Charles V— "Here I stand!"—is matched by the Catholic Thomas More's defiance of King Henry VIII, which cost More his life. At the same time, however, less highly principled forces were at work among both Catholics and Protestants in this great conflict.

The Church in Decay

The firewood for the great religious conflagration had been piling up for two centuries before Luther came on the scene. By the early sixteenth century, the Roman church had once more sunk deep into worldliness. Luther lit the match, but the blaze was ready to roar.

The decline of papal piety and prestige after the great days of Gregory VII and Innocent III had begun with the Avignon exile and the Great Schism of the later Middle Ages (discussed in Chapter 11). During this period, the papacy had first been seen as a tool of French policy, then as bewilderingly divided against itself. Throughout, papal demands for more revenues and charges of secular concerns and luxurious living at the papal court had grown apace. The pontiffs who reestablished a united papacy at Rome in 1417 had continued these unfortunate policies. "The popes of the Renaissance," as the *Catholic Encyclopedia* put it, "had become Italian princes among other Italian princes, who warred and intrigued for worldly interests. Excessive pomp, luxury, and tolerated immorality set the tone of the papal court."[1] The reigns of the Borgia pope Alexander VI and the "warrior pope" Julius II, mentioned in Chapter 12, illustrate the worldliness of the Renaissance papacy.

A similar massive infusion of secularism, ignorance, and selected vices infected the Renaissance church at lower levels. The lavish lifestyles of many cardinals, who lived like great nobles and patronized only the leading courtesans, were among the less edifying sights of Rome. Archbishops, bishops, and others at the top of the church hierarchy were notorious for pluralism (holding more than one post in the church) and absenteeism (actually serving in none of the jurisdictions from which they drew revenues). Further down the scale, monks who lived very well off monastic revenues and priests who lived with women—"clerical marriage" or "clerical concubinage"—were common. Because there were no seminaries for the education of priests, many remained not only ignorant of church doctrine but functionally illiterate. Because humble priests and the vicars who carried out the duties of absentee prelates were extremely poorly remunerated, some took fees for performing church functions—a form of simony. There were even notorious instances of religious fraud, when miraculous relics turned out to be fakes, or when miracle-working holy images turned out to have been manipulated by monks or priests.

Lay piety, by contrast, was spreading in the decades around 1500. The fifteenth century had seen the failure of the conciliar movement to reform the papacy after it had restored the popes to Rome. At the local level, however, the Brethren and Sisters of the Common Life still promoted religious devotion and learning in the Low Countries and in Germany. In Spain, the crown itself sponsored a cleansing of the church. Northern humanists like Erasmus studied the Gospels and satirized the worldly behavior of churchmen. There were still Hussite and Wycliffite heretics in Bohemia and England. There was, in short, a groundswell of popular resentment at the corruption of the church, a growing demand for change.

Some within the church had already spoken up vigorously, even violently, against the state of things. In the Renaissance Florence of the Medici, a hollow-eyed monk named Girolamo Savonarola (1452–1498) kindled an astonishing blaze of medieval piety in the 1490s. Savonarola's passionate sermons sent troops of schoolchildren to collect and burn "vanities," from silks and velvets to works of art. His thunderous denunciations of the reigning pope—the unedifying Borgia pontiff Alexander VI—led to Savonarola's excommunication and eventual execution. Nevertheless, the popular support his protest kindled was a harbinger of things to come.

The firewood was piled high and tinder dry when the German monk Martin Luther came on the scene twenty years later. The only question was whether it was a fire of revolt he would kindle— or an inquisitorial funeral pyre for himself.

1500   **1525**

POLITICAL, MILITARY, AND DIPLOMATIC EVENTS

r. 1509–1547	Henry VIII
r. 1515–1547	Francis I
r. 1519–1556	Charles V
1529–1536	Reformation Parliament
1531	League of Schmalkald
1533–1584	William of Orange

SOCIAL AND ECONOMIC DEVELOPMENTS

1524–1525	Peasants' War
to 1530s	Renaissance popes
1530s–1580s	Reformation popes
1534	Anabaptists in Münster

CULTURE: THE ARTS, PHILOSOPHY, SCIENCE AND RELIGION

1483–1546	Luther
1484–1531	Zwingli
1491–1556	Loyola
1509–1564	Calvin
1515–1563	Castellio
1515–1582	Teresa of Avila
1517	Ninety-five Theses
1521	Diet at Worms
1530	Augsburg Confession
r. 1534–1549	Paul III
1536	Calvin in Geneva
1540	Jesuits recognized

Martin Luther's Religious Crisis

The full open face and generous girth of Martin Luther (1483–1546) in his later years do not look like the stuff of which religious crusaders are made. Pictures of the younger Luther can look a bit more troubled, a little leaner and darker about the eyes. Still, there is little of the Savonarola about the German monk—"the Protestant Hercules"—who shook and then shattered the edifice of Christian unity.

The son of an upwardly mobile German miner of solid peasant stock, Luther had a university education and was destined for law school. Then, at the age of twenty-two, he had an experience that changed his life. Returning to the University of Erfurt in 1505, he was caught in a terrific thunderstorm and, with lightning and thunder crashing around him, cried aloud to the saints that, if he were spared, he would give his life to the church. Such oaths in the grip of a sudden panic were not rare in that age; but young Luther perhaps took the experience more seriously than most. He went on to Erfurt, but instead of law school he entered the highly intellectual order of Augustinian monks.

A closer look at young Luther's character and frame of mind helps us understand this radical shift in direction. To begin with, Luther was a totally committed Christian. Educated in his early years by the Brethren of the Common Life, he was what the twentieth century might call a "true believer," absolutely certain of the truth of his faith. He also had the proverbial mind like a steel trap, quick to grasp abstruse theological concepts and to detect their implications. After joining the elite Augustinians, he continued to earn degrees, and by 1512 he was a theology professor at the University of Wittenberg in Saxony. As he soon demonstrated, he was also immensely eloquent, capable of composing both hymns and diatribes, of writing pamphlets, and of meeting his foes in head-to-head oral

r. 1547–1559   Henry II
r. 1547–1584   Ivan IV
  r. 1556–1598   Philip II
    r. 1558–1603   Elizabeth I
     1559–1589   Catherine de Médicis, queen mother
       1562   French religious wars begin
        1568   Dutch revolt begins
         1571   Lepanto
        1572   St. Bartholomew Massacre

1588   Spanish Armada
1598   Edict of Nantes
1609   Peace in Netherlands

1565–1572   *Oprichniki*

1545–1564   Council of Trent

debates. He was, in short, an extremely formidable man.

He was also a profoundly troubled one. We know this not only from his formal writings but from his "table talk," personal reminiscences recorded by admirers in later life. He had, he said, been convinced in his youth of his own worthlessness, sinfulness, and guilt, certain that God would condemn him to eternal hellfire. Psychohistorians of today, attempting to explain these symptoms in modern terms, have diagnosed a variety of emotional problems including manic-depressive disorders and an identity crisis. Luther himself saw his problem in religious terms, and it was his religious solution to his difficulty that changed history.

To purge himself of this terrible sense of sinfulness, Luther entered a monastery, confessed his modest sins regularly, mortified his flesh with fasts, vigils, and even self-flagellation. Sent to Rome on business for his order, he turned the journey into a pilgrimage. He joked about it later:

> I was a frantic saint. I ran through all the churches and crypts and believed everything, their suffocating lies and falsehoods. I . . . almost regretted that my father and mother were still living, for I would have liked to redeem them from purgatory with my Masses and other good works and prayers.[2]

At the time, as Luther groaned and tossed through sleepless nights, soaked in what he called "the devil's sweat," he was much more deeply concerned than this jocular reminiscence sounds.

Luther found his salvation and began his true life's work while poring over the Epistle of St. Paul to the Romans. Salvation, he suddenly understood Paul to be saying, was "the free gift of God" and came "by faith," not through all the good works that had failed so dismally to free him from his obsessive sense of sin. "Thereupon," he recorded the great moment, "I felt as if I had been born again and had entered Paradise through wide-open gates. Immediately the whole of Scripture took on new meaning for me."[3] Before he was through, it would take on new meaning for half of western Christendom as well.

The Religious Core of Protestantism

Luther was the original voice of the Reformation, and many of his ideas on theological matters were taken up by other leaders. Because religion was such a central concern of the Reformation Age, furthermore, many laypeople were also deeply involved with what may seem to us abstract points of dogma. Sixteenth-century people still memorized lengthy catechisms, listened closely to sermons, and discussed religion seriously and at length. Thus Luther's views had a wide audience and exercised a powerful formative influence on the Reformation mind.

Among Martin Luther's most influential Protestant ideas were his views on salvation, religious authority, the priesthood, and what he saw as the dark role of the popes in history. Luther's moment of truth had come when he discovered that salvation was possible even for sinners through faith in Christ. This doctrine of *salvation through faith* alone contrasted sharply with the church's traditional view that both Christian faith *and* a Christian life were necessary to salvation. For Luther, and for most Protestants, however, salvation came as the free gift of divine grace. Those who had been given this greatest of gifts would be capable of faith, and from faith would spring the life of a true Christian. You could not earn salvation by good works; but through faith, you could see your way to salvation. In Luther's German translation of the Bible, Paul says that salvation comes, not just "through faith," but "through faith *alone.*"

Another key Lutheran view that won almost universal acceptance among Protestants was belief in the unique *authority of the Bible.* The church had for centuries taught that God revealed his will to human beings through a number of authoritative channels. These included not only the canonical books of the Old and New Testaments but also church councils and the official pronouncements of the

popes speaking *ex cathedra,* or "from the chair" of St. Peter. Luther, however, insisted that only the Scriptures had been divinely inspired, and based all his theological views on the Bible. As printed books became cheaper and more readily available in the sixteenth and seventeenth centuries, many middle-class Protestants acquired copies of the Bible in vernacular translations, including Luther's in Germany and the King James version in England. For Protestants, the Bible joined the sermon as the center of Christian worship.

A third crucial Lutheran emphasis was the doctrine of the *priesthood of all believers.* The church had taught that priests possessed special spiritual powers, derived from those of the Apostles and passed on to priests through the "laying on of hands" by a bishop. The unique power to perform sacraments, especially to transform the wine and wafer into the spiritual substance of the body and blood of Christ, seemed magical to many medieval laypeople. Luther, however, declared that all Christians had direct access to God through prayer. All Christians, in this sense, were priests. Those few who bore the title were simply individuals delegated to care for the spiritual needs of the congregation full time; they had no special power denied to any other true believer. This challenge to the traditional position of the priest seemed to question the necessity of the whole hierarchy of the church as mediator between humanity and God.

A larger step in that direction was the doctrine of papal usurpation, which as we see grew directly from Luther's struggle with Rome. Luther never forgot the worldliness of Renaissance Rome as he had seen it, and his disputes with papal emissaries soon led him to question the papal authority that sent them. The pope, Luther and virtually all early Protestants came to believe, had usurped his position as head of the church. He was not even a good priest, let alone the legitimate head of Christendom. In fact, if all the signs were to be believed, he was not only not the vicar of Christ, but the Antichrist long foretold.

Luther's language, often colorful and earthy, was particularly vitriolic in describing his Roman foes. The revenue-mad Roman Curia was made up of "wolves devouring the faithful"; the worldly cardinals were "a nest of crawling worms"; and the pope himself was the Beast of Revelation, "the Whore of Babylon." This millennial sense of being locked in the final conflict with Antichrist infused the Protestant movement with a tremendous fervor.

A number of important Lutheran doctrines were more thoroughly developed or more aggressively urged by other Protestant leaders. Luther's belief in predestination and his doctrine of the "calling" became more central to Calvin's teaching (examined later) than to Luther's own. His challenge to the church's view of the Holy Eucharist, or the communion service, was modest compared to that of Calvin's compatriot Zwingli. Luther's limiting of the sacraments to the two for which he could find biblical warrant—baptism and communion—was common in other movements as well.

Martin Luther's powerful voice is most familiar today from the Bible he opened to Germans for the first time and from such hymns as his "A Mighty Fortress Is Our God," sung in many tongues. But he was a thinker too, a theologian like Augustine or Aquinas, and his crucial role in setting the course of Protestant belief is the core of his claim to have been the indispensable man of the Protestant Reformation.

The Spread of Lutheranism

Certainly he was the core of it, the eye of the hurricane during the first half of the sixteenth century. The reborn Luther's first clash with his ecclesiastical superiors came in 1517, when he challenged what he saw as the unjustified sale of *indulgences*. According to the late medieval doctrine of the "treasury of

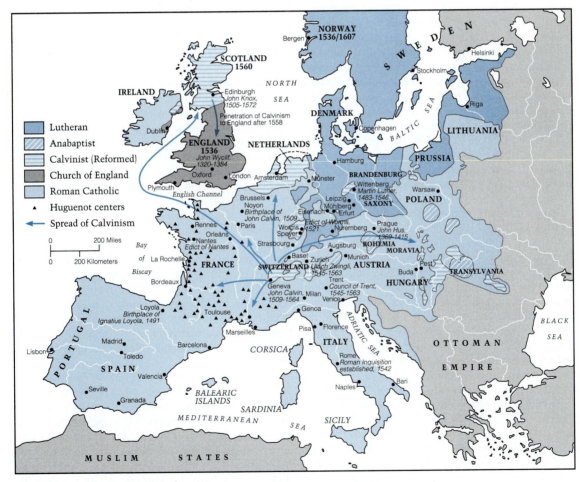

Map 14.1 Catholic and Protestant Centers in Sixteenth-Century Europe

merit," Christians could earn remission of punishment for their sins in purgatory by contributing financially to the good works of the church. By making such contributions, the faithful tapped into the bottomless reserves of merit accumulated by the good works of Christ and the saints. Officially, the church required sincere contrition and repentance by the sinner. As hawked by indulgence "salesmen" like Johann Tetzel (c. 1465–1519), indulgences promised automatic forgiveness even for people, such as beloved relatives, who were currently undergoing punishment in purgatory:

> As soon as the coin in the coffer rings,
> The soul from purgatory springs![4]

Luther was outraged at what he saw as the shameless exploitation of gullible people under the cloak of what to him was an extremely dubious doctrine. In October of 1517, he published his famous *Ninety-Five Theses* against indulgences — according to tradition, by nailing them up on the church door at Wittenberg. The content of these theological propositions left much less of a mark on history than the act itself. Such open challenges to theological debate were not unusual; but this particular challenge marked the beginning of the Protestant Reformation.

Luther's contention that Germans were being bilked under the cloak of false doctrine was widely discussed in the German states, and receipts from the indulgence campaign fell off drastically. In 1518, ordered by a papal legate to withdraw some of his theses as heretical, Luther refused to do so. In 1519, debating the well-known theologian Johann Eck (1486–1543), Luther espoused some of the long-condemned heresies of Jan Hus of Bohemia and dared to suggest that even the pope could be wrong. In 1520 Pope Leo X signed a bull excommunicating Luther from the church. Luther burned it in a public bonfire. In 1521 Emperor Charles V called Luther before an imperial diet, or assembly, at Worms to lay the ban of the Empire on him if he would not recant. Luther replied with his most ringing declaration of defiant faith: "I cannot and will not recant anything, for to go against conscience is neither right nor safe. . . . Here I stand. I cannot do otherwise."[5]

The most likely outcome of Luther's stand against the church was clearly some version of the fate of Hus, burned in 1415, or Savonarola, hanged in 1498. By this time, however, Luther had won powerful protectors among the German princes, notably his own territorial ruler, Frederick the Wise of Saxony (r. 1486–1525). Returning from Worms, the belligerent monk was spirited away to the secluded castle of Wartburg, near Eisenach, where he could carry on his work in safety under the wing of Duke Frederick.

Luther had already completed his three widely read pamphlets of 1520. In *The Freedom of the Christian,* he explained his view of salvation through faith. *The Babylonian Captivity of the Church* challenged the biblical basis of five of the seven sacraments. And the militant tract *To the Christian Nobility of the German Nation* urged the princes to reform the church in Germany and to resist the exactions of a foreign pope. Thanks to the printing press, these and other tracts quickly found a much wider audience than any earlier religious polemics could ever have reached. And at the Wartburg castle in 1521, Luther began the immense task of producing the German translation of the Bible that became his most widely read work and influenced German prose style for centuries.

These were the dramatic years, the years of the Lutheran revolution in the German states. All over Germany, preachers were drawing crowds to hear Luther's reform doctrines, and sometimes to go considerably beyond them. In some places, statues and stained glass windows in churches were smashed by mobs who equated all images with idol worship. In 1522 a group of German knights launched the Knights' War when they rebelled against the archbishop of Trier in the name of their own feudal rights and Lutheran religious independence. In 1524 a great peasant revolt called the Peasants' War broke out in Swabia and spread over much of central and southern Germany, demanding the abolition of serfdom, tithing, the payment of manorial dues, and other medieval hangovers as well as the right to choose their own pastors, as Luther had said. Groups of Protestant extremists called Anabaptists (discussed further on p. 423) rejected infant baptism — one of Luther's two surviving sacraments — and urged such "primitive Christian" practices as common ownership of property. Soon the revolt spread beyond Germany's borders.

Luther, who believed that only salvation and the life to come really mattered, was no political or social radical: in this world, he favored social order and respect for political authority. He therefore urged the suppression of the "thieving and murdering peasants," who were in fact suppressed by their overlords in a brutal campaign that cost many thousands of lives. Luther himself apparently initialed orders for the execution of at least a few Anabaptists. Drawing steadily closer to his princely protectors, he and his followers organized Lutheran churches in Saxony, Hesse, Brandenburg, Prussia, and other north German states, as well as in many imperial cities. The kings of Denmark and Sweden were converted to the new faith and imposed Lutheran reforms on their own churches.

In all the new churches, the Bible was the sole basis for belief and practice, the sermon became the central rite of the church, and priests were allowed to marry. Luther himself married a former nun named Katharina von Bora (1499–1552) and, with their children, established the pattern of the Protestant minister's family. The Lutheran churches all rejected papal authority and recognized the local prince as head of the church. The state church, common all across Europe from the sixteenth through the nineteenth century, was thus a Lutheran contribution.

When at the Diet of Speyer in 1529 a group of German princes signed a "protest" against the decree of an imperial diet prohibiting any further innovations in religion, the wave of religious reform had its name: Protestantism. From the 1530s on, the center of the religious revolt shifted elsewhere, to Switzerland, the Low Countries, France, and Britain. Martin Luther, against all odds, lived to an honored old age, hailed by Protestants as the man who had started it all. He had in fact started more than he knew, and more than he intended.

Secular Sources of Revolt

Luther's case against the sixteenth-century church was a powerful one, powerfully put. But the widespread support he commanded was not entirely rooted in the charges he leveled against the Roman church, or in religious motives of any sort. As with any historic movement of this scope, a variety of causal factors was at work. Besides religious faith, ideological, political, social, and economic factors helped to account for the widespread support of the Protestant cause in northern Europe.

The half-developed ideological force of modern nationalism may be detected behind this German revolt against what many perceived as exploitation of the German states by Italian popes. Luther himself encouraged this feeling in the pamphlet *To the Christian Nobility of the German Nation,* mentioned earlier. Like most early modern national sentiment, this was a negative feeling, an attack on the vices of another people, in this case the Italian leaders of the church. But a similar wave of nationalism greatly increased the strength of the Reformation in the Low Countries, for instance, where Dutch patriots were stirred to resist the Catholic policies of their foreign overlord, the king of Spain.

Another powerful auxiliary force that brought Luther essential support was the political imperative of particularism, the demands of many German rulers for regional autonomy. Since medieval times, the German princes had been asserting their independence of their feudal lord, the Holy Roman emperor. The north German rulers who rallied to Luther's side were in considerable part asserting their political right to decide religious questions for themselves and for their subjects, free of dictation by the Habsburg emperor. Typically, Lutheranism became the church of converted German and Scandinavian rulers, and the maxim *cuius regio eius religio*—roughly "the prince's religion is the people's religion"—became the rule all across the German states. The triumph of Lutheranism in the northern half of the Holy Roman Empire was thus also a victory for political particularism in the Empire.

Other political motives played a part in subsequent Protestant movements elsewhere. In France, for example, both Catholic and Protestant factions were led by ambitious dynasties competing for the throne of France—and as we shall see, the winner, Henry IV, actually changed his religion rather than forgo his political objective.

The social grievances of the peasantry were at least as compelling as their religious commitments in the German Peasants' War of 1524–1525. And there were other religious movements in which social causes loomed large in the course of the Reformation century. A famous Catholic case was that of the so-called Pilgrimage of Grace, a revolt in the north of England that Henry VIII savagely suppressed despite the religious banners borne by the rebels.

Economic motives of the crudest sort also moved some to join the Reformation crusade. Secular princes in the German states had long looked enviously on the wealth of the Empire's archbishops, bishops, and monastic establishments. Some saw Luther's denunciation of the worldly concerns of the church as warrant for the princes themselves to divest the churches in their territories of their wealth and property. Thus, for instance, the grand master of the crusading order called the Teutonic Knights converted to Lutheranism and appropriated the vast properties of the Knights, becoming a very wealthy secular prince, the first duke of Prussia.

A similar interpretation led rulers in other lands, including England and the Scandinavian countries, to move against the wealth of the church. Henry VIII's seizure of the lands of the English monasteries not only filled his own coffers, but enabled him, through judicious distribution of the confiscated property among England's landed aristocrats, to ensure their support for the newly established Anglican church.

Ideology, politics, social grievances, and greed all contributed to the spread of the Reformation. Yet religion was the heart of it, and the religious ideas of Martin Luther were the central cause of the Protestant revolt (see box, "Luther the Revolutionary").

Calvinism and the International Protestant Movement

The rebellious spirit of the Reformation leaped from city to city, from nation to nation across northern Europe. Some countries were missed entirely, and in others the movement made little headway or was stamped out. But within a few years, major outbreaks flared from Switzerland to Britain, with many lesser conflagrations flickering in between. It was clear evidence that the religious needs and resentment of church abuses to which Luther had spoken so eloquently were widespread and deeply felt.

The man who brought some order to this chaos of Reformation upheavals was John Calvin of Geneva. And around the fringes of the Lutheran and Calvinist movements, a host of lesser, even more radical sects proliferated. Altogether, they produced by midcentury a crescendo of trumpets heralding the coming of the New Jerusalem.

Calvin's Theology

Unlike Luther, John Calvin (1509–1564) looked his part. A famous sketch of Calvin preaching, done in his later years, shows the archetypal religious zealot, lean and goat bearded, hollow of cheek and eye. An iron will and an incisive mind, known to college classmates as "the accusative case," Calvin was a man to respect, but not an easy one to love.

The son of a French lawyer with ecclesiastical connections and a devoutly religious woman, young Calvin had a broader, in some ways more sophisticated educational background than the German peasant's son. He studied law as his father had, got a

PROFILES IN HISTORY
Luther the Revolutionary

Martin Luther, who set out to reform the Christian church, ended by inspiring a revolution that left western Christendom divided from that day to this. In this selection from one of Luther's many sermons on the Gospels, the Protestant leader explains he is a revolutionary only in a spiritual sense. He recognizes, as Christ did, the duty of all people to "render unto Caesar that which is Caesar's"—obedience in all earthly affairs. Spiritual convictions, however, could lead to social conflicts; and Luther's movement was sometimes taken up by people driven by more material concerns than Luther's. Charles V's empire was thus torn by violent conflicts, revolts by peasants, knights, princes, and religious extremists like the Anabaptists. Reading Luther's concluding sentence here, can you see any way in which Luther's very passion to "have the truth" might be partially responsible for these other movements which "bathe[d] the world in blood"?

> [Jesus] admitted that he came to make a revolution and yet was not a revolutionary, for the gospel does not come without revolution. "Think you that I am come to bring peace on earth?" He said, "I say no, but division."
>
> In just the same way we [Protestants] are revolutionists now. We preach that everyone should obey his [earthly] lord, and in this we are peaceful and peaceable. . . . We help the emperor in his kingdom and then we upset his kingdom when we say that the Kingdom of Christ is higher than the Emperor Charles. Life and goods we submit in obedience, but we preach the gospel and this divides hearts from hearts. In this comes the revolution, that the father has a different faith from the son. . . . The point is not that children should not obey their parents but that they will believe differently. The gospel is a kingdom, and it effects a revolution, only it is a spiritual revolution. . . .
>
> It is a shame that the world prefers murder, adultery, faithlessness, trickery, guile, lying, and deception to the truth. They would rather bathe the world in blood than have the truth.

Source: Martin Luther, *Luther's Meditations on the Gospel*, trans. and ed. Roland H. Bainton (London: Butterworth Press, 1963), 124–125.

Martin Luther's most important successor in the next generation of Protestant reformers was John Calvin. This portrait shows Calvin about the time he arrived in Geneva, in the 1530's—young, intense, fiercely intelligent and totally committed to his cause.

There were a half-dozen Protestant Swiss cantons by this time, almost twenty years after Luther's Ninety-Five Theses, and Geneva had recently been added to their number. But the conversion, involving a rebellion against the local bishop and the closing of monasteries, had been tumultuous and divisive. One of the leaders of the Geneva Protestants, a red-bearded French radical named Guillaume Farel (1489–1565), saw Calvin—whose intellectual reputation was already spreading—as the man the Geneva reformers needed to organize their victory. The will of God, Farel told the French refugee, had brought him through their city. He must stay and reorder the house of the Lord in Geneva. Calvin did stay, and over the next thirty years he brought order to a much larger sector of Reformation Europe than this single city in the Alps.

The ideas of John Calvin included many of Luther's basic convictions, among them salvation by faith, the authority of the Bible, papal usurpation, and the priesthood of all believers. Calvin, however, gave special emphasis to certain Lutheran and older Christian ideas. Two distinctively Calvinist views, his emphasis on the *sovereignty of God* and his belief in the predestination of each human soul to salvation or damnation, particularly distinguished Calvinism among the Protestant sects.

The center of Calvin's faith was his certainty of God's omnipotence. "God," he wrote, "is the spring and fountain of all life, justice, wisdom, virtue, goodness, and clemency." God's majesty, beneficence, and power towered over the universe. Human beings, by contrast, were utterly powerless: human impotence was a corollary of divine omnipotence. Humanity had also been fatally corrupted by Adam's sin, his presumptuous effort "to raise himself up apart from the Lord." Human depravity was another key Calvinist emphasis: without the gift of divine grace, we were all "sinners from our mothers' wombs . . . all born to the wrath and retribution of God."[6]

On the basis of his conviction of God's omnipotence and human impotence, Calvin became the most vigorous spokesman for *predestination* among the reformers. God the all-knowing, the all-powerful, had predestined each human soul to salvation or damnation:

> The word of God takes root and brings forth fruit only in those whom the Lord, by his eternal election, has predestined to be children and heirs of the heavenly kingdom. To all others (who by the same counsel of

degree from Orléans, and never lost the grasp of legal logic and rigorous organization he had absorbed. He studied ancient languages—his first publication was a humanist commentary on the Roman Stoic Seneca—and Stoic emphasis on duty and suppression of desires became integral parts of Calvin's Christian vision. He studied theology in Paris, became a priest, and was soon interested in the ideas of the reformers.

Sometime in the earlier 1530s, Calvin converted wholly to reform doctrines and soon thereafter joined the streams of religious refugees already in motion across a religiously divided and disordered Europe. In 1536 two actions decided his destiny. He published the first small edition of his book *The Institutes of the Christian Religion,* which in vastly expanded later versions had an immense influence on international Protestantism. And in that same year, he paused for what he intended to be a brief stopover in the Swiss city of Geneva, recently converted to the Protestant faith.

God are rejected before the foundation of the world) . . . nothing but an odor of death unto death.[7]

If this seemed cruel, Calvin pointed out that human wickedness deserved all the punishment it got and it was only thanks to God's amazing grace that any of the seed of Adam were saved. This hard doctrine might have bred apathy or even libertinism, since nothing we did in this life could affect our ultimate destination. In fact, however, the Calvinists' conviction of being themselves "the elect," the chosen few destined for the right hand of the Lord, made them militant crusaders for God's kingdom here on earth.

Calvinist Geneva

Geneva today is an expensively cosmopolitan city on the shores of the bluest of lakes, bustling with international bureaucrats, officeworkers from multinational corporations, students, and tourists. But climb the hill to the Old City and you can walk cobblestoned streets trod by the first reformers and visit the Cathedral of St. Peter where Calvin himself held his audiences enthralled 450 years ago. It is a trip worth taking, if only to see the city that became to sixteenth-century Protestants what revolutionary Paris was during the 1790s, or Stalin's Moscow in the 1930s: the republic of the future, the ideal society realized on earth.

The Calvinist church at Geneva was run by four orders of officials, two clerical orders and two of laypeople. The pastors were the Calvinist priests, possessing no magical powers but charged with leadership, the preaching of sermons, and the care of souls; in fact, these were very powerful people indeed. The teachers were the intellectuals, responsible both for the study of theology and for the teaching of catechisms and creeds to the faithful. Elders and deacons were lay officials, the former responsible for disciplining any of the faithful who fell from grace, the latter caring for the physical fabric of the church and ministering to the sick, the elderly, the infirm.

The civil government of the prosperous city-state of Geneva during Calvin's leadership of the church is sometimes seen as a rare example of a modern theocracy—a state ruled by its priests. The political structure actually functioned more as a close collaboration of church and state than the autocratic rule of the former. Through a cooperative committee of devout laymen and pastors called the *consistory*, however, Calvin wielded immense personal authority over Geneva. Laws were passed making religious and moral offenses civil crimes, and people were punished by the state for questioning the theology of John Calvin.

The black gown of Geneva, worn by Calvin and his fellow pastors, thus stood for a very clearly defined style of life and belief in the middle of the sixteenth century. Calvinists were forbidden to read light literature, attend stage plays, dance or sing popular songs, blaspheme, buy a round of drinks at a tavern, or work on the Sabbath; the penalties for infractions ranged from fines to public exposure in the stocks to imprisonment and worse. And offenses against the faith were even more rigorously punished than moral lapses. Failing to attend church services held several times a week, drowsing through a sermon, preserving holy images, or celebrating "pagan" feasts like Christmas drew reprimands or fines. Even leading citizens who expressed doubt about some of Calvin's views were required to undergo public humiliation. A Spanish fugitive from the Inquisition named Michael Servetus (1511–1553) showed up at Geneva, explained his vaguely Unitarian views, and was promptly put on trial for heresy; he was convicted and burned alive.

Protestant refugees from many lands, however, found Calvin's city a haven of Reformation piety. Deeply stirred by the sobriety of Genevan life and the rigor of Calvinist religion, they took Calvinism back to their own countries when they returned. Calvinist tracts, the Geneva Bible, and Calvin's own *Institutes*, with its detailed instructions for church governance, were read and heeded all over Protestant Europe. The image of the city, its black-gowned pastors, and the teachings of its master spirit dominated the Protestant movement in the later sixteenth century.

By the time John Calvin himself died in 1564, there were Calvinist churches in many lands. Among the most successful were the French Huguenots in Calvin's own homeland, the Dutch Reformed church, the Scottish kirk led by the eloquent John Knox (1513–1572), and the English Puritans, whose day would come in the next century. There were Calvinist congregations also in Germany and Bohemia, and as far east as Poland and Hungary. Everywhere they were militant, demanding change with the fervor of God's chosen. What Luther had begun in Germany, Calvin more than anyone else had turned into a powerful force all across the Western world.

Anabaptists and Other Sects

Luther and Calvin were not the only preachers of the new dispensation. Many others emerged as preachers, prophets, and leaders of religious movements. Some, like Zwingli in Switzerland, were widely recognized as pillars of the Reformation churches. Others, like the Anabaptists, were often condemned in their own time as the lunatic fringe of the movement, though modern scholarship has seen them in a much more positive light. All, however, added to the confusion of voices demanding—and making—changes in the life of faith as the Reformation century roared on.

Ulrich Zwingli (1484–1531) was a contemporary of Luther who paved the way for Calvin and other second-generation Protestant leaders. An Erasmian humanist who had served as a chaplain with Swiss mercenaries, Zwingli challenged the Roman church in the canton of Zurich soon after Luther spoke up in northern Germany. Though Zwingli never founded a church of his own, his views influenced Protestants in a number of other Swiss cities and in southern Germany as well. After laboring for the cause through the 1520s, he was killed in a war between Protestant and Catholic cantons in Switzerland in 1531, five years before Calvin appeared on the scene.

Among Zwingli's most important contributions were his radical view of the Eucharist, or communion service, and his drastic simplification of the church service. He fell out with Luther over the nature of the Mass. Luther had rejected the traditional Catholic doctrine of the transubstantiation of the communion wafer and wine into the spiritual substance of Christ's body and blood, but had adopted an intermediate position, *consubstantiation,* in which Christ is spiritually present but the wafer remains a wafer still. Zwingli departed still further from orthodoxy, seeing the communion service as a purely symbolic act, a commemorative service reminding us of Christ's sacrifice, in which the wafer and wine underwent no mystical transformations at all. Zwingli also provided a model for the stripped-down Calvinist church by insisting that sacred images, candles, incense, and elaborate vestments were all pagan distractions from true piety. His churches, like Calvin's, were simple undecorated buildings with ordinary tables in place of altars. This Protestant trend toward radical simplicity led to waves of iconoclasm—image breaking—in some places, where mobs destroyed treasures of medieval art as emblems of papist idolatry.

Others among the Protestant reformers took a more conciliatory tone. Martin Bucer (1491–1551), a former Dominican who, like Luther, married a nun, helped make Strasbourg a leading Protestant city in the 1520s and then went to England, where he contributed significantly to the development of the Church of England. Bucer also spent many years trying to reconcile the differing religious views of Luther and Zwingli and was a leading shaper of the Helvetic Confession of 1536, a statement of faith for all the Protestant Swiss cantons. Heinrich Bullinger (1504–1575), Zwingli's successor in Zurich, also played a leading part in seeking theological compromises among Protestant leaders, particularly between the Zwinglian tradition and the creeds of Luther and Calvin. Kasper Schwenckfeld (1487–1561), by contrast, objected to both Protestant and Catholic views of the Eucharist and to what he saw as their overconcern with the institutional church and neglect of direct personal revelation. Condemned by all camps, Schwenckfeld wandered Europe preaching an emotional religion of freedom and love and pouring out theological tracts in answer to his many critics.

The most extreme of the new believers, however, were the sectarians now called religious radicals, then often lumped together as *Anabaptists,* a blanket term of condemnation comparable to "Jacobin" or "Bolshevik" in later centuries. Literally, the term meant "rebaptizers" and applied to Protestant groups who challenged the only sacrament besides the Eucharist left by Luther: baptism. Claiming that baptism had no spiritual vitality unless the baptized understood and accepted the teachings of the church—which no baby could do—Anabaptists reserved this rite until adulthood. It may sound like an innocuous doctrine today. But in a period when a substantial part of the population did not survive childhood, it could mean that many would never be baptized at all. And there were even more disturbing beliefs and practices associated with the generic label of Anabaptist.

Some of the sects so described practiced a primitive form of communism, insisting that all worldly goods should be held in common as in the days of the early Christians—though few Anabaptists had much property to share. Some, pointing to biblical instances of polygamy, believed in reinstituting the practice in their own time; others urged that wives, like other forms of property, should be held in common by all. Most rejected both the state and the organized church, withdrawing like monks into sectarian communities, convinced that the Second Coming of Christ was near at hand.

The most notorious religious radicals were the Anabaptists who took over Münster in northern Germany in 1534. Winning power in the city through an appeal to the poor and the humbler craft guilds, they finally drove both Catholic and Lutheran citizens into exile and announced the New Jerusalem. Led by Jan of Leiden (c. 1509–1536), whom they hailed as King David reborn and rewarded with a harem, the Anabaptists of Münster instituted primitive communism and Old Testament polygamy and prepared for the end of the world. It came, in the form of a combined force of Lutherans and Catholics who took the city and massacred the Anabaptists.

The label of Anabaptist, however, covered many other sects whose radicalism was neither violent nor socially divisive. These small groups of peaceful and pious Christians often suffered for the colorful behavior of others. Religious radicals, in fact, were among the first to see religion as primarily a private matter between the worshiper and God, and to espouse such modern principles as toleration, freedom of conscience, and separation of church and state. Such denominations as the Mennonites and Amish, the Baptists and Quakers of today can trace their spiritual ancestry to these quiet unworldly groups who tried to lead Christian lives amid the more strident trumpets of the sects and the drumbeats of resurgent Catholicism.

Protestantism and Society

Protestantism in general has been associated with a variety of social attitudes that began to emerge about this time. We note here the doctrine of the calling, Protestant attitudes toward the family, and the role of women in the Reformation.

An extremely influential Calvinist doctrine focused on the common human problems of getting and spending in this world. This was the Calvinist version of *the calling*. The Roman church had for centuries declared that some few Christians had a divine *vocation*, or "calling," to the priesthood. Protestants, and Calvinists especially, asserted that all Christians had a calling to practice whatever trade they followed in a Christian spirit. Honesty, industry, thrift, sobriety, the letter of the contract or the law all became Calvinist virtues. And businesspeople in many lands, told that they too had a calling and a

way to heaven, found Calvinism a particularly satisfying doctrine.

Protestantism also imputed a particular significance and dignity to the Christian family. The medieval Catholic church had seen celibacy as the noblest human condition, demanding it of priests, monks, and nuns and glorifying the Virgin Mary in a thousand churches. The reformers, by contrast, closed down monasteries and convents, allowed pastors to marry, and largely abandoned the cult of the Virgin. For Luther, marriage was the highest human condition, and the ideal Protestant union was what we now call a "companionate" marriage, in which two helpmeets share interests and work together for the happiness of the family unit. Concern for children and emphasis on family worship and religious training within the family all seem to have received special attention in Protestant homes.

There were limits to the changes wrought by the Reformation, however. The structure of the family, for instance, remained patriarchal, the wife and children subordinate to the will of the father, who, under the new dispensation, was both magistrate and priest to his household. Woman's place was thus still secondary; her principal duty was still the proper and pious rearing of her children.

And yet many courageous and talented women played active parts in the Reformation movement. Luther's wife Katharina von Bora, for example, also served as a local medical healer and faced the very real possibility that, as a heretic, a renegade nun, and the wife of the greatest heretic of them all, she might well end her life dying painfully at his side. Powerful Protestant women also served as patrons of the cause. Thus Jeanne d'Albret (r. 1555–1572), Calvinist queen of Navarre, was an ardent champion of the Huguenots of southern France. Noted for moderation in an age of fanatical religious belief, she was said to have been the only sixteenth-century ruler who executed no one for their religious convictions.

In a few of the radical sects, finally, women became public preachers and leaders. Perhaps the most important such case was that of Margaret Fell (1614–1702), wife and patron of George Fox (1624–1691), who founded the Society of Friends—the Quakers—in seventeenth-century England. Fox found abundant scriptural evidence for women taking active leadership roles in Old Testament times as judges, prophets, and preachers of the Lord's will. Margaret Fell's country estate of Swarthmore became the center of the new sect, and she herself was one of its founders.

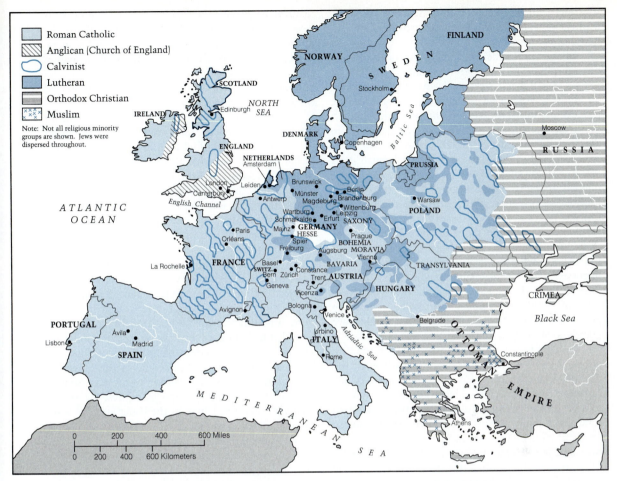

Map 14.2   Centers of Religious Concentration in Europe Toward the End of the Sixteenth Century

The Catholic Reformation

The hunger for religious revival was as strong on the Catholic side of the great sixteenth-century Schism as it was among the Protestants. Long before there were Quakers or Baptists, there were Brethren and Sisters of the Common Life. If Luther's disagreements with Catholicism led him to break with the Roman church, Erasmus, whose witty critique of ecclesiastical wrongdoing had paved the way for Luther, found room for his "philosophy of Christ" within the older church.

The result of this growing demand for spiritual revival in the Catholic church was a great surge of piety and a major reform effort in the later sixteenth century. This movement was in part a reaction to and a counterattack against the Protestant revolt and

is therefore sometimes called the *counter reformation*. As a profound expression of Catholic religious feeling, however, this revival of medieval piety is also often described simply as the Catholic Reformation. Each label expresses a fundamental aspect of the religious rebirth of Roman Catholicism that began in the second quarter of the sixteenth century and had transformed the church by the end of it.

The Reformation Popes

As in past centuries, papal leadership played a crucial part in the Catholic Reformation. After the so-called Renaissance popes of the decades around 1500 came the "Reformation popes" of the half-century after 1530. If widespread popular demand for a return to true piety triggered the reform, vigorous papal reformers organized and increasingly inspired the renewal of the faith.

In many ways the most important of the Reformation popes was one of the first: Paul III (r. 1534–1549). A relatively secular Renaissance character himself, Pope Paul nonetheless inaugurated the moral and spiritual revitalization of the worldly church of Medici and Borgia pontiffs. Like Gregory VII in the High Middle Ages, Paul III appointed men of intelligence and upright character to the Roman curia and to the crucial college of cardinals. These reform-minded appointees both fostered the spread of the Catholic Reformation and ensured a succession of reforming popes to carry on the work. Pope Paul's personal contributions to the Catholic reform also included the recognition of the Jesuit order in 1540 and the calling of the Council of Trent in 1545—both discussed later. Paul's summoning of a council showed particular courage, since the conciliar movement of the fifteenth century had sought to limit the power of the papacy, a development that could have gravely weakened the Catholic Reformation.

Perhaps the most admired of the Reformation popes, Pius V (r. 1566–1572) illustrates how far the Catholic church had moved within fifty years of the Lutheran revolt. Pius himself embodied the new spirit to a far greater extent than had Paul, the child of an earlier and more worldly age. A former Dominican monk, Pope Pius gave much time to prayer, meditation, and pilgrimage, often wore a hairshirt under his papal robes, and washed the feet of beggars. He guided the Catholic Reformation to new heights by publishing new books of prayers and devotions and a new catechism that reflected the reforms of the Council of Trent. By insisting on spirituality and attention to duty from his cardinals and bishops, he revived popular respect for the hierarchy as a whole.

The Rome that Luther visited in 1509 was a worldly Renaissance city ruled by secular and often corrupt princes of the church, a city of great art but little religious spirit. Half a century later, the Rome of the Catholic Reformation was as holy a city in its different way as the Geneva of John Calvin, filled with lay societies devoted to good works and pious prelates dedicated to the greatness of Mother Church.

The Catholic Counterattack

The Catholic side of the great religious revival of the sixteenth century was also, however, a counter reformation, a vigorous attempt to turn back and overcome the Protestant revolt. As such, it involved the mobilization of a number of institutions for struggle as well as for reform. Thus the Catholic Reformation also convened the militant Council of Trent, renewed support for the Inquisition, and developed the Index of Forbidden Books.

The *Council of Trent*, which met off and on for twenty years between 1545 and 1564, was one of the most influential of all church councils. Like that of Nicaea in the fourth century, the Lateran Council in the thirteenth, and the Council of Constance in the fifteenth, this gathering of leading sixteenth-century churchmen was convened to deal with a great crisis in the church. Like these earlier efforts, Trent had its limitations and its failures yet brought major reforms as well.

By and large, the Council of Trent reaffirmed traditional theological views even as it recognized the need for reform in church practice. Thus, for example, the council denied Luther's claim that faith alone was sufficient for salvation, insisting that both Christian faith and good works were prerequisites for admission to the kingdom of heaven. Trent also rejected Zwingli's and Calvin's view of the Mass as a purely symbolic commemoration of the Last Supper, insisting on the real metaphysical presence of the body and blood of Christ in the wafer and the wine. On matters of dogmatic faith, in short, the church would not compromise.

The assembled churchmen, however, did recognize the urgent need for reform in church practice, eliminating the moral lapses that had driven so many into the arms of the Protestants. Trent therefore renewed the old assault on clerical concubinage, simony, nepotism, and other manifestations of worldliness in the lives of the clergy. Keenly aware of the advantages that better education and greater knowledge of Scripture gave to Protestant preachers in the struggle for hearts and minds, the council also decreed the establishment of a new system of seminaries. These institutions trained priests to deal more successfully with their rivals and to communicate the Christian message more effectively to their own congregations.

The Catholic Reformation also offered some important opportunities for women. Roman Catholics, like Protestants, still denied women the right to serve in the priesthood. But whereas Protestants closed down hundreds of convents as they did monasteries, Catholics continued to support these institutions. In convents women held high offices and found opportunities for significant lives beyond the family circle. And the very militancy of the

Catholic Reformation encouraged lives of Christian commitment that earned sainthood for some of these devout women.

For those who rejected the ancient message of the church, on the other hand, the Holy Office of the Inquisition, the system of church courts charged with suppression of heresy, was encouraged to proceed with vigor. The Inquisition had already been revived in the Spain of Ferdinand and Isabella; the reinvigorated Roman Inquisition also proved an effective weapon against Protestants. As in the Middle Ages, the Inquisition of the Reformation period still made use of secret testimony and torture to extort confessions. It still punished heretics with prison and confiscation of property and those who refused to recant or later returned to their heretical beliefs with death. The *auto da fe* ("act of faith") was the public ceremony in which the Inquisition judged and sentenced a heretic. Often culminating in death by fire, this act was one of the most dreadful expressions of what some have termed the last great age of religious faith.

The *Index of Forbidden Books*, finally, was a branch of the Holy Office that proved particularly important in the new age of the printing press. Re-sponding to the large number of books made available by the new print technology, the Index sought to prevent such sources of spiritual and moral contamination as volumes of pornography and magic, Machiavellian political theory, and early modern science from getting into the hands of the faithful. The primary target of the Index of Forbidden Books, however, was the heretical theology of Luther, Calvin, and other leaders of the Protestant Reformation. In all these areas the goal was the same: the prevention of spiritual contamination through exposure to unchristian ideas in printed form.

Loyola and the Jesuits

The Catholic Reformation also produced both new saints and new religious orders in considerable numbers. Prominent among these were two Spanish heroes of the faith, Teresa of Avila (1515–1582) and Ignatius Loyola. St. Teresa (1515–1582) was a Carmelite nun, religious reformer, and mystic visionary. A vigorously practical woman, she developed a rigorous new regimen for Carmelites and traveled

Death by fire, the ultimate punishment decreed by the Inquisition for heretics, is here meted out in a public *auto da fe* or "act of faith." Notice the large crowds, gathered to see this public execution.

about Spain reorganizing convents and founding new ones. Her spiritual voyages of discovery, as recorded in her autobiographical *Life* (1562), in *The Interior Castle* (1577) and other works, described in moving detail the visions she believed brought her into the presence of the risen Christ himself:

> He comes with such majesty that no one can doubt it is the Lord Himself . . . so much the Lord of that inn, the soul, that it seems to dissolve completely and to be consumed in Christ . . . in a rapture or ecstasy, during the enjoyment of which the sight of that Divine Presence is lost.[8]

As much as Luther's moments of revelation over the Scripture, such religious visions were central to the spiritual life of the Reformation century.

Perhaps the most influential saint of the Catholic Reformation, however, was Ignatius Loyola (1491–1556), who was himself the founder of a new order—the Society of Jesus, commonly called the *Jesuits*. A Basque knight from the mountainous border country of northern Spain, Loyola was raised in the centuries-old Spanish tradition of honor and faith. Lamed for life in combat, the Spanish aristocrat shifted the emphasis in his life from chivalric honor to religious faith. But Loyola always saw religion in crusading terms, and he organized the Jesuit order along the military lines of the knightly crusading orders of the Middle Ages. He saw the medieval saints as heroic champions of the faith and sought to emulate their deeds. Taking Christ as his liege lord and the Virgin Mary as the spiritual lady of his heart, he set out to become himself such a militant defender of Holy Mother Church.

After submitting himself to the rigorous austerities of the hermit's life, Loyola went on to study theology in Spain and Paris. He gathered a small band of equally dedicated men around him. During these years—the 1520s and 1530s—he also produced his immensely influential book, the *Spiritual Exercises* (1523–1535), which became the meditation manual of his new order of preaching friars, officially recognized as the Society of Jesus by Pope Paul III in 1540.

Loyola's *Spiritual Exercises* is a four-week course of Christian meditation focused on human sinfulness and on the life, crucifixion, and resurrection of the Savior (see box "Loyola's Spiritual Exercises" for an excerpt from this guide to meditation). This system, involving vivid visualization of a series of spiritual objects, from the pains of hell to the glory of the risen

PROFILES IN HISTORY
Loyola's Spiritual Exercises

St. Ignatius Loyola, founder of the Jesuit order, was also the author of one of the most powerful guides to spiritual meditation ever composed. His *Spiritual Exercises*, still used by Jesuits and others at religious retreats, endeavored to enlist all the powers of the human imagination in strengthening religious convictions and resolve. From these meditations on one's own hopeless sinfulness, this leader of the Catholic Reformation urged the penitent to contemplate with growing fervor and joy the life, passion, and resurrection of Christ, who alone could save us from the punishment our sinful natures so richly deserve.

THE SECOND EXERCISE IS A
MEDITATION UPON SINS

The first point is the review of the sins, that is to say, to recall to memory all the sins of my life, contemplating them from year to year, or from period to period. . . .

The second [point] is to weigh the sins, considering the foulness and malice that each mortal sin committed has in itself. . . .

The third is to consider who I am, abasing myself by comparisons: 1st, what I am in comparison with all men; 2nd, what are all men in comparison with the angels and saints in heaven; 3rd, to consider what is all creation in comparison with God—therefore, myself alone, what can I be? 4th, to consider all my corruption and bodily foulness; 5th, to behold myself as an ulcer and abscess whence have issued so many sins and iniquities, and such vile poison. . . .

The fourth, is to consider who God is, against Whom I have sinned, contemplating His attributes and comparing them with their contraries in myself: His wisdom with my ignorance, His omnipotence with my weakness, His justice with my iniquity, His goodness with my perversity. . . .

The fifth, an exclamation with wonder, with great affection, running through all creatures in my mind, and thinking how they have suffered me to live . . . how the saints have been interceding and entreating for me . . . and the earth [itself], how it has not opened to swallow me, creating new hells that I might suffer in them forever.

Source: Ignatius of Loyola, *The Spiritual Exercises,* trans. W. H. Longbridge (London: Roxburghe House, 1919), 60–63.

Ignatius Loyola is shown, in 1540, receiving the permission of Pope Paul III to establish the Jesuit order. On the right, we see Loyola, who was later canonized, receiving divine inspiration for his work.

Christ, was intended to fortify the Jesuits for the struggle to which they were committed. The result was an elite corps of Catholic crusaders, as dedicated and totally convinced of their own righteousness as the most militant Calvinists were of theirs.

The Society of Jesus was headed by a general who took orders only from the pope and whose commands were in turn obeyed without question by all members. Standards for admission to the order were high, requiring dedication, discipline, and intelligence. Areas in which the society excelled included teaching, foreign missions, and the struggle against what it saw as the heresy of Protestantism. Jesuit schools and colleges came to be recognized as among the finest educational institutions in Europe, providing humanist training in the classics as well as effective religious instruction. Jesuit missionaries carried Christianity to the indigenous peoples of North and South America and to the sophisticated courts of India and China. Within Europe, some Jesuits became spiritual counselors to princes, advising them to take a militant stand on religious issues. Others helped win back Poland and Hungary for the Catholic church; still others traveled in disguise through Protestant England providing an underground church for English Catholics.

The successes and methods of the Jesuits earned them many enemies, among rival Catholic orders as well as among Protestants. They were charged with spreading their views through sophistical argumentation and even deception, with exercising undue influence in high places, and with a willingness to do almost anything to advance their ends. They were also widely feared as the most effective agents of the Catholic counter reformation.

The Nation-States in the Sixteenth Century

It was under such conditions, then, that the sixteenth-century successors to the first new monarchs attempted to govern and expand their nations and to glorify their reigns. For the most part firmly seated on stable thrones, thanks to the labors of their immediate predecessors, rulers like Henry VIII of England, Francis I of France, and Emperor Charles V were able to combine aggressive and costly foreign policies with further drives to strengthen royal authority at home. In the second half of the century, two long-ruling monarchs dominated western European affairs: the Protestant leader Queen Elizabeth I of England, and Philip II of Spain, Elizabeth's great rival and the most militant champion of the Catholic counter reformation. In eastern Europe, meanwhile,

Czar Ivan the Terrible was imposing the most autocratic of all royal governments on Russia. To clarify a complicated picture, the present section focuses on the internal affairs of the several nations. The last section of the chapter outlines the wars and revolutions that convulsed the continent during the sixteenth century.

Henry VIII and the English Reformation

In many ways the most successful sixteenth-century monarchy was Tudor England. Generally united and prosperous, the island kingdom found strong leadership in Henry VIII during the first half of the century and in Elizabeth I during the second half. As historical personalities, they make a striking contrast: the much-married "Bluff Prince Hal," England's Bluebeard, and "Good Queen Bess," the Virgin Queen with her famous red wig. But they had in common the passion for power and the gift for public relations that can make a great politician.

The familiar Holbein portrait of Henry VIII (r. 1509–1547)—hand on hip, glaring out at us, masterful, arrogant, and every inch a king—tells a lot about him; so does the even more familiar tale of his love affair with Anne Boleyn. He was an intelligent, passionate, overbearing man who could also be self-deluding and brutal. And he shook up England as few rulers had before him.

Henry VIII used the treasury surplus that Henry VII had left to fight a couple of quick wars with Scotland and France, and then left affairs of state to his chief minister, Cardinal Wolsey (c. 1475–1530), for the first two decades of his reign. Preoccupied with hunting, feasting, and wenching, Henry had only one problem: his queen, Catherine of Aragon (1485–1536) had not produced a male heir, and only one female one, Mary. The king was already deeply worried about this problem when he fell passionately in love with Anne Boleyn (c. 1507–1536), an ambitious and seductive lady-in-waiting. Unwilling to be merely another royal mistress, Anne demanded a wedding. When she strengthened her claim by getting pregnant, she raised exultant hopes of a male heir—and made marriage essential if the heir was to be legitimate.

In order to marry his paramour, Henry had to get his eighteen-year marriage to Queen Catherine annulled by direct papal dispensation. The pope, however, was under the thumb of Holy Roman Em-

peror Charles V, who was not only highly moral but Catherine of Aragon's nephew. When the situation proved too tricky even for Wolsey, Henry dropped him and turned to two younger men: cunning Thomas Cromwell (c. 1485–1540) and the pious, Protestant-leaning Thomas Cranmer (1489–1556). In a Europe already in an upheaval over the Reformation, their solution seemed just daring enough to work. If Henry declared the English church independent from Rome and himself the head of it, he would be in a position to see to the annulment of his marriage himself and could marry whom he pleased.

To legalize England's secession from the church of Rome, Henry VIII convened what became known as the Reformation Parliament (1529–1536). This long-lived and activist Parliament was soon venting anticlerical feeling rooted in surviving medieval Lollardy (see Chapter 11) and in the Reformation enthusiasms of a group of Cambridge University zealots. Translation of the Bible into English by William Tyndale (1494–1536) and Miles Coverdale (1488–1569) further strengthened support for religious reform in England. Over a period of seven years, then, the Parliament accomplished the king's purpose, and in the process brought the Reformation to England, something the religiously conservative king had *not* intended.

Parliament made it illegal to appeal a case through the ecclesiastical courts to Rome, and a convocation of English churchmen then obediently annulled Henry's marriage. In 1534 the Reformation Parliament made the king "supreme head" of the Church of England, and the Anglican church was born. Thomas Cromwell, Henry's new right-hand man, commissioned to uncover immorality in the English monasteries, promptly closed them down, confiscating their immense lands and wealth. As royal grants spread the confiscated lands among England's ruling classes, furthermore, the aristocracy also acquired a stake in the success of the Reformation. Leading opponents of Henry's claim to rule his church were executed for treason, including Chancellor Thomas More (1478–1535), the humanist, who was subsequently canonized by the Catholic church for his faith. By the conservative Six Articles (1539), however, Henry himself used Parliament to outlaw most of the theological doctrines of Luther and his fellow reformers, leaving the Cambridge radicals and other strong Protestants chafing for further change.

The incremental process of strengthening the government, meanwhile, continued under the second Tudor. Cromwell proved an able administrator who significantly expanded and increased the professionalism of the royal bureaucracy. An evolving Privy (Private) Council debated all important matters in the king's name, and six reorganized bureaus administered the realm according to the king's wishes. Parliament, however, also increased its own power, especially during the seven years of the Reformation Parliament. Legislating matters of immense national interest, working with gentry and burgesses from all parts of the country, members of the House of Commons in particular acquired a growing sense of their own powers, duties, and importance. It was a dangerous development for would-be English absolute monarchs to come.

And what about the amorous king and his problems, Anne Boleyn and her baby? The child, to the king's chagrin, turned out to be another girl—named Elizabeth—and Henry had Anne executed for adultery soon thereafter. He married four more times, divorcing one of these wives, executing another, and losing a third in childbirth. Only the last managed to survive him. From all these later marital ventures came only one child—the male heir he craved, a sickly boy named Edward.[9]

Edward VI (r. 1547–1553) and Mary (r. 1553–1558) are frequently characterized as the "lesser Tudors." In the boy king's brief reign, zealous Reformation preachers and ambitious conspirators at court combined with an economic decline to shake the Tudor throne. The conspirators were frustrated and beheaded, the popular rebellions suppressed. But the boy king died in his teens, having done little but preside over a swing toward doctrinal Reformation in religion.

Queen Mary Tudor aspired to swing the pendulum the other way. Reared in her Spanish mother's Catholic faith, she married the young King Philip II of Spain and tried desperately to restore Catholicism in England. But both moderate Anglicanism and the more radical Protestantism of Edward's reign survived Queen Mary's most determined efforts, including the martyrdom of several hundred Protestants. When she died childless in 1558, the kingdom came into the hands of Elizabeth I, the last child of Henry VIII and the greatest of the Tudors.

Good Queen Bess

Elizabeth Regina—Elizabeth the Queen—looks rather stiff and gaunt in the jewel-encrusted gowns of

Philip of Spain and Queen Mary of England—Queen Elizabeth's sister and predecessor on the English throne—shared a brief unhappy marriage in the 1550's. After Mary's death, Elizabeth succeeded to the English throne and Philip II became her greatest political antagonist for the next forty years.

the royal portraits, and she was never a real beauty even as a girl. She was masterful like her father, prudent and frugal with the public's money like her grandfather, and probably more intelligent then either of these shrewd rulers. She was a great self-advertiser, using jeweled gowns and annual royal progresses through the countryside to stir the admiration and affections of her people, assuring them that she was "a princess to whom nothing . . . was so dear as the hearty love and good will of her subjects."[10] (An excerpt from one of her most rousing speeches is reprinted in the box titled "Queen Elizabeth Rallies Her People.") Frustratingly indecisive, she turned even this quality to her advantage, keeping ambitious favorites and foreign statesmen waiting, fawning, paralyzed while she postponed decisions for months and even years. Though she depended on industri-

PROFILES IN HISTORY

Queen Elizabeth Rallies Her People

Queen Elizabeth's natural flair for public relations led her to appear in armor at the camp where her troops were gathered to repel any Spanish forces landing in the year of the Armada, 1588. In fact, the Spanish fleet had already been turned from Britain's shores by the queen's navy and by a terrific storm at sea. The published account of the royal speech—excerpted here—nevertheless showed the sort of alertness to popularity that made a Renaissance monarch successful as a ruler.

To the Army Gathered at Tilbury to Resist Any Renewed Attempt at Invasion After the Defeat of the Armada, 1588

My loving people, we have been persuaded by some that are careful of our Safety, to take heed how we commit our Self to armed Multitudes, for fear of Treachery. But I assure you I do not desire to distrust my faithful and loving People. Let tyrants fear, I have always so behaved my self the under God I have placed my chiefest Strength and safeguard in the loyal Hearts and good Will of my Subjects, and therefore I am come amongst you, as you see ... being resolved in the midst and heat of the Battle, to live or die amongst you all, to lay down for my God, and for my kingdom, and for my People, my Honor and my Blood, even in the Dust. I know I have the Body of a weak and feeble Woman, but I have the Heart and stomach [Courage] of a King, and of a King of *England* too. ... I my self will take up Arms, and I my self will be your General, Judge, and Rewarder of every one of your Virtues in the Field. ... not doubting but by your obedience ... and your Valor in the Field, we shall shortly have a famous Victory over those Enemies of my God, of my Kingdoms, and of my People.

Source: Alan Glover, ed., *Gloriana's Glass* (London: Nonesuch Press, 1953), 29–30.

VI, and had actually been imprisoned in the Tower of London for alleged involvement in a rebellion against Queen Mary. Neither charge against her was true, but Elizabeth thereafter trod very circumspectly through the Catholic reaction of Mary's days. When she came to the throne at the age of twenty-five, she was a seasoned realist, a Renaissance prince well suited to negotiate the tangled years that lay ahead.

The problems Queen Elizabeth faced were partly inherited, partly rooted in her own times. The question of what sort of church England should have had first been posed under Henry VIII, then answered in radical Protestant terms in Edward's time and in reactionary Catholic terms under Mary. The "Elizabethan settlement" of the Church of England's problems was typically middle of the road. Under Elizabeth, the church retained its hierarchy of bishops and archbishops with the queen at the top as "Supreme Governor," as well as elaborate Catholic liturgies and vestments. At the same time, however, Elizabeth kept the Protestant Prayer Book of Thomas Cranmer and promulgated a set of moderate Protestant doctrines, the Thirty-Nine Articles. It was a compromise settlement, and one that many English Christians could live with.

Like her father, Elizabeth had a political problem with the succession to the throne. Unmarried on her accession, she refused all advice to marry and provide an heir. The danger of chaos and civil war if she died without a clear successor was as great as it had been in Henry's day. Yet she never married and in fact converted her unwed condition into a diplomatic advantage by dangling the possibility of a marriage alliance before one European royal house after another.

A problem that was all her own, however, was that of female governance in her day: how was a woman to rule a court and country dominated by men? Improvising as she went, she soon learned to manipulate rival courtiers, to balance opposing points of view, and to play an elaborate chivalric game in which she was the Fairy Queen, her courtiers her faithful knights. Charming ecstatic crowds and foreign diplomats alike, by turns haughty and gracious with her Parliaments, she invented her own style of government, and she made it work.

Elizabeth's greatest problems were posed by the militancy of the Catholic Reformation and the climax of the religious wars on the continent. Reluctant to become involved in costly foreign adventures, she nevertheless dispatched small expeditionary

ous administrators from the gentry class and especially on the honest advice of Sir William Cecil (1520–1598), Lord Burghley and lord treasurer of the realm, she was, in the end, always the one in charge.

Elizabeth, who had lost her mother to the headsman's ax, had herself been suspected of conspiracy in the brief but tumultuous reign of Edward

forces to support both the Dutch revolt against Catholic Spain and Henry of Navarre (1553–1610), the Huguenot claimant to the French throne about whom we hear more in the next section. At home, meanwhile, Catholic militancy grew in the 1570s and 1580s. The movement centered around the romantic Catholic exile Mary Queen of Scots (1542–1587), who as a direct descendant of Henry VII was next in line for the English throne.

Daughter and heir of James V (r. 1512–1542) of Scotland, Mary had been raised a Catholic in France; she had in fact briefly been queen of that country during the short reign of her husband, King Francis II (r. 1559–1560). But when she returned to rule her own country in 1561, she faced a newly Presbyterian Scottish church and a Scottish nobility that disliked her foreign ways and entourage. Beautiful and intelligent but determined to have her own way, Mary became involved in a series of scandalous love affairs and in increasingly violent confrontations with the Scottish nobles and with the Calvinistic spirit of John Knox. Finally forced to seek asylum across the border in England, the former

queen of France, now deposed queen of Scotland, became the Catholic candidate to replace Queen Elizabeth on the English throne.

Elizabeth prudently had her cousin taken into custody. Supported by Philip of Spain, Catholic militants spawned a series of conspiracies that looked increasingly dangerous. And when Elizabeth was at last prevailed on to order Mary's execution, Philip responded by dispatching the "Invincible Armada" of 1588 against England. This immense force, 130 ships and 25,000 men, was intended to link up with a Catholic rebellion that never materialized and to destroy the greatest Protestant state in Europe. The queen, however, rallied her people, while her most skilled naval commander, Sir Francis Drake (c. 1540–1596), harried the Armada up the English Channel. The English weather did the rest as thunderous seas and a screaming "Protestant wind" sunk a third of the Spanish galleons and sent the rest limping home in defeat.

Besides preserving England from the ravages of foreign wars, Elizabeth presided over a half-century of increasing prosperity. The gentry of Elizabethan

Queen Elizabeth I is shown here surrounded by symbols of her power. Note the crown to her right, the globe under her hand, and the pictorial representation of her naval strength on the wall behind her.

England were serious farmers. They also benefited from a century-long inflation that raised the prices they got for their grain or wool. In addition, members of England's landed aristocracy were quicker than their counterparts on the continent to invest in commercial ventures, thus profiting from the mercantile side of the economy as well.

For the Elizabethan Age saw not only England's rise to naval prominence, but the beginnings of its great commercial outreach. Merchant companies were chartered to trade with the Baltic countries and Russia to the northeast, and with the countries of the Mediterranean and the Levant to the southeast. English fishermen thronged across the North Atlantic to the Newfoundland banks, and salt fish joined woolens as a major export to Europe. English privateersmen like Drake, equipped with licenses to steal from the queen's enemies, seized Spanish merchantmen and raided the coastal cities and islands of Spain and its enormous New World holdings, including Mexico, the Caribbean, and most of South America. England founded no successful overseas colonies of its own in the sixteenth century. But Elizabeth's knighting of Sir Francis Drake on the deck of the *Golden Hind,* in which he had sailed around the world—raiding Spanish colonies all the way—had a symbolic meaning. For the island kingdom would soon begin to build the largest world empire in history.

When Queen Elizabeth died in 1603, her ministers quickly bundled her cousin James VI down from Scotland to take her place on the throne. James, however, lacked her gifts; and as things rapidly came apart in the new century, the hawk-faced old woman in her jeweled gowns quickly became Good Queen Bess, her reign a golden age in the collective memory of her people.

Charles V and the Habsburg Predominance

The house of Habsburg, which governed the largest, most prestigious, and most powerful realms on the continent in the 1500s, also had to bear the brunt of much of the violence of the war-torn Reformation century. The Protestant Reformation began in the Habsburg Holy Roman Empire, and Habsburg Spain soon became the militant champion of the Catholic Reformation. The Habsburgs also ruled the Netherlands, site of one of the most terrible of the wars of religion. Yet despite these and other draining struggles, Charles V's reign in the first half of the century was the high point of Habsburg predominance, while the reign of Philip II in Spain was the climax of that nation's "golden century."

Charles V (r. 1519–1556), Henry VIII's somewhat younger contemporary, was no "bluff prince" like Henry. Small and thin, with a long bony face and sad eyes, Charles had the jutting lower jaw that distinguishes Habsburg portraits from the thirteenth century to the twentieth. Grandson of the knightly emperor Maximilian I and Mary of Burgundy, the heir of Habsburg power over much of Europe was raised in the Netherlands. He inherited the Low Countries in 1506, Spain in 1516, and finally secured election as Holy Roman emperor in 1519—all before he was twenty years old. To this devout, hard-working, duty-bound little man fell the task of governing the largest empire any European prince had ruled since Charlemagne.

In Spain, which proved to be the real power center of the Habsburg domains in the sixteenth century, Charles faced his first great problem: the revolt of the *comuneros.* Arriving in the kingdom he had inherited from Ferdinand and Isabella at the age of sixteen, the new king depended on his retinue from the Netherlands to govern Spain. In so doing, he triggered a widespread revolt of Spanish townsmen, or *comuneros* (members of communes, or incorporated towns), supported at first by much of the Spanish nobility. Beginning as a rebellion against foreign rule and the extension of royal power generally, the *comuneros'* revolt was transformed when the townsmen demanded social reforms as well, particularly challenging the traditional preeminence of the landed aristocracy. The outraged Spanish nobility thereupon turned on their former allies and crushed the *comuneros* themselves.

In response to this revolutionary challenge, Charles and his chief Spanish adviser, the industrious Francisco de los Cobos (d. 1547), constructed an administrative system of unrivaled size and complexity from the Habsburgs' Spanish realms. A central Council of State was established for Spain, the Aragonese holdings in southern Italy, and Spain's growing American colonies. Subsidiary councils, originally developed by Ferdinand and Isabella, were organized into a dual system, some by function—treasury, war, religion—and some by region, including Castile, Aragon, southern Italy, Spanish America, and later the Netherlands. Royal viceroys governed these and other areas in the king's name.[11] After the

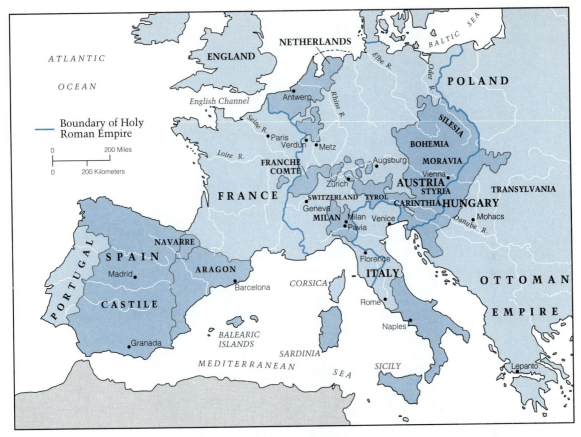

Map 14.3 Empire of Charles V (excluding American colonies)

comuneros' revolt, Charles was careful to staff his government in Spain and its dependencies with Spaniards. Townsmen dominated the councils; nobles filled the viceroyalties.

This administrative structure was riddled with corruption and sometimes nearly paralyzed by delays, caused partly by bureaucratic inefficiency and partly by the slowness of communications in early modern times. But this centralized government gave Charles and his successors real if creaky power in Spain and helped to make Spain the cornerstone of the Habsburg predominance in Europe. It was certainly the most complex and impressive governmental structure in the Renaissance world.

The Holy Roman Empire, the other epicenter of Habsburg interests, was by contrast hopelessly divided and normally out of control, as it had been since its failure to evolve into a nation-state in the

Middle Ages. In the first half of the sixteenth century, this sprawling German empire was torn by a much longer revolt than that of the *comuneros*: the struggle of the Lutheran princes and cities against their Catholic counterparts, and against the Catholic emperor himself.

The German states of the Holy Roman Empire—"the Germanies" as they were sometimes called—included thousands of imperial knights, who held their individual estates directly from the emperor; scores of princes, secular and ecclesiastical; dozens of free cities bound by charter to the crown, and many other noblemen and churchmen. What unifying institutions there were for this medieval agglomeration of territories, including the imperial diet, or assembly, and an imperial council, were controlled by the German princes rather than by the emperor.

Within this feeble political structure, the Lutheran heresy had spread rapidly from one au-

Charles V, founder of the Europe-wide preeminence of the house of Habsburg, was the most powerful ruler in the Western world in the first half of the sixteenth century. The serious-minded Charles ruled the German states, Spain, the Netherlands, parts of Italy and a huge empire in the New World. [Titian. *Charles V*]

tonomous principality and free city to another across north Germany. Luther's Ninety-Five Theses were promulgated two years before Charles V's accession to the imperial throne, and soon thereafter the Knights' War, the Peasants' War, and waves of some-times violent Anabaptist agitation shattered the peace of the Empire. Some Lutherans, led by Luther's moderate-minded lieutenant, Philip Melanchthon (1497–1560), sought reconciliation with both the emperor and the pope. Thus Melanchthon's *Augsburg Confession* of 1530, a statement of Lutheran faith, avoided controversial

theological issues and urged, not secession from the Roman church, but reform of the church as a whole. When Charles V rejected the document out of hand, however, the German princes of the north organized the *League of Schmalkald* in 1531 to defend their interests and their new religion by force.

Charles V's long struggle with Francis I of France—discussed later—and his wars with the Turks prevented him from taking any decisive action against the Protestants for a decade and a half. In 1547, however, imperial armies defeated the Schmalkaldic League in the great Battle of Mühlberg. The emperor's subsequent efforts to impose a Catholic settlement on the Protestant principalities failed, however, despite the best efforts of Melanchthon and equally moderate Catholic prelates to work out a compromise formulation. And in the early 1550s, the Schmalkaldic League reorganized, formed a key alliance with the king of France, and turned the tables on the emperor. Defeated and nearly captured himself, the aging Habsburg ruler finally signed the Peace of Augsburg in 1555. This historic document accepted the right of Protestantism to exist in the Holy Roman Empire, allowed each prince to choose the faith of his own principality *(cuius regio eius religio)*, and recognized the privilege of dissenting subjects to emigrate to another German state in which their creed was the law of the land.

Church bells rang out across north Germany in 1555, hailing the Peace of Augsburg as a victory for Lutheranism and the rights of princes against their emperor. In 1556 Charles V formally resigned all his titles and retired to a monastery in Spain, seeking the peace of soul he had never found in this world.

Philip II and the Greatness of Spain

At the time of his abdication, Charles V divided his vast realms into two parts, surrendering the Holy Roman Empire to his brother Ferdinand, and Spain, southern Italy, the Netherlands, and the New World to his son Philip. Philip II (r. 1556–1598), ruler of the greatest chunk of Habsburg territories, eventually carried the struggle his father had begun against Protestantism into the larger, Europe-wide arena. Once more, however, our focus here is on the domestic affairs of this much maligned king of Spain.

The standard anecdote about the dour Spanish monarch is that he only laughed once in his life—when he heard the news of the massacre of the French Huguenots on St. Bartholomew's Day in 1572. He figures most prominently in histories of the English-

The St. Bartholomew's Day massacre in France in 1572 shows the fanaticism of the Wars of Religion at its worst. Which do you think would be more terrifying to face—official persecution or the hatred of your neighbors?

speaking world as the king who dispatched the Invincible Armada to its doom at the hands of Queen Elizabeth's seamen and the "Protestant wind." In Spanish historiography, by contrast, he is one of the greatest monarchs of Spain's golden century: pious, patriotic, hard-working, dedicated to the job of kingship. With his father's slight build and melancholy temperament intensified by a personal history that included the deaths of many of those he loved, Philip had none of Elizabeth's flair for public relations. But he was a devout Catholic and a natural autocrat, in the tradition of Charles V and the "Catholic kings" before him. His piety led him to pour the blood and treasure of Spain into the religious wars triggered by the Reformation. His autocratic temper compelled him to read and annotate every document and diplomatic report that flowed into Madrid, to decide everything and order everything himself.

Working within the system of government inherited from his predecessors, Philip expanded the Spanish structure of councils and viceroyalties. Noble influence, however, declined, as did that of the various Cortes of Castile, Aragon, and other parts of Spain. In place of these traditional authorities, Philip depended on powerful royal secretaries, typically commoners by birth. These included the small group of industrious advisers popularly called the *junta de noche,* the "night council," who labored away in the palace to advance the king's interests. To staff the sprawling administration inherited from Charles V, Philip turned to university-trained *legados,* officials with legal expertise, who imposed some order on the vast system. Castile, by far the largest, most populous, and wealthiest part of the kingdom, also dominated the government, providing most of its personnel.

Philip II had his victories as well as his defeats. In 1571 his fleets triumphed over those of the Ottoman Turks at Lepanto and temporarily swept the Mediterranean of Muslim raiders. In 1580 Philip seized the small neighboring kingdom of Portugal and its great spice-trading empire in the Far East. In 1591, when Aragon rebelled against the favoritism shown Castile, the revolt was summarily suppressed. Thus the defeat of his Armada in 1588 was a blow, but not a fatal one, to Philip of Spain.

Two major economic problems confronted the king throughout his reign: a massive indebtedness rooted in his endless wars, and the persistent inflation caused by bullion imports from the Americas. The wars and other expenses drained the nation even more rapidly than its vast resources could replenish

it. Owing huge amounts to German and Italian bankers, Philip was three times reduced to declaring the Spanish government bankrupt. More broadly disturbing was the century-long inflation that multiplied prices in Spain four times over. Prices rose for the classic monetarist reason: huge annual imports of silver and gold bullion from Spain's American colonies put too much coinage into circulation without a commensurate increase in production of goods. Too much money chasing too few goods produced a steady rise in prices. Merchants and landowners both profited as the prices they got for what they had to sell went up, while consumers, particularly the poor, suffered.

In the shorter run, however, Spain seemed to be flourishing. Profits from exports of wine and oil, the wool of the high plateau, iron from the north, and Toledo steel for weapons all advanced. Loot from the Aztec and Inca empires, gold and silver from the mines of Mexico and Bolivia, flooded into Spain. But Spanish grandees, unlike the English gentry, had an aristocratic contempt for trade; and Spanish merchants tended to quit business as soon as they had accumulated enough money to buy land and set up as grandees themselves. Foreign merchants, artisans, and bankers thus rapidly took over the Spanish market, providing luxury goods for a ruling class too haughty to provide for itself. And though Philip continued to accumulate wealth through taxes, royal monopolies, and the "royal fifth" he took of all New World treasure, he also continued to spend it in military campaigns against enemies of his country or his church.

Francis I and the French Monarchy

Francis I (r. 1515–1547), the gallant Valois king of France during the first half of the sixteenth century, was a lavish patron of Renaissance art, a lover of tournaments and battles, and a womanizer with a string of beautiful mistresses. Like his contemporary Henry VIII, Francis reveled in Renaissance enjoyment of all the royal pleasures.

Inheriting the refurbished French government of Louis XI, with regular taxation and even a standing army—fifteen thousand men ready for duty every summer, the campaigning season—Francis himself made only modest contributions to the institutional growth of the French monarchy. He did increase the number of civil servants, streamline the treasury, and develop a small council of affairs through which he could govern more directly than through the over-sized grand council he inherited. He also established royal supremacy over the French church through the Concordat of Bologna (1516), an agreement with Pope Leo X giving the French crown the right to appoint bishops and abbots and to enjoy a share of church revenues. Most of Francis's contributions, however, were informal ones, matters of style and expediency rather than reorganization.

Thus, for instance, Francis bound the French nobility to him by heaping provincial governorships, pensions, and other rewards on them and by being a chivalrous comrade-in-arms to France's old "nobility of the sword." He also transformed the sale of government offices from an occasional expedient to a fixed and profitable policy, thus both enhancing royal revenues and opening places in the nation's "nobility of the robe"—especially judgeships—to wealthy bourgeois citizens. He cannily finessed possible challenges to royal power from the French estates general by simply not calling it into session. With the *taille*, or hearth tax, the salt tax, and other revenues his by right, the fortunate Valois ruler, unlike the Tudors across the Channel, had no need to convene representatives of the ruling classes to demand financial appropriations.

The land was large, populous, and generally prosperous through most of Francis's reign, surviving even the immense cost of his Italian wars and his long feud with Emperor Charles V. Inflation did, however, seep across the Pyrenees from Spain, benefiting those with something to sell but hurting the laboring and artisan classes. The burden of taxation also discriminated, falling heavily on peasants and urban craftspeople, while the church, the nobility, and many of the towns enjoyed immunity from taxes.

Francis I of France, a much more colorful and romantic figure than Charles V, fought a long series of wars with Charles to prevent Habsburg encirclement from crushing France. [Jean Clouet. *Francis I of France.* Louvre Museum, Paris, France]

Even in Renaissance France, finally, the divisive impact of the Reformation intruded. In the 1530s and 1540s, the easygoing, intellectually tolerant King Francis allowed the heresy hunters at the Sorbonne to burn Protestant books, execute some Lutherans and Calvinists, and harry many more into exile. If the Habsburg-Valois wars were the central problem of the reign, the rise of Reformation animosities pointed to a more terrible internal struggle to come.

Ivan the Terrible and the Growth of Russian Autocracy

Richard Chancellor (d. 1556), the Elizabethan traveler who visited Russia about the middle of the sixteenth century, did his best to be impressed. He noted the many villages and many famous rivers, like the Volga, and wrote that in Moscow the czar had "a fair Castle, the walls whereof are of brick." Grain and fish, furs and hides were brought to the capital on sleds. But he had to admit that Moscow was "very rude, and standeth without all order," the streets unpaved, the houses low and built of wood, with narrow windows, liable to fire. "I will not stand in description of their buildings," he averred, "because we have better in all points in England."[12]

The isolation and relative backwardness of Russia were still striking in the later sixteenth century, the period of the reign of Ivan IV the Terrible (r. 1547–1584). Ivan's nickname has become a joke—"the Dread" or "Dreaded" is a better translation of *Groznyi*—and his black-robed *oprichniki* guards galloping across the land may sound a bit like a sword-and-sorcery romance. But Ivan, tormented, talented, pious, brutal, and perhaps psychotic, was no joke to contemporaries. And the terror of the *oprichniki*, late in his reign, was all too real.

The most powerful Russian ruler before Peter the Great and Joseph Stalin, Ivan IV came to a hapless throne at the age of three. The result was a traumatic childhood, scarred by bullying, thieving Russian princes and boyars—the ancient independent nobility of Russia—and by the death of his mother, perhaps poisoned, as she struggled to hold his throne for him. Taught and guided thereafter by Metropolitan Makarios (1482–1583), the head of the Russian Orthodox church, Ivan grew up pious, profoundly insecure, determined to crush the boyar nobles and to impose his own absolute rule on the frighteningly chaotic world of his early years.

Ivan's first concern after his coronation as czar at age sixteen, however, was with military conquest and with extending the lands of Muscovy. To the east, he did succeed in pushing down the Volga to the Caspian Sea, defeating the remnants of the Mongols and conquering the khanates of Kazan and Astrakhan. To the west, however, his long campaigns in the Baltic area were frustrated by the power of Poland and Sweden, both strong enough in early modern times to hold the embryonic Muscovite state in check.

It was as a builder of Russian autocracy, however, that Ivan IV carved out his niche in history. Guided by a small group of friends and advisers, the czar imposed a new code of laws on Muscovy as a whole. In 1549 he convened the first *zemsky sobor*, or "assembly of the land," bringing together boyars, bishops, and royal officials, not to advise but to carry out their ruler's will. Like his western European contemporaries, he tried to expand his still modest bureaucracy and forged a small standing army, the musket-armed *streltsy* ("shooters").

More important, his reign saw an acceleration of the process of bringing Russia's princes, boyars, and peasants under more rigorous control. By Ivan's time, all rival princely houses were gone, and the princes of his own blood had definitively lost the right to a share of the family domains. The boyars, denied the right to change overlords by the elimination of other rulers, were also at least nominally the czar's men. In addition, Ivan expanded the system of *pomestie*, or military fiefs, granted to noblemen in exchange for direct service to the crown. The peasant masses of Russia, finally, came under stricter overlordship as Ivan issued an edict forbidding the formerly free peasantry from leaving the estates of their royal or noble masters except during a brief period each year. This limitation was an important step in the growth of serfdom in Russia, an institution that had all but disappeared in western Europe by this time.

The czar's campaign against the boyars reached its climax in the violent period dominated by the *oprichniki* (1565–1572). Created to deal with alleged traitors and with other anticzarist elements, the *oprichniki* have been compared to the political police of modern authoritarian states. In fact, they were members of a unique institution that could have existed only in the still medieval Russia of early modern times. Headquartered at a monastery east of Moscow, they were a special order of armed black-robed royal agents who were given absolute control over the central and northern half of the country. Alternating periods of ecstatic religious devotions with wild orgies, the *oprichniki* were then turned loose on the country where they executed and expropriated the property of boyars and even looted whole cities as punishment for suspected disloyalty. Only after seven years of this reign of terror was the organization disbanded, leaving the ancient boyar aristocracy shattered—for the time at least.

Ivan's last years were filled with capricious cruelty and periods of mental imbalance. His first wife, Anastasia Romanovna (d. 1560), was a woman of character and beauty who restrained some of his worst impulses for many years. After her death, however, he remarried several times, lashed out violently at those around him, killing his own son and striking down others he saw as threats. When he died in 1584, he left Russia filled with discontent and simmering rebellion. But he had also added to the Russian experience of authoritarian government that began with Byzantine and Mongol influences and would continue down to the twentieth century.

The Wars of Religion

The sixteenth century, a time of powerful rulers and consuming religious passions, was also one of the most war-torn centuries. International wars and internal rebellions, many of them rendered more violent by sectarian religious clashes, challenged the best efforts of Europe's rulers. Yet the ambitions and rivalries of monarchs themselves also caused conflict, as did resistance to royal authority by those who saw it as tyranny. Riven by the Habsburg-Valois wars during the first half of the century and the wars of religion in the second half, torn by revolutions and spattered with massacres, the age of Michelangelo and Shakespeare was also perhaps the bloodiest of Western centuries before our own.

The Habsburg-Valois Wars

The central strand of European international relations between the 1490s and the 1550s was the chain of conflict that began with the struggle for Italy and evolved into the prolonged Habsburg-Valois wars. This archetypal dynastic conflict pitted the strengthened monarchies of France and Habsburg Spain against each other, frequently over the wealth of Renaissance Italy.

Both powers had what their rulers regarded as perfectly legitimate claims on major portions of Italy. The house of Aragon, fused with that of Castile in the Spanish monarchy, had ruled parts of Sicily and Naples—the southern half of Italy—since the fourteenth century. In 1494 Charles VIII (r. 1483–1498), the Valois king of France, led a large professional army across the Alps and temporarily occupied Milan, Florence, and Naples, thus vigorously asserting the French right to intervene in the affairs of the peninsula. His successor Louis XII (r. 1498–1515) also intervened in the south, and Spanish and German soldiers were soon fighting there as well.

Italy was the wealthiest and most cultured part of Europe in 1500; but its mercenary companies and city militias proved no match for the large royal armies that were soon marching up and down the peninsula. These armies of the north, on the other hand, had each other to fight as well as the Italians, and they were decimated by disease, desertion, and the great cost of foreign campaigns. Triumphs like Francis I's victory at Marignano in 1515 proved hollow, in the long run leaving the French king's claims no more solid than they had been.

As the sixteenth century advanced, however, the struggle simplified to a basic conflict between the Valois and Habsburg dynasties and shifted north of the Alps, to focus on the virtual Habsburg encirclement of France. This great strategic advantage accrued to the Habsburgs as Charles V first inherited the Netherlands, then the Spanish throne with its claims in Italy, and finally won election to the throne of the Holy Roman Empire in 1519. Threatened by Habsburg power looking down at him from the Pyrenees, the Alps, and across the Low Countries and the Rhineland from Germany, Francis I fought back with more energy than his pleasure-loving image suggested. His worst setback came when he was defeated and captured by Charles V at Pavia in 1525. In the 1540s, Henry VIII, intermittently allied with the emperor, invaded and ravaged large tracts of French territory, while in 1544 Charles's own troops advanced to within 50 miles of Paris. But Francis hung on and in the end preserved the territorial integrity of France despite all Charles V and his allies could do.

The long struggle finally came to an end in the 1550s, when both Francis and Charles were in their graves and their sons, Henry II of France and Philip

II of Spain, had finally wearied of the wars. By the Treaty of Cateau-Cambrésis of 1559, France abandoned Italy to Habsburg Spanish domination, while the French kept claims on key Rhineland outposts, including Metz and Verdun. The Medici and other powerful dynasties also acquired title to new territories in northern Italy.

It was not much for either side after more than sixty years of intermittent struggle. But there was worse to come as the great wars of religion broke over Europe in the 1560s.

The Reformation Wars

Religion and politics made a potent mix in the Age of the Reformation. For sixteenth-century Christians, as we have seen, religious faith was not a matter of opinion but of truth and falsehood; each side was absolutely certain it was right. Protestant and Catholic forces each believed they alone were the legions of the Lord and that their opponents had enlisted under the banner of Satan. The most costly consequences of this revival of the medieval crusading spirit were the waves of religious warfare that began in Luther's day and continued for more than a century.

In the broadest sense, the *wars of religion* encompassed three great waves of religious conflict. A series of relatively small and scattered struggles occurred during the first half of the sixteenth century, including the wars of the Schmalkaldic League in the German states, conflicts between Swiss cantons, and others. In the second half of that century came the great wars of religion in France and the Netherlands and the naval war between Elizabethan England and Philip II's Spain. During the first half of the seventeenth century, finally, religious differences contributed to both the Thirty Years' War on the continent and to England's Civil War. In the remaining sections of this chapter we will concentrate on the bloodiest of these contests, the revolutions in the Netherlands and France in the later sixteenth century. We begin, however, with a few generalizations about all these encounters.

All involved bitter propaganda campaigns, each side condemning the other as heretical and immoral enemies of the true faith. In these wars of words and images, the recently invented printing press played a key role. Religious arguments, suitably simplified, became for the first time accessible to millions through crudely printed tracts and pamphlets, illustrated with woodcut drawings depicting the pope as Antichrist or Luther as a limb of Satan. It was a true struggle for the hearts and minds of the West.

Another feature of the religious conflicts of the Reformation period was the fact that they were frequently civil wars. The Holy Roman Empire, France, the Netherlands, and England were all torn by sectarian strife at one time or another during this century and a half. Nations, towns and villages, even families were thus divided against themselves by religious differences.

International wars between the great powers also figured importantly, however. Neither Philip II nor Queen Elizabeth hesitated to intervene in the civil wars of France or the Netherlands in support of co-religionists. Soon, as we have seen, England and Spain themselves were engaged in sporadic warfare that reached to Spain's overseas colonies and raged up the English Channel and across the Atlantic. In the next century, the Thirty Years' War, which began with a Protestant revolt in Bohemia, soon came to involve virtually all the great powers of Europe.

In all these cases, finally, religious motives were thoroughly mixed with other, more material concerns. Economic and social factors triggered peasant rebellions that took the color of religious revolts. A desire for pillage could inspire such disparate crusaders as Philip II in the Netherlands and the Elizabethan privateers on the high seas. Political rivalries between ambitious dynasts were also often important, as in the French wars of religion, while particularist politics drove the German princes into the wars of the Schmalkaldic League.

This combination of creeds in conflict with more material interests, of propaganda, revolution, and big-power rivalries recurred in various forms throughout modern history. A closer look at these first modern wars of the true believers thus provides a useful foundation for much of what is to come.

The French Wars of Religion

The religious wars in France (1562–1598) were an immensely complicated sequence of civil struggles involving six or seven wars separated by ineffectual truces, four feuding factions ranging from radical Protestant to reactionary Catholic, three French kings, and two generations of leaders. Simplified, these wars were a struggle between Huguenots and Ultra-Catholics. The Ultra-Catholic faction included most of the peasantry, a large part of the urban masses, and probably a majority of the higher nobility, led by the ambitious house of Guise. The Calvinist Huguenots included many bourgeois citizens and a growing portion of the nobility, and were led by the Bourbon dynasty of Navarre, destined to rule France itself for the next two centuries. In between, the rapidly declining royal house of Valois struggled to survive: three feeble kings in succession guided by the strong-willed queen mother, Catherine de Médicis (1519–1589). In its later phases, finally, the civil struggle was exacerbated by the intervention of Philip II on the Ultra-Catholic side and Elizabeth I in support of the Huguenots.

The long civil and religious crisis began to take shape when King Henry II (r. 1547–1559) was killed by a splintered lance in a tournament held to celebrate the Treaty of Cateau-Cambrésis. He left three sons to succeed him: Francis II (r. 1559–1560), a fifteen-year-old who was carried off by illness in a year and a half; Charles IX (r. 1560–1574), a nervous, sickly nine-year-old who died within five years; and Henry III (r. 1574–1589), twenty-three, strong and quick witted, but politically foolish and dissolute even for those times, shocking Catholic and Calvinist alike. To hold the monarchy together through such hopeless reigns became the lifework of their mother, Catherine de Médicis.

A daughter of the great Medici family of Florence, Catherine was a vigorous and intelligent woman and a determined dynast. A foreigner—"the Italian shopkeeper's daughter"—in France and largely excluded from influence during Henry II's life by his powerful mistress Diane de Poitiers (1499–1566), Catherine played a central role in French history during the reigns of her sons. Surrounded by men as ambitious as she was, she was nevertheless all that stood between the crumbling French nation and total collapse.

The Huguenots had hoped for some remission in the persecutions ordered by Francis I, and Catherine in fact issued edicts of toleration in the early 1560s. In 1562, however, François, duke of Guise (1519–1563), after escaping a Bourbon plot, slaughtered a Protestant congregation at Vassy, and the Huguenots sprang to arms. The civil war Catherine had tried to avoid thus broke out; it lasted, with intervening truces, for thirty-five years.

Ambushes and sieges, pitched battles, mob violence, and massacres marked the bloody course of the conflict. Churches were burned on both sides, lands denuded, private scores settled, and personal ambitions advanced in the name of religion. The leaders of the first generation, including the duke of Guise who had initiated the struggle and the militant Huguenot leader Admiral Gaspar de Coligny (1519–1572), were killed in battle or assassinated. The most notorious atrocity of the French wars of religion was the *St. Bartholomew's Day Massacre* in 1572. This horror took place when Queen Catherine, fearing Admiral Coligny's growing influence on young Charles IX, sanctioned a plot by Henry the new duke of Guise (1550–1588) to murder Coligny. The assault soon expanded to include more Huguenot leaders, and mobs began killing Protestants indiscriminately, some three thousand in Paris and several times that in the provinces. The pope had a mass of thanksgiving sung in Rome, and according to the legend, Philip II of Spain laughed.

The seemingly endless bloodshed reached a garish climax in the 1580s War of the Three Henrys. The three were Henry III, the last of the Valois line and unlikely to produce any heirs; Duke Henry of Guise, architect of the St. Bartholomew's Day Massacre and organizer of a nationwide Catholic League against Protestantism; and the knightly, debonair young Henry of Navarre, leader of the militant Huguenot faction after Coligny's death. As heir of the princely Bourbon family, Navarre was also next in line of succession should the Valois dynasty become extinct. In a tangle of shifting alliances and escalating bloodshed, Duke Henry of Guise was murdered at the king's order, Henry III was assassinated by an Ultra-Catholic Dominican monk, and Henry of Navarre declared himself King Henry IV (r. 1589–1610). But when Henry IV learned that Paris, the heavily Catholic capital city of France, would never open its gates to a Protestant ruler, the Huguenot leader abandoned his faith in return for the submission of his new capital. "Paris," he is reputed to have declared, "is worth a Mass."

If Protestants were disturbed by Henry's casual renunciation of his faith, Catholics were soon outraged when the new king issued the Edict of Nantes (1598). This royal dispensation granted the Huguenots religious toleration, civil liberties, and the right to retain their arms and garrison a number of cities for their protection. The religious question flared up again, and Henry IV himself in the end died by violence. But the great wars of religion were over in France after more than three decades of death and destruction.

The Dutch Revolt

The Dutch Revolt (1568–1609) bathed the plush and comfortable Netherlands in blood for more than forty years. And like the French wars of religion, the revolt of the Netherlanders against their Spanish overlords ended without satisfying true believers on either side.

Besides religion, the clash in the Low Countries involved the great wealth of the Dutch and Flemish cities and the local patriotism of their citizens. Mobilized against the increasingly Calvinistic Netherlands were the professional armies of Philip II, their legal ruler who had inherited this portion of the Habsburg domains, along with Spain, from Charles V. Philip, desperate for funds to support his many crusades, tried to squeeze more taxes out of the commercial and industrial cities of his Netherlands provinces. In so doing, he ignored or rode roughshod over the local power structure of these seventeen separate city-states: the elected councils and magistrates of the cities, the respected nobility of the countryside, and the estates general that loosely bound the seventeen states together. As a champion of the Catholic Reformation, Philip also sought to wipe out the Lutheran, Anabaptist, and particularly the new wave of Calvinist heresy spreading rapidly through the Low Countries in the 1560s. A regency council under his sister, Margaret of Parma

(1522–1586), was established to collect the king's taxes. The Inquisition went in to destroy the Calvinist "field preachers," or open-air evangelists. And when he was confronted by a vigorous defense of local liberties led by the nobles, when destructive iconoclastic attacks were mounted on Catholic churches, Philip sent in a Spanish army under the veteran duke of Alva (1507–1582) to maintain order and royal authority in the Netherlands.

Alva, who had fought in the Habsburg-Valois wars and who subsequently seized Portugal for his king, seemed the ideal man to suppress unrest in the Low Countries. He replaced Margaret of Parma's regency with a rigorous council of his own—soon dubbed the Council of Blood by the Netherlanders—and executed thousands for refusing to abide by his decrees. His victims included not only Anabaptists and other Protestants from the lower orders of society, but also leading citizens like the counts of Egmont (1522–1568) and Horn (c. 1524–1568). When Dutch and Flemish nobles petitioned for their rights, Alva dismissed the petitioners as "beggars," a nickname they wore proudly for the rest of the war. In the end, Alva was summoned back to Spain in disgrace, while the revolt raged on.

The Protestant revolt, by condemning the effigies in Catholic churches as "idols," encouraged acts of vandalism like this attack on a church during the Dutch revolt against Catholic Spain. Can you see men breaking stained-glass windows and pulling down statues?

Over four decades, four famous generals in succession were sent out to crush the insurrection. The rebels found a leader in William of Orange (1533–1584), a nobleman widely admired for his wise counsel, who was made stadtholder, or chief magistrate, of the Netherlands in 1580. The Spanish regiments, veterans of many wars and reputed to be the best soldiers of Europe, won almost every battle. But the rebels developed a potent naval arm in the "sea beggars," merchant sea captains turned privateers, who cut the Spanish supply lines by sea and attacked ports held by royal troops.

Violence, inflamed by religious passions on both sides, grew more and more savage. Catholic churches were vandalized by image-breaking mobs, monasteries and convents stripped and closed, bishops imprisoned, priests murdered. To kill a Spaniard, Calvinist preachers told their congregations, was no sin; for the rough-and-ready sea beggars, to kill a priest was half a joke and half a pious act. On the other side, hundreds of Protestants were burned by the Inquisition or executed as traitors by Alva and his successors, while Spanish armies burned and looted the wealthy cities of the Netherlands. The terrible "day of the Spanish fury" at Antwerp, one of the greatest financial and commercial metropolises in Europe, was vividly described by a Protestant source:

> They neither spared age nor fortune . . . person nor country; young nor old; rich nor poor. . . . They slew great numbers of young children. . . . Within three days Antwerp, which was one of the richest towns in Europe, had now no money nor treasure to be found therein, but only in the hands of murderers and strumpets; for every Don Diego must walk jetting up and down the streets with his harlot by him in her chain and bracelet of gold.[13]

On a Sunday in 1584, a Catholic assassin shot William of Orange dead in his own garden; a Protestant multitude watched approvingly while the assassin was publicly tortured to death with red-hot pincers and nearly lynched a woman who was sickened by the spectacle.

The outcome, again, was less a clear-cut victory than a compromise solution. In 1579 the ten southern provinces, where Catholicism was still strong, signed the Treaty of Arras, withdrawing from the rebellion and accepting Spanish protection of their religion against the zealots from the north. The seven northern provinces fought on, finding new leadership in Johan van Oldenbarneveldt (1547–1619). In the 1580s, Queen Elizabeth dispatched modest military aid, and in 1588 a Spanish plan to use troops from the Netherlands under Alexander Farnese (1545–1592), duke of Parma, to invade England was frustrated by the defeat of the Spanish Armada. At an international peace conference in 1609, Oldenbarneveldt won a truce that provisionally recognized the independence of the United (Northern) Netherlands "for purposes of negotiation." Despite renewed fighting in the Thirty Years' War, this became essentially the final settlement. The predominantly Catholic southern states became the Spanish Netherlands, later Belgium. The Protestant northern states emerged as the Dutch Republic—the republic of Rembrandt, the Netherlands of today.

The Birth of Toleration

Somehow, out of this welter of wars and revolutions, persecution and martyrdom, the modest beginnings of modern religious toleration began to appear. This complex shift in the modern religious mind has been attributed to a variety of factors.

The official position of Protestants and Catholics alike during the Reformation was that expressed by the Calvinist leader Theodore Beza (1519–1605): religious freedom was "a most diabolical dogma because it means that everyone should be left to go to hell in his own way."[14] Bitter disputes therefore continued about the right way to salvation, not only between Catholics and Protestants, but within both camps, dividing Jesuits from other Catholic orders, Lutherans from Calvinists, and disputatious theologians within each sect from each other. Meanwhile, religious warfare and persecution also went on, ravaging western Europe.

As early as the middle of the sixteenth century, some few had objected on purely religious grounds to religious persecution. Could God really want such numbers of his creatures to suffer simply because they did not understand his Word properly? Thus Sebastian Castellio (1515–1563) wrote in the 1550s:

> When scourged, spat upon, mocked, crowned with thorns, and crucified shamefully. . . . Thou didst pray for them who did Thee this wrong. . . . [D]ost Thou now

command that those who do not understand Thy precepts . . . be drowned in water, cut with lashes to the entrails, sprinkled
with salt, dismembered with the sword,
burned at a slow fire, and otherwise tortured? Dost Thou, O Christ, command and
approve of these things?[15]

An ancient and powerful current of Christian
opposition to persecution on dogmatic grounds
came from the mystical strain in Christianity. Religious mystics, after all, rooted their faith less in doctrine and dogma than in visionary experience, in direct, often powerfully emotional contact with the
Godhead. Among mystic Catholic saints, visionary
Anabaptists, or Quaker followers of the Inner Light,
religious experience was ineffable—unstatable in
words—so that persecution over differing dogmatic
formulations made little sense.

Outside the religious realm altogether, meanwhile, cosmopolitanism and skepticism began to
emerge as challengers to both doctrinaire religion
and intolerance in its name. Renaissance humanists
had already detected much good in the pagan
philosophers of pre-Christian Greece and Rome, and
such daring spirits among them as Pico della Mirandola had begun to seek truth even in Jewish and
Muslim sources. This cosmopolitan openness even to
non-Christian creeds would not find a significant following in the West until the eighteenth-century
Enlightenment. But it was reinforced, as the sixteenth century advanced, by some degree of familiarity with the very different cultures of Asia and the
Americas. The most celebrated skeptic of the age,
Michel de Montaigne, adopted as his symbol a pair
of evenly balanced scales and the motto, "What do I
know?" Neither people who saw truth in many
creeds nor those who were skeptical about any certain truth could approve of persecuting others for
their beliefs.

Meanwhile, a few politicians began to oppose
religious conflict and repression on purely practical
grounds. The nations were being laid waste, loyal
subjects driven into rebellion, all over religious differences. In the later decades of the century, some
European rulers began to reject policies that produced neither peace nor victory, but only martyrs
(who would not abandon their religious convictions)
and hypocrites (who would only pretend to). Queen
Elizabeth remained a staunch Protestant but tended
to shrug off most controversial doctrines as
"nonessentials" and insisted she would "make no
windows into men's souls" to check on their beliefs.
In France, a faction called *politiques* remained good
Catholics but put the national recovery of their
country first, substituting a political faith in absolute
monarchy for religion as a means of holding the nation together. The Protestant queen of Navarre,
Jeanne d'Albret, issued an edict on freedom of religion as early as 1564. By the end of the century,
many who had wearied of crusades that settled nothing and repression that failed were coming to share
her point of view.

In the seventeenth century, finally, new currents
of ideas, notably the beginning of modern secularism, further advanced the slow process of tamping
down the fires of sectarian enthusiasm that had raged
across Europe for a hundred years. Reflective minds
simply turned to other subjects besides theology.
The scientific revolution, for instance, was advancing
to its climax in the work of Newton. A new interest
in political theory was stimulated by royal absolutism
and the rise of constitutionalism. Modern philosophy
took its beginnings in the 1600s in the thought of
Bacon and Descartes. Religious bigotry still lived,
but Western peoples, weary of religious bloodletting,
grew increasingly willing to let their neighbors follow Christ as they pleased.

A Topical Summary

Religion: The sixteenth century saw a final surge
of medieval religious feeling in the Protestant and
Catholic Reformations. The German monk Martin
Luther ignited the Protestant revolt, protesting the
increasing worldliness of the Roman church and
proposing such new doctrinal emphases as salvation
through faith and the Bible as the sole source of
religious truth. The rigorous mind and organizing talents of John Calvin made the Swiss city of

Geneva a model for Protestant militants everywhere.
The Roman church, meanwhile, responded by generating its own spiritual renewal in the Catholic Reformation. The first Reformation pope, Paul III,
convened the Council of Trent, reinvigorated the Inquisition, and encouraged the labors of the new
Jesuit order, restoring religious piety to the Catholic church and stemming the tide of Protestant
secession.

Politics: Another major trend of the sixteenth century was the continuing development of monarchical government in the European nation-states. Such strong-willed rulers as Henry VIII and Elizabeth I in Tudor England, the Habsburg sovereigns Charles V and Philip II in the German states and Spain, Francis I of France, and Ivan the Terrible in Russia all strove to increase their authority over their people.

War: Many of these rulers mobilized their new powers to fight bloody international wars, like those that pitted the Habsburgs against the Valois dynasty or Elizabeth I against Philip II in struggles that lasted for decades and even generations. Most destructive were the wars of religion, typically civil struggles such as the French religious wars or the Dutch revolt, which divided families, communities, nations, and the Western world itself in terrible ideological conflicts. By the end of the sixteenth century, however, an exhausted Europe began to see the virtue and even the necessity of religious toleration.

Some Key Terms

Anabaptists 423
Augsburg confession 436
authority of the Bible   416
auto da fe 427
comunero 434
consistory 422
consubstantiation 423
Council of Trent 426
cuius regio eius religio 419

diet 435
Index of Forbidden Books 427
Indulgences 417
Jesuits 428
junta de noche 438
League of Schmalkald 436
Ninety-five Theses 418
oprichniki 440

politiques 446
predestination 421
priesthood of all believers 416
St. Bartholomew's Day Massacre 443
salvation through faith 416
sovereignty of God   421
wars of religion 442
zemsky sobor 440

Notes

1. W. S. Barron, "Reformation, Protestant (On the Continent)," *New Catholic Encyclopedia,* vol. 12 (New York: McGraw-Hill, 1967), 183.
2. Quoted in De Lamar Jensen, *Reformation Europe: Age of Reform and Revolution* (Lexington, Mass.: D.C. Heath, 1981), 45.
3. Ibid., 46.
4. Roland H. Bainton, *Here I Stand: A Life of Martin Luther* (New York: New American Library, 1955), 60.
5. Bainton, 144.
6. Calvin, *Instruction in Faith,* vol. 2, trans. Paul Fuhrman (London: Butterworth Press, 1949), 36, 37.
7. Ibid., 38–39.
8. Teresa of Avila, *The Life of Saint Teresa of Avila by Herself,* trans. J. M. Cohen (Harmondsworth, England: Penguin, 1957), 199–200.
9. Modern medical research and various attempts at historical diagnosis of Henry's health problems indicate that, as common sense suggests, the problem was more likely to have been Henry's than that of any of his six wives.
10. Quoted in Lacey Baldwin Smith, *Elizabeth Tudor: Portrait of a Queen* (Boston: Little, Brown, 1975), 118.
11. Charles was King Charles I in Spain, Emperor Charles V in the Holy Roman Empire, and archduke, duke, count, landgrave, and holder of other titles in other parts of his vast domains.
12. "The Book of the Great and Mighty Emperor of Russia," in Richard Hakluyt, *Voyages,* vol. 1 (London and New York: Everyman's Library, 1907), 225–256.
13. George Gascoigne, *The Spoyle of Antwerpe* (London: Richard Jones, 1576), [Bvii recto]–cii recto.
14. In Roland H. Bainton, *The Reformation of the Sixteenth Century* (Boston: Beacon Press, 1952), 211.
15. *On the Coercion of Heretics,* in Roland H. Bainton, *The Age of the Reformation* (Princeton, N.J.: Van Nostrand, 1956), 186.

Reading List

BAINTON, R. H. *Here I Stand: A Life of Martin Luther.* New York: New American Library, 1962. Readable and authoritative, by a leading Protestant scholar. See also E. H. ERIKSON, *Young Man Luther* (New York: Norton, 1962), for an intriguing psychological interpretation.

———. *The Reformation of the Sixteenth Century.* Boston: Beacon, 1956. An earlier version of the Reformation, with much of the flavor of the age.

———. *The Women of the Reformation.* 3 vols. Minneapolis: Augsburg, 1971–1977. Major contributions made by women to the Reformation, country by country.

CAMERON, E. *The European Reformation.* Oxford: Clarendon Press, 1991. Solid survey, emphasizing power of an alliance of clergy and variously motivated secular leaders in launching the Reformation.

DANIEL-ROOS, D. *The Catholic Reformation.* New York: Dutton, 1962. Good overview by a Catholic historian.

DUNN, R. S. *The Age of Religious Wars, 1559–1689.* New York: Norton, 1979. Covers the rise and decline of the sectarian crusading impulse in early modern Europe. See also P. ZAGORIN, *Rebels and Rulers,* 2 vols. (New York: Cambridge, 1982), which classifies rebellions from palace coups to civil wars.

FRIESEN, A. *Thomas Muenzer, a Destroyer of the Godless: The Making of a Sixteenth-Century Religious Revolutionary.* Berkeley: University of California Press, 1990. A collection of useful essays on the intellectual shaping of a religious radical.

GEYL, P. *The Revolt of the Netherlands, 1555–1609.* New York: Barnes and Noble, 1980. Thorough account by a leading Dutch authority.

HELLER, H. *Iron and Blood: Civil Wars in Sixteenth-Century France.* Buffalo, N.Y.: McGill-Queens University Press, 1991. Links the wars of religion to earlier civil strife, emphasizing class conflict rather than religious differences.

HSIA, R. P.-C., ed. *The German People and the Reformation.* Ithaca, N.Y.: Cornell University Press, 1988. Methodologically sophisticated essays on the social history of the Reformation.

KAMEN, H. *The Rise of Toleration.* London: World University Library, 1972. The emergence of the modern view in the aftermath of the religious wars.

KNECHT, R. J. *Francis I.* London: Oxford University Press, 1982. Political history of the reign of the flamboyant French king.

KOENIGSBERGER, H. G., and G. L. MOSSE. *Europe in the Sixteenth Century.* London: Longmans, 1971. Scholarly survey of the period.

LYNCH, J. *Spain Under the Habsburgs.* 2 vols. New York: New York University Press, 1981. Volume 1 of this impressive study covers the century of Charles V and Philip II.

MONTER, E. W. *Calvin's Geneva.* Melbourne, Fla.: Krieger, 1975. The city that became the seedbed of international Protestantism.

NEALE, J. E. *Queen Elizabeth I.* New York: Doubleday, 1957. Classic political biography. For a more recent attempt to deal with the multifaceted queen, see A. SOMERSET, *Elizabeth I* (New York: Knopf, 1991).

O'CONNELL, M. R. *The Counter-Reformation, 1559–1610.* New York: Harper & Row, 1974. Surveys all aspects of the second half of the century.

OZMENT, S. *When Fathers Ruled: Family Life in Reformation Europe.* Cambridge, Mass.: Harvard University, 1983. Draws on personal documents and contemporary books on how to run a household to paint a picture of shared parental authority.

SCARISBRICK, J. J. *Henry VIII.* Berkeley: University of California Press, 1968. Standard life, with the warts left in.

WRIGHT, D. *The Counter-Reformation: Catholic Europe and the Non-Christian World.* New York: St. Martin's Press, 1982. Sees the Catholic Reformation rising from medieval lay piety and perceived threats of Ottoman Turks and other non-Protestant menaces.

Art of the Early Modern Period

Western art during the early modern period included the towering achievements of the Renaissance and Reformation and the impressive baroque and classical art of the age of Louis XIV. From the experimental spirit of the Renaissance and the rediscovered influence of Greco-Roman culture we move through the art of the Catholic Reformation of the sixteenth century and of the absolute monarchs and rising bourgeoisie of the seventeenth century. Here again, stylistic changes blend with the changing themes and concerns of three centuries to produce a unique artistic witness to an age of change.

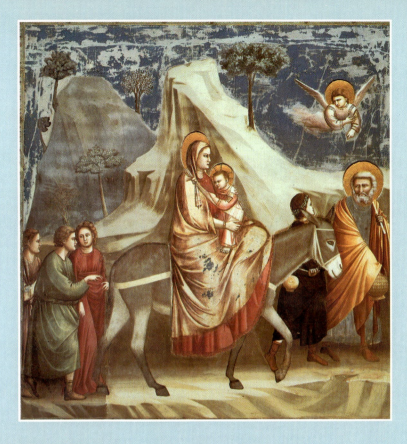

above: GIOTTO DI BONDONE. *Flight into Egypt.* Scrovegni, Padua

Giotto, seen by many as the first distinctively Renaissance painter, produced many moving works like this *Flight into Egypt.* Contrast the Renaissance roundness and solidity of the human figures in this painting with the rather abstract background that is a carryover from medieval art.

left: LEONARDO DA VINCI. *Virgin and Child with St. Anne and Infant St. John the Baptist.* Cartoon. National Gallery, London

Leonardo da Vinci's sketch for his larger painting of the same name defines the figures of the two women and children with his usual subtle manipulation of light and shade. Can you tell from pose and gesture which is Mary, which Jesus, and which the future John the Baptist?

IX

MICHELANGELO BUONARROTI. *Tomb of Giuliano de'Medici.* Medici Chapel, Florence

Michelangelo's tomb sculpture of Giuliano de'Medici depicts the powerful Medici duke costumed like a Roman emperor. Notice, however, that in his Renaissance fascination with human anatomy Michelangelo has effectively rendered the armor transparent, revealing the swelling chest muscles.

below: RAPHAEL (Raffaello Sanzio). *Parnassus.* Stanza di Raffaello, Vatican Museum, Rome

Renaissance enthusiasm for classical culture is strikingly illustrated by Raphael's painting of Parnassus, the home of the Greek Muses, goddesses of the arts and sciences whose mentor was the god Apollo. Interestingly, this painting was created for the pope, in Rome, not for a secular lord of pagan divinities.

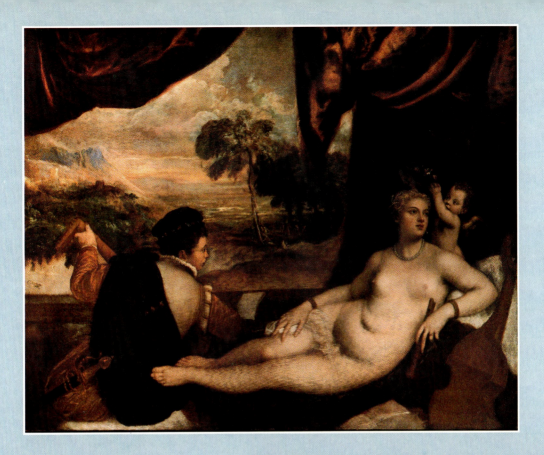

TITIAN (Tiziano Vecellio). *Venus and the Lute Player*. The Metropolitan Museum of Art, Munsey Fund, 1936

A favorite Renaissance subject derived from ancient mythology was the Roman goddess of love, Venus. Titian's *Venus and the Lute Player* couples the beauty of the goddess with an evocation of the art of music.

ARTEMISIA GENTILESCHI. *Judith Slaying Holofernes*. c. 1620. Uffizi, Florence

Artemisia Gentileschi's powerful depiction of Judith's slaying of Holofernes borrows its subject from the story of the Old Testament heroine. The work demonstrates mastery of the dramatic lighting characteristic of mannerist painting.

XI

GENTILE *BELLINI. Procession in St. Mark's Square.*
Accademia, Venice

Gentile Bellini's panoramic painting shows the
square in front of St. Mark's church in Venice
much as it is today. People of the Renaissance
loved parades and pageantry, and though this
is a religious procession, the doge, or duke, of
Venice and many rich merchants have turned
out for it.

EL GRECO (Domenicos Theotocopoulos). *Saint
Jerome As a Cardinal.* Oil on canvas. Musée
Bonnat, Bayonne, France

The unique style of El Greco, with its flame-like
elongated figures and the spiritual power of the
Byzantine tradition he brought with him from
Greece, was ideally suited to this picture of
St. Jerome. He shows Jerome, one of the fathers
of the church and translator of the Bible, in the
red robe of a cardinal.

REMBRANDT VAN RIJN. *The Anatomy Lesson of Dr. Nicolaes Tulp.* 1632. Oil on canvas. Mauritshuis, The Hague

Rembrandt's painting shows the celebrated Amsterdam surgeon *Dr. Tulp* dissecting a corpse for the instruction of his colleagues. This empirical scientific approach was still new in the early seventeenth century when the young Rembrandt created this painting.

FRANS HALS. *Zingara.* Louvre, Paris

Franz Hals' vigorous representations of his Dutch contemporaries combined the passion for realism for which the painters of the Netherlands were renowned with his own lusty vision of life as it was lived in his time.

above: NICOLAS POUSSIN.
Paesaggio con i funerali di Focione. Louvre, Paris

Nicholas Poussin's classical landscapes, although they aimed at naturalistic representation, imbued the countryside of the ancient past with a calm, almost dreamlike quality suitable to images of a vanished golden age.

left: JAN VERMEER.
View of Delft. Mauritshuis, The Hague

Vermeer was a native of the Dutch city depicted in this mid-seventeenth century View of Delft, and he shows it with pride and affection as well as skill. The commercial section is to the left, and the ships that were the lifeblood of Dutch commerce are anchored to the right.

Interior view toward high altar. Abbey of Melk, Austria

Baroque art often consciously combined the skills of the painter, the sculptor, and the architect. Using many-colored marbles, gilded wood, and other expensive materials, baroque artists and artisans sought to create an effect of visual splendor.

Fountain at Château de Versailles, France

The fountain of Versailles epitomized the luxury and splendor of Louis XIV's great palace. What effect do fountains have on the air around them? How do they enliven the view, particularly in a formal park like Versailles?

GIANLORENZO BERNINI. *The Ecstasy of St. Theresa.* Santa Maria delle Vittoria, Rome

Bernini's St. Teresa from the church of Santa Maria delle Vittoria in Rome reveals the Catholic Reformation saint at the moment when, as described in her own spiritual writings, an angel appeared to her and thrust her through with the spear of divine love.

The seventeenth century was a complicated period in Western history. In political, military, economic, and even demographic matters, the 1600s marked a critical stage in the transition from medieval to modern Europe. In both thought and art, this was the brilliant century that brought the scientific revolution to its climax. And on a global scale, this was the period in which the first wave of European overseas empire building reached essential completion. This chapter introduces what has been called the *critical century* in all its complexity. The next two chapters survey the era as a stage in the history of the Western mind and as a phase in the growth of the larger Western world overseas.

The tumultuous period of transition from the medieval to the modern age that began with the Italian Renaissance between 1350 and 1500 and reached its climax in the French Revolution of 1789 passed through a critical phase in the 1600s. During this period, Europe faced a series of crises, ranging from great wars and revolutions to depressions, epidemics, and a resulting social malaise that included a cruel wave of witch hunting. The restoration of order toward the end of the century brought a golden age for Europe's traditional aristocracy. Most important, the "crisis of the seventeenth century" produced two sharply contrasting political solutions: absolute monarchies like that of Louis XIV's France and constitutional monarchies like the government that emerged in England in 1688.

Although the "critical century" is still a theory, this notion that the Western world witnessed a general crisis throughout the seventeenth century offers a useful interpretation of the period between the Renaissance and Reformation of the sixteenth century and the Enlightenment of the eighteenth. This approach also helps us to understand the larger transition between the medieval and the modern West.

This chapter incorporates many of these trends and events into a multifaceted "general crisis" climaxing a long period of tension and escalating violence that began around 1500 and ended with a relative easing of tensions by 1700. During the years around 1650 especially, "Europe entered a new era" with "a change of direction more dramatic than any . . . between the beginning of the Reformation and the French Revolution."[1]

The Crisis of the Seventeenth Century

Europe at the beginning of the seventeenth century was in the grip of a continuing surge of social and religious conflict, originating in the Reformation, that carried on through the first half of the century. Following a savage pandemic of violence around 1650, governments reestablished order—although a broadly different order—in the later decades of the century. Both population growth and economic expansion, meanwhile, leveled off through a series of localized crises during the seventeenth century, not to resume earlier growth patterns until after 1700. In terms of social history, the European aristocracy had come into its golden age of power and prestige by 1700, whereas peasants and urban dwellers had begun to adapt rather more glumly to a new order in which central authority intruded more than ever into local communities.

Defining a crisis is not an easy thing to do. But the sense of mounting tension, followed by crisis and at least some sort of resolution, does seem to recur in one field after another. The crisis may be a war, a revolution, an economic decline, or a savage round of social scapegoating, but the pattern is the same.

War and the State

In the seventeenth century both the scale and effectiveness of military organization and the savagery of warfare expanded dramatically. The brutality of the wars of religion of the later sixteenth century carried over into the decades after 1600. In particular, the Thirty Years' War (1618–1648) was even more devastating to the German states than were the Dutch Revolt and the French wars of religion that had ravaged those areas. In the 1640s and 1650s, a further rash of rebellions and civil wars shook Spain, France, England, and other leading nations, toppling the governments of some states and threatening to fragment others. In the later seventeenth century and the early eighteenth, finally, the wars of Louis XIV and Peter the Great's Great Northern War mobilized armies of unprecedented size for many years. So much great-power violence led to impressive advances in the strength of the armed forces of the Western world, a change so striking it is sometimes called the *military revolution*. And so important were military affairs to the history of this critical century that we begin this chapter with a survey of the growth of armies and navies in the 1600s.

European armies thus multiplied in size, from the 40,000-man Spanish host that had been Europe's largest and best in the sixteenth century to the 400,000-man military establishment of Louis XIV. Undisciplined mercenary companies were replaced by royal standing armies, kept on the government payroll all year round, not just during the summer campaigning season. These evolving military forces had a fixed organizational structure, in which people were promoted on the basis of a combination of aristocratic influence, seniority in service, and skill at soldiering. These new armies stressed drilling to improve battlefield performance and discipline to limit the sort of atrocities that made the Thirty Years' War notorious. Gunpowder weapons, which had supplemented the pike in the sixteenth century, largely replaced it in the seventeenth. Infantry soldiers were equipped with unrifled—hence still rather inaccurate—matchlocks and flintlocks, cavalry often with large one-handed "horse pistols" to be fired from horseback; and both were supported by increasing numbers of lighter, more mobile artillery. Skill in the design and placement of fortifications, in siege warfare, and in military engineering developed steadily. In the new fortifications, projecting bastions were designed to maximize the defenders' field of fire, while attackers made use of complex trench systems and teams of sappers to tunnel under enemy walls and explode or undermine them.

Royal sea power also expanded from the handful of royally owned naval vessels supported by flotillas of privateers developed in earlier centuries to substantial royal navies. Although large sailing ships with two or three gun decks and 75 or 100 heavy guns were built early in the century, the leading role in the later seventeenth century was played by the frigate, a more maneuverable single decker of 300 tons and perhaps 40 guns first introduced by the Dutch. Tactics also changed as the random ship-to-ship encounters of the sixteenth century gave way in the seventeenth to the structured line of battle and to fleet maneuvers requiring a relatively efficient chain of command, discipline, and skilled seamanship.

The aristocracy still filled the large majority of officers' billets on land and sea. The ranks of soldiers and sailors still included large numbers of the very poor, the dregs of the prisons, and impressed men, seized by force and dragooned into the service of the crown. Corruption was still rife, and brutal treatment in the military was if anything increased by the new emphasis on discipline. Nevertheless, the massed power of Europe's military machines, and of

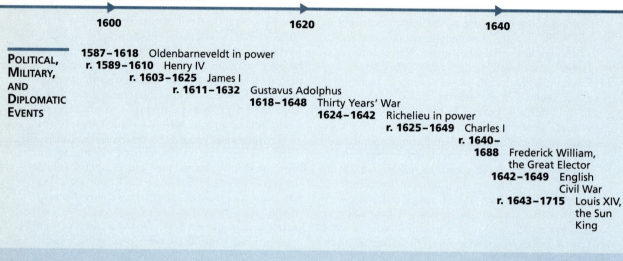

	1600	1620	1640

POLITICAL, MILITARY, AND DIPLOMATIC EVENTS

1587–1618 Oldenbarneveldt in power
r. 1589–1610 Henry IV
r. 1603–1625 James I
r. 1611–1632 Gustavus Adolphus
1618–1648 Thirty Years' War
1624–1642 Richelieu in power
r. 1625–1649 Charles I
r. 1640–1688 Frederick William, the Great Elector
1642–1649 English Civil War
r. 1643–1715 Louis XIV, the Sun King

SOCIAL AND ECONOMIC DEVELOPMENTS

1550–1650 Peak of witch craze
1620–1680 Widespread, intermittent economic depression
1630s–1640s Plague in German states
1640s–1650s "Little Ice Age"

the monarchs who mobilized them, grew steadily through the century.

The impact of military events and organization was so great that some have seen in it both the prime cause and the most important solution of the crisis that shook the social order in the seventeenth century. Wars shattered economies and drastically reduced populations in some regions of Europe. At least through midcentury, some Europeans were so horrified by the intensified level of violence that they feared Western civilization as a whole was grinding itself to pieces. Such fears were particularly widespread when civil wars threatened to tear apart Europe's most substantial centers of social order, the nation-states.

Once the monarchs of the Western world had restored authority, however, military power became a force *for* order instead of disrupting it. The large government expenditures for weapons, uniforms, equipment, and supplies stimulated economies, while weapons development encouraged technological growth. Some historians believe that Louis XIV, Peter the Great, the Habsburg emperors and Prussian kings built up their central governments specifically in order to provide financial revenues, adminis-

trative machinery, and support services for their armies. In any event, the crucial role of warfare and military machines in the history of the modern West was never clearer than in the seventeenth century.

The Thirty Years' War

The Thirty Years' War (1618–1648) began as a civil war between Protestant and Catholic factions within the Holy Roman Empire and ended as an international conflict that involved most of the great powers of Europe. It ravaged the German states of central Europe so terribly that it was sometimes seen as having put Germany a century behind the rest of Europe. It may be seen as the last and goriest of the religious wars—or as the first of the historic series of general European conflicts that included the wars of Louis XIV and Napoleon and climaxed in the two world wars of the twentieth century.

In the half-century after the Peace of Augsburg (1555) that recognized Lutheranism within the Holy Roman Empire and strengthened the indepen-

1660   1680   1700   1720

1648–1653 The Fronde
1649–1660 "Kingless Decade"
1653–1672 de Witt in power
r. 1657–1705 Emperor Leopold I
r. 1660–1685 Charles II
1667–1714 Wars of Louis XIV

r. 1682–1725 Peter the Great
1688 England's Glorious Revolution
1689 Bill of Rights

1700–1721 Great Northern War

1662–1683 Colbert builds mercantilism
1665 Plague in England

dence of the German princes, the religious situation in central Europe had become more complex and more volatile. Calvinism had spread to many states, while militant Jesuits helped to reclaim others for Catholicism. By 1609, two leagues of princes—one Catholic, one Protestant—had been organized within the Empire. Then in 1618 the Habsburg prince Ferdinand, a devout Catholic, became king of Bohemia (today's Czech Republic), which had a substantial Calvinist community. When Ferdinand moved to suppress Protestantism in Bohemia, Bohemian nobles responded by hurling Ferdinand's agents out the window of a castle in Prague. This act, known as the "defenestration of Prague" (from the Latin *fenestra,* for "window") ignited the Thirty Years' War. The Bohemian Calvinists then chose the most militant Protestant prince in the Germanies, Elector Frederick of the Palatinate (r. 1610–1632), in western Germany, as their new king. Ferdinand, meanwhile, was chosen Holy Roman emperor (r. 1619–1637).

In the early phases of the war that followed, Emperor Ferdinand's forces, supported by troops and money from Habsburg Spain, defeated his foes on all fronts. His ally Prince Maximilian of Bavaria

(r. 1597–1651) crushed the rebellious Bohemians at the Battle of the White Mountain in 1620 and overthrew Elector Frederick, whose short reign in Bohemia earned him the nickname of "the Winter King." Frederick's own domain in the Palatinate was conquered and occupied by the Spaniards in that same year.

These striking imperial gains, however, cloaked serious weaknesses. For one thing, Emperor Ferdinand had to depend largely on the armies of his subjects, including the Catholic League of German princes, the Catholic Prince Maximilian, and, most importantly, the opportunistic and brilliant mercenary captain, Albrecht von Wallenstein (1583–1634). These forces lived off the land—Catholic lands as well as Protestant ones—and soon became independent of imperial control, looting and conquering to line their own pockets or advance their leaders' ambitions. Another problem was created by Emperor Ferdinand's growing determination to crush all the Protestant princes, a policy which, combined with his support for Habsburg Spain's attempt to reconquer the Netherlands, aroused the fears of neighboring states, Protestant and Catholic alike. France in particular, guided by the brilliant statesman Cardinal

Richelieu, once more feared Habsburg encirclement, while the newly independent northern Netherlands—the United Provinces—naturally opposed Spanish use of the captured Palatinate as a staging area for Spanish troops coming north from Italy. Both Catholic France and the Protestant Netherlands therefore soon began to subsidize Emperor Ferdinand's Protestant foes. By the 1620s and 1630s, these foes in the field included two ambitious Scandinavian kings, Christian IV of Denmark (r. 1588–1648) and Gustavus Adolphus of Sweden (r. 1611–1632)—both Lutheran, both distrusting Habsburg expansion, and both soon ambi-

tious themselves to seize control of north Germany and the Baltic Sea.

King Christian invaded the northern German states in the later 1620s, but proved unequal to the task and was driven back by Wallenstein, who then invaded Denmark itself. The Swedish monarch, Gustavus Adolphus, however, proved to be made of sterner stuff. A devout Lutheran, a military innovator, and as skillful a field commander as Wallenstein, "the Lion of the North" drove the imperial forces back and won perhaps the greatest victory of the war at Breitenfeld in 1631. King Gustavus had reorga-

Map 15.1 The Thirty Years' War and English Civil War

nized and trained both his infantry and his cavalry with emphasis on battlefield mobility and the use of light artillery. Allied with both Protestant north Germans and some Catholic princes, Gustavus Adolphus pushed into southern Germany and defeated Wallenstein himself at Lützen in 1632—a bloody and ultimately pyrrhic victory, for the Lion of the North himself perished on the field. The enigmatic Wallenstein's ambitions soared, but he was killed in 1634, assassinated at the behest of his apprehensive employer, Emperor Ferdinand.

The surging tides of battle seemed to be turning once more in favor of the emperor. The French and the Dutch, however, contrived to keep the Swedes in the field with money and supplies even after the Swedish king's death. In 1635 France declared war on Habsburg Spain, and in 1636 French armies invaded the Holy Roman Empire to prevent further Habsburg gains. Most of the major powers were thus swept into what became the climactic phase of the Thirty Years' War.

Crisscrossed by warring armies, Germany bled. The new tactics and more effective firepower littered the battlefields with casualties. Foreign and German mercenary armies alike burned crops and villages, slaughtered stock, and tortured and butchered peasants all across central Europe. German cities were pounded by artillery, stormed, sacked, and gutted: at the taking of Magdeburg in 1631, as many as twenty

thousand people were killed in battle or massacred afterward. All told, as much as a third of the population of the Germanies may have died in the thirty-year holocaust.

When peace finally came at Westphalia in 1648 it was a peace involving most of the great powers and a number of the lesser European states. It was also a genuine attempt to settle all outstanding issues in order to prevent the recurrence of such an outbreak of warfare again. France and Sweden, which had pounded away at bleeding Germany the longest, were the biggest winners; the Habsburgs, who had for so long threatened to dominate Europe, were the primary losers.

By the Treaty of Westphalia and the later Peace of the Pyrenees (1659) with Spain, France acquired territory on both its frontiers, including portions of Alsace and Lorraine on its German border. With the decline of Spain and the Habsburgs, France soon emerged under Louis XIV as the greatest power in Europe. Sweden acquired territory on the Baltic and went on to fight an even more titanic struggle with Peter the Great's Russia for domination of the north. The Habsburg emperors, meanwhile, had to acknowledge the legitimacy of Calvinism as well as Lutheranism and Catholicism in the imperial domains. They were also compelled to accept the almost total independence of the German princes, who now added control of their own foreign policy

Jacques Callot's etching, *The Hanging,* was part of a series illustrating the horrors of the Thirty Years' War. Does the fact that all the "thieves" (*voleurs*) portrayed hang like "bad fruit" from the same tree add anything to the impact of this picture? [Jacques Callot.*The Hanging.* The Art Museum, Princeton University, Junius S. Morgan Collection]

to their separate governments, armed forces, coinage, tariffs, and state churches. In addition, the Habsburg rulers recognized the complete independence of the Dutch United Provinces and the Swiss Confederation (today's Netherlands and Switzerland). With the Habsburg attempt to assert imperial authority over central Europe thus decisively defeated, the way was open for the rise of another powerful German dynasty: the Hohenzollerns of Brandenburg-Prussia, the future founders of modern Germany. Meanwhile the Habsburgs built a new Danubian Empire around their remaining stronghold in Austria that included the non-German peoples of Hungary and Bohemia.

Europe as a whole emerged from the carnage of the Thirty Years' War with a revived sense of international order. As the long wars of religion and the duels of the dynasties had demonstrated for two centuries, the old, at least spiritually unified Europe of medieval Christendom was now as dead as the Roman imperial order that had preceded it. Realistic statesmen now thought in terms of an orderly system of national states. Great powers and small were bound by treaty agreements, responsible for maintaining the diplomatic niceties in peace, and obligated to discipline their troops in war. The nations of the West had not only survived a military crisis but had begun to develop a new approach to dealing with international disputes. Though there were plenty of wars down the modern centuries, Western leaders also continued to seek diplomatic solutions to international problems on a Europewide and later a global scale.

The Midcentury Rebellions

The revolutions of the midcentury decades, which coincided with the climax of the Thirty Years' War, constituted as powerful an assault on the unity of the individual nation-states as the long war did on the larger international order. We examine some of these upheavals, including the Fronde in France and the Puritan Revolution in England, in more detail later. Here, however, we will venture a few generalizations on this crisis of national governance between the 1620s and the 1660s.

Since the rise of the new monarchs of the later fifteenth century, the central governments of the European nation-states had resumed their high medieval effort to impose law, order, and royal authority

on the nations they ruled. Throughout the intervening two centuries, rulers had deployed expanding bureaucracies and larger and more effective armies against the traditionally autonomous towns, regions, and above all the independent aristocracy, which still demanded recognition of its time-honored prerogatives and powers. The resulting resentment of the governed against their increasingly powerful monarchical governments reached a climax in the uprisings of the middle seventeenth century.

In a brief overview, these rebellions look like a rather motley array. In France, many elements in society joined the revolt called the Fronde (1648–1653), but nobles recently returned from the carnage in Germany took the lead. In England, Puritan clerics provided spiritual leadership for the revolt of the 1640s, but the gentry, England's country squires, provided the effective leadership of the revolt. During that same decade, Spain was shaken by a struggle in which Castilian domination was challenged by other provinces and regions, including Catalonia, Portugal, and the Spanish-ruled Italian territories of Naples and Sicily. In the United Provinces, the merchant elite, led by the province of Holland, resisted the power of the noble house of Orange, urging a policy of trade and peace against the stadtholders' pressure for Calvinist rigor and war with the Catholic powers. The Thirty Years' War itself was, in its internal imperial dimension, a struggle between the Holy Roman Empire and its nominally subordinate princes and aristocracy. In Poland, a Cossack rebellion cost that country its domination of the Ukraine in 1648. In Russia two decades later, another Cossack revolt freed serfs and ignited peasant rebellions all along the Volga before it was suppressed.

Everywhere, the aggressive centralizing policies of early modern governments thus went through a final time of testing. The results varied from victory for the monarchy, as in France, through an alliance between monarchy and landowning classes, as in England, to a rare victory for the nobles and princes, as in the Holy Roman Empire. Overall, a resolution in favor of the crown in collaboration with the aristocracy was most common.

The victorious monarchies continued to expand their administrative systems: the number of bureaucrats in Europe may have multiplied as much as four times over between the early sixteenth and the later seventeenth centuries. The main purpose of this increasingly elaborate governmental machinery continued to be the collection of revenues and the mobilization of standing armies for war. In addition, however, these strengthened central governments intruded into the lives of provinces and towns to administer royal justice, regulate the economy of the state as a whole, distribute food in time of famine, and in other ways begin the long process of habituating Western peoples to bigger, more powerful government.

With centralizing monarchies thus increasingly accepted in the nation-states and with aristocrats staffing the top spots in government, the structured society that came to be called the *ancien régime*—the "old order" of Western society before the French Revolution—took its final shape. Again the nations of Europe had survived a major crisis—the midcentury revolutions—and Europeans believed a permanent structure had been established in the political order.

Famine, Depression, and Disease

The tendency of twentieth-century historians to seek economic causes for many things is difficult to apply to the crisis of the seventeenth century. There appears to be no clear correlation between the economic doldrums of the century and the wars and revolutions just inventoried. Yet both the demographic and economic trends of the times do seem to have followed the general pattern of crisis, resolution, and acceptance of what was perceived as a new status quo.

The problem for historians seeking to establish a midcentury "crisis" in the economic and demographic history of the period is that famine, depression, outbreaks of plague, and related disasters tended to be localized in an area and to occur at different times in different places. Some historians have seen the greatest economic reverses beginning around 1620, others around 1680, while a few regions, like the Netherlands, enjoyed a golden age of prosperity and growth pretty much throughout the century. If the seventeenth century as a whole is set in the larger context of the early modern period, however, a broad pattern of critical setbacks and survival does emerge.

Overall, the 1600s constituted a period of relative economic stagnation and a striking slowdown in population growth. By contrast with the sixteenth century, with its economic and demographic expansion, and the eighteenth, which saw the agricultural and industrial revolutions and the beginning of the modern population explosion, the 1600s look like grim times indeed.

As in the later Middle Ages, seventeenth-century Europe was visited by a pandemic of disasters. The wars and civil wars we have discussed ravaged agricultural land, ruined prosperous cities, and sometimes made drastic inroads into populations. The central European population may have fallen by as many as six or seven million people, and the economic development of Germany was probably retarded by generations. Outbreaks of plague and related catastrophes killed an estimated half a million Spaniards, a million Italians, and a fifth of the entire Danish population during the century, ravaging such cities as Naples and London with particular ferocity. Local famines were not less brutal simply because they were less widespread. All European agriculture suffered from the so-called Little Ice Age of short, cool growing seasons that was most noticeable in the 1640s and 1650s. Economic downturns may not have been Europewide, but the century as a whole saw a slackening of economic growth and even declines in some fields, from bullion exports to agricultural production. Overall, population, which had doubled in the sixteenth century, scarcely increased by a third in the seventeenth, while agricultural and industrial growth, commercial exchange, and other signs of economic health slumped badly in the 1600s.

In the later fifteenth and sixteenth centuries, the continent had rebounded vigorously from the series of catastrophes that had beset late medieval Europe. In the eighteenth, the West was launched on the unparalleled trajectory of modern growth and expansion. In the disturbed century between, these ascending graph lines wavered, and the Western world seemed as likely to slide backward as to continue its growth. The seventeenth century was thus as critical a century in the material history of the modern West as in the areas of domestic and foreign politics.

The Great Witch Craze

The international military, political, economic, and demographic crisis of the seventeenth century had its social aspects too. The later sixteenth and earlier seventeenth centuries saw the climax of a unique wave

MASTERING OUR WORLD The Power of Witches

The witch hunts of the sixteenth and seventeenth centuries reflected real fear of the magical powers witches were believed to have over the forces of nature. The following sober description of some of these powers comes from a very well-known seventeenth-century handbook on witchcraft, Francesco Maria Guazzo's *Compendium Maleficarum*. The practice of "personalizing" natural misfortunes by blaming them on evil individuals with magical powers is found in many cultures. Can you see peasants who had been victimized by some of the blights listed here feeling at least some psychological satisfaction in knowing whom to blame? How do the "confessions" cited encourage belief on the reader's part?

It is one of the obligations that witches owe to the devil that, when they assemble at the Sabbat, they must show that they have wrought some fresh evil since the last meeting; and if they cannot do so, they do not escape with impunity. And that they may not be able to plead ignorance as an excuse, their evil Master instructs them in all those activities which he demands from them: as in infesting the trees and fruits with locusts, caterpillars, slugs, butterflies, canker-worms, and such pestilent vermin which devour everything, seeds, leaves, and fruit; or in bewitching cattle; or in casting a spell on the crops so that they are destroyed by leeches or wasted in some other way; or in the use of poisons; and [generally,] in working as far as [it] in them lies for the destruction of the whole human race.

For all this we know from their own confessions; as, for example, those of Helena of Armentières at Douzy on the 30th September, 1586; of Anna Ruffa at the same place and time; of Jean the Fisher at Gerbeviller on the 13th May, 1585; of his wife, Colette; and of several others whom we pass over for the sake of brevity.

Source: Francesco Maria Guazzo, *Compendium Maleficarum . . . Showing the Iniquitous and Execrable Operations of Witches Against the Human Race. . . .* trans. E. A. Ashwin (Secaucus, N.J.: University Books, 1974), 22.

of social violence. This was the great surge of witch hunting, the *witch craze* as it is often called, which peaked between 1550 and 1650.

Medieval and early modern witches, sometimes called "wise women" or "cunning men," were probably most often herb healers who combined spells and charms with their folk remedies. Most were women (though about a fifth were men), and more were old than young. Those accused of witchcraft frequently came from the marginal elements of society: beggars, poor widows without families, midwives (commonly blamed for high infant mortality). They were often outsiders in other ways—quarrelsome neighbors, people known to be disrespectful of authority, emotionally disturbed people. Only when a local witch hunt was in full cry did suspicion reach as high as the middle or upper classes of society.

European views of witchcraft had undergone a drastic transformation in the fifteenth century. The Inquisition had decided that witches were actually agents of Satan and as such a major threat to Christendom. Books like *The Hammer of the Witches*

(1487) by Heinrich Kraemer and Johan Sprenger spread the notion that these local weavers of spells and cures had gained their magical powers by swearing allegiance to the Devil. In return, they had received "familiars," demons in the guise of animals, to do their will, as well as the powers traditionally assigned to witches: the ability to conjure up storms, ruin crops, kill livestock, cause illness or death in humans, and transform themselves into animals (see box on "The Power of Witches"). Satan's servants were also believed to rub themselves with a salve that allowed them to fly through the air to the Witches' Sabbath, where they paid obscene homage to the Devil, feasted, danced, and flung themselves into orgiastic sex in defiance of all the laws of God and man.

Using torture to gain confessions to these crimes, both ecclesiastical and civil courts burned or hanged tens of thousands of alleged witches during the 1500s and 1600s. This savage persecution has been interpreted in many ways. It has been seen as an attempt to suppress a genuine witch cult (a view not now generally accepted), as scapegoating of so-

More savagery, as witches die horribly in the fire of persecution while a devil hovers over them. Look closely and you will see another unfortunate about to be beheaded in the background.

cial outsiders made to take the blame for misfortunes like illness or bad harvests, or simply as a form of mass hysteria. The witch craze has also been characterized as an expression of widespread male hatred and fear of women. The box, "Women As Witches," describes one effort to rationalize this persecution of women. Some scholars see the willingness to believe in a diabolical conspiracy of witches as a product of a feverish religious temper. Perhaps three-quarters of the persecutions occurred in the German states, the Swiss cantons, and France, all areas of intense religious conflict, and as Reformation religiosity waned, this brutal campaign against the "witches" also came to an end.

Monarchy and Aristocracy

The impact of monarchical supremacy was felt from the top to the bottom of seventeenth-century society. This section focuses on the social elite, the early modern aristocracy. In the following section, we survey changes in the lives of Europe's masses, rural and urban.

The failure of European aristocrats to halt the rise or limit the power of kings was not followed by the destruction of the landowning elite. Their residual prestige and traditional authority were still too real for this, their value as supporters of the crown too great. The resolution of the centuries-long struggle was thus a partnership, an alliance between monarchy and aristocracy. And while the monarch was clearly the senior partner, the old elite retained and even strengthened its position at the top of the social pyramid, just below the prince.

The source of aristocratic preeminence did shift in the new age. The power of medieval nobles had been based on their landed estates and traditional leadership role in the countryside. The more ambitious early modern aristocrats, by contrast, turned to the crown itself, to royal patronage, offices, court politics, and influence as their new road to supremacy. On this new basis, later seventeenth-century aristocrats particularly continued to dominate most spheres of society. They held the highest positions in government, law, and the diplomatic corps, as well as officer slots in the growing armies and navies. They were appointed to bishoprics, archbish-

PROBING THE PAST
Women as Witches

Alexander Roberts, the author of this seven-teenth-century tract on witchcraft, was a bachelor of divinity and a preacher at King's Lyne, Norfolk. Thus his view on this subject was that of a learned man of his time. Roberts' attempt to explain why more women than men were charged with witchcraft depends heavily on contemporary assumptions about women's "nature." Note the qualities of character that he sees as natural in women, and how he construes each as playing into the Devil's hands. Modern scholarship sees most sex-specific characteristics as learned rather than innate. Can you explain the traits Roberts lists in terms of women's life experience in the seventeenth century or in terms of contemporaneous religious ideas?

> More women in a far different proportion prove Witches than men, by a hundred to one; therefore the Law of God noteth that Sex, as more subject to that sin [*Exodus* 22.18]. . . . neither doth this proceed (as some have thought) from their frailty and imbecility, for in many of them there is stronger resolution to undergo any torment than can be found in man. . . . Therefore the learned have searched out other causes thereof, and among the rest, observed these as the most probable.
>
> First [women] are by nature credulous, wanting [lacking] experience, and therefore more easily deceived.
>
> Secondly, they harbor in their breast a curious and inquisitive desire to know such things as, be not fitting . . . .
>
> Thirdly, their complexion [temperament] is softer, and from hence more easily receive the impressions offered by the Devil; as when they be instructed and governed by good Angels, they prove exceedingly religious and extraordinally devout . . . .
>
> Fourthly, in them is a greater facility to fall, and therefore the Devil at the first took that advantage, and set upon *Eve* in *Adam's* absence. . . .
>
> Fifthly, this sex, when it conceiveth wrath or hatred against any, is implacable, possessed with insatiable desire of revenge. . . and when their power herein answereth not to their will. . . the Devil . . . offereth to teach them the means by which they may bring to pass that rancor . . . nourished in their breasts . . .

Source: Alexander Roberts, *A Treatise of Witchcraft* (London: Samuel Man, 1616), 40–43.

oprics, and other leading places in the state churches of Europe. They dominated the parliaments, estates general, diets, and similar assemblies nominally representing the estates of the realm but actually giving nobles, high churchmen, and upper middle-class citizens a voice in government. Even less ambitious aristocrats in the provinces continued to enjoy exemption from taxation, social prestige, and a good deal of power within the larger framework of royal authority. By combining their medieval prestige and local influence with their Renaissance educations and their new willingness to identify their interests with those of their sovereigns, the aristocrats of the Western world came out on top once more.

They were a varied array of landholding classes. French seigneurs were perhaps the most sophisticated, English gentry the most hardworking farmers, Prussian Junkers the most dedicated state servants. Spanish grandees were most likely to be as poor as they were proud, Russian boyars to be anarchically useless to the state until Peter the Great replaced them with his new "service nobility." Everywhere they were the leading citizens, the most socially respected and politically powerful class of Western society.

The life the nobility led at Louis XIV's court or in Habsburg Vienna was more polite and elegant than that of their medieval ancestors, or even than the lives of Renaissance courtiers a century and a half before. Hunting, dining lavishly, and the fine art of sexual seduction were still primary pastimes. But there were more elegant ways for Europe's "best people" to pass their time now too. Cards, billiards, and sophisticated conversation, plays, concerts, opera, and ballet were more common forms of cultivated entertainment than they had been earlier. Aristocratic women who had once guided medieval "courts of love" or Renaissance courtly conversation now organized elegant literary salons. In these gatherings of sophisticated men and women, intellectual topics were discussed amid the gilt and chandeliers of noble drawing rooms. The "grand tour," introduced in the sixteenth century, also became a standard part of the aristocratic lifestyle. This journey took the European elite from one court or city to another, admiring art and architecture and socializing with the intellectual and social leaders of other lands. Often undertaken in youth, in the company of a tutor, the grand tour could last for months or years. It prepared the hereditary ruling class for the task of managing the affairs of Europe that each generation of aristocrats inherited in turn.

The daily life of a seventeenth-century aristocrat can look as silly in retrospect as that of any group enslaved to fashion and formal conduct. French aristocrats at the court of Louis XIV, for instance, had to learn to rise and remove the hat when receiving a message from the servant of a social superior. They bowed very deeply when encountering footmen bearing food to the royal table, murmuring "the king's meat!" with proper awe and solemnity. To hand Louis XIV his slippers or help him on with even one sleeve of the royal shirt at his ceremonious *levée* each morning was a privilege beyond the wildest dreams of the average baron or marquis. Whatever one thought of such a society, it was clear that a sense of order had thus been restored at least in its upper reaches. At the lower levels, things were not so simple, or so immediately harmonious.

State and Community

In the wake of the political crisis of the seventeenth century, an intrusive order was imposed on the masses of Western people. From peasant villages to bustling cities, Europeans were more regulated, more influenced by outsiders and outside forces than ever before.

Many of the forces that undermined the cohesion of the local community and integrated it into the larger society went back to the Renaissance and Reformation. Expanding Renaissance markets and inflated prices for agricultural products strengthened the profit motive in the villages. The resulting disparities in wealth created rifts between more and less successful peasants. Both Protestant pastors and Catholic Reformation priests, much better trained in theology than most medieval clergymen, strove to weed out local superstitions and unorthodox beliefs during the Reformation century. In so doing, they undermined the shared body of local beliefs that had welded the community together during the Middle Ages. As early as Tudor and Valois times, finally, local landowners began to spend more and more time at the courts of princes or in the fleshpots of the cities, a practice that reached its fullest development in Louis XIV's day. The absence of this traditional elite for much of the year left rural society without its once highly visible leaders.

At the same time, royal officials became more prominent in the provinces as the sixteenth and seventeenth centuries advanced. Royal judges, tax collectors, army recruiters, and other tentacles of the distant capital snaked out through the countryside. Besides ruling and regulating, these officials made efforts to provide local relief for the poor, to suppress vagrancy and begging, to offer food in time of famine, to quarantine those infected with the plague. It was a beginning only, but it represented more of a governmental presence in the farming villages and market towns of Europe than the West had known since Roman times.

Similar processes of integration were felt in the growing cities of Europe. There were now urban complexes of half a million people to be found in western Europe, swollen by a continuing flow of immigration from the countryside. Cities of hundreds of thousands created serious challenges that were met, insofar as they were met at all, by elites and governments. Food for such large numbers was provided by private producers from the surrounding countryside. But water supplies, fire prevention, even modest efforts to clean and police some of the streets were the responsibility of city governments and patrician business elites. Royal governments, meanwhile, increasingly tried to integrate the autonomous chartered towns and cities into the life of the state as a whole. Royal coinage, royal market inspectors, royal regulations began to replace or at least supplement the regulatory functions of local guilds. At the highest level, central governments implemented paternalistic mercantilist policies to foster economic growth—we examine some of these policies in the next major section of the chapter—and fought wars to defend the interests of traders. As government thus intervened directly in the cities, the latter ceased to be independent units of society and became instead parts of larger national communities.

Early reactions to these intrusions of new powers into older local communities tended to be violent. Peasant revolts and urban disturbances could be found practically any year through the sixteenth and earlier seventeenth centuries. Workers rebelled against their masters; peasants burned manor houses. Religious enthusiasts swept town and country into frenzies of sectarian reform or persecution, of image breaking or Anabaptist excesses. And as we have seen, disintegrating communities turned on their own in a fury of witch mania, accusing the herb healers and potion brewers they had once depended on of forming alliances with the Devil and causing illnesses, crop failures, and other misfortunes.

These signs of resentment and resistance to change finally began to diminish during the later seventeenth century. Peasants accepted the new, more centralized order. Urban businesspeople began to think they had a right to the help of government, not only with local problems, but in defending local producers and expanding foreign markets. Once more, a sense of social order triumphed. The ancien régime, headed by hereditary monarchs, was in place across Europe. And it is in the monarchies themselves that we can see the pattern of the century of crisis working itself out politically in some of the great states of Europe.

The Triumph of Absolute Monarchy: France

The odor of politics hangs thick over the seventeenth century. Monarchs in conclave with great ministers of state, leaders in parliaments or estates general all talked the language of power. The winners, successful state builders like Richelieu and Cromwell, stare flintily at us out of darkening portraits. The losers often paid with their lives for their failure.

From these struggles, two fairly stable forms of government emerged in the seventeenth century. In most of the great powers, monarchs prevailed in the particularly impressive form of royal absolutism surveyed in the following sections. In a smaller number, as we see in the chapter's final major section, aristocratic or business elites achieved a level of countervailing power embodied most effectively in the constitutional monarchy. And though the two forms seemed very different and were often in conflict, when the crisis was over, both absolutist and constitutional monarchies had made substantial contributions to the modern age.

"I Am the State"

One of the best ways to get a sense of the scope and splendor of royal absolutism in the seventeenth century is to take a stroll across Louis XIV's vast palace and grounds at Versailles, just outside of Paris. The sweeping green lawns and wooded parklands, the terraces, fountains, paths and statues provide a splendid formal setting for the sprawling palace itself. Within, sumptuous private chambers and spacious public halls all reflect the sense of grandeur that earned for the 1600s the reputation of "the splendid century" in French history.

"L'état, c'est moi!" Louis XIV (r. 1643–1715) is reputed to have snapped when a statesman referred to "the French state" as if the nation were an independent entity: "*I* am the state!" The Sun King's formulation may stand as the central political maxim of the age. From one end of Europe to the other, the monarch was the source of policy, the prop of order, the living embodiment of nationhood in the later seventeenth century. Absolute monarchy, the most widespread political form among the larger states of the seventeenth century, represented the height of royal power. (For some of Louis XIV's views, see the box titled "Louis XIV on the Need for Absolutism.")

After centuries of struggle with the rival claims of institutions and groups that had once been independent powers, absolute monarchs at last seemed to hold the whip hand. State churches were now common, established in Protestant countries by secession from the Roman church, in Catholic ones by *concordat,* or agreement, with the pope. The nobility, although their prestige and power remained great, now derived both from the monarch. Cities and villages, as noted, were brought more closely under royal supervision than ever before.

Absolute monarchs were hereditary rulers who made the extravagant claim to be the first and final source of power in the state. In the absolutist state, both Protestant and Catholic clergymen reasserted with new vigor the medieval doctrine of the divine sanction for royal rule. Expanding bureaucracies and standing armies translated these claims into the facts of power. The nation as a whole looked up in awe — if not always with enthusiasm — to the splendor of the royal courts, housed in vast new palaces like Louis XIV's Versailles, or in cities like Peter the Great's new capital of St. Petersburg. "It is certain," wrote Louis XIV in his carefully prepared set of guidelines for his son and heir,

that in the state where you will reign after me, you will find no authority which is not proud to derive its origins and powers from you. . . . [A]ll eyes are fixed upon the [monarch] alone, all requests are addressed to him alone, all respects are paid to him alone. . . . His favor is regarded as the only source of all good things; . . . all else is cringing, all else is powerless.[2]

It was a hard-won predominance, achieved after centuries of struggle and the critical conflicts of the seventeenth century itself. Let us look at these

Louis XIV, France's Sun King and the greatest of the seventeenth-century absolutists, is shown here with his family. Although such group portraits of royal families made clear that a line of succession had been laid down, they are often less than impressive to later generations. What does this family portrait say to you?

THE RULERS AND THE RULED
Louis XIV on the Need for Absolutism

Louis XIV, the most famous of all absolute monarchs, had a strong sense of his own indispensable place in the state. This conviction, combined with the existence of very real problems, convinced him of his absolute right to rule absolutely. Before he was through, Louis brought the French aristocracy, the royal court, the financial, ecclesiastical, judicial, and administrative establishments all under his control, just as he promised his heir in this early memoir. Due both to the cost of the new power structure and to a series of long and expensive wars, however, the "lower classes" continued to be "burdened with taxes and pressed by extreme poverty."

I began, therefore, to cast my eyes over all the various parts of the state, and not casual eyes, but the eyes of a master, deeply struck at not finding a single one that did not cry out for my attention. . . .

Disorder reigned everywhere. My court, in general, was still quite removed from the sentiments in which I hope that you [my son] will find it. People of quality . . . were always inventing an imaginary right to whatever was to their fancy; no governor of a stronghold who was not difficult to govern. . . .

The finances, which move and activate the whole great body of the monarchy, were so exhausted that there hardly seemed to be any recourse left. . . .

The Church, aside from its usual troubles, after long disputes over scholastic matters that were admittedly unnecessary for salvation [was] finally threatened openly with a schism. . . .

Justice, which was responsible for reforming all the rest, seemed itself to me as the most difficult to reform. An infinite number of things contributed to this: offices filled by chance and by money rather than by choice and by merit; lack of experience among the judges, even less learning. . . .

All these evils, or rather, their consequences and their effects, fell primarily upon the lower classes, burdened moreover with taxes and pressed by extreme poverty in many areas. . . .

Since the principal hope for these reforms rested in my own will, it was first necessary to make my will supreme through conduct that would inspire submission and respect. . . .

Source: Louis XIV, *Mémoires for the Instruction of the Dauphin*, trans. Paul Sonnino (New York: Free Press, 1970), 24–26, 28.

clashes and their consequences in more detail as they were experienced in some of the great nations of Europe: France, Austria, Prussia, and Russia.

Richelieu and the Road to Absolutism in France

Between the end of the French wars of religion in the 1590s and the time when Louis XIV took up his reign in earnest in 1661, well over half a century of tumultuous history elapsed. During this period, three French kings reigned and three able ministers of state made key contributions to the most imposing edifice of royal power in Europe. The mature Louis XIV thus entered into an inheritance shaped by the state-building labors of his predecessors.

Henry of Navarre, founder of France's Bourbon dynasty at the end of the sixteenth century, has a double claim to fame. The first Bourbon both ended the wars of religion and revived the historic drive of the French monarchy to strengthen royal power in the state. As leader of the Huguenots, he was the chivalric "white plume of Navarre," always visible where the fighting was fiercest. As Henry IV (r. 1589–1610), he turned Catholic to win entry into his capital but also issued the Edict of Nantes (1598) granting toleration to Protestants. Thereafter, the benignly bearded, heavy-lidded king became perhaps France's most popular royal ruler, the original coiner of the political slogan "a chicken in every pot" for every French peasant's Sunday dinner. Henry and his finance minister, the duke of Sully (1560–1641), reclaimed wastelands for agriculture, built roads and canals, founded France's silk industry, and even piled up a surplus in the treasury.

To reestablish the authority of the monarchy, Henry IV brought the rebellious "nobility of the sword" into the central Council of Affairs or retired them to their estates with large cash settlements. He allowed the "nobility of the robe," judges and chief administrators, to purchase not only these top offices, but also guaranteed succession to the position for their sons. To undercut the French Estates General, which had been a center of dissent, Henry never convened it at all during his two decades on the throne.

Murdered by a fanatical Catholic in 1610, Henry left nine-year-old Louis XIII (r. 1610–1643) on the throne and a foreign queen mother, Marie de Médicis, to organize a regency. Faced with rule by another foreign queen of the same Italian house as Catherine de Médicis in the preceding century, the

Marie de Médicis, the unfortunate queen of France in the early years of the seventeenth century, faced all the troubles that would lead to the rise of absolute monarchy later in the century. Rivalry between Catholics and Protestants, aristocrats and bourgeois, swirled around her son, Louis XIII, who inherited the throne as a minor.

French nobility grew fractious once more. The Huguenots were restive after the death of their protector. And the Estates General, convened at last in 1614, revealed growing tensions between the aristocracy and the bourgeoisie. For the last two decades of his reign, however, the sickly and unhappy Louis XIII found a royal minister who took up the task of strengthening the monarchy with vigor. Cardinal Richelieu (1585–1642) became one of France's greatest statesmen and by far the most important of those who prepared the way for Louis XIV.

Richelieu sought to bring the French nobility under royal control by requiring the destruction of their fortified strongholds and offering them top jobs in the government, the diplomatic service, and the army. He suppressed growing restlessness among the Huguenots with military force, capturing their garrisoned towns and disbanding the armed companies granted them by the Edict of Nantes, but leaving them their right to freedom of Protestant worship. To advance royal power across the land, finally, Richelieu developed the system of *intendants,* royal

officials who thrust aside local and noble power to collect taxes, administer justice, and generally carry the king's will to distant provinces.

When the all-powerful Richelieu died in 1642 and his ineffective king followed him in 1643, they were succeeded by another royal minor, King Louis XIV, aged five; another "foreign" regent, Anne of Austria; and another powerful royal minister, the Italian-born Cardinal Mazarin (1602–1661), personally groomed for his post by Richelieu. Mazarin, however, was greedier than his illustrious predecessor and less able. Accumulated resentments soon exploded into France's last paroxysm of rebellion before the coming of the Age of Louis XIV in all its authoritarian splendor—the confused and violent midcentury uprising called the Fronde (1648–1653).

Fronde means "sling," the weapon of choice used by Paris streetboys to pelt passing carriages with stones. But the insurrection that drove the boy Louis XIV from his capital and Cardinal Mazarin out of the country was no riot of street kids. Set off by a constitutional dispute between the Parlement of Paris and the crown, the struggle soon expanded to include not only the prestigious Paris Parlement but the provincial parlements as well; some of the highest nobility; the Huguenots; the overtaxed bourgeois of Paris, Bordeaux, and other cities; and peasants caught in a vise of famine and depression that afflicted many parts of the kingdom.

By a combination of military force, lavish bribes, and Machiavellian tactics intended to divide the nobility of the sword from the nobility of the robe, Mazarin gradually reasserted control, and Louis XIV was welcomed back to Paris by cheering crowds in 1652. But the young king never forgot how riotous mobs had broken into the royal palace, or how he was forced to flee from Paris by his own people up in arms. He spent the rest of his long life trying to make sure that such a thing never happened again.

The Sun King

A man of limited intelligence and imagination and no sense of humor, Louis XIV was never really lovable, even in his youth, when he was known as an inveterate womanizer who prowled the palace roofs in search of unbarred windows into ladies' bedchambers. In his later years, under the influence of his devout and dignified mistress and secret wife Madame de Maintenon (1635–1719), the king became increasingly stiff, pompous, obsessed with his own majesty. His narrow religious views led him to the major blunder of revoking the Edict of Nantes in 1685 and expelling fifty thousand highly productive Huguenot families from the country. And his passion for French grandeur and his certainty of his own rights in every international dispute plunged the nation into four immensely costly wars.

Louis XIV was also, however, a serious-minded man, hardworking, with a good memory for detail and a growing determination to make ruling France his full-time occupation. Daily meetings with his chief ministers, close attention even to minor documents, and a firm guiding hand on policy were other qualities of this archetypal royal absolutist. Convinced that God had put him on his throne, he accepted labels like the Sun King or *le Grand Monarque* as no more than his due as ruler of Europe's greatest nation. During a reign of more than seventy years, Louis XIV became a living symbol of monarchical power, a king whose style of governance was widely imitated even by his enemies.

Absolutist government under Louis XIV involved both rigorously curtailing independent authority in his realm and asserting royal authority all across the land. Thus the nobles, summoned to join the social whirl and compete for royal preferment at the palace at Versailles, lost much of their local prestige and influence as their roots in the countryside withered. Towns that had been independently chartered were increasingly run by officials whose positions had been purchased at court, while city guilds became enforcers of economic regulations emanating from the central government. The provincial parlements, which had long claimed the right to pass on the constitutionality of royal edicts in their own provinces, soon became rubber stamps for the king's decrees. The potentially troublesome *Estates General*, where aristocracy, churchmen, and bourgeoisie might offer unwelcome advice to his majesty, was never convened once during the immensely long reign of Louis XIV. The French Catholic church officially formulated its traditional "Gallican Liberties" in Louis's reign, and these formal documents drawn up by the bishops further strengthened the king's claims to control his church and reject papal jurisdiction over French ecclesiastical affairs. Even Louis's economically costly decision to expel the Huguenots may have strengthened the Catholic sovereign's authority over a more homogeneous nation: *un roi, une loi, une foi*—"one king, one law, one faith"— was a French maxim to which Louis firmly subscribed.

On the positive side, absolutism meant many long but apparently quite happy hours for Louis working with his four chief ministries: domestic affairs, finances, international relations, and war. It meant promoting skilled administrators like his finance minister Colbert and his war minister Louvois—both discussed later—to virtually lifetime tenure at the top of the central government. It meant utilizing Richelieu's system of thirty intendants to impose the king's will on the provinces. It meant, in short, battalions if not yet armies of bureaucrats, a mounting flood of paper, and a nation perhaps halfway to the big government of today.

Finally, Louis XIV's absolutism meant the sense of his own greatness that led the Sun King to build the largest palace in the Western world at Versailles. A third of a mile long, with space to house ten thousand people, from princes and ministers of state to valets and scullery maids, the palace of Versailles was set in endless acres of formal gardens, groves, and vistas. Living quarters were actually rather cramped, and the endless ritual that accompanied every moment of the king's day looks oppressive and even ridiculous to us. The lavish meals, entertainments, and ceremonious tone of life may seem almost criminal when we think of the cost of piping water from the Seine to operate hundreds of fountains, the tax revenues burned up in seconds of stunning fireworks displays. But Louis, his ministers, and his masters of the revels knew the importance of cultivating an image of splendor as well as Queen Elizabeth had a century before.

Mercantilism and War

Paternalistic control at home and international predominance in Europe were two central features of the absolute monarchy in France. Nowhere were these elements clearer than in Louis XIV's mercantilistic economic policies and in the wars that did so much to exhaust the nation he was so dedicated to building up.

Jean-Baptiste Colbert (1618–1693), the king's chief minister for economic affairs, was the architect of French *mercantilism,* the most thoroughly worked out such system of government economic regulation in seventeenth-century Europe. A financial genius and a dedicated organizer and planner, Colbert was convinced that government could and should foster economic development. The mercantilist theory, the earliest widely held modern view of economics, asserted that national wealth could be measured in the amount of gold and silver bullion accumulating in the nation.

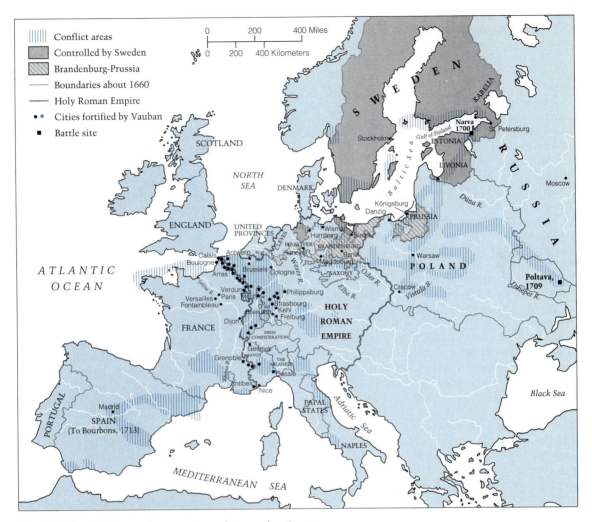

Map 15.2 The Wars of Louis XIV and Peter the Great

To guarantee an inflow of precious metals in the form of coins, national production must rise and exports must exceed imports, the export surplus to be paid for in money. Since mercantilists also believed there was not enough wealth in the world to go around, international economic competition was an essential feature of mercantilism. The accomplishment of all these goals required paternalistic government intervention in the national economy.

To encourage production, Colbert sought to develop such natural resources as timber, minerals, and agricultural land by encouraging reforestation, iron mining, and land reclamation. He fostered profitable luxury trades, importing lace makers and glass-blowers from Venice and converting the Gobelin tapestry works into a state industry famous for furniture as well as for tapestries. To further internal trade, he built roads, bridges, and canals, including one canal that linked the Mediterranean to the Atlantic and was hailed as the greatest engineering feat since ancient Rome.

French explorers had followed Spanish colonizers into the New World in the later sixteenth and early seventeenth centuries, establishing themselves from the Caribbean to Canada. Seeing overseas colonies as an essential part of a closed mercantilist system, Louis's chief minister Colbert committed government funds to develop such profitable colonial agricultural products as sugar, tobacco, and chocolate. He also forbade French colonial trade with foreign powers and required that all shipping between the colonies and France be in French vessels rather than those of competing powers like the Dutch. To protect French industry from foreign rivals, he levied heavy tariffs on imports; to encourage exports, he developed monopolies and state subsidies and imposed quality controls on French goods sold overseas.

With such support and guidance from above, France became the most productive nation in Europe, with the largest acreage of agricultural land, luxury goods admired across the Western world, and the largest population of any great power. All this production and prosperity, however, was sadly drained by the other element in Louis XIV's two-pronged drive for national greatness: the militaristic expansionist drive that produced a new series of exhausting wars during the later seventeenth and early eighteenth centuries.

Louis XIV, seeing himself as heir to the greatness of Charlemagne, aimed at a French predominance over the Western world. Dreaming of commercial and colonial expansion, he came into conflict with the Dutch and others. Seeking defensible frontiers on the Rhine and the Alps, Louis fought France's ancient foes, the Habsburgs, in Spain and central Europe. To overcome both new commercial and colonial rivals and ancient dynastic foes, the French king depended on his dedicated war minister, the marquis de Louvois (1639–1691), his renowned military engineer Sébastien Vauban (1633–1707), and an army that reached the unheard-of size of four hundred thousand men. Thus motivated and equipped, Louis launched war after war to defend his rights and secure his interests in the world.

The other great powers responded to what seemed like unbridled expansionism by organizing a series of coalitions against Louis. These alliances were led by Louis's implacable foe, William of Orange, great-grandson of that William of Orange who had led the Dutch Revolt against Spain, stadtholder of the United Provinces from 1672, and later King William III of England (r. 1688–1702). The result was another in Europe's long sequence of destructive conflicts, leaving France exhausted and the Sun King's own reputation badly tarnished by the time of his death.

Louis's earlier wars actually won him great fame. His armies performed brilliantly in the 1660s and 1670s, though French gains from these wars were

limited. Louis first sent his armies lumbering over his eastern frontier in the 1660s in the so-called War of Devolution (1667–1668) to claim some territories that his legal experts assured him should have "devolved" upon his Spanish queen, Marie-Thérèse, when her dowry was not paid. Frustrated by an alliance he blamed on the Dutch, France's great trade rival, Louis next invaded the United Provinces themselves in the Dutch War (1672–1678). William of Orange, a Calvinist and a constitutional ruler whose power was limited by law, was all the things Louis despised. William organized another coalition against the Sun King, and the ensuing conflict cost the French two of their best generals. By the treaties of Nimwegen (1678–1679), Louis did, however, acquire a number of valuable border fortresses and the territory of Franche-Comté, which barred Spain's corridor from Italy to the Low Countries. It was a clear indication of Spain's decline and the rise of French power.

In the 1680s and 1690s, Louis fought the War of the League of Augsburg (1688–1697), a costly struggle aimed at "reuniting" bits of the Holy Roman Empire to France. Another international alliance against the French king, however, frustrated his designs. During this period, Louis also had to recognize the accession of William of Orange to the English throne in place of the Stuart line of succession that Louis had supported, yet another setback for Louis's hegemonic ambitions.

The climactic and most disastrous of Louis's wars, the War of the Spanish Succession (1702–1714), resulted from the Grand Monarch's most grandiose imperial dream—the establishment of a Bourbon ruler on the throne of neighboring Spain. Such a coup, reversing the Habsburg achievement of the previous century, could have turned the French predominance into an irresistible hegemony of Europe. A fourth coalition, including the United Provinces, England, and the Holy Roman Empire, therefore banded together against the aging French autocrat.

Armies under England's John Churchill, first duke of Marlborough (1650–1722), and the imperial general Prince Eugène of Savoy (1663–1736) defeated the French repeatedly from Blenheim in 1704 to Malplaquet in 1709. These battles could be bloody contests. The Battle of Blenheim, for example, France's first major defeat in the field for half a century, cost Marlborough and Prince Eugène 12,000 men, and the French and their Bavarian allies 18,000 killed or wounded. The total of 30,000 fallen was about as many as the entire Christian West had been able to mobilize for a crusade five centuries earlier.

The peace terms eventually agreed to in 1713 and 1714, primarily at Utrecht, involved the redrawing of a number of European boundaries and ceded some of France's new overseas colonies in Canada and the Caribbean to Britain. Louis XIV's grandson did become Philip V of Spain, but with the condition that the French and Spanish branches of the Bourbon dynasty should never be united—terms Louis could have had before the war broke out.

Famine and plague joined huge war casualties and crushing taxation to bury France under a mountain of woes as Louis's reign neared its end. Yet so great were his resources, so unbending his determination, that he died in 1715 as he had lived—not loved, but securely on his throne, still the incarnation of royal absolutism in Europe.

Absolutism in Central and Eastern Europe

Louis XIV's France was the great exemplar of absolute monarchy in the seventeenth-century West. Many other European sovereigns, however, sought to emulate the Sun King's regime in their own countries. Of these, the Habsburg and Hohenzollern dynasties of German-speaking central Europe and the Russian Empire founded by Peter the Great became in later centuries the most powerful autocracies in Europe.

The New Habsburg Empire

At the beginning of the seventeenth century, Habsburg sovereigns reigned over both the Holy Roman Empire and Spain. By the end of the century, Habsburgs had been replaced by Bourbons on the Spanish throne, and Habsburg imperial authority in German-speaking central Europe was weaker than ever. Yet the Austrian Habsburgs had by 1700 also succeeded in constructing a new and impressive empire for themselves among non-German neighboring peoples.

The decline of the Spanish Habsburgs was one of the most striking features of the seventeenth century. The nation that had towered over Europe in the sixteenth century tumbled into the ranks of the second-class powers in the seventeenth.

The sources of Spain's decline went back at least to Philip II's time. In the century after Columbus, Spain had built the largest overseas empire in the world, but much of the profit had gone to others. Foreign bankers, merchants, and artisans had skimmed off the wealth of Spain's mines and plantations. A ruinous inflation had also accompanied the influx of so much precious metal. Above all, Philip II's enormously costly wars, fought to advance his dynastic interests and to defend the Catholic faith, had exhausted even Spain's vast resources by the end of the seventeenth century.

Under his seventeenth-century successors, Philip III (r. 1598–1621), Philip IV (r. 1621–1665), and Charles II (r. 1665–1700), these trends continued. Declining imports of silver combined with increased taxation to leave the people impoverished. Regional loyalties flamed into open revolt in Catalonia, Portugal, and Spain's Italian holdings, especially during the 1640s. And Philip IV's powerful minister Gaspar de Guzman, count-duke of Olivares (1587–1645), poured the nation's resources into the Thirty Years' War, with results as draining as the wars of Philip II had been. Forced to raise taxes and to borrow heavily, the Spanish crown was soon paying out half of its annual revenues in interest on the national debt. In addition, Spain's once victorious regiments finally began to lose in the field. The Dutch naval victory in the Battle of the Downs (1639) and the crushing French triumph over the Spanish army at Rocroi in 1643 shattered Spain's dream of hegemony over Europe.

In central Europe, the rise of Habsburg and other German absolutism had been repeatedly undercut by princely autonomy, local independence, and geographical and cultural differences. To overcome these handicaps, ambitious German dynasties depended on armed force, on new arrangements with the nobles, and on centralized administrative systems. In the seventeenth century, the Austrian Habsburgs deployed armies to build a new empire on the Danube, came to a profitable arrangement with their aristocracies, and depended increasingly on modern bureaucratic machinery to govern an increasingly diverse group of peoples many of them in the Danube river valley to the south.

The independence of the German princes from the Holy Roman emperor had been established definitively in the Thirty Years' War. From their capital at Vienna, the Habsburgs therefore directed their ambitions toward non-German dependencies: Slavs in Bohemia, Magyars in Hungary, Italians in the

Lombard plain of northern Italy. In 1620 the Bohemians, whose revolt had set off the Thirty Years' War, were decisively defeated in the Battle of the White Mountain. In 1683 Emperor Leopold I (r. 1657–1705), after repelling a last Turkish siege of Vienna, drove the Ottoman Turks out of Hungary and added this territory to his new lands. And in 1713, after the long war with Louis XIV over the Spanish succession, Austria took over the Lombard lands and cities south of the Alps. From these territories, the Austrian rulers fashioned at last the centralized monarchy they had been unable to impose on their fellow German princes in centuries of trying.

The new Habsburg Empire that resulted was a federated state still, with local authority remaining in the hands of the provincial diets or estates general and much power still held by the ancient nobility, especially in Magyar Hungary. But there were centralized bureaus in Vienna directing some administrative, legal, and financial affairs. Austrian settlement in these non-German lands and imperial support for increased noble control of the serf populations that still existed east of the Rhine further strengthened Habsburg power. In addition, this new Danubian Empire increased the leverage of the ancient dynasty in the Holy Roman Empire itself, adding substantially to the remarkable revival of the fortunes of the dynasty.

The Rise of the Hohenzollerns

Within the Holy Roman Empire, the Habsburgs faced a new and potent rival for dominance in central Europe. This was the Hohenzollern dynasty of Brandenburg-Prussia. Stretching east and west across the valleys of the Elbe and the Oder rivers in north Germany, the principality of Brandenburg centered on the town of Berlin, provincial capital of the Hohenzollerns since the fifteenth century. In the course of the seventeenth century, this prominent north German dynasty acquired a number of other scattered territories. These included the Rhineland duchy of Cleves in the west, a stretch of Baltic coastline, and East Prussia in northern Poland. By the end of the century, these noncontiguous holdings added up to more territory than that held by any other German prince except the Habsburg emperor himself. Because the Hohenzollerns were also imperial electors—among the seven rulers who chose the Holy Roman emperors—they would have been men of consequence in the Germanies in any case. In the

middle 1600s, however, Brandenburg-Prussia was ruled by the stern-faced and determined Frederick William (r. 1640–1688), the "Great Elector," who devoted his life to building the family domains into a European great power.

The Great Elector's achievement was one of discipline and determination over circumstance. The lands he inherited were economically poor, geographically divided, politically independent minded, and in 1640 thoroughly ravaged by the Thirty Years' War. Over the following half-century, Frederick William hammered together a well-trained and rigidly disciplined army and built one of the most efficient centralized administrative systems in Europe. The army earned him a profitable place in the diplo-

Frederick William, the Great Elector of Brandenburg–Prussia, is shown here as a young man armed for war. The founder of Hohenzollern greatness did more by his political leadership than by his military skills for the dynasty that ultimately unified modern Germany.

matic intrigues and military struggles of central Europe and gave him a powerful tool to impose his authority on his scattered territories. That authority was then implemented by the effective royal bureaucracy centered in Berlin. His landed aristocrats, the *Junkers,* willingly staffed the higher ranks of both army and administration in return for the Elector's support for their own control over the peasantry. This powerful interlocking alliance proved even more successful at binding geographically separated territories together than the Habsburgs had been at uniting their culturally disparate domains. When the Great Elector's successor, Frederick I (r. 1688–1713), secured the title of king from the Habsburg emperor in return for military support against Louis XIV, the Hohenzollern kings were well positioned to begin the long competition with the emperors that brought them mastery of all Germany two centuries later.

Peter the Great

While Louis XIV made France Europe's greatest power and the Habsburgs and Hohenzollerns dominated central Europe, a nation that would one day be more powerful than any of the others emerged as a great power around 1700: the Russia of Peter the Great (1682–1725).

To western Europeans, Peter was a freak of nature, the "Turk of the North," an apparition out of the barbaric borderlands where Europe and Asia met. To millions of his own shocked and terrified subjects, he was the subverter of old Russian ways and the betrayer of Russian Orthodox tradition. A half-educated giant, almost seven feet tall, and a tremendous eater, drinker, and worker, Peter had a powerful practical intelligence and no patience at all with time-honored traditions. He was possessed by a driving will to change Russia, to turn it from the medieval land of Ivan the Terrible into a modern state second to none in Europe. For three decades, he sought to transform or obliterate old Russian institutions, customs, and beliefs. He has been praised and blamed for what he did to the Russian psyche ever since. What he did to Russian society is less debatable. He found Russia a backwoods anachronism; he laid the foundations for Russian power in the Western world.

The sprawling land he inherited had not stood entirely still since the death of Ivan IV almost a century earlier. There had been a "Time of Troubles"

Peter the Great of Russia looks every inch the self-made emperor, with his cities and the fleet he hoped to build stretching out behind him.

around 1600, a period of economic decline, domestic discord, and foreign invasions climaxing in the temporary occupation of Moscow by the Poles in 1610. After a national movement of Russians of all classes had expelled the Polish invaders, an assembly of notables, the *zemsky sobor,* chose Michael Romanov, a pliable member of a popular boyar clan, as the new czar. The Romanov dynasty thus came to power on the shoulders of a popular movement. It ruled Russia for three hundred years, until the overthrow of the czarist monarchy in 1917.

The first three Romanov czars—Michael (r. 1613–1645), Alexis (r. 1645–1676), and Fyodor III (r. 1676–1682)—proved more modest and tractable than strong leaders. They did, however, preside over national recovery and the beginning of new directions for Russia. Not all the trends they imitated were positive. The *zemsky sobor,* Russia's embryonic assembly of the estates, first summoned in the sixteenth century, essentially ceased to function after the middle of the seventeenth. Its last significant act was to ratify the law code called the *Ulozhenie* of 1649, which completed the process of imposing serfdom on the Russian peasantry after tha medieval institution had died out in western Europe. By allowing the patriarch Nikon (1605–1681) to attempt a moral and spiritual reformation of the Orthodox church from the top down, the first Romanov czars also drove many Russians out of the official church to form a fundamentalist backwoods sect called the Old Believers. More promising for the future, the early Romanovs pursued a policy going back to Ivan the Great and Ivan the Terrible of encouraging foreign tradespeople, artisans, and military officers to settle in Russia, bringing their skills with them. And in wars with Poland and Sweden, then the great powers of eastern Europe, the early Romanovs recaptured much of western Russia and the Ukraine from Poland.

Then in 1682, ten-year-old Peter I came to the throne, under the regency of his sister Sophia and as co-emperor with a feeble-minded half brother, Ivan V (r. 1682–1696). After outmaneuvering these siblings and their supporters to establish his own sole authority and leading a couple of campaigns against the Turks, the young Czar Peter set out on what was to become a legendary European tour of 1697. Fascinated from childhood by the technical skills of the resident foreigners in Moscow's German Quarter, Peter determined to go west himself to see what he could learn. Traveling incognito to avoid wasting time on the formalities normally lavished on a visiting head of state, he visited the Netherlands, England, and other nations in search of practical knowledge of value to Russia. Examining industrial establishments, hospitals, schools, shipyards—he took a job as a carpenter in one such yard—he immersed himself in the practical side of Western culture, endlessly curious, eagerly learning.

Returning home with the beginnings of a vision of the way he wanted Russia to look when he was through, Peter set to work with vigor and a heavy fist. As aware as Louis XIV of the value of symbolism, Peter demanded that his courtiers wear Western clothes and go clean shaven as western Europeans did, and even took the shears to some boyar beards and long-sleeved Russian robes himself. Threatened by a rebellion of the *streltsy*—the musketeer regiments who had become a reactionary force in

Moscow politics—Peter suppressed them brutally, ordering many executions and more than once taking the headsman's ax in his own large hands.

The Founding of Modern Russia

Peter the Great's lifelong efforts to modernize medieval Russia included reforms in government and the military, in religion and society, in economics and technology. Altogether, they added up to the most massive single demonstration of what a dedicated absolute monarch could do to transform his country.

To restructure the face of Russia, Peter needed to bring every Russian under the authority of the crown, the only real force for change in a deeply conservative land. He therefore demanded government service of everyone, from noble to serf. Peasants were most commonly ordered into military service. Many, however, were also mobilized for labor on roads, canals, port facilities, and the czar's new capital at St. Petersburg. The nobility served in special guards regiments or as government officials. Government service by the aristocracy was encouraged by a new Table of Ranks assigning seniority and precedence on the basis of service to the state rather than an ancient boyar name. The resulting *service nobility* earned its place by devotion to Western models and dedicated service to the czar.

The Russian government itself was reorganized. A nine-member Senate served as a regency council during Peter's absences—usually at war—and later acquired important administrative, judicial, and other functions. Russia's several dozen government bureaus were reorganized under a collegial form borrowed from Peter's archenemy, Sweden. Thus departments for finance, foreign affairs, war, and other services were headed by "colleges," or boards, rather than by individual administrators. A system of provinces whose boundaries were drawn in Moscow replaced the traditional territorial divisions. Towns were encouraged to set up their own governing institutions, which could also serve the central government. To cap these changes, Peter arrogated to himself, in his later years, the title of emperor, as more suitable than "czar of all the Russias" to the head of a modern state.

In every aspect of their lives, Peter touched Russians as no czar had done before him. He reformed and expanded taxation until townspeople and peasants felt taxed on everything they used or did, produced or consumed. Even the ancient Russian Orthodox church came more tightly under Peter's control as he abolished the patriarch—the head of the church—and replaced him with a lay *procurator,* the emperor's own appointee, who ran the church virtually as a branch of the government. The economy also felt the impact of Peter's efforts to expand production and trade and to import Western technology. Commerce with western European lands flowed in increased volume through the Baltic ports Peter acquired in war. The iron mines he fostered in the Urals, at the other edge of European Russia, soon became Europe's most productive.

Peter may have made many of these changes, finally, with an eye to strengthening Russia for what was after all his most common year-to-year preoccupation: the wars he fought with the Turks, the Swedes, and others. During the sixteenth and seventeenth centuries, Poland and Sweden were often stronger than Muscovy. To these powerful neighbors, the Russians had lost portions of the Ukraine—the southern grasslands that had been the center of the medieval Kievan Rus—and of the Novgorod area in the north, with its access to the Baltic. The seventeenth-century Romanovs, however, humbled Poland and recovered much of western Russia and the Ukraine in the earlier 1600s. Peter's early efforts to push through the lands held by the Turks in the south to the Black Sea proved a costly failure. But in the north, his tenacity of purpose brought him his greatest success against the Swedish warrior-king Charles XII (r. 1697–1718). Peter fought this "Great Northern War," as he fought the Turks in the south, to reach the seacoast—in this case, the Baltic, with its even more direct access to western Europe. Defeated at Narva in 1700 by Charles XII—a worthy successor to Gustavus Adolphus—Peter reorganized and came back to win a smashing victory at Poltava in 1709. It was the end of Sweden's century of predominance in the north and the beginning of Russia's rise, first to great-power status in the eighteenth century, then to become for a time the most powerful nation in Europe in the twentieth.

On the long stretch of Baltic lands he thus acquired, Peter built his new capital and prime seaport, St. Petersburg. This city was an outstanding illustration of Peter's determination to transform Russia and of the power of absolute monarchy. Built on land conquered by Russian armies, raised on a poisonous swamp by Russian peasant labor at a cost of many lives, the new capital was peopled by reluctant nobles who were simply ordered to build townhouses in the emperor's new city. St. Petersburg thus came into existence, quite simply, because Peter the Great willed that it should. With the passing of generations, it became Russia's great "window on the West," the most civilized of Russian cities, and one of the most beautiful in Europe.

Yet the Russians of Peter's day hated St. Petersburg; and Peter himself, like Louis XIV, was not mourned when he passed to his reward. He died of pneumonia, apparently contracted when he plunged into the surf to help rescue shipwrecked Russian sailors. The man who drove so many to their deaths in war and peace never ordered another man to do what he would not undertake himself. Boyars saw him as a traitor, and Orthodox Old Believers were convinced he was the Antichrist himself. A British observer could only marvel that "the providence of God . . . has raised up such a furious man to so absolute authority over so great a part of the world."[3]

Constitutional Government: England and the Netherlands

In the repeated clashes between the forces of centralization and those who resisted royal power, the centralizers most commonly won out. Absolute monarchy became the archetypal governmental form of the later seventeenth century. In some places, however, those who resisted the further aggrandizement of the monarchy succeeded, sometimes to a surprising degree. In Stuart England and in the United Provinces of the Netherlands, furthermore, the strength of the country gentry and the urban business community paved the way for more democratic forms of government in later centuries.

Toward a More Liberal Order?

It is easy for people of any age to see the problems, conflicts, and great causes of earlier centuries as essentially similar to those of their own time. Easy, but too often deceptive. It is thus tempting to see modern democratic impulses behind seventeenth-century resistance to autocracy—but to do so warps the facts of history.

In the first place, democratic ideas as the nineteenth and twentieth centuries have known them scarcely existed in the 1600s. Moreover, the opposition to royal absolutism came not from the people as a whole but, primarily, from traditional elites defending their own interests and privileges. The *constitutional monarchies* that resulted from these conflicts, finally, were not modern democratic governments, but partnerships between monarchs and traditional ruling classes in the governance of the rest of the nation.

The consequences of aristocratic victories over royal rulers could be both anachronistic and paralyzing. Thus the successful resistance of the German princes to the centralizing efforts of the Holy Roman emperors postponed the unification of Germany for more than two hundred years. In Poland, noble landowners elected the king, and through the unique institution called the *liberum veto,* a single nobleman's negative vote could prevent the royal government from taking any action. Thus the alternative to absolute monarchy could be central government too feeble to function at all.

In at least one important case, however, partial victories for the ruling classes did lead to working partnerships between crown and traditional elites. In the commercially developed North Atlantic powers of England and the Netherlands, the resulting "mixed" system of governance proved both effective and, in the longer term, the harbinger of a more liberal order to come.

England's Long Revolution

A widely reproduced seventeenth-century picture by Cornelius Visscher shows London and the river Thames in the early 1600s. Many vanished landmarks show clearly among the close-packed houses—sights you will not see today as you tour the streets in your bright red double-decker bus: Old London Bridge lined with shops, Old Saint Paul's Cathedral as it looked before the great fire of 1666, even the Globe Theater, where Shakespeare's plays were staged, on the near bank of the river. London in the early seventeenth century was already one of the great cities of the Western world. But it was also the capital of a country on the brink of one of the most violent periods in its history: England's "century of revolution."

In the age of royal absolutism, England's long revolution requires some explaining—and it has had plenty. Some twentieth-century historians, following the trend toward the economic interpretation of history, have seen the conflict in terms of economic

The English parliament, which in the seventeenth century challenged the Stuart kings and began to impose limits on the power of the monarchy.

forces and social classes in conflict, identifying the rebels in socioeconomic terms as gentry and merchants. In contrast, nineteenth-century historians, who were deeply impressed by the increasing role of the House of Commons in English government, tended to see the revolutionary leaders under political labels, as Parliament men and refashioners of the English constitution. Still earlier, it was common to see the English Civil War as above all the Puritan Revolution, identifying the leaders as stiff-necked Calvinist "Roundheads" (from their short haircuts) in the militant Reformation tradition. Many revolutionaries do fit a number of these categories at the same time. Oliver Cromwell, who emerged as the maximum leader of the revolution, was a member of the gentry class, a parliamentary leader, *and* a stiff-necked Puritan. All these interpretations in fact help us to understand the tangle of events that filled four reigns and a decade-long interregnum during the eighty-five years from the accession of James I in 1603 to the deposition of James II in 1688.

Conflicts between ruler and ruled were very likely from the start. Dying without issue in 1603, Queen Elizabeth was succeeded by her cousin King James Stuart of Scotland—ironically the son of her old rival, Mary, Queen of Scots. James I and his descendants, Charles I, Charles II, and James II, lacked both the Tudor gift for public relations and empathy for English ways. They also had to face the piled-up grievances of Puritans, members of Parliament, and others who had not dared confront Queen Elizabeth with their complaints. All four Stuarts, finally, believed totally in royal absolutism and in their own divine right to rule, a view that made compromise extremely difficult as demands for reform escalated toward revolution.

Leadership for the opposition to the crown seems to have come from the gentry. England's thousands of landholding but untitled country squires were a formidable group of men: they were serious farmers frequently involved in business; they were often university educated or trained in law; and they were used to administering their shires as justices of the peace and to serving in the House of Commons. Many of them were also *Puritans,* willing to accept the spiritual guidance of the preachers of a variety of sects who demanded change in the Church of England. Most of the Puritan leaders were militant Calvinists, either Presbyterians who wanted a church modeled on the national church of Scotland or Congregationalists who sought total independence for each congregation. They shared a passion to "purify" the church of surviving vestiges of Catholic practice, such "high church" practices as elaborate vestments, organ music, candles and incense, and militant opposition to moral laxness at court and to such popular practices as maypole dancing and theater going. Some merchants, particularly those from London and the port cities, also joined the opposition. They typically opposed the Stuarts over high taxes and wasteful spending on lavish living at the royal court and on futile foreign wars.

Country squires and other opposition leaders were soon challenging the monarchy on a variety of policies. They spoke for Puritanism against high church tendencies, resisted the "tyranny" of the archbishops and bishops, and even feared a reestablishment of Catholicism in England. They were disgusted with Stuart attempts to draw England closer to such absolutist Catholic states as England's old enemy Spain. They opposed royal attempts to collect taxes not authorized by Parliament. And increasingly, opposition leaders spoke up for the right of Parliament's House of Commons to free elections, free debate, and control of such key matters as taxation and government expenditures.

Both James I (r. 1603–1625) and his successor Charles I (r. 1625–1649) defended their right to rule as continental kings did. James was an irritable and pedantic spokesman for royal absolutism, Charles an emotional believer in high church rule and ritual. Aided by chief ministers like the aristocratic Thomas Wentworth (1593–1641), earl of Strafford, and the militantly high church archbishop of Canterbury William Laud (1573–1645), the early Stuarts responded to parliamentary challenges with vigor. They forbade debates, arrested members, and dissolved parliaments. Charles I tried for over a decade in the 1620s and 1630s to govern by royal prerogative, without summoning Parliament at all, as the Bourbons were doing without the Estates General in France.

Then in 1637, Charles attempted to impose the Anglican prayer book on the rigorously Calvinist Scottish national church. The Scottish lords promptly rose in rebellion—and ignited a civil war in England too.

Cromwell and the English Commonwealth

In need of funds to field an army against his Scottish subjects, King Charles in 1640 summoned what became known to history as the Long Parliament. Once convened, this Parliament remained in intermittent session for most of the next two decades. Inspired by long-term foes of royal autocracy like John Pym (1584–1643), the "uncrowned king of Parliament," the House of Commons used the king's desperate need for funds as a club against him. They forced him to back away from high-handed policies on taxation and governance. They compelled the impeachment and eventual execution of both Wentworth and Laud. They confronted their ruler with a "Grand Remonstrance" (1641), in which they demanded church reform and parliamentary veto power over government appointments. In a final clash, Charles led troops into Parliament himself in an attempt to seize Pym and other radical leaders by force. The radicals escaped, and the parliamentary opposition openly took up arms against the king.

Oliver Cromwell, Lord Protector of the Realm of England, looks soberly and sternly out upon the world. Compare the Puritan Lord Protector's clothing with Marie de Médicis's splendor in the photograph on page 465. [By kind permission of the Master, Fellows, and Scholars of the College of the Lady Frances Sidney Sussex in the University of Cambridge]

In the Civil War (1642–1649) that followed, the king and his hard-riding Cavalier courtiers expected to have it all their own way. The Cavaliers—swashbuckling duelists with flowing locks, real-life English equivalents of the "Three Musketeers"—looked forward to cutting through these stodgy country squires and their holier-than-thou Puritan chaplains like a knife through butter. But Oliver Cromwell (1599–1658), both a Puritan country squire and a successful military commander, organized a disciplined New Model Army whose "Ironside" cavalry—so called because they charged into battle as though bullets would bounce right off them—proved more than a match for the king's Cavaliers. After years of maneuvering and fighting up and down the length of England, Charles's army was defeated, the king captured. Then, to the horror of absolutist Europe, the victorious revolutionaries tried and executed their former monarch in 1649. With the Fronde raging in France and similar outbreaks in other countries, it was the midcentury height of the political crisis of the seventeenth century.

The Cromwellian Commonwealth (1649–1660), a "kingless decade" in the middle of the century of absolute monarchy, astonished the Western world. Of special interest here, the Commonwealth revealed several trends that were found in later ideological revolutions also. These included counterrevolutionary attacks, splits in the ranks of the rebels, and the emergence of a dictator to bring order out of the ensuing chaos.

The public executioner had not raised the bloody head of Charles I above the gaping crowd before his exiled son became Charles II, at least in the minds of royalists. Supporters of the young claimant to the throne regrouped on the other side of the Channel and spent the next decade plotting to restore the Stuart dynasty. Charles himself mobilized attacks on the Celtic fringe of the Commonwealth in Scotland and Ireland. Cromwell beat back all assaults, with such brutality in Ireland as to make a major contribution to the long Irish litany of English oppression. Throughout the kingless decade, royalist efforts to reverse the verdict of the Civil War by force of arms thus failed. Similar counterrevolutionary movements, as we will see, were mobilized against revolutionary regimes in France after 1789 and in Russia after 1917.

A second threat to the success of the English Revolution was the series of splits that fissured the ranks of the victorious rebels themselves. The differences between Presbyterians and Independents on church organization and central discipline surfaced as soon as the common enemy was defeated. Political differences also developed between the gentry leadership, who assumed that England would continue to be guided by its traditional ruling class, and a radical element called the *Levelers*, who dared to dream of a nation ruled by all Christian men. (See the box titled "Cromwell and the Levelers.") There were even a few primitive communists, the so-called *Diggers*, who urged the sharing of property as they believed New Testament Christians had done.

The clearest and most devastating division, however, was that between two power centers: the New Model Army, where radicals found a platform, and the Parliament, whose leadership began to seem too conservative to the soldiers and their general, Oliver Cromwell. The result was a series of defections from and purges of the Long Parliament, until no more than sixty were left, the so-called Rump Parliament, to bring the king to trial before the special court that sentenced him to death in 1649. After

THE RULERS AND THE RULED
Cromwell and the Levelers

Oliver Cromwell, the most successful leader of England's Puritan Revolution and ruler of the nation during the "kingless decade" of the Commonwealth, had no more use for radical democratic notions than the Stuart dynasty he overthrew. Here Cromwell reports on the radical doctrines of "Levelers" in the ranks of the Puritans themselves who felt that the revolution had been betrayed by its own leadership. Why does he suggest that the Levelers are "rustic" country people? Do you know of any other occasions when the rank and file have apparently won their struggle and then felt betrayed by their leaders?

How happy were England were men's design of enslaving her at an end [in 1649, after the defeat of King Charles], how gladly should we here break off, and praise the Lord for his goodness to England? but alas the peoples' hearts are full of grief, and . . . they cry out [that] they are deceived . . . their expectations is frustrated, and their liberty betrayed; they take up David's complaint that it is not an open enemy that enslaves them, not damn Cavaliers . . . but Religious and Godly friends, that have prayed, declared, and fought together for freedom with them, that with their swords have cut in sunder the chains of other Tyrants, and yet now are become the greatest Tyrants over their brethren themselves, which when they can refrain from sighing and sobbing, they in their broken and rustic language thus expatiates: all the form of government [has been] corrupted and abused, the Law and administration perverted, and the peoples' liberties betrayed; it was promised that a new foundation should be laid by an agreement of the people, [based on] such righteous Principles of Justice and common right, that . . . it should be impossible for any Tyrants in this or future generations to introduce bondage upon the people.

Source: Oliver Cromwell, *The Declaration of Lieutenant General Cromwell Concerning the Levelers* . . . n. p., 1649, 5.

1653, finally, Cromwell ruled as lord protector of the Commonwealth, dividing the country into military districts and governing through major-generals in each. Such ideological divisions over power and policy also fissured the French, Russian, and other revolutionary movements in later centuries.

Cromwell represented a familiar type among revolutionary leaders in modern times. A man of rigid discipline and total commitment, sure of his own righteousness, he was as confident of his cause as the "incorruptible" Robespierre of 1789 or the twenty-four-hour-a-day revolutionary Lenin in 1917. Like them, he was willing to employ the most ruthless means to achieve his exalted ends. He saw the slaughter of the Irish supporters of Charles II at the Drogheda garrison in Ireland in 1649, for instance, as "a marvelous great mercy."[4] Like Napoleon and Stalin in those later revolutions, Lord Protector Cromwell turned to stern repression to reestablish order in the land, to become what his enemies called him, the king of the kingless decade.

Cromwell's wars and the changes in government he imposed, however, brought crushing taxes and social turmoil. Puritan efforts to abolish theaters, taverns, and May Day celebrations further angered the citizens. Less than two years after Cromwell's death, one of his own major-generals conspired to turn the nation back over to the Stuart heir, Charles II (r. 1660–1685). The people, who had cheered for the revolution, cheered King Charles back to his kingdom. Cromwell's corpse was disinterred, his head stuck on a pole on top of Westminster Hall in London, where it remained throughout Charles II's reign.[5]

The First Bill of Rights

In 1660 a struggle that had begun in 1603 seemed to have come full circle, ending as it had begun with a Stuart king welcomed into London. Charles II, a romantic but prudent prince, had no desire to go back into exile—and therefore did not press too drastic a reaction on the country. The Anglican church was restored with the monarchy, and Puritans suffered such civil disabilities as being prohibited from holding public office. The pastimes and pleasures the Puritan regime had outlawed were revived, particularly by the pleasure-loving king and his courtiers. Charles, furthermore, had come under Catholic and absolutist influences during his years overseas. He set out to forge an alliance with Louis XIV—who was his first cousin. Raised by a Catholic mother, he was probably converted to Catholicism himself before his death in 1685.

He left the crown to his elderly brother, James II (r. 1685–1688), an avowed Catholic who soon claimed the right to "dispense," or suspend, the laws of the realm and established a 30,000-man standing army to garrison it. The fears of "popery" and royal tyranny that had set the revolutionary spiral in motion at the beginning of the century were thus stirred up once more. Within three years of his accession, James II fell victim to what came to be called the *Glorious Revolution* in English history—the expulsion of the last Stuart king and his replacement by the first real constitutional monarchs, William and Mary, in 1688.

The architects of what was really more a political coup than a popular revolution were the leaders of the second James's parliamentary opposition. By 1688, members of this strong antiroyalist faction were being called *Whigs* by their enemies, while the more conservative defenders of royal policies were labeled *Tories*—colorful tags for Scottish and Irish rogues, respectively. The Glorious Revolution was triggered by the birth of an infant son to James and his Catholic queen, an event that seemed to threaten a long line of Catholic sovereigns on the throne of Protestant England. The Whig leaders reacted by circulating the rumor that the child was not the elderly king's but a commoner's brat smuggled into the queen's bed in a warming pan. They also turned to King James's Protestant sister Mary and her husband William of Orange, stadtholder of the Netherlands, who was both ruler of a constitutional state and the moving spirit behind the international coalition against Louis XIV. William, eager to channel the wealth of England into the struggle against absolute monarchy, landed by prearrangement with a Dutch army. Abandoned even by his Tory supporters, James Stuart fled once more into exile, and William III (r. 1689–1702) and Mary II (r. 1689–1696) were crowned joint sovereigns of England early in 1689.

As a condition of being crowned, however, William and Mary were required to accept a set of English constitutional principles enacted by Parliament in 1689. The Whigs thus pushed through *England's Bill of Rights,* the first such legislation to appear in the Western world. Explicitly or implicitly, this remarkable seventeenth-century document guaranteed many of the rights for which Parliament had been fighting for many decades. The sovereigns were compelled to agree to parliamentary control of government revenues, the right to free elections and regular meetings, freedom of debate, and freedom from arrest during a session. Other supports for the rights of the governed included an independent judiciary in which judges could not be cashiered for their political views; relative freedom of religion; and implied support for the rights of all subjects to life, liberty, and property. William of Orange, who as

stadtholder had functioned for years as constitutional ruler of the Netherlands, was willing to accept these terms. Across the Channel, Louis XIV was horrified that any monarch—even his longtime archenemy William of Orange—would accept a crown at the cost of such constraints on his divine right to rule.

The Glorious Revolution of 1688 and the Bill of Rights of 1689 did not bring democracy to England. The House of Lords, filled with titled noblemen and high churchmen, could still veto any bill passed by the Commons. The House of Commons itself was composed of gentry, merchants, and lawyers elected by a small minority of the population. Nor did the Bill of Rights deprive the crown of power, since the monarchs still retained a preponderance of authority. But what began to grow in 1689 was constitutional monarchy, government by a loose alliance of kings and aristocrats under strict legal limitations. In the following centuries, the English Parliament became both more representative and more powerful; and in the twentieth century a democratic House of Commons became the real seat of power in Britain, the monarchy no more than a symbol of national unity.

The Golden Age of the Dutch Republic

In continental Europe, however, another people had gone even further than the English down the road toward a more liberal political order in the seventeenth century. Culturally and economically, this century was the golden age of the Netherlands, the century of Rembrandt and the Dutch overseas empire. Politically, it was also a time when the United Provinces offered more opportunity for citizen participation than any other power in Europe. Theirs was a political system founded on an immense prosperity and precariously balanced between disunity and autocracy. But it produced a freer, more tolerant society than could be found anywhere else—a freedom that in return made its contributions to the economic progress and the cultural brilliance of the Dutch golden age.

Looking up at the tall, narrow Dutch housefronts as you cruise along an Amsterdam canal today, you will not be as dazzled as you might be by the splendors of Versailles. These gabled residences of the city's seventeenth-century urban patriciate, solidly built and modestly decorated, embody the

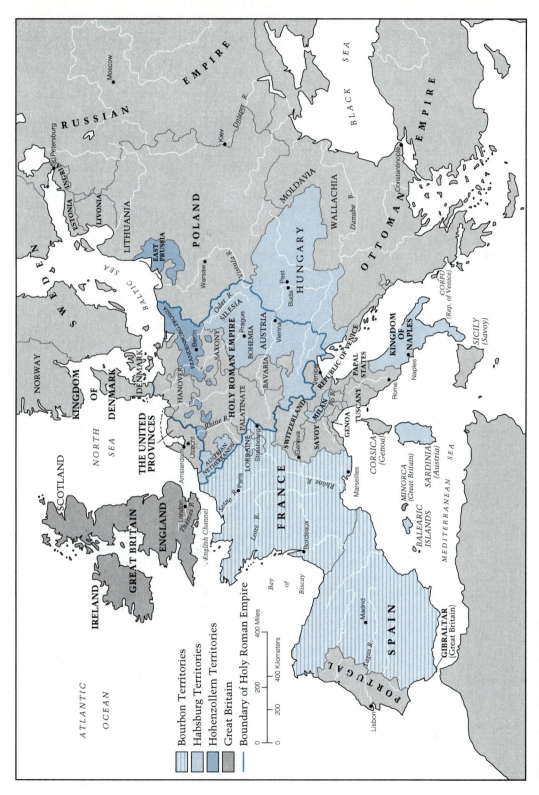

Map 15.3 Europe in 1715

Legend:
- Bourbon Territories
- Habsburg Territories
- Hohenzollern Territories
- Great Britain
- Boundary of Holy Roman Empire

RUSSIAN EMPIRE

Moscow

St. Petersburg

Ingria

Kiev

Dnieper R.

ESTONIA

LIVONIA

LITHUANIA

POLAND

Warsaw

Vistula R.

EAST PRUSSIA

Oder R.

SILESIA

SAXONY

BRANDENBURG-PRUSSIA

Berlin

BALTIC SEA

SWEDEN

NORWAY

KINGDOM OF DENMARK

DENMARK

NORTH SEA

THE UNITED PROVINCES

Amsterdam

Utrecht

AUSTRIAN NETHERLANDS

HANOVER

Rhine R.

PALATINATE

HOLY ROMAN EMPIRE

BAVARIA

BOHEMIA

Prague

AUSTRIA

Vienna

HUNGARY

Buda

Pest

MOLDAVIA

WALLACHIA

Danube R.

BLACK SEA

OTTOMAN EMPIRE

Constantinople

CORFU (Rep. of Venice)

REPUBLIC OF VENICE

Venice

Po R.

MILAN

SAVOY

SWITZERLAND

Geneva

LORRAINE

Strasbourg

Seine R.

Paris

FRANCE

Rhône R.

Marseilles

GENOA

TUSCANY

PAPAL STATES

Rome

KINGDOM OF NAPLES

Naples

SICILY (Savoy)

SARDINIA (Austria)

CORSICA (Genoa)

MINORCA (Great Britain)

BALEARIC ISLANDS

MEDITERRANEAN SEA

SCOTLAND

GREAT BRITAIN

ENGLAND

London

Thames R.

IRELAND

English Channel

Loire R.

Bordeaux

Bay of Biscay

ATLANTIC OCEAN

SPAIN

Madrid

PORTUGAL

Lisbon

Tagus R.

GIBRALTAR (Great Britain)

400 Miles
400 Kilometers
200
200
0
0

479

less ostentatious taste of Europe's most successful middle class. The houses reflect the solid qualities that made their country great.

Economically, centuries of industrial, commercial, and financial development reached their climax in the wake of the successful revolt of the United Provinces against Spain. The tidy, solidly built cities of the northern Netherlands had been a hive of productivity since the High Middle Ages. They were centers of shipbuilding, textile manufacturing, diamond cutting, book publishing, and a dozen other crafts, including the production of Delft china and Dutch gin. The low Dutch polders bloomed beneath the slowly turning windmills. The Dutch city of Amsterdam replaced the Flemish city of Antwerp as Europe's most active financial center, Dutch fishing vessels trolled the North Sea banks, and Dutch merchantmen outnumbered the shipping of all other states combined. In the colonial realm, as we see in Chapter 17, the Dutch shouldered the Portuguese out of southern Asia, competed with the British and the French in North America and the Caribbean, and established one of the West's most long-lasting colonial outposts in South Africa.

The political structure of the Netherlands was an unstable compromise between urban autonomy and domination by the nobility that went back to the relationship between the dukes of Burgundy and the medieval cities of the Low Countries. The seven United Provinces were urban republics with elected councils and magistrates on the medieval pattern. They were loosely joined by an Estates General that had little authority over the affairs of the member provinces.

The Dutch leaders Jan van Oldenbarneveldt, who played a leading part between 1587 and 1618, and Jan de Witt, prominent between 1653 and 1672, guided the United Provinces through some of their most prosperous times. They spoke for the urban patriciate of the cities whose goals were prosperity above all; toleration, which unleashed the productive energies of Protestants, Catholics, and Jews, many of whom migrated to the Netherlands; and control of affairs by the Estates General, where the influence of the urban oligarchy was preponderant.

But there was another center of power in the United Provinces: the noble house of Orange, which had led the northern Netherlands to freedom and enjoyed an aristocratic prestige that went back to the days of the Burgundian dukes. From William the Silent during the sixteenth-century Dutch revolt to the rule of his descendant, the William of Orange who became King William III of England, leaders of this Dutch dynasty were regularly chosen as stadtholders, or overlords, of most of the Dutch provinces.

The goals of the house of Orange, however, differed significantly from those of the industrial, mercantile, and financial elite. The heads of the family tended to be more rigorously Calvinistic than the merchants and more intolerant and fearful of the "Catholic menace," first of Spain and then of Louis XIV's France. They were also typically more eager for war, in which they were the recognized national leaders. An internal tension was thus set up in which power swayed from the stadtholders at the center to the cities and back again through the century.

The Rewards of Freedom

As the English overthrew their monarchs twice in the seventeenth century, so the Dutch Republic went through the same cycle twice during this critical century. It was Holland's Oldenbarneveldt who secured the twelve years' truce with Spain that first recognized the United Provinces in 1609, and it was he who took the leading role thereafter. In 1619, however, the reigning head of the house of Orange, Maurice of Nassau, who dominated affairs from 1618 to 1625, found a religious reason to execute his rival Oldenbarneveldt and plunged the Netherlands into the Thirty Years' War against Spain. As military leaders during this war-torn period, the descendants of William the Silent prevailed for a quarter of a century. As the long struggle wound down in 1648, however, Jan de Witt led the peace forces who subscribed to the Treaty of Münster, finally and permanently accepting the independence of the United Provinces. More than twenty years of peace and prosperity followed under De Witt before Louis XIV broke into the republic in 1672. Outraged at de Witt's lack of preparedness, a mob of his fellow countrymen murdered their venerable leader, and William of Orange took up the reins of leadership for the rest of the century. King of England after 1689 and leader of repeated coalitions against Louis XIV, William also embodied the triumph of centralized authority over the provinces in his own country.

The triumph of Orange, of the executive stadtholders over elected leaders like Oldenbarneveldt and de Witt was, however, more a victory for national unity than for autocracy. Factors that militated against the emergence of absolutism in the United Provinces included the lack of an autocratic royal tradition or a powerful centralized bureaucracy, the economic power of urban mercantile interests, the strength of provincial loyalties, and the relatively high proportion of the citizenry who participated in the political life of these prosperous cities. Religious toleration and cultural pluralism also flourished here as nowhere else in Europe. Many Dutch Calvinists, shrewd businesspeople themselves, saw the value of good minds and welcomed immigrants of any faith: Protestant refugees from Catholic countries, Catholics fleeing Protestant countries, and Jews from everywhere. The latter made the cities of the northern Netherlands Europe's most brilliant center of Jewish culture and productive talent. In this remark-

ably open society, the broader rewards of political freedom might have been discerned generations before they were apparent elsewhere.

The French philosopher René Descartes, one of many freethinkers who sought a haven in the Netherlands, hymned the virtues of the country: "What other place could one choose in the world," he wrote to a friend, "where all the comforts of life . . . may be so easily found as here? What other country where one may enjoy such perfect liberty?"[6] There was a harsher side to the Dutch dominion in its far-flung colonies, where, as we see in a later chapter, they could be as brutal as any other imperialists. But the solid middle-class qualities Descartes applauded—comfort, security, liberty— were major achievements too. In the long run, the modern West looks more like the Dutch Republic than any other seventeenth-century state.

A Topical Summary

POLITICS: The "critical" seventeenth century saw a climactic surge of rebellions and civil wars that fostered the growth of absolute monarchies as a means of restoring order to a battered Europe. Powerful absolutists like Louis XIV in France, the Habsburg and Hohenzollern rulers in central Europe, and Peter the Great in Russia increased royal power at the expense of the traditional prerogatives and liberties of nobles, towns, provinces, and other once autonomous groups and institutions. In England and the Netherlands, by contrast, decades of political struggle produced a rough partnership between the king and Parliament in England, and between stadtholder and Estates General in the Netherlands. In these relations lay the beginnings of modern constitutional government.

Economics: Economic and related problems added

to the social disarray that gripped seventeenth-century Europe. Though commercial states like the Netherlands boomed through much of the century, regional depressions and famines generated much misery for shorter periods. Overall, it was a period of economic stagnation between surges of growth in the sixteenth and eighteenth centuries.

Society: Population growth also leveled off in the 1600s, another slump between two periods of rapid growth. By the end of the century, however, the aristocracy had linked its fortunes to the triumphant monarchies and had entered a golden age of prestige and power. The lower orders, by contrast, became habituated to official intrusions into their lives, and the general malaise stimulated the last large-scale witch hunt in Western history.

Some Key Terms

absolute monarch 462
ancien régime 457
constitutional monarchy 474
critical century 450
Diggers 476
England's Bill of Rights 478
l'état, c'est moi 462
Estates General 466

the Fronde 465
Glorious Revolution 478
intendant 465
Junkers 471
Levelers 476
liberum veto 474
military revolution 451
procurator 473

Puritans 475
service nobility 472
Tories 478
Ulozhenie 472
Whigs 478
witch craze 458

Notes

1. Theodore K. Rabb, *The Struggle for Stability in Early Modern Europe* (New York: Oxford University Press, 1975), 3–4. For a brief summary of the debate over "the crisis of the seventeenth century," see Chapter 2 of this volume.

2. "Mémoires de Louis IV pour l'instruction du Dauphin," trans. Herbert H. Rowen, in H. H. Rowen, ed., *From Absolutism to Revolution, 1648–1848* (New York: Macmillan, 1963), 27, 28.

3. Bishop Gilbert Burnet, in B. H. Sumner, *Peter the Great and the Emergence of Russia* (New York: Collier, 1962), 41.

4. Maurice Ashley, *The Greatness of Oliver Cromwell* (New York: Collier, 1962), 223.

5. Today the lord protector's statue guards the Parliament House in Westminster.

6. Petrus Johannes Blok, *History of the People of the Netherlands,* vol. 4, trans. Oscar A. Bierstadt (New York: Putnam's, 1907), 102.

Reading List

ANDERSON, M. S. *War and Society in Europe of the Old Regime, 1618–1789.* New York: St. Martin's Press, 1988. A useful introduction to a field of growing interest to historians—the role of warfare in Western society.

ASHLEY, M. B. *The Golden Century.* New York: Praeger, 1969. Good place to begin on the seventeenth century.

BRAUDEL, F. *Capitalism and Material Life, 1400–1800.* New York: Harper, 1974. Thoughtful exploration of the material lives of early modern people.

CARSTEN, F. L. *The Origins of Prussia.* Westport, Conn.: Greenwood, 1982. The beginnings of modern Germany, through the Great Elector.

CHURCH, W. F. *The Impact of Absolutism in France.* New York: Wiley, 1969. Materials on the rise of absolutism in seventeenth-century France.

COLE, C. W. *Colbert and a Century of French Mercantilism.* Hamden, Conn.: Archon, 1964. Thorough survey of the mercantile system at its most developed. See also E. F. HERKSCHER, *Mercantilism,* 2d ed. (New York: Macmillan, 1962) for a provocative analysis.

CORVISIER, A. *Armies and Societies in Europe, 1494–1789.* Translated by A. T. Siddall. Bloomington: University of Indiana Press, 1979. The army as an instrument of state power, as part of society, and as a subculture of its own.

DEHIO, L. *The Precarious Balance: Four Centuries of the European Power Struggle.* New York: Knopf, 1962. Long-range perspective on European international relations from the Renaissance to the nineteenth century. See also T. K. RABB, *The Struggle for Stability in Early Modern Europe* (New York: Oxford University Press, 1975), which extends the crisis of the seventeenth century back to the sixteenth, seeing it as a conflict between central government and the regions.

DE VRIES, J. *Economy of Europe in an Age of Crisis, 1600–1750.* New York: Cambridge University Press, 1976. Sees economic growth underlying depression in the critical century.

ELLIOTT, J. H. *Richelieu and Olivares.* New York: Cambridge University Press, 1984. Comparative biographies of the two rival statesmen, seen in the context of their times and the problems each faced.

HILL, H. C. *The Century of Revolution, 1603–1714.* New York: Norton, 1982. Admired overview of the England's "century of revolution," with social and economic emphasis.

———*The World Turned Upside Down.* London: Penguin, 1976. Ideas of the English radicals.

KLAITS, J. *Servants of Satan: The Age of Witch Hunts.* Bloomington: University of Indiana Press, 1985. Synthesizes views of recent scholarship on the great witch hunt.

MOUSNIER, R. E. *The Institutions of France under the Absolute Monarchy, 1598–1789: Society and the State.* Chicago: University of Chicago Press, 1980. Interaction of government and people from the century of Richelieu and Louis XIV to the French Revolution.

RAEFF, M., ed. *Peter the Great Changes Russia.* Lexington, Mass.: D.C. Heath, 1972. Essays on the impact of the controversial founder of modern Russia.

———*The Well-Ordered Police State: Social and Institutional Change . . . in the Germanies and Russia, 1600–1800.* New Haven: Yale University Press, 1983. Comparative study of emerging autocracy, going below institutional structures to administrative routines and political attitudes of elites.

ROOSEN, W. J. *The Age of Louis XIV: The Rise of Modern Diplomacy.* Cambridge, Mass.: Schenkman, 1976. Analyzes the diplomatic system of Louis XIV's day in terms of institutions, personnel, and practice.

STONE, L. *The Family, Sex, and Marriage in England, 1500–1800.* New York: Harper & Row, 1977. Documents a drift in family organization from loose structure through the patriarchal private family of the seventeenth century to a more affectionate nuclear family in the eighteenth.

WEDGEWOOD, C. V. *Oliver Cromwell.* 2d ed. London: Duckworth, 1973. Scholarly, thoroughly readable life of the Puritan leader.

———*The Thirty Years War.* New York: Methuen, 1981. The bloodiest war of the century vividly retold. For a more analytical approach, see T. K. RABB, ed., *The Thirty Years War: Problems of Motive and Effect* (New York: University Press of America, 1981).

WOLF, J. B. *Louis XIV.* New York: Norton, 1968. Impressive political biography.

"'Tis all in pieces," lamented the poet and preacher John Donne, looking around him at the confused and fragmented intellectual world of the early seventeenth century, "all coherence gone."[1] The crisis of the age, which shook society and transformed the state, inevitably had its impact on the thought and art of the period. Sensitive spirits like Donne were no longer able to find answers to all their questions in classical and Christian sources as Renaissance humanists and Reformation preachers had done. They were also challenged by the scientific revolution, which had begun in the middle of the preceding century and reached its climax in the later seventeenth century. Overwhelmed, thoughtful people fumbled for new certainties. As state builders from Louis XIV to Cromwell imposed order on society, so thinkers and artists strove to reassemble an intellectually acceptable picture of the world and of humanity's place in it.

Through their labors the modern Western worldview began to take shape. During the seventeenth century, Western people began to entertain some modern political views, to see the world artistically through realistic eyes, and to understand nature and nature's laws in modern scientific terms. It was only a beginning in all these areas. But it was a level of achievement that has earned for the "critical century" another appropriate label: the "century of genius" in the history of the Western mind.

The Beginnings of Modern Political Thought

The deep political divide between absolutist and constitutional governments in the seventeenth century was reflected in the political thought of the time. From this conflict between the political vision of Louis XIV and that embodied in the English Bill of Rights came the seminal ideas of Thomas Hobbes and John Locke, Hobbes asserting the need for stronger central government, Locke defending the rights of the governed. Both these ideals have echoed down the modern centuries as formulations of two key views of how Western people ought to be ruled or to rule themselves.

The Concept of Sovereignty

The political thought of the age certainly felt the impact of the atmosphere of crisis that enveloped

John Smith. *Sir Isaac Newton.* Mezzotint. Victoria and Albert Museum, London the times. In an age of rebellion and the reassertion of royal power, many political thinkers continued to draw on ancient and medieval ideas, while others found support for their theories in the emerging physical sciences and in new views of human nature. The result was a war of words between rigidly absolutist and radically constitutionalist doctrines in which modern political science was born. We look at the theory of royal absolutism in this section and at constitutionalist ideas in the section that follows.

To support the claims of early modern rulers to unprecedented power over the people, apologists for absolute monarchy drew on sources such as the aristocratic Greek views of Plato and Aristotle, the Roman imperial experience, and the medieval concept of divine right. Views older than Plato that "the people" were sheep in need of a shepherd, or wild beasts requiring a strong hand to tame them, echoed convincingly in the ears of thinkers who had seen the Fronde or the excesses of the Puritan Revolution. Images of Roman imperial grandeur surrounded the Sun King in stone and glowing pigment. Above all,

seventeenth-century thinkers developed and vigorously asserted the medieval concept of the monarch's divine right to rule. Phrases like "God, by whom kings reign" came naturally to their lips.[2] The first principle of government, declared Bishop Jacques Bossuet (1627–1704), court preacher to Louis XIV, is that "royal authority is sacred." King Charles II of England, speaking for the battered Stuart monarchy, said this to a university audience at Cambridge in 1681, only half a dozen years before the Glorious Revolution:

> We will still believe and maintain that our kings derive not their title from the people, but from God; that to him only they are accountable; that it belongs not to subjects, either to create or to censure but to honor and obey their sovereign.[3]

Other political thinkers explored the concept of *sovereignty*, attributing an unprecedented degree of authority to royal government. As a political con-

The all-powerful monarch above in this seventeenth century title page to Hobbes's *Leviathan* shows the monarchy as composed of the subjects whose interests are all served by accepting royal power. The quotation from the Book of Job flanking the crown says that "no power on earth" is comparable to that of the sovereign.

cept, sovereignty had traditionally meant the highest level of authority *within* a particular institution or subdivision of society. The church, the legal system, provinces and towns all had their own sovereign or supreme authorities. In the depths of the French wars of religion, however, Jean Bodin (1530–1596) in his *Six Books on the Republic* (1576) offered a new definition of *maiestas,* or "sovereign authority." Sovereignty for Bodin was no longer relative to a particular subdivision of society, but absolute, supreme over the whole of the body politic. Such absolute sovereignty, furthermore, was necessary to the health of the state, since only *maiestas* could hold together the various component parts of the nation. It was an argument that had as much appeal to the crisis-torn seventeenth century as to the sixteenth, and was freely cited by defenders of absolute monarchy.

The Leviathan State

In a longer perspective, however, the most important supporter of absolutist government was the eccentric English conservative Thomas Hobbes (1588–1679), whose concept of the *Leviathan state* was used later to explain far more authoritarian regimes in our own century. Horrified by the Puritan Revolution in England, Hobbes had fled to France, where his book *Leviathan,* a "Discourse of Civil Government Occasioned by the Disorders of the Present Time," was published in 1651.

Hobbes's view was based not on Christian or classical sources but on the materialistic philosophy that underlay the scientific revolution which, as we see later, reached its apogee in this century. His materialistic analysis produced a grim picture of human beings driven by selfish motives of desire and fear, locked in a perpetual struggle for survival, the "war of all against all." He began his analysis with a look at life in *the state of nature*—a key concept in early modern political thought, meaning the condition in which human beings would live if there were neither government nor laws to restrain them. Hobbes described this condition as bleak and brutal, deprived of the skills and comforts, arts and sciences of civilization. Human life was thus naturally, as an often quoted passage puts it, "solitary, poor, nasty, brutish, and short."

To end this anarchic and mutually destructive situation, Hobbes asserted, human beings sooner or later formulate a *social contract*—another basic conception of modern political analysis. Social contract theory asserts that structured society exists by virtue of a tacit contractual agreement among its people. In Hobbes's view, such a social contract requires the people to surrender all their personal power to a central government that, by ruling over them all alike, will protect them all from each other. Leaving the state of nature behind, people thus create organized society—and absolute sovereignty at the same time. For in order to carry out its primary function of protecting the governed from their own baser instincts, government must have great power. It must possess not only lawmaking and police powers, but control of state revenues, of the armed forces, of the printing press and the pulpit; in short, it must have ultimate authority over every institution and every individual in the state. We are driven by our basic natures, Hobbes said, to erect the *Leviathan state,* a society as powerful and all-encompassing as Leviathan, the biblical monster of the deep—and to more liberal thinkers in later centuries, every bit as frightening (see box, "Hobbes and the Leviathan State").

The absolute monarchs of the seventeenth century understandably preferred divine right and grandiose Roman parallels to Hobbes's grim justification of their supreme power. Later modern political thinkers, however, have made Hobbes's book a classic. And many people since have seen in Hobbes's *Leviathan,* as in Machiavelli's *Prince,* some uncomfortable intimations of the way human beings and human governments too often really are.

Government by Consent of the Governed

In the long run, however, the most influential political thinkers of the seventeenth century proved to be those who spoke for the constitutionalist side in the century's great debate. Phrases and philosophies well known from America's own eighteenth-century Declaration of Independence and Constitution, for example, could be heard on the lips of the Levelers during the English Civil War and from John Locke at the time of the Glorious Revolution.

The *Levelers,* who flourished briefly in the 1640s, got their name from those who charged they wanted to "level" a naturally hierarchic society to confer an unnatural social equality on all people. Part of the extremist fringe in revolutionary England, the Levelers were yeomen farmers and others even lower on the social scale, people who would never serve as magistrates or sit in Commons. But they had heard much talk about "rights"—the rights of Parliament, the rights of judges to try cases without royal interfer-

	1550	1575	1600

POLITICAL, MILITARY, AND DIPLOMATIC EVENTS

r. 1558–1603   Elizabeth I

SOCIAL AND ECONOMIC DEVELOPMENTS

CULTURE: THE ARTS, PHILOSOPHY, SCIENCE AND RELIGION

1540–1600   Catholic Reformation
1543   Copernicus, *On the Revolutions of the Heavenly Bodies*
1543   Vesalius, *On the Structure of the Human Body*

1561–1626   Bacon
1567–1643   Monteverdi
1573–1610   Caravaggio
1577–1640   Rubens
1588–1679   Hobbes
1596–1650   Descartes
1598–1680   Bernini
1606–1669   Rembrandt
1608–1674   Milton
1610   Galileo's telescope

---

ence, the rights of the rather abstract "freeborn Englishmen" the orators defended. Religious Independents (Congregationalists) and leaders among the rank and file of the Puritan Army, these radicals began to demand some rights of their own.

Extremist doctrines commonly voiced by the Levelers included universal manhood suffrage, the elimination of any sort of property qualification for voting, and religious toleration, at least for all Protestant sects. "The poorest he that is in England," thundered Thomas Rainborough in a public debate with Cromwell, "hath a life to live as well the richest he; and truly, sir, I think it is clear that every man that is to live under a government ought first by his own consent to put himself under that government."[4] Men of property themselves and as fearful of anarchy as their royalist opponents were, the leaders of the parliamentary revolution were horrified at these radically democratic demands. Cromwell suppressed the Levelers as firmly as any sovereign in Europe would have done.

John Locke (1632–1704) came several decades after the Levelers, publishing his *Two Treatises of Civil Government* in 1690 and declaring that the work was intended "to establish the throne of our great restorer, our present King, William, to make good his title in the consent of the people . . . the only one of all lawful governments."[5] Locke's epochal *Second Treatise* (though written some years earlier) thus appeared in the wake of the Glorious Revolution that put William and Mary on the throne as England's first real constitutional monarchs. This essay also became the first classic of the liberal political tradition, and Locke the original prophet of government by consent of the governed—though his definition of "the governed" was not so radical as that of the Levelers.

Locke, a physician by training, shared Hobbes's enthusiasm for science and rooted his political theory also in distinctive views of human character, "the state of nature," and an ideal "social contract." Locke's account of all three, however, differed strik-

1642–1649 English Civil War
r. 1643–1715 Louis XIV

1640s The Levelers

1622–1673 Molière
1632–1675 Vermeer
1632–1704 Locke
1639–1699 Racine

1660 Royal Academy of Science

1687 Newton's *Principles of Natural Philosophy*

ingly from the views of his countrymen a couple of generations earlier.

Human character, Locke believed, was not innately selfish and vicious, but infinitely malleable, a *tabula rasa* ("blank slate") on which childhood training, education, and later experience inscribe the character of the adult. Nurture, not nature, said Locke, makes us what we are. This view implied also the doctrine of human perfectibility: the belief that by transforming the social environment, human beings can effectively change human nature—or at least human behavior—and produce a better society, a happier world. It was a vision of humanity that proved central to all the reformist and revolutionary ideologies of the modern world.

In the state of nature, Locke declared, mild-mannered human beings live not in a war of all against all, but relatively peacefully much of the time. Even before the creation of an ordered society, furthermore, humans enjoy both the use of reason and their most precious possessions, their *natural rights,*

particularly the rights to life, liberty, and property (see box, "Locke, Natural Rights, and the Social Contract"). Because intermittent outbreaks of injustice and aggression could occur even in Locke's state of nature, however, institutional support for these rights would in the long run prove beneficial. Thus for the preservation of their natural rights, Locke argued, rational people will enter into a social contract, establishing the state. But this Lockean state will be very different from Hobbes's Leviathan.

Legitimate government, John Locke believed, would be limited in its powers, would be restrained by law, and would exist only by the consent of the people it governed. The powers of the state, far from being absolute, were strictly limited to the protection of the rights of the people. Government was also to be restrained by its own laws, as William and Mary were restrained by the Bill of Rights from ruling by decree or riding roughshod over law and tradition. Above all, any legitimate government should be controlled by the governed themselves, making

THE RULERS AND THE RULED
Hobbes and the Leviathan State

Thomas Hobbes's justification of all-powerful authoritarian government, the sort provided by seventeenth-century absolute monarchs, began with a dark vision of human nature. Human beings "in the state of nature" were driven by greed, fear, or lust for glory and domination of others to exploit or attack each other in an unending "war of all against all." Security and civilization itself thus depended on surrendering all power to "that great Leviathan," the state. Do you agree with Hobbes's analysis of human nature? Which do you think would be worse—the brutish life described here or life under an all-powerful state?

In the nature of man, we find three principal causes of quarrel: First, Competition; Secondly, Diffidence [Fear]; Thirdly, Glory.

The first maketh man invade [others] for Gain; the second, for Safety; and the third for Reputation . . . .

Hereby it is manifest, that during the time men live without a common Power to keep them all in Awe, they are in that condition which is called War; and such a war as is of every man against every man. . . . In such condition there is no place for Industry, because the fruit thereof is so uncertain: and consequently no Culture [Cultivation] of the earth, no Navigation, nor use of the commodities that may be imported by Sea; no commodious Building; no Instruments [Machines] for moving and removing such things as require much force; no account of Time; no Arts; no Letters; no Society; and which is worst of all, continual fear and danger of violent death; and the life of man solitary, poor, nasty, brutish, and short. . . .

The only way to erect such a Common Power as may be able to defend them from the invasion of Foreigners and the injuries of one another . . . is to confer all their power and strength upon one Man or one Assembly of men . . . and therein to submit their Wills every one to his Will and their Judgment to his Judgment. . . . This is the generation [birth] of the great Leviathan . . . of that Mortal God to which we owe under the Immortal God our peace and defence.

Source: Thomas Hobbes, *Leviathan* (London: J. M. Dent, 1914), 64–65, 87, 89–90.

their power felt through an elected legislature like the House of Commons in the English Parliament. And if an illegitimate government arose, one that suppressed rather than protected the natural rights of the governed, then the people had the ultimate "right to revolution," the right to overthrow such a government and replace it with a new one.

Locke saw two other elements as essential to a free society: private property and toleration of dissent. He felt that those who own land or other material possessions have a larger "stake in society" than those who have nothing to lose. An active share in government should therefore be limited to those who, because they owned property, have "something to lose" if society fails to function properly—people with a "stake" in the success of the body politic. Locke also believed strongly, however, in toleration for minority views and in freedom of expression. His support for tolerance was originally intended to apply to religious minorities like the Puritans, but it provided support for freedom of thought more broadly conceived in later centuries.

Expanding Horizons of Art

The arts in the seventeenth century, like so much else, reflected that period's critical place in Western history. Artists and writers looked back for guidance and inspiration to the glories of ancient art the humanists had uncovered and to the religious passions unleashed by the Protestant and Catholic Reformations. Like their predecessors in earlier times, seventeenth-century writers and artists catered to the needs and tastes of church and state. At the same time, however, literature and art responded to the attitudes of increasingly prosperous and educated middle-class Europeans. The result was an expansion of the scope of the arts to reach the middling economic strata whose down-to-earth taste and commonsense view of the world played a more and more important part in the cultural life of the West.

Baroque Art

As the religious passions of the preceding century cooled toward toleration and political thinkers debated the relative merits of absolute and constitutionally limited government, the arts also responded to these trends of the times. This was particularly the

Such a powerful style had an instant appeal to both church and state in a time when both were challenged. Baroque thus became the art of the Catholic Reformation in the later 1500s and of absolute monarchy in the 1600s. Authorized by the Council of Trent to make use of carved and painted images, music, and gorgeous decorations to draw waverers back to the faith, Catholic church leaders built, rebuilt, or refurbished hundreds of baroque churches during the sixteenth and seventeenth centuries. They commissioned thousands of paintings and statues of saints in ecstasy, Mary ascending into heaven, and the Passion of Christ on the cross, all aimed at reviving belief by sheer emotional impact. Royal absolutists built ornate palaces surrounded by vast formal gardens and splendid vistas for the same reason. Such structures served as awesome settings for ceremonies that restored belief, in this case in the sovereigns' authority and divine right to rule. All across Europe, the splendors of baroque churches and palaces, vast paintings, dynamic sculpture, and the cascading sounds of baroque music carried a common message of power and pomp, worldly greatness, and the joys of spiritual surrender.

The baroque style in a variety of media was perfectly suited to these ends. Baroque painting combined drastic foreshortening, asymmetrical composition, bright colors, and swirling movement of draperies and straining limbs. These visually exciting elements were typically organized around an inward-driving diagonal to focus dramatically on a wonder-working saint or a king in his glory. The Flemish master Peter Paul Rubens (1577–1640) thus filled his huge canvases with bodies turning, gesturing, guiding the eye from lower left to upper right through waves of color to a heroic St. Francis, or to Mary offering the infant Jesus to the adoration of the three kings.

In Spain, the court painter Diego Velázquez (1599–1660) and the church artist Bartolomé Murillo (1617–1682) concentrated their great talents in the service of the monarchy and the church. A close friend of Philip IV, Velázquez painted the Spanish Habsburg king, the royal family, and such historic events as *The Surrender at Breda* with an accuracy, powerful composition, and a control of brush strokes that compelled belief. His contemporary Murillo became perhaps the most admired of all baroque religious painters, loved particularly for his moving depictions of the Virgin, from the child Mary to her ascent into heaven.

In Italy, the dramatic paintings of Caravaggio

John Locke founded the liberal tradition in English political thought that became the basis of modern democratic philosophy. It is to Locke that this philosophy owes its emphasis on the rights of the people and on a liberal contract theory of government.

case with later sixteenth- and seventeenth-century styles like the baroque and classicism. Behind the triumphant notes of baroque trumpets, the sweep of St. Peter's Square in Rome, or the fourteen hundred playing fountains of Versailles gleamed the taut calculations of power and politics in an age of crisis.

The word *baroque* may derive from *barroco*, a term of perhaps Arabic origin meaning "an irregularly shaped pearl." Baroque architecture, painting, sculpture, and music did depart from the balanced, logical norms of Renaissance art. It did so in order to stir the emotions rather than to impress the intellect. Its object was to move its audience powerfully by any means possible, from movement and color to sheer breathtaking scale. Baroque art thus answered the uncertainties of the age by an overwhelming assertion of the will: believe, accept, and Donne's disoriented world, "all coherence gone," will make sense once more.

THE RULERS AND THE RULED   Locke, Natural Rights, and the Social Contract

John Locke's view of good government, like Hobbes's, began with humanity in its natural state, before any government existed. Locke, however, saw human beings as essentially good, and emphasized the *natural rights* people enjoyed in the state of nature, including liberty, equality, and property. Government, he said, should be designed to preserve those natural rights. Government policies, furthermore, should be determined, not by an all-powerful individual or group, but by the will of the majority of the people. How does Locke's view of how human beings live without social constraints compare with Hobbes's view of life "in the state of nature?"

> To understand political power aright and derive it from its original, we must consider what state all men are naturally in, and that is a state of perfect freedom to order their actions and dispose of their possessions and persons as they think fit. . . .
>
> A state of equality, wherein all the power and jurisdiction is reciprocal, no one having more than another, there being nothing more evident,

than that creatures of the same species and rank, promiscuously born to all the same advantages of Nature, and the use of the same faculties, should also be equal one amongst another, without subordination or subjection. . . .

Men being as has been said by nature all free, equal, and independent, no one can be . . . subjected to the political power of another without his own consent, which is done by agreeing with other men, to join and unite into a community for their comfortable, safe, and peaceable living one amongst another, in a secure enjoyment of their properties, and a greater security . . . they are thereby presently incorporated and make one body politic, wherein the majority have a right to act. . . .

For when any number of men have, by the consent of every individual, made a community, they have thereby made that community one body, which is only to be governed by the will and determination of the majority. . . . Absolute arbitrary power, or governing without standing laws, can neither of them consist with the ends of society and government, which is to preserve their lives, liberties, and fortunes.

Source: John Locke, *Of Civil Government: Two Treatises* (London and Toronto: J. M. Dent, 1924), 118, 164–165, 186.

(1573–1610) and of Artemisia Gentileschi (1593–1652) exploited realism and violently contrasting chiaroscuro to further intensify the viewer's reactions. Caravaggio (real name Michelangelo Merisi) was himself a violent person, exiled from Rome for killing a man in a brawl. Though his realistic depiction of disciples like St. Matthew as rude peasants disturbed some, his tenebrist (deeply shadowed) chiaroscuro, with its focused lighting and enveloping areas of darkness, stirred powerful emotional responses in many viewers.

Artemisia Gentileschi was the daughter of a well-known artist—the most likely route for a woman into the arts. Like Caravaggio's life, Gentileschi's had its dramatic moments, including her rape by the man her father had engaged to teach her and the humiliation of the resulting trial, in which she— not her attacker—was tortured to ascertain the truth of her testimony. One of the best known artists of her

generation, Gentileschi, like Caravaggio, composed her pictures in dynamic contrasts of light and darkness. Her psychological realism shows in her savage pictures of the biblical heroine Judith decapitating the tyrant Holofernes, images in which some critics have detected a violence born of her own traumatic life experiences.

Baroque sculpture could become almost painterly in its effort to achieve emotionally stirring effects, combining stone, metal, glass, and colored light in an intensely illusionistic art. The famous statue of *The Ecstasy of St. Teresa* by Gianlorenzo Bernini (1598–1680) in the church of Santa Maria della Vittoria in Rome, for instance, features golden metal rays and filtered yellow light from above flooding over the marble figures of the swooning saint, head thrown back, and the smiling angel posed to thrust the arrow of divine love into her heart. A simple bust, like Bernini's of Louis XIV at Versailles,

Velazquez's *Surrender of Breda* shows the climax of the epic siege of that Netherlands city in 1625, during the Thirty Years War. Note both Velazquez's focus on the commanders and the captured city and the air of high seriousness that informs the picture. Paintings of such historic events defined history as the deeds of great leaders.

Bernini's 85-foot *Baldacchino* or tabernacle fills the huge space beneath the dome of St. Peter's. Modeled on the canopy placed over the sacrament, the *baldacchino* matches the immense scale of the expanded baroque St. Peter's.

ing heavily on costume and scenery for their effect, ballets were often performed by noble courtiers and even kings until Louis XIV established the first school to train professional dancers in the 1660s. From this Royal Academy of Dance and its imitators across Europe came rigorously trained, highly athletic artists who could perform feats no dancers had ever before attempted.

The first important opera was the Italian *Orfeo* of Claudio Monteverdi (1567–1643), produced in 1607. Opera developed as a form of musical drama combining choral and solo singing, much as ancient Greek tragedy had done. The powerful solos called *arias* in particular, expressing a character's passion, anguish, or other intense feeling in an intricate flood of melody, tested the range and mastery of the most gifted singers of the age. Though Monteverdi created the first modern operas in Mantua in the early seventeenth century, Jean-Baptiste Lully (1632–1687), a Florentine at the court of Louis XIV, created a French style that rivaled the Italian originals. Built around slender stories and unconvincing characters, baroque opera depended on spectacle and glorious music to hold first courtly and then popular audiences spellbound.

Perhaps most impressive of all, baroque architecture, integrated with sculpture and painting, sounded a powerful reaffirmation of the grandeur of church and state. Ornate and elaborate in Italy, Austria, and Spain, more stately in France, baroque building combined Greek columns and capitals with Roman arches and domes, replaced balanced rectangles with sweeping curves, and aimed at giving a sense of vast spaces mastered by the architect.

Approaching the Karlskirche in Vienna, for example, you may be startled by the enormous, entirely functionless columns in front of the church, displaying the deeds of the Catholic Reformation saint Carlo Borromeo in clear relief. Within, you are engulfed in colored marble, huge paintings, and white statues, their heavy bodies mounting into the dome through golden rays and sculptured clouds aswirl with angels. A single room in the opulent immensity of Versailles, like the Salon of War, blends huge scale with a profusion of art. Dominated by a marble relief of Louis XIV triumphant on horseback, the chamber is resplendent with richly colored paintings, marble fireplaces, huge chandeliers, and carving everywhere, generating awe in even the most footsore visitor. It was the effect the baroque aimed at everywhere—the glory of the re-

could be filled with movement and excitement by the angle of the head, the darting eye, and the tumultuous swirl of hair and cloak about the shoulders.

Baroque music was also eminently suited to the sumptuous culture of court entertainments and gorgeous church ceremonial in which it was born. Richly dramatic church music, dazzling in counterpoint and fugue, made baroque worship a stirring aesthetic experience. Opera and ballet flowered as suitably splendid entertainments for a society of aristocrats and kings. These new forms also mingled the arts—music, dance, drama, and the visual arts of costume design, set design, and scene painting—to produce spectacles of unrivaled splendor.

The first generally recognized ballet was a French court entertainment of the 1580s. Depend-

formed Catholic church, the splendor of the absolutist state.

Classical Art

The diminished exuberance and exalted stateliness of French baroque was due in part to the fact that the France of Louis XIV was the center of another major tendency in the arts of the later seventeenth century: classicism. The term describes a continuing impulse in the arts as a particular seventeenth-century style. In the broadest sense, *classicism* means art bound by its own traditions, art in which beauty is defined in terms of adherence to rules and models inherited from the past. It is not an approach that commands much enthusiasm from twentieth-century audiences. The century of modernism and postmodernism has been one of fermenting change in the arts, a century that glorifies originality, hails innovation, and looks with pity on the "merely derivative" in literature and art. Respect for older styles and formulated rules, however, is at least as common among artists of earlier centuries as is our passion for novelty. And without an appreciation for the enriching impact of tradition on the creative artist, it is impossible to come to grips with the greatness of Racine or Milton, the painting of Poussin, or much of the magnificence of Versailles itself.

The Renaissance had brought the modern West back into contact with its ancient roots, and Renaissance art had profited thereby. Seventeenth-century classicism turned to ancient culture with even greater dedication, building with Greek and Roman columns and capitals, filling pictures and plays with characters out of Greek myth and Roman history, writing epics, lyrics, satires, and tragedies because the ancients had. This century of the restoration of social order was also an age that admired rules and standards in the arts. Drama followed the three unities of action, place, and time derived from Aristotle. Poetry found its ultimate authority in the *Poetic Art* (1674) of Nicholas Boileau (1636–1711), a vigorous defender of classical models against the "moderns." In the arts, Louis XIV became the official patron of the French Academy of Painting and Sculpture in 1667. Here the royal painter Charles le Brun (1619–1690) held regular lecture-discussions of artworks designed to formulate fixed "academic" standards of artistic excellence. Academic training itself helped to shape both artistic practice and public taste, as the French Academy of Literature honed, pruned,

and rendered the French literary language more elegant and precise.

The classic art and literature that resulted cultivated traditional subjects and styles and aimed at refinement, rationality, and high seriousness. Shakespeare's tendency to scatter wit and even ribald humor through his darkest tragedies would have seemed a blasphemous break in the tragic mood to a French classical dramatist like Racine. Often contrasted with the baroque style, classicism sought balance and tranquility where the baroque stressed movement and dynamism; simplicity and clarity where baroque was full of life and action; hardboned structure in contrast to the rich color of the baroque. The surging crowds and driving diagonals of Rubens, for example, vanish in the calm landscapes with a few quiet classical figures of Nicolas Poussin (1594–1665) and Claude Lorrain (1600–1682). In Poussin's arcadian scenes, for instance, a single musing shepherd may be all that breaks the golden-age tranquility of a perfectly balanced landscape of horizontal meadows and vertical trees.

In the classical tragedy of Pierre Corneille (1606–1684) and especially of Jean Racine (1639–1699), noble heroes and heroines discuss their emotional crises—usually involving a clash between love and honor, passion and loyalty—in chiseled diction, balanced rhetorical arguments, and elegant six-beat verse. That such rigorous standards need not drain literature of emotional power is clear in the work of Racine, the most admired of all French dramatists. His tragedy of *Phèdre* (1677), for example, follows the mythic queen of Athens who falls hopelessly in love with her own stepson as she warps and destroys the lives of others.

In England, John Dryden (1631–1700) dominated English letters during much of the later seventeenth century. Popular playwright, master of poetic forms that went back to ancient Greece, and a dry, satiric wit, Dryden illustrated important aspects of the classical mode. As England's poet laureate under Charles II, he wrote a number of dignified dramas like *All for Love*, a soberer version of Shakespeare's passionate *Antony and Cleopatra*. And his translation of Vergil's *Aeneid* was admired for the next two centuries.

Towering over all other English poets of the later seventeenth century, John Milton (1608–1674) has been described as the last great Renaissance writer, as the poetic voice of Puritan England,

and as a clearly baroque poet in the sonorous power of his verse. Yet Milton's deep involvement in all the traditions of the Western past—biblical and Greco-Roman, medieval and Renaissance—makes him a striking exemplar of the classical spirit too.

A pious youth, Milton acquired a classical education at Cambridge, traveled Italy in the afterglow of the Renaissance, and participated as a pamphleteer in the Puritan revolt. He wrote his greatest poems in his later years, however, when he had seen both his revolution and his eyesight fail and had to dictate his lines to the daughters who cared for him. His epic *Paradise Lost* (1667) and his verse drama *Samson Agonistes* (1671) draw on ancient Hebrew and Christian subject matter, the fall of Adam and Eve in the garden of Eden and the last days of Samson, blind and beaten like the poet himself. In form, these great poems reverberate with the classical literary models with which Milton was so familiar. Scenes, characters, speeches, epic similes and mythological allusions, the very Latinate power of the verse itself all echo the great poetry of Western antiquity. And out of all trial and torment comes some of the peace and harmony that was the objective of classicism in that age of crisis. Even the tragic story of Samson, "blind among enemies, O worse than chains," climaxing in victory and death for the hero who pulls the pagan temple down upon him ends on an elegiac note: "calm of mind, all passion spent."[6] It was a resolution that followed crisis, as classicism in general responded to a need for ordered calm after the excitement and dramatic tension of the baroque.

This painting of a woman weighing gold has the realism for which the Dutch painters were famous and the stillness and dignity for which Vermeer's pictures of the Dutch elite are admired. The woman's clothing is quietly costly, her gold and jewels evidence of material wellbeing. [Jan Vermeer. *Woman Holding a Balance*. 1664. Canvas, 16 ¾ × 15". National Gallery of Art, Washington, Widener Collection 1942]

Art for the Middle Classes

In a new wave of art and literature aimed at middle-class Europeans, finally, the century showed a sense of growing confidence, a feeling that the world was good, a worthy stage for the decent lives of decent people. Sensible Englishmen like the diarist Samuel Pepys, solid Dutch burghers like those Rembrandt painted, faced few of the ideological and spiritual torments addressed by political theorists or by the high art of court, church, and academy. But theirs was, in a sense, the art of the future, the culture of the coming bourgeois predominance in the Western world.

The famous "rising middle classes" that had emerged with the towns of medieval times and prospered with the Renaissance economic revival were now a very important—and complex—part of society. From the urban patrician and the high-ranking civil servants at the top through merchants, artisans, doctors, lawyers, and growing numbers of officials, they reached down through the ranks to servants and half-literate clerks at the bottom. This broad middle range of society wanted art to include an exciting narrative, human sympathy, respectability, virtue triumphant. Above all, their view of the world respected the world: the material frame itself, the fascinating variety of people in it, the lives and interesting experiences of real people like themselves. Unlikely to identify with saints in ecstasy or kings in their glory, or to be interested in classical themes, the middle-class public wanted simpler, solider fare. They got it in the English literature of "prose and sense" or the paintings of the Dutch realists of the seventeenth century.

There was clearly a moral dimension to the middle-class view of the world. Good Christian families read their Bibles or attended Mass, prayed and sang hymns. Printed volumes of spiritual edification found substantial numbers of bourgeois readers. In France, Italy, and the Spanish Netherlands, the almost Calvinist vision of the Catholic Cornelius Jansen (1585–1638), stressing human wickedness and the need for divine grace, emphasized rigorous moralism. In England, the middle classes made the *Pilgrim's Progress* (1678) of John Bunyan (1628–1688) one of the all-time English bestsellers. It was an allegory for people seriously concerned about the moral and spiritual dimensions of life, tracing the progress of the pilgrim Christian through life, passing through the Slough of Despond, the Valley of the Shadow of Death, and the worldly temptations of Vanity Fair to reach the Celestial City.

Middle-class literary staples included a flood of books in straightforward prose written by a new class of professional writer. These "Grub Street" literary artisans (so called for the London street where they worked and lived) were not supported by aristocratic patronage like Renaissance writers or like the makers of high culture in their own time, but from the bookshop sale of their works to ordinary people. Adventurous prose fiction, travelers' tales of far places, recent history, biography and autobiography, popular science, and the newly invented newspaper perused over a coffeehouse table—these were what stirred the imaginations of the prosperous and progressive middle ranks. The French comic dramatist Jean-Baptiste Molière (1622–1673) appealed more to the Paris bourgeoisie than to the Versailles courtiers for whom he wrote. These solid citizens immensely enjoyed his satires of social pretense in high society, of religious hypocrisy, and even of the ambitions of some tradesmen to pass as cultured gentlemen. The verbal wit of Molière's *Misanthrope* (1666) and *Bourgeois Gentleman* (1670) was brilliant, but Molière offered high farce too, and he remains to this day the most popular writer of all the galaxy of talent that sought the patronage of France's Grand Monarch.

The greatest example of the sort of painting the middle classes enjoyed and commissioned was the work of the *Dutch realists,* the portraitists and the landscape and still-life painters of the Dutch golden age. These artists offered homely scenes of parlor and kitchen, images of cheese you could pluck off the sideboard, grapes that look good enough to eat. In the level polders, verdant countryside, and tidy towns of the Low Countries, Dutch artists also founded the first famous school of European landscape painters. No mythical gods or heroes were needed to justify these pleasant stretches of country-side with their drifting clouds and shady trees, a cart and horse in the foreground, in the distance a gleam of sunlight off a weathervane or steeple.

Among the leading Dutch painters, Franz Hals (c. 1581–1666) was famed for his vigorous brushwork and vital portraits, particularly of jolly peasants, happy parties, and other scenes from everyday life expressing the cheerful confidence of his people at the height of their golden age. Often compared with Hals was Judith Leyster (1609–1660), a versatile painter of portraits and genre scenes, who excelled in representing the materials and textures of the solid Dutch world around her. She also showed a striking originality of treatment, as in her woman's-eye view of *The Proposition,* an atypical picture showing, not a cheerful prostitute accepting her money, but a woman bent over her needlework, studiously ignoring the lascivious proposals of the man who bends over her. The calm, carefully finished canvases of Jan Vermeer (1632–1675) imparted an almost classical dignity to the lives of the urban patriciate, depicted at such everyday tasks and pastimes as reading a book or writing a letter, playing a meticulously rendered musical instrument or just pouring milk.

But the Dutch golden age left its most moving legacy to future generations in the art of Rembrandt van Rijn (1606–1669). The whole of Rembrandt's seventeenth-century world comes vividly to life in the paintings, prints, and drawings of this, perhaps the most beloved of all the "old masters." There are *Beggars Receiving Alms* at someone's front door and *The Board of the Clothmaker's Guild* meeting around a red-plush covered table, complacent in their suits of sober black. Rembrandt's golden light gleams on the intense faces of the physicians pressing around the pale corpse of *The Anatomy Lesson of Dr. Tulp* and radiates from the quiet face of Christ in *Supper at Emmaus.* Without using pigment at all, Rembrandt could capture in drawings or etchings the colorful streets and synagogues of Amsterdam's Jewish community or freeze forever a simple field of tufted grass or three trees against a flood of light just bursting through the clouds.

The taste that found what it liked in Molière and Rembrandt was that of a productive, prosperous, educated bourgeois public. These middle-class citizens had come a long way from the shops and stalls and muddy lanes of medieval Europe. In the next century, they challenged and in the nineteenth century they replaced the aristocrats who still sniffed at the vulgarity of tradesmen in the age of Louis XIV.

This picture of everyday life in seventeenth-century Spain reveals both Velazquez's precocious genius—he was nineteen when he painted it—and the breadth of his social concern. Done in his early naturalistic style, the picture finds as much seriousness in these ordinary people and their meal as the artist would later see in the deeds of kings and generals.

The Origins of Modern Science

The great breakthrough of this period, however, came not in art or social thought but in science. During the 1500s and 1600s, Western people sought to comprehend the universe as a whole in a new way. The result was the birth of modern science as we know it today.

The scientific revolution, certainly one of the greatest achievements in the history of the Western mind, did not spring full blown from the heads of half a dozen geniuses, from Copernicus in the sixteenth century to Newton in the seventeenth. The roots of early modern science may in fact be traced to several aspects of the cultural life of these two transitional centuries. Let us look at three aspects of the intellectual environment that nurtured the beginnings of modern science: medieval superstition, the inherited worldview of the ancients, and those elements of sixteenth- and seventeenth-century intellectual life that made scientific understanding possible.

Magic and Superstition

The minds of early modern people were open to a broader spectrum of belief than many scientifically educated modern minds are capable of entertaining. Both the unlettered masses and scholars seeking to plumb the secrets of the universe accepted the existence of beings, forces, and powers that later generations have dismissed as figments of the prescientific imagination. Yet it is within this framework of thought that the modern scientific intellect first took shape.

The coming of monotheistic Christianity to the West had never completely eliminated popular belief in supernatural powers other than those sanctioned by the church. Besides the angels, demons, and spirits of the departed sanctified by Christian belief, will-o'-the-wisps hovered in the marsh gas over swamps, and elves and fairies still crept about the fringes of the human world. Even certain human beings called witches (women) or warlocks (men) were believed to have access to secret knowledge of nature or to possess supernatural powers. Filling the role later played by veterinarians, doctors, and sometimes psychological counselors, these village healers brewed herbal medicines that have been found to have genuine medicinal properties. And as we noticed in the last chapter, in these early modern centuries witchcraft was believed to be so real and dangerous that despite the good some did, tens of thousands of these practitioners of the supernatural arts, most of them women, were executed.

More systematic attempts to understand and control the natural world through supernatural powers also flourished, not among the peasantry, but at the top of early modern society. Astrologers studied the properties and motions of the planets, comets, and other celestial bodies to plot personal horoscopes and give public warnings of disaster when comets glowed in the night sky. Alchemists, who had plied their mystical craft in the Middle Ages, continued to seek chemico-magical means of transmuting base metal into gold and to hunt for the philosopher's stone that would lead to spiritual regeneration. Occultists studied the number symbolism of the Pythagoreans and the deeper meanings in Scripture revealed by the tradition of Jewish mysticism called the Cabala. Through such exotic means, some of the most learned and aristocratic of Europeans groped for mystical or magical understanding of the world around them.

Even those educated people with no interest in the occult were likely to see the world primarily in Christian and Platonic terms rather than in merely material ones. Dividing the universe into Platonic ideas and particular things, spirit and matter, they interested themselves in the material world of particulars only insofar as it led to a clearer comprehension of the immaterial realm of ideas and spirit. Like belief in magic spells and number symbolism, this lack of interest in the material world seemed an inhospitable environment for the scientific outlook, which is precisely concerned with explaining the behavior of matter.

Ancient Science

Early modern Europeans did of course have a legacy of scientific understanding at their disposal. Derived for the most part from the ancient Greeks via the Arabs of the High Middle Ages, this body of science had been expanded by a handful of medieval Scholastics and edited by meticulous Renaissance humanists. Empirically, however, it left a good deal to be desired. The astronomy of 1500, for instance, did not accurately predict the observable movements of the heavenly bodies. On the other hand, it did perform a basic function of any worldview: it "made sense" out of the universe around us.

For those few who concerned themselves with such things at the beginning of modern history, then, the physical world looked much as it had in the high medieval centuries. Matter itself was commonly believed to be composed, as some ancient authorities had claimed, of four basic elements: earth, water, air, and fire. These in turn were defined in terms of four fundamental qualities of matter: heat and cold, dryness and moistness. Thus earth was the cold, dry element, water the cold, wet one; air was hot and moist, fire hot and dry. Other features of the material world—hardness and softness, coarseness and fine-grained texture, and so on—were likewise explained by the proportions of the four qualities of all matter in a given material object.

The behavior of matter was also explained for the learned by references to Aristotle and other Greek students of physics, or "mechanics" as the Renaissance called it. According to these ancient authorities, matter moved because it had "impetus." Circular motion was natural to the heavenly bodies, while here on earth the heavier elements (earth, water) naturally tended to descend, the lighter ones (air and fire) to rise.

Living things were also understood by scholarly people in ancient Greek terms, though folk wisdom also contributed, especially in medicine. The biological world was composed of plants, which possessed

Premodern View of the Universe. Note the earth in the center and the zodiacal symbols around the rim.

the quality of life, and animals, which were both alive and conscious. Plants were grouped in families proposed by the Greek Theophrastus, such as trees, shrubs, and herbs, with many subdivisions. Aristotle's classifications of animals on the basis of methods of reproduction also still prevailed: all animals were viviparous (born alive), oviparous (born from eggs), or produced by spontaneous generation (primitive organisms born from slime or ooze). For laypeople, many types of animals, domestic and wild, real and mythological, were described in books called *bestiaries,* in which each creature was also characterized in symbolic terms as illustrating Christian ethical or religious lessons for the human race—a moralizing approach as old as Aesop's fables.

Human beings, unique among created things, possessed immortal souls. But they also possessed physical bodies whose character and health were determined by the mix of the four elements within them. Introduced into human bodies as food, these elements were transformed by the liver into the four bodily fluids called *humors*—blood, phlegm, yellow bile, and black bile, the "melancholy humor." These humors made an individual phlegmatic or melancholy by temperament, healthy or sickly. "Bleeding," a common medical treatment, made good sense as a way of removing impure blood from the system. More common still was the use of herbal medicine, made of garden herbs with medicinal properties both testified to by folk wisdom and spelled out in home-care books called herbals.

The universe itself, finally, was outlined in detail in Ptolemy's *Almagest,* the second-century Alexandrian scientist's cosmology as received through the Arabs. Like medieval scholars, Renaissance thinkers accepted the *geocentric* ("earth-centered") *theory* that the earth was the center of the cosmos. According to this view, the planets, including the sun and moon, moved around the earth in circular orbits while the "fixed stars" were set in an outer sphere between the material world and heaven. Because Ptolemy's theory was wrong, it required many subtle modifications to explain the observed motions of sun, moon, and planets. All these celestial bodies were believed to be made of a different substance from terrestrial matter: either a fusion of all four elements, or a *quintessence* ("fifth essence") finer and purer than earthly matter.

At all levels, finally, the universe was organized according to a broad principle of hierarchy called the *Great Chain of Being.* According to this ancient theory, the cosmos, like human society, was everywhere structured on the basis of higher and lower, superior and inferior, dominant and subordinate. The higher forms of matter were those closer to spirit in their nature; and all groups had their own higher or lower members. Thus earth was the lowest, fire the highest of the elements; animals were higher in the chain of existence than vegetables or minerals. Even within these categories, vestiges of hierarchy remained: the lion was the king of beasts, the oak the noblest of trees, gold the royal metal. It was a premodern scientific vision that drew on ancient and medieval sources, summing up the long Western tradition on the eve of the modern world.

The Need for a New Paradigm

The way from the older science to the new, from Aristotle and Ptolemy to Nicolaus Copernicus and Isaac Newton, was paved by a number of continuing trends and significant new developments in Western thought. Both older approaches and new attitudes toward learning helped to bring about the scientific revolution of the sixteenth and seventeenth centuries.

Some of the roots of modern science may be traced back to the superstitions and pseudosciences just touched on, approaches that mingled mysticism with experiment and empirical observation. Some astrologers did observe the heavens closely and plotted the paths of the planets among the constellations in the effort to calculate their influences on human life. Alchemists undertook long and painstaking experiments in their laboratories, becoming experienced with simple apparatus and knowledgeable of the properties of metals and chemicals. And the prominent sixteenth-century Swiss physician Paracelsus (Theophrastus von Hohenheim, c. 1493–1541), who had a reputation for well-nigh miraculous curative powers, became a pioneer of modern chemotherapy in his advocacy of the use of mercury for the treatment of one of the scourges of the century, syphilis.

Another source of the new science lay in changing modern attitudes toward the inherited body of ancient science. Humanist editions of Aristotle's scientific writings, for instance, sometimes dared to update the master by introducing plants or animals the Greek thinker had never seen, or even by hesitantly pointing out errors that had crept into his work. Some thinkers of the late sixteenth and the seventeenth centuries were willing to challenge and even attempt to go beyond the Greeks and the Romans.

Aristotle was openly rejected by the scientist Galileo, the philosopher Francis Bacon, and others. The broad seventeenth-century dispute over the relative merits of "ancients and moderns" did not demolish the former, as the popularity of classicism in the arts made clear. But the dispute itself indicated a growing confidence that mere modern minds could hope to compete successfully with the giants of antiquity.

Among the earliest believers in the possibility of improving on the ancient knowledge of the material world were technical workers of various sorts. Lacking classical educations these surgeons, ballistics experts, engineers, and others were not overwhelmed by the achievements of the ancients. Impressed by progress in their own trades, such practical men as the surgeon Ambroise Paré saw the possibility of further improvement in the future. From the modest books they produced, the influential philosopher Francis Bacon (discussed later) drew some of his faith in scientific progress. From such views also grew the confidence that modern science could drastically improve our understanding of the world we live in.

Central to the emergence of the new science, finally, was what the philosophical historian of science Thomas Kuhn calls a new scientific *paradigm*. Kuhn borrows the term and the basic concept from the grammatical paradigm, the model conjugation or declension that illustrates the patterns followed by a whole class of verbs or nouns. In the same way, "recognized scientific achievements . . . for a time provide model problems and solutions to a community of scientific practitioners."[7] Breakthrough theories, experiments, or demonstrations capable of serving as new paradigms, many students of the subject feel, are necessary to any significant advance in the sciences.

Such revolutionary shifts in goals and methods are only likely when so many anomalies—failures of accepted theory to explain the observed workings of nature—have piled up that a radical break with past science seems necessary. In Copernicus's day, just such anomalies had accumulated as astronomers tried to use the elaborate Ptolemaic system to explain planetary locations, the sequence of the equinoxes, and other problems. As a colleague of Copernicus's declared, "No system so cumbersome and inaccurate" as the Ptolemaic view, particularly after centuries of revisions and additions, "could possibly be true of nature."[8]

It was time for a radical break with the science of the ancients, for daring assumptions and new methods. From the work of Copernicus and his followers sprang a new scientific paradigm and with it the scientific revolution that is central to the modern mind.

The Scientific Revolution

What is sometimes called the first scientific revolution—our own century has seen the second—was a collection of attitudes toward truth, new research methods, and new conclusions about the natural world. It began with the work of Copernicus in the first half of the sixteenth century and climaxed with the discoveries of Isaac Newton in the second half of the seventeenth. The term *scientific revolution* applies to the work of the scientists who made the discoveries and of the philosophers who explained them, as well as to the spread of the scientific outlook to growing numbers of educated laypeople. It was an international movement, as the Renaissance and Reformation had been, a movement that reoriented the mind of the West as a whole. Where the educated person of the fifteenth century was absorbed by humanistic studies or art and the alert mind of the sixteenth consumed by religious disputes, thinking people in 1700 were increasingly interested in science and the scientific view of the structure of the cosmos. It was a worldview much closer to our own than anything that had come before.

The Copernican Breakthrough

A Pole, a German, and an Italian were the chief contributors to the first century of this explosion of new knowledge. Copernicus inaugurated the great transformation; Kepler methodically elaborated it; and Galileo's combative genius and determination to see with his own eyes advanced the new science in several directions at once.

Nicolaus Copernicus (1473–1543) was the Columbus of the scientific revolution. A Polish clergyman who had studied for a decade in Italy, best known in his own lifetime as a physician, and well versed in law, mathematics, and even economics, Copernicus was a multifaceted intellect of the sort the Renaissance admired. His book *On the Revolutions of the Heavenly Bodies,* on which he labored intermittently for thirty years, was published in 1543, the last year of his life. It is as important a date in the history of modern science as 1492 is in the history of Western global expansion. It was the beginning.

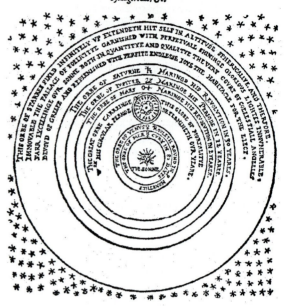

The Copernican Universe. Notice the sun in the center, earth in the third orbit out from the sun.

The revolutionary assertion of the book was, quite simply, that the sun, not the earth, is the center of the universe. Earth, Copernicus suggested, is merely one of the planets, revolving around the sun once a year. It is because our planet rotates on its axis once in every twenty-four hours that the universe as a whole seems to revolve around us. For the better part of two thousand years, the geocentric view had held the field. Now for the first time it was challenged by Copernicus's *heliocentric,* or "sun-centered," interpretation.

In other ways, Copernicus's views were actually rather traditional. He retained such astronomical conventions as circular orbits and the sphere of the fixed stars at the outer edge of the universe. But the heliocentric theory was a red flag to the conservative scientific, philosophical, and religious establishment, and a rallying point for the scientific revolutionaries, for the rest of the century.

The German Johannes Kepler (1571–1630), the next in this succession of scientific geniuses, was a more single-mindedly professional man of science. His career carried him from a post as assistant to Tycho Brahe (1546–1601), the foremost astronomer of the day, to a position as court mathematician to the Holy Roman emperor. Kepler's contributions were based on long years of empirical observation and meticulous mathematical calculation—two keys to the success of the scientific revolution. Yet even in this solid, almost modern-sounding man of science, there was ample evidence of the influence of premodern views. He believed, for instance, in the "music of the spheres" produced by the harmonious movements of the heavenly bodies, and in the possibility that angels rode the planets in their orbits.

Kepler became the first well-known astronomer openly to support the Copernican heliocentric theory. Even more important, he added to it the three laws of planetary motion which, unlike much of Copernicus's theory, have survived intact to the present day. Working with Tycho in the best observatory in Europe, Kepler had collected detailed data on planetary motion for many years, giving him much better evidence to work with than his predecessors had. Like others in the latter part of the century, he was also more willing to break completely with ancient authority than anyone in Copernicus's generation had been. When the observed positions of the planet Mars simply could not be made to fit a circular orbit, as both Ptolemy and Copernicus insisted it must, Kepler took the eminently scientific step of trying another hypothesis. He theorized that the paths of the planets might be ellipses rather than circles. Orbits calculated on the basis of elliptical paths, with the sun at one of the foci of the ellipse, fit his observations. The first law of planetary motion thus entered the astronomy books with impeccable scientific credentials: it fit the facts, and the numbers checked. The other two laws, defining the varying velocity of planets in their orbits and the length of time it takes each planet to revolve around the sun, are even denser with detailed data, mathematical relationships, and scientific concepts as complex as the metaphysics of the ancients.

The Italian Galileo Galilei (1564–1642), the first telescope astronomer and a trailblazer in both physics and astronomy, gave the new movement a genuinely colorful personality. An even more wide-ranging Renaissance man than Copernicus, Galileo studied philosophy and medicine and was a skillful painter and musician. Like Kepler, however, he became a professional mathematician and a passionate advocate of the new science. A university professor in north Italian universities and a protégé of the Medici family of Florence, Galileo published frequently in Italian rather than scholarly Latin, making his treatises accessible to educated nonscientists. When the Inqui-

sition finally reined him in at the end of his long life, the confrontation simply added to the legend of a man who had done more than anyone before him to make the scientific revolution part of the life of the Western mind.

Galileo's earliest formulations, in physics, included the law of the pendulum: he discovered that each swing, whether it covers a longer or a shorter arc of space, takes the same amount of time—the basic principle of the pendulum clock. He also worked out the first hydrostatic balance for establishing the density of an object by weighing it in water. Probably Galileo's most celebrated discovery in physics, however, was the law of falling bodies, which challenged Aristotle's view that heavier bodies fall faster, lighter ones more slowly. By rolling small metal balls down an inclined plane—a kind of controlled free fall—Galileo was able to measure distances covered and times elapsed when an object falls more precisely than anyone before him. He thus demonstrated that all falling bodies, heavy or light, fall at a velocity that accelerates at a rate of 32 feet per second every second. Expressed in the mathematical formula $V = 32n$ (n

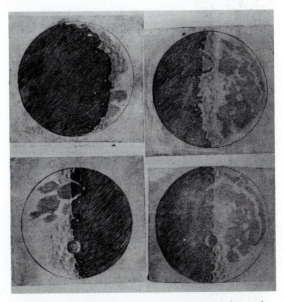

Galileo's drawings of the moon as seen through his telescope in 1610. [*Galileo's telescopes.* Biblioteca Nazionale Centrale, Mueseum of Science, Florence]

Galileo demonstrates the acceleration of falling bodies by rolling small balls down an inclined plane. Such physical experiments, presented before important personages and leading scholars, helped to create an upper-class "scientific culture" in the seventeenth and eighteenth centuries.

being the number of seconds the object falls), this principle, like Kepler's laws of planetary motion, had the quantitative precision of modern hard science.

As an astronomer, Galileo's great contribution was less mathematical than empirical. Learning of the experiments of a Dutch optician in combining lenses in a tube in order to magnify distant objects, Galileo applied the principle to celestial observation and produced the world's first astronomical telescope. His were thus the first human eyes to see the mountains on the moon, sunspots on the sun, the larger satellites of Jupiter, the rings of Saturn, and the multitudes of stars that make up the hazy path of light across the night sky we call the Milky Way.

His announcements of these discoveries, combined with his vigorous defense of the heliocentric theory, brought Galileo into conflict with the scientific establishment and finally to the attention of the Holy Inquisition. Church tradition and even the language of Scripture seemed committed to the view that the earth stood at the center of things while the sun moved through the sky around it. Compelled to recant his heretical views in his last years, Galileo before the Inquisition became a symbol of the modern struggle between free thought and "thought police," of whatever faith or ideology (see box, "Galileo on Science and Scripture").

Newton and the Law of Gravity

Sir Isaac Newton (1642–1727) became for many the master intellect who finally put it all together, explaining the way the universe worked in scientific terms as convincing and coherent as medieval theology and ancient philosophy had been in their day. Science grew and changed drastically over the centuries that followed, and even Newton's master concept, the law of universal gravitation, was restructured by Albert

---

MASTERING OUR WORLD   Galileo on Science and Scripture

In defense of Copernican theories and of his own empirical discoveries with the telescope, Galileo, addressing his patron the grand duke of Tuscany, confronted a problem that bedeviled science for centuries: the apparent conflct between science and religion. Like many scientists, Galileo tried to avoid confrontation by urging that there was no disagreement between scientific discovery and the Bible if the latter was "rightly understood." The religious authorities of his time, however, subsequently compelled him to admit it was his "reading" of the universe, not their reading of Scripture, that was in error. In 1992, however, after a thorough review of the case, the church decided that the seventeenth-century church, not the scientist, had been in error.

> Some years since, as your most Serene Highness well knoweth, I did discover many particulars in Heaven that had been unseen and unheard of until this our age: which as well for their novelty as for certain consequences which depend upon them, clashing with some physical Propositions commonly received by the Schools, did stir up

against me no small number ... they alleged sundry things interwoven with the attestations of the Sacred Scriptures....

Touching this Reason I think it fit in the first place to consider That ... the Sacred Scripture can never lie whenever its true meaning is understood; which I believe none will deny to be many times very abstruse and very different from that which the bare sound of the words signifieth. For instance if ... anyone should constantly confine himself to the naked Grammatical Sense he ... should be forced to assign to God feet, and hands, and eyes, yea more corporeal and human affections, as of anger, of repentance, of hatred....

This therefore being granted, methinks that in the discussion of Natural problems, we ought not to begin at the authority ... of Scripture, but at Sensible Experiments and Necessary Demonstrations: For, from the Divine Word, the Sacred Scripture and Nature did both alike proceed: the first as the Holy Ghost's Inspiration; the second as the most observant Executrix of God's Commands.... Nature being inexorable and immutable, and never passing the bounds of the Laws assigned her....

Source: Galileo Galilei, *The Ancient and Modern Doctrine ... Concerning the Rash Citation of the Testimony of Sacred Scripture in Conclusions Merely Natural and That May be Proved by Experiments ...*, trans. Thomas Salisbury (London: William Layborn, 1661), 427, 432–434.

Einstein in our own century. Yet as a major contributor and as the widely admired embodiment of the scientific spirit, the English scientist deserves his preeminent position in the history of the scientific revolution.

Newton was not particularly good in school, nor was he distinguished as a Cambridge university student in the 1660s. The celebrated episode of the falling apple occurred, if at all, while he was taking tea in a Cambridge garden. But he filed away his unorthodox conclusion—that the force that pulled the apple to the ground might also be the force that bound the planets—for twenty years. Only in 1687, when he was prevailed on by a scientist friend to publish his *Mathematical Principles of Natural Philosophy,* did Newton's name become virtually synonymous with the scientific revolution. As professor of mathematics at Cambridge and virtually lifetime president of the British Royal Society, Newton seemed the incarnation of the scientific spirit. And yet, he remained a man of his age: he never lost his enthusiasm for theology, biblical chronology, and alchemy. Personally an ambitious, arrogant, and contentious man, avid for the fame his discoveries brought him, Newton nevertheless described all his investigations as mere child's play beside "the great ocean of truth" that was yet to be explored.

From a scientific viewpoint, Newton had the two essentials: "a grasp of mathematics" and an understanding of "experiment as a systematic procedure."[9] Among his major achievements are usually listed his development of calculus and his invention of the reflecting telescope, which uses a mirror as well as lenses, as all large modern telescopes do. The first accomplishment was a mathematical breakthrough, the other a great leap forward in empirical observation. Newton's work in optics is often ranked second only to his insights on gravity. By breaking up light through a glass prism into its component chromatic spectrum, he revealed that ordinary white light is in fact composed of all the colors of the rainbow. He also became the father of modern spectroscopic analysis of everything from chemicals on earth to the composition of the most distant stars.

But it was Newton's *law of universal gravitation* that became the linchpin of early modern science. Every object in the universe, he suggested, exerts an invisible attraction on every other chunk of matter. The force of attraction between any two bodies varies directly with the masses of the two bodies: the greater the masses, the more powerful the gravitational pull between them. The force also varies *inversely,* he added with the mathematical precision essential to the new approach, with the square of the distance between the two bodies. Because his formulation could be applied equally to apples and planets, it served as a unifying principle, tying the new physics to the new astronomy. Seen as the binding force that held the universe together, the law of gravity seemed to many to make sense out of the world once more.

Progress in Other Sciences

The major achievements of the scientific revolution came in astronomy and physics, from Copernicus through Kepler and Galileo to Newton. Yet there were advances by other important scientists and in other sciences as well. In this other work too, we have a mix of some very unscientific early modern ideas with some truly remarkable scientific contributions.

Among astronomers and physicists, the Italian Giordano Bruno (1548–1600) and the English scientist William Gilbert (1544–1603) both added significantly to our understanding of the material world while working to varying degrees within the mystical tradition of the sixteenth century. Gilbert's classic study of the compass pioneered in the study of magnetism; yet he also believed in a "world soul" at the heart of the cosmos. Bruno rejected Aristotle, supported Copernicus, and was an early proponent of the view that the traditional sphere of the fixed stars was actually a vast expanse of star-spangled space, that there might in fact be an "infinity of worlds" like our own. But Bruno was also a believer in mathematical magic and in humanity as a microcosm of the universe—a philosopher so unorthodox that he was rejected by the Calvinists, excommunicated by the Lutherans, and finally burned at the stake by the Catholic Inquisition.

In other sciences, the celebrated Swiss physician Paracelsus, already discussed, was an alchemist as well as a celebrated doctor. More important additions to Western scientific knowledge, however, came from the Flemish anatomist Andreas Vesalius (1514–1564) and the English doctor William Harvey (1578–1657). Vesalius's book *On the Structure of the Human Body* (1543) provided the first detailed, empirically accurate study of human anatomy; it was as revolutionary for biology as Copernicus's book of the same year was for astronomy. Harvey, a physician to King James I of England, was the first to offer an accurate description of the functioning of the heart and the circulatory system as a pump and a conduit for the flow of blood through the human body, another major advance.

Abstract mathematics also made striking progress in the sixteenth and seventeenth centuries. Mathematical insights from ancient Greece and medieval Islam and from India by way of the Muslim world had reached Western scholars in the Middle Ages. In the early modern period, however, European thinkers made breakthroughs that form the foundation of mathematics today.

In the sixteenth century, a group of Italian thinkers made major advances in the study of algebra. A single book by Gerolamo Cardano (1501–1576), *The Great Art, or the Rules of Algebra* (1543), summed up the achievements of two generations of Italian mathematicians, stirring wide spread interest in the mysteries of algebraic equations. Later in the century, others further developed the ability to manipulate algebraic variables and symbols and increased Western understanding of decimal fractions.

In the seventeenth century, modern geometry at last moved well beyond Euclid in the work of Newton and the philosophers René Descartes and G. W. Leibniz, both discussed later. Descartes made his greatest scientific contributions in the early development of analytic geometry. Newton and Leibniz were early explorers of the intricacies of calculus. By the end of the century, mathematics had thus far surpassed the work of earlier periods and stood ready to serve the other sciences in centuries to come.

The Philosophers of the Scientific Revolution

Drawing larger meanings from the new science was primarily the work, not of the new scientists themselves, but of the philosophers of the seventeenth century. We have already seen the impact of scientific attitudes on political thought in the ideas of Hobbes and Locke. Other leading thinkers of the period developed even broader views of the world under the influence of the new "natural philosophy," as science was often called. Indeed, the origins of modern philosophy are usually seen in the problems explored, the startling solutions propounded by such thinkers as Descartes, Spinoza, Leibniz, and Francis Bacon.

René Descartes (1596–1650), a Frenchman of independent means who lived most of his productive life in the freer intellectual atmosphere of the Nether-

lands, is often hailed as the founder of both modern philosophy and the stream of philosophic thought called *rationalism*. As a rationalist, Descartes exhibited an immense faith in human reason—in the validity of ideas clearly and distinctly held and logically developed. He also revealed a radical willingness to start over from scratch in the human effort to understand ourselves and our world. His famous maxim, *Cogito, ergo sum*, "I think, therefore I am," summed up the single certainty with which he began his sweeping investigation of the nature of things. All traditional authorities, he declared, even the testimony of our senses *might* be wrong; but the very fact that he could *think* this proved that he, as a thinking center of consciousness, did exist. It was the kind of daring new start that the scientific revolution was making, and it earned his *Discourse on Method . . . Seeking Truth in the Sciences* (1637) an enthusiastic reception from many thoughtful people.

From this single certainty, the existence of the thinking mind, Descartes proceeded to demonstrate the existence of both a highly rational God and of a radically divided world. The universe, he asserted, was composed of two basic substances: mind (imma-

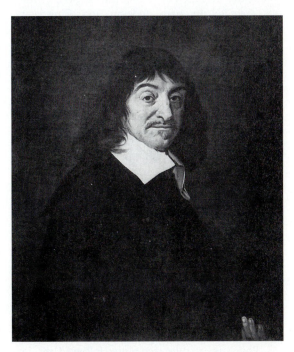

As a philosopher of science and the founder of European rationalism, René Descartes, portrayed here by Frans Hals, was one of the giants of modern philosophy.

terial, "thinking substance") and matter ("extended substance," which occupies space). These two realms of being were so different that it was difficult to see how they could interact at all, as they must in human beings, composed of both mind and matter. But Descartes found a point of interaction for them in the hitherto apparently functionless pineal gland of the human brain. Times had indeed changed: it is difficult to imagine Plato or Thomas Aquinas concerned about the precise part of the human body in which ideas and particulars, soul and body interact; but for the founder of modern philosophy, such a question was only natural.

If Descartes was arguably the most admired philosopher of the age, Baruch Spinoza (1632–1677) was probably the most controversial. A Jewish lens grinder of Amsterdam, the independent-minded Spinoza, like Descartes, benefited from the intellectual toleration of the Netherlands. Deeply impressed by the logical coherence of mathematics, he constructed a system of ethics that sought to be as rigidly logical as Euclid's geometry. Disturbed by the Cartesian problem of interaction between the mental or spiritual world and the world of matter, Spinoza evolved a philosophy resembling pantheism in which both mind and matter were seen as "attributes" of God. Pantheism, heretical in both Judaism and Christianity, seemed one way at least to restore unity to a Cartesian world in which matter, the realm of the sciences, had achieved virtual parity with mind in the Western worldview.

Another radical philosophy seeking to solve the problem of interaction in a metaphysically divided world was that of the great German philosopher Gottfried Wilhelm Leibniz (1646–1716). An intellectual prodigy in his youth, Leibniz became a leading logician and mathematician, the inventor of an early calculating machine, and an organizer of both the Prussian and Russian academies of science. His unique vision posited a universe of *monads,* totally independent centers of consciousness, each a microcosm of the world as a whole, none having any causal contact with the others at all. The appearance of causal interaction, Leibniz declared, was the result of a "preestablished harmony" between their actions that was decreed by God. It was an extreme solution, and with its corollary that the universe God had made must be "the best of all possible worlds," was savagely satirized by Voltaire in the following century.

Philosophers thus sometimes followed the implications of the scientific revolution far from the concrete world of scientific experiment and observation. The leading English thinker of the early seventeenth century, however, made his highly influential contribution precisely by honoring empiricism and glorifying scientific achievement. This was Francis Bacon (1561–1626), essayist, lord chancellor of England, and prophet of a "Great Renewal" in human understanding and control of the world we live in.

A bitter opponent of the logic-chopping authoritarianism of the medieval Scholastics, Bacon spoke for the new thinkers of this pivotal age when he urged the intellectual community "to try the whole thing anew upon a better plan; . . . to commence a total reconstruction of sciences, arts, and all human knowledge."[10] In this call for a new beginning, Bacon was a precursor of Descartes. By contrast with the Cartesian continental emphasis on mathematics and rational clarity, however, Bacon stressed empirical observation and experiment as the road to new truth. He proposed the collection and sifting of evidence, the formation of possible explanations, and the testing of these hypotheses by more empirical evidence before a general theory could be deemed proven. This *inductive* emphasis, building large truths on a foundation of accumulated data, contrasted with the *deductive* method of inferring lesser truths from some larger authoritative proposition. In his fictional account of the utopia he called *The New Atlantis* (1627), the English philosopher stressed the value to society of large-scale state-supported research institutions and insisted that scientists and inventors, not kings and generals, should be recognized as the heroes of the human race.

Above all, Bacon saw the immense power over the world that scientific knowledge could give to humanity (see box, "Bacon on Science and Power"). Through science, he said, we may acquire an unprecedented "dominion over natural things" and "extend more widely the limits of the power . . . of man."[11] Francis Bacon thus became the first prophet of human and scientific progress, envisioning a brave new world of social improvement through research and development. Like a conquistador of the mind, he set a new goal for the Western world: the conquest of nature through science and "the enlargement of the bounds of human empire [control], to the effecting of all things possible."[12]

The Rage for Science

As the seventeenth century advanced, the new science found a growing audience, at least among an educated elite. What classical studies had been to the

MASTERING OUR WORLD
Bacon on Science and Power

Francis Bacon's emphasis on induction—beginning with empirical observation of "the facts of nature" rather than with philosophical or theological theories—represented one of the primary methodological breakthroughs of the scientific revolution. Bacon himself contributed nothing to the new science. But his recognition that, in the case of applied science, "knowledge is power" proved remarkably prophetic. The history of the next four centuries demonstrated that science was indeed destined to become a key shaper of "the real business and fortunes of the human race."

> Being convinced that the human intellect makes its own difficulties, not using the true helps which are at man's disposal, I thought all trial should be made, whether that commerce between the mind of man and the nature of things, which is more precious than anything on earth . . . might by any means be restored to its perfect and original condition. . . . [T]here was but one course left, therefore—to try the whole thing anew upon a better plan, and to commence a total reconstruction of science, arts, and all human knowledge, raised upon the proper foundations. . . .
>
> The completion however of this . . . is a thing both above my strength and beyond my hopes. I have made a beginning of the work—a beginning, I hope, not unimportant—the future of the human race will give the issue—such an issue, it may be, as in the present condition of things and men's minds cannot easily be conceived or imagined. For the matter in hand is no mere felicity of speculation but the real business and fortunes of the human race, and all power of operation. . . . [T]hose twin objects, human Knowledge and human Power, do really meet in one. . . .
>
> And all depends upon keeping the eye steadily fixed upon the facts of nature. . . .

Source: Francis Bacon, *The Great Instauration*, in *Selections*, ed. Matthew McClure (New York: Scribner's, 1828), 3–4, 32.

theories at the Jesuit school he attended. Individual scholars at Gresham's College in London gathered privately to discuss "natural philosophy" in the 1640s. Such leading men of science as Galileo lectured on these subjects at universities. Educational emphasis still fell heavily on Christian teaching and ancient languages, but it was at least possible in seventeenth-century educational institutions to learn something of the scientific breakthroughs that had begun a hundred years before.

Another important source of scientific knowledge was the printed book. As print technology had spread the new learning of the humanists and the religious views of the reformers, so books now played a large part in the success of the scientific revolution. Most important, printing assured the accumulation of the new knowledge: discoveries were not lost, and knowledge of them reached scientists in other parts of Europe through books like those of Copernicus, Galileo, and Newton. In addition, laypeople could get some idea of the new scientific theories, particularly from the works of scientists and philosophers like Galileo, Descartes, or Bacon, who were willing to publish in Italian, French, or English rather than in the scholarly Latin used by Copernicus and Newton.

Scientific societies, finally, came into being in the seventeenth century for the specific purpose of disseminating knowledge to an educated public. The earliest of these organizations were private gatherings, like the Accademia dei Lincei in Rome, founded in 1603, or the meetings at Gresham's College. And in the latter part of the century, rulers like Charles II in England and Louis XIV in France added science to the arts and literature as worthy objects of royal patronage. The Royal Society of London for Improving of Natural Knowledge was thus officially founded in 1660, the Académie des Sciences in Paris in 1666. These organizations brought interested people together at regular meetings to hear and discuss scientific papers or to watch scientific demonstrations. The leading scientists also became fellows of the academies, and their work was often published in the scientific journals the societies sponsored.

In this increasingly hospitable atmosphere, scientific knowledge accumulated rapidly and spread to a small but supportive public. In the next century, we will see, these circles of scientifically informed laypeople grow to include practically minded businesspeople and technicians, with the result that science, technology, and production came together in

Renaissance and religion to the Reformation, a passion for the natural sciences was for the later seventeenth and the eighteenth centuries.

In the 1600s, some educational institutions began to teach modern mathematics and science. Descartes acquired some of the latest mathematical

another great breakthrough—the Industrial Revolution.

The New Worldview

By 1700, then, scientists and philosophers had given the Western world a new vision of the world we live in. The new methods they employed, the conclusions they drew, and the glimpses they had of a universe without limits were key elements in the new scientific paradigm that resulted from the Copernican revolution.

The methodological innovations of the scientific revolution have already been noted. Instead of turning to ancient authority as the inevitable source of truth, the scientific revolutionaries looked at the facts of the physical world around them. Experiment in physics and close observation in astronomy provided an empirical foundation for knowledge that neither ancient philosophy nor medieval theology had possessed. Equally important, the new breed of scientists abandoned the Aristotelian logic practiced by the medieval Schoolmen in favor of the quantitative logic of mathematics. By recording their results in quantitative terms, rather than in terms of vaguely defined "qualities," they gave science a greater degree of precision. And in fact the defining features of modern science became the empirical and quantitative dimensions that distinguished the modern search for truth from that of any other time or place.

Not surprisingly, from these early probes emerged a very quantitative and essentially material vision of the nature of things. Observed in numerical terms, the world came to be seen primarily in dimensions of space and time, its most readily measurable characteristics. Time and space were thus accepted by the modern West as *the* basic dimensions of the physical universe.

The seventeenth century also revived the metaphysical atomism of the Greek Epicureans, especially as presented by the Roman poet Lucretius in *On the Nature of Things*. In this interpretation, the material world was believed to be made of "atoms and the void," minute bits of matter drifting through empty space, bumping and clustering into the larger chunks that compose the physical world as we know it. The real, or "primary," qualities of matter were those of the atoms and their configurations: size, shape, mass, motion, and number (quantifiability). All other apparent qualities—colors, sounds, smells, and other characteristics absorbed by the senses—were dismissed as "secondary," existing only in the mind of the observer, not in the real or objective world at all.

At the level of the infinitely large as well as at the atomic level, the scientific revolution developed a new view of the world. As we have seen, the only real martyr to the scientific faith, Giordano Bruno, was burned for his conviction that there are an infinite number of planets like our own in the cosmos. Without going so far, seventeenth-century astronomers went further than Copernicus had: they rejected the sphere of the fixed stars and projected a much larger size for the universe. Not only the earth, but the solar system itself was looking less and less like the center of God's world, and the stars seemed to stretch on forever, without pattern or obvious meaning.

To some, it was a chilling vision. The French mathematician and religious thinker Blaise Pascal (1623–1662) was deeply disturbed: "The eternal silence of these infinite spaces," he said, "terrifies me." Others saw in Newtonism the basis for a mechanical model of the cosmos, an orderly if rather inhuman universe presided over by a distant, aloof divinity— God the great geometrician who had designed it all. However they responded, theirs was a new and astonishing view of the world we live in. It was to be a crucial Western contribution to the life of the human mind as whole.

A Topical Summary

Politics: The beginnings of modern political thought were stimulated by the political turmoil of the sixteenth and seventeenth centuries. Most serious seventeenth-century political theory, including Hobbes's argument in his *Leviathan,* focused on the concept of sovereignty in an effort to justify strong monarchical government. Locke's *Two Treatises* on government, by contrast, sought to justify the constitutional monarchy just emerging in England, defending limited government and the rights of the governed.

Art: Both dynamic, emotionally compelling baroque art and classicism rooted in tradition responded to the tastes and propaganda needs of the revived Catholic church and the new absolute monarchies.

By contrast, artists like Rembrandt and the Dutch realists produced art that suited middle-class taste in its convincing representations of their everyday world.

Science: Modern science was born from a mass of ancient, often inaccurate scientific ideas, popular magic, and superstition. The Copernican revolution in astronomy, incorporating the work of Kepler, Galileo, and Newton, transformed the Western worldview, replacing a tidy earth-centered universe with a sun-centered planetary system set in an endless field of stars. With additional contributions to physics, some basic biology, and other advances, science began to replace art and religion as a focus for philosophical speculation and educated concern. Newton's formulation of the law of universal gravitation seemed to give scientific order to a disordered cosmos.

Some Key Terms

baroque style 491
classicism 495
cogito, ergo sum 507
deduction 508
Dutch realists 497
geocentric theory 500
gravitation 506
Great Chain of Being 500

heliocentric theory 502
humors 500
induction 508
Levelers 487
Leviathan state 487
monad 508
natural rights 489
paradigm 501

rationalism 507
scientific revolution 502
social contract 487
sovereignty 486
state of nature 487
tabula rasa 489

Notes

1. *An Anatomie of the World: First Anniversary,* line 213.
2. Herbert H. Rowen, ed., *From Absolutism to Revolution, 1648–1848* (New York: Macmillan, 1963), 30.
3. Ibid., 33.
4. John Bowle, *Western Political Thought: An Historical Introduction from the Origins to Rousseau* (London and New York: Methuen and Barnes and Noble, 1961), 345. The "poorest she" is not yet mentioned, and women's political rights were not discussed until the time of the French revolution a century and a half later.
5. In *Locke on Politics, Religion, and Education,* ed. Maurice Cranston (New York: Collier, 1965), 10.
6. *Samson Agonistes,* lines 68, 1758.
7. Thomas S. Kuhn, *The Structure of Scientific Revolutions* (Chicago: University of Chicago Press, 1962), x.
8. Ibid., 69.
9. Jacob Bronowski and Bruce Mazlish, *From Leonardo to Hegel* (New York: Harper & Brothers, 1960), 189.
10. "Proemium" to *Instauratio Magna,* in *The Works of Francis Bacon,* vol. 8, ed. James Spedding (London: Longman, 1857–1874), 18.
11. *New Atlantis,* in *Works,* vol. 8, 260; *Novum Organum,* ibid., vol. 8, 147.
12. *New Atlantis,* in *Works,* vol. 8, 297.

Reading List

ARMITAGE, A. *Copernicus: The Founder of Modern Astronomy.* London: Allen and Unwin, 1933. Still useful older biography.
BAZIN, G. *The Baroque.* New York: Norton, 1978. Stimulating analysis of this complex and controversial phase of Western history.
BURTT, E. A. *The Metaphysical Foundations of Modern Physical Science.* Rev. ed. Garden City, N.Y.: Doubleday, 1931. The philosophical underpinnings of the scientific revolution.
DREYER, J. L. E. *A History of Astronomy from Thales to Kepler.* 2d ed. New York: Dover, 1953. Locates the Copernican revolution in the context of ancient and medieval astronomical and cosmological thought.
FRIEDRICK, C. J. *The Age of the Baroque, 1610–1660.* New York: Harper & Row, 1952. Broadens the scope of the baroque to encompass the tone of society and politics.
GALILEI, G. *Discoveries and Opinions of Galileo.* Edited and translated by S. Drake. New York: Doubleday, 1957. Galileo's vigorous presentation of his controversial views. On the continuing controversies over his ideas,

see C. L. GOLINO, ed., *Galileo Reappraised* (Berkeley: University of California Press, 1966).

GUERARD, A. *France in the Classical Age: The Life and Death of an Ideal.* Rev. ed. New York: Brazillier, 1956. Subtle analysis of the classical spirit in life and art.

HALL, A. R. *The Scientific Revolution, 1500–1800.* Rev. ed. New York: Beacon Press, 1960. Older but still valuable survey, stressing the emergence of the scientific way of seeing the world. H. BUTTERFIELD, *The Origins of Modern Science, 1300–1800,* rev. ed. (New York: Free Press, 1965), puts the discoveries of the sixteenth and seventeenth centuries in a larger framework of thought about nature, from Scholasticism to the Enlightenment.

HOBBES, T. *Leviathan.* Edited by C. B. Macpherson. Harmondsworth, England: Penguin, 1981. Handy edition of the monumental, still surprisingly relevant work.

HUNTER, M. *Science and Society in Restoration England.* New York: Cambridge University Press, 1981. Widely praised account of the absorption of the scientific revolution in later seventeenth-century England.

KEARNEY, H. F. *Science and Change, 1500–1700.* New York: McGraw-Hill, 1971. Good survey of the scientific revolution.

KUHN, T. S. *The Copernican Revolution: Planetary Astronomy in the Development of Western Thought.* Cambridge, Mass.: Harvard University Press, 1957. Thoughtful analysis of the long-range implications of the new scientific paradigm.

LOCKE, J. *Two Treatises of Government.* Edited by P. Laslett.

New York: New American Library, 1966. Seminal essays for the emergence of a more liberal order.

MILTON, J. *The Portable Milton.* Edited by D. Bush. Harmondsworth, England: Penguin, 1976. Reveals the range of thought of the poet of Puritan England.

MOLIÈRE, J. B. de. *The Misanthrope and Other Plays.* Translated by J. Wood. Harmondsworth, England: Penguin, 1959. Accessible English version of Molière's comedies.

SARTON, G. *Six Wings: Men of Science in the Renaissance.* Bloomington: University of Indiana Press, 1957. Probes by an eminent historian of science.

VICKERS, B., ed. *Occult and Scientific Mentalities in the Renaissance.* New York: Cambridge University Press, 1984. Essays drawing a generally sharper distinction between occult studies and early science than do some other scholars.

WEBSTER, C. *From Paracelsus to Newton: Magic and the Making of Modern Science.* New York: Cambridge University Press, 1982. Brief exposition of the close ties many see between magical thinking and the birth of modern science.

WESTFALL, R. S. *Never at Rest: A Biography of Isaac Newton.* New York: Cambridge University Press, 1980. Scholarly life by a leading expert, interweaving scientific, religious, and other strands of his evolving ideas.

WHITE, C. *Rembrandt.* London: Thames and Hudson, 1984. One of many introductions to the life and work, with good reproductions of paintings, prints, and drawings.

Belt mask, c. 1550. Bini tribe, Benin, Nigeria. Ivory, 9⅜". The Metropolitan Museum of Art, New York. Michael C. Rockefeller Memorial Collection.

We come now to the story of how the Western world first turned on a massive scale to confront the rest of the world, setting in motion global changes that are still unfolding today. For us, for whom the rest of the globe is no further away than the nearest television screen, this early modern time seems very remote indeed. It is difficult to imagine a world in which only a tiny handful of Western voyagers had ever ventured beyond Land's End in the west of England or crossed the Urals into the East. Yet that time was only a score of generations ago, a tick of history's clock back to the days of wooden caravels wallowing in heavy seas and plodding caravans along the old Silk Road.

Even while Western peoples struggled with tradition and change through the Renaissance, the Reformation, and the century of crisis, they were thus beginning to reach beyond their first continental base in Europe to the Americas, Africa, and the Far East. This chapter describes this first astonishing wave of Western imperial expansion overseas.

The Beginnings of Western Imperialism

The Western *Age of Discovery,* as it is often called, is actually something of a misnomer: the more recent term *Age of Encounter* comes closer. During the early modern centuries, Europeans did encounter lands and peoples which up to that time they had known only in legend or not at all. In doing so, however, they were "discovering" tracts of land that were not unknown to human beings. Both fully developed civilizations and flourishing village and nomadic societies existed around the world long before Westerners began to intrude on their lives.

This first section briefly surveys that larger world as it was and as it looked to Europeans shortly before 1500. It then looks at the motives that impelled Western people to set out in search of lands beyond the seas, and at the technology and social organization that made these ventures possible. Finally, we outline the phases and forms of the Western conquest of non-Western peoples that resulted and glance ahead at the five centuries of Western colonial expansion that began in the days of Christopher Columbus and ended only yesterday.

The World Beyond the West

In Western civilization textbooks, the West often looks like the center of the world. Understandably, a history of Western peoples, like a history of East Asia, South America, or the United States, must focus on its subject, necessarily reducing the rest of the world to a peripheral role in the story. Unfortunately, this approach sometimes leaves the impression that nothing of importance was happening outside the chosen subject area—here, the Western world. And that was certainly far from true in 1492.

As we saw in the first chapters of this book, history did not begin with the Greeks and the Romans. Three thousand years before the Age of Pericles, cities had been built in ancient Egypt and the Near East. History, furthermore, had continued to advance around the globe while the Western centuries we have been chronicling were unfolding at the European end of Eurasia. By 2500 B.C., cities were being built along the Indus River of northwestern India. By 1500, they were springing up along the Yellow River of northeastern China. Early in the first millennium B.C., there were pyramids in the African Sudan, and Mexican Indians were carving huge and highly realistic stone heads on the shores of the Caribbean. On all habitable continents and countless islands, a wide variety of agricultural, pastoral, and food-gathering societies continued to satisfy the felt needs of their peoples. The world beyond the West, in short, was not a wasteland waiting for Westerners to rescue it from darkness and barbarism, but a rich and varied panorama of nations, cities, villages, high civilizations, and productive preurban cultures.

Even a very rapid survey of the non-Western world on the eve of the Western intrusion should make this clear. When Columbus set sail from Spain, major centers of civilization around the globe included the sprawling Islamic zone, Hindu India and Southeast Asia, China and its sphere of influence in East Asia, and a number of kingdoms and empires in northern Africa, Mexico, and Peru. Nor was Christian Europe obviously the most impressive of the developed civilizations in 1492. The Muslim zone, as we have seen, was then considerably larger than the Christian one, extending from North Africa to Southeast Asia. For many centuries Hindu India had been developing a great civilization of its own, teeming with prosperous trading cities and the cultured courts of cultivated rajahs. Still further east, China,

unified before the time of Christ into an empire as large as most of Europe, was flourishing under the Ming dynasty, powerful enough to send fleets of Chinese junks westward across the Indian Ocean half a century before Vasco da Gama sailed east. The trading cities of East Africa and the empires of the West African grasslands were rich keys to Muslim commerce and African development. Across the Atlantic, the Aztec military machine had unified most of Mesoamerica before 1500, and the Inca emperors ruled the Andes and most of the Pacific coast of South America from their capital in Peru.

In North America and Australia, as well as in many parts of Asia, Africa, and South America, the whole spectrum of preurban, preliterate societies followed their own immemorial ways. Western invaders often dismissed them as uncivilized and even animal-like, less frequently idealized them as noble savages. In fact, these simpler societies, lords of three-quarters of the earth, were both as savage and as sensitive as any other people, accomplished splendid things and perpetrated atrocities, just as Europeans did. There were no more fearsome fighting men than the Mongols of the Eurasian steppes, no greater navigators than the Polynesians of the Pacific, no more amazing survivors than the arctic Eskimos or the Australian Aborigines migrating across the arid outback. And as anthropologists have been learning over the past century or so, the societies of such peoples may be as intricate, their intellectual and spiritual lives as subtle, as those of more economically and politically developed cultures.

In the year Columbus sailed, however, almost all of this larger world, civilized and otherwise, was essentially *terra incognita*, or unknown land, to Western peoples. This was so despite the fact that there had been limited and intermittent contact between the West and some other parts of the globe since ancient times, and despite the considerable amount of conventional knowledge that had piled up over the centuries.

Western Knowledge of the Non-Western World

The West had traded with China through Asian intermediaries since Greco-Roman antiquity. Alexander the Great had marched as far east as northern India in Greek times, and since that time many Asian invaders had come the other way, from Attila the Hun to Genghis Khan. A handful of Western mer-

	1400	1450	1500

POLITICAL, MILITARY, AND DIPLOMATIC EVENTS

1394–1460 Prince Henry the Navigator

1453 Fall of Constantinople to Turks

1492 Ferdinand and Isabella support Columbus
1492–1600 Spanish and Portuguese dominate overseas
1493 Treaty of Tordesillas
r. 1502–1520 Montezuma
1520s Cortés conquers Mexico

SOCIAL AND ECONOMIC DEVELOPMENTS

1488 Dias rounds tip of Africa
1492 Columbus reaches Americas
1497–1499 Da Gama reaches India
1519–1522 Magellan expedition circumnavigates globe

chants like Marco Polo had traveled to China and other parts of Asia in medieval times. Closer to home, Europeans had for more than two thousand years traded and fought with—and learned from—Near Eastern and North African peoples, from the ancient Egyptians and Persians to the Arabs and Turks in the Middle Ages. Nevertheless, military opposition, geographical barriers, and technological limitations had significantly restricted Western contacts with the rest of the world throughout most of history. Distances were too vast, the African Sahara and the arid lands of western Asia too forbidding, the power of their Eurasian and African neighbors more often than not too great. Westward, intrepid Viking voyagers had crossed the Atlantic to North America in the Middle Ages, but again such factors as the stormy ocean and the opposition of indigenous peoples soon extinguished these brief contacts. Throughout their history, then, few Westerners ever left their end of Eurasia at all, and only the most dubious information was available about the world outside.

For the rare scholar with an interest in such speculations, there was the Greek scientist Ptolemy's *Geography*—highly theoretical—and the Roman Pliny's *Natural History,* which included many tall tales about faraway peoples. Some Scholastic thinkers had added views of extra-European geography, again largely speculative, and Marco Polo's report of his travels through Asia was only one of a number of such travelers' tales. Mixed with these, finally, there were some purely fictional travel books masquerading as fact, like the fabulous voyages of "Sir John Mandeville," a fourteenth-century yarn spinner as popular as Marco Polo.

Through this haze of medieval tales and ancient myths, early modern Europeans saw the world outside as a kind of fantasyland. Scholars accepted the ancient Greek view that the earth was a globe, though the average citizen assumed it was flat, as it looked to the casual eye. Even on the best maps, Africa was shown cut off at the equator or curved around to link up with the southern tip of India; Asia was very indistinctly known; and North and South America, Australia, and Antarctica, four of the seven continents, were not shown at all on the European maps available to Columbus at the end of the fifteenth century.

In this fairy tale view of the world, the peoples

1529 Turkish siege of Vienna
r. 1530–1533 Atahualpa
1530s Pizarro conquers Peru

1600–1715 Dutch, French, and
English interlopers
build empires
1602 Dutch East
India Company
1607 Jamestown founded
1608 Quebec founded
1620 Massachusetts
founded

1683 Second Turkish siege
of Vienna

1610 Hudson in Canada

of the rest of the globe were often seen as either vastly superior or horrendously inferior to Europeans. Legends going back to ancient times thus depicted virtuous "noble savages" living on islands as beautiful as paradise; other stories and myths described cannibals, monsters, and mythological beings to be found in India, Africa, and other distant lands. Like distant planets in twentieth-century science fiction, the far places of the earth were lands of marvel to early modern Europeans.

Motives for Imperial Expansion

And yet, in the fifteenth, sixteenth, and seventeenth centuries, Europeans from half a dozen countries set out to find these unlikely countries in earnest. First Portuguese and Spaniards, then Dutch, French, and English—all the major powers of Europe's Atlantic seaboard—dispatched armed flotillas east and west to reach the Indies and Cathay, and then to explore the newfound lands of the Americas. The result was the European Age of Discovery and the first three centuries of Western global imperialism.

It is with the motives of this surge of aggressive expansionism that we are concerned in this section. Most of the hard-bitten men who carried the banners of the West beyond the seas were impelled by one or some combination of three motives. These were desire for material gain, the missionary impulse, or a thirst for fame and reputation—gold, God, and glory.

Thus pithily summarized, these impulses sound simple enough. But what did these abstractions mean to a man like Bernal Diaz, who conquered Mexico with Hernán Cortés and left us an invaluable book about it? To Sir Walter Raleigh, who tried and failed to found an American empire for Queen Elizabeth? To Christopher Columbus himself, whose voyages initiated the first great surge of Western overseas expansion? To appreciate the origins of this first wave of European imperialism, we need to understand the motives of the early imperialists in terms of the age in which they lived.

Greed was a Christian sin in early modern times, but a realist like Bernal Diaz admitted that almost all the conquistadors had their share of it. Golden idols in heathen temples, gold and silver mines, the pearls

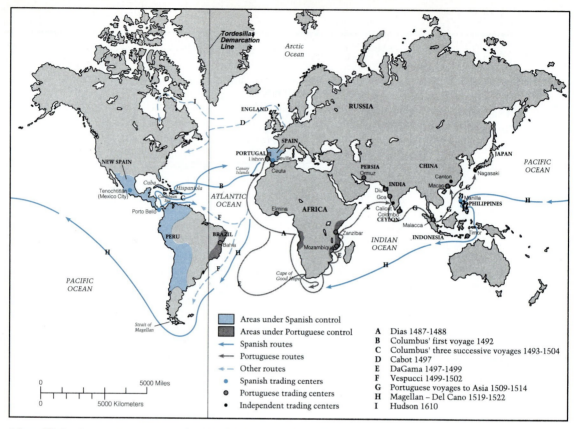

Map 17.1 Europe Encounters the World: Voyages from 1487 to 1610

and precious stones that were rumored to litter the beaches and line the rivers of the New World drew them like a magnet. The most vivid myth of the conquistadors was the dream of El Dorado, the legendary "Golden Man" and his fabulously wealthy city somewhere in South America. The Portuguese mariners who opened up trade by sea between Europe and Asia and the Dutch burghers who founded the first East India Company were drawn by the immense profits to be made from spices and other Eastern imports.

A medieval motive still very powerful in the Reformation century was the missionary urge to convert the pagan masses of the world to Christianity. The religious motive was particularly strong among the Spanish and Portuguese pioneers of imperialism, who had been Europe's earliest crusaders against the Muslims and most militant defenders of the Catholic

Reformation. The Spanish and Portuguese friars who founded missions across the southwestern United States and deep in the jungles of South America, the Jesuits in Canada or China, were spreading Western influence as they spread the Christian creed. But it was the apostolic faith itself that compelled them to undertake such perilous missions to the far places of the earth.

And finally, glory was a powerful motive for these early empire builders. The founders of most early colonies were soldiers, and Renaissance soldiers at that, avid for Renaissance honor, an intoxicating amalgam of medieval chivalric renown and ancient fame. Even so complex a character as Walter Raleigh longed to be hailed by Elizabethan poets and cheered through the streets of London as the founder of an English New World empire. The same sort of lust for honor that led so many cavaliers to seek their reputations in European wars helped inspire Cortés to conquer Mexico and Raleigh to found what became the Lost Colony in North Carolina.

Such motives were often mingled in a single individual. Thus Christopher Columbus urged the economic motive on his patrons, Ferdinand and Isabella, promising the wealth of China, Japan, and the East Indies if they would finance his effort to reach the East by sailing west. But he also seems to have seen himself as doing God's work, carrying the Light of the World across the waters as his namesake, St. Christopher, the patron of all voyagers, had done. And Columbus, grandly styled "the Admiral of the Ocean Sea," worked as hard for the titles and honors he thought were his due as for any pecuniary reward.

Cold-eyed calculators with an eye on the bottom line, saints and fanatics, brave and brutal soldiers, they were a driven, sometimes desperate lot of men. Before their multifarious compulsions waned, they had changed the world forever.

The Technology of Empire Building

Lust for wealth, fame, and converts, however, was not a uniquely European impulse. What transformed these human desires into historic drives were the special advantages enjoyed by the Western world in early modern times.

Some of the most important of these advantages were purely technological. Europe's sturdy little fifteenth-century caravels, combining medieval square sails with triangular lateen ones borrowed from the Arabs, proved remarkably maneuverable oceangoing vessels, capable of tacking across and even into the wind. The galleons of the sixteenth century added bristling gun decks; the lumbering seventeenth-century East Indiamen with their capacious holds multiplied the carrying capacity of European ships. Such steady improvements in design gave the West superiority at sea over all other peoples.

European explorers, traders, and conquerors also developed a number of invaluable navigation aids. The compass was first employed in China, but Europeans perfected it for their own use at the end of the Middle Ages. By means of the astrolabe, an instrument for measuring the altitude of the sun or a selected star above the horizon, Western mariners learned to tell their own latitude north or south of the equator. Using a knotted rope, a floating log, and an hourglass—later a mechanical clock—to estimate the speed with which the ship left the log behind, navigators were able to calculate roughly how far they had progressed in a day—and work out their longitude. In the essential science of map making, European advances included careful coastal charting and such breakthroughs as the *Mercator projection*. The latter, the work of Gerardus Mercator (1519–1594), opened out the curved surface of the earth onto a flat map in such a way as to space the meridians of longitude equally, while parallels of latitude grow further apart north and south of the equator. This projection enabled navigators to plot their bearings as straight lines on the map; it remained the standard projection down to the twentieth century.

A final technological advantage was the rapid improvement of *gunpowder weapons* in the war-torn West. The explosive potential of gunpowder was understood in China before it was in Europe, and the Ottoman Turks leveled what were then the largest siege guns in the world against Constantinople in 1453. From the sixteenth century on, however, European artillery rapidly outdistanced all rivals. Smaller firearms like the cumbersome musket gave Western soldiers at least a psychological advantage from the beginning, and in time provided a devastating advantage in firepower as well. Though other nations, including some Muslim peoples and the Japanese, adopted the new weapons, the West continued to set the global pace in the development of both artillery and small gunpowder weapons.

Not all the elements that promoted Western success were technological, however. As we have seen, European business organization had developed impressively from the commercial revolution of the High Middle Ages on. By pooling the investment capital of many merchants in large joint-stock companies, European traders accumulated sufficient capital to undertake the global ventures of the Renaissance and later centuries. Equipped with efficient business techniques, from bookkeeping methods to large banking institutions, Westerners became worthy rivals of Muslim, Indian, or south Chinese commercial organizations, which had developed independently in the context of their own civilizations. And when we add Western governmental organization, the balance tips decisively to the West. For as we have seen, the European great powers had grown into administratively complex, increasingly powerful institutions, able to mobilize the energies of whole nations for long and costly efforts, from national development and European wars to centuries-long efforts at empire building.

To the strengths derived from technological advances and organizational sophistication, we should add the traditional competitiveness and militarism of many Western peoples. The very fact that Europe was divided, not united as China was, bred an urge for that competitive edge in European traders, military captains, and kings. In a sense, Westerners had been training for this long march against the rest of the world throughout their contentious history. The endless military struggles of the West produced a ruling class habituated to the use of arms, ready to appeal to the ultimate sanction of force against Incas or rajahs beyond the oceans. There were other cultures in 1500 as militaristic as that of the West—the Aztecs and the Japanese samurai, for instance—but none who had the other Western advantages we have described as well.

Thus it is not surprising that by 1600 the Spanish and Portuguese were well established from South America to Southeast Asia, or that by 1700 important parts of North America and South Asia were in the hands of the Dutch, the French, and the English. Western peoples, ever alert to the main chance, had parlayed these temporary advantages into something unique in world history: the domination of the globe by a single one of its major civilizations.

Phases and Forms of Imperialism

The period of spreading *Western global imperialism* lasted some five centuries and involved a variety of forms of Western predominance. This chapter deals only with the earlier phases of this explosion of Western power, from the fifteenth through the seventeenth centuries. Here, however, let us glance briefly ahead in order to put these early centuries of Western expansion in the perspective of the whole astonishing phenomenon of Western overseas empire building.

In some ways, the growing networks of European colonies and trading posts around the world resembled earlier historic empires, in the West and elsewhere. They did, however, exhibit at least one unique feature: they were based for the first time on the mastery of the oceans of the world. The technological advances and economic and political strengths of early modern Europe made it possible for Europeans to dispatch flotillas of sailing ships to

virtually any part of the globe. The result was something very different from the land empires of earlier conquerors like the ancient Romans or Chinese, the Mongols or Incas in more recent centuries. All these highly successful imperial powers had been limited by the reach of armies marching over land. They could conquer their neighbors, but they could not go far beyond. Only the Western imperialism of the period between the fifteenth and twentieth centuries was truly intercontinental in scope—virtually unlimited in its global reach.

Two major phases in the history of Western expansion have been distinguished: the old and the new imperialism. The so-called *old imperialism,* with which we are concerned here, stretched from the late fifteenth century to the late eighteenth, from Columbus's historic voyage of 1492 to the American Declaration of Independence from Britain in 1776. The *new imperialism,* which we discuss in Volume 2 of this book, encompassed the later nineteenth and the first half of the twentieth centuries, from the 1870s to the collapse of the major European overseas empires after the end of World War II in 1945.

Under the rubric of old imperialism, it is easy to distinguish two or three main subdivisions. The pioneers of the Western empire beyond the oceans were the Iberian monarchies, Portugal and Spain, which planted the first colonies and laid the foundations for Western control of world trade during the fifteenth and sixteenth centuries. After 1600, "interlopers," Dutch, French, and English, defied Iberian claims and soon established their own colonies and trading centers around the world. Thereafter, as we will see in Volume 2, the eighteenth century saw a final duel for empire between two of the most successful of Western overseas powers, Britain and France, for imperial supremacy. Throughout this period, finally, Russia was also expanding, though by land rather than by sea, in an eastward sweep across northern Eurasia that was as impressive in its way as the seaborne empires.

Historians have distinguished two major forms of Western expansion during the age of the old imperialism: settlement empires and trading empires. A *settlement empire* meant the establishment of colonies overseas, with European governors and garrisons ruling non-Europeans as well as Western colonists. It meant European-run plantations, mines, fishing and trapping industries, and other profitable overseas ventures. This political and economic restructuring of course required that substantial numbers of European settlers establish themselves in the far parts of the earth. Such colonial empires were most common in the New World. There, in the 1500s, Spanish and Portuguese settled much of South America and Mesoamerica Middle America (Mexico and Central America) and parts of western North America. English, French, and Dutch settlers colonized eastern North America and parts of the Caribbean in the 1600s. Russian expansion across Siberia to the Pacific produced a similar if even more thinly settled empire, led by Cossacks and other frontiersmen.

Trading empires were more common in Asia and Africa. The large and well-established empires that already existed in Asia and the inhospitable geography and disease germs of Africa made conquest and Western settlement much more difficult. Here trading posts, treaties with local rulers, and a relatively modest military establishment proved sufficient to guarantee the European intruders the commercial profits they desired. By such means, Westerners acquired control of the ancient trade between Europe and Asia, and of the new trade in slaves between Africa and their own new Ameri-

can colonies. In the sixteenth century, such a trading empire was established in the East by Portugal. In the seventeenth, the Dutch replaced the Portuguese in the islands of Southeast Asia (Indonesia today), while the French and English began to compete for the profitable trade with Mogul India.

New forms of imperial control evolved further in later centuries. But the Western presence in much of the rest of the world was an accomplished fact in 1715 when Louis XIV died, master of one of the most impressive of Western empires.

The First Global Empires: The Iberians

In the wake of the crumbling of the intercontinental empires in recent decades, both public opinion and scholarly interpretation have turned strongly against Western imperialism in particular and empire in general. Such condemnation of former conquests is natural as the planet's peoples grope toward better ways

The Taj Mahal in Agra, India, built in the early seventeenth century by the Mughal emperor Shah Jahan as a tomb for his beautiful wife, the Mumtaz Mahal. High civilizations existed in many parts of the world when the West began its long campaign of overseas empire building.

of living together in this first age of genuinely global history. Since our goal in this book, however, is simply to comprehend the behavior of earlier generations, it may be best to deal with Western imperialism as objectively as we would the imperial conquests of Assyrians or Aztecs, of Caesar or Charlemagne. For empire building, like warfare and economic exploitation, religion and art, is an important part of the human story.

The Tide Turns Against Islam

There is, however, a sizable chunk of unfinished business to deal with first: the climax of Christian Europe's long feud with the Muslim peoples south and east of the Mediterranean. The last major chapter in that long struggle, which began with the founding of the Arab Empire in the seventh century, came as the West confronted the Ottoman Turks, the most powerful of all Muslim states in the sixteenth and seventeenth centuries.

The *Ottomans,* a nomadic Turko-Mongol people from the steppes of northern Eurasia, had drifted down into the Middle East, converted to Islam, and taken over leadership of the Muslim crusade against Eastern Christendom at the end of the Middle Ages. In 1453 the Ottoman Muhammad the Conqueror had succeeded at last in toppling the Byzantine Empire, Europe's Near Eastern bastion against Asian invasion. By 1500, the Turks had occupied most of the Balkans as well as large portions of the Near East and North Africa. Under Suleiman the Magnificent (r. 1520–1566), the Ottoman Empire loomed like an advancing storm all along the southern and eastern frontiers of the Western world.

Under Suleiman, the greatest of all the Ottoman sultans, the Turkish Empire expanded not only further west to Algeria and south to the Persian Gulf, but northward, pressing up into central and eastern Europe. Ruling the eastern shores of the Adriatic and the northern coasts of the Black Sea, extending their suzerainty as far as the Caspian, the Ottoman Turks threatened the Holy Roman Empire, Poland, and Russia. After crushing a European army at the great battle of Mohács (1526) in Hungary, they temporarily laid siege to the Habsburg capital of Vienna itself (1529). On the sea, Ottoman fleets fought Spanish and Italian armadas up and down the Mediterranean and challenged the newly founded Portuguese Empire for mastery of the Indian Ocean.

Drawing on the resources of western Asia, North Africa, and southeastern Europe, the Ottoman Empire mobilized vast wealth and power. Borrowing autocratic traditions from the Byzantines they had conquered, from their Persian neighbors and rivals within Islam, and perhaps from earlier contacts with China, the Ottomans erected a powerfully authoritarian state. European travelers admired the Ottoman sultan's practice of promoting officials on merit, and they were pleased with the safety of the well-policed roads and impressed by the splendor of the imperial court. Christian sovereigns sought alliances with the Turks against other European rulers, as the Valois kings of France did against the Habsburg emperors. Ottoman attacks on the Holy Roman Empire from the south distracted the emperors from the long struggle with the Protestant princes of north Germany. No Arab or Seljuk Turkish threat in the Middle Ages ever looked more dangerous, no Muslim culture more disturbingly successful, than that of the Ottoman Turks.

Nevertheless, in the seventeenth century the tide turned in favor of the West. After Suleiman's death in 1566, a succession of feeble sultans combined with corruption in court and administration, disunity, and economic decline to undermine the colossus of the Middle East. In 1571, Spanish and Italian fleets administered a stinging setback to Turkish arms in the great naval victory of Lepanto, off the coast of Greece. A century later, in 1683, German and Polish armies broke a second siege of Vienna and decisively turned back what proved to be the last serious Turkish threat to central Europe. Soon thereafter, the Habsburgs pushed the Turks back out of Hungary, while the Venetians established temporary footholds in southern Greece. Shortly before 1700, Peter the Great launched a Russian drive to recapture the northern shores of the Black Sea, an effort that Catherine the Great brought to fruition in the next century.

The 1700s thus saw the beginning of a Western counteroffensive that, over the next two hundred years, reduced Ottoman Turkey to the status of "the sick man of Europe" in the 1800s. In the long struggle between the Western world and the Islamic zone, the initiative had passed decisively to the West.

The Portuguese in Asia

While the Ottoman Turkish tide was being turned back at the eastern end of the Mediterranean, the Iberian powers at the western end were building vaster empires than even that of Suleiman the Magnificent. Of the two new nations of the Iberian peninsula, it was the smaller, Portugal, that took the lead, showing the rest of Europe the way to overseas empire.

The seacoast kingdom of Portugal, in the southwest corner of Europe, was ideally located to lead in transoceanic expansion. Under the able royal house of Aviz, this compact kingdom had established its independence from its much larger Spanish neighbors at the end of the Middle Ages. By 1400, the Portuguese had a centralized government capable of mobilizing the resources that exploration and empire building required. In the early fifteenth century, Prince Henry the Navigator (1394–1460), of the house of Aviz, launched a remarkable early example of a research and development program aimed at pushing back the frontiers of human knowledge—and not incidentally expanding the wealth and power of his own nation.

At Sagres in 1419 Prince Henry established a center to develop ships and maps that enabled Portugal to extend its sway down the coast of western Africa. He had two goals: to make contact with a fabled Christian African ruler called Prester John as an ally against the Muslims, and to take possession of the African mines from which gold had for centuries flowed north across the Sahara in camel caravans. The Portuguese approach was methodical and persevering. Ships were built, maps and reports from merchants, travelers, and other sources carefully collated. Under the patronage of Prince Henry and others, naval expeditions sailed down the African coast. The performance of the vessels and the discoveries of their captains were evaluated, and new expeditions, suitably modified, were dispatched to carry on the work. Decade after decade, the Portuguese added to their store of information about the larger world outside.

Prester John turned out to be a mythical character, commonly identified by historians with the Christian emperor of Ethiopia 2,000 miles to the east. The gold mines of the Guinea coast proved to be real, however, and the Portuguese were importing large quantities of the precious metal by 1500. And in the latter part of the fifteenth century, Prince Henry's successors formulated a new and potentially even more profitable objective: to discover a sea route around Africa to the riches of India and the fabled islands of spices. In 1488 the Portuguese mariner Bartolomeu Dias (c. 1450–1500) reached the Cape of Good Hope at the southern tip of Africa.

In 1497 King Manuel I the Fortunate (r. 1495–1521) sent out four ships under a Portuguese nobleman named Vasco da Gama to round the cape and see what lay beyond.

Vasco da Gama (c. 1460–1524) was tough, shrewd, persistent, brutal—clearly the man for the job. He sailed his little flotilla down the length of Africa, rounded the Cape of Good Hope, and coasted north up the eastern side of the continent to the latitude of modern Kenya. From East Africa, with the help of a Muslim pilot, he crossed the Indian Ocean to the Malabar coast of India. There he reached Calicut, an important link in the Arab trade network that had for centuries linked southern Asia and eastern Africa. As the battered Portuguese vessels dropped anchor in the Indian harbor in May of 1498 two Muslims from North Africa greeted them from a bobbing small boat, calling, "A lucky venture! A lucky venture! Plenty of rubies, plenty of emeralds! You owe great thanks to God for having brought you to a country holding such riches!"[1]

Most Arab traders were not so happy to see these intruders into their ancient preserve. Despite their intrigues, however, and despite the reluctance of the local Indian prince to deal with the Westerners and the contempt Indian buyers showed for European trinkets and trade goods, da Gama managed to assemble a cargo of spices and made his way homeward. Facing hostile natives and pirates, violent storms, dead calms, and scurvy, the Portuguese com-

Calicut, the goal of Vasco da Gama's first Portuguese expedition to India, was one of the many flourishing cities of the Indian subcontinent. In dealing with well-established Asian states like these, Europeans had to ask permission even to trade.

mander kidnapped, cannonaded, and tortured his human foes and doggedly survived the worst that nature could do. Although he lost half his ships and a third of his men, he returned to Lisbon after a two years' voyage with a cargo that sold on the European market for sixty times what the expedition had cost. (See the box titled "Vasco da Gama Goes to India and Back.")

Not surprisingly, the Portuguese mounted new expeditions almost at once. Throughout the sixteenth century, they constructed and ran an extensive trading empire in the Far East. Organized by the grizzled commander Affonso de Albuquerque (1453–1515) around 1510, this zone of Portuguese predominance was an impressive achievement. It included way stations around the coast of Africa, naval bases at key locations around the Indian

Ocean, trading posts on the coast of India, and additional outstations in Southeast Asia and on the south coast of China. In 1500, meanwhile, the Portuguese captain Pedro Cabral (1467–1520) also stumbled across the eastward bulge of Brazil, the beginning of the immense Portuguese colony in South America.

But the Indian Ocean was the heart of Portugal's empire. Seeking to convert this ancient center of commercial exchange into a Portuguese lake, Lisbon determined to seal it off both from the Arabs who had plied these sea lanes for centuries and from interlopers from rival European nations. Pirate ships, competing merchant vessels, even Muslim pilgrim ships on the way to Mecca were summarily burned, their crews and passengers flung into the sea. A few Portuguese priests began trying to con-

MASTERING OUR WORLD   Vasco da Gama Goes to India and Back

These extracts come from the anonymous journal of someone who sailed with Vasco da Gama on the epochal voyage that brought Europe into contact with Asia by sea around Africa six years after Columbus attempted to reach the East by sailing west and found the Americas instead. The first extract describes a predatory assault by the Europeans on Africans, seeking a pilot to guide them on their way. The second emphasizes the fact that Arabs had preceded western Europeans in opening up trade with India by sea and were as ready as the Europeans to resort to aggressive measures to defend their monopoly. The third passage illustrates the dangers all sailors faced in those days: calms, storms, and the scurvy described here.

MOMBASSA TO MALINDI

At break of day we saw two boats (*barcas*) about three leagues to leeward, in the open sea, and at once gave chase, with the intention of capturing them, for we wanted to secure a pilot who would guide us to where we wanted to go. At vesper time we came up with one of them and captured it [with] seventeen men, besides gold, silver, and an abundance of maize [grain]. . . .

IN CALECUT

The moors [Muslims] of the place, who were merchants from Mecca and elsewhere, and who knew us . . . had told the king that we were thieves, and that if we once navigated his country, no more ships from Mecca . . . nor from any other port would visit him. They added that he would derive no profit from this [trade with Portugal], as we had nothing to give, but would rather take away, and that thus his country would be ruined. They, moreover, offered rich bribes to the king to capture and ill us, so that we should not return to Portugal.

ACROSS THE ARABIAN SEA

Owing to frequent calms and foul winds, it took us three months less three days to cross this gulf and all our people again suffered from their gums, which grew over their teeth so that they could not eat. Their legs also swelled, and other parts of the body, and these swellings spread until the sufferer died. . . . Thirty of our men died in this manner . . . and those able to navigate each ship were only seven or eight. . . . Whilst suffering this affliction, we addressed vows and petitions to the saints on behalf of our ships. . . . But it pleased God to send us a wind which in the course of six days carried us within sight of land. . . .

Source: E. G. Ravenstein, ed., *A Journal of the First Voyage of Vasco da Gama, 1497–1499* (London: Hakluyt Society, 1897), 39, 71–72, 87.

vert the Hindu millions of India to Christianity, a futile effort that made the Portuguese unpopular on the subcontinent. But from Angola in Africa to Goa in India and on to Macao in China, Portuguese soldiers, traders, and priests were spreading across the world.

In the long run, however, this pioneering imperial venture faced insuperable problems. Portugal was small, and the East was large: increasingly, numbers told against the Portuguese. The logistics of imperial control also proved tremendously costly in lost ships, in graft, in the sheer expense of maintaining bases and trading posts so far from home. The Portuguese, furthermore, were farmers and soldiers, not merchants, and the commercial exchange they opened up was soon taken over by Italian, Dutch, and German money men more experienced in such matters. By the beginning of the seventeenth century, finally, other European nations could no longer

be kept out of the empire itself: India became an area of French and English predominance; island Southeast Asia became the Dutch East Indies. Though Portugal retained its Brazilian colony and scattered holdings in Africa and Asia, other European architects of empire took the lead in Western overseas expansion.

The Spanish in the New World

During the sixteenth century, the greatest imperial state was clearly Spain, the other Iberian power. As we know, Isabella and Ferdinand financed Columbus's fateful voyage; under Charles V, Cortés conquered Mexico and Pizarro seized Peru; and it was Philip II's galleons that brought back the flow of silver and gold which dazzled all Europe in the 1500s.

This print by Theodore de Bry imaginatively reconstructs Columbus's arrival in the New World. What do the cross being raised on the left and the trade goods being offered by the Native Americans tell us about the motives of the conquistadors? [New York Public Library, Rare Book Division. Astor, Lenox, and Tilden Foundations]

More than anything else, it was the discoveries of explorers and the victories of conquistadors under the Spanish flag that made the sixteenth century Spain's *siglo de oro* or "golden century."

Some evidence suggests that Christopher Columbus (1451–1506) was a physically impressive man with a long face, an aquiline nose, and red hair. Born of ungenteel parents in the ancient Italian port of Genoa, he was self-educated, ambitious, perhaps a bit of a mystic, and, after years at sea, an experienced and instinctive seaman. His knowledge of geography was scrappy, and he became fixated on an erroneous theory that the earth was smaller than most authorities believed, so that China was really within a few weeks' sailing time of Europe—if you sailed west around the world instead of east. He was also, however, a man of dogged determination and inexhaustible persistence, qualities that carried him through years of fruitless petitions for support at the courts of Portugal and Spain, until Ferdinand and Isabella, flushed with victory over the Moors, agreed to find the money he needed to test his theory.

Columbus sailed with a fleet of three small ships in early August of 1492. After a voyage of a bit over two months' duration, including a stop in the Canary Islands, he made his first landfall in the Caribbean at the island of San Salvador (Watlings Island) in the Bahamas. The scene is vivid in every schoolchild's imagination: caravels in the middle distance, men in doublets and hose splashing through the surf to kneel beneath flapping banners to take possession of a wide white beach in the name of the Catholic kings. From further up the palm-fringed shore, naked Indians may be imagined gazing out at the heavy clothing, the glint of swords and muskets, the winged ships on the water—their destiny. "I found very many islands filled with people without number," the Admiral of the Ocean Sea wrote home, "and of them all I have taken possession for their Highnesses, by proclamation and with the royal standard displayed, and nobody objected."[2]

In this and three subsequent voyages, Columbus explored the Caribbean and adjacent coasts of Middle and South America, always under the illusion he was in East Asia. Within a few years, however, Spanish and Portuguese expeditions had discovered Brazil and had sailed far down the Argentine coast; others poked their way up the coast of North America. Geographers and map makers soon realized they were dealing with an unknown land mass, sometimes called *Mundus Novus*—"New World"—and sometimes "America" after the Italian explorer Amerigo Vespucci (1452–1512). Vespucci explored thousands

of miles of the coast of South America and realized within a decade of Columbus's first voyage that this was not Asia, but an unknown continent. Later navigators, still determined to reach the rich markets of the East by sailing west, sought a way around this vast geographical barrier; and in 1520, Ferdinand Magellan (1480–1521) found it.

A Portuguese in Spanish service, Magellan sailed in 1519, equipped by a parsimonious government with five old and battered ships and crews recruited from the dregs of half the ports in Europe, in search of Cathay, the Spice Islands, and the biblical lands of Tarshish and Ophir. The epic voyage of his small fleet, twice as long as da Gama's, took the expedition across the Atlantic, around the southern tip of South America, through what became the Straits of Magellan, and across the wide Pacific. Passing through the Portuguese East Indies (Indonesia today), the survivors crossed the Indian Ocean from east to west, rounded Africa, and headed north once more to Spain. Storms and scurvy, maggoty ship's biscuit and foul water, mutiny, hostile natives and hostile Portuguese all took their toll. Magellan himself was killed in the Philippines. Of all his fleet, only one ship, the tiny *Vittoria* under the Basque captain Sebastián del Cano (1476–1526), and a crew of eighteen, completed the three-year voyage—the first circumnavigation of the earth in human history.

The Spanish Conquistadors

The Spanish monarchy, meanwhile, had been guaranteeing its imperial future against its Portuguese competitors diplomatically. In 1494, after securing a papal decree and renegotiating its contents with the Portuguese, Spain signed the Treaty of Tordesillas with Portugal. The agreement gave Portugal the right to explore, exploit, and colonize everything east of a line that included Brazil, Africa, and Asia to the eastern edge of China. Spain had similar exclusive rights to the west of the demarcation line, which as it turned out meant most of North and South America. No Native Americans, Africans, or Asians, of course, were consulted.

Within a generation, Spanish commanders were conquering a New World empire for Spain. Between 1520 and 1550, as one authority sums it up, "a few thousand down-at-heels swordsmen . . . the products of [Spain's] Moorish wars, possessed themselves of most of the settled areas of both Americas and established the first great European land empire over-

gužmā. mchvácā.

Spanish invaders , accompanied by Indian allies and dogs attack Aztecs. What examples of the savagery of the conquest can you see in this picture?

seas."[3] Theirs was a more orthodox breed of heroics, and a more brutal one. The Aztecs of Mexico and the Incas of Peru, themselves conquering peoples who had only recently imposed their authority on their neighbors, ruled ancient and highly developed civilizations. Cortés, Pizarro, and their mercenary followers destroyed both the rulers and the civilizations.

The *Aztecs* were a military elite who had intrigued and fought their way to mastery of ancient Mexico and part of Central America only a few generations earlier. Their religion required them to sacrifice large numbers of human beings on the altar of the sun in Tenochtitlán, their capital city. Their stone-and-adobe cities, however, were large, beautiful, and cleaner than most European ones, their society almost crime free, the arts and sciences they inherited from Mayan and earlier cultures highly sophisticated. Dominated by priests and nobles, limited by the lack of large beasts of burden and by their failure to develop iron tools, the Aztecs were nevertheless impressive builders and agriculturalists, effective rulers, and fierce fighters.

Against them came, in 1519, "as devoted a gang of desperadoes as ever engaged in a desperate venture," the *conquistadors* ("conquerors") led by Hernán Cortés (1485–1547). Dashing lover, rare university man among the rough men he led, Cortés proved also to be an inspiring and fearless leader, a clever diplomat, and a ruthless conqueror.

With the aid of an Indian woman, Doña Marina, he formed alliances with disgruntled Indian peoples against their Aztec rulers, exploited Mexican legends of returning gods, and maneuvered his way to the heart of Tenochtitlán to seize the person of the Aztec emperor, Montezuma II (r. 1502–1520). Expelled from the city with huge losses following a Spanish massacre of Aztec nobles, Cortés stubbornly regrouped. He turned Spanish troops sent against him by a rival conquistador into reinforcements for his cause; he mobilized his Indian allies, who stuck with him even in defeat. Taking the offensive once more, he returned to cen-

WAR AND PEACE
An Aztec Lament

This Aztec lament for the destruction of Tenochtitlán, "the Venice of the New World," was taken down in the 1520s, only a few years after the Spanish conquest. The shock of the destruction of their land and their own oppressed and helpless condition comes through clearly. What does the Native American poet's choice of things to describe tell you about his or her feelings? Do these images tell you anything about Aztec society?

> And all this happened to us.
> We saw it,
> We are amazed.
> With this lamentable and sad fortune,
> We see ourselves anguished.
> In the roads lie red spears,
> Locks of hair are scattered.
> Roofless are the houses,
> Red with flames are their walls.
>
> Maggots swarm through streets and squares,
> And brains are splashed on the walls.
> Red are the waters, as if they were dyed,
> And when we drink it,
> It is as if we drank saltpetre.
>
> We struck the adobe walls,
> And our heritage was a net full of holes.
> In the shields lay its safeguard,
> But neither with shields can its solitude be
>   sustained.

Source: *MS Anónimo de Tlatelolco* (1528), Bibliothèque Nationale, Paris, in Miguel León-Portilla, ed., *Visión de los vencidos* (Havana: Casa de las Americas, 1972), 220–221.

tral Mexico, crushed the Aztecs, reduced their beautiful capital city to rubble, and established the Spanish colony of New Spain on the ruins of the Aztec Empire.

The feel of the conquest emerges vividly from Cortés's third dispatch to Charles V, telling the bloody story of the capture of Tenochtitlán. (For an Aztec view, see the box titled "An Aztec Lament.") The final clause in particular sums up the impact of the European onslaught in many imperial wars to come:

> Seeing that the enemy was determined to resist to the death, I came to [the conclusion] that they would force us to destroy them totally. This last caused me the greater sorrow, for it weighed on my soul. I reflected on the means I might use to frighten them so that they would realize their mistake and the injury they would sustain from us; and I kept on burning and destroying their houses and the towers of their idols.[4]

Far to the south, the empire of the *Incas* stretched for more than 3,000 miles from what is today Colombia through most of Chile. The empire was bound together by the awesome Royal Road through the Andes, with way stations every few miles and hundreds of suspension bridges swinging over mountain gorges. Indian towns, scattered the length of the realm, "replete with administrative centers and Sun Temples . . . , stone-laid palaces, temples for Sun Virgins, official storehouses, and fortresses, . . . for the sheer mass of building almost equaled the Roman."[5] Having seized power by force even more recently than the Aztecs, the Inca elite had welded many peoples into a centralized state, with a divine emperor, an elaborate administration, and social services that have been compared to those of a modern welfare state.

Into this Andean civilization in 1532 came the grim, illiterate, and thoroughly unprincipled Francisco Pizarro (c. 1475–1541), with his three brothers and a couple of hundred colonial fortune hunters at his back. By exploiting an Indian civil war, by holding the Inca emperor Atahualpa (r. 1530–1533) for a huge ransom and then killing him, and by making murderous use of their superior steel and gunpowder weapons, Pizarro and his conquistadors won a gold-rich empire beyond their wildest dreams. Pizarro himself was murdered less than a decade later in the bloody feuding over the spoils that soon divided the victors. Again, the Indian civilization itself crumbled and vanished, plunging these new subjects of Western rule into centuries of deprivation and misery.

Other would-be conquerors from Castile crisscrossed their newfound lands in search of more Aztec or Inca realms to plunder. Crossing the deserts of the North American southwest or painfully tracing the Amazon to its mouth, they performed prodigies of exploration, but found no more El Dorados. Claiming most of South America, Central America and the Caribbean, and southwestern North America from California to Texas, the Spanish set out to make what they could from the lands and peoples they had conquered.

Climbing up to Machu Picchu today, by train, bus, and foot from the old Inca capital of Cuzco, you get a vivid sense of what these adventurers destroyed. Perched among cloud-crowned peaks high above the jungle floor, Peru's most famous lost city lies roofless and open to the elements now. But its buildings of stones precisely cut, carried to this lofty

The mountain-top city of Machu Picchu, rediscovered in 1911, displays Incan engineering skills. Can you imagine the difficulties of such a building project even today?

pinnacle and fit together so accurately that a knife blade cannot be inserted between them, provide ample evidence of the capacities of the society Western empire builders shattered in these mountain fastnesses.

Spain's American Empire

The political, economic, and social structure of the Spanish Empire in the Americas resulted from a fusing of Old World institutions and ideas with New World realities. The result was the largest and for a while the most profitable Western empire of the old imperial period.

The freebooting rule of the original conquistadors soon gave way to a more bureaucratic structure of government, with its headquarters in Spain, at the great port of Seville and in Madrid itself. From Madrid, viceroys and royal governors were dispatched to the two capitals of Spanish America, the booming colonial metropolises of Mexico City (on the site of the vanished Tenochtitlán) and Lima, Peru, as well as to lesser provincial centers. In the colonies, royal governors were aided by local councils called *audiencias* with advisory and judicial functions. Colonial cities also had local assemblies of their own, like many European cities. Although governors were always Spaniards sent out from Europe, municipal assemblies expressed the views of the Spanish colonial population on matters of public policy. The original Amerindian majority had no more say in how they were governed than the peasant masses of the Old World did.

The Spanish overseas empire was developed in the spirit of European *mercantilism,* which meant paternalistic government regulation. Colonies could not compete with the mother country; they had to provide it with agricultural products and other resources it lacked; and they had to trade exclusively with Spain (see also discussion in Chapter 19). In one way, Spanish America was well suited to mercantilism: the goal of the system was an inflow of bullion to the motherland, and Mexico and Bolivia particularly proved a fabulous source of silver, a "royal fifth" of which went directly to the crown. Colonists, however, could not be prevented from trading with other countries, and smuggling became part of the colonial way of life, as it was in other overseas empires. Economic production, meanwhile, was carried forward under a semimanorial system of land grants called *encomiendas,* in which colonial landholders lived off the labor of Indian fieldhands, cattle herders, or miners. When the Amerindians began to dwindle under the rigors of this system of forced labor, African slaves were imported to take their place, and a plantation system like the one that later evolved in the American south took shape.

Spanish colonial society retained some features of the old country. It was dominated by an elite of royal officials, churchmen, landholders, and merchants in the port cities. Most settlers, however, were farmers, ranchers, miners, shopkeepers, laborers, and servants. And increasing numbers of them were women.

The first European women to settle in the New World were probably the three dozen Columbus brought on his third voyage to the "Indies." In general, European women in Spanish or Portuguese territories were frequently relatives of men settled in the colonies. As in their Iberian homelands, those colonial women often lived cloistered lives, jealously guarded behind high garden walls and shuttered windows. At the same time, there were opportunities and advantages for women in the Iberian colonies. A leading authority on the European conquest of Latin America refers to "many examples of women who fought alongside and encouraged their menfolk, nursed the sick and wounded, and displayed a spirit of exemplary self-sacrifice."[6]

The bulk of the colonial population, male or female, was divided hierarchically along essentially color lines. Descendants of Spanish settlers were the "best people"; *mestizos,* of mixed Spanish and Indian origin, though sneered at by people of unmixed Spanish descent, occupied a productive middle stratum of society; Indians and Africans provided most of the labor force and had the least social prestige.

The fate of the Amerindian peoples of the New World remains one of the most tragic in the whole story of Western global predominance. The so-called *black legend* of particular Spanish cruelty to the Indians, circulated by European enemies of Spanish power, painted a grim picture of hunting, torturing, and burning Indian resisters to death. And there was some substance to it, though Spain was not alone in savage treatment of the Native Americans. More important, however, repressive rule, unfamiliar labor discipline, and above all smallpox and other diseases to which they had no immunities caused Indian populations to decline precipitously. The native population of Mexico dropped from perhaps nineteen million to between two and three million in the course

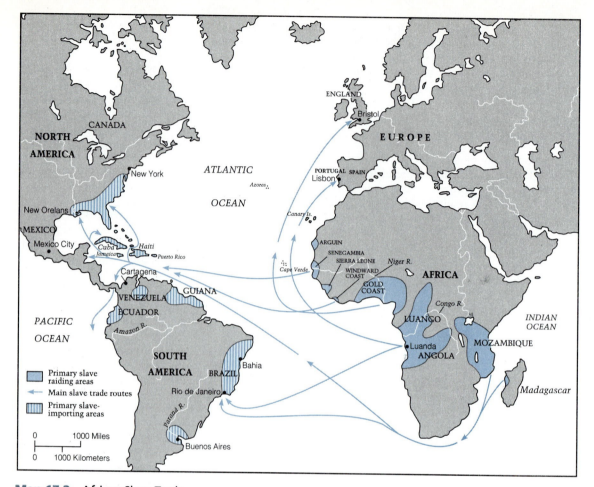

Map 17.2   African Slave Trade

of the sixteenth century, while the Indians of the Caribbean virtually disappeared. Some Spanish churchmen, most notably Bartolomé de las Casas (1474–1566), "Father of the Indians," fought for their interests, and laws were passed protecting the original inhabitants and even making them wards of the crown. The Spanish colonists, however, often ignored such laws, as did Western settlers in many other parts of the world.

The result of the Spanish conquest of so much of Middle and South America was a major extension of the Western world overseas. It was built, like most civilizations up to that time, on the laboring backs of the masses of humanity—in overseas colonies, mostly non-Western masses. From California to Argentina it produced plowed fields and bustling cities, ornate palaces, baroque churches, and dusty missions where Indians and Spaniards prayed together—but to a Christian God.

As the seventeenth century advanced, Spain declined and the Spanish Empire was no longer in the forefront of Western colonial expansion. Spain, as we have seen, was one of the losers in the Thirty Years' War, and faced growing English competition and shrinking revenues from its New World mines. The European preeminence of the Spain of Philip II in the 1500s thus gave way to that of Louis XIV's France in the later 1600s. The Spanish-American Empire remained prosperous enough that other European powers fought for the right to trade with it.

But the Spanish colonies now expanded only slowly on their internal frontiers, while other European powers took the lead in the continuing expansion of the imperial West.

The First Global Empires: The Interlopers

The Spanish and Portuguese, strategically located on southern Europe's westward-jutting Iberian peninsula, were thus the first to carry Western power beyond the oceans in the century after 1492. The North Atlantic maritime powers, however—the Netherlands, France, and England—followed the Iberians onto the world stage around 1600. These were the *interlopers,* intruders into a non-Western world to which the Iberian states claimed exclusive rights. As Spain and Portugal declined in the seventeenth century, these interlopers added more colonies and commercial outposts to the expanding Western hegemony of the globe.

The Dutch Commercial Empire

The Dutch were the first to breach the Iberian monopoly of overseas empire in a large way. With centuries of experience as one of Europe's leading commercial centers and as leaders in seaborne enterprise, the merchants and seamen of the Netherlands were ideally suited to reach beyond the ocean to the world at large. Beginning by marketing the overseas products brought to Europe by the Iberian powers in the sixteenth century, the Dutch began to trade with the outside world directly in the seventeenth. They soon became the world leaders in oceanic commerce.

The Dutch Empire, like that of the Portuguese, was essentially a trading rather than a settlement empire. It differed from Portugal's, however, in being a private enterprise empire, founded by consortia of businessmen organized in great trading companies, rather than by the central government. The Estates General of the United Provinces, like royal governments elsewhere, did charter the East and West India Companies in 1602 and 1621, granting them monopolies of trade in these regions. But it was the initiative, efficiency, and determination of Dutch busi-

nessmen that built the seventeenth-century Dutch supremacy on the seas of the world.

The first Dutch fleets set sail for what were still nominally the Portuguese East Indies in the 1590s. Within a few years, the aggressive Dutch had expelled the Portuguese from island Southeast Asia (Indonesia) and had established themselves as masters of the spice trade.

On the route east, the Dutch established a colony at the southern tip of Africa (the modern Republic of South Africa) that rapidly became a profitable way station for ships of all nations traveling to the Far East. Dutch traders also set up the only Western trading post in Japan before the nineteenth century. But their headquarters in the Far East became the city of Batavia (today's Jakarta) on the island of Java, a tidy port of white high-gabled Dutch houses and canals like those of Amsterdam in the tropical southern seas. If you visit the old port today, you will find its jetty lined with the largest fleet of old-fashioned commercial sailing schooners still afloat, now owned and sailed among the islands of Indonesia by skilled Javanese seamen.

The Dutch West India Company had a harder time of it. Expansive plans to take Brazil and African Angola from the Portuguese and to monopolize the slave trade between Africa and the Americas failed. But Dutch colonies were successfully planted in North America and in the Caribbean. Basing their claims on the explorations of Henry Hudson (c. 1550–1611), an Englishman sailing in Dutch employ, they founded New Netherland in what is today New York State, and demonstrated the celebrated Dutch commercial acumen by buying Manhattan Island from the Indians for gifts and commodities once valued at $24. Further south, the island of Curaçao gave them a valuable base in the Caribbean, an area already settled by Spaniards as well as by English and French interlopers. From these two centers, Dutch traders proceeded to sell better goods at better prices to colonists of all nations in the Americas, in open defiance of the mercantilist closed-empire principle.

"To beat the Dutch" became the dream of European leaders as diverse as Cromwell and Louis XIV. Both absolutist France and constitutionalist England fought essentially commercial wars with the Netherlands in the seventeenth century, and by the end of it, the Dutch Empire was in fact fading. Its small size, like that of Portugal, made it harder for the Netherlands to absorb the inevitable losses that went with such extended commitments. The attrition of repeated wars with European rivals also told. Portugal's recovery of Brazil from the Dutch and the seizure of New Netherland by the English were setbacks from which the Dutch Empire never recovered. They remained masters of the Dutch East Indies and firmly established in South Africa, but from shortly after 1700 on, they ceased to compete with France and England for global supremacy.

The French Mercantilist Empire

French overseas expansion during the old imperial period followed a progression from halfhearted and unsuccessful efforts in the sixteenth century to the most fully developed mercantilist empire of all in the seventeenth. Centrally involved in all the major conflicts of western Europe, the French could not commit themselves to overseas activity as fully as the Iberian powers on the western edge of Europe, or as single-mindedly as the Dutch, whose fundamental activity in the world was commercial exchange. France did make efforts to acquire its share of trade and empire beyond the oceans, particularly in intervals of relative peace, when it was not mired in the Renaissance Italian wars, the wars of religion, or the Thirty Years' War. Only in the seventeenth century, however, under state builders like Cardinal Richelieu and the mercantilist Colbert, did France really begin to construct an overseas empire worthy of the Sun King.

Sixteenth-century French colonial ventures in the Americas, including Huguenot settlements in Brazil and Florida, were destroyed by the Portuguese and the Spanish. Only Jacques Cartier's (1491–1557) explorations of Newfoundland and the St. Lawrence and his founding of Montreal in what became eastern Canada had future significance. Shortly after 1600, Samuel de Champlain (c. 1567–1635) further expanded this wedge into northern North America, founding Quebec and signing treaties of alliance with the Indians around the Great Lakes. But the number of settlers, mostly fur traders and Jesuit missionaries, remained small.

Under Richelieu, these small beginnings in French Canada were expanded somewhat, and profitable Caribbean plantations were established on the islands of Guadeloupe, Martinique, and later Haiti. To work the land in the Caribbean, now bare of its original Native American inhabitants, the French, like the Spanish and the Portuguese before them, imported large numbers of black slaves from Africa.

Louis XIV's great minister Colbert, finally, sought to integrate the American colonies into a unified mercantilist empire. Transferring the Canadian settlements from private operation to royal control, Colbert augmented the population and organized it under landholding seigneurs and peasant tenants, as in France. Explorers like Father Marquette (1637–1675) and the ambitious Robert Cavelier de La Salle (1643–1687), meanwhile, traveled down the Mississippi and claimed this whole swath of inner North America for France, naming it Louisiana after Louis XIV. A broad vision of a French North American presence from the St. Lawrence and the Great Lakes down the Mississippi to the Gulf of Mexico and the Caribbean was thus projected, though settlers on the ground remained few, and claims larger than colonial realities.

In Africa and India also, the French made significant beginnings in the seventeenth century. French traders intruded on Portuguese preserves early in the century, bartering for slaves up the Senegal River in West Africa; French pirates congregated on the huge island of Madagascar off the southeast corner of the continent. More important, the French traded regularly in India after 1600. In the later seventeenth century, the French East India Company established trading posts and bases in India itself, with a center at Pondicherry on the eastern coast. The power of the *Mughal* emperors of India was so great, however, that the interior of the subcontinent remained closed to the French, as to other Europeans. In fact, their position remained that of respectful dependents of Aurangzeb (r. 1658–1707), the last great Mughal ruler, throughout the later 1600s. Here also, however, a French presence was established and ready to expand as the Mughals declined in the following century.

Beginnings of Britain's World Empire

In both East and West, the main competition the French faced was that of the rising imperial power of England. Even slower to start than the French, the English came on with a rush in the seventeenth century once they threw themselves into the empire-building game in earnest.

Sixteenth-century England, for all the Elizabethan heroics of Drake and Raleigh, established no successful colonies overseas. The impulse toward empire, however, was clearly there. Under the Tudors, voyages to the North Atlantic, Greenland, Newfoundland, and the nearby parts of North America were carried out by the Cabots (Genoa-born Giovanni Caboto, c. 1450–c. 1499, and his son Sebastian, c. 1476–1557), by Martin Frobisher (c. 1535–1594), Sir Humphrey Gilbert (c. 1539–1583), and other swashbucklers, but led to no settlements. Sir Walter Raleigh (1554–1618) tried to found a colony on the Outer Banks—islands off the coast of North Carolina—without success. Closer to home, a number of English merchant companies were organized during the century to trade with Russia, the Baltic, and the Levant at the far end of the Mediterranean. And in Ireland, England's "first colony," where English settlers had first established themselves in medieval times, techniques of conquest and settlement were developed that were later applied overseas.

In the sixteenth century, then, England's imperial involvement was largely limited to piracy. Elizabethan privateers raided the Caribbean and prowled the Atlantic, burning Spanish colonial cities and lying in wait for Spanish treasure fleets from the New World or Portuguese spice ships from the East Indies. Sir Francis Drake (c. 1540–1596), the most famous of the sea dogs, became the second captain to circumnavigate the globe in 1580, looting the coasts of Spanish America on the way.

Not until the seventeenth century did English enterprise successfully follow the Dutch and French in shattering the Iberian colonial monopoly and beginning the construction of an English Empire beyond the seas. As in the Netherlands and to a considerable degree in France, English imperialism was undertaken by private companies and individuals, rather than by the crown. In England, these empire builders included not only joint-stock companies of "merchant adventurers" but also groups seeking a religious haven in the New World. And though the royal government did soon impose governors and regulations on the colonies, English settlers remained more self-governing than most.

The first permanent English settlements in what became the United States were established at Jamestown, Virginia (1607) and at Plymouth, Massachusetts (1620). The Jamestown settlement was funded by a commercial corporation, the London Company of Virginia, which hoped to find gold and settled for tobacco, the American south's first plantation crop. The Plymouth colony was set up by a group of Puritan Independents, traditionally known as the Pilgrims, fleeing the religious climate of Stuart England. They were soon absorbed by the Massachusetts Bay Puritans, who arrived later but were

African slaves were the source of much of the labor that produced the Western world's imperial wealth. What story does this label from the finished tobacco product, with its foreground and background figures, seem to tell?

much more numerous. These English efforts north and south both survived, thanks to the rigorous discipline of military commanders like Captain John Smith (c. 1580–1631) in Virginia and the flinty determination of the Puritans in New England. The colonists also had essential early help from neighboring Indian tribes—with whom they were soon at war.

Subsequent English settlements in America followed these two patterns of religious or commercial settlement. Expansion and secession spread Puritans to other New England states; Catholics led by Lord Baltimore (1580–1632) and Quakers under William Penn (1644–1718) sought refuge in Maryland and Pennsylvania, respectively. Meanwhile, speculators undertook to colonize the Carolinas, the Hudson's Bay Company developed settlements devoted to the fur trade in the north, and England took over New Netherland—thereafter New York—in the 1660s. Far to the south, English settlers moved into the West Indies, filling a string of islands from Barbados to Jamaica with slave-operated sugar plantations. English buccaneers also became thick in Caribbean waters during the 1600s, threatening the trade of all nations.

In the Far East too, the English appeared in increasing numbers. A British East India Company, organized in 1600, about the same time as the Dutch and French versions, initiated what became an immensely profitable commerce with the East. English trading posts were established on the west coast of India, across the subcontinent from the French settlements. King Charles II acquired the city of Bombay from Portugal through his marriage with a Portuguese princess in the 1660s. Like the French, however, the handful of English imperialists in India remained mere clients of the Mughal emperors until that powerful dynasty fell into decay after 1700. Thereafter, both the English and the French East India Companies began to involve themselves more aggressively in the political and military affairs of India and to clash with each other for Indian empire.

Women were much more visible in the emerging English Empire than was realized until recently. The first successful English settlement at Jamestown in 1607 soon requested women, hoping their presence would make the male colonists more content to stay on that barbarous shore. By the eighteenth century, there was nothing strange about the petition from the English colony in Georgia for "thirty head of women . . . who would soon get husbands and be an inducement to those soldiers to settle in the colony when the time of their service should expire."[7] The need was not sexual—Western soldiers or settlers quickly found consorts, willing or unwilling, among the indigenous population—but social, the desire to create stable European communities beyond the seas.

Many English immigrants came as part of families. Those who came alone were usually indentured servants, bound to work four or five years to pay for their passage before being free to make their own lives in the colonies. For most, this meant marriage and the establishment of a family, the basic social and economic unit on the frontiers of the expanding West as it was in Europe. Like Spanish women, however, women in England's new colonies also seem to have "played a much greater variety of roles than their contemporaries in England," perhaps because challenging frontier conditions "often made de facto partners of husbands and wives."[8] One still debated thesis suggests that English colonial women were commonly considered "deputy husbands," expected to be able to conduct business for the family just as

the husband did and to carry on a number of trades including "blacksmiths, silversmiths, tinworkers, shoemakers, shipwrights, tanners, gunsmiths, barbers, printers, and butchers, as well as . . . teachers and shopkeepers."[9] (For an account of farming practices by Native American women, see the box titled "Native American Styles of Work.")

England's empire in the old imperial period thus centered in the New World, in the string of colonies running down the east coast of North America and

---

MASTERING OUR WORLD
Native American Styles of Work

The following account of Native American women at work comes from an English colonial woman who lived among the Seneca people in the eighteenth century. As this eyewitness describes it, traditional agricultural work was done primarily by women, rather than by men, as among the English settlers. It was also communal labor, in which the workers planted all the village's fields together, instead of each family planting its own. Can you see grounds for potential misunderstandings and hostility in such seemingly innocuous social differences as these?

In the summer season, we planted, tended, and harvested our corn, and generally had all of our children with us; but had no master to oversee or drive us, so that we could work as leisurely as we pleased. . . . We pursued our farming business according to the general custom of Indian women which is as follows: In order to expedite their business, and at the same time enjoy each other's company, they all work together in one field or at whatever job they may have on hand. In the spring, they choose an old active squaw to be their driver and overseer, when at labor, for the ensuing year. She accepts the honor, and they consider themselves bound to obey her.

When the time for planting arrives, and the soil is prepared, the squaws are assembled in the morning, and conducted into a field where each plants one row. They then go into the next field and plant one across, and so on till they have gone through the tribe.

Source: James Seaver, *Life of Mary Jemison: Deh-he-wa-mis* (1880), quoted in Judith Brown, "Economic Organization and the Position of Women Among the Iroquois," *Ethnohistory*, 17 (1970), 158.

extending into the Caribbean islands. A vigorous town life, crafts, trade, and many farms flourished in Puritan New England, while a single-crop plantation economy emerged in the south and on the islands. It was not as splendid as the baroque churches and ornate colonial palaces of Spanish America to the south, and the English did not get along with the Indians as well as the French north of them did. But there were a quarter of a million English settlers in America already in 1700, and their prosperous colonies were growing fast. In India, meanwhile, the agents of the East India Company could live like rajahs in their trading compounds and come home rich, hailed as "moguls" (Mughals). But the glory days of the company in India still lay ahead. England's star of empire, just beginning to rise, would one day see that country mistress of a quarter of the inhabited earth.

Russia's Eastward Expansion

So far, we have emphasized the unique overseas character of Western imperialism, based on Europe's mastery of the world's oceans. One great exception to this rule must be included here as well: the expansion of Russia across the Eurasian continent to the Pacific.

East of Moscow, east of the Ural Mountains, Eurasia stretched away some 6,000 miles to the Bering Straits. North of the civilized centers of the Middle East, India, and China, these endless reaches of steppe grass, barren tundra, and dark pine forest supported only a scanty population of Mongol tribesmen. It was open country for horsemen, traveled by nomadic herdsmen for many centuries. In addition, a series of great rivers, with their networks of tributaries, offered a water road for those experienced in river transport. A people well suited to both means of moving east were readily available in early modern Russia: the *Cossacks*.

These unique subjects of the autocratic czars lived in independent bands on the steppes. They made their own rules and bought their freedom by serving Moscow as an elite cavalry corps, as ready to repress rebellious Russians as to fight their country's foes. Famous horsemen and skilled river travelers as well, the Cossacks of the Don and Volga river basins and other areas also became the frontier vanguard of Russia's centuries-long eastward expansion.

Under Ivan the Terrible in the later sixteenth century, the Cossack leader Yermak (d. 1584) routed the last Mongol khan and offered western Siberia to the czar. In the seventeenth century, under the early Romanovs, Cossack raiders and fur traders boated and portaged eastward up and down the Russian rivers—the Ob, the Yenisei, the Lena, the Kolyma—to reach the Russian Far East by midcentury. The Cossacks pushed on to explore the Amur River, north of Manchuria. In 1689 the Treaty of Nerchinsk between the Romanovs and the Manchu emperor of China delineated Russia's border with the Chinese Empire a century before the Middle Kingdom, as the Chinese called their ancient realm, officially recognized the existence of any other European power. Further north, Vitus Bering (1681–1741), a Danish navigator engaged by Peter the Great, explored the strait between eastern Siberia and Alaska that was later named for him.

By the early 1700s, Russia had explored and laid claim to more land than any European monarch had ever ruled on the Eurasian mainland. Throughout most of these eastern lands, however, there were very few Russian settlers. The Cossacks and the occasional Russian collector of taxes or tributes from the indigenous population were often looked on more as marauders than as agents of a legitimate government. Independent regimes, especially in central Asia and the Caucasus, still remained for soldiers and proconsuls of empire to conquer in later centuries. Nevertheless, in terms of territory claimed if not yet occupied, Russia in the days of Peter the Great was already the largest country in the world.

Global Plunder

Between the fifteenth and seventeenth centuries, the West moved against the rest of the world as no single civilization had ever done before. The closest parallels, both recent, were the short-lived Mongol Empire of the later Middle Ages, spanning most of northern Eurasia, and the continuing spread of Islam across the Old World. But the commercial and military potential inherent in Europe's predominance on the seas gave Western expansion a unique impact on both European history and the history of the world at large.

In this section we focus on the wide range of benefits accruing to Europe from their new intercontinental empires. For four other continents began to pay tribute to Europe or to trade with it directly again in the sixteenth and seventeenth centuries.

Africa and Asia, North and South America all contributed their share to the growing wealth of the West.

Luxury Goods from Asia

Western imperialism did not always pay as handsomely as empire builders expected, or as critics of the system assumed. It cost a great deal in human and material resources for Western people to impose their will on others. Such costs, as we have seen, in the long run became too great for small nations like Portugal to bear. Even what seemed fabulous gains sometimes had unfortunate side effects, like the inflationary impact of Spanish treasure on Europe, discussed later. Still, there is no doubt that Europe reaped a substantial harvest from its global imperium during the sixteenth and seventeenth centuries.

Having reached the East by sailing east, Europeans had direct access to the luxury goods they had been importing through Asian intermediaries for centuries. From China, for instance, they now imported much larger quantities of silk, porcelain, and tea. From India came cotton textiles in abundance and surprising quantities of precious stones. From the islands of Southeast Asia came the spices that had originally lured the West eastward: cloves, cinnamon, pepper, and other herbs of value both to preserve and to enhance the flavor of European food. From the Middle East and other parts of Asia came coffee and drugs, saltpeter for gunpowder, indigo dye for cloth, and other small but high-value products of the fabulous East.

These luxury goods did more than make life pleasant for an elite: they also had larger effects on Europe's economy and society. For one thing, the tastes Europeans acquired for overseas products led European producers to try to match these non-Western goods. Thus Chinese porcelain, imported for the rich in the 1500s, became accessible to middle-class Europeans in the 1600s and was soon being imitated—though only after years of trying—by manufacturers of "china" dishes in the France of Louis XIV. The manufacture of cotton cloth, imported in large amounts from India in the seventeenth century, was taken up by English textile manufacturers. In the next century, the fast-growing English cotton industry was the first to be transformed by the Industrial Revolution.

Coffee and tea were two other Eastern products to exert transforming influences on Western society.

Imported originally from China, South Asia, and the Middle East, both beverages became national drinks in European countries. Tea shops and coffeehouses, furthermore, became social centers with larger cultural significance for Europe. The coffeehouse in particular developed as a place where people of shared political or religious views or common artistic interests gathered, where news was exchanged, business transacted, opinions formed. Often, too, the tea or coffee was consumed in Chinese porcelain cups with sugar imported from Brazil or the West Indian colonies. The Western way of life was thus reshaped in many subtle ways by this broadened contact with Asia and the world at large.

The African Slave Trade

Africa, which European traders rounded regularly on their way to the East by sea, provided more than way stations for replenishing stores and repairing their battered vessels. African gold and ivory, traditionally exported by West African kingdoms, could now be acquired by Europeans directly, along either the Gold Coast (Ghana today) or the Ivory Coast (still so called) or by penetrating the coastal rain forests to the West African trading city of Timbuktu. Some spices, including pepper and cloves from the island of Zanzibar off the East African coast, were also bought cheap by European merchants and sold for a much higher price in Europe. Almost at once, however, Africa's major contribution to the prosperity of the West became labor—slave labor, bought in Africa and sold in the Americas.

The decimation of Amerindian populations and their inability to adapt to the brutal labor conditions of mine and plantation created a pressing labor shortage in the American colonies. Since few Europeans saw any advantage in moving to the New World to do hard labor in sweltering climates, workers had to be found elsewhere. Within a decade after Columbus's arrival, the first black African slaves were at work in the Americas. From the later sixteenth century on, the slave trade boomed and black Africans poured into the American labor market.

Because the Portuguese had been granted the right to exploit Africa by the Treaty of Tordesillas, they were the first large-scale importers of slaves, particularly for work on their booming sugar plantations in Brazil. The Spanish, however, bought large numbers of Africans; and the interlopers of the seventeenth century, the English, French, and Dutch,

Native American slaves labor in a West Indian sugar mill. Can you follow the process from raw sugar cane in the upper right hand corner to the large jars being carried out for shipment home at the far right?

were soon both trading in slaves and using them to work their own plantations in the Caribbean and the Americas. The famous triangular trade route linking Europe, Africa, and America centered around the slave trade: from Europe, liquor, guns, iron, jewelry, and textiles went to Africa, where they were exchanged for slaves. The slaves were then sold in the New World, where raw materials and such agricultural products as rum, tobacco, and sugar—produced by slave labor—were loaded for European markets.

The brutality of this archetypal example of Western exploitation of the rest of the world has been widely decried. As early as the sixteenth and seventeenth centuries this exploitation was opposed by a few, including Father Las Casas, who had originally favored importing Africans to save the dwindling Native American population from extinction. Given the real labor shortage in the New World, however, and with such European cities as Amster-

dam, Bristol, and Nantes dependent for much of their early prosperity on the slave trade, it is perhaps not surprising that economic forces prevailed over humanitarian considerations.

Apologists for the trade in human beings have pointed out that slavery and slave raiding were established institutions in Africa, as in many other parts of the world. They have not emphasized the great increase in slave taking sparked by the annual visits of European slave ships to the long western coast of Africa, from Senegal to Angola. For more than three centuries, Africans carried off from their villages by slave-raiding neighbors were packed into the European slave ships, two hundred and more into a tiny hold where 10 percent and more could easily die from overcrowding and disease during the Atlantic crossing. The survivors were auctioned off at the slave markets of the West Indies or North or South America, and set to work in the tropical or semitropical colonies of the New World.

In purely economic terms, these African workers contributed greatly to the growth of the colonies of the Western hemisphere. Estimates of the numbers of Africans imported as slaves range from ten to twenty million people over the sixteenth, seventeenth, and eighteenth centuries. By the time of the first national censuses in the 1790s, almost a fifth of the population of the new United States and well over half that of Brazil were at least partially of African descent. It was by any standards a massive addition to the economic life of this first great extension of the Western world overseas.

Commodities from the Americas

Considerably less exciting than Asian luxury goods, and less disturbing than the African contribution, were the dull but immensely profitable exports to Europe from North and South America and the Caribbean. As we will see, these commodities—natural resources and agricultural products that could be grown in the warmer south—made the Americas probably the most valuable of all the colonies in the old imperial period.

An unromantic early lure were the codfish to be found in swarming schools off the Newfoundland Banks and the New England shore. Fish, salted or dried for preservation, was a vital component of the European diet, both for the many religious fast days and for general consumption during the winter. As the herring fisheries of the Baltic Sea were thinning out, English and French vessels swarmed to these new fishing grounds, which proved a rich source of the high-protein food.

Of more debatable value but extremely profitable nonetheless was tobacco. The indigenous Amerindian population grew and smoked the tobacco leaf in many parts of both North and South America, and Europeans soon acquired the habit. The Spanish were the main importers during the sixteenth century, but the English became major producers during the seventeenth. While some saw it as an exotic drug, filthy, poisonous, and tainted by its heathen origins, others claimed medicinal properties for it, presenting it as an ancient Indian remedy for everything from snakebite to toothache. In any event, tobacco soon became a regular part of European theater, tavern, coffeehouse, and even domestic life, another significant addition to Western custom.

A third valuable American product was sugar, as modest seeming today as the spices in our cupboards or the cotton in our clothing, but the support of a booming Brazilian and Caribbean economy in the 1600s. Sugar cane, unlike the tobacco plant, was not native to the New World. It was introduced by the Spanish and Portuguese from Asia, via earlier plantings in the Canary Islands. In Portuguese Brazil and in a number of Caribbean islands, huge sugar plantations worked by large numbers of African slaves became the mainstays of the colonial economy. Brazil provided more than half of Europe's sugar through the first half of the seventeenth century, and sugar continued to dominate the Caribbean economy through most of the 1600s. Used as a sweetener, especially for tea or coffee, sugar was also the basis of other food products. It was commonly shipped home in the form of molasses—like tobacco, believed to have medicinal value—or rum, which became one of the most destructive alcoholic drinks of Europe's poor.

Furs, hides, timber, ships' stores, all added to the profitability of the American colonies. But in these early centuries, the wonderful harvest of metals from the southern half of the New World seemed to dwarf all other gains.

Silver and Gold from Latin America

The flow of precious metals was prodigious by the standards of the Western world thus far. Throughout the sixteenth and the first half of the seventeenth centuries, silver and gold poured into Europe. First taken as booty or in trade, later from the legendary mines of Guanajuato in Mexico and Potosí in Bolivia, Latin America's tribute tripled the European supply of silver and gold in the 1500s. More silver than gold, by far: thousands of tons of silver to hundreds of tons of gold. The European economy, low in precious metals for centuries due to the outflow to Asia for luxury goods, had only begun to make up its needs with late fifteenth-century finds in central Europe. The new flood of bullion from overseas was therefore a powerful stimulus for the European economy.

The first destination for most of the bullion was of course Spain, since the precious metals came from Spanish colonies. But English, French, and Dutch privateers skimmed some of it off between Veracruz and Seville. And much more left Spain to pay the debts incurred by the Western world's greatest power, going either to pay the Spanish crown's debts to German and Italian bankers or to the Spanish armies that were fighting in wars from the Mediterranean to the Netherlands. Much of the bullion bonanza, finally, was paid out to other Europeans for imported goods not produced in Spain. And Spain, having expelled its productive Jewish and Muslim minorities and lived so long on the resources of its colonies, developed few centers of industrial production of its own. Industrious Italian, Dutch, and other European artisans cheerfully supplied Spain's needs—at a price.

The gold and silver thus distributed over the continent had, as noted in an earlier chapter, a powerful inflationary effect, combining with increased demand due to population growth to produce higher prices across much of the continent. This sixteenth-century inflation finished off the late medieval depression and brought—for some at least—a boom comparable to that of the High Middle Ages. The impact was greatest in Spain, where prices tripled, and in France and England, where they doubled over the century. There were also differential class effects. Because prices rose faster than wages, middle-class businessmen profited greatly, especially in labor intensive industries like mining in the Germanies, shipbuilding in the Netherlands, or cloth making in England. Landowners seeking profit from rising cloth prices enclosed their fields and took up sheep raising. Wage workers, however, found that their salaries seldom kept up with inflation, and many peasants were turned out of their villages entirely by enclosures. Once more, the influence of Europe's imperial expansion on European society was extensive and complex.

Western Expansion and Global Power

Less concrete than the material rewards the Europeans reaped in these first imperial centuries was the unprecedented global power this period brought to the West. That power was unparalleled in its worldwide reach. It brought ecological and demographic changes to the world at large. It constructed a global economy and began to spread Western Christianity to peoples on distant continents. In the 1500s and 1600s, it created what some historians have seen as a "world system" with the West at its center.

Ecological and Demographic Impact

Some of the most striking effects of Western imperialism have only been emphasized in recent decades. These effects were ecological and demographic in nature. They included such terrible visitations as the decimation of the Native American population of North America and such long-range benefits as the spread of Indian corn to other peoples around the world. All alike were consequences of the growing Western presence in so many foreign lands.

That presence was not yet the enveloping reality it became in the later nineteenth century and throughout the twentieth century, when Western wars, depressions, ideas, and even tastes did so much to determine the history of the non-Western world. On a map of the Western overseas empires around 1700, it is evident that Europeans were still largely limited to coastal areas or islands, in some places inland rivers or lake shores—areas, in short, that were accessible to their remarkable ships. Even in Latin America, most of the interior was still populated primarily by Amerindian peoples. The most thickly settled parts of North America, the English colonies of the east coast, were scattered patches of towns, villages, and farms with tracts of Indian lands between them. In Africa and Asia, where trading rather than settlement empires were the rule, the intruders were largely confined to isolated trading posts along the coasts.

Nevertheless, the busy little sailing ships that linked this far-flung network moved goods and people around as never before, causing, among other things, unprecedentedly rapid ecological changes. Seeking to make their New World colonies pay, for instance, Europeans transplanted cash crops like sugar, coffee, and cotton from the Old World to the New. They also exported the large domesticated animals, a major lack in the Western hemisphere, including horses, donkeys, cattle, and sheep. From the Americas, finally, they brought back crops that would flourish in various parts of the Old World, including Indian corn, potatoes, tobacco, and other valuable plants. Many of these were soon growing in Asia and Africa as well as in Europe. Again, the impact was eventually immense: Indian corn, originally developed in ancient Mexico, helps to feed half the world's populations today.

Demographic changes were greatest in the Americas. There, the world's most ethnically homogeneous population was replaced by the world's most heterogeneous one. Western wars, mistreatment, and the "biological invasion" of Western disease germs caused a sharp decline in the Native American population. The introduction of African slaves in large numbers established an important new element in the demographic mix. When we add the European invaders themselves, we have a region of the globe uniquely divided among the three main human families: Mongoloid Native Americans, Negroid Africans, and Caucasoid Europeans.

Impact of Western Ideas and Economic Power

Economically, the world also began to feel the weight of the European predominance even this early. On the positive side, commercial exchange on a global basis became possible for the first time, thanks to European merchants and seamen. Ancient Asia experienced only a modest influx of Western products, but Africa got more manufactured goods than ever before, and the Native Americans were introduced to them for the first time. And as overseas imports changed European society, so the introduction of the iron ax into the Brazilian rain forest, or of the horse to the plains Indians of North America, exercised a transforming effect on these cultures.

There was, however, a negative side to the economic picture. In the New World, Western conquest had destroyed the two most developed American empires, stopping their economic evolution in its tracks and condemning masses of Indians to a grim future as second-class citizens in European-dominated lands. In Africa, the ready availability of Western manufactured goods in exchange for slaves both encouraged the economically counterproductive "export" of human labor and discouraged the development of manufacturing in Africa. In Asia, it was another century or two before Western machine-made products began to challenge the ancient craft traditions of India, China, and other lands. But once that happened, Western economic and technological power undermined these ancient economies as well.

Even ideas were transported to new parts of the globe by the Western intrusion. Of these, by far the most important in the period of the old imperialism was the Christian religion. Again, Asia resisted most strongly. The handful of Jesuits in China were largely cocooned in Peking, while the Japanese shoguns became so alarmed at the potentially subversive effect

of the Western religion that they all but destroyed the Christian convert community in Japan. Africa's defenses against Christian missionary activity and other forms of Western penetration consisted of difficult geography and alien microbes. Thick coastal forests and swamps, rivers blocked by rapids or falls, and other geographical barriers combined with malaria, yellow fever, and other germs to which Europeans had no immunities to discourage major efforts at missionary activities. In North America, the Puritans seem to have seen the Indians as limbs of Satan more often than as potential Christians. French Jesuits in Canada and the Spanish mission fathers of California and the Southwest, however, did make many converts to Catholicism. And in Latin America, the Spanish and Portuguese churches and missionary orders exercised an even wider influence, reshaping the religious lives of many of the surviving native population.

The West at the World's Center

For better or worse, by 1700 the world had a center for the first time in its history. This centrality is what we have been describing as an emerging Western or European hegemony. In the most focused sense, the core of this Western global predominance can be located in western Europe. In a broader sense, however, what was beginning was a larger Atlantic-centered Western predominance that lasted throughout modern history.

This Western domination of global affairs has been described by Immanuel Wallerstein as the *modern world system*.[10] In the view of Wallerstein and his adherents, this system is a worldwide network of nations and peoples dominated more by Western economic and political power than by military strength. The "core" of the system was originally the handful of western European Atlantic seaboard nations we have studied in this chapter. In later centuries, however, the core expanded across the Atlantic Ocean to include North America, particularly the United States. The "periphery" of the system was originally composed of European colonies and of other peoples with whom early modern Europeans traded; today it is said to include most of the Third World. Within this "world system," proponents of this theory believe, the West provided capital and control, the rest of the world labor, raw materials, and agri-

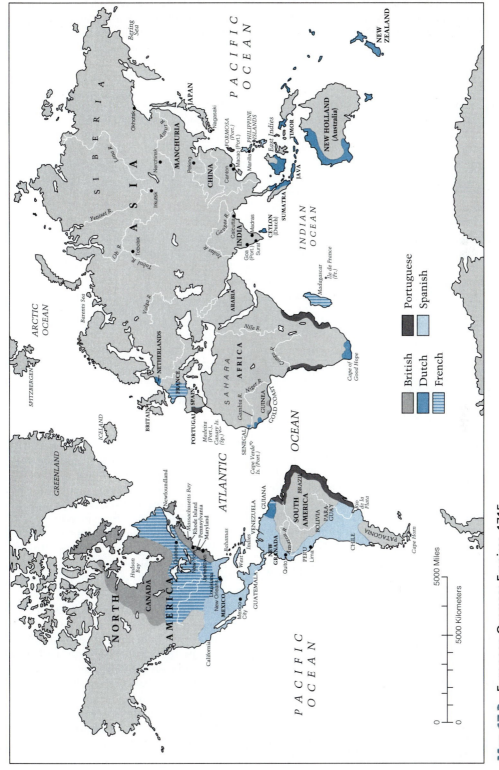

Map 17.3 European Overseas Empires, 1715

Legend:
- British
- Dutch
- French
- Portuguese
- Spanish

ARCTIC OCEAN

SPITZBERGEN

ICELAND

GREENLAND

SIBERIA

Bering Sea

Okhotsk

Nerchinsk

Irkutsk

Tobolsk

Ob R.

Yenisei R.

Tobol R.

Volga R.

Lena R.

Amur R.

ASIA

MANCHURIA

JAPAN

Nagasaki

Peking

CHINA

Canton

FORMOSA (Port.)

Macao (Port.)

PHILIPPINE ISLANDS

Manila

East Indies

TIMOR

JAVA

SUMATRA

CEYLON (Dutch)

Madras

Calcutta

INDIA

Goa (Port.)

Surat

Ganges R.

Indus R.

ARABIA

Nile R.

PACIFIC OCEAN

NEW ZEALAND

NEW HOLLAND (Australia)

INDIAN OCEAN

Île de France (Fr.)

Madagascar

AFRICA

SAHARA

Congo R.

Niger R.

Cape of Good Hope

NETHERLANDS

FRANCE

SPAIN

BRITAIN

PORTUGAL

Madeira (Port.)

Canary Is. (Sp.)

SENEGAL

Cape Verde Is. (Port.)

Gambia R.

GUINEA

GOLD COAST

ATLANTIC OCEAN

Barents Sea

NORTH AMERICA

CANADA

Newfoundland

Hudson Bay

Massachusetts Bay

Rhode Island

Pennsylvania

Maryland

Boston

Jamestown

New Orleans

LOUISIANA

MEXICO

Mexico City

California

GUATEMALA

Bahamas

West Indies

VENEZUELA

GUIANA

NEW GRANADA

Quito

PERU

Lima

Amazon R.

SOUTH AMERICA

BRAZIL

BOLIVIA

PARAGUAY

CHILE

Río de la Plata

PATAGONIA

Cape Horn

PACIFIC OCEAN

5000 Miles

5000 Kilometers

0

0

541

cultural products. Western political hegemony, Western economic exploitation, and Western "cultural imperialism" have thus shaped the global history of the last five hundred years.

Whether this theoretical formulation accurately defines the basic relationship between the West and the rest of humanity over the past five centuries, it does reflect the fact of a growing Western preeminence in modern times. And as we have seen throughout this volume, this wave of Western expansion is only the latest stage in a pattern of Western territorial growth that goes back to our earliest beginnings.

The Western world had been expanding, despite setbacks and periods of paralysis, throughout its history. From a cluster of Greek city-states in southeastern Europe, it had spread around the Mediterranean Sea and thrust north into western Europe in Roman times. During the Middle Ages, Western civilization, though losing its grip on the African and Asian shores of the Mediterranean, had consolidated its position in western Europe and spread through the central and eastern portions of that continent as well. And in early modern times, as we have seen in this chapter, the West expanded once more, this time across the oceans of the world to colonize the Americas and establish commercial beachheads in Africa and Asia.

As we will see in the second volume of this book, Western global expansion had only begun as the seventeenth century drew to a close. But a pattern of imperial conquest, economic penetration, and cultural domination had been established. The future held even more astonishing developments in store, as the West transformed an emerging hegemony into a virtual mastery of the rest of the world in later centuries. It was a global supremacy which, when it ended in the later twentieth century, left the world transformed and evolving in directions undreamed of at the beginning of the modern age.

A Topical Summary

Politics: During the sixteenth and seventeenth centuries, the time of the so-called old imperialism, first the Iberian powers, Spain and Portugal, and then the North Atlantic "interlopers," England, France, and the Netherlands, founded impressive overseas empires. In the sixteenth century, Spain conquered the Aztec and Inca empires and imposed its rule on the southern parts of the New World, while Portugal established commercial colonies in southern Africa, the Indian Ocean, and Southeast Asia. In the seventeenth century, the Netherlands set up trading colonies in South Africa, Southeast Asia, and the Americas, and France and England both established themselves in North America, the Caribbean, and India.

Economics: Europeans reaped lavish rewards from these early intercontinental empires. They imported luxury goods from Asia; sugar, tobacco, and other commodities from North America and the Caribbean; silver and gold from Mexico and South America; and from Africa, slave labor for their New World colonies. Western imperialism also created the first world market in history, both opening the globe to Western exploitation and linking most of the rest of the world in a network of commercial exchange.

Society: Western colonialism transported peoples as well as goods, bringing many Europeans and Africans to the Americas. But many Native American peoples were weakened or destroyed totally by European weapons, forced labor, and European diseases to which they lacked immunity. Europeans took land from its original inhabitants, establishing new, Western-dominated societies. In contrast, traders in Asia and Africa lived largely as clients of local rulers.

Technology: The remarkable success of Europeans in taming the world's oceans and establishing themselves overseas was due in large part to technological advances. In 1500 European ships, navigational instruments, and gunpowder weapons were superior to those of any global competitor of the West. Thus equipped, the West became the first civilization to move confidently across the seas and oceans of the world and to begin the construction of a genuinely global hegemony.

Ecology: A consequence of Western imperialism of great long-range significance was the startling ecological transfer initiated by globe-girdling Europeans. Plants and animals were deliberately transplanted from one part of the world to another—sugar, horses, and cattle to the New World, tobacco, potatoes, and Indian corn to the Old World. An unintended ecological transfer was the passage of disease-causing microbes from Europe to the Americas.

Some Key Terms

audiencia 529
Aztecs 527
black legend 529
conquistador 527
Cossacks 535
encomienda 529
gunpowder weapons 519

Incas 528
interloper 531
mercantilism 529
Mercator projection 519
mestizo 529
modern world system 540
Mughals 532

new imperialism 520
old imperialism 520
Ottomans 522
settlement empire 520
trading empire 521
Western global imperialism 520

Notes

1. E. G. Ravenstein, ed., *A Journal of the First Voyage of Vasco da Gama* (London: Hakluyt Society, 1898), 49.
2. "Columbus's Letter on His First Voyage," in Samuel Eliot Morison, *Christopher Columbus, Mariner* (New York: New American Library, 1955), 149.
3. J. H. Parry, *The Establishment of the European Hegemony, 1415–1715* (New York: Harper & Row, 1961), 60.
4. *Conquest: Dispatches of Cortes from the New World*, ed. Irwin R. Blacker and Harry M. Rosen (New York: Grosset and Dunlap, 1962), 125.
5. Victor W. von Hagen, *Realm of the Incas* (New York: New American Library, 1957), 147, 150.
6. C. R. Boxer, *Mary and Misogyny: Women and Iberian Expansion Overseas, 1415–1815* (London: Duckworth, 1975), 48.
7. Julia C. Spruill, *Women's Life and Work in the Southern Colonies* (Chapel Hill: University of North Carolina Press, 1938), 18.
8. Susan F. Bailey, *Women in the British Empire* (New York: Garland, 1983), 83.
9. Laurel Thatcher Ulrich, *Good Wives: Image and Reality in the Lives of Women in Northern New England 1650–1750* (New York: Oxford University Press, 1983), 35.
10. Immanual Wallerstein's *The Modern World System* (New York: Academic Press, 1974–) has now reached three volumes and the eighteenth century.

Reading List

ANDREWS, K. R. *Trade, Plunder, and Settlement: Maritime Enterprise and the Genesis of the British Empire, 1480–1630.* New York: Cambridge University Press, 1984. Very readable account of voyages by the English to many parts of the world.

BOXER, C. R. *The Dutch Seaborne Empire, 1600–1800.* New York: Humanities Press, 1980. Solid overview by a leading authority. See also J. I. ISRAEL, *Dutch Primacy in World Trade, 1585–1740* (New York: Clarendon Press, 1989).

———. *The Portuguese Seaborne Empire, 1415–1825.* New York: Knopf, 1969. Excellent survey of the achievements of the pioneers of the overseas empire.

CRONON, W. *Changes in the Land: Indians, Colonists, and the Ecology of New England.* New York: Hill and Wang, 1983. An interdisciplinary student-oriented summary of the interaction of cultures and countryside.

CROSBY, A. W. *The Columbian Exchange: Biological Consequences of 1492.* Westport, Conn.: Greenwood, 1973. Highlights microbial interchange and its impact on Amerindian and Western peoples.

DAVIES, K. A. *Landowners in Colonial Peru.* Austin: University of Texas Press, 1984. Good example of the burgeoning literature on the rural landowning elite that dominated colonial Latin American society.

ELLIOTT, J. H. *The Old World and the New, 1492–1650.* Cambridge: Cambridge University Press, 1972.

Essays on the impact of the American colonies on Europe.

GUNDER FRANK, A. *World Accumulation, 1391–1789.* New York: Monthly Review Press, 1978. The consequences of Western capital accumulation and domination of the world market on colonial and other peripheral areas.

LACH, D. F. *Asia in the Making of Europe.* 3 vols. Chicago: University of Chicago Press, 1971–1977. Volume 2 offers encyclopedic treatment of the cultural influence of Asia on sixteenth-century Europe.

LEON-PORTILLA, M. *The Broken Spears: The Aztec Account of the Conquest of Mexico.* Translated by L. Kemp. London: Constable, 1962. History from the viewpoint of the Amerindians of Mexico.

MORISON, S. E. *Admiral of the Ocean Sea.* 2 vols. Boston: Little, Brown, 1942. Classic highly readable account of Columbus's voyages by a mariner and naval historian who explored the fifteenth-century navigator's problems in his own vessel.

PARR, C. M. *So Noble a Captain.* Westport, Conn.: Greenwood, 1976. Magellan and the first circumnavigation of the globe.

PARRY, J. H. *The Age of Reconnaissance.* Berkeley: University of California Press, 1981. The European voyages, by a leading authority. See also his *The Establishment of the European Hegemony, 1415–1715: Trade and Exploration in the Age of the Renaissance* (New York: Harper & Row, 1963).

———. *The Spanish Seaborne Empire.* New York: Knopf, 1966. Sweeping overview of the largest of the early empires.

PRESCOTT, W. H. *The Portable Prescott.* New York: Viking, 1964. Extracts from both his vivid nineteenth-century narratives, *The Conquest of Mexico* and *The Conquest of Peru.*

QUINN, D. B. *North America from Earliest Discovery to First Settlement.* New York: Harper & Row, 1977. Vivid retelling of early Western penetration of North America.

SALE, K. *The Conquest of Paradise: Christopher Columbus and the Columbian Legacy.* New York: Knopf, 1990. Depicts European imperialism as a ruthless ravaging of the planet, perhaps idealizing non-Western peoples in the process. See also F. JENNINGS, *The Invasion of America: Indians, Colonialism, and the Cant of Conquest* (Chapel Hill: University of North Carolina Press, 1975), characterizing the conquest of North America as the devastation of a flourishing Amerindian culture.

SWEET, D., and G. NASH, eds. *Struggle and Survival in Colonial America.* Berkeley: University of California Press, 1981. Biographies of a score of Europeans and Amerindians, illustrating the conflicts between them.

TRUDEL, M. *The Beginnings of New France, 1524–1663.* Translated by P. Claxton. Toronto: McLelland and Stewart, 1973. Good introduction to the beginnings of France overseas.

WALLERSTEIN, I. *The Modern World-System.* Vol. 1, *Capitalist Agriculture and the Origins of the European World-Economy in the Sixteenth Century.* New York: Academic Press, 1974. Widely discussed study of the structure of the global economic hegemony of the West.

Glossary

absolute monarch   European ruler of the seventeenth and eighteenth centuries who claimed absolute authority over his or her people.

Achaean League   Alliance of southern Greek states during the Hellenistic period.

Aetolian League   Alliance of northern Greek states during the Hellenistic period.

agora   Marketplace in a Greek city-state.

Albigensians   Medieval French heretical sect, crushed in the savage twelfth-century Albigensian Crusade.

Anabaptists   Sixteenth-century Protestant religious radicals, many of whom rejected infant baptism.

Antigonid dynasty   Hellenistic rulers of Macedonia following the death of Alexander the Great.

archon   A chief magistrate in ancient Athens.

Areopagus   A high court in ancient Athens.

Arians   Late Roman and early medieval Christian heretics, many of whom were barbarians recently converted to Christianity.

atlatl   Throwing stick used to hurl a spear: the butt of the spear is caught in a thong or notch at one end of the *atlatl* while the thrower grips the other end.

atomism   Ancient Greek theory that all matter is made up of tiny uniform particles called atoms; revived in the seventeenth century by early modern scientists.

atra mors   "Dreadful death," the Latin name for the medieval bubonic plague, mistranslated as the "black death."

auctoritas   Air of authority projected by Roman leaders like Augustus Caesar.

audiencia   Spanish colonial advisory board in Latin America.

Augsburg confession   1530 statement of Lutheran religious views, urging reform of, not secession from, the Roman Church.

Augustan Age   Period of Roman history during which the restored empire was ruled by Augustus Caesar (r. 31 B.C.-A.D. 14).

authority of the Bible   Luther's view that the Bible is the sole source of revealed religious truth.

auto da fe   "Act of faith," the public ceremony in which the Inquisition announced its judgment of a heretic and sentence—often death by fire—was executed by the civil authorities.

autocrat   An authoritarian ruler; also, one of the titles of the medieval Byzantine emperors.

Avignon papacy   Popes resident in Avignon on the southern border of France during the fourteenth century.

Aztecs   Imperial rulers of Mexico from the fifteenth to the early sixteenth centuries.

bailli   Medieval royal officials dispatched to the provinces of northern France.

balance of power   Distribution of power among nations; diplomatic policy of constructing alliances to control powerful and aggressive states, as in fifteenth-century Italy or eighteenth-century Europe.

baroque style   Sixteenth- and seventeenth-century artistic style that sought to stir emotional response through movement, color, and scale.

bastard feudalism   Late medieval corruption of the feudal system, which exaggerated chivalric forms at the same time that it replaced feudal loyalty with cash payments.

Benedictine Rule   Medieval monastic rule laid down by St. Benedict that prescribed poverty, chastity, and obedience.

benefice   A post or appointment in the medieval or early modern church.

benefit of clergy   Medieval Catholic rule that priests could be tried only in church courts.

black figure   Ancient Greek style of vase painting in which the figures were drawn in black on the red clay of the vase.

black legend   Account of the Spanish conquest of the New World in which narrators emphasized the cruelty of the Spanish to the Native American population.

boule   A legislative or administrative council in an ancient Greek city-state.

Bourse   Stock exchange, especially in early modern Europe.

boyar   Russian nobility, especially during medieval and early modern times.

bubonic plague   Contagious disease that killed millions in late medieval and early modern centuries.

Byzantine Empire   The Eastern Roman Empire during the Middle Ages, from the fifth to the fifteenth centuries.

caesaropapism   Church-state relationship in which the state is supreme, as developed in medieval Byzantium.

caliph   "Successor to the Prophet"; a Muslim ruler seen as both political and spiritual head of a Muslim state.

"calling of the princes"   Summoning of Varangian (Viking) rulers to establish order in medieval Russian towns.

canon law   Legal code of the Roman Catholic church.

capitulary   Royal edict in the Carolingian Empire.

Carolingian minuscule   Medieval style of writing in which lower-case as well as capital letters were used for the first time.

cathedral   Church that serves as the seat of a bishop.

Celtic fringe   Celtic inhabitants of the western edge of Europe, especially Scotland, Ireland, and Wales.

century   Hundred-man unit in the Roman army.

chanson de geste   Medieval chivalric epic poem sung by minstrels glorifying the heroism of medieval knights.

chauvinistic nationalism   Aggressive nationalistic policy that often advanced national interests by military means.

chiaroscuro   Use of light and shade in a painting or drawing to create an illusion of three-dimensional reality.

chivalric code   Code of conduct for medieval knights prescribing courage, loyalty, hospitality, and protection of ladies and the church.

church fathers   Leading thinkers in the early Christian church, including St. Augustine, St. Jerome, and Pope Gregory the Great.

ciompi   Rebellious wool workers in Renaissance Florence.

Cistercians   High medieval order of monks famed for spartan living and hard work.

civic humanism   Application of humanistic learning to political and social problems in Renaissance Italy.

civilization   Form of society usually characterized by urban and larger political units, central government, class structure, literacy, metal working, and other features.

classicism   Seventeenth-century style of literature and art that prescribed ancient models and rules for creating beauty.

clientage   Relationship between Romans of higher and lower social class, in which the latter offered the former service and support in return for protection and economic benefits.

cogito, ergo sum   "I think, therefore I am," the French philosopher Descartes's assertion that the fact of human thought proves the existence of human beings.

coloni   Peasants in the later Roman Empire who were bound to their landlords like medieval serfs.

colony   A settlement established by a people in a distant region, as by ancient Greeks around the Mediterranean and by modern Europeans around the world.

comitatus   Among ancient German tribes, a chief's band of fighters sworn to fight and die with him.

comitia centuriata   Roman "assembly of the centuries," in which male citizens were grouped in their military units.

comitia tributa   Roman "assembly of the tribes" in which male citizens were grouped according to place of birth or residence.

commercial revolution   Revival of trade in the High Middle Ages, during which many modern business techniques were developed.

Common Law   English traditional law, dating to medieval times and undergirding the legal systems of other English-speaking countries.

commune   Medieval and early modern town; also, socialistic community in nineteenth and twentieth centuries.

Companions   Macedonian nobles who surrounded the Macedonian king; Alexander the Great's Companions became his officers and comrades in arms in later years.

comunero   Rebellious townsman during reign of Charles V in Spain.

conciliar movement   Effort to resolve problems of the Great Schism in the fifteenth-century Catholic church through a series of church councils.

condottiere   In Renaissance times, an Italian commander of a mercenary military force.

conduct book   Renaissance manual of manners, skills, and qualities of character required of aristocrats.

conquistadores   "Conquerors," the Spanish soldiers who conquered much of the New World for Spain in the sixteenth century.

consistory   Cooperative committee of Calvinist ministers and civic officials in sixteenth-century Geneva.

constitutional monarchy   Royal government in which the monarch accepts legal limits on royal authority and shares power with legislative and other institutions.

consubstantiation   Lutheran explanation of the Mass, asserting that Christ is present, but that the wafer and wine also retain their material substance.

consul   Highest-ranking Roman magistrate during the period of the Republic.

continental rationalism   Continental European philosophical emphasis on rational, rather than empirical, analysis.

Corpus Iuris Civilis   Justinian's Code, the sixth-century Byzantine codification of the Roman Law that became the foundation for a number of European law codes.

cortes   Spanish assemblies or parliaments developed in early modern times.

Cossacks   Tribes of southern Russia; Cossack cavalry were employed by the czars to suppress rebellious Russian peasants.

Council of Trent   Catholic Reformation council convened in the 1540s, 1550s, and 1560s to re-examine doctrines and reform the church.

courtly love   Medieval doctrine urging knightly courtesy, tenderness, and romantic love for his lady as key parts of the chivalric code.

craft guild   Medieval organization of artisans practicing the same craft.

critical century   The seventeenth century seen as a turning point in European history.

Cro-Magnon   A Paleolithic people first found in southwestern France, biologically identical with historic humanity.

Crusader state   Christian state established in the Muslim Near East during the High Middle Ages.

Crusades   Christian military expeditions against the Islamic Near East and North Africa, mostly dating from the late eleventh to the thirteenth centuries.

cuius regio eius religio   Reformation German doctrine that the prince's religion could be imposed upon his subjects too.

curia regis   Medieval royal council.

Cynics Hellenistic Greek philosophers who rejected Greek society and traditional values, preaching total self-sufficiency.

czar Title of Russian monarchs, especially before Peter the Great took the title of emperor.

dance of death Theme in late medieval art showing Death leading all classes of society to the same doom.

Danegeld Tribute paid by early medieval Anglo-Saxon states to Danish Vikings.

Danubian empire Habsburg territories centered on the Danube river valley and inhabited by non-German peoples, including Slavs, Magyars, and Italians.

deduction Form of reasoning that begins with accepted generalizations and infers more specific truths.

Delian League The fifth-century B.C. Greek alliance against Persia, led by Athens, that evolved into the Athenian Empire.

deme An administrative subdivision of ancient Athens and its hinterland.

devotio moderna Late medieval turn toward lay piety and mysticism, especially in the Netherlands and Germany.

diaspora Dispersal of Jewish communities across the Western world, beginning in ancient times.

diet An advisory or legislative assembly of leading citizens or representatives of estates, especially in central or eastern Europe.

Diggers Radical fringe of the Puritan Revolution in England preaching communal ownership of material goods.

divine sanction Royal claim that monarchical government was ordained by God.

djinn Spirits and demons in Arab mythology.

doge Duke of Venice, ruling in conjunction with an assembly of leading merchants.

Dominicans Order of friars founded by St. Dominic in the thirteenth century.

Drang nach Osten German "drive toward the east," into the Slavic lands of eastern Europe, begun in the Middle Ages.

Dutch realists Seventeenth-century Dutch painters famed for realistic rendering of objects and landscapes.

ecclesia The citizens' assembly of ancient Athens.

enclosure Agricultural practice of converting farm land into sheep pastures or commercial grain fields, often causing unemployment and dislocation of the peasants.

encomienda Estate with Indian labor assigned to Spanish conquistadores in the New World.

England's Bill of Rights Statement of the rights of Parliament and the English people imposed on William and Mary by England's "Glorious Revolution" of 1688.

enquêteur Medieval French royal official who oversaw the work of other royal officials in the provinces.

enragés Extremist fringe element in the French Revolution, popular with the *sans-culottes*.

entelechy In Aristotelian philosophy, an indwelling purposiveness or direction of development in nature.

ephor Chief magistrate in ancient Sparta.

Epicureans Hellenistic Greek and later Roman philosophers who saw pleasure and peace of mind as the goals of life.

equestrian Social class that challenged the primacy of the patrician order in ancient Rome.

l'état c'est **moi** "*I* am the State," Louis XIV's famous assertion of the absolute sovereignty of the monarch.

excommunication Expulsion of a sinner or heretic from the Christian church.

fasces Rods and ax carried ahead of a Roman consul as symbols of his power; revived as symbol of the Italian Fascist party in the twentieth century.

feudal lord Medieval noble who could command the loyalty and service of vassal knights.

feudalism Medieval political system built on the exchange of military service and political support for land and serf labor.

fief Land assigned to a vassal by his feudal lord.

First Crusade Christian holy war against Muslims in Palestine, 1095-1099, in which Christian invaders conquered Jerusalem and other cities.

First Triumvirate Informal political alliance of three ambitious Roman politicians, Julius Caesar, Pompey, and Crassus.

formalism Hellenistic Greek school of poetry emphasizing verse forms and ancient models.

Fourth Crusade Christian holy war against Muslims in 1204 that conquered Christian Constantinople instead.

Franciscans Order of wandering friars founded by St. Francis in the thirteenth century.

free company Late medieval band of mercenary soldiers.

the Fronde French revolutionary upheaval in the middle of the seventeenth century.

gens du roi "King's men," French royal officials in the late Middle Ages.

geocentric theory Ptolemy's view that the earth was the center of the universe.

Germanic peoples Preurban tribes who overran the Roman Empire in the fifth century and became ancestors of many later European peoples, including Germans, French, and English.

gerousia The council of elders in ancient Sparta.

ghazi Muslim crusaders and raiders against Byzantium and Christian Europe.

ghetto Jewish section of a medieval or modern city.

Glorious Revolution English Revolution of 1688, establishing constitutional monarchy under William and Mary.

Gnostics Early Christian heretics who believed in a "secret wisdom" about the real nature of Christ.

Golden Bull Fourteenth-century decree by the Holy Roman Emperor granting unprecedented autonomy to the German princes.

Golden Horde The Mongol khanate that ruled late medieval Russia.

golden mean In Aristotelian ethics, virtue seen as the mean between extremes; "moderation in all things."

Gothic style High medieval European artistic style, epito-

547

mized in Gothic cathedrals with their high pointed arches, stained glass windows, and flying buttresses.

gravitation Attraction between particles of matter; explained by Newton in the seventeenth century and by Einstein in the twentieth.

Great Chain of Being Ancient and medieval belief in a hierarchy of being.

Great Schism Split in the Roman Catholic church (1378-1417) in which rival popes claimed headship of the church.

Greek (Eastern) Orthodox Church Eastern European Christian church headed by the patriarch of Constantinople.

Gregorian reform Medieval reform of the Roman Catholic church epitomized by the reign of Pope Gregory VII in the eleventh century.

gunpowder weapons Artillery, muskets, and other weapons that used the power of gunpowder explosions to propel projectiles, transforming warfare in late medieval and early modern times.

hegemony Domination of a country or region by another power.

Hegira Muhammad's flight from Mecca, where he had been rejected, to Medina, where he found many converts.

heliaea courts Large law courts in ancient Athens.

heliocentric theory Copernicus's theory that the sun is the center of the universe.

Hellenes A Greek term for Greeks themselves, based on the belief that all Greeks were descended from the mythical King Hellen of Thessaly.

Hellenistic Age Period of Greek history stretching from the rule of Alexander the Great, fourth century B.C., to the Roman conquest of the Mediterranean, first century B.C.

Hellenistic monarchy Successor states to Alexander the Great's empire, characterized by autocratic power, courtly splendor, and claims of divinity.

Hellenization Spread of Greek civilization, particularly to the Near East and North Africa, during the Hellenistic period.

helot A serf in ancient Sparta.

Heptarchy Seven small Anglo-Saxon kingdoms in early medieval England.

hesychasm The search for inner peace as practiced by Eastern Orthodox monks on Mount Athos, Greece.

Hildebrandine Party Eleventh-century church reformers gathered by Pope Leo X and led by Hildebrand, later Pope Gregory VII the Great.

Holy Roman Empire Loosely organized German empire that was founded in the tenth century and expired in the nineteenth.

homage and investiture Medieval ceremony establishing a feudal relationship between lord and vassal.

hominids The human family, including *homo erectus,* Neanderthal people, and Cro-Magnon people.

hoplite Heavily armed infantry of ancient Greek citizen-soldiers.

humanism Renaissance intellectual movement based on deep study of ancient culture.

humors Bodily fluids believed in medieval and Renaissance times to both determine character and cause illness.

Hussites Followers of Czech reformer Jan Hus, who was burned for heresy in 1415.

ICHTHYS Initials of Greek words for "Jesus Christ, Son of God, Saviour," which spell the Greek word for "fish," the symbol used by early Christian communities to identify themselves.

iconoclastic controversy Dispute over the use of icons in the Greek Orthodox church.

imam Shiite Muslim religious leader.

imperator Imperial title in ancient Rome, denoting possession of imperium.

imperium Political authority to command armies and punish citizens; held by consuls in the Roman Republic and by emperors in the Roman Empire.

Incas Emperors of Peru and neighboring Andean regions in the late fifteenth and early sixteenth centuries.

Index of Forbidden Books Catholic list of writings deemed immoral or irreligious by the church.

Indo-European peoples Language group that originated on the Eurasian steppes and spread from India to Europe.

induction Form of reasoning beginning with detailed data and inferring general truths.

indulgence Remission of punishment for sins granted in return for good works or for monetary contribution to the church during medieval or Reformation times.

insulae Multi-story tenement buildings in ancient Rome.

intendant French government official dispatched to the provinces to impose the authority of early absolutist monarchs.

interdict Papal ban on performing church services, including the sacraments.

interloper "Intruder," term used to describe English, French, and Dutch traders and colonizers who "intruded" into Spanish and Portuguese spheres of influence and empire overseas in the seventeenth century.

investiture controversy Dispute between medieval popes and secular rulers over who had power to invest bishops with their authority and lands.

Islam The religion and civilization of the Muslims, followers of the Prophet Muhammad, from the seventh century to the present.

ius naturale "Natural law," the philosophical foundation for Roman and later legal systems.

ius gentium "Law of the peoples," legal principles originally applied to non-Roman subjects of the Roman Empire and later to citizens as well.

Jacquerie Peasant revolt in France at the time of the Hundred Years' War.

janissary corps Christian converts to Islam serving Ottoman Turks in military and civil posts.

Jesuits The Society of Jesus, an order of friars organized by Loyola during the Catholic Reformation to combat heresy; also known for missionary and educational work.

jihad A Muslim holy war.

joint-stock company Form of business organization in which shares are distributed among a number of investors.

Junkers Prussian aristocracy known for loyalty and efficiency in military and government posts.

junta de noche Philip II's "night council" of special advisors in late sixteenth-century Spain.

justices of eyre Medieval English royal judges dispatched to try cases in the shires under Henry II.

justices of the peace English country gentry who served as royal officials.

kadi Muslim judge adjudicating disputes and trying cases according to Islamic law.

Kievan Rus Medieval Russian state, centered in the southern steppes and ruled from Kiev by Varangian princes.

Koran The Muslim holy book, composed in the early seventh century by the Prophet Muhammad.

kore Archaic Greek statue of a young woman.

kouros Archaic Greek statue of a young man.

largesse Medieval chivalric virtue of offering generous hospitality to guests.

latifundia Large slave-operated Roman estates.

League of Corinth League, organized by Philip of Macedon, that included most of the Greek states.

League of Schmalkald Alliance of German Protestant princes organized in 1531 to defend Lutheran territories against the Catholic Holy Roman Emperor Charles V.

legado Legally trained officials in the Spain of Philip II.

letter of marque Warrant issued to privateering vessels to prey on enemy shipping in early modern times.

Levelers Political democrats in the English Civil War who sought to "level" the social hierarchy.

Leviathan state Hobbes's seventeenth-century vision of the all-powerful state.

Lex Visigothorum Germanic law code issued in the early Middle Ages by the Visigoths.

liberum veto Voting system in the Polish assembly in which a single noble's "nay" could defeat any measure.

liege lord Feudal overlord whose interests a vassal agrees to support first in any dispute.

Linear A and B Forms of writing used by the ancient Minoans and Mycenaeans.

Little Entente Alliance of Czechoslovakia, Romania, and Yugoslavia between the first and second world wars.

liturgy In ancient Greece, a wealthy person's material contribution to the service of the state; in the Christian church, a religious service.

Lollardy Late medieval English heresy based on teachings of Wycliffe.

Lombard League Medieval alliance of northern Italian cities to resist German imperial intrusion.

lugal A king of a Sumerian city state.

ma'at Egyptian principle of justice and order; the spirit in which the pharaohs ruled.

Magna Carta The "Great Charter" forced on King John in 1215 and seen as the foundation of later English liberties.

Manichaeans Early Christian heretics who believed in the equal and opposite power of good and evil in the universe.

maniple Small, independent squads of Roman soldiers deployed for greater flexibility than the massed phalanx allowed.

mannerism Late Renaissance artistic style emphasizing elongated figures, sour colors, and startling lighting effects.

mare nostrum "Our sea," the ancient Roman term for the Mediterranean; revived by Mussolini in the twentieth century.

medieval manor Medieval farming village and surrounding land, run by a knight or noble and operated by serfs.

megalith Large stone erected by prehistoric people for religious or ceremonial purposes.

mentalité The "mentality" or shared ideas and attitudes of a people or group in society.

mercantilism Early modern governmental economic policies seeking to control and develop the national economy.

Mercator projection Mercator's sixteenth-century method of charting the curved surface of the earth on a flat map.

merchant guild Medieval organization of merchants and traders, often the dominant force in medieval cities.

Messiah Among Jews, deliverer of the Jewish people foretold by the Prophets; among Christians, Jesus Christ, the savior of all humanity.

Mesta Medieval and early modern Spanish sheep-herders' organization.

mestizo A Latin American person of mixed Spanish and Native American descent.

metic A foreigner resident in a Greek city-state.

metropolitan A bishop in the Eastern Orthodox church.

mihrab In a mosque, the niche indicating the direction of the city of Mecca, toward which prayers are directed.

military revolution Term sometimes used for the radical changes in military organization, tactics, and technology during the seventeenth and eighteenth centuries.

ministeriale Official of the medieval Holy Roman Empire.

missi dominici Royal emissaries sent out by Charlemagne to keep tabs on the provinces of his empire.

Model Parliament First full Parliament in English history, including townsmen and knights as well as nobles and bishops, summoned by Edward I in 1295.

modern world system Wallerstein's theory that Western imperial domination of the globe was primarily economic and that it divided the world into a prosperous Western "core" and an exploited non-Western "periphery."

monad In Leibniz's seventeenth-century philosophy, one of the independent centers of consciousness of which the universe is made.

Mongols Militant pastoral nomads from the steppes; under Genghis Khan and his successors, the Mongols built an enormous Eurasian empire in the thirteenth and fourteenth centuries.

mosque Muslim house of worship.

Mughals Imperial rulers of India from the sixteenth through the eighteenth centuries.

mystery cults Near Eastern and North African religions emphasizing ecstatic rites and personal salvation that found followers among Greeks and Romans.

natural rights Rights of human beings that governments should not violate; particularly the political rights urged by Locke and expanded by reformers of later centuries.

nave Main hall of a medieval church, from the portals to the altar, where the congregation stood.

Neanderthal Prehistoric people whose traces were discovered in the Neander valley in Germany; the immediate precursors of modern humans.

Neolithic Society of the New Stone Age, when human beings first settled into agricultural villages.

Neoplatonism More mystical "New Platonism" developed by Plotinus of Alexandria in Roman times.

nepotism Advancing the career of a relative; a practice particularly noted in the medieval church.

new monarchs Fifteenth- and sixteenth-century monarchs who revived royal power after late medieval decline.

Ninety-five Theses Luther's list of arguments against the selling of indulgences that was published in 1517 and that launched the Protestant Reformation.

nobility of the robe Early modern French aristocracy that traditionally devoted its energies to law and government.

nobility of the sword Early modern French aristocrats who concentrated on military affairs.

nominalists Late medieval philosophers who dismissed Platonic Ideas as mere "names" for categories of particular things.

northern humanism Renaissance humanism north of Italy, characterized by special concern for Christian classics and morality, and providing background for the Reformation.

oligarchy Rule by a small group or by a particular social class; often rule by the middle classes, as in ancient Greek or medieval European cities.

oprichniki Marauding military order through which Ivan the Terrible imposed his will on sixteenth-century Russia.

Ottomans Steppe nomads who conquered the Byzantine Empire in 1453 and founded the modern Ottoman Turkish Empire with its capital at Constantinople.

palace system The Mycenaean structure of political and military power in ancient Greece.

palazzo Renaissance Italian palace or mansion, the urban residence of a ruler, banker, bishop, or other notable.

Paleolithic Term for the society of the Old Stone Age, when people lived by food-gathering and hunting.

particularism Commitment to the independence and interests of a region, state, or province in a larger political federation, as in the Holy Roman Empire.

pater patriae "Father of his country," title conferred on Augustus Caesar and later Western rulers.

patria potestas In ancient Rome, life-and-death power vested in the male head of the family.

patriarchs Heads of the Eastern Orthodox church; comparable to popes in the Roman Catholic church.

patrician A member of the ancient Roman aristocracy, particularly powerful during the period of the Republic.

pax deorum In ancient Rome, the harmonious relationship between gods and human beings, which was threatened by Christian monotheism.

Pax Romana The Roman Peace in the Western world during the first two centuries A.D.

Peloponnesian League The Spartan-led alliance that fought Athens in the Peloponnesian War.

perioeci The "dwellers around," Sparta's neighbors who were compelled to support Sparta.

perspective Artistic technique for representing three-dimensionality convincingly on a flat surface.

phalanx Military formation involving close ranks and overlapping spears and shields used by ancient Greeks and Romans.

Philippic Speech by the eloquent Athenian orator Demosthenes warning against Philip of Macedon; hence any passionate oratorical denunciation.

phratry Greek youths who ate and fought together as a "brotherhood" before the rise of the Greek city state.

pike Long spear used by early modern infantry soldiers.

plebeians The urban lower classes in ancient Rome.

pneumonic plague Virulent form of the black death affecting the lungs.

pogrom Massacre of Jews, especially in eastern Europe.

polder Dutch agricultural land reclaimed from the sea by a system of dikes.

polis The ancient Greek city-state.

politiques Late sixteenth-century Europeans who favored religious compromise in order to restore political order.

pomestie Fiefs granted to boyars by Russian czars in return for service in the sixteenth century.

pontifex maximus "Chief priest," title conferred on Roman emperors.

power of the purse Authority claimed by the elected House of Commons of the English Parliament to control royal revenues.

predestination Belief that each human soul has been predestined or assigned to heaven or hell; important particularly among Calvinist Protestants.

prévôt Medieval French official under the Capetians.

priesthood of all believers Lutheran doctrine that priests have no special powers and that all believers have direct access to God through prayer.

primogeniture Inheritance of all property by the first-born son.

princeps "First citizen," title of Augustus Caesar and other early Roman emperors.

principate Early imperial period of Roman history when rulers avoided the imperial title by calling themselves "first citizens."

problem of universals Medieval scholastic debate over whether abstract categories are real.

procurator Head of the Russian Orthodox church under Peter the Great and his successors.

prophets Inspired holy men who both condemned and consoled the ancient Hebrews in God's name.

Ptolemaic dynasty Macedonian dynasty that ruled Egypt from the fourth to the first century B.C.

Punic Wars Wars between Rome and the Carthage in the third and second centuries B.C.

Puritans Sixteenth- and seventeenth-century English Protestants, many of them Calvinists, who opposed what they perceived as the immorality and Catholic leanings of the English established church.

putting-out system Early-modern system of production in which merchants organized peasant labor.

Pyrrhic victory Victory so costly as to constitute a defeat, so called after the "victories" of the Greek king Pyrrhus over the Romans in the third century B.C.

quadrivium Four "sciences" studied in medieval schools—arithmetic, geometry, astronomy, and music.

rationalism Belief in the capacity of human reason to understand the world and solve human problems.

realists Medieval scholastic philosophers who believed in the reality of Platonic Ideas; contrast with *nominalists* above.

reconquista Spanish Christian "reconquest" of Spain from the Muslims in the Middle Ages.

red figure Ancient Greek style of vase painting in which the surface of the vase was painted black except for the figures, which were left in the red color of the clay.

Reichstag German legislative assembly.

Renaissance despot Italian Renaissance ruler with no hereditary or religious claim on political power.

Renaissance person Multitalented individual, especially in the Renaissance period.

los reyes católicos The sixteenth-century "Catholic monarchs," Ferdinand and Isabella of Spain.

Roman Civil War The long struggle, combining class conflict with rivalry between ambitious Roman politicians that began with the reform attempts of the Gracchi in 133 and ended with Augustus's victory in 31 B.C.

Roman Empire Rome from the end of the first century B.C. to the fall of Rome in the fifth century A.D., when ultimate political authority was held by the emperors.

Roman legion Primary division of the Roman army consisting of 5000 men divided into ten cohorts.

Roman Republic Rome from the fifth to the first century B.C., when its political life was dominated by the Senate, the assemblies, and elected magistrates.

sacraments Spiritual rites of passage in the Roman Catholic church: baptism, confirmation, marriage, ordination, penance, communion, last rites.

St. Bartholomew's Day Massacre 1572 Catholic massacre of Protestant Huguenots during the French wars of religion.

salvation through faith Luther's belief that Christian faith alone—not faith *and* good works—was necessary for salvation.

satraps Provincial governors in the Persian Empire.

scholasticism High medieval philosophy and theology, rooted in the rediscovery of Aristotle and seeking to explain faith in rational terms.

scientific revolution Beginnings of modern science in the sixteenth and seventeenth centuries; rapid scientific progress in the twentieth century is sometimes described as a "second scientific revolution."

Second Triumvirate Formal political alliance of three Roman rulers, Octavian, Antony, and Lepidus.

Seleucid monarchs Macedonian dynasty that ruled Persia and Syria during the Hellenistic period.

Senate Chief political assembly of ancient Rome, composed of heads of important families and men who had held the chief magistracies.

sénéchal Medieval French official dispatched to the southern provinces to impose royal authority there.

Sephardic Jews Spanish Jews who forged a brilliant medieval culture under Muslim rule.

service nobility Peter the Great's new class of Russian nobility whose high place depended on civil or military service to the state.

settlement empire European colonies where Western people settled in significant numbers, as in the Americas.

sharia Muslim law, based on Koran and Islamic traditions and administered by *kadis*.

shire An English county.

simony In the Christian church, the sin of selling positions in the church.

social contract Formal or tacit agreement by which a people accept a particular government; leading social-contract theorists included Hobbes, Locke, and Rousseau.

Socratic method Questioning and disputation in order to arrive at a higher level of understanding.

sophists Fifth-century Greek philosophers, condemned for using tricky logic to prove that all things are relative and success alone matters.

sovereignty Ultimate authority, particularly in an absolute monarchy.

sovereignty of God Calvin's emphasis on divine omnipotence and the fundamental human duty of obedience to God's will.

sprezzatura Grace of manner with which a Renaissance universal person made many talents look easy.

stadtholder Chief magistrate of the Netherlands in early modern times.

state of nature The human condition outside of organized society and the political state, especially as described by seventeenth- and eighteenth-century political thinkers.

stele Vertical stone slab bearing an inscription or other design.

stigmata The wounds of Christ appearing on the body of a saint or other mystic.

stoa Columned portico used as a public meeting place in ancient Greece.

Stoicism Hellenistic Greek and Roman school of philosophy preaching the value of fortitude, duty, and the brotherhood of all rational beings.

struggle of the orders Conflict between patricians and plebeians in the early centuries of the Roman Republic.

tabula rasa Locke's psychological theory that the human mind is a "blank slate" before experience inscribes ideas and attitudes on it.

taille Medieval French tax imposed on peasantry.

tercio Spanish regiment in the sixteenth century.

Tetrarchy Diocletian's restructuring of Roman government, dividing authority among two *Augusti* and two *Caesars*.

theme system Byzantine system of defense, granting soldiers land in exchange for hereditary military obligation.

Theory of Ideas Plato's philosophical theory that all material things are copies of archetypal Ideas, Forms, or Absolutes that exist in another realm of being.

Third Crusade Christian holy war against Muslims in the Near East, 1189-1191, led by famous warriors like Richard the Lionhearted and Frederick Barbarossa.

Thirty Tyrants Autocratic rulers installed in Athens by Sparta after Sparta's victory in the Peloponnesian War.

tholos Beehive-shaped tombs built in Mycenaean Greece.

Tories Members of the English Conservative party.

trading empire European commercial expansion overseas, achieved through trading posts supported by political alliances and military force, as in India.

triangular trade routes Imperial trade routes carrying manufactured goods to Africa, slaves to the Americas, and agricultural products to Europe.

tribune Roman magistrate representing the interests of the common people.

trireme Ancient Greek warship propelled by three banks of oars.

trivium Three "arts" studied in the Middle Ages—grammar, rhetoric, and logic.

Turko-Mongol peoples Nomadic steppe peoples, including Huns, Turks, and Mongols, who invaded Europe repeatedly from the east.

Twelfth-Century Renaissance Cultural revival of the High Middle Ages, including scholastic philosophy and gothic art.

Twelve Tables Earliest formulation of Roman law, inscribed on twelve wooden tablets in 450 B.C.

Ulozhenie Russian law code of 1649 imposing serfdom on the Russian peasantry.

Unam Sanctam Papal bull issued by Boniface VIII in 1302, claiming supremacy over all secular authorities.

urban patriciate Commercial and financial aristocracy of the towns during medieval and early modern times.

utopia An ideal state or society, usually invented to point up injustices in existing societies; based on More's sixteenth-century book, *Utopia*.

vassal In the feudal system, a knight who pledges military service and support for a more powerful feudal lord in exchange for land, serfs to work it, and the lord's protection.

veche Municipal council in medieval Russian cities.

villas Late Roman agricultural estates in which peasantry surrendered their liberty in return for protection; precursors of medieval manors.

virtù Renaissance quality of character that, combining willpower and skill, made for success.

Waldensians In medieval times, followers of Peter Waldo, considered heretics, who urged poverty and translated the Bible into the vernacular.

War of the Austrian Succession Great-power struggle during the 1740s centering on the effort by Frederick the Great of Prussia to wrest Silesia from Maria Theresa's Austrian inheritance.

wars of religion Wars and civil wars pitting Catholics against Protestants, at their height in the second half of the sixteenth century.

Wars of the Roses Civil wars, 1455-1485, between rival houses of York and Lancaster for the throne of England.

western global imperialism Unprecedented expansion of Western colonial holdings, economic power, and influence around the world between the fifteenth and twentieth centuries.

Whigs English liberal party during the eighteenth and earlier nineteenth centuries.

witch craze Widespread persecution of witches, mostly women believed to have supernatural powers and to be agents of Satan, between the fifteenth and seventeenth centuries.

witenagemot Anglo-Saxon royal council.

zemsky sobor Early modern Russian national assembly of notables, abandoned in the seventeenth century.

ziggurat Mesopotamian temple, pyramidal in shape, with a shrine at the top.

Photo Credits

Chapter 1: page 2, Bildarchiv Preussischer Kulturbesitz; p. 9, American Museum of Natural History; p. 15, Oriental Institute, The University of Chicago; p. 18, Iraq Museum, Baghdad; p. 21, George Holton/Photo Researchers; p. 25, Museum of Fine Arts, Boston; p. 26, Trans World Airlines; p. 30, Israel Ministry of Tourism

Chapter 2: page 36, Reunion des Musées Nationaux; p. 38, Alison Frantz; p. 43, New York Public Library; p. 51, Erich Lessing/Art Resource; p. 54, Museum of Fine Arts, Boston; p. 56, Hirmer Fotoarchiv; p. 57, Bettmann; p. 59, Staatliche Antikensammlungen und Glyptothek, Munich

Chapter 3: page 62, Museo Civico, Bologna; p. 68, Oriental Institute, The University of Chicago; p. 69, G. Hellner/German Archaeological Institute, Athens; p. 70, Mike Andrews/Ancient Art & Architecture Collection; p. 73, Vatican Museums; p. 75, Wadsworth Atheneum, Hartford; p. 81, D.A. Harissiadis; p. 84, Alinari/Art Resource

Chapter 4: page 97, Jo Selsing/Ny Carlsberg Glyptothek, Copenhagen; p. 101, Alinari/Art Resource; p. 105, Bettmann; p. 108, Alinari/Art Resource; p. 109, Alinari/Art Resource; p. 110, Bettmann; p. 113, Ronald Sheridan/Ancient Art & Architecture Collection

Chapter 5: page 119, Art Reference Bureau, NY; p. 123, Villa Giulia Museum, Rome/Alinari/Art Resource; p. 127, Alinari/Art Resource; p. 139, Alinari/Art Resource; p. 142, Vatican Museums, Alinari/Art Resource; p. 147, Alinari/Art Resource; p. 150, Erich Lessing/Magnum Photos

Chapter 6: page 153, Giraudon/Art Resource; p. 158, A.T. Rossano; p. 160, British Tourist Authority; p. 164, Alinari/Art Resource; p. 165, Barbara Malter/Capitoline Museums, Rome; p. 173, Alinari/Art Resource; p. 176, Spanish National Tourist Office; p. 179, Alinari/Art Resource

Chapter 7: page 186, Antikvarisk Topografiska Arkivet; p. 191, BOAC Photograph; p. 194, Walters Art Gallery; p. 197, New York Public Library; p. 206, Bettmann; p. 208, Stadtbibliothek, Trier, Germany; p. 210, Lambeth Palace Library, London; p. 213, British Museum

Chapter 8: page 216, Sovfoto/Eastfoto; p. 222, Alinari/Art Resource; p. 225, Alinari/Art Resource; p. 233, Novosti/Sovfoto; p. 235, Hirmer Fotoarchiv; p. 236, Edinburgh University Library, Scotland; p. 241, Spanish National Tourist Office; p. 243, Hans Patzelt

Chapter 9: page 247, Bildarchiv Foto Marburg; p. 253, Rheinisches Landesmuseum Bonn; p. 255, Bodleian Library, Oxford University; p. 256, French Government Tourist Office; p. 258, Jean Bourdichon/École Nationale Superieure des Beaux-Arts, Paris; p. 263, J. Feuillie/(c) C.N.M.H.S./SPADEM; p. 267, Giraudon/Art Resource; p. 270, British Information Services

Chapter 10: page 281, Lauros-Giraudon/Art Resource; p. 286, Ambrogio Lorenzetti/National Gallery, London; p. 291, Alinari/Art Resource; p. 296, British Museum; p. 302, Ewing Galloway, NY; p. 303, Lauros-Giraudon/Art Resource; p. 305, Bettmann

Chapter 11: page 317, Giraudon/Art Resource; p. 323, Alinari/Art Resource; p. 324, Bayerisches Staatsbibliothek; p. 326, Bibliotheque Nationale; p. 328, Giraudon/Art Resource; p. 330, Giraudon; p. 336, Snark International/Art Resource; p. 344, Florence, Bargello

Chapter 12: page 355, National Gallery, London; p. 357, Giraudon/Art Resource; p. 359, British Museum; p. 360, New York Public Library Picture Collection; p. 361, Herzog Anton Ulrich-Museum Braunschweig; p. 365, Alinari/Art Resource; p. 367, Bettmann; p. 374, Stock Montage

Chapter 13: page 378, Reunion des Musées Nationaux; p. 383, Giraudon; p. 385, National Gallery, London; p. 391, Bettmann; p. 399, Alinari/Art Resource; p. 400, Anderson/Art Resource; p. 401, Alinari/Art Resource; p. 406, Italian State Tourist Office; p. 407, Alinari/Art Resource

Chapter 14: page 421, Musée Historique de la Reformation, Geneva; p. 427, Giraudon; p. 429, Stock Montage, Inc.; p. 433, Cooper-Bridgeman Library (Collection Thyssen-Bornemisza); p. 436, Art Reference Bureau/Art Resource; p. 437, André Held; p. 439, Louvre Museum; p. 444, Archiv fur Kunst und Geschichte, Berlin

Chapter 15: page 449, Giraudon/Art Resource; p. 455, Princeton University; p. 459, Mansell Collection; p. 463, The Wallace Collection; p. 470, Bettmann; p. 471, New York Public Library Picture Collection; p. 474, Folger Shakespeare Library; p. 476, University of Cambridge

Chapter 16: page 484, Art Resource; p. 491, New York Public Library Picture Collection; p. 493, Museo del Prado; p. 503, Scala/Art Resource; p. 504, Alinari; p. 507, New York Public Library Picture Collection

Chapter 17: page 521, Air India; p. 523, Ronald Sheridan/Ancient Art and Architecture Collection; p. 525, New York Public Library; p. 527, Historical Pictures Collection/Stock Montage; p. 528, Ewing Galloway; p. 533, Granger Collection; p. 537, New York Public Library Picture Collection

Inserts: page IV, top, Richard Carafelli; p. VI, Wim Swaan; p. VII, top, Bridgeman/Art Resource; p. VII, bottom, © Ara Güler, Istanbul; p. VIII, left, Alinari/Art Resource; p. XV, bottom, The Image Bank; Scala/Art Resource; p. I, bottom; p. II, top; p. III, bottom; p. IV, bottom; p. IX, top; p. X, top and bottom; p. XI, bottom; p. XII, top; p. XIII, bottom; p. XIV, bottom; p. XVI; Art Resource, p. III, top; p. V, bottom; p. VIII, right; p. IX, bottom; p. XIV, top; p. XV, top; Erich Lessing/Art Resource, p. XII, bottom; p. XIII, top

Index

Gaius, *See* Gracchus, Gaius
Galen, 112, 305
Galileo (Galileo Galilei), 501, 503–5, 506, 509
Galleons, 365, 519
Gattamelata (Donatello), 406
Gauls, 128
Gelasius I, pope, 208
Genesis (Michelangelo), 403
Geneva, Calvinist church at, 422
Gentiles, mission to, 176–77
Gentileschi, Artemisia, 492
Geography (Ptolemy), 516
Georgics (Vergil), 174
Germania (Tacitus), 175
German Peasants' War, 418, 419
Germany:
    kingdoms, in Early Middle Ages, 194–96
    medieval (map), 276
    Roman Empire, Germanic invasions of (map), 167
    society, in Early Middle Ages, 166, 191–94
    under Holy Roman Empire, 273–79
Gerousia, 47, 76
Gibbon, Edward, 169
Gilbert, Humphrey, 533
Gilbert, William, 506
Giotto di Bondone, 400
Glaciers, and Paleolithic period, 6, 7
Glorious Revolution, 478, 486, 487
Gnostics, 180
Godfrey of Bouillon, 312
God-kings (Egypt), 21–22
Golden Bull, 342
Golden Hind, 434
Golden Horde, 338–40, 373
Golden Horn (harbor), 226
Golden mean, 85
Gospels, 180
Gothic Age, 300–308
    architecture/art, 302–4
    culture, 300–302
Goths, 166
Government by consent of the governed, 488–90
Gracchus, Gaius, 134, 135–37
Gracchus, Tiberius, 134, 135–36
Grand Monarque, Le See Louis XIV, king of France
Grand Remonstrance, 475
Great Art, or the Rules of Algebra (Cardano), 507
Great Chain of Being, 500–501
Great Charter, 271–72
Great Greece, 123
Great Northern War, 451
Great Schism, 334–35, 367
Greece:
    classical age, 45, 48, 62–91, 108
    early Greeks, 36–61
    See also Athenian democracy; Athenian Empire; Classical Greeks; Early Greeks; Greek Awakening; Greek Dark Age; Hellenistic Age; Macedonia/Macedonians
Greek Aegean (map), 47
Greek Awakening, 45–52, 54, 75, 79, 93, 113, 144, 211
    colonies, 48, 49 (map)
    commercial expansion, 49–50
    revival, sources of, 45–46
    tensions/reforms, 50–51
    tyrants, 51–52
Greek city-state, 13, 14–15, 45, 46
    political power in, 46, 47–48
Greek Dark Age, 44–45, 50, 52, 53, 54, 56, 57, 75, 76

Greek (Eastern) Orthodox church, 221
    schism between Roman Catholic church and, 227
Greek hegemony, 94–96, 98 (map)
Greek naval war, 69–70
Gregorian reforms, 288, 293
Gregory of Tours, 212
Gregory I the Great, pope, 207–9, 211
Gregory VII, pope, 275, 277, 278, 288–90, 333, 413
Gregory IX, pope, 288
Gregory XI, pope, 334
Groote, Gerard, 335
"Grub Street" literary artisans, 497
Gudea of Lagash, 16
Guicciardini, Francesco, 364, 392
Guide of the Perplexed (Maimonides), 308
Guidi, Tommaso, 400
Guilds, 255, 257–60, 299, 324, 343, 362
Gunpowder weapons, 451, 519
Gustavus Adolphus, king of Sweden, 454–55, 473
Gutenberg, Johannes, 395
Guzman, Gaspar de, count-duke of Olivares, 469

Habsburg dynasty, 342, 362, 375, 452, 469–70, 522
    Maximilian I, 333
    new Habsburg Empire, 469–70
    and the Reformation, 434–37
Habsburg-Valois wars, 441–42, 444, 522
Hadrian, 160–61, 171, 173
Hadrian's Wall, 160, 161
Hagia Sophia, 228, 234, 235 (illus.)
Hals, Franz, 497
Hamilcar, 131
Hammer of the Witches (Kraemer/Sprenger), 459
Hammurabi of Babylon, 13, 16, 22
Hammurabi's Code, 16, 31
    and women, 16, 17
Handbook of the Christian Knight, The (Erasmus), 392
Hannibal, 131, 132, 390
Hanseatic League, 314, 324, 360
Hardraada, Harold, king of Norway, 268
Harold the Saxon, 268
Hasdrubal, 132
Hatshepsut, 23
Hebrews, *See* Judaism/Jews
Hegemony, 94–96, 98 (map)
Hegira, 236
Helen of Troy, 38, 54
Heliaea courts, 51
Hellenes/Hellenism, 39, 52
Hellenistic Age, 93, 101–14
    arts, 107–9
    culture, 107–14, 115
    economics, 104–6, 114
    Hellenization of the East, 106–7
    literature, 109–11
    monarchies, 101–7
    monarch's "Friends," 104
    new rulers, image of, 103–4
    philosophy, 112–14
    religion, 112–14
    royal cults, 104
    science, 111–12
    social tensions, 106, 114
    successor states, 102–3
    technology, 114
Hellenistic monarchies, 102 (map), 103–4

Hellenization:
  of the East, 106–7
  of Roman, 143–45
Hellespont, 64, 67, 74, 77, 99
Helots, 47
Henry of Guise, duke of Guise, 443
Henry the Lion, duke of Saxony, 278, 309
Henry the Navigator, prince of Portugal, 370, 523
Henry II, king of France, 268, 269, 270–71, 441, 443
Henry III, Holy Roman emperor, 288
Henry III, king of France, 443
Henry IV (Henry of Navarre), king of France, 433, 443
Henry IV, Holy Roman emperor, 275–77, 290
Henry V, king of England, 328, 329–30, 331, 341
Henry VI, king of England, 329, 331–32
Henry VII, king of England, 363, 369–70
Henry VIII, king of England, 394, 404, 413, 419–20, 429,
    430–31, 432
Hera (Greek god), 144
Heraclitus, 56, 83
Heraclius I, 223
  theme system, 223
Hereditary succession, 261
Heresy, in Christian church, 180–81, 284–86, 335–37
Herod I the Great, 148
Herodotus, 66, 69, 82–83, 87
Hesiod (poet), 44, 45, 54
Hesychasm, 338
High Middle Ages, 247–80, 365–66, 519, 539
  chivalric epics, 306–7
  Christianity/Christian church, 292
  city life, 296–99
  Crusader States, 312–14
  Europe, medieval expansion of, 308
  European revival, 248–52
  feudal monarchy, 260–73
  Gothic Age, 300–308
  Holy Roman Empire, Germany under, 273–79
  knights/nobles, 294–96
  peasant life, 296–99
  Reconquista, 308–10
  scholastic thought, 305–6
  social organization, 292–300
  troubadour poetry, 306–7
  Twelfth-Century Renaissance, 304
Hildebrand, 288–89
Hildebrandine party, 288–89
Hildegard of Bingen, 293
Hipparchus, 52, 112
Hippias, 51–52, 71
Hippocrates, 111–12, 305
Histories (Polybius), 109
History of Italy (Guicciardini), 364, 392
History of Rome (Appian), 136
History of Rome from Its Foundations (Livy), 127, 128
History of the Franks (Gregory of Tours), 212
Hittites, 3, 25, 27–28, 30
Hobbes, Thomas, 485, 488–90
  and the Leviathan state, 490
Hohenstaufen dynasty, 277, 278
Hohenzollern dynasty, 469, 470–71
Holbein, Hans (the Younger), 404
Holy Office of the Inquisition, 288, 427
Holy Roman Empire, 250, 273–79, 373, 452–56, 522
  Barbarossa, Frederick, 277–79
  birth of, 273–75
  Charles IV, 342
  Charles V, 418, 429, 436–37, 441, 444

decline/fall of, 435–36
emperor-pope struggles, 275–77
Frederick I, 275, 277, 471
Frederick II (Stupor Mundi), 275, 277–79, 304, 309, 342
Frederick III, 333
Germany under, 273–79
Henry III, 288
Henry IV, 275–77, 290
Leopold I, 470
Ottoman attacks on, 522
Otto the Great, 275, 309
Holy Trinity with The Virgin and St. John (Guidi), 400
Homage and investiture, ceremony of, 203–4
Homer, 38, 53, 54, 55, 57–59, 87, 109–10, 111, 145
Hominids:
  defined, 5
  migration of, 5–7
Homo erectus, 5
Homo habilis, 5, 11
Homo sapiens, 5
Hoplite, 45
Horace, 174
Horus (sky god), 21, 24
House of Commons, 273, 342, 474, 475, 478, 487
House of Habsburg, 434, *See also* Habsburg dynasty
House of Lords, 273, 342
Hudson, Henry, 531
Huguenots, 442–43, 465, 466, 532
Humanists/humanism, 389–95
  classics, rediscovery of, 389–90
  Erasmus, Desiderius, 391–92, 394
  northern humanism, 191
  Petrarca, Francesco, 390
  Pico della Mirandola, Giovanni, 390
  schools/theories of education, 394–95
  social thought, 392–94
  Valla, Lorenzo, 390–91
Humbert (Cardinal), 289
Hundred Years' War, 318, 325, 327–33, 341, 369
  bastard feudalism, 331
  cause of conflict, 327–28
  Edward III, 327, 328–29
  Henry V, 328, 329–30
  Joan of Arc, 327, 328, 329–30
  map, 332
  mercenaries, 330
  monarchies, challenge to, 331–33
Huns, 166–67
Hus, Jan, 335, 336–37, 418
Hussite religious revolt, 373, 413
Hyksos, 23

Iberians, 520, 521–31
  Portuguese in Asia, 522–25
  Spain's American Empire, 529–31
  Spanish conquistadors, 526–29
  Spanish in the New World, 525–26
"Iceman, The," 11
ICHTHYS (fish), 178
Iconoclastic controversy, 223
Idylls (Theocritus), 111
Illiad (Homer), 38, 58
Imams, 241
Imitation of Christ (Kempis), 335
Imperator, 159
Imperialism, *See* Western imperialism
Imperium, 125, 155
Inanna (Sumerian goddess of love), 18, 19

Marduk (patron god of Babylon), 18, 64
Margaret of Parma, 444
Marie of Champagne, 295–96
Marie-Thérèse, 468
Marius, 137–38
Marquette, Father, 532
Marriage of Giovanni Arnolfini and Giovanna Cenami (van Eyck), 355
Mars (Roman god), 144, 146
Martel, Charles, 202, 239
Martin V, pope, 335
Mary II, 478
Mary of Burgundy, 375
Mary, Queen of Scots, 433, 475
Mary Tudor, queen of England, 431
"Mask of Agamemnon," 37
Massacre of St. Bartholomew's Day (Coligny), 443
Mathematical Principles of Natural Philosophy (Newton), 506
Mathematics, achievements in, 507
Matilda of Anjou, 269
Matthias Corvinus, king of Hungary, 373
Maurice of Nassau, 480
Mausolus, 104
Maximilian I, Austrian Habsburg emperor, 333
Maximilian of Bavaria, 453
Mazarin, (Cardinal), 465
Mecca, 236, 242, 243, 524
Medea (Euripides), 82
Medes, 28, 63
Medici family, 360–62, 368, 389, 442
    Cosimo de', 362, 363, 368
    Giovanni di Bicci de', 368
    Lorenzo de' (the Magnificent), 363, 364, 368, 400
Medieval society, 202–7
    feudal system, 202, 203–5
    manor, 205–7
    successor states, 202–3
Meditations (Marcus Aurelius), 161
Melanchthon, Philip, 436
Menander, 109–10, 145
Menes, 22
Mercator, Gerardus, 519
Mercator projection, 519
Merchant guilds, 257, 362
Merisi, Michelangelo, *See* Caravaggio
Mesopotamia, 3, 14–19, 38, 313
    first cities, emergence of, 14
    hero tales, 19
    lugals, 15
    religion, 18
    Sumer, city-states of, 14–15
    ziggurats, 15, 25
Messiah, 148, 150
    and Judaism, 148–49
Mesta, 357
Mestizos, 529
Metamorphoses (Ovid), 174
Metic, 80
Michael (Romanov), czar of Russia, 471
Michael VIII Paleologus, 338
Michelangelo, 85, 352, 353, 398, 404, 408
    paintings, 402
    sculpture, 406–7
Middle Kingdom Egypt, 22–23
Mibrab, 244
Miletus, 64–65
Military revolution, 451–52

Miltiades, 66–67
Milton, John, 495–96
Ministeriales, 277
Minnesingers, 307
Minoans/Minoan Empire, 37–43, 48, 53–54
    commerce, 41
    culture, 41–42
    disappearance of, 42
    history, periods of, 40
    map, 42
    women, 54
Misanthrope (Molière), 497
Missi dominici, 202–3
Mithras (god), 29, 147, 148
Mithridates, 138
Model Parliament, 273
Modern political thought, beginnings of, 485–90
Modern science:
    origins of, 499–502
    superstition/pseudoscience as roots of, 501
Mohács, battle of, 522
Molière, Jean-Baptiste, 497
Mona Lisa (da Vinci), 398, 402
Monasteries, 283–84
Mongols/Mongol Empire, 191, 337–41, 370
    Golden Horde, 338–40
Monks, 209–11
Monotheism, 29–33
Monteverdi, Claudio, 407, 494
Montezuma II, 527–28
Moors, 370
More, Thomas, 392, 393–94, 404, 413, 430
Moses, 30, 31
Moses (Michelangelo), 407
Mosques, 244
Mughal emperors, India, 532, 534
Muhammad, 200, 223, 235, 236–37, 239
Muhammad II, 340–41
Muhammad the Conqueror, 522
Mühlberg, Battle of, 437
Munster, Treaty of, 480
Murillo, Bartolomé, 491
Music:
    baroque, 491, 494
    Renaissance, 407–8
Muslims, 234, 240–44, 250, 252, 262, 309, 312, 337–41, 518, 522, 524
    Abbasids, 239–40
    caliphs, 239–40, 243
    divisions/schisms, 240–41
    Islam, 234, 237, 240, 241–42, 300
    jihad, 237–38
    Koran, 236, 237
    Mecca, 236, 242, 243, 524
    mosques, 244
    Muhammad, 200, 223, 235, 236–37, 239
    Muslim Zone (map), 238
    Shiites, 239, 240–41, 312
    Sunni, 239, 240–41, 312
    Umayyads, 239–40
Mycenaeans, 43–45, 48
    Lion Gate, 43–44
    map, 42
    military oppression in, 43
    palace system, 43
    tholos, 43
Mystery cults, 113, 147–48
Mysticism, 335–37

566

Woman Weighing Gold (Vermeer), 496
Women:
  and Catholic Reformation, 426–27
  colonial, 529
  convent life, 210–11
  as food gatherers, 9
  and Hammurabi's Code, 17
  Hebrew, 31
  medieval, 207
  in Paleolithic period, 8
  and the Renaissance, 382–83
  of Sparta, 76
Works and Days (Hesiod), 44, 45
Writing, 13, 19
  cuneiform script, 19
  Phoenician alphabet, 28
Wycliffe, John, 335, 336–37

Xerxes, 67–68

Yahweh, 30–33, 148
Yaroslav the Wise, 233–34, 337
Yermak, 535
Yersinia pestis, See Black Death

Zemsky sobor, 440, 471–72
Zeno, 113–14
Zenobia, queen of Palmyra, 164
Zeus, king of the gods, 53, 54–55, 88, 101, 108, 109, 112, 144, 148
Ziggurats, 15, 25
Zoe, 225
Zoroaster, 29
Zoroastrianism, 286
Zwingli, Ulrich, 417, 423